2 CORINTHIANS

Baker Exegetical Commentary on the New Testament

ROBERT W. YARBROUGH
AND JOSHUA W. JIPP, EDITORS

Volumes now available

Matthew *David L. Turner*

Mark *Robert H. Stein*

Luke *Darrell L. Bock*

Acts *Darrell L. Bock*

Romans, 2nd ed. *Thomas R. Schreiner*

1 Corinthians *David E. Garland*

2 Corinthians *George H. Guthrie*

Galatians *Douglas J. Moo*

Ephesians *Frank Thielman*

Philippians *Moisés Silva*

Colossians and Philemon *G. K. Beale*

1–2 Thessalonians *Jeffrey A. D. Weima*

James *Dan G. McCartney*

1 Peter *Karen H. Jobes*

1–3 John *Robert W. Yarbrough*

Jude and 2 Peter *Gene L. Green*

Revelation *Grant R. Osborne*

George H. Guthrie (PhD, Southwestern Baptist Theological Seminary) is professor of New Testament at Regent College in Vancouver. He previously taught at Union University. Guthrie is the author of numerous books and articles, including commentaries on Hebrews and James, and was a translator or consultant on four Bible translation projects. He is currently spearheading a biblical literacy effort to help churches train their members more effectively in reading the Bible well.

2 CORINTHIANS

GEORGE H. GUTHRIE

Baker Exegetical Commentary on the New Testament

Baker Academic
a division of Baker Publishing Group
Grand Rapids, Michigan

Published by Baker Academic
a division of Baker Publishing Group
P.O. Box 6287, Grand Rapids, MI 49516-6287
www.bakeracademic.com

Printed in the United States of America

Library of Congress Cataloging-in-Publication Data
Guthrie, George H., 1959–
    2 Corinthians / George H. Guthrie.
        pages cm. — (Baker exegetical commentary on the New Testament)
    Includes bibliographical references and index.
    ISBN 978-0-8010-2673-7 (cloth)
    1. Bible. Corinthians, 2nd—Criticism, interpretation, etc. I. Title. II. Title: 2nd
Corinthians. III. Title: Two Corinthians.
    BS2675.52.G88 2015
    227′.307—dc23   2014036494

19   20   21   7   6   5   4   3   2

To Chuck Maxwell
and the Pastoral Leadership Team
of Northbrook Church

sincere
sent by God
living before God
in Christ

(2 Cor. 2:17b)

Contents

Series Preface

The chief concern of the Baker Exegetical Commentary on the New Testament (BECNT) is to provide, within the framework of informed evangelical thought, commentaries that blend scholarly depth with readability, exegetical detail with sensitivity to the whole, and attention to critical problems with theological awareness. We hope thereby to attract the interest of a fairly wide audience, from the scholar who is looking for a thoughtful and independent examination of the text to the motivated lay Christian who craves a solid but accessible exposition.

Nevertheless, a major purpose is to address the needs of pastors and others involved in the preaching and exposition of the Scriptures as the uniquely inspired Word of God. This consideration affects directly the parameters of the series. For example, serious biblical expositors cannot afford to depend on a superficial treatment that avoids the difficult questions, but neither are they interested in encyclopedic commentaries that seek to cover every conceivable issue that may arise. Our aim, therefore, is to focus on those problems that have a direct bearing on the meaning of the text (although selected technical details are treated in the additional notes).

Similarly, a special effort is made to avoid treating exegetical questions for their own sake, that is, in relative isolation from the thrust of the argument as a whole. This effort may involve (at the discretion of the individual contributors) abandoning the verse-by-verse approach in favor of an exposition that focuses on the paragraph as the main unit of thought. In all cases, however, the commentaries will stress the development of the argument and explicitly relate each passage to what precedes and follows it so as to identify its function in context as clearly as possible.

We believe, moreover, that a responsible exegetical commentary must take fully into account the latest scholarly research, regardless of its source. The attempt to do this in the context of a conservative theological tradition presents certain challenges, and in the past the results have not always been commendable. In some cases, evangelicals appear to make use of critical scholarship not for the purpose of genuine interaction but only to dismiss it. In other cases, the interaction glides over into assimilation, theological distinctives are ignored or suppressed, and the end product cannot be differentiated from works that arise from a fundamentally different starting point.

The contributors to this series attempt to avoid these pitfalls. On the one hand, they do not consider traditional opinions to be sacrosanct, and they are certainly committed to doing justice to the biblical text whether or not it supports such opinions. On the other hand, they will not quickly abandon a long-standing view, if there is persuasive evidence in its favor, for the sake of fashionable theories. What is more important, the contributors share a belief in the trustworthiness and essential unity of Scripture. They also consider that the historic formulations of Christian doctrine, such as the ecumenical creeds and many of the documents originating in the sixteenth-century Reformation, arose from a legitimate reading of Scripture, thus providing a proper framework for its further interpretation. No doubt, the use of such a starting point sometimes results in the imposition of a foreign construct on the text, but we deny that it must necessarily do so or that the writers who claim to approach the text without prejudices are invulnerable to the same danger.

Accordingly, we do not consider theological assumptions—from which, in any case, no commentator is free—to be obstacles to biblical interpretation. On the contrary, an exegete who hopes to understand the apostle Paul in a theological vacuum might just as easily try to interpret Aristotle without regard for the philosophical framework of his whole work or without having recourse to those subsequent philosophical categories that make possible a meaningful contextualization of his thought. It must be emphasized, however, that the contributors to the present series come from a variety of theological traditions and that they do not all have identical views with regard to the proper implementation of these general principles. In the end, all that really matters is whether the series succeeds in representing the original text accurately, clearly, and meaningfully to the contemporary reader.

Shading has been used to assist the reader in locating salient sections of the treatment of each passage: introductory comments and concluding summaries. Textual variants in the Greek text are signaled in the author's translation by means of half-brackets around the relevant word or phrase (e.g., ⌜Gerasenes⌝), thereby alerting the reader to turn to the additional notes at the end of each exegetical unit for a discussion of the textual problem. The documentation uses the author-date method, in which the basic reference consists of author's surname + year + page number(s): Fitzmyer 1992: 58. The only exceptions to this system are well-known reference works (e.g., BDAG, LSJ, *TDNT*). Full publication data and a complete set of indexes can be found at the end of the volume.

Robert Yarbrough
Robert H. Stein

Author's Preface

Most commentators have agreed that 2 Corinthians, this letter of the apostle's broken yet buoyed heart, presents a work on which a commentator can easily break his or her heart and head. With good reason, in the preface to his Word Biblical Commentary, Martin (1986: x) describes it as "both the paradise and the despair of the commentator," and Danker (1988: 550–51), one of Martin's reviewers, laments, "A modern interpreter has about as much chance to comprehend all the nuances in 2 Corinthians as an Amish farmer to comprehend a Doonesbury comic strip." Certainly, 2 Corinthians can seem to be an exegetical quarry with luminous veins of gold surrounded by almost impenetrable rock. Thus those who take up the book must do so, to borrow wording from Paul's hardship list in chapter 6, "in great endurance; in troubles, hardships and distresses; even in exegetical beatings, interpretive imprisonments and emotional riots." Indeed, walking with Paul in these pages must be done "in hard work, sleepless nights and hunger for understanding" (cf. 2 Cor. 6:4–5). As noted by Furnish (1984: 3), "No Pauline letter requires more of its readers," but he adds encouragingly that no Pauline letter "offers more of a reward to those who apply themselves carefully to its interpretation." Here we have a good reason for taking up the study of this difficult book. The pain brings a reward.

Yet there are various ways to "apply" oneself to the interpretation of 2 Corinthians and many good tools with which to do so, which presses a question, voiced by a lady at church just last week: "Why another commentary on 2 Corinthians?" especially with so many outstanding commentaries already on the shelf? It is a good question, and in various forms the question has become a cliché among commentators on biblical books, has it not? We seek to justify our efforts. But for me, on many mornings over the past few years, as I have stared alternately at the Greek text, an open commentary, and the computer screen, it has been a very personal question. I have reached the age at which giving a significant portion of my life to any project is not done lightly— "Teach us to number our days" (Ps. 90:12 NIV). Furthermore, work on this book in particular took me away from my normal paths of deeper research on the New Testament. In other words, I had a lot of work to do just to get up to speed on basic discussions surrounding such a wonderfully complex letter—and the contours of this letter in particular don't lend themselves to easygoing! Nevertheless, at the end of the journey I am deeply grateful to Baker Academic not only for inviting me to this project but also for being exorbitantly patient while waiting for its completion. I am thankful to make it through the process for many reasons, but I will mention three.

First, I needed to study 2 Corinthians in greater depth for my own growth, understanding, and edification. To attempt to teach is to learn. To articulate, one must grapple. Although I will spend the rest of my life trying to grasp all the nuances, those elusive subtleties Danker mentions above, the commentary has been a good beginning for me personally, and I hope that other beginners will join me in the journey of discovery. I also hope to delve more deeply into this book in the years to come. In line with the BECNT series, I have worked from the Greek text of the NT, and I normally have begun with my own exegesis and translation before taking up secondary literature, although my exegesis and translation have been informed and constantly adjusted on the basis of the excellent body of literature we now have on the book. My dialogue partners have consisted of a core of commentators and analysts, primarily from the English-speaking world, as well as pertinent primary sources from the Second Temple period, whom I thought would be at least somewhat accessible and helpful to most educated pastors. I make no claim to have covered all the bases on each passage. Even with the generous concessions of my editors, I constantly fought the battle between depth and word count, and too often word count won. It astounds me that one could write a commentary of this length and still live primarily in what seems "the shallows," merely skimming the surface of what needs to be addressed! Thus my hope is that the commentary will serve its readers as it has served me—that it will offer a helpful beginning track, a starting point, for a lifelong study of this rich and complex book.

Second, in spite of the wealth of scholarly resources we now have at our disposal, 2 Corinthians needs and rewards continued study. While not rivaling its older sister, 1 Corinthians, the past four decades have witnessed an increasingly rich flow of rigorous and reflective commentaries, stimulating monographs, and insightful articles on this "second" (which most think is actually the fourth) letter to ancient Corinth. Commentaries like those by Thrall, Harris, Barnett, and Furnish are erudite and expansive, inviting pastors and other students of the Word to a veritable word feast on this book. Yet as I hope to demonstrate at points in this volume, all that could be said has not been said: a fresh look at certain interpretive issues in 2 Corinthians can contribute to a needed, ongoing conversation. This is a great joy in biblical studies—we are always learning and discovering, and that process takes place in community and, at times, amid a cacophony of voices, some barking a bit against particular assumptions expressed by others. I am thankful to have invested time in this project because, at least in a modest way and at least at a few key junctures, I think I have something to say and want to contribute to the conversation. For instance, my interpretations of 2 Cor. 2:14–16 and 3:7–18—both sticky interpretive wickets in their own ways and massively important to Paul's message—attempt to offer pertinent bits of background information that have failed to make it into contemporary discussions. Thus

I hope in some small way to stir up the interpretive pot, not for the sake of novelty but to vie for a fresh reflection on Paul's thought and intended impact.

Third, and in some ways most important, we in the modern church desperately need 2 Corinthians. Barrett (1982: 1) has noted, "If Romans gives us the most systematic presentation of Paul's theology, it is nevertheless from the Corinthian Epistles that we gain the most complete and many-sided picture of how Paul believed that his theological convictions should be expressed in the life of a church." Consequently, we need to hear 2 Corinthians, know it, and take it very seriously as we reflect on how Christian ministry is to be done in the world. Sitting at the feet of this apostle at this painful, critical juncture in his ministry, we find theological and pastoral rhetoric of great beauty and breathtaking depth pouring from a treasure-laden-though-cracked vessel. Harris (2008: 434) has declared that 2 Corinthians, though not normally bearing the label, should be considered "the pastoral epistle *par excellence*." I agree, for the words of 2 Corinthians embody a pastoral strategy, both elegant and wise, that seeks to draw a wandering congregation close, close to their apostle and his mission, and thus close to the true gospel and the true Christ.

And the words draw us. At times and places in the twenty-first century, we the church are wanderers, false teachers, faithful or faithless sufferers, fellow-workers with Paul, disillusioned ministers or congregations, opponents of the true gospel, polished and competitive and powerful public speakers, or powerless leaders who long for status and popularity and social significance like a dehydrated, dying person longs for water. Especially in the American church, we too easily drift into ruts of power, posturing, position, and presentation as the pragmatic backbone of ministerial effectiveness, and 2 Corinthians offers a sobering, loud, cautionary voice against such an approach to ministry. Further, the cultural climate of power and presentation often finds many faithful pastors emotionally battered and burdened under their own perceived limitations. Others face real persecution, brought to bear in various manifestations, and are exhausted emotionally and physically. Thus my hope and prayer is that what is written here may be used to give strong encouragement to those in ministry who find themselves deeply discouraged by opposition in its various forms.

Many people deserve thanks for their parts in bringing this book to completion. I deeply appreciate Moisés Silva, former editor of the series, for the initial invitation, and Bob Yarbrough has served as an encouraging and competent editor in coaching me through to the end. Baker's Jim Kinney has been wonderfully gracious and patient in the face of too many delays, and Wells Turner, the technical editor at the publishing house, has been ever quick to respond, generous in his direction, and encouraging with feedback.

My administrators at Union University, including President David Dockery (now president of Trinity International University), Provost Carla Sanderson, and Dean Gregory Thornbury (now president of The King's College, New York), have always been great encouragers of my work and have a clear-eyed vision for rigorous academic work done for kingdom purposes; further, they facilitate the space needed to get that work done. In addition the university committee granting research leaves has granted me leaves at two critical stages of the commentary—the very beginning and the very end—for which I am deeply thankful. I have taken both of those leaves at Tyndale House in Cambridge, England. As I sit now at desk 14, surrounded by one of the top biblical studies libraries in the world and looking out on a beautiful summer day, I am deeply grateful to be here. The staff and community of Tyndale House embody the work of biblical studies done in community, for the church, to God's glory and the advancement of his cause in the world. My own Christian community too, Northbrook Church, has prayed for me, encouraged me, and treated my ministry as an extension of its own.

Finally, I must express special gratitude to my wonderful family. My children, Joshua and Anna, have grown up as I have written this commentary; they have been interested, supportive, and my partners in play. Anticipating meals out or movies or even just walks around the yard has gotten me through some days that demanded raw diligence in the books. And words for my Pat fail me. Partner in all ministries. Best friend. Deepest love, save One. Thank you, dear wife, for your wonderfully substantive part in this project. As these "tents" continue to fray, may we never give up, may our inner persons be renewed day after day, and may we be pleasing to him until what is mortal is swallowed up by life (2 Cor. 4:16–5:5).

George H. Guthrie
Tyndale House
Cambridge, England
August 2013

Abbreviations

Bibliographic and General

//	parallel
א	Codex Sinaiticus
A	Codex Alexandrinus
acc.	accusative case
AD	*anno Domini*, in the year of the Lord
ANRW	*Aufstieg und Niedergang der römischen Welt: Geschichte und Kultur Roms im Spiegel der neueren Forschung*, edited by H. Temporini and W. Haase, part 2: *Principat*, 7.1 (Berlin/New York: de Gruyter, 1979)
ASV	American Standard Version
b.	Babylonian Talmud
B	Codex Vaticanus
BC	before Christ
BDAG	*A Greek-English Lexicon of the New Testament and Other Early Christian Literature*, by W. Bauer, F. W. Danker, W. F. Arndt, and F. W. Gingrich, 3rd ed. (Chicago: University of Chicago Press, 2000)
BDF	*A Greek Grammar of the New Testament and Other Early Christian Literature*, by F. Blass and A. Debrunner, translated and revised by R. W. Funk (Chicago: University of Chicago Press, 1961)
C.E.	Common Era
cent.	century
CEV	Contemporary English Version
cf.	*confer*, compare
chap(s).	chapter(s)
CIJ	*Corpus inscriptionum judaicarum* (Rome, 1936–)
CNTUOT	*Commentary on the New Testament Use of the Old Testament*, edited by G. K. Beale and D. A. Carson (Grand Rapids: Baker Academic/Nottingham, UK: Apollos, 2007)
Darby	Darby Translation, by John Nelson Darby (1890)
DBI	*Dictionary of Biblical Imagery*, edited by L. Ryken, J. Wilhoit, and T. Longman (Downers Grove, IL: InterVarsity, 1998)
DJBP	*Dictionary of Judaism in the Biblical Period*, edited by J. Neusner and W. S. Green (New York: Macmillan Library Reference, 1996)
DJG	*Dictionary of Jesus and the Gospels*, edited by J. B. Green, S. McKnight, and I. H. Marshall (Downers Grove, IL: InterVarsity Press, 1992)
DNTB	*Dictionary of New Testament Backgrounds*, edited by C. A. Evans and S. E. Porter (Downers Grove, IL: InterVarsity, 2000)
DPL	*Dictionary of Paul and His Letters*, edited by G. F. Hawthorne and R. P. Martin (Downers Grove, IL: InterVarsity, 1993)
EDNT	*Exegetical Dictionary of the New Testament*, edited by H. Balz and G. Schneider, 3 vols. (Grand Rapids: Eerdmans, 1990–93)

e.g.	*exempli gratia*, for example
esp.	especially
ET(s)	English translation(s) or versification
ESV	English Standard Version
fig(s).	figure(s)
frg(s).	fragment(s)
GELNT	*Greek-English Lexicon of the New Testament: Based on Semantic Domains*, by J. P. Louw and E. A. Nida, 2nd ed., 2 vols. (New York: United Bible Society, 1999)
Geneva	Geneva Bible (1599)
GNT	Good News Translation
Goodspeed	*The Bible: An American Translation*, by J. M. P. Smith and E. J. Goodspeed (Chicago: University of Chicago Press, 1931)
hapax	hapax legomenon, a term occurring only once
HBD	*Holman Bible Dictionary*, edited by T. Butler (Nashville: Holman Bible Publishers, 1991)
HCSB	Holman Christian Standard Bible
h.t.	homoeoteleuton (omitting text due to similar endings nearby)
i.e.	*id est*, that is
KJV	King James Version
Knox	Knox Version, translated from the Latin Vulgate by Ronald Knox
LEH	*Greek-English Lexicon of the Septuagint*, compiled by J. Lust, E. Eynikel, and K. Hauspie, rev. ed. (Stuttgart: Deutsche Bibelgesellschaft, 2003)
lit.	literally
LSJ	*A Greek-English Lexicon*, by H. G. Liddell, R. Scott, and H. S. Jones, 9th ed. (Oxford: Oxford University Press, 1940)
LSJSup	*Greek-English Lexicon Revised Supplement*, edited by P. G. W. Glare and A. A. Thompson (Oxford: Clarendon, 1996)
LXX	Septuagint (the Old Testament in Greek)
m.	Mishnah
𝔐	majority text
Message	Eugene H. Peterson, *The Message* (Colorado Springs: NavPress Publishing Group, 1993–2004)
Moffatt	James Moffatt, *The Bible: A New Translation* (1926, 1935)
MS(S)	manuscript(s)
MT	Masoretic Text
NA[27]	*Novum Testamentum Graece*, edited by Eberhard Nestle, Erwin Nestle, B. Aland, K. Aland, J. Karavidopoulos, C. M. Martini, and B. M. Metzger, 27th ed. (Stuttgart: Deutsche Bibelgesellschaft, 1993)
NA[28]	*Novum Testamentum Graece*, edited by Eberhard Nestle, Erwin Nestle, B. Aland, K. Aland, J. Karavidopoulos, C. M. Martini, and B. M. Metzger, 28th ed. (Stuttgart: Deutsche Bibelgesellschaft, 2012)
NAB	New American Bible
NASB	New American Standard Bible (1960–77)
NASB[95]	New American Standard Bible (1995)
NBD	*New Bible Dictionary*, edited by J. D. Douglas, D. R. W. Wood, N. Hillyer, and I. H. Marshall (Leicester, UK/Downers Grove, IL: InterVarsity, 1996)
NDBT	*New Dictionary of Biblical Theology*, edited by T. D. Alexander and B. S. Rosner (Downers Grove, IL: InterVarsity, 2000)

NEB	New English Bible
NET	New English Translation
NETS	*A New English Translation of the Septuagint*, edited by A. Pietersma and B. G. Wright (New York: Oxford University Press, 2007; 2nd, corrected printing, 2009, http://ccat.sas.upenn.edu/nets/edition/)
NewDocs	*New Documents Illustrating Early Christianity: A Review of the Greek Inscriptions and Papyri Published in 1976*, edited by G. H. R. Horsley (North Ryde, NSW: Ancient History Documentary Research Centre, Macquarie University, 1981–)
NIDNTT	*The New International Dictionary of New Testament Theology*, edited by C. Brown and D. Townsley (Exeter, Devon, UK: Paternoster, 1986)
NIV⁸⁴	New International Version (1973, 1978, 1984)
NIV	New International Version (2011)
NKJV	New King James Version
NLT	New Living Translation (1996)
NLT²	New Living Translation, 2nd ed. (2004, 2007)
*NPNF*¹	*Nicene and Post-Nicene Fathers of the Christian Church*, edited by P. Schaff, first series, 14 vols. (repr., Grand Rapids: Eerdmans, 1952–57)
NRSV	New Revised Standard Version
n.s.	new series
NT	New Testament
OT	Old Testament
OTP	*The Old Testament Pseudepigrapha*, edited by J. H. Charlesworth, 2 vols. (Garden City, NY: Doubleday, 1983–85)
𝔓	papyrus, as for 𝔓⁴⁶
PG	Patrologia graeca, edited by J.-P. Migne, 161 vols. (Paris, 1857–66)
Phillips	*The New Testament in Modern English* (J. B. Phillips, 1958, 1973)
pl.	plural
pp.	pages
P.Cair.Zen.	*Zenon Papyri: Catalogue général des antiquités égyptiennes du Musée du Caire*, edited by C. C. Edgar (Cairo: Inst. Français d'Archéologie Orientale, 1925–)
P.Mich.	*Michigan Papyri*, vol. 1: *Zenon Papyri*, edited by C. C. Edgar (Ann Arbor, 1931)
P.Oxf.	*Some Oxford Papyri*, edited by E. P. Wegener (Leiden: Brill, 1942–48)
P.Oxy.	*The Oxyrhynchus Papyri* (London: Egypt Exploration Society in Graeco-Roman Memoirs, 1898–)
P.Ryl.	*Catalogue of the Greek and Latin Papyri in the John Rylands Library, Manchester* (Manchester: Manchester University Press, 1911–52)
P.Sorb.	*Papyrus de la Sorbonne*, vol. 1, edited by H. Cadell (Paris 1966)
P.Stras.	*Griechische Papyrus der Kaiserlichen Universitäts- und Landesbibliothek zu Strassburg*, edited by F. Preisigke (Leipzig: Hinrichs, 1906–).
REB	Revised English Bible
RSV	Revised Standard Version
t.	Tosefta
TCNT	Twentieth Century New Testament (1904)
TDNT	*Theological Dictionary of the New Testament*, edited by G. Kittel and G. Friedrich, translated and edited by G. W. Bromiley, 10 vols. (Grand Rapids: Eerdmans, 1964–76)
Tg.	Targum

Theod.	Theodotion (version of the Greek Old Testament)
TNIV	Today's New International Version
Tyndale	Tyndale Bible, translated by William Tyndale (16th cent.)
UBS[4]	*The Greek New Testament*, edited by B. Aland et al., 4th rev. ed. (Stuttgart: Deutsche Bibelgesellschaft, 1994)
v(v).	verse(s)
v.l.	*vario lectio* (variant reading)
Voice	*The Voice Bible* (Nashville: Nelson, 2012)
Webster	Noah Webster's limited revision of KJV (1833)
Williams	C. B. Williams, *The New Testament: A Translation in the Language of the People* (Boston: Bruce Humphries, 1937; rev. ed., Chicago: Moody, 1950)
x	times (e.g., 2x = two times)
YLT	Young's Literal Translation

Hebrew Bible

Gen.	Genesis	2 Chron.	2 Chronicles	Dan.	Daniel
Exod.	Exodus	Ezra	Ezra	Hosea	Hosea
Lev.	Leviticus	Neh.	Nehemiah	Joel	Joel
Num.	Numbers	Esther	Esther	Amos	Amos
Deut.	Deuteronomy	Job	Job	Obad.	Obadiah
Josh.	Joshua	Ps(s).	Psalm(s)	Jon.	Jonah
Judg.	Judges	Prov.	Proverbs	Mic.	Micah
Ruth	Ruth	Eccles.	Ecclesiastes	Nah.	Nahum
1 Sam.	1 Samuel	Song	Song of Songs	Hab.	Habakkuk
2 Sam.	2 Samuel	Isa.	Isaiah	Zeph.	Zephaniah
1 Kings	1 Kings	Jer.	Jeremiah	Hag.	Haggai
2 Kings	2 Kings	Lam.	Lamentations	Zech.	Zechariah
1 Chron.	1 Chronicles	Ezek.	Ezekiel	Mal.	Malachi

Greek Testament

Matt.	Matthew	Eph.	Ephesians	Heb.	Hebrews
Mark	Mark	Phil.	Philippians	James	James
Luke	Luke	Col.	Colossians	1 Pet.	1 Peter
John	John	1 Thess.	1 Thessalonians	2 Pet.	2 Peter
Acts	Acts	2 Thess.	2 Thessalonians	1 John	1 John
Rom.	Romans	1 Tim.	1 Timothy	2 John	2 John
1 Cor.	1 Corinthians	2 Tim.	2 Timothy	3 John	3 John
2 Cor.	2 Corinthians	Titus	Titus	Jude	Jude
Gal.	Galatians	Philem.	Philemon	Rev.	Revelation

Josephus

Ant.   *Jewish Antiquities*   *J.W.*   *Jewish War*

Philo

Abr.	Abraham	*Migr.*	The Migration of Abraham
Agr.	Agriculture	*Mos.*	The Life of Moses
Alleg.	Allegorical Interpretation	*Plant.*	Planting
Cher.	The Cherubim	*Post.*	The Posterity of Cain
Conf.	Confusion of Tongues	*Prelim. Studies*	The Preliminary Studies
Contempl.	The Contemplative Life		
Creat.	Creation of the World	*Prov.*	Providence
Decal.	The Decalogue	*QG*	Questions and Answers on Genesis
Drunk.	Drunkenness		
Emb.	Embassy to Gaius	*Rewards*	Rewards and Punishments
Etern.	The Eternity of the World	*Sacr.*	Sacrifices of Cain and Abel
Flight	Flight and Finding	*Spec. Laws*	The Special Laws
Good Free	That Every Good Person Is Free	*Unchang.*	God Is Unchangeable
		Virt.	On the Virtues
Jos.	The Life of Joseph	*Worse*	That the Worse Attacks the Better

Rabbinic Tractates

The abbreviations below are used for the names of the tractates in the Mishnah (indicated by a prefixed *m.*), Tosefta (*t.*), Babylonian Talmud (*b.*), and Palestinian/Jerusalem Talmud (*y.*).

Ber.	Berakot
Mak.	Makkot
Šeqal.	Šeqalim
Yeb.	Yebamot

Qumran/Dead Sea Scrolls

1QH	Hodayot (Thanksgiving Hymns)
1QM	Milḥamah (War Scroll)
1QS	Rule of the Community (1QS)
1QSa	Rule of the Community (1Q28a)
4QM	4Q491 (War Scroll variant; cf. 1QM)
4Q174	4QFlorilegium
4Q504	4QWords of the Luminaries

Other Jewish and Christian Writings

Add. Dan.	Additions to Daniel
Add. Esth.	Additions to Esther
Apoc. Mos.	Apocalypse of Moses
Bar.	Baruch
2 Bar.	2 Baruch (Syriac Apocalypse)
3 Bar.	3 Baruch (Greek Apocalypse)

1 Clem.	1 Clement
Comm. 2 Cor.	Pelagius, *Commentary on the Second Epistle to the Corinthians*
Comm. 2 Cor.	Theodoret of Cyr, *Commentary on the Second Epistle to the Corinthians*
Comm. Paul's Ep.	Ambrosiaster, *Commentary on Paul's Epistles*
Deut. Rab.	Deuteronomy Rabbah
Eccl. Hist.	Eusebius, *Ecclesiastical History*
1 En.	1 Enoch (Ethiopic Apocalypse)
2 En.	2 Enoch (Slavonic Apocalypse)
Ep.	*Epistle/Letter*, by the named author
1 Esd.	1 Esdras (in the Apocrypha)
2 Esd.	2 Esdras (= 4 Ezra)
Exod. Rab.	Exodus Rabbah
Gen. Rab.	Genesis Rabbah
Hom. 2 Cor.	John Chrysostom, *Homilies on 2 Corinthians*
Hom. Gen.	John Chrysostom, *Homilies on Genesis*
Hom. Heb.	John Chrysostom, *Homilies on Hebrews*
Hom. in 2 Cor. 11:1	John Chrysostom, *Homily on 2 Corinthians 11:1*
Hom. Lev.	Origen, *Homily on Leviticus*
Jdt.	Judith
Jos. Asen.	Joseph and Aseneth
Jub.	Jubilees
Let. Aris.	Letter of Aristeas
Let. Jer.	Letter of Jeremiah (= Bar. 6)
1–4 Macc.	1–4 Maccabees
Midr. Tadshe	Midrash Tadshe
Odes	Odes of the Greek Church et al. (in Rahlfs, *Septuaginta*, vol. 2)
Ord. Levi	Ordinances of Levi
Pr. Azar.	Prayer of Azariah (Odes 7)
Pr. Man.	Prayer of Manasseh (Odes 12)
Pss. Sol.	Psalms of Solomon
Sg. Mos. Deut.	Song of Moses in Deuteronomy (Odes 1)
Sib. Or.	Sibylline Oracles
Sipre Deut.	Sipre Deuteronomy
Sir.	Sirach (Ecclesiasticus)
T. Ab.	Testament of Abraham
T. Iss.	Testament of Issachar
T. Job	Testament of Job
T. Jud.	Testament of Judah
T. Levi	Testament of Levi
T. Naph.	Testament of Naphtali
T. Reu.	Testament of Reuben
T. Sim.	Testament of Simeon
T. Sol.	Testament of Solomon
Tob.	Tobit
Wis.	Wisdom of Solomon

Classical Writers

Aem.	Plutarch, *Aemilius Paullus*
Ages.	Plutarch, *Agesilaus*
Agr.	Cicero, *On the Agrarian Law*
Alex.	Plutarch, *Alexander*
Ant.	Plutarch, *Antonius*
Antid.	Isocrates, *Antidosis (Oration 15)*
Aph.	Hippocrates, *Aphorisms*
Apoph. lac.	Plutarch, *Apophthegmata laconica*
Arch.	Cicero, *Pro Archia*
Att.	Cicero, *Epistles to Atticus*
Bell. civ.	Appian, *Civil Wars*
Bell. Mith.	Appian, *Mithridatic Wars* (in *Roman History*)
Ben.	Seneca, *Benefits*
Brut.	Cicero, *Brutus*
Caes.	Plutarch, *Caesar*
Cat. Maj.	Plutarch, *Cato the Elder*
Cat. Min.	Plutarch, *Cato the Younger*
Catullus	Catullus, *Poems*
Cic.	Plutarch, *Cicero*
Cleom.	Plutarch, *Cleomenes*
Comp. Pel. Marc.	Plutarch, *Comparatio Pelopidae et Marcelli*
Comp. Thes. Rom.	Plutarch, *Comparatio Thesei et Romuli*
Controv.	Seneca the Elder, *Controversies*
Cor.	Demosthenes, *On the Crown*
Cor.	Plutarch, *Marcius Coriolanus*
Crass.	Plutarch, *Crassus*
Cyn. Ep.	Diogenes of Sinope (?), *Cynic Epistles*
Cyr.	Xenophon, *Cyropaedia (The Education of Cyrus)*
De or.	Cicero, *De oratore (The Orator)*
De pace	Demosthenes, *De pace (On the Peace)*
De re milit.	Vegetius, *De re militari (On Military Matters)*
Dep. Schol.	Lucian of Samosata, *The Dependent Scholar*
Dial.	Tacitus, *Dialogues*
Disc.	*Discourses*, by the named author
Ep.	*Epistle/Letter*, by the named author
Ep.	Seneca, *Moral Epistles*
Epid.	Hippocrates, *Epidemics*
Fab.	Plutarch, *Fabius Maximus*
False Emb.	Demosthenes, *False Embassy*
Fam.	Cicero, *Epistulae ad familiares (Letters to Friends)*
Flam.	Plutarch, *Titus Flamininus*
Fug.	Lucian of Samosata, *Fugitivi (The Runaways)*
Geogr.	Strabo, *Geography*
Gymn.	Philostratus, *Gymnastica (Gymnastics)*
Hell.	Xenophon, *Hellenica*

Hermot.	Lucian of Samosata, *Hermotimus* (*Rival Philosophies*)
Hist.	Herodotus, *Histories*
Hist.	Polybius, *The Histories*
Hist. Rom.	Livy, *History of Rome*
Inst.	Quintilian, *Institutio oratoria* (*The Orator's Education*)
Issues	Hermogenes of Tarsus, *Legal Issues* (*Staseis*)
Jupp. trag.	Lucian of Samosata, *Juppiter tragoedus* (*Zeus Rants*)
Leg.	Plato, *Leges* (*Laws*)
Leg. Man.	Cicero, *Pro Lege Manilia*
Leis.	Seneca the Younger, *To Serenus on Leisure*
Libyca	Appian, *Carthaginian Affairs* (in *Roman History*)
Lucil.	Seneca the Younger, *Moral Letters to Lucilius*
Lyc.	Hyperides, *Pro Lycophrone*
Mach.	Athenaeus Mechanicus, *On Machines*
Mar.	Plutarch, *Marius*
Marc.	Porphyry, *Letter to His Wife, Marcella*
Max. princ.	Plutarch, *Maxime cum principibus philosophiam esse*
Med.	Marcus Aurelius, *Meditations*
Mor.	Plutarch, *Moralia*
Mulier. virt.	Plutarch, *Mulierum virtutes* (*The Virtues of Women*)
Nat.	Pliny the Elder, *Natural History*
Nub.	Aristophanes, *Nubes* (*Clouds*)
Off.	Cicero, *De officiis* (*On Duties*)
1–3 Olynth.	Demosthenes, *1–3 Olynthiac*
Op.	Hesiod, *Opera et dies* (*Works and Days*)
Or.	*Orations/Speeches*, by the named author
Pel. War	Thucydides, *Peloponnesian War*
Phil.	Diogenes Laertius, *Lives of Eminent Philosophers*
Phoen.	Euripides, *Phoenician Maidens*
Plac. philos.	Pseudo-Plutarch, *Placita philosophorum* (*Opinions of Philosophers*)
Plat. Q.	Plutarch, *Platonic Questions*
Pol.	Aristotle, *Politics*
Pol.	Plato, *Politicus* (*Statesman*)
Pomp.	Plutarch, *Pompeius*
Pun.	Appian, *Punic Wars*
Pyth. Life	Iamblichus, *Life of Pythagoras*
Quaest. conv.	Plutarch, *Quaestionum convivialium libri IX*
Quaest. nat.	Plutarch, *Quaestiones naturales*
Quint. fratr.	Cicero, *Letters to His Brother Quintus*
Rect. rat. aud.	*Plutarch, De recta ratione audiendi* (*Listening to Lectures*)
Regum	Plutarch, *Sayings of Kings and Commanders*
Rep.	Cicero, *The Republic*
Res. gest.	Augustus, *Res gestae divi Augusti* (memorial inscription)
Resp.	Plato, *Respublica* (*Republic*)
Rhet.	Aristotle, *Rhetoric*

Rhet. praec.	Lucian of Samosata, *Rhetorum praeceptor* (*Professor of Public Speaking*)
Rom. Ant.	Dionysius of Halicarnassus, *Roman Antiquities*
Rom. Q.	Plutarch, *Roman and Greek Questions*
Sat.	Juvenal, *Satires*
Sert.	Plutarch, *Sertorius*
Soll. an.	Plutarch, *De sollertia animalium* (*On the Intelligence of Animals*)
Symp.	Xenophon, *Symposium*
Ti. C. Gracch.	Plutarch, *Tiberius et Caius Gracchus*
Tib.	Suetonius, *Tiberius*
Val. Max.	Valerius Maximus, *Memorable Deeds and Sayings*
Verr.	Cicero, *The Verrine Orations*

Transliteration

Hebrew

א	ʾ	בָ	ā	qāmeṣ
ב	b	בַ	a	pataḥ
ג	g	הַ	a	furtive pataḥ
ד	d	בֶ	e	sĕgōl
ה	h	בֵ	ē	ṣērē
ו	w	בִ	i	short ḥîreq
ז	z	בִ	ī	long ḥîreq written defectively
ח	ḥ	בָ	o	qāmeṣ ḥāṭûp
ט	ṭ	בוֹ	ō	ḥōlem written fully
י	y	בֹ	ō	ḥōlem written defectively
כ/ךְ	k	בוּ	û	šûreq
ל	l	בֻ	u	short qibbûṣ
מ/ם	m	בֻ	ū	long qibbûṣ written defectively
נ/ן	n	בָה	â	final qāmeṣ hē ʾ (בָה = āh)
ס	s	בֶי	ē	sĕgōl yōd (בֶי = ēy)
ע	ʿ	בֵי	ē	ṣērē yōd (בֵי = ēy)
פ/ף	p	בִי	î	ḥîreq yōd (בִי = îy)
צ/ץ	ṣ	בֲ	ă	ḥāṭēp pataḥ
ק	q	בֱ	ĕ	ḥāṭēp sĕgōl
ר	r	בֳ	ŏ	ḥāṭēp qāmeṣ
שׂ	ś	בְ	ĕ	vocal šĕwāʾ
שׁ	š			
ת	t			

Notes on the Transliteration of Hebrew

1. Accents are not shown in transliteration.
2. Silent šĕwāʾ is not indicated in transliteration.
3. The spirant forms ב ג ד כ פ ת are usually not specially indicated in transliteration.
4. Dāgēš forte is indicated by doubling the consonant. Euphonic dāgēš and dāgēš lene are not indicated in transliteration.
5. Maqqēp is represented by a hyphen.

Greek

α	*a*	ζ	*z*	λ	*l*	π	*p*	φ	*ph*
β	*b*	η	*ē*	μ	*m*	ρ	*r*	χ	*ch*
γ	*g/n*	θ	*th*	ν	*n*	σ/ς	*s*	ψ	*ps*
δ	*d*	ι	*i*	ξ	*x*	τ	*t*	ω	*ō*
ε	*e*	κ	*k*	ο	*o*	υ	*y/u*	ʽ	*h*

Notes on the Transliteration of Greek

1. Accents, lenis (smooth breathing), and *iota* subscript are not shown in transliteration.
2. The transliteration of asper (rough breathing) precedes a vowel or diphthong (e.g., ἁ = *ha*; αἱ = *hai*) and follows ρ (i.e., ῥ = *rh*).
3. *Gamma* is transliterated *n* only when it precedes γ, κ, ξ, or χ.
4. *Upsilon* is transliterated *u* only when it is part of a diphthong (i.e., αυ, ευ, ου, υι).

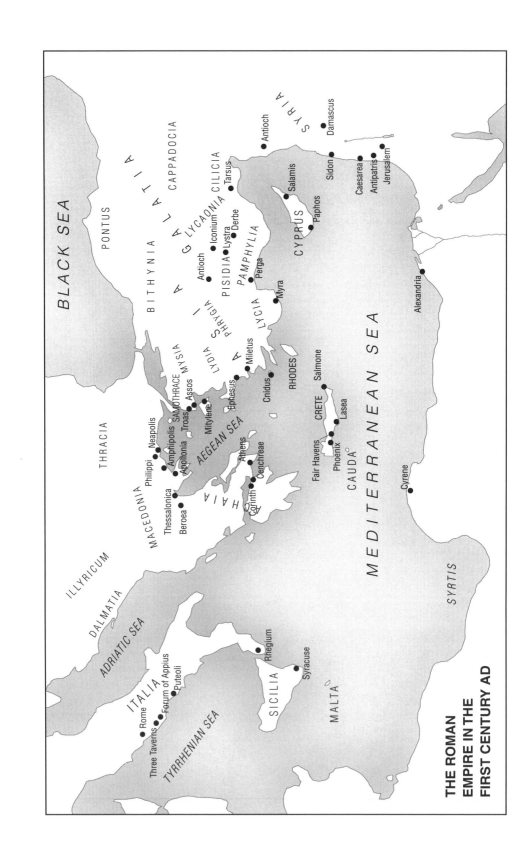

THE ROMAN
EMPIRE IN THE
FIRST CENTURY AD

Introduction to 2 Corinthians

In a monograph on 1 Corinthians, Stephen Pogoloff (1992: 273) writes, "As historians, we search for clues to further enrich and constrain our imaginations in order to revise our narrative both to satisfy our critical convictions and to provide more meaningful readings of the text." Normally, the introduction to a critical commentary seeks to organize such "clues" around topics such as authorship, date, destination, and structure—presenting the facts, or at least reasonable speculations, offered by scholars toward a more intelligible reading of the text. "And this we will do if God permits." But I want to start our study by inviting you into an imaginative reading of the story behind 2 Corinthians, a story grounded in the data both *behind* (the cultural and historical backdrop of Corinth) and *within* the biblical book. Pogoloff's words describe the "historical" dimensions of this bit of historical fiction, which I'm using to serve a pedagogical purpose by pulling us into Corinth of the mid-first century, a place of vivid sights and smells, powerful cultural dynamics, and heated relational tensions. In the balance of the introduction, we will sort out which aspects of the narrative rest on a firm historical footing, but for now, enter with me into the world of Paul's Corinth.

As he stepped onto the gravel of the Lechaeum road, heading south from the Asclepion back to the forum, Stephanas was still a bit rattled by the meeting, not used to such a confrontational discussion with such a powerful man. "Why in the world does Lucius want to meet at the Asclepion?" his wife, Alba, had wondered that morning as they had breakfast in the garden. From the slight rise on which their Craneum neighborhood sat, the view of Corinth spread out before them in all its vastness like a giant patchwork quilt draping the landscape, flowing down to the Lechaeum port.

Stephanas loved this city. It was flourishing, and his business had flourished along with it. The wild mix of travelers, tourists, merchants from all of the world, ports crammed with exotic goods, new buildings going up as the great men tried to outdo each other, their wonderful, plentiful baths and springs, their enviable sewage system. . . . Horace had written, "It is not the privilege of every man to visit Corinth."[1] But here Stephanas lived. He perhaps was not one of the elite, but as a successful merchant Stephanas felt great pride in this wealthy city of thousands. There were the desperately poor, of course,

---

1. Horace, *Ep.* 17.36.

a number of them now associated with the church, but opportunities for the population generally were greater in Corinth than in most places. And since Paul had come with the gospel, Stephanas saw his place and his prosperity—his purpose in the world—in a very new light.

Of course Stephanas knew why Lucius Domitius Felix had chosen the Asclepion. It was a lovely place, the complex dedicated to the healing god. Stephanas had attended weddings there from time to time. Out from the city center and near the northern wall, the temple grounds were beautifully groomed, comfortable, and quiet. But there was more. It was an obvious way of pushing back, not even a veiled attempt at pushing back. When Paul's letter had arrived last year, Lucius had heard it read and then read it himself. In that letter the apostle had answered many of the church's pressing questions, including the one about eating meat from a temple. So Lucius was quite aware of Paul's perspective. The Asclepion was a nice place to eat, of course, one of the nicest in the city. But the temple meat roasting in that temple was not the draw for Lucius. No. The Asclepion was a defiant retreat of sorts at which to talk about Lucius's ongoing "concerns" about Paul, concerns that had been building ever since the "undignified tentmaker," who "dirtied his hands with manual labor," had refused Lucius's patronage.

So as he kicked gravel along the Lechaeum road, some 400 paces farther into the city's heart, he thought back through the day and how that difficult conversation had unfolded. That morning Stephanas had walked from home to the city center to conduct business before the meeting. Having passed Maximos's tavern on his left, he entered the Forum from the southwest end. He had greeted Erastus briefly. The city treasurer, walking briskly past the area in front of Apollo's and Aphrodite's temples, was on his way to an office in the South Stoa, weaving through a crowd of shoppers, priests, tourists, and merchants heading in all directions. The Forum, almost 200 paces long and some 125 paces deep on the west end, was massive by anyone's estimation, a wide-open space of buzz and bustle. As he continued, Stephanas made a quick stop at a banker in one of the Forum's center shops, and then on to a jeweler to pick up a gift for his daughter Theodora, whose twelfth birthday was coming up on Kalends Octobris (Oct. 1).

He had seen Achaicus and Chloe talking just across the Forum's east end, near the Peirene Fountain. Stephanas made his way over to them and told them about the meeting that was to take place with Lucius, asking for prayer. Each of the three had been staunch defenders of Paul and had spoken out boldly during Titus's recent visit. Following that gut-wrenching letter from Paul, they had drawn most of the house churches firmly to the apostle's side. But none of them embraced the illusion that tensions in the church were laid to rest. Matters were so complex, so difficult to work through, what with people coming and going in the household groups throughout the city and region. The church was still very young, not quite five years old, and the blend of classes, education, cultural backgrounds, personalities, and levels of spiritual maturity could be dynamic but fragile. The majority of the house groups in the city, as well as those from Tenea, Cenchreae, and Cromna, resolutely made a fresh commitment to the apostle and his mission. Unfortunately, the group at Crommyon had remained cold toward Paul (several who continued in sexually immoral behavior were in that house), as had the small group led by Lucius's steward and, of course, the group of students from the school of Alexandros, among whom was Lucius's oldest son. But generally, the response to Paul's heartrending letter had been positive, and Titus left two weeks later to give the apostle that news.

So this morning, as the sun had climbed toward noon, Stephanas had continued his walk toward the Asclepion, past the North Market and the Theater, out through blocks of shops and homes, finally arriving at his destination. Lucius had reserved a private room and had ordered food. He had with him David and Samuel, "wise professional speakers," as Lucius liked to refer to them, men who had even won some notoriety in rhetor competitions at the games last spring. They and a number of their disciples had arrived from the East two years ago, shortly before Paul had arrived in Ephesus, bringing with them recommendation letters from obscure church leaders back east. Like Apollos, David and Samuel obviously had advanced training in rhetoric; they were good speakers, by most standards of the culture. But unlike the Alexandrian, the content of their "preaching" always seemed "Spiritless," devoid of the gospel message and power. Though words about Jesus and the gospel were used at times, there was no substance to the teaching: no clear doctrine, no ethical foundations for living. Their speaking entertained but did nothing to promote mission, or righteous living, or community. It just seemed to focus mainly on the exalted Jesus as a means of glory, success, and status. Some had been taken in and were increasingly under their harsh influence, and now these impressive public speakers were aligned with Lucius.

The meeting had not gone well. The arguments against Paul, presented by Lucius and the other two, had sounded wonderfully reasonable; Stephanas had heard most of them before. They claimed that the church was acting unwisely, unreasonably. Paul's critics sounded hurt, offended by the apostle's arrogance, his inattention to social conventions, his teachings, and especially his "wishy-washy character." In short, they tagged Paul as a weak, ineffective leader who had brought on the current "crisis" in the church. David and Samuel appealed to Stephanas's Jewish background, a heritage they shared and of which they were very proud. Honestly, Stephanas felt bullied, cowed by the confrontation, glad when the meeting was behind him. Although the majority of the church were firmly committed to the apostle, these pockets of opposition were worrisome; powerful and gifted people were involved.

As he continued now back south, into the city's heart, Stephanas had business at his warehouse that called for his attention. He needed to check on a shipment of Italian lamps that should have arrived in port yesterday, and he wanted Crestus to follow up on an order of glazed bowls from the physician's consortium. Stephanas stopped at the public latrine and felt like visiting the baths, to wash away the tension of the last hour. If only dealing with

Paul's opponents could be so easy! He wished the apostle would come back to Corinth, or at least send another letter.

The danger of labeling something "historical fiction" is that the second word in the designation may be confused for the first—that is, reading fictional elements as historical. So let me sort things out a bit. In the preceding narrative, the descriptions of Corinth and the region to which it belonged are based on solid archaeological evidence, and the cultural climate of Roman Corinth has also been extensively studied by scholars, being drawn from both inscriptional evidence and other primary-source pieces of literature. References to the comings and goings of Paul, Timothy, and Titus—as well as Paul's ongoing correspondence with the Corinthians—are based on statements drawn from Acts, 1 Corinthians, 2 Corinthians, and Romans. As explained below, the exact chronology of Paul's ministry has been greatly debated; attempting to put together the puzzle of his movements and length of stays in various places is a great deal of fun, though beastly difficult at points. Nevertheless, most of the general movements depicted in our narrative and the people involved as Paul's associates, including Achaicus and Chloe, rest on solid footing (if one is willing to accept the Acts accounts as well as the Corinthian Letters as historically reliable).

Erastus normally has been considered a believer, who also was a city official in Corinth, though some scholars have recently questioned whether he was really a believer, suggesting instead that he was simply a high-ranking friend of Paul (Friesen 2010). We know that members of the household of Stephanas were the first to respond to Paul's missionary outreach in the region (1 Cor. 1:16; 16:15) and that Stephanas himself later joined the apostle for a time in Ephesus (1 Cor. 16:17). But beyond the fact that he had a "household" (which may point to a certain level of wealth) and was one of Paul's trusted associates in Corinth, we know nothing. Lucius is a completely fictional character, as are the public speakers, David and Samuel. We know that Paul had opponents in Corinth and have some knowledge of their patterns and concerns, but Paul purposefully does not dignify his opponents by naming them.

Thus the physical and cultural contexts of Corinth, the general development of Paul's interactions with the Corinthians, and the identity of some of his key associates from Corinth all rest upon historical fact. Other elements of my narrative, particularly the situation of Stephanas and Paul's opponents, embody dynamics in the Corinthian church that are hinted at in the NT but remain in the realm of speculation. So having walked the roads of Corinth in our imaginations, let us now discuss the typical introductory matters of this rich and difficult letter, beginning with a closer look at Paul, the letter's author.

Paul in Mid-First Century AD

The Greek term Παῦλος (*Paulos*), "Paul," stands as the first word in ΠΡΟΣ ΚΟΡΙΝΘΙΟΥΣ Β′ (*PROS KORINTHIOUS B*), the letter commonly known as

2 Corinthians. Most consider the letter's authorship to be undisputed, though debate swirls around virtually every other aspect of this complex book's background and content. Over the past two millennia the apostle Paul has been called many things by people, "most of them nasty," according to some (Crossan and Reed 2005: ix). Ernst Renan (1869: 126) famously labeled the apostle an "ugly little Jew." In contradistinction to Jesus, he often has been portrayed as the true "founder of Christianity as a new religion," a perverter of the Jesus movement (Klausner and Stinespring 1946: 303–4). Others have named him "A Radical Jew" (Boyarin 1994: title), "The Fifth Evangelist" (A. Hunter 1980: 1), "the thirteenth witness" (Burchard 1970: 173), the preeminent symbol of early Gentile Christianity (J. Becker 1989: 1), "the first Christian theologian" (Hengel and Schwemer 1997: 1), moreover "the greatest and the most influential of all Christian theologians" (M. Hooker 2003: 150), and even "the man-mountain" around which theologians have walked for centuries, a mountain never scaled (Horrell 2006: 1). Still others have embraced the apostle as an object of deep affection and even love (Bruce 1977: 15); in fact, early church father John Chrysostom confessed, "I love all the saints, but I love most the blessed Paul, the chosen vessel, the heavenly trumpet, the friend of the bridegroom, Christ" (*Hom. in 2 Cor. 11:1* 1 [15.301]).[2]

Second Corinthians presents us with the apostle's most deeply personal book, a book written in the heat and hurt of crisis, and one that delves most deeply into Paul's theology of Christian ministry. When he wrote 2 Corinthians, Paul probably had been a follower of Jesus Christ for a little over two decades. Morna Hooker (2003: 149) reminds us, "To understand Paul, we need to endeavour to see him, as far as is possible, in terms of his own time and situation, and to ask why he felt so passionately about his calling and why he reacted as he did." So let's review a few things about our apostle, moving from his broader context to the matters that define him more specifically, noting especially how these characteristics are reflected in 2 Corinthians.

Man of the Greco-Roman World

First, *Paul was a man of the Greco-Roman world and a citizen of the Roman Empire*. The apostle Paul was a man of his world, a world that had inherited a great many values, perspectives, and its common language from the Greeks, and one that was shaped, in terms of daily existence, by the political structures of the Roman Empire. His ability to communicate in the Greek language and Greek educational values played a part in making the apostle a man who could communicate well, even powerfully, with churches throughout the Mediterranean world, and he primarily used Greek translations of the Jewish Scriptures. But it was the Pax Romana, the "Roman Peace" established under the rule of Augustus, as well as the Roman roads and relatively safe sea travel (during sailing season) that facilitated the establishment of and ongoing communication with those churches.

2. As quoted in Mitchell 2000: 1; on John Chrysostom and Paul, see esp. 1–33.

Via Acts, Paul says that he was born a Roman citizen (22:27–28) and that citizenship protected Paul from certain forms of punishment and afforded him certain rights, which he often seized upon for the advance of the gospel (16:37–38; 22:26–29; 25:10–12; 26:32). In addition, Paul's Roman citizenship may have given him a certain level of credibility with leading men in Corinth, like Erastus (Rom. 16:23), for the city had been established in the previous century by Julius Caesar as a Roman colony, and the Corinthians still prided themselves on their connections to Rome. His citizenship may also have given Paul an advantage when he was brought up on charges by Jewish leaders in Corinth before the proconsul Gallio (Acts 18:12–17), who seems to have legally recognized the Christian movement, in tandem with Judaism, as a *religio licita*, which would have made the church's members exempt from normal imperial religious expectations (Winter 1999).

Acts also tells us that the apostle was a citizen of Tarsus in Cilicia (21:39; 22:3), one of the great educational centers of the world at that time. His upbringing in Tarsus, whose gymnasium was on the Cydnus River, probably gave Paul a grounding in a well-rounded education, perhaps even training in rhetoric (see Witherington 1995: 44–48), a supposition that seems validated in sections of text like 2 Cor. 10–13.[3] Strabo writes that the people of Tarsus had not only committed themselves to philosophy and education, exceeding even Athens and Alexandria, but they also loved learning and often completed their education abroad (*Geogr.* 14.5.12–13), as Paul did (Acts 22:3).

In addition Tarsus was known both for linen woven from flax grown in its fertile plain and for a local material called *cilicium*, woven from goats' hair and used to make materials that offered protection from cold and wet weather (Bruce 1977: 35). Thus the apostle may have learned the craft of tentmaking (Acts 18:3) in his hometown. With this skill the apostle was able to support himself in his travels throughout the Greco-Roman world. As an occupation, tentmaking was quiet, portable, and universally needed (Murphy-O'Connor 1983: 192). Paul would have been able to service people who were traveling by land or ship, hucksters who needed coverings for their wares, and shop owners or city leaders buying awnings for shops or public buildings in various cities around the Mediterranean (Pliny the Elder, *Nat.* 19.23–24). Tentmaking would have been grueling and exhausting work (1 Thess. 2:9; 2 Thess. 3:8), but the craft would also have provided the apostle with opportunities to talk to people and preach the gospel. Paul may have even used his workshop at points as a house church (Murphy-O'Connor 1983: 195–96).[4] At the same

---

3. In most English translations (ETs) of 2 Cor. 11:6, Paul seems to deny that he has had formal training in public speaking. Yet, as explained in the comments on that verse, the word ἰδιώτης (*idiōtēs*, amateur) could be used to speak of those trained in rhetoric, who for the good of the community choose not to use that skill for personal advancement (Winter 2002: 224–25; e.g., Philo, *Agr.* 143; Isocrates, *Antid.* 201, 204).

4. There were several market areas in Corinth where Paul might have worked. The North Market, e.g., had been completed not long before Paul arrived in the city. Around a central square were forty-four shops. Paul seems to have lived and worked with Aquila and Priscilla

time, Paul's manual labor would have been disdained by some as unbefitting a gentleman and community leader. Cicero (*Off.* 1.150–51), for instance, contrasted intelligent work that makes a contribution to society with vulgar trades, suggesting that manual laborers live like mere slaves. This prejudice may be reflected in passages like 2 Cor. 11:7–11, where Paul defends his decision to refuse payment for his speaking services.

A Messianic Jew

Second, *Paul was Jewish and understood Judaism to have been fulfilled in Jesus the Messiah*. Although some scholars have suggested that Paul turned his back on Judaism, seen as a dark previous life set over against the real life he had after his Christian reorientation (e.g., J. Becker 1989: 34), recent scholarship, both Jewish and otherwise, has been increasingly aware of the apostle's Jewishness as key to his identity (Frey 2008: 285–88). Paul was a well-educated, widely traveled denizen of the Greco-Roman world and unarguably the key missionary to the Gentiles in the early Jesus movement. But the apostle's self-identity and his mission were driven by his Jewish heritage and understanding of the world. As one scholar states, "When Paul talks about his moorings, he boasts of his Jewish heritage and his learning in Judaism (Gal. 1.14; Phil. 3.5f.). Even after his conversion, he continues to think of himself as a Jew (2 Cor. 11.21–26; Rom. 11.1, 13f.)" (Koenig 1979: 38). Indeed, Paul converted from rejecting Jesus to confessing Jesus as Lord (Phil. 2:9–11), from a life dead in sins to a new-covenant life in the Spirit (2 Cor. 3:4–6; Rom. 8:1–4). Yet his conversion should not be seen as from "Judaism" to "Christianity," but from one type of Judaism to another (Frey 2008: 321). For Paul's Scriptures, his interpretive methods, his theology, and his goals for his mission all have their origin and foundation in the bedrock of his Jewish faith.

Paul describes himself as having been "zealous" for his ancestors' traditions, advancing the form of Judaism in which he had been raised (Gal. 1:13–14). He had been "circumcised the eighth day; of the nation of Israel, of the tribe of Benjamin, a Hebrew born of Hebrews; regarding the law, a Pharisee; regarding zeal, persecuting the church; regarding the righteousness that is in the law, blameless" (Phil. 3:5–6 HCSB). In 2 Corinthians he calls himself a Hebrew, an Israelite, and "the seed of Abraham" (11:22). He had grown up in the Diaspora and would continue to have connections with Tarsus in his adult life (Acts 9:30; 11:25), but he was trained, probably beginning in his teen years, in Jerusalem under the rabbi Gamaliel (Acts 22:3). Paul founded churches throughout the Mediterranean world yet also interacted with and

---

when he arrived in Corinth (Acts 18:1–3). Normally a hired person slept in the workroom, while the owner slept with his family in the loft above. The shops of the North Market had a single unglazed window centered above the shop entrance (which was about 7.5 feet wide). The shops were of uniform size, 13 feet high, and about 12 feet deep. The width of a shop would be about 9–13 feet. Often there was a communicating window or door with the shop next door (Murphy-O'Connor 1983: 194–95).

raised support for the mother church back in Jerusalem (e.g., Acts 21:15–20; 1 Cor. 16:1–2; 2 Cor. 8–9), which for Jews was the center of the world.

In the mid-first century and in the wake of Claudius's edict expelling Jews from Rome, people like Priscilla and Aquila had almost certainly swelled the numbers of Jews in Corinth (J. Wiseman, *ANRW* 504). When he came to that city, the apostle "reasoned in the synagogue every Sabbath and tried to persuade both Jews and Greeks," confessing Jesus as the Messiah (Acts 18:4–5). Thus the apostle's missionary methods show a profound connection to his Jewish heritage and broader associations, and the connection is theological and biblical rather than merely pragmatic. Some synagogue members believed, including the leaders Crispus (Acts 18:8; 1 Cor. 1:14) and Sosthenes (Acts 18:17; 1 Cor. 1:1), but to a great extent the apostle's message was rejected by many of his Jewish discussants. Toward the end of his first visit to Corinth, Jewish leaders of the city attacked Paul, bringing him before Gallio, a tactic that failed miserably (Acts 18:12–17). Still later, at the end of his third visit to Corinth, the Jewish leaders again plotted against the apostle, causing him to change his plans for travel (20:3). But almost certainly, even by fellow Jews, Paul was not perceived as promoter of a religion other than Judaism. Rather, Gallio had it right. Paul's conflict with the Jewish synagogue in Corinth was an internecine struggle. Paul's gospel was grounded in the Jewish Scriptures and what God had done among his people in the promised land; his gospel was centered in the death and resurrection of the Jewish Messiah, Jesus, and was for the Jewish people first. But Paul understood that not only were the life, death, and resurrection of Jesus decisive in the history of Israel; they also shaped the key eschatological event for understanding what God was doing in the world and thus reflect "a salvation-historical perspective in which the coming of Christ is seen to be the climactic fulfillment towards which the whole history of Israel has been leading" (Ciampa and Rosner 2010: 10). Ultimately, that salvation-historical perspective points beyond Israel to the whole of humanity.

A Uniquely Called Apostle

This brings us to our final point about Paul: within the early Jesus movement, *Paul was a uniquely called apostle and church planter, the preeminent Christian missionary to the Gentiles.* When Paul was confronted by Christ, his calling was unique, being both an "apostle" who was born "at the wrong time," that is, selected by Christ in a fashion quite out of step with the rest of the apostles (1 Cor. 15:8), and the apostle chosen specially to reach the Gentiles (Rom. 11:13; Gal. 2:8; 1 Tim. 2:7). We should not see this mission to the Gentiles as a pragmatic Plan B, launched upon Jewish rejection of Jesus as Messiah; rather, it should be understood as a part of God's comprehensive agenda, revealed in the OT and fulfilled in Christ (Goldsworthy 2000: 15). Paul Barnett, for instance, has pointed out that "Paul saw his own role more distinctly than any other leader we meet in the NT, apart from Christ himself. Based on the Damascus event and his subsequent career, Paul appears to have regarded himself and his life's work in fulfillment of a number of OT texts," including Isa. 49:6; 42:6–7. The Isaiah passages, for instance, speak of a servant who is made a "light" to the nations (2 Cor. 4:6; Barnett 2008: 118–19). A nuanced reading of Paul's interaction with the Isaiah material suggests that Paul did not self-identify as Isaiah's servant but rather as a herald of the Servant, Jesus, thus as "a servant of the Servant" (Gignilliat 2007: 51–52, 108–42). That Servant's ministry would not be limited to the Jewish people but would have international impact, as expressed in Isaiah's prophecy and fulfilled in Paul's mission.

What, then, was at the heart of Paul's gospel service to the Gentiles? In Romans, Paul himself tells us of his agenda for his missionary ministry: "to bring about the obedience of faith among all the Gentiles on behalf of his name" (Rom. 1:5 NET). Brian Rosner has suggested that this "obedience of faith" may be understood as centered in the glory of God, as we see, for example, in 2 Cor. 3:7–18 and 4:4–6. As demonstrated in the commentary on these passages, the theme of God's glory is complex and rich, speaking not only of the manifestation of God's presence and the proclamation of God's "fame," but also of the transformation of people so that they reflect God's character and values. Rosner (2011: 168) writes, "There is good evidence to conclude that divine glory is woven into the fabric of Paul's missionary theology and practice. It sets in motion his mission to the Gentiles, directs his missionary movements, interprets his experience of missionary suffering and gives focus to his aim to see believers transformed 'from glory to glory.'" Further, glory is brought to God and his people are glorified by God "having acted and . . . acting through Christ's life, death, resurrection/exaltation and present reign as Lord over all creation to set things right" (Ciampa 2011: 190). People who respond in faith to the good news found in Jesus Christ are delivered from both the guilt and the power of sin. They are justified and transformed by God's power, are set free, and foreshadow the very transformation of the heavens and the earth in the new creation (2 Cor. 5:17). Paul's missionary strategy centers on the simultaneous proclamation of this gospel and establishment of gospel-centered churches throughout the Mediterranean world. For reasons that become clearer as we learn about this intriguing ancient city, the apostle chose Corinth as a key station for the development of this mission.

The City of Corinth

Political and Cultural Backdrop

Corinth's history, development, and role in the ancient world owe a great deal to the city being strategically situated on an isthmus joining the Greek mainland to the Peloponnese.[5] In this attractive spot, the city began to flourish in the seventh century BC under Periander, a leader who governed Corinth

---

5. For general introductions on the ancient city of Corinth, see esp. J. Wiseman, *ANRW* 438–548; Murphy-O'Connor 1983; Engels 1990; and Thiselton 2000: 1–17.

around 625–583 BC, the same period when Jeremiah was carrying out his lament-filled, prophetic ministry under the shadow of Babylon's invasion of the land of Judah. Founding new colonies around the Mediterranean and thus increasing trade, Corinth grew in wealth and was on the rise as a major economic center.

Three centuries later, however, Corinth was caught in a political tug-of-war between Macedonia and the newly formed Achaian League. In 243 BC, Aratus of Sikyon liberated the city from a century of Macedonian domination and took it into the Achaian League. Yet just two decades later (222 BC), the city returned to Macedonian control (J. Wiseman, *ANRW* 451–54). When the Macedonians were defeated by the Romans in 197 BC, Corinth was returned to the Achaian League and played a significant role in the league through the first half of the second century BC. But the relationship between the Achaian League and Rome gradually deteriorated over that period. The Achaians interpreted the "freedom" they had been granted by Rome more literally, while the powers in Rome stayed politically engaged in the region. In Corinth and much of Greece, popular hostility against the Romans was on the rise. In 147 BC, the Romans sent an embassy to settle a dispute between Sparta and other members of the Achaian League. In a surprise move, the Romans suggested that many of the league's key cities, including Corinth, declare independence, effectively calling for the dissolution of the Achaian League, a proposal harshly rejected by the Greeks. The meeting ended when the Achaians angrily left the meeting and had all the Spartans arrested. Rome was insulted by this response to its "suggestion." Then at a critical meeting in the spring of 146 BC, the Achaian League declared war against Rome's ally, Sparta, which made war with Rome inevitable (J. Wiseman, *ANRW* 459–61). The Romans answered by sending the consul Lucius Mummius by sea and Metellus overland to crush the Greek rebellion. On the Isthmus of Corinth, a ramshackle army under the Achaian general Diaeus was destroyed by Mummius's larger and better-equipped force. Corinth was sacked and burned, many of its buildings destroyed, its men killed, and women and children sold into slavery. Thus Greek Corinth, "the Light of all Greece" (Cicero, *Leg. Man.* 5), came to an end (Engels 1990: 14–16).

After a century of desertion, the strategic position of the city was recognized by Rome, leading to Corinth's rebirth as a Roman colony. Refounded by Julius Caesar shortly before his assassination in 44 BC, the former site of the Greek city was named Colonia Laus Julia Corinthiensis (Colony of Corinth in Honor of Julius [Thiselton 2000: 3]). As noted by Strabo (*Geogr.* 8.6.23; Clarke 1993: 9–10), the population of the new Roman colony was made up largely of freedmen (those liberated from slavery),[6] as well as transplanted soldiers (*Geogr.* 17.3.15; Plutarch, *Caes.* 57.8), urban tradesmen, and laborers (Thiselton 2000: 3). Corinth seems to have become the administrative capital of the province in 27 BC (Gill 1994: 449) and thus was home to the proconsul

---

6. In Paul's day many inscriptions paid tribute to freedmen who had risen in the world and undoubtedly had an impact on Corinth's cultural climate (Savage 1996: 37).

(e.g., Gallio for one year during Paul's first sojourn in the city; Acts 18:12). Under Roman rule the city was governed by four magistrates (two *duoviri* and two *aediles*, all elected annually) and other city officials, along with a city council (Barnett 1997: 2). During the reigns of Augustus and Tiberius, the city again began to thrive economically and develop as a commercial capital of the region.

As a prominent Roman colony established to foster a reverence for Roman power and culture, the city would have been perceived on the surface to be "geographically in Greece but culturally in Rome" (Garland 1999: 21). Yet, on closer inspection, it seems that the colony was neither completely Roman nor Greek in cultural orientation.[7] In a recent monograph on the social and ethnic origins of Roman Corinth, Benjamin Millis (2010: 34–35) reflects:

> Corinth was a Roman colony: its political structure, its position within the province of Achaia, the architectural form of the city center, the layout of the colony, and not least its strong political allegiance were all wholly Roman. This very Roman city, however, had strong, even dominant, Greek roots, some of which were manifest in the mediating role Corinth played between east and west. This was a city and a population which was capable, whether consciously or not, of presenting different faces in different circumstances and contexts. The Roman face appears most obviously in public display in Roman contexts in the city center, where anything else would have been inappropriate and out of place. In sharp contrast, private contexts present a very different and notably Greek face. This conclusion is not meant to imply that the *romanitas* of the colonists was a veneer or a facade to be shed at will but that this group of people had found a way to navigate effectively between both worlds. . . . This was a city which presented itself as a new foundation while simultaneously laying claim to the past, providing a focal point for the mixing of Greek and Roman cultures at a major crossroads in the eastern Mediterranean. It was, in short, a nexus of old and new, conquered and conquerors, Greek and Roman.

Richard Oster (1992: 54) concurs: "It would be a grave error to suppose that the inhabitants of colonial Corinth lived in a setting which was mono-cultural and homogeneous at the time of nascent Christianity." This intersection of the Roman and Greek worlds was embodied in the city's unique geographical situation on the Isthmus of Corinth, which also contributed significantly to its rapid economic development in the first century AD.

Paul's Corinth: A Thriving, Wealthy City

Strabo attributed Corinth's great wealth to it being "master of two harbours" (*Geogr.* 8.6.20). The man-made port of Lechaeum, one of the largest in the

---

7. Latin was the dominant public language of Roman Corinth for at least the first 150 years of its existence (from 44 BC): Latin inscriptions outnumber Greek ones by a ratio of about 25 to 1. Only inscriptions related to the Isthmian Games, held every two years, are exclusively in Greek (Millis 2010: 23). Yet Paul's Letters were written in Greek, as were graffiti and various types of personal marks, including those of masons and manufacturers (Millis 2010: 26–29).

Roman world (only the ports at Rome, Ostia, and Caesarea were bigger), was roughly 1.8 miles north of the Corinthian forum and on the Gulf of Corinth (Engels 1990: 214n72; Murphy-O'Connor 1983: 16). The smaller port of Cenchreae lay a little less than 6 miles to the east, on the Saronic Gulf. Connecting these two gulfs, the isthmus measures just 3–4 miles wide at its most narrow point. The two ports thus served as a unique crossroads,[8] providing Rome with a shortcut[9] to the ports of Asia and the Eastern Mediterranean. Consequently, Corinth served as a major distribution center both for the Greek mainland and the Peloponnese. Goods could be imported and exported, both east and west, as well as north and south (J. Wiseman, *ANRW* 445–46). In this way, Corinth functioned as a major commercial intersection in the ancient world.

Immediately surrounding Corinth stood a zone of villas, gardens, and prosperous farmsteads, while further out from this zone, there were towns, villages, and occasionally isolated farmhouses (Engels 1990: 24). Within a fifteen-mile radius, those towns and villages, which had constant interaction with Corinth itself, included Nemea, Cleonae, Tenea, Examilia, Cromna, Cenchreae, Isthmia, Scheonus, and Crommyon. People in the broader region considered themselves Corinthians, identifying readily with their much larger neighbor.

Some have celebrated the fertility of Corinth's coastal plain (Furnish 1988: 17). Cicero (*Agr.* 1.5; 2.51) calls the land of Corinthia "most excellent and

8. A portage road, the Diolkos (= "across"), was built in the sixth century BC and was used at points to transport cargo from one gulf to the other. From ancient times there were plans to build a canal across the span (only the emperor Nero and, perhaps, Demetrius Poliorcetes actually initiated digging), but that dream was not realized until 1893 (J. Wiseman, *ANRW* 441–42). Almost all modern works on Corinth or the Corinthian Letters note the extensive use of the Diolkos and mention that ships were transported overland regularly, but this view has been called into question in a number of recent studies suggesting that the Diolkos was not used to transport ships (except on rare occasions, then mostly warships) and had a rather limited use in the transport of cargoes (e.g., Lohmann 2013; Pettegrew 2011). This does nothing, however, to reduce the importance of Corinth as a vast emporium serving as a conduit of merchandise between its two harbors and thus the two gulfs. Strabo (*Geogr.* 8.6.20) explains: "Corinth is called 'wealthy' because of its commerce, since it is situated on the Isthmus and is master of two harbours, of which the one leads straight to Asia, and the other to Italy; and it makes easy the exchange of merchandise from both countries that are so far distant from each other."

9. This route saved six days of sailing around the Peloponnese, avoiding the treacherous winds and currents of Cape Malea. Engels (1990: 50–51) notes that the winds in December and January often exceed Beaufort force 6 (over 30 mph), a hazardous condition for ancient ships, and even in summer, winds can reach that velocity 25–30 percent of the time. This is in the general vicinity where Paul's ship, bound for Rome, was caught in a violent storm (Acts 27:13–19) and driven all the way to Malta off Sicily. Again, Strabo (*Geogr.* 8.6.20) explains the strategic nature of Corinth as follows:

And just as in early times the Strait of Sicily was not easy to navigate, so also the high seas, and particularly the sea beyond Maleae, were not, on account of the contrary winds; and hence the proverb, "But when you double Maleae, forget your home." At any rate, it was a welcome alternative, for the merchants both from Italy and from Asia, to avoid the voyage to Maleae and to land their cargoes here. And also the duties on what by land was exported from the Peloponnesus and what was imported to it fell to those who held the keys.

productive" and "rich and fertile." This almost certainly refers to the land west of the city, cut through by the Nemea River,[10] yet recent studies have shown that Corinth could not have subsisted on its agricultural base, but rather was oriented to service and trade (Engels 1990: 121–42). One of the driest sites in southern Greece, the Corinthia has an average annual rainfall of about fifteen inches; thus both streams and wells in the region can run dry in the summer months (Engels 1990: 12). Yet the city was exceptionally well supplied with water, having vast underground reserves, indeed, one of the most extensive watering systems in the ancient world (Landon 2003: 43). The Corinthians rightly celebrated their abundant supply of fresh drinking water, their baths and fountains, and their enviable sewage system.

Looming over the Corinthia region, the Acrocorinth sits just south of the ancient city, rising up over 1,800 feet. From its lower slopes on the north, Corinth spread north, across two descending plateaus, toward the port at Lechaeum (Lechaion). The heavy fortification wall, which originally surrounded the heart of the city, had been over 32,000 feet (6.2 miles) in circumference and anchored to the fortifications on the summit of the Acrocorinth.[11] The main part of the city covered an area of about 1.5 square miles (Murphy-O'Connor 1983: 58). In short, Corinth was a large, thriving city by ancient standards, with a population during Paul's day estimated at about 80,000, plus another 20,000 people in the rural areas outside the city (Engels 1990: 84); perhaps one-third of the population consisted of slaves (Garland 1999: 23). In addition, Corinth attracted not only merchants but also tourists and other travelers on a regular basis. Every two years the numbers of travelers making their way to the city swelled as large crowds were attracted to the Isthmian Games (Strabo, *Geogr.* 8.6.20), a popular religious and athletic festival involving, for instance, musical and literary competitions, contests in public speaking, contests involving horses (e.g., chariot races, skills in chariot driving, men leaping on and off both horses and chariots), various kinds of footraces, the pentathlon, and boxing. The festival was a boon to the Corinthian economy and image as a major tourist destination.

In the early 50s AD, when Paul arrived in Corinth, the city was at the pinnacle of its development and would have struck a visitor with its size, its beauty, and, perhaps most of all, its wealth (Strabo, *Geogr.* 8.6.23; Aristides, *Or.* 46.27; Alciphron, *Ep.* 3.24.3).[12] Impressive buildings and statues made of

---

10. Yet Strabo (*Geogr.* 8.6.23) describes the terrain immediately around the city and toward the Isthmus as "not very fertile, but rifted and rough; and from this fact all have called Corinth 'beetling,' and use the proverb, 'Corinth is both beetle-browed and full of hollows.'" Commenting on this, Murphy-O'Connor (1983: 66) reports, "The soil is thin, and erosion damage very noticeable; jagged edges of limestone project above the worn surface of the soft marl."

11. See esp. color figs. 3 and 7 in Gregory 1993: 16–18, which depict the original layout of the city by the Romans. By Paul's time the wall was in great disrepair, as were the two additional parallel walls that ran northward, connecting the city proper with its northern port on the Gulf of Corinth (Murphy-O'Connor 1983: 58; J. Wiseman, *ANRW* 440–41).

12. This context of wealth also was home to the egregiously poor. Alciphron (*Ep.* 3.60) comments, "I learned in a short time the nauseating behavior of the rich and the misery of the poor."

various hues of marble, exotic woods, and various kinds of stone and adorned with bronze would have been everywhere one turned. Some of the most impressive buildings would have been in the vicinity of the massive Forum, an area almost 600 feet long. Looking around, the visitor would have seen the huge South Stoa, the largest in the Roman world, which ran the length of the Forum, with the Acrocorinth rising up behind it. The North Stoa on the Forum's opposite side was not as long but was equally impressive. Engels (1990: 60) suggests that about 76,000 square feet of building space was devoted to stoas and shop structures in the central, excavated part of the city. At the Forum a visitor would have seen the Julian Basilica, temples to Apollo and Aphrodite, the Peirene Fountain, and the statue of Athena. Just off the Forum were the Archaic Temple and, to the west, the Temple of the Imperial Cult. Besides these, there were at least five public baths, numerous fountains, other temples, a library, lawcourts, latrines, rooms to rent, monuments to celebrated people, many schools, shops of various kinds, bronze works, pottery works, the Jewish synagogue (Acts 18:4), and large market areas. Making his way to the northwest of the Forum, our visitor might stop by the theater, which could seat 15,000 people. Out toward the Acrocorinth, this person may have walked by handsome homes adorned with mosaics and frescos. Throughout this bustling city, the visitor would see crowds of travelers, merchants, shoppers, worshipers, and tourists from Rome, Alexandria, Sardinia, North Africa, Italy, Spain, Syria, Judea, Anatolia, and from all over Greece.

Either at the warehouses near the ports, the warehouses in the city, or the market areas throughout the city, visitors might have encountered cooks, prostitutes, entertainers, doctors, barbers, travel guides, wagon drivers, leatherworkers, rope makers, bankers, merchants selling perfumes or ceramic goods, blacksmiths, jewelers, architects, tentmakers, bakers, farmers selling produce or animals, carpenters, masons, stonecutters, road builders, shoemakers, embroiderers, or those carrying out dozens of other occupations. People would have been able to buy every good imaginable, including spices, silks, imported wines (Williams 1993: 38), precious stones, olive oils, copper and tin ingots, clothing, and shoes (Engels 1990: 57–58). A visitor would have been able to worship at one of the many temples, get a haircut, wash at one of the public baths or even in a swimming pool, or eat a meal in a public tavern.

In short, the city was filled with a dazzling array of colors, smells (both pleasant and unpleasant), and experiences. The city was a large, international, pluralistic, wealthy center of commerce, and a political hub for the Roman Empire; these characteristics do serve as important backdrops for the interpretation of our letter. But to understand certain dynamics at play in 2 Corinthians, we also need to understand cultural values fostered in this ancient city, especially as they relate to leadership.

The Corinthian Context and Leadership Values

The Corinthian Letters make clear that the church in this impressive first-century city was racked with problems, and scholars increasingly attribute many of the problems to the Corinthian cultural and social values by which the lives of these young believers had been shaped. In short, "many of their faults can be traced to their uncritical acceptance of the attitudes, values, and behaviors of the society in which they lived" (Ciampa and Rosner 2010: 4).[13] In 2 Corinthians, Paul seems especially concerned with misconceptions of leadership, a concern carried over from 1 Corinthians (1:12–17; 3:1–15; 4:1–7), as he vies for the authenticity and authority of his mission in the city. Momentarily and more specifically, we will address the identity of Paul's opponents in Corinth (see "Paul and His Opponents at Corinth" below), but here we seek to present the cultural value-set according to which those opponents apparently worked.

The Greco-Roman world celebrated the attainment of "glory" and "honor"[14] and emphasized the corresponding avoidance of "shame" in a leader of society. "Honor" has been defined as "the value of a person in his or her own eyes . . . *plus* that person's value in the eyes of his or her social group. Honor is a claim to worth along with the social acknowledgement of worth" (Malina 1983: 27), a concept also associated with "glory." If an individual had honor, that brought honor or glory to their family, clan, group, and city. Correspondingly, if a person was shamed by some activity or event or association, the shame transferred also to that person's associations. Denizens of Greco-Roman culture competed against one another (cf. 2 Cor. 10:12) for the attaining of honor so that they might rise in social status, in the public perception of worth. In fact, social competition for increased honor was a key element and a distinctive feature of Greek culture (Jewett 2003: 552).

Andrew Clarke (1993: 25) notes that, especially in an urban culture like Corinth's, "Social progression was inevitably the goal of most." People were bent on climbing the ladder of success, or more specifically for that society, "the ladder of social status"; so in line with their cultural values, the Corinthians were competing for social status. Many of the freedmen who had risen in status

13. Ciampa and Rosner (2010) cite Vander Broek (2002: 27–28), who states,
> Each of the community problems Paul needed to address grew out of the Corinthians' inability to let the gospel message fully reshape their gentile, Greco-Roman lives, whether because they misunderstood that message or because they rejected it outright. They were Hellenists through and through, and this eschatological, cross-centered, body-affirming Jewish sect called Christianity demanded that they enter another theological and ethical world. It is no surprise that these residents of Corinth would seek rhetorical wisdom, be unconcerned with immorality and the preservation of the body, be infatuated with asceticism and spiritual empowerment, and preserve the distinctions between rich and poor. The Corinthians were simply trying to be Christians with a minimal amount of social and theological disturbance.

Winter (2001: 43) points especially to the educational backdrop of the culture: "The Christian community was influenced by the secular educational mores of Corinth."

14. In 2 Corinthians, Paul does not specifically use the Greek term we normally translate as "honor" (τιμή), but the word does occur elsewhere in Paul, including Romans and 1 Corinthians (Rom. 2:7, 10; 9:21; 12:10; 13:7; 1 Cor. 6:20; 7:23; 12:23–24). The antithetical word ἀτιμία is found at 2 Cor. 6:8 and 11:21. In 2 Corinthians Paul prefers to speak of δόξα (glory, e.g., 1:20; 4:15, 17; 6:8; 8:19, 23). He also uses δόξα extensively in 3:7–4:6; for the association of glory and honor in the Greco-Roman world, see, e.g., Plutarch, *Rom. Q.* 1.13; *Mulier. virt.* 16; *Cor.* 4.3.

through acquisition of wealth and position, still faced "status inconsistency" when compared to wealthy, high-status Romans (Pogoloff 1992: 273). So people in Corinthian culture desperately engaged in "boasting" and other forms of self-promotion to raise their own status or "glory" in the world (Thiselton 2000: 12–13).[15] Thus Witherington notes that "in Paul's time many in Corinth were already suffering from a self-made-person-escapes-humble-origins syndrome" (Witherington 1995: 20) and were seeking to overcome that syndrome.

Numerous factors contributed to a person's rank in the Greco-Roman world of the first century AD. A person's "power" referred to their ability to achieve certain goals in the society. Paul, by contrast, always places emphasis on God's power, even couched in the context of his own weakness (2 Cor. 1:8; 4:7; 6:7; 8:3; 12:9, 12; 13:4). Skill in rhetoric also could increase one's honor and status (Stansbury 1990: 278). Accordingly, that Paul was accused of poor public speaking was a way of shaming him (2 Cor. 10:10). Other dynamics that increased status included occupation, wealth or income, education and knowledge, religious or moral integrity, one's position in a family or ethnic group, or status in the local community (Meeks 1983: 54). Thus Paul in effect acts counterculturally when he chooses an occupation involving manual labor (11:7–9), denies income that would be provided by a patron (11:7), and downplays his own education (11:6). It may be that his opponents sought to lessen his status by questioning his moral integrity (1:12, 17) and his status as an apostle (11:5). Perhaps some in Corinth were struggling with Paul because his actions and patterns of leadership did not reflect a person seeking high status in Corinth's cultural milieu. In fact, he preached that true "glory," rather than being possessed by a gifted few, was for all believers and was a result of knowing Christ (3:17–18).

Finally, the Corinthians of the first century were enamored with wealth as contributing to one's social status. They were "impressed with material splendour and intent on raising their standing in the world," and, among other things, were famous for being "'ungracious . . . among their luxuries' (Alciphron, *Ep.* 3.15.1) and for 'assuming airs and priding themselves on their wealth' (Dio Chrysostom, *Or.* 9.8)" (Savage 1996: 36). In short, for the Corinthians wealth was a preeminent value, tied to getting ahead in the world, and this was true especially for those who aspired to leadership in the society (Clarke 1993: 25, 39). Clarke (1993: 10–11) has shown that the leadership structure in Corinth was made up of wealthy political leaders who provided massive resources to fund all kinds of civic needs, and they did this to advance their own popularity and power. Thus leadership was expensive and elitist. One moved up the ranks of leadership and power by having money and spending it on those under one's leadership. So it is not difficult to see why Paul

15. From the Corinth agora, e.g., the inscriptions to Babbius provide a good example of benefaction and self-promotion: "Gnaeus Babbius Philinus, aedile and pontifex, had this monument erected at his own expense, and he approved it in his official capacity of duovir" (as quoted in Murphy-O'Connor 1983: 27).

did not measure up to the cultural ideals. Not only does Paul reject financial remuneration for himself, but he also asks the rank-and-file members of the church to contribute money for the collection in Jerusalem (2 Cor. 8–9)! Given their cultural background, this must have seemed odd to many of the relatively new believers in Corinth.

Based on his extensive study of leadership patterns in the Corinthian context, Clarke (1993: 129) asserts that the Corinthians were using "secular categories and perceptions of leadership in the Christian community." In short, in the apostle's seeming humility (even humiliation, 12:21), his taking on the role of a servant, his rejection of patronage and the concomitant rejection of financial gain, and his refusal to advance his status by use of rhetorical skills, he stood in violation of key leadership values and principles embedded in the Corinthian culture. The apostle, on the other hand, presents to the Corinthians an alternative: a theocentric and biblical vision of authentic leadership.

Paul's Relationship with the Corinthians

As we read 2 Corinthians, it seems these tensions with the Corinthians had come to a head. Before probing those tensions further and addressing how Paul seeks to address them in our letter, we need to review the apostle's history with this church, placing the historical moment of this letter's production in historical context.[16] What follows is one possible scenario based on the data we have in Acts and our two extant Letters to the Corinthians. Admittedly, this recounting of events is rather "tight," and the apostle may have stayed in certain locations for additional months or an additional year. Nevertheless,

---

16. In this running account of Paul's movements (following the chart below), I have placed the dates in italics so the reader can track the progression more easily. On Pauline chronology, see Jewett 1979a (in its other iteration as Jewett 1979b); Hyldahl 1986; Riesner 1998; D. Campbell 2002; and for 2 Corinthians specifically, the introductions of the major commentaries. Beyond "anchor" events such as Paul's interaction with Gallio (Acts 18:12–17) and places at which we are given specific reference points from the annual calendar (e.g., 1 Cor. 16:8; Acts 20:6), the normal seasons for shipping offer some help in determining the apostle's movements, though Paul seems to have traveled during periods that were less safe, and sea travel always had its hazards (2 Cor. 11:25b–c). Hesiod said no one should sail except for fifty days a year, in July and August (*Op.* 663–65). Although Hesiod is quite conservative, the heart of the main shipping season consisted of the summer and a few weeks before and after it. Through much of the year, the seas were mostly deserted, and the ports went into hibernation. In general, shipping shut down from mid-November to mid-March; from September 14 to November 11 and from March 10 to May 27 were periods also considered very dangerous for travel by ship (Vegetius, *De re milit.* 4.39; Pliny the Elder, *Nat.* 2.47). Paul normally seemed to spend the winter months away from the road (Riesner 1998: 308–9). The rabbis advised travel by sea only between Pentecost and the Feast of Booths (May to the end of October). Storms were certainly a problem on the seas, yet in an age when sailors plotted their courses by landmarks or the sun by day and the stars by night, visibility was an even greater concern. Cloudiness in fall or spring was a serious threat, since ships could drift off course and wreck in unknown waters. Consequently, good weather was critical. In addition, during the summer months Mediterranean winds are northerly (i.e., coming from the north), which would make for a quick trip from Rome to Alexandria, e.g., but would work against a ship traveling north from Alexandria to Rome (Casson 1974: 150).

the itinerary below offers a reasonable sequence of events in the apostle's interaction with the Corinthian church.[17]

A Chronology of Paul's Interaction with the Corinthians

spring 50 (March?)	Paul arrives in Corinth for the first time.
summer 51 (July?)	Paul is brought before Gallio.
autumn 51 (September?)	Paul leaves Corinth, sailing for Syria, arriving by mid-October.
late spring 52 (May?)	Paul arrives in Ephesus for a period of extensive ministry.
summer or autumn 52	Paul receives news of the Corinthians and writes the "Previous Letter" (1 Cor. 5:9).
autumn 52	Apollos joins Paul in Ephesus.
summer/autumn 53	Paul writes 1 Corinthians and sends it to Corinth (Timothy sent to Macedonia).
early spring 54	Timothy arrives in Corinth, finding the church in disarray.
late spring 54 (May?)	When shipping opens, Paul travels to Corinth for the "sorrowful visit" (2 Cor. 2:1), then returns to Ephesus.
summer 54	In Ephesus, Titus reports to Paul, who writes the "sorrowful letter" (2 Cor. 2:3–4).
late summer 54 (Aug.?)	The riot in Ephesus precipitates Paul leaving the city after teaching for two years and three months (Acts 19:8–10).
autumn–winter 54/55	Paul ministers in Troas, then Macedonia, where he writes 2 Corinthians.
winter–autumn 55	Paul evangelizes in Macedonia and Illyricum (Rom. 15:19).
autumn/winter 55	Paul makes his way back through Macedonia to Greece.
January–March 56	The apostle stays for three months in Corinth and writes Romans.
spring 56 (end of March?)	A plot causes Paul to abort a trip back to Syria by sea and reroute travel through Macedonia.
April 56	Paul sails, leaving Philippi after the Feast of Unleavened Bread (Acts 20:6) on a trip that takes him back to Jerusalem, where he is taken into Roman custody.

The Church Established

Paul probably arrived in Corinth the first time early in *AD 50*, perhaps in *March*,[18] when winter weather would have given way to the beginnings of

17. The identification of specific months in the chronology are meant to be suggestive rather than exact, mere approximations, but at points they are based on normal shipping seasons. Dates such as when Paul arrived in Ephesus the first time or the length of Paul's ministry in Macedonia and Illyricum are debated and could add months or years to this chronology. Also, Luke's language is notoriously inexact when dealing with periods of time. When in Acts 18:18 he says that Paul stayed "quite a few days" (ἡμέρας ἱκανάς, *hēmeras hikanas*), e.g., does that mean something like a few weeks or a few months? What we present here, then, is an approximate chronology, meant to be suggestive of the general time frames surrounding the apostle's ministry.

18. March AD 50 + eighteen months (Acts 18:11) + "quite a few days" (18:18) would still allow Paul to sail in fall of 51.

spring, making travel south from Macedonia to Greece easier. The apostle lived with Priscilla and Aquila, who shared his occupation of tentmaking and who had recently been expelled from Rome under the Edict of Claudius (Acts 18:2–3). Most scholars date the expulsion in AD 49 or the first month of AD 50 (Jewett 1979b: 36–38). Silas and Timothy came south from Macedonia and joined Paul in the Corinthian ministry. Together they founded the church through the preaching of the gospel (Acts 18:5; 2 Cor. 1:19). The result was that "many of the Corinthians, when they heard, believed and were baptized," including a prominent man named Titius Justus and Crispus, the synagogue leader (Acts 18:7–8 HCSB). After ministering in Corinth for over a year, in *summer of AD 51* Paul was brought before Gallio at the judgment seat in the Forum. Gallio served as proconsul of Greece from July 1 in AD 51 to June 30 in 52 (Murphy-O'Connor 1983: 164–69). Perhaps the Jewish leaders in Corinth brought the apostle before the proconsul in *July*, shortly after Gallio took office, thinking the new administrator might be sympathetic to their concerns (cf. Acts 25:1–2). They were mistaken (18:14–16).[19] After Paul had stayed on in Corinth for a number of days, he, Aquila, and Priscilla sailed to Ephesus from the port at Cenchreae, perhaps in *late September 51* (18:18). He then sailed on to Caesarea, traveling from there up to Jerusalem and arriving by *mid-October*.[20] This ended what we normally refer to as the "Second Mission Journey."

The Move to Asia

From Jerusalem, Paul traveled north to Antioch in *late fall of 51*, shortly after the time that eloquent Apollos took up his ministry in Corinth (Acts 19:1). The apostle then traveled on through South Galatia and Phrygia, visiting the churches there (18:22–23) before moving to set up residence in Ephesus. The trip from Jerusalem to Ephesus (1,120 miles) would have taken sixty to ninety days on foot. But with wintry conditions (in the Taurus range and the Anatolian highlands), Paul would have had to overwinter somewhere, and he did spend some time in ministry. So he probably reached Ephesus in *late spring of the year AD 52* (Riesner 1998: 313). Priscilla and Aquila were already in the city, having been left there by Paul at the end of the previous mission trip (Acts 18:18, 21). For the first three months in Ephesus, the apostle preached boldly in the Jewish synagogue. But then he moved to the lecture hall of Tyrannus and spent two years of exceptionally powerful and productive ministry there as all Asia heard the Word of God preached (19:8–20). After Paul was established in Asia, perhaps that first *summer or fall* in Ephesus, he received news of the Corinthians and wrote them "not to associate with sexually immoral people" (1 Cor. 5:9). At some point during the Ephesian ministry, he was

---

19. Sosthenes, the leader of the synagogue in Corinth, was beaten in front of the judge's bench (Acts 18:17) and later came to Christ (1 Cor. 1:1), as had Crispus, the leader who preceded him (Acts 18:8; 1 Cor. 1:14).

20. Riesner (1998: 313) suggests that it would have taken no more than about fourteen days for Paul to travel from Corinth to Caesarea.

joined by Sosthenes (1 Cor. 1:1), as well as Stephanas, Fortunatus, Achaicus (16:17), Timothy, and Erastus (Acts 19:22; 1 Cor. 4:17; 16:10). As early as *autumn of 52* (or as late as *spring of 53*), Apollos, after just a few months of ministry in Corinth, had left the city and joined Paul in Ephesus, perhaps due to the factionalism inspired at least in part by his ministry (1 Cor. 1:12; 3:4–6, 22; 4:6; 16:12).

1 Corinthians

About halfway through his time in Ephesus, in *summer or early autumn 53*, Paul wrote 1 Corinthians, and he may have sent the letter by ship with Stephanas, Fortunatus, and Achaicus, or perhaps with Titus (2 Cor. 8:6, 16–17) before sea travel closed for the season (1 Cor. 16:17; Furnish 1984: 28). This was before the apostle had made definite plans to carry the collection to Jerusalem personally (16:3–4). At the time of writing, Paul planned to stay in Ephesus until after *Pentecost of 54* because the ministry was going so well (16:8–9), but he was also open to an earlier trip if necessary (4:18–19). So his plan was to visit the Corinthians after traveling through Macedonia in *late spring or early summer of 54*. He hoped to stay with them perhaps through the winter months of the following year (AD 54–55; 1 Cor. 16:5–9). Part of the purpose of Paul's trip to Corinth was to take up a collection for the believers in Jerusalem (16:1–4). In the meantime, perhaps in *autumn of 53*, before he sent 1 Corinthians by ship, Paul sent Timothy on a trip, probably through Macedonia, that would include Corinth. But he anticipated that the letter would reach them first (1 Cor. 4:17; 16:10–11).

A Painful Visit and a Painful Letter

Evidently, when Timothy arrived in Corinth, perhaps in *early spring of 54*, things were not well in the church, and at least some of Paul's directions in 1 Corinthians had not been acted upon. There were, for instance, those who continued to be involved in sexual immorality and divisiveness (2 Cor. 12:21). The false teachers were gaining in influence (as is clear from the opponents reflected in 2 Corinthians; e.g., 10:2, 12; 11:19–21). So it is possible that as soon as shipping opened in *late spring of 54*, Timothy headed to Ephesus to report to his apostle (or perhaps he sent a letter). Paul immediately left for Corinth for a grievous, crisis visit (2 Cor. 2:1–2),[21] which disrupted his previously made plans of traveling first through Macedonia before going to Corinth (1 Cor. 16:5–6). Perhaps during this visit Paul told the Corinthians that he would return to them in the months to come, travel on to Macedonia, and then come back through their city on his way to Judea.[22] The apostle may

21. It would have taken Paul anywhere between three to four days and two weeks to get to Corinth from Ephesus (Casson 1974: 150–51).

22. The other alternative is that the crisis visit is the first leg of the plan of which Paul speaks in 2 Cor. 1:15–16, with the apostle cutting the trip short by heading back to Ephesus early (Hafemann 2000: 86). This is an attractive position, but the problem with this view is twofold. First, if Paul left Corinth for Ephesus, instead of continuing on to Macedonia, his plan reflected in

have seen in the Corinthian situation a need to spend more time with a church in crisis. Yet his expressed purpose for this planned double visit to Corinth was to receive financial help for the trip to Macedonia and, on the way back through Corinth, to receive help for the trip to Jerusalem, offering the Corinthians a double opportunity to participate in giving (2 Cor. 1:15–16). Yet those plans never materialized.

During this crisis visit to Corinth, the apostle experienced emotional turmoil and even humiliation; in short, the confrontation with the church was deeply painful, though Paul was patient even as he warned those who were living in sin (2 Cor. 2:1–4; 12:21; 13:2). Either before or shortly after he traveled back to Ephesus,[23] the apostle was openly attacked, and the majority of members in the church failed to respond appropriately by defending their apostle (2:5–11).[24] As noted by Fee (1978: 538), Paul now had two problems: First, he needed to set things right with the church in Corinth. Second, he needed to follow through in a way that would not jeopardize the collection for Jerusalem.

So to address the first problem, in the *summer of 54, the apostle sent Titus to Corinth with the painful letter* mentioned in 2 Cor. 2:3–4. In this letter he may have informed the church that he had changed back to his original travel plans and would not be visiting them before going to Macedonia (1:15–16). Rather, Paul planned to go through Macedonia and then to Corinth to accomplish the second need related to the collection (2 Cor. 8:19), in effect returning to the previous itinerary mentioned in 1 Cor. 16:5–6. Thus Paul "resolved in the Spirit to pass through Macedonia and Achaia and go to Jerusalem" (Acts 19:21 HCSB). At that time he also sent Timothy and Erastus on ahead to Macedonia (19:22). As these plans solidified in the apostle's mind and heart, he evidently had changed his mind about allowing the Corinthians to appoint those who would deliver their part of the collection to Jerusalem (1 Cor. 16:3), for there is no mention of such representatives in 2 Cor. 8:16–24.

---

2 Cor. 1:15–16 was changed at that point. Yet Paul makes clear that the motive for the change was to avoid a second painful visit to Corinth. This is possible, but it seems awkward that he would speak of a second visit while still on the first. Second, the crisis visit was probably made in haste, with the apostle not having ample opportunity to wrap up his ministry in Ephesus, for the itinerary of 2 Cor. 1:15–16 has little place for Paul to resolve ministry needs and responsibilities in Corinth before going back to Jerusalem (although he could have stopped briefly near Ephesus, as reflected in Acts 20:17–38).

23. Harris's position, that the offender denounced Paul after the apostle had traveled back to Ephesus, makes good sense. As Harris (2005: 226–27) points out, it seems less likely that Paul "had ignominiously retreated to Ephesus, an insulted and broken man, only later to accomplish by letter and the intervention of his delegate Titus what he had earlier failed to achieve in person." If Paul had experienced a public collapse and retreat, the threat of his impending visit in 2 Cor. 13:10 would ring quite hollow. Further, the apostle's assurance to Titus at 7:13–15 would have fallen flat in the face of such a failure in Corinth.

24. It is most likely that the apostle was attacked by a person who had high social status, which would explain why most of the congregation was shocked into silence, failing to confront the attacker until after the reception of the sad letter (2 Cor. 2:4).

Transitions and the Writing of 2 Corinthians

Late in the summer or early fall of 54, a little over two years after Paul had arrived in Asia (Acts 19:10), the situation in Ephesus deteriorated, as reflected in Acts 19:23–41. Luke does not tell us about the "affliction" Paul experienced in Asia (2 Cor. 1:8–11), but it is a viable option to conclude that it happened during this "major disturbance about the Way" (Acts 19:23; see the comments on 2 Cor. 1:8). Regardless, that uproar caused by Demetrius and the craftsmen seems to have precipitated Paul's departure from the city (Acts 20:1). The apostle left Ephesus, ministering in Troas for a brief time (2 Cor. 2:12). While there he had evidently expected to meet Titus, who was returning from delivering the painful letter; not finding his young protégé, the apostle continued on to Macedonia (2:12–13). As Paul describes this period, he had no rest in his spirit but was troubled and fearful (2 Cor. 7:5–7); understandably, he would have still been traumatized by the experience of his severe "affliction" during which he had stared death in the face (1:8). The apostle finally found emotional relief and God's comfort in Titus's arrival (in Philippi?), for the young man brought a generally good report concerning the Corinthians' response to the painful letter (7:7–13).[25] He also must have met Timothy at about this time (2 Cor. 1:1) in Macedonia and started what may have been a multiweek process of *writing 2 Corinthians, perhaps in the fall or winter of 54,* a little over a year after the church had received 1 Corinthians (2 Cor. 8:10). In winter or early spring, the apostle sent Titus, along with two other brothers (2 Cor. 8:16–24), to Corinth with 2 Corinthians.

Ministry in Macedonia, Illyricum, and Corinth

At Acts 20:2 Luke records, "and when he had passed through those areas and exhorted them at length, [Paul] came to Greece" (HCSB). For the sake of space, Luke often telescoped his narrative, omitting material that did not concern him (Keener 2012: 101), and he seems to do so here. For Paul took time to write a rather lengthy letter, and he sent a team bearing that letter ahead to Greece.[26] Since Paul stayed in "those areas" after writing the letter, it is reasonable to conclude that he was carrying out ministry there, especially since Luke tells us he "exhorted them at length" (Acts 20:2). But from a brief statement in Rom. 15:19b, it seems that the apostle also journeyed west to the region of Illyricum to preach the gospel there (so Bruce 1990: 93; P. Walker

---

25. Generally speaking, Titus's report had been encouraging. The younger minister had been received well and could speak of the Corinthians' conformity to Paul's wishes and their "longing" for the apostle (e.g., 2 Cor. 7:7, 15). At the same time, some of them had been offended by the severe letter he had sent (7:8), and his back-and-forth approach to his travel plans did not inspire confidence (Furnish 1984: 141).

26. Doing so, the apostle evidently wished to accomplish at least two things. First, he was seeking to thwart the work of his opponents (2 Cor. 11:12–15) and restore the Corinthians to a full commitment to his apostolic mission (7:2; 10:6; on which see below). Second, he exhorted the Corinthians not only to restart the collection but also to complete it (8:11; 9:3–4), which would have taken time.

2012: 8–10; Keener 2012: 248)[27], and such travel and ministry would have taken time. In that passage, written from Corinth once Paul arrived back in Greece, the apostle states, "As a result, I have fully proclaimed the good news about the Messiah from Jerusalem all the way around to Illyricum" (HCSB). Allan Chapple (2013: 35) concludes that "Illyricum" here refers to Dalmatia (southern Illyricum), that Paul ministered there for at least several months, and that his mission to the Roman province[28] of Illyricum was meant as a prelude to the apostle's ministry in Rome, perhaps even a preparation for ministry in Spain. Such a time in Latin-speaking Illyricum would have put the Roman church on his heart, which would then explain his soon-to-be-written Letter to the Romans from Corinth.

It seems at least possible, then, that Paul spent the next year, from *the winter of 54–55* and through *autumn of 55* ministering in Macedonia and Illyricum. Given his normal practice, the apostle probably had fellow workers with him from Macedonia (and perhaps other places, as he moved west (2 Cor. 9:4; Acts 20:4). After ministering in Illyricum, he probably passed back through Macedonia on his way to Corinth, for he seems to have arrived around *the beginning of January 56*, an unlikely time for a sea voyage south along the western coast of the peninsula. The apostle then spent three months in Corinth, from *January to around the end of March 56*, and wrote the book of Romans during that time. Luke tells us that Paul had planned to set sail for Syria, perhaps after sea travel opened in mid-March, but the plan was thwarted due to the Jewish leaders' plot against him in Corinth (Acts 20:3). So Paul and his ministry team traveled back to Macedonia instead, leaving Philippi after the Feast of Unleavened Bread and eventually making their way to Jerusalem (20:7–21:15). As far as we know, Paul never again visited the church in Corinth, although 2 Tim. 4:20 hints that he may have.

The Letter We Call 2 Corinthians: Its Form and Purpose

One Letter, Two, or More?

Thus far in the introduction, we have written of 2 Corinthians as a single "letter," sent at a particular time. The reality is, however, that since the time

---

27. See esp. Jewett and Kotansky's excellent discussion (2007: 911–14) of καὶ κύκλῳ μέχρι τοῦ Ἰλλυρικοῦ (*kai kyklō mechri tou Illyrikou*) in Rom. 15:19, lit., "and in a circle until Illyricum": My chronology allows several months for this in the summer and fall of 56 C.E. after meeting Titus in Macedonia (2 Cor 7:5–16); the later tradition of the Pauline school associated Titus with Dalmatia, which is part of Illyricum (2 Tim 4:10). The founding visit to Illyricum would have immediately preceded Paul's return for the final winter in Corinth—when Romans was written. Since Paul usually missionized in important urban centers, it is likely that he worked in Epetium, Salona, Tragurium, or Scodra, of which the latter would have been most easily accessible from Macedonia. (2007: 913–14)

28. Chapple (2013: 20) argues that Paul's reference in Rom. 15:19 is not just to the Illyrian region, on the north side of the western section of the Via Egnatia, from the vicinity of Lychnidos to the Adriatic, as with, e.g., Hengel and Schwemer 1997: 261.

of Johann Salomo Semler in the late eighteenth century (Semler 1776),[29] and especially since Adolf Hausrath's (1870) short monograph on 2 Corinthians a century later (ET of the title: The four-chapter letter of Paul to the Corinthians), many scholars have seen this work as a patchwork of more than one letter, pieced together by an editor once all the parts had been written. At a number of places in the letter, the transitions, either in subject matter or tone, seem abrupt. For instance, based on the shift in tone at 10:1, many have suggested that our 2 Corinthians was redacted out of two letters, chapters 1–9 and chapters 10–13. Still other "fragments" have been identified in relation to 2:14–7:4 (the earliest "letter," some suggest), 6:14–7:1 (which some do not believe is Pauline), and in relation to chapters 8 and 9 (which some understand to be two distinct letters). The suggestions vary widely,[30] but it is common to divide the letter into two, or as many as five, or even six fragments.[31]

Although space does not allow a thorough treatment of all the proposed theories, some of their aspects will be addressed in the exegetical reflections of the commentary. Nevertheless, at this point it may help to briefly summarize the most common reasons for assessing 2 Corinthians as a composite of multiple letters by considering the most commonly proposed divisions.

1. *The seams at 2:13/2:14 and 7:4/7:5.* In 1894 (513–14) Johannes Weiss first suggested that 2 Cor. 1:1–2:13/7:5–16 constituted a single, independent letter. More recently, L. L. Welborn (1996: 583) defended Weiss's proposal on the basis of the coherence of 1:1–2:13 and 7:5–16, analyzed in terms of Greco-Roman literary thought and practice. Welborn concludes that the two passages were originally contiguous, vindicating Weiss in his assessment. Welborn's (1996: 562–69) strongest argument has to do with the continuity of the material from 2:12–13 to 7:5, in which he points out that the parallelism and even the shifts from singular to plural and from πνεῦμα (*pneuma*, spirit) to σάρξ (*sarx*, flesh) are not compelling arguments against the original juxtaposition of these passages (as suggested, for instance, by Garland 1999: 34). Welborn is correct, of course, that parallelism and repetition form a part of good Greek style. However, elements arranged to craft parallelism may at times be "distant," separated by intervening text, to mark or set off movements in a discourse. This is the case, for instance, with the uses of inclusio peppered throughout the book, as well as occurrences of what I have referred to as "parallel introductions" (4:1//4:16; 11:30–31//12:1–3; 12:14//13:1).

Moreover, distant parallels at times can be used in biblical literature to resume a topic that had been abruptly left earlier in a work. In Hebrews, for

---

29. As Betz and MacRae (1985: 4) detail, the groundwork for Semler's study was laid by his teacher, Siegmund Jacob Baumgarten, whose commentary on the Corinthian letters Semler published posthumously.

30. For an overview of the discussion on partitioning theories, see Bieringer 1996b; Furnish 1984: 30–48; Martin 1986: xl–xlvi; Peterson 1998b: 39–51; and the extensive treatment by Harris 2005: 8–51.

31. For a five-letter hypothesis, see, e.g., E.-M. Becker 2004: 66; and for a six-letter proposal, note Taylor 1991: 71.

instance, each shift from exposition on Christ to hortatory material and then back to exposition on Christ is marked by "distant hook words" (that is, words used at the end of one section of exposition and at the beginning of the next section of exposition to "stitch" the two units together thematically). Thus, as the author returns to his christological discussion after a brief hortatory unit, he picks up where he left off in the previous christological argument (Guthrie 1994: 96–99).[32] Rather than an indication of document "fragments," this use of parallelism thus forms a particular literary strategy.[33]

We may well suggest that Paul's departure from his travel narrative at 2:14 and that narrative's resumption at 7:5 also has a strategic literary purpose.[34] The apostle leaves the Corinthians "hanging" with his restless departure for Macedonia recounted at 2:12–13. He does not resume the narrative until 7:5 for at least three reasons. First, the section of text on "authentic ministry" at 2:14–7:4 constitutes the heart of 2 Corinthians, as the apostle offers a robust defense of authentic Christian ministry. The interruption of his travel narrative serves to set off, and thus draw special attention to, that section of text.[35] Second, that treatment of "authentic ministry" in 2:14–7:4 has a great deal to do with the tensions and suffering inherent in following Christ through the world (e.g., 4:7–18; 5:1–10; 6:3–10), and the ministry moment *before* the coming of Titus embodies that tension and suffering. Thus the bracketing of 2:14–7:4 with statements about lack of rest at 2:13 and 7:5 are entirely in accord with a key characteristic of authentic ministry. Third, we may further suggest that Paul delays the happy resolution of tension found in the coming of Titus until (our) 7:5–16, because he was not yet ready to talk about the collection (chaps. 8 and 9), a topic in which the younger minister figures prominently (8:6, 16–24; 9:3–5). Thus the coming of Titus (7:6), as well as the happy news

32. This happens in Hebrews at 1:14/2:5; 2:17–18/4:14–16; and 5:10/7:1. In each case there are also hook words that tie each unit of exposition to the hortatory unit that immediately follows it, and the hortatory unit to the unit that resumes the exposition.

33. In Hebrews, e.g., the author introduces Jesus's appointment as high priest in the order of Melchizedek at 5:1–10, but then shifts abruptly to an extended hortatory section (5:11–6:20). Following the exhortation, he resumes his treatment of the Son's appointment by focusing on the superiority of Melchizedek (7:1–10; Guthrie 1998: 252). The resumption of the earlier exposition is clear and purposeful, riveting the audience's attention on the need for the exposition that has already been introduced (Heb. 6:1–3). Ancient preacher John Chrysostom (*Hom. Heb.* 12, on Heb. 7:1–10, in PG 63:423) recognized the rhetorical effect, noticing that, following the blistering though mitigated exhortation of 5:11–6:20, the hearers of Hebrews would have listened attentively to the speaker when he resumed his discussion of Melchizedek at Heb. 7:1.

34. In the commentary, by appealing to Quintilian (*Inst.* 4.3.14–17), we suggest that Paul uses a form of digression, to rivet the attention with supportive but varied material. Welborn (1996: 566–67) denies that the category is appropriate in this case, but he suggests that specific terminology and procedure should be followed with a true digression. However, we may recognize that while Paul draws on certain rhetorical techniques, he does not seem compelled to follow them slavishly but shapes them to his own purposes. Quintilian notes many ways of digressing.

35. As Quintilian (*Inst.* 4.3.14–17) explains, digressions "serve to refresh, admonish, placate, plead with, or praise the judge." Here Paul makes a personal and theological case for the authenticity of his ministry.

he brought, news that allowed Paul to praise the Corinthians exuberantly (7:7, 11, 13–16), paved the way for a renewed emphasis on the collection.

In addition, as has often been noted, reading a decisive break between 2:13 and 2:14 and between 7:4 and 7:5 seems ill-advised given the continuity between 2:12–13 and 2:14–17 and between 7:4 and 7:5–16. With the former "seam," we have the hook words or themes of "Christ" (2:12, 14), travel (2:12–13, 14), preaching (2:12, 14, 17), and the message preached (2:12, 14). At 7:4 and 7:5–16 we find the themes of "confidence" (7:4, 16), "boasting" (7:4, 14), "encouragement" (7:4, 7, 13), and "joy" (7:4, 13), as well as a description of Paul's afflictions (7:4, 5). The idea that an editor crafted 7:4 specifically to smooth a transition back into 7:5 and following should be seen as "a counsel of desperation," to use Thrall's (1982: 109–10) nicely turned phrase. Contra Welborn (1996: 577), it certainly cannot be fairly claimed that "2:14–7:4 . . . is unrelated to its present context." At both its beginning and ending, the section weaves seamlessly into what goes before and what follows, however abrupt these seams may seem on the surface. In short, the material at these seams satisfies Welborn's criteria of continuity and connectedness. Thus we reject the view that reads 2:14–7:4 as an interposed letter fragment inexpertly embedded in 2 Corinthians.

2. *The "interpolation" at 6:14–7:1.* Some scholars have argued that the unit at 6:14–7:1,[36] coming near the end of the apostle's treatise on authentic ministry, is either the fragment of a letter that Paul mentions in 1 Cor. 5:9 (e.g., Hurd 1965: 135–39; Jewett 1978: 389–444), or a fragment that did not originate with Paul at all (e.g., Betz 1973: 88–108;[37] Fitzmyer 1961). The objections raised against this part of 2 Corinthians are, for instance, that it doesn't fit logically into the flow of argument for the whole letter, or that it does not match the apostle's other writings, having a great number of hapax legomena and correspondences to the Qumran literature.

But with its treatment of pagan temple worship, others have read the passage as profoundly integrative with the surrounding material (see esp. Scott 1992: 217–20; as well as Beale 1989; Goulder 1994a). In fact, Paul's call for a "moral conversion" (Matera 2003: 160) of a church so inundated with the

36. In 2 Cor. 6:14–7:1 Paul presents a highly crafted, logically developed series of exhortations, with various types of support material. Rhetorical questions, theological assertion, and a string of OT quotations having to do with restoration—all work to reinforce, or provide the bases of, or restate the exhortations and call the Corinthians to separate from worldly relationships, which defile them and hurt their relationship with God. Paul wants them to be restored to the true worship of the living God, mediated through the apostle's mission.

37. Betz (1973: 108) suggests that the fragment originated with Paul's opponents and concludes: Paul must have been the embodiment of everything that the Christians speaking in 2 Cor 6:14–7:1 warned against. For them, his "freedom" from the law must have been nothing but the committing of those who followed him to the realm of Beliar and the turning of Christ into a "servant of sin" (Gal 2:17). In fact, the Paul of Galatians, building the entire salvation by God upon "faith" and "Spirit," looks very much like a radical pneumatic, not far from gnosticism. The conclusion is unavoidable that the theology of 2 Cor 6:14–7:1 is not only non-Pauline, but anti-Pauline.

values of its Greco-Roman context, one can argue, quite literally strikes at the "heart" of the Corinthians' need (cf. 12:21)—if they are indeed going to open their hearts in a fresh way to their apostle (6:11–13; 7:2–4). Their "affections" hold them back (6:12), and Paul addresses their affections through this string of OT texts on restoration to the true worship of God.

Further, as James Scott (1992: 216) has pointed out, since the combination of Scripture citations forms a unity within 6:14–7:1, and the use of Scripture we find here stems from a Christian perspective, the Qumran proposal begins to fade in credibility.[38] Further, at 5:20–21 Paul calls for the Corinthians to "be reconciled to God" on the basis of the gospel, in which "we might become the righteousness of God" in Christ. As Thrall (1977: 144–46) observes, this reference to God's righteousness and the appeal not to receive God's grace in vain (5:21–6:1) anticipate very particularly the content of 6:14–7:1, with its call to holy living. The passage, in fact, should be seen as an appropriate and resounding climax of the apostle's call for the Corinthians to recommit themselves to his ministry, for the path to full reconciliation with him and the path to full restoration to the true worship of God are one and the same.

3. *2 Corinthians 8 and 9 as separate letters.* A number of scholars have argued that chapters 8 and 9 constitute two letter fragments.[39] Bultmann (and Dinkler 1985: 256), for instance, states that 2 Cor. 9 could not possibly follow chapter 8 for the following reasons. (1) The phrase at 9:1, Περὶ μὲν γὰρ τῆς διακονίας (*Peri men gar tēs diakonias*, Now on the one hand about this ministry) clearly forms an introduction of a theme just taken up, whereas chapter 8 has already been treating the theme. (2) The description τῆς διακονίας τῆς εἰς τοὺς ἁγίους (*tēs diakonias tēs eis tous hagious*, this ministry to God's people; lit., the saints/holy ones) is odd given the fact that Paul has already described the ministry clearly in chapter 8. (3) The περισσόν μοί ἐστιν τὸ γράφειν ὑμῖν (*perisson moi estin to graphein hymin*, it is redundant for me to write to you further) again sounds as if a new theme is being initiated. (4) That 9:2 describes the eagerness of the Corinthians as boastworthy does not match chapter 8, where the Macedonians are the ones who serve as the model. This seems backward to Bultmann, who thinks chapter 9 must have been written first. And finally, (5) 8:20 depicts a different purpose for sending the brothers than does 9:3–5. The former suggests that Paul's motive had to do with guarding his nonembezzling reputation; the latter points to the practical work of gathering the collection. Yet Bultmann admits that these verses could be reconciled.

In spite of such concerns, a strong case can be made for the unity and yet the unique functions of chapters 8 and 9 in the development of 2 Corinthians. For instance, Stowers (1990), who investigates ninety uses of περὶ μὲν γάρ

---

38. Scott (1992: 216) takes on the alleged Qumranisms directly.

39. Thus, e.g., Bornkamm 1965: 31–32; Betz and MacRae 1985: 141–44; Jewett 1978: 389–444; Georgi 1986: 17; Bultmann and Dinkler 1985: 256. The proposals concerning when and why each letter was written vary widely. For an overview, see Taylor 1991: 69n2.

outside the NT, makes a strong case that 9:1 actually refers back to the content of chapter 8. Also, Garland (1999: 400) has pointed out an extensive inclusio bracketing the beginning and end of 8:1–9:15, pointing to the two chapters as a literary unit. To his list of five elements we add four others:[40]

τὴν χάριν τοῦ θεοῦ (*tēn charin tou theou*, the grace of God; 8:1; 9:14)

δίδωμι/δωρεά (*didōmi/dōrea*, I give/gift; 8:1; 9:15)

δοκιμή (*dokimē*, test; 8:2; 9:13)

ἡ περισσεία/περισσεύω (*hē perisseia/perisseuō*, the overflow/I overflow; 8:2; 9:12)

ἁπλότης (*haplotēs*, generosity; 8:2; 9:11, 13)

κοινωνία (*koinōnia*, sharing; 8:4; 9:13)

διακονία (*diakonia*, ministry; 8:4; 9:12–13)

δέησις/δέομαι (*deēsis/deomai*, request/I request; 8:4; 9:14)

ἅγιος (*hagios*, saint; 8:4; 9:12)

These extensive parallels provide further evidence of the literary unity of 2 Cor. 8–9, and movements within these two chapters show continuity. For example, as will be explained further in the commentary, 8:16–9:5 deals with Titus's mission. Having dealt with the "who" of the trip in 8:16–24, the words of 9:1–5 offer an explanation of "why" Paul has sent these brothers on ahead to deal with the collection. The section comprising 9:6–15 then offers encouragement by treating both the resources that God will provide the Corinthians for their giving and the promised results. Thus, it is ill-advised to depict these two chapters as somehow separate entities.[41]

4. *The "break" between chapters 9 and 10.* Of course, one of the most obvious shifts in 2 Corinthians comes at the transition from chapter 9 to chapter 10; the view that chapters 1–9 and 10–13 constitute two separate letters is widely held and published (Taylor 1991: 68). Some who hold this view believe the first nine chapters were written first and the final four sometime later, perhaps after Paul had received additional, disturbing news from Corinth (e.g., Furnish 1984: 44–45; Martin 1986: xlvi). Others suggest that the content of 10–13 mark it as the earlier production, perhaps the sorrowful letter mentioned in 2:3–4 (e.g., F. Watson 1984; Taylor 1991: 71).

40. Garland (1999: 400) does not include the following (with two parallels based on cognate relationships) in his list: δίδωμι/δωρεά, *didōmi/dōrea*, I give/gift (8:1; 9:15); δέησις/δέομαι, *deēsis/deomai*, request/I request (8:4; 9:14); ἅγιος, *hagios*, saint (8:4; 9:12); κοινωνία, *koinōnia*, sharing (8:4; 9:13).

41. Betz and MacRae (1985: 142) have carried out one of the most extensive analyses of the two chapters. Though they conclude that the content of chaps. 8 and 9 point to two separate letters, they believe that they may have been sent at the same time, one addressing Corinth and the other Achaia generally. But as Murphy-O'Connor (1991b: 78) has suggested, Betz and MacRae have demonstrated only that these two sections of the book formally follow the pattern of administrative letters in dealing with an administrative issue, the collection for the saints.

Generally, those who hold the two sections apart as separate letters point out the positive tone of chapters 1–9, replete with expressions of joy, relief, and confidence in the Corinthians, in contrast to the harshness of 10–13. How can the "I am glad to say that I have complete confidence in you!" of 7:16 be reconciled with the sobering warning of 12:20, "For I am afraid that perhaps when I come I will find you to be not the sort of 'you' I want you to be," and with the exhortation of 13:5, "Test yourselves to see whether you are in the faith!"? It seems, then, that in contrast to the first nine chapters of the book, the final four seem full of "jarring sarcasm, violent self-defence, fierce accusation of others" (R. Hanson 1961: 16). Further, Furnish (1984: 30–32) notes that while the earlier chapters of the book do not make reference to an impending visit (indeed, they explain why Paul had *not* come to visit!; 1:15–16), the final chapters of the book speak straightforwardly about the apostle's intention to travel to Corinth. Also, chapters 1–9 seem to speak of an earlier visit of Titus (7:7, 14), but the latter chapters imply a second visit of the young minister (12:18a). Also, the latter chapters, with their acerbic tone, would destroy the goodwill that Paul sought to build with the friendly, conciliatory tone of chapter 9. Finally, Furnish (1984: 30–32) suggests, chapters 1–9 are filled with use of the first-person plural, whereas chapters 10–13 have Paul speaking in the first-person singular.

Yet the position that chapters 1–9 and chapters 10–13 form a unified letter has always had its champions,[42] and there seems to be a current trend back toward viewing the book as a unity (Harris 2005: 42–43).[43] Numerous arguments have been marshaled in this direction (e.g., Garland 1999: 38–44; Harris 2005: 42–51; Hall 2003: 86–128; Long 2004). For instance, the abrupt change in tone can be explained variously. Paul may have been traveling when he started composition, and the writing of the letter may have taken days if not weeks. Perhaps the apostle received an alarming report from Corinth that caused him to shift the tone of the letter's end rather decisively. Once a letter was prepared, adjustments could be made. For instance, in one of his letters Cicero says, "I wrote to you above that Curio was very cold; well, he is warm enough now; . . . he had not done so before I wrote the first part of this letter" (*Fam.* 8.6.5). In fact, "It was not uncommon for an author's tone to change

42. See the helpful history overview of those defending the unity of the book in Betz and MacRae 1985: 27–35. Betz's treatment largely focuses on German scholarship, but it demonstrates well that a significant contingent of critical scholars have found partitioning theories on 2 Corinthians to be less than convincing.

43. It is often recognized that no existing textual tradition presents 2 Corinthians as anything other than a unified whole (Hall 2003: 86), and that we have no patristic evidence that the book is made up of fragments. This is true and has some significance. We must take seriously the form of the document we have before us. However, since the earliest data on the existence of 2 Corinthians we have comes in the mid-second century, with allusions in Polycarp and an inclusion of the book in Marcion's canon (Harris 2005: 2–3), it leaves open the possibility that another form or forms of the book existed very early in the collection process. Such a view, however, apart from the literary theories mentioned above, remains pure speculation since 2 Corinthians has come down to us as a whole.

or his opinion to shift in a postscript. Something happened, news arrived, the situation shifted, and the author needed to clarify, modify or change his view on the matter. A writer needed to soften (or stiffen) his tone in light of some new information" (Capes, Reeves, and Richards 2007: 79).

A number of recent works, however, have suggested that Paul's abrupt change in tone at 10:1 was rhetorically strategic, rather than merely circumstantial, as the apostle turned to focus quite specifically on his opponents in Corinth. Leaving such an offensive until the end was rhetorically appropriate (e.g., Young and Ford 1987: 28, 37–38, 43–44; Danker 1991; Hall 2003: 89–91; Witherington 1995: 429–32). For instance, Demosthenes, toward the end of his *Second Epistle*, shifts the tone of his work to address his opponents directly (Young and Ford 1987: 37). In his final movement he writes, "Now thus far I am appealing to you all, but for those in particular who are attacking me in your presence I wish to say a word" (*Ep.* 2.26; N. W. De Witt and N. J. De Witt 1949: 225). He goes on to argue that the enmity of certain men should not be allowed to prevail (*Ep.* 2.26). This form of apology has at least some analogy to 2 Corinthians, in which Paul continues to address the church generally but foregrounds his opponents in a heated defense from chapter 10 onward.[44]

Others have not only answered the alleged contradictions between chapters 1–9 and 10–13 but have also demonstrated the extensive continuity between the two sections of the letter in terms of vocabulary and controlling themes (see esp. Barnett 1997: 19–23;[45] Harris 2005: 44–51;[46] Garland 1999: 40–44).[47] Moreover, James Scott (1998: 5) has observed that the discourse flow of 2 Corinthians has three main movements, each preparing for Paul's third visit to Corinth in a different way. Chapters 1–7 present a rigorous defense of the authenticity of his apostolic ministry in the face of criticisms leveled against him (e.g., 1:12–2:13), the difficulty of his second visit (2:1–11), and the opponents in the community (2:17; 5:12; 6:8; 6:14–7:1). Thus Paul spends a good bit of time reflecting on the difficulties of recent months, seeking full reconciliation with

---

44. The complexity of the Corinthian church has at times been given too little attention in discussions of the letter's complicated makeup. It should not be surprising that a church spread throughout a large city, and perhaps throughout the broader region in which that city was located (see the comments at 1:1 on σὺν τοῖς ἁγίοις πᾶσιν τοῖς οὖσιν ἐν ὅλη τῇ Ἀχαΐᾳ, *syn tois hagiois pasin tois ousin en holē tē Achaia*, along with all God's holy people throughout Achaia), would have various factions (1 Cor. 1:10–11!) and subgroups that the apostle may need to address in various ways.

45. Barnett (1997: 18–19), e.g., observes that throughout the letter, Paul makes powerful appeals to the Corinthians (2 Cor. 5:20–6:2; 6:11–7:1; 10:1–2; 12:11–13; 13:5–11); foreshadows his upcoming visit, when he will correct some attitude or action in the church (2:1, 3; 9:4; 10:2, 6; 11:9; 12:14, 20, 21; 13:1, 2, 10); and uses distinctive vocabulary.

46. Harris (2005: 47–48), e.g., notes verbal echoes from chaps. 1–9 in 10–13 at 3:9/11:15 ("ministry of righteousness"); 2:17/12:19 ("we speak before God in Christ"); 1:17/10:2 ("from worldly motives"); 6:13/12:14 ("to/for children"); 3:2/12:11 (on endorsement); 4:2/12:16 (Paul as a "crafty" fellow who manipulates by selling God's Word).

47. Garland (1999: 40–44) notes, e.g., the subject of boasting (1:12, 14; 5:12; 10:8, 13, 15–16, 17–18; 11:10, 12, 16–18, 30; 12:1, 5–6, 9), sincerity of his conduct (1:17; 2:17; 4:2; 6:3–10; 7:2; 10:2; 12:16–18), not "according to the flesh" (1:17; 4:2; 5:16; 10:2–4; 12:16); etc.

the Corinthians. In the second movement, chapters 8–9, the apostle specifically challenges the church to get busy with the collection for the saints and to do so now in preparation for his coming visit. Chapters 10–13, moreover, prepare for that visit by taking on the opponents quite directly.

From another perspective, Thomas Schmeller has analyzed the "closeness" of Paul to the Corinthians in chapters 1–9 over against the "distance" in chapters 10–13 in terms of both relationship and situation. Schmeller, following Vegge (2008: 254–359), suggests that both the positive statements in 1–9 and the harsh, critical statements in 10–13 are overstated for rhetorical effect; they thus have a pragmatic function. Vegge suggests that both the statements of "closeness" and "distance" are meant to motivate the Corinthians from the two vantage points. But Schmeller (2013: 81), in contradistinction from Vegge, proposes, "The transition to a more critical tone does not necessarily point to the beginning of a new letter but has more to do with Paul's attempt to deal with the same situation, albeit in two different ways, in order to fulfill two related and yet distinct aims." The situation to which Schmeller refers has to do with the collection for Jerusalem. He suggests that chapters 1–9 prepare for Titus's visit, but 10–13 prepare for Paul's own visit to Corinth. Titus's earlier visit had been successful, while Paul's earlier visit had been a disaster. Also, in chapters 1–9 Paul sets the tone for an appropriate communion between the church in Corinth and the church in Jerusalem. In chapters 10–13, according to Schmeller, the apostle confronts opponents who would challenge his mediation between these two churches. Thus, rather than signaling two letters, the change in tone at 10:1 points to a shift in ways that Paul addresses the situation in Corinth. In 1–9 he prepares for the coming of Titus, while in 10–13 he prepares for his own coming and a final reconciliation (Schmeller 2013: 81).

One final point can be noted in defense of the letter's unity: the last section (chaps. 10–13) closes with a passage that mirrors no fewer than nine terms and phrases found in 1:1–7, forming a striking inclusio (on its use, see Guthrie 1994: 76–89) that brackets the beginning and ending of the letter. The parallel terms (or cognates) are as follows:

Parallel Term	1:1–7	13:11–13
ἀδελφός (adelphos, brother)	1:1	13:11
παρακαλέω (parakaleō, I comfort)	1:4, 6	13:11
αὐτός (autos, same)	1:4, 6	13:11
εἰρήνη (eirēnē, peace)	1:2	13:11
θεός (theos, God)	1:1, 2	13:11
forms of ὑμεῖς (hymeis, you [pl.])	1:2, 6, 7	13:11, 12, 13
οἱ ἅγιοι πάντες (hoi hagioi pantes, all the holy people)	1:1	13:12
χάρις (charis, grace)	1:2	13:13
κυρίου Ἰησοῦ Χριστοῦ (kyriou Iēsou Christou, the Lord Jesus Christ)	1:2, 3	13:13

This use of inclusio seems to thwart those who propose that these closing verses, in their original literary context, function only as the conclusion to chapters 10–13. Further, the suggestion that 13:11–13 did not originally belong to 13:1–10 (on which see Thrall 2000: 900) seems highly doubtful given the lexical cohesion between the two units.[48]

For any competent resolution, the details of the discourse and the case for continuity or discontinuity must be made in the process of exegesis and discourse analysis. The approach taken in this commentary assumes the unity of the book, believing that the discourse, while containing great difficulties for interpretation, throughout sustains certain topics such as Paul's treatment of "commendation" and "boasting." There also is great benefit in assessing Paul's posture toward God, toward the Corinthians, and toward the opponents in evaluating the unity, progression, and logic of the book. This will be treated further in the section below (see "The Message and Intent of 2 Corinthians").

The "Voice(s)" with Which Paul Writes 2 Corinthians

The interplay of first-person singular verbs and pronouns and first-person plural verbs and pronouns in 2 Corinthians raises the question With whose "voice" does Paul speak? When speaking in a "plural voice," does the apostle use a "literary" (or "epistolary") plural, by which "we" represents singular "I"? Or does he speak to the Corinthians both personally (i.e., "I") and as part of a larger ministry team (i.e., "we")?[49]

The convention of the literary plural in Greek writings was on the rise in the Hellenistic period (e.g., in Cicero and Josephus; see Lyons 1985: 42–53), and Paul seems to use it at points (Rom. 2:2; 3:19; 7:14; 8:22, 28; see Thrall 1994: 105). However, the question for 2 Corinthians remains whether Paul in his use of plural forms normally intends to speak of himself as a representative of a larger ministerial group, or whether he uses the first-person plural as a literary device by which he simply means "I." The fact that the apostle names a cosender (1:1) doesn't help us much in and of itself since he also names cosenders in 1 Corinthians, Galatians, Philippians, and Philemon, but then proceeds to speak in the first-person singular. It may be noteworthy

48. Elements include forms of λοιπός (13:2, 11), χαίρω (13:9, 11), αὐτός (13:4, 11), θεός (13:4, 7, 11, 13), ὑμεῖς (throughout), πᾶς (13:1, 2, 12, 13), κύριος (13:10, 13), and Ἰησοῦς Χριστός (13:5, 13).

49. E.g., in the benediction of 1:3–7, there is some question about to whom the first-person plural pronoun refers. This use of the plural is sustained all the way through 1:14 and then reactivated at various points in following chapters. Is this a reference to the general Christian community (i.e., "who encourages us as believers in every affliction"), specifically to Paul's ministry team (i.e., "who encourages me and my coworkers in every affliction"), or only to Paul himself—and thus an epistolary, or literary, use of the plural (i.e., "who encourages me in every distressing situation")? The question has no easy resolution. In 1:3–7 plural forms of ἐγώ are used eight times, and in verses 6–7 Paul uses the pronoun or the first-person plural form of the verbs to place the "we" over against "you" references to the Corinthians. Therefore it seems that Paul's use of "we" does not include the Corinthians at this point but accomplishes one of two things. Either he is referring to himself with an epistolary use of the plural, or he is referring to himself and others who are part of his ministerial circle, most immediately Timothy, Silvanus, and Titus.

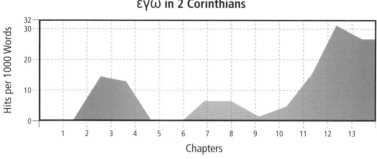

Figure 1 **Occurrences of the Singular Pronoun ἐγώ in 2 Corinthians**

that 1 and 2 Thessalonians, books that include both Timothy and Silvanus as coauthors (1 Thess. 1:1; 2 Thess. 1:1; cf. 2 Cor. 1:19), are oriented to the use of first-person plural. But what is striking about the authorial voice in 2 Corinthians is the alternation back and forth between singular and plural. Lyons (1985: 14) notes, "The uneven distribution of the first person singular and plural in Paul's letters and the frequent and often inexplicable alternation between the two make it extremely improbable that the fact of co-senders significantly influences his use of 'we.'"[50] How, then, might we understand the apostle's interesting mix of singular and plural? Does the phenomenon have anything to tell us about Paul's approach to ministry as reflected in this book? The issue is notoriously difficult, but I offer the following points for consideration:

1. Notice that although both singular and plural pronouns and verb forms are found throughout the book, chapters 1–9 clearly favor the plural, while chapters 10–13 have a preponderance of the singular.[51] For instance, Paul uses singular forms of the pronoun ἐγώ (egō, I/me) 64 times in 2 Corinthians,[52] with a higher concentration of these occurring in the final four chapters of the book (1:17, 19, 23; 2:2–3, 5, 10, 12–13; 6:16–18; 7:4, 7; 9:1, 4; 10:1; 11:1, 9–10, 16, 18, 21–23, 28–30, 32; 12:6–9, 11, 13, 15–16, 20–21; 13:3, 10), as seen in figure 1.[53]

By contrast, ἐγώ occurs in plural forms 108 times in 2 Corinthians, with only 14 of these found in chapters 10–13[54] (1:2–8, 10–12, 14, 18–22; 2:14;

50. The uneven distribution also speaks against dividing the letter neatly into "we" and "I" sections, such as with Murphy-O'Connor (2010: 6), who identifies "broad patterns" and their exceptions. Further, this movement back and forth between singular and plural is unique to the Corinthian correspondence and Colossians (Verhoef 1996: 422).

51. This is one reason some suggest that chaps. 1–9 and 10–13 are two separate letters (e.g., Furnish 1984: 32). Murphy-O'Connor (2010: 11–12) understands the "we" sections to indicate that Paul's letter found in 2 Cor. 1–9 is coauthored with Timothy. The uses of the singular "I" are read as eruptions into an otherwise consistent pattern of speaking of the coauthors in the plural.

52. In four of these, God is the speaker (6:16–18; 12:9).

53. Notice, e.g., the consistency with which Paul speaks in first-person singular in the "Fool's Speech" of 11:22–12:10.

54. Of these, only two occurrences are in chap. 11 and none in chap. 12.

3:2–3, 5–6, 18; 4:3, 6–7, 10–14; 4:16–5:2; 5:5, 10, 12, 14, 16, 18–21; 6:11–12, 16; 7:2–7, 9, 12–14; 8:4–7, 9, 19–20, 22–24; 9:3–4, 11; 10:2, 4, 7–8, 13, 15; 11:12, 21; 13:4, 6–7, 9).

Figure 2 **Occurrences of ἐγώ in Plural Constructions in 2 Corinthians**

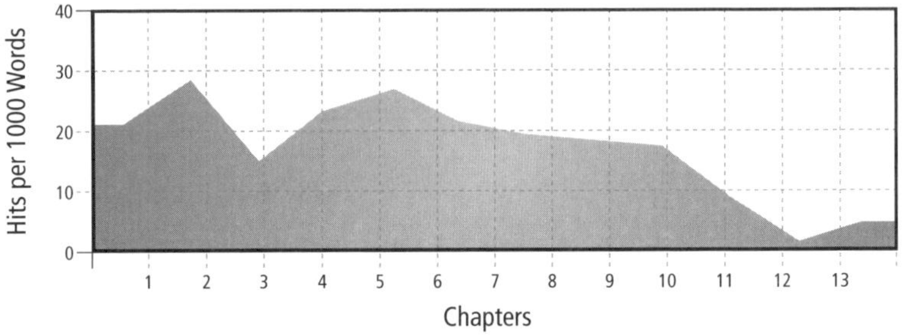

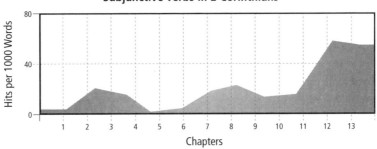

We find similar patterns when we consider verbal forms. Verbs in the indicative or subjunctive moods occur in first-person singular forms 145 times in the book, with only a little over one-third of these found in the first nine chapters (1:13, 15, 17, 23; 2:1–5, 8–10, 13; 4:13; 5:11; 6:2, 13, 16–18; 7:3–4, 8–9, 12, 14, 16; 8:3, 8, 10; 9:2–5; 10:1–2, 8–9; 11:2–3, 5, 7–9, 11–12, 16–18, 21, 23–25, 29–31; 11:33–12:3; 12:5–11, 13–18; 12:20–13:2; 13:6, 10).

Figure 3 **Occurrences of Singular Indicative and Subjunctive Verbs in 2 Corinthians**

By contrast, first-person plural forms of indicative or subjunctive verbs appear 94 times in the letter, only 21 of these occurring in chapters 10–13 (1:4, 6, 8–10, 12–14, 24; 2:11, 15; 2:17–3:1; 3:4–5, 12; 3:18–4:2; 4:5, 7, 11, 13, 16; 5:1–4, 6–9, 11–13, 16; 5:20–6:1; 6:9, 16; 7:1–2, 13–14; 8:1, 5, 18, 21–22; 9:4; 10:3, 11–14; 11:4, 21; 12:18–19; 13:4, 6–9).

Thus we have a clear *general* pattern in the book that must be taken into consideration. If we reckon all thirteen chapters to form a single letter, why does the apostle transition at 10:1 to speak predominantly in a "singular" voice? It is striking that he begins the section with "Now I, Paul, personally appeal to you," and such a personal appeal fits the preponderance of the

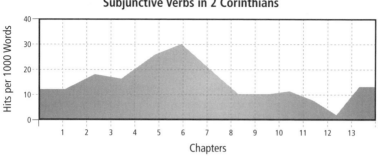

Figure 4 **Occurrences of Plural Indicative and Subjunctive Verbs in 2 Corinthians**

first-person forms in these last chapters of the book. Might it be that the use of the first-person forms in the first nine chapters also marks especially "personal" statements in some way?

2. At times Paul clearly uses the plural to refer to himself and his ministry team. This seems to be the case especially when he speaks of ministry in general, either principles that govern his mission, or patterns of ministry practice. The most obvious case is found in 1:18–19, where the apostle shifts from the singular to the plural to include Timothy and Silvanus as coproclaimers of God's word: "On the contrary, as God is faithful, *our* word to you is not a contradictory 'yes' and 'no'! For Jesus Christ, the Son of God, who is among you through *our* preaching, that is through me and Silvanus and Timothy, was not a confusing 'Yes and No,' but in Him has become a resounding 'Yes!'" Here Paul clearly uses the plural pronoun to speak not only of himself but also of a broader team of ministers. Also, notice that when at 1:24 he states, "Not that we dominate you with regard to your faith, but we work together for your joy; for you stand in faith," the Greek noun συνεργοί (*synergoi*, workers) is plural. Paul shifts from first-person singular in 1:23 and then back to first-person singular in 2:1, and he does so, not to employ a literary plural but to make a reference to his broader ministry team. Further, at 3:2 the apostle depicts the Corinthians as a recommendation letter "written on our hearts" (ἐγγεγραμμένη ἐν ταῖς καρδίαις ἡμῶν, *engegrammenē en tais kardiais hēmōn*), and the word rendered "hearts" (ταῖς καρδίαις) is plural. Similarly, at 3:6, speaking of himself and his ministry team, Paul writes, "who also made us competent as ministers of a new covenant," and the word rendered "ministers," διακόνους (*diakonous*), is plural in form. These seem to be clear cases where Paul has his broader ministry team in mind.

3. At times the first-person plural is used of all believers or for Paul, his ministry team, and the Corinthians inclusively. For instance, the apostle's mention of the anointing and sealing of the Spirit at 1:21–22 can be understood as referring to all believers. The πάντες (*pantes*, all) at 3:18 clearly indicates that the pronoun ἡμεῖς (*hēmeis*) that precedes it is an inclusive "we," speaking of all those who participate in the liberating new covenant. Further, 5:10 clearly speaks of a mandatory appearance at Christ's judgment seat for all people

(Garland 1999: 74), and Paul seems to refer to all believers when at 6:16 he notes that "we are the temple of the living God" (ἡμεῖς γὰρ ναὸς θεοῦ ἐσμεν ζῶντος, *hēmeis gar naos theou esmen zōntos*). Finally, at 7:1 he seems to make an appeal that encompasses his ministry team and the Corinthians when he writes, "Therefore, dear ones, since *we* have promises like these, *we* should wash ourselves clean from every impurity of the flesh and spirit, making *our* holiness complete in the fear of God."

4. Cranfield (1982: 286) considered it a virtual certainty that Paul at times used the literary plural, a conclusion with which Lyons (1985: 15) agrees: "That 'we,' at least sometimes, means only 'I' cannot be avoided." Accordingly, at least some of the occurrences of the first-person plural in 2 Corinthians seem to be epistolary or literary plurals. For example, Thrall (1994: 106) suggests that the ἡμᾶς (*hēmas*) at 10:2, given the presence of the singular verbs in 10:1–2, almost certainly is epistolary, and this may well be the case. But it should be noted that this use of ἡμᾶς initiates uses of the plural that continue through verse 7, and it is at least possible that the switch to the plural with the pronoun in verse 2 has been effected because the apostle now speaks of patterns of ministry evident in his ministry team. On the other hand, in 10:10 Paul seems to speak of statements made about him personally, and the follow-up use of the plurals in 10:11 ("we say"/"we do") seem to be examples of literary plurals. Other examples of literary plurals have been suggested, for instance, at 2:14–16 (Hafemann 1990b: 12–15); 7:12–14; and 11:6 (Thrall 1994: 106–7). In most cases, however, these *could* be read as references to both Paul and his broader ministry team.

5. There are spans of discourse in 2 Corinthians where the singular and plural forms are used quite consistently, and these may offer further clues for our query. At 2:14–6:15 we find no occurrences of the first-person singular pronoun and only four uses of first-person singular verbs in the indicative or subjunctive moods.[55] Of those four occurrences, two are in quotations (4:13; 6:2) and two are personal interjections by which Paul expresses hope or intense emotion (5:11; 6:13). This consistent use of the plural (with the exception of the interjection at 1:13) is also true of 1:1–14.[56] So the letter

55. In reality the pattern holds all the way through 7:2. The occurrences of the singular pronoun and singular forms of the verbs in the quotation of 6:16–18 have God speaking. Only at 7:3–4, in the apostle's final appeal of the section, does he revert to the singular.

56. I respectfully disagree with Harris (2005: 140–41) on a number of counts. It does not seem obvious that Paul shares a general principle in 1:4 applicable "primarily to himself" (this could include his ministry team). Further against Harris, I think it entirely conceivable that the intense experiences described in 1:8–11 could have been an experience shared by Paul and his coworkers. Moreover, 2:12–13 and 7:5–6 do not refer to "the same events," but rather to a sequence of events, the first focused on leaving Troas and the second on entering Macedonia. In my opinion, it does not seem to be a given that both must be referring to Paul alone. In 2:12–13 Paul may use the singular because he is in the process of defending the decisions he has made in recent months. At 7:5–6 the plural pronoun might indicate that Paul has met and traveled with companions as he moved into Macedonia. It seems that at least Timothy and Erastus were waiting for him there (Acts 19:22); others from Derbe and Asia are named as traveling with him

opening (1:1–2), the prologue (1:3–11), what many consider the letter's thesis statement (1:12–14), and the letter's theological heart (2:14–7:4)—all these are dominated by Paul's "plural voice."

By contrast, the use of plural referents almost completely falls away in the heart (and heat!) of chapters 10–13. It should be remembered, as noted above, that Paul introduces chapters 10–13 as a *personal* appeal (10:1), marking a clear shift in the discourse. It may be suggested that the dominance of the first-person singular in 10–13 is consonant with this section being a personal appeal in which Paul speaks primarily for himself. Between 10:15 and 13:4, plural forms of ἐγώ only occur at 11:12, 21, and first-person plural forms of the verb in the indicative or subjunctive moods appear only at 11:4, 21 and 12:18–19.[57]

6. So how might we read this data? It seems, first of all, that the alternation between singular and plural in the book must be more than an offering of literary variety. This is clearly the case with points 2 and 3 above. Second, it may be suggested that the plural by which Paul refers to both himself and his ministry team can be considered the default voice in the book. The naming of Timothy as cosender, while of little significance on its own, must be read alongside the naming of Timothy and Silvanus as fellow preachers to the Corinthians at 1:18–22 and subtle references to a plurality of ministers at 1:24; 3:2; and 3:6. Accordingly, it seems significant that 1:1–14 and 2:14–6:15, where the apostle offers respectively the introduction and heart of his letter, he lays before the Corinthians praise to God for deliverance in the midst of ministry, as well as the principles and patterns of ministry as lived out by his ministry team.

On the other hand, the middle section of the apostle's confrontational discourse in 2 Cor. 10–13 finds Paul mounting a personal defense of his ministry in which he personally goes toe-to-toe with his opponents in Corinth, defending his own actions. Correspondingly, shifts to the first person throughout the book seem to be triggered by

    a. interjection of personal exclamations (e.g., 1:13; 5:11; 6:13),
    b. defense of personal decisions or actions (e.g., 1:15–17; 1:23–2:4; much of chaps. 10–13),
    c. statements of his own interaction with the Corinthians (e.g., 2:5–11; 6:13; 7:3–4, 8–12; 8:8), and
    d. forms of personal history or testimony (e.g., 2:12–13; 8:3).

as he left Corinth, journeying back through Macedonia (Acts 20:4–5), and perhaps they have been with him from the beginning of the trip, though this is by no means clear. In any case, at 7:2–16 the use of the plural pronoun is mixed with the use of first-person singular forms. This might be the epistolary plural at work, with Paul referring to himself alone, but the back-and-forth nature of Paul's use of the singular and plural in the chapter could also be a mix of the apostle referring to himself and to his ministry team.

57. At 11:4 Paul may revert to the plural due to the topic of proclamation, harking back to earlier references to the preaching of his team (e.g., 1:19; 2:17). At 12:18–19 the apostle uses the plural to speak of himself and Titus as a ministry team.

In other words, when Paul turns to his own defense or notes his personal thoughts or actions, he departs from a default orientation in which he, as a general pattern, writes as a part of his broader ministry team.

These patterns are not rigorously followed by the apostle. At times the movement between plural references that include himself and his team members and those that speak of himself in the singular seems fluid. But the shift to first person, rather than a specific literary strategy, highlights the very personal nature of Paul's appeal in this letter. This personal orientation grows in the final four chapters of the book because Paul confronts the unrepentant with his imminent return. In other words, when the apostle's personal relationship or interaction with those in Corinth is foregrounded, and especially when it is more confrontational, he seems to revert to the singular. Elsewhere, it seems he speaks with a plural voice primarily as a way of including his ministry team in his statements.

The apostle Paul understands himself to be unique, and he speaks at times of his own responsibility, or accusations made against him personally, or actions he has personally carried out. Yet ministry to Paul is carried out as part of a larger team, as his mission practices strongly indicate. The "we" of ministry carried out as a team must be considered a significant "voice" in 2 Corinthians alongside the "I" of Paul's personal plans, experiences, perspectives, authority, and defense. The lines between the singular voice and the plural voice are neither rigidly firm, nor are they nonexistent. Paul's concept of ministry posture and practice presents a mixture of his unique role and responsibility as apostle and spiritual father to the Corinthians and his partnership as part of his mission team. This, I suggest, is why 2 Corinthians is written with a mix of singular and plural voices.

2 Corinthians as Reflecting a Relational Network

For those who understand the letter as a patchwork of fragments written at various times and for various purposes, there exists no single purpose and perhaps no unifying message(s) in our canonical 2 Corinthians. But since we consider the book a unity, we need to assess the discourse as a whole, seeking to make sense of the apostle's approach, his message(s), and his intent. A number of analyses of the discourse or its parts are on offer, including a study of the rhetorical form,[58] the literary structure,[59] and its thematic development,[60] and these all prove helpful in various ways. But I wish to offer a slightly different perspective, one that is complementary to other analyses and especially oriented to analyzing the network of relationships reflected in 2 Corinthians. For whatever else we may say about the letter, it may be suggested that the

---

58. As, e.g., by Witherington 1995: 333–36; Long 2004; Young and Ford 1987: 28, 37–38, 43–44; Danker 1991; Hall 2003: 89–91. See the comments by Harris 2005: 105–10.

59. Especially in analyzing the letter or part of it in terms of its chiastic structure (e.g., Segalla 1988; Blomberg 1989; Garland 1999: 422–23).

60. See, e.g., Hafemann 2000: 37–39; Furnish 1984: xi–xii; Matera 2003: 8–9; Barrett 1973: 51–52.

relational tension between Paul and the Corinthian church (and the Corinthian interlopers) does much to shape this letter. Whether he is appealing for sensitivity to his suffering (e.g., 1:8–11), explaining his decisions (1:12–2:4), commending to the Corinthians his mission's authentic embodiment of Christian ministry (2:14–7:4), promoting the collection (chaps. 8–9), or confronting the Corinthians about his opponents (chaps. 10–13), the apostle addresses various aspects of his relationship with the church and their relationship to his mission. Therefore, one approach to grasping the book's reason for being is to analyze the relational network reflected in its pages.

1. *Paul and his God.* Our letter to the Corinthians manifests a profound "Godward" grounding in the apostle's life and ministry. Paul begins with a self-identification that he is an apostle "by God's will," who writes to "God's church," expressing grace and peace "from God our Father and the Lord Jesus Christ" (1:1–2). In the face of the afflictions Paul has faced, it is God whom the apostle blesses as the God of supreme encouragement (1:3–7; 7:6), and it is God who delivers, who gives perspective in the face of severe suffering, and on whom Paul has set his hope for the future (1:8–11). Paul and his ministry team conduct their ministry by God's grace and with God-given straightforwardness and sincerity (1:12), as well as by God's anointing and strength (1:21).

Paul preaches the gospel of God's Son, Jesus Christ, in whom all God's promises are fulfilled (1:19–20). God leads his ministers in triumphal procession of this gospel in Christ, and as these ministers proclaim the gospel in the world, they "are a fragrance of Christ to God," for which Paul gives thanks (2:14–16). The apostle speaks, not "twisting" God's Word as a huckster (2:17; 4:2), but as having been "sent by God, living before God, in Christ" (2:17). Since he lives with a posture "before God" (2:17; 4:2) and speaks "in the sight of God" (12:19), he can appeal to God as his witness (1:23), as well as commend himself to people (4:2). He has supreme confidence "through Christ toward God" (3:4), not on the basis of his own abilities, but on the basis of new-covenant, Spirit-enabled competence that comes from God (3:4–6). Paul and his team preach the gospel of God in the world, for they have seen and been transformed by the glory of God in the face of Christ (3:17–18; 4:6).

As God's ministers who preach God's message, Paul and his team suffer, in part so that it might be manifested that the power displayed in their ministry has its source in God (4:7–11). Thus he only boasts in God (10:17–18) and only about his weaknesses (11:21–12:10). In fact, suffering for the sake of God's gospel is building up a tonnage of glory in the unseen, eternal realm (4:16–18); indeed, God prepares his servants for that realm by making for them a "building from God," an eternal, heavenly residence (5:1). Paul lives with a longing to please and be with the Lord (5:8–9), with an appropriate "fear" before God and openness toward God (5:11). In fact, even when he is misunderstood as being out of his mind, Paul lives for God (5:13), constrained by the love of Christ (5:14). God has reconciled Paul and his ministry team to Christ and given them the ministry of calling others to be reconciled to God. Thus they serve as Christ's ambassadors (5:18–21) and commend themselves in every way as God's ministers in the world (6:3–10). God's grace flows through them (8:1; 9:8, 14), and the result is great thanksgiving and glory to God (9:11–13).

To this end, Paul has been given authority from God to minister to and build up the Corinthian church (10:8, 13; 13:10). Correspondingly, this means that with the very power of God he confronts those who threaten the Corinthian church through false ministry (10:3–6). In fact, Paul preaches God's gospel free of charge to make a clear distinction between himself and the false ministers (11:7–12). Ultimately he prays to God that the Corinthians will be restored and unified in the true gospel so that the God of love and peace will be with them (13:7, 11, 13). In short, Paul's profound Godwardness stems from God being the source, the primary audience, and the ultimate goal for all the apostle is and does. Before God, he lives out and preaches the gospel from God, ministering and suffering for God, to bring about reconciliation between people and God, all to God's glory.

2. *Paul's commitment to and concern for the Corinthians.* This is why Paul ministers to the Corinthians. He has been given the ministry to them by God himself, who assigned Corinth as an area of influence for which Paul was responsible (10:13–14), to the end that he would use this authority to build up the Corinthians in the faith (10:8; 12:19; 13:10). *Thus, in every way the ministry he does is "for" the believers in Corinth* (4:14; 5:13), "in order that when the grace has spread dynamically through many people, it might cause thanksgiving to overflow to God's glory" (4:15). If he and his ministry team suffer affliction, it is for their "encouragement and salvation" (1:6–7); death works in Paul, but life in the Corinthians (4:12). Further, the apostle and his coworkers have lived out a particular pattern of life and ministry toward the Corinthians, and Paul longs for the Corinthians to understand and to be proud of him and his mission (1:12, 14). Paul and his fellow workers do not dominate the faith of the Corinthians but work for their joy (1:24), for Paul loves the Corinthians (11:11) and wants them to know it (2:4). Indeed, rather than acting as dominating "lords," he and his fellow ministers are the Corinthians' "slaves" for the sake of Jesus (4:5). Moreover, the forgiveness he has offered to the offender mentioned in 2:5–11 has been offered for the sake of the Corinthians, so that the community of faith might not be exploited by Satan (2:10–11). This posture toward the Corinthians stems in part from parental concern, for Paul sees the Corinthians as his spiritual children (6:13; 12:14). This is why his heart has been opened wide to them (6:11); thus they are in the "hearts" of Paul and his fellow ministers, "to the point of dying together or living together" (7:3).

At the same time, *the apostle has specific concerns about the Corinthians*; all is not completely well in the church. This is why the apostle is "jealous" about them "with a jealousy from God" (11:2). Their recent actions suggest that at least some of the Corinthians don't fully understand Paul and his team (1:13–14; 5:11). Their misunderstanding of the apostle may also have been contributing to the tentative nature of their obedience, for Paul has felt the need to "test" them to see the extent of their obedience (2:9) and the genuineness of their love (8:8; 12:15). He wanted them to be clear about their devotion to him (7:12), and at least part of the community responded well to at least one of his tests of devotion, communicated through his grievous letter (7:11). Yet this does not negate the fact that in their relationship with Paul, they have been keeping their hearts closed, held back in their affections, and thus not living in a healthy, open relationship with him and his mission (6:11–13). Their lack of resolute commitment to the apostle and his mission may also be why they have faltered in following through on the collection for Jerusalem (8:10–11).

This coolness of affections toward the apostle has been due in part to their participation in relationships with unbelievers (6:14), which has led to moral impurity (7:1). In fact, Paul is concerned that some among their number will not have repented of their sexual immorality by the time he arrives and that he will find "dissension, jealousy, fits of rage, selfish ambitions, slanderous words, gossiping, swelled heads, and chaos," which would shame Paul and grieve him deeply (12:20–21). Furthermore, the apostle has great concerns that the false teachers are deceiving them, leading them away from right thinking and pure devotion to Christ (1:3). At least some of the Corinthians are giving too much of a place to the interlopers and their teachings (11:4). It cannot be assumed that all of those in the church at Corinth are in the faith (13:5). Consequently, he prays for their full restoration (13:9).

3. *Paul and his opponents at Corinth.* In a real sense, the false teachers at Corinth are not a part of his "relational network," but they do hover menacingly in the background of this letter. The nature and the extent of opposition to Paul at Corinth has long been a complicated debate. Various views include that the opponents were Judaizers, gnostics, Divine Men, Pneumatics, Jewish-Christian Sophists, or some combination of the above.[61] It seems that questions about the apostle and his mission were being raised by a vocal minority (cf. 2:6) within the church at Corinth, persons who may have been made up of several factions, as well as by interlopers who had presented themselves as alternate "apostles." It is hard to distinguish the concerns of each group, for they probably formed a coalition against Paul, playing off one another (Scott 1998: 11). It is not surprising that in a church made up of house churches spread across a geographical area (1:1), response to Paul was mixed.

Let's first consider concerns about Paul that seem to be reflected in 2 Corinthians[62] and the counterconcerns raised by Paul himself. It seems that

61. For an extensive bibliography on the debate, see Bieringer, Nathan, and Kurek-Chomycz 2008: 209–14. For introductions, see Barnett, *DPL* 644–53; Harris 2005: 67–87; Martin 1986: 336–42; and esp. Sumney 1990: 77–86, who vies for a minimalist approach to historical reconstruction.

62. John Barclay (1987: 74) has suggested that "mirror reading" is both essential and extremely problematic: such a reading, trying to piece together a specific concern or heresy from what is said in a letter, can lead to exegetical romance rather than an accurate assessment of the text. Garland (2003: 13) offers this appropriate caution on mirror reading:

> Since Paul reacts to what the Corinthians are saying, it seems imperative to try to reconstruct what they were thinking so as to understand better his responses. The method used, mirror-reading—reading what Paul says as in some measure mirroring what the Corinthians have said—is fraught with the danger of making mistakes, as the reasoning

opposition to Paul focused on the validity of his apostleship and the conduct of his ministry, and Paul has similar concerns that he expresses about his opponents. In fact, four general areas of criticism provide a framework for the opposition raised against the apostle and the counterconcerns reflected by Paul in 2 Corinthians. These are (a) what constitutes appropriate validation of an apostle, (b) the manifestations of true apostolic ministry, (c) remuneration for ministry, and (d) ministerial integrity.

3a. *Validation of ministry.* First, it seems that Paul's opponents suggested that he lacked the credentials of a valid minister or apostle (3:1–3; 12:12). At 3:1–2 the apostle writes, "We are starting to recommend ourselves to you again. Or do we, like some, need letters of recommendation to you or from you?! You yourselves are our letter of recommendation, written on our hearts, known and read by everyone." As explained in the commentary, 3:1a can be read as an affirmation of self-recommendation, as the apostle subtly rebukes the Corinthians because he needs to go through a process that should be unnecessary at this point in their relationship. The contrast here (ἤ, $\bar{e}$, or) is with the need to produce letters of recommendation, as had supposedly been produced by the opponents, alluded to as "hucksters" in 2:17, when they arrived in Corinth. The apostle points out that his ministry stands validated by the only letter of recommendation he needs—the Corinthians themselves. The validity of authentic ministry manifests in those to whom ministry is carried out.

The interlopers claimed to be apostles (11:13), servants of Christ (11:23) and of righteousness (11:15). They were either claiming to be or being heralded as "superapostles" (11:5, 12; 12:11) who were on par with or superior to Paul (11:12). They were Hebrews (11:22), probably from Palestine. But they were seeking to validate and evaluate ministry on the basis of comparison and inappropriate boasting (10:12; 11:21b–23a), commending themselves (4:5; 10:12) by touting their own competence (3:4–6), outward appearance (5:12; 10:1), and eloquence of speech (10:10; 11:6). In other words, they sought

---

is necessarily circular. . . . When such reading is carried out injudiciously, the text can become the servant of preconceived impressions. The interpreter can read too much into what Paul says, read in his or her own biases, and misread Paul's argumentation in a particular passage. Too often in the interpretation of [1 Corinthians] mirror-reading has been used incautiously and overconfidently. The forces shaping the Corinthians' thoughts and actions have been attributed to a particular theological aberration rooted in Gnosticism, Jewish wisdom theology, or an "over-realized eschatology." One theological misconception, however, is unlikely to explain the sundry problems Paul addresses in the letter. If Paul thought that a misrepresentation of the gospel he first preached to them lay behind their problems, then, Pickett (1997: 44–45) reasonably asks, "Why did he not provide them with a more explicitly theological corrective as he does, for example, in Galatians?" It is far more likely that the influences on them were more amorphous and that their behavior was swayed by culturally ingrained habits from their pagan past and by values instilled by a popularized secular ethics.

Our goal in this section is to attempt to discern dynamics in Corinth that are clearly reflected in the text and to probe possible cultural contexts in which such concerns might have been fostered. However, we also want to live within the limits of our data and not overinterpret based on a particular theory of the opponents.

public validation, with personal honor and glory, on the basis of their own accomplishments—even at times claiming the accomplishments of others (10:13–17; 11:12).

By contrast, Paul commends himself (3:1; 4:2; 5:12; 6:4; 10:18; 12:11), boasting only in the Lord and knowing that ultimately only the Lord's commendation matters (10:17–18). Rather than his own abilities and gifts (3:4–6), the apostle commends himself by a display of the truth (4:2) and the condition of his heart before God (2:17; 3:2–3; 5:12; 6:11; 7:3). He does not proclaim himself but Jesus as Lord (4:4–6), and he considers suffering a key validating mark of authentic ministry (4:7–11; 6:4–10), for suffering manifests the power of God (4:7; 12:9–10; 13:3–4). This brings us to a second area of concern expressed in 2 Corinthians.

3b. *Manifestations of true apostolic ministry.* Paul's opponents seem to suggest that the apostle does not manifest divine power in a way that an apostle should (12:12; 13:3), and perhaps that he does not have appropriate spiritual experiences (12:1). Thus he is considered an impostor (6:8), inferior (11:5; 12:11), unimpressive in terms of public presence (10:1, 10) and ineffective, having failed in his ministerial duties (13:4–6). He has to resort to intimidation through his letters (10:9). Elsewhere, it seems he has been accused of being domineering in posture (1:24; 10:8), of restricting the Corinthians (6:12), of not loving them (11:11), and of taking advantage of them (7:2; 12:1).

But Paul suggests that his opponents are the false apostles, as can be seen clearly from their ministry practices and teaching. They are false teachers who minister on the basis of human standards (5:16; 11:18), distorting God's Word (4:2) and offering thoughts "raised up in opposition to knowledge about God" (10:4–5). Paul is deeply concerned that they are seducing the Corinthians away from pure devotion to Christ, preaching another Jesus, a different spirit, a different gospel (11:3–4). Further, they devour, dominate, capture, and slap the Corinthians in the face (11:20).

Paul, on the other hand, manifests the power of God in suffering and in authentic ministry to the Corinthians and in the world (1:12; 3:2–3; 4:11–18; 10:3–4; 13:4). He serves as an ambassador for Christ, to bring about reconciliation between God and people (5:18–6:2). God leads him through the world in a triumphal procession, celebrating Christ. Paul proclaims the gospel in a way that divides humanity, speaking sincerely, as one who is in Christ, sent from God, and living before God (2:14–17). Thus the gospel and its impact manifests authentic Christian ministry as people are brought into new covenant relationship with God (3:12–18).

3c. *Remuneration for apostolic ministry.* It is clear that one of the chief concerns on the part of Paul's opponents is his refusal to receive pay for the ministry he carries out in Corinth (11:7, 9–11; 12:13). It is likely that Paul's manual labor was seen as inappropriate and shameful for one supposed to be a leader and public figure. Yet Paul insists that this "boast" of his will not be stopped because it is a key mark distinguishing his ministry from the false apostles (11:12). The false teachers, on the other hand, seem to have accepted patronage in Corinth, for they preach for pay (2:17) and devour the Corinthians in the process (11:20).

3d. *Ministerial integrity.* It seems that in some ways Paul and his mission have been accused of lacking integrity. At 1:12 he insists, "Now we are proud of this and say so with a clean conscience: we have lived a pattern of life in the world and especially toward you, which is characterized by straightforwardness and sincerity that come from God, a pattern not based on human wisdom but lived out by God's grace." Paul may simply be asserting his integrity and that of his ministry team as a foundation for the self-recommendation he offers as the letter develops. Yet, with the explanation of his change of itinerary at 1:15–20, the apostle seems at great pains to defend his actions as above reproach. At verse 17 he writes, "Therefore, certainly you don't think I was being wishy-washy when I planned to do this?" Concerning his travel decisions, he feels the need to make a solemn oath before God, "Now, I call upon God as my witness" (1:23). He insists that he and his fellow ministers have turned their "backs on the shameful things people hide, not living by tricks" like his opponents (4:2). In fact, he considers the opponents to be "false," deceitful workers simply masquerading as apostles of Christ (11:13–14). They are masters of deception (11:3, 15), who will be judged according to their actions. Lacking integrity, they have invaded Paul's ministry territory and claimed responsibility for the fruit there (10:13, 15–16). By contrast, it is Paul and his mission who minister in absolute integrity, appealing to the consciences of people and living openly before God (1:12, 14; 2:17; 4:2; 5:11; 6:3–4; 7:2; 8:20–21; 12:17–18).

Sumney concludes that these contrasting visions of apostolic ministry lie at the heart of problems in Corinth,[63] and Harris (2005: 72–73) agrees with this assessment:

> As we have delineated all these charges and countercharges, it all comes down to this. Paul's opponents regarded themselves as ἀπόστολοι Χριστοῦ [*apostoloi Christou,* apostles of Christ] (11:13) and Paul as a πλάνος [*planos*], an imposter (6:8). Paul viewed himself as an ἀπόστολος Χριστοῦ (1:1) and his rivals as ψευδαπόστολοι [*pseudapostoloi,* false apostles] (11:13). The Corinthians were faced with rival apostolates. There can be no doubt that the primary and immediate aim of Paul's rivals was to undermine and destroy his reputation and apostolic authority and thus subvert his gospel. What they taught and did was calculated to bring about Paul's downfall, at least at Corinth, and to establish their own credentials as authentic servants of Christ.

We might further add that the function of chapters 10–13 in our letter is Paul's attempt to attack head-on the influence of the false apostles among a recalcitrant minority in the church and to reestablish a full commitment to his mission in the city.

---

63. Sumney (1999: 130–31) believes chaps. 1–9 and 10–13 constitute two different letters, but he concludes that, generally speaking, the concerns about the opponents and Paul's answers to them are fairly closely aligned in the two parts of 2 Corinthians.

What then of the more specific orientation of these opponents? Among the positions on offer, it seems that the best case has been made for the opponents as Jewish-Christian ministers working under strong influences of the Sophist tradition.[64] Conflict between philosophers and Sophists dated to several centuries before Paul, the Sophists being renounced by Socrates, for instance, for their rhetorical techniques (Thrall 2000: 679). The Sophists were professional educators and traveling speakers who sought pay for their services. At times they embraced philosophical relativism, placing more emphasis on the glory and profit of winning arguments than on proclaiming truth. By the time of the Second Sophistic, the emphasis was on a Sophist teacher being "a virtuoso rhetor with a big public reputation" (Bowersock 1969: 13–14).

Munck (1959: 152–54) suggested that Sophist influence may have been in play in Corinth, as seen in the Corinthian craving for applause, and his lead has been followed by commentators such as Gordon Fee (1987: 49, 80, 94). Winter (2002) has now demonstrated that there is a great deal of evidence for a vibrant Sophist movement in the first century AD and specifically in Corinth. Philo has a great deal to say about Sophists,[65] as do P.Oxy. 2190 and Dio Chrysostom (Winter 2002: 19–39, 48–54), the latter bearing witness to the Corinthians' enthusiasm for Sophist speakers (Winter 2002: 135) and describing the competitive nature of their oratory: "That was the time, too, when one could hear crowds of wretched Sophists around Poseidon's temple shouting and reviling one another, and their disciples, as they were called, fighting with one another, many writers reading aloud their stupid works, many poets reciting their poems while others applauded them" (*Or.* 8.9).

As reflected in 2 Corinthians, the emphases on public appearance, social status, powerful oratory, words of worldly "wisdom," style over content, pay for speaking, boasting about achievements, public applause,[66] and the competitive nature of the opponents[67]—all these match characteristics of the Sophist movement. Winter (2002: 234–35) suggests that Sophists were already present

64. As suggested by Barrett (1971) and Barnett (*DPL* 649–50; 1997: 35), it may be that these ministers were Judaizers, but it is questionable whether the references to "stone tablets" (3:3), the "letter" that kills (3:6), the old-covenant ministry of death (3:7–8), and the claim to be "ministers of righteousness" (11:15) are sufficient evidence to make that judgment. Paul's evocation of old-covenant imagery in 3:3–18 may simply be the offering of biblical reflection on the nature of new-covenant ministry as an answer to any alternate form of so-called ministry.

65. There are some forty-eight references to Sophists in Philo's works (e.g., *Creat.* 157; *Alleg.* 3.232; *Cher.* 10; *Worse* 35, 38–39, 41–42, 71–72; *Post.* 86, 131, 150; *Jos.* 103, 106; *Mos.* 1.92; 2.212; *Rewards* 58; *Contempl.* 4, 31; *Etern.* 132; *QG* 3.27, 33, 35).

66. Quintilian (*Inst.* 2.2.9–12), a contemporary of Paul, speaks against "mutual and indiscriminate applause" that tends toward the theatrical and is the "worst foe of genuine study" in a school. "But in the schools today we see boys stooping forward ready to spring to their feet: at the close of each period they not merely rise, but rush forward with shouts of unseemly enthusiasm. Such compliments are mutual and the success of a declamation consists in this kind of applause. The result is vanity and empty self-sufficiency" (cf. 2 Cor. 3:4–6 on self-sufficiency).

67. With reference to 1 Corinthians, Thiselton (2000: 15) states, "Thus there grew up a pragmatic concern with who had the best performance, who was winning in the marketplace."

in Corinth when 1 Corinthians was written,[68] and 2 Cor. 10–13 reflects the full blossoming of their impact in the church. His suggestion that Paul's words in the Corinthian correspondence constitute an anti-sophistic stance makes good sense, and Winter's suggestions are bolstered and furthered by Clarke (1993: 129–31), who has demonstrated that the sophistic interlopers fostered in the Corinthian church an intrusion of secular leadership values, which Paul must combat. A sophistic approach to public leadership would have greatly appealed to the Corinthians—indeed they embraced these fools!—but Paul says that this approach to ministry constitutes pure foolishness and must not be tolerated (11:19–20). One wonders if there aren't parallels in the modern church that need similar attention!

The Message and Intent of 2 Corinthians

As described above, Paul's immediate relational network provides one framework for understanding the main message and ultimate intent of 2 Corinthians. In spite of the tensions in their relationship, the majority in the church at Corinth had responded well to the apostle's leadership—at least to a certain extent and in response specifically to the concerns in the painful letter of 2:3–4/7:8 (1:14; 2:6; 7:7). Now he wanted the church to move to complete obedience (10:6) and those who had yet to repent to do so (7:1; 12:20–21). He also wanted the church to follow through on their commitment to the collection for the saints in Jerusalem (chaps. 8–9) and to reject the so-called "ministry" of the interlopers. To these ends, Paul attempted to answer various charges leveled against him and, correspondingly, to commend his ministry to the Corinthians, drawing the church back into a healthy relationship with himself, his mission, and God. The book has been notorious for the circuitous development of its themes, prompting the many theories concerning patched-together fragments. Yet, from certain perspectives, there is a logic to its development.

In the overview that follows, notice two primary dynamics, the "context" and the "core content" of the apostle's communication. First, the theme of "travel" provides one important structural framework for an analysis of the book's discourse. Travel in this sense is the "geographical context" of the conversation—which is not surprising since Paul was traveling when he wrote the book. Paul begins the letter's main body by explaining his travel decisions (1:15–2:11). The apostle brackets the great central section of the letter with the "absence" and then "presence" of Titus in Paul's move to Macedonia (2:12–13; 7:5–7). That central section, the book's theological heart (2:14–7:4), is launched with an image of God as leading the apostle and his fellow ministers in triumphal procession through the world as proclaimers of the gospel (2:14–16). As Paul addresses the Corinthians' commitment to the collection, Titus is again present with them (8:16–24) in preparation for the coming of

---

68. Thus the apostle's manner when he first came to Corinth presents a firm decision not to follow sophistic patterns (1 Cor. 2:1–5; Winter 2002: 151).

the absent apostle (9:3–5). Finally, chapters 10–13 are also bracketed by the twin themes of Paul's absence and presence (10:1, 11; 13:1–2, 10),[69] for his confrontation of the false teachers constitutes a key point in preparation for his imminent return.

If travel forms the context or framework of his communication, the content has to do largely with the network of Paul's immediate relationships described above, that is, with God, Paul's concern for the Corinthians, the authenticity of Paul's ministry (communicated in part by his suffering as he travels around), and how the Corinthians should respond in this ministry moment. Paul does not have a direct relationship with the interlopers, who are always in the background but do not become the main topic until chapters 10–13. Even then, he does not address them directly but addresses the Corinthians concerning the false teachers. Yet notice that Paul's commendation of his own ministry is woven throughout the book. At every point in this letter, we are presented with the apostle's appropriate boasting in the Lord, which often means his boasting in suffering. Notice also that Paul constantly appeals to the Corinthians, through various means exhorting them to return to a healthy relationship with their apostle. Thus the backbone of the book unfolds as follows:

Absence and Presence in the Structure of 2 Corinthians

Context (Travel)	Content
The Letter Opening and Prologue (1:1–11)	
While Paul was absent	God: Praised for his redemption of suffering
	Paul: Encouraged and brought to complete dependence on God
	Corinthians: Treated as part of Paul's ministry
Why Paul Did Not Come Directly to Corinth (1:12–2:13)	
Why Paul was absent; Titus absent	God: Has strengthened and anointed Paul for ministry
	Paul: Has acted with complete integrity and for the Corinthians
	Corinthians: Have misunderstood and needed a test
Paul's Ministry of Integrity (2:14–7:4)	
What Paul has been doing while absent	God: Leads Paul's mission through the world, transforming people by the gospel
	Paul: Proclaims the gospel, commending his ministry in every way, and suffers as Christ's ambassador of reconciliation
	Corinthians: Should be reconciled to God and reject unhealthy relationships
When Titus Arrived in Macedonia: The Happy Result When the Corinthians Respond Well (7:5–16)	
When Paul found Titus	God: Encouraged Paul and clarified things for the Corinthians
	Paul: Encouraged and rejoiced at Titus's coming and news
	Corinthians: Grief led to repentance

69. In fact, inclusios built on the themes of "presence" and "absence" bracket the units at the beginning and end of 2 Cor. 10–13 (excluding the closing in 13:11–13). This should be seen as a significant structural marker.

Context (Travel)	Content
	How to Prepare for Paul's Coming (Part 1): Again Take Up the Ministry of Giving (8:1–9:15)
Titus present to prepare for Paul's coming	God: God's grace manifests in giving
	Paul: Has sent Titus to prepare this ministry
	Corinthians: Prepare by reinitiating the collection
	How to Prepare for Paul's Coming (Part 2): Reject the False Teachers, Embrace Paul (10:1–13:13)
Paul absent but will be present soon!	God: Has assigned Paul the ministry in Corinth, bears witness to Paul
	Paul: Boasts in God, especially in his own weaknesses
	Corinthians: Should reject the false teachers and test themselves

Following the letter opening, the apostle offers a benediction, praising God for encouragement and for God's work in the midst of suffering (1:3–7). The testimony of 1:8–11 offers a specific example of how God had redeemed suffering in the life of the apostle and his fellow ministers. The weakness of suffering in Asia, where Paul was confronted with his own limitations, manifested God's strength. Thus the prologue (1:3–11), with its emphasis on God's work through affliction, highlights a dominant theme for the book. Yet it also invites the Corinthians into the messy mix of Paul's ministry. Already Paul draws the wayward church close with his words, speaking of them as those who share in his sufferings (1:7) and offer prayer to God on his behalf (1:11). Thus the prologue begins with a positive focus on God, on God's work in and through affliction, and on the Corinthians' need to share in Paul's mission.

Yet this invitation to draw close brings to mind the jarring tension that has invaded the apostle's relationship with this church, and in the next movement the apostle confronts that tension head-on (1:12–2:11). Since concerns have been raised about his change in travel itinerary, Paul defends his recent decisions as being carried out with complete integrity (1:12–2:4). His confident testimony of a clear conscience and his desire to be understood by the Corinthians (1:12–14)—what some consider the book's thesis statement—presents another key theme of the book. The apostle has acted with complete integrity, but because they have not understood him and his mission (1:14), pain has entered his relationship with the church. This painful conflict in his relationship with the Corinthians was manifested in a painful visit (2:1), a decision not to come to Corinth as planned (1:23; 2:1–2), and a painful letter (2:3), evidently having to do with an offender who had caused a great deal of pain to the community (2:5–11).

Second Corinthians 2:12–13 functions to effect a transition, picking up the "travel" explanations of 1:15–2:5, introducing the alternate itinerary the apostle had followed (2:12–13), and anticipating the resolution of Paul's travel narrative at 7:5–7. This transition in 2:12–13 and the resolution in 7:5–7 form a bracket and thus set in great relief the theological heart of the book, which focuses on the nature of Paul's authentic ministry (2:14–7:4). In this section Paul carries out a form of self-recommendation (3:1; 4:2; 5:12; 6:4), explaining how his mission, as they travel through the world, spreads the aroma of knowledge about God through the gospel (2:14–16). Paul and his fellow workers are distinct from hucksters who preach for profit, because Paul and his team are from God, live before God, and speak with sincerity in Christ (2:17).

Thus the Corinthians themselves are the only recommendation letter Paul needs (3:1–3), for he and his team are true ministers of the new covenant, which transforms people (3:4–4:6). Gospel ministry, moreover, involves sacrifice and suffering. The treasure resides in terra-cotta so that the life of Jesus can be manifested through suffering and God will be glorified (4:7–15). The frailty of the minister's life also turns his or her focus to the eternal, unseen world (4:16–18) and ultimately the resurrection from the dead (5:1–10). Paul lives openly before God and the Corinthians, and he and his fellow workers are driven by the call of God and the gospel (5:11–15). It is on the basis of this ministry of reconciliation, drawing people to right relationship with God through Jesus Christ, that Paul calls the Corinthians to be reconciled to God through being reconciled to his ministry (5:16–6:2). All of Paul's life and ministry—including his sufferings—commends his ministry to the Corinthians (6:3–10), and he pleads with them to open their lives to him (6:11–13). But since they are limited by their own affections, he uses Scripture to exhort them to turn again to the true worship of God and abandon spiritually unhealthy relationships with unbelievers (6:14–7:4).

At 7:5 the apostle resumes his travel narrative. He has allowed the hearers to live with the unresolved tension embodied in 2:12–13 (the absence of Titus), for authentic ministry lives in suffering and tension. But now the tension is resolved for at least two reasons: (1) Paul celebrates that the majority in the community have responded well to his painful letter. Their repentance has paved the way for their reengagement with Paul's mission through the collection. In addition, the God of all encouragement (1:3–7) has encouraged Paul by the Corinthians' response, showing that God is working in their community (7:7, 12, 13–16). (2) Paul has delayed his account of Titus's coming, for it is only now that he is ready to reintroduce their need to engage in the collection for the saints (chaps. 8–9). So he has sent Titus to them again, along with two other brothers (8:17–19, 22), in preparation for Paul's return to Corinth (9:3–5).

But in preparation for Paul's return to the city, there is a final great need. The foolishness surrounding the false apostles has gone on long enough. So Paul, in a personal appeal, confronts the Corinthians' toleration of these interlopers in no uncertain terms. His apostolic power and authority will be manifested when he returns (10:1–10; 13:1–4). He makes his principles about wrongheaded boasting and games of classification and comparison abundantly clear. Paul will not play by the interlopers' rules; instead, he only boasts in the Lord (1:12–18). But then, in a grand parody of the false teachers' foolish boasting, the apostle does speak a bit of foolishness. He "celebrates" the Corinthians' amazing "tolerance" for the interlopers (11:1–4) and boasts that he has preached to the Corinthians free of charge, for that makes a clear distinction between him and the false apostles (11:5–15). The pinnacle of his "foolishness" is the grand Fool's Speech of 11:22–12:10, in which he turns boasting on its head by boasting about his weaknesses. Why has he been so foolish? The Corinthians, who should have commended him, drove him to it (12:11–13). So in preparation for his coming, they should repent and embrace his ministry, which is for building them up (12:14–13:10). Paul then closes, reiterating themes from the letter opening and prologue, longing for the Corinthians' maturity, unity, and right relationship with God (13:11–13).

In short, the message of 2 Corinthians is that Paul commends his ministry to the Corinthians as one of integrity. Appointed by God, under the lordship of Christ, and suffering in his proclamation of the gospel, Paul calls the Corinthians to repent from unhealthy relationships and embrace his authentic apostolic leadership. Their appropriate response will be seen, on the one hand, by again taking up the collection for Jerusalem, and on the other hand, by resolutely rejecting the ministry of the false teachers.

Outline of the Book

I. The letter opening and prologue (1:1–11)
    A. Letter opening (1:1–2)
    B. Prologue (1:3–11)
        1. Praise God for his encouragement! (1:3–7)
        2. Paul's recent deliverance (1:8–11)
II. The integrity of Paul's ministry (1:12–7:16)
    A. Why Paul did not come directly to Corinth (1:12–2:13)
        1. The integrity of Paul's recent actions (1:12–14)
        2. Misunderstanding Paul's change of travel plans (1:15–22)
        3. Why Paul changed his travel plans, part 1: Confrontation would have been painful for the Corinthians (1:23–2:11)
            a. A painful visit and a painful letter (1:23–2:4)
            b. Forgive the one who caused the pain (2:5–11)
        4. Why Paul changed his travel plans, part 2: An open door and an absent coworker (2:12–13)
    B. Paul's reflections on authentic ministry (2:14–7:4)
        1. Paul commends his authentic ministry (2:14–4:6)
            a. Led in Christ's triumph (2:14–16a)
            b. Qualified for ministry (2:16b–3:6)
            c. The better ministry of the Spirit (3:7–18)
            d. A ministry of integrity (4:1–6)
        2. The suffering involved in Paul's authentic ministry (4:7–5:10)
            a. Treasure and terra-cotta (4:7–15)
            b. Perspective in the midst of suffering (4:16–18)
            c. Longing to be "fully clothed" (5:1–10)

3. "Respond to authentic ministry": A series of exhortations to the Corinthians (5:11–7:4)
    a. An opportunity for the Corinthians (5:11–13)
    b. The ministry of reconciliation (5:14–6:2)
    c. The impeccable apostolic credentials of Paul's mission (6:3–10)
    d. A call for open hearts and pure lives (6:11–7:4)
C. When Titus arrived in Macedonia: The happy result when the Corinthians respond well (7:5–16)

III. The ministry of giving (8:1–9:15)
A. Paul's exhortation to finish the collection (8:1–15)
B. Titus's mission (8:16–9:5)
C. Reflections on resources for giving and the results (9:6–15)

IV. Paul confronts the malignant ministry of his opponents (10:1–13:13)
A. Present or absent, Paul's authority is the same (10:1–11)
B. Proper and improper boasting (10:12–18)
C. Paul boasts like a fool to stop the false apostles (11:1–12:13)
    1. Bear with me, not them (11:1–4)
    2. Paul and the "superapostles" (11:5–15)
    3. Embracing fools (11:16–21)
    4. Paul's countercultural "Fool's Speech," part 1 (11:22–29)
    5. Paul's countercultural "Fool's Speech," part 2 (11:30–12:10)
    6. Epilogue to the "Fool's Speech" (12:11–13)
D. Preparation for the third visit (12:14–13:10)
    1. Concerns related to the third visit (12:14–21)
    2. The third visit as stern accountability (13:1–10)
E. Closing exhortations, greetings, and benediction (13:11–13)

I. The Letter Opening and Prologue (1:1–11)

The German poet Johann Wolfgang von Goethe once wrote, "Letters are among the most significant memorial[s] a person can leave behind them," and the statement certainly rings true in the case of the apostle Paul. The apostle's ministry ranged over a vast geographical area, and long-distance communication played a vital role in his work. No medium for that communication has had a more lasting impact than that of the apostle's letters, and his letters present certain patterns in terms of form.

In the Greco-Roman world, letters often were papyrus scrolls—though brief notes were scribbled on a variety of materials—with an outside address to which the letter was to be sent. The text on the "inside" of the letter often started with a "prescript," or letter opening; just as today we may open a letter with "Dear _____," letters of Paul's day also often followed a standard format of a *superscriptio* (the sender's name in the nominative form), an *adscriptio* (the name of the addressee in the dative), and finally a *salutatio* (a greeting in the infinitive) (Klauck and Bailey 2006: 17–18). The apostle follows this pattern as he opens 2 Corinthians:

superscriptio	Paul, an apostle of Christ Jesus by God's will, and our brother Timothy,
adscriptio	to God's church in Corinth, along with all God's holy people throughout Achaia:
salutatio	Grace and peace to you from God our Father and the Lord Jesus Christ!

Notice the rhythmical balance of this brief opening, in which we are presented with four pairs: Paul and Timothy; the church in Corinth and God's holy people throughout Achaia; grace and peace; and finally, God our Father and the Lord Jesus Christ.

In the first century the letter opening often was followed by a *proem*, or prologue, which served to make a transition to the letter body. Paul's prologue has two movements, a benediction praising God for encouragement (1:3–7), followed by an account of a recent, harrowing brush with death and the celebration of God's deliverance of the apostle and his coworkers (1:8–11). Early in the development of the use of epistolary prologues, we find the *formula valetudinis*, which Seneca the Younger (*Ep.* 15.1) described as "a custom which survived even into my lifetime. They would add to the opening words of a letter, 'If you are well, it is well; I also am well'" (as quoted in Klauck and Bailey 2006: 21). So, fundamental to the prologue was a statement of how things were going in the life of the writer, and this constitutes part of the content of Paul's prologue in 2 Corinthians, since he informs the Achaians about tribulations that have affected his life and ministry.

The prologue also could include expressions of thanksgiving and references to prayer (Klauck and Bailey 2006: 42), both of which are also included in 2 Cor. 1:3–11. Paul expresses thanks in the form of his benediction (1:3–5) and mentions the thanks that will be given as a result of the Corinthians' answered prayers (1:11). It may also be that the element of "remembrance" of someone before the gods lies behind Paul wanting the Corinthians to not "be unaware of," or perhaps "take lightly," the apostle's great affliction experienced in Asia (1:8).

A. Letter Opening (1:1–2)

Paul crafts the opening we have in 2 Cor. 1:1–2 in line with a pattern commonly used for letter prescripts in the first century, but the demands of his ministry, as well as his theological convictions, have shaped that formal pattern in nuanced ways (O'Brien, *DPL* 553; Stirewalt 2003: 25). The letter opening in 1:1–2 marks 2 Corinthians as an official letter sent by a person in an official capacity to a group of people under that person's authority (Stirewalt 2003: 3, 9, 33–34). In an official letter, a writer of the period would normally self-identify, naming rank or position, the addressee(s), and perhaps a cosender. An opening also expressed greetings (χαίρειν, *chairein*).[1] Here Paul, who identifies his role as an apostle of Christ Jesus, with Timothy as cosender of the letter, writes to the believers in Achaia, addressing them with "grace and peace," which come from God the Father and the Lord Jesus.[2]

Exegesis and Exposition

[1]Paul, an apostle of Christ Jesus by God's will, and our brother Timothy, to God's church in Corinth, along with all God's holy people throughout Achaia. [2]Grace and peace to you from God our Father and the Lord ⌜Jesus Christ⌝!

As in his normal pattern of letter writing, Paul begins his salutation by identifying himself as the sender, and this is the only time in the book, other than at 10:1, that he mentions himself by name. Παῦλος (*Paulos*), of course, is the Greek rendering of his Hebrew name "Saul" (שָׁאוּל, *šāʾûl*), given him at birth (Acts 13:9).[3] To make his identity more specific, Paul adds, "an apostle of Christ Jesus," a designation he uses in the salutations of seven other letters (Rom. 1:1; 1 Cor. 1:1; Gal. 1:1; Eph. 1:1; Col. 1:1; 1 Tim. 1:1; 2 Tim. 1:1).[4]

    Paul seems to have used the term ἀπόστολος (*apostolos*) in at least three ways. In line with the broad use of the cognate verb form in the Greek OT, it could refer to one sent as a messenger or a representative to carry out a task. For example, 2 Cor. 8:23 speaks of the brothers with Titus, to whom Paul refers

1:1

---

1. At times the sender and addressees were presented in inverse order: "To B, from A."
2. There was no public postal system, so Paul sent his letters with associates, who would read the letter to the assembled group addressed and answer questions on behalf of the apostle (Klauck and Bailey 2006: 60–65; Richards 2004: chaps. 11–12).
3. As Harris (2005: 128) reports, Jews who assumed a Greek name commonly took a moniker that sounded similar to their original Hebrew or Aramaic name.
4. Paul does not use the term "apostle" in the salutations of 1 and 2 Thessalonians, Philippians, or Philemon (1 Thess. 1:1; 2 Thess. 1:1; Phil. 1:1; Philem. 1).

as "messengers of the churches" (ἀπόστολοι ἐκκλησιῶν, *apostoloi ekklēsiōn*).[5] Second, the term seems to be used in a semitechnical sense of those directly associated with the Twelve or Paul, who also carried out a significant ministry in the church. Here we can name Barnabas (1 Cor. 9:5–6), Andronicus and Junia[s] (Rom. 16:7), James brother of the Lord (1 Cor. 15:7; Gal. 1:19), and perhaps Apollos (1 Cor. 4:6–9). Finally, as here in 2 Cor. 1:1, ἀπόστολος seems to be used in a distinct sense of the Twelve and Paul, as those directly commissioned by the Lord for a unique, authoritative role in the early church (Harris 2005: 128; 1 Cor. 9:1; 15:3–9; Gal. 1:17).[6] In this vein Paul writes 2 Corinthians as an "apostle" of Christ, and his role as an apostle serves as one very large foundation stone in his rhetorical strategy embodied in this letter, since the Corinthians need to respond well to his apostolic leadership.[7]

That he is an apostle "of Christ Jesus" (Χριστοῦ Ἰησοῦ, *Christou Iēsou*) can be taken as a genitive of relationship or perhaps source ("from Christ Jesus"), that is, Paul is sent from Messiah Jesus as his official representative. Yet Paul also adds to his salutation the phrase "by God's will" (διὰ θελήματος θεοῦ, *dia thelēmatos theou*), a favorite expression for describing the nature of his apostleship (1 Cor. 1:1; Eph. 1:1; Col. 1:1; 2 Tim. 1:1). When διά (*dia*) is used with the genitive, as here, it can communicate the "circumstance by which something is accomplished" (BDAG 224). So it is "by God's will," that is, at the initiative of God himself, that Paul is an apostle.[8] Since this phrase is used in tandem with Χριστοῦ Ἰησοῦ, Paul actually points to a joint commissioning in which both Jesus and God the Father are involved.[9] Elsewhere in 2 Corin-

---

5. Also see Phil. 2:25, where Epaphroditus is called a "messenger" (ἀπόστολος, *apostolos*).

6. Paul's situation was unique even in comparison with the Twelve, since his commissioning came later than theirs (1 Cor. 15:8) and carried with it a specific call to minister to the Gentiles (Gal. 1:16; 2:7; Rom. 1:1–6; 11:13; 2 Cor. 10:13–16; Eph. 3:1–2). The Damascus-road experience seems to have marked Paul profoundly (Kim 1985; 2002), shaping his understanding of his apostolic ministry in a way that gave him security, direction, and a reference point from which to evaluate those ministering to the churches. He was set apart uniquely for the gospel, to bring about the obedience of the Gentiles (Rom. 1:1–6; 11:13). In spite of the uniqueness of his apostolic commissioning, however, Paul saw his role clearly as on equal grounds with the Twelve in terms of authority and significance, although he considered himself least among them because he had persecuted the church (1 Cor. 15:9).

7. In the context of 2 Corinthians, the apostle characterizes his ministry as clearly authentic over against the false apostles (2 Cor. 11:13), with that authenticity in part manifested by signs and wonders that accompanied his ministry (2 Cor. 12:12). Further, it was not by vote of human authority, nor by career-track plans that Paul took up his apostolic ministry. Rather, he was "captured and constrained by God's sovereign call" (Garland 2003: 25), appointed and set apart as an official representative "of Christ Jesus by God's will."

8. The phrase can, however, also be used to describe God's guidance as ministry is carried out (Rom. 15:32) or to describe God's providential work in a church that has shown wholehearted dedication to the cause of Christ (2 Cor. 8:5).

9. Showing further the close association of the first and second persons of the Trinity in Paul's commissioning, at 2:17 Paul can say he speaks ἐκ θεοῦ κατέναντι θεοῦ ἐν Χριστῷ (*ek theou katenanti theou en Christō*, from God, before God, in Christ), with "God" being the source of Paul's ministry in this passage, as well as the one to whom Paul truly answers, and "Christ" described as the one with whom Paul lives in profound relationship (see 2:14–17 below).

thians, of course, the apostle also emphasizes his work as by the power of the Spirit (3:3, 6, 8; 6:6; 13:13), and he ends the letter with a beautiful, three-part blessing invoking the work of Jesus the Christ, God the Father, and the Holy Spirit (13:13). Thus the triune God's sovereign will forms the basis and context for Paul's work as an apostle.

Further, Paul writes with "our brother Timothy" (Τιμόθεος ὁ ἀδελφός, *Timotheos ho adelphos*) as his cosender.[10] Although elaborate speculation has been offered concerning Timothy being named here,[11] that he also is so named in five other Pauline letters (1 and 2 Thessalonians, Colossians, Philemon, and Philippians) again suggests that this has more to do with a general practice of Paul than an attempt specifically to bolster Timothy's status before the Corinthians, though the young man has suffered some difficulty in ministry to this church (1 Cor. 16:10–11). Against those who suggest that Timothy's image needed rehabilitating with the Corinthians, Furnish (1984: 104–5) suggests that his inclusion as cosender actually demonstrates the opposite—that he still has standing with that church. Keener (2005: 20–21) notes, moreover, that mention of composite authorship could simply serve as a means of special greetings in ancient letters (see also Thrall 1994: 82), and in this vein the mention of Paul's younger protégé served as a natural reminder to the congregation of Timothy's ministry to them.[12]

With the *adscriptio* Paul addresses 2 Corinthians "to God's church in Corinth, along with all God's holy people throughout Achaia." He uses the phrase "God's church" (τῇ ἐκκλησίᾳ τοῦ θεοῦ, *tē ekklēsia tou theou*) nine times in his writings (1 Cor. 1:2; 10:32; 11:16, 22; 15:9; 2 Cor. 1:1; Gal. 1:13; 1 Thess. 2:14; 2 Thess. 1:4). The term ἐκκλησία is used some one hundred times in the Greek OT and translates קָהָל (*qāhāl*),[13] often referring to the assembly of the

---

10. As with the article in 1:1 that precedes ἀδελφὸς, the definite article can at times function as a possessive pronoun (D. Wallace 1996: 215–16). Paul also refers to Timothy as "Timothy the brother" at Col. 1:1; 1 Thess. 3:2; and Philem. 1. In Acts and Paul's Letters, approximately 100 people are named as associates of Paul in his ministry (E. E. Ellis, *DPL* 183), but none are closer to Paul than Timothy, whom he calls his "dear and faithful son in the Lord" (1 Cor. 4:17; also Phil. 2:22; 1 Tim. 1:18; 2 Tim. 1:2). A native of Lystra (Acts 16:1), Timothy was born of a Jewish mother named Eunice (evidently a devout believer; 2 Tim. 1:5) and a Greek father (Acts 16:1), and by Paul's second mission trip he had already established a strong reputation as a follower of Christ (Acts 16:2). Further, Timothy's ministry found endorsement in the context of prophetic pronouncements and the laying on of hands by leaders of the church (1 Tim. 1:18; 4:14; 2 Tim. 1:6). On Timothy's role in Paul's mission, and specifically in his ministry to the Corinthians, see Ollrog 1979: 185–87.

11. The great early preacher John Chrysostom (*Hom. 2 Cor.* 1.2) says, "By associating Timothy with himself, Paul increased respect for him and displayed his own great humility, since Timothy was far less well known than Paul" (Bray 1999: 194). On Paul's use of coauthors, see Richards 2004: 33–36.

12. Windisch and Strecker (1970: 33) note that in a Jewish context, this general practice of naming a cosender might be related to the legal requirement of Deut. 19:15, that testimony should be confirmed by at least two witnesses. In this sense, the cosender functions to attest the fact of the letter's origin and message.

13. The word can, e.g., refer to an assembly brought together for counsel, war, or for a religious festival. It is often used of an organized group of people, including the nation of Israel,

Lord, but the phrase "assembly of God" seems to occur only at Neh. 13:1, although the LXX translation there reads ἐκκλησία θεοῦ (*ekklēsia theou*), not using the articles commonly found in Paul's construction (the exceptions in Paul occur at 1 Tim. 3:5, 15). Nevertheless, Paul seems to equate the church with eschatological Israel, the people of God in whom the promises of old find their fulfillment through Messiah Jesus. The church is the new-covenant assembly of the Lord (P. T. O'Brien, *DPL* 126; e.g., Deut. 23:1–3; 1 Chron. 28:8; Mic. 2:5), and here, the church of God as it finds expression at Corinth.

With reference to his addressees, the apostle also adds "along with all God's holy people throughout Achaia" (σὺν τοῖς ἁγίοις πᾶσιν τοῖς οὖσιν ἐν ὅλῃ τῇ Ἀχαΐᾳ, *syn tois hagiois pasin tois ousin en holē tē Achaia*). The word rendered "God's holy people" has often been translated "saints." Yet the term does not refer to a superspiritual group, as the word "saints" has been used at times both in Roman Catholic ecclesiology and in a different way in popular English parlance. Rather, this Greek term refers to "those who, by their commitment to Christ, are set apart for the service of God" (Furnish 1984: 100). The term, used with reference to God's people, derives from LXX usage of the adjectival noun ἅγιος (*hagios*), which renders קָדוֹשׁ (*qādôš*), having to do with being set apart, or holy. In its use for Christian believers, it is associated with God's election of his people, his setting them apart as a distinct community for himself, their separation from sin, and thus their holiness (Harris 2005: 134).

The phrase ἐν ὅλῃ τῇ Ἀχαΐᾳ (*en holē tē Achaia*, throughout Achaia) suggests to Witherington (1995: 354) that 2 Corinthians was intended to serve as a circular letter, and the lack of personal greetings at the end of the letter would seem to support this. Yet it may be simply that the city of Corinth, as capital of the province, would see a constant interaction between the believers in the city proper and those from towns throughout the immediate area. In fact, J. Wiseman (*ANRW* 446) notes that "Citizens of all the towns of the Corinthia evidently considered themselves, throughout most of antiquity, citizens of Corinth."[14] Knowing this, and perhaps mindful of other congregations such as the one in Cenchreae, Paul may have addressed his letter accordingly. The apostle's use of πᾶσιν and ὅλη certainly suggests an awareness of a number of Christ-followers outside of Corinth, but we know specifically only that there were Phoebe and the church at Corinth's eastern port, Cenchreae (Rom. 16:1), and some, including Dionysius the Areopagite and Damaris, at Athens (Acts 17:34). Beyond these locations, there may have been churches at Lechaeum, the western port of the isthmus, only about two miles to the north of ancient Corinth's center.[15] But there were other towns nearby as

---

the community of Jerusalem, a group of angels, or an assembled multitude. Another common term used for translating this Hebrew verb is συναγωγή (*synagōgē*, assembly/synagogue).

14. J. Wiseman offers the caveat, "Only Tenea offers evidence of independence (spiritually or politically) from Corinth at any time."

15. Strabo (*Geogr.* 8.6.22) mentions that not many people lived there, but this reflection occurs well before Paul's time.

well, including Sicyon, Isthmia, Crommyon, Schoenus, Cleonae, and Tenea (Murphy-O'Connor 1983: 7).

Paul's use of this broad address may suggest that the problems plaguing the church in Corinth have spread beyond the city's boundaries, the influence of his opponents having a more regional effect. Indeed, in answer to the question "Why address the entire region?" John Chrysostom (*Hom 2 Cor.* 1.2) suggests, "The reason, I think, is that they were all involved in a single, common problem and were therefore all in need of the same remedy" (Bray 1999: 194). As today, church scandals or conflicts need little publicity to spread far and wide. The "geography" of the challenges to the apostle's ministry at Corinth would have made his task of unifying the church that much more difficult.

Paul greets this body of believers with "grace and peace." The whole of verse 2 forms a balanced structure, with four words per line:[16]

1:2

χάρις ὑμῖν καὶ εἰρήνη	*charis hymin kai eirēnē*	grace to you and peace
ἀπὸ θεοῦ πατρὸς ἡμῶν	*apo theou patros hēmōn*	from God our Father
καὶ κυρίου Ἰησοῦ Χριστοῦ	*kai kyriou Iēsou Christou*	and the Lord Jesus Christ

"Grace and peace" are directed to the Corinthians and expressed as coming from God the Father and the Lord Jesus Christ. Paul uses the highly stylized wording "grace to you and peace" in the salutations of Romans, 1 and 2 Corinthians, Galatians, Ephesians, Philippians, Colossians, 1 and 2 Thessalonians, and Philemon (Rom. 1:7; 1 Cor. 1:3; 2 Cor. 1:2; Gal. 1:3; Eph. 1:2; Phil. 1:2; Col. 1:2; 1 Thess. 1:1; 2 Thess. 1:2; Philem. 3). This "wish" is also used in the salutations of 1 and 2 Peter as well as John's greeting to the churches in Rev. 1:4, indicating that the phrase was broadly used in Christian circles.

Hellenistic letters commonly opened with "greetings" (χαίρειν, *chairein*; cf. Acts 15:23; 23:26; James 1:1).[17] In Christian letters the standard χαίρειν changes to the term χάρις and combines with the common Jewish greeting of "peace" (*shālôm*), reflecting Christianity's deep roots both in its experience of God's grace through the person of Jesus Christ and its Jewish sociocultural context and heritage. Used as it is here in 2 Corinthians, this expression of grace and peace reflects God's gift of well-being promised in the gospel, which is the true peace conveyed graciously by God through Christ.

These spiritual blessings can come only "from God our Father and the Lord Jesus Christ." It seems clear grammatically and contextually that "God our Father" and "the Lord Jesus Christ" are coordinate and that the single use of the preposition ἀπό extends to both, indicating Father and Son as together the source of grace and peace (on the grammar, see Harris 2005: 135–36).

---

16. Harris (2005: 135–37) observes that the nouns "grace" and "peace" lack the article "because they occur in a common, stereotyped expression and because abstract nouns are generally anarthrous when they express a quality without a particular reference to specific, concrete expressions of that quality."

17. On the reason why the letter form may have used the infinitive in this way, see Klauck and Bailey 2006: 18–19.

The confession of God as "our Father" may go back to Jesus's crafting of the Lord's Prayer (Matt. 6:9–13) and, in any case, participates in a rich early Christian heritage of reference to the fatherhood of God in relationship to his children (e.g., 1 Cor. 8:6; 15:24; Gal. 1:4; 4:6; Eph. 1:3, 17; 4:6; Phil. 2:11; Col. 3:17; James 1:27; 1 John 2:14). Paul mentions God as Father four additional times in this letter (2 Cor. 1:3 [2x]; 6:18; 11:31).

The title κύριος (*kyrios*), used of Yahweh in the Greek OT, is Paul's favorite title for Jesus and stems not only from the very earliest Christian communities but also reaches back into the life and ministry of Jesus himself.[18] As Barnett (1997: 62–63) points out, this claim of Jesus as the source of "grace and peace" would have been shocking in a first-century Jewish context.[19] Such radical association of the covenant God of the Jewish Scriptures with "the Lord Jesus Christ" bears witness to how dramatic a shift in worldview Paul received in his encounter with Christ on the Damascus road (Barnett 1997: 62). Paul understands Jesus to be directly associated with God the Father, so, as elsewhere in Paul, grace and peace come from the Lord Jesus Christ (1 Cor. 16:23; 2 Cor. 13:13; Gal. 6:18; Phil. 4:23; 1 Thess. 5:28) as well as from God the Father.

Reflection

The elements that shape the letter opening reveal a man who understands his primary orientation and loyalties to be otherworldly. George MacDonald (1867: 61) once wrote, "We are dwellers in a divine universe where no desires are in vain, if only they be large enough." Paul writes as a man of great "desire," great commitment to the ministry God has assigned to him. Thus he lives under the highest possible commission, a commission from the Lord of the universe, Jesus, by virtue of the very will of God. God's will gives the impetus for Paul communicating to God's church, and he communicates "grace and peace" that originate with God, divine gifts of which we all stand in need. So the letter opening communicates a thorough God-centeredness for Paul—he understands himself to be part of God's plan, writing to God's people on the basis of God's work of grace and peace. Therefore, he also writes as a person of profound relationships, his unique relationship with God through Christ Jesus forming the basis for his relationship with Timothy as his partner in ministry and the Achaians as a part of God's church.

18. The Gospels display a varied use of κύριος, at times referring to God the Father (e.g., Matt. 1:20; 2:15; 4:7; Luke 1:11–16), at times with the common cultural meaning of "sir" or "master" (e.g., Matt. 6:24; 8:2, 6; 10:25; 13:27; Mark 13:35; Luke 7:6), and at times with reference to Jesus as sharing in God's identity (Matt. 3:3; 7:22; 12:8; and esp. Matt. 22:43–45//Mark 12:36–37//Luke 20:42–44).

19. Both Larry Hurtado (1998: 93–128, 108–17) and Richard Bauckham (1999: 45–77) have made strong cases for Jesus's identity with God in earliest Christianity, based in part on the use of OT passages that speak of God as "Lord" being appropriated by the earliest Christians to refer to Christ.

Additional Notes

1:1. The origin of the term "apostle" (*apostolos*), as used in the NT, has been much debated. In broader Greco-Roman culture, the term could be used of an expedition (Demosthenes, *3 Olynth.* 3.5) or a delegation (Josephus, *Ant.* 17.300), though in literary Greek of the first century, the term is rare. In LXX Codex Alexandrinus, the noun *apostolos* occurs only once, at 1 Kings 14:6, in the story of the sick child, where the prophet Ahijah, having been warned by God concerning a visit from Jereboam's wife, says, "I am sent [ἐγώ εἰμι ἀπόστολος, *egō eimi apostolos*] to you with bad news." Yet the verbal cognates of the noun occur almost 700 times (either as forms of *apostellein* or *exapostellein*), which in all but a handful of cases translate the Hebrew שָׁלַח (*šālaḥ*, to send) and most often refer to a person sent by another to accomplish some task. This seems to have led to a later use in rabbinic literature, where the noun *šālîaḥ* came to speak of a commissioned surrogate, one who carried the authority of the sender (e.g., *m. Ber.* 5.5). Though disputed, it is possible that the concept of the *šālîaḥ*, rendered as ἀπόστολος, was already in use among first-century Hellenistic Jews and thus formed a backdrop to its use in the NT (Barnett 1997: 45–47; Spicq 1994: 1.186–90).

1:2. Witnesses A D G K L Ψ read Ἰησοῦ Χριστοῦ (*Iēsou Christou*), reflected, for instance in the KJV. To be preferred, the reading Χριστοῦ Ἰησοῦ (*Christou Iēsou*) follows early witnesses such as 𝔓[46] and B.

B. Prologue (1:3–11)

Leo Tolstoy writes, "It is by those who have suffered that the world has been advanced" (quoted in Yancey 1990: 143). Accordingly, those of us who minister to other Christ-followers often suffer in the course of ministry. Such suffering can pummel our perspective, straining both our relationship with God and our relationships with others in the church. But, as Paul models for us in the prologue to 2 Corinthians, the pain of our afflictions does not need to result in relational breakdown and bitterness. Suffering can actually drive us to God, into deeper community with others who suffer, and even to a celebration of God's encouragement, a type of encouragement only experienced fully in the crucible of affliction.

As Paul writes the prologue for 2 Corinthians, he introduces rich reflection on God's redemption of suffering, a key theme for the book. The apostle and his coworkers have been deeply bruised by recent experiences, with fresh emotional and spiritual wounds still stinging. Yet instead of bitterness and regret, the apostle offers one of the most beautiful and beloved passages in the NT, turning his suffering into a song of thanks to God and an appeal for continued partnership with the Corinthian church. The prologue divides nicely into two main movements. In the first (1:3–7) we find a beautiful, encouraging benediction. In this benediction Paul blesses God for his encouragement in the midst of affliction (1:3). Then he points to the purposefulness of the affliction (1:4–6) and notes the special fellowship the experience of suffering forges between his mission and the Corinthians (1:7).

In the second movement of the prologue (1:8–11), Paul shares overtly about his recent brush with death. The apostle doesn't want the Corinthians to take lightly the affliction he has endured in Asia (1:8), and he points to how God redeemed his suffering by causing Paul and his mission team to abandon trust in themselves and to trust only in God, "who raises the dead" (1:9). He also expresses hope about God's continued deliverance (1:10) and the Corinthians' help through prayer (1:11). Notice how the prologue begins and ends with God being celebrated (1:3, 11). Also, both halves of the prologue trumpet God's redemption of afflictions (1:4, 6, 9), and both halves end with a focus on Paul's partnership with the Corinthians (1:7, 11). Thus through both praise (1:3–7) and appeal (1:8, 11), the apostle strategically opens his heart to the Corinthians, sharing out of his pain and laying a foundation for the relational rebuilding he hopes to accomplish with the Achaian church through this letter.

1. Praise God for His Encouragement! (1:3–7)

In this first movement of the prologue, Paul accomplishes several things. First, he uses a thoughtful benediction to model for the Corinthians a proper Christian response to suffering, blessing God for the encouragement experienced amid great persecution (1:3). Second, Paul explains that his experience of persecution was purposeful. It enables him to draw on the encouragement he has received from God and pass it on to others, including the Corinthians (1:4–6). Third, the experience of suffering and encouragement allows the apostle to forge a deeper connection with the Corinthians (cf. 1:11), appealing to their common fellowship in both suffering and encouragement (1:7). Such a connection is vital for what Paul wants to accomplish with his letter (Hafemann 2000: 58–59, following O'Brien 1977: 263), which in part is to woo the Corinthians back into a solid relationship with himself as their apostle. As noted in the introduction, the apostle's change in itinerary seems to have put a strain on his relationship with some in the church. So, even in this opening benediction, Paul begins the task of vindicating his integrity (P. Hughes 1962: 9) and calling the Corinthians back into a sound relationship with himself. The unit can be outlined as follows:

a. Blessed be our compassionate, encouraging God! (1:3)
b. Purposeful affliction (1:4–6)
c. The fellowship of suffering and encouragement (1:7)

Exegesis and Exposition

³Blessed be the God and Father of our Lord Jesus Christ, the compassionate Father and the God who offers every possible encouragement! ⁴He encourages us in all our affliction, so that we might be able to encourage those experiencing any affliction with the encouragement by which we ourselves are encouraged by God. ⁵Because just as the sufferings of Christ spill over toward us, to the same degree, through Christ, our encouragement overflows. ⁶Now, if we are afflicted, it is for your encouragement ⌐and salvation, or if we experience the encouragement that follows the affliction— both result in your encouragement, which is at work as you endure the same kinds of sufferings that we suffer. ⁷Indeed, our hope for you is resolute⌐, knowing that as you share our experience of sufferings, so also you share our experience of encouragement.

a. Blessed Be Our Compassionate, Encouraging God! (1:3)

Paul often begins his letters with a salutation (e.g., Rom. 1:1–7; 1 Cor. 1:1–3; Phil. 1:1–2; Col. 1:1–2) followed by giving thanks to God for those to whom he is writing (e.g., Rom. 1:8; 1 Cor. 1:4–9; Phil. 1:3–5; Col. 1:3–8). At times he also includes prayers for the congregation (e.g., Rom. 1:9–10; Phil. 1:9–11; Col. 1:9–14). In the prologue of 2 Corinthians (1:3–11), he seems unusually preoccupied with his own experience (and perhaps that of his ministry team?),[1] focusing on how God has encouraged him and requesting prayers for himself (1:3–5, 11; Harris 2005: 138). Given what the apostle has recently experienced, it is no wonder that he focuses on that experience of affliction and requests prayer. But, as already mentioned, this benediction has a rhetorical purpose as well. Paul wants the Corinthians to understand these experiences as one explanation for his change of travel plans (cf. 1:12–20). According to his account in verses 8–11, Paul has recently been deeply challenged emotionally and threatened physically, having come through a terrifying time of intense persecution. The apostle describes this experience as overwhelming, bringing him to the brink of despair and a certain inability to cope with the situation. Death seemed imminent.

Yet, in spite of all he has been through, Paul begins this difficult letter to a difficult congregation at a difficult time in his ministry by praising God: "Blessed be the God and Father of our Lord Jesus Christ, the compassionate Father and the God who offers every possible encouragement!" The apostle expresses this blessing with εὐλογητός (eulogētos), a term having to do with being "worthy of praise or commendation" (GELNT 430).

The verb of being (εἰμί) is understood, and the sentence may be read either as a proclamation (i.e., as indicative, "God is blessed") or as an exclamation (i.e., as optative, "Blessed be God!" or "May God be blessed!").[2] The expression follows roughly a common formula found in Jewish prayers of the era, the בְּרָכָה (bĕrākâ, blessing), such as the Eighteen Benedictions (the Shemoneh Esreh; lit., Eighteen), which repeats "Blessed are You, Lord" (Instone-Brewer 2004: 41–42).[3]

But the Jewish Scriptures serve as the real backdrop for Paul's expression of blessing. This construction, εὐλογητός + an understood verb of being, is quite common in the LXX, and either "God" (e.g., Gen. 14:20; 1 Kings 5:21 [5:7 ET]; 1 Esd. 4:40; Pss. 17:47; 65:20 [18:46; 66:20 ET]), or "the LORD" (e.g., Gen. 24:31; Exod. 18:10; Ruth 4:14; 1 Sam. 25:39; 2 Sam. 6:21 [not in ET]; 1 Kings 8:56; 1 Esd. 8:25; Pss. 27:6; 30:22 [28:6; 31:21 ET]), or some variation of the two terms together (e.g., Gen. 9:26; 24:27; 1 Sam. 25:32; 2 Sam. 18:28; 1 Kings 1:48; 8:15; 2 Chron. 2:11 [2:12 ET]; 6:4; Ezra 7:27; Ps. 40:14 [41:13 ET]) announces that God is the object of blessing. Thus, when Paul refers to

---

1. On the use of the first-person plural in 2 Corinthians, see the introduction, plus the first additional note on 1:8 at the end of this unit.

2. Barrett (1973: 58) suggests that it is somewhat immaterial whether we read the blessing as indicative or optative, though the Jewish liturgical context favors the former.

3. The Eighteen Benedictions is also known as the Shemoneh Esreh (Eighteen), the Tephillah (Prayer), or the Amidah (Standing), because one stands to say the prayer (Instone-Brewer 2003: 25–29).

the "God" (θεός) of our "Lord" (κυρίου), he uses terms taken directly from a common way of blessing God in the Scriptures.

But why begin the letter with this beautiful, effusive blessing? Welborn (2001: 58) suggests that by use of the blessing, Paul not only expresses his own heartfelt praise but also mentors the Corinthians in proper Christian response to suffering:

> By employing the form of the εὐλογία, Paul is able to locate the source of the emotion he feels, not in the giftedness of the Corinthians, but in the fullness of his own heart, which overflows with praise for unexpected deliverance. Like the Psalmist of old, Paul declares God "blessed" because of the consolation he has personally experienced in the midst of affliction.

According to Welborn (2001: 57–59), Paul uses the benediction as a launching point, developing the letter by dramatizing the transformation of "despair" into "hope," of "sorrow" into "love," and of "fear" into "joy." Thus by example he calls the Corinthians to consider their own response to the circumstances in which they find themselves, challenging them to bless God in the midst of suffering.

The object of the benediction is "the God and Father of our Lord Jesus Christ" (ὁ θεὸς καὶ πατὴρ τοῦ κυρίου ἡμῶν Ἰησοῦ Χριστοῦ, *ho theos kai patēr tou kyriou hēmōn Iēsou Christou*). When Paul blesses "the God and Father," he crafts a smooth transition from the end of the salutation in verse 2, where the apostle refers to "God our Father" (see comments on v. 2). Yet, unlike the blessings of broader Judaism, Paul refers also to the Lord Jesus. Such a christologically oriented version of the formula is found elsewhere in the NT at Eph. 1:3 and 1 Pet. 1:3, mirroring Paul's words here.[4] At 2 Cor. 11:31, Paul refers to "the God and Father of the Lord Jesus" (ὁ θεὸς καὶ πατὴρ τοῦ κυρίου Ἰησοῦ, *ho theos kai patēr tou kyriou Iēsou*) as "the eternally blessed One" (ὁ ὢν εὐλογητὸς εἰς τοὺς αἰῶνας, *ho ōn eulogētos eis tous aiōnas*), echoing the benedictory words of 1:3. Second Corinthians is profoundly "Christ-centered."[5] At times Paul points to his solidarity with Jesus in his suffering (1:5; 4:10–11, 14; 8:9; 10:1; 12:10), but he also makes much of Jesus as the exalted Lord (1:14; 2:14; 4:5, 14; 5:8, 10–11; 10:5, 8). This double look at Jesus gives strong encouragement to the believer experiencing difficulties and is instructive for us. When we experience suffering, we need to think much on and pray much to our Lord Jesus, who also suffered but now reigns as Lord of the universe. All the enemies hurting us will be put under his feet. Both our shared experi-

---

4. Elsewhere in the NT, God is called "the blessed One" (τοῦ εὐλογητοῦ, *tou eulogētou*) at Mark 14:61, used as a periphrasis for God's name, and Luke 1:68 where, on the lips of Zechariah, "the Lord, the God of Israel" is called blessed because he has visited his people and provided them with redemption. The use in Luke conforms to LXX phraseology (e.g., 1 Kings 1:48; 2 Chron. 2:11 [2:12 ET]; 6:4; Ps. 71:18 [72:18 ET]). The term finds expression over seventy times in the LXX.

5. See 2 Cor. 1:1–3, 5, 14, 19, 21; 2:10, 12, 14–15, 17; 3:3–4, 14, 16–18; 4:4–6, 10–11, 14; 5:6, 8, 10–11, 14, 16–20; 6:15, 17–18; 8:5, 9, 19, 21, 23; 9:13; 10:1, 5, 7–8, 14, 17–18; 11:2–4, 10, 13, 17, 23, 31; 12:1–2, 8–10, 19; 13:3, 5, 10, 13.

ence with Jesus in suffering and his status as the exalted Lord should give us encouragement!

Paul specifically notes that Jesus is "our" (ἡμῶν, hēmōn; genitive of relationship) Lord, perhaps placing emphasis on his solidarity with the Corinthians under the lordship of Christ.[6] Yet in the first part of the benediction, focus rests on the Father as the one who provides encouragement, or comfort, for his people.[7] The phrase ὁ πατὴρ τῶν οἰκτιρμῶν (ho patēr tōn oiktirmōn, or "the Father of mercies") conveys that God is a "compassionate Father." As noted in the comments on verse 2, the fatherhood of God finds rich expression in biblical tradition. God is called the "one Father" (Mal. 2:10; Matt. 23:9; 1 Cor. 8:6; Eph. 4:6) and even the more intimate "Abba"[8] (Mark 14:36; cf. Rom. 8:15; Gal. 4:6). He delights in claiming his people as his children (1 John 3:1), and as a good Father, he provides necessities for his sons and daughters (Matt. 6:25–34), as well as good gifts (Luke 11:11–13) and discipline for their training (Prov. 3:12; Heb. 12:5–11; DBI 274–75).

Moreover, God is compassionate, expressing concern over the difficulties faced by his people. The term οἰκτιρμός (oiktirmos), used approximately thirty times in the Greek OT and five times in the NT (Rom. 12:1; 2 Cor. 1:3; Phil. 2:1; Col. 3:12; Heb. 10:28), almost always occurs in the plural form, as here,[9] and communicates a concern for the troubles of another person, expressed variously in English translations as "pity," "mercy," or "compassion." Paul certainly has in mind a rich Jewish tradition that speaks of God's encouragement of his people in the midst of their suffering. In that tradition one finds exhortations to embrace trials as an opportunity to see God work, both in circumstances and in the hearts of his people. For instance, God's remnant will be purified through their struggles (Isa. 48:10–11) as he redeems situations, carrying his people through the water and fire of troubles and bringing them out to a place of prosperity (Ps. 66:12). God's encouragement for his people as they struggle with difficulties in life can be seen in Abraham, Job, and Joseph, among many others, who, resolute in faith and commitment, received

6. As noted, the benediction in Eph. 1:3 exactly mirrors this form in 2 Cor. 1:3; in Ephesians, Paul also places a great deal of emphasis on unity (e.g., 4:1–16).

7. The reference to God as a "compassionate Father and the God who offers every possible encouragement" reverses the uses of "God" and "Father" in the first part of the verse, forming a chiastic structure (an abba pattern) that rolls off the tongue to the ear:

A   ὁ θεὸς καὶ (ho theos kai, the God and)

  B   πατὴρ τοῦ κυρίου ἡμῶν Ἰησοῦ Χριστοῦ (patēr tou kyriou hēmōn Iēsou Christou, Father of our Lord Jesus Christ)

  B′ ὁ πατὴρ τῶν οἰκτιρμῶν καὶ (ho patēr tōn oiktirmōn kai, the Father of compassion and)

A′ θεὸς πάσης παρακλήσεως (theos pasēs paraklēseōs, God of all encouragement)

8. This was a family word that expressed a degree of intimacy; although Jeremias's ET as "daddy" has been criticized for being too simplistic, the unusual nature of this designation as used by Jesus, as well as its intimacy, seems clear (L. W. Hurtado, DJG 275; Jeremias 1971: 56–68, 178–203).

9. The exceptions are Zech. 1:16; 7:9; 12:10; cf. 4 Macc. 6:24; Sir. 5:6; Bar. 2:27; and, in the NT, Col. 3:12.

strong encouragement. Especially apt, Ps. 103:13 combines these concepts of fatherhood and compassion, reading, "As a father has compassion on his children, so the Lord has compassion on his faithful followers" (NET).[10]

As we face harsh circumstances in life, we may be tempted to doubt God's attention, feeling as if God has abandoned us to our difficulties. Yet here in 2 Cor. 1:3 Paul reminds us of this aspect of our Father's character: our cries are answered by his compassion, the natural concern of a father for his children.

Also, God offers encouragement. The theme of encouragement dominates these five verses of the benediction, with the noun παράκλησις (paraklēsis, encouragement, comfort) used six times and its verbal cognate another four. Given Paul's use of both noun and verb throughout his writings, it constitutes an important theme for the apostle. If 2 Corinthians can be tagged as his letter of encouragement, 1:3–7 offers the apostle's finest piece on the topic (Hafemann 2000: 59).[11] The word παράκλησις could be used with the sense of "comfort" and is translated in this way, for instance, by most English versions, including the HCSB, NET, ASV, KJV, NASB, NIV, and NLT. Yet the term can carry the sense of an "act of emboldening another in belief or course of action," thus "encouragement" (BDAG 766), which seems as appropriate as "comfort" for a situation in which difficulties are being faced. Elsewhere, at 7:4, 7, 13 the word again could be translated either with the sense of "comfort" or "encouragement," but at 8:4, 17 only the latter would seem appropriate, as Paul prompts someone to action (i.e., "encouragement" or "exhortation").[12] Also, the verb form in 2 Corinthians often carries this overtone of encouraging a person to take action (2:8; 5:20; 6:1; 8:6; 9:5; 10:1; 12:8, 18; 13:11), and in these passages a rendering of "comfort," as commonly used in English, won't do. As David Garland (1999: 60) aptly observes concerning the sense of the "comfort" to which Paul refers in 1:3–7,

> The comfort that Paul has in mind has nothing to do with a languorous feeling of contentment. It is not some tranquilizing dose of grace that only dulls pains but a stiffening agent that fortifies one in heart, mind, and soul. Comfort relates to encouragement, help, exhortation. God's comfort strengthens weak knees and sustains sagging spirits so that one faces the troubles of life with unbending resolve and unending assurance.

10. The LXX (Ps. 102:13 [103:13 ET]) uses the cognate verb form οἰκτίρω (oiktirō), rather than the noun, to convey the concept of compassion.

11. Elsewhere in 2 Corinthians, the concept occurs evenly spread throughout, with clusters of occurrences in chaps. 7–8: 2:7–8; 5:20; 6:1; 7:4–13; 8:4, 6, 17; 9:5; 10:1; 12:8, 18; 13:11. In Paul's other writings, the noun occurs another nine times (Rom. 12:8; 15:4–5; 1 Cor. 14:3; Phil. 2:1; 1 Thess. 2:3; 2 Thess. 2:16; 1 Tim. 4:13; Philem. 7), and the verb another thirty-six times (Rom. 12:1, 8; 15:30; 16:17; 1 Cor. 1:10; 4:13, 16; 14:31; 16:12, 15; Eph. 4:1; 6:22; Phil. 4:2 [2x]; Col. 2:2; 4:8; 1 Thess. 2:12; 3:2, 7; 4:1, 10, 18; 5:11, 14; 2 Thess. 2:17; 3:12; 1 Tim. 1:3; 2:1; 5:1; 6:2; 2 Tim. 4:2; Titus 1:9; 2:6, 15; Philem. 9–10).

12. An author can use a term variously in a writing, but my point here is that Paul employs the term with the meaning of "encouragement" elsewhere in this letter.

Therefore, here we opt to translate the word with the sense of "encouragement," which communicates "the lifting of one's spirits" (as does the English term "comfort") but also hints at effecting a forward-looking, strengthening sense of hope for what lies down the road.

That God is the God of "all" (πάσης, *pasēs*) encouragement might be a temporal reference to encouragement given at all times (e.g., "an ever-encouraging God"), but perhaps preferred, given what follows in the immediate context, it also might point to the comprehensive nature of God's encouragement of his children—"every possible encouragement" (Harris 2005: 142–43). This corresponds to the use of ἐν πάσῃ τῇ θλίψει (*en pasē tē thlipsei*, in any affliction) in the next verse, a reference to a wide variety of difficulties in the face of which encouragement is needed.[13] For Paul, moreover, such encouragement extends beyond an emotional and spiritual uplift and at times includes the actual deliverance from harm, which will be Paul's focus in 1:10 (so Barrett 1973: 60). Of course, Paul also has experienced the type of encouragement that gave him courage to stand in the face of unrelenting hardship and danger, as the hardship lists of 2 Corinthians so well attest (e.g., 4:8–11; 6:4b–10; 11:23b–33; 12:10).

As we face the sometimes crushing discouragement of day-to-day ministry, are we living in and living out the benediction of 2 Cor. 1:3? Do we see God, the Father of our Lord Jesus, as compassionate and the Supreme Encourager? Are we characterized by "blessing" him amid very difficult periods of ministry?

b. Purposeful Affliction (1:4–6)

1:4 Paul continues his description of our compassionate, encouraging God: "who encourages us in all our affliction." The substantival participle ὁ παρακαλῶν (*ho parakalōn*, the one encouraging), which we have translated "who encourages," introduces this further description of the one called "Father" and "God" in the previous verse. God provides this strong encouragement "in all[14] our affliction" (ἐπὶ πάσῃ τῇ θλίψει ἡμῶν, *epi pasē tē thlipsei hēmōn*), and Paul certainly has in mind God's encouragement in the thick of the persecution through which he has just lived (1:8–11). Kierkegaard (1956: 278–79) states, "When one preaches Christianity in such a way that the echo answers, 'Away with that man, he does not deserve to live,' know that this

---

13. The end of 1:3 and the beginning of verse 4 craft another chiastic relationship:
   A God of
      B all encouragement
      B′ who encourages us in
   A′ all our difficulties

14. The preposition ἐπί + the dative can be used to communicate a wide array of possible meanings and is rendered by most English versions with a local sense ("in all our"; so ESV, HCSB, NASB, NLT², NIV, NET). Yet the construction can also carry a nuance of "perspective," such as "with regard to," or a temporal sense as "upon every occasion of our affliction" = "every time we experience affliction" (BDAG 363–67).

is the Christianity of the New Testament. . . . Capital punishment is the penalty for preaching Christianity as it truly is." So here in the benediction, Paul's words about affliction anticipate the fuller explanation of his troubles recounted in 1:8–11.

The term we have rendered here as "affliction"[15] (θλῖψις, *thlipsis*) occurs rarely in extrabiblical Greek, where it carries the sense of "pressure." In the biblical literature, however, the word could refer to the troubling circumstances or events that bring about intense distress (so "oppression," or "affliction," or "persecution," as in Acts 11:19 and perhaps in our immediate context at 2 Cor. 1:8) or the inward emotion of anguish or deep distress itself, produced by harsh outward circumstances. In the NT this distress often has to do with living under persecution.[16] Paul uses the term nine times in 2 Corinthians[17] and another fifteen times elsewhere in his writings, in places referring to harsh difficulties in life (e.g., Rom. 2:9; 8:35; 1 Cor. 7:28; Phil. 1:17) and often specifically referring to a context of persecution (e.g., Eph. 3:13; Col. 1:24; 1 Thess. 1:6; 3:3).[18] The point of Paul's praise is that God always meets us in our affliction, counterbalancing the affliction with strong encouragement.

The encouragement God brings to Paul and his ministry team, however, does not end with him but instead has a greater purpose in the community of faith: "so that we might be able to encourage those experiencing any affliction with the encouragement by which we ourselves are encouraged by God" (εἰς τὸ δύνασθαι ἡμᾶς παρακαλεῖν τοὺς ἐν πάσῃ θλίψει διὰ τῆς παρακλήσεως ἧς παρακαλούμεθα αὐτοὶ ὑπὸ τοῦ θεοῦ, *eis to dynasthai hēmas parakalein tous en pasē thlipsei dia tēs paraklēseōs hēs parakaloumetha autoi hypo tou theou*). The implication of this part of the verse is fairly straightforward. The experience of being encouraged by God in the midst of harsh ministry situations has served the purpose ("so that")[19] of enabling Paul to offer encouragement to others. There are two sides to this coin of encouragement: the side that identifies with the suffering of another person, and the side that takes the opportunity to offer encouragement.

On the one hand, those in Christian ministry who have suffered have resources to empathize with and minister to those who are scarred. Charles Spurgeon (1960: 221–22) shares poignantly from his own experience:

15. θλῖψις refers to "trouble that inflicts distress, oppression, affliction, tribulation" or the "inward experience of distress, affliction, trouble" (BDAG 457). The ET "troubles" (so, e.g., NLT², NIV, NET) has such a broad semantic range in English that it often does not carry the hard edge of "tribulation" or "oppression," and Paul certainly has persecution in mind. Although "affliction" is not a word people commonly use in modern English, it carries the sense of "troubles" inflicted on a person, which Paul seems to have in mind in 2 Corinthians.

16. θλῖψις is used over one hundred times in the LXX and a total of forty-five times in the NT.

17. In 2 Cor. 1:4 (2x), 8; 2:4; 4:17; 6:4; 7:4; 8:2, 13.

18. Rom. 2:9; 5:3 (2x); 8:35; 12:12; 1 Cor. 7:28; Eph. 3:13; Phil. 1:17; 4:14; Col. 1:24; 1 Thess. 1:6; 3:3, 7; 2 Thess. 1:4, 6.

19. In 1:4, εἰς (*eis*) + the infinitive (δύνασθαι, *dynasthai*) + the infinitive's subject in the acc. case (ἡμᾶς, *hēmas*)—such a phrase is a standard way of expressing purpose: "so that we might be able."

One Sabbath morning, I preached from the text, "My God, My God, why hast Thou forsaken Me?" and though I did not say so, yet I preached my own experience. I heard my own chains clank while I tried to preach to my fellow-prisoners in the dark; but I could not tell why I was brought into such an awful horror of darkness, for which I condemned myself. On the following Monday evening, a man came to see me who bore all the marks of despair upon his countenance. His hair seemed to stand up right, and his eyes were ready to start from their sockets. He said to me, after a little parleying, "I never before, in my life, heard any man speak who seemed to know my heart. Mine is a terrible case; but on Sunday morning you painted me to the life, and preached as if you had been inside my soul." By God's grace I saved that man from suicide, and led him into gospel light and liberty; but I know I could not have done it if I had not myself been confined in the dungeon in which he lay. I tell you the story, brethren, because you sometimes may not understand your own experience, and the perfect people may condemn you for having it; but what know they of God's servants? You and I have to suffer much for the sake of the people of our charge.

As we continue to track with Paul's thought, notice yet two points about this enabling that Paul celebrates. First, it covers any (πάσῃ, *pasē*) affliction that fellow believers might encounter—so the encouragement is comprehensive in scope. Second, Paul's emphasis is on the encouragement rather than on the suffering, and the encouragement the apostle offers comes via the same encouragement he himself has received. The preposition διά (*dia*) plus the genitive case here communicates instrumentality or the circumstance by which something is brought about. In other words, Paul would not be able to encourage the Corinthians in their experiences of affliction if he were not already experiencing[20] such encouragement from God.

1:5 The ὅτι (*hoti*, because) at the beginning of verse 5 serves to mark the beginning of an explanation, specifically an explanation of the first part of verse 4, the thought that God encourages Paul and his associates "in all our affliction." The construction καθὼς ... οὕτως (*kathōs ... houtōs*, just as ... so also) indicates that there is a correlation between Paul's suffering and the encouragement he has received from God. The extent to which he has experienced affliction has been matched at every point by God's encouragement, and the degree to which he has suffered is indeed great. In fact, Christ's sufferings (τὰ παθήματα, *ta pathēmata*), he suggests, "overflow toward us." Ancient authors used a form of the term περισσεύω (*perisseuō*) at times to speak of having an abundance of something, or a lot left over (e.g., the pieces of bread remaining after Jesus fed huge crowds, Matt. 14:20; 15:37; Luke 9:17; John 6:12–13). In the experience of his ministry, Paul says, there is a superabundance of sufferings, and he bears elegant witness to the fact elsewhere (2 Cor. 4:8–11; 6:4–10; 11:23–29; 12:10): numerous times he was beaten, stoned, shipwrecked, pressured, imprisoned, hungry, sleepless, slandered, near death—and in danger at sea, in riots and

---

20. The verb is present tense, thus having imperfective aspect. So Paul experiences encouragement as an ongoing reality.

rivers, in both city and country, from both Gentiles and his own people, and from exposure to the elements.

Obviously, Paul was well acquainted with suffering. Yet what does he mean by the sufferings "of Christ"? Numerous suggestions have been made (see the additional notes), but perhaps it is best to read this genitive form as reflecting the Christian's identification with Christ in his sufferings, that is, the sufferings experienced "in association with Christ."[21] It may well be that this perspective was birthed in Paul's experience on the Damascus road, where Jesus asked him, "Why are you persecuting me?" (Acts 9:4). Out of this experience, Paul came to understand persecution against Christ's people, Christ's body, as a direct assault on Christ himself, as Christ's people follow Christ's path of suffering in identification with him. Thus, for Paul to be beaten constituted both a continued assault on Christ and the apostle's identification with the preeminent Righteous Sufferer.[22] For Paul, then, being in a world hostile to Christ means an experience of overflowing difficulties in life and ministry. Yet these sufferings highlight the authentic connection Paul has with Jesus and thus, over against the false teachers, the validity of his ministry. He has suffered with Jesus while they "stayed home and stayed safe" (P. Hughes 1962: 9).

Yet the encouragement Paul has experienced in his sufferings as Christ's person in a hostile world was just as abundant as the sufferings experienced. In fact, the encouragement resulted from the sufferings and met the sufferings point for point in every way. Thus it is only in the experience of suffering that we find the answer to suffering; in great suffering one experiences great encouragement from the Lord. For it is the Lord himself who suffered for us and now not only identifies with us in our suffering on his behalf but also provides encouragement to match the suffering.

In what we have as verse 6, Paul draws an inference from verses 4–5: God's   **1:6**
economy of suffering surrounding Paul's ministry accomplishes a win-win situation for the Corinthians. The apostle states, "If we are afflicted, it is for your encouragement and salvation, or if we experience encouragement . . .—both

---

21. This interpretation of 1:5 reads the genitive τοῦ Χριστοῦ (*tou Christou*) as a genitive of association, that is, the sufferings experienced "in association with Christ."

22. Consequently, Paul himself could desire to know "the fellowship of his sufferings, being conformed to his death" (Phil. 3:10) and could boast, "In my flesh, for his body the church, I am filling up what is lacking in Christ's afflictions" (Col. 1:24), and "I carry Jesus's marks on my body" (Gal. 6:17). When in Colossians Paul writes that he fills up "what is lacking," he is not speaking in the sense of atonement, which for him has been decisively accomplished. Rather, suffering continues in the world until Christ's coming, and those who are Christ's, who follow his path, naturally follow in the rejection he faced and the concomitant sufferings. Christ identifies with such people. Bruce (1971: 178) puts it well, "Christ, who suffered personally on the cross, continues to suffer in his people on earth so long as the present aeon lasts." Correspondingly, for believers to suffer persecution constitutes solidarity with Christ. In suffering for him, as they are persecuted for his name, Christians also suffer with him and he with them. Instead of standing with the world over against the cross, shouting against Jesus (Matt. 27:38–44), we stand with him at the cross of suffering, identifying with our Lord. As Heb. 13:13 says, "Therefore, we must go outside the camp to him, bearing his disparagement he experienced."

result in your encouragement." As Harris (2005: 147) states, the combination of εἴτε . . . εἴτε (*eite . . . eite*) does not communicate a situation in which mutually exclusive alternatives are presented. Rather, Paul has in mind events occurring in succession: the experience of difficulties and the encouragement that follows. In verse 4 we translated the two occurrences of θλῖψις (*thlipsis*) as "affliction." Here we have the cognate verb θλίβω (*thlibō*), which can mean "to press together," or "compress," but here, given the context, it also carries the sense of "to trouble," "oppress," or "afflict"; Paul is alluding to the persecution he has experienced (BDAG 457).

If Paul and his ministry team experience affliction, that affliction is "for"[23] the Corinthians' encouragement and salvation. How, then, has Paul's persecution worked for "encouragement and salvation"? Suffering can be a discouraging experience for a community. As the Corinthian community witnesses Paul's persecution (detailed in 1:8–11) and his subsequent encouragement, they realize that they are part of a larger project of God, with a purpose that makes sense of their own experience of persecution. Paul, via his experience of encouragement in his sufferings, has been equipped to communicate encouragement to the Corinthian church. Also, this results in their "salvation" (σωτηρία, *sōtēria*), a term that could refer to "deliverance" or "preservation," in the sense of physical escape—but most often in Paul it refers to the deliverance that Christ brings about in the gospel (Rom. 1:16; 10:1, 10; 11:11; 13:11; Eph. 1:13; Phil. 2:12; 1 Thess. 5:8–9; 2 Thess. 2:13; 2 Tim. 2:10; 3:15). The term occurs in only two other passages in 2 Corinthians (6:2; 7:10), both of which also seem to refer to dimensions of deliverance brought by the gospel.[24] The Corinthians have experienced salvation because of Paul's ministry of the gospel, and that ministry has involved affliction. Thus the affliction has been endured, in part, so that they might know the salvation effected by God through Christ. As Paul points out later in the letter, death is at work in him, so that life might be at work in the Corinthians (4:12).

So authentic Christian ministry involves both affliction and encouragement, but both can result in encouragement for those on the receiving end of the ministry. This can be seen more clearly when considering contrast and correspondences in the structure of verse 6 (see fig. 5).[25]

The contrast is seen by the bracket on the left side of the diagram (C), a contrast between the ministry experiences of affliction and encouragement. Moreover, both of these dimensions of the experience of persecution result

---

23. The preposition ὑπὲρ (*hyper*) + the genitive serves here to mark the experience of affliction as in the interest of the Corinthians (BDAG 1030).

24. In mentioning their "salvation" in the context of persecution, Paul may be crafting a play on words similar to that found in Phil. 1:19, 28, where he speaks of his own imprisonment and deliverance (1:19) and then the destruction of the Philippians' opponents over against the Philippians' salvation (1:28). So here the Corinthians' "salvation"—their ultimate deliverance through the gospel—ironically comes in connection with Paul's experience of persecution.

25. To make the structural dynamics clearer in the English version of the diagram, I have departed from my smooth ET of the verse at the beginning of this section.

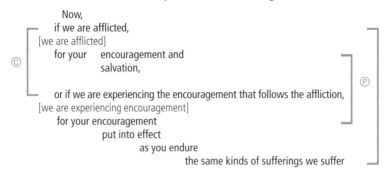

Figure 5 **Contrasts and Parallels in Paul's Description of His Sufferings**

in encouragement, as seen by the parallel lines in the diagram, marked by the bracket to the left of *P*. Further, the suffering Paul experiences in his ministry corresponds to the suffering faced by the Corinthians themselves, as seen by the parallel between "if we are afflicted" at the beginning of the unit and "the same kinds of sufferings that we suffer" at the end of the unit.

Therefore the "encouragement" received by the Corinthians as a result of Paul's experience of harsh circumstances parallels the encouragement the Corinthians receive while enduring the same kinds of suffering that Paul and his missionary team experienced. The present participle (the form is genitive feminine singular) τῆς ἐνεργουμένης (*tēs energoumenēs*, being at work) is attributive, delimiting τῆς . . . παρακλήσεως (*tēs . . . paraklēseōs*); it is translated like a relative clause: "the encouragement, *which is at work*." The preposition ἐν (*en*) works with the word rendered "endurance" (ὑπομονῇ, *hypomonē*) to reflect the circumstance or condition under which the Corinthians' encouragement is put into effect: "as" they "endure the same kinds of sufferings" that Paul and his associates suffer. Thus they benefit from the apostle's ministry to them, but they also stand with him in the experience of Christians suffering for the sake of the gospel and receive encouragement from God. The only way the Corinthians could experience this type of encouragement is in the crucible of persecution. With reference to the "suffering" endured by the Corinthians, it may be that Paul, in part, has in mind the pressure put on those who stand with him over against his opponents at Corinth, but that is not clearly indicated by the text.

c. The Fellowship of Suffering and Encouragement (1:7)

The Corinthians' endurance in sufferings actually gives Paul hope as he looks forward with confidence or expectation, and his hope is "resolute." The term βεβαία (*bebaia*), a predicate adjective describing the hope, had various connotations in the ancient world, speaking for instance of something that is reliable or does not disappoint. In this sense the word is used in Heb. 6:19 of an anchor that does not give way but rather provides stability. So too, the

1:7

term could communicate "persistence over time" or "something in force" or "valid." Here Paul probably means that the hope he has is firm or unwavering (so the HCSB and NIV, "firm"; the NET, "steadfast"; or the NASB[95], "firmly grounded") and will not lead to disappointment. This matches a general hopefulness that pervades 2 Corinthians (P. Hughes 1962: 15–16). Even in the face of continuing opposition—an attempt at usurping his authority by a vocal minority in the church—Paul expresses confidence in the ultimate response from the Corinthians, this perhaps especially in light of Titus's recent visit to Corinth (7:6–7, 13–16). In short, he has confidence that many of them are true Christ-followers, sharers in his ministry and the sufferings and comfort that go with it.

What, then, is the basis for this hope? Ultimately Paul's hope is in God and in the work God has already done in this church. As he says in 1:21: "Now God himself is the one strengthening us with you in our relationship with Christ." Paul believes the Corinthians are Christ's "letter . . . written . . . with the Spirit of the living God" (3:3). At 1:7 the participle εἰδότες (eidotes) is causal, "since we know." As they endure suffering, standing with Paul and his mission, experiencing the fellowship of both suffering and encouragement,[26] the Corinthians manifest something about themselves: they are authentic Christ-followers. Thus suffering in the cause of Christ and the encouragement that comes as one endures the suffering serve as validating marks of true Christianity. We have noticed that Paul's sufferings are to be directly identified as the continuing sufferings of Christ, as a hostile world beats against the Lord's body. As the Corinthians experience the same kinds of sufferings faced by Paul, they too share in Christ's overflowing sufferings, and this serves to validate their Christian experience.

Reflection

As Paul models an appropriate response to suffering, his words in 2 Cor. 1:3–7 resonate with beauty and power, and it is easy to understand why this benedictory celebration of God's character has meant so much to suffering Christians through the ages. The apostle praises God the Father of our Lord Jesus because of God's compassion and encouragement; and if we are engaged in Christian ministry, we desperately need both. Once such compassion and encouragement are received, we also need to be characterized by "blessing" God. God's good gifts should elicit praise. Moreover, God should be praised as "Redeemer" of our sufferings, for he enables Paul and his ministry team to minister encouragement to others out of the encouragement they themselves have experienced. The Corinthians are thus encouraged with the same type of encouragement that Paul receives and are marked as a true community of faith; the pattern of suffering and

---

26. The construction ὡς . . . οὕτως (hōs . . . houtōs) points to a correlation between the fellowship of sufferings and the fellowship of encouragement.

encouragement tags them as involved in an authentic form of Christian *koinōnia*, or partnership.

Additional Notes

1:5. *"The sufferings of Christ."* There have been numerous suggestions for the best interpretation of the phrase "the sufferings of Christ" in verse 5 (Harris 2005: 145–47; Thrall 1994: 107–10). Harris is correct to emphasize that this cannot refer to the atonement, a decisively accomplished event for Paul (Rom. 6:10), and a possessive genitive ("the sufferings personally experienced by Christ") does not seem to be the emphasis, for here in 2 Corinthians there is a strong note of solidarity between Christ and those who follow him.

So to what might the phrase refer? First, the genitive could be read, though with difficulty, as a genitive of agency or source ("sufferings from Christ"), Christ being the origin of the Christian's sufferings. Yet this reading does not seem to do justice to the context and is by no means obvious. Second, in apocalyptic Judaism of the NT era, there existed the concept of the "messianic woes," the birth pangs that would lead into the messianic age (Isa. 26:17; 66:8; Jer. 22:23; Hosea 13:13), and some have suggested that Paul has this concept in mind. Yet, if this is the case, Christ's death and resurrection have radically altered the concept from the broader Jewish conception. The culmination of the Messiah's woes on the cross is now experienced by his followers, who in union with him share in his sufferings by their own sufferings on his behalf. Yet in their sufferings and in union with him, believers also share in Christ's resurrection glory (Beker 1980: 146; Dubis 2002: 172–85; Grabbe 2000: 119).

Thrall (1994: 108) notes that the idea may be seen in 4:11 but questions whether the genitive form in and of itself can carry the message. However, Christian suffering as identification with Christ need not be tied solely to the "messianic woes" paradigm. As Christians participate with Christ, who was the ultimate "righteous sufferer," standing with God and for God in an era of increasing opposition to God's ways, they too will share in the Righteous Sufferer's sufferings. This could be seen as a third position. Fourth, growing out of his Damascus road experience of the exalted Christ, Paul, understanding believers to be the body of Christ in profound union with Christ through the Spirit, may regard believers' sufferings as both a continuation of and a supplement to Christ's sufferings. This interpretation has often been understood in terms of a mystical relationship, but this need not be the grid through which the body imagery is read. A fifth view suggests that the idea of the imitation of Christ could be in play. Yet the *imitatio* theme does not occur elsewhere in 2 Corinthians, and, as Thrall notes, this injects a volunteerism into the immediate context, which does not seem to be natural to it.

There is considerable overlap among several of these positions, but, in light of the broader context of Paul's writings, it seems that the third and fourth positions have the most validity. Paul seems to address suffering due to identification with Christ and Christ's continued presence in, and working through, the sufferings of his followers.

1:6–7. The reading represented by NA²⁸ has strong support ([𝔓⁴⁶: h.t. παθημ. vs 6/7] ℵ A C P Ψ 0121 0243 104 365 [629 1175] 1739 1881 *pc* r vg [syᵖ] co; Ambst) and crafts an important connection between verses 6 and 7. As noted by Metzger (1994: 505–6), the other variants seem to have resulted from homoeoteleuton and later attempts at correcting the accidental omissions.

2. Paul's Recent Deliverance (1:8–11)

So much of modern ministry revolves around the public presentation of our strengths. Churches want pastors who are powerful communicators, exceptional administrators, and motivational leaders. Yet when it comes to relationships with people, our trials, limitations, failures, and weaknesses often play a significant role in building bridges. Indeed, vulnerability stands out as one of the most basic ingredients in relationship building or repair. For through sharing with another person our pain, our own limitations, or our needs and hopes, we extend an offer: "Hear me. Embrace me. Help me. Walk with me, and allow me to walk with you in community." Paul extends such an invitation to the Corinthians in 2 Cor. 1:8–11.

Thus far in 2 Corinthians we have worked our way through the letter opening (1:1–2) and the first half of the prologue (1:3–7). As the apostle moves into the latter half of the prologue, he carries over a number of themes from his grand statement of praise. Here Paul continues to speak about "affliction" (1:4, 8); in fact he sets the tone for a book that often highlights the suffering involved in authentic Christian ministry (e.g., 4:7–18; 6:4–5, 8–10; 7:5; 11:23–33; 12:7–10). Further, he celebrates "God," the encourager of 1:3–4, now spoken of as the deliverer in 1:9–10. And Paul expresses his hope about the future (1:7, 10; Barnett 1997: 81). Both movements of the prologue end with Paul making specific reference to the Corinthians themselves, expressing his hope for them first as they share in his sufferings and second as they share in his ministry through prayer.

If verses 3–7 break out in a general song of praise, Paul now points to a specific instance for which he is thankful to God. Grammatically, the passage divides into two main movements. The first (1:8), anchored in the statement "we do not want you to take lightly . . ." (Οὐ γὰρ θέλομεν ὑμᾶς ἀγνοεῖν, *Ou gar thelomen hymas agnoein*), expresses Paul's desire that the Corinthians be cognizant of and thoughtful about the θλῖψις (*thlipsis*), the "affliction" he has endured in Asia. The second movement (1:9–11), initiated with a contrastive use of the conjunction ἀλλά (*alla*, "yet") at the beginning of verse 9, consists of Paul's explanation of the redemptive purpose for "the verdict of death" (τὸ ἀπόκριμα τοῦ θανάτου, *to apokrima tou thanatou*), as he calls it (1:9), his proclamation of God as deliverer (1:10), and his hope for the Corinthians' role as prayer partners in his ongoing ministry (1:11). These verses develop as follows:

    a. An extraordinary affliction (1:8)
    b. The purpose of the affliction (1:9)
    c. Deliverance by God (1:10)
    d. Prayer partnership (1:11)

These four verses also present us with a number of interpretive challenges, not least of which is the exact nature of Paul's θλῖψις that he experienced in Asia. What was this harsh trial, this "horrible death" (τηλικούτου θανάτου, *tēlikoutou thanatou*), out of which God delivered his missionaries? Was it persecution, illness, or something else? Paul is graphic without being explicit about the nature of the trial. Much clearer is that the apostle grasps and proclaims the great spiritual benefit that sprouted and has taken root in the rocky soil of harsh troubles: the experience serves as an assault on self-reliance and an impetus for trusting God as the great deliverer from death. Some claim that the embattled apostle strategically uses the account of his afflictions to invite the Corinthians into a closer alliance with himself and his mission through prayer.[1] The vulnerability expressed here also serves as part of a larger rhetorical strategy: Paul is presenting the Corinthians with cogent reasons for his recent change in itinerary.

Exegesis and Exposition

[8]Now brothers and sisters, ⌜we do not want⌝ you to take lightly ⌜ ⌝ the tremendous affliction that happened to us in Asia, that we were oppressed to an extraordinary degree, beyond our ability to deal with the situation, so that we experienced deep despair, to the point that we thought we were going to die. [9]Yet we ourselves had this verdict of death in ourselves in order that we might not trust in ourselves but rather in God, who raises the dead. [10]He rescued us out of ⌜such horrible brushes with death⌝, and ⌜he will rescue us⌝—that is, we have placed our hope in him ⌜that he also⌝ will deliver us in the future as the need arises—[11]with you also joining in helping us through prayer, in order that many people might give thanks to God on ⌜our⌝ behalf for the gift given to us through the cooperation of many.

a. An Extraordinary Affliction (1:8)

The conjunction γάρ (*gar*), positioned postpositively at the beginning of verse 8, ties 1:8–11 somewhat loosely, albeit purposefully, to the first part of the prologue (1:3–7).[2] The heart of the main clause—"We do not want you to   **1:8**

---

1. In fact, John Chrysostom (*Hom. 2 Cor.* 2.2) writes that if the Corinthians identified his comfort with theirs, this thought would encourage them but also "get them to accept his absence from them more easily" (Bray 1999: 196–97). This is in line with Quintilian's (*Inst.* 4.1.23) instruction that in a difficult situation, "an appeal to compassion with regard to what we have suffered in the past or are likely to suffer" is appropriate (cf. Welborn 2001: 39; Witherington 1995: 356–57). Further, Welborn (2001: 39–47) notes the appeal to pity (ἔλεος, *eleos*) seen in his suffering at 1:3–7 and his experience of persecution at 1:8–11, the mistreatment by his opponents in 2:5–11, and his anxiety of separation from his friends at 2:4, 12–13; 7:5. He proposes that Paul's attempt to elicit pity suggests that Paul holds an ambivalent attitude toward the Corinthians, since, as noted by Aristotle (*Rhet.* 2.8.6), those between two extremes feel pity. Welborn comments, "Evidently, Paul regards the Corinthians as no longer antagonistic, but not yet supportive; no longer skeptical, but not yet confident."

2. Thrall (1994: 114) renders the sense as follows: "I talk about our suffering, for we have just experienced an almost fatal affliction."

---

take lightly" or "We do not want you to be ignorant" (Οὐ . . . θέλομεν ὑμᾶς ἀγνοεῖν, *Ou thelomen hymas agnoein*)—constitutes a widely used convention in ancient letters, expressing a desire for the audience to be aware of some fact or event, and Paul uses variations on the formula at a number of points in his letters (Rom. 1:13; 11:25; 1 Cor. 10:1; 12:1; 1 Thess. 4:13) (Furnish 1984: 112).[3] In every case, he attaches the affectionate term ἀδελφοί (*adelphoi*), which in Paul's use seems to be a part of the formula. Employing the address here, he continues a pattern of verbally drawing the Corinthians to himself.[4] We translate the word *adelphoi* as "brothers and sisters" since it was used in the ancient world with reference to men and women in a religious fellowship.[5]

Paul does not offer specifics about the ordeal mentioned in verse 8 but simply refers to it as "the affliction" (τῆς θλίψεως, *tēs thlipseōs*). This probably means that the Corinthians already knew about it (Barrett 1973: 63–64). In the first century the word ἀγνοεῖν (*agnoein*) could carry the sense "to pay little or no attention to," "not to recognize," "to disregard," or "to ignore" (BDAG 12).[6] Using a negated form of this term, Paul expresses his desire for the Corinthians to consider carefully the severity, the result, and the implications of his great affliction in Asia. In our translation, therefore, we render Paul's desire as "we do not want you to take lightly the tremendous affliction that happened to us in Asia." So it is not their ignorance of the affliction that concerns Paul, but rather their perspective on the affliction and its implications (Thrall 1994: 114).[7] Perhaps knowing something of his troubles, they had failed to take those troubles with the utmost seriousness they deserved and consequently failed to assess the negative impact the affliction had on his recent travel decisions.

"Asia" was a Roman senatorial province that took in most of western Asia Minor, along with islands such as Rhodes and Patmos off the coast in the Aegean Sea, with Ephesus as the provincial capital (Furnish 1984: 113; Garland 1999: 73). The general reference to "Asia" probably means that Paul speaks of an experience outside the city of Ephesus (cf. 1 Cor. 15:32; 16:8; Furnish 1984:

---

3. The first-person plural form occurs here and at 1 Thess. 4:13. Yet cf. 1 Cor. 11:3; Gal. 1:11; Phil. 1:12, which use a singular verb form and a more positive statement of what Paul wishes his readers "to know."

4. At 1:7 Paul has identified them with himself in suffering and encouragement, and in 1:11 he presumes that they will stand with him in prayer. Thus, throughout the prologue, Paul embraces the Corinthians and invites them to embrace him in return.

5. Thus Jesus refers to all those who are devoted to him as "brother" or "sister" (Matt. 12:50; Mark 3:35), especially those who are his disciples (Matt. 28:10; John 20:17).

6. In the first century, the verb ἀγνοεῖν (*agnoein*, be ignorant), used sixteen times by Paul (Rom. 1:13; 2:4; 6:3; 7:1; 10:3; 11:25; 1 Cor. 10:1; 12:1; 14:38 [2x]; 2 Cor. 1:8; 2:11; 6:9; Gal. 1:22; 1 Thess. 4:13; 1 Tim. 1:13), could be used absolutely (e.g., 1 Cor. 14:38; 2 Cor. 6:9), or followed by περί (*peri*, concerning; 1 Cor. 12:1; 1 Thess. 4:13), ὅτι (*hoti*, that; as in Rom. 1:13; 1 Cor. 10:1), or a word in the acc. (e.g., 2 Cor. 2:11); yet 2 Cor. 1:8 is the only case where it is qualified by ὑπέρ (*hyper*, about, concerning; Harris 2005: 153).

7. Thrall notes that Bultmann (1910: 13, 65) regards the expression as comparable to the phrase μή σε λανθανέτω (*mē se lanthanetō*; lit., let it not escape you) in Epictetus *Disc.* 1.1.11; 5.29.

113), since otherwise he probably would have mentioned that city by name. By the time he wrote 2 Corinthians, Paul had faced a great deal of trouble while carrying out his ministry in this region (Yates 1981: 241). In 1 Cor. 4:9 he notes the ignominy of the apostolic ministry—apostles are like condemned men—and in 15:32 he writes of battle with "wild animals" in Ephesus, probably a reference to opponents of the gospel rather than literal beasts. Later in 2 Corinthians, Paul provides an extensive, sobering list of the harsh realities experienced in his mission work (2 Cor. 11:23–29), and just months later he applauds Priscilla and Aquila for risking their necks for him (Rom. 16:4; which certainly means his neck was at risk as well!). Certainly, trouble was Paul's constant companion.

Yet the reference to Paul's ordeal in Asia seems to suggest this affliction was exceptional in its impact on him and his coworkers. Given the "normal" afflictions suffered by the apostle, this experience must have been challenging in the extreme. But beyond a general reference to severe difficulties, to what might this θλῖψις refer? With Bruce (1971: 179) we must confess, "The task of identifying it calls for speculation beyond the exegete's province." Paul simply says too little about it to make a firm identification of that "horrible death" (τηλικούτου θανάτου) from which God delivered him. Perhaps, however, we can narrow the possibilities a bit. The suggestions offered by commentators can be grouped into three general categories: a psychological struggle, a serious illness, or persecution.

1. Some have suggested that Paul was under such great duress due to his strained relationship with the Corinthians that he felt he was going to die. This struggle has been seen variously as caused by the rebelliousness of the Corinthians, turmoil caused by his opponents in Corinth, or Paul's own regret at having been so harsh in his correspondence with the church (Talbert 2002: 165). For instance, Fredrickson (2000) understands Paul's "sentence of death" in verse 9 as Paul's self-recrimination over the harsh letter he had sent to the Corinthians. In favor of such psychological views on the affliction, the phrase ἐν ἑαυτοῖς (en heautois, in ourselves) can be read as indicating an internal struggle.

Yet if Paul's struggle here is primarily psychological, why the emphasis on the threat to Paul's life? This interpretation does little to explain God's deliverance of the apostle from a "horrible death." Further, as Thrall observes, the reference to the place of Paul's struggle as "in Asia" would seem somewhat irrelevant for a psychological affliction (Thrall 1994: 114–15). Therefore, the view that Paul's affliction here is primarily psychological stands as the least likely.

2. The view that the affliction refers to a serious, potentially fatal illness is more likely and more popular with modern interpreters (e.g., Barrett 1973: 64). The verb ἐβαρήθημεν (ebarēthēmen, we were oppressed) in the papyri can refer to sickness;[8] like the psychological position, this view could explain

---

8. Yet, as Garland (1999: 74–75) notes, it can be used as well of dissipation and sadness, misfortune and injustice, financial burdens, and social burdens.

ἐν ἑαυτοῖς as referring to an internal struggle, since an illness is an embodied condition. Further, Paul's use of the perfect tense in verse 9 (τὸ ἀπόκριμα τοῦ θανάτου ἐσχήκαμεν, *to apokrima tou thanatou eschēkamen*, we had this verdict of death) could indicate that the death sentence remained with (or in) Paul, and this could be read as consonant with the thorn in the flesh in 2 Cor. 12:7 (Witherington 1995: 361–62). Finally, referring to "God" as the one "who raises the dead" forms a common OT encouragement for those facing severe sickness (Thrall 1994: 114–15).

Yet there are problems with this view as well. The word θλῖψις is not Paul's normal word for illness (Garland 1999: 74–75). Further, it is difficult to see how a severe illness corresponds to the "sufferings of Christ" (1:5), a phrase used in the context of several references to "affliction," and here too the mention of the location "in Asia" would seem somewhat irrelevant, especially if Paul has in mind a recurring illness. The ἐν ἑαυτοῖς has other possible explanations, as discussed below, and the perfect form of ἐσχήκαμεν might be read as aoristic, referring primarily to the period of his time in Asia. Finally, the thorn of 12:7 is notoriously obscure, and there are great dissimilarities between our passage under consideration and that one (Thrall 1994: 114–15).

3. This brings us to the third and most likely interpretation: Paul's affliction in Asia refers to some form of severe persecution, perhaps mob violence or an imprisonment that Paul thought would lead to his death. Some have identified the θλῖψις with Paul's struggle with beasts in Ephesus (1 Cor. 15:32); yet he seems to be speaking of a more recent event. It could be the riot in Ephesus recounted in Acts 19:23–40 (Barnett 1997: 83), but if so, Luke certainly has played down the danger the situation posed for Paul (Matera 2003: 43), and no direct violence against the apostle is recorded. Nevertheless, that the disciples and city officials urge Paul not to enter the theater (Acts 19:30–31) could be read as connoting a dangerous situation. This would not be the first time that Luke telescoped material in Acts. Other scholars suggest the affliction corresponds to the first two chapters of Philippians, written during an Ephesian imprisonment, and the correspondences are striking.[9] Although it is true that the references to a life-threatening situation and hope in God fit this scenario, the states of mind reflected in the two books seem quite disparate, and many argue against an Ephesian origin for Philippians. Hemer (1972: 104–5) has shown, furthermore, that τὸ ἀπόκριμα (*to apokrima*) of 1:9 should not be read as judicial, which lessens the likelihood that Paul speaks here of an imprisonment truncated by a stay of execution.

9. Furnish (1984: 123) notes the following: (1) both Philippians and our passage mention a life-threatening situation (cf. Phil. 1:20–23; 2:12–18); (2) Philippians notes the presence of Timothy, whom Paul has named as cosender of 2 Corinthians (Phil. 2:19–23); (3) that Titus is not with Paul accords with Phil. 2:20, which states that no one is with him except Timothy; (4) Paul's intention to go to Philippi when released (Phil. 2:24) matches Paul's trip to Macedonia following his affliction of 2 Cor. 1:8; and (5) Timothy is named as cosender of 2 Corinthians, which corresponds to Paul's plan to follow the young minister to Macedonia as soon as he could (Phil. 2:19–24).

Another angle on the persecution view suggests that perhaps Paul's affliction refers to intense opposition from fellow Jews (Garland 1999: 74–75). That he was in conflict with the broader Jewish community in Asia is clear (2 Cor. 11:24). Paul's ministry must have had a strongly deleterious impact on Jewish outreach and the stability of the Jewish communities in the region. Shortly after this time, the Jews plotted against Paul (Acts 20:3, 19; 21:11), and it was the Jewish community from Asia that instigated his arrest in Jerusalem (21:27).[10]

After considering everything, we cannot go beyond the evidence in identifying the affliction, but the evidence seems to suggest some form of violent persecution.[11] Ambrosiaster, in his *Commentary on Paul's Epistles*, comments, "Paul means that there was such a violent upsurge of evil against preachers of the faith that death was staring them in the face. . . . Their affliction was so great that they would not have withstood it if God had not been with them" (Bray 1999: 197).

In the balance of 2 Cor. 1:8, Paul provides graphic testimony to the intensity of this experience of persecution. The second-aorist passive verb ἐβαρήθημεν (*ebarēthēmen*, we were oppressed) stands at the heart of the ὅτι clause, which explains some of what the "affliction" in Asia consisted.[12] This verb can carry the idea of being "pressed down" with a weight, "weighed down," or "burdened," and, for instance, could refer to being fatigued, having eyelids heavy with sleep (e.g., Matt. 26:43; Mark 14:40; Luke 9:32). Yet the word also can connote a mental or psychological burden experienced by those facing trouble, injustice, or financial strain (BDAG 166). Here Paul seems to use the word for being emotionally oppressed,[13] rendered variously by English translations as being "burdened" (NASB, NET, ESV), under "pressure" (NIV, TNIV), or emotionally "crushed" (NRSV, NLT).

Further, Paul accentuates the degree to which he was oppressed with the phrase καθ' ὑπερβολὴν ὑπὲρ δύναμιν (*kath' hyperbolēn hyper dynamin*, to an extraordinary degree, beyond our ability to deal with the situation).[14] The

---

10. Yates (1981: 241–43) understands the affliction as centered around the law/gospel controversy erupting from Paul's ministry in Ephesus.

11. Especially from the catalog of troubles at 2 Cor. 11:23–29 and Paul's statement that he has been "near death many times" (ἐν θανάτοις πολλάκις, *en thanatois pollakis*; 11:23), it is clear that Luke was selective in recounting the apostle's experiences. As already noted, the "affliction" Paul mentions here in 2 Cor. 1 was exceptional, but the telling of this tale may not have fit into Luke's immediate purposes for Acts.

12. The clause reads as providing an explanation rather than as marking causality.

13. If indeed Paul's "affliction" is persecution, the term "oppression" might take a step toward inferring an agent(s) behind the affliction.

14. Paul may have moved the phrase forward in the ὅτι clause (in 1:8) for emphasis; it is balanced in number of syllables (the two clauses each have ten syllables), with the ὥστε clause that follows the verb providing a stylistic eloquence to the description:

καθ' ὑπερβολὴν ὑπὲρ δύναμιν (*kath' hyperbolēn hyper dynamin*, we were oppressed to an extraordinary degree, beyond our ability)

ἐβαρήθημεν (*ebarēthēmen*, to deal with the situation),

ὥστε ἐξαπορηθῆναι ἡμᾶς (*hōste exaporēthēnai hēmas*, so that we experienced deep despair)

word ὑπερβολή speaks of a remarkable quality, or a state of excess to an extraordinary degree. In other words, the oppression Paul faced was extraordinary, even for an apostle who had faced extensive difficulties. Indeed, it was ὑπὲρ δύναμιν (beyond our ability), to which we have added for clarification, "to deal with the situation." Paul and his ministry team had been pushed by this affliction to their limits and beyond.

The ὥστε (hōste, so that) clause expresses the result of this oppression: ἐξαπορηθῆναι ἡμᾶς (exaporēthēnai hēmas), "we were experiencing deep despair."[15] The verb occurs only here and at 2 Cor. 4:8 in the NT, and elsewhere in the biblical literature only at Ps. 88:15 (87:16 LXX).[16] In the ancient world the word communicated a state of perplexity, embarrassment, doubt, or despair—to be psychologically at a loss. Further, the extent to which this was the experience of Paul and his fellow missionaries was καὶ τοῦ ζῆν (kai tou zēn), "even of life."[17] When he says that they despaired even of life, he means that their situation was so desperate that they thought they were going to die. Elsewhere in 1:8–11, this threat is expressed as a "verdict of death" (τὸ ἀπόκριμα τοῦ θανάτου, to apokrima tou thanatou) and "such a horrible death" (τηλικούτου θανάτου, tēlikoutou thanatou), and Paul celebrates God as the One who raises the dead (τῷ ἐγείροντι τοὺς νεκρούς, tō egeironti tous nekrous).

b. The Purpose of the Affliction (1:9)

1:9
Yet God has a way of turning desperate situations inside out, turning perplexity to perspective, restoring one's life from the darkest of pits, and granting a sense of purpose to even the most harrowing of life's traumas. So in 1:9 Paul turns to an explanation of why he and his fellow missionaries had been pushed beyond their own resources—it was so that they might abandon self-reliance entirely, placing all their trust in God, who alone has the power to raise the dead. Some commentators read the conjunction ἀλλά (alla) as ascensive (indeed), reinforcing what Paul has just said about the extent of his despair (Furnish 1984: 113; Harris 2005: 155; Lambrecht 1999: 20),[18] but it may be better to render the conjunction as communicating a sharp contrast ("yet," "but"), highlighting the demarcation between the despair experienced in the face of imminent death and the purposefulness of such an experience once God grants perspective on the situation (Barrett 1973: 64).[19]

The construction αὐτοὶ ἐν ἑαυτοῖς (autoi en heautois) is intensive, "we ourselves in ourselves." Paul uses the phrase ἐν ἑαυτοῖς on five occasions (Rom. 1:27; 8:23; 2 Cor. 1:9; 10:12; 1 Thess. 5:13). In every case, he could be speaking of an "internal reality" within the person or persons spoken of, or

---

15. The acc. as subject of the infinitive is a common construction in the NT.
16. "Poor I am and in troubles from my youth, and after being exalted I was humbled and became perplexed" (Ps. 87:16 NETS [88:15 ET]).
17. The conjunction καί is intensive, translated as "even," and the articular infinitive is epexegetical, expressing the depth of Paul's despair.
18. Also, the NASB, NET, ESV, NIV, NRSV.
19. The HCSB reads "However," and the NLT, "But as a result."

as a dynamic that exists "among" a group of persons, and this seems to be the case especially with 1 Thess. 5:13: "Be at peace among yourselves." Romans 1:27 offers the closest parallel to the use at 2 Cor. 1:9. It too could be read as communal—"and received among themselves the appropriate penalty for their error"—although it is more likely that Paul refers to God's judgment being carried out in their bodies (Moo 1996: 116). Yet even if, as suggested in the introduction, we read the plural here in 2 Cor. 1:9 literally rather than literarily, Paul probably emphasizes a common, internal conviction shared by those who were being persecuted. Thus we translate this part of the passage as "we ourselves had this verdict of death in ourselves."

Both translators and commentators often render τὸ ἀπόκριμα τοῦ θανάτου (*to apokrima tou thanatou*) as "death sentence" or "sentence of death" (e.g., Barnett 1997: 81; Barrett 1973: 57; Furnish 1984: 108; Garland 1999: 72; Martin 1986: 12; HCSB, NASB, ESV, NIV, NRSV). Eugene Peterson's *The Message* reads transculturally, "We felt like we'd been sent to death row." Yet Hemer (1972: 104–5) argues persuasively that ἀπόκριμα, as used in proconsular Asia around the time of the writing of 2 Corinthians, is not a judicial metaphor connoting a death sentence. Rather, ἀπόκριμα became "an official decision" or "verdict" in answer to a petition. Thus Paul and colleagues probably were not under a literal death sentence but perhaps had[20] received a negative answer to their request for protection or release from prison, and thus they felt that their lives were threatened.[21]

The apostle now shares the key spiritual insight that had come out of this harrowing experience. The brush with death occurred "in order that we might not trust in ourselves" (ἵνα μὴ πεποιθότες ὦμεν ἐφ᾽ ἑαυτοῖς, *hina mē pepoithotes ōmen eph' heautois*).[22] Severe crises have a way of putting life, and our limited resources, into perspective. Dorothy Sayers (Sayers and Jellema 1969: 27) reflects on what war can do for Christian faith:

> In ordinary times we get along surprisingly well, on the whole, without ever discovering what our faith really is. If, now and again, this remote and academic problem is so unmannerly as to thrust its way into our minds, there are plenty of things we can do to drive the intruder away. . . . But to us in wartime, cut off from mental distractions by restrictions and blackouts, and cowering in a cellar with a gas mask under threat of imminent death, comes in the stronger fear and sits down beside us. "What," he demands rather disagreeably, "do you

20. The perfect verb ἐσχήκαμεν (*eschēkamen*) may be read as aoristic, that is, a dramatic or historical perfect (e.g., Furnish 1984: 113).

21. See, e.g., Harris 2005: 156. The suggestion of Fredrickson (2000: 103) that the "'sentence of death' is self-recrimination over the severity of this letter [i.e., the harsh letter], whose effects on the congregation in Corinth he would not know until he met Titus," seems most unlikely in light of Paul's emphasis on death in the passage.

22. The periphrastic construction (the perfect form of the participle + the present subjunctive form of the verb of being) basically carries a present force in this case: "in order that we might not continue trusting in ourselves," the second perfect of πείθω (*peithō*) having the present meaning "depend on," "trust in" (Thrall 1994: 119).

make of all this? What do you believe? Is your faith a comfort to you under the present circumstances?"

Accordingly, Paul and his companions found themselves embattled in some extreme way that pushed them to the very limit of their emotional and physical resources. They had been confronted with the complete inadequacy of self-reliance when facing so formidable an enemy as death. They learned that the principle of "God-reliance" is the higher path for God's people. What Paul found was that letting go of self-reliance also meant letting go of the despair—the natural by-product of dependence on so limited a resource as oneself. As Barnett (1997: 66) declares, "Christian discipline means, for an apostle and for the church as a whole, a progressive weakening of man's instinctive self-confidence, and of the self-despair to which this leads, and the growth of radical confidence in God."

The confession of God as the one "who raises the dead" may allude to the Jewish prayer known as the Eighteen Benedictions (see comments on 1:3), which all observant Jews of the era said three times per day. In the second of these benedictions, we find a prayer to God that reads, "You are powerful, humbling the proud; strong, and judging the violent; alive forever, raising the dead, . . . sustaining the living, reviving the dead. . . . Blessed are you, Lord, reviving the dead." The allusion is even more pertinent if Paul and his colleagues are facing persecution in some form, since the benediction begins by confessing God as "humbling the proud . . . and judging the violent." Surely for Paul, this prayer has been infused with new meaning by the resurrection of Christ (Hafemann 2000: 64). Paul has come to realize that Christ-followers live by resurrection power that, while having Easter and the Coming as its prime points of reference, impregnates the nitty-gritty realities of day-to-day existence with supernatural power for living "today" in light of "that day" (Barnett 1997: 88). As John Chrysostom (*Hom. 2 Cor.* 2.4, in *NPNF*[1] 12:279; cited by Bray 1999: 198) writes:

> Although the resurrection is a thing of the future, Paul shows that it happens every day. When a person is delivered from the gates of death, it is really a kind of resurrection. The same thing can be said of those who have been delivered out of serious illness or unbearable trials.

c. Deliverance by God (1:10)

1:10   Speaking of God, Paul in verse 10 reflects on God's deliverance of him and his associates: "He rescued us out of such horrible brushes with death, and he will rescue us—that is, we have placed our hope in him that he also will deliver us in the future as the need arises." Thus 2 Cor. 1:10–11 serves as the climax of the book's benedictory prologue (1:3–11), and as Matera (2003: 44) observes, the understanding of God as the deliverer from death, which has been initiated in verse 9 and continues here, "underlies all that Paul writes in 2 Corinthians," since God's deliverance serves as a primary validation of

God's call and work in and through the apostle. The relative clause of which verse 10 consists, where Paul confesses that God has delivered him and his coworkers "out of such a horrible death," points to the constant peril matched by constant help from God woven into Paul's experience of ministry. The verb ῥύομαι (*rhyomai*), used three times in verse 10—the first an aorist and the others future in form—could mean to "rescue from danger," "save," "deliver," or "preserve" (BDAG 908). It is the same term used, for instance, in the plea for deliverance from evil (or the evil one) in the Lord's Prayer (Matt. 6:13) and in the verbal abuse hurled at Jesus on the cross: "He has put His trust in God; let God *rescue* Him now—if He wants Him! For He said, 'I am God's Son'" (Matt. 27:43 HCSB; Ps. 22:8 [21:9 LXX]). Paul uses the word a dozen times in his writings (Rom. 7:24; 11:26; 15:31; 2 Cor. 1:10 [3x]; Col. 1:13; 1 Thess. 1:10; 2 Thess. 3:2; 2 Tim. 3:11; 4:17, 18) but only in this verse in 2 Corinthians.

Yet, why the repetition of "he will deliver us," the second qualified with the expression of hope in God?[23] Murray Harris (2005: 159) suggests that here we have a case of *epidiorthōsis* (also known as *correctio*), which constitutes the amending of a term or phrase just used. In this case Paul seemingly does not want to be heard as being presumptuous, as stating emphatically that God's future deliverance is as good as certain. Thus he qualifies his confidence in God's rescue with "that is, we have placed our hope in him that he also will deliver us in the future as the need arises."[24] Paul cannot be certain about God's deliverance, but he can be certain about God as the appropriate object of the believer's hope. To hope (ἐλπίζω, *elpizō*) in God's deliverance or salvation, as Paul expresses his resolve here, especially echoes the psalms (Pss. 7:1; 22:5, 9; 25:20; 31:1; 37:40; 91:14 [7:2; 21:5, 9; 24:20; 30:2; 36:40; 90:14 LXX]).

Of course, this hope in God has been vindicated by Paul's recent experience of deliverance. What Paul and his companions have been delivered out of (ἐκ, *ek*) is "such a horrible death" (τηλικούτου θανάτου, *tēlikoutou thanatou*). To be "delivered out of death" (the verb ῥύομαι in combination with ἐκ θανάτου) is a common confession found in the LXX (Add. Esth. 4:8; Tob. 4:10; 12:9; Pss. 32:19; 55:14; 88:49 [33:19; 56:13; 89:48 ET]; Prov. 10:2; 23:14; Job 5:20; 33:30; Hosea 13:14; Let. Jer. 35 [36 ET]; Add. Dan. 3:88 Theod. [Pr. Azar. 66]). The adjectival pronoun τηλικοῦτος (*tēlikoutos*), which we translate as "so horrible," adds intensity to the phrase and can be used to mean "so large," "so great," "so important," or "so mighty," referring to size (e.g., James 3:4) or, as here, to degree (see also Rev. 16:18; Heb. 2:3). The word suggests that Paul,

---

23. The awkwardness of the repetition of the future form ῥύσεται (*rhysetai*, "he will deliver us") has caused some turbulence in the textual tradition, as witnessed to by the variants here. See the second additional note on 1:10 for comments.

24. Our ET "that is" brings out the abrupt qualification as Paul uses *epidiorthōsis*, correcting a previous statement to ensure hearers' understanding. The καί likely is adverbial, communicating an additive relationship ("also"). God has delivered in this recent situation, and the hope is that he will also deliver in the future; the adverb ἔτι (*eti*, yet, still) communicates continuance. Paul places his hope in God that the deliverance he and his ministry team have experienced will continue "as the need arises" in days to come.

no stranger to life-threatening situations, was taken aback by the intensity of this particular threat. Yet the intense threat served to focus these ministers, with proportional intensity, on God as deliverer and object of their hope.

d. Prayer Partnership (1:11)

1:11   With 1:11 the apostle turns to a role the Corinthians themselves can play in the unfolding drama of his ministry: "with you also joining in helping us through prayer, in order that many people might give thanks to God on our behalf for the gift given to us through the cooperation of many." As we have seen, Paul often prays for the congregation to whom a letter is sent and requests prayers for himself at the close (Rom. 15:30–32; 1 Thess. 5:25; Philem. 22). Yet, breaking with that normal pattern, here at the book's beginning, on the doorstep of the letter's main body, he invites the Corinthians to pray for him. Here again, Paul draws them into participation with (and thus validation of) his ministry. Doing so, "Paul shrewdly provides the Corinthians, many of whom have criticized him, with yet another opportunity to align themselves with him rather than criticize him" (Matera 2003: 44). As Furnish (1984: 125) observes, their response to this request will signify something about them; this may be more on Paul's mind than the effect of their prayers. As he draws the Corinthians into this work of ministry and into prayer and thanks to God, it also certainly has a sanctifying impact, that of reversing "the effects of sinful self-dependence and self-glorification in their lives" (Hafemann 2000: 65).

A genitive absolute (συνυπουργούντων καὶ ὑμῶν, *synypourgountōn kai hymōn*), translated as "with you also joining God in helping," dominates the part of the verse prior to the purpose clause. The verb συνυπουργέω could connote "to join in helping," or "to cooperate with." Although there is no overt mention of God here, the act of joining in helping is with reference to God's work of deliverance in the previous verse. Through prayer the Corinthians will join God in acting on behalf of Paul and his fellow workers. It is an amazing truth that God has invited us to participate in his work in the world through prayer.

In the balance of the verse, Paul uses a purpose clause to explain why the Corinthians should pray for his mission: "in order that many people might give thanks to God on our behalf for the gift given to us through the cooperation of many." Some interpret the two occurrences of "the many" as the majority of the Corinthians, who have reaffirmed their commitment to Paul and his mission, rejecting the advancement of the rebellious person(s) who had stood against the apostle (e.g., Martin 1986: 16; 2 Cor. 2:6; 7:12). Yet perhaps Paul has in mind the wider impact of their future support and participation in the broader, regional work of God (e.g., 8:24–9:2). As he experiences God's gift (τὸ εἰς ἡμᾶς χάρισμα, *to eis hēmas charisma*, "the gift given to us") of deliverance in the future, many people—the Corinthians and others in the region—will be prompted to thank God, just as many have participated (διὰ πολλῶν, *dia pollōn*, through many) in the deliverance through prayer.

The phrase ἐκ πολλῶν προσώπων (*ek pollōn prosōpon*; lit., "out of many faces," but ET as "by many people") can be understood as (1) many people raising their faces to God in thanks, (2) simply a reference to "many persons," or (3) metaphorically as a graphic way of speaking of the role played by the Corinthians, the "faces" painting a word picture of the roles taken by actors in a play (Thrall 1994: 124–25). The term πρόσωπον is popular with Paul, used twenty-three times in his letters and extensively in 2 Corinthians (2:10; 3:7, 13, 18; 4:6; 5:12; 8:24; 10:1, 7; 11:20). It can refer to the face, the countenance, one's personal presence, an embodied person, or appearance. In this book Paul uses the term quite variously as referring to a literal face (3:7, 12, 18; 4:6; 11:20), outward appearance (5:12; 10:7), or personal presence (2:10; 8:24; 10:1). Although the language here is ambiguous, Paul may have in mind a picture of many people raising their faces in thanks to God (cf. 3:18). This seems the most straightforward interpretation based on the context. Thus Paul ends the benediction where he started it, with praise and thanks being given to God.

Reflection

In 2 Cor. 1:8–11 Paul calls on the Corinthians to take seriously the exceptional affliction experienced by him and his coworkers in Asia. Pointing to the effect of that experience, he testifies that God used the deep despair to bring the apostle and company to a place beyond their own limited resources. Indeed, they thought they were going to die. Yet, in facing death they were also driven to a deeper level of trust in God and his resurrection life. The experience in Asia, moreover, had given Paul a posture of trust that would carry him into the future, as other challenging situations would present themselves. But the apostle names the Corinthians as prayer partners in the deliverance he and his mission team would continue to experience by God's grace and to God's glory.

If you and I are to live effectively for Christ in this world of swirling, striking, sometimes debilitating forces—and lead others under our ministry influence to live effectively—we must come to grips with the objective reality of limits on our resources as human beings and confront the concomitant despair head-on. We can no more master certain forces of this fallen world, under our own power, than we can leap over the Himalayas or swim from Hawaii to Hong Kong. For Christ-followers the lesson by which we confront the grim realities of our limitations constitutes a special, though often oddly wrapped, gift from God, for we are introduced to despair, which in turn can lead us to greater understanding of God himself. Have you been brutally confronted with your own limitations? If this drives you to a deeper level of trust in God, it is a gift. Yet for creatures created and destined for joy, this can be quite a shock. In the face of overwhelming persecution or other threats to life and limb, we may at times struggle deeply with despair.

As I write these words, my wife and I have a friend, an aid worker in Asia, who has been kidnapped and suspected dead for the past three months. I have prayed for her and thought about her often during these days. What must she feel, or have felt, in her captivity? What waves of despair must have come over her at times. Certainly she has been pushed beyond the limits of her own resources. Yet, knowing her, I suspect that she was pushed right into the arms of the God who raises the dead. N. T. Wright (1995: 71) states, "We are not to be surprised if living as Christians brings us to the place where we find we are at the end of our own resources, and that we are called to rely on the God who raises the dead." This is normal Christianity, and this—despite the horrors that at times lurk along the way as we journey toward resurrection—is the most blessed place in the world to be. A. W. Tozer (1961: 53) writes, "How completely satisfying to turn from our limitations to a God who has none."

Additional Notes

1:8. The reading of the first-person singular, θέλω, has weak attestation (K *pc* bo) and probably was introduced, in part, because in this section Paul tends to switch back and forth between speaking in first-person singular and first-person plural. A scribe also may have felt that the first-person singular made Paul's appeal more personal.

1:8. The variant περί has a number of weighty MSS in its favor, including ℵ A C D, and follows Paul's normal pattern of following θέλω/θέλομεν ὑμᾶς ἀγνοεῖν with περί, but it certainly is the easiest reading, and thus points to ὑπέρ (supported by $\mathfrak{P}^{46vid}$ B Ψ among others) as the preferred reading (so Harris 2005: 151).

1:10. There is a good bit of textual turbulence in verse 10, the text containing three difficult variants. The first concerns the reading τηλικούτου θανάτου, which has the weight of external manuscript evidence in its favor (supported by ℵ A B C D and others). This swayed the majority of the UBS Committee in favor of the singular readings (Metzger 1994: 506). The plural forms (τηλικούτων θανάτων), on the other hand, are attested by the early witness $\mathfrak{P}^{46}$ (as well as 630 *pc* d [lat] sy; Or^{1739mg} Ambst) and constitute the more difficult reading since people normally die only once! Also, Paul uses the plural form at 11:23. Thus Thrall (1994: 121) prefers the plurals. Yet Paul may have been influenced here in his choice of the form by his reference to death in the previous verse, which also is genitive singular in form. Thus the "verdict of death" (ἀπόκριμα θανάτου) in verse 9 would find an echo in the "horrible death" (τηλικούτου θανάτου) in verse 10. Based on this and the weight of the manuscript evidence, the singular is to be preferred.

1:10. The textual variants related to forms of the verb ῥύομαι probably point, in part, to scribes having a level of discomfort with what they perceived as needless repetition, which certainly would explain the omission of the second occurrence in some manuscripts (A D* Ψ ar b sy^p; Ambst). The second use of the verb in this verse occurs in third-person singular future form, and this reading has the weight of strong external evidence in its favor ($\mathfrak{P}^{46}$ ℵ B C P 0209 33 81 365 1175 *pc* t vgst co). The adjustment of this form to present tense (κ. ῥύεται; D^2 F G 0121 0243 1739 1881 𝔐 vg^{cl}; Or Did) almost certainly was done to create a sequence, built on the three occurrences of this verb, from past, to present, to future (Metzger 1994: 506). However, this disrupts Paul's use of *epidiorthōsis*, a rhetorical technique explained in the comments above.

1:10. The third important variant in verse 10 concerns the three particles [ὅτι] καὶ ἔτι. The ὅτι is omitted in $\mathfrak{P}^{46}$ B D* 0121 0243 1739 1881 *pc*; Did, yet retained in ℵ A C D^2 Ψ 33 𝔐 f t vg (sy^p), so the external evidence for the omission is strong. Yet the three particles together, a somewhat awkward construction, would explain why scribes might drop the ὅτι. Also, if the ὅτι were not present in the original, this would disrupt the rhetorical effect of *epidiorthōsis*, since a full stop would occur after ἠλπίκαμεν.

1:11. Both ἡμῶν (𝔓⁴⁶ᶜ ℵ A C D* G Ψ 1739 Old Latin vg syrᵖ, ʰ copˢᵃ, ᵇᵒ goth arm *al*) and ὑμῶν (𝔓⁴⁶* B Dᶜ K P 614 *al*) have strong witnesses in their favor, but as noted by Metzger and the UBS committee (Metzger 1994: 507), the latter does not fit the context well and should be attributed to scribal error.

II. The Integrity of Paul's Ministry (1:12–7:16)

There can be no more basic ingredient to an authentic, Spirit-empowered ministry than the integrity of the minister, an integration of spiritual commitments, motives, actions, attitudes, and posture toward God and others. Unfortunately, the church has always had its Elmer Gantry–type characters, whose commitments and motives are questionable at best, whose actions and attitudes are sub-Christian, and whose posture toward God and others reeks of arrogance rather than spiritual brokenness and humility. As we see in 2 Corinthians, Paul wrestled with the infiltration of such characters into the church, yet—and this must have caused him intense pain and distress—found himself on the receiving end of pointed fingers and having to defend himself against charges of misconduct and false motives.

Having penned the letter's opening (1:1–2) and prologue (1:3–11), Paul moves into the body of the letter, with 2 Cor. 1:12, and he begins by defending a recent change in plans. Apparently the apostle had had a rough period in his ministry (1:8–11), and his difficulties as well as his opportunities (2:12) had forced him to change a previously made itinerary. At least some of the Corinthians read this change as showing a wishy-washy character and count his sufferings as demonstrating a lack of God's blessing on his ministry. These assumptions—combined with his sometimes abrasive style of ministry, his supposed lack of rhetorical skills, and the turbulence in his recent interactions with the Corinthian church—have raised questions for some about the integrity of his apostolic ministry as a whole (Garland 1999: 84). Their misunderstanding of their apostle has introduced pain into the relationship. Thus the apostle takes a bulk of 2 Corinthians to defend the integrity of his ministry, beginning with explanations of why he did not come to them when planned (1:12–2:13). He then moves to a more direct treatment concerning the nature of authentic Christian ministry (2:14–7:16).

A. Why Paul Did Not Come Directly to Corinth (1:12–2:13)

At 2 Cor. 1:12–2:13 the apostle begins by defending the integrity of his ministry in a statement that should be read as the book's main thesis (1:12–14). Then the question of why he did not come to Corinth as originally planned is discussed in three movements. First, Paul addresses a wrongheaded view of why his itinerary had changed: some thought he was vacillating, demonstrating a confused or indecisive character that says both "yes" and "no" at the same time (1:15–22). Rather, the apostle asserts that his character stands as rock-solid as the gospel he has preached.

The second movement of this section (1:23–2:11) addresses the first of two reasons Paul did not travel to Corinth as expected. Simply put, the trip would have caused pain to the Corinthians (1:23; 2:1). In other words, the wounds in their relationship, which were appropriate to the chastising and "test" (2:9) the Corinthians needed at the time, were still open "soul sores," and the apostle did not want to rub spiritual salt in their wound. Paul's mention of the sorrow caused by the confrontational visit and letter (1:2–2:4), moreover, gives rise to discussion of a person who evidently had triggered much of the immediate friction between Paul and the church (2:5–11). The majority had played their part in punishing the person, and the apostle now expresses his forgiveness and urges the Corinthians to offer comfort and a reaffirmation of the wrongdoer (2:7–8).

Finally, Paul addresses a second primary reason he did not stick to his original plans. In 2:12–13 he explains that when he traveled to Troas, he had an opportunity to go directly to Macedonia. Paul was restless in spirit because Titus did not meet him in Troas, and Paul evidently felt compelled to go and find Titus, which is what happened (7:5–7).[1]

---

1. The references to Macedonia in 1:15–16 and again in 2:13 form an inclusio, or bracket, around this section where Paul explains his change of plans, clearly marking it as a unit.

1. The Integrity of Paul's Recent Actions (1:12–14)

In *The Scarlet Letter* Nathaniel Hawthorne (2008: 118) writes, "A pure hand needs no glove to cover it." There are many places in 2 Corinthians where Paul in a sense raises his "ungloved hand" and proclaims his integrity before God, the church, and the watching world, and his words challenge us to consider the integrity of our own ministries. At 2 Cor. 1:12–14 we find a foundational statement on the apostle's integrity, indeed the book's thesis statement (Garland 1999: 83–84; Matera 2003: 47; Mitchell 1991: 200).[1] The three verses thus set the stage for both Paul's explanation concerning why he did not come directly to Corinth as previously planned (1:15–2:13) and his fuller treatment of the nature of authentic ministry (2:14–7:16).

With a clean conscience, Paul expresses godly pride in what God has accomplished in his ministry, since his pattern of life has been characterized by being aboveboard and has been marked with a sincerity that could only come from God (1:12). This straightforwardness also characterizes the apostle's Letters to the Corinthians: they contain no hidden messages between the lines (1:13a). The Corinthians seem to have a partial understanding of Paul and his ministry, but Paul wants them to understand him fully. In short, Paul wants to be read accurately, which, hopefully, will take place as they read what follows. If that happens, the Corinthians will be as proud of their apostle at the appearing of Jesus as he is of them (1:13b–14). This brief unit may be outlined as follows:

a. The integrity of Paul's mission (1:12)
b. An appeal for understanding (1:13–14)

Exegesis and Exposition

[12]Now we are proud of this and say so with a clean conscience: we have lived a pattern of life in the world and especially toward you, which is characterized by ⌜straightforwardness⌝ and sincerity that come from God, a pattern not based on human wisdom but lived out by God's grace. [13]For we do not write anything to you ⌜other than what⌝ you read, indeed, other than what you can understand! I hope that you really will understand us completely, [14]just as you have understood us partially, so that you will be proud of us, just as we will be proud of you on the day of ⌜our⌝ Lord Jesus.

1. Matera (2003: 47) labels the passage as an exordium of the book's main body. Elsewhere the theme is reiterated at 5:11–12.

a. The Integrity of Paul's Mission (1:12)

At times in the NT, γάρ (*gar*) does not carry a causal force ("for," "since") but rather indicates that a new unit has begun ("now"), and this is the case here (see BDAG 189; Furnish 1984: 126; contra Plummer 1915: 23). Paul begins the passage by expressing pride in the pattern of life[2] maintained by himself and his associates.[3] The idea of "boasting" or being "proud" (καύχησις, *kauchēsis*) grates on modern, Western sensibilities, as it did at times in ancient Greco-Roman culture.[4] But, in addition to Paul's utilization of certain Greco-Roman conventions, an important, biblical backdrop lies behind the apostle's pride here. The Jewish Scriptures use the noun καύχησις and its cognate verb (καυχάομαι, *kauchaomai*)[5] to describe two types of boasting: the first a foolish pride in human abilities or accomplishments (e.g., Judg. 7:2; 1 Sam. 2:3; Jer. 12:13; Ezek. 24:25) and the second an appropriately placed celebration of the Lord's character and works (e.g., 1 Chron. 16:35; 29:13; Ps. 5:11 [5:12 LXX]; Prov. 16:31). In the NT, *kauchēsis* finds expression only once outside of Paul, where it is used pejoratively: "But as it is, you boast in your arrogance. All that kind of boasting is evil" (James 4:16). Yet, of the ten times Paul takes up the word (Rom. 3:27; 15:17; 1 Cor. 15:31; 2 Cor. 1:12; 7:4, 14; 8:24; 11:10, 17; 1 Thess. 2:19), six of these in 2 Corinthians, all but two uses (Rom. 3:27; 2 Cor. 11:17) carry a positive sense of glorying in what God has done. In short, Paul only wishes to glory in the Lord (1 Cor. 1:29, 31; 2 Cor. 10:17) or in the Lord's cross (Gal. 6:14). In the present verse Paul celebrates the integrity with which God has worked in and through his ministry.

For Paul, this boasting is in line with "the witness of" his and his mission team's "conscience" (τὸ μαρτύριον τῆς συνειδήσεως ἡμῶν, *to martyrion tēs syneidēseōs hēmōn*), which I have translated as "and say so with a clean conscience." The word rendered "witness" (μαρτύριον, *martyrion*), used nineteen

1:12

---

2. Similarly, Demosthenes begins his *Second Epistle* by appealing to his conduct in public life (*Ep.* 2.1; 2.9).

3. Paul begins and ends the unit with something he considers the object of an appropriate boast (καύχησις/καύχημα, *kauchēsis/kauchēma*), forming an inclusio marking off the unit as distinct. In the ancient world, writers marked their texts with structural devices such as inclusio, much as authors today use subheadings to mark the development of a discourse. For more on such structural features, see Guthrie 1994: 11–16, 55–58.

4. For the wide-ranging, pejorative uses of καύχησις and its cognates in Greco-Roman literature, see Spicq 1994: 2.295–302. Keener (2005: 159) notes that boasting was frowned upon unless properly justified (see also Roetzel 2007: 130). For boasting in the Greco-Roman context, see the nice overview by D. F. Watson (2003: 94), who explains, "Paul's understanding of boasting is a unique mix of boasting as understood within Judaism and within the dominant Greco-Roman culture. Paul uses boasting in the situations prescribed as appropriate by the Greco-Roman culture, and he uses boasting according to its conventions for those situations. However, his understanding of the content of boasting itself is borrowed from his Jewish heritage and his newfound faith in Christ."

5. Paul uses the verb thirty-five times, and twenty of these are in 2 Corinthians, marking it as a very important concept for the apostle in this writing. Only two uses are found outside the Pauline literature, both in James (1:9; 4:16).

times in the NT[6] but only here in 2 Corinthians, communicates the concept of a testimony or proof. Here Paul's conscience has taken the witness stand to affirm the integrity of his actions. The conscience (συνείδησις, *syneidēsis*) speaks of an awareness of something, especially an awareness of the difference between right and wrong in one's own actions, that is, "the human faculty of critical self-evaluation" (Furnish 1984: 127).[7]

We may question whether a person's conscience is a good guide for patterns of life and ministry. As Best (1987: 16) states, "Many of those who have misled others in religion have been most sure they themselves were led by God"; and Mark Twain's character Huck Finn comments, "It don't make no difference whether you do right or wrong, a person's conscience ain't got no sense, and just goes for him anyway. If I had a yaller dog that didn't know no more than a person's conscience does I would pison him. It takes up more room than all the rest of a person's insides, and yet ain't no good, nohow" (Twain 2009: 175). Yet Paul speaks of conscience in a way that makes it a more reliable guide than might seem obvious at first glance, for he appeals to conscience as he looks to God (Furnish 1984: 129–30) and submits to God's norms for life and conduct. In fact, in these three brief verses we see interweaving references to God's character (he is the source of "straightforwardness and sincerity"), the minister's general pattern of life and ministry as being lived according to God's norms, as well as the apostle's motives and desires (that the Corinthians understand him and boast in the right things). These form a powerful reality that stands witness before a watching world and church. Paul's conscience, however clear, does not have the ability to clear him of others' accusations (1 Cor. 4:4); it merely bears witness to the fact that Paul has lived consistently in line with God's character and God's ways. This is the basis for the apostle's confidence (Garland 1999: 89).

We too will be able to appeal to a clear conscience only so far as we are characterized by a posture bowed before the Lord God and a pattern of life lived according to God's ways. So the witness of the conscience as used by Paul should not be interpreted in merely a subjective sense of right and wrong, but rather as tethered to the objective reality of God's work in and through the apostle, the outward actions bearing witness to and manifesting the inner spiritual realities in the apostle's life and ministry (4:2; 5:11; Hafemann 2000: 82).[8]

6. Matt. 8:4; 10:18; 24:14; Mark 1:44; 6:11; 13:9; Luke 5:14; 9:5; 21:13; Acts 4:33; 7:44; 1 Cor. 1:6; 2 Cor. 1:12; 1 Thess. 1:10; 1 Tim. 2:6; 2 Tim. 1:8; Heb. 3:5; James 5:3; Rev. 15:5.

7. Spicq notes that the first use of the term in the papyri is from AD 59, shortly after Paul wrote 2 Corinthians. A former soldier, Lucius Pamiseus, was violently kicked by a donkey being led by a slave. The slave fled, being "aware" (κατὰ συνήδεσιν, *kata sunēdesin*) of his crime (Spicq 1994: 3.333). Margaret Thrall (1967–68), however, has shown that Paul employs the term beyond normal secular usage of the day, which thought of "conscience" as focused only on oneself and only related to past actions. She demonstrates that Paul, rather, can use the concept of conscience with reference to the actions of others and as a moral guideline for future actions.

8. Since his life and ministry manifest the truth, Paul can also appeal to the consciences of others on this objective basis. At 4:2 the apostle writes, "In God's sight we commend ourselves to every person's conscience by an open display of the truth" (HCSB).

The ὅτι (*hoti*, that) clause presents the content, or substance, of the witness given by Paul's conscience (Harris 2005: 185). Paul and his associates have "lived a pattern of life in the world, and especially towards [the Corinthians], which is characterized by straightforwardness and sincerity that come from God." The word ἀνεστράφημεν (*anestraphēmen*) serves as the main verb and thus the heart of the ὅτι clause. In the ancient world the term had a broad semantic range and, for instance, could mean to "overturn," "spend time in a location," "associate with someone," or "return" (BDAG 72). However, for the two centuries prior to the time Paul wrote this book, the word had been used in broader Greek culture to refer to patterns of ethical conduct (Plummer 1915: 25). Here it speaks of living a pattern of life according to certain principles.[9] Thus we translate the verb as "we have lived a pattern of life."

Four phrases beginning with ἐν flank this main verbal idea:

> we have lived a pattern of life
> > by straightforwardness and sincerity (ἐν ἁπλότητι καὶ εἰλικρινείᾳ,
> > > *en haplotēti kai eilikrineia*)
> > not based on human wisdom (οὐκ ἐν σοφίᾳ σαρκικῇ, *ouk en*
> > > *sophia sarkikē*)
> > by God's grace (ἐν χάριτι θεοῦ, *en chariti theou*)
> > in the world (ἐν τῷ κόσμῳ, *en tō kosmō*)

The explanation of the content of the witness given by Paul's conscience begins by describing the manner in which his ministry team has lived: ἐν ἁπλότητι καὶ εἰλικρινείᾳ τοῦ θεοῦ (*en haplotēti kai eilikrineia tou theou*).[10] The term ἁπλότης speaks especially of personal integrity manifested in word or action and can connote "simplicity," "sincerity," "uprightness," "frankness," or "generosity" (BDAG 104). Paul uses the word five times in 2 Corinthians (here and at 2 Cor. 8:2; 9:11, 13; 11:3), and three times elsewhere (Rom. 12:8; Eph. 6:5; Col. 3:22), in every case speaking of actions that demonstrate laudable heart attitudes.

Εἰλικρίνεια, similarly, speaks of "sincerity" or "purity of motives." In Greco-Roman literature it involves being "pure" or "without mixture," in the way we might speak of gold that is unalloyed, wine that has not been mixed with water, or air that has not been polluted with noxious fumes. Thus, beginning in the classical period, it began to be associated with integrity and sincerity (Spicq 1994: 1.420–21). Those who live in this manner have nothing to hide, no shifty motives lurking in the shadows of their actions.

---

9. Aside from variants that occur at Matt. 17:22 and John 2:15, ἀναστρέφω occurs nine times in the NT (Acts 5:22; 15:16; 2 Cor. 1:12; Eph. 2:3; 1 Tim. 3:15; Heb. 10:33; 13:18; 1 Pet. 1:17; 2 Pet. 2:18). Based on context, the term can be used either positively (as in 2 Cor. 1:12) or negatively, of an undesirable pattern of life, as in Eph. 2:3, and in Gal. 1:13 with the cognate noun.

10. There is some question whether the first of these two descriptors, ἁπλότητι, is original to the book, or whether the textual variant ἁγιότητι (*hagiotēti*, holiness) is to be preferred. Although the evidence is quite balanced (see the first additional note on 1:12), our ET reflects the former word. The NLT[2], NASB, and NIV, e.g., follow the variant ἁγιότητι.

Further, the phrase τοῦ θεοῦ (*tou theou*) delimits both "straightforward-ness" and "sincerity" and may be understood as a genitive of source (Plummer 1915: 23). Thus these character qualities are understood as ultimately having originated with God himself, an interpretation further supported by the phrase ἐν χάριτι θεοῦ (*en chariti theou*), with "by the grace" understood as communicating "means" or instrumentality. It is by means of "the grace of God" that Paul's ministry manifests its candidness and sincerity.

Both the phrase translated "characterized by straightforwardness and sincerity that come from God" and the phrase "by the grace of God" are set in contrast to the phrase rendered "not by human wisdom."[11] In his Letters to the Corinthians, Paul often contrasts appropriate patterns of Christian living with living "according to the flesh"[12] or "according to the world"[13] (Hafemann 2000: 81), or with a wisdom "of this age" (1 Cor. 1:20; 2:6, 8; 3:18; 2 Cor. 4:4).[14] Here he almost certainly has in mind those fleshly, false teachers of the sophistic tradition who are drawing on their earthbound rhetorical skills to lead the Corinthians astray (Witherington 1995: 362). Rather than depending on such "wisdom," the apostle works solely by the grace of God.

Paul's integrity has been such that it functions as a living witness "in the world" (ἐν τῷ κόσμῳ, *en tō kosmō*), a witness to the veracity of his message. "The world," after all, is the context for Paul's ministry and message of reconciliation of the world to God (2 Cor. 5:19). He expands this thought, however, by stating that the exemplary pattern of life lived by his ministry team should have been most evident to the Corinthians. The phrase περισσοτέρως δὲ πρὸς ὑμᾶς (*perissoterōs de pros hymas*, especially toward you) suggests that the Corinthians have had a better vantage point than people in general, and thus more abundant evidence of the integrity of Paul's ministry. After all, he had lived with them for eighteen months during his second mission journey (Acts 18:11). Thus they should be able to affirm his integrity without reservation, for they had witnessed it firsthand and over an extended period of time.

b. An Appeal for Understanding (1:13–14)

1:13 In verse 12 Paul has just written a general statement about his integrity and that of his mission. Now he puts a particular manifestation of his integrity to the

---

11. Paul especially likes to use the word εἰλικρίνεια in contrast to negative motives or characteristics. At 1 Cor. 5:8 he contrasts the "unleavened bread of sincerity and truth" (ἀζύμοις εἰλικρινείας καὶ ἀληθείας, *azymois eilikrineias kai alētheias*) with the "old yeast of evil and wickedness," and at 2 Cor. 2:17 the apostle contrasts the sincerity (εἰλικρινείας) with which his ministry team proclaims the gospel, over against the motives of the hucksters, who peddle the Word of God for their own profit.

12. See, e.g., 2 Cor. 1:17; 5:16; 10:2; Rom. 8:3–17; Gal. 5:13–26; Eph. 2:1–3.

13. See, e.g., 1 Cor. 1:20; 2:12; 3:19; also Eph. 2:2; Titus 2:12.

14. Savage (1996: 159) notes that Paul's reference to a wisdom "of this age" is used "to draw our attention to the general intellectual climate of the day, the social atmosphere of the first century, the sort of competitive and self-serving outlook which . . . the Corinthians would have imbibed as naturally as the air they breathed. It is this outlook which Paul attributes to Satan. It is this outlook which is blinding people to Christ."

Corinthians: "For we do not write anything to you other than what you read, indeed, other than what you can understand!" (οὐ γὰρ ἄλλα γράφομεν ὑμῖν ἀλλ' ἢ ἃ ἀναγινώσκετε ἢ καὶ ἐπιγινώσκετε, *ou gar alla graphomen hymin all' ē ha anaginōskete ē kai epiginōskete*). Stated positively, Paul means, "Everything we write to you is stated plainly, just what you read and can easily grasp." Some of the Corinthians, perhaps, were overinterpreting his words, reading motives into his messages, motives that were not there. It is dangerous to question a person's integrity because we have *read into their words* questionable motives!

Whereas the γάρ (*gar*, now) that begins verse 12 functions as a loose connector to what goes before, the γάρ (for) at the beginning of verse 13 is more explanatory in force, playing off Paul's claim of integrity in verse 12. Further, Paul explains that his writings to the Corinthians are nothing other than what they can "read and . . . understand";[15] the apostle uses a clever play on words with the verb forms ἀναγινώσκετε (read)[16] and ἐπιγινώσκετε (understand/know).[17] Paul's point is that his writings are transparent, written with integrity, with no hidden agendas, and therefore are part of the general pattern of life and ministry that he and his associates have lived. The integrity of the letters flows from and reflects the general integrity of his life. Paul simply writes in the same manner that he lives—straightforwardly. Understanding what he writes, therefore, should also be straightforward if the Corinthians will but give the writings a real hearing.

The letter continues, "I hope that you really will understand us completely, just as you have understood us partially" (ἐλπίζω δὲ ὅτι ἕως τέλους ἐπιγνώσεσθε, καθὼς καὶ ἐπέγνωτε ἡμᾶς ἀπὸ μέρους, *elpizō de hoti heōs telous epignōsesthe, kathōs kai epegnōte hēmas apo merous*). The apostle briefly switches from the first-person plural form of the verb, which has been constant in the book to this point, to the first-person singular (ἐλπίζω, I hope), a switch that might be meant to express the intensity of Paul's personal desire for the Corinthians to understand him.[18] At this point τέλος (*telos*, end, completely) could be understood in two primary ways. First, it could be taken as a reference to the parousia of Christ

15. The construction in Greek (its first part is classical in expression) has caused some turbulence in the textual tradition (see 1:13 in additional notes). The ἄλλα is a neuter plural acc. from ἄλλος (*allos*) and means "other things." So Paul has not (οὐ, *ou*) written "other things," alluding possibly to what others had accused him of saying in his letters. Then ἀλλ' ἤ (*all' ē*) means "except" and is equivalent to εἰ μή (*ei mē*). The ἅ is a relative pronoun introducing the relative clause. The comparative particle ἤ (*ē*, or) is used in conjunction with an intensive use of καί (*kai*, indeed). So our ET reads, "We do not write anything to you other than what you read, indeed, other than what you can understand!"

16. Many in the congregation would not have been able to read the Letters of Paul themselves, but they were read aloud in the congregation; the practice of reading out loud, even in private, was the norm in the Greco-Roman world. Paul almost certainly refers to this public reading of his letters.

17. This would be much like pairing the English words "apprehend and comprehend" (Furnish 1984: 130–31; Harris 2005: 187). The present-tense form of these verbs can be read as gnomic, referring to Paul's ongoing correspondence with the Corinthians, including past letters and the one we have as 2 Corinthians.

18. For more on the use of singular and plural in 2 Corinthians, see the introduction.

(thus "end" as in "end of the age"). In that case, Paul would be expressing his hope for the Corinthians' endurance in understanding his mission and, more importantly, the mission's gospel. Yet the term probably should be read in this context as meaning "completely" or "fully," since it stands in contrast to ἀπὸ μέρους (apo merous, partially) at the end of the following clause (Furnish 1984: 126, 128). Thus, when the apostle writes "I hope that you really will understand us completely," he expresses a longing that the true nature of his ministry will come into full focus for the Corinthians.

1:14 The καθώς (kathōs, just as) clause, "just as you have understood us partially," further hints at the current status of Paul's relationship with the Corinthian church. Positive steps had been taken toward normalization of the relationship (Bieringer 1996a: 33). Yet further steps were needed for the relationship to be fully healthy.

> Paul had reason for joy (7:7, 9, 13e, 16). Yet on a deeper level he remains troubled. His converts have yet to grasp the full significance of his ministry. . . . They understand it only in part. . . . While they have demonstrated a zeal for him by renouncing the so-called "offender" (cf. 7:5–13a), it was merely a superficial response to the forcefulness of his letter. As pertains to his meekness and humility, they remain disturbed and unimpressed (10:1). (Savage 1996: 68)

This may be why we seem to get mixed signals from Paul concerning his relationship with the Corinthians (Matera 2003: 49–50). Is he filled with joy, or still concerned to a certain degree? The answer is "yes" to both questions, depending on the particular community dynamics under consideration at the moment. What Paul is after, therefore, is that the church would fully embrace him, his mission, and thus his gospel. Their vacillation between him and other voices vying for a following is distracting at best and destructive in its most insidious forms.

What then might express the essence of Paul's desire for their understanding? In short, that when measured against the backdrop of Christ's coming, both Paul and the Corinthians might have a common boast, specifically, what God has worked in and through their relationship. The term καύχημα (kauchēma) is a cognate of καύχησις, used at the beginning of this unit (v. 12),[19] and often carries a slightly different nuance. Yet here the two terms are roughly synonymous, both speaking of the content or object of the boasting: what God has accomplished through the gospel (Harris 2005: 184).

Some OT prophets proclaimed a "day" or "days" of the Lord that would herald judgment for the Lord's enemies and a time of redemption for his people (e.g., Amos 8:9–11; 9:9–12; Isa. 2:2–21; Joel 1–3). The Israelites of Amos's day, for instance, put their hope in the day of the Lord, thinking it would be a day of light for them, but their hope was misplaced because of

---

19. As noted above, the two words form an inclusio, or sandwich structure, marking off 1:12–14 as a unit.

their unrighteousness (Amos 5:18). For Paul and the NT generally (e.g., 1 Cor. 1:8; 5:5; 1 Thess. 5:2; 2 Thess. 2:2; 2 Pet. 3:10), "the day" is the day of Christ's return and therefore an object of great hope. Part of that hope for Paul is that he and the Corinthians will be able to make a mutual boast on that day, that they will be able to take pride in Paul and he will be able to take pride in them.

Reflection

When John Stott was rector of All Souls Church in London, Billy Graham preached a crusade that filled Wembley Stadium night after night. Stott puzzled over why Graham was able to attract such crowds when the churches of that great city were half empty week after week. Stott reflected, "The answer I gave myself was this: I believe that Billy was the first transparently sincere preacher these people have ever heard" (Dudley-Smith 1999: 298–99). In commenting on the story, R. Hughes (2006: 42) writes, "We need preachers whose sermons are like thunder because their lives are like lightning!" Certainly Paul's life and ministry shone with brilliant integrity, which undergirded all he did, including his writing of letters like 2 Corinthians, and Paul wanted the Corinthians themselves to grasp the fact. He was a man under orders and under a Truth.

In *The Book of Merlyn: The Unpublished Conclusion to The Once & Future King*, T. H. White (1977: 112) wrote of one of his characters:

> He caught a glimpse of that extraordinary faculty in man, that strange, altruistic, rare, and obstinate decency which will make writers or scientists maintain their truths at the risk of death. "*Eppur si muove*," Galileo was to say; "it moves all the same." They were to be in a position to burn him if he would go on with it, with his preposterous nonsense about the earth moving round the sun, but he was to continue with the sublime assertion because there was something which he valued more than himself. The Truth. To recognize and to acknowledge What Is. That was the thing which man could do, which his English could do, his beloved, his sleeping, his now defenceless English. They might be stupid, ferocious, unpolitical, almost hopeless. But here and there, oh so seldome, oh so rare, oh so glorious, there were those all the same who would face the rack, the executioner, and even utter extinction, in the cause of something greater than themselves. Truth, that strange thing, the jest of Pilate's.

In 2 Cor. 1:12–14 Paul proclaims his own integrity and that of his mission. God is the source of their exemplary pattern of life in the world, and that pattern should have been abundantly clear to the church at Corinth. And Paul's Letters to the Corinthians, as an extension of the apostle's ministry, also are expressions of utmost integrity. Paul does not insinuate or craftily obscure his messages, forcing his readers to look between the lines for his *real* intent! Rather, he desperately wants to be understood by the Corinthians! He wants them to be proud of him, embracing him and his ministry, so he can in turn be proud of them on the day of the Lord Jesus.

Additional Notes

1:12. Each variant at this point in the text, ἁπλότητι (straightforwardness) and ἁγιότητι (holiness), has a good bit of evidence in its favor, and it is difficult to determine which is original to 2 Corinthians. As pointed out by Metzger (1994: 507), the variant may have arisen by a misreading of letters (ΑΠΛΟΤΗΤΙ vs. ΑΓΙΟΤΗΤΙ), yet this is inconclusive since the misreading could have gone either way. External evidence strongly favors ἁγιότητι (𝔓⁴⁶ ℵ A B C K P Ψ 0121 0243 *al*), over against the Western-Byzantine witnesses for ἁπλότητι (ℵ² D F G 𝔐 lat sy), but various levels of context tip the balance in the favor of ἁπλότητι for the following reasons: (1) the meaning "straightforwardness" fits the immediate context better than "holiness"; (2) while ἁπλότης occurs several times in 2 Corinthians (8:2; 9:11, 13; 11:3), ἁγιότης is never used by Paul elsewhere; if 1:12–14 is the thesis of the book, as we have maintained, it would explain why the word shows up at points throughout the book; (3) it is ἁπλότητι that gives rise to other variants in the textual tradition (πραότητι 88 635 and σπλάγχνοις eth). Therefore, although the decision is difficult, the weight of the contextual matters seems to be paramount.

1:12. Four phrases beginning with ἐν flank the main verb of the ὅτι clause (the words here given in the order found in the Greek text):

manner	By [ἐν] straightforwardness and sincerity that come from God,
contrast/means	not by [ἐν] human wisdom, but
contrast/means	by [ἐν] God's grace,
main assertion	we have lived a pattern of life
place/general	in [ἐν] the world, and
specific	especially toward you.

The first of these phrases speaks of the manner in which Paul and his ministry associates have lived, "by straightforwardness and sincerity" that have God as their source. The second, which begins with "not," stands in contrast to the manner of life demonstrated in Paul's mission: "not by human wisdom." This phrase shifts slightly to a focus on the "means" by which one might live, the apostle hinting at the "wisdom" by which his opponents have carried out their "ministry." The phrase "by human wisdom" then is set in strong contrast (ἀλλ᾽) to the following phrase, "by God's grace." The phrase "by straightforwardness and sincerity that come from God" and the phrase "by God's grace" stand somewhat in parallel to one another but present different nuances on God's role in the life of authentic ministry: the first emphasizes the manner of life that has been lived, and the second emphasizes the means by which life has been lived. The final phrase beginning with ἐν, "in the world," shifts attention to the place where Paul's pattern of life has been lived out and speaks of the "general" context of Paul's ministry. The phrase "especially toward you" provides further emphasis that Paul's ministry has focused on the Corinthian church and shifts focus to the more specific context of the Corinthian church.

1:13. The series of words ἀλλ᾽ ἤ ἅ, read by ℵ B C D² Ψ 1881 𝔐, is awkward, resulting in some witnesses dropping ἀλλά (F G), some dropping ἤ (𝔓⁴⁶ 33. 945. 1505 *pc* sy), and some omitting ἅ (D* 0243 1739 *pc*). Alexandrinus (A) drops both ἤ and ἅ.

1:14. The external evidence for keeping ἡμῶν (ℵ B F G P 0121 0243 6 33 81 104 365 630 1175 1739 1881 2464 *al* lat sy^{p.h**} co) slightly outweighs the evidence (𝔓^{46vid} A C D Ψ 𝔐; Ambst) for omitting the pronoun, although normally the shorter reading would be preferred. Further, the formula τοῦ κυρίου ἡμῶν Ἰησοῦ is rare and thus less likely to have been crafted by a copyist (Harris 2005: 184). For further discussion of the title "our Lord Jesus," see J. Elliott 2003: 6.

2. Misunderstanding Paul's Change of Travel Plans (1:15–22)

Samuel Johnson (2003: 57) once wrote, "There can be no friendship without confidence, and no confidence without integrity." In 2 Corinthians Paul seeks to reestablish the Corinthians' confidence by shoring up their understanding of his integrity; after proclaiming the integrity of his ministry (1:12–14), Paul now addresses a misunderstanding about why he did not stick with previously communicated travel plans. Thus the apostle moves from speaking about the integrity he has maintained as a general pattern of life, to defending his integrity in a very specific instance. Evidently some in the Corinthian congregation have used the apostle's recent change in plans to question his dependability. As we shall see, Paul largely makes a defense of his integrity on theological grounds. In order for us to gain a clearer picture of the charge Paul addresses in this passage, however, it may be helpful to put the current passage in historical context before we proceed to a detailed exegesis.[1] Here is a brief review of the chronology outlined in the commentary's introduction.

While Paul was in Ephesus in the summer or autumn of AD 53, he sent what we know as 1 Corinthians to the church in Corinth. He told the Corinthians of his intention to stay in Ephesus until Pentecost and then travel through Macedonia on his way to see them. He hoped to stay with them perhaps through the winter months of the following year (in 54–55; 1 Cor. 16:5–9). Part of the purpose of Paul's planned trip to Corinth was to take up a collection for believers in Jerusalem (16:1–4).

However, these plans started to go awry early in the spring of 54, when Timothy visited the Corinthians on behalf of the apostle. The young man found the Corinthian church in great disarray, with little or no progress having been made in response to 1 Corinthians. So Timothy left Corinth for Ephesus once shipping was possible; there he provided Paul with the bad report concerning the church's current state. To address the problems there, Paul changed his original plans for travel and went straight to Corinth in late spring of 54. Since it was late spring, the apostle easily booked passage over to Corinth and made what has come to be known as "the sorrowful visit" (2 Cor. 2:1–2). Perhaps at that time Paul told the Corinthians he would return to them in the months to come, travel on to Macedonia, and then

---

1. The following overview serves as a condensed version of the chronology treated in the commentary's introduction. For further details on a reconstruction of Paul's interaction with the Corinthians, see the introduction.

come back their way on his way to Judea. This is the plan he mentions in 2 Cor. 1:15–16.[2]

The apostle's time with the Corinthians went badly. After this crisis visit in the spring of 54, Paul faced personal and public criticism and abuse from a vitriolic church member (2:1–5), who seems to have had some support from a minority in the congregation. The majority stood by in silence and allowed the accuser to criticize Paul openly, neither supporting the apostle nor disciplining his critic (2:5; 7:12).

After returning to Ephesus, Paul received a report about the public criticism and fired off a "painful" letter (2:4) to address the problems made clearer by his sorrowful visit and especially to confront the congregation on their poor handling of the public disturbance that had taken place when the offender had his say. Probably through this letter, or perhaps by word of the letter carrier, the Corinthians learned that Paul had shifted back to his original travel plans, unwilling to visit the Corinthians until he was sure the problems between him and the congregation had been worked out. He did not want to make another "sorrowful visit" (2:1). According to the new travel itinerary, he would travel through Macedonia before possibly coming to them.[3] Thus the severe letter took the place of the promised trip to see them. Consequently, if the relational tensions were worked out, he would be visiting them after passing through Macedonia and much later than they had anticipated. This disappointed the Corinthians and was used by some to question Paul's actions and even his integrity. In the autumn of 55, Titus reported this response to Paul when they met in Macedonia shortly before the writing of 2 Corinthians (2 Cor. 7:8–13a).[4]

2. Philip Hughes (1962: 32–33) understands our "plan B," which includes a double visit to Corinth, to be Paul's original plan, supplanted by the plan he communicates in 1 Cor. 16. The problem with this view is at least twofold. First, at 2 Cor. 1:15–16, where he speaks of the double visit, Paul clearly is defending himself against a charge of vacillation. This suggests that a change to a plan involving the double visit has taken place, so this would not have been Paul's original plan. Second, at 1 Cor. 16:5–9 (our "plan A"), Paul has made no definite plans to go to Jerusalem with the offering for the Jerusalem church. Yet 2 Cor. 1:15–16 makes clear that Paul now plans to go to Judea himself. As Bruce (1971: 180–81) notes, "This indicates that the plan of a double visit to Corinth was subsequent to that of a single visit announced in 1 C. 16:5–7." Hafemann suggests that the painful visit was the first leg of the itinerary described in 2 Cor. 1:15–22 (and this may be true). In his understanding, Paul returned to Ephesus instead of going on to Macedonia and then coming back through Corinth a second time. Hafemann (2000: 86) posits that Paul returned to Ephesus "rather than going on directly to Macedonia and then risking yet another such 'painful visit' (2:1)" by coming back to Corinth at that time. In Hafemann's view, Paul cut short that plan by returning to Ephesus.

3. See the comments below on 2:3, where Paul writes, "I indicated this very thing," speaking of his decision not to stay with the "double visit" plan to see the Corinthians both on his way to and on his return from Macedonia.

4. Generally speaking, Titus's report had been encouraging. The younger minister had been received well and could speak of the Corinthians' conformity to Paul's wishes and their "longing" for the apostle (e.g., 7:7, 15). At the same time, some of them had been offended by the severe letter he had sent (7:8), and his back-and-forth approach to his travel plans did not inspire confidence (Furnish 1984: 141).

This brings us to Paul's rejoinder in 2 Cor. 1:15–22. Specifically, the apostle explains that he had intended to visit the Corinthians first, passing through their area on his way to Macedonia, then coming back through Corinth after his work in Macedonia had been completed (1:15–16). A second stop in Corinth also would facilitate the journey he planned to make to Judea. Paul categorically denies that he was being fickle, acting like a worldly person, when he made these plans (1:17). The Corinthians should intuitively realize this as they consider God's character—especially his faithfulness—and the very nature of the gospel that Paul and his ministry team preached to the Corinthians (1:18–20). God's promises do not vacillate; they should understand that the integrity of the gospel message through Jesus relates directly to the integrity of Paul. So the apostle appeals to what the Corinthians know of God, the gospel, and the transformation they themselves have experienced; he further appeals, calling them to trust his integrity as he carries out the very ministry that brought them the gospel of God.

Based on this reading, the passage can be outlined as follows:

a. Paul's plans (1:15–16)
b. Paul accused of fickleness (1:17)
c. Paul's character: Grounded in God's faithfulness (1:18–22)
    i. God's faithfulness (1:18)
    ii. God's promises fulfilled in Christ (1:19–20)
    iii. Expressions of God's faithfulness to us (1:21–22)

In this way, here at the beginning of the main body of 2 Corinthians, the apostle answers the charge of worldly fickleness. The passage has much to say to us concerning how we use our words in the context of ministry, the integration of our integrity and the proclamation of God's good news, and how we answer unfair charges in the context of the local church.

Exegesis and Exposition

[15]With this confidence I intended to come to you first, so that you might have a second ⌜opportunity for benefit⌝, [16]namely, passing through your area on the way to Macedonia and again from Macedonia to return to you and to be sent on by you to Judea. [17]Therefore, certainly you don't think I was being wishy-washy when I planned to do this? Or that I make plans like a worldly person, so that I say ⌜"absolutely" and "no way"⌝ in the same breath? [18]On the contrary, as God is faithful, our word to you is not a contradictory "yes" and "no"! [19]For Jesus Christ, the Son of God, who is among you through our preaching, that is, through me and Silvanus and Timothy, was not a confusing "Yes and No," but in him has become a resounding "Yes!" [20]For in relation to him, every last one of God's promises receives "yes" for an answer. That is why also through him the "Amen" is offered in response through us to God, for his glory. [21]Now God himself is the one strengthening us with you in our relationship with Christ, and

he is the one who anointed us. [22]He also sealed us and gave us the down payment of the Spirit in our hearts.

a. Paul's Plans (1:15–16)

1:15   Paul begins this unit by lining out the travel plans he had intended to follow before his plans changed, as well as his motivation for those initial plans. We first need to ask to what the apostle refers when he writes "With this confidence" (ταύτῃ τῇ πεποιθήσει, *tautē tē pepoithēsei*). Among the NT authors, Paul alone uses the term translated "confidence" (2 Cor. 1:15; 3:4; 8:22; 10:2; Eph. 3:12; Phil. 3:4),[5] which speaks of trusting in, or having assurance about, a person or situation. Here Paul expresses confidence not in the Corinthians' understanding of him (1:13b–14), as many commentators claim (e.g., Harris 2005: 192; Kruse 1987: 73; Martin 1986: 23; Scott 1998: 37; Thrall 1994: 136); although the Corinthians understand Paul partially, a full understanding on their part is primarily a future hope. Rather, his confidence is in his own integrity and the clear sense that God has led him in his decision making (1:12–13a); grounded in his integrity and the knowledge that God was leading him in his life and ministry, Paul made his plans (Hafemann 2000: 83).[6]

A second interpretive question concerns which word in the sentence the term πρότερον (*proteron*, first) should be associated with grammatically. The word, generally translated as "earlier" or "formerly" when speaking of a period of time, could be understood as delimiting ἐβουλόμην (*eboulomēn*, I intended), meaning that Paul had "intended previously" to visit the Corinthians twice (NASB[95]; Message; Thrall 1994: 136). However, given the context, πρότερον should be taken with the infinitive ἐλθεῖν (*elthein*, to come), for in the next breath the apostle mentions that he had planned a "second" (δευτέραν, *deuteran*) opportunity for their benefit and thus would visit them "again" (πάλιν, *palin*) after traveling to Macedonia (v. 16). Thus we translate the clause, "I intended to come to you first" (Furnish 1984: 133).

Third, Paul explains why he had planned to travel first to the Corinthians on his now-abandoned itinerary, and he does so in the form of a purpose clause: "so that [ἵνα, *hina*] you might have a second opportunity for benefit." But what does the apostle mean by a second (δευτέραν, *deuteran*)[7] χάριν? The term χάριν, used 155 times in the NT—100 of these in Paul's writings—had a broad range of possible meanings in the NT world.[8] In 2 Cor. 1:15, modern

---

5. It occurs only once in the LXX, at 2 Kings 18:19, where the king of Assyria asks Hezekiah, "What is your source of confidence?" Spicq (1994: 3.78–79) notes that Josephus uses it six times with the meaning of "assurance" or "boldness" (in a quarrel, *Ant.* 11.299); of confidence in oneself (19.317), or one's strength (1.73), in weapons or money (3.45); this confidence can be inspired by someone else's posture (5.74) or by God himself (10.16).

6. Paul also uses the word to speak of personal confidence in 3:4 and 10:2.

7. Thus Δευτέραν refers to something that follows whatever is "first" in a series. It can be used adjectivally, as here, or adverbially as in "a second time" (BDAG 220).

8. These include, e.g., a form of attractiveness (graciousness, charm, winsomeness), a benevolent disposition toward someone (favor, grace, gracious care/help, goodwill), an act of

translations render it variously as "benefit" (HCSB, NIV, TNIV, KJV), "bless-ing" (NASB, NLT, NLT², CEV); "favor" (NRSV), "pleasure" (Tyndale), and "grace" (ESV). In inscriptions and the secular writings of the period, χάριν is fairly synonymous with a benefit or a show of favor and especially connotes an act of kindness offered by a friend, a prince, or even the gods. Here in our passage under consideration, it carries this sense of "benefit," in short, "any gift, present, pardon, or concession that is granted freely, out of one's good-ness" (Spicq 1994: 3.501–2). Paul states that through his previous itinerary, he wanted to give the Corinthians a second opportunity for benefit by visiting them twice in one trip.

Yet, is this "opportunity for benefit" some form of ministry or kindness that Paul wished to impart to the Corinthians, or is it an opportunity for them to participate in ministry? Fee (1978; followed by Garland 1999: 98; and Martin 1986: 24) has suggested the latter, arguing, among other points, that Paul's stays in Corinth would be too brief for substantive ministry, and the use of χάρις at 8:7 speaks of the contribution of the Corinthians as a "gracious gift." The strength of this interpretation is that it reflects what Paul overtly states in the next verse, that he wished to go to Macedonia with the help of the Corinthians, and after returning to Corinth a second time, would also receive their help in support of his trip to Jerusalem (contra Furnish 1984: 133; Thrall 1994: 138). Paul wanted to give them a double opportunity to be blessed by expressing generosity.

Paul details the now-abandoned itinerary in verse 16, with the verse's structure crafted around three primary verbal ideas:[9]

1:16

      through your area
1. passing
      on the way to Macedonia and again

      from Macedonia
2. to return
      to you and

3. to be sent on
      by you
      to Judea.

Notice that each of the three stages of travel mentioned includes a reference to the Corinthians ("your area," "to you," "by you"), geographical movement ("passing," "to return," "to be sent"), and a geographical reference ("Mace-donia," "Macedonia," "Judea"). The first verb, presented in infinitive form

---

kindness (favor, gracious deed/gift, benefaction), or a response to generosity (thanks, gratitude; BDAG 1079–81).

    9. The use of καί (*kai*) after the end of 1:15 is exepegetic, unpacking the idea of a "second opportunity for benefit" by linking verse 15 to the detailed itinerary of verse 16.

(διελθεῖν, *dielthein*, "to pass through"), simply means that Paul intended to make a stopover in Corinth on his way to Macedonia, the Roman senatorial province to the north of Achaia. While traveling from Corinth into Macedonia, the apostle probably intended to visit Berea before picking up the Via Egnatia at Thessalonica and heading east on that prominent roadway to Philippi. Once his ministry in the province was finished, Paul explains, he would again travel south to Corinth for a second visit with the church. This second visit had a practical purpose: Paul would be "sent on" by the Corinthians to Judea,[10] so that there he might deliver the funds collected for the Jerusalem church. Although the verb προπέμπω (*propempō*, sent on) could mean "to accompany," as in Acts 20:38, here it means "to assist in making a journey," that is, to support travelers on a trip by sending with them food, money, companions, or other aids to travel (BDAG 873; 1 Cor. 16:11; 1 Macc. 12:4; 1 Esd. 4:47).

b. Paul Accused of Fickleness (1:17)

1:17 Having laid out the motives that played a part in his crafting the now-ditched itinerary—he wanted the Corinthians to be blessed twice and to have the opportunity to participate in helping him in his travels to Jerusalem (1:15–16)—in verse 17 Paul categorically denies that his change of plans (from those communicated in 1 Cor. 16:5–9) was due to a flaw in his character. He shapes his denial in the form of two rhetorical questions, each of which expect a negative answer:[11] "Certainly you don't think I was being wishy-washy when I planned to do this? Or that I make plans like a worldly person, so that I say 'absolutely' and 'no way' in the same breath?"

Among commentators it is a matter of some debate exactly of what the apostle has been accused. Is it that Paul was being blasé about his relationship with the Corinthians (Garland 1999: 98–99)? Or are they accusing him of being obstinate in a fleshly way, so that when he says, "Yes (I am going to do such and such)" it means "Yes!," and he is not open to change? On this latter reading, Paul's primary point would be to counter this accusation by implying that his itinerary ultimately is not up to him but up to the Lord.[12]

Much better is the interpretation that Paul is being accused of a fleshly, self-centered sort of waffling, by which his plans changed according to his personal whims. In other words, some are accusing him of lacking a reliable

---

10. As Harris notes, "Judea," rather than a reference to the whole of Palestine, refers here to the southern province in Palestine, as distinct from Samaria and Galilee to the north, Peraea to the east, and Idumea to the south (Harris 2005: 194).

11. Rhetorical questions are a stylistic way of making an assertion. The μήτι (*mēti*) marks the double question as anticipating a negative response and makes the stylistic assertion more emphatic than a simple negation; thus our addition of "certainly" in the ET.

12. Witherington (1995: 363) follows Young and Ford (1987: 102) in this interpretation. As Thrall (1994: 140) notes, the main objection standing in the way of this interpretation is that Paul emphasizes his constancy in the following verses, not his flexibility.

character, reading him as moved more by the winds of his circumstances and personal wishes than by his previous commitments.[13]

The term ἐλαφρία (*elaphria*) is cognate to ἐλαφρός (*elaphros*), which carries the idea of "light" in terms of weight and therefore something that is "insignificant." From the time of Homer, it also could connote quickness or nimbleness and thus came to be used to describe impulsive behavior or impetuousness. Ἐλαφρία is a hapax in biblical literature and is not found outside the Bible prior to the Christian era. Yet, in line with its cognate, the word communicates thoughtlessness, frivolousness, and instability, thus the idea of "vacillation" or being "wishy-washy" (BDAG 314; *GELNT* 88.99).

So the Corinthians' problem with Paul was that his change of plans from the original version to the now-abandoned double visit, and back again to the original,[14] indicated a certain instability, and therefore an undependability of character. In short, they have accused Paul of waffling on his commitments. In 1:15–22 Paul addresses their concern, to begin with, by pointing out that the plans he had made were made for their benefit (v. 15); therefore they were not made lightly. He goes on to explain that the further shift in plans also was made, following the painful visit, with them in mind. The apostle simply did not want to cause them further sorrow (1:23–2:2). Yet the characterization of Paul as fickle was there, passed around like so much fetid garbage among at least some of the Corinthians.

Paul describes the type of vacillation of which he is being accused as making "plans like a worldly person" (κατὰ σάρκα βουλεύομαι, *kata sarka*

13. To grasp the weight of the accusations against Paul, we need to understand that not only was fickleness an offense to Jewish and early Christian values; the flaw also was broadly condemned in the Greco-Roman world, especially among leaders. Keener (2005: 159) explains,

Ancient literature regularly condemns fickleness and unreliability while praising those who keep their word even under duress. Many thought fickleness inappropriate for a virtuous person (Maximus of Tyre 5.3); the Roman world despised it in leaders. Those who changed stated plans had to explain their reasons and prove that they were not fickle . . . ; one might argue that it is impossible to foresee the future (Libanius *Declamation* 36.42; 44.50–52, 61) or that one was avoiding danger (Cicero *Att.* 3.4). Failure to carry through on one's word led to ridicule (e.g., Suetonius *Tib.* 38); keeping an agreement despite another's failure was honorable (Iamblichus *Pyth. Life* 30.185).

This view of fickleness being strongly held in the general, secular environment of the day perhaps forms a broader backdrop for the rumblings against Paul in Corinth, since, as noted in the commentary's introduction, the Corinthians were oversensitive to the mores of the cultural climate of their day. Yet, for the apostle, such a characterization constituted a theological issue, for fickleness was both worldly (1:17b) and out of line with the character of God and God's gospel (1:18–21).

14. It is possible, as Harris notes, that the Corinthians did not know that Paul had now changed from "Plan B" (the double visit) back to "Plan A," but upon receiving 2 Corinthians they would have learned of this second switch. Thus they were accusing him of the switch from Plan A to Plan B, and Paul realizes that when they learn of yet another switch, back to Plan A, they will have even more fodder for accusation (Harris 2005: 196). It seems more likely, however, that the Corinthians already knew of the switch back to Plan A, since the apostle is keen to explain why he has not come directly to them (1:23–2:2).

bouleuomai). The phrase κατὰ σάρκα presents a uniquely Pauline expression,[15] used by the apostle in his writings twenty times.[16] The phrase connotes dynamics associated with human existence. This is most straightforward when Paul uses the phrase to speak of one's heritage (e.g., Rom. 1:3; 4:1; 9:3) but also occurs when he speaks of the vantage point of human perspective (1 Cor. 1:26; 2 Cor. 5:16; Eph. 6:5; Col. 3:22). The apostle also uses the phrase to speak of worldly patterns of life as set over against the life directed by the Holy Spirit (e.g., Rom. 8:4–5, 12–13; 2 Cor. 10:2–3; 11:18), and that seems to be how he employs the phrase here in 2 Cor. 1:17. In effect he is writing to the Corinthians, "Do you really think I live like an ungodly person?" In 1:12 he has already stated that he has conducted himself in the world "not by human wisdom, but by God's grace," and this rhetorical question builds on that confident assertion.

The ἵνα clause carries a consecutive force ("so that"), expressing the result that would be the outcome of such a worldly mode of planning: "so that I say 'absolutely' and 'no way' in the same breath?" The double ναί (*nai*, yes) followed by the double οὔ (*ou*, no) has been read variously as an oath, an expression of flattery, and an emphatic answer of "yes!" and "no!" given either in the same breath or one after the other.

Welborn (1995a: 48–49) has championed the first of these positions, proclaiming, "Paul says: 'You suspect me of acting insincerely; you accuse me of vacillation and self-interestedness; you deem me untrustworthy. As a result, I am like a man who must continually seek to establish the truth of his statements by employing what amounts to an oath.'" It is true that Paul's words here seem to echo the words of Jesus (Matt. 5:37) and his half brother James (James 5:12), given in teachings that deal directly with taking an oath. Yet, rather than the double "yes" and double "no" standing for a single concept of making an oath, the context of our passage seems to set the "yes" over against the "no" in the next two verses.

Peter Marshall (1987: 70–90) suggests the "yes, yes" and "no, no" are stock answers of a flatterer, who gives responses according to the need of the moment, so that he says "yes" to one group and then "no" to another (see also Talbert 2002: 136). On this reading, Paul simply shapes his answers at any given time according to what various groups would want him to say, regardless of his true motives and commitments. Garland (1999: 100) is correct, however, in pointing out that this position fails to explain the doubling of the "yes" and "no." We might add—in light of the sorrowful visit and the severe letter (2:1, 4) through which Paul harshly confronted the Corinthians—that it is difficult to believe they conceived of Paul as a "yes man"!

The better position is to take the double "yes" and double "no" as emphatic, straightforward, contradictory answers, which we have translated

---

15. The similar κατὰ τὴν σάρκα is found in John 8:15.
16. Rom. 1:3; 4:1; 8:4–5, 12–13; 9:3, 5; 1 Cor. 1:26; 10:18; 2 Cor. 1:17; 5:16 (2x); 10:2–3; 11:18; Gal. 4:23, 29; Eph. 6:5; Col. 3:22.

as "absolutely" and "no way."[17] While it is true that the phrase "in the same breath" is not in the Greek text, as commentators countering this view point out, the juxtaposition of the opposite answers can be understood as implying that Paul has been accused of talking out of both sides of his mouth. Thus at least some of the Corinthians have denounced him for lacking integrity, a moral vacuousness in which he could say "absolutely" and "no way" to the same question (here: "Am I coming to visit you first?"). This interpretation fits the broad context of 2 Cor. 1:12–7:16, which treats "The Integrity of Paul's Ministry."

c. Paul's Character: Grounded in God's Faithfulness (1:18–22)

i. God's Faithfulness (1:18)

Paul strategically begins verse 18 by shifting the focus from his own faithfulness to the faithfulness of God: πιστὸς δὲ ὁ θεὸς (*pistos de ho theos*, on the contrary,[18] as God is faithful).[19] The apostle uses these same words to appeal to the faithfulness of God at two other places in the Corinthian correspondence (1 Cor. 1:9; 10:13),[20] but in each of these other cases a relative clause follows on the heels of the confession of God's faithfulness ("God is faithful, who . . ."). The presence of ὅτι suggests that Paul's wording in 1:18 expresses an oath (Harris 2005: 199),[21] comparable to "As surely as God is faithful" (so ESV, NLT[2], NIV, NRSV), or "with God as my witness."[22] Thus Paul appeals

             1:18

---

17. See Wenham (1986: 271–72), who suggests that Paul's opponents accused Paul of twisting the famous words of Jesus on oath-speaking to his own end as a two-faced liar.

18. The use of δέ (*de*), a conjunction in the postpositive (i.e., not occurring first in the sentence) position at the beginning of verse 18, is contrastive, and the context heightens the contrast, so that we have translated the conjunction as "on the contrary."

19. Here 2 Cor. 1:18 effects a smooth transition between the second movement of this unit, "Paul Accused of Fickleness" (1:17), and the third (1:18–22), in which the apostle makes a theological defense of his actions. In 1:18 Paul's denial that he uses both "yes" and "no" in the same breath (this time each word used only once) continues the thought of verse 17. His exclamation "God is faithful" introduces the heart of his theological defense, which argues for Paul's good character based on the character of God. An argument from greater to lesser was a common rhetorical tool of the day, which assumed that if something is true in a more important situation, it certainly holds true in a lesser situation. Notice also that with 1:18 the apostle shifts back to use of the first-person plural, in part because he now emphasizes the preaching of the gospel to the Corinthians (v. 19), an activity participated in by Paul and his associates Timothy and Silvanus.

20. He also uses variations of this confession at 1 Thess. 5:24 and 2 Thess. 3:3, in which God is referred to as ὁ καλῶν ὑμᾶς (*ho kalōn hymas*, the One who calls you) and ὁ κύριος (*ho kyrios*, the Lord) respectively.

21. Harris (2005: 199) points to the following passages that include a ὅτι oath formula: 2 Cor. 1:23; 11:10; Rom. 14:11 (citing Isa. 45:23); Gal. 1:20; Rev. 10:6.

22. Kruse (1987: 74) writes,

> Paul uses oaths quite often in his letters (cf. Rom. 1:9; Gal. 1:20; 2 Cor. 1:23; 11:10, 31; Phil. 1:8; 1 Thess. 2:5, 10) when he wants to defend or lay heavy stress upon the truth of his assertions. This suggests that in the early church Christ's words against swearing in Matthew 5:33–37 were understood as a criticism of the improper use of oaths, rather

---

strongly to God as the one before whom he lives with integrity (cf. 2:17), pointing to God as the ultimate witness of his motives and actions. In light of what follows in verse 19, this appeal constitutes more than just a call for the Corinthians to trust him in this isolated incident. Rather, Paul suggests that his personal faithfulness stands grounded in the very faithfulness of God. His mission, his decisions, his pattern of life, and therefore his words are not perfect, but they so rest on the bedrock of the character of God and are so in sync with God's gospel that Paul can speak of the integrity of his words and commitments with the utmost confidence.

The apostle continues, "Our word to you is not a contradictory 'yes' and 'no.'" With the term rendered "word" (λόγος, *logos*) the apostle intends a play on words that associate Jesus with "the word" of the Gospel of John (Barnett 1997: 103). Perhaps paralleling the Johannine "The Word became flesh," here Paul proclaims that the Word, Jesus Christ the Son of God, became "yes"! Thus, as Calvin notes, Paul focuses his defense on God's faithfulness to the gospel rather than Paul's own person, for the integrity of the gospel is his ultimate concern.[23]

ii. God's Promises Fulfilled in Christ (1:19–20)

1:19   So verse 19 confidently asserts, "For Jesus Christ, the Son of God, who is among you through our preaching, that is, through me and Silvanus[24] and Timothy,[25] was not a confusing 'Yes and No,' but in him has become a resounding 'Yes!'" Jesus, the Son of God, had come among the Corinthians via the preaching of Paul and his companions, Silvanus and Timothy, during Paul's second mission trip (Acts 18:1–18a). This word of the gospel preached to the Corinthians was not an uncertain "Yes" and "No," not filled with contradictions or wracked with uncertainty, with God giving a promise one minute and taking it back in the next. Rather, the word of promise, that word of which Jesus is the heart, the author, the content, the subject, the perfecter, and the relational goal, has been answered with a resounding "Yes!" by God. It has become "yes" in

---

than their prohibition. According to Matthew 26:63 Christ himself was prepared to be placed under oath when answering the question of the high priest.

23. Elsewhere (Gal. 1:8–9) the apostle is so bold as to pronounce an anathema on even an angel of heaven who dares to subvert the true gospel! Calvin (1964: 20) proclaims that the only reason Paul can do this is because he knows that God is the author of the gospel and its ultimate defender.

24. Before the second mission journey, Paul chose Silvanus, also known as Silas, as his traveling companion (Acts 15:40–41). A prominent leader and prophet (15:32) of the Jerusalem church, Silvanus had been one of two persons sent to Antioch with Paul and Barnabas to deliver the decision reached by the apostles and elders at the Jerusalem Council (15:22). On the second journey, Silvanus and Paul were imprisoned in Philippi (16:19, 25, 29), accosted in Thessalonica (17:4), and sent to Berea (17:10). After being left behind in Macedonia, Silvanus and Timothy later joined Paul shortly after the apostle arrived in Corinth (18:5). At about this time, Silvanus joined Paul and Timothy in writing to the Thessalonians (1 Thess. 1:1; 2 Thess. 1:1) and later is named as Peter's amanuensis in writing the letter 1 Peter (5:12).

25. For a summary on Timothy's life and place in Paul's mission, see the comments on 1:1.

him (ἐν αὐτῷ, *en autō*), that is, in relation to Jesus. Christ is—has been and continues as[26]—God's yes to the question of whether human beings can be saved from the devastating power of sin.

So in 1:20a Paul exclaims, "For in relation to him, every last one of God's promises receive 'yes' for an answer." This exclamation stands joined to the previous verse by the conjunction γάρ (*gar*), which here serves as a marker of clarification (BDAG 189). The central element that adds clarification to the previous verse is "the promises of God," the promises implied in verse 19. The term ὅσαι (*hosai*), translated here as "every last one," communicates extent or comparative quantity. This is another way of saying that all of God's covenant promises poured out graciously on the human race have crescendoed, with Jesus as their answer. Preeminently, the promise to Abraham of blessing for all the nations of the earth (Gen. 12:3; 18:18; Gal. 3:16; Eph. 1:13; 3:6), the promises to David concerning his messianic descendant (2 Sam. 7:12–16; 1 Chron. 17:11–14; Pss. 89:3; 132:11; Isa. 11:1–5, 10; Jer. 23:5–6; 30:9; 33:14–18; Ezek. 34:23–24; 37:24; and Rom. 1:4), and the promise of a new covenant given through Jeremiah (31:31–34)—all have their fulfillment in Christ.

1:20

The latter half of verse 20 centers around the little phrase τὸ ἀμήν (*to amēn*, the amen), taken from the worship context of the early church. In early church worship, praise was offered through Christ to God and confirmed by the congregation answering "Amen!" (Kruse 1987: 75).[27] The word, a transliteration of the Hebrew (אָמֵן, *'āmēn*), functions in the biblical literature as a strong affirmation of something said.[28] In Paul's writings "amen" might occur at the end of a benediction (e.g., Rom. 15:33 or 1 Cor. 16:24, v.l.), or a doxology (e.g., Rom. 11:36; Gal. 1:5), or a prayer of thanks (e.g., 1 Cor. 14:16). At times, moreover, the apostle uses the affirmation strategically, as here, in contexts in which he wants to promote unity in the face of relational strain (cf. Gal. 1:5), inviting the whole community to speak with one voice in response to the gospel that reconciles.

In 2 Cor. 1:20 this "Amen" of public worship functions as the grammatical center around which four crisp, three-syllable phrases in verse 20 revolve:

26. The force of the perfect-tense γέγονεν (*gegonen*) points to an ongoing state of affairs.
27. See Rom. 1:25; 9:5; 11:36; 15:33; 16:27; 1 Cor. 14:16; 2 Cor. 1:20; Gal. 1:5; 6:18; Eph. 3:21; Phil. 4:20; 1 Thess. 3:13; 1 Tim. 1:17; 6:16; 2 Tim. 4:18; Heb. 13:21; 1 Pet. 4:11; 5:11; 2 Pet. 3:18; Jude 25; Rev. 1:6–7; 3:14; 5:14; 7:12; 19:4; 22:20. Notice that the "amen" formula normally follows an expression of glory or honor to God.
28. In the OT, "amen" might be used to endorse a curse (e.g., Num. 5:22; Jer. 11:5), or a prayer, or word of praise (e.g., Neh. 8:6; Ps. 41:13; 106:48). By the first century AD the use of the amen formula had become well established in Jewish liturgy, with the congregation answering words of prayer with "Amen!" (J. L. Wu, *DPL* 558–59). Christ often opened a solemnly spoken declaration with an "amen" ("truly"; Matt. 5:18, 26; 6:2, 5, 16; 8:10; Mark 3:28; 8:12; 9:1; Luke 4:24; 12:37; John's Gospel presents a double amen: 1:51; 3:3, 5, 11; 5:19, 24–25; 6:26, 32, 47, 53; 8:34, 51, 58; 10:1, 7; 12:24; 13:16, 20–21, 38; 14:12; 16:20, 23; 21:18), and Revelation refers to Christ as "the Amen" at 3:14.

also* through him	καὶ δι' αὐτοῦ (*kai di autou*)
the "Amen"	τὸ ἀμὴν (*to amēn*)
to God,	τῷ θεῷ (*tō theō*)
for his glory	πρὸς δόξαν (*pros doxan*)
[is offered in response] through us	δι' ἡμῶν (*di hēmōn*)

*This use of καί is adjunctive ("also") and connects the phrase ἐν αὐτῷ (in him) earlier in the verse with the δι' αὐτοῦ here: "For in relation to him every last one of God's promises receives 'yes' for an answer. That is why also through him the 'Amen' is offered."

These four phrases proclaim Christ's agency in bringing about the fulfillment of God's promises, God as the receiver of the "Amen" offered in worship, "glory" as the goal of that worship, and believers as the agents of worship.

1. *Christ is the agent who has made it possible for us as the church to experience the fulfillment of the promises of God.* The "yes" of God only comes in relation to Jesus, and it is through him, the agent who has accomplished the establishment of the new covenant (2 Cor. 3:3–4; 5:18), that we experience the gospel. Thus we can only respond to God's promises with the "Amen" through Christ. He is the only way. Salvation cannot be found through anyone or anything else (Garland 1999: 103).

2. *The "Amen" of response to the gospel is proclaimed in worship to God.* In the context, Paul has been speaking about the faithfulness of God (1:18), who in accord with his promises (1:20a) sent his Son, Jesus Christ (1:19a), to fulfill those promises. That fulfillment had been preached to the Corinthians as the good news (1 Cor. 1:17; 4:15; 9:12–23; 15:1; 2 Cor. 2:12; 4:3–4; 8:18; 9:13; 10:14, 16; 11:4, 7), and in response to the revelation of the gospel, they turn to God in worship, with "Amen!"

3. Further, this "Amen" is *for God's glory*. In the NT, πρός + the accusative serves to mark movement or orientation toward someone or something and, specifically, can communicate a goal, as in an intended purpose for something (BDAG 874). When Paul writes that the Amen is "for God's glory," he means that as the church worships, offering the Amen up to God in response to the fulfillment of his promises through Christ, it does so with the purpose of giving God glory for what he has done.

4. *The Amen is offered in response "through us, the church."* The ἡμῶν (*hēmōn*) could be taken as a reference to Paul and his associates, as in verse 19. Yet here Paul transitions to an emphasis on the church as a whole, as is clear with the list of spiritual realities mentioned in verses 21–22. Further, the phrase δι' ἡμῶν should be understood as relating most directly to τὸ ἀμήν, rather than to πρὸς δόξαν. It is not that the glory comes "through us," but that the "Amen" is offered up through us, resulting in glory being given to God.[29]

29. Why then does Paul not follow "the Amen" immediately with "through us"? The answer probably has to do with the crafting of a chiastic structure. Notice that the διά phrases (*dia . . . ,*

This dynamic network of relationships can be diagrammed as follows:

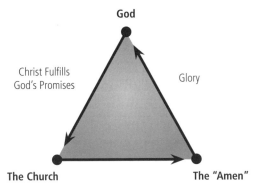

Figure 6 **The Dynamic Relationship between God and the Church**

God

Christ Fulfills God's Promises

Glory

The Church

The "Amen"

iii. Expressions of God's Faithfulness to Us (1:21–22)

The unit concludes with a series of affirmations celebrating what God has done on behalf of those who are in Christ: "Now God himself is the one strengthening us with you in our relationship with Christ, and he is the one who anointed us. He also sealed us and gave us the down payment of the Spirit in our hearts." The ἡμᾶς σὺν ὑμῖν (*hēmas syn hymin*, us with you) makes it clear that Paul has the whole church in mind, and he crafts his words in this way to appeal to the solidarity that he has with the Corinthians in Christ.[30] To achieve this end, however, the focus remains squarely on God himself as the one establishing, anointing, sealing, and giving the down payment of the Spirit. In fact, Fee (1994: 289) marks this passage as "one of the most God-centered, God-focused paragraphs in the Pauline corpus."[31]

1:21

"through him," "through us") begin and end this portion of Scripture. The two phrases having to do with direction ("to God," "for his glory") form the second and third of the four phrases. Thus an *a-b-b-a* pattern is produced.

30. Notice that the apostle has used a similar approach in every unit thus far in the book (1:3–7, 8–11, 12–14), beginning each unit with a focus on what has taken place in his ministry but ending with a reference to his relationship with the Corinthians. At 1:7 he ends with "knowing that as you share our experience of sufferings, so also you share our experience of encouragement"; at 1:11, "you also joining [God] in helping us"; and at 1:14, "so that you will be proud of us, just as we will be proud of you."

31. Structurally, the four participles are arranged in two pairs, the article (ὁ, *ho*, the one) at the beginning of each pair carrying over to the second participle of the pair:

ὁ δὲ βεβαιῶν ἡμᾶς σὺν ὑμῖν εἰς Χριστὸν καὶ χρίσας ἡμᾶς θεός (*ho de bebaiōn hēmas syn hymin eis Christon kai chrisas hēmas theos*, Now God himself is the one strengthening us . . . who anointed us),

ὁ καὶ σφραγισάμενος ἡμᾶς καὶ δοὺς τὸν ἀρραβῶνα τοῦ πνεύματος ἐν ταῖς καρδίαις ἡμῶν (*ho kai sphragisamenos hēmas kai dous ton arrabōna tou pneumatos en tais kardiais hēmōn*, He also sealed us . . . and gave us the down payment of the Spirit).

The verb βεβαιόω (*bebaioō*) could be used as meaning, "to make sure," "confirm," "authenticate," "guarantee," "carry out," "strengthen," "establish," or "put beyond doubt" (BDAG 172; Spicq 1994: 1.280–83).[32] Spicq (1994: 1.281) gives the example of a magistrate who had promised to hand out beef upon his entrance to office and then carried out (ἐβεβαίωσεν, *ebebaiōsen*) his promise.[33] Yet here in 2 Cor. 1:21, believers are the "object" of God's work of strengthening, or perhaps securing (as at 1 Cor. 1:8; Col. 2:7), and this work is "Christward" (εἰς Χριστόν, *eis christon*), growing toward Christ in ongoing relationship development and confirmation. Notice also that the participle is present tense,[34] indicating that this work of strengthening is ongoing in the life of believers. Using the same term in an earlier Letter to the Corinthians, Paul had proclaimed, "He will also strengthen you to the end, making you blameless in the day of our Lord Jesus Christ" (1 Cor. 1:8). Therefore, God is in the process of strengthening or firming up the commitment of believers as they grow in relationship with Christ.

Second, Paul writes, "and he is the one who anointed us." As with the final two participles, the term rendered "anointed" (χρίσας, *chrisas*) is an aorist in form, in context pointing to something that has already taken place. In other words, God's ongoing work of strengthening his people has its bedrock foundation in God's original work of grace in their lives—that work of the Spirit through the gospel (2 Cor. 3:3, 8).[35] The Spirit, first of all, has anointed the church; the apostle is making a play on the words Χριστόν (*christon*, Christ, the Anointed One) and χρίσας. In the LXX this term speaks of the leaders of God's people being anointed with oil as they entered their offices (e.g., Aaron and his sons as priests, Exod. 28:41; 29:7; Saul, David, and Solomon as kings, 1 Sam. 9:16; 16:12; 1 Kings 1:39; Elisha as prophet, 1 Kings 19:16). In the Gospels and Acts, the Spirit is said to have anointed Jesus for his ministry (Luke 4:18; Acts 4:27; 10:38). One of the images of the coming of the Spirit on believers is that the Spirit would be "poured out" on them (Isa. 32:15; Acts 2:33; 10:45), which may suggest the idea of anointing. As God's Spirit-indwelled heirs, believers are anointed for their royal role in kingdom service (Thrall 1994: 155).

1:22   Third, at the beginning of 1:22, Paul celebrates the fact that God has sealed (ὁ . . . σφραγισάμενος, *ho . . . sphragisamenos*) those who are in Christ. The

---

Thus Paul pairs the concepts of "strengthening" and "anointing," followed by a pairing of "sealing" and "giving the down payment."

32. The author of Hebrews uses the adjectival cognate of βεβαιόω at 2:2 and 9:17 and the noun form at 6:16, all in the context of legal overtones, and there may be legal overtones of "guarantee" in Paul's use here. In broader Christian literature, the word group serves to speak of the early Christian message as offering permanence and stability for the faith of believers (see *EDNT* 1:210–11).

33. This is the sense of Rom. 15:8: "For I tell you that Christ has become a servant of the circumcised on behalf of God's truth to confirm the promises made to the fathers" (NET).

34. The aspect is imperfective, depicting an "incomplete" action in context.

35. The idea communicated is "having anointed, sealed, and given the pledge of the Spirit in our hearts, he is strengthening us and you."

word picture stems from a common aspect of ancient culture, the use of seals of various kinds and for various purposes. From the OT era onward, seals were widely used in the Middle East and made of various materials, such as wood, stone, terra-cotta, and often semiprecious stones; these were pressed into clay or wax to leave the seal's image. Some were cylindrical in form, and others had a stamp form. Some hung on a cord around the neck (e.g., Gen. 38:18) or on a pin attached to one's clothing. Others were attached to a ring that was worn on the arm or finger (Jer. 22:24).

Seals could be used as a mark of authority, as when Joseph received authority from Pharaoh (Gen. 41:42); or security, as when Daniel was sealed in the lions' den (Dan. 6:16–17) or Jesus's tomb was sealed (Matt. 27:66).[36] Seals also could mark authenticity, as with a sealed letter (1 Kings 21:8; Esther 3:12), the imagery of Abraham's circumcision as a confirmation of his righteousness (Rom. 4:11), or the Corinthians as showing the validity of Paul's ministry (1 Cor. 9:2). Further, seals could be used to represent identity or ownership. In Song of Songs 8:6, for instance, the woman asks her lover to place her as a seal on his arm and heart, the figure representing both permanence and closeness of relationship. The image of the seal also can represent preservation, as when Isaiah commands God's law to be sealed among the disciples (8:16; *DBI* 766–67; *NBD* 1070–73). The image as used in 2 Cor. 1:22 speaks most particularly of God's ownership of his people, and therefore their authenticity and security as his inviolable possession (Harris 2005: 207). Thus God's people have been sealed, marking their identity and guaranteeing their final inheritance (Fee 1994: 292–93).

Finally, the apostle writes, "He also . . . gave us the down payment of the Spirit in our hearts." The word picture of a "down payment" (τὸν ἀρραβῶνα, *ton arrabōna*)[37] also was associated with legal language in the first century. In contracts that involved the sale of goods or the buying of services, a down payment, or initial installment, guaranteed that the one receiving a partial payment would receive the full measure as described in the legal agreement. Garland (1999: 106–7), following Kerr (1988), has pointed out that the translation "pledge" is misleading, for in the ancient world a pledge served more as collateral for something promised and could be taken back at a later date. This would be similar to pawnshop transactions today, in which people hand over their possessions for a time until they are financially capable of reclaiming them. Such an analogy does not do Paul's language justice! Rather, τὸν ἀρραβῶνα communicates a transaction in which there are obligations on both sides.

For Paul, the Holy Spirit, who has entered the lives of believers, serves as this down payment. The genitive form, τοῦ πνεύματος (*tou pneumatos*, of the Spirit), is appositional, meaning "the down payment, *which is* the Spirit." Paul

---

36. A letter also could be secured with a clay or wax seal, or a cord or clay could be stretched across the crack of a door to keep it from being opened.

37. Also rendered as a "pledge" (NASB, Message, Moffatt) or "first installment" (NLT, NRSV, Williams) or "deposit" (NIV).

is not suggesting that believers receive part of the Spirit in this age and the rest of the Spirit in the next. Rather, the indwelling Spirit serves as a guarantee of the believer's full inheritance.

This rich, graphic imagery—strengthening, anointing, sealing, and giving the down payment of the Spirit—plays a significant, climactic role in the immediate context. Here Paul vies for the Corinthians' trust, calls for them to affirm his integrity, by moving from a basic overview of his plans (1:15–16) to a denial that he was vacillating when he made those plans (1:17), and finally to a theological defense of his own integrity (1:18–22). Thus far, that defense has pointed to the faithfulness of God (1:18) and the fulfillment of God's promises in Christ (1:19–20). Brilliantly, Paul climaxes his theological explanation with an appeal the Corinthians must acknowledge—the foundational yet ongoing work of the Holy Spirit in their lives. The apostle proclaims that to validate the integrity of his ministry, the Corinthians need only to look in the mirror. To deny the validity and integrity of Paul's ministry would be to deny their own spiritual existence. As those being strengthened, as those who have been anointed and sealed and have received the down payment of the Spirit upon believing the gospel, their life in the Spirit points to the faithfulness of God, and Paul's ministry was carried out in the context of living faithfully before the faithful God. Paul's integrity is bound up in the integrity of the very gospel he has preached.

Reflection

With 2 Cor. 1:15–22 Paul lines out his recent travel plans related to Corinth (1:15–16), addresses the accusation that he had been fickle in the planning process (1:17), and explains to the Corinthians that his character and that of his mission are grounded in the very faithfulness of God (1:18–22). He beautifully celebrates the stability in life and ministry provided by God's promises (1:19–20) and bears witness to the pattern of God's faithfulness to his mission and to the Corinthians (1:21–22). Yet consider Paul's position for a moment. These words were written at a distance, in an attempt to diffuse false accusations that were being made about his motives. We can learn something from both Paul's theology and his example.

Certainly, having one's integrity unfairly called into question constitutes one of the most difficult experiences in ministry. To feel emotionally stripped and exposed to the brutal, false blows of a gossip or liar can test our character in the extreme, especially when we have no immediate way to address the accusations. With the psalmist we may pray urgently (Ps. 17:1–3, 9 NET):

LORD, consider my just cause!
Pay attention to my cry for help!
Listen to the prayer
I sincerely offer!
Make a just decision on my behalf!
Decide what is right!

You have scrutinized my inner motives;
you have examined me during the night.
You have carefully evaluated me, but you find no sin. . . .
Protect me from the wicked men who attack me. . . .

Several years ago I had a colleague, a professor at an institution in another state, whose theological position on a certain issue was called into question. The man is a person of utmost theological integrity and thoroughly orthodox. Yet the accusations were broadcast publicly via radio and thus in a way that was beyond my friend's ability to give any kind of response. His character was maligned. The accuser perpetrated an egregious power play, momentarily damaging my friend's reputation and his ministry. Understandably, my friend struggled emotionally and spiritually with the situation. Thankfully, with time his integrity was vindicated and the long-term effect of the accusations was minimal. The patterns of his life and teaching bore bright witness to his character.

In 2 Cor. 1:15–22 Paul sets his honest patterns of life over against the dishonest words of his accusers. In the face of the accusations, *he lays before the church the facts of the situation, explaining that he was working for their benefit*. For Paul, a minister for whom integrity was of utmost importance, the righting of the Corinthians' misperception about his motives regarding his changed travel plans constituted a matter of some urgency, for the spiritual health of the church was at stake. So also, when accused, we need to check our own motives and ask, "Why do I want vindication? Is it because of my own sense of well-being, or is it for the sake of the church and the cause of Christ?"

Notice also that Paul *points to the theological foundation of his ministry's integrity*. Thus the stability of his ministry was grounded in the character of God, rather than just the actions of him and his associates. Our deep-seated confidence in the faithfulness of God will both keep us on the path of integrity and encourage us when that path gets rough. Paul's defense ultimately rested in the integrity of God and the gospel, as witnessed to in his wholehearted, whole-life commitment to the God of the gospel. It doesn't necessarily follow that a minister of the gospel never makes a mistake in speech; Paul does not argue for his perfection but rather that he *knows* he has lived a general pattern of life before God with utmost integrity. He cannot conceive of intentionally breaking his word, or shifting plans on the basis of emotional waffling. It is not in him to do so because his character is shaped, ordered by the God of integrity, who fulfills all his promises.

Today we need men and women, both "professional" and "lay" ministers, who are people of resolute integrity, who can appeal to their God, his gospel, and their patterns of life in the same breath with quiet confidence. We need ministers who can live transparently, in glass houses, without the constant fear of a rain of shards shattering the illusion of a godly character.

Only lives lived by the principles of God, grounded in the gospel of God, empowered by the Spirit of God, and under the watchful love of God—only such lives can do so.

Additional Notes

1:15. As noted by Metzger (1994: 508), χάριν (ℵ* A C D G K Ψ 33 1739 Byz Lect it vg syr[p, h] cop[sa] arm), perhaps under the influence of 2:3, appears to have been modified by a scribe to read χαράν (ℵ[c] B L P 88 614 915 2005 cop[bo] al). Yet the evidence for χάριν is substantial, being both stronger and wider than the alternative (Harris 2005: 191), and the change could have been due to transcriptural error, since the words differ in only one letter (Thrall 1994: 137; Windisch and Strecker 1970: 61–62).

1:17. Some ancient scribes evidently shortened the reading τὸ ναὶ ναὶ καὶ τὸ οὒ οὒ to a single ναί and a single οὒ (𝔓[46] 0243 6 424[c] 1739 *pc* lat; Or[1739mg]), probably to assimilate to similar forms in verses 18 and 19. Some have defended the shorter reading on the basis of the doubling of each word being an assimilation to Jesus's words at Matt. 5:37. Yet the doubling is the more difficult reading, has stronger manuscript support, and makes good sense in context (Harris 2005: 191).

3. Why Paul Changed His Travel Plans, Part 1: Confrontation Would Have Been Painful for the Corinthians (1:23–2:11)

Authentic ministry leadership demands careful communication, especially when relationships have become strained or have deteriorated. Healthy relationships run on the twin tracks of trust and understanding. Many ministries have been shipwrecked on the rocks of poor communication.

As we saw in 1:12–14 the apostle proclaims the integrity of his ministry, and in 1:15–22 he addresses a misunderstanding of his recent change in travel plans. Now, in 2 Cor. 1:23–2:13 Paul tries to help the Corinthians understand why his travel plans had changed. Hopefully the truth would snuff out unhealthy speculations concerning his motives. The section has two main movements, 1:23–2:11 and 2:12–13. The first of these submovements also has two parts. In the first, 1:23–2:4, Paul explains that his recent change in plans was made in light of his earlier visit to Corinth, a painful visit that stung him, and in light of the painful letter to the church, which had been written through a flood of tears.

a. A Painful Visit and a Painful Letter (1:23–2:4)

Having affirmed his own character (1:12–14) and the theological dimensions of his relationship with the Corinthians (1:15–22), Paul now appeals to an emotional dimension. The unit coheres especially around the topic of emotional pain caused by Paul's previous letter and visit. It was for the Corinthians' good that the apostle had changed his itinerary; he did not want to cause them—and thus himself—further emotional grief. The painful visit, combined with the harsh letter that followed, had distressed Paul deeply, and he longs for his relationship with the Corinthians to produce joy instead of sadness. In short, he wants to move the relationship out of its current relational rut. As he closes this unit, Paul tries to clarify how emotionally difficult the recent breakdown in their relationship with him has been for him. Rather than feeling triumphant over his wielded authority, the whole experience has been gut-wrenching, breaking his heart, and he wants them to know that his motivation for writing has always been love.

These verses may be analyzed as follows:

  i. Why Paul did not come as planned (1:23)
 ii. The nature of Paul's authority (1:24)
iii. Paul's strategic decision (2:1–3)
 iv. Paul's gut-wrenching letter (2:4)

Exegesis and Exposition

1:23Now, I call upon God as my witness, the reason I did not return to Corinth was to spare you. 24Not that we dominate you with regard to your faith, but we work together for your joy; for you stand in faith. 2:1ᴦForᴧ I made a resolute decision not to come to you again in a way that would produce emotional turmoil. 2For if I upset you, who will cheer me up, if not you—the very ones I hurt!? 3I wrote about this very thing in my last letter, in order that when I arrive, ᴦI might not beᴧ made sad by the ones who ought to give me joy, trusting in all of you that we have a common source for joy. 4For as I wrote my last letter to you, the experience was gut-wrenching, heartbreaking, accomplished through a flood of tears. My motive was not to hurt you but that you might know the very great love that I have for you.

i. Why Paul Did Not Come as Planned (1:23)

Wishing to drive home the real reason he had changed his travel plans, the 1:23
apostle makes what amounts to a solemn oath before God: "Now, I call upon
God as my witness." The language here stems from lawcourts of the day,
and the gravity of the oath is reflected in two parts. First, God is appealed
to as a witness: in a sense the apostle asks God to take the witness stand on
his behalf. The main verb, ἐπικαλοῦμαι (*epikaloumai*, I call upon) was used
variously in the ancient world to appeal to a higher judicial authority, to call
someone as a witness, or to invoke God or the gods (BDAG 373). The Lord
God, supreme judge of all, who knows all the corners of a person's heart,
whose discerning Spirit probes all motives and sorts all intentions, is therefore
also incomparable as a witness—a witness who puts to rest the need for any
other. Second, the phrase we have translated "as my witness" could more
literally be rendered as witness "about my life" (ἐπὶ τὴν ἐμὴν ψυχήν, *epi tēn
emēn psychēn*), or even "against my life,"[1] suggesting that Paul is submitting
himself before God as judge and even putting his life on the line if he is lying
(Hafemann 2000: 87).

What then was the apostle's true motive for his change of plans? He wanted
to spare the church. Paul uses the same verb (φείδομαι, *pheidomai*, to spare)
twice elsewhere in 2 Corinthians and four other times in his writings (Rom.
8:32; 11:21 [2x]; 1 Cor. 7:28; 2 Cor. 12:6; 13:2). For instance, in Rom. 8:32
Paul uses the term to make clear allusion to what God did not do—keep
his Son from judgment on the cross: "Indeed, he who did not *spare* his own
Son, but gave him up for us all . . ." (NET). Further, speaking to Gentiles
at Rom. 11:21, Paul states, "For if God did not *spare* the natural branches,
perhaps he will not *spare* you" (NET). Thus he reminds the Gentiles, as they
consider the "fallen" state of Israelites who have yet to believe in Messiah
Jesus, that humility is always in order for those who receive God's grace.
So, once again, "sparing" has to do with escaping punishment or judgment
in some way. The closest parallel to the passage under consideration comes
later in 2 Corinthians: "When I was there the second time, I warned those
who sinned before and all the rest, and although I am absent right now, I
warn them again. When I return, I will not spare you" (2 Cor. 13:2). Simply
put, if repentance does not take place, the apostle is going to confront and
discipline those continuing in sin. Thus, in 2 Cor. 1:23 Paul tells the Corinthians that he did not stay with the two-visit itinerary in order to refrain
from confronting and disciplining those who persisted in sin. This certainly
was a case in which Paul was exercising wisdom as to the timing of such a
confrontation, rather than questioning its appropriateness (as is made clear
in 13:2).

---

1. The rendering "about my life" carries the sense of "with reference to" and "against
my life," a note of "hostile intent." These are just two of the many uses of ἐπί + the acc.
(BDAG 366).

ii. The Nature of Paul's Authority (1:24)

1:24   Yet this immediately raises a question concerning the nature and exercise of Paul's authority, and 1:24 makes clear that the apostle anticipates the question: "Not that we dominate you with reference to your faith, but we work together for your joy." The graphic term κυριεύω (*kyrieuō*) means to exercise authority over or rule over someone or something; thus it is used of military leaders and monarchs who make a grab for land, property, or persons (Spicq 1994: 2.351). In the LXX the term translates the Hebrew word מָשַׁל (*māšal*). It seems significant that the term finds expression some eighty-four times in the Hebrew Bible and yet is used of God's rule only once (2 Chron. 20:6). Throughout the OT, and in contrast to the benevolent rule of God as king, the Greek verb often carries a pejorative nuance: it frequently occurs in contexts describing some form of punishment, as earthly powers dominate those under their authority (LXX: e.g., Gen. 3:16; Exod. 15:9).

In the NT, Jesus states, "The kings of the Gentiles dominate them [κυριεύουσιν, *kyrieuousin*], and those who have authority over them are called 'Benefactors'" (Luke 22:25 HCSB), and this too probably carries a pejorative overtone (cf. Mark 10:43; Acts 19:16; 1 Pet. 5:3). Such a mode of governing people stands in contrast to the servant leadership commanded of those in the Christian community (Luke 22:26).

Thus, the term κυριεύω (*kyrieuō*) can connote the nuance of dominating someone or ruling over them harshly, and that is the sense used here. We must make a distinction between the domination of which Paul speaks and legitimate apostolic authority, which he certainly is not denying. Rather, he denies an inappropriate, dominating posture toward the Corinthians—"Not that we dominate you,"[2] understanding his relationship with them to be paternal and filled with grace (6:13; 11:2; 12:14–15; Barnett 1997: 115–16). It is the false ministers of Corinth who enslave and exploit the church (11:20).

More specifically, Paul denies that he dominates the Corinthians with reference to their faith.[3] There have been a number of suggestions as to what this might mean (Thrall 1994: 161), but it probably is not best to understand Paul's reference to faith simply as a general reference to their experience as a Christian community (i.e., "My holding you accountable does not constitute my inappropriately dominating you in the context of Christian community"). Rather, the second reference to faith in this last verse of the chapter ("for you stand in faith") suggests that the apostle has something more in mind. Although "faith" or "trust" (πίστις, *pistis*) can refer to the body of Christian teaching (e.g., Rom. 1:5; Gal. 1:23; Jude 3), here Paul seems to place the em-

---

2. Here Paul uses a rhetorical technique known as *epidiorthōsis* (*correctio*), by which an author corrects a previous statement in order to keep his hearers from misunderstanding him (Harris 2005: 159).

3. In the NT, the verb κυριεύω normally is associated with a genitive of person. Therefore, as with our ET, it is best to render πίστις (*pistis*, faith) as a genitive of reference, rather than as delimited by ὑμῶν (*hymōn*, i.e., your faith; Furnish 1984: 139).

phasis on the Corinthians' personal response of faith toward God, and the phrase τῇ . . . πίστει (tē . . . pistei) should be read as a dative of means, faith being understood as the means by which the Corinthians are able to stand. The verb ἑστήκατε (hestēkate, you stand), perfect tense in form, implies a state of being steadfast. So the Corinthians remain steadfast as the church of Jesus Christ by a response of faith or trust. Such trust, by its very nature, cannot be coerced and does not stem from fear. Instead, it has right relationship as its source and "joy" as its outcome.

Thus Paul and his associates[4] work together for the Corinthians' joy; the phrase τῆς χαρᾶς ὑμῶν (tēs charas hymōn) is understood to be an objective genitive—their work produces joy in the Corinthians. The goal and outcome, therefore, is not control, but the joy of a trusting relationship with God. Here, stated plainly, is one of the chief aims and marks of authentic Christian ministry, the engendering of joy in those to whom one ministers. That joy comes by the recipients of ministry—in this case the Corinthians—being rightly related to God and therefore being rightly related to Paul and his ministry team.

iii. Paul's Strategic Decision (2:1–3)

With the first three verses of chapter 2, Paul explains that he did not come to them as he had planned, because he was determined not to exacerbate an already-difficult situation: "For I made a resolute decision not to come to you again in a way that would produce emotional turmoil." The first part of the verse, "For I made a resolute decision" (Ἔκρινα γὰρ ἐμαυτῷ τοῦτο, Ekrina gar emautō touto), could also be rendered (lit.) as "For I judged this in myself." The verb κρίνω can carry more judicial overtones, or imply criticism of a person or situation, or simply mean "to select" someone or something. Yet here the term refers to using one's good judgment, coming to a decision after thinking matters through carefully (BDAG 568). The reflexive pronoun ἐμαυτῷ (in myself) seems to be included by Paul for intensity, thus our inclusion of the word "resolute" in the translation. Rather than basing his decision on the whim of a moment, the apostle had thought matters through and had come to the conviction that his plans needed to be adjusted.

Why? Because to return as planned to the Corinthians "would produce emotional turmoil" (ἐν λύπῃ, en lypē). An antithesis of joy, the term λύπη refers to distress, grief, or sorrow and is associated with various experiences of pain. For instance, translators of the Greek OT use the term for the "pains" associated with childbirth (Gen. 3:16) or the burdens of people wrestling crops from the dirt of a fallen world (Gen. 3:17; 5:29). This noun and its cognates can point

2:1

---

4. The two uses of the first-person plural in 1:24 (inherent in the verb forms κυριεύομεν [kyrieuomen, we dominate] and ἐσμεν [esmen, we are]) almost certainly refer to Paul and his coworkers. That they are συνεργοί (synergoi, fellow workers) makes clear that Paul is not using a literary "we" to speak of himself alone. Nor, as with most ET (e.g., ESV, HCSB, NIV, NRSV, NLT), does the συνεργοί refer to the Corinthians as Paul's coworkers for the Corinthians' joy. Rather, Paul and his ministry team, including Timothy and Silvanus (named in 1:19), are coworkers in working for the joy of the Corinthians.

to deep sadness in the form of emotional torment (Bar. 2:18; Sir. 30:21; Matt. 26:37) and can manifest itself in bitterness (Matt. 26:38), groaning (Isa. 35:10; Ps. 55:2; Wis. 11:12), and as Paul mentions momentarily, tears and anguish (2 Cor. 2:3–4). As those who have experienced real grief know, it drains one of strength (Sir. 38:18), burdens the mind, and "dries out the bones" (as we say in contemporary American culture, "I feel emotionally spent"; Prov. 15:13; 17:22; Spicq 1994: 2.417–18). Few experiences in church life are as difficult as the soul-draining sadness of relational conflict and tension. While noting that the Corinthians' sorrow, which became a godly grief (2 Cor. 7:10), *had* been productive in leading them to repentance, Paul simply wasn't ready to step back into the fray just yet.

2:2 Speaking transparently in verse 2, Paul lays out his own emotional stake in his recent travel decisions: "For if I upset you, who will cheer me up, if not you—the very ones I hurt!?" Notice, first of all, the repetition of γάρ (*gar*, for), the conjunction used here and at the beginning of the previous verse. This use of γάρ in verse 2 shows that Paul is elaborating on his explanation initiated in verse 1. In verse 2 he explains that "to inflict pain on the Corinthians at that time would have effectively dried up the very source of his own happiness—the Corinthians themselves" (Harris 2005: 217)! Those in Christian community have lives that are intertwined, the emotional state of the community being inextricably related to the emotional state of the leaders. Thus Paul notes that if he upsets the Corinthians, there will be no one in the church to "cheer" him during his visit. This word εὐφραίνω (*euphrainō*) means "to cheer up," "to cause to rejoice," to make someone "glad." Thus it, along with the noun we translate "joy," sits across the table of emotions from the "grief" or "sorrow" about which the apostle has been speaking. Paul naturally wants a healthy relationship with the Corinthians, the type of relationship that will be joyful rather than sorrowful.

2:3 When in verse 3 the apostle comments, "I wrote about this very thing"[5] (ἔγραψα τοῦτο αὐτό, *egrapsa touto auto*), he almost certainly refers to his motives for not coming as planned (the dominant topic in this paragraph), communicated in the previous, "severe" letter that had been sent to the congregation. As we consider bits and pieces scattered throughout 2 Corinthians, the apostle's motives for writing are expressed variously: that they might know the love he has for them (2:4), that he might test their character and obedience (2:9), and to help them realize their zeal for him as their apostle (7:12). These reasons are varied, but they are interrelated rather than contradictory (Matera 2003: 60). Upon reflection, they are the normal motivations one might see in a concerned parent, or in this case a concerned apostle. He appeals to the bonds of their relationship, the mutual feelings of love and earnestness forged with this congregation.[6]

---

5. Our ET of the Greek at this point makes the allusion more overt: "I wrote about this very thing in my last letter."

6. David Hall (2003: 224–26) has suggested that this severe letter was what we have as 1 Corinthians. Yet the way Paul speaks of the letter in 7:11–13 certainly sounds as though it had one primary topic, not the multiple topics that we now have in 1 Corinthians.

The ἵνα (*hina*, in order that) clause explains the negative (μή, *mē*, not) purpose for what Paul had written the congregation, and it is somewhat an inverse statement of his rhetorical question of the previous verse. He delayed the visit because he did not want to hurt the ones who might cheer him up: "in order that when I arrive, I might not be made sad by the ones who ought to give me joy" (ἵνα μὴ ἐλθὼν λύπην σχῶ ἀφ' ὧν ἔδει με χαίρειν, *hina mē elthōn lypēn schō aph' hōn edei me chairein*). The aorist participle, ἐλθών, is temporal, "when I come": Paul refers to the time of his arrival in Corinth. Here to "have sadness" (λύπην σχῶ, *lypēn schō*) is set over against "to give me joy" (με χαίρειν, *me chairein*). The Corinthians would be the source (ἀφ' ὧν, *aph' hōn*) of one or the other. The perfect participle πεποιθώς (*pepoithōs*) should be understood as causal (so, e.g., HCSB, NET), "since I trust," or "trusting in all of you."

So in verses 2 and 3, Paul acknowledges that the Corinthians should give him joy rather than grief, but he suggests that this is only possible to the extent "that we have a common source for joy" (ὅτι ἡ ἐμὴ χαρὰ πάντων ὑμῶν ἐστιν, *hoti hē emē chara pantōn hymōn estin*; more lit., that my joy is of all of you). The conjunction ὅτι (*hoti*) probably should be read as marking the content of Paul's trust, as expressed in our translation: he writes that he is confident "that we have a common source for joy." In other words, his relationship with the Corinthians can only go forward on a common set of values, common commitments, and therefore, a common source of joy. At the time of writing the letter, Paul trusted that the congregation shared his values and thus his joys.[7]

iv. Paul's Gut-Wrenching Letter (2:4)

Also, analogous to the experience of a parent or anyone confronting a recalcitrant person they love, the process of confrontation can be difficult, as Paul expresses in verse 4. The apostle uses three graphic descriptors for his experience of writing the severe letter: "the experience was gut-wrenching, heartbreaking, accomplished through a flood of tears." As shown in the diagram below, the first two of these descriptions stand in parallel, and the third expresses the circumstance in which Paul wrote (but might also have a spatial meaning—he wrote while looking through a literal veil of tears!).[8]

2:4

The experience was gut-wrenching	ἐκ πολλῆς θλίψεως
and heartbreaking,	καὶ συνοχῆς καρδίας
as I wrote my last letter to you,	ἔγραψα ὑμῖν
accomplished through a flood of tears.	διὰ πολλῶν δακρύων

7. The perfect active participle πεποιθώς (*pepoithōs*, trust, believe) delimits the verb ἔγραψα, expressing the circumstances under which Paul wrote the letter.

8. Windisch and Strecker (1970: 82) say that the use of ἐκ (*ek*, out of) suggests a state of mind that led to the writing of the letter, and the use of διά (*dia*, through) points to accompanying circumstances (see also Thrall 1994: 170).

The first of these descriptions we have seen before and will see again in 2 Corinthians, for the apostle describes his process of writing the letter as ἐκ . . . πολλῆς θλίψεως (*ek . . . pollēs thlipseōs*; 2 Cor. 1:4, 8; 4:17; 6:4; 7:4; 8:2, 13). Here the term refers to that experience of internal turmoil, discomfort, or trouble that accompanies a distressing situation (cf. Phil. 1:17). As in our translation, we might say the experience of writing the letter was "gut-wrenching." Paul was deeply distressed and must have agonized over the letter.

The second description (συνοχῆς καρδίας, *synochēs kardias*) speaks of the intense sadness the whole situation had caused the apostle. The word συνοχή could be used of a prison or place of confinement but here refers to a person experiencing "a high degree of anxiety, distress, dismay," or "anguish" (BDAG 974). This anguish further is described as being "of heart" (καρδίας), referring generally to the inner life.[9] Thus the first two descriptions stand in parallel relationship and are fairly synonymous; Paul stacks one on the other to emphasize the depth of his anguish, his inner turmoil that accompanied the letter.

Third, the inner turmoil manifested in an external response, for the letter was "accomplished through a flood of tears" (διὰ πολλῶν δακρύων, *dia pollōn dakryōn*, through many tears). As noted above, διά plus the genitive can communicate attendant circumstances (BDF 119; i.e., "I wept as I was writing") but here may also have spatial overtones as the apostle writes through a flood or "curtain" of tears.

Finally, Paul explains his motive for writing in contrasting statements:

My motive was	not to hurt you but
	that you might know the very great love that I have for you.

The double use of ἵνα (*hina*, that) in verse 4 sets up the contrasting purpose clauses. Paul did not write the letter to hurt the Corinthians. The verb λυπέω (*lypeō*), here in aorist-passive subjunctive form, could be used in the ancient world for causing severe mental or emotional distress, irritating, insulting, or offending (BDAG 604). Of the fifteen times Paul uses this verb, twelve occur in 2 Corinthians, all of which are used as the apostle reflects on the recent unhappy conflict between himself and the church (2 Cor. 2:2, 4–5; 6:10; 7:8–9, 11). In essence, the apostle writes that his motive was not to distress the Corinthians. Later in the book he explains that λύπη can be used by God to bring about repentance (7:9–10), but here in 2:4 his focus is on pain as an end in itself (Harris 2005: 221). Paul was not acting out of fleshly retaliation, merely wishing to distress or offend the Corinthians.

9. The term καρδία (*kardia*, heart) is used some 156 times in the NT and another 912 times in the LXX. The closest parallels to Paul's language here are found in Sirach, which speaks of a wound of the heart (πληγὴ καρδίας, *plēgē kardias*, 25:13, 23), pain of heart (ἄλγος καρδίας, *algos kardias*, 26:6), and sorrow of heart (λύπη καρδίας, *lypē kardias*, 38:18). In this case the genitive may be considered descriptive or perhaps, as with our ET, an attributed genitive: "a broken heart."

Rather, the apostle says he wrote "that you might know the very great love that I have for you," the most overt statement of Paul's feelings for and commitment to the community at Corinth (Furnish 1984: 160). Paul crafts this explanation of his true motive in a way that expresses his love in no uncertain terms. First, in the Greek text τὴν ἀγάπην (*tēn agapēn*, the love) unexpectedly precedes ἵνα γνῶτε (*hina gnōte*, in order that you might know) and stands in a position immediately following the strong contrastive ἀλλά (*alla*, but). Paul positions "the love" in this way for the sake of emphasis (P. Hughes 1962: 54). It is a first-century, grammatical way of highlighting an especially important point or concept.

Second, the adverb περισσοτέρως (*perissoterōs*, especially, how much more) offers an intense way of expressing comparison or heightened emphasis (meaning "all the more," "very intensely," or "especially"). Yet the word can be understood as functioning in several ways here:[10] (1) as adding intensity to the noun ἀγάπην, (2) as delimiting the verb γνῶτε, or (3) as delimiting the verb ἔχω (*echō*, I have) along with the prepositional phrase εἰς ὑμᾶς (*eis hymas*, for you). The first could be translated, "the very great love that I have for you," and this is possible, but the adverb is positioned within the relative clause and seems to relate more easily to the other terms within that clause. The second suggestion above, while attractive, also seems less likely due to the adverb's lack of proximity to that verb. Those who adopt the third interpretation normally translate the clause as "the love that I have especially toward you." Most recent translations prefer the first interpretation (e.g., HCSB, NLT[2], ESV, NIV, NRSV), understanding the adverb to directly intensify the noun "love," while others prefer the third interpretation (e.g., NASB, NET, KJV). Grammatically, the third interpretation is preferred, but the sense of the text is rendered more smoothly from Greek as if the adverb were directly describing the word "love": "the very great love I have for you."

10. Paul uses περισσοτέρως seven times in 2 Corinthians (1:12; 2:4; 7:13, 15; 11:23 [2x]; 12:15), in three cases accompanied by a prepositional phrase involving the pronoun ὑμᾶς (*hymas*, you; 1:12; 2:4; 7:15). The difficulty of discerning the exact grammatical function of the term here is exacerbated by the fact that the adverb was in a state of flux in general use, the comparative form being used as a superlative with elative force (BDF 32–33). In almost every case in 2 Corinthians, the word can mean something to the effect of "even more" or "to a great degree" (e.g., 1:12; 7:13, 15). In 2 Cor. 2:4, περισσοτέρως stands in the middle of a relative clause that relates to the term ἀγάπην, and some commentators have understood the adverb to delimit and intensify the concept of love (i.e., "the intense love"). Yet, as noted in the comments, grammatically περισσοτέρως occurs more in the proximity of the verb ἔχω (*echō*, I have), and thus other scholars have taken the adverb to relate directly to this verb. If this is the case—and it does seem grammatically more probable—it might appear to create another problem. Is the apostle saying that he has a special love for the Corinthians when compared to other churches (e.g., "that I have especially for you"; Barrett 1973: 88; Matera 2003: 57)? Probably not. A better interpretation reads the intensification as relating to the great degree of love that Paul has for the Corinthians, rather than his love for them in comparison to others. Thus Martin (1986: 30) translates the clause, "that I have in great measure for you." In this line, the clause also could be read as carrying a temporal note: "that I have for you now more than ever." If this is what Paul wishes to express, he says in effect, "Our recent struggles have not lessened my love for you but stoked my love to a greater intensity!"

Paul is not saying that he loves the Corinthians more than others. Rather, he wrote his "last letter" to the Corinthians as an expression of love, hoping that they would understand the great degree of his love for them. Thus our translation reads, "that you might know the very great love I have for you." Our interpretation stands more closely to option 3 above as to grammatical relationships, but closer to option 1 in terms of the sense of what Paul intended to communicate.

Thus, from 2 Cor. 1:23–2:4 Paul offers several points of explanation to the Corinthians related to his change of itinerary and the subsequent harsh letter he had sent them. In 1:23 he explains why he did not keep his scheduled itinerary. In the next verse (1:24) the apostle offers a disclaimer concerning his relationship to the Corinthians: he does not wish to dominate them spiritually. Verse 1 of chapter 2 explains that part of the reason Paul changed his travel plans was to keep from exacerbating an already-difficult situation with the Corinthians, fearing that an untimely visit would only escalate the conflict between them. Finally, he opens his heart to the church, explaining that the severe letter he had written had been horribly difficult for him to write; yet rather than being driven by a vengeful spirit, he had written that letter out of a deep love for the church.

Reflection

In 1:23–2:4 Paul offers the Corinthians a partial explanation of why his travel itinerary had changed, explaining that he wanted to spare them (1:23). Immediately he clarifies that his reference to "sparing" them wasn't meant to imply that his work as their apostle consists of him dominating them spiritually. Rather, everything in his ministry is meant to work for their joy as they "stand in faith" (1:24). Further, Paul explains what he means by "sparing" them, specifically that he did not want to act in a way that would upset them again, knowing that their emotional turmoil would also upset him (2:1–2). Evidently he had written about that motive of sparing them in his previous, "severe" letter (2:3), a letter that was terribly difficult for him to write. His description makes it clear that the crafting of that letter was emotionally draining, reflecting a crisis in his relationship with the Corinthians (and thus in their relationship with God). It must have been a very harsh letter since they read it as hurtful, but Paul explains that it was really an expression of love (2:4).

Paul exhibits a healthy approach to ministry leadership and authority. Notice that he seeks to foster healthy communication and rejects a dominating spirit. His goal is not to control but to work for their joy in the faith. He obviously cares deeply about the congregation, being motivated by love, and he wants to refrain from actions that would cause a great deal of emotional turmoil.

Today there exists confusion concerning the concept of authority. "To have authority" must not be confused with what might be called "authoritarianism." True, biblical authority is derived from God, for he has given people in leadership as gifts to the church (Eph. 4:11–12), but this is a servant leadership, focused not on self-exaltation or power as an end in itself but rather on the needs of others. The power of authentic leadership authority is wielded for the protection and building up of God's people. It is tenderly tough for the well-being of others.

Joe Belz (2006: 3) describes good leadership in this reflection:

> The sentence still jumps out at me from the middle of an editorial in the *Wall Street Journal*. It's been half a decade since I read it, but it was one of those electric expressions that you can't forget: "People want to be lightly governed," the writer said, "by strong governments."
>
> That's what you've wanted since you were a small child. You wanted your dad to be big and strong and able to do anything you could think of—except that, when he dealt with you, it had to be with gentleness and tenderness. You wanted a policeman on the corner tough enough to handle any neighborhood bully, but who would also hoist you to his shoulders and help you find your parents when you got lost in the crowd.
>
> Lots of muscle; lots of restraint. There's an innate yearning in almost all of us for that rare combination. When evil people rise up, we want a government with the clout to back them down. Yet we never want that clout turned on us.
>
> In the final analysis, people want to be lightly governed by strong governments because that's how God governs. The omnipotent ruler of the universe is also the one who invites us tenderly: "Come unto me, all you who are weary and heavy laden, and I will give you rest. Take my yoke upon you, and learn from me, for I am gentle and humble in heart, and you will find rest for your souls. For my yoke is easy, and my burden is light [Matt. 11:28–30]."

This is the type of leadership Paul exhibits in 2 Corinthians. He deals with the Corinthians forcefully because a great deal is at stake. He yearns for them to be right theologically and right relationally. Yet he seeks their submission to the truth and to God, not their subjugation to him as their apostle.

Additional Notes

2:1. It is probable that scribes failing to recognize the logical progression from 1:24 to 2:1 replaced γάρ with δέ (ℵ A C D^{b, c} [D^{gr*} τε] G K P Ψ 614 most Old Latin vg syr^p al). Although the support for γάρ among the witnesses consists primarily of proto-Alexandrian and later Alexandrian witnesses, and various versions ($\mathfrak{P}^{46}$ B 31 33 1739 it r syr^{h, pal} cop^{sa ms}, bo al), it is the more difficult reading and plays a vital role in marking 2:1 as providing the explanation needed in the context (Harris 2005: 211; Metzger 1994: 508).

2:3. The present subjunctive ἔχω has a variety of witnesses in its favor (ℵ² C D F G 𝔐), but the aorist subjunctive σχῶ has far superior external evidence ($\mathfrak{P}^{46}$ ℵ* A B P Ψ 0243 0285 6 33 81 365 630 1175 1505 1739 1881 2464 pc) and thus is preferred.

b. Forgive the One Who Caused the Pain (2:5–11)

One of the most unsettling matters in the life of any church has to do with carrying out church discipline in relation to a church member. As Paul continues to reflect on the pain surrounding his relationship with the Corinthians, in 2:5–11 he turns attention to the situation involving an unnamed offender. In the history of the church, the offense in mind has been understood variously, the traditional position being that Paul here speaks of the incestuous brother dealt with in 1 Cor. 5:1–5.[1] Yet, with most modern interpreters, we follow another route, understanding the offender to be an unnamed combatant who had taken Paul on publicly during the apostle's last visit to Corinth and thus had prompted the severe letter mentioned in 2:3–4 (for a fuller discussion of the evidence, see the additional note on 2:5–11).

At first blush the relationship of this unit to the broader context, which constitutes Paul's defense of his recent decisions, might not seem obvious. Yet, once understood, the apostle's rationale for addressing the situation with the offender at this point in the letter becomes clear. In 1:23–2:4 the apostle has just discussed his previous letter (what often is called "the severe letter") and the pain surrounding it. Then 2 Cor. 2:5–11 continues to discuss the letter (2:9) and the twin subjects of pain and grief (2:5, 7). In our passage at hand, the apostle has moved from a general discussion of his motives concerning his itinerary (1:15–2:2) and the severe letter (2:4), to addressing, in a strikingly sensitive manner, the Corinthians' response to a person who, at least for a moment, stood at the chaotic center of their relationship with Paul.

This subunit develops in three primary movements. First, in 2:5 Paul raises the subject of the unnamed offender and points out that the grief caused by the incident really constitutes a community issue, not just a personal issue for the apostle himself. Second, in verses 6–8 Paul observes that the punishment of the offender has worked, and it is time for the community to offer strong encouragement and forgiveness so that the person might not be overwhelmed. Finally, in verses 9–11 the apostle mentions yet another motivation at work in his writing of the severe letter: he wrote to test the Corinthians' obedience. He states strongly that he has forgiven the offender, and he has done this for the good of the community, not wanting Satan the schemer to exploit the situation. Thus the unit may be outlined as follows:

---

1. For a recent defense of this position, see Hall 2003: 227–35.

i. The grief caused by the offender (2:5)
ii. Encourage the offender (2:6–8)
iii. Other reasons for forgiveness (2:9–11)

Exegesis and Exposition

[5]Now if anyone has caused grief, he has grieved not only me, but to a certain extent—not to be burdensome—[he has grieved] all of you. [6]The punishment carried out by the majority was sufficient for a person in this situation; [7]so that now, ⌜instead, you⌝ should extend grace and encouragement to him, in order that he might not be consumed by overwhelming sadness. [8]So I urge you to affirm your love for him. [9]For I also wrote to test you, to see ⌜the extent of your obedience⌝. [10]But now, whoever you forgive, I forgive. Indeed, whatever I myself have forgiven—if I have forgiven anything—is for your sakes before Christ, [11]in order that we might not be exploited by Satan. For we know the way he thinks.

i. The Grief Caused by the Offender (2:5)

With the conjunction δέ (*de*), Paul connects this new unit, which coheres around his discussion of "the offender," to what has gone before, signaling a mild shift in the topic. The conditional clause (Εἰ . . . τις λελύπηκεν, *Ei . . . tis lelypēken*, if anyone has caused grief) raises the subject of a person who had indeed caused a great deal of grief in the Achaian community. Three points can be made about the wording here. First, in 2 Corinthians the apostle often refers to his opponents as "someone" or "anyone" (τις, *tis*) rather than naming names (2 Cor. 3:1; 10:2, 7, 12; 11:16, 20–21; 12:6).[2] So the way the apostle refers to the offender may offer a bit of evidence concerning the nature of the offense, specifically, that we are dealing with one of Paul's opponents, perhaps a local Corinthian rather than one of the interlopers.

Second, the conjunction εἰ (*ei*) points to a real condition: Paul is not raising the possibility of an offense taking place; rather, he specifically puts the real situation forward for the Corinthians to address. Third, the aspect of the perfect-tense verb suggests there exists an ongoing state of grief surrounding the situation; the grief lingers, perhaps causing a sense of unsettledness in the community. To deal kindly with an offender, as Paul does here, does not involve downplaying the sin and its consequences—the consequences in the community still are blatantly obvious. Rather, Paul faces squarely the consequences of the person's offense, yet leads the Corinthians in a process of restoration.

Following the conditional clause, the apostle offers a disclaimer: "he has grieved not only me" (οὐκ ἐμὲ λελύπηκεν, *ouk eme lelypēken*). There are times when Paul uses the negative, not with an absolute meaning (i.e., "not at all") but in a way that expresses a relative sense (i.e., "not primarily," "not only"; see 1 Cor. 1:17; 2 Cor. 7:12; Harris 2005: 223), and this is one of those

2:5

---

2. The indefinite reference may suggest a sensitivity on Paul's part (Thrall 1994: 171).

times; hence our addition of "only" to the translation. There are those who take Paul's statement literally as disclaiming that he had been hurt personally, and this interpretation at times is tied to the understanding that the offender was the incestuous brother of 1 Cor. 5 (e.g., P. Hughes 1962: 64). Yet, why would Paul present such a declamation at all if he had not been offended? The apostle's statement of forgiveness in verse 10 also suggests that Paul had been hurt in the matter, though there too the language is muted ("if I have forgiven anything"), and Paul says his forgiveness was given for the sake of the Corinthians.

The conjunction ἀλλά (alla, but) obviously is contrastive, but there is some question as to the function of the prepositional phrase ἀπὸ μέρους (apo merous, partially, to a degree), a phrase the apostle has already used at 1:14.[3] Does the phrase delimit "he has grieved not only me" (as with the KJV, Tyndale)[4]? If so, Paul would be downplaying the grief caused him personally (i.e., "he has grieved me only to a certain extent"). The better reading of the grammar, however, understands the prepositional phrase to define the grief experienced by the Corinthians: "he has grieved not only me, but to a certain extent [he has grieved] . . . all of you."[5] The Corinthians don't feel the full force of grief felt by Paul, for Paul was the one directly assaulted. Nevertheless, as 7:7, 11 make clear, they were grieved by their own mishandling of the situation (Barrett 1973: 89; Harris 2005: 224; Thrall 1994: 172).

Finally, we have translated the ἵνα (hina, in order that) clause with "not to be burdensome" (ἵνα μὴ ἐπιβαρῶ; hina mē epibarō). Among ancient authors the verb ἐπιβαρέω (epibareō) spoke of burdening someone or weighing them down. Picture a slave carrying a huge bundle on his back. Thus the term could be used to describe various burdens one might need to bear. At 1 Thess. 2:9 and 2 Thess. 3:8, Paul states that he and his ministry team worked with their own hands because they did not want to "burden" the Thessalonians with their living expenses. Here the apostle perhaps uses the word with the sense of "in order not to heap up too great a burden of words" (BDAG 368); given the context, the idea of verbally "being hard on" someone, or "burdensome," probably is not far from the mark. In Appian's Bell. civ. 3.2.17, for instance, Octavius uses the term in appealing to Antony "not to be hard on us." Paul, broaching a sensitive issue with the Corinthians, may be saying that he does not wish to burden them further with a point he most certainly made in his

---

3. At 1:14 it clearly means "partially," for it is in contrast to the idea of the Corinthians understanding Paul "completely." Similarly, the phrase ἐκ μέρους (ek merous) can be used to mean "partially" (e.g., Philo, Mos. 2.1).

4. The KJV reads, "But if any have caused grief, he hath not grieved me, but in part: that I may not overcharge you all." Similarly, Tyndale offers, "If eny man hath caused sorow the same hath not made me sory but partely: lest I shuld greve you all."

5. Eugene Peterson's Message reads, "I want you to know that I am not the one injured in this as much as, with a few exceptions, all of you" (also Plummer 1915: 52, 56). The phrase can be read temporally: "[he has grieved] all of you for a while." Yet the use just a few verses earlier at 1:14 gives the more confident nod to the idea of "partially" or "to some extent."

previous correspondence. He simply wants the Corinthians to own the fact that the troublesome person had in reality injured the whole community, not just their apostle. Further, the form ἐπιβαρῶ is present active subjunctive, used here with the negative in a preventative sense. Thus Paul wants to stop short of pressing the issue and burdening the Corinthians more than is necessary at this point.

ii. Encourage the Offender (2:6–8)

In the following three verses, Paul declares that the punishment that has been carried out by the church has been enough to accomplish its goal of bringing about repentance and that it is now time to offer forgiveness, comfort, and a reaffirmation of love to the offender. The punishment (ἐπιτιμία, *epitimia*) carried out against "a person in this situation"[6] evidently had been the withdrawal of fellowship,[7] and Paul comments now, "That's enough." The term ἱκανός (*hikanos*) can carry the sense of "considerable" (e.g., Mark 10:46; Luke 7:12; Acts 11:24, 26; 19:26) or "appropriate," "competent," or "qualified" (Matt. 3:11; Mark 1:7; Luke 3:16; 1 Cor. 15:9; 2 Cor. 2:16; 3:5). Yet here it communicates that the punishment has been "sufficient," and it could have overtones of either degree (i.e., intense enough) or time (i.e., long enough). That the punishment had been carried out by "the majority" (ὑπὸ τῶν πλειόνων, *hypo tōn pleionōn*) speaks of intensity: to have the bulk of one's community confront one with discipline would be sobering. Further, Paul's reference to "the majority" also hints that a faction exists that did not support the disciplinary action. Nevertheless, given the offender's repentance implied in the passage, Paul's point is clear. The punishment has worked, and it is time to embrace the brother, welcoming him back into the fellowship.

2:6

Verse 7 begins with ὥστε . . . μᾶλλον (*hōste . . . mallon*, so that . . . rather), "so that" showing the needed result at this point in their relationship with the brother, and "rather," or "instead," suggesting that their posture toward the brother needs to change. The Corinthians have followed Paul's lead in terms of doling out church discipline; now it is time to follow his lead in extending forgiveness and restoration (Hafemann 2000: 89). They have turned away from the offending brother. Now they should turn toward him in love. Thus Paul exhorts the Corinthians to open their arms and lives in forgiveness, comfort, and reaffirmation.

2:7

---

6. In 2:6, τοιοῦτος (*toioutos*) can refer to a person or thing mentioned in a given context ("a person like this"). We have translated it with an emphasis on the situation since Paul's concern is not with the type of person represented by the offender but rather with a person in this kind of circumstance.

7. The withdrawal of fellowship was also known, e.g., in the Qumran community. Thus 1QS 7.15–19 says that a person who has slandered his companion shall be excluded from the meal of the congregation for a year and do penance, and the person who has spoken against the congregation shall be expelled permanently. Further, whoever has murmured against the authority of the community is to be expelled permanently (see comments by Furnish 1984: 161).

Forgiveness constitutes one of the most salient motifs in the biblical literature and thus is foundational for true Christian community. John Stott (1992: 48) reports that when a leading British humanist was interviewed on television, in a moment of surprising frankness, she said, "What I envy most about you Christians is your forgiveness. I have nobody to forgive me." Here Paul doesn't use the more common ἀφίημι (aphiēmi), which occurs some 143 times in the NT. Rather, he calls for forgiveness by employing the word χαρίζομαι (charizomai), a term that could communicate the idea of giving something graciously or freely as a favor, to cancel a debt, or as here, to be gracious by forgiving someone for a wrong committed (BDAG 1078). Paul encourages the Corinthians, who have applied appropriate pressure to the offending brother in confrontation, now to adopt a gracious posture toward him, to "extend grace."

Appropriate confrontation appeals to a person to repent and communicates consequences of continued misbehavior. The punishment had consisted of withdrawing a key aspect of community—the ready fellowship of brothers and sisters in Christ. Yet forgiveness must give, not merely take away. God has extended grace toward us, so forgiveness must be a fundamental aspect of our relationships with one another in the body of Christ, the extension of grace to one another.

Although παρακαλέω[8] (parakaleō) can mean "to exhort" or "request," or even "comfort," the context seems to demand a translation at this point that emphasizes the idea of encouragement,[9] even more so than the idea of "comfort" (the term preferred by almost all modern ETs).[10] Comfort could be understood as offering emotional salve for the wounds incurred from confrontation and punishment; but what this person needs is "not some tranquilizing dose of grace that only dulls pains but a stiffening agent that fortifies one in heart, mind, and soul" (Garland 1999: 60). The offender needs the encouragement of a warm, open, welcoming posture on the part of the community.[11] In another place Paul writes, "Therefore welcome one another as Christ has welcomed you, for the glory of God" (Rom. 15:7 ESV).

Further, this action needs to be taken on the part of the Corinthians in order that the brother "might not be consumed by overwhelming sadness." The verb καταποθῇ (katapothē) is an aorist passive subjunctive form of καταπίνω (katapinō), which could be used to mean "swallow," "drink down," "swallow up," "drown," or "destroy." Polybius, for example, a writer of the second and third centuries BC, writes of a city that was swallowed up by the

8. The verb is used 18 times in 2 Corinthians, at 1:4 [3x], 6; 2:7–8; 5:20; 6:1; 7:6–7 [3x], 13; 8:6; 9:5; 10:1; 12:8, 18; 13:11.

9. In the next breath Paul, using the same verb, writes, "So I urge you" (2:8).

10. So, e.g., the HCSB, NASB, NET, NLT, ESV, and NIV.

11. See the discussion on "encouragement" at 1:3. BDAG 765 notes that in several places the word "appears to mean simply treat someone in an inviting or congenial manner, someth[ing] like our 'be open to the other, have an open door': invite in, conciliate, be friendly to or speak to in a friendly manner" (see Luke 15:28; Acts 16:39; 1 Cor. 4:13; 1 Thess. 2:12; 1 Tim. 5:1).

sea (*Hist.* 2.41.7). At 1 Cor. 15:54, Paul alludes to Isa. 25:8, writing that in the resurrection death will be "swallowed up" in victory; later in 2 Corinthians, Paul writes of mortality being "swallowed up" in life (2 Cor. 5:4). Here, however, the term at least connotes being consumed with something and perhaps carries the idea of being destroyed. Paul is concerned that "excessive" (πε-ρισσοτέρᾳ, *perissotera*) sadness might engulf the offender, drowning him in a sea of remorse. This would be both unfortunate and inappropriate, given the person's repentance. Once repentance has been expressed, further discipline "would be strictly punitive," leading to a sort of grief that is worldly and finds no relief in God's redemptive approach to sin (cf. 7:9–11; Furnish 1984: 162).

Third, therefore, the Corinthians are to affirm their love for the offender. The term κυρόω (*kyroō*), used in the NT only here and at Gal. 3:15,[12] could be used to mean "to confirm, ratify, validate," or "to make legally binding," as in the Galatians passage. During the first century, it was used in this way of wills, treaties, decrees, and bills of sale.[13] Yet it could also mean, "to come to a decision in a cognitive process, conclude," or "decide in favor of" (BDAG 579), and that may well be the sense here. Paul exhorts the Corinthians to make a conscious decision to embrace the brother in love. John Chrysostom, who interpreted our passage as referring to the incestuous brother of 1 Cor. 5, nevertheless has pertinent words concerning the nature of reaffirmation of love: "In other words, reveal your friendship as certain, unshakable, fervent, ardent and fiery; present your love with the same strength as the previous hatred" (*On Repentance and Almsgiving* 1.3.22; Bray 1999: 206). In another place, the church father remarks, "Paul asks the Corinthians not only to lift the censure but also to restore the man to his former status, for to punish a man without healing him means nothing" (*Hom. 2 Cor.* 4.4; Bray 1999: 207).

2:8

iii. Other Reasons for Forgiveness (2:9–11)

In the final movement of this unit, Paul reveals another aspect of his motives in writing to the Corinthians: "For I also wrote to test you" (or, "that I might know [γνῶ, *gnō*] your character"). His instructions concerning church discipline were meant to test the Corinthians to see whether they would follow his instructions. The word δοκιμή (*dokimē*), used only by Paul in the NT (Rom. 5:4; 2 Cor. 2:9; 8:2; 9:13; 13:3; Phil. 2:22), had to do with a process of testing, often involving an ordeal that demonstrated the nature of one's character. Thus a "test" in this sense manifests character. Paul uses the term later in 2 Corinthians of the Macedonian churches, whose test resulted in joy and generosity (8:2). Further, the apostle wanted "to see the extent" of the Corinthians' "obedience" (εἰ εἰς πάντα ὑπήκοοί ἐστε, *ei eis panta hypēkooi este*). The conditional εἰ shows that their complete obedience was not a foregone conclusion and overtly portrays the tension that existed between Paul

2:9

---

12. "When a covenant has been ratified, even though it is only a human contract, no one can set it aside or add anything to it" (Gal. 3:15 NET).

13. See Belleville (1996: 75), who follows Johannes Behm's article (*TDNT* 3:1098–99).

and this problematic congregation. The tension also stems from the extent of their obedience—would it be εἰς πάντα, "unto all," "compete"? Partial obedience is disobedience. Church discipline cannot be conducted halfway, since its effectiveness depends in part on a clearly defined and united stand in relation to the offender.

2:10-11   In verses 10 and 11 the apostle concludes the unit with further reflections on forgiveness. The conjunction δέ (*de*) is additive, showing progression from the past test to the current status of the situation, and carries a hint of contrast: "but now." In light of the Corinthians' response to his instructions and the brother's repentance, Paul assures the church that he fully supports extending forgiveness to the offender and joins in that offering of forgiveness.

He explains further, "Indeed,[14] whatever I myself have forgiven—if I have forgiven anything—is for your sakes before Christ." In essence the apostle here explains what drives him as he works toward reconciliation in this unfortunate episode in the life of the church. Rather than self-centered vindication, Paul is driven by a desire to see good result for the church, his brothers and sisters in Christ. He writes, "What I myself have forgiven [ἐγὼ ὃ κεχάρισμαι, *egō ho kecharismai*] . . . is for your sakes before Christ" (δι' ὑμᾶς ἐν προσώπῳ Χριστοῦ, *di' hymas en prosōpō Christou*). This statement reiterates Paul's act of forgiving the offense,[15] states that he has forgiven for the sake of the Corinthians,[16] and expresses his posture "before Christ." All that he does, he does with an attitude and posture reflecting that he is a man living under the lordship of Christ, before the living Christ as his audience, and for Christ's church.

The conditional clause that stands at the heart of the sentence, "if I have forgiven anything" (εἴ τι κεχάρισμαι, *ei ti kecharismai*), seems oddly dismissive or even uncertain at first blush. Yet, rather than communicating uncertainty, this conditional clause expresses Paul's pastoral sensitivity; the conditional clause is used to understate Paul's role in the whole affair. Harris (2005: 232) calls this a "dismissiveness born of pastoral tact." It simply is another way Paul attempts to tone down the emotional intensity that had infused the situation.

Paul has already identified one reason the church should extend forgiveness and comfort to the offender: so that the person would not be drowned by excessive sorrow (v. 7). Yet, in addition to this personal reason, the apostle names a second, corporate reason the Corinthians should work for full reclamation of the brother: it will work against Satan's agenda of exploiting Paul and the congregation. The verb πλεονεκτέω (*pleonekteō*) could be used to mean "to take advantage of, exploit, outwit, defraud," or "cheat" (BDAG 824). Paul uses the word three times elsewhere in 2 Corinthians and once in

---

14. In the construction καὶ γάρ (*kai gar*), the γάρ probably carries the dominant force, for the connection is for the sake of explanation. Yet the additive sense of καί seems to play a role as well. The term "indeed" is used in the ET, leaving the explanatory force of the whole as implicit to Paul's statement (see BDF 235–36).

15. The ὅ (*ho*, what) is neuter singular acc. and refers to the offensive act.

16. In 2:10, διά (*dia*) + the acc. indicates cause and can be translated "because of," "on account of," or "for the sake of."

1 Thessalonians (2 Cor. 7:2; 12:17–18; 1 Thess. 4:6); in each case it can be understood to speak of unfairly taking advantage of another person. In short, forgiveness frustrates the plans of Satan, who wants to use people and situations for ill. The word νόημα (*noēma*) can refer to a thought or "the way" one processes thought with the mind. Thus we render the text here, "for we know the way he thinks." Given the way Satan schemes for the disunity of the church, forgiveness and reconciliation provide beautiful strategies for disrupting his evil, church-dissolving schemes.

Reflection

With 2 Cor. 2:5–11 the apostle Paul deals straightforwardly with the restoration of a person who had caused a great deal of relational pain in the community. The focus here is on restoration through forgiveness, but we also see the situation as reflective of at least two forms of tension between Paul and the congregation. First, the situation precipitated by "the offender" provides one specific example of someone in the community coming into direct conflict with Paul. We do not know the specific offense, but our passage seems to indicate that Paul himself had been verbally attacked in some way. Second, that the Corinthians needed a "test" to ascertain "the extent" of their "obedience" points to the fact that among some in the congregation, the apostle's authority had been questioned or downgraded. The difficult situation with the offender gave the Corinthians an opportunity to live out an obedience to Paul's apostolic authority.

I suggest that how we today deal with community-damaging sin and restoration of a sinner still constitutes a matter of apostolic authority, yet most churches have little concept of appropriate church discipline. Consequently, the backstory to Paul's words in 2 Cor. 2:5–11 may seem harsh to some and rather primitive. Yet, from a biblical perspective, church discipline constitutes a profound expression of grace: it offers a healthy form of accountability, which leads to healthy patterns of Christian living. It is one of the gifts of true biblical community. The church father Basil writes in *The Long Rules* (question 7, in PG 31):

> Community life offers more blessings than can be fully and easily enumerated. It is more advantageous than the solitary life both for preserving the goods bestowed on us by God and for warding off the external attacks of the Enemy. . . . For the sinner, moreover, the withdrawal from his sin is far easier if he fears the shame of incurring censure from many acting together—to him, indeed, might be applied the words: "To him who is such a one, this rebuke is sufficient which is given by many"—and for the righteous man, there is a great and full satisfaction in the esteem of the group and in their approval of his conduct (Bray 1999: 206).

There are churches that, thinking themselves "grace" oriented, never confront even blatant and public sin. This might be due to a lack of community maturity, the distraction of "more pressing" matters, being emotionally manipulated, or more likely, a mistaken view of grace as only forgiving and never formative. Yet those who do not have the grace of this pattern of confrontation-consequences-repentance-restoration never know the outcome of true restoration, and the church is crippled on numerous levels.

On the other hand, churches that practice church discipline with zeal, reveling in confrontation, celebrating their boldness in handing out consequences, must be rigorously guarded against Satan's ploys, making sure that the discipline truly is an expression of love and restoration, rather than simply punitive. The Corinthians were in danger of giving Satan an opportunity by truncating the process of repentance and restoration, punitively glorying in the repentance while neglecting the restoration. This too is inadequate and cripples the church on many levels. In *Mere Christianity*, C. S. Lewis (2001: 117) writes:

> Christianity does not want us to reduce by one atom the hatred we feel for cruelty and treachery. We ought to hate them. Not one word of what we have said about them needs to be unsaid. But it does want us to hate them in the same way in which we hate things in ourselves: being sorry that the man should have done such things, and hoping, if it is anyway possible, that somehow, sometime, somewhere, he can be cured and made human again.

True church discipline, therefore, must not be neglected but must always be given in love, given with appropriate measures, and given for the purpose of renewal and restoration. This does great damage to the schemes of the adversary.

Additional Notes

2:5. On the division of the apodosis in 2:5: Most scholars divide the apodosis of verse 5 (οὐκ ἐμὲ λελύπηκεν ἀλλὰ ἀπὸ μέρους ἵνα μὴ ἐπιβαρῶ, πάντας ὑμᾶς) as delineated in the comments above. However, given the lack of punctuation in the ancient Greek text, other possibilities exist.[17] First, the οὐκ ἐμὲ λελύπηκεν can be read as a question ("If anyone has caused grief, has he not grieved me?") anticipating the answer "yes!" The ἀλλά and following would then constitute a separate sentence. Yet, as Thrall notes, this disrupts both the contrast between the "me" and "you," as well as the grammatical construction οὐκ . . . ἀλλά, which is a favorite of Paul's. A second possibility would be to place commas after μέρους and πάντας, reading, "He has not grieved me primarily, but in part, so that I may not burden all you." Yet this construction is quite unnatural to Greek grammar. Finally, one could read the text as containing a break after ἀπὸ μέρους: "He has not grieved me primarily, but partially—that I might not load you all down with an excessive burden."[18] Here Paul would be easing the minds of the Corinthians with regard to his own suffering in the matter. Yet Thrall is correct that οὐκ ἐμέ and ἀπὸ μέρους should not be seen as presenting an antithesis between Paul feeling

17. Here the discussion follows Thrall 1994: 172–73, who presents three primary options.
18. This, e.g., is the approach of KJV, "But if any have caused grief, he hath not grieved me, but in part: that I may not overcharge you all," which seems to follow Tyndale, "If eny man hath caused sorow the same hath not made me sory but partely: lest I shuld greve you all."

deep grief in the matter, over against him feeling a partial burden. All in all, the division as presented in this commentary's ET seems to be preferable.

2:5–11. Who is the offender? Various suggestions have been made concerning the identity of the "offender" Paul mentions in 2:5–11. Several points are clear. (1) The offender seems to have been a single person within the Corinthian community, who in some way clashed with and attacked Paul. (2) The person's actions had adversely affected the whole community. (3) The offense seems to be of an interpersonal rather than a theological nature. The passage concerns an event that caused grief and church discipline, and now it highlights the need for forgiveness and restoration. (4) The church at Corinth had acted on Paul's exhortation and now needs to express love to the offender (Garland 1999: 119–21).

Many commentators in the history of the church, reading 1 and 2 Corinthians in their canonical context, understandably identify the offender with the incestuous brother of 1 Cor. 5:1–5.[19] In 1 Cor. 5 the apostle calls the church to discipline the man, who was having sexual relations with his father's wife. Such a person certainly would be a cause of grief to the whole community, since their reputation would be negatively affected by the person (1 Cor. 5:2). Satan also is mentioned in both the 1 Corinthians passage and 2 Cor. 2:11. In 1 Corinthians the offender was to be handed over to Satan for "the destruction of the flesh." In our passage at hand, the Corinthians are to guard against Satan taking advantage of the situation. Thus, upon this reading 2 Cor. 2:5–11 constitutes a follow-up on one of the critical situations addressed in 1 Corinthians. Garland (1999: 121–22) has recently tried to reinvigorate this position.

However, most modern interpreters reject this interpretation as not fitting numerous details of the text.[20] First, Paul here uses extraordinary sensitivity in addressing the status of the offending brother. Tertullian first suggested that Paul's attitude and the lightness with which he calls for a new attitude toward this person do not fit the gravity and offensiveness of the sin of incest. Second, in 1 Cor. 5 Paul had called for the Corinthians to turn the offender over to Satan for the destruction of the flesh (1 Cor. 5:5), and this seems in stark contrast to a brief withdrawal of fellowship. Further, that extreme measure could not have been handed down simply to "test" the Corinthians (2 Cor. 2:9). Third, the offense to which Paul alludes in 2 Cor. 2:5–11 seems to be directly related to Paul himself and probably constituted a personal attack on the apostle. If not, why would Paul state, "He has not grieved me primarily" (οὐκ ἐμὲ λελύπηκεν, ouk eme lelypēken)? The offender of 1 Cor. 5, on the other hand, offended through a gross pattern of life, and there is no indication in 1 Corinthians that Paul was attacked by the incestuous person. Fourth, Paul's references to Satan have quite a different tenor in the two passages. In 1 Corinthians, Satan is a tool for disciplinary action (5:5). In 2 Corinthians he is presented as a schemer who could twist an evil advantage by a failure of the parties to reconcile with the offender (see esp. the discussion by Garland 1999: 119–20).

In rejecting the traditional view that the offender was the incestuous person of 1 Cor. 5, scholars offer other nuanced proposals. Margaret Thrall, who admits that any alternative suggestion is "more speculative," suggests, for instance, that the offender, a member of the church, had stolen money that a member of the congregation had given to Paul for the collection (2 Cor. 8–9). She points out

19. In addition to ancient commentators such as John Chrysostom (*On Repentance and Almsgiving* 1.3.22) and Theodoret of Cyr (*Commentary on the Second Epistle to the Corinthians* 297), among those who hold to some form of the traditional position is Kruse (1987: 41–45), who suggests that the incestuous brother committed a second offense by publicly spurning Paul's authority (see also P. Hughes 1962: 59–65; and more recently, Garland 1999: 121).

20. Among those who diverge from the traditional position on various grounds are Thrall 1994: 68–69; Barrett 1973: 91; Martin 1986: 34; Windisch and Strecker 1970: 237–39; Barnett 1997: 124, who suggests that the person may have been connected with sexual aberrations in Corinth or supported temple attendance in the city; Furnish 1984: 164–68.

that such an offense fits the term ἀδικέω at 7:12, the offender would be someone subject to the church's disciplinary action, such an offense could be righted by the confession of the thief, and the congregants could prove their innocence in the matter (Thrall 1994: 68–69). Yet it might be suggested that this view stretches the evidence beyond what is clearly stated in the text. For one thing, the statement in 7:12, ἕνεκεν τοῦ ἀδικηθέντος (because of the one wronged), might be taken as a self-reference by Paul, if he is speaking euphemistically (as he does in 2:5–11) and does not necessarily refer to a third party. Finally, nothing in the text suggests that the offense involved money.

Other suggestions are that the offender was one of the false apostles, a visitor to the community, who had been stirring up trouble in the Corinthian church and took a bold public stance against Paul on the apostle's recent visit (Barrett 1973: 91; Martin 1986: 34), or that the offender was the person discussed in 1 Cor. 6:1–8, who took his brother to court (Windisch and Strecker 1970: 237–39). Yet there is a reason why most modern commentators opt for a position that is more ambiguous, that the offender was an unnamed perpetrator, from within the church at Corinth, who had verbally attacked Paul in public. Further, Harris (2005: 226–27) makes a reasonable case that the person had not confronted the apostle while Paul was in Corinth, but had mounted a public opposition between the time of Paul's painful visit and his severe letter. Anything beyond this skirts too near the realm of speculation.

2:7. The reading μᾶλλον ὑμᾶς has the most evidence in its favor (𝔓⁴⁶ ℵ C Ψ 0243 0285 1739). Some manuscripts have μᾶλλον following ὑμᾶς (e.g., D F G 33), and others omit μᾶλλον altogether (e.g., A B Jerome), but it seems more likely that μᾶλλον was accidentally omitted in some manuscripts and later reintroduced after ὑμᾶς in others (Metzger 1975: 576).

2:9. There exists a good bit of volatility in the textual tradition at the beginning of what reads as a conditional clause in the standard texts (εἰ εἰς πάντα ὑπήκοοί ἐστε). In variations, εἰ is omitted (e.g., 𝔓⁴⁶ 1505), perhaps due to its juxtaposition with εἰς, and replaced with ἦ (e.g., A B 33) or ὡς (e.g., 460 1836). Yet the external evidence for εἰ is quite strong (ℵ C D F G Ψ 0243 0285 1739 1881 𝔐 lat sy sa? bo), and read thus, the conditional clause makes good sense.

4. Why Paul Changed His Travel Plans, Part 2: An Open Door and an Absent Coworker (2:12–13)

My family and I recently read the novel *Jane Eyre* by Charlotte Brontë. Published in the fall of 1847, the story follows a young orphan girl through early years of abuse in the home of an aunt, through her development and maturation at a boarding school, and finally to her role as a governess in the grand home of Mr. Edward Rochester, a house of opportunity and secrets. The novel focuses beautifully on redemption, especially in relation to Mr. Rochester. This man, bitter and broken, opens his life in a fresh way to love and ultimately to God. In fact, the conclusion of the novel, zeroing in on two men in Jane's life, the devastated Mr. Rochester and the resolute missionary, St. John (pronounced "sin gin"), crescendos with focus on divine grace and providence.

Since reading the book, my wife, Pat, and I have watched two film adaptations, the best of which was the very good four-hour BBC version. We enjoyed it a great deal. Although even the most faithful movie adaptation cannot offer the depth of experience plumbed in reading a great novel, the main factor missing from the BBC adaptation was the "God factor." God was there, in small dialogue asides, but the resolution of the story rested more on the fulfillment of surprising human relationships than on the surprise of being rescued by God from one's own self-centeredness and depravity. You don't understand *Jane Eyre* as originally written until you understand God as a key character in the plot.

With the account at 2 Cor. 2:12–13 of the apostle's trip north from Ephesus to Troas and then on to Macedonia, we now come full circle in Paul's explanation concerning his change of travel plans, an explanation that now turns to an opportunity opened to him by the Lord.[1] The Lord's leadership of Paul, as described here and echoed in the triumphal procession imagery of 2:14–16, is central to the apostle's defense of his actions. Christ is the one who has determined his itinerary. According to the apostle, the God factor must be put in the mix for an accurate assessment of Paul's character and ministry decisions.

As we have already observed, the Corinthians were quite disappointed in the apostle's travel decisions, with some even accusing him of being fickle. In vindicating himself, Paul has defended his integrity (1:12–14), addressed a potential misunderstanding of his motives and character (1:15–22), and

---

1. See the reconstruction of the events that lie behind Paul's change in plans above in the introduction ("Paul's Relationship with the Corinthians").

explained his true motive for not coming to Corinth as planned: he did not want to exacerbate an already painful situation, alluding both to his painful visit to the Corinthians as well as the painful letter he had sent them (1:23–2:4). He has further exhorted the Corinthians to forgive and embrace the brother who had precipitated the great grief experienced by the community, so that the brother would not drown in a sea of regret and so that he himself and the Corinthian church might not be exploited by Satan (2:5–11).

It might seem to be an abrupt shift as Paul again turns to the specifics of his itinerary, but the mention of his trip to Troas and the continuation of his journey as he travels to find Titus in Macedonia serve two purposes, one informational and the other having to do with the structure of the letter. From the standpoint of information, 2 Cor. 2:12–13 provides another plank in the defense Paul builds in explaining why he did not come to Corinth as previously planned. He writes that he was propelled north from Ephesus to Troas on a gospel mission. While there, two factors spurred him to travel on to Macedonia. First, when he did not find Titus in Troas, perhaps being worried that things had gone badly in Titus's trip to Corinth, Paul became restless in spirit. Second, however, it seems that the Lord had changed his travel plans by giving him an opportunity for ministry in Macedonia, a point that we will need to unpack in our treatment of the text. Add this to Paul's discernment that, given the state of things in Corinth, a premature trip back to that city would only exacerbate an already tense and difficult situation, and his explanation for his change in plans is complete. Hopefully this full explanation would help the Corinthians "understand" the dynamics that caused his change of itinerary and the fact that he had acted with integrity (1:12–13) and under the Lord's leadership.

Structurally, 2:12–13 frames the section on Paul's explanation concerning why he changed his itinerary, an explanation that started in earnest at 1:15–16. There he tells the Corinthians that he had intended to travel to them first, planning to pass through Corinth on the way to Macedonia and again to travel to them from Macedonia. In 2:12–13 he again talks about Macedonia as important to his itinerary, and the language of geographical movement, "coming" and "going," plays a key role. Thus Paul starts and ends his rigorous defense of his actions with statements concerning his specific itinerary.

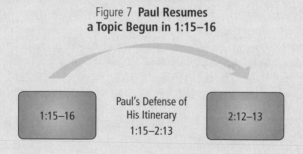

Figure 7 **Paul Resumes a Topic Begun in 1:15–16**

| 1:15–16 | Paul's Defense of His Itinerary 1:15–2:13 | 2:12–13 |

Moreover, 2 Cor. 2:12–13 also forms a wonderfully crafted transition that both opens the way for what follows in 2:14–17 and yet anticipates the resumption of the travel narrative at 7:5–6.[2] Both 2:12–13 and 7:5–6 make reference to the apostle coming to Macedonia, to the apostle not having rest (ἔσχηκεν ἄνεσιν, *eschēken anesin*), and to Titus. This structural framing of the great center section of the book, in which Paul presents a profound discourse on the nature of authentic ministry, demonstrates a rhetorical crafting of 2 Corinthians that must be grasped in order to deal adequately with the question of the book's unity.[3]

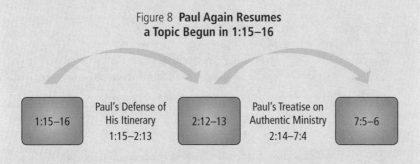

Figure 8 **Paul Again Resumes a Topic Begun in 1:15–16**

Further, as demonstrated by the diagram that follows,[4] conjunctions evenly divide the unit into three movements, the first and last addressing respectively Paul's move to Troas and the trip on to Macedonia. At the

2. I refer to this transition technique elsewhere as "distant hook words" (see Guthrie 1994: 96–100). With distant hook words, an author resumes an earlier discussion in a discourse, clearly marking the resumption with distinct parallel elements shared by the two passages. For another reading of the transition here, see Barnett (1997: 133). On this reading, 2:14–7:4 is a *digressio*, a "digression" that Paul sets in high relief with the travel narrative (Matera 2003: 64). Murphy-O'Connor (1985: 102) has attributed the digression to Paul's thought patterns naturally moving from Macedonia, to the health of the Macedonian churches, then to the nature of apostolic ministry; yet something more rhetorically strategic seems to be in mind. In ancient oratory, digressions were used, not to distract from the main topic at hand, but rather to rivet the attention (Quintilian, *Inst.* 4.3.14–17). So the digression from 2:14–7:4 must not be read as off topic. Rather, greater focus is afforded this great central section of the book, which addresses the nature of authentic ministry, by the "brackets" framing it. The travel narrative leaves off at the end of 2:13 and then resumes at 7:5, not because letter fragments have been stitched together randomly, but as a result of the apostle crafting the letter in a way that would highlight both the reasons for his change in itinerary and his theological reflections on the nature of authentic ministry.

3. Failing to grasp the significant structural roles played by 2:12–13, Héring (1958: 32), e.g., suggests that these verses originally went before 7:5–16, and Windisch and Strecker (1970: 93) say that 2:12–13 should come after 2:4.

4. The diagram that follows places the main clauses on the far left. Conjunctions are indented from the left margin, and both participle clauses and prepositional phrases are indented after the verbs they delimit. When the passage is grammatically diagrammed, one immediately notices three sets of parallels in the passage: (1) the balance of Ἐλθὼν . . . εἰς τὴν Τρῳάδα at the beginning and ἐξῆλθον εἰς Μακεδονίαν at the end of the unit; (2) the parallel εἰς prepositional phrases in 2:12; and (3) the parallelism between τῷ πνεύματί μου and τῷ μὴ εὑρεῖν με Τίτον τὸν ἀδελφόν μου in 2:13.

center of 2:12–13, then, stands "the open door" and Paul's confession of restlessness:

> Now (δὲ, *de*)
>> when I came (Ἐλθὼν, *elthōn*)
>>> to the region of Troas (εἰς τὴν Τρῳάδα, *Trōada*)
>>> for the gospel of Christ (εἰς τὸ εὐαγγέλιον τοῦ Χριστοῦ, *eis to euangelion tou Christou*),
> and then (καὶ, *kai*)
>>> a door of opportunity having been opened to me by the Lord (θύρας μοι ἀνεῳγμένης ἐν κυρίῳ, *Thyras moi aneōgmenēs en kyriō*),
>> I found no rest (οὐκ ἔσχηκα ἄνεσιν, *ouk eschēka anesin*)
>>> in my spirit (τῷ πνεύματί μου, *tō pneumati mou*)
>>> since I did not find my brother Titus (τῷ μὴ εὑρεῖν με Τίτον τὸν ἀδελφόν μου, *tō mē heurein me Titon ton adelphon mou*),
>> on the contrary (ἀλλὰ, *alla*),
>>> having told them good-bye (ἀποταξάμενος αὐτοῖς, *apotazamenos autois*),
>> I traveled (ἐξῆλθον, *exēlthon*)
>>> into Macedonia (εἰς Μακεδονίαν, *eis Makedonian*).

Notice that there are two main clauses in the passage, translated, "I found no rest" (οὐκ ἔσχηκα ἄνεσιν) and "I traveled" (ἐξῆλθον). It seems, then, that the focus of the passage is on the apostle's restlessness that played a part in his moving from Troas on to Macedonia. Thus understood, the travel itinerary seems to unfold in three steps:

a. The trip to Troas (2:12a)
b. Paul's restlessness: An open door and an absent coworker (2:12b–13a)
c. The trip to Macedonia (2:13b)

Let's consider the details of Paul's narrative.

Exegesis and Exposition

¹²Now when I came to the region of Troas for the gospel of Christ, and then a door of opportunity having been opened to me by the Lord, ¹³I found no rest in my spirit since I did not find my brother Titus; on the contrary, having told them good-bye, I traveled into Macedonia.

a. The Trip to Troas (2:12a)

2:12a   The conjunction δέ (*de*) is mildly contrastive and marks the beginning of a new unit as the apostle transitions from his exhortation for the Corinthians to forgive and embrace the offender who had caused so much pain (2:5–11).

Now Paul refers to his trip to Troas with the aorist participle Ἐλθὼν (*Elthōn*), and it probably should be understood as temporal ("when I came"), simply associating the apostle's restlessness with a particular time and place.[5] The reference to "Troas" is articular (τὴν Τρῳάδα, *tēn Trōada*) and may refer to the region as a whole (as suggested by Thrall 1994: 182–83; see the additional note on 2:12). But the article is also used at Acts 20:6, where the city probably is in view (Furnish 1984: 168). In any case, the importance of the city of Troas to Paul's travels finds ample expression in Acts, and the city was strategic geographically from the standpoint of travel. Thus there is little doubt that the city, which Strabo calls "one of the notable cities of the world" (*Geogr.* 13.1.26), was a focus of Paul's time in the area.

Troas was the main seaport in Mysia in northwest Asia Minor and had a population of about 30,000–40,000. The city had been founded before 300 BC by Antigonus, a successor to Alexander the Great, and was located about 10 miles south-southwest of the city of Troy (Ilium). It was not until Augustus made the city a Roman colony that the designation "Troas" became its commonly used name. The city was in a strategic location since it was used to reach Neapolis in Macedonia, from which the Via Egnatia (a major Roman highway) could be taken toward Rome. Thus it was an ideal spot for ministry that would have a high impact in that part of the world. On one occasion while in Troas, Paul had had a vision of a man from Macedonia who pleaded with him to bring the gospel to what we now call Europe (Acts 16:8–11), and the apostle's trips often took him through this city in his travels. Perhaps for some years Paul had desired to do more extensive ministry in the Troas (or Troad) region (Acts 20:5–13; 2 Tim. 4:13; Barnett 1997: 134; *HBD* 1374; *NBD* 1211–12).

Although he may have been driven out of Ephesus (Acts 19:23–41; Harris 2005: 236), Paul tells us what primarily brought him to Troas: he came there "for the gospel of Christ" (εἰς τὸ εὐαγγέλιον τοῦ Χριστοῦ,[6] *eis to euangelion tou Christou*), the preposition εἰς marking the purpose or desired end for which the apostle made the trip.[7] This partly explains why he had traveled some 250 miles to the north, away from Corinth and the Corinthians who awaited his arrival, on a route that almost tripled the miles he would have traveled if he had gone to the Corinthians directly by ship. Christ's gospel demanded it. Paul is not under his own authority but, rather, is a man under Christ's authority. He does not serve his own cause but the cause of the gospel.[8] Thus ministry at times demands flexibility, a willingness to move in unexpected ways under the

---

5. The adverbial participle delimits the perfect active indicative verb ἔσχηκα (*eschēka*, I have/found), from ἔχω (*echō*, have).

6. The genitive τοῦ Χριστοῦ probably should be considered an objective genitive, that is, the "gospel about Christ."

7. Barrett (1973: 94–95) suggests that Paul has gone to Troas out of anxiety that perhaps bandits have waylaid Titus on the road. However, Paul's statement is clear: he did not go primarily to find Titus, but rather "for the gospel."

8. References to the gospel occur seven times in the rest of the letter: 4:3–4; 8:18; 9:13; 10:14; 11:4, 7.

Lord's leadership. The call to go north for the sake of the gospel preempted the apostle sticking to a previously communicated itinerary, and this insight forms the capstone to his defense of his changed itinerary.

b. Paul's Restlessness: An Open Door and an Absent Coworker (2:12b–13a)

2:12b–13a   Paul continues with a grammatically interesting explanation that we translate, "and then a door of opportunity having been opened by the Lord" (καὶ θύρας μοι ἀνεῳγμένης ἐν κυρίῳ, *kai thyras moi aneōgmenēs en kyriō*).[9] It may be that the "open door" refers to the warm reception the apostle received in Troas (Harris 2005: 237), but the text may be read a bit differently, as we shall see in a moment. Notice that Paul did not open the door, but it was opened for him (a passive form of the participle), specifically "by the Lord" (ἐν κυρίῳ, *en kyriō*). So Paul was acting on an authority higher than his own. Elsewhere the apostle uses the imagery of the "open door" at 1 Cor. 16:9 and Col. 4:3, and it is used likewise at Rev. 3:8. In Paul's use the word picture speaks of opportunity for the advancement of the gospel. *Where* was the opportunity of which he writes? To answer that question we need to consider the role played by the conjunction καί (*kai*).

Commentators almost universally understand Paul's opportunity to refer to ministry in Troas (e.g., Barnett 1997: 135; Lambrecht 1999: 33); some suggest that the καί be read concessively ("although a door stood open"; so, e.g., Barrett 1973: 94; Harris 2005: 235; ESV, NET). Upon this reading, Paul came to Troas and had a wide-open opportunity for ministry there. Yet, upon not finding his coworker Titus, he became restless in spirit as he worried about the outcome of Titus's mission in Corinth. So he pushed on to Macedonia, thinking perhaps that it was too late in the season for Titus to travel by sea. The grammar of the passage certainly can be read in this way. Yet would Paul really abandon a fruitful opportunity for the gospel because of discomfort over not finding Titus? It could be, as some suggest, that he communicates in this way for rhetorical effect (i.e., "you Corinthians have disrupted effective ministry by your relational mess!").

However, the καί could be considered as continuative, as communicating a consecutive event: "and then a door of opportunity having been opened to me by the Lord." Read in this way, the open door came subsequent to Paul's arrival in Troas. Now that open door *could* refer to opportunities in the Troad region. But the text could also be understood as referring to an open door to move on to Macedonia.[10] Read in this way, the apostle learned of an opportunity for significant ministry *in Macedonia*, and his restlessness was due *both* to the

---

9. The construction is a genitive absolute, which often communicates a temporal idea (D. Wallace 1996: 654–55). Further, the participle ἀνεῳγμένης is perfect passive in form, indicating a present state of affairs relative to the situation spoken of in the context.

10. The stative aspect of the participle indicates that Paul is grappling with an open opportunity staring him in the face.

opportunity and the absence of his coworker.[11] The main clause "I found no rest in my spirit" (οὐκ ἔσχηκα ἄνεσιν τῷ πνεύματί μου, *ouk eschēka anesin tō pneumati mou*), is flanked by the "open door" and by Titus's absence:

> A door of opportunity having been opened to me by the Lord,
> I *found no rest* in my spirit
> since I did not find my brother Titus.

It is clear that the apostle's restlessness of spirit continued until he met Titus in Macedonia (7:5–6). Could it be that the door opened by the Lord was for his departure to Macedonia, perhaps to go there to further his gospel ministry, and his unrest in not finding Titus led Paul to act on the opportunity? We do not know why Titus had been delayed in his travel, but it seems obvious that Paul had expected his younger fellow minister and was disturbed when he did not turn up on time. In any case, the apostle's statement that he "found no rest" is telling and adds to an overall picture of Paul being upset over the situation with the Corinthians (Thrall 1994: 186). However, it may also be that opportunity in Macedonia beckoned to him, as suggested by the glowing report of the churches in Macedonia at 8:1–4. The opportunity, however, coincided with great affliction (7:5), as ministry opportunity often does.

c. The Trip to Macedonia (2:13b)

The final clause of verse 13 is connected to what goes before by the contrastive conjunction ἀλλά (*alla*). Furnish (1984: 170) suggests that the contrast is with the previously mentioned "open door," and this may be. But after a negative, ἀλλά can mean "on the contrary" or "rather," and it may be that the apostle contrasts "not finding rest" and moving on to Macedonia, the two independent clauses in the unit: "I found no rest in my spirit . . . ; on the contrary, . . . I traveled into Macedonia." Those to whom he said "good-bye" (ἀποταξάμενος αὐτοῖς, *apotaxamenos autois*) must refer to the believers in Troas (see Acts 18:18, 21). As Barnett explains, travel was greatly affected by the seasons of the year. Perhaps winter had set in and closed the seas to travel by ship (except for coastal travel). The apostle knew that if Titus had not arrived at that point, his young associate would need to travel overland. So Paul moved north to Macedonia (Barnett 1997: 136–37). Hopefully, having read the extensive explanation we have as 2 Cor. 1:15–2:13, the Corinthians understood why.

2:13b

Reflection

There are a couple of points of which we should take special note as we consider 2 Cor. 2:12–13. First, however his detractors in Corinth read the

---

11. The τῷ μὴ εὑρεῖν με Τίτον τὸν ἀδελφόν μου (*tō mē heurein me Titon ton adelphon mou*, since I did not find my brother Titus) is the only place in the NT where we have the articular infinitive + the dative communicating cause (BDF 207).

situation, Paul's change of plans coincided with his engagement in gospel mission. For us, this does not mean that ministry can be used as an excuse for not keeping one's commitments, or that relationships can be sacrificed on the altar of ministry (too many families have played the role of sacrificial lambs due to such a perspective). But gospel ministry at times demands flexibility, both on the part of ministers and on the part of those in their network of relationships. Such flexibility demands maturity and good communication. Notice that Paul seems to work very hard at communicating with the Corinthians, some of whom have been offended by his decisions, *for the sake of the gospel in Corinth as well* (11:1–6). So all that he does, whether adjusting his travel plans or explaining why he has done so, is for the sake of the gospel.

Second, the leadership of the Lord and the purposefulness of gospel ministry are not guarantees of emotional peace. Paul was unsettled when Titus did not show up in Troas, and his initial experiences in Macedonia were anything but peaceful (7:5). God encouraged the apostle when Titus finally showed up, but 2 Corinthians evinces a great deal of anxiety on Paul's part (e.g., 1:8–9; 11:27–28). He was not debilitated by it, but he was affected, driven to deeper dependence on God. Thus we should not read a lack of emotional peace as an indication that God has not led us in our ministries. We sometimes are led to difficult places for the sake of the gospel. Anxiety may simply be a normal part of life in such places.

Additional Note

2:12. Since the article is normally omitted in the use of place names, and Paul normally omits the article when speaking of cities, there is some debate concerning whether τὴν Τρῳάδα refers to the city of Troas or the surrounding region, called "the Troad." Harris points out that the city's full designation was Ἀλεξάνδρεια (ἡ) Τρῳάς ("the Trojan Alexandria"), so the word Τρῳάς serves an adjectival function, requiring the article. Of the six references to Troas in the NT, two have an article (Acts 20:6; 2 Cor. 2:12),[12] and these two can be explained as referring back to a previous reference to the city, either in the text (in the case of Acts 20:6) or in a mutually understood fact (as here in 2:12, since it is assumed the Corinthians had known Titus was to meet Paul at Troas). Further, Harris suggests, it would be more likely that Paul would designate a city where he and Titus would meet, rather than the more general region (Barrett 1973: 93–94; Harris 2005: 236; Windisch and Strecker 1970: 94).

Yet, Thrall demurs regarding this interpretation, suggesting that the region is in view. She reasons that the articular form may indeed indicate that the region as a whole is in view: when the apostle refers to cities or towns, he almost always omits the article[13] but normally includes it when referring to broader areas.[14] She notes that the primary objection to interpreting this as referring to the region is that Paul is speaking of the city as the place he had planned to meet

12. The four anarthrous occurrences are Acts 16:8, 11; 20:5; 2 Tim. 4:13.
13. As with Antioch at Gal. 2:11; Damascus at 2 Cor. 11:32; Gal. 1:17; Ephesus at 1 Cor. 15:32; 16:8; and Jerusalem at Rom. 15:19; 1 Cor. 16:3; Gal. 1:17; etc.
14. Thus Asia at Rom. 16:5; 2 Cor. 1:8; Achaia at 1 Cor. 16:15; and Macedonia and Achaia at 1 Thess. 1:7.

Titus, and that he would not have been so ambiguous in referring to their meeting place as to name a whole region. Yet she goes on to point out that in 7:5–6 the apostle is equally vague in referring to Macedonia as the place where they eventually met. That they had specific cities upon which they had agreed does not necessitate that Paul refer to those cities in the letter (Thrall 1994: 182–83).

B. Paul's Reflections on Authentic Ministry (2:14–7:4)

After the salutation (1:1–2) and prologue (1:3–11) open the door to 2 Corinthians, and the apostle's defense of his changed itinerary (1:12–2:13) moves the reader into the entrance hall, at 2:14 we step into the very heart of the letter's structure. The section reaching from 2:14 to 7:4 exudes a theological richness and depth of reflection on the nature of Christian ministry unparalleled in the NT. Some commentators tag 2:14–7:4 as a digression (Harris 2005: 240; P. Hughes 1962: 76), and the term applies in the sense of a shift in topic that will come back eventually to its point of departure. For Paul brackets the whole of 2:14–7:4 by references to Titus, Macedonia, and his own restlessness (2:12–13; 7:5–7). Yet the term "digression" must not be taken to mean "off topic."[1] Indeed, the section grounds the whole of 2 Corinthians, giving the letter its theological center of gravity.

Since Paul abruptly leaves off speaking about Titus at 2:12–13 and as abruptly resumes the topic at 7:5–7, some scholars deem this section a piecemeal fragment in some editor's literary patchwork (see the section on "One Letter, Two, or More?" in the introduction). Yet this powerful treatise on the nature of authentic ministry integrates purposefully with the whole of chapters 1–7, building on Paul's explanation of recent events and building toward his assault on the "false apostles" (2 Cor. 10–13; see Keener 2005: 163). As Matera (2003: 66) puts it, in this movement of the book, Paul offers the Corinthians "a compelling reason to boast in him as their apostle rather than to criticize and compare him unfavorably with the intruding apostles who have come to Corinth, with whom he will deal in chapters 10–13."

The opponents of Paul had claimed superiority in public presentation (1 Cor. 2:1; 2 Cor. 10:10), but Paul provides a poignant treatment of the theological, ethical, and spiritual superiority of true Christian ministry, which exhibits a posture of submission to God, is lived out with integrity before people, and is

---

1. Ancient rhetoric applauded the strategic use of *digressio*. Digressions were used in ancient oratory, not to distract from the main topic at hand, but rather to refresh the hearer in the midst of a logically developing argument and to rivet the attention with supportive but varied material. Quintilian (*Inst.* 4.3.14–17) writes of effective digressions:

> There are so many different ways of diverging from the straight path of a speech. . . . When these are subordinate to Arguments involving similar subjects, they are not felt as Digressions, because they cohere with the whole; but many such passages are inserted with no such coherence with the context, and serve to refresh, admonish, placate, plead with, or praise the judge. Such things are countless. . . . One who breaks off in the middle must get back quickly to the point where he left the main track. (Russell 2002: 291–93)

driven by the Spirit-empowered message of reconciliation. In 2:14–7:4, therefore, Paul appeals to the Corinthians via thoughtful reflection and testimony. The section consists of three primary movements: a treatment of the dynamics of authentic Christian ministry (2:14–4:6), the suffering intrinsic to authentic ministry (4:7–5:10), and finally, Paul's appeal to the Corinthians to respond appropriately to him and his ministry team as those who represent ministry as it should be lived out before God (5:11–7:4).

1. Paul Commends His Authentic Ministry (2:14–4:6)

In 2:14–4:6 Paul delineates the dynamics that identify an authentic ministry, earmarks that have characterized the apostle and his mission team. By setting before the Corinthians the distinguishing marks that contrast his ministry with that of the interlopers, Paul moves the Corinthians toward a proverbial fork in the road. Choosing to whom they will listen and whom they will follow is not a choice between valid expressions of Christian leadership. Rather, they choose between the valid and invalid, the Christ-sent and the self-promoting, the Spirit-endowed and the spiritually vacuous, the ministry of integrity and the work of hucksters (2:14–17).

Jan Lambrecht has demonstrated that Paul crafted the whole of 2:14–4:6 with a multilevel, chiastic structure built around contrasts (Bieringer and Lambrecht 1994: 257–94):[1]

A *Christian ministry* (2:14–3:6)
    a Ministers (2:14–17)
        b Corinthian community (3:1–3)
    a′ Ministers (3:4–6)
B *The two ministries* (3:7–18)
    1. Old and new ministries (3:7–11)
        a *A minori ad maius* reasoning (3:7–9)
            b Statement (3:10)
        a′ *A minori ad maius* reasoning (3:11)
    2. Moses and Paul, Israelites and Christians (3:12–18)
        a We (ministers; 3:12–13a [13b])
            b They (Israelites; 3:14–16 [17])
        a′ We (Christians; 3:18)
A′ *Christian ministry* (4:1–6)
    a We (ministers; 4:1–2)
        b They (Israelites; 4:3–4)
    a′ We (ministers; 4:5–6)

1. On the extensive lexical and conceptual parallels between 2:14–3:6 and 4:1–6, see the additional note on 2:14–16a. Bieringer and Lambrecht (1994) have been followed by numerous commentators, often with slight modifications (e.g., Garland 1999: 137–39; Harris 2005: 241; Thrall 1994: 189–90). For alternatives on this reading of the structure, see Belleville 1991: 177–79; Furnish 1984: 185–86.

Thus, in 2:14–4:6 Paul begins with a proclamation concerning the integrity and impact of true Christian ministry, progresses to a theological treatise contrasting two types of ministries, then returns to the topic of integrity and impact. On this reading, 3:7–18 provides the theological grounding for a ministry of integrity and impact as described in 2:14–3:6 and 4:1–6.

Yet this span of 2 Corinthians contains some of the more difficult exegetical conundrums in this difficult letter. The section begins with a riveting use of the Roman *pompa triumphalis*, an elaborate parade celebrating a victorious Roman general. Paul's itinerate ministry—and even the changes he has made in relation to his trips to Corinth—is not the helter-skelter wanderings of a confused and incompetent leader. Rather, Paul has made the decisions he has because he is being led by God. Paul uses this cultural icon of the triumph to paint a word picture depicting the impact made by authentic proclamation of God's word (2:14–16). A key question concerns what the apostle intends to communicate by this imagery, and the suggestions made by scholars on this point vary considerably. Yet it is clear that the picture of authentic ministry painted with the triumphal-procession imagery brings to Paul's mind the stark contrast between the ministry of preaching as carried out by his mission and that of hucksters who preach for profit (2:17).

Chapter 3 has been especially knotty for interpreters. Hays (1989: 123) states, "Unfortunately, 2 Corinthians 3, though squeezed and prodded by generations of interpreters, has remained one of the more inscrutable reflections of a man who had already gained the reputation among his near-contemporaries for writing letters that were 'hard to understand' (2 Pet. 3:16). It is hard to escape the impression that, to this day, when 2 Corinthians 3 is read a veil lies over our minds."[2] In that chapter Paul begins by contrasting letters of commendation (which he does not need) with the Corinthians themselves as a living letter (3:1–3), but then the image shifts as Paul draws a contrast between the new-covenant ministry of the Spirit and "the ministry of death, chiseled in letters on stone" (3:6).

With 3:7–18, the expositional heart of this section, the apostle takes up the veiling of Moses's face as recounted in Exod. 34 LXX. That old-covenant speaking of God's Word through a veil he contrasts with the new-covenant ministry in which the veil has been ripped away, with all God's people being transformed by the glory of the Lord (3:7–18). What does Paul intend by the contrast, and what is the significance of the veil imagery employed in 3:12–18? What does he mean at 3:17, where he says, "The Lord is the Spirit"? These are but a few of the questions we must address in the latter part of 2 Cor. 3.

In 4:1–6 the apostle returns to numerous themes from 2:14–3:6, as well as terminology used in 3:7–18. So 4:1–6 serves as somewhat of a conceptual net, pulling together numerous threads woven through the whole of the section. He writes of perseverance in integrity (4:1–2), of why the gospel is not grasped

---

2. Sloan (1995) agrees that 2 Cor. 3 contains special challenges for the interpreter but suggests that Hays (1989: 123) in part struggles to see through a veil of his own making.

by those on their way to destruction (4:3–4), and he addresses the true goal of Christian preaching (4:5–6). In this way 2 Cor. 4:1–6 serves as a powerful and appropriate conclusion on the dynamics that mark the authentic Christian ministry of Paul's mission.

Although 2:14–3:6 probably should be considered a single unit in terms of the book's structure[3]—indeed, it lies at the theological heart of the book[4]—there seems to be expositional benefit in unpacking the unit in two parts, 2:14–16a on the triumphal procession, and 2:16b–3:6 on adequacy for ministry.

3. Many of the words in 2:14–3:6 are echoed in 4:1–6, and therefore 2:14–3:6 seems to be a cohesive unit. In 2:14–3:6, Paul snatches a mix of word pictures from his world to depict clearly and concisely the integrity, impact, and qualifications necessary for true Christian ministry.

4. Concerning 2:14–3:3, Hafemann (1990b: 1–2) declares, "II Cor. 2:14–3:3, being part of the 'theological heart' of II Corinthians, is both a thesis-like compendium of Paul's self-conception as an apostle, as well as a classic presentation of his corresponding apologetic for the authority and validity of his apostolic ministry."

a. Led in Christ's Triumph (2:14–16a)

When speaking to my university students, it is a safe bet to incorporate into a lecture some analogy drawn from J. R. R. Tolkien's *Lord of the Rings*. The story hits so many life themes with which we can readily identify, and there are at least three reasons why Tolkein's ubiquitous trilogy, originally intended as one very long novel, works so well and appeals so much. First, it presents an epic clash between good and evil, populated with homey and humorous hobbits, set in contrast to the overwhelming darkness of Mordor. Second, in Frodo, the work presents us with an unexpected antihero, who wins the day not because of great skills but because of calling, integrity, relentless courage, and community (epitomized in Frodo's faithful friend, Samwise Gamgee). Third, the story works so well because one crystal clear objective for the antihero's story emerges. The whole tale is driven by the quest to get to Mordor, or better yet, the antiquest of getting rid of the ring. Frodo is not just wandering around the world. He is going somewhere particular, and he has a particular task. The clarity and integrity of his mission guide him even through the fogs of mind-numbing fatigue, brutal enemies, and growing terror of the Eye.

In our ministries in the world, we must come to grips deeply and clearly with our true purpose, our objective, our Mordor (and I know that some of the ministries in which we serve at times feel like Mordor). All kinds of objectives will present themselves as we go through life—whether comfort, money, popularity, fame, a position, academic recognition, book sales, or just survival—and we will be tempted constantly to wander about the world, searching for legitimacy, affirmation, comfort, reward, security, Twitter followers, "likes" on Facebook, hits to our blogs, and other forms of visibility that tell us we are OK, that we are significant. We need to have before us constantly why we are doing the things we are doing and what stands at the heart of our gospel calling. Here 2 Cor. 2:14–16a serves as an excellent, perspective-giving plumb line.

As we turn to the text of 2 Cor. 2:14–16a, we encounter at least three key interpretive issues.[1] First, what is the meaning of θριαμβεύω (*thriambeuō*; often translated as "lead in triumph")? Does Paul have a Roman triumphal procession in mind? If so, how does he use the imagery, and what is the extent of that imagery? Does it extend through 2:16, or does Paul shift to another metaphor? Second, what is the significance of the twin terms ὀσμή/εὐωδία (*osmē*/*euōdia*, aroma/fragrance) in the extended word picture? Are

---

1. For a more detailed, technical treatment of this passage, see Guthrie 2015.

the terms simply synonymous? Are these images used consistently, only in relation to the Roman triumph, or does Paul mix his metaphors, shifting to OT sacrificial imagery? Third, and most significant, where does Paul see himself and his ministry in this imagery, and what is the relationship between his metaphorical description of himself, his mission, and the other referents in the passage, most particularly "those being destroyed" and "those being saved"?

These verses are analyzed as follows:

i. Celebrating God's triumphant gospel (2:14a)
ii. Gospel ministry as incense bearing (2:14b–15a)
iii. The gospel as the dividing line of humanity (2:15b–16a)

Exegesis and Exposition

[14]Yet thanks be to God, who always leads us in triumphal procession in Christ and makes known through us the aroma of knowledge about him everywhere we go. [15]For we are a fragrance of Christ to God among those who are being saved and among those who are being destroyed. [16]To some we are a stench arising ⌜from⌝ death and leading to death, to others an aroma arising ⌜from⌝ life and leading to life.

i. Celebrating God's Triumphant Gospel (2:14a)

2:14a   As we have already seen, in 2:12–13 Paul recounts the restlessness he experienced when he did not find Titus in Troas and reports that this restlessness, and perhaps an opportunity for ministry, prompted him to continue on to Macedonia. With 2:14, however, the apostle shifts rather abruptly to an expression of thankfulness to God.[2] The "Yet" of our translation renders a contrastive use of δέ (de), highlighting the juxtaposition of Paul's unsettledness in Macedonia and his thankfulness for the continued work of God through his ministry.[3] Paul has great confidence that the events of his life are under the Lord's direction. He is not simply wandering around the Mediterranean, as some of his opponents have probably suggested. Rather, he is led by God, under the triumphant lordship of Christ, for the cause of the gospel. The phrase translated as "thanks be to God" (τῷ . . . θεῷ χάρις, tō . . . theō charis) also occurs in various configurations (Rom. 6:17; 7:25; 1 Cor. 15:57; 2 Cor. 8:16; 9:15),[4] each expressing gratefulness for some aspect of God's work. The

2. Thrall has made a strong case for the strategic nature of this shift (Thrall 1982; 1994: 20–25), placing the burden of proof on those who suggest that the shift points to a letter fragment running from 2:14–7:4. On the strategic use of *digressio*, see Keener 2005: 163–64.

3. Indeed, Paul's thankfulness at 2:14 anticipates the resumption of his travel narrative at 7:5–7 and the relief expressed there, relief both from seeing Titus and from hearing his good news concerning the Corinthians' response to Titus's ministry.

4. In four of the six occurrences τῷ θεῷ follows χάρις, but here as in 1 Cor. 15:57, the order is reversed. Moving τῷ θεῷ forward could be for emphasis, but the order may simply be literary variation. It is difficult to discern a comparatively heightened emphasis on God here and

term χάρις had a broad range of meanings in the first century, communicating, for instance, graciousness, attractiveness, favor, grace, help, or as here, an attitude of thankfulness. So Paul suddenly erupts with an expression of thanks to God. Further, he expresses a foundational reason he is thankful to God with τῷ πάντοτε θριαμβεύοντι ἡμᾶς ἐν τῷ Χριστῷ (*tō pantote thriambeuonti hēmas en tō Christō*, who always leads us in triumphal procession in Christ).

Here is where interpretation of this passage becomes a bit dicey: scholars are anything but unified when it comes to the meaning and significance of the word θριαμβεύω. Generally speaking, most agree that what Paul has in mind, in some way, is the Roman parade, given to a triumphant general, upon an especially significant victory on behalf of Rome. A few scholars, such as Egan (1977), demur, suggesting, for instance, that Paul has some other cultural image in mind. But both the extensive, normal use of the verb (mostly in the form of a participle or an infinitive) and its cognate noun in the Greco-Roman world, plus the widespread public reports of the *pompa triumphalis* as a major cultural artifact,[5] have rightly overruled such suggestions.

So first of all, in crafting his word picture, Paul clearly has in mind the Roman practice of triumphal processions, elaborate parades celebrating victory, in which a Roman general was the focus of attention (P. Marshall 1983; Versnel 1970; Williamson 1968). As described in Versnel's monograph, which has now become a modern classic on the topic, the main components of such a procession were as follows. Of the triumphator himself, Versnel (1970: 56–57) writes:

> The victorious general whom the senate had granted the right to a triumph, entered Rome standing on a high, two-wheeled chariot, the *currus triumphalis*, which was drawn by four horses. Under the chariot, which was decorated with laurel-branches, a phallos had been fastened, whilst reports moreover speak of bells and whips being tied to the chariot. The triumphator is clothed in the *vestis triumphalis*: the *tunica palmata*—thus called after the palm-branches embroidered on it—and the *toga picta*, a name it owed to its rich embroidery, according to Appian, in the form of gold stars. Both garments were purple, and there is reason to assume that originally the toga was purple all over and that the gold-coloured ornaments were a later addition. On his head the triumphator, and his military suite, wore the *corona laurea*, the symbol of the triumph, and for this reason often called *corona triumphalis*.

Later in the monograph, Versnel (1970: 95) describes aspects of the parade itself:

> The part of the procession which entered the city ahead of the triumphator's chariot gave the spectators an idea of the victory. Not only were spoils of war carried along—weapons, gold, silver and jewellery—but also pictures of battle-scenes, of towns conquered, and boards with the names of the peoples

---

at 1 Cor. 15:57. Rather, the phrase as a whole, in whichever configuration, communicates an expression of thankfulness to God.

5. E.g., Plutarch, *Aem.* 5.5; 35.2; *Ti. C. Gracch.* 2.17.1; *Mar.* 24.1; 27.5; Appian, *Bell. civ.* 2.13.93; 4.6.38.

subjugated. . . . The gifts of honour presented by the conquered peoples, originally laurel-wreaths, later on gold wreaths, were shown. White oxen, to be
sacrificed to Iuppiter, were brought along. The procession marched to a flourish
of trumpets. . . . Aromatic substances were also carried. The chained prisoners,
the most prominent of whom were as a rule killed in the dungeon before the
sacrifice was made to Iuppiter, walked right in front of the *currus triumphalis*.
The triumphator was preceded by the lictors in red war dress with *laureate fas-
ces*. The magistrates and the senate also walked ahead of the chariot with the
triumphator and his small children. Older boys accompanied the triumphator
on horseback, as did his officers. The chariot was followed by the Romans who
had been liberated from slavery, wearing the pileus of the *liberti*. The soldiers,
wearing laurel-wreaths on their heads and singing songs deriding their com-
mander, brought up the rear.

Writers of ancient Greco-Roman literature record over three hundred such
processions, and depictions occur in paintings and plays and on coins, cups,
arches, statues, medallions, and columns of the era (P. Marshall 1983: 304),
demonstrating that the *pompa triumphalis* was part of the cultural fabric
of the time. This was, to draw an analogy from the American context, the
Super Bowl parade of the Greco-Roman world.[6] Thus the imagery as used
by Paul was widely recognized in first-century Corinth and serves as a potent
word picture.

The question remains, however, what precisely does Paul intend to communicate when he uses the word θριαμβεύω? We need to take some time in
unpacking this interpretive conundrum, for the import of the whole passage
rides on it. For a thorough summary of various positions on offer, see, for
example, Furnish (1984: 174–75) and Hafemann (1990b: 17–19), who reports,
"Almost all commentators since Findlay have simply chosen either to ignore the
significance of the meaning of the word altogether 'by vague generalizations
which rob the metaphor of all precision and vividness,' or to modify the meaning itself in order to bring it in line with their theological convictions" (18).

A look at a standard lexicon for NT Greek (BDAG 459) presents six possible
meanings of the word on offer in the history of interpretation:

1. to lead in triumphal procession (as a captive); or God's victory over hostile
   forces (Col. 2:15)
2. to lead in triumph (e.g., a general leading his troops; e.g., NASB[95])
3. to cause to triumph (e.g., Tyndale, KJV, Calvin, etc.)
4. to triumph over (Col. 2:15?)
5. expose to shame (e.g., P. Marshall 1983)
6. display, publicize, make known (e.g., HCSB)

    6. As one of my former students was carrying out her student teaching, her pupils asked if
she had watched the Super Bowl. When she replied no, they could hardly believe anyone was so
culturally illiterate! The Super Bowl and its parade are ubiquitously known in modern American
culture, just as the triumphal procession was woven into the public consciousness of the Greco-
Roman world of Paul's time.

This array of nuances is reflected in the various ways the term finds expression in modern English translations of 2 Cor. 2:14:

has made us his captives and continues to lead us along in Christ's triumphal procession (NLT[2])

who always leads us as captives in Christ's triumphal procession (NIV)

For in union with Christ we are always led by God as prisoners in Christ's victory procession (GNT)

who in Christ always leads us in triumphal procession (ESV)

God leads us from place to place in one perpetual victory parade. (Message)

who always leads us in triumphal procession in Christ (NET)

who always leads us in triumph in Christ (NASB[95])

thankes be vnto God which alwayes geveth vs the victorie in Christ (Tyndale)

Now thankes be unto God, which always maketh us to triumph in Christ (Geneva)

which always causeth us to triumph in Christ (KJV)

God always makes it possible for Christ to lead us to victory (CEV)

who always marches us to victory under the banner of the Anointed One (Voice)

who always puts us on display in Christ (HCSB)

Duff (1991) has proposed that the image is intentionally complex, even ambivalent, and to a certain extent this may account for the wide variety of understandings of this image. Nevertheless, many recent interpreters have embraced one of the several variations on the first of BDAG's options, suggesting that Paul depicts himself as a defeated captive paraded by God through the world. For example, Thrall (1994: 194–95), Harris (2005: 243), Hafemann (1990b: 10–34), Garland (1999: 142–43), and Witherington (1995: 367–68) all affirm this interpretation in some form. Hafemann (1990b: 23–34), in line with a brutal aspect of the ancient processions, goes so far as to suggest that Paul presents himself as being led to death, since the most notorious captives often[7] were sacrificed to Jupiter at a strategic point in the procession. Barnett (1997: 148–51), who also sees the image as pointing to the prisoners of war in the parade, nevertheless understands the image as complex, communicating aspects of both triumph and antitriumph, both victory and the humiliation of suffering. Further, he rightly emphasizes that the triumph must be read in conjunction with the images of aroma and fragrance.

Furnish (1984: 173, a caveat on 175) understands the image primarily to communicate that the apostolic ministry involves one being put on public display, and P. Marshall (1983) emphasizes the nuance of social shame. Barrett disagrees with the Paul-as-captive interpretation: "In this verse he is describing

---

7. Beard (2007: 129–30) notes that actual accounts of captives being executed are infrequent.

himself and his colleagues as collaborating with God, and not as exposed by him to disgrace." In spite of the lack of lexical evidence, Barrett (1973: 98) proposes that the apostle depicts himself as a "victorious soldier" led along in the celebratory train of his victorious Lord.

So both translations and interpretations track along various lines of thought, but at present the dominant view seems to be that the apostle paints himself as a defeated captive, led along in chains and humiliation, in the cause of Christ. This interpretation rests on two foundation stones. First, accounts of the Roman Triumph in both Greek and Latin literature at times include the fate of the captives taken from the opposing army, and the treatment of the captives can form a centerpiece of the narrative. This is quite understandable. Those who had been conquered were an object of terror and hatred for what they would have done to Rome and her people if they had won the war. In ancient accounts, the relief on the part of the citizens of Rome is palpable, painted in rapturous detail.[8] Thus, central to the parade celebration was a gloating over the enemy. In some accounts, the leaders of the opposing side are front and center in the celebration. For instance, Strabo (*Geogr.* 12.3.6) writes of the fate of Adiatorix, tetrarch of the Galatians:

> But Adiatorix, the son of Domnecleius, tetrarch of the Galatians, received from Antony that part of the city which was occupied by the Heracleiotae; and a little before the Battle of Actium he attacked the Romans by night and slaughtered them, by permission of Antony, as he alleged. But after the victory at Actium he was led in triumph and slain together with his son. (Jones and Sterrett 1954: 379)

And Cicero (*Verr.* 5.77):

> Why, even triumphing generals, who keep enemy leaders alive for some time in order to have them led in the triumphal procession, so as to enable the people of Rome to enjoy the fine sight and reap the reward of victory—even they, as their chariots swing round to leave the Forum for the Capitol, bid their captives be led off to prison, and the day that ends the authority of the conqueror also ends the lives of the conquered. (Greenwood 1953: 555)

So in Greco-Roman literature, captives from the enemy army at times serve as a focal point in the descriptions of the triumphal procession, and those captives at times were killed at a culminating point of the parade.

---

8. Thus, e.g., Appian, *Pun.* 20.134:
   When the people of Rome saw the ship and heard of the victory early in the evening, they poured into the streets and spent the whole night congratulating and embracing each other like people just now delivered from some great fear; . . . no other war had so terrified them at their own gates as the Punic wars, which ever brought peril to them. . . . Pondering on these things, they were so excited over this victory that they could hardly believe it, and they asked each other over and over again whether it was really true that Carthage was destroyed. (H. White 1912: 639–40)

Laying a second interpretive foundation stone, scholars point out that in the Corinthian correspondence Paul emphasizes his position as apostle as a position of shame, compulsion, even captivity and death (P. Marshall 1983: 313–16). One thinks of 1 Cor. 4:9, "For I think that God has exhibited us apostles as last of all, like men sentenced to death, because we have become a spectacle to the world, to angels, and to men" (ESV); and of 2 Cor. 4:10, "We are always carrying around the death of Jesus in our bodies." Consequently, many today conclude that in 2 Cor. 2:14–16 Paul, having been conquered by the triumphant Christ, presents himself as one of the captives being led through the world in a parade of death for the sake of the gospel. The position makes sense in the broader context of 2 Corinthians, a letter so often focused on suffering in the course of ministry (Hafemann 2000: 109).

Yet through the centuries some, in spite of passages like 1 Cor. 4:9 and 2 Cor. 4:10, have struggled with this interpretation as theologically jarring. Why would the apostle depict himself in such a debased manner, as even an *enemy* of God? It is one thing to say that he had been God's enemy (Rom. 5:8, 10) and that he suffers humiliation on behalf of Christ, but quite another to suggest that Paul still lives in the status of a defeated enemy of God, even if speaking figuratively. Would this not be playing into the hands of the Corinthian opponents?

But aside from theological indigestion, the dominant interpretation at present does not rest easily with certain lexical and grammatical aspects of our passage, and we need to probe the details of the text to see if we might have other options for hearing the text well.

First, in terms of lexical and grammatical dynamics here, Hafemann (1990b: 31) suggests that the word θριαμβεύω "with prepositional phrases to indicate its object or with a direct object alone, *always* refers to the one who has been conquered and is subsequently led in the procession, and never to the one who has conquered or to those who have shared in his victory (e.g., his army, fellow officers, etc.)." Yet, we must evaluate Hafemann's assertion carefully, since our database of the verb being used in this grammatical construction is quite small, *at most* four to five instances out of over sixty occurrences of the verb, most of which are in participial form or rendered as an infinitive.[9] In fact,

---

9. In supporting his strongly worded statement, Hafemann (1986: 33) references only one example from Plutarch (*Comp. Thes. Rom.* 4.4), on which see below, and the 1968 article by Williamson (1968: 319–20), who in turn references the lexicons by Liddell and Scott and by Bauer. Williamson himself notes that the evidence when dealing with θριαμβεύω followed by a direct, *personal* [emphasis mine] object is "limited." In addition to Col. 2:15, he mentions Liddell and Scott's three cases from Greco-Roman literature (Plutarch, *Comp. Thes. Rom.* 4; *Cor.* 35; *Ant.* 84) and, in further discussion, two examples from Bauer's lexicon, both from Plutarch (*Pomp.* 83.3 [= *Agesilaus and Pompey* 3.2.10]; *Aratus* 54.8). Of these five references, the two noted in Bauer (Plutarch, *Pomp.* 83.3; *Aratus* 54.3 [54.8 is a misprint]) and Plutarch's *Comp. Thes. Rom.* 4 are the only texts that roughly match the pattern (θριαμβεύω in the active + direct object) that we find in 2 Cor 2:14. It should be noted, however, that *Comp. Thes. Rom.* 4 may not refer to captives being led in a triumphal procession parade. Further, Plutarch's *Cor.* 35.3 has a passive participle in the one instance, and in the second the object of the triumph occurs in a prepositional phrase. In

it simply is not true that this grammatical form is limited to cases involving captives in a procession,[10] and the vast majority of uses of the verb in Greco-Roman literature speak of a triumph without any reference to the captives at all. If we expand our data to include roughly synonymous phrases using the cognate noun,[11] which occurs extensively, and perhaps the corresponding Latin verb,[12] we find that *conceptually* triumphators often are depicted as leading diverse groups of people, not just doomed captives, in their triumphal parades.

For example, Plutarch (*Regum* 76.6–7), a Greek historian born north of Corinth in AD 46, writes of Scipio the Elder, a Roman general during the Second Punic War:

> When the Carthaginians had been utterly overthrown, they sent envoys to him to negotiate a treaty of peace, but he ordered those who had come to go away at once, refusing to listen to them before they brought Lucius Terentius. This Terentius was a Roman, a man of good talents, who had been taken prisoner by the Carthaginians. . . . Terentius marched behind him in the triumphal procession, wearing a felt cap just like an emancipated slave. (Babbitt 1927: 166–67)

Here Terentius, who had been enslaved by the Carthaginians and then was liberated by Scipio, was led by Scipio in triumphal procession. Terentius marched in honor of "the Roman Hannibal," as Scipio was sometimes called, celebrating his newfound freedom. Many other examples could be given, and I will offer a few more below.

For now, let me emphasize that contextually—in the broader descriptions of the parade in texts such as those by Appian, Plutarch, Livy, Josephus, Dionysius, and Juvenal—multifarious descriptions of the participants in the triumphal procession parades are made abundantly clear.[13] So it is not the case

---

Plutarch's *Ant.* 84.4 Cleopatra (via a passive participle) enjoins Antony not to allow himself to have a triumph celebrated over him in her person (μηδ᾽ ἐν ἐμοὶ περῐ́δῃς θριαμβευόμενον σεαυτόν). To these we join Breytenbach (1990) in adding Appian (*Bell. Mith.* 11.77) and Strabo (*Geogr.* 12.3.35), both of whom provide good examples of the θριαμβεύω + direct object construction. Yet, having reviewed all of the references, Breytenbach (1990: 262) concludes, "Only one relevant instance [he refers here to the text from Strabo] is known where the form θριαμβεύειν + τινά is used in an expression that undoubtedly refers to captives being led in triumph." His assessment may be a bit conservative, but it illustrates that we are dealing with a *very* limited body of data. Again, out of *over sixty* occurrences of the verbal forms of θριαμβεύω in Greco-Roman literature, *at best* we find four, or perhaps five, cases in which θριαμβεύω is used in a construction paralleling Paul's use in 2 Cor 2.14 to refer to captives in a triumphal procession.

10. The pattern of θριαμβεύω + a direct object (though not a personal object) is also found in several places in the literature without reference to the defeated captives in the parade (e.g., Plutarch, *Regum* 82.22; *Max. princ.* 23.2.1; Appian, *Bell. civ.* 2.15.101). Thus the statement that the verb "with prepositional phrases to indicate its object or with a direct object alone, *always* refers to the one who has been conquered and is subsequently led in the procession" does not hold true.

11. E.g., Plutarch, *Aem.* 30.1–2; 31.1; 32.1; *Ant.* 12.1.

12. E.g., Livy, *Hist. Rom.* 2.16.1; 3.63.9; Cicero, *Off.* 2.28.

13. E.g., Plutarch, *Mar.* 27.5–6; Appian, *Bell. civ.* 2.13.93; *Pun.* 9.66; Livy, *Hist. Rom.* 45.40; Juvenal, *Sat.* 10.38–45. Consequently, Hafemann (1990b: 33) simply overstates the case when

that when an ancient author uses the term or its cognates, one automatically and only thinks about the captives in the procession. In fact, Paul's emphasis seems to be elsewhere, as we see when we consider the structure and syntax of the passage. Note the structure:

δὲ (*de*, yet)
Τῷ . . . θεῷ χάρις (*tō . . . theō charis*, thanks be to God)

  πάντοτε (*pantote*, always)
τῷ . . . θριαμβεύοντι (*tō . . . thriambeuonti*, leading in triumphal
                                                                    procession)
    ἡμᾶς (*hēmas*, us)
    ἐν τῷ Χριστῷ (*en tō Christō*, in Christ)
καὶ (*kai*, and)
    τὴν ὀσμὴν τῆς γνώσεως αὐτοῦ (*tēn osmēn tēs gnōseōs
                      autou*, the aroma of knowledge about him)
  φανεροῦντι (*phanerounti*, manifesting)
    δι' ἡμῶν (*di' hēmōn*, through us)
    ἐν παντὶ τόπῳ· (*en panti topō*, everywhere we go)
ὅτι (*hoti*, for)

Χριστοῦ (*Christou*, of Christ)
εὐωδία ἐσμὲν (*euōdia esmen*, we are a fragrance)
τῷ θεῷ (*tō theō*, to God)
      ἐν τοῖς σῳζομένοις (*en tois sōzomenois*, among those
                                          being saved)
      καὶ (*kai*, and)
      ἐν τοῖς ἀπολλυμένοις (*en tois apollymenois*, among those
                              who are being destroyed).
        οἷς μὲν ὀσμὴ ἐκ θανάτου εἰς θάνατον (*hois
              men osmē ek thanatou eis thanaton*,
              to some we are like a stench arising
              from death and leading to death),
        οἷς δὲ ὀσμὴ ἐκ ζωῆς εἰς ζωήν (*hois de osmē ek
              zōēs eis zōēn*, to others an aroma aris-
              ing from life and leading to life).

Observe several things about the way the apostle has crafted his text. First, the present participles τῷ . . . θριαμβεύοντι and φανεροῦντι are parallel

he says that "all the evidence points to the conclusion that there is only one basic and common meaning for this term available in the time of Paul, namely, that of the triumphal procession in which the conquered enemies were usually led as slaves to death, being spared this death only by an act of grace on the part of the one celebrating the triumph." Hafemann is correct that the term was used of the triumphal procession (though it was also used more generally of simply "winning a victory" over someone), but suggesting that the verb was primarily meant to communicate leading a captive in the parade to death overreaches the evidence.

grammatically and offer descriptions of God (Τῷ . . . θεῷ). The first of these participles is delimited by three elements. God "always" (πάντοτε) leads Paul and his mission in triumphal procession. The ministry and God's leadership over the ministry encompass the whole of the apostle's life. This is no part-time endeavor. Further, Paul says that God leads "us" (ἡμᾶς), referring to himself and his mission, and Paul and his team are led "in Christ" (ἐν τῷ Χριστῷ), perhaps speaking of his ministry as being grounded in his relationship to Christ as the ultimate cause of the mission (C. Campbell 2012: 143).

Concerning the phrase ἐν τῷ Χριστῷ, Scott (1996: 265–70) has offered a critical corrective, insisting that the metaphor of "triumphing" foundationally speaks of God as the triumphator, a point too often neglected in the history of interpretation. Scott helpfully draws a parallel between the triumphator's chariot in the *pompa triumphalis* and God's throne chariot in Jewish tradition, a throne chariot early Christianity conceived as *shared with the Christ in exercising sovereignty over the world*.[14] So when Paul crafts his word picture, stating that God leads the Pauline mission in triumphal procession "in Christ," he expresses a theology of God's sovereign victory in Christ through the gospel (cf. Rev. 5:8–13) and Christ's leading of the mission as its Lord (2 Cor 1:1; 2:12; 4:5). After all, the glory of God is seen in the face of Christ (2 Cor. 4:6). We suggest, therefore, that Christ is identified with God as triumphator in Paul's metaphor. As the Roman Triumph proclaimed the glory of the triumphator, so the Pauline mission proclaims knowledge about Christ.

In parallel fashion, the second participle, φανεροῦντι, also is delimited by three elements in the sentence. The object of the manifestation is "the aroma of knowledge about [Christ]" (τὴν ὀσμὴν τῆς γνώσεως αὐτοῦ). This aroma is manifested "through us" (δι' ἡμῶν), again a reference to Paul and the mission team, and the manifestation occurs "everywhere we go" (ἐν παντ' τόπῳ). Further, although the participle φανεροῦντι could be taken as adverbial—communicating the result of the first participle or, perhaps, the circumstances surrounding it—we read the construction as an example of Sharp's rule of the article, understanding φανεροῦντι as substantival. God is the one both leading in triumphal procession and manifesting the aroma. So our translation reads, "Yet thanks be to God, who always leads us in triumphal procession in Christ and makes known through us the aroma of knowledge about him everywhere we go."

Further, the present-tense form of the participles, with their imperfective aspect, in conjunction with πάντοτε (always) and the phrase ἐν παντὶ τόπῳ (in every place) highlight God's work through Paul and his ministry team in toto, as a constant, ongoing work of God throughout the broader Mediterranean world. Thus the result of God leading Paul and his ministry team in triumphal procession is that God manifests through them τὴν ὀσμὴν τῆς

---

14. On Christ sharing God's throne as a mark of his identification with the one true God of Israel, see Bauckham 2008: 172–81.

γνώσεως αὐτοῦ (the "aroma" or "smell" of knowledge about him) in every place. Thus, the images of leading in triumphal procession and manifesting the aroma are directly associated, having to do with the proclamation of the gospel in the world. Generally, in the Corinthian correspondence, the term γνῶσις speaks of a more general knowledge about spiritual matters or truth.[15] Yet here, the "knowledge about him" is specifically knowledge about God's salvation, the light that "has shone in our hearts" through the glorious gospel seen in the face of Christ (2 Cor. 4:6; 10:5; see Luke 1:77–78).

ii. Gospel Ministry as Incense Bearing (2:14b–15a)

Second, from the structure of the passage it is clear that the dominant image in 2:14–16a, which permeates the whole of the passage, has to do with this "aroma" manifested by the ministry. The "aroma" (ὀσμή) is introduced in 2:14 and then expanded upon in 2:15–16a. Notice that ὅτι (*hoti*) constitutes the bridge from verse 14 to verses 15–16a. As with most translations, we render ὅτι as "for," taking it as causal but loosely so.[16] What then is the semantic relationship between these two parts of the passage?

2:14b–15a

The apostle specifically picks up on and expands the word picture of the manifestation of the aroma mentioned in verse 14, unpacking the effect of his ministry on those being saved and those being destroyed. Paul begins this unpacking with "we are a fragrance of Christ to God" (Χριστοῦ εὐωδία ἐσμὲν τῷ θεῷ, *Christou euōdia esmen tō theō*). The genitive "of Christ" (Χριστοῦ) may be a genitive of source (from Christ),[17] and the dative "to God" (τῷ θεῷ) a dative of termination. It is a fragrance (εὐωδία) that ultimately has its source in Christ and rises up to God. This imagery adds a directional dimension to Paul's word picture, for now the fragrance ascends to God. The apostle has not left the outward focus of the "aroma" of the gospel in 2:14, for in 2:15–16a the fragrance that rises up to God is also described as an aroma that has great impact on people in the world. Rather, the apostle has merely added to the metaphor, showing a profoundly close relationship between the "aroma" of the gospel itself and the pleasing "fragrance" of authentic apostolic ministry before God. In fact, the two are so closely associated as to be inseparable. Paul identifies himself and his ministry so closely with his message because his entire existence revolves around the proclamation of the crucified and risen Christ, and this ministry flows from a profound orientation to pleasing God. The correspondences and the slightly different directional orientation between 2:14 and 2:15–16a may be seen in figure 9.

15. See 1 Cor. 1:5; 8:1, 7, 10–11; 12:8; 13:2, 8; 14:6; 2 Cor. 6:6; 8:7; 11:6.

16. Robertson (1934: 962) notes that ὅτι often presents a rather loose form of subordination, bordering on parataxis, simply developing a thought with another point. Another option here is to read the ὅτι as introducing the *content* of that for which Paul gives thanks: "Yet thanks be to God . . . that we are a fragrance of Christ to God among those . . ." There are parallels to this reading of χάρις/εὐχαριστέω + τῷ θεῷ (or a reference to God) + ὅτι in the apostle's writings (e.g., Rom. 6:17; 1 Tim. 1:12; 1 Cor. 1:14).

17. It could also be an objective genitive, "about Christ" or perhaps "in celebration of Christ."

Figure 9 **Differing Directional Orientations**

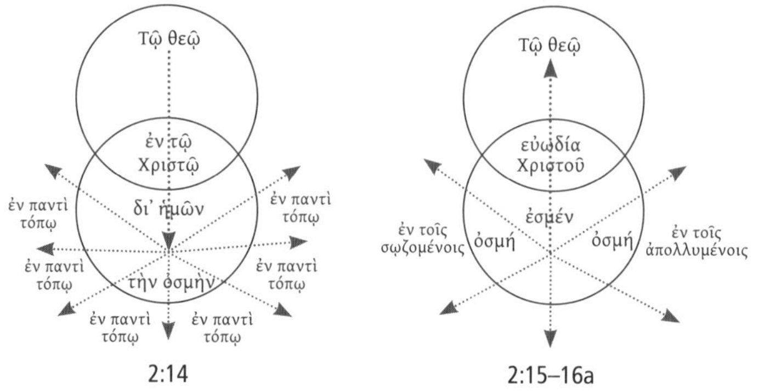

Further, the image of an aroma wafting out over people and simultaneously rising up to God is consistent with what we know of Roman triumphal processions of the era, and it is clear that incense played a significant role in such celebrations. In his description of the *pompa triumphalis* presented above, Versnel (1970: 95) notes that "Aromatic substances were also carried" in the parade. For instance, Appian describes features of the triumphal procession: "Next came *a large number of incense bearers*, and just after *the fragrances* the general himself on a chariot inscribed with various designs, wreathed with gold and precious stones . . ." (*Pun.* 9.66, my translation). In this case the incense bearers in the parade hold pride of place, marching right in front of the triumphator himself. Dionysius of Halicarnassus (*Rom. Ant.* 7.72.13) tells of the Roman triumph: "and after these groups of dancers came a crowd of lyre players and a lot of flute players, and after them the people taking care of the incense censers in which aromatic herbs and frankincense were burned to produce fragrant smoke along the whole route" (my translation). And in Horace's poetic *Odes* (4.2.50–51) we read of all the citizens of the city offering incense upon Caesar's triumphant return to the city:

> You will celebrate festivals and public
> games for the answer to the city's prayers,
> brave Augustus's return, and no lawsuits
> heard in the Forum.

> Then, if something I sing deserves hearing, my
> best voice will join in, and "O glorious
> sun, worthy of praise," I will gladly chant for
> Caesar's homecoming.

> As you lead the way, "Hail, God of Triumph,"
> we shall sing more than once, "Hail, God of Triumph,"
> all the citizens, and to the kind gods shall
> offer our incense.

Further, in Josephus's account of the *Jewish War* (7.72) we note that upon Vespasian's homecoming in Rome, he was called "Savior" (σωτῆρα, *sōtēra*), and the city was filled with incense like a temple (though admittedly this occurred in a general party atmosphere rather than a Triumph parade). In addition to these literary examples of the importance of incense in celebration of victory, the incense bearers as a significant part of the triumphal procession appear in art, such as the famous frieze on the Arch of Titus, in which people carrying incense baskets and burners appear.

In line with these data, we suggest that Paul overtly identifies himself and his gospel ministry not with the doomed captives of the triumphal procession but with the incense bearers, and we suggest that the word picture permeates the whole of 2:14–16a. A host of interpreters stand opposed to this reading of the text. For instance, based on the move in verse 15 to the "fragrance" of Paul's ministry rising up to God, along with the use of the semantically related terms ὀσμή and εὐωδία, Hafemann (1990b: 35–44) and others (e.g., Thrall 1994: 198; Harris 2005: 248) posit that Paul here, having begun with triumphal procession imagery, now shifts to the imagery of OT sacrifice. To evaluate this interpretation, we need to probe the use of the terms ὀσμή and εὐωδία in the literatures of the ancient world.

First, let us consider the LXX. The words ὀσμή and εὐωδία are paired fifty times in the LXX, and in all but one occurrence the pairing appears in a distinct formula, ὀσμὴν (or ὀσμὴ/ὀσμῆ) εὐωδίας, which describes a pleasing aroma of sacrifices offered up to God.[18] For example, Gen. 8:21 speaks of Noah's burnt offering with the words "and when the Lord smelled the pleasing aroma [ὀσμὴν εὐωδίας], the Lord said in his heart, 'I will never again curse the ground. . . .'" The formula most often occurs in the Pentateuch and in the context of the cultic worship of Israel. Ezekiel (e.g., 20:28) adapts the formula mostly to speak of pagan worship practices involving sacrifices. In the NT, Paul twice takes up this formula in his letters, where he clearly crafts an image of sacrifice (Eph. 5:2; Phil. 4:18).

Only in Sir. 24:15 in the LXX does the pair uncharacteristically appear outside the formula, the terms placed in a parallel relationship:

> Like the spices cinnamon and camel's thorn
> I have given an aroma [ὀσμὴν],
> and like high-quality myrrh
> I distributed a fragrance [εὐωδίαν],
> like galbanum and onycha and myrrh oil,
> indeed like the vapor [ἀτμὶς] of frankincense in a tent.

This passage stands as part of the fifth of Sirach's vignettes in which Wisdom is personified, and Sirach draws the language from descriptions of the

---

18. E.g., Gen. 8:21; Exod. 29:18, 25, 41; Lev. 1:9, 13, 17; 2:2, 9, 12; 3:5, 11, 16; 4:31; 6:8, 14; 8:21, 28; 17:4, 6; 23:13, 18; Num. 15:3, 5, 7, 10, 13–14, 24; 18:17; 28:2, 6, 8, 13, 24, 27; 29:2, 6, 8, 11, 13, 36; Jdt. 16:16; Sir. 24:15; 50:15; Ezek. 6:13; 16:19; 20:28, 41; Dan. 4:37.

anointing oil used in Israel's cultic worship (Exod. 30:31–35; Sinnott 2005: 123–25). Sirach thus suggests a priestly and liturgical role for Wisdom, but the imagery, drawing on ὀσμή and εὐωδία in parallel fashion to speak of the delightful smells of cultic fragrances, connotes anointing rather than sacrifice.[19] Thus the pattern of ὀσμὴν εὐωδίας as a *terminus technicus* for the pleasing aroma of sacrifices is broken both in terms of form and connotation.

The OT Pseudepigrapha presents the formula in three places. The occurrences at T. Levi 3.6 and Ord. Levi 30 follow the septuagintal norm, speaking of sacrifices. At T. Ab. 16.8 we find an account of Abraham being visited by Death personified, and Death is said to give off "a pleasing odor" (ὀσμὴ εὐωδίας). This part of the narrative, however, occurs in the long recension, which in its current form in all likelihood stems from a late date (Allison 2003: 40). Philo uses our two terms in combination at two points in his writings. In the first, the formula ὀσμὴν εὐωδίας follows the biblical norm and speaks of sacrifices (*Prelim. Studies* 1.115). In the second, the words are used in the same context, apart from the septuagintal formula, to speak of the fragrance of beautiful flowers (*Prov.* 2.71).

The septuagintal formula does not occur in Greco-Roman literature (though see the variant in Aristotle, *Rhet.* 1.11.5), but writers of that literature employ the two terms often in the same context to connote a wide array of smells and fragrances.[20] Thus, in considering both the biblical and extrabiblical literature of the era, where ὀσμή and εὐωδία occur together in the formula ὀσμὴν εὐωδίας, the author uses the formula very specifically to speak of the aroma of sacrifices. In cases where the two words occur together but apart from this formula (as at 2 Cor. 2:14–16a), the author has other types of smells in mind.

Further, we should note the common use of each of these terms individually in literature outside the NT. For instance, in eight places authors of the LXX employ εὐωδία alone, and a few of these speak of sacrifical imagery; others refer simply to a pleasing fragrance.[21] Moreover, Philo uses εὐωδία five times, always referring simply to a fragrant smell or incense (*Creat.* 165; *Alleg.* 1.42; *Drunk.* 87; *Dreams* 1.178; *Abr.* 148), and this pattern matches what we

---

19. Hafemann (1990b: 42–43) sees Sir. 24:15 as the "crucial link for understanding Paul's use of this terminology in 2 Cor. 2:14–16a," for he suggests that "here, as in 2.14ff., the *terminus technicus* has been split up, but the two terms have nevertheless retained their sacrificial meaning" (42). Yet, the language here is of anointing oil and not sacrifice. Rather than claiming that the septuagintal formula normally used of sacrifice (ὀσμήν εὐωδίας) has been "split up," perhaps we should conclude that it is not present because sacrifice is not in view. Instead, the use of our terms in Sir. 24:15 accords well with the broad use of these terms in all literature of the period where the septuagintal formula is not employed.

20. E.g., Plutarch, *Quaest. conv.* 1.8.3; *Quaest. nat.* 23; Lucian, *Fug.* 1; Xenophon, *Symp.* 2.2; Aristotle, *Rhet.* 1.11.5.

21. In Dan. 2:46 LXX (Theod.) εὐωδία is used with reference to a grain offering and incense. At 1 Esd. 1:13, Ezra 6:10, and Sir. 35:5 the term speaks of the pleasing smell of sacrifices, and at Sir. 38:11 a fine flour offering seems to be in view. Sirach 45:16 describes a pleasant smell associated with incense. In both Pss. Sol. 11.5 and Bar. 5:8 we find εὐωδία denoting the fragrance of trees.

find in dozens of uses in the broader Greco-Roman literature.[22] Thus, in the literature of the period, εὐωδία when used alone most commonly refers to a variety of pleasant fragrances, a handful of cases in the LXX referring to the fragrance of a sacrifice of some kind.

The term ὀσμή, on the other hand, occurs alone only one time with reference to sacrifices (Lev. 26:31). And in this case, the smell is not pleasant but rather a "stench" to God, which is probably why the word is employed. For unlike εὐωδία, ὀσμή boasts a semantic range that includes bad smells as well as good. Accordingly, the writers of the biblical text use this word to refer to various smells, both good and bad. For instance, at Gen. 27:27 ὀσμή connotes the "smell" of Esau's clothing, and at Exod. 5:21 the leaders of the Israelites complain to Moses that he has made them "stink" (τὴν ὀσμὴν ἡμῶν) before Pharaoh. At Tob. 8:3 and in 2 Macc. 9:9–10, 12 the word communicates the terrible stench of dead fish or dead people. In Song of Songs the word is used of the wonderful fragrances associated with romance (Song 1:3–4, 12; 2:13; 4:10–11; 7:9, 14). In Isa. 3:24 ὀσμή refers to a pleasant scent, but in 34:3 it communicates the stink of the wounded or dead.[23] Thus, in the biblical literature, when ὀσμή is used outside the formulaic combination with εὐωδία, it almost always refers to a smell, either pleasant or rank, and at times the word is associated with death, as at 2 Cor. 2.15–16a. Moreover, Philo uses ὀσμή another nineteen times to speak of the ability to smell, good smells, or very bad smells. Philo never employs the term outside the septuaginal formula to speak of the aroma of sacrifices.[24] In short, in all of the literatures consulted, ὀσμή consistently connotes either a pleasant smell or a very bad one, but authors never take up the word alone to speak of the pleasing aroma of sacrifice.

It may be suggested that at 2 Cor. 2:14–16a Paul does not use the septuagintal formula ὀσμὴν εὐωδίας, which he employs elsewhere to speak of sacrifices, because he does not wish to craft an image of the cultic sacrifices of Israel in this case. Rather, the apostle takes up ὀσμή at 2:14 and 2:16a because in his cultural milieu the term, when used outside the *terminus technicus* ὀσμὴν εὐωδίας, commonly refers to a smell either good or bad, and this serves the purposes of his imagery well. Having crafted a triumphal procession word picture in 2:14, which highlights the "incense" of the gospel (τὴν ὀσμὴν τῆς γνώσεως αὐτοῦ) as central to the work of God through the Pauline mission, the apostle then elaborates in 2:15–16a, expanding the image of an "aroma" from 2:14 by introducing the semantically related term εὐωδία and then unpacking the sense of ὀσμή, utilizing both its positive and negative connotations. Thus Paul continues the triumphal procession imagery but now introduces

---

22. E.g., Plutarch, *Quaest. conv.* 1.6.1; 4.2.2; 5.8.1; *Alex.* 4.1; Xenophon, *Symp.* 2.3; Lucian, *Jupp. trag.* 44; Polybius, *Hist.* 12.2.

23. There are twenty-three cases where ὀσμή is used apart from εὐωδία. Other occurrences include Job 6:7 (smell of a lion); 14:9 (smell of water); Sir. 39:14 (incense); Jer. 25:10 (perfume); 31:11 (aroma of Moab); Dan. 3:94 (smell of smoke).

24. *Alleg.* 3.235; *Cher.* 117; *Sacr.* 23, 44; *Post.* 161; *Plant.* 133; *Drunk.* 106, 190–91; *Conf.* 52; *Migr.* 188; *Flight* 191; *Dreams* 1.47–49, 51; *Mos.* 1.105; *Good Free* 15; *Contempl.* 53.

elements of contrast, the contrast between a positive smell and a stench and the contrast between life and death (Martin 1986: 47–48).

Consequently, those who hold that ὀσμή conjures sacrificial imagery in 2 Cor. 2:14b–16a must explain how the image of a *negative* smell, perceived as such by people heading to destruction, fits our data on sacrificial imagery of the OT—especially when the apostle uses the term apart from the septuagintal formula commonly employed in the biblical literature to speak of sacrifice. Rather, it seems that having invoked triumphal procession imagery, the apostle stays with that imagery all the way through 2:16a, evoking the incense offered to the gods in the parade. Two other bits of information strongly suggest that we follow this course of interpretation. Specifically, we need to consider the images of "those being destroyed" and "those being saved" and whom these images represent in Paul's extended word picture.

iii. The Gospel as the Dividing Line of Humanity (2:15b–16a)

2:15b–16a The imagery of the passage depicts the gospel as wafting like incense out over the world "among those who are being saved and among those who are being destroyed" (ἐν τοῖς σῳζομένοις καὶ ἐν τοῖς ἀπολλυμένοις, *en tois sōzomenois kai en tois apollymenois*). This "aroma of knowledge about" Christ (2:14), now expressed as a "fragrance of Christ" (2:15), rises up to God, even as it has an effect on people in the world. As the apostle is "among" (ἐν, *en*, which communicates a locative sense) the masses of humanity, the gospel ministry has an effect on "those who are being saved" that is different from the effect on "those who are being destroyed" (2:16). The correlative construction in 2:16 (οἷς μέν ... οἷς δέ, *hois men ... hois de*; lit., to whom on the one hand ... to whom on the other hand), which I translate "To some ..., to others," compares and contrasts the positive effect of the gospel on the saved and the adverse effect on those being destroyed.

As the apostle continues to appropriate the imagery of the triumphal procession, it is clear that "those who are being destroyed" (τοῖς ἀπολλυμένοις, *tois apollymenois*) alludes to the captured enemies on display in the parade.[25] For the captives in the Roman triumph, the fragrance of the triumphator's celebration was a smell "arising from death and leading to death" (ἐκ θανάτου εἰς θάνατον, *ek thanatou eis thanaton*). The preposition ἐκ communicates source, specifically the image of death as the source of a bad, pungent ὀσμή (Tob. 8:3; 2 Macc. 9:9–10, 12; Isa. 34:3). The captives in the triumphal procession would remember the smell of death, the death of friends and comrades back on the field of battle. Yet we have already reported that death often awaited the captives being paraded through the streets of Rome. Accordingly, εἰς θάνατον may be read as speaking of termination—those being destroyed are heading to death. Thus, for them, the incense celebrating the triumphator's victory stinks, reminding them of the death that awaits them at a climactic moment in the parade.

25. For background on the captives in the parade, see esp. Hafemann 1990b: 19–29.

Paul uses this imagery of "those being destroyed," for whom the smell of the gospel and gospel ministry stinks of death, to speak of those who do not respond well to the good news about Christ. Thus understood, the ἐκ θανάτου communicates that the gospel stinks to them because they are spiritually dead. Their spiritual faculties do not have the ability to "smell" appropriately, if you will. They cannot enjoy the sweet smell of Christ. In fact, evoking another sense, the sense of sight, the exact same wording (ἐν τοῖς ἀπολλυμένοις) is used at 4:3 of those for whom the gospel is veiled. Also, the "smell" of the gospel and gospel ministry anticipates (εἰς θάνατον) their own destruction in judgment.

Thus it is vital to recognize that in this imagery of 2 Cor. 2:15–16, Paul actually *distinguishes himself and his ministry from those who "are being destroyed," who are spiritually aligned with death*, a point that speaks quite loudly against the interpretation that he sees himself as represented by the captives in the triumphal procession.

But what of the image of those "who are being saved"[26] (v. 15), for whom the gospel is "an aroma arising from life and leading to life" (v. 16)? Forms of the verb σῴζω (*sōzō*) and its cognates permeate Greco-Roman literature, including accounts of victory in war. For instance, Vespasian is hailed as "Benefactor" and "Savior" (τὸν εὐεργέτην καὶ σωτῆρα, *ton euergetēn kai sōtēra*; Josephus, *J.W.* 7.71–72) on his return to Rome. The language of salvation can speak of deliverance,[27] for instance the deliverance of fugitives (Demosthenes, *De pace* 18). As with 2 Cor. 2:15–16a, Greco-Roman writers often utilize this "salvation" language in contrast with θάνατος and/or forms of ἀπόλλυμι.[28] This use of "salvation" language accords with a particular aspect of the Roman triumphal procession, although the commentaries are fairly silent on the allusion.

I have already noted Plutarch's account of Terentius, who, after being rescued from Carthaginian captivity, followed Scipio the Elder in his Triumph

---

26. Seneca (*Ben.* 2.11.1–2) also seems to use the imagery of triumphal procession metaphorically:

> He wants to cry out like the man who, after being saved from the proscription of the triumvirs by one of Caesar's friends, because he could not endure his benefactor's arrogance, cried, "Give me back to Caesar!" How long will you keep repeating: "It is I who saved you, it is I who snatched you from death"? Your service, if I remember it of my own will, is truly life; if I remember it at yours, it is death. I owe nothing to you if you saved me in order that you might have someone to exhibit. How long will you parade me? How long will you refuse to let me forget my misfortune? In a triumph, I should have had to march but once!

What should be noted here is that the braggart parades the unfortunate speaker as one he has saved. It is not clear that the person is being saved from being a paraded captive in a triumphal procession. It seems, rather, that the allusion is to the parading of a liberated person in a figurative sense.

27. E.g., Plutarch, *Regum* 39.6; 72.2; *Sert.* 15.1; *Cat. Min.* 62.3; 71.2; *Comp. Pel. Marc.* 3.1; *Fab.* 9.2; *Apoph. lac.* 2.38.4; Polybius, *Hist.* 11.9.

28. Plutarch, *Apoph. lac.* 2.22; 2.23.1; *Crass.* 25.11; Dionysius of Halicarnassus, *Rom. Ant.* 8.12.4; Herodotus, *Hist.* 3.14.11; Plato, *Leg.* 5.728b. Also see Philo, *Cher.* 130; *Alleg.* 3.225; *Flight* 27; and the LXX: Wis. 18:5–7; Amos 2:14–15; Jer. 31:8.

(Plutarch, *Regum* 76.6–7). Similarly, the colonists of Placentia and Cremona, rescued from Gallic captivity, wore the *pileus* in the triumphal procession of Gaius Cornelius (Livy, *Hist. Rom.* 33.23.1–6),[29] as did over a thousand Roman citizens who were saved from slavery in Greece by Titus Flamininus, a Roman general in the early second century BC. According to Plutarch (*Flam.* 13.3–6), the freed Romans, in celebration of their liberation, marched as the centerpiece in the triumphal procession of the general who had saved them:

> The Achaeans voted Titus many honours, none of which seemed commensurate with his benefactions except one gift, and this caused him as much satisfaction as all the rest put together. And this was the gift: The Romans who were unhappily taken prisoners in the war with Hannibal had been sold about hither and thither, and were serving as slaves. In Greece there were as many as twelve hundred of them. The change in their lot made them pitiful objects always, but then even more than ever, naturally, when they fell in with sons, or brothers, or familiar friends, as the case might be, slaves with freemen and captives with victors. These men Titus would not take away from their owners, although he was distressed at their condition, but the Achaeans ransomed them all at five minas the man, collected them together, and made a present of them to Titus just as he was about to embark, so that he sailed for home with a glad heart; his noble deeds had brought him a noble recompense, and one befitting a great man who loved his fellow citizens. This appears to have furnished his triumph *with its most glorious feature* [emphasis added]. For these men shaved their heads and wore felt caps, as it is customary for slaves to do when they are set free, and in this habit followed the triumphal car of Titus. (Perrin 1921: 361–62; see also Plutarch, *Regum* 77.2; Livy, *Hist. Rom.* 34.52.11–12)

In these passages, we read of Romans who, having been enslaved in a foreign country, are liberated, saved by a Roman general; after being set free, they marched in triumphal procession in celebration of their liberator.[30] Although commentators have failed to recognize the connection between "those being saved" in 2:15–16a and the liberated in the *pompa triumphalis*, the implications for our interpretation of the passage are significant.

In 2 Cor. 2:14–16a, Paul's use of the triumphal-procession imagery is both vivid and consistent, crafting a powerful word picture to describe both the nature and the effect of authentic ministry. The correspondences between the Roman triumphal procession and authentic Christian ministry may be seen in figure 10.

The apostle's grand metaphor and message in 2 Cor. 2:14–16a may be summed up as follows. God in Christ, stands as the cosmic triumphator, who leads the apostle in a triumphal procession through the world. Paul and his mission are analogous to the incense bearers in the parade, for through them God spreads the gospel, the "aroma of knowledge" about Christ, "everywhere" the

---

29. Livy emphasizes that it was the throng of those liberated from captivity, *not the enemy captives*, who were the focus of attention in the parade.

30. On the possible associations of the triumphator as "savior," see Versnel 1970: 393–95.

Figure 10 **Roman Triumphal Procession
and Authentic Christian Ministry Compared**

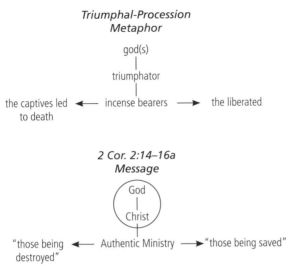

*Triumphal-Procession
Metaphor*

god(s)
|
triumphator
|

the captives led ← incense bearers → the liberated
to death

*2 Cor. 2:14–16a
Message*

God
|
Christ
|

"those being ← Authentic Ministry → "those being saved"
destroyed"

apostle goes. Further, as Paul lives a Christ-centered life before God, the fragrance of true gospel ministry rises up like pleasing incense to God (even as the incense of the Roman procession was regarded as rising to the gods), while having a dichotomizing effect on those with whom the ministry comes into contact. In the apostle's metaphor, "the ones being saved" brings to mind those who had experienced "salvation" through the victory of the Roman general. These are analogous to people who have responded positively to the gospel and thus have experienced salvation through Christ. "The ones being destroyed," on the other hand, evokes the image of the doomed captives of the *pompa triumphalis*, serving as an analogy to those who reject Paul's gospel. For those being saved, the apostle's authentic ministry and its message carry the sweet scent of life, but for those being destroyed, Paul's ministry and message "stink" of death. Thus, Paul's use of the triumphal-procession metaphor in 2 Cor. 2:14–16a offers a coherent, consistent, and balanced word picture that speaks of the nature of authentic Christian ministry and the effect of this gospel ministry in the world.

Reflection

The emphasis in 2:14–16a as a whole lies on Paul's authentic ministry, specifically, his proclamation of the gospel word[31] and its effect. In other words, *Paul's primary purpose for the image of triumphal procession centers in the effect of the gospel, preached from the standpoint of ministry integrity,*

31. Note esp. that this ministry spreads "the aroma of knowledge about him." At 2:17 Paul makes clear that he has in mind speaking the Word as the centerpiece of his ministry.

as Paul is led by God, in relationship with Christ, throughout the world. That integrity flows in part from Paul's posture of submission before God, as will be emphasized further in 2:17, but the emphasis in Paul's use of the extended metaphor has to do with the effect of authentic ministry of the Word on various groups with which it comes in contact.

Thus God's Word, rather than being static, serves as a dynamic force in the world, like rain or fire, like a sword or a smashing rock (Heb. 4:12; Isa. 55:11; Jer. 23:29). Ministry of the Word is more than a word of *explanation*. It is a word either of salvation or devastation, dividing humanity in two parts; for it demarcates two realms of existence, one in which life is lived in covenant with the benevolent triumphator (God), and one as a life of spiritual death under his judgment. Covenant or condemnation thus hangs over two different responses to the gospel message when ministry is carried out with authenticity and integrity. This means that by its very nature authentic ministry will sound like bad news to a significant portion of humanity, and this should not surprise us. Negative reactions to Christian ministers come from various quarters and for various reasons, some of them deserved, but we need to remember that certain negative reactions actually serve as a marker of authentic ministry (cf. Matt. 10:24–25). For authentic ministry by its very nature proclaims a message that divides, that demarcates human beings according to two very different destinies. In a famous passage C. S. Lewis (2009: 46) reminds us, "There are no ordinary people. You have never talked to a mere mortal. Nations, cultures, arts, civilizations—these are mortal, and their life is to ours as the life of a gnat. But it is immortals whom we joke with, work with, marry, snub, and exploit—immortal horrors or everlasting splendours." Therefore the passage confronts us with a weighty issue: What effects do our ministries have in the world? Do we live in such a way that our ministries are a sweet fragrance to God and at the same time a dynamic that leads people to life or death?

Additional Notes

2:14–16a. Jan Lambrecht (1994a: 261–62) has identified the following parallels between 2:14–3:6 and 4:1–6:

4:1	διακονία	3:6	διάκονος (3:3, διακονηθεῖσα)
	οὐκ ἐγκακοῦμεν	3:4	πεποίθησιν . . . ἔχομεν
4:2	δολοῦντες	2:17	καπηλεύοντες
	τὸν λόγου τοῦ θεοῦ		τὸν λόγου τοῦ θεοῦ
	ἐνώπιον τοῦ θεοῦ		κατέναντι τοῦ θεοῦ
	τῇ φανερώσει	2:14	φανεροῦντι (3:3, φανερούμενοι)
	συνιστάνονττες ἑαυτούς	3:1	ἑαυτοὺς συνιστάνειν
	πρὸς πᾶσαν συνείδησιν ἀνθρώπων	3:2	ὑπὸ πάντων ἀνθρώπων
4:3	ἐν τοῖς ἀπολλυμένοις	2:15	ἐν τοῖς ἀπολλυμένοις

4:5	ἑαυτούς	3:1	ἑαυτούς
	δούλους (ὑμῶν)	3:6	διακόνους (καινῆς διαθήκης)
	κηρύσσομεν	2:17	λαλοῦμεν
4:6	ἐν ταῖς καρδίαις ἡμῶν	3:2	ἐν ταῖς καρδίαις ἡμῶν (2:14, δι' ἡμῶν)
	πρὸς φωτισμόν	2:14	φανεροῦντι
	τῆς γνώσεως . . . τοῦ θεοῦ		τῆς γνώσεως αὐτοῦ

Thus Paul brackets the whole of the section by use of extensive parallelism. This means that the apostle uses the triumphal-procession imagery at 2:14–16a to launch a more extended reflection that extends through 4:6. The function of the parallelism is especially to mark 4:1–6 as picking up and reiterating the primary themes introduced in 2:14–3:6. Such parallelism also serves to mark 4:1–6 as part of the unit beginning at 2:14. In 3:7–18 the theological treatise on the contrast between old-covenant ministries and new-covenant ministries provides the theological basis for the assertions made about valid ministry in 2:14–17 and 4:1–6.

2:16. The double use of the preposition ἐκ is omitted by the witnesses D F G K L Ψ 365[(*).c] 1241 1505 2464 𝔐 latt sy; Ir[lat], a scribe perhaps thinking that the idea of source, communicated by the preposition, did not sit well with the concepts of life and death. In any case, the external evidence for the inclusion of the preposition is very strong (𝔓[46] ℵ A B C 0243 33 81 104 630 1175 1739 [1881] 2464 *pc*; Cl).

b. Qualified for Ministry (2:16b–3:6)

As we come to 2 Cor. 2:16b–3:6, we are confronted with the issues of quali-fication and validation in ministry. What constitutes a truly competent ministry? In our home my family has a "memorials table" that sits in the middle of our gathering room. Our table is about two feet tall and three by three feet wide. With a glass top and wooden drawers beneath the glass, it is filled with things that remind us of moments in which God has worked meaningfully in our lives. There is a tiny newborn's hospital bracelet, re-minding us that God spared my life in 1959, when I was born ten weeks early, had one lung working, and was deemed unlikely to live, according to the doctors. There are pictures of my children's baptisms, a brick from our first home, and a piece of glass from when an F4 tornado caused $45 million in damage to our university but killed no one. Also in the table sits a letter, in which Dr. William Lane celebrated preliminary work I had done on the structure of the NT book of Hebrews. I had called Bill out of the blue, introduced myself, and asked him if he would interact with me on my work (at that point he was finishing his two-volume Word Biblical Com-mentary on Hebrews). He graciously agreed and went on to be the external reader for my dissertation. But his letter was wonderfully encouraging. He commended the work (even though it disagreed with a position he had been teaching for years) and ended up including nineteen pages from my work in the introduction to his commentary. His commendation also opened the door for the later publication of my dissertation.

Through the years, I have had the opportunity to commend the work of others. Each year my students ask me to fill out letters of recommenda-tion, either to a church, to a business where they are applying for work, or perhaps to a graduate program. When those of us who are professors write such letters, we are saying in effect, "I think this person has basic spiritual, intellectual, social, and ministerial competences to do what will need to be done, to be what a church or ministry or business or academic institution will need the applicant to be." I also have written dozens of blurbs for book jackets and have evaluated numerous book manuscripts submitted for publication. It is a joy when a book is so well done that I can commend it with enthusiasm.

As we have seen, in 2:14–16a Paul uses the imagery of triumphal pro-cession in part to proclaim the impact of authentic ministry in the world. To some the proclamation of the gospel "stinks" of death; to others the gospel carries the aroma of life. Thus the gospel serves as a dividing line for humanity. To have such a role in the world constitutes a grave, daunting responsibility, and the apostle responds, "Who is qualified for this role?!" Thus Paul in essence raises the issue of qualification for ministry, and he will follow almost immediately with the issue of commendation in ministry. Paul's ministry is set apart from the hucksters, false ministers who preach for profit; their whole approach to a life of "ministry" differs from Paul's style in the most fundamental ways. Paul speaks with integrity, having been sent by God, and lives with a posture of reverence before God and in profound relationship with Christ.

Therefore, being sent by God and being accountable to God, Paul at 3:1–6 turns to the issue of commendation and competence for ministry. We need to address what the apostle intends to communicate with the first clause of chapter 3, which most read as a rhetorical question anticipating a negative answer. As we will see, the apostle often speaks positively in the book about self-recommendation. So how are we to understand his words at this point? And how do his words about commendation here relate to his references to self-recommendation as he continues with the letter?

From the second clause in 3:1, it is clear that Paul does not perceive himself as needing letters of commendation to or from the Corinthians. Indeed, the work of the Spirit in their lives constitutes the only letter of recommendation the apostle needs. Paul is confident of the authentic ministry accomplished in the lives of the Corinthians, not because of his own competence to accomplish such but because God has made him competent for the task and has worked through the Spirit, rather than through "the letter," to bring it about. This dichotomy between the "Spirit who brings life" and the "letter" that "kills" in 3:6 needs to be probed, for it has been much debated.

This movement of the book breaks down as follows:

i. Who is qualified for gospel ministry? (2:16b)
ii. Hucksters versus God-centered ministers (2:17)
iii. Self-recommendation and letters of commendation (3:1–3)
iv. The confidence of a truly competent ministry (3:4–6)

Exegesis and Exposition

2:16b And who is qualified for this role?! 17For we are not like ⌜so many⌝, hucksters who peddle the Word of God to make money; rather, we speak with integrity, indeed, as those sent by God, living before God, in Christ.

3:1We are starting to recommend ourselves to you again! Or do we, like some, need letters of recommendation to you or from you?! 2You yourselves are our letter of recommendation, written on ⌜our⌝ hearts, known and read by everyone, 3making it clear that you are a letter produced by Christ, prepared by us, written not with ink but with the Spirit of the living God, not on stone tablets but on ⌜tablets of human hearts⌝. 4Now we have this kind of confidence through Christ toward God. 5Not that we are qualified because of ourselves to consider anything as coming from ourselves, but our competence is from God, [6]who also made us competent as ministers of a new covenant, not of the letter but of the Spirit. For the letter kills but the Spirit produces life.

i. Who Is Qualified for Gospel Ministry? (2:16b)

2:16b The apostle concludes his treatment of God as triumphator and the effect of Paul's ministry with the question, "And who is qualified for this role?!" (καὶ πρὸς ταῦτα τίς ἱκανός; *kai pros tauta tis hikanos?*). That is, who is adequate or competent to proclaim the gospel, the good news that serves as the dividing line for all of humanity? This question embodies a "stupendous claim" (Barnett 1997: 155), a "horrifying truth" (Barrett 1973: 102), indeed a profoundly staggering, deeply sobering reality. Those who proclaim the gospel participate in cosmic-sized matters, spiritual life and death, liberation and destruction. Who can be considered adequate for such a role? This may be *the* key question of the whole book, for Paul seeks to establish the fundamental difference between his gospel ministry and the misguided "ministries" of those who seek to lead the Corinthians in his absence. The God of the universe has called Paul to proclaim his message in the world, to celebrate his triumphant Christ by the power of the Spirit, to build Christ's church through the proclamation of the true gospel. Later in the book he points out that the interlopers of Corinth preach a different Jesus, a different gospel, and bring with them a different spirit (11:4).

The term ἱκανός can range in meaning from "sufficient" (cf. 2:6) or "adequate" (in terms of the degree or amount of something) to "considerable," "large," or "numerous" (e.g., Luke 8:32; 23:9). When speaking of a person's abilities or status, the word connotes capability, qualification, or worthiness. Philo, for instance, who uses the term over 140 times in his writings, notes that by seven years of age a person is able to speak well because he is "competent" in dealing with nouns and verbs (*Alleg.* 1.10), and John the Baptist could proclaim that he was not "qualified," or perhaps "worthy," to loose Jesus's sandals (Matt. 3:11; Mark 1:7; Luke 3:16; Spicq 1994: 2.217–19). At 1 Cor. 15:9 Paul writes that he is not "worthy" to be called an apostle since he has persecuted the church. In 2 Cor. 2:16 the term seems to carry the sense of qualification or capability. Paul answers this question, "Who is qualified?" in the broader context: "Not that we are qualified in ourselves to consider anything as coming from ourselves, but our competence is from God" (3:5). So his answer rings out, "We are—but only because of the new-covenant work of God in and through us!"

ii. Hucksters versus God-Centered Ministers (2:17)

2:17 Paul's dramatic depiction of God's proclamation of the gospel through his ministry leads to a contrast with the false teachers with whom he is forced to deal at Corinth. He distinguishes himself from them by saying, "For we are not like so many, hucksters who peddle the Word of God to make money." The use of γάρ (*gar*, for) is explanatory, expanding on Paul's implied answer to his question at the end of verse 16. He offers a negative explanation (i.e., what he is *not* like) followed by a series of positive descriptors that characterize his ministry. The comparison as a whole is set up by an initial use of ὡς (*hōs*, like), which the apostle answers in contrast with parallel ἀλλ' ὡς (*all' hōs*, rather/indeed) clauses in the latter half of the verse. When Paul speaks of "the many" (οἱ πολλοί, *hoi polloi*), a common term that when used with the article could mean "the many" or "the majority," he has the false teachers in mind (11:4, 13), and this designation suggests that their number was significant. Although it could speak of "the majority," Paul is characterized by using οἱ πολλοί to refer to a large number of people (Rom. 5:15, 19; 12:5; 1 Cor. 10:17).

Paul describes these false teachers as "peddling" or "huckstering" the Word of God. The verb καπηλεύω (*kapēleuō*), expressed in a present active participle, occurs only here in biblical literature. Its cognate noun (κάπηλος, *kapēlos*) could be used in a general sense of a small shopkeeper, a retailer, a reseller, a peddler, a secondhand dealer, or a merchant—but in the broader literature of the period, these Greek terms came to carry a pejorative sense of the backstreet peddler carrying on an illicit business, cheating people for his own profit (Sir. 26:29; Hafemann 1990b: 115–17; Spicq 1994: 2.254). Lucian, for instance, writes figuratively of questionable teachers: "The philosophers sell their teaching like tavern keepers, and most of them [οἱ πολλοί] mix their wine with water and misrepresent it" (*Hermot.* 59; see also Isa. 1:22 LXX). Thus Paul points to the dark shadow of inappropriate motives hanging over the heads of the Corinthian interlopers.

Paul contrasts the hucksters' approach to ministry with his own. The latter half of verse 17 coheres around the main verb, λαλοῦμεν (*laloumen*, we speak), and the whole therefore describes Paul's preaching of God's word.[1] This description consists of parallel clauses, each introduced with ἀλλ' ὡς to express strong contrast in comparison to the hucksters just described:

ἀλλ' ὡς	ἐξ εἰλικρινείας	*all' hōs*	*ex eilikrineias*
ἀλλ' ὡς	ἐκ θεοῦ	*all' hōs*	*ek theou*
	κατέναντι θεοῦ		*katenanti theou*
	ἐν Χριστῷ		*en Christō*
λαλοῦμεν		*laloumen*	

The ἀλλ' ὡς ἐξ εἰλικρινείας points to the sharp contrast between Paul's motives and those of the word peddlers. The term εἰλικρινεία speaks of sincerity or purity of motives (1 Cor. 5:8; 2 Cor. 1:12), which is an essential aspect of

---

1. Grammatically, one could take the second ἀλλ' ὡς alone as relating to the verb, with the parallel use of ἀλλ' ὡς functioning to distinguish between two different aspects of Paul's ministry, his conduct generally and his preaching (so Harris 2005: 255, but see footnote 76). Yet the context suggests that Paul especially has in mind his proclamation of the Word; hence we should likely understand the second use of ἀλλ' ὡς as a marker of intensity or elevation—referred to in Greek grammar as being rhetorically ascensive.

"Christian existence in its relation to God and to people. It is not so much the absence of duplicity or hypocrisy as [it is having] a fundamental integrity and transparency" (Spicq 1994: 1.420). Paul has already emphasized the good conscience with which he has conducted his ministry (1:12), and this serves as a related concept, emphasizing that what drives Paul is pure.

The second ἀλλ᾽ ὡς intensifies Paul's claim (i.e., "indeed") and also clarifies the impetuses for his preaching (λαλοῦμεν, *laloumen*) with sincerity. It is a sincerity born of the origin of Paul's ministry (ἐκ θεοῦ), his posture of accountability to God (κατέναντι θεοῦ), and the profundity of his relationship with Christ (ἐν Χριστῷ). First, Paul claims to speak ἐκ θεοῦ. Including our current passage, the phrase finds expression in Paul nine times (Rom. 2:29; 1 Cor. 2:12; 7:7; 11:12; 2 Cor. 3:5; 5:1, 18; Phil. 3:9), either as here or with the article preceding θεοῦ. In every case the phrase speaks of something that has God as its source, something that comes *from* God, as at 2 Cor. 3:5, where Paul suggests that his competence for ministry comes "from God." In the current context this points to God as the source of Paul's preaching ministry. In contrast to the interlopers, it is God's commission that drives him in his ministry, rather than personal profit (1:1–2). The implication is that the false teachers were sent by someone or something else, other than God. The phrase puts the question to those of us who claim to be ministers of the gospel: Who sent you? We are all driven by something, sent by someone into our seminary training, into the ministry we serve, into our tasks of ministry on any given day. Who sent you?

Second, Paul speaks κατέναντι θεοῦ, "before God." Although the phrase as expressed here only occurs elsewhere at 2 Cor. 12:19[2]—where Paul also defends his preaching: "We speak before God, in Christ"—the concept has a rich biblical backdrop. For instance, Josh. 24:1 reports that Joshua brought together the tribes of Israel at Shechem, calling the leaders to present themselves "before God." Speaking of a pattern of life, as Paul does here, Ps. 56:13 reads, "For You delivered me from death, even my feet from stumbling, to walk before God in the light of life" (HCSB). Also, 2 Kings 3:14 records that Elisha, speaking to kings of his day, says, "As the Lord of Hosts lives, I stand before him" (LXX: ᾧ παρέστην ἐνώπιον αὐτοῦ, *hō parestēn enōpion autou*). In his use of the phrase, what Paul especially has in mind has to do with a gravity of posture, a profound sense of accountability to God for the ministry he conducts. Paul lives out his ministry with reverence and humility, keenly aware, as Milton put it, that he was "ever in the great Taskmaster's eye."[3] The phrase prompts us to reflect on the question: "Before whom do you stand as you minister?" Are you and I primarily performing for people, or living in a submissive posture before God?

---

2. The LXX, e.g., uses variously the prepositions ἀπέναντι, ἐνώπιον, ἐναντίον, πρός (*apenanti, enōpion, enantion, pros*) + the acc., or the words πρὸ προσώπου (*pro prosōpou*), in phrases that speak of someone being "before God." The NT renderings of the concept are equally varied.

3. The much more common Pauline term is "before God" or "before the Lord," using the word ἐνώπιον (*enōpion*): Rom. 3:20; 14:22; 1 Cor. 1:29; 2 Cor. 4:2; 8:21; Gal. 1:20; 1 Tim. 2:3; 5:4, 21; 6:13; 2 Tim. 2:14; 4:1.

Third, Paul speaks ἐν Χριστῷ, a favorite phrase that the apostle uses variously but with strongly relational overtones. The sense can be more corporate, as "in the body of Christ," but here the sense seems to be more individualistic. It may be understood as a dative of association, "in relation to Christ." What Paul does in his preaching is far more than simply preach a message *about* Christ Jesus. Rather, he preaches the message about Christ, from the standpoint of a profound relationship *with Christ*. After all, he is an apostle *of Christ*. This final prepositional phrase raises a key question: With whom are you associated? Ministry must be carried out from the standpoint of a profound personal relationship with Jesus Christ.

iii. Self-Recommendation and Letters of Commendation (3:1–3)

In 3:1–6 Paul moves to the issue of self-recommendation and the imagery of 3:1
recommendation letters. He thus continues the train of thought already begun in 2:17: What legitimizes a Christian ministry claiming to be "sent by God, living before God, in Christ" (2:17; Barnett 1997: 162)? In a programmatic article in 1942, Ernst Käsemann suggested that what was at stake in Paul's conflict with the interlopers of Corinth was Paul himself—more specifically, his legitimacy as an apostle. Almost a half century later, Scott Hafemann played off Käsemann's article in one of his own titled "Self-Commendation and Apostolic Legitimacy in 2 Corinthians: A Pauline Dialectic?" (Hafemann 1990a). Hafemann affirmed Käsemann's view that "Paul defended himself by reestablishing the rules of the game and thereby redefining those eligible to play it." Hafemann observed that in Käsemann's view, "Paul insisted on a 'heavenly criterion' of dependence upon the crucified Lord now risen, which in turn demanded as its corollary a divinely inspired discernment in the Spirit for its evaluation" (66). The weaknesses of Paul shifted the perspective from earthly, cultural values to a heavenly perspective that could only be discerned spiritually. Hafemann pointed out, further, that the various ways Paul speaks of commendation and boasting in the book seem at points to contradict each other, but he champions the view that "self-commendation" constitutes "the key to understanding the focus of Paul's apologetic in 2 Corinthians" (69), a view I wholeheartedly endorse. In fact, as Linda Belleville (1989) has also suggested, aspects of this letter seem to fit the form and flow of a letter of self-recommendation.

But here we are confronted immediately with 2 Cor. 3:1. Most translate the first clause of verse 1 as a rhetorical question, with which the apostle asks, "Are we beginning to recommend ourselves to you again?"

Are we beginning to commend ourselves again? (ESV, HCSB, NASB, NIV, NET)

Are we beginning to praise ourselves again? (NLT[2])

Do we begin again to commend ourselves? (KJV)

Are we once again bragging about ourselves? (CEV)

Is this going to be more self-advertisement in your eyes? (Phillips)

Are we back to page one? Do we need to gather some recommendations to prove our validity to you? (Voice)

Does it sound like we're patting ourselves on the back, insisting on our credentials, asserting our authority? (Message)

Tyndale alone takes the clause as a statement rather than a rhetorical question: "We begyn to prayse oure selves agayne."

Ancient authors used this word translated "to recommend" (συνιστάνειν, *synistanein*) to communicate a range of ideas, including "to put or fit together," "to unite," "to consist of," "to introduce," "to recommend," "to prove to be," "demonstrate," or "to provide evidence of some characteristic" (*EDNT* 3:308; BDAG 972). In the NT the term occurs sixteen times, only twice outside of Paul's writings (Luke 9:32; 2 Pet. 3:5). In the Pauline literature nine of the occurrences are in 2 Corinthians (2 Cor. 3:1; 4:2; 5:12; 6:4; 7:11; 10:12, 18 [2x]; 12:11), and the word weaves one of the most important threads through this book. In fact, it may be suggested, this concept of "commending" constitutes the letter's raison d'être, for the apostle earnestly seeks to convince the Corinthians to embrace his ministry wholeheartedly.

Most commentators, however, in line with the translations noted above, embrace the clause as a rhetorical question anticipating a negative answer. On this understanding, the μή in the following, parallel clause, reaches back to the first clause, marking the first clause as also anticipating a negative answer (e.g., Harris 2005: 258). In other words, Paul here denies that he is recommending himself again. Read this way, it seems that the apostle contradicts himself as he uses the word in the following chapters, at one moment insisting that he is not commending himself to the Corinthians (3:1; 5:12; cf. 10:18) and in the next breath proclaiming that he does commend himself (4:2; 6:4), or that the Corinthians should have recommended him (12:11). So what are we to make of the apostle's varying statements? Is Paul contradicting himself? I suggest that he is not and that the clause in 3:1 should be read, with Tyndale, as Paul offering a self-recommendation, albeit hesitantly and somewhat with tongue in cheek. Three points support this assertion: the cultural context, the literary context, and the grammar of the passage.

1. *Cultural context.* To automatically read an act of self-recommendation pejoratively[4]—as do versions like NLT[2], CEV, Phillips, and Message—is to

---

4. Some commentators, reading the words as a rhetorical question, have understood the question to display a touchiness on Paul's part, referring to a confrontation in which Paul has responded to a rebuke concerning some expression of his strong, boastful personality. On this discussion, see Furnish 1984: 192–93; P. Hughes 1962: 85. As Keener (2005: 220–21) points out, many prominent rhetoricians of the Greco-Roman world looked down on self-praise and warned against it (e.g., Plutarch, *Plat. Q.* 1.2; *Cic.* 24.1–2). At the same time, it was culturally appropriate to appeal to one's deeds in the face of criticism; this was a form of apologetic self-recommendation (e.g., Demosthenes, *Cor.* 299–300; *False Emb.* 174; Cicero, *Fam.* 5.12.8) and seen as rhetorically appropriate.

be unaware that in the first century self-recommendation was an appropriate, widely accepted form of self-representation (Garland 1999: 154; P. Marshall 1987: 91–93, 124, 271). In one form of self-recommendation, an individual establishes a new relationship with friends or associates, introducing himself and seeking a mutual relationship of trust with the party addressed.

Epictetus (*Disc.* 2.3.2–3) notes Diogenes of Sinope's demurring when someone asked of him a recommendation letter, and he inadvertently affirms self-recommendation:

> That is an excellent answer of Diogenes to the man who asked for a letter of recommendation from him: "That you are a man," he says, "he will know at a glance; but whether you are a good or a bad man he will discover if he has the skill to distinguish between good and bad, and if he is without that skill he will not discover the facts, even though I write him thousands of times." For it is just as though a drachma asked to be recommended to someone, in order to be tested. If the man in question is an assayer of silver, you will recommend yourself. (Oldfather 1925: 231–33)

Self-recommendation was similar to a letter of recommendation but without third-party involvement. With self-recommendation one presented credentials or personal testimony with the goal of establishing a reciprocal, trust-based relationship (P. Marshall 1987: 66–73). From the use of the word πάλιν (*palin*), "again,"[5] at 3:1a, it seems that Paul had offered the Corinthians a self-recommendation in the past, probably when he first came to Corinth.

There is, however, another occasion when self-recommendation was appropriate, for the convention could be brought into play to help restore a strained relationship. This form of "apologetic self-commendation," as P. Marshall (1987: 66–73) calls it, is exactly what Paul carries out in the following chapters, defending himself in light of public criticism. Thus when Paul writes, "We are beginning to recommend ourselves to you again," he intimates, "We seem to need to go through the process of establishing our relationship again—and I have some things to say in light of the accusations that have been made against me and my ministry!" As Theodoret writes, "Paul is telling the Corinthians that they should have been commending him without any reminders of this kind" (Bray 1999: 212). His relationship with the Corinthians had long been established. After all, he was their spiritual father (1 Cor. 4:14–15), God's apostle whom God sent to establish their church (1:1), and he had conducted himself in a manner that warranted their trust. Therefore when he states, "We are beginning to commend ourselves again," he asserts categorically that he sees the need to revisit the issue of their mutual trust, in spite of the fact that he and the Corinthians should be past that relational milestone. They should not be listening to criticism against him, but given that they are, he will

---

5. The term πάλιν delimits the complementary infinitive συνιστάνειν (*synistanein*, to recommend) rather than the main verb Ἀρχόμεθα (*Archometha*, We are starting). He is not asking whether he is beginning again, but whether he is beginning "to recommend himself again."

provide an answer, albeit reluctantly. So his statement that he is commending himself to them again, rather than a denial of inappropriate action on his part, constitutes a use of a common cultural convention and an open rebuke of the Corinthians. But there is a second point concerning why 3:1a should be read as a statement rather than a rhetorical question.

2. *Literary context.* The broader literary context of the book suggests that Paul consistently uses the concept of self-recommendation positively. First, notice that Paul has just stated very positive things about himself in 2:17, contrasting the pattern of his ministry with those hucksters who peddle the Word of God for profit. This is appropriate self-recommendation, a self-recommendation grounded in a Godward life and ministry.

Also, notice how Paul uses the word we translate as "recommending" in the remainder of the book. At 4:2 he writes, "We recommend ourselves to every person's conscience as we live before God." How does Paul recommend himself? In 4:2–6 he says, "We have turned our backs on the shameful things people hide, not living by tricks, nor twisting God's Word"; "We live before God"; and, "We preach Christ as Lord and ourselves as your slaves." At 5:12, the apostle states, "It is not *really*[6] that we are recommending ourselves to you again; rather, we are giving you an opportunity to boast on our behalf." It may well be that this "opportunity" (ἀφορμήν, *aphormēn*) arises as Paul gives the Corinthians information with which to answer the objections to his ministry. Giving them *content* with which to boast on his behalf, it may be suggested, is the same as Paul commending himself. What he means here is that the Corinthians have put him in an awkward position. It is not really that he is trying to reestablish his apostolic relationship with them, for Christ has already made him their apostle. But they have forced him to act like he needs to go through the process of self-recommendation again. What does Paul say for himself and his mission in the passage?

Our lives stand open to God. (5:11)

We appeal to people's consciences. (5:11)

We boast in heart, not in appearances. (5:12)

We serve God and others. (5:13)

These declarations may be straightforwardly read as self-commendatory.

---

6. The text at 5:12 reads, οὐ πάλιν ἑαυτοὺς συνιστάνομεν ὑμῖν ἀλλὰ ἀφορμὴν διδόντες ὑμῖν καυχήματος ὑπὲρ ἡμῶν (*ou palin heautous synistanomen hymin alla aphormēn didontes hymin kauchēmatos hyper hēmōn*). The addition of "really" in our ET stems from the context. This is similar to 1 Cor. 11:20, where the apostle writes that when the church comes together οὐκ ἔστιν κυριακὸν δεῖπνον φαγεῖν (*ouk estin kyriakon deipnon phagein*, it is not to eat the Lord's Supper; 1 Cor. 11:20). A number of versions appropriately render the verse as "it is not really to eat the Lord's Supper" (e.g., HCSB, NET, NLT[2], NRSV). Of course they were eating the Lord's Supper when looked at in a surface manner. Paul's point is that the actions did not match the reality of what truly was occurring. This is also the case with 2 Cor. 5:12.

At 6:4 we read, "But we are recommending ourselves in every way as God's ministers." In the broader context of that passage (6:3–10), the apostle explains how he and his ministry team commend themselves: "in a great deal of endurance, in afflictions, in crises, in stressful situations, in beatings, in being put in jail, in mobs, in hard work, in sleepless nights, in times of hunger, in sincerity, in knowledge, in patience, in kindness, in the Holy Spirit, in genuine love, in the word of truth, in the power of God; through weapons of righteousness." Further, at 7:11 Paul writes to the Corinthians, "In every way you have recommended yourselves as pure in this matter," again using the term συνίστημι in a positive way.

At 10:12–13 the apostle contrasts his form of self-recommendation with that of the false ministers in Corinth:

> For we wouldn't dare to classify or compare ourselves with any of those who are commending themselves. Here's the difference: when they measure themselves, using themselves as the standard, and compare themselves with one another, they are clueless. We, on the other hand, refuse to boast beyond proper limits but boast within the boundaries of the assignment God has given us.

There are two important points to be made here. First, Paul treats self-recommendation and boasting as roughly synonymous. Second, note that *Paul does boast*, but he does so appropriately, based on the essential point: "It is not the one commending himself who passes the test, but the one whom the Lord commends!" (10:18). So Paul's words at 10:12–13 are not a denial of self-recommendation, but rather a denial of *inappropriate* self-recommendation, which involves games of classification and comparison.

Finally, at 12:11, Paul exclaims, "I have made a fool of myself; you yourselves drove me to it. Actually, I should have been commended by you." In other words, he has been commending himself, but that should not have been necessary. The Corinthians should have been recommending him.

What these uses of the word and Paul's constant self-recommendation suggest is that there are appropriate and inappropriate forms of self-recommendation. Notice that the way Paul commends himself in 2 Corinthians, as we have looked at the uses of the word in the book, is very God centered and very ministry centered. There is nothing here that is self-centered or self-promoting. Paul's self-recommendation, in other words, is really a commendation of God's work and God's ministry accomplished in the world. This is made even more sure as we turn to the remainder of our passage.

Yet Paul walks the edge of a ministerial knife. He is pushed by the circumstances to recommend himself and thus the true ministry of God, but he believes it should not be necessary. He will also enter into boasting later in the book, but he is a very reluctant boaster. In both cases he does not want to be mistaken as playing by the interlopers' rules. Thus it may be maintained that godly self-recommendation in 2 Corinthians is seen as a positive enterprise (Belleville 1996: 88) that should be unnecessary in the case of Paul's relationship with this church. As Didymus the Blind comments, "Paul gently expresses his surprise that the Corinthians are still unaware of the implication of his apostleship" (Bray 1999: 212). But there is a final piece of evidence that supports the translation of 3:1a as a statement rather than as a rhetorical question anticipating a negative answer: the grammar.

3. *Grammar*. Fitzgerald (1988: 187) suggests that when Paul speaks negatively about self-recommendation, he places the pronoun before the verb for emphasis (as here in 3:1); then the pronoun follows the verb when Paul writes positively of self-recommendation. However, I agree with Thrall (1994: 218) that it seems artificial to make a distinction, sometimes on the basis of word order (e.g., Harris 2005: 259), between bad forms of self-recommendation and appropriate forms. After all, the "again" (πάλιν) in 3:1a suggests that Paul has participated in such commendation before.

In the second part of the verse, we find further insight on the grammar. The apostle asks, "Or[7] do we, like some, need letters of recommendation to you or from you?!" As reflected in our translation, the negative μή (*mē*) anticipates a negative answer from the second clause,[8] and some commentators suggest that the μή in the second clause of 3:1 should be read back into the first clause. But this does not seem to work grammatically. Rather, the natural way to read the grammar is to read the first clause in the verse as a statement and the rhetorical question that follows as a contrast.

We are starting to recommend ourselves to you again!

  or

do we, like some, need letters of recommendation to you or from you?!

The contrast here stands between Paul's self-recommendation and the need for letters of recommendation. In other words, Paul is saying with the contrast, "or isn't my self-recommendation enough?!"

The "like some" (ὥς τινες, *hōs tines*) almost certainly alludes to the Corinthian interlopers (Barnett 1997: 159; Belleville 1996: 88; P. Hughes 1962: 85), called "hucksters" in the previous verse, who were recommending themselves and perhaps came with letters of recommendation as well (10:11–12).[9] It may

---

7. The conjunction ἤ (*ē*) indicates an alternative and at times was used at the beginning of a rhetorical question in a series (e.g., Matt. 26:53; Rom. 3:29; 1 Cor. 6:9; 2 Cor. 11:7).

8. This is also reflected in NET and NRSV. The NET reads, "We don't need letters of recommendation to you or from you as some other people do, do we?"; and the NRSV, "Surely we do not need, as some do, letters of recommendation to you or from you, do we?"

9. In Paul's discussion at 10:12, his problem with the false teachers is not their use of the convention of self-recommendation but rather that they have engaged in a game of comparison based on a misunderstanding of Christian ministry. Paul's self-recommendation, by contrast, is based on the fruit of his life and ministry. Further, in the introduction to his commentary, Barrett (1973: 40–41) suggests that the interlopers have received their letters from leaders at the church in Jerusalem (though in his comments on 3:1 [1973: 106] he merely mentions "recognized authorities" without naming a place of origin). But as Furnish points out, why then would they need letters from the Corinthians as well? It could be that the letters they

be inferred from the term rendered "we . . . need" (χρῄζομεν, *chrēzomen*) that the "some" Paul has in mind indeed do need such letters (Barnett 1997: 161–62).

By Paul's day, letters of recommendation (one was a συστατικὴ ἐπιστολή, *systatikē epistolē*) had been used in broader Greco-Roman culture for several centuries, and ancient manuals on letter writing describe their crafting (Furnish 1984: 180). Such letters were provided to persons traveling to a new location, to formally introduce them to those who might help them in some way, perhaps providing hospitality or employment. Based on a social system in which one honored friends or relatives in good standing, or demonstrated loyalty to patrons, it was hoped that such a letter would be responded to positively by the recipients (W. R. Baird Jr. 1961: 168–69). For instance, in a letter, dated about AD 25, a man introduces his brother to acquaintances, appealing to them for a good response: "Heraklides, who is delivering the letter to you, is my brother. Therefore I beg you as urgently as possible to consider him introduced (to you). I have also asked my brother Hermias to inform you about him by letter. You will do me the greatest possible favor if he wins your consideration" (P.Oxy. 292; Keyes 1935: 35). It is clear from the NT that personal recommendations via letters also played a role in the early churches. For instance, 3 John in part should be considered as a letter of recommendation. Further, Luke makes reference to letters introducing a person or persons in Acts 9:2; 15:25–27; 18:27; and 22:5, and Paul himself includes a recommendation of Phoebe at Rom. 16:1–2.[10] Thus Paul is not adverse to the use of formal introductions in line with the conventions of the day. Rather, in 2 Cor. 3:1 he objects to the *need* for such letters in his relationship with the Corinthians. He needs neither to bring a recommendation letter to them (since his relationship with them is well established), nor does he need a letter from them in order to carry out his broader ministry.

One reason Paul does not need a letter of recommendation is that he already   3:2
has one—the work of God in the Corinthians themselves: "You yourselves are our letter of recommendation" (ἡ ἐπιστολὴ ἡμῶν ὑμεῖς ἐστε, *hē epistolē hēmōn hymeis este*). Using the image of "letter" metaphorically, Paul suggests that the Corinthians, as the fruit of his ministry, provide the only authenticating

---

carry are from other Hellenistic congregations (Furnish 1984: 192–93), or that the letters originated with another church in Judea or from the Pharisaic branch of the Jerusalem church, which insisted on careful observance of the Mosaic law as essential for salvation (Harris 2005: 260). For more on this matter, see "Paul and His Opponents at Corinth" in the introduction. Further, that Paul mentions letters from the Corinthians as well does not necessarily mean that the false teachers have now left. Rather, Paul anticipates that they will maintain their pattern of acquiring such letters on their departure from Corinth (Furnish 1984: 192–93; Thrall 1994: 220–21).

10. Harris (2005: 260) also includes Paul's recommendation of Timothy (1 Cor. 16:10–11), Titus and his traveling companions (2 Cor. 8:22–23), Tychicus (Eph. 6:21–22; Col. 4:7–8), Mark (Col. 4:10), and Onesimus (Philem. 10–12, 17–19). However, it is not clear that these involve formal introductions of someone to a person or church. Rather, they may be read as general acts of speaking on behalf of someone.

credentials he needs (cf. 1 Cor. 9:2).[11] Interpreting Paul, John Chrysostom (*Hom. 2 Cor.* 6.1–2) observes:

> "If we needed to be commended to others," he says, "we would have produced you before them rather than a letter." . . . Here Paul bears witness not only to their love but also to their good works, since by their behavior they can demonstrate to everybody the high worth of their teacher. What letters would have done to gain respect for the apostle, the Corinthians achieve by their life and behavior. The virtues of disciples commend the teacher more than any letter. They are an epistle of Christ, having the law of God written in their hearts. God wrote that law, but Paul and his companions prepared them to receive the writing. For just as Moses hewed stones and tables, so Paul shaped their souls. (Bray 1999: 212–13)

This letter he describes as "written on our[12] hearts" (ἐγγεγραμμένη ἐν ταῖς καρδίαις ἡμῶν, *engegrammenē en tais kardiais hēmōn*). In 2 Corinthians, the apostle has much to say about the heart (καρδία, *kardia*), using the image eleven times (2 Cor. 1:22; 2:4; 3:2–3, 15; 4:6; 5:12; 6:11; 7:3; 8:16; 9:7). The heart often represents the center and source of a person's inner life, including emotions, volition, and thinking (BDAG 508). Thus, for instance, Paul writes of deep emotion, the anguish of heart he felt when he confronted the Corinthians in a difficult letter (2:4), and he can use the image as well in referring to a person's integrity or commitment (5:12; 6:11; 8:16; 9:7). He notes that the heart is the place where the Spirit works (1:22; 3:3), and as such it is the place where spiritual illumination must take place (3:15; 4:6).

Here in 3:2 and in 7:3, when he says that the Corinthians are "written on our hearts,"[13] the apostle speaks of his love for and commitment to these fellow believers, expressed through authentic ministry to them. Accordingly, Paul describes the hearts of his ministry team as the scribal writing desk upon which the Corinthians had been written. The verb ἐγγράφω (*engraphō*) can refer to recording information, writing things down, or making an inscription (BDAG 270). Paul could be alluding to a new-covenant reality reflected in Jer. 31:33 (38:33 LXX), the law written on the heart, which will be contrasted with the ministry of "stone tablets" in the next verse.[14] Yet here Paul refers to the Corinthians themselves as written on the hearts of Paul and his fellow ministers, not the law or the ways of God written on the Corinthians' hearts.

---

11. The pronoun ὑμεῖς (*hymeis*, yourselves) intensifies Paul's statement.

12. Following ℵ and a few minor witnesses, in 3:2 the RSV has "your" (*hymōn*, ὑμῶν) hearts. See the additional note on 3:2 for the text-critical issue.

13. The stative aspect of the perfect participle ἐγγεγραμμένη suggests that the Corinthians have been written on the hearts of Paul's ministry team but also continue to be written on the hearts of Paul and his associates in an ongoing way. In other words, his ministry of love and commitment toward them continues, and thus continues to be authenticated through the church in Corinth.

14. Or perhaps the exhortation of Prov. 3:3 to write mercy and faithfulness on the tablet of one's heart.

Thus Paul uses the imagery of "having been written on our hearts" to communicate another specific reality: the work of the Spirit in and through him as he ministers lovingly to the Corinthian believers.

Further, remember that a letter of recommendation normally was given to persons being recommended, in order that they might present the letter for validation at an appropriate time. Thus Paul, expressing his love and devotion to the Achaian church, infers that he carries the Corinthians with him (Matera 2003: 77), like a letter of recommendation, but in his heart, in his deepest affections and commitments. Christ has done an authentic, spiritual work in the Corinthians,[15] yet in Paul as well. For, as the Spirit has worked through him to minister to the Corinthians, the Spirit has also worked in Paul, fostering a ministry heart of concern, compassion, and commitment toward them. Paul is not an opportunist ministering for his own profit (2:17), nor a hireling merely fulfilling an assigned drudgery. He is a called, deeply committed minister of Jesus Christ, who loves Christ's church.

Although this metaphorical Corinthian Letter has been written on his heart, in the depths of Paul's person, the letter is not hidden away there. Rather it is "known and read by everyone" (γινωσκομένη καὶ ἀναγινωσκομένη ὑπὸ πάντων ἀνθρώπων, *ginōskomenē kai anaginōskomenē hypo pantōn anthrōpōn*). The present[16] passive participles rendered "known and read" are cognates and, like the perfect participle ἐγγεγραμμένη, are grammatically related to the term ἐπιστολή (letter). These images have to do with the ongoing openness of authentic ministry, its public platform as the life of the church plays out before a watching world. Paul's ministry of integrity is "known" (2:4, 9; 3:2; 5:16, 21; 8:9; 13:6) in that it is there in plain view, made public, for those who can or will notice or recognize it. Since reading was normally done aloud, this image too speaks of the public nature of Paul's Corinthian ministry. The fruit of genuine ministry, initiated by God, is that it is transparently authentic before the world and understood for what it truly is. Thus in verse 2 Paul proclaims that the Corinthians have been "written," and they are "known" and "read," a natural progression from the foundational work of Paul's ministry to its ongoing public witness.

In verse 3 the apostle continues, "making it clear that you are a letter produced   **3:3** by Christ, prepared by us, written not with ink but with the Spirit of the living God, not on stone tablets but on tablets of human hearts." The conjunction

---

15. As noted by Barnett (1997: 164), given the spiritual immaturity, the "disloyalty, fickleness, and waywardness" of the Corinthian church, it is remarkable that Paul celebrates them here as a commendatory letter. Yet the apostle does so on two bases, first that God has indeed done a work in them, but primarily on the basis of the authenticity of his own ministry to them. He knows that the gospel ministry he has carried out has been a powerful, gospel-imbued work, and this is the main point of his statement here.

16. The present-tense participles communicate imperfective aspect: the Corinthians are portrayed as currently and in an ongoing way living out a public witness to the validity of Paul's ministry.

ὅτι (*hoti*) goes untranslated in our rendering, but it is explanatory,[17] marking Paul's statement in verse 3 as a clarification of his proclamation of verse 2. As Paul's ministry to the Corinthians is perceived rightly, something becomes clear (φανερούμενοι, *phaneroumenoi*; cf. 2:14; 4:10–11; 5:10–11; 7:12; 11:6). This work of ministry, embodied in the Achaian church, spoken of metaphorically as a "letter," really originates with Christ, not with the apostle himself. Some have taken the genitive Χριστοῦ (*Christou*) as objective, that is "a letter about Christ," but it more likely proclaims the true originator of this letter, the primary agent by whom it has come into being, since the descriptors that follow all have to do with the letter's production. In fact, Daniel Wallace's (1996: 104–5) category "genitive of production" seems fitting: "You are a letter produced by Christ." In keeping with the figurative language used by the apostle thus far in the chapter, the Corinthians as his letter of recommendation have been produced not by Paul himself but rather under the initiative and authority of Christ (cf. 1:1). This places Paul's ministry in sharp contrast to those who bring credentials from human agents (i.e., the "some" of 3:1). Paul's letter of recommendation, the Corinthians themselves, has been produced by the Lord Christ.

Although Christ alone stands as the ultimate authority and source of Paul's ministry to the Corinthians, the apostle hastens to point out his own role in the process, stating that the "letter" was "prepared by us" (διακονηθεῖσα ὑφ' ἡμῶν, *diakonētheisa hyph' hēmōn*), perhaps casting himself in the role of an amanuensis, or "secretary." Humanly speaking, Paul founded the church at Corinth and thus, as their "father" in the faith, not only was he there at their birth as a community, but as a good parent, the apostle also continues to care for them (1 Cor. 4:15). The verb διακονέω (*diakoneō*) has a wide range of meanings in literature of the first century but generally connotes the idea of rendering a service or help of some kind (e.g., Matt. 25:44). Such service could be that of an intermediary or agent (e.g., 1 Pet. 1:12), and that sense almost certainly exists here, since Paul acts on behalf of Christ in ministering to the Corinthians. In a related nuance, the term also could be used to refer to ministry carried out in an official capacity (e.g., 1 Tim. 3:10), and using this word, or the word's cognates, Paul has much to say on Christian ministry in the verses and chapters that follow (3:6–9; 4:1; 5:18; 6:3–4; 8:4, 19–20; 9:1, 12–13; 11:8, 15, 23). So given the "letter" imagery, how might the term best be translated in 2 Cor. 3:3?

Some have opted for the general sense of "cared for by us" (NASB), or as the NIV[84] and NIV put it, "the result of our ministry," an updated rendering of the more archaic "ministered by us" (KJV, ASV, Tyndale). Other translations, in keeping with the letter-writing imagery, go with "produced by us" (HCSB) or "prepared by us" (NLT, NRSV), and still others understand the word as referring to the delivery of the letter ("delivered by us," RSV, ESV, NET, NEB).

---

17. The ὅτι functions very similarly to the ὅτι at the beginning of 2:15, offering a clarification of what has just been said.

The unadorned conciseness of Paul's language thwarts us somewhat at this point, but given the context, it is reasonable to suggest that Paul conceives of himself as Christ's secretary, the agent used by Christ in the production of this Corinthian "letter."[18] Thus we translate the phrase "prepared by us," which leaves the image appropriately vague (Thrall 1994: 225) while at the same time noting the apostle's significant role. Some might object that this interpretation conflicts with the role of the Spirit in the next phrase—translated by some as "*by* the Spirit of the living God"—but as noted below, Paul contrasts the Spirit with the "ink" used in the writing process, rather conceiving of the Spirit as the writer of the letter.

This brings us to the "media" used in the writing of Christ's letter, and lining out the structural parallelism in the text offers a helpful beginning place for unpacking the imagery:

written not with ink but	ἐγγεγραμμένη οὐ μέλανι ἀλλὰ *engegrammenē ou melani alla*
with the Spirit of the living God,	πνεύματι θεοῦ ζῶντος, *pneumati theou zōntos,*
not on stone tablets but	οὐκ ἐν πλαξὶν λιθίναις ἀλλ' *ouk en plaxin lithinais all'*
on tablets of human hearts.	ἐν πλαξὶν καρδίαις σαρκίναις. *en plaxin kardiais sarkinais.*

As noted by Hafemann (2000: 117), the contrast between "ink" and "the Spirit" is a contrast of means, whereas the contrast of stone tablets and hearts presents a contrast of sphere. When the apostle writes that the means (or instrumentality) by which Christ's ministry has been accomplished among the Corinthians is "not written with ink," he uses a word picture from literary practices of the day. Ink (μέλαν, *melan*) in the first century most often was black, made by combining soot and gum (thus the word's derivation from the adjective "black," μέλας), and was applied with a reed pen to papyrus, the most common writing material of the era.[19] "Ink" clearly parallels πνεύματι (*pneumati*), "with [or by means of] the Spirit." In keeping with the letter imagery and the structure of the passage, as well as Paul's scriptural allusions at this point, the phrase should be translated as communicating means/instrumentality ("with the Spirit") rather than agency ("by the Spirit").[20]

Further, "the Spirit" as used here in 3:3 echoes an important thread in OT prophecies concerning the ministry of the Spirit in effecting new or renewed

18. On the role of secretaries in the ancient world, see Klauck and Bailey 2006: 55–60.
19. On the materials used in the writing process in the first century, see Klauck and Bailey 2006: 44–54.
20. Paul uses the term πνεῦμα seventeen times in 2 Corinthians; ten of these refer to the Holy Spirit (1:22; 3:3, 6, 8, 17 [2x]; 18; 5:5; 6:6; 13:13). Here the Spirit is referred to as "the Spirit of the living God," paralleling Paul's reference to God as "living" at 6:16, "For we are the temple of the living God." In the OT, God is proclaimed as "living" in confessions of his active presence among his people (e.g., Deut. 5:26; Josh. 3:10; 1 Sam. 17:26, 36; 2 Kings 19:4, 16; Pss. 42:2; 84:2; Isa. 37:4, 17; Jer. 10:10; 23:36; Dan. 6:20, 26; Hosea 1:10).

covenant relationship between God and his people. In passages such as Isa. 44:3; Ezek. 39:29; and Joel 2:28–29, the prophets announce that the Spirit will be poured out on God's people; the Joel proclamation is taken up by Peter on the day of Pentecost (Acts 2:17–21). Other portions of Scripture, however, use the language of the Spirit being "put/placed" on or in people (e.g., Num. 11:29; Isa. 42:1; 63:11), and chief among these for our consideration are a pair of passages from Ezekiel (11:19; 36:26–27), for these combine the gift of the Spirit (or at points "a new spirit") with a promise that speaks of stony hearts in contrast to hearts of flesh:

> I will give them one heart and I will put a new spirit within them; I will remove the hearts of stone from their bodies and I will give them tender hearts. (Ezek. 11:19 NET)

> I will give you a new heart, and I will put a new spirit within you. I will remove the heart of stone from your body and give you a heart of flesh. I will put my Spirit within you; I will take the initiative and you will obey my statutes and carefully observe my regulations. (Ezek. 36:26–27 NET)

In the first of these passages, one can read the term "spirit," which parallels the "new heart" in the previous clause, as referring to the human spirit, the seat of moral will and thought. Pointing to a new covenant between God and his people, Ezekiel builds on the words of his contemporary Jeremiah, who spoke of the need for a "single heart" (Jer. 32:39) by adding reflection on the need for a new spirit and a heart of flesh that will replace the peoples' heart of stone (Block 1998: 352–53). Yet, in the second of these Ezekiel passages (36:26–27), this prophecy concerning a "new spirit" merges with the promise of God's Spirit being placed within his people. Block (1998: 355–56) comments:

> Concomitant with the heart transplant, Yahweh will infuse his people with a new spirit, his Spirit. On first sight, the present juxtaposing of *rûaḥ* [spirit] and *lēb* [heart] in such precise, if chiastic, parallelism suggests that "spirit" and "mind/ heart" should be treated as virtual synonyms. However, the synonymity is seldom exact in Hebrew parallelism, and here the terms are associated with different prepositions. The new heart is given to (*nātan lĕ*) the Israelites, but the spirit is placed *within* (*nātan bĕqereb*) them. This distinction is confirmed by the manner in which vv. 26b–27 elaborate on the two statements. The provision of the new heart involves a removal of the petrified organ and its replacement with a heart of flesh, the source of which is unspecified. But the new spirit placed inside Israel is identified as Yahweh's *rûaḥ* (v. 27), which animates and vivifies the recipients.

Echoing Ezek. 36:26–27, yet using the image of the Spirit being written on the heart, Paul points to authentic Christian ministry in which God places the Spirit of God in the hearts of his people.

But, as already noted, the image of the Spirit as performing a heart transplant in believers is conflated with the image of "writing on the heart," a word picture that seems to have its source in the prophet Jeremiah. Accordingly, Paul's letter metaphor may have brought to the apostle's mind another potent new-covenant passage, Jer. 31:31–34 (38:31–34 LXX): "'Instead, this is the covenant I will make with the house of Israel after those days'—the LORD's declaration. 'I will place My teaching within them and write it on their hearts. I will be their God, and they will be My people'" (Jer. 31:33 HCSB).[21] Jeremiah's use of writing imagery also concerns the effect of spiritual renewal on the hearts of Yahweh's people, a renewal that issues in dynamic relationship. Significantly for our understanding of 2 Cor. 3, Jeremiah has the law written on the hearts of new-covenant people. So it seems that Paul primarily borrows from Jeremiah the image of writing on the hearts. Thus, when in 2 Cor. 3:3 he pictures the Spirit not as writer but as the written message, he offers a reflection of the Spirit's work in the life of a new-covenant believer, bringing together images from both Ezekiel and Jeremiah.

In the ancient world, a stone "tablet" (πλάξ, *plax*) could be used for inscriptions. This sphere of the "tablets of human hearts"[22] as the authentic place of Christian ministry stands in contrast to "stone tablets."[23] Exodus 31:18 refers to the "tablets of stone" inscribed by "the finger of God," and Paul probably merges allusions at this point: the replacement of stony hearts (Ezek. 36:26–27) dovetails with the writing of the law (Jer. 31:33) on the tablets of stone (Exod. 31:18). These latter two allusions mark a turning in Paul's imagery to the topic of the law, anticipating the Spirit/letter contrast in 3:6 and the contrast between new-covenant ministry and Moses's ministry through a veil in 3:7–18.[24]

---

21. See also Jer. 17:1: "The sin of Judah is written with an iron stylus. With a diamond point it is engraved on the tablet of their hearts and on the horns of their altars" (HCSB).

22. Translated variously as "human hearts" (NASB, NET, NLT, NIV, NRSV), "hearts of flesh" (HCSB, ASV), "fleshly tables of the heart" (Tyndale, KJV, Darby, Webster), "on tablets of flesh, that is, of the heart" (NKJV). In other places, Paul employs the term σάρκινος (*sarkinos*) to contrast human life as oriented to the flesh as opposed to life in the Spirit (e.g., Rom. 7:14; 1 Cor. 3:1).

23. Elsewhere in the NT, πλάξ is used only at Heb. 9:4, the stone tablets of the covenant in the ark of the covenant: LXX in span from Exod. 32–34 and Deut. 4–10 (e.g., Exod. 31:18; 32:15; 34:1, 4; Deut. 4:13; 5:22; 9:9–11; 10:1, 3; 1 Kings 8:9).

24. Hafemann (2000: 117) suggests that the contrast should not be conceived as an authentic, internal work ("written with the Spirit of the living God . . . on tablets of human hearts") in contrast to an external work of legalism ("on stony hearts"):

> Paul's contrast is not an abstract one between "outward" and "inward," between "externality" and "internality," between "ritualism" and "a living experience of the Spirit," or between "rigidity" and "spontaneity," etc., as is often suggested. Nor is Paul making a negative statement about the nature or content of the law by associating it with "stone," which seems to be the common denominator undergirding these interpretations. The reference in 3:3 to the "tablets of stone" is part of a long tradition in which this designation is at the least a normal, neutral way of referring to the law, and more likely functions to emphasize its permanence, divine authority, honor, and glory (cf. 3:7, 9, 11!).

Thus, according to Hafemann, Paul's reference to the "tablets of stone" should not be taken as pejorative, for the law came with glory (3:7–11). Rather, with the reference to "tablets of stone," Paul highlights two spheres of the work of ministry, building on the ministry of the

iv. The Confidence of a Truly Competent Ministry (3:4–6)

3:4   In the first three verses of chapter 3, Paul's assessment of his ministry might sound arrogant in its claims and resolute confidence—Paul does, after all, claim to be a coworker with God! So with verse 4 the apostle explains the basis for his expressed confidence. The apostle uses the noun πεποίθησις (*pepoithēsis*) six times in his writings, four of these in 2 Corinthians (1:15; 3:4; 8:22; 10:2; Eph. 3:12; Phil. 3:4). In literature of the first century, the word connotes a state of certainty about something, to the point that one has confidence or trust in a person or outcome (BDAG 796). Elsewhere in 2 Corinthians, Paul states that he is confident about the integrity (1:15) and performance (10:2) of his ministry, and he reports a brother's confidence in the Corinthian church (8:22).

Reflecting on what he has just written in 2:14–3:3 (the referent for the word τοιαύτην, *toiautēn*, this kind, such), at 3:4 Paul expresses an unflinching trust that the source (Christ), effect (the work of the Spirit), validation (the fruit among the Corinthians), and orientation (toward God) of his ministry all mark the authenticity of his work[25] and are summed up with two phrases, "through Christ" and "toward God." That Paul's confidence is "through Christ" (διά τοῦ Χριστοῦ, *dia tou Christou*) suggests that Christ stands as the primary agent[26] of Paul's confidence, since Christ has sent him and enabled him in this work of ministry. He ministers with the confidence of one who knows the authority, agenda, and abilities of the One by whom he has been sent. The phrase rendered "toward God" (πρὸς τὸν θεόν, *pros ton theon*; so NASB, NRSV, HCSB; the KJV, ASV, and Tyndale have the similar and nicely phrased "to God-ward") is expressed by other translations with "in God" (NET, NLT), or "before God" (NIV). Yet the wording "toward God" probably captures the sense of the Greek phrase best. While at places in the NT the phrase can communicate intimacy of relationship (e.g., John 1:1–2, "with God"), in the vast majority of NT occurrences it communicates an action directed to God or done with reference to God, such as prayer (Acts 4:24; 12:5; Rom. 10:1; 15:30; 2 Cor. 13:7; Phil. 4:6), faith (1 Thess. 1:8), confidence (1 John 3:21), having a clear conscience or peace (e.g., Acts 24:16; Rom. 5:1), turning to God from idols (1 Thess. 1:9), or rendering service (Heb. 2:17; 5:1). This makes the translation "in God" (NET, NLT) highly unlikely, and although the idea "before God" (NIV) is attractive, Paul has already used the term κατέναντι (*katenanti*, before) to express that idea in the immediate context (2:17). When he says he has confidence "toward God" at 3:4, the apostle speaks of God as the one to whom he ultimately is answerable.

---

old-covenant era, contrasting it with true new-covenant ministry in order to magnify the greater glory of the latter.

25. Furnish (1984: 196) notes, "The apostle's parenthetical reflections in 3:1–3 will have served only to accentuate the question he himself has posed in 2:16b and to which he has not yet actually responded: How can anyone presume to be fit to take up the kind of responsibilities which have been envisioned in the grand affirmation of 2:14–16a, and which Paul believes he and his associates have fulfilled in Corinth specifically (3:1–3)?"

26. Often διά + the genitive communicates agency ("by" or "through").

With verse 5 the apostle again quickly qualifies the confidence he expresses in   **3:5**
verse 4, stating that rather than a personal boast, this God-centered origin and
orientation of his ministry constitutes a confession of his own inadequacy.
This confession Paul organizes around a pair of contrasts (in vv. 5–6), each
having a disclaimer followed by a contrasting statement:

> [5]Not that we are qualified because of ourselves (οὐχ ὅτι ἀφ᾽ ἑαυτῶν ἱκανοί
> ἐσμεν, *ouch hoti aph᾽ heautōn hikanoi esmen*) . . . ,
>
> but our competence is from God (ἀλλ᾽ ἡ ἱκανότης ἡμῶν ἐκ τοῦ θεοῦ, *all᾽
> hē hikanotēs hēmōn ek tou theou*), . . .
>
> [6]Not of the letter (οὐ γράμματος, *ou grammatos*)
>
> but of the Spirit (ἀλλὰ πνεύματος, *alla pneumatos*)

It is probably for emphasis that Paul places the negative οὐχ (*ouch*, not) first
in the Greek sentence that comprises most of verses 5–6. The term ἱκανός
(*hikanos*) was used variously to refer to that which is sufficient or adequate
in terms of degree (e.g., something that is enough), or measuring up to a
standard in terms of what is "fit, appropriate, competent, qualified, or able"
(BDAG 472; Spicq 1994: 2.217–22). Paul seems to have in mind the idea of
being competent or qualified to carry out a role as a proclaimer of God's
gospel in the world (2:16).[27] This interpretation fits well the broader context
in which letters of recommendation are under discussion. Using this adjective
and two cognates—the noun ἱκανότης (*hikanotēs*, fitness, capability, qualification) and the verb ἱκανόω (*hikanoō*, to cause to be sufficient/qualified; BDAG
472–73)—the apostle asserts in no uncertain terms that he is not qualified,
or competent, in himself to carry out the ministry in which he participates.
His disclaimer would have placed his attitude and posture in direct contrast
to the self-competent false teachers at Corinth (10:12).

Further, it may be that Paul's statement here, that he is "unqualified" in
and of himself,[28] serves as an allusion to the call and ministry of Moses, the
intermediary who helped establish the old, Sinai covenant between God and
his people. When God appoints Moses as his spokesman before the Israelites
and their Egyptian masters, the LXX records Moses's reply as οὐχ ἱκανός
εἰμι (*ouch hikanos eimi*, I am not qualified), the same adjective Paul uses here
in verse 5 (Exod. 3:11; 4:10). God answers, "'Who gave a mouth to man, or
who makes a person mute or deaf or seeing or blind? Is it not I, the LORD?
So now go, and I will be with your mouth and will teach you what you must
say'"(Exod. 4:11–12 NET). Thus God makes the inadequate to be adequate,

27. Spicq (1994: 2.219) explains that "it is Philo who fleshed out the sense of *hikanos* as
'capable of' in applying it to people; he gave it the nuances of being apt, particular to (*Spec.
Laws* 4.188), equal to ([*Emb.*] 257), gifted for, in a position to do (*Flight* 40); seeds 'are capable
of producing plants like those which produced them'" (*Unchang.* 40; *Drunk.* 212; *Cher.* 65).

28. In our translation, we render ἀπό as "because" with the sense of oneself being the origin
or cause of being qualified for ministry (BDAG 106).

the unqualified to be qualified, the incompetent to be competent, and this pattern dominates as one considers the call of other great leaders throughout redemptive history.

In verse 5 the phrase ἀφ' ἑαυτῶν (*aph' heautōn*, because of ourselves) parallels the phrase ἐξ ἑαυτῶν (*ex heautōn*, out of [from] ourselves), and both contrast with ἐκ τοῦ θεοῦ (*ek tou theou*, from God). At first blush, it may seem difficult to sort out the nuanced differences between Paul's use of ἀπό and ἐξ in the first two of these phrases. Yet, the first prepositional phrase probably denies that the apostolic team should be understood as the precipitating *cause* of their personal adequacy for ministry (see BDAG 106.5), while the latter denies that Paul and his mission could be seen as the ultimate source or origin of "anything" (τι, *ti*) that would seem to validate their ministry as competent. The λογίσασθαί τι ὡς ἐξ ἑαυτῶν (*logisasthai ti hōs ex heautōn*, to consider anything as from ourselves) makes clear that those who see themselves as "competent" or "qualified" consider[29] at least some[30] aspects of their qualifications as originating in their own gifts and resources. By contrast, Paul points to God as the true source, both immediate and ultimate, for his adequacy in ministry.[31] Thus Paul's ministry draws on and flows from the sufficiency of God.

3:6   Eschatologically the apostle and his team have been "made competent" by God (ἱκάνωσεν[32] ἡμᾶς, *hikanōsen hēmas*, made us competent) as "ministers of a new covenant" (διακόνους καινῆς διαθήκης, *diakonous kainēs diathēkēs*) established by Christ's death and carried forward under Christ's lordship (Hafemann 2000: 127–28).[33] The genitives καινῆς διαθήκης (of a new covenant) delimit the word διακόνους (ministers) and may be read as attributive,[34] communicating an innate quality of ministry. In contradistinction from his opponents, Paul and his team are "new-covenant ministers."

Consequently, Paul's appeal to his authority and status as a minister of Christ rests in his "inadequate adequacy," the call and enabling of God for

29. The aorist infinitive λογίσασθαι has to do with reckoning, calculating, or thinking in a certain way.

30. This is the opposite of Paul's proclamation, which is that he doesn't consider anything (τι) that qualifies him for ministry as originating in himself.

31. God was confessed to be the truly sufficient One in Jewish theology of the day (e.g., Philo, *Alleg.* 1.44, who speaks of God as being "sufficient" [ἱκανός] unto himself).

32. The perfective aspect of the aorist suggests that Paul's competence is an accomplished fact, a work of God in the apostle upon his calling to this ministry. The Lord has commissioned Paul, established him (1:21) and anointed him (1:21), and given him authority to minister to the Corinthians (10:8; 13:10). Paul has this ministry in accordance with God's mercy (4:1); he is an ambassador for Christ, entrusted with the message of reconciliation (5:19).

33. Hafemann (2000: 127–28) follows Sandnes (1991: 7–8, 64–69), who makes the case that Paul's self-understanding as an apostle is expressed in terms of prophetic motifs, the apostle seeing himself in continuity with the OT prophetic tradition (e.g., Rom. 1:1–5; 1 Cor. 2:6–16; 2 Cor. 4:6; Eph. 2:19–3:7; 1 Thess. 2:3–8).

34. This is also referred to as a "Hebrew genitive" or a "genitive of quality" (D. Wallace 1996: 86–87). Among other points Paul wishes to make, there exists a qualitative difference between his ministry and that of his opponents.

a very particular kind of ministry. Thus, while there are parallels with the ministry of Moses, the apostle's ministry has a different orientation than that mediator of the Sinai covenant. This constitutes a main point as the apostle focuses on the contrast between Moses's ministry and authentic Christian ministry in 3:7–18. The apostle uses the noun διάκονος (*diakonos*, minister, servant) five times in 2 Corinthians (2 Cor. 3:6; 6:4; 11:15 [2x], 23), the term διακονία (*diakonia*, ministry, service) another twelve times (2 Cor. 3:7–9 [4x]; 4:1; 5:18; 6:3; 8:4; 9:1, 12–13; 11:8), and the verbal form three times (2 Cor. 3:3; 8:19–20); thus the ministry motif weaves a significant thread through the book. We are, after all, in a section of the letter that treats Paul's understanding of true Christian ministry, and that ministry works from the standpoint of the new covenant.

The reference to the "new covenant" has as its backdrop Jer. 31:31–34 (38:31–34 LXX), the OT promise introduced with "'Indeed, a time is coming,' says the LORD, 'when I will make a new covenant with the people of Israel and Judah.'" That covenant would involve knowing the Lord, the internalization of the laws of God, and the decisive forgiveness of sin, realized in the new-covenant sacrifice of Christ on the cross (Heb. 8:7–10:18). Thus Christ held up the cup at the Last Supper, saying, "This cup is the new covenant established by My blood; it is shed for you" (Luke 22:20 HCSB; 1 Cor. 11:25), and Paul's ministry proclaims that same covenant. Therefore, true Christian ministry constitutes a particular type of covenant ministry, within the new covenant established by the death of Jesus. This is Paul's gospel and his profound orientation in relation to the Corinthians as the apostle appeals to them on the basis of new-covenant realities (see Lane 1982).

The final part of verse 6 reads, "not of the letter but of the Spirit. For the letter kills but the Spirit produces life." The parallels in the passage may be laid out in an *abab* pattern as follows:

A   οὐ γράμματος ἀλλὰ (*ou grammatos alla*)
  B   πνεύματος· (*pneumatos*)
      γὰρ (*gar*)
A′ τὸ . . . γράμμα ἀποκτέννει (*to . . . gramma apoktennei*),
      δὲ (*de*)
  B′ τὸ . . . πνεῦμα ζῳοποιεῖ (*to . . . pneuma zōopoiei*).

The genitives γράμματος and πνεύματος elaborate on the immediately preceding καινῆς διαθήκης. This ministry "of the new covenant" is, therefore, "of the Spirit," that is, carried out by the agency of the Spirit, a point that Paul will speak to in much greater detail in the next unit (3:7–18). The "Spirit" is the "Lord" referred to in Exod. 34:34, the Lord who brings freedom and works transformation in the glorious, unveiled people of the new covenant (3:17–18). By contrast (ἀλλά), Paul's ministry is οὐ γράμματος, not oriented to the agency of the "letter." He explains (γάρ) that "the letter kills but the Spirit produces life."[35]

What does the apostle mean by this contrast? Generally speaking, interpreters through the millennia have answered this question in one of three primary veins. Especially in the earliest centuries of the church, the "letter" at points was understood as a literalist approach to reading the text of Scripture, and "the spirit" was interpreted as reflecting a spiritual discernment of the Scripture's true meaning. For instance, in his work *First Principles* (1.1.2), Origen writes, "The letter means what is material and the spirit what is intellectual, which we also call spiritual," and elsewhere he suggests:

> For even in the Gospels, it is "the letter" that "kills." Not only in the Old Testament is "the letter that kills" found; there is also in the New Testament "the letter that kills"—that one who does not spiritually perceive what is said. For, if you follow according to the letter that which is said, "Unless you eat my flesh and drink my blood," this "letter kills." (*Hom. Lev. 7.5.5*; Bray 1999: 217–18)

Second, since the time of the Reformation the spirit/law dichotomy has been understood as communicating a radical dualism between the new covenant and its older predecessor, with the old covenant seen as functioning to produce condemnation and death, and the new covenant functioning to bring justification and life (e.g., Grindheim 2001). This interpretation focuses on the abrogation of the old covenant as that which has been replaced by the new in the history of redemption.

Rather than setting up a radical dualism, a third position sets forth the two covenants as in a continuum and the contrast expressed in 2 Cor. 3:6 as a contrast between those who attempted to keep the law apart from the work of the Spirit, and new-covenant people who have the ability to fulfill the law because of the Spirit. Augustine seems to agree with this understanding: "How does the Spirit give life? By causing the letter to be fulfilled, so that it may not kill" (*Sermons for Easter Season* 251.7); and, "He gives by the Spirit; for the law without grace makes sin abound, and the letter without the Spirit kills. He commands so as to make us learn how to ask the help of grace when we try to obey his commandments and in our weakness fall wearied under the law, and also to make us grateful to him who helps us if we have been able to perform any good work" (*Ep. to Hilarius* 157).

As we evaluate these positions, a few preliminary observations are in order. First, the term "covenant" (διαθήκη, *diathēkē*) provides the framework for

---

35. This deceptively straightforward passage, along with the unit of text that follows (3:7–18), has generated expansive, multifaceted discussions from the earliest Christian centuries. Yet, in spite of vigorous and widely published debates, it remains what many see as the stickiest wicket in Pauline theology. To what exactly does Paul refer when he speaks of the letter and Spirit in 2 Cor. 3, and why does he place them in a contrasting relationship here? Hafemann (1995: xiii) observes, "This seemingly proverbial, thesis-like statement and the context within which it is found epitomize why Second Corinthians has come to be known as both 'the paradise and the despair of the commentator'" (see also Martin 1986: x).

Paul's contrast between the letter and Spirit, as noted in the second and third of these positions. Second, although the reference to the new covenant as being "of the spirit" (πνεύματος, *pneumatos*) could possibly be anthropological, the reference to "the Spirit of the living God" in 2 Cor. 3:3 and to the Spirit as giving life later in verse 6 (as well as in 3:17–18) points to the Holy Spirit as the active agent in providing new-covenant experience. Third, with the double reference to the "letter," the apostle seems to have made a complete transition away from his "letter of recommendation" imagery that dominates the first three verses of the chapter, for here he uses a different term (γράμματος, *grammatos*, rather than ἐπιστολῶν, *epistolōn*) and points to a different function: the "letter kills." The terseness of Paul's statement suggests that he describes a fundamental dynamic of the old-covenant context, but the debate concerns the nature of that dynamic.

So how might we understand this contrast between the ministry carried forward under the agency of "the letter" and that carried out under the agency of "the Spirit"? First, when Paul says that "the letter kills," he does so out of his reading of the OT narratives. Here I agree with Francis Watson (2004: 277):

> For him, the law that brings with it the conditional offer of life is overtaken by the realities of sin and death, so that those who are under law are under its curse. Paul makes this claim not because of his prior dogmatic commitments, but because he has read and noted the scriptural stories that tell of the law's disastrous impact on its first addressees, who rebel against it and who are doomed to die in the wilderness in consequence. Other interpreters appear to skirt around the fact that the post-Sinai history of Israel in the wilderness is a history of catastrophe. For Paul, this represents an act of interpretive repression. It is the narratives of the Torah itself that lead him to claim that "the letter kills."

We can contrast an orientation to letters being inscribed on tablets of stone (3:3), then, with transformation of human hearts by the Spirit (2 Cor. 3:3; 4:6; F. Watson 2004: 312–13). Although this insight assumes that Paul writes out of deep reflection on the OT text, I prefer to think of this as a Spirit-oriented hermeneutic, in addition to a theologically oriented hermeneutic. It is as much relational as textual in its orientation. The Spirit orientation that Paul has experienced through the new covenant affects the way the text is read and illumined in Christ (3:14–15).

Second, however—as will become much clearer in our treatment of 3:7–18—the comparison here has more to do with *contrasting approaches to ministry* and the *outcomes of those ministries*, rather than with successive dispensations of the old covenant over against the new covenant. It is the new covenant that makes authentic Christian ministry possible, powerful, and productive (3:3, 6). The contrast in 2 Cor. 3 is not *primarily* with the old covenant per se but with the ongoing attempt to minister apart from the work of the Spirit and through a veil that lies over peoples' hearts (3:14–15). The "letter," then, refers to an attempt to minister or engage the Scriptures apart from the new-covenant work of the Spirit. That form of ministry "kills" just as it did in the old-covenant era. The present-tense verb ἀποκτέννει (*apoktennei*), like its counterpart ζῳοποιεῖ (*zōopoiei*), is a gnomic present (Harris 2005: 273). Those who experience that form of ministry are perishing (4:3) until the light of the new-covenant, life-giving Spirit breaks through in the gospel of Christ.

In the next unit the point the apostle makes builds as Paul points to the fact that Moses himself experienced the ministry of the Spirit, who transformed him as he met face-to-face with the Lord. Thus the ministry of the glorious, transforming Spirit existed in the old-covenant era, as Paul himself makes clear in 3:7–11. What Paul will show in the next unit is that this glorious experience of the life-giving Spirit was never meant to be limited to Moses himself (thus the new covenant was anticipated all along). Paul's boldness stems from the fact that Christ, through the new covenant, powerfully rips away the veil separating people from the presence of God (3:12). In other words, real transformation is possible because people may experience the presence of the Lord through the power of the life-giving Spirit (3:17–18).

Reflection

One of Paul's primary concerns in 2 Corinthians has to do with qualification for ministry. Who is qualified to participate with God, proclaiming his humanity-dividing gospel to the world (2:16b)? In 2 Cor. 2:16b–3:6 the apostle makes clear that only ministers of integrity qualify: those who are sent by God, live before God, and have a true relationship with Christ (2:17). Thus human letters of recommendation pale in significance before the open "letter" of a community's new-covenant transformation by the Spirit of the living God (3:1–3). Consequently, such a transformation, carried out under the lordship of Christ and the heart-changing, life-giving power of God's Spirit, marks a ministry as authentic and the minister as "qualified" before God. By its nature, then, authentic ministry is based in the work and competence of God, rather than in human qualification (3:4–6). The false ministers of Corinth, though having some form of human credentialing, are not sent from God (2:17), do not work by the Spirit, and do not have the fruit of authentic ministry. Thus they are not qualified to be ministers at all. Only ministers of the new covenant are qualified to minister to the Corinthians or anyone else.

From the beginning of the Christian movement, hucksters have tried to pass themselves off as Christian ministers. A few years ago our drama department at Union University performed Molière's play *Tartuffe*. As the play begins, a well-off man named Orgon takes into his home and confidence a man of seemingly great religious devotion. His name is Tartuffe. In fact, Tartuffe is a scheming hypocrite, a huckster of the first order, which some in the household discern from the start. Tartuffe is finally shown to be false when he tries to seduce Orgon's wife, as Orgon himself hides under a table. In that scene, Tartuffe says, "Your scruples, Madam, are easily overcome. You may be sure of the secret being kept, and there is no harm done unless the thing is bruited about. The scandal which it causes constitutes the offence, and sinning in secret is no sinning at all" (Molière 1879: 440). So Tartuffe is exposed as false. Yet, by this point, he has legal control of Orgon's finances and family, and is about to steal all of Orgon's wealth and marry his daughter. Thankfully, the king intervenes, and Tartuffe is condemned to prison. The false minister is caught and gets his just deserts. By analogy, in 2 Corinthians Paul alludes to false teachers who have sneaked into the house, so to speak. They have jeopardized Paul's authority and seduced some of his spiritual children, all the while offering themselves as fully qualified to minister to the Corinthians.

For those in the church today who wish to minister to others, the apostle's words in 2 Cor. 2:16b–3:6 offer much food for thought. How do *we* think about our qualifications for ministry? Are those qualifications oriented to human institutions, gifts, talents, positions, and credentials, or do we see our primary qualification as from God, by God's power, in God's work, and the fruit of authentic ministry carried out faithfully over time? In Paul's cultural context the interlopers appealed to their letters of recommendation as validating their positions vis-à-vis the Corinthian church. Thus human authority lay at the center of their conception of validity. This is not to say that human institutions and credentials have no place in the church. Such *can* serve as safeguards against hucksters who would infiltrate the church. Yet every authentic Christian ministry will have its primary orientation to God and will evaluate itself primarily in terms of the work of God.

Second, therefore, we might also consider the fruit of our ministries, not in terms of nickels and noses (numbers and size being a very American standard of measure), but in terms of the work of Christ through the Spirit in people's lives. In Charles Dickens's work *Barnaby Rudge*, a character named Gabrielle says to a traveler, "To be plain with you, friend, you don't carry in your countenance a letter of recommendation" (Dickens 2003: 27). Paul might ask us if the communities to which we minister carry in their countenance an authenticating "letter of recommendation," the new-covenant work of God's Spirit on human hearts. The true "proof of the pudding is in the eating." Real ministry from God will be self-authenticating in the lives of those who are transformed by the gospel.

Additional Notes

2:17. In spite of several strong witnesses ($\mathfrak{P}^{46}$ D F G L 6 326 614^s 630 945 1505 *al* sy) for λοιποί, the variant πολλοί has stronger Alexandrian support (ℵ A B C Ψ 0243 33 1739 1881 𝔐 lat co; Ir Ambst Did) and support that is more geographically distributed (Harris 2005: 242). From Paul's broader usage, neither the use of πολλοί (1 Cor. 16:9; 2 Cor. 11:18; Phil. 3:18; Titus 1:10) nor λοιποί (Gal. 2:13; Eph. 2:3; 1 Thess. 4:13; 5:6; 1 Tim. 5:20) could be said to be more characteristic of the apostle. However, πολλοί (the many), referring to a group of false workers, makes more sense in context than λοιποί (the rest).

3:2. Following ℵ and a few minor witnesses, the RSV has "your" (ὑμῶν) hearts, but the witnesses for "our" (ἡμῶν) are much stronger ($\mathfrak{P}^{46}$ A B C D G K P etc.), and Paul states at 7:3, "for I told you before that you are in *our* [ἡμῶν] hearts." The confusion probably stemmed from the ambiguity of Paul's metaphorical language at this point.

3:3. The evidence for the reading πλαξὶν καρδίαις σαρκίναις is weighty and beyond dispute (ℵ A B C D F G *al*). It is much preferred over variants with the genitive καρδίας (F Ψ 629 945 1505 latt [sy^p]; Ir^{lat} Eus), an obvious scribal error.

c. The Better Ministry of the Spirit (3:7–18)

Of Christian ministry, Richard Baxter (1821: 120) once said, "It is no easy matter to speak so plain that the ignorant may understand us, so seriously that the deadest hearts may feel us and so convincingly that contradictory cavaliers may be silenced." In other words, communication, especially communication of spiritual truth in a world of spiritual barriers, has its challenges. Sometimes we sense we are speaking to veiled hearts. The glory of God is not easily perceived. Thus powerful, life-changing proclamation of God's Word must be carried out under the enabling, new-covenant work of the Spirit. The tool kit of human talent alone will not do, offering but a false confidence to the preacher of the gospel.

The span of 2 Corinthians extending from 2:14–4:6 concerns "dynamics of authentic ministry." As we have seen, Paul employs the word picture of a recommendation letter in 3:1–3, suggesting that the work of his mission among the Corinthians is self-authenticating; the Corinthians are the only recommendation letter he needs. The "letter" imagery, however, begins to shift in verse 3 with mention of writing done "by the Spirit of the living God" on human hearts, a clear allusion to new-covenant realities. The allusion blossoms in verse 6, as Paul defines his ministry as "of a new covenant" and explains the contrast between a ministry of "the letter," which kills, and the ministry of "the Spirit," who gives life.

With 3:7–18 the apostle now explores that contrast by offering what has been called "an allusive homily" (Hays 1989: 132) on the glory and veiling of Moses's face.[1] The apostle's comments here are profoundly oriented to his reading of the OT text, particularly the LXX version, and his conclusions can be understood as drawn responsibly from that text, without fanciful exegetical footwork (Dumbrell 1986: 190; Hafemann 1995: 189–254; F. Watson 2004: 290). Grounded in Scripture, the apostle suggests that his ministry manifests the glorious, new-covenant work of the Spirit and the very presence of God; it thus stands as superior to any ministries that attempt to work apart from the Spirit's new-covenant enabling (3:4–6).[2]

---

1. This section has generated a great deal of scholarly discussion. E.g., see Abernathy 2000; Baker 2000; Belleville 1991; Dalton 1987; Duff 2004; Dumbrell 2002; Dunn 1970; Dupont 1949; Fitzmyer 1981; Grindheim 2001; Hafemann 1992; 1995; Hanson 1980; Hasitschka 1999; Kayama 1990; Lambrecht 1983; Nayak 2002; Randrianarimalala 1996; Sloan 1995; Starnitzke 1999; Stegemann 1986; Stockhausen 1989; Ulonska 1966; Unnik 1963; Wong 1985.

2. Some have suggested Paul's "argument from lesser to greater" in 3:7–11 and his treatment of the veil in verses 12–18 stand as a polemic against his opponents and their teaching. It is reasoned that perhaps the false teachers have held up Moses as a model for spirituality and ministry—that he was more "glorious" than Paul—and that Moses's law should be seen

The homily clearly constitutes Paul's reflections on Exod. 34:29–35 and falls nicely into two primary movements. The first (vv. 7–11), based on Exod. 34:29–30, 35, focuses on the theme of "glory" (δοξάζω, *doxazō*, in the OT passage), with Paul arguing for the greater glory of the new-covenant ministry. The second movement (vv. 12–18), which includes more personal language (Matera 2003: 85), comments on Exod. 34:33–35, a passage dealing with the repeated veiling of Moses's face (Harris 2005: 276). Here the apostle treats "the veil" as a barrier standing between people and the glory of God. He contrasts the repeated veiling of Moses, as well as the "veiling" of the hearts and minds not yet transformed by the new covenant, with the unveiling of hearts and minds by Christ in that covenant.

In 3:7–18 Paul builds on the hearers' veneration for Moses in order to celebrate the value, power, and extent of new-covenant ministry, which the apostle's ministry embodies. In Exod. 34:29–35 the shining of Moses's face in part authenticates the old covenant delivered by Moses (Dumbrell 1986: 181); similarly, the abundance and extent of the glory of God's presence experienced by those in the new covenant provide dynamic authentication of Paul's ministry. The implication is that if old-covenant ministry was authentic, Paul's ministry certainly is authentic and has a far greater effect and extent.

Thus the unit falls in two main submovements:

i. The greater glory of new-covenant ministry (3:7–11)
ii. Veiled and unveiled people (3:12–18)

Exegesis and Exposition

[7]Now if the ministry of death, engraved in ⌜letters⌝ on stones, was attended by glory—with the result that the children of Israel were not able to continue looking at

---

as the true guide for Christian life. Perhaps there even was a midrashic treatment of Exod. 34 with which or to which Paul was responding (e.g., Barnett 1997: 178; Belleville 1996: 96; Georgi 1986: 264–71; Schulz 1958; Thrall 1994: 246). Yet as Garland (1999: 169) and others point out, the suggestion, to a certain degree, rests on speculation, for nowhere does the apostle make this polemic overt. Paul's "adequacy" for ministry (3:5) and the "openness" with which he conducts his ministry (3:12) seem to be the touchstones of this section. The flow of thought instead suggests that Paul defends the boldness with which he addresses the Corinthians (see the comments on 3:12; 4:1–2) as an aspect of his overall portrayal of authentic ministry. Yet the concerns in our broader context almost certainly mean that Paul has the false teachers at least in mind (e.g., 2:17–3:1). We can agree that the emphasis here seems to be on Paul's rigorous defense of his conduct of ministry, rather than an outright attack on his opponents (Hafemann 1996: 290–91). Thus we should see Paul's description of authentic ministry as foregrounded in this passage, with only hints of polemic against the false teachers (Furnish 1984: 242–43). Garland (1999: 169) wisely states, "Since this text is not an overtly polemical section which castigates opponents, the best procedure for understanding it is to try to grasp its internal logic within its own context. Interpreting what Paul says against some contrived, hypothetical scenario regarding a prior background for the exegesis of Exodus 34 or the reconstruction of the teaching of imagined opponents will only lead us far afield."

the face of Moses because the glory of his face was being made inoperative—⁸how could the ministry of the Spirit not be attended by glory to a greater degree? ⁹For if ⌐in the ministry⌐ characterized by condemnation there was glory, to a much greater degree the ministry characterized by righteousness overflows with glory. ¹⁰For really, in this situation, what had been glorified now has no glory at all because of the glory that outshines it. ¹¹For if that which was being made inoperative was through glory, to a much greater extent the ministry that remains is attended by glory.

¹²Therefore, since we have this kind of hope, we conduct our ministry with a great deal of openness, ¹³in contradistinction to Moses. He kept putting a veil over his face with the result that the children of Israel did not look with sustained attention unto the completion of what was being made inoperative. ¹⁴Rather, their minds were hardened. For, until this very day, when the old covenant is read, that same veil remains unmoved, because it can only be made inoperative in Christ. ¹⁵Indeed, right up to the present time, when Moses is read, a veil drapes their hearts; ¹⁶but when a person turns to the Lord, the veil is removed. ¹⁷Now "the Lord" is the Spirit, and where the Spirit of the Lord is, there is ⌐freedom⌐. ¹⁸⌐All⌐ of us, with unveiled faces observing the Lord's glory as in a mirror, are being transformed into the same image from glory to glory, just as from the Lord who is the Spirit.

i. The Greater Glory of New-Covenant Ministry (3:7–11)

Among his arsenal of rhetorical arguments, a rabbi in the ancient world could   **3:7–8**
use "an argument from the lesser to the greater," one of the seven hermeneutical principles traditionally attributed to Rabbi Hillel.[3] This argument normally began with an appeal to a biblical fact to which the readers or hearers would readily agree, but this "lesser situation" was used as a stepping-stone to a "greater" point made by the teacher.[4] Here 2 Cor. 3:7–8 presents a somewhat rambling conditional clause, which in fact offers an argument from lesser to greater. In verse 7 Paul draws from Exod. 34:29–35 for the "lesser" point in his argument, focusing on the glory of Moses's face. As he continues his argument in verse 8, he moves to the "greater" point, that the new-covenant ministry of the Holy Spirit is attended by more glory.

The apostle begins verse 7 with a conditional clause: "Now if the ministry of death, engraved in letters on stones, was attended by glory" (Εἰ δὲ ἡ δια-κονία τοῦ θανάτου ἐν γράμμασιν ἐντετυπωμένη λίθοις ἐγενήθη ἐν δόξῃ, *Ei de hē diakonia tou thanatou en grammasin entetypōmenē lithois egenēthē en doxē*). The conjunction δέ effects a mild transition to the new unit, and the

---

3. Referred to as *qal wāḥômer* (the light and the heavy), *a fortiori* (to the greater), or *a minore ad maius* (from the lesser to the greater).

4. Hebrews repeatedly uses this technique to set up strong exhortations or warnings. See, e.g., the argument at Heb. 10:28–29, which runs as follows: (a) under the old covenant death was the punishment for those who rejected the law of Moses; (b) those who reject the superior Son of God and his new covenant thus insult the Spirit of grace and are deserving of more severe punishment than the disobedient who rejected the law under the old covenant. Other examples of *qal wāḥômer* are found at Heb. 2:2–3; 9:13–14; 12:9, 25.

condition (Εἰ), anchored with the aorist passive indicative ἐγενήθη, describes a historical reality upon which Paul wants to build his argument: the glorious ministry of Moses as he interacted both with the Lord and with the people of Israel (Exod. 34:29–35). Of the thirty-four uses of the term διακονία in the NT, twenty-three are found in Paul, and twelve of these are in 2 Corinthians (3:7–9 [4x]; 4:1; 5:18; 6:3; 8:4; 9:1, 12–13; 11:8). In this letter, the cognate noun, διάκονος (*diakonos*), occurs five times (2 Cor. 3:6; 6:4; 11:15 [2x], 23), and the verb διακονέω (*diakoneō*) three times (2 Cor. 3:3; 8:19–20). So "ministry" constitutes a key theme for 2 Corinthians. The word could be used to speak of "aid," "service," "support," "an office," an "assignment," or "mediation" (BDAG 230). Paul uses the term for work done in the service of Christ and for Christ's church.

In our passage the apostle's focus rests on contrasting types of ministry, rather than on the general contrasts between the old and new covenants, and it is critical that we grasp this point.[5] Notice the generous references to ministry in this section. The two covenants offer two contexts for ministry, but the emphasis rests on the contrasting ministries, which Paul lays out in parallel fashion in 3:6–9:

the ministry of the letter (3:6) versus the ministry of the Spirit (3:6)

the ministry of death (3:7) versus the ministry of the Spirit (3:8)

the ministry of condemnation (3:9) versus the ministry of righteousness (3:9)

The apostle's reflections are not primarily about the old covenant per se being done away with, although the demise of that institution is inherent in Paul's words; the Scriptures are, after all, called τῆς παλαιᾶς διαθήκης (*tēs palaias diathēkēs*, of the old covenant) in verse 14. But Paul is particularly focused on the superiority of his new-covenant form of ministry, and specifically on the proclamation of the Word of God under the power of the Spirit.

Here Paul has in mind Moses's ministry, which he calls a ministry "of death." Whether the genitive form (θανάτου) is understood as an objective genitive, a ministry that produces death (e.g., NLT[2], NIV, NET); or as an

---

5. In our span of text running from 2:14–4:6, notice esp. Paul's repeated references to ministry, most often the ministry of preaching. In the imagery of triumphal procession at 2:14–16, we saw depicted the dichotomous effect of his gospel ministry that wafts out over the world like incense. In 2:17 is an emphasis on how Paul speaks in contrast to the false teachers at Corinth peddling the Word. In 3:6 Paul celebrates being a new-covenant minister of the Spirit, whom God has made competent for the task. This is contrasted with being a minister of the death-dealing letter. Just beyond our passage, at 4:1 the apostle writes, "Since we have this ministry in accordance with the mercy we have received, we do not give up." This is contrasted with those who minister "by tricks, . . . twisting God's Word" (4:2). Paul, by public proclamation of the truth, commends himself to every person's conscience as he lives before God (4:2). In this section, Paul seems especially interested in a ministry of the Scriptures. In 3:14–16 he refers specifically to the reading of those Scriptures, the impossibility of them being communicated effectively while a veil lies over the heart, and the power of the ministry of the Word when a person turns to the Lord, who is the Spirit.

adjectival genitive, a ministry associated with or characterized by death (e.g., ESV, HCSB, NASB[95])—Paul's point is that the "law engraved in letters on stones" was deadly, an assertion that would have puzzled some of his Jewish contemporaries.[6] Yet the OT context bears out Paul's assertion. At the giving of the law, anyone who crossed the boundaries around the mountain died (Exod. 19:12), and death was the punishment for a wide variety of transgressions (e.g., Exod. 21:12, 14–17, 28–29; 22:2, 19; 31:14–15).[7] Theologically, Paul holds that the old covenant and its law, by their very nature, were associated with death.

Further, when he refers to Moses's ministry as a ministry "engraved in letters on stones,"[8] the allusion points to God's personal engraving of his law on the stone tablets, which served as the epitome and a physical representation of the covenant and as such were placed in the ark (Exod. 24:12; 25:16; 31:18; 32:15). In Deut. 9:9, 11 the tablets are called the "tablets of the covenant" (לוּחֹת הַבְּרִית, *lûḥōt habběrît*). Most immediately the apostle has in mind the momentous event of Moses coming down from the mountain with "the tablets of the testimony" (לֻחֹת הָעֵדֻת, *luḥōt hāʿēdut*) in hand (Exod. 34:29), tablets that had been engraved by God himself (34:1). This ministry written on stones stands in sharp contrast to the ministry in which God writes on human hearts (2 Cor. 3:3).

Nevertheless, this ministry of death "was attended[9] by glory" (ἐν δόξῃ). The "glory of God" constitutes one of the richest of biblical images. The Shekinah of God descended on the tabernacle at its dedication, the presence of God filling the tent with glory. The glory was manifested further in the cloud that led the Israelites in the wilderness and the pillar of fire at night (Exod. 40:34–38).

In secular Greek usage, the term δόξα spoke of a sentiment, opinion, or thought (e.g., Plato, *Pol.* 260; Philostratus, *Gymn.* 17). When held in relation to a person, the word could connote one's fame or reputation, normally used in a positive sense (Demosthenes, *2 Olynth.* 2.15), and often in inscriptions or the

---

6. Jesus said to the Jewish leaders, "You pore over the Scriptures because you think you have eternal life in them, yet they testify about Me" (John 5:39 HCSB); later rabbis proclaimed that the law was meant to give life to God's people (e.g., Exod. Rab. 41.1). See Barrett 1973: 115; Hafemann 1995: 273.

7. See further, e.g., Lev. 20:2, 4, 9–13, 15–16, 27; 24:16–17, 21; 27:29; Num. 1:51; 3:10, 38; 15:35–36; 18:7.

8. In 2:7 the perfect passive participle ἐντετυπωμένη (*entetypōmenē*) speaks of something being carved, impressed, or "engraved." The preposition ἐν could communicate either instrumentality or manner at this point, whereas the dative λίθοις (*lithois*, stones) could be a dative of place (i.e., where the letters were written) or perhaps a dative of material, that is, "The dative substantive denotes the material that is used to accomplish the action of the verb" (D. Wallace 1996: 169–70).

9. The phrase in Greek (3:7) is ἐγενήθη ἐν δόξῃ (*egenēthē en doxē*). The aorist passive form of γίνομαι (*ginomai*) could refer to the beginning of the covenant, e.g., "came with glory" (NASB, HCSB, ESV) or "began with glory" (NLT[2]). However, the emphasis of the context does not seem to be on inauguration of the covenant, but on the general era of the old covenant. Thus Tyndale simply translated the phrase as "was glorious." With Harris (2005: 280), our ET reads "attended by glory."

papyri it means "esteem" or "honor";[10] similarly, at 1 Cor. 4:10 Paul contrasts the Corinthians as "glorious" (the cognate adjective ἔνδοξοι, *endoxoi*) with his ministry as "dishonored" (ἄτιμοι, *atimoi*), and at 2 Cor. 6:8 "dishonor" (ἀτιμίας, *atimias*) is contrasted with "glory" (δόξης, *doxēs*). Thus the ideal of δόξα or *gloria* (Latin) in the Greco-Roman world has been undervalued as a backdrop of Paul's words in our passage.[11] The old Republican perspectives of glory and the celebration of glory in the Roman imperial cult in the first Christian century would have made personal glory and the glory of family, city, and empire a high value in Corinthian culture. Cicero claims that the best leaders possess the noble virtue of *gloria* and are led and nurtured by it (*Arch.* 26; *Rep.* 5.7.9). Judge (1966: 38–39) adds:

> By New Testament times the predominant Stoic school of philosophy had raised the estimate [of the value of glory] to a very high level, apparently in response to the cult of glory among the Roman nobility. It was held that the winning of glory was the only adequate reward for merit in public life, and that, given the doubt as to the state of man after death, it was the effective assurance of immortality. It therefore became a prime and admired objective of public figures to enshrine themselves, by actually defining their own glory, in the undying memory of posterity. What was more, a man was thought the meaner for not pursuing this quest for glory. . . . Self-magnification thus became a feature of Hellenic higher education, and by no means merely a caricature of its aims.

This does not mean that Paul's primary orientation in 2 Cor. 3:7–18 focuses on glory as reflected in the broader Greco-Roman culture. He certainly is well aware of the cultural value, and it seems likely that the opponents are caught up in the pursuit of glory.[12] We suggest that Paul offers his biblical reflection as a countercultural alternative that democratizes the attainment of glory as for all people of the new covenant (3:17–18), not just special leaders, a glorified few. If this is accurate, the apostle addresses a cultural value by offering a thoroughgoing biblical treatment of the concept of glory. Again, Paul's primary purpose, rather than polemical, is to demonstrate his own ministry as grounded in biblical principles, but the false teachers will be shown in poor light by contrast.

In terms of the biblical literature, Spicq (1994: 1.364) notes that the semantic development of δόξα is "probably the most extraordinary in the Bible." With the exception of Eccles. 10:1 LXX, the term never means "opinion" in that

10. E.g., δόξα is associated with honor in Plutarch, *Rom. Q.* 1.13; *Mulier. virt.* 16; *Cor.* 4.3. The concept of δόξα is widespread in the writings of Plutarch, who, when Paul wrote 2 Corinthians, was a child growing up in a wealthy family in Chaeronea, a town about 50 miles north of Corinth.

11. See esp. Harrison (2009: 329), who states, "It is a curiosity of Romans scholarship that the Roman context of glory has been overlooked in discussions of Paul's use of δόξα and its cognates," noting that the focus normally and understandably has been on the Jewish background of the word.

12. Plutarch (*Cat. Maj.* 22.2), e.g., speaks of Carneades as a charming, powerful public speaker whose speaking had δόξα that was equal to its power.

body of writings. Most often it translates כָּבוֹד (*kābôd*) in the OT, a word grounded in the idea of "heaviness" or "weightiness," and thus can communicate respect, reputation, riches, splendor, glory, honor, majesty, or dignity.[13] God's glory can be directly related to his mighty acts on behalf of his people (e.g., LXX: Exod. 14:18; 16:7; Isa. 12:2; 35:1–4; Ezek. 39:21–29), and this active intervention of God may be related directly to the manifestation of his presence (Isa. 40:5).[14]

Significantly for our passage at hand, when Moses went up on the mountain of God at the time of covenant making, prior to the construction of the tabernacle, "the glory of the LORD settled on Mount Sinai. . . . The appearance of the LORD's glory to the Israelites was like a consuming fire on the mountaintop" (Exod. 24:16–17 HCSB). Later, after the original tablets had been broken and the people had been punished for their rebellion in Moses's absence, Moses asked to see God's glory (33:18); God fulfilled his request in 34:1–9, the encounter from which Moses emerged with a glowing face (34:29; *DBI* 330).[15]

13. In recent years good work has been done on the concept of glory. Hamilton (2010: 56) defines God's glory as "the weight of the majestic goodness of who God is, and the resulting name, or reputation that he gains from his revelation of himself as Creator, Sustainer, Judge, and Redeemer, perfect in justice and mercy, loving-kindness and truth." Hamilton (2010: 58–59) goes on to outline, in seven points, how God's glory "functions as the center of and organizing principle for biblical theology."

14. Morgan (2010) describes the "enormous" challenge of defining the glory of God and suggests the following on how glory functions in the biblical narrative (summarized here):

1. Glory is used as a designation for God himself.
2. Glory sometimes refers to an internal characteristic, an attribute, or a summary of attributes of God.
3. Glory as God's visible and active presence.
4. Glory as the display of God's attributes, perfections, or person.
5. Glory as the ultimate goal of the display of God's attributes, perfections, or person (that is, God's name, his renown).
6. Glory sometimes connotes heaven, the heavenly, or the eschatological consummation of the full experience of the presence of God.
7. Giving glory to God may also refer to appropriate response to God in the form of worship, exaltation, or exultation.

Morgan (2010: 159) says these multiple meanings are distinct but related: "The triune God who is glorious displays his glory, largely through his creation, image-bearers, providence, and redemptive acts. God's people respond by glorifying him. God receives glory and, through uniting his people to Christ, shares his glory with them—all to his glory." Thus Morgan proposes that the nuances of glory in the biblical story, all central to that story, may be summarized as glory possessed, glory purposed, glory displayed, glory ascribed, glory received, and glory shared. In trying to wrap our minds around the glory of God, we can certainly confess with John Owen, "How little a portion is it of him that we can understand! His glory is incomprehensible, and his praises unutterable" (*The Glory of Christ* [1684], quoted in Morgan 2010: 153).

15. In the Qumran literature the glory of God on the face of Moses serves as a manifestation of God's presence, but it also parallels Adam being fashioned in the image of God's glory (4Q504). The parallel between Adam and Moses may also be seen in rabbinic texts such as Deut. Rab. 11.3 and Midr. Tadshe 4 (see Orlov 2007). At points in Second Temple Judaism, the hope

Moses's face shone with the glory of God as a direct result of being in the presence of the Lord.[16] In the LXX, Exod. 34:29 reads, "Now as Moses came down from the mountain, he was holding the two tablets in his hands. When he came down from the mountain, Moses did not know that the skin of his face shone because he had been speaking with him" (my ET). Thus the lawgiving moment of the old covenant was "attended by glory." This manifestation of glory gives Paul a launching point for his argument and constitutes a main theme of 2 Cor. 3:7–11. Paul uses the noun form of the word δόξα eight times, evenly spread throughout these five verses, and the verbal form twice (v. 10). Clearly this is the apostle's main theme in this passage. His point, in part, has to do with the difference in degree of glory between Moses's covenant and the new covenant.

According to Paul, what happened (ὥστε, *hōste*)[17] when the "glorified" Moses came down from the mountain was that "the children of Israel were not able to continue looking at the face of Moses, because the glory of his face was being made inoperative" (ὥστε μὴ δύνασθαι ἀτενίσαι τοὺς υἱοὺς Ἰσραὴλ εἰς τὸ πρόσωπον Μωϋσέως διὰ τὴν δόξαν τοῦ προσώπου αὐτοῦ τὴν καταργουμένην, *hōste mē dynasthai atenisai tous huious Israēl eis to prosōpon Mōuseōs dia tēn doxan tou prosōpou autou tēn katargoumenēn*). The apostle's point is simple and picks up on the emphasis of the OT passage:[18] Moses covered his

was that humanity would be restored to the likeness of God's glory as reflected in Adam (see Fletcher-Louis 2002: 91–97).

16. Duff (2004: 318) notes, "When Paul speaks of 'glory' (δόξα) in connection with his own as well as the Mosaic ministry, he refers to the presence of God as mediated through each of these διακονίαι."

17. I take ὥστε (*hōste*) in 3:7 to express "actual result" (BDAG 1107).

18. The point of the passage is not that they were dazzled by the sight (though see Philo, *Mos.* 2.70, who states that the Israelites could not look at the brightness of Moses's face, which shone like the sun), nor that the veil was put in place because they were afraid (contra Garland 1999: 170), although they were afraid of him initially (Exod. 34:30). Nor was the veil placed over the face of Moses to protect the people from being consumed by God's judgment, an interpretation based on the broad context of Exod. 32–34 but not noted in the immediate passage (Hafemann 1995: 278–86). See the article on Moses's shining face by Philpot (2013: 11), who makes the case that Moses's shining face functions to show the goodness and grace of God to the Israelites, to remind them of God's presence, to distinguish Moses in terms of status, and to facilitate a transition from the rebellion narrative found in Exod. 32–34; the purpose of the veil, according to Philpot (2013: 9), was simply to cover Moses's face. As Francis Watson (2004) points out, no explanation is given in the OT text concerning why Moses veiled his face. Exodus 34:30–32 seems to suggest that the fear of the Israelites was overcome prior to the veil being put over Moses's face. Later, in verse 35, Moses veils himself but with no reference to fear on the part of the Israelites. The OT text simply places emphasis on the continued process as Moses veils and unveils his face. F. Watson (2004: 292) goes on to suggest that "the veil serves to conceal Moses' face only at those times when he is not fulfilling his role as mediator of God's commandments." The NETS version of the LXX text reads, "And when he came out, he would tell all the sons of Israel what the Lord commanded him. And the sons of Israel saw the face of Moyses that it was charged with glory, and Moyses put a covering over his face until he went in to converse with him" (Exod. 34:34b–35). Harris's (2005: 277) ET reads the καί at the beginning of the final clause in 34:35b LXX as communicating result ("and so"), rather than marking a simple consecutive event. This is possible but by no means clear. The καί may be a simple connection

face because it was glowing, and since he covered it, the Israelites were not able to continue staring at this amazing sight. Moses habitually covered his face with a veil until he would go in to speak to the Lord again (Exod. 34:35). The verb ἀτενίζω (atenizō) means "to look at something intently" or to "stare at it" (BDAG 148). The perfective aspect of the infinitive ἀτενίσαι (atenisai) depicts holistically the inability of the Israelites to gaze at the sight, but the sense of the verb may suggest that the original witnesses of Moses's shining face were not able to have an ongoing, unimpeded view because of the veil that Moses put over his face. In short, they were not allowed to stare at his face.

But this brings us to one of the most debated terms in the passage, κατ-αργέω (katargeō), found in participial form in verse 7 and again in verse 11. The evidence shows that the verb καταργέω (katargeō), presented here as a present participle (τὴν καταργουμένην, tēn katargoumenēn), could be used variously in the first century to mean "to use up," "exhaust," "waste," "make ineffective," "invalidate," "to cause something to be abolished or set aside," or "to be discharged" or "released from an obligation" (BDAG 525).[19] Paul uses the term extensively,[20] almost always with the sense of something being "canceled" or "made inoperative," and here in 2 Cor. 3:7–18 he uses it four times, at 3:7, 11, 13–14.[21] Clearly the participle in verse 7, τὴν καταργουμένην, delimits the noun τὴν δόξαν. A popular rendering of the participle in 2 Cor. 3:7 is "fading":

> because of the glory from his face—a fading glory— (HCSB)
> because of the glory of his face, fading as it was (NASB[95])
> even though the brightness was already fading away (NLT[2])
> because of its glory, transitory though it was (NIV)

Some form of this translation is also followed by commentators such as Harris (2005: 280) and Belleville (1991: 204–5; 1996: 99).[22]

---

to the next thing that happened in the narrative. The LXX text is ambiguous as to exactly when Moses veiled his face in his ongoing interaction with the Lord and with the people. Exodus 34:34a NETS reads, "But whenever Moyses would enter in before the Lord to speak with him, he would remove the covering *until coming out*" (italics mine). The text seems to indicate that Moses veiled himself *after* speaking to the people (Dumbrell 1986: 181).

19. See esp. Hafemann (1995: 301–9): of the 1,300 occurrences of καταργέω from the fourth century BC to the fourth century AD, "only 16 are found in literature outside the NT and its circle of influence."

20. His twenty-five uses of καταργέω are in Rom. 3:3, 31; 4:14; 6:6; 7:2, 6; 1 Cor. 1:28; 2:6; 6:13; 13:8 (2x), 10–11; 15:24, 26; 2 Cor. 3:7, 11, 13–14; Gal. 3:17; 5:4, 11; Eph. 2:15; 2 Thess. 2:8; 2 Tim. 1:10.

21. As noted in the exegesis that follows, Paul employs καταργέω to speak of "the glory" (3:7), the old-covenant ministry (vv. 11, 13), and of the veil that lies over the hearts of unbelievers (v. 14), so the nuances of meaning he intends can be difficult to discern.

22. Uncharacteristically, Harris (2005: 284) bases his rendering of the participle on contextual nuance rather than the semantic range of the term as used in the first century—this in spite of the fact that he delineates that range of meaning, which does not include "fade." Thrall (1994: 237) translates the term as "in process of effacement."

Yet a growing number of scholars have challenged this rendering as insupportable.[23] For example, after reviewing classical and Septuagintal usage,[24] the uses in the NT outside of 2 Cor. 3,[25] and finally, the uses in 2 Cor. 3:7–18, Garrett (2010: 739–46) makes a sound case that the term never means "fade away" and normally carries the sense "to render powerless" or "make inoperative."

Paul uses the word four times in our passage, and I think he does so very consistently with the sense "to make inoperative." At 3:7 the term is used to describe the "glory" of Moses's face. A straightforward reading of Exod. 34:29–35 tells us what happened to the glory on Moses's face. It was made inoperative by the veil placed over his face. Thus we translate 3:7, "the children of Israel were not able to continue looking at the face of Moses because the glory of his face was made inoperative." In other words, the glory was snuffed out by the veil, and according to the narrative, this happened over and over again. Moses would remove the veil when he was in the presence of the Lord and put it back on when he was in the presence of the people.

The apostle continues his argument from lesser to greater, with "the greater" situation presented in verse 8: "How could[26] the ministry of the Spirit not be attended by glory to a greater degree?" What makes the new covenant ministry "greater"—μᾶλλον (mallon) means "to a greater or higher degree"—is that it is "the ministry of the Spirit" (ἡ διακονία τοῦ πνεύματος, hē diakonia tou pneumatos), and in the following verses Paul gives reasons why the ministry of the Spirit is greater, but the contrast inherent in verses 7–8 lays the foundation. At verse 6 Paul has already said that "the Spirit produces life." Correspondingly, here the ministry of the Spirit is set over against the "ministry of death." So the ministry of the Spirit is greater in part because, rather than dealing out death, it makes people alive.

3:9 Further, the Spirit's ministry, which is "characterized by righteousness" (τῆς δικαιοσύνης, tēs dikaiosynēs), "overflows with glory" (περισσεύει . . . δόξῃ, perisseuei . . . doxē), but by contrast the old-covenant ministry, "characterized by condemnation" (τῆς κατακρίσεως, tēs katakriseōs), was merely attended by glory (to a much lesser degree). The term κατάκρισις (condemnation) refers to "a judicial verdict involving a penalty" (BDAG 519) and only occurs in the NT here and at 2 Cor. 7:3. The genitive form may be taken as "adjectival," that

---

23. E.g., Baker 2000: 3–15; Hafemann 1992: 37–40; 1995: 301–9; 2000: 147–48; Hays 1989: 133–35.

24. See, e.g., Euripides, *Phoen.* 751–53; Athenaeus Mechanicus, *Mach.* 4.6; Ezra 4:21, 23; 5:5; 6:8.

25. In addition to Paul's use of the term elsewhere (see earlier note), see also Luke 13:7; Heb. 2:14.

26. The form of εἰμί (*eimi*, be) in 3:8 is future tense, given with the time of Moses as its point of reference, since the new covenant would come, from the perspective of Moses's day, in the future. Paul proclaims that if the old covenant came with glory, it is only logical that the new covenant that would come through the ministry of Christ, by the power of the Spirit, would be attended by a greater degree of glory. In the remainder of 3:7–18, Paul offers his argument to demonstrate the strength of his argument.

is, the ministry was characterized, or marked by, condemnation. What Paul almost certainly means is that although there was glory during[27] the time of the old covenant, specifically on the face of Moses, that covenant also came with a host of laws that were attended by penalties, and the Israelites experienced those penalties. We have already seen that Paul understands the law of that covenant as deadly (3:6), given in the context of a ministry of death (3:7). One does not need to look far into the broader context of Exod. 34:29–35 to find a great deal of "condemnation." In 34:7, when the Lord passes before Moses as he was on the mountain receiving the tablets of the covenant, the Lord proclaims that "he will not cleanse [καθαριεῖ, kathariei] the guilty, bringing the guilt of the fathers upon the children, and the children's children, to the third and fourth generation." Immediately following the statement in Exod. 34:35 that the Israelites saw the glorified face of Moses, Exodus records the lawgiver's words concerning observance of the Sabbath: "Everyone who does work on it must die" (Exod. 35:2). Thus Moses's ministry was characterized by condemnation, even though it was attended by glory, as seen in his face.

By contrast, the ministry of the Spirit is "characterized by righteousness," the genitive here too being taken as an adjectival genitive, expressing an innate quality. The term δικαιοσύνη (dikaiosynē) has generated a great deal of discussion among commentators on Paul's theology.[28] Yet we are given help in discerning the nuance at this point by Exod. 34:6–7 LXX, which offers the only use of the term in the immediate context of the OT passage to which Paul primarily orients his discussion, and the use there perhaps points us in the direction intended by the apostle. As the Lord passes before Moses—again, the passage depicts the critical moment at which the requirements of the covenant were being conveyed to Moses on the mountain—he says, "The Lord God, compassionate and merciful, patient and full of mercy and true, and maintaining righteousness [δικαιοσύνην, dikaiosynēn] and accomplishing mercy for thousands, taking away lawlessness and unrighteousness [ἀδικίας, adikias] and sins." The Lord removes unrighteousness and sins; the Lord expresses extensive mercy and compassion. This confession comes in the same breath with proclamation of God as a Lord who maintains "righteousness," expressed *in the context of the giving of the covenant*. As Moo (1996: 80)

---

27. The textual variant in the dative form (τῇ διακονίᾳ, tē diakonia, in the ministry) is preferable in 3:9; the dative may indicate time, although in Koine Greek this means of expressing a temporal frame of reference is increasingly being replaced by ἐν (en, in) + the dative (D. Wallace 1996: 155). See the additional note on 3:9 weighing this variant.

28. Thus, e.g., BDAG 247 states,

> In Pauline thought the intimate association of God's interest in retaining a reputation for justice that rewards goodness and requites evil, while at the same time working out a plan of salvation for all humanity, complicates classification of his use of δικαιοσύνη. On the one hand, God's δ. is pardoning action, and on the other [it is] a way of sharing God's character with believers, who then exhibit righteousness in the moral sense. God achieves this objective through exercise of executive privilege in dispensing justice equitably without reference to νόμος by making salvation available to all humanity.

On the NT theology of righteousness, see esp. the treatment of Moo 1996: 79–89.

notes, δικαιοσύνη language in Paul "has its context in the covenant and designates most often that form of life which is the Israelite's appropriate response to the covenant." What is critical for Paul is that the old covenant, in and of itself, was not able to attain to this ideal. Only in the new covenant has the law been written on the hearts of believers; thus, only in the new covenant is righteousness realized and condemnation averted.[29] This righteousness, which here is contrasted with condemnation, certainly is forensic, having to do with "forgiveness, acquittal, or vindication" (Barnett 1997: 184–85), but also issues in righteous living.[30]

Further, this ministry of righteousness "overflows with glory." Authors of the ancient world could use the term περισσεύω (perisseuō), as here, to mean "to be extremely rich" in something, or "abundant."[31] Paul's logic goes as follows. Moses's face shone because he had been in the presence of the Lord. Yet it was a glory suppressed (by the veil) and limited to Moses himself. By contrast, under the new covenant the presence of the Lord, through the ministry of the indwelling Spirit, is manifested in every person involved in that covenant (3:17–18). So, unlike the restricted reach of the glory of God on Moses's face, the new-covenant glory "overflows." The apostle develops this thought further as his discussion goes forward.

3:10 In verse 10 Paul now expands on his reiteration of the a fortiori argument in verse 9. Here the apostle underlines the very great difference in the degree of glory between the two contexts of ministry: "For really, in this situation, what had been glorified now has no glory at all because of the glory that outshines it" (καὶ γὰρ οὐ δεδόξασται τὸ δεδοξασμένον ἐν τούτῳ τῷ μέρει εἵνεκεν τῆς ὑπερβαλλούσης δόξης, kai gar ou dedoxastai to dedoxasmenon en toutō tō merei heineken tēs hyperballousēs doxēs). The conjunctions καὶ γάρ at the beginning of this verse break the highly crafted pattern found in the conditional clauses of verses 7, 9, and 11, for in verse 10 the apostle comments on the superabundance of glory celebrated in verse 9.

The "situation" (ἐν τούτῳ τῷ μέρει) Paul has in mind is the comparison between the glory found on the face of Moses at the giving of the law and the glory found on the faces of Christ's followers under the new covenant. The main clause of the verse is made up of a perfect passive participle[32] form of

---

29. Dumbrell (2002: 68) is correct in suggesting that to a great extent Paul is interested in the effect or efficacy of the two covenants in the lives of individuals.

30. In the Corinthian correspondence, forensic uses of δικαιοσύνη and cognates seem to be foundational for relationship, with ethical uses indicating a result of the Christian's relationship with God. See 1 Cor. 1:30; 4:4; 6:11; 2 Cor. 5:21 for forensic uses, and 2 Cor. 6:7, 14; 9:9, 10 for moral/ethical uses (Barnett 1997: 185–86).

31. Paul uses περισσεύω twenty-six times: Rom. 3:7; 5:15; 15:13; 1 Cor. 8:8; 14:12; 15:58; 2 Cor. 1:5 (2x); 3:9; 4:15; 8:2, 7 (2x); 9:8 (2x), 12; Eph. 1:8; Phil. 1:9, 26; 4:12 (2x), 18; Col. 2:7; 1 Thess. 3:12; 4:1, 10.

32. It may be, as Dumbrell (2002: 74) suggests, that in using the perfect form of the participle, Paul has in mind the old covenant as still on offer in Corinth. However, from a linguistic standpoint, Paul might also be referring to the glory borne witness to and still shining in the text of Scripture.

the verb δοξάζω (doxazō) acting as the subject, and a third-person singular perfect passive indicative form of the same word providing the main verbal idea: "What was having been glorified now has no glory at all."

When Paul refers to "what was having been glorified" that "now has no glory," of what does he speak? In the Greek OT and the form of the participle here, we find the answer. At Exod. 34:29b we read: "Now as he was descending from the mountain, Moyses did not know that the appearance of the skin of his face was charged with glory while he was speaking to him" (NETS).[33] And Exod. 34:35 reads, "And the sons of Israel saw the face of Moyses that it was charged with glory, and Moyses put a covering over his face until he went in to converse with him" (NETS).[34] In both of these verses it was Moses's face that was "glorified" (δεδόξασται, dedoxastai) and, just as in 2 Cor. 3:10, a perfect passive form of the verb δοξάζω (doxazō) is used. In verse 29 it is "the appearance of the complexion of his face" (ἡ ὄψις τοῦ χρώματος τοῦ προσώπου αὐτοῦ, hē opsis tou chrōmatos tou prosōpou autou) that is glorified. In verse 35 it is simply "the face of Moses" (τὸ πρόσωπον Μωυσῆ, to prosōpon Mōysē) that is charged with glory. Note that the perfect passive participle used in Exod. 34:30 is in the feminine form because its referent is ἡ ὄψις, the appearance of the complexion (τοῦ χρώματος) of his face, ἡ ὄψις being feminine in form.

Back in our passage, the perfect passive participle in this case serves as the subject of the sentence, and it is neuter in form. Why is the participle neuter here? Because it has a specific referent in context (the gender agrees with the word to which it refers). It is not "the ministry" to which it refers, for that word is feminine in form. It is not the covenant, for that word too is feminine. Paul refers here to the same word referred to in Exod. 34, for "what was having been glorified" that "now has no glory at all" is Moses's face. Notice the double reference to the neuter noun πρόσωπον in 2 Cor. 3:7.

Why, according to Paul, did Moses's face no longer have glory (for it had glory in the OT passage)? Two reasons. First, simply, the glory was "made inoperative," snuffed out by the veil. Second, however, Paul plainly states that it was because it is so outshone by the glory of the new-covenant ministry. It is outshone both by extent and therefore by degree. In terms of extent, the glory of Moses's face was limited to one person. The new-covenant ministry is "to a much greater degree" (v. 8), it "overflows," and it "far outshines [the glory of Moses]" (v. 9), because "all of us, with unveiled faces observing the Lord's glory . . . are being transformed" into glorious people (v. 18). This is both a

---

33. καταβαίνοντος δὲ αὐτοῦ ἐκ τοῦ ὄρους Μωυσῆς οὐκ ᾔδει ὅτι δεδόξασται ἡ ὄψις τοῦ χρώματος τοῦ προσώπου αὐτοῦ ἐν τῷ λαλεῖν αὐτὸν αὐτῷ (katabainontos de autou ek tou orous Mōysēs ouk ēdei hoti dedoxastai hē opsis tou chrōmatos tou prosōpou autou en tō lalein auton autō).

34. καὶ εἶδον οἱ υἱοὶ Ισραηλ τὸ πρόσωπον Μωυσῆ ὅτι δεδόξασται, καὶ περιέθηκεν Μωυσῆς κάλυμμα ἐπὶ τὸ πρόσωπον ἑαυτοῦ, ἕως ἂν εἰσέλθῃ συλλαλεῖν αὐτῷ (kai eidon hoi huioi Israēl to prosōpon Mōysē hoti dedoxastai, kai periethēken Mōysēs kalymma epi to prosōpon heautou, heōs an eiselthē syllalein autō).

superabundance of glory in terms of extent (it reaches farther) but also degree (there is a lot more of it). The glory of Moses's face was quashed, snuffed out by a veil. So naturally, the constantly shining faces of new-covenant ministers and those to whom they minister will far outshine his face.

To draw an analogy,[35] imagine a large, dark room with no windows, in which a 40-watt bulb has been inserted into a lamp in the middle of the room. The lamp is turned on, and the "glory" of that 40-watt bulb shines brightly amid the darkness. Further, imagine that a person repeatedly comes in to put a cover over the bulb, dousing the light. But suddenly dozens and dozens of spotlights with thousands of watts of power are brought into the room. When the spotlights are turned on, not only is the whole room bathed in an intense light, but the glory of the 40-watt bulb, when it is not covered, has been completely lost in the overwhelming and constant glory of the spotlights. So also the glory of the new-covenant ministry so outshines that of the old that the glory on Moses's face no longer seems glorious at all by comparison.

Here Paul does not negate the significance of the glory in Moses's ministry. After all, it *was* a manifestation of Moses having been in God's presence. Rather, he builds on the significance of that important dynamic in Israel's story, using it as a theological stepping-stone to show the much greater degree of glory under the new covenant. In fact, as we shall see, God intended a much greater glory for his people all along.

3:11   Finally, verse 11 expands (γάρ, *gar*) the apostle's discourse by reiterating the argument of verse 9, but with nuanced changes: "For if that which was being made inoperative was through glory, to a much greater extent the ministry that remains is attended by glory" (εἰ γὰρ τὸ καταργούμενον διὰ δόξης, πολλῷ μᾶλλον τὸ μένον ἐν δόξῃ, *ei gar to katargoumenon dia doxēs, pollō mallon to menon en doxē*). Paul now replaces a description of Moses's ministry as "the ministry characterized by condemnation" (3:9) with "that which was being made inoperative" (τὸ καταργούμενον). This is Paul's second use of the verb καταργέω (*katargeō*).[36] Here it is used in the form of a substantival participle, translated "that which was being made inoperative." Notice that the gender of the passive participle is neuter, so it has a neuter referent. In fact, its gender, voice, and number all parallel τὸ δεδοξασμένον in the previous verse, which we have already suggested parallels the tense and voice of the same verb in the LXX text, which clearly refers to Moses's face. What then does Paul mean in verse 11 that Moses's face was being made inoperative? Again Exod. 34:35: "And the sons of Israel saw the face of Moyses that it was

---

35. Calvin (1964: 46) draws an analogy using the moon and stars as compared to the sun, but he misreads Paul's intention by suggesting that the contrast is between the law and the gospel: "Just as the moon and the stars, though they are themselves bright and spread their light over all the earth, yet vanish before the greater brightness of the sun, so the Law, however glorious in itself, has no glory in the face of the Gospel's grandeur."

36. As explained above, in the first century καταργέω could be used variously to mean "to use up," "exhaust," "waste," "make ineffective," "invalidate," "to cause something to be abolished or set aside," or "to be discharged" or "released from an obligation" (BDAG 525).

charged with glory, and Moyses put a covering over his face until he went in to converse with him" (NETS). So his face was made "inoperative" in the sense that the glory was snuffed out.

What, then, might Paul mean when he says that Moses's face was "through glory"? I suggest that διά with the genitive serves as a marker of instrumentality or circumstance whereby something is accomplished or effected. I think this may refer to the glory that Moses experienced every time he entered the presence of God. Moses's being in the presence of God's glory rendered his face glorious, and thus it was "through glory"—a thought that parallels what Paul will say about new-covenant believers in 3:18. Beholding the glory of the Lord makes one glorious.

In the apodosis of the sentence, "the ministry characterized by righteousness" of verse 9, Paul now describes as "the ministry that remains" (τὸ μένον, *to menon*; v. 11). The present participle of μένω (*menō*) also has been translated variously as that which "remains" (NASB[95], NET, NLT[2]), "endures" (HCSB), "lasts" (NIV, TNIV), or "is permanent" (ESV, RSV). Whereas Moses's ministry was provisional, designed to be for a limited period of time, the new covenant constitutes the culmination of God's plan for his people and therefore will not be terminated. The apostle lives and ministers in the vibrant context of this new covenant. Moreover, to a much greater degree (πολλῷ μᾶλλον, *pollō mallon*) than the old covenant, the new dispensation of ministry is "attended by glory" (ἐν δόξῃ, *en doxē*); here Paul echoes the same phrase used twice in verses 7–8 and thus forms an inclusio marking off verses 7–11 as a unit of thought. In the next section, the apostle explains in further detail why the new covenant was more glorious than the old, now focusing on the extent of the glory.

ii. Veiled and Unveiled People (3:12–18)

Paul now turns from focusing on the different degrees of glory in the two ministries to a consideration of the veil that covered the face of Moses. The apostle begins this part of his homily on Exod. 34:29–35 by again contrasting the two ministries but this time taking up the difference between the veiled faces of Moses and his inheritors and the "unveiled faces" (v. 18) of Paul and new-covenant believers. The apostle begins, "Therefore, since we have this kind of hope, we conduct our ministry with a great deal of openness" (Ἔχοντες οὖν τοιαύτην ἐλπίδα πολλῇ παρρησίᾳ χρώμεθα, *Echontes oun toiautēn elpida pollē parrēsia chrōmetha*).

Of what is Paul speaking when he says that his conduct of ministry is in some way grounded in his possession of (ἔχοντες) "this kind of hope" (τοιαύτην ἐλπίδα)? The conjunction translated "Therefore" (οὖν, *oun*) points us back to the previous unit, where Paul has proclaimed in no uncertain terms the vastly greater glory of the new-covenant ministry as compared to the ministry of Moses (3:7–11). The message that the ministry of the new covenant is "much greater" than the old-covenant ministry of Moses, therefore, gives hope because

3:12–13

it demonstrates that Paul's ministry rests on the ongoing and developing work of God in the world, which is carried out by the new-covenant power of the Spirit (3:17–18). Thus, in 3:12–18 the apostle offers the implications of the argument from lesser to greater carried out in 3:7–11.

In accordance with the new-covenant work of the Spirit, Paul carries out his "ministry with a great deal of openness." In the first century the verb χράομαι (chraomai) could be used to speak of "using" something or "acting" in a certain way, and Paul employs the word with the latter nuance both here and elsewhere in the book (2 Cor. 1:17; 13:10; BDAG 1088).[37] Specifically, Paul compares his ministry to Moses's ministry, for Moses "acted" not with openness, but with a "closed" posture, veiling himself repeatedly as he related to the people to whom he was ministering. So, "in contradistinction to Moses" (οὐ καθάπερ Μωϋσῆς, ou kathaper Mōysēs) the ministry of the new covenant is conducted with "a great deal of openness" (πολλῇ παρρησίᾳ, pollē parrēsia). The word παρρησία can speak of "boldness," "courage," or "confidence of posture" (e.g., Heb. 10:19), or speech that is "outspoken," "frank," or "plain." Garland (1999: 181) helpfully explains that the word refers

> to the right to speak freely and openly and to give frank criticism to cultivate moral improvement. Paul is talking about speech, not just his behavior. The word's usage had shifted from meaning freedom of speech in a political context to personal candor, speaking directly and bluntly. Boldness related to freedom of speech and had to do with "speaking without restraint about the most painful things," "not mincing words." It was, however, the characteristic of the true friend and not the flatterer (see 1 Thess. 2:2; Philem. 8; Phil. 1:20).

Thus, here Paul has in mind the "openness" of his ministry in general and particularly his frankness in speaking to the church at Corinth about their situation (BDAG 781).[38] His ministry is not veiled. Correspondingly, just a few verses later, in 4:2 he writes, "We have turned our backs on the shameful things people hide, not living by tricks, nor twisting God's Word; rather, by public proclamation of the truth we commend ourselves to every person's conscience as we live before God." So his ministry goes forward "with a great deal of openness" in terms of straightforward speaking of the truth, but this is possible because no veil impedes the communication. The veil is ripped away by the Lord when the gospel is received (3:16). Hearts thus are no longer draped in a veil (3:14, 16), and the new-covenant ministers, preaching in

37. Also, by use of this term the apostle seems to signal for us that he is still living in the Greek version of the OT text. There the text speaks of the χρώματος (chrōmatos), the complexion or color of Moses's face. Since χράομαι and χρώματος are two words that sound almost the same, Paul seems to be engaging in wordplay. Moses performed his ministry with a change of χρώματος on his face. Now, Paul says, we χρώμεθα, "conduct," or carry out, our ministry with glowing faces (3:12).

38. In this regard, see esp. the cogent discussion of Garland (1999: 180–83), where he provides extensive background to the virtue of plain speaking among friends in the Greco-Roman context.

the freedom of the Spirit, also minister unveiled, with their communication enabled by the Spirit (3:17–18).

Among commentators there exists a great debate concerning the meaning of the remainder of verse 13. The verb ἐτίθει (*etithei*, put, place) should be read as an iterative imperfect (i.e., "kept putting a veil"), for the OT text states that Moses had a pattern of veiling and unveiling himself (Exod. 34:33–35). Then Paul comments on the outcome of Moses veiling himself: "with the result[39] that the children of Israel did not look with sustained attention." The verb ἀτενίζω (*atenizō*), used earlier at 3:7 in the same aorist infinitive form, does not merely mean "to look" or "see" (contra HCSB, NLT, TNIV). Rather, the word "expresses curiosity" and refers to "attentive and prolonged visual observation of an object," or "an insistent fixing of the attention" (Spicq 1994: 1.227–28; NET, ESV, NIV; Luke 22:56; Acts 3:12; 10:4). From the OT text it is clear that the visage of Moses's face was alarming to the Israelites initially (Exod. 34:30). However, the OT passage also seems to indicate that Moses's activities, specifically his interactions with the Lord and the Israelites, settled into a pattern of veiling when he was before the people and unveiling when he went in to speak to the Lord. The main point seems to be that their viewing of his face was repeatedly interrupted by the placing of the veil over his face, and thus they were not able to look at his face in a sustained way. This understanding accords with Paul's emphases in the passage before us.

We now come to the more debated aspects of the verse, which we have translated, "unto the completion of what was being made inoperative." Two sticky interpretive issues present themselves here. First, what does the apostle mean by the τέλος (*telos*) of what was made inoperative? Second, to what is he referring when he writes τοῦ καταργουμένου (*tou katargoumenou*)?

Consider the second question first. Here, in the form of a present passive participle (τοῦ καταργουμένου), it delimits the word τέλος. As with the previous uses by Paul in the immediate context, the word refers to something made inoperative (3:7, 11), and we translate it as past tense because the time frame is past relative to Paul. Again the participle is neuter, and the thing being made inoperative is the neuter term translated as "face" (τὸ πρόσωπον, *to prosōpon*) just a few words earlier. So again, it is Moses's face that is being "made inoperative" in the sense that the glory of his face is being suppressed. But of what does the apostle speak when he writes of the τέλος? The word carries a fairly broad semantic range[40] and has been variously understood here as referring to the "end" or "termination" of something (e.g., KJV, HCSB,

---

39. Although the construction πρὸς τό (*pros to*) + infinitive can connote purpose (as reflected in almost every modern ET of 3:13), it also may simply communicate the result of some action (D. Wallace 1996: 611; Zerwick 1963: 135). Nevertheless, even if the construction expresses purpose here, all that is added to the discussion is the question of Moses's motive for veiling himself, a question that the Exodus passage does not answer.

40. E.g., "end," "termination," "cessation," "close," "conclusion," "goal," "outcome," "rest," "remainder," or "a tax;" as an adverb to mean "finally," "in the end," "to the last" (BDAG 998). See esp. the discussion in Hafemann 1995: 347–62.

NASB, TNIV, NRSV, YLT, Darby), or the "result" or "outcome" of something (e.g., NET, ESV).

Yet the meaning and significance of the term is highly debated. Numerous suggestions have been made. Harris (2005: 299) helpfully delineates these for us in two primary categories:

> Teleological sense: goal, purpose, significance
> Temporal sense: end, termination, cessation

The dominant view in the recent history of interpretation has been to understand the word to refer "to Moses's practice of hiding from Israel the fact that the glory on his face was coming to an end (τὸ τέλος) because of its fading nature (τοῦ καταργουμένου)" (as explained and criticized by Hafemann 1995: 347). Others have interpreted the τέλος as referring to what Moses intended to accomplish through putting a veil over his face: to hide from Israel the ultimate significance of the glory on his face, which was in some way a reflection of Christ and/or his gospel (A. Hanson 1965: 27–29; Martin 1986: 68). However, I agree with Hafemann (1995: 357–58) that the understanding of τέλος that accords with Paul's reading of Exod. 34, the passage to which he orients his discussion, is that of "outcome" or "result." Where I differ with Hafemann, however, is the nature of this "outcome." For Hafemann (1995: 358) reads the outcome as "the death-dealing judgment of the glory of God upon his 'stiff-necked' people as manifested in the old covenant." Yet this interpretation misses a more straightforward and less complex reading.[41]

I suggest that we take a bit different course and consider the phrase εἰς τὸ τέλος as a whole, a phrase that occurs only here in the NT.[42] In fact, this phrase is found only three times in ancient Greco-Roman literature, fifty-six times in the superscriptions of certain psalms (as for Pss. 4; 5; 6; etc.), where the NETS translates it as "regarding completion," twice in the LXX (Josh. 3:16; and in an alternate reading of Dan. 11:13), and once in the Pseudepigrapha (Sib. Or. 12.140). In every case it seems clear that the phrase has to do with the "completion" of something. For example, Plutarch (*Soll. an.* 1.22) speaks positively of the work of the deity as he uses birds to give people direction through soothsaying: "so that [the god] uses some birds to cut short, others to speed enterprises and inceptions to the destined end [εἰς τὸ τέλος]" (Cherniss and Helmbold 1957: 413).

41. I suggest that most contemporary interpretations of the passage have overinterpreted the passage, missing the more straightforward sense of Paul's reading the veil as a barrier to the glowing of Moses's face, which in turn was a manifestation of the presence of God.

42. Here I am concerned with the exact phrase εἰς τὸ τέλος, not the more common εἰς τέλος, which usually means "in the end" or "finally" and occurs at Matt. 10:22; 24:13; Mark 13:13; Luke 18:5; John 13:1; and 1 Thess. 2:16. However, the sense we are suggesting has some correspondence to the nuance in 1 Thess. 2:16, if in that verse the term is translated with the sense "completely" (e.g., NET).

So, what if we translate this phrase in 2 Cor. 3:13 as having to do with something done "unto completion," or "to the designed end," specifically the completion of something to be initiated in relation to Moses's glorified face? In the text, after all, Moses dons a veil so that the children of Israel would not be able to look at the "glorious complexion of his face," or simply his glorified face. So what might it mean that Paul ministers "in contradistinction to Moses. He [Moses] kept putting a veil over his face with the result that the children of Israel did not look with sustained attention unto the completion of what was being made inoperative"?

Earlier in the narrative, as expressed by the Greek translation of Exodus at 33:16 we may find the answer.[43] There Moses pleads with God to go with the children of Israel up to the land of promise, for God's judgment on the golden-calf incident was that he was not going with the people (see the end of Exod. 32 and the beginning of Exod. 33). Moses continues in 33:16, and a translation of the LXX reads:

> "And how shall it be truly known that I have found favor with you, both I and your people, other than if you go along with us? And *we shall be glorified, both I and your people,* above [in comparison to] all the nations that are on the earth" [καὶ ἐνδοξασθησόμεθα[44] ἐγώ τε καὶ ὁ λαός σου παρὰ πάντα τὰ ἔθνη, *kai endoxasthēsometha egō te kai ho laos sou para panta ta ethnē*]. Then the Lord said to Moyses, "Even this word that you have spoken, I will do for you. For you have found favor before me, and I know you above all others." (Exod. 33:16–17 NETS, emphasis added)

It is clear from this passage that according to the LXX, Moses anticipated a particular outcome of the presence of God among his people: God would dwell among his people and *glorify them* along with Moses. I believe that what Paul is saying in 2 Cor. 3:13 is that this anticipation, because of the hardness of the hearts of the people, was cut short and not brought to completion. The veil then becomes symbolic of a dull heart that does not grasp God's purposes nor

---

43. Moberly (1983: 66–75) notes that the content of Exod. 33:12–23 "is the most dense and compressed in the whole of [chaps.] 32–34." Yahweh will make the people of Israel distinctive by his presence, but Moses still realizes that the problem of sin may undo the whole. What is needed is a deeper revelation of God's character as gracious and merciful (33:19; 34:6–7).

44. The verb is a cognate with δοξάζω (*doxazō*, in Exod. 34:29, 35) and overlaps with it semantically. In 33:16–17 ἐνδοξάζω renders the Hebrew term וְנִפְלֵינוּ (*wĕniplênû*), a Niphal perfect of פלה, which means "to be treated as distinct or excellent, or to be wonderful." ἐνδοξάζομαι means "to be honored, held in high esteem, or be glorified." It may be that the LXX translators, under the influence of δοξάζω at 34:29, 35, rendered the Hebrew to reflect the overarching theme of glorification in the broader context. Wevers suggests that the LXX Exodus translators have taken MT's וְנִפְלֵינוּ as וְנִפְלָאנוּ (*wĕniplē'nû*) and points out that the Vulgate reads *glorificemur* at this point (Wevers 1990: 550). Interestingly, one version of the Targum on the verse also reflects the tradition of glorification. An ET of that Targum on the verse reads, "But by what shall it be known now that I have found grace and mercy before you, I and your people? Is it not when the glory of your Shekinah leads with us, and signs and wonders are done with us, me and for your people, more than all the people on the face of the earth?" (Tg. Onkelos on Exod. 33:16).

enjoy the outcome of being a people who know God's presence. In short, the people fail to embrace the fullness of the glorious relationship that God desires with them; this, for Paul, is analogous to those up to his day who fail to grasp the gospel because the veil still stands between them and the manifestation of God's glory in the gospel of Christ, as we see in the next verse (3:14; 4:6).

Consequently, the apostle speaks of the glowing of Moses's face as the limited outcome—one that terminated with Moses himself. A key here is to understand the veil as a barrier standing between the people and the manifestation of God's presence. When Paul writes, "[Moses] kept putting a veil over his face with the result that the children of Israel were not able to keep looking attentively unto the completion of what is being made inoperative," he simply means that the veil cut off their experience of God's manifest presence on Moses's glorious face (Baker 2000: 13–14).[45] They were cut out, closed off, refused access (Dumbrell 2002: 78). This then stands in bold contrast to the new covenant, where the veil has been taken away by Christ and there is free and open access to the presence of God by the indwelling Spirit (3:14–18), the thought to which the apostle turns next.

3:14–16   Moses's veiling, thus, relates to a deleterious effect on the Israelites: "Rather, their minds were hardened" (ἀλλὰ ἐπωρώθη τὰ νοήματα αὐτῶν, *alla epōrōthē ta noēmata autōn*). Paul begins verse 14 with the conjunction ἀλλά (*alla*, here translated as "rather"), used contrastively, and the contrast is with what *would* have been if the Israelites had been afforded a sustained view of the glory on Moses's face, spoken of in the previous verse. The hardening or dulling of the mind stands in contrast, then, to an open-faced experience of the glory of God.

It is interesting that in this context Paul uses the word πωρόω (*pōroō*) to speak to the motif of "hardness" or of being "stiff-necked," concepts found in Exod. 32–34 as well as passages such as Jer. 5:21–24, and Ezek. 12:2 (Stockhausen 1989: 135–46). The word itself, however, is found in the LXX only at Job 17:7, which does not seem to be a relevant backdrop for our passage. A better parallel, the use of the verb at John 12:40,[46] plays a part in John's quotation of Isa. 6:10, an extraordinarily important passage in the ministry of Christ and the earliest Christians (see Mark 4:12; 8:17–18; Acts 28:26–27): "He has blinded their eyes and hardened [ἐπώρωσεν] their hearts, so that they would not see with their eyes or understand with their hearts, and be converted, and I would heal them" (HCSB). In the context, John reports on the refusal of those under the voice of Jesus's ministry to believe in spite of the many miracles he had done. Notice that in John's version of the Isaiah

---

45. My understanding of the passage was arrived at independently of Baker but parallels his understanding of the text to a certain degree.

46. On the form of the passage and John's use of πωρόω, see Barrett 1978: 431–32; Keener 2003: 2.883–84. It is likely that John 12:40 provides a fairly loose rendering of the Hebrew of Isa. 6:10, since the quotation is closer to the MT, but he also may shape his paraphrase based on his own theological emphases. In John, those who exhibit faith can see God's glory in Jesus's signs (2:11; 11:40).

passage, πωρόω speaks of "hardness" of heart and parallels the blinding of eyes. Yet the "hardened heart" is in contrast with "understand with their hearts, and be converted."

So here in 2 Cor. 3:14–16 Paul has in mind the dulling of the spiritual perception of the Israelites, a spiritual hardness or blindness of heart. In verses 14b–16 he unpacks this hardness in parallel[47] fashion, speaking of (a) a time frame for this spiritual condition, (b) the problem, and (c) the solution:

	2 Cor. 3:14b	2 Cor. 3:15–16
Time frame:	Until this very day when the old covenant is read,	Right up to the present time when Moses is read,
Problem:	that same veil remains unmoved,	a veil drapes their hearts;
Solution:	because it can only be made inoperative in Christ.	but when a person turns to the Lord, the veil is removed.

The conjunction γάρ (*gar*) in verse 14b facilitates a transition from Paul's reflection on the OT text to the current spiritual situation of those who do not yet know Christ. What follows the transition is an analogy between the spiritual condition of the Israelites of Moses's day, symbolized by the veil on Moses's face, and the spiritual condition of those who have yet to have their hearts transformed by the Spirit of the new covenant.

First, *the time frame*. Verse 14b reads, "until this very day, when the old covenant is read" (ἄχρι . . . τῆς σήμερον ἡμέρας . . . ἐπὶ τῇ ἀναγνώσει τῆς παλαιᾶς διαθήκης, *achri . . . tēs sēmeron hēmeras . . . epi tē anagnōsei tēs palaias diathēkēs*). The general historical time frame extends from the time of Moses right to the present, as expressed by the parallel in verse 15: "Indeed, right up to the present time" (ἀλλ᾽ ἕως σήμερον ἡνίκα, *all' heōs sēmeron hēnika*). More specifically, however, Paul is concerned with a person's ability to "hear" the truth of the gospel in the Scriptures. In verse 14 he expresses this more particular time frame with "when the old covenant is read" and in verse 15 with "when Moses is read"[48] (ἂν[49] ἀναγινώσκηται Μωϋσῆς, *an anaginōskētai Mōysēs*).[50]

47. The conjunction ἀλλ᾽ (*all'*) at the beginning of 3:15 we render "indeed," for, underscoring the use of the same conjunction at the beginning of verse 14, ἀλλά here is rhetorically ascensive. This double statement serves to amplify 3:14–16 as at the heart of Paul's concern in this portion of the letter.

48. This "reading" of Moses, moreover, constitutes a proclamation of the true Word of God. When the Scriptures detailing the Sinai covenant are read in the synagogue, God's Word goes forth. Thus Moses should not be perceived as "the problem" in Paul's interpretation of the OT narrative (so Calvin 1964: 47; John Chrysostom, *Hom. 2 Cor.* 7.3, in Bray 1999: 220).

49. The particle offers an aspect of contingency in the verbal idea. Specifically, Paul has in mind those times when people are hearing the OT text read.

50. The temporal use of the prepositional phrase ἐπὶ τῇ ἀναγνώσει (*epi tē anagnōsei*, [lit.] upon the reading) in 3:14, and ἂν + the imperfective aspect of the present passive subjunctive verb ἀναγινώσκηται (*an anaginōskētai*) in 3:15—both communicate that what Paul has in mind is an ongoing situation.

The problem, however, is that "the same veil . . . remains unmoved" (τὸ αὐτὸ κάλυμμα . . . μένει, μὴ ἀνακαλυπτόμενον, *to auto kalymma . . . menei, mē anakalyptomenon* [3:14]), that is, "a veil drapes their hearts" (κάλυμμα ἐπὶ τὴν καρδίαν αὐτῶν κεῖται, *kalymma epi tēn kardian autōn keitai* [3:15]). In the veiling of Moses, the Israelites' carnal minds were left without spiritual understanding; when Moses put a veil over his face, cutting off the Israelites from the glory manifested in his ministry, they were kept from perceiving the true import of the glory on Moses's face—that God's ultimate goal was for his covenant people to experience his presence and thus his glory. This would be at the heart of the new covenant, a covenant in which all of the covenant people would "know the Lord" and have their hearts transformed (Jer. 31:31–34), when all would be able to go boldly behind the tabernacle curtain (which also stands as a barrier) into the holiest place of the Lord because their sins have been forgiven decisively (Heb. 10:19–20). Correspondingly, in the synagogues of the first century, when people hear the old covenant read and understand it as the apex of God's intentions for his people, they are blinded to the significance of Christ's new covenant.[51] Thus the κάλυμμα, the "veil," functions as a barrier. When Paul writes that the veil is "the same" one (τὸ αὐτό) as on Moses's face (2 Cor. 3:14), he speaks typologically. He does not mean the actual, physical veil worn by Moses is passed around the Mediterranean in his day! Rather, the veil represents the spiritual obstruction that blinds those who have yet to respond to the new covenant and truly grasp God's glorious gospel. This obstruction lies over their hearts (τὴν καρδίαν αὐτῶν, v. 15) because their hearts have yet to be transformed. In essence Paul strongly suggests that just as the Israelites of Moses's day could not see the glory of God due to a barrier, so too those who fail to see the glory of Christ reflected in those Mosaic Scriptures are blinded to the ultimate import of those Scriptures; the veil remains; it drapes (κεῖται, *keitai*) their hearts.

Third, Paul offers *the solution*: that veil, that barrier of the heart and mind, can only be removed in Christ. The word καταργέω, which we have translated "made inoperative" (καταργεῖται, *katargeitai*) and has figured so prominently in 3:7–18 thus far, we encounter once more in 3:14b. Here Paul crafts a play on the imagery of "nullification." In Moses's ministry the glory on the mediator's face was "made inoperative" each time Moses put on the veil (3:7, 11). Yet in Christ[52] the veil itself is made inoperative, or "removed" (περιαιρεῖται, *periaireitai*), as Paul states in verse 16. Both καταργεῖται and περιαιρεῖται are present passive verbs, presupposing the Lord as the agent of change. Moreover, the imperfective aspect of the verbs works in context to speak of an ongoing occurrence. This nullification or removal of the veil happens "when a person

---

51. As Dumbrell (2002: 66) notes, Paul's concern in part is not with the Mosaic age but with those who wish to carry the Mosaic age into his own age.

52. Here ἐν Χριστῷ (*en Christō*) may be read as communicating relationship, "in relationship with Christ." Paul uses the construction six times in 2 Corinthians (2:17; 3:14; 5:17, 19; 12:2, 19). As we have seen, the construction ἐν τῷ Χριστῷ also appears at 2:14, as well as elsewhere in Paul: 1 Cor. 15:22; Eph. 1:10, 12, 20; 3:11.

turns to the Lord" (ἡνίκα . . . ἐὰν ἐπιστρέψῃ πρὸς κύριον, *hēnika . . . ean epistrepsē pros kyrion* [v. 16])—and Paul clarifies to whom "the Lord" refers in the next verse. His allusion here perhaps works on three levels:

> Moses going into the presence of the Lord in Exod. 34:34: "But whenever Moses went in before the LORD to speak to him, he removed the veil."[53]
>
> Paul's personal experience on the Damascus road (Barnett 1997: 184).
>
> All those who turn to the Lord through the new-covenant gospel.

Thus understood, Moses's removal of his veil in the presence of the Lord forms the foundational word picture to describe the essence of the new-covenant gospel, a reality that Paul himself has experienced on the Damascus road and one that he sees taking place time and again as people turn to the Lord of the gospel. The new covenant means that people have an open-faced relationship with the Lord in which that which separated them from the presence of God and his glory has been removed. Most immediately for Paul, the veil represents disbelieving the gospel of Christ (3:14; 4:4; Rom. 11:23). Moses, the covenant mediator, removed his veil as he turned to the presence of the Lord, and his face shone with the glory of God. In the new covenant, the Lord removes the veil draped over the hearts of unbelievers so that they might see the glory of God in the face of Christ (4:4–6).

When Paul writes, "'The Lord' is the Spirit,"[54] he comments on the term κύριος (*kyrios*) as used in the OT context (thus our use of quote marks in the ET). The apostle points out that "the Lord" alluded to in the previous verse (2 Cor. 3:16) and spoken of in the OT context (Exod. 34:34) actually is the Holy Spirit.[55] Paul, therefore, understands the references to "the Lord" in the Exod. 34 narrative as being references to the Holy Spirit as present among the Israelites. The Pentateuch speaks of the Spirit as filling the craftsmen who worked on the tabernacle (Exod. 31:3; 35:31) and of the Spirit coming on the leaders of Israel so that they prophesied (Num. 11:17, 25–26, 29). Paul seems to understand God's descent onto Mount Sinai (Exod. 24:15–18), his traveling among and instructing the Israelites (e.g., Exod. 33:3, 7–11; Neh. 9:20; Isa.

3:17–18

---

53. Exod. 34:34 LXX: ἡνίκα δ' ἂν εἰσεπορεύετο Μωυσῆς ἔναντι κυρίου λαλεῖν αὐτῷ περιῃρεῖτο τὸ κάλυμμα (*hēnika d' an eiseporeueto Mōysēs enanti kyriou lalein autō periēreito to kalymma*).

54. For a discussion of the various proposals, see Harris (2005: 309–12), who states, "Few sentences in the New Testament have prompted more debate than this linguistically simple statement" (309–10). Harris explains that there exist two dominant views: (1) "the Lord" refers to the risen Lord Jesus; (2) clarifying 3:16, "the Lord" spoken of in the OT context refers to the member of the Godhead we name as the Holy Spirit—the view adopted by a host of recent interpreters (e.g., Belleville 1991: 261–62; 1996: 110; Furnish 1984: 202, 212; Hafemann 1995: 397–400; 2000: 160).

55. Contra, e.g., Calvin (1964: 48–49), who reads "The Lord is the Spirit" as "Christ is the life of the Law" or "the spirit of the Law" in the sense that the law "will come alive and be life-giving only if it is inspired by Christ."

63:11), and his descent on the tabernacle in the cloud (Exod. 33:9–11) to be the Spirit coming into the camp. Thus it makes sense that the person of the Holy Spirit met with Moses on the mountain.

The apostle goes on to assert "and where the Spirit of the Lord is, there is freedom" (οὗ δὲ τὸ πνεῦμα κυρίου, ἐλευθερία, *hou de to pneuma kyriou, eleutheria*). This second half of the verse has no verb: the verb of being is to be understood. The phrase πνεῦμα κυρίου occurs twenty-five times in the LXX (e.g., Judg. 3:10; 11:29; 13:25; 1 Sam. 10:6; 11:6; 2 Sam. 23:2; 1 Kings 18:12; 2 Chron. 15:1; 18:23; Mic. 2:7; 3:8; Isa. 61:1; Ezek. 11:5; 37:1), and only elsewhere in the NT in Luke-Acts (Luke 4:18; Acts 5:9; 8:39). But the use in Acts 5:9 helps confirm the identity of "the Lord" in the first half of the verse, for in Acts 5 "testing the Spirit of the Lord" (5:9) parallels lying "to the Holy Spirit" (5:3).

Paul uses the term "freedom" (ἐλευθερία, *eleutheria*) to speak of various forms of liberty (Rom. 8:21; 1 Cor. 10:29; 2 Cor. 3:17; Gal. 2:4; 5:1, 13). Here he means primarily an open relationship with God once the Lord has removed the "veil" of unbelief. The thought conceptually parallels the idea of the "openness" (παρρησία, *parrēsia*) of Paul in his ministry. A veil restricts neither his life nor his ministry, and the gospel he proclaims liberates new-covenant believers through the power of the Spirit.

Verse 18 makes clear that the "freedom" Paul has in mind is a direct result of a person being "unveiled": "All of us, with unveiled faces observing the Lord's glory as in a mirror, are being transformed into the same image from glory to glory, just as from the Lord who is the Spirit" (ἡμεῖς δὲ πάντες ἀνα-κεκαλυμμένῳ προσώπῳ τὴν δόξαν κυρίου κατοπτριζόμενοι τὴν αὐτὴν εἰκόνα μεταμορφούμεθα ἀπὸ δόξης εἰς δόξαν καθάπερ ἀπὸ κυρίου πνεύματος, *hēmeis de pantes anakekalymmenō prosōpō tēn doxan kyriou katoptrizomenoi tēn autēn eikona metamorphoumetha apo doxēs eis doxan kathaper apo kyriou pneumatos*). Given the context, the conjunction δέ (*de*)[56] indicates a simple continuation of thought: Paul now comments on the nature of the freedom of which he speaks in verse 17. The "all[57] of us" (ἡμεῖς . . . πάντες) refers to those who are members of the new covenant, who are under the ministry of the Spirit (3:8). The plural pronoun ἡμεῖς (*hēmeis*) plus πάντες (*pantes*) places the new-covenant glory in stark contrast to the old *as to the extent of the glory*. Under the old covenant, Moses's face alone, when it was unveiled, reflected the glory of the Lord. Under the new covenant, all members of the covenant have "unveiled faces observing the Lord's glory as in a mirror" (Renwick 1991: 159).

The word "unveiled," a perfect participle that delimits "face," stems from the verb ἀνακαλύπτω (*anakalyptō*), which commonly expresses the act of unveiling or uncovering something. Xenophon (*Hell.* 5.4.6), for instance, writes of a group of conspirators who were disguised as women and would strike their

---

56. The conjunction is left untranslated in this commentary since it does not add to the sense of continuation in the passage at this point.

57. The πάντες is omitted by 𝔓⁴⁶.

targets as they threw off their veils. In the LXX the word most often refers to the uncovering of a body part (e.g., Isa. 3:17; 20:4), as it does in the case of Moses's unveiling as he went into the presence of the Lord. Yet, as we have seen, in 2 Cor. 3:14–18 Paul has shifted to a figurative use of the word "veil," one that for Paul reflects a typological parallel to the veil on Moses's face. New-covenant believers, therefore, have "unveiled faces" because through the work of Christ, by the ministry of the Spirit, they have believed the gospel borne witness to first in Moses (3:14; 4:4). Their hearts, on which the Spirit has now written (3:3), as well as their faces, have been unveiled. Unveiled hearts allow the message to be heard, understood, and responded to. Unveiled faces have open access to God's presence and thus are contemplating the glory of the Lord (4:6) as they are in a constant process of transformation by the Spirit.

The present middle participle κατοπτριζόμενοι (*katoptrizomenoi*), rendered in our translation as "observe . . . as in a mirror" (κατοπτρίζω, *katoptrizō*), has at times been translated with the sense of "reflecting like a mirror" (e.g., Belleville 1991: 279–81; HCSB, NET, NLT, NIV[84]) or "beholding as in a mirror" (e.g., Furnish 1984: 202; NASB[95], NRSV).[58] The former would mean that the new-covenant believer reflects the Lord's glory to others, even as Moses did upon his initial descent from the mountain. But the primary idea communicated by the verb has to do with looking at something intently; thus the word rests in the same semantic domain as ἀτενίζω (*atenizō*), "to look at intently," used earlier in the context (3:7, 13; e.g., Matera 2003: 96–97; RSV, ESV, Tyndale). Thus the new-covenant believer, liberated from the heart veil, "observes" the Lord in his glory (4:6). Nevertheless, the verb also can carry the nuance of observing in a way analogous to seeing a reflection in a mirror (e.g., Diogenes Laertius, *Phil.* 2.33; 3.39; Pseudo-Plutarch, *Plac. philos.* 3.5). Thus Paul could mean that as we see the glory of God in the face of Christ, we constantly are exposed to the Lord's glory, and this comports with 4:6 in the immediate context: "For God, who said, 'Let light shine out of darkness,' is the one who shined in our hearts to give us the light of the glorious knowledge of God in the face of Christ" (2 Cor. 4:6 NET). Christ himself radiates the Shekinah glory.[59] And we experience this glorious observation through the presence and work of "the Lord," the Holy Spirit. Further, as Moses met with God, experiencing the presence of God directly, he was transformed by the glory he witnessed (Lambrecht 1994b). This fits the concept in the ancient world, and the broader NT, of transformation by observation (see, e.g., 1 John 3:2).

Thus Paul proclaims that new covenanters have an ongoing, unimpeded, face-to-face relationship with God: they constantly gaze at the Lord's glory by the work of the Spirit in their lives. The result is that they "are being transformed into the same image." The verb μεταμορφόω (*metamorphoō*)—which

---

58. This is the only time κατοπτρίζω occurs in biblical literature; the term κάτοπτρον (*katoptron*, mirror; Exod. 38:26 LXX [38:8 ET]) is a cognate of this verbal form.

59. Heb. 1:3 states that the Son is the "radiance of the glory" (ἀπαύγασμα τῆς δόξης, *apaugasma tēs doxēs*), imagery indicating close association of the Son and the Father. The Son radiates the Shekinah; he does not merely reflect it.

means "to change in a manner visible to others, be transfigured," or "to change inwardly in fundamental character or condition, be changed, be transformed" (BDAG 639)—only finds expression four times in the biblical literature: twice in relation to the transfiguration accounts in Matthew (17:2) and Mark (9:2), once in Romans (12:2), where Paul speaks of the Christian's transformation by mind renewal, and here. As Moses was changed by his encounter with God (Exod. 34:29–30), so those of the new covenant are changed by their experience of the presence of God through the ministry of the Spirit. When the apostle writes that that change is "into the same image" (τὴν αὐτὴν εἰκόνα, *tēn autēn eikona*), he is not speaking of "the same image as each other" (Belleville 1991: 296), but rather a transformation into the image of the glory of God that we are "observing." Ferguson (1996: 139–40) observes:[60]

> In Scripture, image and glory are interrelated ideas. As the image of God, man was created to reflect, express and participate in the glory of God, in miniature, creaturely form. Restoration to this is effected through the Spirit's work of sanctification, in which he takes those who have distorted God's image in the shame of sin, and transforms them into those who bear that image in glory.

Initially, while in the earthly body, the transformation is internal: since Christians today do not shine outwardly like Moses, this transformation is inward (4:16) as God changes us in accord with the "new creation" (5:17), through transformation of the mind (Rom. 12:2), heart, and character. Outward manifestations of this inward transformation, in Christlike character and actions, certainly reflect the glory of God (Harris 2005: 315–16). So, as we live in the new-covenant presence of God, observing his glory, we manifest God's presence and his communicable attributes.

This work, inaugurated when a person enters upon new-covenant relationship with God, is ongoing (note the imperfective aspect of the present participles in this verse) and will be consummated at the end of the age. Horton (2008: 21) comments:

> Through the Spirit, all that is done by Christ for us, outside of us and in the past, is received and made fruitful within us in the present. In this way, the power that is constitutive of the consummation (the age to come) is already at work now in the world. Through the Spirit's agency, not only is Christ's past work applied to us but his present status of glory in glory [also] penetrates our own existence in a semirealized manner. The Spirit's work is what connects us here and now to Christ's past, present, and future. . . . The Spirit shapes creaturely reality according to the archetypal image of the Son.

As God shares his glory with us as his creatures, he enables us to live as fully human image bearers of the living God (Morgan 2010: 186).

---

60. I am indebted to Chris Morgan (2010: 185–86) for alerting me to the following quotes by Ferguson and Horton.

The phrase "from glory, to glory" could be understood as "from one degree of glory to the next" (ἀπὸ δόξης εἰς δόξαν, *apo doxēs eis doxan*; so, e.g., ESV, Message, NLT², NRSV, NIV, NET), expressing the idea of progression, indicating that the transformation of the believer is an ongoing, dynamic reality, from "the initial glory already received through regeneration *to* final glory to be gained at the parousia" (Harris 2005: 316). The final stage will be the believer putting on a "body of glory" (Phil. 3:21; cf. Col. 3:4) through resurrection, a body made ready for "the ecology of heaven" (Harris 2005: 316–17). This accords with Marvin Pate's (1991: 22, 115–16) suggestion that the glory lost in the fall will be restored ultimately in the resurrection from the dead (5:1–5). In the heavenly Jerusalem, believers will experience the glory of God in all its brilliance; there will be no need for the sun or the moon, for God's glory, and that of the Lamb, will light up that city (Rev. 21:11, 23–24), and the nations will walk by that light. The believer, however, not only will see the glory of God but also will reflect the glory of God in astounding brilliance.

Yet it may also be that the two phrases, ἀπὸ δόξης and εἰς δόξαν, communicate respectively the source of the glory and the result. The first of these phrases parallels "just as from the Lord who is the Spirit" (καθάπερ ἀπὸ κυρίου πνεύματος, *kathaper apo kyriou pneumatos*). The word καθάπερ (just as) has to do with appropriate correspondence, indicating that which is fitting. The reference to "the Lord who is the Spirit"[61] harks back to verse 17, where "the Lord" of the Exodus passage is said to be referring to the Holy Spirit. Thus "from the Lord," an allusion to the OT context and Moses's experience, parallels "from glory." Thus understood, Paul is saying that the Christian's transformation by being in the presence of the Lord parallels Moses's transformation by the Spirit. So the "source" of the glory that new-covenant believers experience is ἀπὸ δόξης, that is, "from the glory of the Lord." We are made glorious by our observation of the Lord's glory as we experience his presence. But we also arc transformed εἰς δόξαν, "to glory," just as Moses was.

Reflection

A rich and difficult unit, 2 Cor. 3:7–18 begins with an "argument from lesser to greater," championing the greater glory of new-covenant ministry (3:7–11). Paul's point is not that Moses's ministry was bad and Paul's ministry is good. Rather, the apostle builds on the Spirit's good work in the ministry of Moses, a work that "glorified" Moses as the mediator who enjoyed God's presence. Moses experienced the glory of God—but the other Israelites did not. So in terms of extent and therefore degree, the glory experienced by people in the ministry of Moses was profoundly limited; the veil on Moses's face cut them off from the glory altogether. On the other hand, since the Israelites under Moses's ministry did not know the presence and glory of God through the Spirit, Moses's good ministry

---

61. Many translate the phrase as "the Spirit of the Lord," but as Harris (2005: 317) points out, this is grammatically unlikely.

was for them a "ministry of death" (3:7) and a "ministry characterized by condemnation" (3:9). New-covenant believers, however, experience "glory to a greater degree" (3:8), indeed "to a much greater degree" because they are benefactors of a ministry that produces "righteousness" in the hearts of God's people, and the glory overflows (3:9).

The second movement of the unit (3:12–18) draws out implications of the argument from lesser to greater. New-covenant ministry is not veiled like Moses's ministry (3:13); rather, grounded in the hope-full, new-covenant ministry of the Spirit, Paul and his ministry partners conduct ministry with great openness (3:12). People in Paul's world who have yet to be transformed by Christ, through the new-covenant work of God's Spirit, still have hardened minds and veil-draped hearts that fail to understand the gospel as witnessed to by Moses (3:14–15). It is when a person turns to the Lord, opening their lives to the Holy Spirit, that the veil over the heart is removed in Christ (3:16–17). People transformed by the experience of God's glory in the gospel then can experience the ongoing transformation of God's Spirit as they live life in the presence of God (3:18).

In some ways, this passage is about transcending spiritual barriers through Spirit-empowered ministry. Augustine (*Letter to Honoratus* 140.10) and Jerome (*Homily* 66, on Psalm 88) compare the veil on Moses's face and the veil of the temple (Bray 1999: 222–23); although there is not a direct correlation here, there is an analogy. For example, Hebrews makes much of the new covenant, the Day of Atonement offering of Christ (who is both the sacrifice and the high priest) as removing the veil (καταπέτασμα, *katapetasma*, curtain) of the tabernacle, opening the way for all believers to enter directly into the very presence of God in the holy of holies (Heb. 10:19–20). In 2 Cor. 3:12–18, on the other hand, as Christ removes the veil (κάλυμμα, *kalymma*) that naturally drapes the human heart, he extends the glory and presence of God to all believers. The difference is a matter of perspective, but in both, a barrier between people and God is being removed. At least in part, Paul's point is that the breaking down of the barrier between people and God, the veil that drapes the human heart, must be a work of God, through the medium of Spirit-enabled ministry. Ministry carried out apart from the Spirit has less ability to effect spiritual change than a gnat has to break through an iron door.

James Davison Hunter (2010: 222–23) is concerned that the church of the West now finds itself mired in a media-driven culture.

> Reality becomes constituted by the ephemera of image, representation, and simulation. Pseudo-intimacy with well-known personalities provides the primary form and style of communication for a population hungry for significance. Here too the message is fragmented, creating a context in which the distinctions between simulated and lived realities are largely dissolved. . . . How much spiritual fruit actually comes from the frenetic symbolism created by these media is debatable, but there is no question that in all of these

1. Paul Commends His Authentic Ministry
  c. The Better Ministry of the Spirit
                                  2 Corinthians 3:7–18

ways, these technologies unwittingly weaken the connective tissue "between word and world."

While not buying into his whole program (indeed, I don't recognize myself nor Union University, where I teach, in Hunter's description of evangelicals and their lack of emphasis on vocation), I think Hunter has a very good point. In our celebrity-driven culture, media drives celebrity and celebrity drives media. While media offers amazing means of communication for the sake of the kingdom—I benefit greatly from well-done blogs that put me in touch with important trends, books, audios, and movements—if we are not careful, we can grow inordinately fixated on the power of the uniquely "glowing face," if you will, those persons who seem to be especially touched by God for broad impact. Personally, we may become so caught up in our public and publicized ministries, in terms of the numbers of hits on our blogs or the number of followers on Twitter, that we actually begin to *dis*integrate in terms of more biblical forms of ministry. Such disintegration may cause us to forget that *Spirit-empowered men and women are God's primary media through which ministry is accomplished.*

Speaking of a biblical form of leadership, J. Hunter (2010: 260) declares:

> It is . . . the antithesis of celebrity, a model of leadership that many Christians in prominent positions have a very difficult time resisting. Celebrity is, in effect, based *on an inflated brilliance*, accomplishment, or spirituality generated and perpetuated by *publicity*. It is an artifice and, therefore, a type of fraud. Where it once served power and patrons, in our own day it mainly serves itself and its pecuniary interests. Celebrity must, of necessity, draw attention to itself. (emphasis added)

In his contrast of ministry styles and orientations, Hunter offers a cautionary word. We appropriately celebrate those who minister the Word of God to us uniquely in the power of the Spirit. But we need to be careful not to turn them into celebrities. For those of us who are blessed with some form of public ministry, we must live in the text and in authentic Christian community in such a way that image, the "inflated brilliance," gives way to interpersonal reality of a people being constantly transformed by a true, sacrificial interface with real people who, in normal life and normal everyday community, share the glory of the Spirit of the living God.

In 2 Corinthians, Paul seems to be dealing with a form of celebrity culture. Perhaps, as discussed in the introduction to this commentary, these are some form of Judaizers, teachers of Tanakh with a showy, public, "Christian" veneer, who carry out their ministries under the influence of first-century Sophist values. Paul says that for all their "skills" in public speaking (10:10; 11:6) and their claims to be ministers of Christ (11:23), they actually are preaching a different Jesus, a different gospel, and are ministering by a different spirit (11:4). May we never settle for a "ministry of the glowing face" that settles for celebrity rather than new-covenant transformation by the Spirit of God.

Additional Notes

3:7. The term γράμμασιν at 3:7 forms a hook word with the reference to the two uses of γράμμα in 3:6, making a smooth transition from 3:6 to this new unit.[62] Under the influence of the singular forms in verse 6, some ancient manuscripts read the word as singular in verse 7 as well (B D*·ᶜ F G *pc* syᵖ). However, the plural form is the stronger reading ($\mathfrak{P}^{46}$ ℵ* A B C D* F G P 0243 6 33 81 630 1739 *pc*; Or Epiph). In both the MT and the Greek OT, emphasis is placed on God writing "the words" (τὰ ῥήματα, הַדְּבָרִים; Exod. 34:1, 28) on the stone tablets.

3:9. Some ancient manuscripts read ἡ διακονία (B D² 1881 𝔐 ar f vg bo) or simply διακονία (81 629* 1505 2464 *pc*), but the evidence is much earlier and broader for the dative τῇ διακονίᾳ ($\mathfrak{P}^{46}$ ℵ A C D* F G Ψ 0243 33 104 326 630 1175 1739 *pc* (b) sy sa; Ambst Pel), and it is the more difficult reading. As Harris (2005: 281) notes, the use of the dative breaks the pattern of the word in the nominative case in verses 7–9, and both the dative of possession and the locative dative are rare in the NT.

3:17. At 3:17 the text reads οὗ δὲ τὸ πνεῦμα κυρίου, ἐλευθερία, and the final term here evidently seemed somewhat abrupt to some ancient scribes, who felt compelled to add ἐκεῖ before the word (ℵ² D¹ F G Ψ 1881 𝔐 lat syʰ sa; Epiph). Yet the evidence for ἐλευθερία alone is much stronger ($\mathfrak{P}^{46}$ ℵ* A B C D* 0243 6 33 81 1175 1739 *pc* r syᵖ bo) and thus preferred (Metzger 1994: 509).

3:18. The πάντες is omitted by $\mathfrak{P}^{46}$.

---

62. On the use of hook words in the NT, see Guthrie 1994: 96.

d. A Ministry of Integrity (4:1–6)

In 2 Cor. 4:1–6 Paul concludes his treatment of the dynamics that mark a ministry as authentic (2:14–4:6) by echoing numerous themes from 2:14–3:6. These echoes include references to "ministry" (3:6; 4:1), "the Word of God" (2:17; 4:2), a posture "before God" (2:17; 4:2), manifestation of the truth (2:14; 4:2), the abuse of God's Word (2:17; 4:2), "commending ourselves" (3:1; 4:2), "people" (ἀνθρώπων, anthrōpōn) before whom ministry is accomplished (3:2; 4:2), those who are being destroyed (2:15; 4:3), speaking or preaching the gospel (2:17; 4:5), "Christ" (2:15; 4:5), "ourselves" (3:1; 4:5), "in our hearts" (3:2; 4:6), and "knowledge" of God (2:14; 4:6).[1]

Yet in 4:1–6 we also find echoes of prominent themes from 3:7–18, including the "ministry" in which Paul is involved (3:8; 4:1) and the "veiling" of the gospel as it comes to unbelievers (3:14–15; 4:3–4), whose minds have been blinded (3:14; 4:4), causing them not to see the light of the gospel (3:13; 4:4). Other important parallels include "face" (3:13, 18; 4:6), "Christ" (3:14; 4:4), "heart" (3:15; 4:1, 6), "the image of God" (3:18; 4:4), and especially "the glory" (3:7–11, 18; 4:4, 6) of "the Lord" (3:16–18; 4:5).

In short, to express salient features of his argument, in 4:1–6 Paul pulls together threads from the tapestry on authentic ministry he has woven since 2:14. In this unit he moves from a declaration of perseverance in integrity (4:1–2), to an explanation of why, in spite of his ministry's integrity, the gospel is not grasped by those on their way to destruction (4:3–4), to the true object and basis of Christian preaching (4:5–6). Thus 2 Cor. 4:1–6 functions as a powerful crescendo on the dynamics that mark authentic Christian ministry and proclamation (2:14–4:6). An outline of the passage is as follows:

  i. Perseverance of an authentic ministry (4:1–2)
 ii. Why the gospel is "hidden" to some (4:3–4)
iii. The object and basis of authentic ministry (4:5–6)

Exegesis and Exposition

[1]Because of this, since we have this ministry in accordance with the mercy we have received, ⌜we are not giving up⌝. [2]On the contrary, we have turned our backs on the shameful things people hide, not living ⌜by tricks⌝, nor twisting God's Word; rather, by public proclamation of the truth we ⌜commend⌝ ourselves to every person's

---

1. To a great extent based on Lambrecht (1994a: 261–62), although I have added the reference to "Christ" and omitted other parallels proposed by Lambrecht that I do not see as true parallels.

conscience as we live before God. ³Now even if our gospel is hidden, it is hidden among those who are being destroyed, ⁴among whom the god of this world has blinded the minds of the unbelieving with the result that they don't see the light emanating from the gospel, which is Christ's glory; he is the image of God. ⁵For we are not preaching ourselves, but Jesus Christ as Lord, and ourselves as your slaves for the sake ⌐of Jesus⌐. ⁶Because God, the one having said, "Light will shine out of darkness!" has shone in our hearts the light, which is the personal comprehension of God's glory in the face ⌐of Christ⌐.

i. Perseverance of an Authentic Ministry (4:1–2)

4:1 Paul begins 4:1–6 with the retrospective (Harris 2005: 322; Martin 1986: 76) phrase that expresses a causal relationship with what has gone before: διὰ τοῦτο (dia touto), "for this reason" or "because of this" (διά + the acc. communicates cause). Of what does Paul speak when he refers to τοῦτο (touto, this)? The referent would have been somewhat ambiguous if the apostle had not followed with the participial clause ἔχοντες τὴν διακονίαν ταύτην (echontes tēn diakonian tautēn, since we have this ministry), which reiterates the causal idea and points to his treatment of ministry in the whole of 2:14–3:18.² As we have seen, this span of 2 Corinthians presents the foundation of Paul's apology (his case) for the authenticity of his ministry, describing it in part as glorious, of the new covenant, and by the power of the liberating Spirit of God.

Moreover, his call to this ministry (2:17) stems not from his own adequacy (2:16, 3:5) but is "in accordance with the mercy" he has received from God (καθὼς ἠλεήθημεν, kathōs eleēthēmen).³ The καθώς clause may communicate a causal idea (i.e., "since we have experienced mercy"; BDAG 494), but a "comparison" probably is in view. The ministry of Paul accords with—is harmonious with, or consistent with—God's generous act of showing the apostle mercy. The apostle's reference to God's mercy here (cf. Rom. 11:31) reminds us that Paul received entrance into the new covenant and his call to ministry at the same time, even while he was on a murderous rampage against the church, persecuting those who would become his brothers and sisters in Christ (Acts 9:1–19). Yet God had mercy on Paul, calling him to Jesus Christ and to a new-covenant ministry in that glorious confrontation on the Damascus road (Barnett 1997: 212).

Therefore the apostle's call to ministry by God's mercy, along with the nature of that ministry to which he has been called, form a powerful basis for perseverance: "we are not giving up!" (οὐκ ἐγκακοῦμεν, ouk enkakoumen).⁴

2. So Thrall 1994: 298. Calvin (1964: 51) states that "this ministry" refers to "the ministry whose excellence he has just been extolling in such magnificent terms, whose power and usefulness he has so fully expounded."

3. Paul uses the verbal form of the word rendered "mercy" (ἐλεέω, eleeō) at Rom. 9:15, 18; 11:30–32; 1 Cor. 7:25; 2 Cor. 4:1; Phil. 2:27; 1 Tim. 1:13, 16. The perfective aspect of the aorist form at 4:1 could reflect the event of Paul's conversion and call, but this is not certain.

4. Barrett (1973: 128) translates οὐκ ἐγκακοῦμεν as "We do not neglect our duty." Our ET, "We are not giving up," seeks to make the imperfective aspect of the present tense a bit more overt.

After giving an extensive account of the difficulties faced in his ministry, Paul repeats this declaration at 4:16a, forming a "parallel introduction" that effects a smooth transition to the next major section of the discourse (4:16–5:10).[5] The verb ἐγκακέω (enkakeō) is fairly rare and appears only here in Paul, at 4:16, and at Gal. 6:9; Eph. 3:13; and 2 Thess. 3:13. In the Galatians passage and in 2 Thessalonians, the word has to do with "growing tired" of doing what is good, and in Eph. 3:13 it communicates the concept of discouragement. Thus, in Paul ἐγκακέω has to do with "letting up," "losing heart," or "shrinking back,"[6] perhaps with the related idea of "being remiss in one's duty" (Thrall 1994: 299–300). As Spicq (1994: 1.399) puts it, the term connotes

> relaxing one's efforts, losing heart in the midst of difficulties, letting go, inter-
> rupting one's perseverance before attaining one's goal; giving up rather than
> continuing the fight. Hence, on the moral level, the exhortation is to overcome
> lethargy, boredom, duration, even distress in tribulation; one must not give in
> to the apparent uselessness of appeals to God and succumb to exhaustion, but
> on the contrary overcome fatigue and continue without yielding or softening.

In 2 Corinthians Paul has thus far noted the very great difficulties attending his ministry, mentioning his troubles (1:4), particularly the affliction he experienced in Asia, which threatened his life (1:8). He has obviously experienced relational friction with the Corinthians (2:1–10) and emotional turmoil at moments of uncertainty in his ministry (2:12–13). Moreover, in this letter he soon turns to the troubles assaulting him from every side, which constitute a constant dance with death as he carries out his ministry (4:7–15). The temptation to quit or become timid must at times have been a very real tug to Paul. Yet the apostle stands resolute, determined not to give up or give in to the pressures involved in carrying out his ministry.

The ἀλλά (alla, on the contrary) at the beginning of verse 2 effects a sharp contrast. Rather than giving up, Paul and his coworkers remain on a path of ministry integrity (cf. 1:12); in speaking of this integrity, he first points to patterns of behavior on which he has turned his back: "We have turned our backs on the shameful things people hide, not living by tricks, nor twisting God's Word" (ἀπειπάμεθα τὰ κρυπτὰ τῆς αἰσχύνης, μὴ περιπατοῦντες ἐν πανουργίᾳ μηδὲ δολοῦντες τὸν λόγον τοῦ θεοῦ, apeipametha ta krypta tēs aischynēs, mē peripatountes en panourgia mēde dolountes ton logon tou theou).

The word ἀπεῖπον (apeipon),[7] found only here in biblical literature, means "to disown" or "to renounce" something. What Paul and his ministry

4:2

---

5. On the use of parallel introductions, see Guthrie 1994: 104–5.
6. Perhaps in contrast to the "boldness" of which Paul speaks at 3:12 (Furnish 1984: 245).
7. This may be an example of an ingressive aorist, with the apostle expressing "the entrance into a state" (D. Wallace 1996: 558). The perfective aspect, however, underscores Paul's posture toward such patterns of life in a comprehensive way.

associates have renounced are "the shameful things people hide"[8] (τὰ κρυπτὰ τῆς αἰσχύνης). The apostle has in mind the practices of "hucksters" (2:17), who get ahead in the world by sneaky actions, for which they ought to be ashamed. These practices are hidden, not in the sense of being out of the public eye, but in the sense that they constitute deceit, a misleading "ministry." Even those who practice such shifty "ministry" know that exposure of their true motives would mean a loss of influence. Although the adjective κρυπτός (*kryptos*), employed here as a direct object, can at times be used of the condition of the heart,[9] Paul seems to place emphasis on patterns of behavior, and this is made clear by the three participial clauses that follow; these expand on Paul's rejection of shameful patterns of ministry. Authentic ministers (1) do not live by pedagogical tricks, (2) do not twist God's Word, but rather (3) live out a pattern of life and ministry that is commendable.

First, Paul and his associates are "not living by tricks" (μὴ περιπατοῦντες ἐν πανουργίᾳ, *mē peripatountes en panourgia*). NT authors consistently use the term πανουργία (*panourgia*) pejoratively to describe cunning word-and-idea crafters, who skew the truth to their own ends (e.g., Luke 20:23; 1 Cor. 3:19; 2 Cor. 11:3; Eph. 4:14). The preposition ἐν may be interpreted as communicating "means" (i.e., "by"). The present participle περιπατοῦντες (walking) indicates that the apostle is concerned with craftiness as an ongoing pattern of life and ministry,[10] and he sees this pattern as characterizing false ministers. Their ministries reek of false motives and the crafty massaging of words to garner a following.

Second, in line with his rejection of pedagogical trickery, the apostle and his coworkers do not distort the Word of God: "nor twisting God's Word" (μηδὲ δολοῦντες τὸν λόγον τοῦ θεοῦ, *mēde dolountes ton logon tou theou*). Used only here in the NT and just twice in the LXX (Pss. 14:3 [15:3 ET]; 35:3 [36:3 ET]), the verb δολόω (*doloō*)[11] means "to make false through deception or distortion" or "to adulterate" something (BDAG 256). With this description, how inauthentic ministers carry out their pedagogical tricks comes clearly

---

8. More literally, "the hidden things of shame." The genitive τῆς αἰσχύνης is descriptive: the actions that Paul describes are "shameful," or perhaps "disgraceful" (Thrall 1994: 303). The word is used similarly of false teachers in Phil. 3:19: "Their end is destruction; their god is their stomach; their glory is in their shame" (HCSB). For the various ways of reading the genitive here, see Harris (2005: 324), who in the end opts for an adjectival reading: "underhand and disgraceful ways."

9. The adjective κρυπτός at times is used with reference to the hidden condition of a person's heart (e.g., Rom. 2:29; 1 Pet. 3:4). At 1 Cor. 4:5, e.g., Paul writes, "Therefore don't judge anything prematurely, before the Lord comes, who will both bring to light what is hidden in darkness and reveal the intentions of the hearts. And then praise will come to each one from God" (HCSB).

10. The image of "walking" is one of Paul's favorites for describing patterns of life: Rom. 6:4; 8:4; 13:13; 14:15; 1 Cor. 3:3; 7:17; 2 Cor. 4:2; 5:7; 10:2–3; 12:18; Gal. 5:16; Eph. 2:2, 10; 4:1, 17; 5:2, 8, 15; Phil. 3:17–18; Col. 1:10; 2:6; 3:7; 4:5; 1 Thess. 2:12; 4:1, 12; 2 Thess. 3:6, 11. The imperfective aspect of the participle further supports the ongoing pattern reflected in the image.

11. Harris (2005: 325) points out that the cognate noun δόλος (*dolos*) refers to "bait" for fish, thus anything used to deceive, or any trick.

into view. They distort or twist the Word, misleading people by a pretense of leading them to the authoritative revelation of God. This is the Word as a power tool, a tool of manipulation, rather than a gift for spiritual maturation. For in the mouths of the false ministers, the Word of God has been mixed with and molded to fit wrong teachings. Thus the false teachers use the Word as an instrument to their own ends, as a means to bolster their influence rather than to better the church.

Third, the apostle now sets the pattern of his ministry in stark contrast to the trickery and Word twisting of false ministers. At the heart of Paul's description of his authentic ministry stands an important motif for 2 Corinthians. The apostle writes, "By public proclamation of the truth we commend ourselves to every person's conscience as we live before God" (τῇ φανερώσει τῆς ἀληθείας συνιστάνοντες ἑαυτοὺς πρὸς πᾶσαν συνείδησιν ἀνθρώπων ἐνώπιον τοῦ θεοῦ, *tē phanerōsei tēs alētheias synistanontes heautous pros pasan syneidēsin anthrōpōn enōpion tou theou*).

Paul has already used the term συνίστημι (*synistēmi*) at 2 Cor. 3:1, and he will employ it in the balance of the book at 5:12; 6:4; 7:11; 10:12, 18; and 12:11. Thus the concept, which has to do with relationship building, or bringing people together as friends in a trusting relationship (BDAG 972), provides us with an important thread that weaves its way through the book. As noted in the introduction and in our discussion of 3:1, Paul's commending of himself and his ministry to the Corinthians lies at the heart of his purpose for this letter.[12] Here, as he continues to describe his resolute commitment to the ministry, he details the *means* by which he and his coworkers commend themselves, the *audience* addressed by the commendation, and their *posture* before God as he and his coworkers carry out authentic ministry.

The commendation is accomplished "by public proclamation of the truth" (τῇ φανερώσει[13] τῆς ἀληθείας). A lost and blinded world does not know the truth. Thus truth must be disclosed or announced to the lost; the dative φανερώσει communicates the means by which this is accomplished. This public proclamation of the truth contrasts with a ministry that tricks people and twists God's Word. The problem is that those who do not believe, who are on their way to destruction, have minds blinded to the gospel (4:3–4), and they hear the truth as a death knell (2:15–16). Yet it is through the public proclamation of the truth that unbelievers become believers, that those on their way to destruction are liberated, that the blind can see spiritually. In short, the Spirit of God uses the proclamation of the truth to work transformation, to take away the

---

12. See under the heading "The Message and Intent of 2 Corinthians" in the introduction and the comments on 3:1.

13. In our context, Paul uses this concept of "announcement" or "disclosure" (BDAG 1049) with reference to the preaching and teaching of God's Word. In contrast to its cognate verb (φανερόω), which occurs 49 times in the NT, the noun only occurs twice in the NT, here and at 1 Cor. 12:7. Contra Martin (1986: 78), who says φανέρωσις "is a favorite Pauline expression in this letter," by which he must be referring to the use of the noun in conjunction with the cognate verb, which occurs nine times in the letter (2 Cor. 2:14; 3:3; 4:10–11; 5:10–11 [3x]; 7:12; 11:6).

veil over hardened hearts (3:13–16). Thus the proclamation of the liberating truth of the gospel serves as an authentication of Paul's mission—indeed, it is the only recommendation he and his coworkers need (Furnish 1984: 246). Those who are right-minded recognize Paul's work of gospel preaching as worthy of commendation because it leads to a transformation that ultimately can only be accomplished by God.

As to audience, Paul and his coworkers commend themselves "to every person's conscience." At 1:12 the apostle has already declared that he carries out his ministry with a sound conscience, and at 5:11 he expresses his hope that the consciences of the Corinthians bear witness to his integrity in ministry. Here he speaks in general terms of his public ministry, appealing to the consciences of all[14] people of discernment, wherever he may encounter them. As noted in the comments at 1:12, the conscience speaks especially of an awareness of the difference between right and wrong in one's own actions (Furnish 1984: 127), or "the capacity for moral judgment" (Barrett 1973: 129). Unlike the tangled webs woven by false ministers, authentic Christian ministry weaves a tapestry of motives, actions, and fruit that presents a consistent picture of integrity before self, before others—whether a particular community or people in general—and before God.

Thus finally, Paul reiterates (see 2:17) that his ministry is carried out as he lives "before God" (ἐνώπιον τοῦ θεοῦ). As in 2:17, the phrase speaks of one's posture, the conducting of ministry with a profound sense of answering directly to God for one's actions.

An African proverb says something to this effect: "I want to live in a house with no walls," meaning a life of complete openness to others, having nothing to hide. Authentic ministry embraces such a life. No walls of deception, of hidden motives or shifty actions, no walls that stand between the minister and his own conscience, or between the minister and the people inside or outside the reach of ministry. And there must not be "walls" between the minister and God. Such a minister, who lives with integrity in the proclamation of the gospel, should be commended and embraced by the people of God.

ii. Why the Gospel Is "Hidden" to Some (4:3–4)

4:3 In the letter, Paul in no uncertain terms has already stated that his ministry is "open," having at its center a very public proclamation of the gospel. His ministry is public like a triumphal procession is public (2:14–16), his face is "unveiled" as he speaks God's message of truth (3:12–13), and his actions are laid bare before his own conscience, before the consciences of others, and before God. Yet a publicly and authentically proclaimed gospel does not necessarily mean that gospel will be "heard" and received. So the apostle goes to the heart of the problem of "good news" that is not received as such: "Now even if our gospel is hidden, it is hidden among those who are being destroyed" (εἰ δὲ καὶ ἔστιν κεκαλυμμένον τὸ εὐαγγέλιον ἡμῶν, ἐν τοῖς ἀπολλυμένοις ἐστὶν

---

14. In 4:2 πᾶσαν (*pasan*, all) stands forward within its phrase for emphasis.

κεκαλυμμένον, *ei de kai estin kekalymmenon to euangelion hēmōn, en tois apollymenois estin kekalymmenon*).

When Paul writes, "Now even if our gospel is hidden," he is not stating a hypothetical situation. Rather, εἰ plus the periphrastic construction (ἔστιν κεκαλυμμένον)[15] assumes a real situation, as the apostle makes clear in the words that follow. Indeed, some have eyes blinded to the gospel. Further, when Paul refers to "our gospel" (τὸ εὐαγγέλιον ἡμῶν), the possessive pronoun may indicate that he is answering a charge that has been laid at his feet: "Paul, your form of the gospel is so obscure!" or perhaps, "Your weaknesses overshadow your message!" This charge certainly could have been leveled at the preacher by the false teachers (Collange 1972: 131–32), or by the unbelieving Jewish community in Corinth, for whom Christ would have been a stumbling block (1 Cor. 1:23; so Thrall 1994: 305; cf. Acts 18:4–6). In any case, the possessive pronoun certainly refers to the distinctive form of the gospel as preached by Paul and his coworkers and contrasts with the "different gospel" preached by the false ministers in Corinth (2 Cor. 11:4).

The apostle answers that the hiddenness of the gospel cannot be attributed to his lack of rhetorical skill nor to the weakness of his gospel. Rather, its obscuring has to do with the spiritual condition of unbelievers and the "god of this world" (4:4), who blinds the minds of unbelievers. In this sense the "veil" draping the hearts of unbelievers is satanic (3:15; 10:3–12), facilitated by the "servants of Satan" in Corinth (11:14–15). Thus, neither Paul nor the gospel he preaches can be faulted that there are those for whom his message is obscure. The obscurity is due to a spiritual condition of those who are being destroyed (i.e., under judgment). As Hodge (1994: 84) puts it poetically, "The sun does not cease to be sun although the blind do not see it." To make this point, the apostle both continues the veil imagery begun in the previous unit at 3:14–15 (especially picking up on the spiritual blindness discussed there) and addresses a general theological motif that he covers elsewhere: the spiritual realities of a fallen world in which the advancement of God's kingdom is opposed by spiritual forces.

Consequently, the gospel is "hidden" or "not known" (καλύπτω, *kalyptō*) because of the spiritual condition of those who are perishing. The verb καλύπτω can carry the sense of causing something to be covered (e.g., Matt. 8:24; Luke 8:16; James 5:20; 1 Pet. 4:8), but here the word communicates that the gospel is concealed, hidden, or kept secret (e.g., Matt. 10:26; Luke 23:30; BDAG 505). The consequence follows that those to whom the gospel is hidden are on their way to destruction. At times Paul uses the term rendered "destroyed" (ἀπόλλυμι, *apollymi*) to speak of a person being hurt spiritually, as when a weaker brother or sister is caused to stumble (1 Cor. 8:11), but the word more often refers to those facing the devastation of divine judgment (1 Cor. 10:10; 2 Cor. 2:15; 2 Thess. 2:10). Thus Paul's use here recalls the triumphal-procession imagery of those being led away to destruction, for whom the gospel smells like death

---

15. The present-tense verb of being + the perfect participle is equivalent to a perfect-tense verb.

remembered and death to come (2:16). It is among (ἐν, *en*, used spatially) this group of people that Paul's gospel is cloaked.

4:4 Moreover, there exists an insidious spiritual force working among those who are perishing, especially against their understanding of the gospel message, for "the god of this world has blinded the minds of the unbelieving" (ἐν οἷς ὁ θεὸς τοῦ αἰῶνος τούτου ἐτύφλωσεν τὰ νοήματα τῶν ἀπίστων, *en hois ho theos tou aiōnos toutou etyphlōsen ta noēmata tōn apistōn*). Although this use of ὁ θεός (*ho theos*, god) for Satan is unique to the NT, and some commentators suggest the phrase "the god of this age" refers to the one true God (e.g., Scott 1998: 85; John Chrysostom, *Hom. 2 Cor.* 8.2),[16] the reference here almost certainly is to the Enemy (Hafemann 2000: 177–78; Thrall 1994: 308). In calling Satan a "god," the apostle does not ascribe divine status to the evil one but rather speaks of the functional status given him and the subordination of the fallen world to him.[17] The phrase is comparable to John's "ruler of this world" (John 12:31; 14:30; 16:11). Ever since the fall, this "god" has beclouded the Word of God (Gen. 3:1), blinding the minds (1 John 2:11) of those who do not believe.[18] Thus peoples' minds constitute one very significant battleground in the cosmic conflict between God's gospel and the twisted machinations of the god of this world (2 Cor. 2:11; 3:14; 4:4; 10:5; 11:3).

The result (εἰς τό, *eis to*) for those under the voice of Paul's preaching is that "they don't see the light emanating from the gospel, which is Christ's glory" (εἰς τὸ μὴ αὐγάσαι τὸν φωτισμὸν τοῦ εὐαγγελίου τῆς δόξης τοῦ Χριστοῦ, *eis to mē augasai ton phōtismon tou euangeliou tēs doxēs tou Christou*). Used transitively, the aorist infinitive αὐγάσαι (*augasai*) refers to something that is seen with clarity (Philo, *Mos.* 2.139; BDAG 149). The references to "light" and "Christ's glory," moreover, continue the imagery from Exod. 34 expounded in 3:7–18. Thus they point to the Shekinah glory of God that, among many functions, manifests Christ's presence. Of course, people come to know that Presence by the gospel. Thus, when the apostle refers to "the light of the gospel," he speaks especially of God's revelation of truth concerning his righteousness

---

16. Scott (1998: 85) points out that Dan. 5:4 LXX and Tob. 14:6 (in Codex Sinaiticus) both refer to God as "the God of the age." By the end of his discussion, however, he admits that Second Temple Jewish texts speaking of Belial as ruler of the age and the one who leads people's hearts off God's path make the interpretation in our passage difficult.

17. The τοῦ αἰῶνος (*tou aiōnos*) can be considered a genitive of subordination (D. Wallace 1996: 103). This theology expresses the conceptual framework of apocalyptic Judaism, which worked on the basis of three primary dualities: (a) the heavenly over against the earthly realm; (b) the "now" of the current age (which may variously be spoken of as the "last days" inaugurated by Messiah [e.g., Heb. 1:2] or as an evil age [Gal. 1:4]), set over against the age to come; and (c) those under the rule of God, over against those who oppose God's rule. Basically, when Paul calls Satan "the god of this world," he observes that during this stage of history, Satan exercises a powerful counteraction to God's work in the world. It is a counteraction doomed to failure, but it is effective in blinding those who are unbelievers.

18. In calling the lost "unbelievers" (τῶν ἀπίστων, *tōn apistōn*), Paul uses a term to which he is especially partial in the Corinthian correspondence (1 Cor. 6:6; 7:12–15; 10:27; 14:22–24; 2 Cor. 4:4; 6:14–15; cf. 1 Tim. 5:8; Titus 1:15).

and salvation that are proclaimed in the gospel, with "gospel" as a genitive of source: "the light emanating from the gospel" (Barnett 1997: 218).

On one level, "light" here represents truth, for it is the "minds" of the unbelieving that have been blinded. In the OT, the concepts of "light" and "truth" often are associated, as at Ps. 43:3, where the psalmist prays to God, "Send out your light and your truth," or at 119:130, where God's words are said to give light and impart understanding. God's Word is a light to the path (119:105) and can give light to the eyes (19:8). Elsewhere in the NT, Peter can describe the prophetic word as "a lamp shining in a dark place" (2 Pet. 1:19).

Paul now stacks up genitives with τῆς δόξης τοῦ Χριστοῦ, literally, "the glory of Christ." The genitive τῆς δόξης can be interpreted as epexegetical (Martin 1986: 75, 79) and related to this "light" emanating from the gospel. It is light, "which is Christ's glory."[19] In other words, "Christ's glory" is the light that emanates from the gospel. And the genitive τοῦ Χριστοῦ may be understood as communicating the source of the glory. The light emanating from the gospel is the same as the glory emanating from Christ.

Further, Paul writes of Christ, "He is the image of God" (ὅς ἐστιν εἰκὼν τοῦ θεοῦ, hos estin eikōn tou theou). The relative clause constitutes a focal reflection on the glory Christology that infuses 2 Cor. 3:7–4:6. According to Ceslas Spicq (1994: 1.418),

> The image of something is its expression, the thing itself expressed. . . . By the incarnation, Christ manifests the Father (cf. Col 2:9—"in him dwells bodily [by the incarnation] all the fullness of the godhead"). In and by his image, God becomes visible. The emphasis falls simultaneously on the equality, if not identity (consubstantial will be the word) of the eikōn with the original, and on the authentic representativeness of Jesus.

What the apostle does with this terse proclamation is to make a direct relationship between the glory of the Christ and the person of God the Father.[20] The statement parallels other NT confessions of Jesus as the image or in the form of God (e.g., Col. 1:15; Phil. 2:6; cf. Heb. 1:3), but here the emphasis is on the glory that has been under discussion since the previous unit, and that glory is witnessed especially in the proclamation and reception of the gospel that heralds the crucified and resurrected Lord. Jesus's identity is revealed by his glory, and that glory is directly related to the image of the Father; all this parallels, for instance, the twin confession of Heb. 1:3: ὃς ὢν ἀπαύγασμα τῆς

---

19. This seems to be a prudent interpretation in view of the parallels between 4:4 and verse 6, where "the light" and "the personal comprehension of God's glory" are also identified. Here in verse 4 the term "glory" (τῆς δόξης, tēs doxēs) belongs with τοῦ Χριστοῦ (tou Christou, of Christ) rather than being an attributive genitive related to "gospel" (i.e., "the glorious gospel," NET).

20. Paul probably draws upon the background of the Jewish conception of wisdom, which was understood to reflect the image of God: "For she is a breath of the power of God and an emanation of the pure glory of the Almighty; therefore nothing defiled gains entrance into her. For she is a reflection of eternal light and a spotless mirror of the activity of God and an image of his goodness" (Wis. 7:25–26 NETS).

δόξης καὶ χαρακτὴρ τῆς ὑποστάσεως αὐτοῦ (*hos ōn apaugasma tēs doxēs kai charaktēr tēs hypostaseōs autou*), which can be translated as "who, being the radiance of the glory and the exact representation of his nature." Here the glory of the Son and the "representation" are paired, as they are in 2 Cor. 4:4. That the Son is the "representation" (i.e., the "image") of the Father stands as a confession of direct identity. We might say that, analogous to a human biological relationship between a father and son, the image of the Father is "stamped" on the face of the Son. When you see the Son, you see One with a direct relationship to the Father.

But the glory is revealed as it emanates from the gospel, at the heart of which is the crucifixion and resurrection. The apostle certainly is aware of the paradoxical nature of "glory" being found in crucifixion (e.g., 4:7–15; 12:9–10; 13:4). Yet he not only embraces the paradox but also uses it as a foundation for both his apostolic role and the Christian life (Furnish 1984: 248–49). Paul further reflects on the glory of the gospel that proclaims Christ in verse 6, discussed below.

iii. The Object and Basis of Authentic Ministry (4:5–6)

4:5   In 2 Cor. 4:5–6 Paul provides the church with striking encapsulations on the nature of Christian preaching (4:5) and the glory of that ministry's gospel (4:6)—"It would be hard to describe the Christian ministry more comprehensively in so few words" (Barrett 1973: 134). In verse 5 the apostle writes, "For we are not preaching ourselves, but Jesus Christ as Lord, and ourselves as your slaves for the sake of Jesus" (Οὐ γὰρ ἑαυτοὺς κηρύσσομεν ἀλλὰ Ἰησοῦν Χριστὸν κύριον, ἑαυτοὺς δὲ δούλους ὑμῶν διὰ Ἰησοῦν, *Ou gar heautous kēryssomen alla Iēsoun Christon kyrion, heautous de doulous hymōn dia Iēsoun.*).

In Greco-Roman culture, self-aggrandizement—the gaining of honor, position, and prestige via one's communication abilities—was a high value among some groups of the day. As discussed in the introduction to this commentary, Paul's opponents probably were from the Sophist tradition, as Bruce Winter (2002: 244) has shown, for whom "elitist training was the ideal or even an essential prerequisite for the high teaching or preaching office of the church." For the Sophists, preaching was an opportunity to parade one's superiority and perhaps gain an office of influence.[21] Thus Paul's "weaknesses," his constant afflictions (4:7–11; 6:4–10; 11:23–33), his lack of charging for his services, and his unimpressive public speaking would all suggest that the apostle was unfit for leadership according to the value system of his opponents. Yet Paul glories in his impediments. More than simple humility, the apostle embraces humiliation, for it forces him to "a radical reliance on Christ" (Knowles 2008:

21. Winter points to Philo (*Emb.* 167), who notes that there are Jews of his day who pursue teaching positions, not for virtue's sake, but "with no lighter motive than parading their superiority or from desire of office under our rulers." Roetzel (2007: 69), citing Dio Chrysostom (*Or.* 8.11), points to the Sophists "who proclaim themselves . . . just as the Olympian heralds proclaim the victors."

147). His weaknesses put greater attention on Christ, the true focus of Christian preaching.

No, Paul and his associates "are not preaching"[22] themselves; they preach "Christ Jesus as Lord."[23] This confession stands at the center of early Christian confession of Jesus's identity and position in the universe (e.g., Rom. 10:9; 1 Cor. 12:3). Christ, the Crucified, has been exalted to the right hand of Power in the universe and thus is Lord (Phil. 2:9–11). He is the true ruler of the world. To accept his gospel of salvation also means to be enslaved under his benevolent lordship (which is true for all believers: 1 Cor. 7:22b–23), and this means that Paul and his associates are Christ's slaves (Rom. 1:1; Phil. 1:1). Yet, not only are Paul and his coworkers slaves of Christ himself, but "for the sake of Jesus" they also are "slaves" or "servants" of those to whom they minister, willing to "spend and be spent up" (12:15) for those who belong to Christ (Barrett 1973: 134).[24] The phrase "for the sake of Jesus"[25] (διὰ Ἰησοῦν, *dia Iēsoun*) points to the fact that while Paul is a "slave" of the Corinthians, they are not his Lord: Jesus is his Lord (Harris 2005: 333). Paul and his mission do all that they do in submission to the exalted Lord, by whom they are constantly being transformed (3:17–18). This servant orientation of his apostleship grounds his motives and his posture toward the Corinthians in Christ's virtues. This is the upside-down orientation of true Christian leadership. Instead of advancing the kingdom by power, true leaders advance God's kingdom by sacrificial service.

In verse 6 the section concludes with a powerful proclamation of the gospel's glory. The content of the verse parallels (and contrasts) the reflection in verse 4 on those blinded by "the god of this world." **4:6**

2 Cor. 4:4	2 Cor. 4:6 (lines are numbered and reordered)
the god of this world	[1]God, the one who said, "Light will . . . ,"
has blinded	[2]has shone
the minds of the unbelieving	[3]in our hearts
with the result that they don't see	[5]which is the personal comprehension
the light emanating from the gospel,	[4]the light,
which is Christ's glory;	[6]of God's glory
he is the image of God.	[7]in the face of Christ.

Whereas those facing destruction have minds blinded by the evil one so that they cannot see the light of the gospel of Christ's glory, God has shone

22. In this instance, the present tense reflects an ongoing practice, an event that occurs regularly, and thus may be considered a "customary" or "habitual" use of the present; see D. Wallace 1996: 521.

23. See Harris's (2005: 332) eight theological implications of this Christian confession.

24. Paul's words call to mind the imagery of footwashing in John 13, where Jesus turns the concept of leadership on its head, calling for true leaders to take the role of abased servants. This is cruciform leadership, defined by a downward mobility.

25. Here διά + the acc. can communicate "cause," explaining variously the reason something takes place or exists, or as here, something that has been done "for the sake of" someone else, especially a divinity (BDAG 225).

in the hearts of those belonging to the new covenant, gifting them with the light of the knowledge of God's glory as seen in the face of Jesus Christ. To gain a full-orbed appreciation for the richness of Paul's words, we need to probe more deeply the conceptual well from which he draws.

Savage (1996: 111) suggests that with 4:6 we have come to the verse in 2 Corinthians that sheds the most light on Paul's understanding of the glory surrounding Christian ministry, through which God's gospel light shines in human hearts. First, the apostle relates this act of God shining light into dark hearts directly to God saying, "Light will shine out of darkness!" (ἐκ σκότους φῶς λάμψει, *ek skotous phōs lampsei*). Most scholars believe Paul draws this reflection as a loose citation from Gen. 1:3 (e.g., Furnish 1984: 251; Thrall 1994: 138), which reads:

> וַיֹּאמֶר אֱלֹהִים יְהִי אוֹר וַיְהִי־אוֹר (*wayyōmer 'ĕlōhîm yĕhî 'ōr wayhî-'ōr*)
> καὶ εἶπεν ὁ θεός Γενηθήτω φῶς. καὶ ἐγένετο φῶς. (*kai eipen ho theos Genēthētō phōs. kai egeneto phōs.*)
> And God said, "Let there be light, and there was light"

In its favor, the καὶ εἶπεν ὁ θεός at the beginning of the Greek rendering of Gen. 1:3 roughly parallels Paul's ὁ θεὸς ὁ εἰπών at the beginning of 4:6. Yet the clause φῶς λάμψει in 4:6 is future indicative rather than the command we find in Gen. 1:3, and the "Light will shine" proclamation is in a form more associated with prophecy (Savage 1996: 111–14). We should note, moreover, that the clause φῶς λάμψει occurs in biblical literature only at Isa. 9:1 LXX:

> ὁ λαὸς ὁ πορευόμενος ἐν σκότει, ἴδετε φῶς μέγα· οἱ κατοικοῦντες ἐν χώρᾳ καὶ σκιᾷ θανάτου, φῶς λάμψει ἐφ' ὑμᾶς (*ho laos ho poreuomenos en skotei, idete phōs mega; hoi katoikountes en chōra kai skia thanatou, phōs lampsei eph' hymas*)
> O you people who walk in darkness, see a great light! O you who live in the country and in the shadow of death, light will shine on you! (NETS)

The context in Isaiah anticipates a future beyond the time of Israel's exile and is ripe with messianic passages. These include passages that speak of the child named Immanuel (7:14), the One who would be the stone of stumbling (8:14–15), and the promise of the child who would be Wonderful Counselor, Almighty God, Everlasting Father, and Prince of Peace, who would bring in an age of renewal and the messianic kingdom (9:6 [9:5 LXX]; Blomberg, *CNTUOT* 18). Moreover, Matthew proclaims that Isa. 9:1–2 was fulfilled in Jesus at the dawn of his public ministry (Matt. 4:14–16).

Paul uses Isaiah extensively, quoting from that prophet more than any other OT writing, and he often uses Isaiah to rebuke spiritual blindness,[26] a key motif

---

26. Savage (1996: 113) notes four places in Paul where Isaiah passages cluster to address the condition of unbelievers: Rom. 2–3; 9–11; 1 Cor. 1–2; and 2 Cor. 3–4.

in 2 Cor. 3:12–4:6. Further, the topics of "light," "darkness," "blindness,"[27] and "glory," among others, are key themes for Isaiah, being used more than in all of the other prophets together. The word δόξα, for instance, occurs sixty-eight times in the Greek version of Isaiah.[28] After studying the concept of "glory" in that prophet, Savage concludes, among other points, that the glory of the Lord constitutes a dynamic of God's eschatological kingdom, in which blindness will be turned to sight as God's people witness his glory (e.g., Isa. 35:2–5).[29] Significantly, given our context in 2 Corinthians, the ones who see God's glory also will reflect that glory (Isa. 60:1; 58:8; 4:2; 2 Cor. 3:17–18). Furthermore, this eschatological light, according to Isaiah, will usher in a time of new creation (Isa. 42:9; 43:19; 48:6–8; 62:2; 2 Cor. 5:17), which will be a time of sight for blinded eyes, deliverance, and salvation (Savage 1996: 115–26).

It may be that what we have in Paul's allusion is a conflation of the Genesis passage and the one from Isaiah, with the former being read in light of the latter (Harris 2005: 334; Scott 1998: 88). If this is the case, then the apostle uses these twin images—God's giving creation's light and the light of re-creation in his new, eschatological age—to speak of the dawning of light in the human heart through the gospel. In 2 Cor. 4:6, this eschatological light of a new era of God's work has shone "in our hearts" (ἐν ταῖς καρδίαις ἡμῶν) to bring "the light, which is the personal comprehension of God's glory."

For Paul, as in much of the biblical literature, the problem of the sinful human condition apart from God may be described as a problem of the heart (Rom. 1:21, 24; 2:5; Eph. 4:18), and in 2 Corinthians he has already declared that a veil lies over the hearts of unbelievers (2 Cor. 3:15). Correspondingly, the answer to the human condition at times is expressed in terms of heart transformation (Rom. 2:29; 5:5; 6:17; 10:9–10; 2 Cor. 1:22; Gal. 4:6; Eph. 3:17; 1 Thess. 3:13), a central dynamic of the new covenant (Jer. 31:31–34; Heb. 8:7–13), as Paul notes in 3:4–6.

What has been shone in our hearts through the gospel is "the light," expressed with πρὸς φωτισμὸν (pros phōtismon) in the Greek text; πρός plus the accusative serves as a marker of movement or orientation toward someone or something (BDAG 874) and here communicates a point of reference: "with reference to the light of." In other words, the apostle, having used the analogy of creation's light, now narrows the focus to a very particular reference, a particular form of "light," the knowledge of the gospel. This light, moreover, is "the personal comprehension of God's glory." Here we read the genitive τῆς γνώσεως (tēs gnōseōs, the knowledge) as epexegetical, meaning "the light,

27. "Blindness" has already been raised by Paul in 2 Cor. 4:4. In the LXX, Isaiah is replete with references to the malady of spiritual blindness: 29:18; 35:5; 42:7, 16, 18–19; 43:8; 56:10; 59:10; 61:1.
28. Savage (1996: 113) puts the number at seventy-one times.
29. Matera (2003: 101), citing J. Louis Martyn (1997: 92), notes the inextricable link in Paul's thought between epistemology and eschatology, "so that those who stand at the turn of the ages are granted a new means of perception."

which is the personal comprehension"; and the sense of "knowledge" has relational overtones, rather than mere cognitive assent to God's existence.

What is known, or personally grasped, is "God's glory" (τῆς δόξης τοῦ θεοῦ, *tēs doxēs tou theou*), which is closely associated with personal relationship with God—the experience of his presence. Finally, this "light, which is the personal comprehension of God's glory," is found "in the face of Christ" (ἐν προσώπῳ Χριστοῦ, *en prosōpō Christou*),[30] whom Paul has proclaimed as "the image of God" (4:4). According to Isaiah's prophecy, God had turned his face away from Israel (8:17; 54:8; 59:2). But in Christ, God has turned his face to his people. This confession lies at the heart of the gospel. Human beings were created in the image of God (Gen. 1:26), but in the fall the glory attending that image has been lost (Rom. 3:23). Yet, through Christ's obedience to the Father, the curse has been reversed (Rom. 5:12–21), and the glory has been restored through Christ, our "new Adam" (1 Cor. 15:49; Bruce 1971: 196).[31] Moreover, God predestined believers to be conformed to the image of the Son (Rom. 8:29; Matera 2003: 102). This is "the same image" into which new covenanters are being transformed, "from glory to glory" (2 Cor. 3:18). This in large part stands as a major foundation stone in Paul's commendation of his apostolic ministry, for the gospel preached by Paul and his coworkers brings about real change (3:18). His gospel manifests the glory of God by focusing on the glory seen in the face of Christ, who then glorifies his new-covenant people.

Reflection

In 2 Cor. 4:1–6 Paul grounds his perseverance in authentic Christian ministry in the mercy of God (4:1), a mercy manifested in the transformational, new-covenant glory of God (3:7–18), seen ultimately in the face of Jesus (4:6). Since he has experienced this transformation himself and lives out his ministry before God, the apostle proclaims this glorious gospel with integrity, making a clear distinction between his mission and the so-called "ministry" of the false teachers at Corinth (4:2). Not everyone embraces Paul's gospel, since "the god of this world" has "blinded the minds of the unbelieving," "those who are being destroyed" (4:3–4). But their response to Paul is not the main issue. He and his ministry team do not preach themselves. The response of people to Jesus is the main issue, for Paul preaches "Jesus Christ as Lord." To experience the "light" of the gospel, people must personally comprehend "God's glory in the face of Jesus Christ" (4:5–6).

The apostle's words in 4:1–6 offer at least five key principles for conducting ministry. First, those of us who wish to proclaim the gospel authentically should remember that *authentic ministry rests on the mercy of God*.

30. On the omission of Ἰησοῦ (*Iēsou*, Jesus) here, see the additional note on 4:6.

31. Thrall (1994: 310) notes the rabbinic idea that Adam's face was so brilliant that it outshone the sun and comments that if this is in Paul's mind at 4:4, "Paul is saying that it is in Christ as the second Adam that this original glory has been restored. Christ as the εἰκὼν τοῦ θεοῦ [*eikōn tou theou*, image of God] is Christ as true man."

Ambrosiaster (*Comm. Paul's Ep.*, 2 Cor. 4:1) says, "Paul attributes his perseverance not to human merit but to the mercy of God, which first cleanses a person, then makes him righteous, adopts him as a son of God and endows him with a glory like the glory of God's own Son" (Bray 1999: 227). Thus our preaching of the gospel will only be authentic inasmuch as we *have embraced the gospel* and *continue to experience gospel mercy* in our own lives.

Second, *authentic proclamation of the gospel must be practiced with integrity*. In Ps. 78:72, the psalmist celebrates David as a leader who shepherded the people of Israel with both a "heart of integrity" (כְּתֹם לְבָבוֹ, *kětōm lĕbābô*) and "skillful hands" (וּבִתְבוּנוֹת כַּפָּיו, *ûbitbûnôt kappāyw*). The use of skills in preaching, without integrity, leads to an inevitable twisting of God's Word and shame, for the minister must preach and live "before God" and in a way that the truth proclaimed "commends" the minister to every person's conscience.

Third, we do well to remember that *authentic proclamation of the gospel will be rejected by those who have blinded minds*. This explains one reason why our preaching seems less than "successful" at points, but it can be profoundly discouraging, as Spurgeon (1954: 156–57) explains:

> Passionate longings after men's conversion, if not fully satisfied (and when are they?), consume the soul with anxiety and disappointment. To see the hopeful turn aside, waxing more bold in sin—are not these sights enough to crush us to the earth? The kingdom comes not as we would, the reverend name is not hallowed as we desire, and for this we must weep. How can we be otherwise than sorrowful, while men believe not our report, and the divine arm is not revealed?

Yet our sorrow must be mixed with cosmic realism, recognizing that preaching the gospel, by its very nature, involves spiritual forces beyond us. God alone can shine light into the human heart, giving sight to those blinded by the god of this world. We therefore must preach in full dependence on the Lord, in the power of the Spirit.

Which brings us to a fourth point: *we minister as servants*, first of the Lord Jesus, but also of those to whom we minister. On this point John Chrysostom (*Hom. 2 Cor.* 8.3) reflects, "I am a servant. I am but a minister of those who receive the gospel, transacting everything for Another, and for his glory doing what I do" (Bray 1999: 230). Our preaching of the gospel *can* be carried out for self-advancement, but we must not preach in this way or for this reason. We must preach as an act of service.

Finally, *we must preach Jesus Christ, as both Lord and the manifestation of the glory of God*. Only here do we find the true gospel, the good news of God's design for the ages, the climax and ultimate culmination of his grand Story that he has written on the world. In all its dimensions, God's glory must be personally comprehended in the face of Jesus Christ or not seen at all.

Additional Notes

4:1. The stronger reading here is ἐγκακοῦμεν ($\mathfrak{P}^{46}$ ℵ A B D* F G 33 81 326 1175 2464 *pc* co), ἐκκακοῦμεν having later and more narrow support (C D² Ψ 0243 1739 1881 𝔐). According to BDAG 272, the two words have much semantic overlap ("to lose heart"), but Thrall (1994: 299) points out that LSJ suggests the former means to "behave remissly in a thing."

4:2. At 12:16 the use of the adjective cognate to πανουργία seems to indicate that Paul's opponents had accused him of being "tricky" or "crafty." Barrett (1973: 128) notes that the word is used by Galen and others with the sense of adulterating medicines. Philo uses the word twenty-four times, mostly in vice lists or in comparison of virtues over against patterns of wickedness. For instance, he reports that the philosophers use it in criticism of the Sophists, saying that they have called their trickery "wisdom": "not that philosophy which the existing sophistical crowd of men pursues (for they, studying the art of words in opposition to truth, have called crafty wickedness, wisdom, assigning a divine name to wicked action)" (*Post.* 101; see also *Worse* 71).

4:2. The reading συνιστάνοντες has support from $\mathfrak{P}^{46}$ B P 0243 630 1175 1505 1739 1881 *pc*; while the variant συνιστάντες is found in ℵ C D* F G 33 81 326 *pc*. These verbs συνιστάνω and συνίστημι are synonyms. Both Harris (2005: 321) and Thrall (1994: 300) note that the latter variant probably resulted from parablepsis, in which a copyist's eye jumps over the second ν.

4:5. Although many translations render δοῦλος as "servants" (e.g., NLT, NLT², ESV, NIV, TNIV, Tyndale), the Greek term refers to a person who is enslaved. Modern use of "servant" for "slave" has more to do with slavery in American history and patterns in Bible translation than an accurate assessment of the term's use in the first century AD. Further, the term δοῦλος, in an Oriental context (as opposed to Hellenistic), could connote "humble service" (BDAG 260).

4:5. Both Alexandrian and Western texts (A*vid B Dᵍʳ Gᵍʳ) support the reading Ἰησοῦν. The variant Ἰησοῦ does have early support but is slightly weaker ($\mathfrak{P}^{46}$ ℵ* Aᶜ C 33 1739 itᵈ, ᵍ, ʳ vg copˢᵃ, ᵇᵒ Marcion), and the acc. form is also found at 4:11. The other readings, various forms of Χριστός, clearly are secondary (Harris 2005: 322; Metzger 1994: 509–10).

4:6. Since it is highly unlikely that a scribe would drop the Ἰησοῦ in either of the longer variants—Ἰησοῦ Χριστοῦ ($\mathfrak{P}^{46}$ ℵ C H Ψ 0209 1739c 𝔐 t vgᵐˢˢ sy), and Χριστοῦ Ἰησοῦ (D F G 0243 630 1739* 1881 *pc* lat; Ambst)—the shorter Χριστοῦ (A B 33; Tert) is preferred. The shorter reading has significant support, although the support for Ἰησοῦ Χριστοῦ is more extensive. As Metzger (1994: 510) points out (though this was a minority opinion on the committee), the shorter reading best explains the existence of the two longer alternatives.

2. The Suffering Involved in Paul's Authentic Ministry (4:7–5:10)

In the previous section (2:14–4:6), Paul offers a detailed explanation of what constitutes an authentic ministry and how one should persevere in it. Who is qualified? Not the hucksters, who peddle God's Word for profit. Rather, Paul and associates, who have been sent by God and who speak with integrity and reverence "before God," are presented as authentic ministers (2:17; 4:1–2). They are competent ministers of the new covenant, who have ministered to the Corinthians by the power of the Spirit and thus need no letters of recommendation (3:1–6). Further, in 3:7–18 the apostle presents a powerful overview of new-covenant ministry, focusing on the glory that manifests God's presence, showing through an a fortiori argument that the glory of the new-covenant ministry shines greater than that of the old, both in terms of the degree and the extent of that glory (3:7–11). Also, Paul emphasizes *the limitation*, the nature of the old-covenant ministry as having to do with barriers, over against the "openness" and "freedom" that new-covenant believers experience (3:12–18). Finally, in 4:1–6 the apostle returns to the theme of integrity, proclaiming that a sound, new-covenant ministry does not distort God's Word but rather offers the truth straightforwardly in such a way that the minister commends himself to people's consciences in God's sight as he preaches Christ as Lord.

Now the apostle turns to the paradoxical fact that the glory of the new covenant gospel moves out into the world via "jars of clay," who are fragile and often suffer as they carry out their ministries. In the first movement of this new section (4:7–15), Paul speaks of the difficulties faced in ministry but insists that the suffering experienced by authentic ministers has a purpose: the advancement of the gospel in the world.

From a human perspective, it might seem that the intensity of suffering faced by Paul and his coworkers would be devastating. Yet, as Paul explains in the second movement of the section, rather than being destroyed by the traumas faced in ministry, true Christian ministers experience renewal (4:16), and the suffering faced in ministry has a personal outcome: the building up of an eternal "tonnage of glory" that makes suffering pale by comparison. Finally, the "eternal" glory brings to mind the eternal realm, on which true ministers focus their attention (4:18).

In the third movement of the section (5:1–10), Paul explains the hope that authentic ministers have in the face of suffering and death, and he uses word pictures such as "house," "tent," and "building" to talk about the contrast and relationship between the earthly body of suffering and the heavenly body that will be put on at the resurrection of the dead (5:1–5). Out of this discussion of death and resurrection, the apostle writes openly about his longing to be with Christ and his desire to be pleasing to him (5:6–10).

a. Treasure and Terra-Cotta (4:7–15)

There are many ironies wrapped up in true Christian ministry, not least of which is that God delivers his glorious gospel treasure in pots made of dirt, his transformative life in cracked and crumbling caskets. In speaking of his sufferings in ministry, Richard Baxter (1998: 28), the Puritan church leader and hymn writer, declared:

> These, with the rest which I mentioned before, when I spake of my infirmities, were the benefits which God afforded me by affliction. I humbly bless his gracious Providence, who gave me his Treasure in an Earthen Vessel, and trained me up in the School of Affliction, and taught me the Cross of Christ so soon; that I might be rather *Theologus Crucis*, as Luther speaketh, than *Theologus Gloriae*; and a Cross-bearer, than a Cross-maker or Imposer.

In 2 Cor. 3, the apostle commends the new-covenant ministry of the Spirit, who brings life, in contrast to the ministry of the letter, which brings death (3:6). Here in 4:7–15 he turns this formula inside out, proclaiming that the "dying" and "death" of the Christian minister lays the foundation for people to experience the life-giving ministry of the Spirit. In other words, the suffering that Paul experiences as a normal course in his ministry, rather than invalidating his work,[1] serves as another mark of authenticity, for he follows the pattern of his crucified Lord.

The unit unfolds in four movements. First, in 4:7 Paul uses a striking word picture to explain why God uses the frailty of human vessels, "jars of clay," to advance the gospel. He does so to make clear the true source of gospel power: God himself. Second, in 4:8–11, the apostle provides the first of four "hardship lists" in the book (cf. 6:4b–10; 11:23b–33; 12:10) to communicate both the normalcy of suffering in the course of Christian ministry and the endurance experienced as one relies on God. Verses 10–12 embody the third movement of the unit and play off a pattern witnessed in the gospel story: Jesus's death on the cross was prerequisite for resurrection life. This pattern holds true for ministry as well. A minister of Jesus must be bodily "carrying around the death of Jesus" (4:10) and "handed over to death because of Jesus" (4:11) so that Jesus's life might be experienced by people. Tersely put, ministers die so that people can live (4:12). But this does not bring about despair. Rather—and this constitutes the fourth movement

---

1. As noted in the introduction, the false teachers at Corinth may have pointed to Paul's sufferings as a sign that his ministry is not valid, that it is not blessed by God. Paul turns this accusation inside out, proclaiming that suffering serves as a validating characteristic of authentic ministry.

of the unit (4:13–15)—this pattern of a faith-full (4:13), "dying" ministry leads to two happy results: (a) the resurrection of the minister along with those who have believed in Jesus (4:14), and (b) thanksgiving will "overflow to God's glory" (4:15). So we can outline the unit in this way:

i. Introduction: We are purposeful pots (4:7)
ii. Hardships and God's help (4:8–9)
iii. Death leads to life (4:10–12)
iv. Faith, communication, and the spread of the gospel (4:13–15)

Exegesis and Exposition

[7]But we have this treasure in jars of clay, in order that this extraordinary power might be seen for what it is, power that comes from God and not from us. [8]In every way we are being afflicted but not restricted, baffled but not to the point of despair, [9]abused but not abandoned, knocked down but not terminated; [10]we are always carrying around the dying of Jesus in our ⌜body⌝, in order that also the life of Jesus might be made known through the medium of our body. [11]For we who are alive are constantly being handed over to death because of Jesus, in order that also the life of Jesus might be made known by means of our mortal flesh. [12]Therefore death is at work in us, but life in you. [13]But since we have the same spirit of trust in accordance with what has been written, "I trusted, therefore I spoke," we also trust, therefore we also speak, [14]knowing that the one who raised ⌜Jesus⌝ also will raise us with Jesus and present us with you. [15]For all things are for your sake, in order that when the grace has spread dynamically through many people, it might cause thanksgiving to overflow to God's glory.

i. Introduction: We Are Purposeful Pots (4:7)

4:7   Paul ushers in 4:7–15 with a striking word picture: "but[2] we have this treasure in jars of clay" (ἔχομεν δὲ τὸν θησαυρὸν τοῦτον ἐν ὀστρακίνοις σκεύεσιν, *echomen de ton thēsauron touton en ostrakinois skeuesin*). The apostle speaks of "the personal comprehension of God's glory,"[3] mentioned in verse 6, as a

2. Based on the context, the conjunction δέ (*de*), carries at least a note of contrast ("but" in the ET), for the focus now shifts from the glory of the new covenant to the minister's human frailty in the face of suffering and death.

3. Here τὸν θησαυρόν functions as the direct object in the sentence. Commentators have made various suggestions as to the exact referent for "this treasure" (τὸν θησαυρὸν τοῦτον, *ton thēsauron touton*), some proposing that Paul has in mind the ministry as a whole (3:7–9; 4:1); others, the knowledge of God's glory mentioned in the previous verse (v. 6); still others, the gospel itself (4:3–4). A similarly worded clause occurs at 4:1, where the apostle writes, "Since we have this ministry" (ἔχοντες τὴν διακονίαν ταύτην, *echontes tēn diakonian tautēn*), and the two clauses may serve as parallel introductions to the two successive units (Savage 1996: 164). However, this literary parallel need not suggest an exact conceptual parallel between the two verses. If immediate context is given weight (but see the suggested referent for the parallel clause at 4:1), the apostle most immediately has in mind "the light, which is the personal comprehension of God's glory in the face of Christ" mentioned in verse 6. Understood thus, the

"treasure" (τὸν θησαυρόν).[4] Although the Greek word translated "treasure" can refer to a repository where something is kept (e.g., a box, a chest, or a storeroom), here the term refers to the thing of great value put in such a place or container for safekeeping. In other words, to grasp the gospel and personally come to know the God of glory—to have one's blinded mind cleared to understand and one's veiled heart uncovered—is of inestimable value.

Yet, rather than a gilded box, God entrusts[5] this treasure to fragile "containers,"[6] "jars of clay" (ἐν[7] ὀστρακίνοις σκεύεσιν). Paul anticipates a time when he will have a body made for another world (1 Cor. 15:35–58; 2 Cor. 5:1–4), but that time is not yet. The "earthly house" of which he speaks in the next chapter consists of crumbling clay, of groaning, disintegrating mortality, in which the Christian minister must live by faith rather than sight (2 Cor. 5:4–7; Garland 1999: 220).[8] Paul's word picture capitalizes on a common aspect of everyday life. Clay jars were unexceptional, affordable, disposable, and put to a wide variety of uses in the ancient world.[9] As mass-produced, throwaway containers for the general population, they were both fragile and expendable. Paul's emphasis, however, seems to rest on the idea of fragility (contra Barrett 1973: 137–38) and perhaps the unassuming "ordinariness" of clay containers, rather than suggesting that the human minister is of little value or disposable (Fitzgerald 1988: 167–68).[10] After all, the verses that follow

---

glory experienced through the gospel is shown to "shine out from cracked pots" as Jesus's life is made visible (4:11). Yet for Paul, his ministry, the gospel he preaches, and the glory attending the knowledge of that gospel—all these are so intertwined as to be inseparable.

4. NT authors use θησαυρός (thēsauros, treasure) seventeen times, with fourteen of these occurring in the Gospels (Matt. 2:11; 6:19–21; 12:35 [2x]; 13:44, 52; 19:21; Mark 10:21; Luke 6:45; 12:33–34; 18:22), twice in Paul (the other is at Col. 2:3), and once in Heb. 11:26. Jesus uses the word to speak of material things (e.g., Matt. 6:19; 13:44) and metaphorically to speak of spiritual valuables (Matt. 6:20; 19:21; Mark 10:21; Luke 12:33).

5. Harris (2005: 339) notes that the present-tense verb ἔχομεν (echomen, we have), rather than denoting personal ownership, communicates the idea of guardianship or being a trustee.

6. Like the word for "treasure," a σκεῦος (skeuos) could be a material object, sometimes a jar, dish, vessel, or container. Yet, as here, it could speak figuratively of a human being used as an "instrument" or "vessel" for some purpose (BDAG 927).

7. The preposition is used spatially here ("in").

8. The background of Paul's thought lies neither in gnostic thought, nor in Cynic-Stoic philosophy, but rather in Paul's profound orientation to the OT literature (Furnish 1984: 278; Garland 1999: 220), in which man is understood as made from the earth (Gen. 2:7) and has been shaped by God, the master potter (Job 10:9; Isa. 29:16; 41:25; 45:9; 64:8; Jer. 18:1–10; Rom. 9:21–23). Thus Paul is not interested here in contrasting the mortal body with the immortal soul (Bieringer and Lambrecht 1994: 314).

9. The suggestion that the clay lamps produced in Corinth lie behind Paul's imagery (e.g., Bruce 1971: 197) is probably off the mark, since such lamps, though shining light, did not contain treasure.

10. Some point to Leviticus, where the writer speaks of an "earthen pot" as being used by the priest to offer sacrifice; such containers are expendable and should be broken when they become ritually unclean (Lev. 6:28; 11:33; 14:50; 15:12; Furnish 1984: 253). The imagery of humans as clay pots occurs elsewhere in the biblical literature. Especially relevant are passages that speak of humans as made from the earth (Gen. 2:7), which return to earth (Gen. 3:19; Eccles. 3:20), and which during their lives are shaped by God, the master potter (Job 10:9; Isa. 29:16; 41:25;

focus on death, mortality, and vulnerability (vv. 8–11), physical bodies that are wearing away (v. 16). Speaking of this passage, John Chrysostom (*Hom. 2 Cor.* 8.3) writes, "He used the term *earthen* in allusion to the frailty of our mortal nature and to declare the weakness of our flesh. For it is no better than earthenware, which is soon damaged and destroyed by death, disease and even variations of temperature. The power of God is most conspicuous when it performs mighty works by using vile and lowly things" (Bray 1999: 232). As clay pots, the apostle and his coworkers crack and crumble; they are made from the earth and return to the earth (Gen. 3:19).

Yet this juxtaposition of treasure and terra in the minister has a profound purpose (ἵνα): "in order that this extraordinary power might be seen for what it is, power that comes from God and not from us" (ἵνα ἡ ὑπερβολὴ τῆς δυνάμεως ᾖ τοῦ θεοῦ καὶ μὴ ἐξ ἡμῶν, *hina hē hyperbolē tēs dynameōs ē tou theou kai mē ex hēmōn*). The problem with gilded boxes is that their shine can distract from the glory of the treasure they contain.

The beauty of containers made of earth is that their very weakness and baseness focus attention on God's extraordinary "power" (τῆς δυνάμεως). Paul has already described at length the life-giving, freedom-bringing Spirit's power to effect transformation under the new covenant (3:6, 17–18). God in Christ rips away the veil of blindness that lies over the human heart (3:14), allowing God's gospel "light," "the personal comprehension of God's glory," to shine in (4:6). Paul describes this power of God as "extraordinary"[11] (ὑπερβολή) in quality: the term connotes a "state of exceeding to an extraordinary degree" (BDAG 1032). He already has described the "glory" of the new-covenant ministry as "much more" (3:7–11) and as "overflowing" (3:9). Now he reflects on the extraordinary nature of the power that can lift the veil from the human heart (3:15), giving spiritually blinded minds sight (4:4, 6) and transforming believers "from glory to glory" (3:18).

The fragility of the human minister thus serves to keep the focus on the God of the gospel, not his messenger. We read the verb of being, ᾖ (*ē*) as connoting recognition (i.e., "might be seen for what it is"). Savage (1996: 166–67) suggests that the significance of the verb of being, rather, is that it communicates a reality, rather than a perception, that in a minister of weakness the power can only "be" of God (2 Cor. 12:1–10). Yet I maintain that the source of the gospel's power is "from God" (τοῦ θεοῦ)[12] apart from any human agent (μὴ ἐξ ἡμῶν). Paul's point has to do with *recognition* of that fact. So Paul's

---

45:9; 64:8; Jer. 18:1–10; Rom. 9:21–23). On various uses of the image in ancient literature, see Thrall 1994: 322.

11. In this case τῆς δυνάμεως is an attributed genitive, since ἡ ὑπερβολή functions as an attributive adjective. It is an "extraordinary" power.

12. Perhaps the genitive τοῦ θεοῦ (*tou theou*, of God) is meant to communicate possession (Harris 2005: 341). While it is true that God is the only one who has the power of which Paul speaks, the contrastive parallelism with μὴ ἐξ ἡμῶν (*mē ex hēmōn*, not from us), which clearly communicates the idea of source, should be given greater weight.

ministry is profoundly God-centered, not self-aggrandizing, like the message of his opponents.

ii. Hardships and God's Help (4:8–9)

Paul heads the hardship list[13] of 4:8–11 with a pair of clauses that read, "In every way we are being afflicted but not restricted" (ἐν παντὶ θλιβόμενοι ἀλλ' οὐ στενοχωρούμενοι, *en panti thlibomenoi all' ou stenochōroumenoi*). The phrase translated "in every way" (ἐν παντί) probably stands at the front of the list for emphasis and to keep from interrupting the rhythmic flow of the list itself. The list is made up of four terms describing the afflictions encountered in Paul's ministry, each of which is answered by a qualification that puts Paul's suffering in perspective:

4:8

being afflicted	but not restricted
baffled	but not to the point of despair
persecuted	but not abandoned
knocked down	but not terminated

All of the participles describing the challenges of those involved in Paul's ministry are present tense in form, indicating that Paul has in mind common, ongoing experiences, and thus are "customary" uses of the present tense (see D. Wallace 1996: 521).[14] The difficulties surrounding his ministry go with the territory; they constitute a normal dynamic in authentic ministry. From Paul's perspective, such afflictions have characterized his ministry in the past and certainly will continue.

The apostle begins his list: "We[15] are being afflicted" (θλιβόμενοι). The verb θλίβω (*thlibō*) and its cognate noun make up Paul's favorite word group for

13. The list of the troubles faced by the apostle and his associates found in 4:8–9 is the first of four such lists in 2 Corinthians. Thrall (1994: 326) suggests that Paul's language is biblical but that the structure of his presentation of these hardships is drawn from the rhetoric of his own day. Such hardship lists were common in the ancient world among philosophers, but the Cynics and Stoics of the day had perspectives quite different from those of Paul. Epictetus (*Disc.* 1.24.1), e.g., emphasizes that hardships demonstrate the moral fortitude of a person, and Seneca (*Ep.* 71.26) boasts of the sage's indestructibility. Paul, on the other hand, emphasizes human weakness as revealing God's power and never boasts of his own character as the source of ministry success. In fact, the assaults of life serve to move the minister to greater dependence on God (2 Cor. 1:9). The philosophers of the age boast of emotional equilibrium amid hardships and downplay their sufferings as trivial, but Paul's God-centered perspective faces his afflictions squarely and demonstrates an emotional transparency. The depths of his difficulties demonstrate the extent of God's power (Barnett 1997: 228–29; Garland 1999: 225–26).

14. Grammatically, we could read these participles, as well as the present participle περιφέροντες (*peripherontes*, carrying around) in 4:10, as delimiting ἔχομεν (*echomen*, we have) in 4:7. Yet in 2 Corinthians Paul commonly uses participles that are syntactically absolute, standing in for the indicative (e.g., 5:12; 7:5; 8:19–20, 24; 9:11, 13), and this seems to be the case here (see Harris 2005: 342, who follows P. Hughes 1962: 141).

15. The first-person plural verb (ἔχομεν) and the first-person plural pronoun (ἡμῶν) in the previous verse establish the subject for the participles in 4:8–9; Paul refers to himself and his ministry team.

describing the trials and persecutions he has experienced in ministry and find expression in 2 Corinthians a dozen times.[16] In the ancient world, authors could use the word to refer to various kinds of pressure or constriction, including being pressed in a crowded social situation (e.g., Mark 3:9), or, as here, being afflicted or oppressed (e.g., Lev. 19:33; Deut. 28:53; 1 Thess. 3:4; 2 Thess. 1:6–7; BDAG 457). It is likely that the apostle uses this term first in the list as an all-inclusive descriptor of the very great troubles surrounding his mission. These troubles have been experienced "in every way,"[17] which speaks to the extent and the variety of difficulties Paul has encountered, fulfilling the exalted Jesus's words concerning "how much" Paul would suffer for the Name (Acts 9:16).

Paul qualifies the observation "we are being afflicted" with "but not restricted" (ἀλλ' οὐ στενοχωρούμενοι, *all' ou stenochōroumenoi*). Overlapping semantically with θλίβω, the verb στενοχωρέω (*stenochōreō*) means "to confine or restrict to a narrow space, crowd, cramp, confine," or figuratively, "to be distressed" (i.e., to be emotionally cramped; BDAG 942). The only other place it occurs in the NT is at 6:12, where Paul writes, "You are not held back by us, but you are held back by your affections." In the LXX the word occurs four times (Josh. 17:15; 4 Macc. 11:11; Isa. 28:20; 49:19), for the most part speaking of spaces or places that are too small. In modern English translations, the most popular rendering of the term is "crushed" (e.g., HCSB, NET, NLT[2], ESV, NIV), but this does not seem to be Paul's intent, given the normal use of the word in the ancient world and use of the word at 6:12. Here it probably connotes the idea of being confined or limited in one's activities, thus in our translation "restricted." Calvin (1964: 59) understood the apostle's assertion here to mean that the Lord always provided him with a means of escape. The apostle states that his ministry involves a great deal of pressure, but this has not led to a cessation or limitation of his ministry.

The second pair of descriptors states that Paul and coworkers are "baffled but not to the point of despair" (ἀπορούμενοι ἀλλ' οὐκ ἐξαπορούμενοι, *aporoumenoi all' ouk exaporoumenoi*). The first of these terms, ἀπορέω (*aporeō*), occurs six times in the NT (Mark 6:20; Luke 24:4; John 13:22; Acts 25:20; 2 Cor. 4:8; Gal. 4:20) and has to do with being confused or uncertain, to be at a loss concerning why something is taking place or how to respond (BDAG 119). For example, the term describes the perplexity of the women confronted with the resurrection as they went to the tomb and did not find Jesus's body (Luke 24:4); it also is used of Festus being at a loss to understand the dispute between Paul and the Jewish leaders from Jerusalem (Acts 25:20). Further, Paul is clearly exasperated when he uses the term at Gal. 4:20 to confess he is "baffled" about the Galatians. Thus the term has to do with a state of mental confusion or uncertainty about something. Accordingly, Paul comments to

---

16. The verb θλίβω is used three times in 2 Corinthians (1:6; 4:8; 7:5), the cognate noun another nine times (1:4 [2x], 8; 2:4; 4:17; 6:4; 7:4; 8:2, 13). For more on the use of the term by Paul, see the comments on 1:4, 6.

17. The apostle repeats the exact clause, ἐν παντὶ θλιβόμενοι, at 7:5, which might be another use of "parallel introductions."

the Corinthians that he has faced times of uncertainty or perplexity, times in which he has been "baffled."

Yet such momentary confusion has not led to a state of utter perplexity or "to the point of despair" (ἐξαπορούμενοι), the verb connoting a more intense form of psychological perplexity or doubt.[18] Polybius, for instance, uses the term to describe being lost to the point of hopelessness (*Hist.* 3.47.9) or being in a state of despair (3.48.4). The apostle must mean that he has not been drawn into an *ongoing* state of despair, or that he was not touched by such a state at present, for, using the same word, he has already noted at 1:8 that the extraordinary persecution he faced in Asia had brought him and his ministry team to a point where "we experienced deep despair, to the point that we thought we were going to die." The key is that God delivered him in that situation, and consequently delivered him from the momentary despair. It may be that the "move from 1:8 to 4:8 shows that Paul learned his lesson in Asia" (Hafemann 2000: 183), that momentary perplexity should never give way to despair.

Third, Paul states that he and his ministry team were "persecuted but not abandoned" (διωκόμενοι ἀλλ᾽ οὐκ ἐγκαταλειπόμενοι, *diōkomenoi all' ouk enkataleipomenoi*). The former term can mean "to pursue," "to move rapidly toward an objective," "to drive away," or "to persecute" someone. The apostle uses the word with the sense of "to move toward," for instance, at Phil. 3:14,[19] and in passages like Rom. 12:13b, Paul employs the term with the sense "pursue," as he instructs the Romans to "pursue hospitality." Yet in roughly half of the times Paul takes up this word, it carries the meaning "to persecute," as it does here. To mention just a few of the forms in which Paul was persecuted, at 6:4–10 he lists beatings, imprisonments, riots, slander, and chastening, and at 11:23–28 he further reports that he faced death on numerous occasions, received 39 lashes five times, was beaten with a rod three times, and was stoned (e.g., Acts 14:19). The extent to which Paul faced persecution is daunting.

Yet, as he reflects in 2 Cor. 4:9, God has not abandoned him. The verb, in participial form here and rendered "abandoned" (ἐγκαταλείπω, *enkataleipō*), occurs ten times in the NT, half of these occurring in quotations from the LXX that speak of God's comfort/support (or lack of it) in the face of trials.[20] It speaks of forsaking, abandoning, or deserting someone. For instance, the term finds expression at Heb. 13:5, where the author speaks of God's faithfulness in the face of money matters: "Your conduct must be free from the love of money and you must be content with what you have, for he has said, "I will never leave you and I will never abandon [ἐγκαταλίπω] you" (NET). However,

4:9

---

18. Notice that the second descriptor (ἐξαπορέω, *exaporeō*) is an intensification of the first (ἀπορέω).

19. He writes, "With this goal in mind, I strive toward [διώκω, *diōkō*] the prize of the upward call of God in Christ Jesus" (NET).

20. The term ἐγκαταλείπω is common, used 174 times in the LXX; see, e.g., Gen. 28:15; Deut. 31:6, 8; 1 Chron. 28:20; Pss. 26:9; 36:25, 28, 33; 37:22; 70:9, 18; 118:8; 139:9 (ET: 27:9; 37:25, 28, 33; 38:21; 71:9, 18; 119:8; cf. 140:8); see Scott 1998: 104.

as here, most uses of the word come in contexts that speak of abandonment or God's vigilant care in the face of potential harm (Acts 2:27, 31; 2 Tim. 4:10, 16), the most striking of which is Jesus's cry of dereliction from the cross, "My God, my God, why have you forsaken me?" (Matt. 27:46//Mark 15:34). Here, positively stated, Paul celebrates that in the face of persecution, God has always stood with him. He may be echoing uses of the term in the Psalms, where a psalmist praises God as a God who does not abandon the righteous (e.g., Ps. 37:25, 28, 33 [36:25, 28, 33 LXX]).

Finally, Paul proclaims that he has been "knocked down but not terminated." The graphic imagery could be from the backdrop of athletics, either wrestling ("throw down") or boxing ("knock down"), but the image could as well be taken from a military context, in which a person is thrown to the ground and then killed (Harris 2005: 344). Thus the verb καταβάλλω (*kataballō*) means to hit with enough force to be knocked or struck down (BDAG 514).[21] Paul's words here might be literal, since he would have been knocked to the ground repeatedly in the course of being persecuted (e.g., Acts 14:19–20). Yet he qualifies such brutality with "but not terminated" (ἀλλ᾽ οὐκ ἀπολλύμενοι, *all᾽ ouk apollymenoi*). The apostle has already used the word ἀπόλλυμι (*apollymi*) twice in 2 Corinthians (authors use the term ninety times in the NT), both times to speak of those lost without the gospel (2:15; 4:3). The sense here may also be eschatological, that Paul will not perish as the lost are perishing (thus Barnett 1997: 234); however, the apostle could also be referring to personal ruin or, more likely given the verses that follow, martyrdom for the faith, since the term can refer to dying (Epictetus, *Disc.* 2.19.16; Matt. 8:25; 26:52; Luke 15:17). The Lord had been faithful to save him out of the threats to his life, and Paul was confident that such deliverance would continue (1:10). Yet, as he describes in the next three verses, death was a constant companion, shadowing the steps of his mission.

iii. Death Leads to Life (4:10–12)

4:10 In verse 10 the apostle continues expounding on apostolic suffering for the sake of the gospel by highlighting the dynamics of "death" and "life" as manifested in ministry. Ministers toil on a path of death so that those to whom they minister can experience life. The contrast, indeed the paradoxical relationship, between death and life in the crucible of authentic Christian ministry (4:10–12) serves as a theological comment on the ministerial sufferings described in 4:8–9. These dynamics of life and death, furthermore, are expressed in three parallel assertions, which can be diagrammed as follows:

> always
> **we are . . . carrying around the dying of Jesus in our body,**
> in order that also the *life* of Jesus might be made known

---

21. The only other place καταβάλλω is used in the NT is at Heb. 6:1, with the alternative meaning of "laying a foundation."

                                                 through the medium
                                                 of our body.

For
         constantly
we who are alive are . . . being handed over to death
          because of Jesus,
             in order that also the *life* of Jesus might be made known
                                                      by means of
                                                      our mortal flesh.

Therefore,   death is at work   in us, but
             life   in you.

Notice the contrast between life and death in each of these main clauses. The first two of these assertions, moreover, have a pronounced parallelism:

2 Cor. 4:10	2 Cor. 4:11
always	constantly
we are	we are
carrying around the dying	being handed over to death
of Jesus	because of Jesus
in order that also the *life* of Jesus	in order that also the *life* of Jesus
might be made known	might be made known
through the medium of our body	by means of our mortal flesh

In the first statement (4:10), Paul proclaims that he and those alongside whom he ministers are "always carrying around the dying of Jesus in our body" (πάντοτε τὴν νέκρωσιν τοῦ Ἰησοῦ ἐν τῷ σώματι περιφέροντες, *pantote tēn nekrōsin tou Iēsou en tō sōmati peripherontes*). The adverb translated "always" (πάντοτε, always, at all times) refers to the state of constant threat under which the apostle ministers. Notice the parallel between this adverb and the phrase ἐν παντί (*en panti*, in every way) at the beginning of verse 8, and the adverb ἀεί (*aei*, constantly), which begins verse 11.[22] These suggest that suffering is "the essential and continuing characteristic of apostolic service" (Furnish 1984: 283). For the Christian minister, suffering constitutes a normal characteristic of authentic ministry.

Paul's word for "death" (νέκρωσις, *nekrōsis*) in this first statement is rare in the NT, occurring only here and at Rom. 4:19. It speaks of "deadness, dying, or putting to death."[23] Translators and commentators are divided as to its significance: some suggest that the emphasis is on the process of dying (e.g., NASB, Tyndale, Message, Barrett 1973: 139–40; P. Hughes 1962: 141; Thrall 1994: 331–33), and others insist that Paul must have in mind the state of death, as at Rom. 4:19 (where the deadness of Sarah's womb is the topic), but here

---

22. The first of these is modal, and the two that follow are temporal. All three stand forward in their part of the successive sentences for emphasis.
23. The cognate verb, νεκρόω, is found at Rom. 4:19; Col. 3:5; and Heb. 11:12.

specifically with the death of Jesus (τοῦ Ἰησοῦ) in view (Collange 1972: 155; *EDNT* 2:462). The former view is likely preferable: Paul speaks of the process of Jesus's suffering in his passion, and the apostle seems to be emphasizing a process, an ongoing condition of his own life, in which, following the pattern of suffering modeled by his Lord, he constantly suffers abuse and is confronted by the prospect of death.[24] He writes that he and his ministry associates are "carrying around" (περιφέροντες, *peripherontes*)[25] this process of suffering "in our[26] body" (ἐν τῷ σώματι, *en tō sōmati*) in the sense that the suffering involved in Christian ministry is embodied, experienced in physical bodies, "jars of clay." God transports the treasure of the gospel via clay jars, and the jars become battered in the process.

Paul continues by communicating the purpose of these sufferings: "in order that also the life of Jesus might be made known through the medium of our body" (ἵνα καὶ ἡ ζωὴ τοῦ Ἰησοῦ ἐν τῷ σώματι ἡμῶν φανερωθῇ, *hina kai hē zōē tou Iēsou en tō sōmati hēmōn phanerōthē*). The conjunction ἵνα marks the clause as expressing this "purpose," and καὶ (also) is additive, grammatically linking the concepts of "carrying around the dying of Jesus" and making "known" the "life of Jesus." This "life of Jesus" does not refer merely to Jesus's earthly life and ministry but rather to both the "life" experienced by the resurrected Jesus—the living Lord!—and the life offered to people by the risen Jesus, through the new-covenant ministry of the Holy Spirit (3:6).[27] Both the suffering and the manifestation of Jesus's life take place "in our body,"[28] but the former is prerequisite for the latter. Apostolic suffering is necessary for the advancement of the gospel in the world. For people to experience Jesus's life, the apostle constantly experiences "dying."

4:11 Verse 11 restates the basic assertions of verse 10: "For we who are alive are constantly being handed over to death because of Jesus, in order that also the life of Jesus might be made known by means of our mortal flesh." Paul uses the phrase "we who are alive" (ἡμεῖς οἱ ζῶντες, *hēmeis hoi zōntes*) in exactly

---

24. At 1 Cor. 15:30–31a and Rom. 8:36b we find parallels to at least an aspect of Paul's thought at this point. In the first passage he says, "Why too are we in danger every hour? Every day I am in danger of death!" (NET); in the second he quotes Ps. 44:22 (43:23 LXX), "For your sake we encounter death all day long" (NET). Here the apostle speaks broadly of the wear and tear of the adversities that accompany apostolic ministry, rather than specifically of mere mortality. Furnish (1984: 284) rightly distinguishes between Paul's thought here and Seneca's "We die every day" (*Ep.* 24.19), which refers to the gradual breaking down of the body with age.

25. Like the present participles in the previous two verses, περιφέροντες can be considered syntactically independent, standing in for an indicative verb, and the present form may be interpreted as "customary," in the context playing a part in depicting suffering as a normal circumstance of Christian ministry.

26. The personal pronoun ἡμῶν (*hēmōn*, our) does not occur until later in the verse, but it is understood here.

27. Here we read Ἰησοῦ as a subjective genitive.

28. The first use of ἐν τῷ σώματι in 4:10 is spatial, while the second can be read as instrumental, "via the medium," the point being that the life of Jesus is made known to other people by the apostle and his mission.

the same form as at 1 Thess. 4:15, 17, where he speaks of those who remain alive on earth until the coming of the Lord. The phrase also occurs in the Greek text of Ps. 115:17–18 (113:25–26 LXX), as the psalmist contrasts the dead and the living: "The dead will not praise you, O Lord, nor will all who go down to Hades. But we that are alive [ἡμεῖς οἱ ζῶντες] will bless the Lord, from now on and forevermore" (NETS).

Thus Paul seems to mean that he and his ministry team are alive, but this is juxtaposed with the constant threat of death. In other words, in Christian ministry "facing death is a part of life," or "we who have yet to die, constantly face death." When Paul speaks of "being handed over to death because of Jesus" (εἰς θάνατον παραδιδόμεθα διὰ Ἰησοῦν, *eis thanaton paradidometha dia Iēsoun*), the language brings to mind the betrayal of Jesus to crucifixion (e.g., Matt. 20:18; 1 Cor. 11:23). As Paul and associates proclaim the good news (in which the death of Christ is prominent), they suffer for it, sharing in the sufferings patterned by their Lord as their story is patterned after his. So the sufferings play a key role in both manifesting and delivering the gospel. The apostle states this purpose similarly to the ἵνα clause in verse 10: "in order that also the life of Jesus might be made known." How are people to know of the resurrection life of Jesus? Is it not by the carrying forth of the gospel into a hostile world, where the bearers of good news suffer for the telling of it? In verse 11 Paul expresses the "embodiment" of the sufferings a bit differently than in verse 10, for now the term "flesh" (σαρκί, *sarki*) replaces "body" (σώματι, *sōmati*), and he adds that the "flesh" is τῇ θνητῇ (*tē thnētē*), "mortal." These changes underscore "the transitory, creaturely, and weak nature of the body that, paradoxically, is the very place where Jesus' powerful risen life is on display" (Harris 2005: 349).

When in verse 12 Paul writes, "Therefore death is at work in us, but life in you," he means, "We are dying, but you are living" (ὥστε[29] ὁ θάνατος ἐν ἡμῖν ἐνεργεῖται, ἡ δὲ ζωὴ ἐν ὑμῖν, *hōste ho thanatos en hēmin energeitai, hē de zōē en hymin*). The apostle points out that his ministry functions as the means by which the Corinthians have experienced the gospel life of Jesus. That death "is working" (ἐνεργεῖται) in the apostolic ministers is equivalent to what Paul has already said in verses 10–11 about a "dying" ministry and simply means that their lives are patterned after that of their suffering Lord. The "life" (ἡ . . . ζωή) at work in the Corinthians speaks of spiritual life afforded the Corinthians by the proclamation of the gospel under the power of the Spirit.

4:12

Thus verses 10–12 proclaim that the apostolic ministry of Paul is the vehicle by which both the death and the life of Jesus are proclaimed to the world (and particularly to the Corinthians). The suffering of Paul and his coworkers, in which the threat of death is ever present, is in accordance with the suffering of Jesus unto death. The suffering of Jesus made the gospel possible and is at the heart of that gospel; the suffering of Paul and all authentic ministers makes

---

29. When used with an independent clause, as here, ὥστε means "therefore," "so," or "for this reason" (BDAG 1107).

it possible for the gospel to spread in the world so that people might know of both the death and the resurrection life of Christ. Paul and company thus carry around the death of Jesus in their bodies in two ways: they fill up the sufferings of Christ, and they proclaim the death as a message, mediated through frail bodies. Yet ultimately this message in broken vessels manifests resurrection life. This is another way of saying that the power of God is manifested in jars made of earth (v. 7). Yes, Paul and his coworkers are persecuted and vulnerable, but the outcome is the spreading of the gospel with its message of life.

iv. Faith, Communication, and the Spread of the Gospel (4:13–15)

4:13 The speaking involved in spreading the gospel has gotten Paul into a great deal of trouble, indeed a life of troubles (4:8–9), even a life of "dying," described reiteratively in the previous three verses (4:10–12). Why would someone embrace a life and ministry characterized by such affliction? The apostle has already stated twice in the previous verses, "in order that also the life of Jesus might be made known" (4:10–11) and, further, that the Corinthians themselves might experience life (4:12). Now he expands upon these allusions to the spread of the gospel, explaining that his continued involvement in the gospel ministry has three interrelated bases. First, he finds affirmation in the Scriptures for continuing to speak on the basis of faith (v. 13). Second, there is a life beyond the life of dying experienced in his present ministry (v. 14). Third, Paul celebrates the fact that the dynamic spread of the gospel will lead to greater glory to God (v. 15), which is worth the cost paid in authentic ministry.

1. So, Paul first points to an OT text with which he resonates: "But since we have the same spirit of trust in accordance with what has been written, 'I trusted, therefore I spoke,' we also trust, therefore we also speak" (Ἔχοντες δὲ τὸ αὐτὸ πνεῦμα τῆς πίστεως κατὰ τὸ γεγραμμένον· Ἐπίστευσα, διὸ ἐλάλησα, καὶ ἡμεῖς πιστεύομεν, διὸ καὶ λαλοῦμεν, *Echontes de to auto pneuma tēs pisteōs kata to gegrammenon; episteusa, dio elalēsa, kai hēmeis pisteuomen, dio kai laloumen*). The conjunction δέ (but) is mildly adversative,[30] and the participle Ἔχοντες ("since we have") introduces the cause, or grounds, for the affirmations later in the verse, "We also trust, therefore we also speak" (Thrall 1994: 337–38). Further, Ἔχοντες (*Echontes*) takes as its grammatical object "the same spirit of trust" (τὸ αὐτὸ πνεῦμα τῆς πίστεως) that introduces faith's role in the proclamation of the gospel. The apostle reflects that "since" he and fellow ministers "have the same spirit of trust" he sees reflected in the Scripture (Ps. 116:10 [115:1 LXX]), speaking follows naturally on the heels of belief or trust. The reference to "spirit" (πνεῦμα) probably is not a reference to the Holy Spirit (contra, e.g., Barrett 1973: 142), but rather a disposition reflected by the psalmist. Such a use of "spirit," for example, occurs at 1 Cor. 4:21 and Gal. 6:1, where Paul speaks of a "spirit of gentleness." The disposition here, however, is a spirit "of trust" (τῆς πίστεως), which means a spirit

---

30. Death is at work in Paul (4:12), but he trusts God for both resurrection and the fruitfulness of his ministry.

of "faith"[31] or "belief" in God. This life of "trust" then forms the foundation of a life of proclamation, and Paul suggests this posture accords with (κατά, in accordance with) what he sees revealed in the posture of the psalmist.

Paul quotes part of the Greek version of Ps. 116:10 (115:1 LXX), the whole of which reads, "Hallelouia. I believed; therefore I spoke, but I, I was brought very low" (NETS). The broader context of the psalm perhaps illuminates why Paul's mind was drawn here.[32] In addition to the sigh "I was brought very low" in 116:6 (114:6 LXX), the psalmist confesses that he had been "brought low," but the Lord saved him; and 116:8–9 (114:8–9 LXX) says that he had been "delivered . . . from death" and will be pleasing to the Lord "in the country of the living." Further, at 116:15 (115:6 LXX) the writer declares that the "death of his devout ones" is "precious before the LORD." Thus the context of the quotation contains rich reflection on the Lord's deliverance out of difficulties and death, the very topics Paul has been discussing since 4:7. This section of the psalms must have been comforting to Paul, and here he also finds a deep resonance with the faith and the resulting expression of faith portrayed by the psalmist: "We also trust, therefore we also speak."

2. Second, in 2 Cor. 4:14 the apostle focuses on a theology of resurrection as **4:14** providing him with confidence while he faces the threat of death. He writes, "knowing that the one who raised Jesus also will raise us with Jesus and present us with you" (εἰδότες ὅτι ὁ ἐγείρας τὸν κύριον Ἰησοῦν καὶ ἡμᾶς σὺν Ἰησοῦ ἐγερεῖ καὶ παραστήσει σὺν ὑμῖν, *eidotes hoti ho egeiras ton kyrion Iēsoun kai hēmas syn Iēsou egerei kai parastēsei syn hymin*). In other words, Paul's boldness and endurance stems from his relationship with God, whose work in this world includes the defeat of death and hope of a future that transcends the present afflictions he experiences in his ministry, even if those afflictions lead to a premature death (4:16–18).

Like ἔχοντες at the beginning of verse 13, the εἰδότες (knowing) is causal, expressing another basis for the apostle's bold speaking, and the ὅτι introduces the "content" of what Paul knows. What Paul knows is that just as God, the one who raises the dead (1:9), raised the Lord Jesus, so he will resurrect those who believe in the resurrected Lord. Jesus, and even his disciples, had raised the dead in his earthly ministry (e.g., Matt. 10:8; 11:5; Luke 7:22), reviving those who would die again. Yet with Jesus's resurrection, a new form of being raised to life was initiated, one in which the perishable becomes imperishable, the dishonor of death becomes glorious, the weak becomes powerful, the

---

31. The word πίστις (*pistis*, faith, trust) is a favorite for Paul, who uses it 142 times. Although he uses the term variously, here he speaks of trust in God. I prefer the ET "trust" over "faith" at this point since the latter has come to reflect an existential "leap" against the facts for many modern English speakers. The biblical concept of faith, rather, constitutes a "step into the light," a trust in God on the basis of what God has revealed as true about himself.

32. See the alternative suggestion by Stegman (2007), who poses that Paul practices "christological ventriloquism," reading the psalm as though uttered by Christ. Thus Paul quotes the psalm, claiming for himself a relationship with the Spirit of faithfulness and thus practices the faithfulness demonstrated by Jesus.

natural is transformed to a spiritual body, never to die again (1 Cor. 15:42–44), the mortal being swallowed up by life (2 Cor. 5:4). Thus Jesus's resurrection forms an essential aspect of the "good news" (1 Cor. 15:4), for there exists a dynamic relationship between Christ's resurrection and that of his followers.

This is what Paul means in verse 14, where he writes that God "will raise us with Jesus" (ἡμᾶς σὺν Ἰησοῦ ἐγερεῖ). Paul expresses this confession variously as Christ being the "first fruits of those who have fallen asleep," or the resurrection coming "through a man," namely, Jesus, the second Adam (1 Cor. 15:20–21, 23, 45). Our victory over death comes "through our Lord Jesus Christ" (15:57), and this gives stability to our present life (15:58). As Harris notes, therefore, "with Jesus" does not mean "at the same time with" (for the resurrection of Jesus lies in the past), nor "in the company of," nor even simply "in union with" Jesus. Rather—and here Harris points to Plummer (1915) and Bruce (1971)—the sense "may be paraphrased 'in the wake of Jesus' resurrection,' 'to share Jesus' resurrection,' or 'in virtue of his resurrection'" (Harris 2005: 353). The general resurrection from the dead, which will take place upon Jesus's return, has been initiated and foreshadowed in the resurrection of Christ.

At that time, the apostle says, God will "present us with you" (παραστήσει σὺν ὑμῖν). Throughout the letter thus far, Paul has spoken of himself and his ministry team vis-à-vis the Corinthians. He has already stated that he anticipates being proud of the Corinthians, and them being proud of those who have ministered to them, in the day of the Lord Jesus (1:12, 14), and here again he expresses his confidence that the church to whom he writes will persevere in the true faith. Thus the presentation of which he speaks in verse 14 is God's presentation of his church before himself and his Son at the end of the age.

4:15   3. With verse 15 Paul gives yet a third reason why he goes forward with his ministry in the face of daunting difficulties: his ministry to the Corinthians is productive, ultimately resulting in glory given to God: "For all things are for your sake, in order that when the grace has spread dynamically through many people, it might cause thanksgiving to overflow to God's glory" (τὰ γὰρ πάντα δι' ὑμᾶς, ἵνα ἡ χάρις πλεονάσασα διὰ τῶν πλειόνων τὴν εὐχαριστίαν περισσεύσῃ εἰς τὴν δόξαν τοῦ θεοῦ, ta gar panta di' hymas, hina hē charis pleonasasa dia tōn pleionōn tēn eucharistian perisseusē eis tēn doxan tou theou). Accordingly, as depicted in the diagram below, the apostle refers to the Corinthians as those advantaged by his ministry, the purpose of his ministry, and its goal:

2 Cor. 4:15	For all things are
Advantage	for your sake,
Purpose	in order that the grace . . . might cause thanksgiving
Goal	to the glory of God

When he writes "all things" (τὰ πάντα), he speaks of the totality of his ministry—his preaching and teaching, his interactions with the Corinthians, and the suffering he endures in the normal course of his travels throughout the Mediterranean world. Yet, as seen in the phrase "for your sake" (δι' ὑμᾶς),[33] he specifically has in mind his ministry to the Corinthians. Thus his statement somewhat reiterates verse 5, where he has already said that he and his coworkers are the Corinthians' "slaves." His motives in all that he does, in other words, are pure motives oriented to the advancement of God's kingdom in the lives of those to whom he ministers.

This gospel orientation becomes clearer as Paul marks the purpose of his ministry (ἵνα, in order that) as having to do with "grace" (χάρις) that has "spread" (πλεονάσασα). The term rendered "grace" expresses various ideas in its eighteen occurrences in 2 Corinthians.[34] Already, for instance, he has used the word in his introduction (1:2, "grace and peace"), as the basis of his ministry conduct toward the Corinthians (1:12, "by God's grace"), and with the sense of "thanks" given to God (2:14). Elsewhere in the book he speaks of "grace" as that which enabled the Macedonians to give elaborately (8:1), as the "privilege" of being involved in that ministry (8:4), and as an expression of God's favor (e.g., 9:8, 14; 12:9; 13:13). Here Paul probably has in mind God's favor as expressed in and embraced by means of the gospel, as that message spreads to more and more people (Furnish 1984: 287).

In the first century, the verb πλεονάζω (*pleonazō*), here in the form of an aorist active participle, could connote the idea of growth, increase, abundance, to have more and more of something, and even to have something in super-abundance (BDAG 824). Although it can be used transitively (and thus could be read as grammatically related to τὴν εὐχαριστίαν, thus "when the grace has spread thanksgiving"), the word normally is used intransitively in the NT,[35] and the word order supports this reading of its use here (Harris 2005: 355). Further, as our translation reflects, the participle should be read temporally and as referring to the whole impact of the spread of God's grace:[36] "when the grace has spread dynamically." The phrase διὰ τῶν πλειόνων (through many people; lit., through the many) should be understood as communicating agency (through the agency of many people) rather than as referring to spatial extension (throughout many people).[37]

Finally, the aorist active subjunctive verb, περισσεύσῃ (cause to overflow) has τὴν εὐχαριστίαν (thanksgiving) as its object: "might cause thanksgiving to overflow." When used transitively, the verb means to cause something to exist in abundance" or "abound" or "overflow," and Paul uses the word

---

33. At this point διά + the acc. communicates "advantage," something done "for the sake of" someone.

34. For χάρις, see 2 Cor. 1:2, 12, 15; 2:14; 4:15; 6:1; 8:1, 4, 6–7, 9, 16, 19; 9:8, 14–15; 12:9; 13:13.

35. Harris (2005: 355) traces the uses of πλεονάζω also at Rom. 5:20; 6:1; 2 Cor. 8:15; Phil. 4:17; 2 Thess. 1:3; 2 Pet. 1:8.

36. The verb can be read as a constative aorist, viewing the action as a whole.

37. Paul uses this term variously. At 2:6 the apostle employs the word to refer to the "majority" group among the Corinthians, and at 9:2 he makes reference to the Macedonians. Neither is the case here, which is more in line with 1:11, where Paul has in mind large numbers of fellow believers out in the world.

extensively in 2 Corinthians (1:5; 3:9; 4:15; 8:2, 7; 9:8, 12). What the apostle has in mind is that as he carries out his ministry to the Corinthians, in spite of the hardships that ministry entails, grace spreads through (and thus to) more and more people. As the grace of the gospel makes its impact, this produces overflowing thanksgiving as people respond to God's favor, and such thanksgiving gives God glory, that is, God's fame spreads. Thus the suffering that Paul and his fellow ministers experience in the course of authentic ministry not only manifests the glory of the gospel (4:4–6) but also results in greater glory being given to God.

Reflection

For Christian ministers caught in the constant turmoil of afflictions and persecution, Paul offers a welcome dose of perspective. Our existence as fragile "jars of clay" (4:7) may be difficult, but it is purposeful, for our fragility automatically points away from ourselves as "the source" to God himself (4:7). That the apostle Paul suffered so extensively, yet over and again saw God's help mitigating the disabling impact of those afflictions (4:8–9), should offer us encouragement and prompt us to reflect on God's varied deliverances in our own sufferings. If you are reading this commentary, you probably are still "in the game," continuing in ministry in spite of the difficulties you have faced, and that in itself presents a reason to praise God. Paul also reminds us that the spiritual life brought to the lost comes via "dying" ministers, who follow the example of their Lord (4:10–12). "We experience dying" in order that people can live. Woe be to the minister or ministry that is always and only about winning, progressing, moving up, getting, succeeding—in short, "living!" Finally we "die" as we speak and explain God's Word, but we speak and die in great hope, for "Christ is risen!" heralding our own resurrection and that of those to whom we minister, and the gospel advances in the world, bringing thanks and glory to God (4:13–15).

The daughter of missionaries to the Congo Republic recounted to Leith Anderson (2004) how as a little girl she had participated in a celebration of the 100th anniversary of missionaries coming to the Congo Republic. Speeches were given, music was played, and at the end of the day a very old man stood before the crowd to speak. He said that when the missionaries first came, the people thought them odd and their message suspicious. The tribal leaders, seeking to test the missionaries, slowly poisoned them to death over a period of months, even years. Children of the missionaries died one by one, but the missionaries stayed and proclaimed the gospel, even as they died. The old man commented, "It was as we watched how they died that we decided we wanted to live as Christians." Death leads to life.

As we conclude this unit, we might pray this prayer with Blaise Pascal:

I ask you neither for health nor for sickness, for life nor for death; but that you may dispose of my health and my sickness, my life and my death, for your glory. . . . You alone know what is expedient for me; you are the sovereign master; do with me according to your will. Give to me, or take away from me, only conform my will to yours. I know but one thing, Lord, that it is good to follow you, and bad to offend you. Apart from that, I know not what is good or bad in anything. I know not which is most profitable to me, health or sickness, wealth or poverty, nor anything else in the world. That discernment is beyond the power of men or angels, and is hidden among the secrets of your Providence, which I adore, but do not seek to fathom. (via Yancey 1990: 112)

Additional Notes

4:7. The imagery of "containers made of earth" to speak of the baseness, sinfulness, and mortality of humans appears in the Qumran literature (e.g., 1QS 11.22; 1QH 9 [formerly 1].21–22; 11 [3].20–21; 12 [4].29; 18 [10].5; 19[11].3; 20 [12].24–31; 5.20–21 [13.15–16]; Furnish 1984: 253).

4:10. Several witnesses read τοῖς σώμασιν (ℵ 0243 326 1739 1881 *pc* r t vg sy^p bo^pt; Or), a scribe perhaps altering the original to clarify that the "body" in mind is not the body of Jesus but the "bodies" of Paul and his ministry team.

4:14. Since there exists a diversity of important, early witnesses supporting the longer reading, which includes κύριον (e.g., ℵ C D F G Ψ 1881), the UBS Editorial Committee opted for this reading over the shorter τὸν Ἰησοῦν (𝔓^46 B [0243 33] 629 [630]), explaining the latter as an assimilation to Rom. 8:11a. Metzger (1994: 510–11), however, demurred regarding the decision, on the strength of the strong Alexandrian witnesses for τὸν Ἰησοῦν, as well as witnesses of other textual traditions, and the scribal tendency to expand divine titles for Jesus. Harris (2005: 339) adds the insight that the simple title Ἰησοῦς often occurs in the immediate context (4:10a–b, 11a–b, 14b). Thus the shorter reading is preferred.

b. Perspective in the Midst of Suffering (4:16–18)

Paul's life and ministry show that eternity already breaks in on the harsh, cruel fallenness of this present, temporary age. We see God's glory breaking in. Alfred Delp, a German Jesuit priest martyred by the Nazis for his stand against their ruthless regime, writes:

> Space is still filled with the noise of destruction and annihilation, the shouts of self-assurance and arrogance, the weeping of despair and helplessness. But round about the horizon the eternal realities stand silent in their age-old longing. There shines on them already the first mild light of the radiant fulfillment to come. From afar, sound the first notes as of pipes and voices, not yet discernible as a song or melody. It is all far off still and only just announced and foretold. But it is happening today. (via Gerson 2008: 453)

This eternal working its way into the temporal gives great hope and thus perseverance, as Paul celebrates in 2 Cor. 4:16–18. This is the second movement in the apostle's treatment of "The Suffering Involved in Paul's Authentic Ministry" (4:7–5:10), and it forms a hinge-type transition between 4:7–15, which speaks of the constant sufferings of Paul and his coworkers, and 5:1–10, which anticipates a time in the future when mortality will be "swallowed up by life" (5:4). Our passage bridges the two by speaking of *perseverance* in the present condition of "wasting away," coupled with a *perspective* that focuses on what is eternal, knowing that a "tonnage of glory" is being built up in the spiritual realm (Matera 2003: 114; Thrall 1994: 347). In this way, Paul continues to reflect on realities that put suffering in perspective. He especially stresses that suffering is productive in quite an extraordinary way. This powerful unit develops a series of contrasts, an outline of which can be depicted as follows:

  i. Outer physical deterioration and inner spiritual renewal (4:16)
 ii. Momentary, light suffering and an eternal fullness of glory (4:17)
iii. Temporary "seen" things and the eternal unseen things (4:18)

Several questions are raised by the passage. In verse 16, for instance, what exactly does Paul mean when he speaks of ὁ ἔξω ἡμῶν ἄνθρωπος (*ho exō hēmōn anthrōpos*), literally, "our outer man"? Is this the "outer self" (ESV), or synonymous with the physical body (NET), or should we interpret the phrase some other way? How then should we understand the contrasting phrase having to do with the "inner person" (HCSB) in the same verse?

Further, what did Paul have in mind when he spoke of the tremendous "tonnage of glory" (4:17) being built up by his sufferings? These and other questions are addressed below.

Exegesis and Exposition

[16]For this reason, we are not giving up. On the contrary, even though from the standpoint of our current physical existence we are wasting away, who we are on the inside is being renewed day after day. [17]For ⌜our⌝ momentary, light bundle of affliction produces for us—in a way both breathtaking and immeasurable—an eternal tonnage of glory. [18]This is why we are not paying special attention to the things that are seen, but rather the things that are unseen. For the things that are seen are here today and gone tomorrow, but the things that are unseen are eternal.

i. Outer Physical Deterioration and Inner Spiritual Renewal (4:16)

The inferential conjunction διό (*dio*, for this reason) begins the transition to Paul's new train of thought and alludes back to the spiritual posture expressed in the previous passage (4:7–15), especially the apostle's confidence that the suffering he and his coworkers have experienced has worked to the furthering of God's work in the world. Paul effects the transition further by repeating the words οὐκ ἐγκακοῦμεν (*ouk enkakoumen*, we are not giving up), a statement of persevering confidence he expresses earlier at 4:1.[1] So Paul perseveres in his ministry in part because he sees the events taking place around him—even those events that are painful and seemingly destructive—from a spiritual vantage point. Now in 4:16–18 that vantage point finds a different focus but beautifully expresses Christian hope and its sister, Christian faith.

    4:16

From the perspective of outward appearances, Paul and his mission don't seem to be faring too well. The lists of hardships given in 2 Corinthians (4:8–11; 6:4b–10; 11:23–33; 12:10) bear witness to the brutal physical and emotional pressures brought to bear against the advancement of the gospel. Yet the apostle insists that Christ-followers perceive greater realities than those that are obvious. Like Elisha, whose servant only saw the armies of Syria surrounding the city and not the greater number of horses and chariots of fire in the hills surrounding the Syrians (2 Kings 6:15–19), Paul incessantly points the Corinthians to the greater spiritual realities behind what could be understood as a discouraging situation. Is he tempted to give up in the face of the brutal nature of authentic ministry? He answers, "On the contrary, even though from the standpoint of our current physical existence we are wasting away, who we are on the inside is being renewed day after day" (ἀλλ' εἰ καὶ ὁ ἔξω ἡμῶν ἄνθρωπος διαφθείρεται, ἀλλ' ὁ ἔσω ἡμῶν ἀνακαινοῦται ἡμέρα καὶ ἡμέρᾳ, *all' ei kai ho exō hēmōn anthrōpos diaphtheiretai, all' ho esō hēmōn anakainoutai hēmera kai hēmera*).

---

1. See the comments on 4:1 about this verb, which has to do with losing heart, becoming discouraged or tired, perhaps with reference to one's duty.

The construction ἀλλ᾽ εἰ καὶ (*all᾽ ei kai*, on the contrary, even though) expresses both a strong contrast (ἀλλ᾽, on the contrary) and concession (εἰ καί, even though). As for the latter, Paul concedes that from the standpoint of current physical existence, he and his mission team are "wasting away." The part of the sentence that reads ὁ ἔξω ἡμῶν ἄνθρωπος (*ho exō hēmōn anthrōpos*) has been rendered variously as the "outer person" (HCSB), the "outer man" (NASB, Tyndale), the "outer self" (ESV), the "outer nature" (NRSV), the "physical body" or "bodies" (NET, NLT[2]), or "outwardly," in terms of perception (NIV).

What Paul speaks of here is who one is perceived to be from the standpoint of outward appearances, so it constitutes more than just the physical body (Garland 1999: 240; Thrall 1994: 349–50).[2] Certainly this aspect of the apostle's life is "wasting away" from the persecution Paul suffers. The term διαφθείρεται (*diaphtheiretai*), a present passive verb, refers to something being spoiled or destroyed through corrosion of some kind. For instance, at points in ancient literature the verb speaks of rust eating into iron, or of moths eating clothing (BDAG 239; Philo, *Abr.* 11; Luke 12:33). Thus Paul uses the term to continue his discussion of the ongoing process of death experienced as one lives for Christ (4:10–12). Paul admits that life in a fallen, death-impregnated world is no party. This may be discouraging at points, but not only is it not debilitating, the outward appearance of deterioration also masks a vibrant, spiritual, internal renewal taking place in Paul and his fellow workers. Thus Paul's brutal circumstances also are not indicative of a lack of spiritual power on his part, as some in Corinth may have been suggesting.

The strong contrast expressed ("on the contrary"), as shown by the repetition of ἀλλ᾽ in the second half of verse 14, is between giving up ("we do not give up") in the face of the brutality of physical existence and the renewal mentioned in the words that follow. In other words, spiritual renewal trumps quitting. The term ἀνακαινόω (*anakainoō*, to renew) finds expression in the NT only here and at Col. 3:16,[3] and Paul describes this renewal as both internal and ongoing. The ὁ ἔσω ἡμῶν (*ho esō hēmōn*) stands in contrast to ὁ ἔξω ἡμῶν ἄνθρωπος and speaks of the inner person, "one's unseen personality, visible only to God and (in part) to oneself"; since it is experiencing renewal, it is equivalent to "the new man/self" of Eph. 4:24 (Thrall 1994: 350). As Paul here refers to the inner being, the word ἄνθρωπος is understood, but the apostle refers to this inward, spiritual reality very much as at Rom. 7:22 and Eph. 3:16, both of which speak of τὸν ἔσω ἄνθρωπον (*ton esō anthrōpon*), "the inner person." Furthermore, this renewal is taking place "day after day"

2. We need to avoid the temptation to read into Paul's language here a Platonic division of the body and soul, which sees the former as a throwaway container for the latter.

3. "[You] have been clothed with the new man that is being renewed in knowledge according to the image of the one who created it" (Col. 3:10 NET). Although ἀνακαινόω does not occur in the LXX, translators there use the cognate verb ἀνακαινίζω five times (1 Macc. 6:9; Pss. 38:3; 102:5; 103:30 [39:2; 103:5; 104:30 ET]; Lam. 5:21), but only three of these occurrences are used positively to speak of a renewal that God brings about.

(ἡμέρᾳ καὶ ἡμέρᾳ, *hēmera kai hēmera*) and thus is ongoing. In other words, the persecution against Paul and his mission might be consistent, but the spiritual renewal taking place amid that persecution is incessant. Concerning this renewal, Ambrosiaster comments, "In times of persecution the soul advances. Every day it adds something more to its experience of faith" (Bray 1999: 236).

ii. Momentary, Light Suffering and an Eternal Fullness of Glory (4:17)

Yet, not only is there a stark contrast between inner and outer realities in the apostle's experience, but there also exists a striking contrast between the "momentary, light bundle of affliction" that Paul faces in the course of ministry and the "eternal tonnage of glory" that far outweighs it. The conjunction γάρ (*gar*) anticipates the further explanation of why Paul and his ministry team do not lose heart (4:16). First, Paul describes the affliction (τῆς θλίψεως, *tēs thlipseōs*)[4] he has experienced in the course of his ministry as both παραυτίκα (*parautika*, momentary) and ἐλαφρόν (*elaphron*, light, insignificant). The first term, a temporal adverb used here adjectivally,[5] normally connotes something happening "immediately" or "for the time being" (BDAG 772). So the apostle puts his suffering in perspective by noticing that it will not last forever but rather is a momentary reality to be endured for a relatively short period of time. It contrasts with that which is "eternal" (αἰώνιον, *aiōnion*) just a few words later.

Second, he labels the affliction as "insignificant," or "light"; here the adjective ἐλαφρόν is used as a substantive and sets up a contrast with βάρος (*baros*, weight, tonnage) later in the verse. The term finds expression elsewhere in the NT at Matt. 11:30, where Jesus declares that his yoke is easy and his load, or burden, "light." Ancient authors used the word to speak of things light in weight, but this literal meaning came to have a figurative counterpart, speaking as it does here in 2 Cor. 4:17 of something considered unimportant or insignificant (BDAG 314). Yet, although Paul uses the word figuratively, he does so by painting a word picture of something lightweight, over against something of astounding weight, thus our translation "light bundle."

Furthermore, this light bundle of affliction produces something for those carrying it. Here Paul taps a broader Jewish theological tradition concerning the benefit of trials, a tradition expressed elsewhere in the NT (e.g., James 1:2–4; Rom. 5:2–5; 1 Pet. 1:6–7).[6] The verb κατεργάζομαι (*katergazomai*), which

---

4. For more on the use of θλῖψις in 2 Corinthians (1:4, 8; 2:4; 6:4; 7:4; 8:2, 13), see the comments at 1:4. Here the genitive can be interpreted as attributed, with the head noun (ἐλαφρόν) acting as an attributive adjective. On this use of the genitive, see D. Wallace 1996: 89–90.

5. The adverb παραυτίκα should be read as having an adjectival function. A similar construction, where the article is followed by postpositive γάρ, which in turn is followed by an adverb used adjectivally, is found elsewhere in Exod. 9:14 LXX: ἐν τῷ γὰρ νῦν καιρῷ ἐγὼ ἐξαποστέλλω πάντα τὰ συναντήματά μου (*en tō gar nyn kairō egō exapostellō panta ta synantēmata mou*, For at the present time I am sending out all my encounters [NETS]).

6. For more on God's redemption of sufferings, see the comments on 1:3.

Paul uses extensively, has to do with accomplishing or producing something, or bringing something about,[7] and the pronoun ἡμῖν (*hēmin*) that follows it is used with the sense of advantage ("for us"). This production, moreover, is "in a way both breathtaking and immeasurable" (καθ᾽ ὑπερβολὴν εἰς ὑπερβολήν, *kath' hyperbolēn eis hyperbolēn*). The repeated term speaks of something extraordinary in quality and/or extent (BDAG 1032), and Paul has already used the phrase καθ᾽ ὑπερβολήν at 1:8 to describe the extreme persecution he had faced in Asia and ἡ ὑπερβολή at 4:7 to speak of God's extraordinary power. The repetition here probably underscores both the astounding character (καθ᾽, according to; thus "breathtaking") and the extent (εἰς, unto; thus "immeasurable") of the way suffering is productive.

What the afflictions accompanying his mission produce for Paul and his coworkers is "an eternal tonnage of glory" (αἰώνιον βάρος δόξης, *aiōnion baros doxēs*). The term βάρος (*baros*), which we have translated "tonnage," could be used by writers of the ancient world to mean "a burden" that is oppressive, or "a claim to importance," but here it speaks positively and almost lyrically of the "fullness" or "weight" of an accumulated "mass" of glory (BDAG 167).[8] What Paul has in mind with this word picture seems to be that the glory gained, by the comparatively insignificant amount of suffering that produces it, staggers the imagination.

We have already noted the rich, multidimensional use of "glory" (δόξα, *doxa*) in the biblical literature (see the discussion above at 3:7–8). Among other nuances, God's glory is shared with his people, and this seems to be in mind at 4:17. In Jesus's high-priestly prayer of John 17:22, Jesus says he has given his disciples the glory that the Father gave him, and Peter speaks of himself as a "sharer" of God's glory that will be revealed (1 Pet. 5:1). Elsewhere Paul himself writes that God calls us into his glory (1 Thess. 2:12), a glory that one can obtain (2 Thess. 2:14) because God's gospel wisdom was meant for our glory (1 Cor. 2:7–8), and our resurrection bodies will be raised in glory (15:42–58). As we saw at 2 Cor. 3:17–18, new-covenant believers are already being transformed into that glory (Morgan 2010: 170–71). Further, this "tonnage of glory" is "eternal" (αἰώνιον, *aiōnion*), in contrast to the "momentary" nature of the suffering.

iii. Temporary "Seen" Things and the Eternal Unseen Things (4:18)

4:18   In light, then, of the spiritual renewal that Paul and his coworkers experience while suffering for the gospel (v. 16), and the amazing productivity of that suffering as it yields an eternal, exorbitant "tonnage of glory" (v. 17)—now

---

7. In the NT, twenty of the twenty-two occurrences of κατεργάζομαι are found in Paul's writings (Rom. 1:27; 2:9; 4:15; 5:3; 7:8, 13, 15, 17–18, 20; 15:18; 1 Cor. 5:3; 2 Cor. 4:17; 5:5; 7:10–11; 9:11; 12:12; Eph. 6:13; Phil. 2:12). The other two occurrences are James 1:3 and 1 Pet. 4:3.

8. The Hebrew word כָּבוֹד (*kābôd*) can mean either "weight" or "glory," and it may be that Paul coined the phrase "the weight of glory" (so Harris 2005: 362, following Collange 1972: 177).

2. The Suffering Involved in Paul's Authentic Ministry
b. Perspective in the Midst of Suffering
2 Corinthians 4:16–18

the apostle expresses his posture toward the "seen" things of the world over against the eternal "things that are unseen." In 2 Corinthians we have already noticed Paul's gravity of posture toward God himself (e.g., 2 Cor. 1:23; 2:17), as he lives "before God." Such a posture speaks of both his reverence toward God and his sense of accountability to God as the One who called him to his ministry. Yet his reverent posture before God also indicates Paul's primary orientation to the spiritual realm as determinative for his actions. The apostle's identity, his motivation, and the ultimate results of his work all flow from this spiritually oriented view of things.

The concept of posture in 4:18 is related, pointing to realms of reality and their relative influence on Paul: "This is why we are not paying special attention to the things that are seen, but rather the things that are unseen" (μὴ σκοπούντων ἡμῶν τὰ βλεπόμενα ἀλλὰ τὰ μὴ βλεπόμενα, *mē skopountōn hēmōn ta blepomena alla ta mē blepomena*). The present participle translated "paying special attention" derives from the verb σκοπέω (*skopeō*), which can be used to mean "to look out for," "notice," or "pay careful attention to" (BDAG 931) and has to do with giving special scrutiny to or being thoughtfully aware of something. Elsewhere, for example, Paul uses the term when exhorting the church to watch out for false teachers (Rom. 16:17), to watch out for one's own temptation while restoring a fallen brother (Gal. 6:1), and to pay special attention to the interests of other people in the church (Phil. 2:4). The participle grammatically relates to κατεργάζεται (*katergazetai*), the main verb in verse 17, and has been variously interpreted as temporal (i.e., "while we are not paying special attention to"; NASB), conditional ("provided our eyes are fixed"; REB), causal ("because we are not"; NET, NRSV), attendant circumstance ("as we are not"; ESV), or result[9] ("with the result that"). The construction is an irregular genitive absolute since the pronoun ἡμῶν (*hēmōn*) has the same referent as the ἡμῖν (*hēmin*) at the end of the previous verse. This strengthens the relationship between the two verses. Nevertheless, as a genitive absolute, the construction gives a note of grammatical independence to the participle (Harris 2005: 363). In this case the logical step from verse 17 to verse 18 is plausibly one of explanation (not a category normally associated with adverbial participles), as Paul explains why he focuses attention on the unseen realm rather than on the seen realm. A number of translations render this sense with "So we do not focus on what is seen" (e.g., HCSB, NLT[2], NIV, TNIV), which is the same sense as our translation, "That is why we are not paying special attention to the things that are seen." Paul's explanation stands that since suffering in the visible, temporary world produces immeasurable glory in the eternal, unseen world, the logical place on which he and his coworkers focus their attention is on the latter rather than on the former.[10]

9. Some commentators mark the versions that read "so we do not" as "result," but as explained below, such a rendering should be read as expressing accordance, not result.

10. The closest parallel to the apostle's statement about the seen and unseen realms is Heb. 11:3, which reads, "By faith we understand that the universe was created by the word of God, so that what is seen has been made from things that are not visible" (HCSB).

Reflection

Paul's reflections in 2 Cor. 4:16–18 speak of enduring suffering in light of a greater reality. As he has made clear in 4:7–15, authentic ministry involves suffering, a type of suffering that is profoundly purposeful. The gospel and the cause of Christ in the world move forward in fragile vessels. In verses 16–18 Paul offers further perspective on suffering. It may look as if he and his fellow ministers are "wasting away" physically, but the outward appearance belies the greater reality, both the daily renewal and the "tonnage of glory" being built up. Golden-tongued John Chrysostom (*Homily on Genesis* 25.17) comments on the passage:

> Such, after all, is the way with good people: when they endure something for his sake, far from attending to the appearance of what occurs, they understand the reason behind it and thus bear everything with equanimity. Likewise Paul, the teacher of the Gentiles, identified imprisonment, arraignment, daily peril, all those many unbearable hardships as light burdens, not because they really were so by nature but because the reason behind their happening produced such an attitude in him that he would not turn back in the face of these oncoming threats. (Bray 1999: 237)

Perspective shapes response. The apostle doesn't focus on the things that can be seen from the standpoint of outward appearance. Rather, he focuses on the eternal. Paul's confident theology, his way of interpreting the world—his "worldview," we would say today—shapes his values and therefore his approach to life. The pain of temporal sufferings has little value. The "glory" of God has much. For the reader of this text (or the preacher/teacher), the text earnestly asks: What do we hold as of ultimate value? How does this shape our response to suffering?

Additional Note

4:17. The ἡμῶν following θλίψεως is omitted by the significant witnesses 𝔓⁴⁶ B, probably in an attempt to avoid repetition of the pronoun, used twice in the previous verse, an additional time in verse 17, and again in verse 18. Yet its inclusion has strong external support (א C^vid D F G Ψ 0243 33 1739 1881 𝔐 latt sy^h; Or) and should be retained. The pronoun underscores the personal nature of the afflictions faced by Paul and his coworkers.

c. Longing to Be "Fully Clothed" (5:1–10)

With 5:1–10 we come to one of the most discussed and debated passages in 2 Corinthians.[1] Here Paul continues his treatment of the sufferings surrounding authentic ministry (4:7–5:10). As we have seen, in 4:7–15 the apostle speaks of the daily grind of suffering and "death" experienced by those engaged in authentic ministry, and 4:16–18 forms a transition from that topic to a focus on eternal realities that offer perspective in the face of afflictions. Now in 5:1–10 the section on suffering arrives at a fitting crescendo: Paul explains how the unseen realm mentioned at 4:18 relates to the ultimate hope of those often caught in the tumultuous mill of ministry.[2] That hope is the resurrection from the dead, and Paul uses the word pictures of a "house," a "tent," a "building," and an "outer garment" to speak of the transition from our earthly bodies to a body "not made with hands" (5:1).[3]

The passage develops in two movements. The first (5:1–5) focuses on the resurrection body, and the second (5:6–10) deals with Paul's longing to be with the Lord and his aspiration to be pleasing to the Lord, whether in

1. For a recent history of interpretation, see Pate 1991: 1–21.

2. The explanatory role of 5:1–10, in relation to the two preceding units (4:7–15; 4:16–18), may be seen in part by the uses of conjunctions marking explanation peppered throughout: γάρ (gar, for; v. 1), καὶ γάρ (kai gar, moreover; v. 2), καὶ γάρ (v. 4), γάρ (v. 7), διὸ καί (dio kai, for this reason; v. 9), γάρ (v. 10). At 5:1, γάρ does not herald a mere addition of thought (so the NIV, Tyndale) but points to the ground or basis of Paul's words in 4:16–18. Paul stands confident in his present situations in life, partly on the basis of his convictions about the future (Barrett 1973: 150; Hafemann 2000: 207).

3. Ellis (1960) has proposed an alternative reading of the passage, one that understands Paul's words to refer to the corporate identity of believers in Christ. Ellis understands the building imagery in the passage to allude to the Jewish temple as a symbol for the church universal and bases the position, in part, on parallels between 5:1 and Mark 14:58. What Paul has in mind, in this view, is the incorporation of people into the body of Christ. Rather than the individual's experience of death, Paul refers to the process of dying (4:7–11, 16–18). The "clothing" imagery, rather than referring to the resurrection body, refers to "putting on Christ" (e.g., Rom. 13:14; Gal. 3:27; Eph. 4:22–24; Col. 3:9–10). The "nakedness" of 5:3 does not refer to being without a body but to the shameful state of being without Christ at the judgment. Although the view has merits, Hafemann correctly points out that this interpretation does not explain Paul's longing for the "dwelling" (5:2), nor does it read 5:1 adequately as an anticipated event in the future. For a development of Ellis's view, see the monograph by Marvin Pate (1991: 22), who ties the passage to Paul's Adam-Christology and understands the "nakedness" of 5:3 to refer to Adam being stripped of glory after the fall. The idea is that man's glory experienced by Adam, which was lost, has been reestablished by Christ. This view ties into the context of 2 Corinthians (e.g., 3:17–18, where the new-covenant believer is being transformed "from glory to glory") much more neatly than does Ellis's interpretation. For more on this position, see Hafemann's review of Pate's treatment (Hafemann 1994).

the earthly body or the heavenly. The passage may be broken down further as follows:

i. A confident confession (5:1)
ii. Groaning and desiring a heavenly residence (5:2–5)
iii. Being "at home" and "away" (5:6–8)
iv. Always accountable to God (5:9–10)

As often noted, an important theological question here is whether the apostle's eschatology reflected in this passage differs from that of 1 Cor. 15. Gillman (1988: 439–41) has helpfully delineated three main categories of answers to that question: (1) the apostle's theology has shifted between the writing of 1 Corinthians and the writing of 2 Corinthians; (2) in both passages Paul is speaking of the general resurrection at the end of the age; and (3) the apostle is really addressing two different topics, perhaps 1 Cor. 15 focusing on individual resurrection of the body, while 2 Cor. 5 focuses on a "collective reality" having to do with the body of Christ. The view reflected in this commentary is that Paul has not changed his theology between the writing of these two letters to the Corinthians. Rather, whereas 1 Cor. 15 focuses on the resurrection body, in our passage Paul speaks both of an "intermediate state" (being present with Christ between the time of one's death and the final resurrection at the end of the age) and of the receiving of a resurrection body at the second coming of Christ.

As NT theologian Oscar Cullmann (2000: 3–5) noted decades ago, the question of "what happens to a believer upon death" has profound significance for the average Christ-follower, for the answer to the question reflects one's understanding of the Gospel—what God is up to in the world—as well as one's understanding of the nature of Christian hope. The passage before us gives us a rich reflection on that question, certainly one of the richest reflections on the nature of Christian hope in the NT. If we engage in Christian ministry, we live in a state of "groaning" (5:2) and "longing" (5:6), and in this passage Paul gives voice to both—and the answer to both.

Exegesis and Exposition

[1]For we know that if our earthly residence, a tent, is torn down, we have a building from God, a residence not made with hands, eternal in the heavens. [2]Moreover, in this tent we groan, greatly desiring to put on our habitation from heaven, [3]⌜assuming that⌝, ⌜putting it on⌝, we will not be found inadequately dressed. [4]For indeed, while we are in this tent we groan because we are burdened; it is not that we want to be undressed, but rather to be fully clothed, in order that what is mortal might be swallowed up by life. [5]Now God is the One who has prepared us for this very event and given to us the down payment of the Spirit. [6]Therefore, always being confident and understanding that as long as we are at home in the body we are absent from the Lord— [7]for we walk by faith, not by what can be seen— [8]we are confident, I say,

and would rather be away from the body and at home with the Lord. ⁹For this reason, we aspire to be pleasing to him, whether we are at home or absent. ¹⁰For we must all appear before the judgment seat of Christ, in order that each one might be paid back in accordance with the actions done while in the body, whether good or ⌐bad⌐.

i. A Confident Confession (5:1)

The apostle begins with the confession "For we know" (Οἴδαμεν, *Oidamen*),   5:1
which points to a fundamental, theological conviction of Paul's Christian faith.[4] To "know" something, in the sense expressed here, means more than having information, or having a theoretical understanding of some concept. Rather, Paul *knows* about the resurrected body because of his encounters with the resurrected Christ (Acts 9:1–9; 2 Cor. 12:2–9). He also had heard much about Jesus's resurrection from the first eyewitnesses (1 Cor. 15:3–8), and he has a solid theology of resurrection. What he knows—ὅτι (*hoti*) introduces the *content* of this knowledge—is "that if our earthly residence, a tent, is torn down, we have a building from God."

Notice that in this verse three interrelated metaphors are used to speak of the physical existence experienced in this earthly (ἐπίγειος, *epigeios*)[5] life and the immortal body that Paul anticipates: a residence, a tent, and a building. The first two of these are grammatically related in a direct way. The word for "tent," τοῦ σκήνους (*tou skēnous*), is in the genitive case and delimits the word we translate as "residence" (οἰκία, *oikia*), or (lit.) "the residence of a tent."[6] In other words, Paul speaks of the body as "a residence," but clarifies this general metaphor with a more specific one, the body as a "tent." So the body is "a residence that is a tent,"[7] perhaps hinting at ideas of insecurity and impermanence of human physicality (Barrett 1973: 151).[8] As here, in Isa. 38:12 LXX death is described as someone "taking down a tent" (ὁ καταλύων σκηνήν, *ho katalyōn skēnēn*). Keeping with the metaphors, the verb καταλύω (*katalyō*, destroy, demolish, dismantle) could be used to speak of demolishing a building (e.g., Matt. 24:2; Mark 13:2; Luke 21:6) or dismantling a tent (BDAG 521), and Paul uses this imagery to speak of death.

Yet, "if"[9] death comes to the believer before Christ returns, "we have a building from God." As noted in our introductory remarks on this unit, numerous

---

4. Of course, the Christian concept of resurrection flows from broader Jewish theology of the day, but the resurrection of Christ gave specificity to the Christian understanding of that doctrine. On both the view of resurrection in broader Judaism and in Paul, see, e.g., Wright 2003: 129–206, 361–71.

5. The term ἐπίγειος often speaks of "what is characteristic of the earth as opposed to heavenly" (BDAG 368).

6. Similar wording occurs at 1 Chron. 9:23, where the tabernacle is in view: ἐν οἴκῳ τῆς σκηνῆς (*en oikō tēs skēnēs*, in the house of the tent [NETS]).

7. Understood as a genitive of apposition, also called an epexegetical genitive.

8. For references in ancient literature to the body as tent, see Windisch and Strecker 1970: 158–59.

9. The condition applies to whether the believer will die an earthly death or be alive at the return of Christ (so Barnett 1997: 257). As usual, ἐάν (*ean*) + the aorist subjunctive is a third-class

interpretations are on offer in explanation of this assertion (Thrall 1994: 363–68; Gillman 1988: 439–41), since the wording is ambiguous both in terms of the exact nature of the "building" and the exact time it will be received.[10] Whereas the verb καταλύω connotes dismantling, the term translated "building" (οἰκοδομήν, *oikodomēn*) speaks of a structure that stands as the end result of a building process (BDAG 696), and Paul points out that this heavenly building originates with God (ἐκ θεοῦ, *ek theou*). The image brings to mind Jesus's words of comfort in John 14:2, "I am going away to prepare a place for you" (HCSB).[11] Accordingly, Paul proclaims that this building is a "residence not made with hands, eternal in the heavens."

The description "not made with hands" (ἀχειροποίητος, *acheiropoiētos*) implies "not made by human effort or ability" and speaks of something that only God can do. Paul uses the term at Col. 2:11 in discussing spiritual circumcision of the fleshly self, and at Mark 14:58 the witnesses against Jesus say they heard him claim that he would tear down the current temple and rebuild one "not made with hands."[12] I (and others) suggest that "a house not made with hands" refers to an immortal body, which only God can provide to the believer at the resurrection of the dead.[13]

Moreover, the apostle characterizes this house (i.e., the heavenly body) as being "eternal" and "in the heavens." The attributive adjective translated as "eternal" (αἰώνιον, *aiōnion*) helps tie the apostle's words to the previous passage, since in 4:17 he writes of "the eternal tonnage of glory," and at 4:18 he points out that the "unseen" things are "eternal." The eternal residence of which Paul speaks stands in stark contrast to the "earthly," mortal body, the container "made of earth" (4:7), a temporal vessel subject to death. That

---

condition and here can communicate a note of uncertainty about something that still seems likely. Paul is not sure whether he will die before the return of Christ, but he may see the event as likely. On the third-class condition, see D. Wallace 1996: 696.

10. For a sorting out of the key exegetical issues here, see Licona 2010: 426–36; Wright 2003: 364–71.

11. Yet this does not suggest that Paul believes a person's resurrection body already resides in heaven (contra Witherington 1995: 391). Rather, Paul believes the earthly body will be transformed into a resurrection body (1 Cor. 15:42–44). The language of "we have" is "the language of hope" (Barnett 1997: 259).

12. Hebrews uses the same concept at 9:11, 24, but does so with the phrase οὐ (*ou*, not) + a form of χειροποίητος (*cheiropoiētos*, made with hands). Also, see Chen (2013), who argues that anticipation of a heavenly sanctuary, made by God himself, stands as an early theological concept in the Jewish Scriptures.

13. Cullmann (2000: 17) states, "Because resurrection of the body is a new act of creation which embraces everything, it is not an event which begins with each individual death, but only at the End. It is not a transition from this world to another world, as is the case of the immortal soul freed from the body; rather it is the transition from the present age to the future. It is tied to the whole process of redemption" (see also Cullmann 2000: 23–27 on the intermediate state). Other views, e.g., include that "the body" refers to the church (as with Ellis's view described above in the footnotes of the unit introduction), to the heavenly temple in the new Jerusalem or the new Jerusalem itself (Furnish 1984: 294), or to the heavenly mansion prepared by Christ (John 14:2–4; see Barnett 1997: 258).

the location of this residence will be "in the heavens" (ἐν τοῖς οὐρανοῖς, *en tois ouranois*) suggests that the body will be made suitable for that realm of existence (1 Cor. 15:47–50). Wright (2003: 367) emphasizes that the phrase "in the heavens" does not refer to Christians simply "going to heaven" after death. Rather, he speaks of a body fit for the future, the new heavens and new earth. This is what Paul means at 1 Cor. 15:50, when he writes, "Now this is what I am saying, brothers and sisters: Flesh and blood cannot inherit the kingdom of God, nor does the perishable inherit the imperishable" (NET).

Some scholars suggest that Paul's language at 2 Cor. 5:1–10 differs much from what we find in 1 Cor. 15 and that Paul certainly must have shifted his position on life after death altogether, opting rather for a Greek idea of a disembodied immortality (Boismard 1999: 82). Yet we need to avoid the temptation to read into Paul's language a Platonic division of the body and soul, which sees the former as a throwaway container for the latter. Rather, Paul speaks of phases in the Christian experience, involving (1) an earthbound, deteriorating body, (2) a second phase for those who go to be "with Christ" upon death,[14] and (3) a final phase in which that body will be transformed (or "swallowed up," 5:4) by resurrection life. In Paul's understanding, there is a profound continuity, both physically and spiritually, between his life now and his life after death. To die will be to transition to be "with the Lord" (5:8–9), but there will also be a "life after life after death," as Wright (2003: 86) has put it, when the mortal puts on immortality through the resurrection. These phases give the apostle clear-eyed perspective as he faces the challenges of his ministry.

ii. Groaning and Desiring a Heavenly Residence (5:2–5)

In verse 1 Paul lays out his theme for what he discusses in the balance of the passage: earthly, bodily existence set over against the body that Paul anticipates receiving in the resurrection, a body made by God, one that is both "eternal" and "heavenly." He now addresses his perspective on each body and explains specifically his groaning in the earthly body and longing for the heavenly body. In verses 2–4 the apostle describes the "groaning" experienced in the earthly body (5:2) and explains that this groaning stems from the burden of earthly existence (5:4). The groan-producing difficulty of life, moreover, plays a part in stoking a desire for "our habitation from heaven," and, still with the tent imagery in mind, Paul shifts his metaphor slightly to speak of the heavenly

5:2

14. Paul describes this phenomenon elsewhere as being "with Christ" (σὺν Χριστῷ, *syn Christō*; Phil. 1:23), or to be "asleep" (τοὺς κοιμηθέντας, *tous koimēthentas*; 1 Thess. 4:14). Speaking of personal eschatology, Barnett (1997: 259) states,

> Paul does not set a timetable of personal eschatology, so that any reconstruction is to a degree speculative. It appears to be true both that (1) the deceased believer is "with the Lord" at his coming (1 Thess. 4:17), and that (2) at death he/she has "depart[ed]" to be "with Christ" (Phil. 1:23). It would seem to follow, therefore, that some kind of "independent state" exists between a person's death and the general resurrection. This appears to be what Paul is stating in v. 8, "to be away from the body" is to be "with the Lord."

body as something put on as an overgarment, one that will make the believer adequately dressed for eternity (5:3). He further explains that the desire for the resurrection body is not simply a desire to be rid of a body (as in Platonic thought), but rather a desire that the earthly, mortal body might be swallowed up by the heavenly (5:4).

Thus continuing[15] the discussion in 5:2, he writes, "In this tent we groan, greatly desiring to put on our habitation from heaven." Alluding to "the tent" mentioned in verse 1, Paul identifies the locus of his groaning simply as ἐν τούτῳ (en toutō, in this).[16] The verb στενάζω (stenazō) could be used in the ancient world to speak of "complaining" but here connotes an involuntary response, a sigh or groan, upon encountering some difficulty in life (BDAG 942),[17] and the imperfective aspect of the present-tense verb suggests an ongoing life experience.

When life gets excruciatingly hard, a person naturally longs for relief, and in verse 2 the apostle explains that he greatly desires to put on his resurrection body. While the verb ἐπιποθέω (epipotheō, desire), here presented as a present participle, had a range of meanings in antiquity, expressing earnest desire or even anxiety, Paul uses the word positively to speak of longing or desire, most often of his (or a coworker's) longing to see members of the church in various places (Rom. 1:11; 2 Cor. 9:14; Phil. 1:8; 2:26; 1 Thess. 3:6; 2 Tim. 1:4).[18] Yet here he longs for the resurrection body, and he describes the putting on of that glorified body in a vivid, though mixed, metaphor as the longing "to put on" (ἐπενδύσασθαι, ependysasthai) "our habitation from heaven" (τὸ οἰκητήριον ἡμῶν τὸ ἐξ οὐρανοῦ, to oikētērion hēmōn to ex ouranou). The aorist infinitive[19] can be read as shifting the imagery slightly, portraying the immortal body as clothing of a sort, as "an imperishable topcoat" (Belleville 1996: 134). Yet the object of the infinitive continues to employ "housing" imagery, since τὸ οἰκητήριον refers to a "dwelling" or "habitation." We end up with "a residence" that one "wears" like clothing.

Normally one builds a house or tent, moving in and out of it. Paul wants to speak both of the constancy of an immortal body as a dwelling place (the parallel here is to the earthly body as a tent; one does not move constantly in

15. It seems that in 5:2 καὶ γάρ continues the explanatory pattern established by the γάρ in 5:1, adding additional information ("for also," "moreover").

16. This demonstrative pronoun is neuter, matching τοῦ σκήνους in the previous verse.

17. Specifically, in 5:4 Paul uses στενάζω in tandem with "being burdened" (βαρούμενοι, baroumenoi), experiencing the pressures of life in a way that leads to onerous physical or emotional weariness. In 2 Cor. 1:8, the only other place in the book where Paul uses the term βαρέω to speak of being burdened, he tells the church that he and his coworkers were "oppressed to an extraordinary degree" and even thought they were going to die.

18. Spicq (1994: 2.60) notes, "Thus St. Paul marked *epipotheō* and its derivatives with his personality, imbuing them with a lively sensibility. Sometimes they suggest an urge, an inclination; sometimes a fervent tenderness, an emotion that grips the heart; always love, always a favorable sense. These nuances are, moreover, those of *potheō* and *pothos*."

19. The infinitive is complementary, working with the participle ἐπιποθοῦντες (epipothountes) to communicate the idea of "greatly desiring to put on."

and out of that "dwelling"; Paul will move out of his only once!) and of the immortal body as a "place to be," or a place to "have one's existence." On the other hand, writers of the ancient world described the body as clothing (e.g., Seneca the Younger, *Lucil.* 66.3; Epictetus, *Disc.* 1.25.21; Marcus Aurelius, *Med.* 10.1), and death could be seen as undressing (Philo, *Alleg.* 2.56; Porphyry, *Marc.* 33.501–5; see Keener 2005: 180). Using a cognate of ἐπενδύομαι, at 1 Cor. 15:53, the apostle writes, "For this perishable body must put on the imperishable, and this mortal body must put on immortality" (1 Cor. 15:53 NET). With regard to the immortal, resurrection body, believers will be "cloaked about" with a "residence," a place to be. In verse 1 the apostle has already mentioned that his heavenly residence will be "from God" (ἐκ θεοῦ); similarly, he now says its origin is "from heaven" (ἐξ οὐρανοῦ). In both cases he simply means that an immortal body will have its origin in God and be made for an immortal realm.

The chapter's third verse has generated a good bit of discussion among commentators, who have various ways of reading Paul's intent here. Before we can interpret the words, we must make decisions about which words are original to the text, since there is a good bit of textual turbulence in the verse. First, does Paul's statement begin with εἴπερ καί (*eiper kai,* since, if indeed), as read in some manuscripts, or εἴ γε καί (*ei ge kai,* assuming that, even if), as in other witnesses (see the first additional note on 5:3)? Following Harris (2005: 368), we opt for the latter, translated as "assuming that." In short, although both readings are found elsewhere in Paul,[20] the latter is the more difficult, and thus a scribe would have been more likely to bring this more difficult reading in line via a construction with εἴπερ, which was more commonly used in Koine Greek. Further, Thrall (1962: 82–97; 1994: 376) has gone to great lengths to demonstrate that the construction εἴ γε καί in Paul communicates a strong note of confidence in the assertion being made. With these words Paul introduces an assumption that he is making and in essence underscores that assumption's veracity.

Second, does the apostle write ἐκδυσάμενοι (*ekdysamenoi,* taking it off; Belleville 1996: 134; NRSV), referring to the mortal body? Or does he write, "putting it on" (ἐνδυσάμενοι, *endysamenoi*), speaking of the resurrection body? Details of our reasoning may be found in the second additional note on 5:3, but in short, the latter has much stronger external and internal evidence (despite the majority of the UBS committee reading this form of the text as banal and tautologous; see Metzger 1994: 511) and is to be preferred (so most modern translations, including HCSB, NASB, NET, NLT[2], ESV, NIV/TNIV). Also, Paul likes this word very much, using it most often to speak of "putting on" the new person in Christ (Rom. 13:12, 14; Gal. 3:27; Eph. 4:24; 6:11, 14; Col. 3:10, 12; 1 Thess. 5:8). As noted above, at 1 Cor. 15:53–54 he also uses the word to describe the "putting on" of the resurrection body.

5:3–4

---

20. See εἴπερ at Rom. 3:30; 8:9, 17; 1 Cor. 8:5; 15:15; 2 Thess. 1:6; and εἴ γε at Gal. 3:4; Eph. 3:2; 4:21; Col. 1:23; and possibly Rom. 5:6 (if one opts for the textual variant there). See the first additional note on 5:3.

If these textual decisions are correct, then in 2 Cor. 5:3 the apostle writes, "assuming that, putting it on, we will not be found inadequately dressed." The primary assertion has to do with putting on, or being clothed with, the resurrection body at the end of the age. In a Jewish apocalyptic vein, Paul anticipates that climactic, decisive event that will usher in a new age and thus a new existence for the people of God. In the language adopted by Paul in this passage, the resurrection will involve a "putting on" of a new body. The verb ἐνδύω (endyō), which means simply "to put on clothes," is a more basic form of its cognate, ἐπενδύομαι, which appears in verses 2 and 4. As noted above, the latter communicates the idea of putting on an overgarment.[21] Paul offers a parenthetical correction to head off a potential misreading of his statement in 5:2, and the key to unlocking his meaning focuses on the use of γυμνός (gymnos). In the NT, writers use the word variously to speak of being inadequately clothed (Matt. 25:36, 38, 43–44; James 2:15), being completely bare (Mark 14:51–52), being partially clothed (John 21:7), and being spiritually vulnerable (Heb. 4:13; Rev. 3:17; 16:15). In another passage on the resurrection body (1 Cor. 15:37), Paul speaks of the earthly body as a "bare kernel" (γυμνὸν κόκκον, gymnon kokkon).

What might Paul mean when he asserts that when the heavenly body has been put on, believers will not be found "naked," or as we translate the word, "inadequately dressed"? In Greek philosophy, the body was seen as a burdensome weight to be shed by the soul.[22] For instance, Wisdom of Solomon, an apocryphal book that combines Jewish piety and Greek philosophy, reads, "For a corruptible body burdens the soul, and the earthly tent weighs down a mind full of cares" (9:15). Consequently, death was seen as the deliverance of the soul from the body, and γυμνός was used to describe this separation of the soul from the body. Rather than this Platonic worldview, however, Paul writes from a Jewish apocalyptic worldview, using the image of nakedness to speak of the intermediate state between the believer's death and the resurrection of the dead at the end of the age. For the apostle, a transition takes place at death in which the earthly body is abandoned for a time. In the presence of Christ the believer enters a temporary disembodied state, a "nakedness," awaiting the heavenly building—that is, the transformation of the earthly body—to be received at the general resurrection from the dead. Anticipation of this "nakedness" seems uncomfortable for Paul, he does not want to be "undressed," but his emphasis here is on his anticipation of the resurrection body.

Our passage brings to mind Jesus's story of the wedding guest who was not dressed properly and was thrown out on his ear (Matt. 22:11–14). Certainly

21. For the idea of someone being clothed with heavenly glory, see, e.g., 2 En. 22.7–10, where God commands Michael to remove Enoch's earthly clothing, anoint him with oil, and clothe him with the glory of God (see the discussion in Scott 1998: 128).

22. Although, as Barrett (1973: 153) notes, the common person probably did not have such lofty views of the disembodied state. For the variety of perspectives on the nature of "souls" and bodies in the Greco-Roman world, see Keener 2005: 177–78.

an ethical dimension plays a part in the apostle's discourse at this point, for he soon speaks of standing before Christ in the judgment (5:10).[23] Yet at present the apostle is concerned with the bodies of believers, and his point is that the resurrection body will fully fit him and all Christ-followers for eternity. Paul assumes that at the resurrection of the dead, he and other believers will be found adequately clothed with their resurrection bodies. This is that for which he longs—"to be fully clothed, in order that what is mortal might be swallowed up by life." Thus the glory lost in the fall will be fully restored (cf. 2 Cor. 3:17–18) in the transformation that takes place at the resurrection of the dead (Pate 1991: 22, 115–16).[24]

In the first century, the word καταπίνω (*katapinō*) could be used as meaning "to drink down" or "swallow up" something, but it also developed a figurative meaning, "to destroy completely" by devouring. For instance, the term could be used to speak of a wild animal devouring its prey (Tob. 6:2), or of the waves of the sea swallowing up a drowning person (Polybius, *Hist.* 2.41.7; Philo, *Virt.* 201). Paul uses the word two other times, both of which are in the Corinthian correspondence. At 1 Cor.15:54 he quotes Isa. 25:8 in his treatment of the resurrection body, celebrating that death will be "swallowed up" in victory. The other occurrence we have already seen is in 2 Cor. 2:7, where Paul demonstrates great pastoral sensitivity, concerned that a fallen brother not be "swallowed up" by grief.

The resurrection does not involve a mere laying aside of one body for another, as could be inferred from the imagery of 5:1, 4. Rather, in the resurrection the earthly body is transformed, swallowed up, in the process of resurrection. It may be that we have here an echo of Isa. 25:8, quoted in 1 Cor. 15:54 as "Death has been swallowed up in victory" (HCSB).[25] The apostle's thoughts in our passage at hand and in 1 Cor. 15:54 parallel quite closely: the perishable will put on the imperishable, the mortal will put on immortality. As Paul uses the language here, he seems to place stress on continuity, rather than on destruction of the mortal by the immortal. With the coming of "life" at death, the believer's salvation will be fully consummated, and physical life here will be taken up into a resurrection life.

23. Some read Paul's use of "naked" here as coming out of the Jewish disposition toward nakedness in general. Although the Greeks found the naked body glorious, the Jews considered it shameful outside of the marriage relationship. Used figuratively in our passage at hand, Paul's reference to nakedness can be read as a reference to being found spiritually lacking, shown to be wanting in the face of judgment. One thinks immediately of the naked shame of Adam and Eve at the fall (Gen. 3:7, 10–11; see also passages such as Isa. 20:2–5; 47:3; Ezek. 16:36–39; Hosea 2:3, 8–13; Mic. 1:8, 11; Rev. 3:17; 16:15; 17:16). Pate (1991: 22, 115–16) goes so far as to tie Paul's words here to Adam being stripped of glory, a glory that has been restored in Christ.

24. For the idea of "nakedness" as an image of Adam losing his glory, being "undressed," see 3 Bar. 4.16; 2 En. 22.8; Gen. Rab. 20.12.

25. Paul's quotation of the Isaiah passage in 1 Cor. 15:54 differs a great deal from the LXX text, and he may be using another Greek translation of the passage, which reflects a tradition also adopted in Revelation (21:4). See Ciampa and Rosner (*CNTUOT* 747), who follow Stanley (1992: 210–11).

5:5   Verse 5 points out that this process of the mortal body being swallowed up by resurrection life is according to God's plan. God has prepared the believer for "this very event" (αὐτὸ τοῦτο, *auto touto*; lit., this very thing), referring to the resurrection from the dead. God is the One "who raises the dead" (1:9), a truth made strikingly immediate to the apostle during the crisis in Asia. With the same word here translated "prepared" (κατεργάζομαι, *katergazomai*), at 4:17 Paul has already noted that "our momentary, light bundle of affliction profusely produces [κατεργάζεται] for us . . . an eternal tonnage of glory," and this too speaks of a process designed by God in readying the believer for eternity.

     In broader NT theology, the coming and work of the Spirit of God formed a cornerstone of eschatology. In the last days, the Lord would pour out his Spirit on his people (Isa. 44:3; Ezek. 39:29; Joel 2:28–29; Acts 2:17–18), indwelling them as he had the tabernacle of old. The "Spirit orientation" of Paul's theology becomes clear when we consider that he refers to the Holy Spirit some 112 times (*DPL* 405). In 2 Cor. 3 he has already pointed out that the new-covenant ministry is a ministry of the Spirit of God. The Spirit writes the reality of the gospel on the hearts of believers (3:3), giving them life and freedom (3:6, 17). At 2 Cor. 1:22 Paul has already proclaimed that God "also sealed us and gave us the down payment of the Spirit in our hearts." The word translated "down payment" at 5:5 (ἀρραβών, *arrabōn*) is the same as that at 1:22 and in Eph. 1:14. As explained in our comments on 1:22, the term was associated with legal language in the first century. In contracts involving the transfer of goods or services, a down payment guaranteed the transfer of those goods or services as described in the legal agreement.[26]

     The teaching that God has given believers the Spirit as a down payment flows from Paul's teaching on the resurrection, and at least two points should be noted in relation to this aspect of the apostle's theology. First, his words do not mean that the Spirit is parceled out in stages, part of the Spirit given in this age and the rest given at the second coming! Rather, Paul intends a word picture communicating assurance that present realities foreshadow future realities. Since Christ-followers are indwelled by the Spirit (Rom. 8:9), the relationship with the Spirit bears witness to the fruits yet to come in that relationship. Second, in this passage the reference to the Spirit as down payment stands in direct theological relationship to the resurrection. We experience the power and presence of God now, through the Spirit, and thus anticipate the consummation of God's power and presence at the end of the age, through the resurrection.

iii. Being "At Home" and "Away" (5:6–8)

5:6–7   At 5:6 the apostle begins a second submovement of 5:1–10 in which he speaks of implications (οὖν, *oun*, therefore) of the theology expressed in 5:1–5: his confidence in life and his longing to be with Christ. Paul's confidence does

---

26. See Garland (1999: 106–7) and Kerr (1988) for arguments against translating ἀρραβών as "pledge."

not consist of an arrogant presumption on his part, but rather arises from what God has revealed to be true about himself, about human beings, and about life in the world. God has given his revelation through the created order (Rom. 1:18–20) and through the Scriptures (e.g., Rom. 1:2; 15:4; 2 Tim. 3:16), but preeminently in the person of his son, Jesus Christ (e.g., Rom. 16:25–26; 1 Cor. 15:3–4; Gal. 3:8, 22). Further, Paul's own experience of the resurrected Christ on the road to Damascus (Acts 9:1–9, 16), along with subsequent words of encouragement from God,[27] certainly gave him ongoing courage in the face of the troubles he experienced.

The word translated "being confident" (θαρροῦντες, *tharrountes*) means to be convinced about something, to be bold or courageous (BDAG 444), and Paul's life is always (πάντοτε, *pantote*) characterized by such confidence. The apostle uses the term θαρρέω only in 2 Corinthians, taking it up four additional times in the verses and chapters that follow (2 Cor. 5:8; 7:16; 10:1–2). In the immediate context this confidence is reiterated at the beginning of 5:8 with a present active indicative form of the verb, the apostle picking up the idea of confidence expressed at the beginning of 5:6. Again, Paul's theology forms the bedrock foundation for this confident posture in life. He is bold in his relationship with God, because of what God has revealed and accomplished through the gospel, and his boldness toward the Corinthians has this same, unshakable foundation. Some in their community undoubtedly mistook this confidence for arrogance, but Paul was compelled in his life posture because he knew the gospel about which he preached to be true. He had the boldness of a man who knows he is right!

An aspect of his theology, however, understood that life here on earth involves an absence from the exalted Lord (v. 6): "understanding that as long as we are at home in the body we are absent from the Lord" (καὶ εἰδότες ὅτι ἐνδημοῦντες ἐν τῷ σώματι ἐκδημοῦμεν ἀπὸ τοῦ κυρίου, *kai eidotes hoti endēmountes en tō sōmati ekdēmoumen apo tou kyriou*). The conjunction ὅτι introduces the content of what Paul knows or understands (εἰδότες). He understands that "to be at home in the body" is to be "away/absent from the Lord." The verb ἐνδημέω (*endēmeō*) means "to be at home," thus "to be in a familiar place." Ἐκδημέω (*ekdēmeō*) is its opposite, "to be away." So, as long as Paul is "at home" in his mortal body, he is "away from" the presence of the Lord. This does not mean that Paul doubts the presence of Christ, through the Spirit, in the believer's life prior to death or the parousia (Gal. 2:20). Rather, believers have a relationship with Christ, inaugurated in the new covenant by the ministry of the Spirit, that will change both spatially and qualitatively at death and will be consummated at the resurrection from the dead. By definition, the fellowship that believers have with Christ in the earthly body is partial, obscured, shadowed by a fallen world, and stands in contrast to the

---

27. Upon the founding of the church at Corinth, e.g., the Lord gave Paul strong encouragement to keep on preaching and teaching: "Then the Lord said to Paul in a night vision, 'Don't be afraid, but keep on speaking and don't be silent'" (Acts 18:9 HCSB).

fullness and glory of the face-to-face relationship with Christ that will follow in the next life (Garland 1999: 264–65). The dim will give way to clarity. The darkness and confusion of this veil of tears will drop away before the glory of the unveiled Presence.

Paul understands that his current condition means to be absent from Christ. Thus in verse 7 the Christ-follower's pattern of life (περιπατοῦμεν, *peripatoumen*, we walk) must be "by faith, not by what can be seen" (διὰ πίστεως γὰρ περιπατοῦμεν, οὐ διὰ εἴδους, *dia pisteōs gar peripatoumen, ou dia eidous*). In the modern era, "faith" often is confused with "a blind leap into the dark," but this is not the biblical concept of faith, nor is it what Paul communicates here. The modern misconception comes from a naturalistic view of the world that suggests God does not intervene, indeed cannot intervene in the cause-and-effect systems of the physical order. Thus a person must take a leap against, or in the face of, what modern science tells us is true. Biblical faith, on the other hand, constitutes a "step into the light," holding that bold steps are in order because God has revealed what is true about himself, the world, and life in the world (Heb. 11:1–2). When Paul says that we walk "by faith" (a genitive of means, "by means of faith"), he insists that his pattern of life is governed by what God has revealed as true about life: in other words, he trusts God, based on revelation.

This faith, moreover, contrasts with walking "by what can be seen" (also a genitive of means): the word εἴδους (*eidous*) refers to the "form," or "appearance" of something. At present Paul cannot see Jesus, or God the Father, or the Spirit, or the spiritual realm, but he trusts God in any case. His focus of life rests on the unseen, eternal realities, known through God's revelation, even though he cannot physically see those realities (4:18). This is what it means to walk by faith—to trust God on the basis of what God has revealed to be true.

5:8   Paul's confidence rests on such faith, and he reiterates that confidence at the beginning of 5:8. The fact that he physically cannot see such spiritual realities does not diminish his confidence in the least. Yet in spite of his confidence, he admits that he "would rather be away from the body and at home with the Lord" (εὐδοκοῦμεν μᾶλλον ἐκδημῆσαι ἐκ τοῦ σώματος καὶ ἐνδημῆσαι πρὸς τὸν κύριον, *eudokoumen mallon ekdēmēsai ek tou sōmatos kai endēmēsai pros ton kyrion*). The verb εὐδοκοῦμεν speaks of being pleased with something (and thus here a "preference"), and Paul plays off this word in the next verse, confessing that he wants to be "pleasing" (εὐάρεστοι, *euarestoi*) to Christ.

To be "away from the body" refers to death. When he writes of being "at home with the Lord," he indicates his understanding that to die, for the believer, is to step into the presence of Christ. As Plummer (1915: 150) notes, Paul assumes the believer is conscious upon death, "conscious of the Lord" (Phil. 1:20–23; Luke 23:43; Acts 7:59); otherwise death would be a condition worse than this life with regard to his relationship with Christ. Although Paul may have the whole of the afterlife in mind—to know the Lord's presence upon death (if death comes before Christ does) and in the resurrection to follow—he probably here has in mind the intermediate state between death and resurrection, since in the resurrection believers will be reunited with their earthly bodies, albeit in a transformed state. As N. T. Wright (2003: 367) observes,

> This is about as explicit as he gets on the question of an "intermediate state"; clearly he believes that people in such a state will be happy and content. But, precisely because Paul is still thinking in a very Jewish manner, his preference is for the final state, in which one will be given a new body to be put on over the top of the present one, clothing the Messiah's people in a new kind of physicality whose main characteristic is incorruption.

Paul has no death wish, but he does know the nature of Christian hope (1:10) and has a clear-eyed theology that gives him a foundation for living boldly and ministering confidently in the world.

iv. Always Accountable to God (5:9–10)

Paul's emphasis on a coming day on which he will transition to a resurrection body also brings to mind the tribunal of Christ, before which every believer will appear and give an account of actions done in life on earth. In Paul's understanding, recompense will be made to each person individually, primarily having to do with receiving commendation or the withholding of commendation. The passage clearly demonstrates the connection between the ethical/ spiritual choices of the present life and the response of Christ, both in the present life and the future judgment.

5:9

Thus the apostle's discussion of death (5:1–8) and especially his thoughts on being "away from the body and at home with the Lord" (5:8) give rise to Paul's statements concerning his desire to please Christ and his awareness of a coming judgment: "For this reason, we aspire to be pleasing to him, whether we are at home or absent" (διὸ καὶ φιλοτιμούμεθα, εἴτε ἐνδημοῦντες εἴτε ἐκδημοῦντες, εὐάρεστοι αὐτῷ εἶναι, *dio kai philotimoumetha, eite endēmountes eite ekdēmountes, euarestoi autō einai*).[28] Early in its development, φιλοτιμέομαι (*philotimeomai*, aspire) could have negative connotations of being inappropriately ambitious, or in a positive sense, "to show patriotic zeal" (Harris 2005: 404). By the first century the word could be used, for instance, of wealthy persons "aspiring" to outdo other wealthy persons in rendering philanthropic service (BDAG 1059). In addition to our verse under consideration, Paul employs the word positively two times to speak of "aspiring" or "considering [something] an honor," each having to do with a pattern of life or service (Rom. 15:20; 1 Thess. 4:11). In Rom. 15:20 Paul aspires "to preach the gospel where Christ has not yet been named," and at 1 Thess. 4:11 he exhorts the believers of Thessalonica "to aspire to lead a quiet life, to attend to your own business, and to work with your hands." What the apostle aspires to at

---

28. The addition of καί (*kai*) at the beginning of 5:9 strengthens the inferential conjunction (διό, *dio*): the construction suggests that what follows is a "self-evident" inference (BDAG 250).

2 Cor. 5:9 is "to be pleasing to him" (the present infinitive of εἰμί [*eimi*] plus the adjective εὐάρεστος [*euarestos*]). The adjective εὐάρεστος occurs eight times in Paul (Rom. 12:1–2; 14:18; 2 Cor. 5:9; Eph. 5:10; Phil. 4:18; Col. 3:20; Titus 2:9) and once in Hebrews (13:21). With the exception of Titus 2:9, the apostle uses the term to speak of pleasing God. Moreover, it is clear that Paul desires to please Christ in the present life as well as when he is "with the Lord" upon death, and ultimately when he stands before Christ's tribunal[29]—"whether we are at home or absent," that is, whether at home in the earthly body or departed through death to be with Christ.

5:10 Furthermore, the desire to be pleasing to Christ (v. 9) finds its basis[30] in the theology expressed in verse 10: "For we must all appear before the judgment seat of Christ, in order that each one might be paid back in accordance with the actions done in the body, whether good or bad." The word βῆμα (*bēma*, judgment seat) originally referred to "a step" made by a foot, and then a measurement, less than the space covered by taking a stride (as at Acts 7:5). Yet the term came to be used of a platform that had steps by which a person would ascend to the top, or especially a judicial bench where judgments were made (BDAG 175).

Nine of the twelve uses in the NT refer to a Roman seat of judgment, occupied by such as Pilate, Herod, Caesar, or Gallio (Matt. 27:19; John 19:13; Acts 12:21; 18:12, 16–17; 25:6, 10, 17). The occurrences in Acts 18 form somewhat of a backdrop for our discussion, since about four years prior to the writing of 2 Corinthians, Paul was brought before Gallio, who sat on a βῆμα in the city of Corinth. We know that the judicial bench referred to in Acts was located on the south side of the city, near a statue of Athena and just west of a row of shops (Furnish 1984: 301a; Murphy-O'Connor 1983: 24–25). In a context addressing believers who were criticizing other believers, Paul uses the term at Rom. 14:10, where he writes, "For we will all stand before the tribunal of God" (HCSB), and at 14:12 he expands the thought with "So then, each of us will give an account of himself to God" (HCSB). It is significant that in our passage under consideration, the βῆμα is the judgment seat "of Christ" (τοῦ Χριστοῦ, *tou Christou*). There exists no tension between this confession at 5:10 and that of Rom. 14:10, for the apostle elsewhere notes that Christ is the Father's agent in carrying out the judgment (Acts 17:31; Rom. 2:16).

So it is before Christ that all "must appear." The combination of the passive infinitive φανερωθῆναι (*phanerōthēnai*) and δεῖ (*dei*, must, it is necessary) communicates a strong note of accountability. In contexts speaking of judgment, the former term refers either to "appearing" to give an account of oneself (as in Rev. 3:18) or to be vindicated (Col. 3:4) or to having one's works publicly exposed (e.g., 1 Cor. 4:5; Eph. 5:13–14). Given the double use of φανερόω (*phaneroō*) in the next verse (2 Cor. 5:11), the former meaning

---

29. The present tense of the infinitive, along with the reference to being "at home," suggests that Paul believes a Christian can please Christ in the present life.

30. In its postpositive position at the beginning of 5:10, γάρ has an explanatory function.

seems in order here. Moreover, the πάντας ἡμᾶς (*pantas hēmas*, we all) suggests that the judgment is comprehensive, that is, involving all the persons in a given group, and ἕκαστος (*hekastos*, each one) indicates that scrutiny will apply to each individual rather than consisting of a summary judgment on that group of people.

Yet, are we speaking of all people or Christ-followers in particular? Commentators have been divided on the matter, but there are reasons for embracing the latter position. First, the logical relationship between this verse and the previous one, as well as the broader context, points to believers, who will be resurrected (v. 5) and desire to "please the Lord." Second, the pronoun ἡμᾶς (*hēmas*) most naturally refers to Paul and his fellow Christians (Thrall 1994: 394). Finally, at Rom. 2:7–10, where Paul addresses the more comprehensive judgment of both believers and unbelievers, he clearly refers to two categories of people, not the two types of action we see in the present verse (Harris 2005: 406).

So Paul desires to please God in light of the fact that there will come a time when all Christ-followers will appear before Christ's tribunal. The purpose (ἵνα, *hina*) for that appearance finds expression in the clause "in order that each one might be paid back in accordance with the actions done while in the body, whether good or bad." The verb κομίζω (*komizō*), when in the middle voice, as here, communicates the idea of getting or receiving back something that is owed or deserved (BDAG 557). This recompense (Barrett 1973: 149; Martin 1986: 96; Thrall 1994: 357) by Christ has been interpreted in at least two primary veins. One view understands believers to have been brought into relationship with Christ by grace but kept in, or judged, by works. In this interpretation, one's keeping of the law ends up being the final measure of eschatological salvation.[31] Yet this view must be ruled out in light of Paul's treatment of justification, not least in the immediate context, in which the apostle proclaims a reconciliation to God in which sins are no longer counted against those in the new covenant (5:19, 21), those who have been made the righteousness of God in Christ (Barnett 1997: 276).

The other interpretation, then, is to understand the "recompense" in terms of evaluation rather than condemnation (Rom. 5:16, 18; 8:1; 1 Cor. 3:10–15; 4:5). Certainly there seem to be various levels of commendation (e.g., Luke 12:42–44), but rewards (one aspect of recompense) in Paul seem to have to do with "the enjoyment of all the blessings that are in Christ and the future tangible recognition of service in the furtherance of the gospel" (*DPL* 819). These rewards play a part in motivating those who have been saved to live well for Christ in the world, reminding believers that God has saved us to participate in the advancement of his cause in the world. On

---

31. So, e.g., Sanders (1977: 543), who states, "The point is that God saves by grace, but that within the framework established by grace he rewards good deeds and punishes transgression." See also Thrall (1994: 395), who leaves open the possibility that a Christian's unrighteous works could threaten his or her salvation.

the other hand, "suffering loss" may be a form of recompense for believers who do not live well for the Lord (1 Cor. 3:15), who, though forgiven, will experience a forfeiture of reward or privilege (Harris 2005: 408). Both reward and the withholding of reward, therefore, seem to play a role in motivating believers concerning their choices in life. We trust in God's grace for salvation and live for his pleasure, anticipating his pronouncement "well done" as commendation for how we have lived for him. Paul Barnett (1997: 277) puts it well:

> The sure prospect of the judgment seat reminds the Corinthians—and all believers—that while they are righteous in Christ by faith alone, the faith that justifies is to be expressed by love and obedience (Gal. 5:6; Rom. 1:5), and by pleasing the Lord (v. 9). Our "confidence" that we will be "with the Lord" (v. 8) is to be held in tension with the "fear of the Lord" (v. 11), from which we serve him. Confidence, while real, does not empty service of sobriety.

In line with this interpretation of the judgment seat, we understand the phrase διὰ τοῦ σώματος (*dia tou sōmatos*) to be temporal, "while in the body" (so NET, NIV), that is, during one's time on earth, not actions "done by means of the body" (Plummer 1915: 158). Further, πρὸς ἃ ἔπραξεν (*pros ha epraxen*) communicates the idea of "accordance," suggesting that Christ's recompense will be according to what a person has accomplished during earthly life. So Christ's judgment is specific to each individual and has a basis in what each person has done. Finally, the adjectives ἀγαθόν (*agathon*, good) and φαῦλον (*phaulon*, worthless) speak of two categories of the "actions done while in the body," the first connoting that which is good, useful, or beneficial, and the second that which is of a low standard or inferior. Since Paul has shifted from plural (τά, *ta*, the things) to singular adjectives at this point, Plummer (1915: 158) suggests that the apostle has in mind the judgment of one's life or character as a whole, rather than individual acts.

Reflection

Christ-followers live in a perpetual tension between the "now" of fragile, earthly existence and the "not yet" of our hoped-for, future, resurrection life in the presence of God.[32] The apostle Paul constantly faced the onslaught of physical persecution, a form of being "torn down," threatened with the prospect of death. So he says, "We groan" (5:2, 4), longing for the burden of mortality to be "swallowed up" by life immortal. Yet Paul is confident because he knows that if he dies before the coming of Christ, he will be with Christ (5:6–8), and he knows that God has a resurrection body for him at the end of the age (5:1–4). In fact, the Spirit serves as a down payment in anticipation of these realities (5:5–6). It would be preferable to shake off this tent, this earthbound residence. That time will come (5:7–8), and

---

32. For more on this theological framework, see Lincoln 1981.

whether in this life or the next, Paul wants to be pleasing to the Lord, ready to stand before his judgment seat (5:9–10).

When we are confronted with our own mortality, as Paul had been at this stage in his life, the encounter may have at least two effects. First, it puts the "heavenly" realm front and center in our thoughts, and second, it tests our theology. Paul's theological presuppositions come through strongly in these words of longing for the resurrection body. Here we see again the integration—the integrity—of Paul's theology, his life, and his ministry. What he believes, what he longs for, and what he does all blend in the mix of life, and we can ask ourselves whether this integration characterizes our lives as well.

All of us face an "undressing" at death. At the moment that death may seem more distant or immanent, depending on our current circumstances—a cancer patient or persecuted pastor in a third-world country may groan more deeply under the burden of mortality right now, and they thus, by faith, may long for resurrection life. But sooner or later all of us—our theology, our confidence—will be put to the test. The burdens of physical existence tend to be clarifying, crystallizing Christian hope of resurrection, bringing it into focus. Our physical trials force us to assess our longings. If we understand the great Christian hope, we long not for a disembodied existence, a "less-than-we-are-now" form of ghostly fluttering among the clouds. We long for transformation, resurrection life in the new heavens and earth, mortality swallowed down, deferring to immortality. Southern agrarian Wendell Berry writes:

> Imagine the dead waking, dazed, into a shadowless light in which they know themselves all together for the first time. It is a light that is merciless until they can accept its mercy. . . . In it, they are loved completely, even as they have been, and so are changed into what they could not have been, but what, if they could have imagined it, they would have wished to be.

Additional Notes

5:3. Here εἴπερ καί is in 𝔓⁴⁶ B D F G 33 1175 *pc*, but εἴ γε καί in א C K L P 049 1 6 69. Following Harris (2005: 368), we opt for the latter, translated as "assuming that." Both readings appear elsewhere in Paul, εἴπερ at Rom. 3:30; 8:9, 17; 1 Cor. 8:5; 15:15; 2 Thess. 1:6; and εἴ γε at Gal. 3:4; Eph. 3:2; 4:21; Col. 1:23; and possibly Rom. 5:6 (if one opts for the textual variant there), but the latter is more difficult; thus a scribe likely brought this more difficult reading in line by using εἴπερ, more common in Koine Greek.

5:3. Does the apostle write ἐκδυσάμενοι (having taken it off; Belleville 1996: 134; NRSV, NA²⁷; D*·c ar f⁵; Marcion Tert Spec), referring to the mortal body? Or does he write ἐνδυσάμενοι (putting it on), speaking of the resurrection body? The latter has much stronger external support (𝔓⁴⁶ א B C D² Ψ 0243 33 1739 1881 𝔐 lat sy co; Cl). The UBS committee argued that the internal evidence favors ἐκδυσάμενοι, since with ἐνδυσάμενοι "the apostle's statement is banal and even tautologous, whereas with ἐκδυσάμενοι it is characteristically vivid and paradoxical ('inasmuch as we, though unclothed, shall not be found naked')" (Metzger 1994: 511). However, the reading ἐνδυσάμενοι can be interpreted as playing a part in a parenthetical statement, correcting a possible misinterpretation of verse 2 (so Harris 2005: 368). Thus the reading ἐνδυσάμενοι is to be preferred (so most modern translations, including HCSB, NASB, NET, NLT^2, ESV, NIV/TNIV). As pointed out in the comments, Paul likes this word very much, using it most often to speak of "putting on" the new person in Christ (Rom. 13:12, 14; Gal. 3:27; Eph. 4:24; 6:11, 14; Col. 3:10, 12; 1 Thess. 5:8). At 1 Cor. 15:53–54 he also uses the word to describe the "putting on" of the resurrection body.

5:10. Although κακόν has strong external support ($\mathfrak{P}^{46}$ B D F G Ψ 𝔐; Cl), φαῦλον (ℵ C 048 0243 33 81 326 365 630 1739 [1881] *pc*) is the preferred reading since it is more difficult. The former term is common in Paul when paired with ἀγαθόν in an antithesis, whereas the latter only occurs in an antithesis with ἀγαθόν elsewhere in Paul at Rom. 9:11 (it appears as a stand-alone term at Titus 2:8).

3. "Respond to Authentic Ministry": A Series of Exhortations to the Corinthians (5:11–7:4)

In 2 Cor. 2:14–7:4 Paul presents his defense of authentic ministry in an attempt to win the Corinthians over to a solid commitment to him and his mission (and thus to a renewed commitment to the true gospel). Having explicated the dynamics of true, Christian ministry in 2:14–4:6 and the suffering involved in such a ministry in 4:7–5:10, the apostle now builds on these theological foundations by offering a series of strong exhortations directed at the Corinthian church—it is time for them to begin thinking about their response to his words! Barrett (1973: 163) rightly calls the first movements of this section (5:11–21) "one of the most pregnant, difficult, and important in the whole of the Pauline literature." Here we find powerful, beautiful expressions of God's gospel and a portrayal of Paul's role as God's ambassador in proclaiming it. The series of units extending to 7:4, moreover, has a logical progression.[1]

First, in 5:11–13 the apostle begins by asserting again his posture toward God, his posture toward people generally, and his posture toward the Corinthians. Mindful of God's judgment (5:10), he has appropriate fear of the Lord, and he lives a life "open to God" (5:11). This gives a proper grounding for persuading people through the preaching of God's Word. Yet Paul's real agenda for this series of exhortations is to challenge the Corinthians to respond to his ministry (5:12–13).

Second, it seems clear from 2 Corinthians as a whole that the crisis with the false teachers involves, among other dynamics, inappropriate bases for evaluating leadership of the church. So in 5:14–17 Paul details the implications of a christocentric ministry and life for the way a person approaches life and evaluates others. Christ's death and resurrection change everything

---

1. Contra Boers (2002: 545–47), who, in dialogue with Hans Windisch and Rudolf Bultmann, concludes that the question of the contextual relationship of 5:14–6:2 to the passages that surround it is unanswerable. Windisch and Strecker (1970: 202, 203, 220) suggest that the units running from 5:11–6:10 have been misarranged, and they attempt to put the units back in an order that shows more thematic continuity. What stands against this proposal, however, is the unidentified motivation of the editor to rearrange Paul's original flow of thought. Jan Lambrecht sees a three-step development in the section running from 5:11 to 6:10 (Bieringer and Lambrecht 1994: 364–65):

    A self-defense (5:11–13)
      B emissary of Christ (5:14–21)
    A′ self-defense (6:1–10)

I suggest that B in this scheme might extend through 6:2, for 6:1–2 continues Paul's plea for the Corinthians to be reconciled to God, as expressed in 5:20.

(5:14–15), so that judgments according to the flesh have been made obsolete (5:16–17). Paul asserts that when a person has embraced the lordship of Christ and Christ's gospel, one's world is seen from the standpoint of new creation.

Third, the apostle develops this hortatory section further with 5:18–6:2, where he hits on the book's central purpose, reconciliation of the Corinthians to God (and to his mission). It is no accident that Paul's defense of his ministry has come to this point, offering a powerful summary of the gospel as a message of reconciliation (Roetzel 2007: 81–82), for the gospel itself has reconciliation at its heart and forms the basis for the Corinthians themselves being reconciled to God.

Fourth, in the four subunits of exhortation running from 6:3–7:4, the apostle weaves assertions of his own integrity (6:3–10; 7:2), with clearly stated pleas for openness to him, his mission, and ultimately to God (6:11–13; 7:3–4). The exhortations also contain a corresponding challenge to turn away from those who are adulterating the Corinthians' spiritual lives (6:14–7:1).

Thus this series of exhortations (5:11–7:4) begins with Paul's ministry orientation (as he relates to God, to people generally, and to the Corinthians particularly) and an explanation that he is providing the Corinthians with the means to answer the interlopers who are criticizing him. The section continues with a treatment of appropriate bases for evaluation (of Paul and other ministers) and moves to pleas for reconciliation. Paul pleads with the Corinthians primarily on the bases of the gospel and his own integrity. Finally, he calls for an appropriate response from the Corinthians.

a. An Opportunity for the Corinthians (5:11–13)

In some ways, 2 Cor. 5:11–13 again reiterates the letter's main theme found in 1:12–14 (Garland 1999: 268), for here again Paul speaks of boasting, an appeal to conscience, and the manifestation of the truth, in short, the appropriateness of his motives and actions before God and before other people. In fleshing out these themes, Paul actually speaks of himself in this passage as relating to three parties: God, people in general, and the Corinthians in particular, and he has spoken of his relationship with each at earlier points in the book. He has written of his posture before God (5:11), for instance, at 1:23; 2:17; 3:4; and 4:2, each of which points to the validity of Paul's ministry on the basis of his relationship with God. The openness of his ministry before a watching world (5:11) finds expression, for example, at 3:2, where he describes the ministry accomplished among the Corinthians themselves as a letter that people can read; and at 4:2, where, by the proclamation of the truth, he and his coworkers commend themselves "to every person's conscience." Finally, in 5:12–13 we see a window on the situation behind this letter. Paul clearly expresses his motive for writing—he attempts to draw the Corinthians to an understanding of himself and his mission, in part that they might be able to come to his defense before those evaluating his ministry improperly. Others might question Paul's mental state, but the Corinthians must understand that his ministry flows from his commitment to God and his commitment to them as God's church (5:12–13).

The unit can be outlined as follows:

  i. The openness of Paul's life (5:11)
 ii. Paul's hesitant self-recommendation (5:12)
iii. The state of Paul's mind (5:13)

Exegesis and Exposition

[11]Therefore, knowing the fear of the Lord, ⌜we appeal to⌝ people, but our lives stand open to God; but I hope that who we really are has been made clear to your consciences also. [12⌜ ⌝]It is not *really* that we are recommending ourselves to you again; rather, we are giving you an opportunity to boast on ⌜our⌝ behalf, in order that you might have something to use against those boasting in appearance and ⌜not in⌝ heart. [13]For if we are out of our minds, it is for God, or if we are of sound mind, it is for you.

i. The Openness of Paul's Life (5:11)

5:11   The conjunction οὖν (*oun*, therefore), which ties this new unit to what has gone before, functions both inferentially and transitionally. Inferentially, the "fear of the Lord" that Paul experiences and his "appeal to people" relate very directly to the judgment seat of which he speaks in the previous verse; that judgment looms large on the far horizon of life, providing a point of reference for life and ministry now. Yet the word also plays a part in crafting a transition to this new section as the apostle moves from his previous discussions of authenticity and suffering in ministry to this series of direct appeals to the Corinthians.

Paul uses the word οἶδα (*oida*, to know) over one hundred times in his writings, sixteen times in 2 Corinthians. In this book, he uses the term to speak of what someone "knows" concerning basic facts (9:2; 11:11, 31), or with the sense of knowing or recognizing a person (5:16; 12:2–3); yet as we have seen at numerous points, the apostle also employs the word to speak of knowing certain theological truths (2 Cor. 1:7; 4:14; 5:1, 6). Here, however, Paul "knows" something from experience—he knows what it means to fear the Lord. In the NT the "fear of the Lord" (τὸν φόβον τοῦ κυρίου, *ton phobon tou kyriou*) expresses an appropriate reverence and awe that stem from God's mighty acts (*EDNT* 3:429). Yet, rather than debilitating, such reverence reverberates through an appropriate faith, ultimately manifesting a trust in God as one reflects upon the awesome dimensions of God's power. This reverence for God, moreover, motivates Paul for ministry as he appeals to people on God's behalf.

In the remainder of verse 11 the apostle presents his mission, motivated by this dynamic reverence for "the Lord," in relation to three parties: people generally, God, and the Corinthian church. Paul's ministry exists to proclaim the truth of the gospel, and he does this everywhere he goes, as he and his associates "appeal to people." Although it has a broad semantic range, the word πείθω (*peithō*) here means "to cause to come to a particular point of view or course of action" in the sense of "to convince," "to persuade," or "to appeal." In other words, at the heart of his ministry and out of reverence for the Lord, Paul seeks to convince people of the veracity of the gospel message so that they respond to it, submitting their lives to Jesus as their Lord.

Second, such a ministry demands a certain posture toward God—it is, after all, God's gospel and God's ministry to which Paul and his associates have been called. Thus the apostle emphasizes such a posture time and again throughout the book (e.g., 1:23; 2:17; 3:4; 4:2). Because he understands his mission to be one of complete integrity, with no shady motives or moves, Paul can write, "Our lives stand open to God" (θεῷ . . . πεφανερώμεθα, *theō . . . pephanerōmetha*). The verb[1] has to do with that which is revealed, made public, or known, and with the exception of the use at 5:10, he employs the word in 2 Corinthians to speak either of the manifestation of the gospel to

---

1. The perfect-tense form πεφανερώμεθα indicates that Paul understands this posture before God as characterizing his ministry in the past and continuing to characterize his ministry at present. This posture constitutes a "state" in which his ministry functions.

the lost, the manifestation of what is true about himself, or the manifestation of what is true about the Corinthians (2 Cor. 2:14; 3:3; 4:10–11; 5:11; 7:12; 11:6). Thus the word has relational overtones as used by Paul and connotes the reality about a situation or person being made clear to another. He categorically states that his life stands as an "open book" before God, nothing hidden, nothing of which to be ashamed, nothing found but an integrity of character and purpose.[2]

Finally, in verse 11 Paul turns to the issue of the Corinthians themselves and their view of him: "but I hope that who we really are has been made clear to your consciences also." The apostle hopes (ἐλπίζω, *elpizō*), or trusts, that the letter he writes has done its work and clarified the integrity of his ministry for the Corinthians. He has worked at this agenda especially since 2:14, and he continues in the units that follow (see esp. 6:3–10). We have seen the word συνείδησις (*syneidēsis*, conscience) twice before in 2 Corinthians (1:12; 4:2) and noted that it has to do with "the inward faculty of distinguishing right and wrong," or "moral consciousness" (BDAG 967; see the discussion at 1:12). Rather than appealing to the Corinthians for approval, however, he appeals to them to recognize the spiritual realities of his ministry, that he has been called by God and that they are called to the true God and the true gospel through Paul's ministry. The apostle's outward actions, his patterns of life and ministry, bear witness to and manifest the truth, and Paul hopes the Corinthians will be spiritually discerning enough to recognize it.

ii. Paul's Hesitant Self-Recommendation (5:12)

In the comments on 3:1 we suggest that Paul's references to self-recommendation weave an important thread through the book (3:1; 4:2; 5:12; 6:4; 7:11; 10:12, 18; see the comments on 3:1 for the background of this concept), and at points he *seems* to contradict himself. As a case in point, the statement here at 5:12 appears to be an overt denial of self-recommendation. Yet I suggest that the apostle consistently offers self-recommendation, and our current passage is no exception; in fact, he clearly uses 2 Corinthians to a great extent to recommend himself quite forcefully. Normally the self-recommendation of his ministry comes via his exemplary patterns of life and ministry (4:2; 6:4), and yet, given the current crisis with the Corinthians, Paul has been forced to commend his ministry to them very directly and overtly. The seemingly mixed signals in this regard, however, stem from the fact that his self-recommendation is offered with two particular reservations. First, the Corinthians should not have put him in his current position of needing to commend himself to them (12:11). The validity and spiritual integrity of his ministry should be beyond question for the Corinthian church, and the interlopers in Corinth should not

5:12

---

2. The word speaks more of Paul's posture than of God's ability. We do understand theologically that God knows all things: "No creature is hidden from Him, but all things are naked and exposed to the eyes of Him to whom we must give an account" (Heb. 4:13 HCSB). However, what the apostle addresses here has to do with his own posture of openness toward God.

have been able to call the apostle's ministry into question. Second, he does not want to be mistaken as offering the same type of self-recommendation as carried out by those false teachers at Corinth, a self-recommendation that involves "boasting in appearance," as stated here, with classification and comparison as the standards of evaluation rather than being grounded in God's approval (10:12, 18).

Now this interpretation seems to hit a snag with 5:12, for at first blush his statement in this verse seems to constitute a clear denial of self-recommendation: "We are not recommending ourselves to you again" (οὐ πάλιν ἑαυτοὺς συνιστάνομεν ὑμῖν, *ou palin heautous synistanomen hymin*). Yet this seemingly straightforward denial must be read in light of the statement that follows, which the apostle sets in contrast to it. He follows with "rather, we are giving you an opportunity to boast on our behalf" (ἀλλὰ ἀφορμὴν διδόντες ὑμῖν καυχήματος ὑπὲρ ἡμῶν, *alla aphormēn didontes hymin kauchēmatos hyper hēmōn*). The conjunction ἀλλά (but, rather) marks a contrast, and the present active participle διδόντες (giving) may be read as independent, standing in for an indicative verb.[3] That participle, moreover, has ἀφορμήν as its object, a word that refers to an "occasion," or "opportunity," and among NT writers,[4] is used only in Paul (Rom. 7:8, 11; 2 Cor. 5:12; 11:12; Gal. 5:13; 1 Tim. 5:14; BDAG 158). So in the writing of this letter, Paul understands himself to be presenting the Corinthians (ὑμῖν, the indirect object) with a particular opportunity, and that opportunity he further defines as καυχήματος ὑπὲρ ἡμῶν, "of boasting on our behalf." In other words, Paul is saying, "Rather than a formal self-recommendation, I am giving *you Corinthians* what you need to answer the interlopers' objections to me." Thus we translate his statement as "It is not *really* that we are recommending ourselves to you again; rather, we are giving you an opportunity to boast on our behalf." In what goes before in the letter, Paul has lined out both the nature of authentic ministry and extensive evidence that his mission lives up to a very high standard. The Corinthians have the content with which to boast on behalf of Paul and his mission. In giving the Corinthians this content, he has, in fact, been commending himself, but he suggests that he does not need to do so in a formal manner. Their relationship has already been established by Christ.

Having defined his actions, the apostle then explains *why* (ἵνα, *hina*) he has provided the Corinthians with such extensive evidence with which they can boast on behalf of him and his mission: "in order that you might have something to use against those boasting in appearance and not in heart" (ἵνα ἔχητε πρὸς τοὺς ἐν προσώπῳ καυχωμένους καὶ μὴ ἐν καρδίᾳ, *hina echēte pros tous en prosōpō kauchōmenous kai mē en kardia*). The term πρός plus the accusative (τούς . . . καυχωμένους) may speak of conscious purpose, but it

---

3. On this fairly rare use of the participle, see D. Wallace 1996: 653.

4. The word ἀφορμή occurs in the LXX only at 3 Macc. 3:2; Prov. 9:9; Ezek. 5:7. At Prov. 9:9, e.g., we read, "Give a wise person an opportunity, and he will become wiser; inform a just person, and he will continue to receive" (NETS).

probably marks a hostile relationship in this case ("to use against those boasting"; see BDAG 874.3dα). Paul also contrasts his form of boasting, which he describes as "in heart" (ἐν καρδίᾳ), with the opponent's boasting, which is "in appearance" (ἐν προσώπῳ; lit., in face). In both cases the preposition ἐν can be read as marking a "standard," that is, "according to the standard of the heart/appearance."[5] Thus the apostle contrasts the inner integrity of his ministry with a surface and appearance-oriented performance of the interlopers. For Paul in 2 Corinthians, the heart often is the locus of the true work of God (1:22; 2:4; 3:2–3, 15; 4:6; 5:12; 6:11; 7:3; 8:16; 9:7). Later in the letter, at 10:7, he chides the Corinthians for evaluating the situation in the church in a way that depends on outward appearance.

Thus read, Paul's words in 5:11–12 suggest that his actions in 2 Corinthians *do constitute what would normally be done in a self-recommendation*: the apostle is presenting the Corinthians with arguments that defend his character, his actions, and his motives. Yet this "self-recommendation" he has been carrying out via the book is not really a *true* self-recommendation, which is offered as a person comes for introduction to a person or community (thus the statement at 3:1 really constitutes a rebuke). Rather, Paul's purpose for the "self-recommendation" he carries out in the book is to offer an answer to those who have been openly critical of his ministry; it is a "self recommendation" type of boasting, but has a different purpose.[6] Therefore, we have translated the first statement in the verse as "It is not *really* that we are recommending ourselves to you again."

iii. The State of Paul's Mind (5:13)

The fact is that Paul, in offering what could be understood as a self-recommendation, could be tagged as crazy. Yet, "if we are out of our minds," he writes, "it is for God." Here again we find the apostle's Godward orientation in life. From Paul's standpoint, his life and his pattern of ministry can only be explained on the basis of it being "for God,"[7] for the sake of service and devotion to the one, true God.

5:13

Of course, others did not read the man this way, perhaps suggesting that his behavior (and perhaps his oratorical style)[8] was erratic, unpredictable to the

---

5. On this use of the preposition, see D. Wallace 1996: 372.

6. In line with this interpretation but with a slightly different read (as meant to be "non-sophistic"), Witherington (1995: 393) states, "While he is in fact commending himself, Paul says he is not (v. 12a), by which he means that he is doing so in an inoffensive and rhetorically nonsophistic way. The goal of this self-recommendation is that the converts have a reason to be proud and to boast about his ministry and not be ashamed of it."

7. Probably Θεῷ (*theō*, for God) should be understood as a dative of advantage. It may be, however, that Paul has in mind how he carries on his ministry "with reference to God" (dative of reference) in the sense that "these matters are between him and God" (so Bruce 1971: 207).

8. Harris notes that the terms ἐξίστημι (*existēmi*, be out of one's mind) and σωφρονέω (*sōphroneō*, be in one's right mind) were used in the rhetorical handbooks with reference to improper over against proper oratorical style. Thus Paul, in part, may be defending himself against the accusation that his public speaking is not up to par (see Harris 2005: 418).

point of indicating mental and/or emotional instability (see the comments on 1:15–22). At issue may be the (intense and emotional) way Paul is responding to the Corinthian crisis.

With the exception of two cases, all of the occurrences in the NT of the verb rendered "out of our mind" (ἐξίστημι, existēmi) carry the sense of being "astounded," and those described thus normally are astounded because a miracle has been performed.[9] Yet at Mark 3:21, where Jesus's family members respond to him negatively, intending to restrain him, and here at 2 Cor. 5:13, the word communicates the idea of being "out of one's senses," or "having lost the ability to reason soundly." This may be a reference to Paul's ecstatic experiences (Bruce 1971: 207). Thus, John Chrysostom (*Hom. 2 Cor.* 11.2) interprets Paul's words here as meaning, "Even if people think he is mad, everything he does is for the glory of God" (Bray 1999: 245). Or put another way, the apostle asserts ironically, "If we have lost our ability to reason soundly as we relate to you (as some claim), at least we are crazy people committed to God and his agenda!"

Then, playing off the idea of mental instability, he proclaims, "If we are of sound mind, it is for you." In contrast to an instability in reasoning ability, to be of sound mind (σωφρονέω, sōphroneō) means to be able to think in a sane, rational manner, to be sensible, or to keep one's head (BDAG 986).[10] The apostle declares that if his actions point to a sane and rational response to the Corinthians' situation, that response stems from a desire to benefit the Corinthians themselves.[11] "In short," Paul claims, "however you read me and my mission—as acting irrationally or rationally—be assured of this: I do what I do out of a resolute commitment to God and to you, God's church."

Reflection

Imagine a moment of conflict in your church. Relationships have become messy, misunderstandings have developed, people are beginning to form sides, and you are being accused in some way of lacking integrity in the matter. You are puzzled by this since you have been ministering in this context for a while, and you feel your conduct has always been aboveboard. In fact, you feel deeply hurt by the accusations that are being leveled at you, and you very much wonder why those to whom you have ministered faithfully, those for whom you have sacrificed a great deal, those whom you *know* have benefited from your ministry and who, by most indications, believe in your ministry—why they *do not step forward in your defense*. You are

9. All the NT uses of ἐξίστημι except this one occur in the Gospels and Acts (Matt. 12:23; Mark 2:12; 3:21; 5:42; 6:51; Luke 2:47; 8:56; 24:22; Acts 2:7, 12; 8:9, 11, 13; 9:21; 10:45; 12:16).
10. Mark 5:15; Luke 8:35; Rom. 12:3; 2 Cor. 5:13; Titus 2:6; 1 Pet. 4:7. The word is used, e.g., at Mark 5:15//Luke 8:35 of a man delivered from demon possession, who now is in his "right mind." At Rom. 12:3; Titus 2:6; and 1 Pet. 4:7 the word has more to do with being "sober-minded" in life.
11. The dative plural, ὑμῖν (hymin, for you), should be read as a dative of advantage.

being put in a position of defending yourself, a terribly awkward position, when others should be stepping up to vindicate you.

In point of fact, you may not need to imagine this scenario: you may have lived it. One of the most painful experiences in ministry leadership consists of unfair accusations against you being met by silence from those to whom you have poured out your life. Thankfully, you are not the first leader to experience this particular form of pain. In our passage at hand, Paul models for us ways to handle the moment.

Make sure your perspective is oriented to fearing the Lord, not people. Fear God. Appeal to people. Live "open to God." Have a life and words that speak to the consciences of people. If we reverentially live our lives "open to God," we will have the grounding from which to meet unfair opposition. And that orientation will not only help us to live lives that are worthy of defense, but also will help us see the elements of truth in the criticism. We may need to assess whether the evidence for our vindication is not obvious to others; we may need to repent of patterns in our leadership that have been hurtful and build a ministry life that people find easy to celebrate. Do we boast "in heart"? Or do we, like Paul's opponents, boast in surface matters (e.g., great speaking ability, growth of the church, a contingent of passionate followers)? At our deepest level, do we do whatever we do—read by some as crazy and others as sane—for God and the church? If we can answer those questions affirmatively, with integrity, then we have a basis for appealing to people, like Paul did, from a position of trust in God and confidence in our public witness.

Additional Notes

5:11. Some manuscripts have the hortatory subjunctive πείθωμεν (let us appeal to; $\mathfrak{P}^{46\ 99}$ P Ψ 629 2464 *pc* vg^ms), but the present-indicative form (gnomic in syntax) probably is original, for Paul is testifying of his actions.

5:12. Desiring a smoother transition, it is understandable why some witnesses have γάρ (D² K L P 048 33 365 630 1175 1241 1505 𝔐 sa), but the evidence for its exclusion is much stronger ($\mathfrak{P}^{46}$ ℵ B C D* F G Ψ 0243 81 104 326 1739 1881 2464 *pc* latt sy bo).

5:12. The reading of ὑμῶν, which garners strong external support ($\mathfrak{P}^{46}$ ℵ B 33 *pc* g vg^ms) over against ἡμῶν, seems to be so difficult as to override our normal nod to *lectio difficilior potior* (preference for the more difficult reading). As Harris points out (2005: 412), here we have a case in which the difficult reading is so difficult as to be virtually impossible. It is hard to conceive of Paul encouraging the Corinthians to boast about themselves!

5:12. In place of μὴ ἐν ($\mathfrak{P}^{46}$ ℵ B 0243 33 81 104 365 630 1175 1505 1739 1881 2464 *pc*) some manuscripts read οὐκ ἐν (D* F G) or οὐ alone (C D² Ψ 𝔐), but μή ἐν has the much stronger support, and as a general rule in Koine Greek, οὐ negates the indicative, while μή normally negates the remaining moods, including the infinitive and the participle (in this case καυχωμένους; see BDF 220).

b. The Ministry of Reconciliation (5:14–6:2)

In the first movement of the section (5:11–13), Paul declares that his life stands open before God and before the Corinthians, who should affirm his motives and the integrity of his ministry. The reference to "those boasting in appearance and not in heart" (5:12) again points to the interlopers, simultaneously lurking in the shadows (2:17; 4:2) and commanding the spotlight (11:5–6) of the Corinthian church. The false apostles offer a form of ministry that Paul categorically rejects as inappropriate.

In the movement of the section to which we now turn, the apostle asserts that the true gospel compels Paul to conduct his ministry as he does and places all who confess Christ's name under Christ's lordship. He presents the heart of that gospel, "one died on behalf of all, which means that all died" (5:14), and a key purpose of the gospel, "in order that the living might no longer live for themselves but for him who died and was raised for them" (5:15). In unpacking these proclamations, we need to ask to whom the "all" refers. Paul states further that, by the gospel's new creation, the old patterns and posturing of the world have been nullified: "New things have come." This offers a new perspective on God, ministry for God, and the dynamic of reconciliation. But we need to assess whether by "new creation" Paul refers to individual soteriology or eschatology, or whether he speaks of Christ as initiating the transformation of the whole cosmos through the transformation of individuals.

Beginning with 5:18 Paul focuses on reconciliation as a description of what God accomplishes through the gospel, using this as a basis for appealing to the Corinthians for their reconciliation to him, his ministry, and ultimately to God (5:20). In the passage we can identify four key themes (adapted from Turner 1989: 94–95):

God's initiation of reconciliation (5:18–19, 21)
Christ's mediation of reconciliation (5:18–19, 21)
Paul's proclamation of reconciliation (5:18, 20)
A plea for the Corinthians' appropriation of reconciliation (5:20; 6:1–2)

In probing Paul's words at this point, we need to assess, among other interpretive issues, the origin of Paul's concept of reconciliation and why he thinks the Corinthians need to be reconciled to God. Does he not believe they are true Christ-followers? Or does his purpose for this language lie elsewhere? An outline of the unit may be depicted as follows:

i. Ministry compelled by Christ's love (5:14–15)
ii. A new basis for evaluation (5:16–17)
iii. God's program of reconciliation and Paul's mission (5:18–19)
iv. Paul's plea to the Corinthians: "Be reconciled to God!" (5:20–6:2)

Exegesis and Exposition

5:14For the love of Christ constrains us, because we have come to this conclusion: that ⌜ ⌝ one died on behalf of all, which means that all died. 15And he died on behalf of all, in order that the living might no longer live for themselves but for him who died and was raised for them. 16So, from this point on, we don't understand anyone from a worldly perspective. ⌜Even if⌝ we have understood Christ from a worldly perspective, now we no longer understand him in this way. 17So if anyone is in Christ, he is a new creation; the old things have passed away, behold ⌜new things⌝ have come into being.

18Now all this is from God, who reconciled us to himself through Christ and has given us the ministry of reconciliation; 19—that God was in Christ reconciling the world to himself, not reckoning their transgressions against them—and having placed in us ⌜the word⌝ of reconciliation. 20⌜Therefore⌝ we are Christ's ambassadors. Certain that God himself is exhorting through us, we plead on Christ's behalf, be reconciled to God! 21The One who has never known sin, he made sin on our behalf, in order that we might become the righteousness of God in him. 6:1So, because we are fellow workers with him, we also strongly urge you not to receive God's grace in vain. 2For he says, "At the time of favor I listened to you, and on the day of salvation, I helped you." Pay attention! Now is the "preeminent time of God's favor!" Pay attention! Now is the "day of salvation"!

i. Ministry Compelled by Christ's Love (5:14–15)

Paul begins the unit by explaining (γάρ, *gar*) why he characterizes his min-   5:14–15
istry as consisting of this dual, interrelated devotion—a devotion to God as
his Lord and to the Corinthians as those to whom he ministers (5:13): "the
love of Christ constrains us." Most commentators interpret τοῦ Χριστοῦ (*tou
Christou*) as a subjective[1] rather than an objective[2] genitive, reading the phrase
to refer to "the love Christ has for us," rather than "our love for Christ," and
this seems to be the best interpretation on at least two primary grounds. First,
the immediate context emphasizes Christ's sacrificial death on the cross for
his people. Later in this verse, Paul confesses "that Christ died for all," and
in the next verse, "he died on behalf of all," and that act of giving himself in
death for the benefit of "all" certainly constitutes Christ's expression of love.
Second, in Paul's writings, when a personal use of the genitive follows on the

---

1. See, e.g., Thrall 1994: 408–9; Plummer 1915: 173. Furnish (1984: 309) lays out an extensive and convincing argument for reading τοῦ Χριστοῦ as a subjective genitive (see Gal. 2:20).
2. See, e.g., Héring 1958: 50. Spicq (e.g., 1994: 3.341) at times reads τοῦ Χριστοῦ as a "comprehensive genitive" that is both subjective and objective.

heels of the word ἀγάπη (*agapē*), as it does here, the construction speaks of the person "having or showing love, not the one receiving it" (Harris 2005: 418).[3]

Yet, what does the apostle mean that Christ's love "constrains us"? The verb συνέχω (*synechō*) occurs twelve times in the NT (Matt. 4:24; Luke 4:38; 8:37, 45; 12:50; 19:43; 22:63; Acts 7:57; 18:5; 28:8; 2 Cor. 5:14; Phil. 1:23). In the ancient world the word could connote something "held together," such as a fabric held together and stitched, or the universe being held together by the Lord (Wis. 1:7). The term also could mean "to hold together" in the sense of shutting or stopping something up (Ps. 68:16 [69:15 ET]; Isa. 52:15; Pss. Sol. 17.19; Acts 7:57). Other meanings include, "to press hard," "torment," or "guard." Although shades of some of these meanings may be reflected in the use at 2 Cor. 5:14, in this context commentators and translators normally interpret συνέχω either as communicating the sense of "to compel" (NKJV, NIV, NRSV) or "to control" (NLT, NASB, ESV, RSV). The first emphasizes urgency, and this may be involved in what Paul intends to communicate. The apostle experiences an urge to fulfill his mission given him by the Lord. The latter meaning, however, connotes restraint, which seems to be an emphasis in the broad semantic range of the term and seems appropriate in context. The English word "constrain," used in a number of older translations (YLT, Darby, KJV, ASV), carries both the sense of control and compulsion. The love of Christ, as expressed in the gospel, has taken hold of Paul, puts limits on his actions, and moves him in specific directions, constraining his course of actions in the world, calling him to a self-sacrificial love patterned by Christ himself. He has been boxed in and set on a particular course by the gospel and now lives only "for him who died and was raised" for him (5:15). In other words, he is a man under orders and cannot cavalierly set his own agendas in life and mission. This gospel constrains, boxing out self-indulgent self-love.

The clause κρίναντας τοῦτο (*krinantas touto*) may be read as causal: "because we have come to this conclusion." The verb (κρίνω, *krinō*), here in the form of an aorist participle, could be used by authors of the time to communicate the idea of arriving at a decision, a judgment, a conviction, or a conclusion. The question "At what conclusion has Paul arrived?" finds its answer in the balance of verse 14: "that one died on behalf of all, which means that all died" (ὅτι[4] εἷς ὑπὲρ πάντων ἀπέθανεν, ἄρα οἱ πάντες ἀπέθανον, *hoti heis hyper pantōn apethanen, ara hoi pantes apethanon*). For Paul, the second of these clauses, introduced by ἄρα (*ara*, consequently), may be inferred from the first. If Christ died on behalf of all, this means that all died with him.

At least two theological convictions find voice in these twin, logically connected confessions. The first expresses Christ's death as "on behalf of," or

---

3. In support of this point, Harris (2005: 418) lists Rom. 5:5; 8:35, 39; 15:30; 2 Cor. 8:24; 13:13; Eph. 2:4; 3:19; Phil. 1:9; Col. 1:8, 13; 1 Thess. 3:6; 2 Thess. 1:3; 3:5; Philem. 5, 7. He also observes that in no case is Christ ever the object of believers' ἀγάπη. Other scholars, such as Spicq (1965: 88; 1994: 3.341) and Collange (1972: 253) understand τοῦ Χριστοῦ at 5:14 to carry both an objective and a subjective sense.

4. The ὅτι clause expresses the content anticipated in the pronoun τοῦτο.

"for the sake of" all.[5] The grammatical construction ὑπέρ (*hyper*) + the genitive, where the genitive represents a group of people, connotes an action or event done in the interest of that group ("for, in behalf of, for the sake of someone;" BDAG 1030). Significantly, the construction finds expression in statements concerning sacrifice (Acts 21:26; Eph. 5:2; Heb. 9:7). A phrase similar to this one in 2 Cor. 5:14 occurs at Rom. 5:8, where Paul proclaims that Χριστὸς ὑπὲρ ἡμῶν ἀπέθανεν (*Christos hyper hēmōn apethanen*, Christ died on our behalf). Further, the language of "one" (εἷς) and "all" (πάντων) seems to invoke Paul's Adam-Christ theology (Bieringer and Lambrecht 1994: 377–78; Pate 1991: 139–40) and the concept of corporate solidarity, whereby the one and the many are identified. In this way we see a foreshadowing of a more full-blown theology that the apostle pens in his letter to the Romans, produced a year or so later (so Barnett 1997: 291).

Yet, as Harris (2005: 421) notes, this raises the question of the exact referent (or referents) for "all." Is Paul speaking of "all" humanity or "all" believers? In answering this question, we first should notice that since forms of πάντες (*pantes*) occur three times in verses 14–15, they should be understood as having the same referent. Second, to these references to "all" in verse 15 Paul adds a reference to "the living" (οἱ ζῶντες, *hoi zōntes*) who, having died, no longer live for themselves. The addition of this reference seems to have the purpose of making a distinction between the "all" and another group (in this case a subgroup), "the living," which most naturally refers to believers, those who have experienced new life in Christ. So the "all" refers to all people, and "the living" refers to believers. This insight is made more sure by the phrase in verse 15 that states, "who died and was raised for them" (τῷ ὑπὲρ αὐτῶν ἀποθανόντι καὶ ἐγερθέντι, *tō hyper autōn apothanonti kai egerthenti*), since Christ's resurrection is never said to have been accomplished on behalf of humanity in general (Harris 2005: 421).

But what does Paul mean when he writes, "which means that all died" (ἄρα οἱ πάντες ἀπέθανον, *ara hoi pantes apethanon*)?[6] The particle ἄρα (*ara*) introduces an inference ("consequently," "which means that") or perhaps a result (i.e., "with the result that"), and the key here is to understand the corollary between the two parts. That Christ "died for all" means that the atonement has been accomplished in such a way that Christ has died on behalf of all humanity (thus contra the concept of a limited atonement). He shared in the death (but not the sin), which all human beings share (Heb. 9:27–28), brought into the world by Adam's sin (Rom. 5:12, 14). Moreover, he drank of that death on behalf of all humanity; therefore, in that sense all humanity died that day in Christ's substitutionary experience of the condemnation that had passed from Adam to all humanity (Rom. 5:18). Yet this does not mean

---

5. The phrase certainly includes the idea of representation but also should be understood as including the idea of substitution (Witherington 1995: 394).

6. See the review of literature by Thrall (1994: 409–11), who explains six interpretations on offer.

that all humanity lives as a result of that death. "The living" live under the lordship of Christ (2 Cor. 5:14–15), having entered into new covenant with him (3:6); they have had the veil of separation removed from their hearts (3:14) and have received "the abundance of grace and the free gift of righteousness" (Rom. 5:17); it is they, "the living," whom Christ's death has liberated (2 Cor. 3:17) and benefited. Humanity in general is condemned, existing in a living death, headed for physical death (broadcast in Christ's death on the cross), and destined for destruction via God's judgment (2 Cor. 2:15; 4:3). To benefit from Christ's substitutionary death, the "all" must repent and believe the gospel.

At the beginning of verse 15, by repeating the clause translated "he died on behalf of all" (ὑπὲρ πάντων ἀπέθανεν, *hyper pantōn apethanen*), the apostle underscores the thought and goes on to explain the purpose of Christ's sacrificial death: "in order that the living might no longer live for themselves but for him who died and was raised for them." The false teachers of Corinth practice a worldly form of self-aggrandizement and one-upmanship politics in the church, seeking to win advantage over Paul in terms of church leadership. In no uncertain terms Paul wishes to show that such a posture runs counter to the very essence of what it means to belong to Christ. Christ died in order to win for himself a people, referred to here as "the living" (οἱ ζῶντες, *hoi zōntes*), who no longer would live for themselves, but rather for him. The pronoun ἑαυτοῖς (*heautois*, for themselves), which refers to believers, and the substantive participles referring to Christ as "him who died and was raised" (τῷ . . . ἀποθανόντι καὶ ἐγερθέντι, *tō . . . apothanonti kai egerthenti*) are datives of advantage. In other words, believers no longer live for the purpose of advantaging themselves—the natural course of human nature since the fall—but rather live for the advantage of Christ and his agenda for the world. This is what Paul means in verse 13 when he states that his actions, his very persona, exist "for God" and "for you." God and God's gospel ministry constitute Paul's life purpose and, indeed, the purpose of every believer. Believers do not live for themselves. Church leaders, therefore, do not carry out ministry for their own advantage.

ii. A New Basis for Evaluation (5:16–17)

5:16   Paul's intention for this unit becomes even clearer with the next two verses, which have to do with not recognizing or endorsing people on fleshly bases. He begins with a general principle expressing an implication or consequence (ὥστε, *hōste*, for this reason, so) of believers now living for Christ: "So, from this point on, we don't understand anyone from a worldly perspective." The verb translated "understand" (οἶδα, *oida*) has to do with "having information about" or "knowing" something. It could be used with the sense of intimacy of relationship, the knowledge of how to do a task, to grasp the meaning of something (perhaps through experience, as at 5:11), to recall, or to honor/respect based on merit (BDAG 693–94). Our translation at this point reflects the sense of "understanding" or "grasping the meaning" of something, for Paul has in mind one's bases of evaluating another person. Since every believer now lives for Christ, under Christ's lordship, evaluation of people "with respect to the flesh" no longer can be considered appropriate (cf. Rom. 14:4).

At times the apostle uses the words κατὰ σάρκα (*kata sarka*, with respect to the flesh),[7] a distinctly Pauline turn of phrase, to refer to physical descent (e.g., Rom. 1:3; 4:1; 9:3, 5; 1 Cor. 10:18), to being human (1 Cor. 1:26), or to that aspect of human nature by which a person acts in a worldly, inappropriate way rather than according to the Spirit (e.g., Rom. 8:4–5, 12–13). Paul uses the phrase four times elsewhere in 2 Corinthians with this final meaning (1:17; 10:2–3; 11:18), and this seems to be the sense in 5:16 as well. So, the gospel and living for Christ have precluded believers from evaluating others on worldly, fleshly terms.

Paul admits that in the past he has evaluated Christ in a worldly manner— "Even if we have[8] understood Christ from a worldly perspective"[9] (εἰ καὶ ἐγνώκαμεν κατὰ σάρκα Χριστόν, *ei kai egnōkamen kata sarka Christon*)—but insists that he does not know Christ on these terms any longer. With the first of these statements, the apostle almost certainly refers to his understanding of Christ before his conversion,[10] for in the next verse (v. 17) the "new creation" becomes the dividing point between a worldly way of evaluation and a new perspective "in Christ." Evaluation of Christ himself on worldly terms may be seen as the preeminent absurdity, for Paul had been confronted by Christ the Lord on the road to Damascus, and all his misjudgments lay shattered in the dust. The encounter put the lie to the adequacy of understanding people on fleshly bases, and Paul's reflection seems at least to hint at the irony of judging the exalted Christ!

The ὥστε (*hōste*, so that) clause at the beginning of verse 17 stands in parallel with the ὥστε clause in verse 16, both of which follow from the idea that those who are now alive in Christ no longer live for themselves:

5:17

> So, from this point on, we don't understand anyone from a worldly perspective. (5:16)

> So, if anyone is in Christ, he is a new creation. (5:17)

To be "in Christ," a phrase used seventy-six times in Paul, has been understood variously: it should probably be interpreted as a dative of association, "in relation to Christ." If any person has a relationship with Christ, "he is a

---

7. Paul uses κατὰ σάρκα twenty times in his letters: Rom. 1:3; 4:1; 8:4–5, 12–13; 9:3, 5; 1 Cor. 1:26; 10:18; 2 Cor. 1:17; 5:16 (2x); 10:2–3; 11:18; Gal. 4:23, 29; Eph. 6:5; Col. 3:22.

8. Clearly, based on its contrast with "now no longer" (νῦν οὐκέτι, *nyn ouketi*), the perfect-tense form should be read as consummative, referring to a process completed in the past (D. Wallace 1996: 577).

9. Keener (2005: 185) correctly objects to the view that Paul here denies interest in the historical Jesus (a view espoused by Bultmann, Conzelmann, et al.). Such a view reads modern existential concerns into Paul, who to the contrary was most interested in historical information about Jesus.

10. As Garland (1999: 282–85) states; see his discussion of the phrase.

new creation" (καινὴ κτίσις, *kainē ktisis*). A verb must be supplied in this terse assertion (which simply reads, "new creation"), and some translations have rendered it as a personal reference to the "anyone" (τις, *tis*) in Christ ("he is a new creation"; e.g., Witherington 1995: 395; NASB, NET, NLT, NLT², NIV, ESV; cf. Eph. 4:24). Jewish teachers of a later period could apply new-creation language to those experiencing personal renewal (perhaps proselytes), as well as to Israel's experience of forgiveness on the New Year's festival or on the Day of Atonement (Keener 2005: 185).

Others, however, have taken the new creation to refer to the new created order established by Christ (e.g., "there is a new creation"; Roetzel 2007: 80–81; NRSV, HCSB, TNIV),[11] which certainly takes in believers as newly created but places the phrase in a broader, eschatological context. The new bases for understanding others stems not simply from the individual person who has been transformed by the gospel but also from the kingdom values put in place under Christ's rule; a new eschatological order has been brought in. The love of Christ constrains (5:14); those alive in Christ live for Christ by Christ's principles and mandates. The old, worldly ways of evaluating others have passed away, with the old system of self-centeredness. Thus, understanding others "according to the flesh" must be counted among "the old things" that "have passed away." Rather, people should be understood in light of the risen Christ and his gospel, and this new basis for understanding should be counted among "the new things" that "have come into being." Given the Corinthians' present dalliance with false teachers, the new creation has implications for how they should understand ministry and the false teachers' criticisms of Paul.

iii. God's Program of Reconciliation and Paul's Mission (5:18–19)[12]

5:18-19 The "all this" (τὰ . . . πάντα, *ta . . . panta*) with which the apostle launches verse 18 refers especially to the grand confession of verse 17—God has brought about the new creation via Christ. This new creation comes "from God" (ἐκ τοῦ θεοῦ,[13] *ek tou theou*), and in bringing about new creation, God has accomplished two things immediately relevant for Paul's discussion. First, he has "reconciled us to himself through Christ," and second, he has "given us the ministry of reconciliation." The "us" (ἡμᾶς, *hēmas*) to whom Paul refers in the first half of the verse seems to be the apostle himself and his coworkers,

11. See references to new creation at Isa. 65:17; 66:22; 1 En. 72.1; Jub. 1.29; 4.26; 2 Bar. 44.12.

12. Some suggest that Paul has incorporated traditional material into the treatment of reconciliation at 5:18–21. Martin (1986: 138–40), e.g., has discerned such material on three bases: (1) the appeal to the Corinthians to be reconciled to God (v. 20) seems more appropriate to unbelievers than to established believers; (2) the literary structure of the section seems to reflect a carefully crafted "piece of soteriological credo," or confessional statement; and (3) the lines of 5:19b (μὴ λογιζόμενος αὐτοῖς τὰ παραπτώματα αὐτῶν, *mē logizomenos autois ta paraptōmata autōn*) and 5:20c (δεόμεθα ὑπὲρ Χριστοῦ, καταλλάγητε τῷ θεῷ, *deometha hyper Christou, katallagēte tō theō*) seem to be out of place. Yet Martin's proposals have not found wide acceptance among commentators.

13. This construction is a genitive of source.

for in the latter half of the verse God is said to have given "to us" (ἡμῖν, *hēmin*) the ministry[14] of reconciliation. In verse 19 he makes clear that reconciliation has a much broader scope (i.e., "the world"), but here he expresses the natural order of personal reconciliation before ministry proclamation. One must be reconciled to God before one can participate in the ministry of reconciliation. In Paul's case, the call to the latter followed immediately on the heels of the former (indeed, the sequence is hardly discernible): the apostle to the Gentiles was called in the same moment he was converted on the road to Damascus (Acts 9:1–19).

The concept of reconciliation, expressed in this passage in both verbal and noun forms, presents an important theological idea, though it receives relatively little press biblically. Among the writers of the NT, the verb (καταλλάσσω, *katallassō*) occurs only in Paul (2 Cor. 5:18–20 [3x]; 1 Cor. 7:11; Rom. 5:10 [2x]). Similarly, the noun (καταλλαγή, *katallagē*)[15] occurs twice in our passage (2 Cor. 5:18–19) and twice in Romans (5:11; 11:15).

Reconciliation has to do with "reestablishment of an interrupted or broken relationship," or the "exchange of hostility for a friendly relationship" (BDAG 521). This idea occurs also in pagan authors, and C. Breytenbach (1989: 100) has suggested that the politico-diplomatic context of Hellenistic peace treaties offers a backdrop to Paul's words in 2 Cor. 5. Yet Spicq (1994: 2.262) remarks, "Secular parallels can hardly shed light on the theological elaboration of so specifically Christian a reality as the reconciliation of God with humans." I. Marshall (1978) looks to 2 Maccabees especially for a theological origin of Paul's teaching on reconciliation (2 Macc. 1:5; 7:33; 8:29), for there God is reconciled to his people by their prayers or will be reconciled at the completion of the process of punishing his people. Yet Paul's use of reconciliation language is unique, for here it is not that God is reconciled to people but that God takes the initiative to reconcile human beings to himself: it is human beings who are in need of an act that will reconcile them to God (Kim 1997: 362). Thus Kim (1997: 368–71, 382) argues persuasively that "Paul developed his soteriological metaphor 'reconciliation' from his own Damascus

14. Bieringer (1994: 428) notes that Paul's ministry involved presenting to people the salvation that God brought about in Christ, not simply as a disseminator of information, but as one personally involved in the process of reconciliation as he appeals to people to respond to God's initiative. It may be that Paul continues to have Moses in mind as carrying out a ministry of reconciliation, to which Paul's ministry stands in typological relationship (cf. 3:6–9; 4:1). Scott (1998: 137–38) notes that both Philo (*Mos.* 2.166) and Josephus (*Ant.* 3.315) present Moses as a "reconciler" in the golden-calf incident of Exod. 32.

15. The use at Isa. 9:4 (9:5 ET) is the only occurrence of the noun in the LXX: "because with reconciliation they shall repay every garment and cloak acquired by deceit, and they will be willing to do so even if they have been burned by fire" (NETS). An obscure use of the cognate verb also occurs at Jer. 31:39 (48:39 ET). The cognates διαλλάσσομαι (*diallassomai*, be reconciled; e.g., Matt. 5:24) and διαλλάγη (*diallagē*, reconciliation) occur at various places in the biblical literature (the verb: Matt. 5:24; Judg. 19:3; 1 Sam. 29:4; 1 Esd. 4:31; 2 Macc. 6:27; Job 5:12; 12:20, 24; 36:28b; Wis. 15:4; 19:18; the noun: Sir. 22:22; 27:21), and the verb ἀποκαταλλάσσω (*apokatallassō*, reconcile) occurs at Eph. 2:16; Col. 1:20, 22.

experience," for 2 Cor. 5:11–21 is full of allusions to that encounter on the road.[16] Almost certainly, the use of the concept in the broader cultural contexts of his day was known and understood by Paul, but he seems to have developed the concept in his own way to express the unique work that God had done through Christ, a work he had experienced firsthand on a dusty road near Damascus.

As used by Paul, "reconciliation" assumes that a state of hostility exists between God and humans, who apart from God's action are considered "sinners" and "enemies" (Rom. 5:1–11). God acted to bring about reconciliation through Christ (Rom. 5:1–2, 6, 8, 10–11; 2 Cor. 5:19) and specifically worked through Christ to deal with the problem of sin (2 Cor. 5:19), in order to bring people back into relationship with himself (cf., 1 Pet. 3:18). This is how God "reconciled the world to himself," by "not reckoning their transgressions against" those in Christ (5:19).

"Transgressions" (παραπτώματα, *paraptōmata*)—a word that occurs in the NT mostly in plural form, as here in verse 19 (e.g., Matt. 6:15b; Mark 11:25, 26; Rom. 4:25; 5:16; Eph. 1:7; 2:5; Col. 2:13)—constitute "a violation of moral standards, offense, wrongdoing," or "sin" (BDAG 770). Such violations normally are committed by people against God, even as Adam sinned against God (e.g., Wis. 10:1; Rom. 5:15). Yet, because of Christ's death (2 Cor. 5:21), transgressions are not counted against those in relationship with him. The term λογίζομαι (*logizomai*) could be used in a mathematical sense, "to count," "calculate," or with the sense of an evaluation or estimation based on a calculation (BDAG 597). Thus God has not counted or reckoned transgressions against those in Christ, thus making it possible for them to be in right relation to God.

As noted above, Paul places a great deal of emphasis on God's role in reconciliation. The gospel was God's idea and his work. It is God who has "placed in us the word of reconciliation" (5:19). He does the reconciling and the calling to ministry. Thus it is God's program, his agenda, that stands behind Paul and his ministry. Various explanations can be offered for why ministers do what they do in the world, and Paul stands accused by troublemakers of a variety of motives (e.g., 1:12–22; 12:19). Yet he wishes to make clear the true origin and driving force of his mission. The true gospel proclaims what God has done and is doing in the world, not what any person seems to be accomplishing; if understood rightly, the gospel ministry must be grasped as radically God-centered. Thus God stands behind Paul's gospel, Paul's ministry, and Paul's approach to the proclamation of the gospel through his ministry.

---

16. Kim (1997) proposes that the use of the language in 2 Cor. 5, moreover, stems from Paul's desire to defend himself against opponents who railed against the apostle's past (and thus his present claim to apostolic leadership), calling him an enemy of Christ and the church. Thus it is out of Paul's own experience and in answer to the interlopers in Corinth that he crafts his "reconciliation" theology. This proposal makes a great deal of sense, especially since Paul's theological reflection occurs in the context of his defense of his ministry.

iv. Paul's Plea to the Corinthians: "Be Reconciled to God!" (5:20–6:2)

The implication (οὖν, *oun*, therefore) of God calling Paul and his coworkers   **5:20**
to the gospel ministry is that he and his coworkers "are Christ's ambassadors"
(πρεσβεύομεν, *presbeuomen*): they carry out their ministry "on Christ's behalf"
(ὑπὲρ Χριστοῦ, *hyper Christou*). The term πρεσβεύω (*presbeuō*) originally was
related to the concept of "being older" (cf. the cognate πρεσβύτερος, *presby-
teros*, elder); as a general pattern, officials were appointed from among the
elders of a people, since age was valued as a basis for wisdom and judgment.
So by the first century the term came to be used in a technical sense for one
who serves as an ambassador or envoy, who travels and represents another in
an official capacity (BDAG 861). For instance, it is used in inscriptions of the
era to speak of the emperor's legates (Thrall 1994: 436). Paul's use of this word
picture would have carried strong implications for the Corinthians, for in the
ancient world, an ambassador's role was seen as sacrosanct. In the political
realm, those to whom an ambassador was sent understood that he was to be
treated well and with respect. Dire consequences fell upon those who abused
an ambassador (Garland 1999: 295).

Yet Paul's role as ambassador stands as strikingly different from ambassadors in the political realm of his day. The normal pattern of diplomacy
involved the lesser political powers sending their ambassadors to the greater
political powers before whom they would plead their cases. For instance,
Roman emperors often received ambassadors from subject lands.[17] Yet in the
gospel we see an amazing reversal. The all-powerful God sends his ambassadors, seeking reconciliation with those whom he has created but who lack
a relationship with him.

The clause translated "certain that God himself is exhorting[18] through us"
(ὡς τοῦ θεοῦ παρακαλοῦντος δι᾽ ἡμῶν, *hōs tou theou parakalountos di' hēmōn*)
consists of ὡς plus a genitive absolute construction. When this occurs, it communicates "subjective motivation," and here, rather than "mere supposition"
("as though," "on the pretext that"), it communicates "actual fact" ("since,"
"in the conviction that"; Harris 2005: 446)—thus the translation "Certain."
Paul has a firm conviction that God speaks his message of reconciliation
through him. This conviction serves as the basis for his exhortation, his plea
to the Corinthians to be reconciled with God.

---

17. Garland (1999: 296) notes Augustus's boast in *Res gest*. 31: "Royal embassies from India,
never previously seen before any Roman general, were often sent to me. Our friendship was
sought through ambassadors by the Bastarnians and Scythians and by the kings of the Sarma-
tians, who live on both sides of the Don river, and by the kings of the Albanians and of the
Iberians and of the Medes."

18. For the use of παρακαλέω (*parakaleō*, encourage, exhort) in 2 Corinthians, see the
comments at 1:3 and the footnote there. The concept (verb or noun) occurs evenly spread
throughout, with clusters of uses in chaps. 7 and 8, plus 2:7–8; 5:20; 6:1; 7:4–13; 8:4, 6, 17; 9:5;
10:1; 12:8, 18; 13:11. In Paul's other writings, the noun occurs another nine times and the verb
another thirty-six times.

Yet, why would Paul speak to the Corinthians as those in need of reconciliation to God? Elsewhere he seems to assume that they are believers, and the words here most naturally read as addressed to unbelievers (Bruce 1971: 210). Some understand the statement as a general reference to Paul's preaching of the gospel, which involves the plea "Be reconciled to God," and 6:1 to be directly addressed to the Corinthians (Thrall 1994: 437–38). But this approach makes too sharp a division between 5:20–21 and 6:1–2, where Paul urges the Corinthians not to receive God's grace in an empty manner. Barnett's (1997: 311) understanding seems better, for he reads the verse as a call for the "Corinthians to be restored in their relationships with God." He goes on to suggest that due to the influence of the false teachers (2:17; 11:4), the Corinthians had drifted from a firm adherence to the apostle's gospel and had been called to question the ministry of the apostle himself (3:5–6; 4:2–12; 5:11–13; 6:3–10; 7:2–4). In the immediate context, therefore, he calls for them to embrace the reconciliation offered in the gospel.

Commenting on the relationship between the reconciliation of the world to God and relational reconciliation among believers, Turner (1989: 93) explains:

> Those who receive reconciliation have already received a taste, token, or guarantee of God's future work in their lives and in the universe as a whole. They also individually begin to model the kind of peaceful relationships in every area of life which God has ordained for the eschaton. Paul's strained relationship with the Corinthians is a serious aberration from this ideal, and he desperately desires to resolve the hostility.

In other words, the Corinthians' alienation from Paul says something about their relationship to the gospel: they are out of step with gospel realities. Thus, that some of the Corinthians are still not fully reconciled to Paul manifests a turbulence in their relationship with God, and that fact *might* indicate that they do not have a relationship with God at all.

We need to remember that just as with modern churches, the ancient churches involved a mix of people, the spiritual conditions of whom certainly were quite varied. In commenting on "the church at Corinth," it seems too easy for commentators to make sweeping generalizations about the spiritual state of "the Corinthians." Yet the individuals in that church probably ranged from those deeply committed to Christ to those who had little or no spiritual commitment at all. The data seems to indicate that some in the church were more aligned with Paul and his gospel (e.g., 7:8–9), and others had distanced themselves from Paul and hence from his gospel (e.g., 10:2). Thus Paul's call for reconciliation would have had a varied relevance for those addressed by the letter. Perhaps some needed to embrace the gospel. Others needed to examine themselves to see whether they were in the faith (Rom. 8:9, 17; 11:22). Later in the book, Paul raises the possibility that, while he generally assumes they are indwelled by Christ, some of them "might fail the test" (2 Cor. 13:5b). Still others needed to take a firm stand with Paul and confess their reconciliation to God as described in Paul's gospel.

The final verse[19] of chapter 5 has somewhat a formulaic cadence and grandeur, **5:21** perhaps because, as suggested below, the apostle is reflecting deeply on a grand passage of Scripture: Isa. 53. The flow and conceptual structure of the verse is depicted in figure 11.[20]

Figure 11 **The Flow of Thought in 5:21**

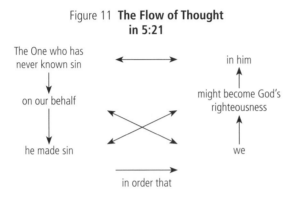

The apostle begins this theologically packed proclamation with a confession of Christ's sinlessness. It was a widely disseminated tradition in earliest Christianity that Jesus was sinless (John 7:18; 8:46; 14:30; 1 John 3:5, 7; Heb. 4:15; 7:26–28; 9:14; 1 Pet. 1:19; 2:22; 3:18), a claim made all the more pointed by the fact that many of the church's leaders were drawn from Jesus's family members or closest associates. Thus, Paul begins verse 21 with "the One who has never known sin" (τὸν μὴ γνόντα ἁμαρτίαν, *ton mē gnonta hamartian*). The verb γινώσκειν (*ginōskein*) connotes knowledge that has been acquired by personal participation; while the expression presents a timeless truth, the emphasis rests on Christ's sinlessness in his incarnation (Harris 2005: 450). The significance of this fact for the present verse has to do with Christ being a fit, "unblemished," substitutionary sacrifice for sins (Bruce 1971: 210; Martin 1986: 135), which Paul states as "he [God] made sin on our behalf."[21] This is another way of saying that Christ died "for sins" in the sense of Christ dying as a sacrifice for sins (Rom. 3:22–25; 5:6–8; 14:15; 2 Cor. 5:14–15; Gal. 1:4; 2:20; 3:13; 1 Thess. 5:9–10; 1 Tim. 2:6), delivering the reconciled from the consequences

19. Of this verse, Boers (2002: 530) writes, "The final christological statement in v. 21 is syntactically unconnected to what precedes and thematically does not continue the theme of God's reconciliation of vv. 18–20; it refers to Christ in completely unrelated terms as having been 'made sin' so that believers would become 'God's justice in him.'" On the contrary, rightly understood, the content of 5:21 serves as a resounding, climactic note on Paul's treatment of reconciliation.

20. Similar to, but distinct from, Harris's two analyses (2005: 449). The diagram here follows the phrase and clause order of the Greek text.

21. For an account of the variety of ways this clause has been interpreted, see Bieringer and Lambrecht 1994: 473–95.

of sin.[22] Martin (1986: 144) comments, "The elements are presented in their bare simplicity. The sinless Christ took our condemnation, that for us there might be condemnation no more." Gregory of Nazianzus (*Theological Orations* 5) put it this way: "But look at it in this manner; that as for my sake he was called a curse who destroyed my curse, and sin who takes away the sin of the world, and became a new Adam to take the place of the old, just so he makes my disobedience his own as head of the whole body" (Bray 1999: 253).

Yet it should be emphasized that the third-person singular verb form ἐποίησεν (*epoiēsen*) points to God the Father's initiative in assigning Christ the role of sin-bearer, even as we remember that Christ's sacrificial death was an expression of Christ's love (5:14). In other words, Father and Son are of one mind and purpose in the act that reconciles humans to himself. In speaking of Christ's identification with the reconciled, the purpose of this act (ἵνα) was "in order that we might become the righteousness of God in him." "The righteousness of God" stands as one of the most debated concepts in NT theology. Concerning its comprehensive scope in the NT, Bird (2008: 94) comments, "The 'righteousness of God' is an all-encompassing act that implements the entire plan of salvation, including justification, redemption, atonement, forgiveness, membership in the new covenant community, reconciliation, the gift of the Holy Spirit, power for a new obedience, union with Christ, freedom from sin, and vindication at the final judgment." So what does Paul mean when in 2 Cor. 5:21 he says, "that we might become the righteousness of God in him"?

To begin with, a key here is the little phrase "in him" (ἐν αὐτῷ, *en autō*). It is in relation to, or in identification with, Christ that believers become the righteousness of God. Harris (2005: 456), following Hoad (1957) and Barnett (1997: 313), has convincingly argued that Isa. 53 lies behind Paul's words at this point. That passage expresses the ideas of identification, substitution, and transformational interchange, which also lie at the heart of 2 Cor. 5:21.

Parallels between the two passages may be depicted as follows:

Christ sinless	"because he committed no lawlessness, nor was deceit found in his mouth." (Isa. 53:9 NETS)
Christ made sin on behalf of others	"This one bears our sins" (Isa. 53:4 NETS)
	"But he was wounded because of our acts of lawlessness and has been weakened because of our sins; upon him was the discipline of our peace; by his bruise we were healed. All we like sheep have gone astray; a man has strayed in his own way, and the Lord gave him over to our sins. . . . He himself shall bear their sins. . . . His soul was given over to death, and he was reckoned among the lawless, and he bore the sins of many, and because of their sins he was given over." (Isa. 53:5–6, 11–12 NETS)
The result	"to justify a righteous one" (Isa. 53:11c)*

*The Hebrew has more the sense "By his knowledge shall the righteous one, my servant, make many to be accounted righteous" (Isa. 53:11 ESV).

22. For an accessible treatment, see Bird 2008: 79–80.

The description of the Suffering One in Isa. 53 certainly includes the idea of substitution, and this is expressed in Paul's words ὑπὲρ ἡμῶν (*hyper hēmōn*), which connote advantage but more than mere advantage. In describing what Christ has done for believers, some have used the language of "transference" or "imputation." For this passage I think "transformational interchange" works better than these descriptions; although I think 5:21 plays a part in a broader theology of imputation, it does not express imputation specifically. Paul has in mind an interchange that works for transformation, for this is why the reconciled can serve as a presentation of God's righteousness to the world. It is more than positional, though it is positional ("in him"): it is transformational, as those of the new covenant are changed from glory to glory (3:18). M. Hooker (2008: 373) observes:

> Nevertheless, it is "we" who become the righteousness of God, and that righteousness should therefore be revealed in the lives of all believers, not just those of the apostles. If Christ is the source of "righteousness and sanctification" (1 Cor 1:30), then those who, in him, become what he is, should also embody righteousness and sanctification. Perhaps this explains why Paul goes on, in 6:14–7:1, to urge Christians to live holy lives.

Christ the sinless One, through identification with us, took sin on himself and died, serving as our sin sacrifice. We the unrighteous, through relationship with Christ, take on God's righteousness, are reconciled to God, and transformed as newly created, new-covenant people in the world. In other words, because of our identification with Christ, we as the new-covenant people of God are in right standing before God and are an expression of God's righteousness before the world.

The first two verses of chapter 6 serve as the applied conclusion to Paul's   **6:1-2**
theological reflections on reconciliation begun at 5:18, with several elements pointing back to the treatment of reconciliation.[23] Paul is a "fellow worker" (συνεργοῦντες, *synergountes*) with God since God has given him and his co-workers responsibility for the ministry of reconciliation (5:18) and the word of reconciliation (5:19). Thus, in strongly urging (παρακαλοῦμεν, *parakaloumen*) the Corinthians to respond to the message of the gospel (6:1),[24] Paul works as a conduit, with God exhorting through him (ὡς τοῦ θεοῦ παρακαλοῦντος δι' ἡμῶν, *hōs tou theou parakalountos di' hēmōn*) those in need of reconciliation

---

23. On grammatical grounds, some commentators insist that these verses must be the introduction to what follows, with παρακαλοῦμεν serving as the main verb delimited by the participles in 6:3–4, but this is not the case. In fact, from a pragmatic standpoint, the participles of 6:3 do not sit well with the verb παρακαλοῦμεν in 6:1 since they represent Paul's move to defend the general characteristics of his ministry, while the exhortation of verse 1 offers a pointed exhortation based on the theological substance of 5:18–21.

24. Paul wields παρακαλέω (*parakaleō*, urge) and παράκλησις (*paraklēsis*, encouragement) in various ways, and clusters of such use occur in chaps. 7–8, plus 2:7–8; 5:20; 6:1; 7:4–13; 8:4, 6, 17; 9:5; 10:1; 12:8, 18; 13:11. In Paul's other writings, the noun occurs another nine times and the verb another thirty-six times (see comments on 1:3 with the footnote there).

(5:20). Finally, Paul now expresses God's act of reconciliation through the gospel (5:18–21) as "the grace of God" and "salvation" (6:1–2). Yet, not only do these first two verses of chapter 6 provide a resounding, practical call to respond to the message of reconciliation found in 5:18–21; they also do so by working together in a logical relationship, with 6:2 functioning as the Scriptural reinforcement of the exhortation given in verse 1.

From the standpoint of grammatical structure, the conjunction δέ (*de*, so) links 6:1 to what has gone before, but καί (*kai*, also), rather than joining in this grammatical task, is used in an adjunctive sense, semantically pointing from the verb παρακαλέω back to the use of the same verb (in participial form) in 5:20: "we also strongly urge you." So in one breath Paul proclaims that God exhorts people through him and his coworkers (5:20), and in the next breath he states that he and his coworkers exhort the Corinthians to receive God's grace appropriately, in a way that bears spiritual fruit (6:1). Perhaps this is the most significant contextual signal that when Paul speaks of himself as a "fellow worker" (the referent is ambiguous in the Greek text), he has God in mind as the one with whom he cooperates in ministry (1 Cor. 3:9; Barrett 1973: 183). Furthermore, the participle συνεργοῦντες (*synergountes*) may be read as causal ("because we are fellow workers with him"): Paul points to his coworker status with God as the basis upon which he exhorts the Corinthians. Repeatedly in this letter the apostle reminds this wayward church that his words to them do not rest in his own authority, but in the authority of God, who has called him, appointed him to his ministry, sent him to the Corinthians, and speaks through him the reconciling word of salvation.

So Paul strongly urges the Corinthians "not to receive God's grace in vain" (μὴ εἰς κενὸν τὴν χάριν τοῦ θεοῦ δέξασθαι ὑμᾶς, *mē eis kenon tēn charin tou theou dexasthai hymas*). As seen from the seventeen other uses of χάρις in the book (1:2, 12, 15; 2:14; 4:15; 8:1, 4, 6–7, 9, 16, 19; 9:8, 14–15; 12:9; 13:13), the term can bear several meanings.[25] For instance, "grace" serves as the foundation for appropriate ministry and a contrast to fleshly wisdom (1:12), as a "benefit" experienced by the Corinthians via Paul's ministry (1:15), as an expression of graciousness (8:4, 7), or as an expression of thanks (8:16). Here Paul writes of God's gracious act of reaching out to the unreconciled with the gospel of salvation. This is especially clear in light of the content of 5:18–21 and the terms "salvation" and "help" in the quotation that follows in 6:2.

Given the present crisis in his relationship with the Corinthians (see the introduction), Paul worries that some among their number might end up responding to the gospel in a way that will be unfruitful. The word κενός (*kenos*) can refer to an empty object, such as an empty building (Josephus, *J.W.* 2.636) or an empty jug (Judg. 7:16). It can also speak, for instance, of being "empty-handed" when one comes to God (Exod. 23:15; 34:20; Deut.

---

25. The term χάρις could be used by ancient authors with the sense of graciousness, attractiveness, charm, winsomeness, a beneficent disposition toward someone, favor, grace, gracious care/help, goodwill, (a sign of) favor, a gracious deed/gift, benefaction, thanks (BDAG 1079–81).

16:16; Sir. 35:4 [35:6 ET]), or of someone being sent away "empty-handed" when they were supposed to have collected fruit (Mark 12:3; Luke 20:10–11). This moves us closer to the meaning at 6:2, for the term could be used with the figurative meaning "useless, without effect or result, in vain" (Deut. 32:47; Isa. 32:6; 1 Cor. 15:14), and this fits with the construction εἰς + the accusative (κενόν). Thus the term speaks of a foolish response that fails to lead to an intended result (Spicq 1994: 2.303–10).

There is some question as to the time frame Paul has in mind when he speaks of accepting the grace of God. Is he referring to a response they have made in the past (cf. 11:4; mistakenly suggested by some on the basis of the aorist form δέξασθαι), or does the verb carry more of a "global" or timeless sense of the response they had in the past, continue to have, and will have in the future (similarly Thrall 1994: 451)? The latter seems to be the case and points to the tension in discerning a person's spiritual condition: someone may seem to be standing with the community of faith, but only ongoing response and fruit give indication of where the person stands in relationship with God (Guthrie 1998: 134–38, 141–43). In other words, for some an encounter with the gospel comes to nothing. The apostle's concern is that, given a wrong turn in the Corinthians' response to his ministry, they could be led down an "empty" road to a spiritually barren land. His call to them, therefore, constitutes a challenge to return spiritually to a posture of complete acceptance of Paul and his gospel (6:11–13).

This call he reinforces (γάρ, gar) with a quotation of Isa. 49:8a: "'At the time of favor I listened to you, and on the day of salvation, I helped you.' Behold, now is 'the time of favor'; behold, now is the 'day of salvation'!" Notice first that the introductory formula, "He says" (λέγει, legei), presents the quoted words as if they are falling from the Lord's lips. This was a common means of introducing Scripture in Hellenistic synagogue sermons of the day and points to a view of God's Word as perennially "in play" and relevant (Heb. 4:12). Here Paul takes this introductory formula directly from Isaiah, who introduces the portion quoted here with οὕτως λέγει κύριος (houtōs legei kyrios, thus says the Lord). Isaiah 49:8 comes from a section in Isaiah (49–55) on the character, role, and challenging ministry of "the Servant of the Lord." Specifically, the verse sits in a passage (49:7–12) that focuses on the Servant's role and the results of his ministry (Smith 2009: 54, 349–54). The passage is significant for Paul's agenda at this point, tying the apostle's words to the broader redemptive drama found in Isa. 40–66, declaring how a covenant-keeping God draws a wayward people back to himself (Gignilliat 2007: 57–107).

In this word from God, God promises a time of his "favor" (רָצוֹן, rāṣôn; δεκτῷ, dektō), a day of "salvation" (יְשׁוּעָה, yěšûʿâ; σωτηρίας, sōtērias). The Greek term δεκτῷ delimits καιρῷ (kairō, time) and may be interpreted as referring to an "acceptable" time (that is, God's appointed time; HCSB, NASB, NET), or the time of God's "favor" (ESV, NIV; BDAG 217). An edge is given to the latter rendering, for it parallels the day of God's "salvation," on which God "helped" (ἐβοήθησα, eboēthēsa, gave assistance, aid) his Servant. The "time of" God's "favor" thus speaks of the time at which God heard (ἐπήκουσα, *epēkousa*) his Servant cry for help and favored him with deliverance. God will respond positively to his Servant—the parallel statement underscores the strong assurance given—but the time frame remains imprecise in the OT context. It is critical to understand, however, that the Servant of the Lord in this passage is closely associated with, and at points representative of, the broader people of God. Indeed, he "is the concrete means by which God's relationship with Israel is embodied and manifest" (Seitz 1994: 430).[26] Thus the prophecy speaks specifically to God's deliverance of the Servant but more broadly to his deliverance of his people.

Yet Paul knows the outcome of Isaiah's prophecy. Ultimately the words were fulfilled in the ministry of Jesus, the Servant, who has accomplished reconciliation between God and people through his death and resurrection (2 Cor. 5:14–15).[27] It is significant that in the next breath (49:8b), Isaiah says that the Servant will be appointed as a "covenant for the people" (לִבְרִית עָם, *librît ʿām*; the LXX reads εἰς διαθήκην ἐθνῶν, *eis diathēkēn ethnōn*), for Paul makes much of the new-covenant ministry established by Jesus (2 Cor. 3:6, 14), a ministry in which Paul participates as Jesus's ambassador of reconciliation. Thus Paul's ministry works as an extension of Jesus's ministry, calling the Corinthians to hear in a fresh way this word from the Lord initially given in Isaiah.[28]

Having quoted the OT passage, Paul is now applying it in pesher style[29] and draws out the implications of the Isaiah passage as immediately relevant and applicable to the Corinthians: "Pay attention! Now is the 'preeminent time of God's favor!' Pay attention! Now is the 'day of salvation'!" Notice the repetition of ἰδοὺ νῦν (*idou nyn*, pay attention now) at the beginning of each of these parallel lines. The first ἰδού functions to rivet the listeners' attention on what is about to be said, exhorting in effect, "Pay attention to this!" The second word, νῦν, presents the word of exhortation from the OT text as immediately relevant to the Corinthians, answering the question "When is this time of salvation?" The answer is "Right now!" Paul reckons that he and the Corinthians live in a new-covenant era (3:6), inaugurated by the death and resurrection of Jesus, bringing salvation to the renewed people of God based on Christ's sacrifice (5:14–15, 21). Yet this opportunity demands response,

26. See Seitz's discussion (1994: 430) of the complex mix in this section of the Lord addressing Israel as a nation and also addressing the Servant.

27. At Luke 4:18–19 Jesus defines his ministry by quoting Isa. 6:1–2a, which speaks of "the favorable year of the Lord" (ἐνιαυτὸν κυρίου δεκτὸν, *eniauton kyriou dekton*), a parallel statement to that given at Isa. 49:8.

28. Much has been made of Paul's use of the Servant Songs material in Paul's Epistles and Acts. As already noted in the commentary, Paul sees in Jesus's ministry a paradigm of his own. Yet Harris (2005: 460–61) correctly cautions against reading Paul's use of Isa. 49:8 here as a signal that Paul understands the words of Isa. 49 as paradigmatic of his own relationship with the Corinthian church (so Lane 1982). As Harris suggests, the words of the Isaiah passage, rather than speaking of Paul's own experience, speak to the Corinthians' experience and need to respond wholeheartedly to the gospel.

29. On pesher as an appropriation technique, see P. Balla, *CNTUOT* 768.

and the implication is that the Corinthians should respond positively, in this opportune time, to the living Word of God!

As in the quotation from Isaiah, the time is described as "favorable," but whereas the apostle uses the term δεκτῷ in the quotation, he now takes up an intensified cognate, εὐπρόσδεκτος (*euprosdektos*). Spicq (1994: 2.137) comments, "The choice of the compound form is surely intentional, and it must be given an intensive value. . . : 'Now, at the present, is a very favorable time, the most acceptable time there is.'" Thus we have translated the exclamation as "Now is the preeminent time of God's favor!" The second line reiterates that now is the era of God's salvation. God's grand deliverance of his people has been realized in the person and work of his Son, Jesus, who has reconciled people to God. This word of salvation should not be treated lightly but must be fully embraced by the Corinthians.

Reflection

Paul draws near the climax of his extended reflections on authentic ministry (2:14–7:4), building a substantive case for his full reclamation of the Corinthians to his mission, a case both personal and profoundly theological. In our passage at hand, he digs down to what may be considered the central foundation stone upon which he stands against the alienation and fragmentation of the Corinthian church: God's ministry and message of reconciliation. Packer (1961: 43–44) explains Paul:

> His royal Master had given him a message to proclaim; his whole business, therefore, was to deliver that message with exact and studious faithfulness, adding nothing, altering nothing, and omitting nothing. And he was to deliver it, not as another of man's bright ideas, needing to be beautified with the cosmetics and high heels of fashionable learning in order to make people look at it, but as a word from God, spoken in Christ's name, carrying Christ's authority, and to be authenticated in the hearers by the convincing power of Christ's Spirit.

It is "to be authenticated in the hearers" and in their relationships. Certainly this message lies at the heart of ministry in the church, but the church itself, composed as it is of people, is messy. People skew messages, both in their thinking and their living. In fact, the church's context, our fallen world, is at its very core a place of strained, shattering, and shattered relationships, and our mess blurs the message. We need the message to attend to our mess. As Tripp (2002: 116) states, the church is "a conversion, confession, repentance, reconciliation, forgiveness and sanctification center, where flawed people place their faith in Christ, gather to know and love him better, and learn to love others as he designed."

The fact is, "the word of reconciliation" really is our only hope. We cannot deliver ourselves from sin and its devastating power. Solzhenitsyn (1974: 168) writes of the sinfulness of human nature: "If only there were evil people somewhere insidiously committing evil deeds, and it were necessary only to separate them from the rest of us and destroy them. But the line dividing good and evil cuts through the heart of every human being." We all are sinners and in need. We cannot put things right with God. This word of our need for reconciliation will continue to be a strikingly unpopular message with the world, for it presupposes sin and the will of God, and our need for Christ, and a very particular vision of what he is about in the world. So be it. It is the only message upon which a Christian life and Christian ministry can be built. There is no other Christianity. Stott (1971: 96–97) ends his chapter on the death of Christ with this quote from Richard Hooker (1888: 490–91), a sixteenth-century English theologian: "Let it be counted folly, or phrensy, or fury, or whatsoever. It is our wisdom, and our comfort; we care for no knowledge in the world but this, that man hath sinned, and God hath suffered; that God hath made himself the sin of men, and that men are made the righteousness of God." Amen.

Additional Notes

5:14. The addition of εἰ by some witnesses (א² C* 048 0243 81 104 365 629ᶜ 630 1175 1739 ℓ 249 *pm* f vg sa boᵐˢ) clearly is secondary.

5:16. There exist a variety of derivatives from the strongly supported reading εἰ καὶ (𝔓⁴⁶ א* B D* 0225 0243 33 326 1739 1881 ℓ 249; Eus), including καί εἰ (F G), εἰ δέ (K), and εἰ δὲ καί (א² C² D¹ L P Ψ 81 104 365 630 1175 1241 1505 2464 𝔐 syʰ).

5:17. The external evidence for the preferred reading καινά (new things) is both early and of high quality (𝔓⁴⁶ א B C D* F G 048 0243 629 1175 1739 ℓ 249 vgˢᵗ co; Cl). Metzger (1994: 511) explains:

> Since the following sentence begins with τὰ δὲ πάντα, one could argue that the original reading was καινὰ τὰ πάντα (Dᶜ K P Ψ 629 Byzᵖᵗ *Lect* syrʰ goth ethᵖᵖ Marcion *al*) and that the reading καινά originated when the eye of a scribe accidentally passed over the first τὰ πάντα. Such an explanation, however, does not account for the reading τὰ πάντα καινά.

The reading τὰ πάντα καινά also is clearly secondary (6 33 81 365 614 630 1241 1505 1881 *pm* ar b vgᶜˡ; [Ambst]).

5:19. It is understandable why scribes either would replace the preferred reading τὸν λόγον with τὸ εὐαγγέλιον (𝔓⁴⁶), or supplement it, εὐαγγελίου τὸν λόγον (D* F G [d]), to overtly identify the message of reconciliation with "the gospel."

5:20. Based on the strength of the external evidence, οὖν should be retained (𝔓³⁴ א B C D² K L P 048 33 81 104 365 630 1175 1241 1505 1739 1881 2464 𝔐 vg sy) rather than omitted (as with 𝔓⁴⁶ D* F G Ψ).

c. The Impeccable Apostolic Credentials of Paul's Mission (6:3–10)

Rather abruptly, it seems, Paul shifts from a call for the Corinthians to be reconciled to God, to a catalog of his credentials as an apostle. Yet this list of the characteristics that mark his mission should be seen as very much in sync with a primary topic of this entire subdiscourse of the book (2:14–7:4), "Paul's Reflections on Authentic Ministry." In the more immediate context (5:11–7:4), this passage fills out the point notably underlined in 5:12, that Paul was giving the Corinthians an opportunity to be proud of him and was providing them with answers for those who criticized the apostle and his ministry. In short, the list of *circumstances* surrounding his ministry, *means* of accomplishing his ministry, and *perceptions* of his ministry found in 6:3–10 all offer a natural continuation of a discussion that focuses on "the ministry of reconciliation" given him by God (5:14–6:2); reconciliation is costly on numerous levels, including the level of frontline ministry. After explaining the motivation, the basis, the heart, and the implications of that ministry, Paul now offers a resounding picture of what is involved in the carrying out of such a ministry. Suffering, character, the power of God, and varied responses by those who hear the message mark his apostleship as genuine.

This catalog of hardships is one of four in the book (4:8–11; 6:4b–10; 11:23b–33; 12:10; cf. Rom. 8:35b; 1 Cor. 4:10–13; Phil. 4:12), and along with the list at 11:23b–33 it provides the most extensive overview of dynamics that marked Paul's work for the gospel. In chapter 11 the apostle shapes the list in terms of narrative, recounting his memories of various hardships; here 6:3–10 presents us with a structurally crafted passage of elevated style. Through rhythmic repetitions the apostle drives home a balanced picture of true ministry. Generally speaking, most commentators agree on the manner in which the structure of the passage should be understood:[1] an introduction (6:3–4a), followed by four movements (6:4b–5, 6–7a, 7b–8a, 8b–10) marked by both thematic development and a switch from the preposition ἐν (*en*, in) in the first two movements, to διά (*dia*, through) in the third,

---

1. E.g., Furnish 1984: 353–59; Harris 2005: 465–66; Martin 1986: 161–64; Thrall 1994: 453–54. Harris notes that there is movement from "circumstances" (6:4b–5) to "means" (6:6–7a), to an item that functions to communicate "means" in the third movement (6:7b), then back to "circumstances" (6:8a). Prudently, however, Harris reflects Moule's (1959: 196) caution: "II Cor. vi.4–10 is an impassioned and almost lyrical passage, where precision in the interpretation of the prepositions is probably impossible because the 'catalogue' has lured the writer into repeating a preposition in some instances where in sober prose it might have been unnatural."

and finally to ὡς (hōs, as) in the fourth. The first movement recounts nine hardships presented in three triads of ἐν phrases (6:4b–5). The second has a list of eight dynamics that enable ministry, also in the form of ἐν phrases (6:6–7a). The third movement is shorter and marked by the preposition διά. This third movement presents another enablement of ministry ("weapons of righteousness") and then two contrasting circumstances that surround ministry (6:7b–8a). The final movement rounds off the list with seven ὡς phrases presenting antitheses in ministry (6:8b–10). This schema can be seen in the left-hand column in the table below.

Yet there are other ways of reading the structure and development of this list. For instance, in addition to the structural analysis presented above, Harris (2005: 466–67) also provides an analysis by content, in which Paul moves from a list of "outward circumstances" (6:4b–5), to "qualities of character" (6:6), to "spiritual equipment" (6:7), to the "vicissitudes of ministry" (6:8–10). In Harris's analysis by content, as well as the grammatical analysis above, the phrase ἐν ὑπομονῇ πολλῇ (en hypomonē pollē, in great endurance) is considered part of the introduction to the list (6:3–4a), where Paul denies that his ministry has been offensive and claims, rather, that the ministry carried out by his mission has been completely commendable.

However, if instead the phrase ἐν ὑπομονῇ πολλῇ is considered part of the list,[2] other structural possibilities present themselves. As depicted in the right-hand column of the chart below, the list divides evenly into three main movements, each of which has two submovements. The first movement, marked by ἐν + dative, recites ten "circumstances" surrounding ministry, the first four being general circumstances (6:4b) and the last six more specific situations (6:5). The second movement, also marked by ἐν + dative, lists eight "manners and means" of ministry, the first four covering various manners in phrases composed of two words each (6:6a), and the last four "means" or enablements expressed in phrases of three words each (6:6b–7a). Finally, the last movement mirrors the first, with ten "contrasts" experienced in ministry: the first is another "enablement for ministry" (6:7b); the next are two more circumstances experienced in ministry (6:8a); and the last are seven "paradoxical perceptions" of Paul's ministry (6:8b–10). This final movement of ten divides into the first three, expressed by διά + genitive constructions; and the last seven, presented via ὡς + nominative constructions. Furthermore, if the first of these movements is divided into general and specific circumstances, then

---

2. It is true that Paul's endurance certainly characterizes all of the ministry described in the rest of the list (2 Cor. 1:6; 12:12), and yet this may be why he uses the phrase to head the list. It also is true that the nouns through 6:5 are plural, and thus ἐν ὑπομονῇ πολλῇ, as singular, does not fit that pattern. However, ὑπομονή normally occurs in singular form (the only exception in the Greek OT and the NT is 4 Macc. 7:9), and the addition of πολλῇ to the noun gives the sense of the endurance of which he speaks as occurring over a period of time in many circumstances.

we have a list of four, followed by a list of six, eight, and ten respectively, although the divisions between the various subgroupings are not clearly marked and should not be overstressed.

Generally speaking, however, Paul may be understood as moving in this list from the circumstances surrounding his ministry (the first ten), to the manner in which his ministry was conducted and the means by which it was effective (the next eight), and finally to the contrasts experienced in authentic ministry (the final ten).

The general consensus on the structure of 2 Cor. 6:4b–10	An alternate reading of the structure of 2 Cor. 6:4b–10
Ministry Hardships:	*Four General Circumstances:*
In General	
in a great deal of endurance,	in a great deal of endurance,
in afflictions,	in afflictions,
in crises,	in crises,
in stressful situations,	in stressful situations,
At the Hands of Others	*Six Specific Circumstances:*
in beatings,	in beatings,
in being put in jail,	in being put in jail,
in mobs,	in mobs,
In the Normal Course of Ministry	
in hard work,	in hard work,
in sleepless nights,	in sleepless nights,
in times of hunger,	in times of hunger,
Dynamics that Enable Ministry:	*Eight Manners and Means of Ministry:*
	Manner
in purity,	in purity,
in knowledge,	in knowledge,
in patience,	in patience,
in kindness,	in kindness,
	Means
in the Holy Spirit,	in the Holy Spirit,
in genuine love,	in genuine love,
in the word of truth,	in the word of truth,
in the power of God;	in the power of God;
Instruments and Circumstances:	*Ten Contrasts in Ministry:*
Means	*Means*
through the weapons of righteousness for the right hand and the left,	through the weapons of righteousness for the right hand and the left,
Circumstances	*Circumstances*
through honor and disrespect,	through honor and disrespect,
through slander and good report,	through slander and good report,
Antitheses in Ministry	*Contrasting Perceptions*
as deceivers, yet true,	as deceivers, yet true,
as unknown, yet well known,	as unknown, yet well known,
as dying and, behold, we live,	as dying and, behold, we live,

Instruments and Circumstances (cont.):	Ten Contrasts in Ministry (cont.):
as disciplined and yet not being killed,	as disciplined and yet not being killed,
as experiencing deep sorrow but constantly rejoicing,	as experiencing deep sorrow but constantly rejoicing,
as poor but making many rich,	as poor but making many rich,
as having nothing, yet really possessing everything.	as having nothing, yet really possessing everything.

I have chosen to structure the unit as follows:

i. Introduction to the hardship list (6:3–4a)
ii. General and specific circumstances (6:4b–5)
iii. The manner and means of Paul's ministry (6:6–7a)
iv. Contrasts in ministry (6:7b–10)

Exegesis and Exposition

[3]We make it a point not to offend anyone in any way, so that the ministry ⌐ ¬ won't be criticized, [4]but we are ⌐commending¬ ourselves in every way as God's ministers, in a great deal of endurance, in afflictions, in crises, in stressful situations, [5]in beatings, in being put in jail, in mobs, in hard work, in sleepless nights, in times of hunger, [6]in purity, in knowledge, in patience, in kindness, in the Holy Spirit, in genuine love, [7]in the word of truth, in the power of God; through weapons of righteousness for the right hand and the left, [8]through honor and disrespect, through slander and good report, as deceivers, yet true, [9]as unknown, yet well known, as dying and behold, we live, as ⌐disciplined¬ and yet not being killed, [10]as experiencing deep sorrow, but constantly rejoicing, as poor but making many rich, as having nothing and yet really possessing everything.

i. Introduction to the Hardship List (6:3–4a)

6:3   In 2 Cor. 6:3–4a Paul presents the introduction to his hardship list. Grammatically, Paul's statement seems strangely abrupt and disconnected from what has preceded it, since its verbal elements are participles yet do not delimit a main verb. Here we have a case, as occurs at a number of points in 2 Corinthians, where a participle stands in for a main verb. Paul seems to use this grammatical setup for the passage as a device that initiates the elevated style of the list itself. The contrasting participles, with their accompanying phrases and their objects, set a singsong rhythm that works nicely with the repetitive elements that follow on their heels in the list, and the contrast in this introduction anticipates the ten contrasts that end the list in verses 7b–10:

We make it a point not to offend anyone in any way, . . . *but* we are commending ourselves in every way.

Verse 3 first expresses Paul's intention for his ministry (carried out with his coworkers) to be characterized by appropriate behavior.[3] The term προσκοπή (*proskopē*, cause for offense) has to do with "an occasion for taking offense" or "making a misstep" (BDAG 882). Paul is not speaking of the "offensiveness" of the gospel to the spiritually blind (e.g., 1 Cor. 1:23) but rather of inappropriate actions, missteps, or misjudgments that offend cultural or moral sensibilities. He denies that through his actions or patterns of ministry he has given people a legitimate cause to be offended (cf., e.g., 2 Cor. 1:12–13). In this sense he has offended "no one in any way." Yet the purpose clause that follows gives the participial clause a note of intentionality; thus our translation: "We make it a point not to offend anyone in any way." The double negative, Μηδεμίαν ἐν μηδενί (*Mēdemian en mēdeni*, no one in any way) may be moved forward in the sentence for emphasis, constituting a firm denial on Paul's part that his actions and patterns of ministry are offensive in any conceivable sense or to any person who looks at those actions and patterns appropriately.

In the form of a purpose (ἵνα, *hina*) clause, Paul next explains his motive for living out such an exemplary ministry: "so that the ministry[4] won't be criticized." The negated (μή, *mē*) verb μωμάομαι (*mōmaomai*), here in a third-person singular aorist passive subjunctive form ("it might not be"), connotes finding fault with, criticizing, censuring, or blaming someone or something (BDAG 663). It occurs elsewhere in the NT only at 8:20,[5] where Paul speaks of taking along a traveling companion as a precaution, so that no one would find fault with his handling of the money given by his churches as a gift to the Jerusalem church. Thus in Christian ministry exemplary patterns of life and ministry provide a frontline defense against unnecessary criticism.

If verse 3 expresses Paul's determination that his mission will not cause others   **6:4a** to stumble, verse 4a presents the flip side of the coin:[6] "but we are commending ourselves in every way as God's ministers." So not only have Paul and his coworkers not acted inappropriately in carrying out their ministry; abundant evidence also points to their laudatory patterns of life and ministry. When Paul proclaims that they are "commending" (συνιστάντες, *synistantes*) themselves, he picks up a vitally important thread that has been woven through the book (3:1; 4:2; 5:12; 7:11; 10:12, 18; 12:11), one that lies at the heart of the apostle's intentions for 2 Corinthians (see the comments on 3:1 and 5:12). This letter plays an important part in commending Paul's mission to the Corinthians, arguing for their full affirmation of the apostle, his ministry, and his gospel.

Given the present context, take note of two points. First the phrase "in every way" (ἐν παντί, *en panti*) serves as the true introduction to the extensive list

---

3. The present participles in 6:3–4 may be considered "customary" presents, speaking of patterns of behavior.

4. A textual variant adds the word "our" (ἡμῶν, *hēmōn*), so many ETs include "our" in the verse (e.g., NET, NLT[2], ESV, NIV, NRSV). See the additional note on 6:3.

5. The term μωμάομαι also occurs in the LXX at Prov. 9:7; Wis. 10:14; Sir. 34:18.

6. The conjunction ἀλλά (*alla*, but) is highly contrastive in this case.

that follows. Through a wide variety of circumstances, in ways appropriate for a Christian minister, and by powerful ministry enablements, Paul and his coworkers present themselves as God-sent, God-empowered ministers of the highest order. The term translated "commending" here carries the nuance of providing "evidence of a personal characteristic or claim through action" (BDAG 972). These circumstances, the aspects of Paul's approach to ministry, the "tools" that enable him to minister, and even the varied perceptions of his work provide evidence of his mission's authenticity. Unlike the false teachers, Paul's work of ministry consists not of flowery oratory in cushioned contexts. Rather, his ministry is difficult and elicits varied responses. A comprehensive look at the apostle's ministry leads to the conclusion that Paul and his coworkers are "God's ministers" (θεοῦ διάκονοι, *theou diakonoi*). With the genitive form θεοῦ, Paul might mean to communicate that he and his mission belong to God (possession) or that they are sent from God (source), but either way, God stands behind Paul's ministry.

The apostle's opponents may have been arguing that Paul's ministry presented an uneven picture, one that called into question whether his mission really was from God. After all, "troubles," "beatings," "jail," "disgrace," perceived "deception," "punishment," "sorrow," and "poverty" may not seem to be hallmarks of an influential, effective, and "blessed" work. In presenting the following list as credentials for authentic ministry, however, the apostle offers a countercultural picture of "success" when it comes to carrying out God's work in the world, one that follows in the footsteps of the Suffering Servant, whose authentic ministry led to a cross. Such a ministry makes clear the power of God rather than the prominence of an individual. In carrying around "the dying of Jesus" in his ministry, Paul points to Jesus's life in a way that marks his ministry as an exemplar of true Christian mission (4:7–12).

ii. General and Specific Circumstances (6:4b–5)

6:4b   The first four descriptors in the list present a general picture of difficult circumstances[7] surrounding the apostle's ministry:

in a great deal of endurance	ἐν ὑπομονῇ πολλῇ (*en hypomonē pollē*)
in afflictions	ἐν θλίψεσιν (*en thlipsesin*)
in crises	ἐν ἀνάγκαις (*en anankais*)
in stressful situations	ἐν στενοχωρίαις (*en stenochōriais*)

We have seen the first two earlier in the book. Paul opens 2 Corinthians with a beautifully articulated blessing, praising God for his encouragement amid affliction (1:3–7). At 1:6, using a similar prepositional phrase as in 2 Cor. 6:4, the apostle notes that the Corinthians also experience encouragement as they embrace endurance of the same kinds of sufferings (ἐν ὑπομονῇ τῶν

---

7. The ἐν + the dative construction communicates the idea of "sphere," and here the spheres mentioned are circumstances or experiences.

αὐτῶν παθημάτων, *en hypomonē tōn autōn pathēmatōn*; 1:6) Paul suffered. Later in the book, in yet another passage speaking to the validation of Paul's ministry, he writes in 12:12, "The signs of an apostle were performed among you in all endurance" (ἐν πάσῃ ὑπομονῇ, *en pasē hypomonē*). In our passage under consideration, Paul describes the endurance demanded by his ministry as "a great deal of" or "much" (NASB) or "great" endurance (e.g., HCSB, NIV, NLT², ESV, NRSV). Endurance involves holding out or bearing up in the face of hardships of various kinds (BDAG 1039). Such endurance presents the manner in which he engages the "troubles," "pressures," and "stressful circumstances" that follow in the list; thus it serves as a fitting header for the list.

In the blessing of chapter 1, Paul also mentions "affliction" (1:4), a theme reiterated throughout the first eight chapters of the book (1:8; 2:4; 4:17; 6:4; 7:4; 8:2, 13). As noted in the comments on 1:4, the word rarely occurs outside of biblical Greek, and in the biblical literature it could refer to difficult circumstances or "troubles" (so the NIV) that bring about distress, such as forms of oppression or persecution, or the inward emotion of anguish produced by such difficult circumstances. The NT authors often use the word with reference to persecution. Thus the NET renders the word at this point as "persecutions."[8]

Next Paul mentions that he has faced "crises," or "pressures" (ἀνάγκαις, *anankais*; 9:7; 12:10), and "stressful situations" (στενοχωρίαις, *stenochōriais*; 12:10), terms that appear again in the brief difficulties list at 12:10. The first word could be used to speak of pressure or some form of constraint or necessity brought to bear in a situation.[9] Thus it could connote compulsion by torture, or as something understood to be necessary given a certain set of circumstances (e.g., the common use in Hebrews, e.g., 7:12, 27; 9:16, 23). Paul uses the word more generally to speak of trouble or a calamity leading to emotional distress—what we might refer to as a "crisis." The second term (στενοχωρίαις) refers to "a set of stressful circumstances, distress, difficulty, anguish," or "trouble" (BDAG 60–61, 943).[10] Outside of 2 Corinthians, Paul uses this word only in Romans, where he writes, on the one hand, of the "distress" that evil people will eventually face (2:9) and, on the other, of the inability of "difficulties" to separate the child of God from the love of Christ (8:35). In both cases our word follows immediately on the heels of the word θλῖψις (*thlipsis*, affliction), which here occurs just two words back in the list. Together the terms translated in 2 Cor. 6:4 as "afflictions," "crises," and "stressful situations" present a multifaceted picture of the stress-infused

---

8. The word θλῖψις is used over one hundred times in the LXX and a total of forty-five times in the NT.

9. The term ἀνάγκη appears seventeen times in the NT: Matt. 18:7; Luke 14:18; 21:23; Rom. 13:5; 1 Cor. 7:26, 37; 9:16; 2 Cor. 6:4; 9:7; 12:10; 1 Thess. 3:7; Philem. 14; Heb. 7:12, 27; 9:16, 23; Jude 3.

10. This noun occurs thirteen times in the LXX: Deut. 28:53, 55, 57; Add. Esth. 11:8; 14:1; 1 Macc. 2:53; 13:3; 3 Macc. 2:10; Wis. 5:3; Sir. 10:26; Isa. 8:22–23; 30:6.

challenges, indeed the tapestry of trials that were part and parcel of the apostle's mission.

6:5   Now Paul's list of hardships moves from the general to the specific, and this subgroup of six phrases can be divided evenly into two groups of three:

Persecution	Other ministry challenges
in beatings,	in hard work,
in being put in jail,	in sleepless nights,
in mobs,	in times of hunger,

"In beatings, in being put in jail," and "in mobs" describe specific situations in which the apostle and his fellow ministers faced persecution, unjust abuse at the hands of others, and the first two, "beatings" (πληγαῖς, *plēgais*) and being thrown in jail (φυλακαῖς, *phylakais*), are also mentioned in the hardship list at 11:23b–33. The third (ἀκαταστασίαις, *akatastasiais*) refers to disturbances or tumults and probably points to mob violence. Luke's reports that Paul often faced beatings, attacks by mobs, and being put in prison (Acts 13:50; 14:19; 16:22–23; 17:5; 18:12; 19:29–30; 21:30–36; 23:35) highlight normal dangers that followed in the wake of the countercultural gospel, a message that at times unsettled the established powers of official Judaism and Rome.

The next three phrases, "in hard work, in sleepless nights," and "in times of hunger," refer to challenges that characterize normal situations faced in missionary ministry. All three of the experiences listed in the second group of three are also found in the hardship list of 11:23b–33. The first term, κόπος (*kopos*), could refer generally to discomfort, distress, or trouble (e.g., NET, "troubles"), but most take it here to speak of burdensome work or labor (e.g., NASB, HCSB, NLT², ESV, NIV), and rightly so, since the apostle uses the word with this meaning at a number of points in his writings (1 Cor. 3:8; 15:58; 2 Cor. 10:15; 1 Thess. 1:3; 2 Thess. 3:8). As Paul moved from place to place in the Mediterranean world, he was carrying out cross-cultural ministry, working hard to build relationships with leaders in his young churches, evangelizing the lost, conducting theological training of new believers, corresponding with his network of churches, and often supporting himself while doing all of the above! Hard work indeed.

The second term in this subgroup of three, ἀγρυπνία (*agrypnia*), could connote either sleeplessness or a deep concern of the kind that might keep one up at night (BDAG 16), but it probably refers to the former. Much less common than κόπος, we find this term for sleeplessness only here and in another hardship list at 11:27. The third term, νηστεία (*nēsteia*), could be interpreted as a reference to fasting (so Tyndale; cf. Luke 2:37; Acts 14:23; 27:9), but it probably refers to times that Paul went hungry. Both here in chapter 6 and in 2 Cor. 11:27 the stringing of the three experiences—hard work, sleeplessness, and hunger—seem to stress the depletion of physical resources that happens as Paul pours himself out in ministry.

iii. The Manner and Means of Paul's Ministry (6:6–7a)

If the first ten phrases in Paul's description present a picture of the challenges **6:6** surrounding authentic ministry, the next eight delineate first the manner in which Paul's mission has been carried out (6:6a) and then the means (6:6b–7a) by which his ministry has been enabled. The first group consists of the preposition plus a single word, and each of the four phrases in the second group have a two-word description (in Greek) of the means for ministry:[11]

Manner	Means
in purity,	in the Holy Spirit,
in knowledge,	in genuine love,
in patience,	in the word of truth,
in kindness,	in the power of God

Ἁγνότης (*hagnotēti*), a rare term found in the biblical literature only here and at 11:3, refers perhaps to purity of behavior or motive (i.e., "sincerity"), but the word is so little used that it is hard to pinpoint the exact nuance. At 11:3 (if those manuscripts that contain this variant are followed) Paul uses the term in tandem with ἁπλότης (*haplotēs*), which speaks of simplicity or sincerity. The context of 11:3 puts both terms as opposites of corruption, pointing to sincerity and a chaste devotion to Christ; so perhaps we are not much off the mark with the translation "purity." The term translated "knowledge" (γνῶσις, *gnōsis*), on the other hand, finds wide expression in Paul[12] and has already been used twice in this book, both times in contexts dealing with the knowledge of God (2 Cor. 2:14; 4:6).[13] At 2:14, for instance, Paul uses the figure of burning incense in a triumphal procession in speaking of the proclamation of the gospel as "making known . . . the aroma/smell of knowledge about him." In the contexts at 4:6 and 11:6 it seems that when Paul uses the term γνῶσις, he means knowledge of the gospel. The description might seem a bit out of place with the other three characteristics in this group of four, until we understand that for Paul knowledge of God is a proper understanding of who God is but much more than that. As explained in the comments on 4:6, "knowledge of God" has relational overtones; it is a knowledge that is personally grasped as one experiences the presence of the Lord through the transforming work of Christ. This is not "knowlege-as-instrument" but "knowledge" as a person

---

11. The ἐν + dative construction communicates a dative of manner in the first group of four phrases and dative of means in the second group of four. As D. Wallace (1996: 161–62) notes, ἐν serves as the workhorse among the prepositions of the NT, occurring over 2,700 times. Normally we would translate a dative of manner with the English preposition "with," and for a dative of means use "by," "by means of," or "with." Yet the style of Paul's list thrums with the repeated preposition through the first eighteen phrases, and staying with the ET "in" maintains a sense of this aspect of the list's crafting.

12. Used twenty-three times in Paul's writings: Rom. 2:20; 11:33; 15:14; 1 Cor. 1:5; 8:1 (2x), 7, 10–11; 12:8; 13:2, 8; 14:6; 2 Cor. 2:14; 4:6; 6:6; 8:7; 10:5; 11:6; Eph. 3:19; Phil. 3:8; Col. 2:3; 1 Tim. 6:20.

13. The term γνῶσις is also used at 2 Cor. 8:7; 10:5; and 11:6.

shaper. Thus someone who has a knowledge of God has a character shaped by that relationship.[14]

Further, the apostle and his ministry team have conducted their ministry with "patience" (μακροθυμία, *makrothymia*) and "kindness" (χρηστότης, *chrēstotēs*). The former refers variously to remaining calm "while awaiting an outcome," "patience," or "endurance." It also can connote enduring while being provoked in a difficult situation. The latter term, translated here as "kindness," speaks of doing what is good or right in relation to others and can refer to being helpful, beneficial, kind, or generous (BDAG 612, 1090). Both terms are used of God and of appropriate responses as believers interact with one another. The terms occur together in the "fruit of the Spirit" list of Gal. 5:22–23 and in the exhortation at Col. 3:12 to "clothe yourselves with" certain qualities that make for healthy community.[15] Thus in living out patience and kindness, believers emulate the character of God, who is patient and kind. Paul and his mission appropriately model these characteristics as normal for an authentic ministry and here speak of them as patterns that characterize their activities.

Hence purity, knowledge, patience, and kindness present the manner in which authentic ministry is carried out; then "in the Holy Spirit, in genuine love, in the word of truth," and "in the power of God" point to the means by which ministry works effectively. For the apostle Paul, true Christian ministry cannot progress on the basis of human activity alone; fundamentally it is a God-ordained, God-empowered, and God-sustained work, and so he sees himself as inherently inadequate for the task. God has made Paul and his coworkers adequate as ministers of the new covenant (3:5–6).

In 2 Corinthians Paul has already placed a great deal of emphasis on the role of the Spirit in the Christian life and in the work of true ministry (1:22; 3:3, 6, 8, 17–18; 5:5). Some commentators have remarked on how strange it is to find a reference to the Holy Spirit in this list (e.g., Plummer 1915: 196); yet Paul speaks here of all the varied facets of authentic ministry, and the third member of the Trinity stands at the heart of the work. Under the new covenant, the Spirit transforms human hearts, giving life and freedom (3:3, 6, 17). Further, Christ-followers experience relationship with the Spirit as a down payment of the eschatological inheritance to come (5:5).

At first blush, "in genuine love" seems to be another character quality rather than a ministry enablement. Yet "love" sits naturally following reference to the work of the Holy Spirit, since love is one fruit of the Spirit and the hallmark

---

14. In American evangelical culture we might say, "That person knows God," speaking not of their theological understanding but of their personal experience of relationship. This appraisal is not intended to make a dichotomy between theology and experience but suggests that a robust relationship should flow out of right theology.

15. "Patience" is used of God at Rom. 2:4; 9:22; 1 Pet. 3:20 and of Christ at 1 Tim. 1:16; 2 Pet. 3:15, and God is said to be kind at Rom. 2:4; 11:22; Eph. 2:7; Titus 3:4. The NT authors write of patience, e.g., as a defining characteristic of Christian behavior at Gal. 5:22; Eph. 4:2; Col. 1:11; 3:12; and of kindness at Gal. 5:22; Col. 3:12.

of Christian conduct in the NT (Gal. 5:22; Rom. 12:9–21; John 13:34–35). Also, at 2:4 Paul underscores that love serves as a driving force in his ministry to the Corinthians. Indeed, Christ's love constrains Paul, guiding him in the ministry God has given him to do. This love, moreover, he describes as "genuine" (ἀνυπόκριτος, *anypokritos*),[16] being authentic, without pretense. In other words, the displays of, or expressions of, affection line up with a sincerity concerning the relationship: "one does not play-act in brotherly relationships" (1 John 3:18; Spicq 1994: 1.135).

The final two phrases beginning with the preposition ἐν (*en*) sit at the beginning **6:7a** of verse 7: "in the word of truth, in the power of God." Now "the word of truth" (λόγῳ ἀληθείας, *logō alētheias*) could be rendered as "truthful speech" (thus ἀληθείας read as an attributive genitive; so, e.g., ESV, NET, NIV, NRSV), and Paul certainly spends a good deal of time in 2 Corinthians defending his integrity in terms of what he has said (e.g., 1:17–18; 7:14; 12:6). Yet there are good reasons for understanding this phrase to refer to the apostle's proclamation of the gospel. First, three times elsewhere in his writings, Paul refers to "the word of truth" (τὸν λόγον τῆς ἀληθείας, *ton logon tēs alētheias*;[17] Eph. 1:13; Col. 1:5; 2 Tim. 2:15). In Eph. 1:13 and Col. 1:5 the phrase is associated with the proclamation of the gospel, and in 2 Tim. 2:15 it means the whole of Christian teaching. Second, the three other times in 2 Corinthians where Paul crafts a phrase using λόγος (*logos*, word) plus a genitive singular term to describe the word, he is referring to the Word of God, particularly God's message of the gospel. In fact, at 2:17 and 4:2 Paul writes of "the Word of God" (τὸν λόγον τοῦ θεοῦ, *ton logon tou theou*), and at 5:19 of "the word of reconciliation" (τὸν λόγον τῆς καταλλαγῆς, *ton logon tēs katallagēs*). Finally, at 4:2 Paul also refers to "the manifestation of the truth" (τῇ φανερώσει τῆς ἀληθείας, *tē phanerōsei tēs alētheias*) in the context of speaking about authentic proclamation of God's Word. Thus it seems best to understand the phrase at 6:7 as "the word of truth," as referring to the proclamation of God's Word, rather than truthful speech.

The final "in" phrase in the list refers to God's power. At three critical junctures in 2 Corinthians, Paul juxtaposes God's power with human weakness. At 4:7 he writes, "But we have this treasure in jars of clay, in order that this extraordinary power might be seen for what it is, power that comes from God and not from us." Thus the frailty of human experience manifests God's power. Similarly, Paul speaks out of his own experience in 12:8–9, where he writes of his request to God that his thorn in the flesh might be removed. The response was not what Paul wanted. The apostle explains: "But He said to me, 'My grace is sufficient for you, for power is perfected in weakness.' Therefore, I will most gladly boast all the more about my weaknesses, so that Christ's

---

16. Used elsewhere in the NT at Rom. 12:9; 2 Cor. 6:6; 1 Tim. 1:5; 2 Tim. 1:5; James 3:17; 1 Pet. 1:22.

17. As Harris (2005: 476) points out, the anarthrous expression should not be distinguished in meaning from the articular renderings of the phrase.

power may reside in me" (HCSB). Thus weaknesses facilitate power. This paradigm was truly fleshed out in the ministry and passion of Jesus, as Paul writes in 13:4: "He was crucified in weakness, but He lives by God's power. For we also are weak in Him, yet toward you we will live with Him by God's power" (HCSB). Thus the paradigm of "weakness" existing in dynamic relationship to "power" stands behind Paul's understanding of the power of God as it works in Christian ministry. Yet, with our phrase under consideration the apostle also could have in mind specifically manifestations of the miraculous, as at 12:12, but his primary point certainly is that authentic ministers carry out a work enabled by the power of God, and the broader context places that enablement as in concert with the minister's weaknesses.

iv. Contrasts in Ministry (6:7b–10)

6:7b Thus far in this section, Paul has rhythmically drummed home his list by using prepositional phrases beginning with ἐν (*en*). Now he shifts stylistic gears to use phrases beginning with διά (*dia*), and the first of these reads "through weapons of righteousness for the right hand and the left" (διὰ τῶν ὅπλων τῆς δικαιοσύνης τῶν δεξιῶν καὶ ἀριστερῶν, *dia tōn hoplōn tēs dikaiosynēs tōn dexiōn kai aristerōn*). This phrase serves as a hinge in the list, continuing the subtopic on enablements for ministry—the use of διά here is instrumental (by)—but using a different preposition and also initiating a new subtopic on contrasts in ministry (marked by contrasting elements separated by the conjunction καί, *kai*).

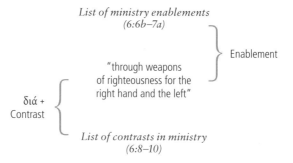

Figure 12 **Enablement and Contrast in Paul's Ministry**

The word ὅπλον (*hoplon*) could be used to mean "tool" (as probably at Rom. 6:13), but given Paul's employment of the term again at 2 Cor. 10:4,[18] in a context that clearly speaks of warfare, it should be understood as referring to "weapons," and more specifically spiritual weapons. Now these are described as "weapons of righteousness," and there are several ways of

---

18. The passage reads, "for the weapons of our warfare are not human weapons, but are made powerful by God for tearing down strongholds. We tear down arguments" (2 Cor. 10:4 NET).

interpreting the phrase "of righteousness" (Harris 2005: 477), among which four are most compelling:

1. As a descriptive genitive, or more particularly, an attributive genitive: "righteous weapons"
2. As an epexegetic genitive: "weapons that consist of righteousness"
3. As an objective genitive: "weapons that promote righteousness"
4. As a subjective genitive: "weapons that flow out of righteousness" (or from the Righteous One)

Given the greatly varied use of "righteousness" (δικαιοσύνη, *dikaiosynē*) in Paul, it is difficult to decide between these options. I am not convinced that the parallel with the genitives of Eph. 6:11, 13 ("armor of God") is close enough to tip the balance in favor of option 4 (contra Harris 2005: 477), although the weapon imagery draws a clear parallel to Eph. 6:11–17, and the context emphasizes ministry as enabled by God. On the other hand, perhaps Paul simply attributes righteousness to the weapons he has in mind (thus option 1). Accordingly, the apostle may be asserting that the "tools of his trade" (to mix our metaphors here) are of an exemplary character when compared to those of his opponents. Further, Harris probably is correct that the imagery finds its greater focus in the references to "the right hand and the left." A sword and a shield are the two weapons mentioned in Eph. 6, one for the right hand and the other for the left, one primarily for attack and the other primarily for defense. If these are the weapons in mind, they give a balanced picture of ministry as both a spiritual offensive and a defensive endeavor. Nevertheless, this brief phrase offers no certainty in the matter beyond conjuring an image of multiple and righteous weapons for conducting spiritual warfare (Barrett 1973: 188; P. Hughes 1962: 231). What is certain is that Paul and his fellow workers stand well equipped to carry out their fight for the faith.

Contrasting circumstances that show the variability of ministry comprise the remainder of the list. Thus the first two of these phrases continue the use of διά, now connoting circumstances Paul has experienced in ministry: "through honor and disrespect, through slander and good report" (διὰ δόξης καὶ ἀτιμίας, διὰ δυσφημίας καὶ εὐφημίας, *dia doxēs kai atimias, dia dysphēmias kai euphēmias*). Paul arranges these phrases in an ABBA pattern as follows:

6:8

A through honor and
  B disrespect,
  B′ through slander and
A′ good report

Thus far in 2 Corinthians, Paul has used the term δόξα (*doxa*, glory) theologically to speak of the honor or praise due God (e.g., 1:20; 4:15), or more prominently, of the Shekinah glory of God's presence (3:7–11, 18; 4:4, 6).

Here, however, he uses the term with reference to honor or fame in the eyes of people, stemming from a person's status or performance (BDAG 257). It has to do with being seen as important or significant, a cut above the crowd. Its opposite then is ἀτιμία (*atimia*), "dishonor" or "disrespect,"[19] being treated as unimportant, insignificant.[20] In the natural course of Christian mission, Paul at times was honored as a significant person, perhaps in his broader contexts of Greco-Roman culture (as a Roman citizen, for instance) and Judaism (as a rabbi), as well as in the church. Yet from his account of his ministry and the picture we see in Acts, both those inside and outside the church disrespected Paul throughout his ministry.

The values system of Greco-Roman society held honor as of great worth for positioning and advancement socially or politically and avoided shame at all costs. Although Paul does not hesitate to point out those things that are truly shameful, as we have seen, his use of honor/shame language has been shaped by biblical and theological categories that turn the Greco-Roman value system on its head. The apostle does not buy into the power and so-called wisdom of the culture; instead, he points to the weakness and foolishness of the cross, and to the role of believers as "the foolish" who shame "the wise." Great honor is given to those parts of the body of Christ that lack honor, and the power of authentic Christian ministry is the power of the Holy Spirit (Rom. 12:10; 1 Cor. 1:18–2:5; 6:5; 12:22–24).

The next pair, "through slander and good report," are closely related to honor and shame (as the ABBA pattern shows) but involve how others speak about Paul and his mission. The terms in Greek, δυσφημίας (*dysphēmias*) and εὐφημίας (*euphēmias*), form a phonetic play on words, based as they are on the same root word but with a different prefix. The former has to do with defamation or damaging another person's reputation or character; it is found only here in the NT.[21] By contrast, the latter term refers to speaking positively about someone or something, or giving a good report (BDAG 265, 414). It too occurs only here in the NT at 2 Cor. 6:8. So Paul has experienced the circulation of both slander and good reports concerning his ministry.

What follows now are seven paired antitheses, each introduced by ὡς (*hōs*), which functions as a "marker introducing the perspective from which a person, thing, or activity is viewed or understood" (BDAG 1104). The first member of each pair notes the perception of those looking in on Paul's mission from the outside, and the second member its antithetical counterpart. The second member of each pair, for the most part, offers Paul's assessment of the more

19. This term ἀτιμία appears elsewhere in Paul at Rom. 1:26; 9:21; 1 Cor. 11:14; 15:43; 2 Cor. 11:21; 2 Tim. 2:20. Paul's other terms to speak of shame are αἰσχύνη (*aischynē*; as at 2 Cor. 4:2) or its cognate verb καταισχύνω (*kataischynō*; Rom. 5:5; 9:33; 10:11; 1 Cor. 1:27; 11:4–5, 22; 2 Cor. 7:14; 9:4), "to put to shame" or "disgrace;" ἐντροπή (*entropē*; 1 Cor. 6:5; 15:34), which speaks of shame or humiliation, or its cognate verb ἐντρέπω (*entrepō*; 1 Cor. 4:14; 2 Thess. 3:14; Titus 2:8).
20. On honor and shame in Greco-Roman culture, see, e.g., Winter 2002: 71–72.
21. The word δυσφημία does occur in the LXX at 1 Macc. 7:38; 3 Macc. 2:26.

important reality that counters what he sees as a false (e.g., "as deceivers") or more often, a limited perspective.

The perception	The antithesis
as deceivers	yet true
as unknown	yet well known,
as dying	and behold, we live,
as disciplined	and yet not being killed,
as experiencing deep sorrow,	but constantly rejoicing,
as poor	but making many rich,
as having nothing	yet really possessing everything.

In other words, as people observe Paul's mission, evaluating the activities and events surrounding his ministry, they often have and express a limited and thus incomplete perspective on that mission and ministry. From what we have seen thus far in 2 Corinthians, such perceptions were in the air in Corinth and too often taken seriously by members of the church.

Some considered Paul and his coworkers as "deceivers" or "imposters" (πλάνοι, *planoi*),[22] steering the gullible in wrong directions. In speaking to Pilate and using this same term, the chief priests and Pharisees called Jesus, whom they had crucified, a deceiver (Matt. 27:63), one who, from their perspective, had led people astray. Certainly Paul faced many opponents who considered him to be morally, socially, or theologically twisted and even dangerous. Yet the apostle denies this, asserting that he and his coworkers are ἀληθεῖς (*alētheis*), a term that can be translated as "true," "honest," or "genuine," meaning that Paul and his fellow missionaries work with utmost integrity, faithfully steering people in the right direction. Since in the immediate context the apostle has spoken of "the word of truth" (v. 7, ἀλήθεια), it is not too much to suggest that Paul's "true" manner of life and ministry flows from his orientation to the gospel as the true word from God. He has already asserted that he manifests the truth (4:2) and in the next chapter will assert that he speaks truthfully to the Corinthians (7:14; cf. 11:10; 12:6; 13:8). Paul is no imposter; rather, he embodies genuineness and authenticity as a minister.

Most modern English translations render the second pair "as unknown, yet well known" (ὡς ἀγνοούμενοι καὶ ἐπιγινωσκόμενοι, *hōs agnooumenoi kai epiginōskomenoi*; e.g., NASB, NET, NLT, NIV, NRSV; see Gal. 1:22, where Paul, using the passive participle, speaks of being "unknown" to the churches of Judea), and it may mean that he and his coworkers were not widely recognized "in the public world of learning and politics, and were not sought after like the famous rhetoricians" (Thrall 1994: 464–65). The contrast to this idea of public obscurity might be that Paul is well known among the churches, or

6:9

---

22. The word can be used as an adjective (1 Tim. 4:1, "deceitful spirits") or a substantive, as here.

that he is well known by God himself (e.g., 1 Cor. 13:12). This interpretation fits the whole list's general orientation to what seems to be broad public perceptions of Paul's ministry. Yet Barrett may be correct that the sense rather has to do with being perceived as "unrecognized" in terms of his apostleship, over against being "recognized" as a bona fide apostle. This makes a good bit of sense against the backdrop of 2 Cor. 10–13, which pits Paul's position against the interloping false apostles (Barrett 1973: 189). It also fits well with the descriptions of Paul's experience immediately preceding this description, so that the progression would be "through slander, . . . as deceivers, . . . as unrecognized."

As suggested by many commentators (e.g., Harris 2005: 481–83), the third and fourth pairs of antitheses echo Ps. 117:17–18 LXX (118:17–18 ET).

2 Cor. 6:9	Ps. 117:17–18 NETS
as *dying* and behold, we *live*,	I shall not *die*, but I shall *live* and recount the deeds of the Lord.
as *disciplined* and yet *not being killed*	In disciplining the Lord *disciplined* me, and to *death he did not surrender me*.

As Harris points out, this psalm, a song of great victory in the face of opposition,[23] serves as the climax of the Egyptian Hallel (Pss. 113–18), sung at the great Jewish festivals in the first century and thus a very familiar part of Scripture to Jesus and the writers of the NT. Earlier in the psalm, the singer celebrates, "In affliction [ἐν θλίψει, *en thlipsei*; see 2 Cor. 6:4] I called on the Lord, and he hearkened me into a spaciousness. The Lord is a helper to me; I will not fear what a person may do to me. The Lord is a helper to me, and I, I shall observe my enemies. It is better to trust in the Lord than to trust in a person" (Ps. 117:5–8 NETS). Just a few verses later, the psalm speaks of the rejected cornerstone: "A stone which the builders rejected, this one became the chief cornerstone" (117:22 NETS). Thus it is not surprising that Paul would be quite familiar with the psalm, nor that he would echo the psalm as he meditated on the variabilities of his own ministry.

The antithesis of "dying" with "behold, we live" (ὡς ἀποθνήσκοντες καὶ ἰδοὺ ζῶμεν, *hōs apothnēskontes kai idou zōmen*) continues a death-life thematic thread that the apostle weaves through the letter (2 Cor. 1:9–10; 4:11–12; 5:8; 7:3; 11:23). For instance, Paul set a vulnerable tone for the letter in the prologue (1:8–11), writing of his and his coworkers' experience of deep despair "to the point that we thought we were going to die." Yet this seeming verdict of death occurred so that they would trust in the Lord of life, who rescued them out of this brush with death. As with Ps. 117:17 LXX, so here in 6:9 the

---

23. Paul begins his move toward wrapping up this center section of the book as he started it in 2:14–17, with triumphant military language. Harris (2005: 483) states of Ps. 117 LXX, "It is a processional thanksgiving liturgy, celebrating a God-given military victory. In the presence of the congregation the king testifies to Yahweh's powerful intervention in answer to prayer when he and his army were confronted in war by a confederacy of nations."

sense of the contrast seems to be straightforward: Paul is constantly exposed to death, but by God's grace he is still alive.

The echo of the psalm continues with "as disciplined and yet not being killed" (ὡς παιδευόμενοι καὶ μὴ θανατούμενοι, *hōs paideuomenoi kai mē thanatoumenoi*) The word παιδεύω (*paideuō*) could be used by ancient authors to refer to the process of educating, instructing, or training by which the person will be able to make sound choices. Further, it can refer to punishment at the hands of those wielding a whip, and the discipline here almost certainly alludes to persecution at the hands of opponents. Thus some translations render the word with the sense of being "scourged" or "beaten" (e.g., NET, NLT[2], NIV; 2 Chron. 10:11, 14; Luke 23:16, 22), and scourging at times was carried out prior to execution, or in a way that led to the death of the person being beaten—thus Paul's addition of "yet not being killed." Later in the book he mentions that in the course of his ministry he has been whipped five times, beaten with rods three times, and stoned once (11:24–25).

However, especially in light of Ps. 117:18 LXX, Paul probably has in mind the movement of a greater hand behind the strikes and stripes of human punishment, for παιδεύω in the biblical literature often refers to the discipline of the Lord (Pss. 6:2; 37:2 [38:1 ET]; 140:5 [141:5 ET]; Prov. 3:11–12; 1 Cor. 11:32; Heb. 12:5–11; Rev. 3:19). Thus in Jewish thought and particularly in the NT stands a rich tradition of the Lord's discipline coming to his child in the form of persecution or other difficulties. The discipline should be understood, therefore, as a means of spiritual formation rather than as punitive.[24] Paul has faced persecution, which he receives as the Lord's discipline, but these assaults have not yet resulted in the apostle being killed.

The fifth antithesis, "as experiencing deep sorrow, but constantly rejoicing" **6:10** (ὡς λυπούμενοι ἀεὶ δὲ χαίροντες, *hōs lypoumenoi aei de chairontes*), presents two experiences of which Paul speaks elsewhere. He had faced grief when a coworker was sick (Phil. 2:27), and the spiritual lostness of his fellow Israelites caused him intense sorrow (Rom. 9:1–4). Yet, closer to home for the Corinthians, an earlier visit to their city had been full of sorrow and an earlier letter to their church sorrow-soaked with the apostle's tears (2:1–4).

However, the apostle chose joy in the midst of his sorrows. Most of the twenty-nine occurrences of the verb χαίρω (*chairō*) in Paul find him rejoicing over various circumstances in his churches or exhorting believers to rejoice.[25] For instance, he exhorts the Romans to "Rejoice in hope" (12:12) and "Rejoice with those who rejoice" (12:15); later in 2 Corinthians he challenges the hearers to rejoice (13:11); in Philippians, the book that reflects Paul's posture of chosen joy more than any other, he models and encourages the Philippians to rejoice (Phil. 2:17–18, 28; 3:1; 4:4, 10). Thus Paul seems to understand

---

24. On such discipline in the literature of Judaism and the broader Greco-Roman culture, see Croy 1998.

25. See χαίρω in Rom. 12:12, 15 (2x); 16:19; 1 Cor. 7:30 (2x); 13:6; 16:17; 2 Cor. 2:3; 6:10; 7:7, 9, 13, 16; 13:9, 11; Phil. 1:18 (2x); 2:17–18, 28; 3:1; 4:4 (2x), 10; Col. 1:24; 2:5; 1 Thess. 3:9; 5:16.

rejoicing as volitional and as a hallmark of Christian discipleship. His letters witness to the fact that he has practiced rejoicing "constantly" (ἀεί, *aei*) in his own life (2 Cor. 6:10).[26]

The sixth pair of antitheses, really a paradox in this case, states, "as poor but making many rich" (ὡς πτωχοὶ πολλοὺς δὲ πλουτίζοντες, *hōs ptōchoi pollous de ploutizontes*); the first term is used quite literally of lacking financial resources, and the latter is used figuratively of an abundance of spiritual resources. In various places Paul affirms this perception of poverty, agreeing that he and his fellow workers live on meager resources (e.g., 11:7–10), and he clearly sees this pattern as a characteristic of authentic apostolic ministry in general (Rom. 8:35; 1 Cor. 4:11–12; 2 Cor. 11:27; Phil. 4:11–12). Ironically, it may be that the Corinthian interlopers understood Paul's "failure" to ask for support from the church as a tacit admission that he lacked apostolic authority (Furnish 1984: 359). It seems more likely, however, that the opponents in Corinth evaluated the quality and effectiveness of the apostle's ministry according to the financial resources (or lack thereof!) generated by his ministry. If we are correct that these opponents were Sophists, the emphases on popular public performance and remuneration were understood as synergistic dynamics in the life of a successful public speaker (Winter 2002: 222–23, 224–25, 228).

In broader Hellenistic-Jewish culture, we see approximate parallels to Paul's words on this paradox of meager material resources set over against wealth. For instance, at one point Philo (*Good Free* 77) describes the Essenes: "For while they stand almost alone in the whole of mankind in that they have become moneyless and landless by deliberate action rather than by lack of good fortune, they are esteemed exceedingly rich, because they judge frugality with contentment to be, as indeed it is, an abundance of wealth" (Colson 1941: 55). What is unique here in Paul's words at 2 Cor. 6:10, however, is the emphasis on one's poverty as *enriching others* (Furnish 1984: 359). Paul has told the Corinthians that he is in a process of dying that they might really live: his life is poured out for them so that they might know real life (4:11–12). This "sacrifice for the good of others" mentality follows the pattern learned from Jesus, who was made poor that others might be made rich: "For you know the grace of our Lord Jesus Christ, that although he was rich, he became poor for your sakes, so that you by his poverty could become rich" (2 Cor. 8:9 NET). The long lists of ministry hardships in Paul demonstrate in no uncertain terms that authentic Christian ministry is costly to the minister. Yet it is a price paid with a purpose of advancing the kingdom of God in the lives of others. To be right in the middle of God's will, living out the cause of Christ, having a positive and eternal impact on those for whom Christ died—Paul embraces all this as of inestimable value. This is why in his final antithesis he can say that he and his fellow missionaries rightly may be perceived "as having nothing and yet" in

---

26. Garland (1999: 313) follows A. Hanson (1987: 69) in showing the parallels between Paul's hardship list of 2 Cor. 6:3–10 and the joy expressed/proclaimed in the Beatitudes.

reality they are "really possessing everything."[27] The parallel in wording in the Greek text shows an intensification from the first participle, ἔχοντες (*echontes*, having) to the second, κατέχοντες (*katechontes*, possessing). Following Furnish on the intensification (in his notes, not his translation), we translate the second as "really" possessing all things to drive home the emphasis, and perhaps the lasting nature of that possession is also in view.[28] Nevertheless, Paul's point certainly is that to have Christ is to have all (cf. Rom. 8:32). As C. S. Lewis (2009: 34) famously writes, "He who has God and everything else has no more than he who has God only."

Reflection

In speaking of the apostle's hardships listed in our passage, golden-tongued John Chrysostom (*Hom. 2 Cor.* 12.2) states, "Any one of these things is intolerable, but taken together, think what kind of soul is needed to endure them" (Bray 1999: 257). This may be why Paul in his commendation (6:3–4a) mixes the endurance required by a swirling blizzard of hardships (6:4b–5) and God-empowered character (6:6–7a) as key elements that mark an authentic ministry. By its nature, ministry means vulnerability to hardships; hardships test and shape character, and character undergirds endurance in hardships (Rom. 5:3–5). Today authentic ministry still demands vulnerability and character, whether in the Mediterranean, Chicago, Beijing, or Nairobi.

In the afterword of his book about the doomed ship *Andrea Gail*, Junger (2009: 227) writes, "Fishing continues to be one of the easiest ways in America to die while earning a paycheck. The yearly fatality rate for commercial fishermen is thirty to forty times the national workplace average." Yet fishermen die—are willing to put themselves in harm's way—because what they are after, by its very nature, demands a certain detachment from security. They have to get "out there" to catch fish, out there in the elements, in the deep, unpredictable, sometimes overwhelmingly violent ocean. We too have to get "out there," in places of vulnerability to hardships, to "fish" for people.

A number of years ago, when my son, Joshua, was seventeen, he traveled to Sudan, into a war zone. Joshua had started a ministry called "Dollar for a Drink," which raised money for freshwater wells in Sudan, and he traveled to Sudan to meet the team responsible for installing the wells. Pat and I, as his parents, went through that two-week period of Joshua's trip in a cloud of vulnerability. For the first time in his life, we could not get to Joshua if he needed us. We could not protect him if he was threatened. But you can't raise kids up to advance the kingdom of God in the world and then say, "But I didn't mean *there*."

Paul's words raise for us the question of our vulnerability and character in our ministries. To what vulnerabilities are we being called to reach the

---

27. For Greco-Roman parallels to Paul's words in this final antithesis, see Furnish 1984: 348.
28. Other nuances of the verb are "holding fast" or "keeping in one's possession" (BDAG 533).

unreached? To what illusions of "safety" are we clinging? The irony is that in the end our gospel-fueled vulnerabilities lead to us "having all things." A God-centered vulnerability that leads to character is the only way to live as God's minister in the world. Again John Chrysostom (*Hom. 2 Cor.* 12.4) writes, "People outside the church may think we are sorrowful, but in fact we are always rejoicing. We may look poor, but in fact we have enormous riches, both spiritual and physical. As usual, the Christian life is the exact opposite of what it appears to be on the surface" (Bray 1999: 258).

Additional Notes

6:3. Paul clearly commends the mission carried out by himself and his coworkers, so some witnesses (D F G 629 1505 it vg^ww sy co; Ambst) add ἡμῶν following ἡ διακονία to bring greater clarity to what is implicit in this introductory statement and expressed more overtly in the next verse (the use of ἑαυτούς, ourselves). Thus many ETs include "our" in rendering the verse (e.g., NET, NLT[2], ESV, NIV, NRSV).

6:4. Three synonymous verbs meaning "to commend" are in play in the variants at 6:4: συνιστάνω, συνίστημι, and συνιστάω. At 4:2 we noted that the variant συνιστάνοντες (from συνιστάνω) had greater support, and it may be that it is original here (so Harris 2005: 467), with the variant συνιστάντες (from συνίστημι; 𝔓^46 ℵ* C D* F G 0225 0243 33 81 1739 1881*vid; Cl) resulting from parablepsis (the scribe skipping over a ν, leading to the shorter reading). However, here the external support for συνιστάνοντες (B P 104 1175 1505) is not as strong and widespread as the same reading at 4:2 (𝔓^46 B P 0243 630 1175 1505 1739 1881), nor as strong as that for συνιστάντες. If συνιστάνοντες is the preferred reading at 4:2, the same reading here may have resulted from scribes wishing to bring the reading at 6:4 in line with that at 4:2. Thus NA^27 and NA^28 may be correct in preferring the reading συνιστάντες. In any case the reading συνιστῶντες (ℵ^2 D^2 K L Ψ 048 365 630 1241 2464 𝔐; from συνιστάω) has no other firm Pauline parallels and is clearly secondary both at 4:2 and here (so Thrall 1994: 300).

6:9. The reading παιδευόμενοι (being disciplined) clearly has the stronger external support (B 𝔓^46 ℵ C D^2 K L P Ψ 049 075 1 6 33 69) over against πειραζόμενοι (being tested; D* F G it; Ambst). It may be that a scribe balked at the idea of the apostle "being disciplined," finding the idea of him "being tested" more palatable (so Harris 2005: 467).

d. A Call for Open Hearts and Pure Lives (6:11–7:4)

In his *Treatise concerning Religious Affections*, Jonathan Edwards (1825: 332) writes, "If the moral beauty of God be hid, the enmity of the heart will remain in its full strength. No love will be enkindled; the will, instead of being effectually gained, will remain inflexible. But the first glimpse of the moral and spiritual glory of God shining into the heart produces all these effects as it were with omnipotent power, which nothing can withstand." This is another way of saying that "holiness, in the fear of God" (2 Cor. 7:1) serves as a foundation for right Christian living. In 6:11–7:4 Paul summons the Corinthians to that holiness, simultaneously calling them away from unholy relationships.[1] Such relationships deaden their spiritual sensibilities, including their discernment about Paul and his mission.

So, following Paul's extensive list detailing his ministry's impeccable apostolic credentials, we come to a series of powerful, emotional appeals from the apostle's heart. Here we find both a turning point in the letter and one of the clearest indications of the occasion that prompted Paul to write. At the heart of the apostle's conflict with the Corinthian church lies a moral crisis, since at least a subgroup within the church had not repented of their immorality (12:21), and repentance from that immorality stands as a key point on the road to reconciliation with the apostle and his ministry. As Matera (2003: 160) states concerning 6:14–7:1,

> Paul's call for reconciliation requires a moral conversion on the part of the Corinthians, and what he writes here anticipates what he will deal with in chapters 10–13. To summarize, the material of this section is the climax of Paul's exposition of his apostolic ministry, inasmuch as it calls the Corinthians to be reconciled with Christ's ambassador.

Three interrelated units, 6:11–13; 6:14–7:1; and 7:2–4, provide for us a window on this situation, a clear view of the moral battle that Paul is waging for the heart of the Corinthian church. In the first and last of these units, the apostle makes a heartfelt plea for this church to open up to him—to embrace unreservedly his true ministry of the true gospel—as he has approached them with an open heart, ministering to them freely, consistently, sacrificially. In the middle of the three units, the apostle challenges the Corinthians to eschew inappropriate relationships with

---

1. On concepts of corporate holiness as reflected in 6:14–7:1, see Adewuya 2003.

unbelievers, calling them to move away from relationships that are hurting their spiritual lives by inhibiting a wholehearted embrace of Paul and his mission. So here we have an ABA pattern in the development of this series of units:

i. (A) A plea for openness (6:11–13)
ii.   (B) A plea for purity (6:14–7:1)
iii. (A′) A plea for openness resumed (7:2–4)

Exegesis and Exposition

⁶:¹¹We have spoken openly to you, Corinthians; ⌜our⌝ heart stands wide open! ¹²You are not held back by us, but you are held back by your affections. ¹³Now as a fair return on our investment—I am talking to you as if you were my children!—make room for us in your hearts!

¹⁴Stop being in incompatible relationships with unbelievers. For what do righteousness and lawlessness have in common? Or what kind of close relationship does light have with darkness? ¹⁵What harmony is there between ⌜Christ⌝ and ⌜Beliar⌝? Or what part of the life God has given his people does a ⌜believer⌝ have in common with an unbeliever? ¹⁶In what way can God's temple and idols come to an agreement? For ⌜we are the temple of the living God⌝, just as God said, "I will live among them and walk around, and I will be their God, and they will be ⌜my⌝ people." ¹⁷Therefore, "Come out from among them and separate yourselves from them, says the Lord, and don't touch that which is unclean, and I will welcome you." ¹⁸And, "I will be your father, and you yourselves will be my sons and daughters, says the almighty Lord." ⁷:¹Therefore, dear ones, since we have promises like these, we should wash ourselves clean from every impurity of flesh and ⌜spirit⌝, making our ⌜holiness⌝ complete in the ⌜fear⌝ of God.

²Make room for us! We haven't mistreated anyone; we haven't corrupted anyone; we haven't taken advantage of anyone. ³I am not saying this to condemn you, for I have told you before that you are in our hearts to the point of dying together or living together. ⁴I have spoken to you with great openness; I boast a great deal about you to others. I am very encouraged. In the midst of all our troubles, I am ecstatic with joy.

i. A Plea for Openness (6:11–13)

With the list of 6:3–10 Paul drums home a long, carefully crafted reflection of perceptions of his mission, as well as the dynamics that truly characterize his mission. But now he suddenly breaks that rhythm with an appeal that seems to burst from his heart: the apostle directly addresses the hearts of his hearers. It is almost as if he blurts out, "What more could I say?! What further evidence do you need of the integrity of my ministry?!" The appeal at 6:11–13 consists of three brief movements corresponding to the three verses in the unit. First, in verse 11 Paul in no uncertain terms asserts the posture he and his fellow workers have maintained toward the Corinthians: "We have spoken openly to you, Corinthians; our heart stands wide open!" Paul's ministry to the Corinthians can be characterized as one of openness. Second, in verse 12 the apostle assesses why the Corinthians have been held back in their relationship with him and his mission, in spite of the openness of Paul's ministry to them: "You are not held back by us, but you are held back by your affections." Their attitudes and actions toward Paul and his mission have been restrained relationally due to their affections. Finally, with verse 13 Paul calls for a response: "Now as a fair return on our investment—I am talking to you as if you were my children!—make room for us in your hearts!" The apostle desires that the Corinthians respond to him and his coworkers as he and his coworkers have related to the church—with wide-open hearts.

Paul normally addresses readers of his letters directly with the vocative **6:11** ἀδελφοί (*adelphoi*, brothers [and sisters]), but here he addresses the church as Κορίνθιοι (*Korinthioi*, Corinthians). There are only two other cases where Paul calls the members of a church by their particular collective designation (Gal. 3:1; Phil. 4:15), and all three occurrences seem to be charged with emotion.[2] The use of Κορίνθιοι marks this passage as elevated in emotion, noticeable even in one of Paul's most emotionally charged letters (Thrall 1994: 468–69). The apostle thus expresses heartfelt concern for the congregation (Matera 2003: 161).

The apostle points out the openness with which he and his fellow workers have ministered to the Corinthians, both in terms of what they have said and the affections that have driven them. The expression with which Paul begins the unit, translated "We have spoken openly to you" (Τὸ στόμα ἡμῶν ἀνέῳγεν πρὸς ὑμᾶς, *To stoma hēmōn aneōgen pros hymas*; lit., our mouth has been and is[3] open to you), probably does not carry the sense "I have let my tongue run away with me" (contra Barrett 1973: 191), as if the apostle suddenly realizes he has gotten carried away with the list we have in 6:3–10. Rather, Paul states straightforwardly that his communication with the Corinthians has been characterized by openness.[4] He uses an idiom that speaks of free, sincere communication, and he probably refers not merely to the part of his letter immediately preceding this passage, nor even the whole of what he has written thus far in the letter, but generally to the posture he has maintained in his relationship with the Corinthians all along.

2. With the Galatians passage, the emotion is frustration; with the vocative at Phil. 4:15, the emotion seems to be one of warmth and appreciation. On reading the significance of emotions as expressed by authors of the NT, see M. Elliott 2006.

3. The perfect-tense verb reflects the current state of Paul's relationship with the Corinthians. He can say that to this point his relationship with them has been marked by integrity in the way he has communicated with them.

4. Paul has spent a good deal of space in the letter thus far defending the general pattern by which his ministry has been characterized (e.g., 1:12, 23–24; 2:17; 3:3–5; 4:2, 5; 5:11; 6:3), and such a key turning point in his discourse might be expected to reiterate a key theme or themes from earlier in the book.

The parallel statement that follows on the heels of this one (our heart stands wide open, ἡ καρδία ἡμῶν πεπλάτυνται, *hē kardia hēmōn peplatyntai*) communicates, again idiomatically, Paul's deep affection for this church.[5] The verb πλατύνω (*platynō*), here a third-person singular perfect middle indicative form,[6] has to do with something being expanded, broadened, or widened. Think of a road that has been widened so it can accommodate more traffic.[7] Yet here Paul's heart has been widened or enlarged: his affections are given freely. At 3:2 he has already explained that they are the only letter of recommendation he needs, written on his heart. His ministry to them flows from this intimacy of relationship, this deep affection grounded in the gospel, by which God transforms the heart (4:6). So the apostle holds up the "heart" as transformed by the power of God and also representative of human affection that flows from a right relationship with God and others. Paul's ministry to the Corinthians, fueled by a deep relational connection born of the love of Christ (5:14), knows no restrictions. Speaking of 6:11, John Chrysostom (*Hom. 2 Cor.* 13.1) writes, "Paul means by this that he talks to the Corinthians freely, as he would to people whom he loves. He holds nothing back and suppresses nothing. Nothing is wider than Paul's heart, which loved all the believers with all the passion which one might have toward the object of one's affection" (Bray 1999: 260). Thus, the tension in his relationship with this church cannot be due to his relational posture toward them, since he and his coworkers are holding nothing back. The problem must lie with the Corinthians themselves, as we see in verse 12.

6:12   This contrast, between Paul's openness and the posture of the Corinthians themselves, comes to the fore in verse 12, which speaks of the role of their affections in the current relational breakdown. They are holding back in the relationship; the emotional connection between them and their apostle has been weakened. Paul now assesses what holds the Corinthians back in their relationship with him and his mission, and the assessment is communicated tersely in parallel statements:[8]

οὐ	στενοχωρεῖσθε	ἐν	ἡμῖν
δὲ	στενοχωρεῖσθε	ἐν τοῖς σπλάγχνοις	ὑμῶν

5. As Thrall (1994: 469) notes, the phraseology used, which speaks of an enlarged heart, has two parallels in the LXX (Deut. 11:16; Ps. 118:32 [119:32 ET]), neither of which seems relevant for Paul's assertion in 2 Cor. 6:11. Paul seems simply to confess that he has come to have great affection for the Corinthians. On the use of expressions of affection in skillfully crafted appeals among ancient writers, see Keener 2005: 191.

6. The term καρδία is singular and thus takes a singular form of the verb. The perfect form plays a part in communicating that this openness, rather than a decision of the moment, constitutes an established state of existence: this has been and is a standard posture maintained by Paul and his fellow workers.

7. The sister term πλατεῖα (*plateia*) can refer to a wide road or street (e.g., Matt. 6:5; 12:19). The cognate πλάτος (*platos*) connotes "breadth," while another cognate, πλατύς (*platys*), means "broad" and can speak of a wide gate, as at Matt. 7:13 (*EDNT* 3:101).

8. I have repositioned postpositive δέ to make the parallelism clearer.

ou	*stenochōreisthe*	*en*	*hēmin*
de	*stenochōreisthe*	*en tois splanchnois*	*hymōn*
not	You are held back	by	us
but	you are held back	by affections	your

We have seen the verb στενοχωρέω (*stenochōreō*) before, at 4:8, and these are the only two occurrences of the verb in the NT.[9] As noted in the comments on 4:8, the word means "to confine or restrict to a narrow space, crowd, cramp, confine," or figuratively, "to be distressed" (i.e., to be emotionally cramped) (BDAG 942). Here we find the conceptual contrast to the "wide open" (πεπλάτυνται, *peplatyntai*) posture of Paul's heart proclaimed in the previous verse. Clearly the apostle asserts that the Corinthians are not emotionally boxed in or held back in their relationship with himself and his associates by his or his associates' actions, attitudes, or affections (ἐν ἡμῖν, *en hēmin*, by us). The problem lies in the affections of the Corinthians. In broader Greek literature, the term σπλάγχνον (*splanchnon*) could refer to the inner parts of the body, including the heart, lungs, stomach, spleen, liver, kidneys, and intestines. But, as with use of the word "heart" in modern English, the term was used figuratively in our literature to speak either of the seat of the emotions or more particularly of the emotions themselves. Thus in the NT σπλάγχνον can speak of love, affection, mercy, or compassion (e.g., Luke 1:78; Phil. 1:8, 2:1; Col. 3:12; Philem. 7; 1 John 3:17). Paul uses the word again at 2 Cor. 7:15 to speak of Titus's growing affection for the Corinthians as he remembers the way they welcomed him.

So the problem with the Corinthians is what we might call a "heart problem": their heart lacks commitment to Paul and his mission. They have become emotionally entangled with someone or something that has dampened their affection for the apostle and his ministry. Paul apparently addresses the entanglement in the next unit (6:14–7:1) and then, at 7:2, resumes his appeal that they open their hearts to him.

Offering a solution to the Corinthians' "heart" problem, Paul very directly **6:13** calls for a response. Thus far in the letter the apostle has sustained a variety of diplomatic approaches to commending himself to the Corinthian church. He has appealed to them emotionally,[10] sharing openly with the Corinthians concerning his sufferings (e.g., 1:8–11); he has offered explanations for his actions (e.g., 1:15–16); he has reflected elaborately on a theology of authentic Christian ministry (e.g., 3:7–18); and he has given an extensive list of his ministry experiences (e.g., 6:3–10). Now the apostle speaks baldly, stating in no uncertain terms what he wants this church to do, dampened as it is in its

9. In the LXX στενοχωρέω occurs five times (Josh. 17:15; Judg. 16:16 [B]; 4 Macc. 11:11; Isa. 28:20; 49:19), for the most part speaking of spaces or places that are too small.

10. The use of emotional appeal, or pathos, was a well-honed skill among ancient rhetoricians and could be used in expressing affection (e.g., 6:11–13; 7:2–4) as well as indignation (6:14–7:1). On the use of pathos at this point in 2 Corinthians, see Keener 2005: 190–91.

affections toward him and his fellow ministers: "make room for us in your hearts!" (πλατύνθητε καὶ ὑμεῖς, *platynthēte kai hymeis*).

First of all, Paul sets up this exhortation by appealing to the Corinthians on the basis of what would be an appropriate exchange, or reciprocation, in the situation (τὴν δὲ αὐτὴν ἀντιμισθίαν, *tēn de autēn antimisthian*, Now as a fair return on our investment). The term ἀντιμισθία was used in the first century to refer to a reciprocal transaction, an appropriate recompense, where someone receives what is deserved, either positively as here, or negatively in the sense of punishment (e.g., Rom. 1:27). In the ancient world, generosity was to be answered with reciprocity (Matt. 5:46–47; Xenophon, *Cyr.* 6.1.47; Keener 2005: 191). Paul is saying that, given the affection he and his ministry team have lavished on the Corinthians, it is only appropriate that they should return the affection in kind.[11]

Using a parenthetical statement, Paul then appeals to the Corinthians on the basis of his relationship with them as a spiritual parent. The apostle is not speaking down to them here, as if they are babies (Barnett 1997: 337). Rather, he appeals to the church on the basis of his apostolic ministry to them, as their "spiritual father" who brought them the gospel (12:14–15; Gal. 4:19; 1 Tim. 1:2, 18). The thought stands right in line with 1 Cor. 4:15, where Paul had previously written to them, "For you can have 10,000 instructors in Christ, but you can't have many fathers. For I became your father in Christ Jesus through the gospel" (HCSB). One of the duties of parents is to teach their children about what is fair in various situations of life. So Paul talks to the Corinthians as his spiritual children, calling for a fair exchange, challenging them to follow his example and open their hearts widely to him and his ministry, even as he and his associates have lavished their affections on the church.

ii. A Plea for Purity (6:14–7:1)

As we near the end of the apostle's extensive reflections on authentic ministry (2:14–7:4), we encounter a passage that, as noted in the introduction to the commentary, some have labeled out of place, an interpolation plopped down in the middle of a naturally progressing argument. As explained briefly in the introduction, there are good arguments against this perspective: the passage may be read as integrative with the surrounding material (see esp. Beale 1989; Goulder 1994a; Webb 1993: 14, 27–30). In fact, it is "the carefully structured, closely argued, and theologically rich climax" to this great midsection of the letter (Hafemann 2000: 277). Momentarily, I will offer such a reading, but before turning to a more detailed explication of the text, we need to grasp the big picture of what and how Paul communicates in this passage.

---

11. The τὴν . . . αὐτήν (*tēn . . . autēn*) perhaps should be considered an acc. of reference, "with reference to the same," meaning something that is "comparable" or "equivalent" (Thrall 1994: 450).

As seen in the table below, 6:14–7:1 presents a highly crafted, logically developed series of exhortations, accented by various types of support material. Through rhetorical questions, theological assertion, and a string of OT quotations having to do with restoration to the true worship of God (Garland 1999: 336–37, following Olley 1998), Paul reinforces (even restates) the exhortations, calling the Corinthians to separate from worldly relationships, which defile them and hurt their relationship with God, and to embrace the true worship of the living God, mediated through the apostle's mission.

Paul exhorts his readers at the beginning, middle, and end of the passage, underscoring the hortatory nature of this passage. The lead exhortation to eschew mismatched relationships gathers reinforcement from five rhetorical questions, each calling for a ringing, negative answer. These rhetorical questions drum home the incompatibility of God's people living in intimate partnership with unbelievers, who are aligned with lawlessness, darkness, Beliar, and idols.

The mention of idols in the last of the rhetorical questions gives rise to the theological assertion in verse 16b, "For we are the temple of the living God." Thus these passages are set in a worship context. The following string of OT quotations and allusions (vv. 16c–18) reinforces ("just as God said") the theological assertion about worship and coheres around two interrelated ideas. The first of these expresses a dominant biblical theme, *God's presence among his people*, which flows from the temple theology just expressed in verse 16b. Notice that the OT texts underscoring this theme of "presence" are highly relational in nature and constitute the promises of which the apostle speaks in 7:1 ("since we have promises like these"):

> "I will live among them
>   and walk around,
> and I will be their God
>   and they will be my people." (Lev. 26:11–12; Ezek. 37:27)

and

> "I will welcome you."
> And "I will be your father,
>   and you will be my sons and daughters." (Ezek. 20:41; 2 Sam. 7:14)

Paul expresses the second idea, that intimacy with God demands *separation from that which is unclean*, with the quotation of Isa. 52:11, a triple exhortation given by the Lord to "come out," "separate yourselves," and "don't touch that which is unclean." This hortatory part of the string of OT texts gives rise to the final exhortation, presented in 7:1: "We should wash ourselves clean from every impurity of flesh and spirit." In short, Paul calls believers to be a separate, holy people in order to have right relationship with God.

Exhortation	⁶:¹⁴Stop being in incompatible relationships with unbelievers.
Reinforcement (with five questions)	For what do righteousness and lawlessness have in common?
	Or what kind of close relationship does light have with darkness?
	¹⁵What harmony is there between Christ and Beliar?
	Or what part of the life God has given his people does a believer have in common with an unbeliever?
	¹⁶In what way can God's temple and idols come to an agreement?
Theological Assertion	For we are the temple of the living God,
Reinforcement using a catena of OT passages (four promises; Lev. 26:11–12; Ezek. 37:27)	just as God said, "I will live among them
	and walk around,
	and I will be their God
	and they will be my people.
Three additional exhortations flowing from the promises (Isa. 52:11)	¹⁷Therefore, "Come out from among them and
	separate yourselves from them, says the Lord,
	and don't touch that which is unclean,
Three additional promises (Ezek. 20:41; 2 Sam. 7:14)	and I will welcome you."
	¹⁸And, "I will be your father
	and you yourselves will be my sons and daughters, says the almighty Lord."
	⁷:¹Therefore, dear ones,
Basis	since we have promises like these,
Concluding Exhortation	we should wash ourselves clean
Extent	from every impurity of flesh and spirit,
Result	making our holiness complete
Posture	in the fear of God.

What, then, is the purpose of this unit in context? How does it fit with Paul's original intent and crafting of this part of the book? In much of 2 Corinthians, Paul has been pleading for the Corinthians to embrace his ministry wholeheartedly, unreservedly, and to see themselves as partners with him in that authentic ministry. In 6:11–13 his pleading becomes especially personal as the apostle calls for a mutual commitment to an open-hearted relationship. So a ministry partnership, one of intimacy and integrity, seems to be Paul's longing. But something keeps the Corinthians back from this free and open-hearted relationship: their affections. Now these twin concerns of partnership and affections give rise to 6:14–7:1. Just as the right relational commitments can have happy results, bad relationships have had deleterious results, and thus the Corinthians are not where they should be in relation to Paul, nor in relation to God.

Admittedly, the shift between 6:13 and 6:14 is abrupt, but as pointed out above, scholars have offered much evidence that the unit need not be seen as out of step with Paul's thought. It may be, therefore, that Paul incorporates a bit of a sermon he had composed and delivered previously (such a catena of OT texts occurs as an aspect of first-century preaching; see, e.g., Heb. 1:5–14),[12] thinking that this powerful, practical exhortation fit the need of the moment. Read thus, the unit forms a resounding, climactic appeal, rounding off the apostle's extended discourse in which he attempts to draw the Corinthians away from spiritually poisonous relationships and back into the solid, relational context of his ministry.

The unit begins with "Stop being in incompatible relationships with unbelievers" (Μὴ γίνεσθε ἑτεροζυγοῦντες ἀπίστοις, *Mē ginesthe heterozygountes apistois*), which Barrett (1973: 195) paraphrases colorfully: "You must not get into double harness with unbelievers." The negative Μή, in conjunction with the periphrastic present construction, could either mean "stop" or "don't begin," but the context argues for the former. Paul has just said that the Corinthians' "affections" hold them back from fully embracing the apostle and his mission (6:12), and the balance of the passage speaks as if the addressees need cleansing (6:17; 7:1). The present imperative verb γίνεσθε (*ginesthe*) contributes the voice of command to the construction. The present active participle ἑτεροζυγοῦντες (*heterozygountes*), from the verb ἑτεροζυγέω (*heterozygeō*), occurs only here in the biblical literature, but the sense is clear, and the word has an identifiable OT backdrop. A cognate adjective, ἑτερόζυγος (*heterozygos*) occurs in Lev. 19:19, a verse prohibiting the mixing of things—crossbreeding livestock (lit., breed with one of a different yoke), sowing a field with two types of seeds, wearing clothing made of two types of material. A parallel passage in Deut. 22:10 LXX reads, "You shall not plow with an calf and a donkey together" (NETS).[13] The calf was considered a clean animal and the donkey an unclean animal (Craigie 1976: 290). Perhaps the Israelites were not to mix livestock, seeds, and fabric as a living picture of separation and purity, reminding them not to mix socially or religiously with people of the land (Merrill 1994: 299–300).

Corresponding to this OT backdrop, according to Spicq (1994: 2.80–81), ἑτεροζυγέω as used in 2 Cor. 6:14 connotes pulling "the yoke in a different direction than one's fellow," and thus, figuratively, "mismate," or "make a mismatched covenant."[14] He comments, "Just as in a yoked team the difference between two mismatched animals keeps them from pulling the yoke in the same way and with the same force, so also is an alliance between light and

6:14

---

12. On Hebrews as a first-century sermon, see Guthrie 1994: 32, 115; 2004: 430.
13. Derrett (1978) has suggested that our passage is a midrash on Deut. 22:10.
14. Spicq (1994: 2.80–81) points to a use of the cognate adjective, attested once in the papyri, where the property of a person named Demetrius was confiscated, including "two unmatched vases" (P.Cair.Zen. 59038, 12).

darkness unimaginable—between Christ and Belial, between pagans and believers in their practical living." Translations have varied in how to communicate this sense. The NET and NLT[2] have focused on the concept of partnership ("Don't become partners with," NET; "Don't team up with," NLT[2]), but this leaves aside the sense of incompatibility. From the five rhetorical questions that follow in verses 14b–16a, the emphasis seems to be on association or relationship or agreement, rather than having a common work.[15] The HCSB and the NRSV capture the nuance of incongruity with "Do not be mismatched," but this fails to include the sense of involvement in relationship (two inanimate objects can be mismatched). The ESV, NIV, and Tyndale all leave the figurative language in place, for example, "Do not be unequally yoked" (ESV). It might be preferable to use either this more formal equivalence approach, or a functional equivalence alternative, as with our "Stop being in incompatible relationships with unbelievers." But how is such an exhortation to be applied?

The use of the term ἄπιστος (unbeliever) appears thirteen other times in 1 and 2 Corinthians, all of which seem to refer to unbelievers in general, those outside of the faith.[16] Seemingly, then, Paul calls for the Corinthians to put a stop to relating to unbelievers inappropriately.[17] More specifically, some have understood the ἀπίστοις (*apistois*) to be the opponents of Paul (e.g., Keener 2005: 193; Collange 1972: 305–6), and thus Paul would be calling for them to turn away from these interlopers, embracing Paul and his mission instead of leaders who were influencing them negatively, and this certainly fits with a prominent theme of 2 Corinthians. Later in the letter Paul says these false teachers preach "another Jesus" and a "different gospel" (11:4), so it is not hard to see how Paul might label them "unbelievers."

As discussed in the commentary's introduction, the interlopers, who gave Paul such grief, had been profoundly influenced by the sophistic tradition and thus had adopted worldly patterns of life and ministry. Among the Corinthians their ministry has promoted a moral corruption that comes from embracing the values of unbelievers. The false teachers have entangled members of the

15. At Eph. 5:5–11, where he also contrasts light and darkness, Paul uses the term συμμέτοχοι (*symmetochoi*; 5:7) to speak of inappropriate partnership: "Therefore, do not become their partners. For you were once darkness, but now you are light in the Lord. Walk as children of light—for the fruit of the light results in all goodness, righteousness, and truth—discerning what is pleasing to the Lord. Don't participate in the fruitless works of darkness, but instead, expose them" (Eph. 5:7–11 HCSB).

16. See ἄπιστος in 1 Cor. 6:6; 7:12–15; 10:27; 14:22–24; 2 Cor. 4:4; 6:14–15.

17. As 1 Corinthians indicates, Paul does not intend for members of the church to cut off all association with unbelievers (1 Cor. 5:9–11). The problem stems from the Corinthians adopting the moral standards of the world (2 Cor. 7:1). The affections of the Corinthians have been corrupted morally, and their sin is affecting their relationship with God and his apostle. First Corinthians gives plenty of evidence that members of the church have been morally compromised at points (1 Cor. 6:1–11; 6:12–20; etc.) and that such moral compromise has negatively affected their spiritual discernment. They are "influenced by the flesh and behaving like unregenerate people" (1 Cor. 3:3 NET). So Paul calls them to disassociate from unbelievers, not in the sense of their influence on unbelievers for the sake of the gospel, but in the sense of unbelievers' immoral influence on the Corinthians.

church with the worldly ways of unbelief, and the Corinthians need to make a decisive choice to separate from them.

Now Paul reinforces his exhortation to separate from incompatible relationships with unbelievers by crafting five rhetorical questions, questions both conceptually and structurally parallel (6:14b–16a). The rigorous parallelism creates a rhythmic cadence.

γὰρ						
τίς	μετοχὴ	δικαιοσύνῃ	καὶ	ἀνομίᾳ,	ἢ
τίς	κοινωνία	φωτὶ	πρὸς	σκότος;	δὲ
τίς	συμφώνησις	Χριστοῦ	πρὸς	Βελιάρ,	ἢ
τίς	μερὶς	πιστῷ	μετὰ	ἀπίστου;	δὲ
τίς	συγκατάθεσις	ναῷ θεοῦ	μετὰ	εἰδώλων;
gar						
tis	*metochē*	*dikaiosynē*	*kai*	*anomia,*	*ē*
tis	*koinōnia*	*phōti*	*pros*	*skotos?*	*de*
tis	*symphōnāsis*	*Christou*	*pros*	*Beliar,*	*ē*
tis	*meris*	*pistō*	*meta*	*apistou?*	*de*
tis	*synkatathesis*	*naō theou*	*meta*	*eidōlōn?*

For
what do righteousness and lawlessness have in common?
Or what kind of close relationship does light have with darkness?
[15]What harmony is there between Christ and Beliar?
Or what part of the life God has given his people does a believer have in common
   with an unbeliever?
[16]In what way can God's temple and idols come to an agreement?

The five questions are opened with γάρ, the conjunction introducing theological reinforcement, or explanation, of the exhortation just given. Notice the relationship between the conjunctions joining the five rhetorical questions as the apostle alternates between ἤ and δέ.[18] Notice also the pattern of elements joining the contrasting elements in each question: καί, πρός, πρός, μετά, μετά. Finally, the verb of being (ἐστι, *esti*) must be provided for each of the questions. All of this adds up to make the unit highly crafted and rhetorically pleasing. Functionally, the rhythmic drumming of these rhetorical questions serves to drive home the main point: the essential incompatibility of the people or ways of God with people and ways aligned with godlessness.

The first rhetorical question, "For what do righteousness and lawlessness have in common?" anticipates a resounding "None!" as the answer. Righteousness (δικαιοσύνη) here refers to "the quality or characteristic of upright behavior" (BDAG 248), or ethical conduct, and it is set over against ἀνομία (lawlessness), living with no regard for God's laws. This antithesis appears in

---

18. The movement back and forth between these two conjunctions seems to be primarily stylistic, rather than intended to pair rhetorical questions 1 and 2, and questions 3 and 4.

the Psalms, contrasting the righteous and the wicked (Pss. 1; 11; 34 [1; 10; 33 LXX]; Barnett 1997: 346). Jesus has harsh prophetic words for the lawless at the end of the age (Matt. 7:23; 13:41) and says that lawlessness will increase dramatically at the end, causing the love of many to grow cold (Matt. 24:12). Paul also associates ἀνομία with the end of the age in 2 Thess. 2:3, 7 as he speaks about the "man of lawlessness" and "the mystery of lawlessness." Elsewhere Paul equates lawlessness with moral impurity (Rom. 6:19; Titus 2:14). The term μετοχή (*metochē*) has to do with "sharing" or "participation," and its cognate μέτοχος can refer to a companion or business partner. Paul's point is that right and wrong, morality and immorality, have nothing in common.

Next Paul asks, "Or what kind of close relationship does light have with darkness?" Again, the implied answer is "There is none!" The apostle has already made much of the contrast between light and darkness, a contrast that weaves a thread through the NT literature.[19] At 4:6, with a backdrop of the Shekinah glory in new-covenant ministry just presented (3:7–18), Paul proclaims, "God, the one having said, 'Light will shine out of darkness!' has shone in our hearts the light, which is the personal comprehension of God's glory in the face of Jesus Christ." God's light dispels spiritual darkness; it does not have κοινωνία (*koinōnia*) with the darkness. The two are antithetical. The term κοινωνία overlaps semantically with μετοχή, connoting sharing or association. Yet when used in conjunction with the preposition πρός (*pros*), it carries a nuance of intimacy or close relationship (so Robertson 1934: 625). Again, the main point is that spiritual light and spiritual darkness do not mix; the former completely drives out the latter.

6:15   A third rhetorical question, at the beginning of verse 15, reads, "What harmony is there between Christ and Beliar?" Συμφώνησις (*symphōnēsis*), found only here in the biblical literature, would normally mean "the accord between two voices singing together" or "agreement."[20] The thought has to do with two people working together in a coordinated way and on a common task. So Paul asks how there could be this kind of "harmony" between Christ and Beliar. In early Judaism the name "Belial" may have been coined as a name for Satan by conflating an OT word for "worthlessness" (בְּלִיַּעַל, *bĕlîyaʿal*) with the name of the pagan god Baal. "Beliar," a common variant, was also used of Satan, one ancient text emphasizing that a person must choose between God and Beliar (T. Naph. 2.6; 3.1; Keener 2005: 194). Again, it makes no sense to think of Christ and Beliar as cooperating or in agreement on any agenda!

Hitting close to Paul's main application, the fourth rhetorical question reads, "What part of the life God has given his people does a believer have

---

19. Matt. 4:16; 6:23; Luke 11:35; John 3:19; Acts 26:18; Rom. 2:19; 13:12; Eph. 5:8; 1 Thess. 5:5; 1 Pet. 2:9. At 1 Thess. 5:5 Paul writes to the Thessalonians, "For you are all sons of light and sons of the day. We're not of the night or of darkness" (HCSB).

20. Spicq (1994: 3.324–25) notes that in Plato (*Leg.* 3.689d) the cognate συμφωνία (*symphōnia*) can connote agreement or harmony of relationship, and the Stoics define the term as an "agreement" of teaching related to life. Further, the papyri use this cognate with the sense of "covenant" or "agreement."

in common with an unbeliever?" The first three questions have intimated respectively that believers and unbelievers have different moral values, belong to different spiritual spheres, and serve different masters. The apostle now states the case baldly: believers and unbelievers have no common share in God's gift of spiritual life. Thus they have no common ground on which to build their most intimate relationships. The term μερίς (*meris*) could be used by an ancient author to speak of a "part," a "share," or a "portion" (BDAG 632). For instance, Peter rebukes Simon, the Samaritan sorcerer who sought to buy the ability to "give" the Holy Spirit: "You have no share [μερίς] or part [κλῆρος, *klēros*, a share, portion] in this matter because your heart is not right before God!" (Acts 8:21 NET). Similarly, Paul tells the Colossians that God the Father "has enabled you to share in the saints' inheritance [τὴν μερίδα τοῦ κλήρου, *tēn merida tou klērou*] in the light" (Col. 1:12 HCSB). This pairing of μερίς with κλῆρος occurs twenty-three times in the LXX, always speaking of a part or allotment given by the Lord (e.g., Deut. 10:9; 12:12; 14:27, 29; 18:1; Josh. 18:6; 19:9; Wis. 2:9; Isa. 57:6; Jer. 13:25). What the Lord gives to the believer is different from what he gives to the unbeliever, and a "part" given the believer, by its very nature, cannot be shared by an unbeliever.

The apostle finally comes to the end of this string of rhetorical questions, asking, "In what way can God's temple and idols come to an agreement?" The term rendered "agreement" (συγκατάθεσις, *synkatathesis*) has to do with a pact or a relationship arrived at by mutual consent. One of the darkest moments of the OT era was when, in the temple of the Lord, King Manasseh built altars to the heavenly host and set up a carved image of Asherah (e.g., 2 Kings 21:3–7). The writer of 2 Kings says that this was a greater evil than that done by the nations the Lord had destroyed and displaced in favor of the Israelites (21:9). The temple of God and idols don't mix. Accordingly, here in 2 Cor. 6:16 Paul asserts that the people of God cannot make a pact with idols. In 1 Corinthians Paul has already used the "temple" metaphor to speak of the people of God as the dwelling place of God (1 Cor. 3:16–17; 6:19–20), and here he states succinctly, "For we are the temple of the living God" (see Webb 1993: 32–33). This theological assertion both rounds off the series of rhetorical questions and leads into the catena of OT texts, serving as a literary hinge between the two.[21]

6:16a–b

Paul now reinforces the theological assertion of 6:16b with a string of OT passages centering on the themes of God's presence among his people and the consequent need for sanctification.[22] Each OT passage has been carefully chosen from a context emphasizing appropriate worship of the one true God over against pagan worship, with the passages strongly exhorting the people of God to separate from idolatry (so Garland 1999: 336–37) so God will restore them to proper relationship with himself. The introductory formula, "just as

6:16c

---

21. On the use of intermediary transitions, see Guthrie 1994: 105–11.
22. On the use of these OT quotations in 2 Cor. 6:16–18, see P. Balla, *CNTUOT* 769–74.

God said" (καθὼς εἶπεν ὁ θεὸς, *kathōs eipen ho theos*) is not characteristic of Paul's Letters and, indeed, in this exact form, does not occur elsewhere in the NT (but see the similar formula at 4:6; Thrall 1994: 477). However, presenting Scripture as falling from the lips of God was common in Jewish synagogue homilies of the Hellenistic world (Thyen 1955: 69–74), perhaps suggesting that Paul could be incorporating in his letter a part of a sermon he had preached in the past.

The first of the OT quotations comes from a conflation of Lev. 26:11–12 and Ezek. 37:27, brought together at least in part on the basis of verbal analogy.[23] The passages come together in a triple promise:

> "I will live among them
>   and walk around,
> I will be their God,
>   and they will be my people."

Notice that the promise of God's presence is followed by a double promise concerning relationship.

There are at least three interesting points to note from the context of Lev. 26:11–12, which give the OT passage strong ties with Paul's discussion at this point in the letter. First, Lev. 26 begins with commands against idolatry and commands to observe the Sabbaths and respect God's sanctuaries. The warning against idolatry and a concern for the true place for the worship of God match the last of Paul's rhetorical questions (2 Cor. 6:16a). Second, Lev. 26:11–12 serves as a capstone on a long series of promises (Lev. 26:3–12) to those who obey the commands of Lev. 26:1–2, and in our string of OT quotations, Paul clearly highlights God's promises as a significant basis for his exhortations ("since we have promises like these," 2 Cor. 7:1a). Third, in Lev. 26:13 LXX God reminds the Israelites of the foundation of their relationship with him in the exodus from Egypt. The text reads, συνέτριψα τὸν δεσμὸν τοῦ ζυγοῦ ὑμῶν (*synetripsa ton desmon tou zygou hymōn*, "I have shattered the bond of your yoke," NETS). Of course this brings to mind Paul's exhortation to not be "unequally yoked" with unbelievers (2 Cor. 6:14).

The context of Ezek. 37:27, the prophet's vision of the valley of dry bones, also has a number of connections with 2 Cor. 6:14–7:1. The prophetic word concerns God's lavish promises, a cleansing from idolatry and lawlessness (τῶν ἀνομιῶν αὐτῶν, *tōn anomiōn autōn*), God's dwelling place among his

---

23. Perhaps these two passages were originally brought together by common emphases (promises, prohibition of idolatry, etc.) and the rabbinic principle of verbal analogy. Both passages in the LXX combine future forms of the verbs with forms of the pronoun αὐτός (*autos*). Yet the parallels are also conceptual. In the Greek text of each, the term διαθήκη (*diathēkē*, covenant) is closely associated with the promise of God dwelling among his people (Ezek. 37:26). In fact, Lev. 26:11, instead of saying that God would place his tent or dwelling among them (as in MT), reads, καὶ θήσω τὴν διαθήκην μου ἐν ὑμῖν (*kai thēsō tēn diathēkēn mou en hymin*, I will place my covenant among you).

people, and a climactic statement on the Lord as the one sanctifying his people (Ezek. 37:23–28 LXX).

Thus, while neither of these conflated passages matches the wording of our quotation in 2 Cor. 6:16 perfectly, each brings rich contexts to bear in service of Paul's exhortation.[24] God promises that he will be present among his people, that he will be their God and they his people. *Presence* and *identification* both are emphasized in the context of covenant (cf. Jer. 31:31–34). These constitute twin aspects of healthy relationship, which God promises to those who heed the call to sanctification.

Verse 17 begins with the inferential conjunction διό (*dio*, therefore, for this reason), pointing to a logical relationship between the quotation just given and the quotation of Isa. 52:11 that now follows. The promise that God will live among his people and will be their God (6:16) provides a basis for the exhortation quoted in 6:17: **6:17–18**

> "Come out from among them
> and separate yourselves from them, says the Lord,
> and don't touch that which is unclean."

This triple exhortation stems from a passage in Isaiah[25] celebrating the redemption of Israel, its salvation by which God has delivered the people from captivity among the unclean and uncircumcised (52:1–2). The prophecy points out that this is not the first time God has delivered his people: they had been enslaved in the past by the Egyptians and the Assyrians (52:3–4). Yet, in spite of their rebellion against God, a rebellion that has again put a yoke around their necks (52:2, 5), God in his mercy brings salvation, restoring the people to his presence; so it is a time for joy and celebration (52:6–10). God promises to reign over them (52:7), and God's presence among them is expressed with "the Lord will go before you, and the Lord God of Israel is the one who gathers you together" (52:12 LXX).

It is in this context where we find the triple exhortations Paul appropriates for his word to the Corinthians. The passage in Isaiah reads,

> ἀπόστητε ἀπόστητε ἐξέλθατε ἐκεῖθεν
> καὶ ἀκαθάρτου μὴ ἅπτεσθε,
> ἐξέλθατε ἐκ μέσου αὐτῆς ἀφορίσθητε,
> οἱ φέροντες τὰ σκεύη κυρίου. (Isa. 52:11 LXX)

> *Apostēte apostēte exelthate ekeithen*
> *kai akathartou mē haptesthe,*

---

24. On the view that for the ancient audience, OT quotations intentionally brought to mind a broader OT context, see Guthrie, *CNTUOT* 920; Carter 2000: 505–6.

25. On the impact of Paul's reading of Isa. 40–66 as driving his theology of new creation and reconciliation in 2 Cor. 5:17–7:1, see Beale 1989. Beale's interpretation fits well the restoration theme evident in the catena of OT texts in 6:14–18. Beale reads this digression as strategic to Paul's theological purpose in this section of 2 Corinthians.

exelthate ek mesou autēs aphoristhēte,
hoi pherontes ta skeuē kyriou.

Depart, depart, go out from there,
and touch no unclean thing;
go out from the midst of it; be separated,
you who carry the vessels of the Lord. (Isa. 52:11 NETS)

The terminology here has to do with religious ritual and calls for "an absolute separation from evil" (Oswalt 1998: 372). The delivered Judeans are commanded to leave a context in which they are defiled by sin; they are to touch nothing that is unclean. Oswalt proposes that the emphasis on ritual defilement, rare in Isaiah, suggests that the focus of the passage is release from spiritual bondage, rather than physical bondage. Further, the context suggests that it is not only the priests and Levites who carry the vessels of the Lord,[26] which had been taken in the sacking of the temple. Rather, the whole people of God carry out the vessels (Oswalt 1998: 372–73).

In appropriating the passage as an exhortation for believers generally, Paul paraphrases, highlighting aspects of the passage and dropping the reference to those who carry the Lord's vessels:

ἐξέλθατε ἐκ μέσου αὐτῶν καὶ ἀφορίσθητε,
    λέγει κύριος,
καὶ ἀκαθάρτου μὴ ἅπτεσθε. (2 Cor. 6:17)

Exelthate ek mesou autōn kai aphoristhēte,
    legei kyrios,
kai akathartou mē haptesthe.

"*Come out* from among them and *separate* yourselves from them,
    says the Lord,
and *don't touch that which is unclean.*"

In the sentence, the apostle moves forward the exhortation to "separate" (ἀφορίσθητε, *aphoristhēte*) from those who are not God's people, pairing it with the exhortation to "come out," both of which communicate an idea of spatial movement, but in Paul's use here they especially are relational. From a biblical standpoint, separation naturally takes place at various stages in the relationship between God's people and those who do not know God. At times the ungodly hate the followers of Christ and separate themselves (ἀφορίσωσιν ὑμᾶς, *aphorisōsin hymas*, they exclude you) from them (Luke 6:22). At other times, as here in 2 Cor. 6:17, believers are to put distance between themselves

---

26. For places in the OT where the Levites "carry," or "take up," the Lord's vessels, see Num. 1:50–51; 4:12, 15; 1 Kings 8:3–4. See also Motyer 1993: 421.

and the ungodly (Acts 19:9).[27] At the end of the age God himself will separate out the evil from the righteous as a shepherd separates sheep and goats (Matt. 13:49; 25:32). Thus, Paul wants to emphasize the need for the Corinthians to separate from those who defile them by dragging them into "unclean" patterns of life. Consequently, the third exhortation says, "Don't touch that which is unclean."

The writers of the Gospels use the term "unclean" (ἀκάθαρτος, *akathartos*) especially to describe evil spirits (e.g., Matt. 10:1; 12:43; Mark 1:23, 26–27). Peter's response concerning the "unclean" animals in his vision of Acts 10 points to the greater backdrop of instructions concerning ritual defilement under the Sinai covenant (Acts 10:14, 28). Yet, among the writers of the NT era, the word could also be used with reference to moral impurity generally (Eph. 5:5; Rev. 17:4), and this seems to be the import here. The Isaiah passage, put down with Paul's pen, calls for the Corinthians to come out from those who are corrupting them morally and to side decidedly with Paul, his mission, and his gospel.

When the Corinthians respond well to the promise in 6:16 and the triple exhortation of 6:17, God, the almighty Lord, promises to welcome them, living among them as their father (6:17c–18):

"And I will welcome you."
[18]And, "I will be your father,
and you yourselves will be my sons and daughters,
    says the almighty Lord."

As with the bringing together of Lev. 26:11–12 and Ezek. 37:27 as a word of promise in 2 Cor. 6:16, Paul now conflates Ezek. 20:41 LXX and 2 Sam. 7:14 (with, perhaps, the ascription "says the almighty Lord" stemming from 2 Sam. 7:8 LXX), presenting another triple promise that balances nicely the triple exhortation just given in 6:17 and the previous promise in 6:16. As with the triple OT promise quoted in 6:16c, here too we find a promise of God's presence, followed by a double promise of relationship or identification.

	2 Cor. 6:16c (Lev. 26:11–12; Ezek. 37:27)	2 Cor. 6:17c–18 (Ezek. 20:41; 2 Sam. 7:14)
Presence	"I will live among them and walk around, and	"and I will welcome you."
Relationship	I will be their God, and they will be my people."	And, "I will be your father, and you yourselves will by my sons and daughters, says the almighty Lord."

In accordance with the emphases we have already noted in this string of OT texts, the context of Ezek. 20:41 speaks of God bringing his people out

---

27. Peter's error, recounted in Gal. 2:12, was inappropriately separating himself from Gentile fellow believers as if they were unclean.

from among the peoples of the earth (20:34), sorting out the impious and rebellious among them (20:38). The whole people of God will be set apart as acceptable to the Lord (20:40), and they will remember and turn away from the things that made them unclean (20:43–44). So God calls his people out from the place of their uncleanness, calling them into the promised land, where they will experience his presence. This is a microcosm of a key theme of the Bible, and thus of Paul's gospel: the people of God enter God's presence and—miracle of miracles—he welcomes them.

What is more, God welcomes his people, not as mere slaves to be cared for and utilized in the advancement of some work, but as a father welcoming his sons and daughters to the family gathering. The covenants of the OT era generally ran along family lines, God working through generations of families (Gen. 13:16; 17:5–6). The allusion to 2 Sam. 7:14 stems from the Nathan oracle, and in its original context reads, "I will be a father to him, and he shall be a son to me" (NETS; LXX: ἐγὼ ἔσομαι αὐτῷ εἰς πατέρα, καὶ αὐτὸς ἔσται μοι εἰς υἱόν, *egō esomai autō eis patera, kai autos estai moi eis huion*). The original word concerned God's covenant promise of close relationship to David's heir and forms the basis for subsequent OT passages that focus on the father-son relationship between Yahweh and David's son (1 Chron. 17:13; 22:10; 28:6; Ps. 2:7): God promises a covenant love toward David's house (Ps. 89:28–35).

This promised covenant love laid the groundwork for what would develop into Israel's hope for a future king who would carry on the Davidic line and inherit the covenant promises (Isa. 11:1–5; Jer. 23:5; 33:15; Amos 9:11; Zech. 3:8; 6:12; Bateman 1997: 158–59). Some in ancient Judaism found in 2 Sam. 7 a basis for belief that the Messiah would be God's son (4Q174 frg. 1 1.10–11; Heb. 1:5). What is more, the family relationship grounded in God's relationship with the Davidic heir was expanded to include the whole nation (Jer. 31:9) and, in the NT, the new-covenant people of God. Thus, for example, Hebrews proclaims that the Son of God is not ashamed to call the new covenanters siblings (Heb. 2:11; Matt. 12:48–49). Believers, whether described as being born or adopted, are part of God's family (Gal. 4:1–7; 6:10; Eph. 1:5; 1 Pet. 1:23; 4:17; 1 John 3:9) and now coheirs with the Messiah (Rom. 8:17). Thus, here in 2 Cor. 6:18, the promise of 2 Sam. 7:14, originally spoken of the Davidic heir, is expanded to include all of God's sons and daughters.[28] Moreover, Paul has shaped the words of the allusion to be very personal. The third-person pronouns "him" (αὐτῷ, *autō*) and "he" (αὐτός, *autos*) of 2 Sam. 7:14 have been replaced with the personal address "you" (ὑμῖν/ὑμεῖς, *hymin/hymeis*): "I will be a father to you, and you yourselves will be my sons and daughters."

The string of OT passages comes to a conclusion with the words, "says the almighty Lord," an ascription at 2 Sam. 7:8 LXX taken from the beginning

---

28. The addition of "daughters" (θυγατέρας, *thygateras*) probably comes from the LXX of Isa. 43:6, which reads, "Bring My sons from far away, and My daughters from the ends of the earth" (HCSB).

of the Nathan oracle. The word παντοκράτωρ (*pantokratōr*) speaks of God as awesome, all-powerful, the One who can "take hold" (κρατέω, *krateō*) of "all things" (πάντα, *panta*), or exercise his authority over all things (Harris 2005: 511).[29] In the context of 2 Sam. 7 "the almighty Lord" speaks of God's ability to accomplish great things on behalf of David, his anointed one. Thus the title fits well at the conclusion of a string of exhortations and promises to the sons and daughters of God. There is both a solemnity and a sublimity to the title "almighty Lord." He is the awesome One whose exhortations we must take seriously—we should be sobered by them—and yet, he can accomplish all that is needed on our behalf.

The promises concerning the identification of God with people and God's pres-   **7:1**
ence among people have a demand, a hortatory requirement, that God's people be holy, separate from the world, cleansed from impurity. Having presented a rich mix of exhortations, rhetorical challenges, and promises (6:14–18), Paul now builds on them with a concluding exhortation: "Therefore, dear ones, since we have promises like these, we should wash ourselves clean from every impurity of flesh and spirit, making our holiness complete in the fear of God" (Ταύτας οὖν ἔχοντες τὰς ἐπαγγελίας, ἀγαπητοί, καθαρίσωμεν ἑαυτοὺς ἀπὸ παντὸς μολυσμοῦ σαρκὸς καὶ πνεύματος, ἐπιτελοῦντες ἁγιωσύνην ἐν φόβῳ θεοῦ, *Tautas oun echontes tas epangelias, agapētoi, katharisōmen heautous apo pantos molysmou sarkos kai pneumatos, epitelountes hagiōsynēn en phobō theou*). There are at least four points to notice about this summary exhortation found in 7:1.

First, the inferential conjunction οὖν (*oun*) forms the bridge to this concluding thought, transitioning to this clear statement of the main implication of what has just been said. "Imperative rests on indicative, 'ought' upon 'is'" (Barnett 1997: 356). In other words, the promises lay the foundation for how the Corinthians should respond. The "promises" (τὰς ἐπαγγελίας, *tas epangelias*) to which the apostle refers are those quoted in the previous unit (6:16c, 17b–18) concerning God's relationship with his people and his presence among them. These promises give the basis for the exhortation that follows. Promises serve to motivate. Longing for God's presence, desiring a right relationship with him in which he welcomes us as sons and daughters, lays a foundation for holy living.

Second, notice that Paul addresses the Corinthians as ἀγαπητοί (*agapētoi*), a common form of address when exhortation is being given, but also an affectionate form of address. That he calls them "dear ones" gives insight into the constancy of Paul's love for and commitment to these believers in spite of the irritations of dealing with problem people. But it also has theological overtones. The Corinthians are not loved ones because of stellar behavior but rather because they are God's loved, covenant people (Hafemann 2000: 288).

29. The only other place the term is found in the NT is in Revelation, where the word is paired with θεός (*theos*), the Lord being addressed as "God almighty!" (Rev. 1:8; 4:8; 11:17; 15:3; 16:7, 14; 19:6, 15; 21:22).

Third, the clear call of the entire unit is that the Corinthians must cleanse themselves from every form of uncleanness, and the apostle probably has in mind the immoral patterns that had plagued the church, yet especially the improper association of certain members with Paul's opponents, with whom they are in incompatible relationships (6:14a). The verb καθαρίσωμεν (*katharisōmen*) is first-person plural aorist active subjunctive, a form appropriately used by a preacher exhorting a congregation, a form by which he identifies with those being addressed (cf., e.g., Heb. 2:1; 4:1, 14, 16). Moreover, they are to cleanse themselves from "every impurity of flesh and spirit." The term μολυσμός (*molysmos*) refers to defilement in a religious or moral sense. Used only here in the NT, the word shows up three times in the LXX. At 1 Esd. 8:80 (NETS) we read, "The land that you are entering to possess is a land polluted with the pollution [μεμολυσμένη μολυσμῷ, *memolysmenē molysmō*] of the aliens of the land, and they have filled it with their uncleanness" (= 1 Esd. 8:83 NRSV). In context, the passage concerns the intermingling of the Israelites, along with their rulers, priests, and Levites with foreigners in the period following the Babylonian captivity (1 Esd. 8:69–70 [8:66–67 LXX]). At 2 Macc. 5:27 one reads of Judas Maccabee's retreat to the wilderness to escape the forced hellenization under Antiochus.[30] Finally, Jer. 23:15 offers a powerful word in a prophetic denunciation of the false, adulterous prophets of Jerusalem who, speaking their own words rather than the Lord's words (23:16), had polluted the whole land. Fitting for Paul's concerns here, each of these examples addresses inappropriate relationships (at times inappropriate leaders) that have a negative effect on relationship with God.

Thus, the Corinthians are to cleanse themselves from *every* (παντός, *pantos*, every, the whole) bit of contamination; this is the extent to which they are to strive for holiness in light of the elaborate promises of God. The genitives that follow, σαρκός and πνεύματος (*sarkos, pneumatos*), are attributive,[31] speaking of sins of the physical body and sins of the spirit. Rather than communicating a dichotomy between sins of the flesh and of the spirit, the apostle simply challenges the Corinthians to be holistic in their resolve to reject sinful patterns of life. In other words, everything sinful, whether matters of the spirit or matters of the physical body, must be rejected by the sons and daughters of God.

Fourth and finally, holiness is "completed" as we have a proper reverence for God. The participle ἐπιτελοῦντες (*epitelountes*) is an adverbial participle of result. The word ἐπιτελέω (*epiteleō*) could be used with the sense "to finish" something (e.g., 1 Esd. 4:55; 6:27; Rom. 15:28; Phil. 1:6) or "to fulfill a purpose" (1 Pet. 5:9), but here the term seems to communicate the idea "to complete, accomplish, perform, or bring about a result" (BDAG 383). So, as

30. "But Ioudas Makkabaios, with about nine others, got away to the wilderness and kept himself and his companions alive in the mountains as wild animals do; they continued to live on what grew wild so that they might not share in the defilement [τοῦ μολυσμοῦ, *tou molysmou*]" (2 Macc. 5:27 NETS).

31. On the attributive genitive, see D. Wallace 1996: 86–88.

believers cleanse themselves "from every impurity of flesh and spirit," this results in them "making . . . holiness complete," removing sinful patterns of life so that one's patterns of life are characterized as being set apart for God.[32] And they do this "in the fear of God" (ἐν φόβῳ θεοῦ, *en phobō theou*).

In the NT the idea of fearing God expresses an appropriate reverence and awe, which stem from God's mighty acts and accompany faith (*EDNT* 3:429). Neither mere caution nor a debilitating terror, the term communicates an emotional state in which one reflects upon the awesome dimensions of God's power and is appropriately sobered. Holiness of life stems from reverent reflection on the devastating gravity of being out of step with God's will. Paul has already communicated a good deal about the appropriate posture for Christian ministers as they live by God's grace (1:12), with God as their witness (1:23), before God (2:17), and in God's sight (4:2). Indeed, Paul ministers in "the fear of the Lord" (5:11): his life and ministry are permeated by the gravity of his calling, the awesomeness of the God he serves. So too the Corinthians must live out their calling to holiness with deep reverence for God, who gives promises but also strong warnings of the consequences of turning away from the gospel of grace, turning to devastating patterns of sin.

iii. A Plea for Openness Resumed (7:2–4)

At this point, Paul renews his call, made a few moments before (6:11–13), for the Corinthians to open up to him relationally: "Make room for us!" At 6:13 he used the word πλατύνω (*platynō*) to communicate the idea of "enlarging" their hearts toward him. The word here is χωρέω (*chōreō*), "to contain" or "have room for."[33] So they need to close down the "border crossings" of their hearts transversed by the false teachers, the interlopers contaminating their spiritual lives, and at the same time open up the heart boundaries that are keeping them from a free and open relationship with Paul and his fellow workers. As a basis for this call to openness, the apostle boldly rebukes the Corinthians, asserting, with a skillful use of repetition,[34] that he and his fellow ministers have done nothing to warrant the closed attitude of some in the church:

7:2

> We haven't mistreated anyone;
> οὐδένα ἠδικήσαμεν (*oudena ēdikēsamen*)
>
> we haven't corrupted anyone;
> οὐδένα ἐφθείραμεν (*oudena ephtheiramen*)

32. The term ἁγιωσύνη (*hagiōsynē*) means "holiness" and is found only in Paul in the NT (Rom. 1:4; 2 Cor. 7:1; 1 Thess. 3:13); in the LXX the word occurs five times (2 Macc. 3:12; Pss. 29:5; 95:6; 96:12; 144:5 [30:4; 96:6; 97:12; 145:5 ET]).

33. The word finds expression at John 2:6, e.g., where the stone water jars contained 20–30 gallons each. Mark 2:2 offers a better parallel here: "So many people gathered together that there was no more room, not even in the doorway, and He was speaking the message to them" (HCSB).

34. The repetition of οὐδένα (*oudena*, [in] nothing) at the beginning of each clause is called anaphora. Notice that each verb ends with -αμεν (*-amen*), a use of homoeoptoton. The combination of the two forms of repetition makes for a pleasing literary "ring" when read or heard.

we haven't taken advantage of anyone
οὐδένα ἐπλεονεκτήσαμεν (*oudena epleonektēsamen*)

The language may betray at least aspects of the accusations made against Paul by his opponents, but the words here are more likely Paul's way of pointing a finger at outcomes of his opponents' ministry.

To "mistreat" (ἀδικέω, *adikeō*) is a general term (Thrall 1994: 481) meaning to treat someone wrongly or unjustly, thus harming them (BDAG 20). For example, Paul uses the term in tandem with "cheating" at 1 Cor. 6:8: "But you yourselves wrong and cheat, and you do this to your brothers and sisters" (NET); and in 2 Cor. 7:12 he refers to the harm done by an unnamed offender, probably the same one mentioned in 2:5–11.[35] Thus the upshot of the word has to do with poor treatment. Perhaps the harshness of Paul's past rebukes (2:1–3; 7:8) had been construed as abuse by some, but the apostle categorically denies that he has acted unjustly.

Harsher still, φθείρω (*phtheirō*) could be used by ancient authors with the sense of "to cause harm to in a physical manner or in outward circumstances, destroy, ruin, corrupt," or "spoil" (BDAG 1054). Here Paul might have in mind the moral corruption that comes from false teaching (so the NLT[2]: "led anyone astray"; cf. 1 Cor. 15:33), or a form of punishment so harsh that it leads to destruction (1 Cor. 3:17; Jer. 13:9 LXX). If moral corruption is the idea, the denial may relate to accusations against Paul that he had bamboozled the Corinthians in relation to the collection for the saints at Jerusalem (8:20; 12:17). In any case, Paul denies having corrupted anyone.

Πλεονεκτέω (*pleonekteō*), the third term in this triad of denials, has to do with exploiting, defrauding, or taking advantage of someone (BDAG 824). The suggestion may have been made that Paul's mission, rather than serving the Corinthians, sought to use them for his own personal gain (12:16–19). Ironically, the "ministry" of the opponents seems to have been characterized by the "peddling" of the Word for personal profit (2 Cor. 2:17).

7:3   Paul's intention in using such strong language is not to hurt the Corinthians. He does not want to "condemn" them. The construction is the negated λέγω (*legō*, I speak), followed by the preposition πρός (*pros* + acc., for the purpose of), plus the noun κατάκρισις (*katakrisis*, condemnation). The sense is "I am not saying this to pass judgment on you," or "to accuse you." Paul does not make such strident denials to put them in their place spiritually, to condemn them, nor to put them on the defensive. Rather, his words are an expression of love and service.[36] He is ready "to die or live with" them (συναποθανεῖν καὶ συζῆν, *synapothanein kai syzēn*). The expression Paul uses here seems to have been a common way in Greco-Roman culture of referring to the abiding

---

35. See other examples of ἀδικέω in Paul at 2 Cor. 7:12; Gal. 4:12; Col. 3:25; Philem. 18.

36. Such a caveat—proclaiming that what was written was not intended to stir negative emotions but rather an expression of love—was commonly used in the ancient world among writers like Cicero (*Fam.* 2.4.2; Keener 2005: 197).

nature of real friendship (Furnish 1984: 367). The apostle certainly expresses his commitment to the Corinthians relationally. He will walk with them in Christian community in all its aspects, saying, "We are in the struggles of life and death together." He is willing to give up time, effort, and resources now or to give up life itself to walk with them as their devoted father-minister.

Yet, given the context of the broader letter, which speaks so much of a theology of life and death (2:16; 4:10–12; 5:14–15; 6:9), the apostle uses this expression of friendship from a particular theological vantage point. For the believer, both death and life are aspects of a true ministry, true community, and a true walk with God. Thus Paul's expression of friendship, that he is ready to die or live with the Corinthians, is undergirded with a robust theology of relationships in Christ.

The final word of this section, in which Paul makes such fervent appeals to the Corinthians, has four affirmations. Verse 4 reads, "I have spoken to you with great openness; I boast a great deal about you to others. I am very encouraged. In the midst of all our troubles, I am ecstatic with joy." The first affirmation expresses Paul's openness (παρρησία, *parrēsia*) toward the Corinthians, which he describes as extensive (πολλή, *pollē*, great, much). The term παρρησία, which the apostle has already used at 3:12 with reference to his new-covenant ministry, can mean "frankness" or "outspokenness," in terms of one's speech; or "boldness," "courage," or "confidence," especially in the presence of someone of high rank. Most translations render the word "confidence" (HCSB, NASB, NET, NLT², NIV). Given the context, however, Paul seems to be reiterating the openness of his posture toward the Corinthians, expressed at the beginning of this section with "We have spoken openly to you" (6:11a). This is another way of saying that his communication with the Corinthians has been frank or, perhaps, bold (so the ESV; cf. the use of the word at 3:12; Thrall 1994: 485).

7:4

But not only has Paul been open with the Corinthians; he also is proud of them and has spoken positively about them: "I boast a great deal about you to others." Boasting (καύχησις, *kauchēsis*) has to do with the pride one has in something or someone; as we saw at 1:12, the word can be used positively or negatively.[37] Paul uses the term and the cognate verb several times in this book (the noun: 1:12; 7:4, 14; 8:24; 11:10, 17), and the uses of the noun at 7:14 and 8:24 closely parallel the use here in 7:4, suggesting that Paul has in mind his boasting about the Corinthians to others. The preposition ὑπέρ (*hyper*, about) plus the genitive (ὑμῶν, *hymōn*, you) can function as a "marker of general content," meaning "concerning" or "about." So the boast of which Paul speaks has been extensive (πολλή, *pollē*, a great deal) and about the Corinthians.

Often a wise leader knows how to blend words of confrontation with words of encouragement; and here, as he concludes his great treatment of authentic ministry and turns toward the book's next section, Paul ends on

---

37. For the positive and negative uses of καύχησις in the LXX as well as the broader Greco-Roman world, see the comments on 1:12 and Spicq 1994: 2.295–302.

a note of encouragement: "I am very encouraged. In the midst of all our troubles, I am ecstatic with joy." Thus the apostle acknowledges the difficulties that have surrounded his ministry, but he also expresses his hope and joy. The reference to "encouragement" (παράκλησις, *paraklēsis*) returns to a key theme for Paul, one with which he launched the book (1:3–7).[38] That he is "ecstatic with joy" renders the words ὑπερπερισσεύομαι τῇ χαρᾷ (*hyperperisseuomai tē chara*); this verb is found in the NT only here and at Rom. 5:20: "But where sin multiplied, grace *multiplied even more*" (Rom. 5:20 HCSB). Throughout the book thus far, Paul has been quite open about the challenges surrounding his ministry (this term θλῖψις, *thlipsis*, occurs at 1:4, 8; 2:4; 4:17; 6:4; 7:4; 8:2, 13). Yet his joy runs high, and he explains why in our next section of the letter.

Reflection

To love God is to love and long for holiness. To embrace inappropriately that which is unholy constitutes a withdrawal from God, God's gospel, God's ways, God's people, and God's true mission in the world. Here we discern the reason Paul has brought his theologically robust treatise on authentic ministry to a climax by focusing on purity and withdrawal from entanglements with unbelievers. Christ-followers must follow Christ in the world (where else?) and must engage unbelievers with the gospel of salvation (who else?). But Paul knows that entanglements of impure affections, values, commitments, worldly philosophies, and perspectives are to the true God's holiness as oil is to water: they cannot mix. Thus, if not checked and dealt with, impurity drives a person away from authentic ministry, from the distinctiveness of countercultural Christianity. Augustine writes:

> Now I speak to the true Christians. If you believe, hope and love otherwise [than the pagans do], then live otherwise and gain approval for your distinctive faith, hope and charity by distinctive actions. Pay attention to the apostle when, in earnest admonition, he says: "Do not bear the yoke with unbelievers. For what has justice in common with iniquity? Or what fellowship has light with darkness? . . . Or what part has the believer with the unbeliever? And what agreement has the temple of God with idols?" (*New Year's Day* 198.3; Bray 1999: 261–62)

The problem with a heart full of the world's spiritual contamination, as Paul's urgent appeal makes clear, is that such a heart has no room for God, nor for a truly God-centered ministry. As with Jesus's parable of the sower (Mark 4:1–9), the seeds of God's good Word fall into a life that is hardened, shallow, or congested, but the heart has no room for it. No place for God

---

38. For the use of παράκλησις in Paul and particularly in 2 Corinthians, see the comments on 1:3.

to "walk around" and be God in the person's life. No place to live like a son or daughter relating to the heavenly Father. No place for the words and ministry and love of an apostle. The heart is closed because of impurity, and the heart too often is impure because of bad relationships.

Missionary martyr Jim Elliot (1978: 135) once wrote,

> Sacredness is an aspect this people never assumes toward anything. In a rebellious reaction to Victorian prudishness, they revel in bald frankness which enervates moral consciousness. Tragedy is that I feel it affecting me. We have a noncommittal morality. Nothing is so bad, and nothing is so good. Everything is a muddle of both.

If that was true in the mid-twentieth century, what about our generation? The only answer—the only answer there has ever been for believers in the world—is to "come out from among them and separate yourselves from them, says the Lord, and don't touch that which is unclean," not in the sense of asceticism or withdrawal from the world, but in the sense of our deepest inner commitments and the patterns of our lives. To such, the God who walks around among his people responds, "I will welcome you."

Additional Notes

6:11. The reading ὑμῶν (after καρδία) has some external support in its favor (ℵ B 0243 1881 2464) but does not make sense in the context and may have resulted from a scribe mishearing the pronoun because of the word's pronunciation. Paul's exhortation has to do with their hearts being closed, and the stative aspect of the verb in context does not seem to be referring only to a time in the past (as in "in the past your heart was wide open!"). Thus the reading ἡμῶν ($\mathfrak{P}^{46c*}$ F C D[1,2] K L P Ψ 323 440 630 1270 049 075 1 6) is preferred.

6:15. At 6:14–16a Paul lays out pairs of contrasts, asserting the incompatibility of true Christ-followers with unbelievers. Generally the first member in each of these pairs is in the dative case. In verse 15, however, the preferred reading Χριστοῦ ($\mathfrak{P}^{46}$ ℵ B C P 0243 33 326 1739 1881 lat; Cl Ambst), a genitive in form, breaks the pattern (the genitive may be read as a genitive of source; "harmony initiated by Christ"?). The inferior reading Χριστῷ (D F G K L Ψ 81 104 365 630 1175 1241 1505 2464 𝔐 sy) probably resulted from a scribe conforming Χριστοῦ to the general pattern of using the dative for the first member in each pair.

6:15. Scribes obviously were confused by the preferred reading Βελιάρ ($\mathfrak{P}^{46}$ ℵ B P C 1881 1175 330 33); some manuscripts read Βελιάν (D K Ψ 6 [b] vg[ms]) and others Βελιάβ (F G d) or Βελιάλ (lat; Tert).

6:15. The genitive Χριστοῦ earlier in the verse has given rise to the inferior reading πιστοῦ (B 33) over against the preferred dative form πιστῷ.

6:16. In *A Textual Commentary*, Metzger and the UBS editorial committee (Metzger 1994: 512) give the reading ἡμεῖς γὰρ ναὸς θεοῦ ἐσμεν (B D* L P 6 33 81 [104] 326 365 1175 1881 2464 co; Or) a B rating on the basis of its strong support by both Alexandrian and Western witnesses and the probability that it gave rise to the reading ὑμεῖς γὰρ ναὸς θεοῦ ἐστε ($\mathfrak{P}^{46}$ C D[2] F G K Ψ 630 1241 1505 𝔐 lat sy; Tert), the latter influenced by 1 Cor. 3:16 and verses 14 and 17 in our present context.

Readings with the plural ναοί (ℵ* 0243 1739; Cl) are secondary adjustments to bring the term in line with plural forms of the pronoun and verb.

6:16. Based on external and internal support, μου ($\mathfrak{P}^{46}$ ℵ B C I^vid P 0243 33 81 1175 1739; Cl Or) is preferred over μοι (D F G K L Ψ 0209 104 365 630 1241 1505 1881 2464 𝔐 latt sy co; Tert Eus Epiph).

7:1. Clearly secondary readings, $\mathfrak{P}^{46}$ reads πνεύματι in place of πνεύματος, ἁγιωσύνης in place of ἁγιωσύνην, and ἀγάπη instead of φόβῳ.

C. When Titus Arrived in Macedonia: The Happy Result When the Corinthians Respond Well (7:5–16)

We now come to the resumption of Paul's travel narrative. After the apostle has instructed on the nature of authentic ministry, and woven this instruction with exhortations and praise (2:14–7:4), he gets back to where he left off at 2:13:

2 Cor. 2:12–13

[12]Now when I came to the region of Troas for the gospel of Christ, and then a door of opportunity having been opened to me by the Lord, [13]I found no rest in my spirit since I did not find my brother Titus; on the contrary, having told them good-bye, I traveled into Macedonia.

2 Cor. 7:5–6

[5]Even when we came into Macedonia, we were not able to rest at all but were hounded by trouble in every way, conflicts on the outside, fears on the inside. [6]But God, the one who encourages the discouraged, encouraged us by Titus's arrival. . . .

Notice that in each passage Paul mentions

a. that he "came into" (forms of ἔρχομαι, *erchomai* + εἰς, *eis*) a new area,
b. that he specifically traveled into Macedonia,
c. that he experienced certain negative emotions, and
d. that Titus was anticipated (2:12–13) and then joined him (7:5–6).

These connections between the two passages might be referred to as "distant hook words [catchwords],"[1] signaling to the first hearers of the letter that Paul had again picked up his travel narrative (contra Welborn 1996: 559–83). Far from indicating that 2 Corinthians is a patchwork of correspondence

---

1. On the use of distant hook words, see Guthrie 1994: 96–100. It is also interesting, however, to notice the mix of singular and plural pronouns in the two passages, singular in 2:12–13 and plural in 7:5–6 (and there is a mix in 7:7). Harris (2005: 524) and Barrett (1973: 206) conclude that Paul speaks of himself in both passages, but Furnish (1984: 385–86) disagrees. Paul seems to move fluidly back and forth between reflections as an individual and reflections offered from the perspective of one who is part of a broader group, and this seems to be manifested especially in passages like 7:7.

fragments,[2] the use of this literary device shows a high level of crafting, a shaping of the letter on Paul's part. The material running from 2:14–7:4 rivets attention on the heart of Paul's concern—that the Corinthians recognize and embrace the kind of authentic Christian ministry embodied in Paul and his fellow workers. Yet that extended, embedded discourse is what Paul sandwiches between the bookends of a step-by-step travel narrative. Why?

Paul's situation, described in 2:12–13, has a healthy amount of tension built into it. That moment in Macedonia, highlighted in 2:12–13, provides a snapshot of how difficult this period of ministry was for the apostle. As he unpacks various dimensions of authentic ministry in the following chapters, the tension built into this snapshot sets the tone for the picture of true ministry as *revealed in brokenness, persecution, and even death.* The false ministers, with whom Paul vies for the affections and allegiance of the Corinthians, neither understand nor display real Christian ministry, which enters into the suffering of Christ for the sake of the church. Will the Corinthians ultimately follow these false ministers or Paul? Will the suffering of the apostle be exacerbated or eased by this church?

Though tension still remains, as the apostle resumes his travel narrative, he communicates at least a partial answer to these questions, mitigating this tension; for Titus came and brought a very encouraging report about the Corinthians. Thus, 2 Cor. 7:5–16 focuses on (1) the encouraging report Paul has received from Titus, that the Corinthians have received the harsh letter well (7:6–7), (2) Paul's reflections on the positive effects of the letter (7:8–13a), and (3) Titus's joy at the Corinthians' response (7:13b–16). Therefore, the section can be outlined as follows:

1. Causes of discouragement and encouragement (7:5–7)
2. The positive effects of Paul's harsh letter (7:8–13a)
3. Titus's joy (7:13b–16)

So, after focusing so much on the hardships of his ministry to this point in the letter, Paul now turns to the flip side of the ministerial coin. Ministry certainly is hard and "deadly," but it also has a tremendous temporal reward: joy. Notice how the themes of "sorrow" and "joy" are balanced in this section (7:7, 9, 13b; Harris 2005: 523). The experience of being used by God to minister to a Christian community produces great returns as that community opens up to God and responds appropriately to godly exhortation. In now celebrating the positive response of the Corinthians to Titus's visit,

---

2. For more on the topic, see the introduction to the commentary. Keener (2005: 198) notes that pages would be mixed more easily in later codices than in first-century papyri, but by that later period the organization of the letter would have been too widely known for an alteration to have been made, and in any case, there exists no manuscript tradition that has the parts of 2 Corinthians rearranged or missing. Stylistic arguments have also been made in favor of the book's unity, including the fact that 7:5–16 echoes elements in 6:11–13 and 7:2–4 and seems to carry the same emotional intensity (Keener 2005: 198; Lambrecht 1999: 133).

the apostle relieves some of the tension in the previous chapters, reinforces their good response to his rebuke, and prepares to challenge the Corinthians to follow through on their commitment to the collection for the saints, which Titus will collect (2 Cor. 8–9; Garland 1999: 350). In fact, 7:5–16 plays an important role in laying a foundation for the remainder of the letter and the apostle's eventual return to Corinth (9:4; 10:2, 6; 12:14, 20–21; 13:1–2, 10). In praising them, expressing his joy in their good responses and his confidence in them, Paul prepares for further exhortations to come in the letter (Barnett 1997: 365) and further ministry to them in person.

Thus, as we consider 2 Cor. 7:5–16, we certainly find ourselves at both a literary and a relational crossroads. Literarily, with the resumption of Paul's travel narrative, we should be caused to think, "Why did he craft the letter in this way?"[3] The apostle had strategically sent his painful letter with Titus as an envoy, rather than making the trip to Corinth himself, thinking that the former course would do more good (2:1)! He seems quite anxious about the outcome of his letter and here is obviously relieved by the outcome. Yet, in 2 Corinthians, Paul delays his celebration of the Corinthians' response to Titus until he has unpacked a defense of his actions (1:12–2:13) and a discourse on the nature of authentic ministry (2:14–7:4). Paul then chooses another crossroads, this critical and relational intersection in his ongoing saga with the Corinthians, as the focus of the literary piece in 7:5–16. Only now does he let the church in on the joy he received from their response to his harsh letter. What all of this tells us is that the apostle is thoughtful, careful, even strategic in communicating with the Corinthians during this difficult time in his relationship with them. His correspondence is organized to have a particular effect.

Following Paul's example, perhaps those of us in ministry today, when faced with a difficult moment vis-à-vis a congregation, should think more strategically about how to lead the congregation through the process of reconciliation. Are there moments when our personal presence is demanded? Should we send an "envoy," or perhaps write out our thoughts in a letter? We especially should think carefully about issues of timing. Choosing when we should rebuke and when we should relieve the relational tension present with celebration seems critical to the outcome of difficult situations.

Exegesis and Exposition

[5]Even when we came into Macedonia, we were not ⌐able⌐ to rest at all but were hounded by trouble in every way, conflicts on the outside, ⌐fears⌐ on the inside. [6]But God, the one who encourages the discouraged, encouraged us by Titus's arrival—[7]and not only by his arrival, but also by the encouragement he received from you. For he

---

3. Of course, this is assuming the unity of the book, as argued in the introduction to this commentary.

told us about your deep desire, your mourning, your enthusiastic concern for me, with the result that I rejoiced even more.

[8]For even though I upset you by my letter, I don't regret it. And yet, I did regret it for awhile (even if the effect was only momentary, ⌐ ¬ I see that that letter made you sad). [9]Now I am glad about it, not because you were upset but because you were upset to the point of repentance! For you were upset in a way that God wanted you to be, with the result that you did not experience loss in any way because of us. [10]For this grief according to God's will ⌐produces¬ repentance that leads to salvation, with no regrets, but worldly sorrow is deadly. [11]For recognize how great an effect this very experience of grief ⌐ ¬ according to God's will has had on you: your eagerness, as well as your defense of yourselves, indeed your indignation, fear, yearning, enthusiasm, and even your execution of justice! In every way you have shown yourselves to be innocent in this matter. [12]Consequently, although I wrote to you, I did not write because of the wrongdoer, nor for the sake of the person who was wronged, but so that your eager devotion to us might be made clear to you before God. [13a]This has been encouraging.

[13b]And in addition to the personal encouragement we experienced, we were especially delighted to see Titus's joy, since all of you have refreshed his spirit. [14]For if I have boasted a bit to him about you, I was not shamed by your response. Rather, just as everything we said to you was true, so our boasting to Titus about you turned out to be true as well. [15]And now his affection for you is even greater as he remembers the obedience of you all, how you received him with fear and trembling. [16]I am glad to say that I have complete confidence in you!

1. Causes of Discouragement and Encouragement (7:5–7)

What the apostle sets before us in the remainder of chapter 7 has three movements (7:5–7; 7:8–13a; 7:13b–16). In the first, Paul shares causes of both discouragement and encouragement from his time in Macedonia (7:5–7). Travel into the region proved to be difficult. When the apostle arrived, he was met with external conflicts and plagued by his own fears (v. 5). But the great God of encouragement, whom Paul so beautifully celebrates at the beginning of 2 Corinthians (1:3–7), provided strong encouragement in the person of Titus, both by the young minister's arrival and his report about the Corinthians' response to Titus's visit.

7:5   Paul now resumes his travel narrative, picking up where he left off at 2:12–13: "Even when we came into Macedonia." The construction καὶ γάρ (kai gar, indeed, for indeed, even) is quite common in the NT, with thirty-nine occurrences, thirteen of which appear in the Corinthian correspondence.[4] Here it functions to provide a logical connection between verses 4 and 5. At the end of verse 4 Paul mentions "all our troubles" (πάσῃ τῇ θλίψει ἡμῶν, pasē tē

---

4. In 1 Cor. 5:7; 7:5; 8:5; 11:9; 12:13–14; 14:8; 2 Cor. 2:10; 3:10; 5:2, 4; 7:5; 13:4. The construction can hardly bear the weight of effecting a connection back to 2:13, as suggested by Thrall. Paul accomplishes that feat with distant hook words that signal to the reader a resumption of the travel narrative.

thlipsei hēmōn), and now he goes back to his recent experience in Macedonia as an example of such difficulties.

As far as we know, the apostle had first come to Macedonia on his second mission trip (Acts 16:9–12) and had a fruitful ministry there, finding natural connections for church planting (16:15; 17:4, 12). He spoke affectionately of the Macedonians in his writings (1 Thess. 1:3; Phil. 4:1), and seemed to enjoy traveling through the region (Acts 20:1; 2 Cor. 1:16). As we see in 2 Cor. 8, the Macedonians eagerly supported Paul's mission and his work of raising money for the believers in Jerusalem (2 Cor. 8:1–4), and several Macedonians served as fellow workers in his ministry (Acts 19:29; 20:4; *NBD* 711). Barnett (1997: 368–69) proposes Philippi as the most likely place of Paul's rendezvous with Titus, due to the apostle's close relationship with the church there, which he had planted some six years earlier (Phil. 4:14–16). Thus it may be that he wrote 2 Corinthians from Philippi.

Yet the recent trip into Macedonia was not happy at first. Remember that the previous spring (AD 54) Timothy had visited the Corinthians, found the situation in the church to be a mess, and took a troubling report to Paul. The apostle followed up with a "sorrowful visit" that spring (2 Cor. 2:1–2), which involved a difficult, public interchange with a vitriolic church member (2:1–5). Wounded, he then returned to Ephesus. Since that time, Paul had changed his plans and sent a harsh letter via Titus (2:4). The change of plans raised questions in the mind of some concerning his dependability (1:15–22). So he sent Titus, as his official envoy,[5] to the Corinthians to assess the state of things.

As Paul writes 2 Corinthians, it is now autumn/winter AD 54/55, and at 7:5 he shares with the Corinthians his experience of coming into Macedonia as he makes his way back to them: "We were not able to rest at all but were

---

5. On the use of official envoys in the Greco-Roman world and particularly Paul's mission, see esp. Mitchell (1992), who contests Funk's (1967) conclusions concerning the three forms of apostolic parousia: the apostle's physical presence, an envoy, and a letter. Funk suggests that the three forms stood in a hierarchical relationship to one another in terms of value and effectiveness, with "presence" being the most effective. Mitchell (1992: 642) debates this conclusion:

> I would like to argue that we must question the assumption that Paul sent envoys and wrote letters as only "inadequate substitutes" for his own physical presence because of the busyness of his schedule. Is it not more likely the case that in certain instances Paul sent envoys or letters (or both) to represent him because he thought that they might be more effective than a personal visit in dealing with a particular situation that was facing a church? It is quite possible that we have a Pauline corpus in the first place because of the relative ineffectiveness of Paul's personal presence and his own creative recognition of that limitation.

Mitchell concludes, based partially on 2 Cor. 7, that the apostle used associates as envoys according to the conventions of his culture, namely, that an envoy should be received in a proper manner according to the one who sent him and that the envoy acts as an official representative of the person who sent him (1992: 661–62). In other words, the apostle sees himself as effectively working with the Corinthians via envoys and letters. In this regard, see also L. Johnson (2006) on Paul's adaptability and how his unique relationship with the Corinthians may have affected his modes of communication. These issues raise interesting questions regarding the interaction of church leaders today with those they seek to lead.

hounded by trouble in every way, conflicts on the outside, fears on the inside."
No doubt the stress of not connecting with Titus when he expected to meet
him was burdening Paul greatly (2:13). He and his fellow workers were not able
to rest (7:5b), finding no relief from incessant challenges (οὐδεμίαν ἔσχηκεν
ἄνεσιν ἡ σάρξ ἡμῶν, more directly, "Our flesh had no rest"). The reference
to "flesh" (σάρξ, sarx) speaks of the frailty and vulnerability of human life in
the face of physically and emotionally draining circumstances (12:7), and the
apostle had faced a series of compounding challenges prior to this point (4:8–9).

The conjunction ἀλλ' (all') contrasts relaxation with being "hounded by
trouble in every way" (ἐν παντὶ θλιβόμενοι, en panti thlibomenoi; 7:5c). As we
have seen earlier in the book, the verb θλίβω (thlibō; 1:6; 4:8) and its cognate
noun (θλῖψις, thlipsis; 1:4, 8; 2:4; 4:17; 6:4) are favorite terms for Paul when
he is speaking about affliction generally, yet he can also use this verb to speak
of persecution (e.g., 1 Thess. 3:4; 2 Thess. 1:7). The verb can describe either
outward circumstances or an inward anguish, so it is interesting that Paul mentions both in the next breath. The "conflicts on the outside" (ἔξωθεν μάχαι,[6]
exōthen machai) and "fears on the inside" (ἔσωθεν φόβοι,[7] esōthen phoboi),
rather than an attempt to neatly define the types of trouble Paul experienced,
are—along with the phrase "in every way" (ἐν παντὶ, en panti)—a manner of
stating that his difficulties had been significant and various. As noted above,
the prepositional phrase "in every way" echoes ἐπὶ πάσῃ τῇ θλίψει ἡμῶν (epi
pasē tē thlipsei hēmōn) at 7:4, providing what might be called a hook word,
or catchphrase, transitioning from the digression back to the travel narrative. Yet this little phrase also echoes the references to "in every affliction"
(ἐπὶ πάσῃ τῇ θλίψει ἡμῶν, epi pasē tē thlipsei hēmōn) and "any affliction"
(ἐν πάσῃ θλίψει, en pasē thlipsei) at 1:3b–4. This offers more evidence that
here we have a significant turning point in the book. Paul not only picks up
his travel narrative. He also makes literary connections back to the letter's
introduction, evoking both the pain and celebration reflected there. In short,
these descriptions of conflicts and emotional turmoil, which are painted as
both external and internal, express that the apostle had a difficult time of it
during this period of ministry, and the trouble had taken its toll (cf. 1:8–11).
But the experiences also served to drive Paul deeper in his experience of God,
as is underscored in the next verse.

These words ought to be deeply encouraging to those involved in ministry
today. As we consider Paul's circumstances, and especially his emotional state
as he entered Macedonia, we again are reminded that sincere, committed,
Spirit-enabled ministry does not provide immunity from fear and discouragement. R. Kent Hughes (2006: 148) calls this period of Paul's ministry the
"Macedonian misery," and certainly those involved in ministry have visited

6. In the NT literature (here; 2 Tim. 2:23; Titus 3:9; James 4:1) μάχη (machē) occurs only in
the plural and "only of battles fought without actual weapons." Thus it means "fighting, quarrels,
strife, disputes" (BDAG 622). See Furnish (1984: 386), who translates the word as "disputes."
7. The plural form here is preferred over the singular found in some MSS. See the third additional note on 7:15.

that cloud-darkened land. Working with people in the cause of Christ has tremendous rewards, with great joy, but it can be accompanied by great occupational hazards such as stress, discouragement, and even depression. For as Christian ministers we not only carry the weight of our own spiritual struggles and failures but also work with spiritually dysfunctional people who at times kick against us as we try to lead them toward growth. To the shock of his congregation in 1866, C. H. Spurgeon confessed, "I am the subject of depressions of spirit so fearful that I hope none of you ever gets to such extremes of wretchedness as I go to" (R. Hughes 2006: 147). If a Paul or a Spurgeon faced moments of discouragement and depression, we should not count those conditions as abnormal to our occupation. Thankfully, Paul did not stay there, and that too gives us hope.

At this point in the passage, the conjunction ἀλλά (*alla*) does heavy lifting in shifting the semantic center of gravity to a positive tone. In 7:5 we have already picked up echoes from the book's opening benediction, and now Paul revisits another topic from 1:3–7, his celebration of God as the Grand Encourager, and the topic of "encouragement" will continue through 2 Cor. 8. At 1:3b–4, he had described God as "the God who offers every possible encouragement! He encourages us in all our affliction, so that we might be able to encourage those experiencing any affliction with the encouragement by which we ourselves are encouraged by God."

7:6

As noted in the comments on the benediction at 1:3–7, the theme of encouragement permeates that passage, παράκλησις (*paraklēsis*, encouragement, comfort) used in noun form six times, and in its verbal cognate another four. These cognate terms are part of the apostle's common stock, yet are most showcased in 2 Corinthians, his "letter of encouragement" (Hafemann 2000: 59).[8] As noted in our comments on chapter 1, the word could be used with the sense of "comfort." Yet, generally speaking, Paul's use of the word in this letter should be read as referring to an "act of emboldening another in belief or course of action," thus "encouragement" (BDAG 766). Paul consistently uses the verb form in 2 Corinthians with the sense of encouraging a person to take action (2:8; 5:20; 6:1; 8:6; 9:5; 10:1; 12:8, 18; 13:11).

Specifically, here God is said to encourage "the discouraged" (τοὺς ταπεινούς, *tous tapeinous*), a word used at seven other points in the NT to speak of a posture of humility (Matt. 11:29; Luke 1:52; Rom. 12:16; 2 Cor. 10:1; James 1:9; 4:6; 1 Pet. 5:5). For instance, both James 4:6 and 1 Pet. 5:5 quote Prov. 3:34 LXX: "God opposes the proud but gives grace to *the humble*." Later in 2 Corinthians, at 10:1, the apostle writes of himself as "I who am *humble* among you in person, but bold toward you when absent" (2 Cor. 10:1 HCSB). Thus the NT often uses ταπεινός as the opposite of pride. Yet the emphasis in

---

8. As noted in our treatment of 1:3–7, the concept appears evenly spread throughout 2 Corinthians, with clusters of occurrences in chaps. 7 and 8: 2:7–8; 5:20; 6:1; 7:4–13; 8:4, 6, 17; 9:5; 10:1; 12:8, 18; 13:11. In Paul's other writings, the noun occurs another nine times, and the verb another thirty-six times. See comments on 1:3 and the footnote there.

our present context seems to be on a humility, a lowliness of spirit, brought about by the hammering of difficult circumstances, especially discouragement. Specifically, Paul alludes to Isa. 49:13 LXX, which reads,

ἠλέησεν ὁ θεὸς τὸν λαὸν αὐτοῦ καὶ τοὺς ταπεινοὺς τοῦ λαοῦ αὐτοῦ παρεκάλεσεν.
(ēleēsen ho theos ton laon autou kai tous tapeinous tou laou autou parekalesen.)
God has had mercy on his people and he has comforted the humble of his people. (NETS)

Thus God encourages "the discouraged," and the encouragement given to Paul and his companions by God came wrapped in two packages: the arrival of Titus and the news that Titus carried (1:6b–7).

7:7 Titus was a Gentile believer and a fellow worker trusted by Paul (2 Cor. 8:23), having accompanied the apostle and Barnabas to Jerusalem during the Gentile controversy reflected in Galatians (2:1, 3). He is not mentioned in Acts, and after Galatians he next appears in 2 Corinthians (2:13; 7:6, 13–14; 8:6, 16, 23; 12:18) as a main liaison with the congregation. From the glimpses of Titus in this letter, he seems to have been a man of great integrity, tact, and administrative abilities. Paul's relief and encouragement at Titus's arrival say much about the value the apostle placed on his young partner in ministry.

Yet Paul also was greatly encouraged by Titus's report. As today, writers in the ancient world could worry about how their letters might be received (Cicero, *Quint. fratr.* 2.16.5; Keener 2005: 199), and news that the correspondence had been well received brought relief. This was the case with Paul at the arrival of Titus. The structure of the passage is as follows:

	ἐν τῇ παρουσίᾳ Τίτου,
οὐ μόνον δὲ	ἐν τῇ παρουσίᾳ αὐτοῦ
ἀλλὰ καὶ	ἐν τῇ παρακλήσει
	ᾗ παρεκλήθη
	ἐφ' ὑμῖν

	en tē parousia Titou,
ou monon de	*en tē parousia autou*
alla kai	*en tē paraklēsei*
	hē pareklēthē
	eph' hymin

	by the arrival of Titus,
and not only	by his arrival
but also	by the encouragement
	with which he was encouraged
	by you

The three prepositional phrases ("by") form the backbone, and ἐν + the dative forms communicate the means by which encouragement was delivered.

The "not only . . . but also" construction (οὐ μόνον δέ . . . ἀλλὰ καί) has the effect of building on the emotion of Paul's encouragement at Titus's coming, adding to it the additional factor of the Corinthians' good response to the young minister's intervention on behalf of the apostle. Further, here again we have an echo of a dynamic seen in 1:3–7. In that benediction at the letter's beginning, Paul had spoken of encouragement as passed on by a recipient to another recipient. God encourages Paul and his fellow ministers in all their affliction, so that they in turn can encourage others who are suffering (1:4). Here at 7:7, the Corinthians encouraged Titus, who in turn was able to offer encouragement to Paul. Clearly the apostle's concept of encouragement is that it is spiritually "contagious," by its nature spreading to others in need of encouragement.

Paul goes on to detail three specifics from Titus's report: "he told us about your deep desire, your mourning, your enthusiastic concern for me." The translation "your deep desire" renders the term ἐπιπόθησις (*epipothēsis*), found in the NT only here and a few verses later in verse 11;[9] the word can refer to a "yearning, desire for," or "longing" (BDAG 377). At 5:2 and 9:14 Paul uses the cognate verb to speak of the longing to be clothed with the heavenly dwelling (5:2) and the longing for the Corinthians on the part of the Jerusalem believers, to whom the Corinthians had ministered through giving (9:14). In the present context the "deep desire" of the Corinthians seems to be for a reconciliation with their apostle, as the other two terms indicate. That the Corinthians had entered into "mourning" (ὀδυρμός, *odyrmos*) shows that they grasped the wrong that had been done to Paul or perhaps their grief over the strained relationship (Thrall 1994: 489). The NLT, for instance, translates the term thus: "How sorry you were about what had happened." The only other occurrence of the word in the NT comes at Matt. 2:18, where Jer. 31:15 [38:15 LXX] is quoted, but it illustrates well the grief inherent in the term: "A voice was heard in Ramah, weeping, and great *mourning*, Rachel weeping for her children; and she refused to be consoled, because they were no more" (HCSB).

Third, Titus reported that the Corinthians had given enthusiastic attention to Paul's concerns: "your enthusiastic concern for me" (τὸν ὑμῶν ζῆλον ὑπὲρ ἐμοῦ, *ton hymōn zēlon hyper emou*). Finally, they had awakened to the need to rivet serious, focused attention on the concerns raised by the apostle. While the word ζῆλος (*zēlos*) could be used to speak of intense negative feelings (e.g., 12:20), the context here suggests, rather, that strong positive emotions are in view, for the word can also connote "intense positive interest in something, . . . marked by a sense of dedication" (BDAG 427). This, for instance, is the sense of the word when used later in the letter at 9:2 with reference to the Corinthians' zeal to participate in giving to the saints at Jerusalem, and at

---

9. The cognate verb occurs thirteen times in the LXX: Deut. 13:9 (13:8 ET); 32:11; Pss. 41:2 (2x); 61:11; 83:3; 118:20, 131, 174 (42:1; 62:10; 84:2; 119:20, 131, 174 ET); Odes 2.11; Wis. 15:19; Sir. 25:21; Jer. 13:14; and nine times in the NT, including twice in 2 Corinthians: Rom. 1:11; 2 Cor. 5:2; 9:14; Phil. 1:8; 2:26; 1 Thess. 3:6; 2 Tim. 1:4; James 4:5; 1 Pet. 2:2.

11:2, where the apostle speaks of a godly zeal. What Titus's report brings out is that the Corinthians are indeed dedicated to Paul, and that is the key to the apostle's encouragement. The result (ὥστε, *hōste*) was that he "rejoiced even more." Paul uses the verb χαίρω (*chairō*) twenty-nine times in his letters to speak of a posture of gladness or joy. The word can communicate, as here, a natural response to good things the Lord has done (Rom. 16:19; 1 Cor. 7:30; 16:17; 2 Cor. 7:9; Phil. 1:18; 1 Thess. 3:9) but often carries a note of volition. Rejoicing is a Christian habit to be embraced by those who see God working in their circumstances in the world (Rom. 12:12, 15; 2 Cor. 7:16; 13:9, 11; Phil. 1:18; 2:17–18; 3:1; 4:4; 1 Thess. 5:16).

Thus this first movement of 7:5–16 resumes Paul's travel narrative from which he departed after 2:13, tells the Corinthians specifics about the difficulty of the beginning days in Macedonia, and especially focuses on the great joy the apostle has experienced with the arrival of Titus and his news of the Corinthians' good response to Titus's visit and Paul's harsh letter.

2. The Positive Effects of Paul's Harsh Letter (7:8–13a)

The second movement in this section (7:8–13a) treats the positive effects of the harsh letter Paul had sent earlier. The apostle acknowledges that his letter had upset the Corinthians, and he admits that for a brief time he did regret the sorrow he had caused them (7:8). However, that brief regret had quickly given way to joy as the man of God realized the effects the letter had produced. He was not glad that they were upset, but he recognized that these negative emotions drove them to repentance, which is exactly what God wished to happen (7:9). This kind of grief "according to God's will" is profoundly different from the sorrow that is produced by the world and is deadly (7:10). In fact, the grief caused by Paul's harsh letter had quite an impact on the Corinthians, moving them to address the situations Paul had raised in the letter (7:11). Ultimately, this is why Paul wrote—not because of the wrongdoer, nor for the sake of the person who had been wronged (probably himself), but to show the Corinthians their eager devotion to their true apostle. Paul was encouraged by the outcome (7:12–13a).

7:8–9b As we have seen in the previous unit (7:5–7), where Paul renews his travel narrative from which he had departed after 2:13, the apostle entered Macedonia in an emotional state, haunted by personal fears exacerbated by difficult circumstances. Yet Paul's emotions changed dramatically when Titus arrived with news of the Corinthians' positive response to his visit and Paul's harsh letter.

In 7:8–13a Paul focuses on the positive effects of his harsh letter to the church at Corinth. He has spoken of this letter earlier, at 2:4: "For as I wrote my last letter to you, the experience was gut-wrenching, heartbreaking, accomplished through a flood of tears. My motive was not to hurt you but that you might know the very great love that I have for you." Now, with 7:8–13a, Paul returns to the topic of this difficult letter and its affect on the Corinthian church. Verse 8 begins with "For even though I upset you by my letter, I don't regret it." The conjunction ὅτι (*hoti*, for) facilitates Paul's transition to the topic of the severe letter. Yet ὅτι functions causally to introduce an explanation as the apostle tells the Corinthians why he has such joy, as described at the end of verse 7, even as they have been agonizing over the sharp rebuke he sent earlier.

The apostle first acknowledges that they had been upset by the letter (εἰ καὶ ἐλύπησα ὑμᾶς ἐν τῇ ἐπιστολῇ, *ei kai elypēsa hymas en tē epistolē*), but then immediately denies that he regrets sending the hurtful correspondence (οὐ μεταμέλομαι, *ou metamelomai*).[10] The term λυπέω (*lypeō*) has to do with stirring up negative emotions on the part of another person and could speak of irritating, offending, insulting, or making a person very sad (BDAG 604; Spicq 1994: 2.417–22); Paul has already mentioned that both he and the Corinthians have been grieved by their previous interactions, and he did not wish to repeat the experience (2 Cor. 2:2, 4–5). Yet the precipitating event that gave rise to the conflict had injected grief into the relationship, and that grief would of necessity run some course, either for ill or good.

In certain situations when one party has caused another party pain, the appropriate response would be regret (μεταμέλομαι), and Paul admits that, having sent his harsh letter, he did feel regret temporarily (εἰ καὶ μετεμελόμην . . . νῦν, *ei kai metemelomēn . . . nyn*). The term μεταμέλομαι has a great deal of semantic overlap with μετανοέω (*metanoeō*, repent) and its cognate noun μετάνοια (*metanoia*, repentance), the latter used in verse 9. Both words can communicate some form of changing one's mind or having changed feelings about a situation. So we have here a play on words. Paul softens the sting of his earlier rebuke by admitting that their sadness, though "only momentary" (πρὸς ὥραν ἐλύπησεν ὑμᾶς, *pros hōran elypēsen hymas*, v. 8b), did cause him *regret* for a brief period, but this changed with the news that the Corinthians had been brought to *repentance* (v. 9b). "Now," he writes, "I am glad about it," not at the distress the letter caused but that they were upset to the point of turning from their previous attitudes and actions.

Speaking of the paradox of Paul rejoicing in the sadness of the Corinthians, John Chrysostom (*Hom. 2 Cor.* 15.1) writes, "Like a father who watches his son being operated on, Paul rejoices not for the pain being inflicted but for the cure which is the ultimate result. He had no desire to cause harm for its own sake" (Bray 1999: 266). And Augustine (*Sermons for Easter Season* 254.4) draws an analogy between sorrow and dung. Used in the wrong place and in the wrong way, both lead to uncleanness; but used appropriately, both produce fruit. Thus Christians should grieve as we live as fallen creatures in a fallen world. This is the way of spiritual fruitfulness (Bray 1999: 267). Thus a key point must not be missed here. The present happy state of the Corinthians corresponded directly to the unhappy confrontation carried out by their apostle. Paul had performed one of the most difficult tasks in ministry—confronting the church at Corinth and demanding that they adjust their attitudes and actions so as

---

10. The grammar here proves a bit difficult and, as mentioned in the additional note on 7:8, must be unraveled in tandem with decisions about the text form at this point.

to align with the apostle's ministry and his gospel. Both the stress of waiting for a response as he entered Macedonia and the joy that accompanied the church's response delivered by Titus *were the result of a risky, tremulous courage.* Paul had been willing to do the hard thing. He insisted that he be heard, not out of self-interest but out of his responsibility as the spiritual father of that difficult congregation. Biographer John Pollock tells of a moment in the ministry of George Whitefield, who as he was preaching "noticed an old man settling down for his accustomed, sermon-time nap." As the sermon rose in intensity, Whitefield addressed the sleeper: "'If I had come to speak to you in my own name, you might rest your elbows upon your knees and your heads on your hands, and go to sleep! . . . But I have come to you in the name of the Lord God of hosts, and (he clapped his hands and stamped his foot) I *must* and I *will* be heard.' The old man woke up startled" (Pollock 1972: 248). Paul had shaken the Corinthians awake with his letter, and the positive outcome he recounts in verse 9 continues.

7:9c–11   Now the apostle offers a series of three clauses introduced by γάρ (*gar*), which explain why he rejoices (harking back to the note sounded at the end of v. 7) in the particular kind of sadness the Corinthians have experienced. First, their emotion of being upset was in accordance with God's will, so the situation was not one of emotional abuse on the part of Paul: "For you were upset in a way that God wanted you to be, with the result that you did not experience loss in any way because of us." The Corinthians were "upset" (Message), or "made sad" (NET) or "sorry" (KJV, NIV),[11] but their grief was redeemed and thus productive because it was "according to God's will" (κατὰ θεόν, *kata theon*). The phrase, underscored by being repeated in verses 10 and 11, means being aligned with God's will.[12] In 7:10c it is contrasted with a worldly grief (τοῦ κόσμου λύπη, *tou kosmou lypē*)—one at odds with and out of sync with God's will and thus producing negative effects (Barnett 1997: 374).

That they were not hurt by the situation (ἐν μηδενὶ ζημιωθῆτε ἐξ ἡμῶν, *en mēdeni zēmiōthēte ex hēmōn*, you did not experience loss in any way because of us) has been understood in various ways. The word ζημιόω (*zēmioō*) could be used by authors in the ancient world to describe the experience of some type of punishment or loss so that a person suffered or was injured or harmed in some way (BDAG 428; Spicq 1994: 2.157–58). But does Paul mean that, ultimately, he did them no real harm (perhaps by failing to come to them), or that some significant harm was avoided because they were brought to repentance? The latter could be the case.[13] Philip Hughes (1962: 269–70), for instance, suggests

---

11. Here is the second-person plural aorist passive indicative form of λυπέω (*lypeō*), already discussed in verse 8.

12. The versions communicating that the sorrow is in line with God's will (so NASB⁹⁵, NLT², HCSB, NIV) seem better than "godlike" or "godly" (so ESV, Tyndale, NRSV, KJV) since the latter could be understood as a sorrow expressed by God, and God's own "sorrow" does not lead God to repentance. Interestingly, the HCSB, NASB⁹⁵, NLT², and the NIV mix the two renderings.

13. The verb ζημιόω could be used with this latter sense, as seen in Philo (*Virt.* 182): "Those who rebel against divine law come into grave danger for the body and the soul."

that what the Corinthians had been on the verge of losing was eternal reward, which would have been forfeited in their case if the apostle had not done the difficult task of confronting them:

> In building upon the foundation of Jesus Christ, which he as a wise master-builder had laid, it was his earnest desire that they should build with enduring and precious materials—gold, silver, precious stones—and not with perishable and worthless materials—wood, hay, stubble, which would be consumed in the day of testing and cause them to suffer loss, by which he means the loss not of salvation but of reward (1 Cor. 3:10–15). Not content with having laid the saving foundation, he is aware of his solemn responsibility, as a diligent pastor and apostle, for the care and guidance of those whom he had brought to a knowledge of the gospel. Accordingly he was determined, by God's grace, to allow neither concern for their feelings nor unwillingness to give offense to preponderate in such a way as to make him keep silence, instead of dealing with them as a faithful father, and thereby to jeopardize their spiritual well-being.

This interpretation seems appropriate in light of the contrast with "salvation" (εἰς σωτηρίαν, *eis sōtērian*) mentioned in verse 10. Yet, though not unrelated to P. Hughes's interpretation, this portion of text could also be read in a more down-to-earth manner, that Paul's interaction with the Corinthians could have led to further bitterness and brokenness in their relationship with the apostle. In other words, they could have responded in a worldly manner, with a worldly sorrow as the result (Thrall 1994: 492). Thankfully that unhappy outcome was avoided.

Thus, second, the grief "according to God's will" (v. 10) experienced by the Corinthians was the kind that leads to repentance, a repentance that in turn results in salvation. Such grief has no regrets and sharply contrasts with a worldly grief, which leads to death. Speaking of the latter, John Chrysostom (*Hom. 2 Cor.* 15.2) writes, "Worldly sorrow . . . is regret for the loss of money, reputation and friends. That kind of sorrow merely leads to greater harm, because the regret is often a prelude to a thirst for revenge. Only sorrow for sin is really profitable" (Bray 1999: 266).

With the third γάρ clause (v. 11), Paul appeals directly to the Corinthians' experience: "For recognize how great an effect this very experience of grief according to God's will has had on you: your eagerness, as well as your defense of yourselves, indeed your indignation, fear, yearning, enthusiasm, and even your execution of justice!" These seven terms suggest that the Corinthians recognized the gravity of the situation and their need to address it aggressively.

The word σπουδή (*spoudē*) can refer to "haste" or quick action, especially when preceded by μετά (*meta*, with; Mark 6:25; Luke 1:39). Yet, as in the case of our current context, the word also connotes "eager commitment" or "diligence" in carrying out an obligation (BDAG 939).[14] The apostle appreciates

---

14. This is the common sense of σπουδή in the NT letters: Rom. 12:8, 11; 2 Cor. 7:11–12; 8:7–8, 16; Heb. 6:11; 2 Pet. 1:5; Jude 3. Notice that the apostle employs the term three times

this virtue and uses the word again, praising the Corinthians in the following verse for their "eager devotion" (7:12) and later in 8:7, in a list of ways they excel spiritually. In fact, according to his explanation in 7:12, the whole point of his harsh letter was so that the Corinthians themselves might get in touch with their "eager devotion" to Paul. Evidently, once Titus had laid the situation before the Corinthians, the fire of their devotion to Paul had been relit.

Notice that each following term in this series of descriptions (v. 11) is introduced by the conjunction ἀλλά (alla), employed not in its common contrastive role, but rather in a way that is rhetorically ascensive: "as well as, indeed, even" (BDAG 45 4b).[15] The second term in this list, ἀπολογία (apologia), refers to a defense, either in a court of law, before an official (e.g., Acts 25:16; 2 Tim. 4:16), spoken (e.g., Acts 22:1), or written (e.g., 1 Cor. 9:3), explaining one's actions or circumstances. Probably what is in mind here is the Corinthians' explanation concerning their attitudes and actions related to the offender spoken of in 2:5–11, and perhaps especially the attention they had now given to the situation.

The third word in this list, ἀγανάκτησις (aganaktēsis), only occurs here in the biblical literature. The cognate verb can communicate a range of emotions, including displeasure, annoyance, indignation, anger, even rage (Spicq 1994: 1.5–7).[16] Here the noun may be rendered "indignation," and it may be that the Corinthians' indignation was over how Paul had been treated.[17]

A much more common term, φόβος (phobos) could be used by ancient authors to refer to intimidation (1 Pet. 3:14) or a force that is appropriately terrifying or sobering. In relation to God, the word speaks of a deep, awe-inspirited reverence, as at 2 Cor. 5:11, where the apostle writes of "the fear of the Lord" as he reflects on the accountability before God inherent in ministry (EDNT 3:429). Yet the word also can refer to fright/fear (so, e.g., HCSB, NASB, ESV) in the face of life circumstances, or alarm (so, e.g., NET, NLT²,

---

in 2 Cor. 8 (8:7, 8, 16). Here the word has been translated variously as "diligence" (HCSB, Tyndale), "earnestness" (NASB, NLT², ESV, NIV), and "eagerness" (NET). Some versions make this term the main topic of the sentence, the primary object, which then is more clearly defined by the list that follows: "For consider how much diligence this very thing—this grieving as God wills—has produced in you" (HCSB). However, in 7:11 this term is immediately followed by ἀλλά (alla) and the series of comparable descriptions, suggesting that σπουδή is the first term of the list. Thus a better ET reads, "For see what this very thing, this sadness as God intended, has produced in you: what eagerness, what defense of yourselves" (NET).

15. In my ET, I have tried to reflect the ascensive dynamic by the use of each of these terms, without the prose being rigid in reflecting each use of ἀλλά: "your eagerness, as well as your defense of yourselves, indeed your indignation, fear, yearning, enthusiasm, and even your execution of justice!"

16. The cognate verb occurs seven times in the NT and only in the Gospels: Matt. 20:24; 21:15; 26:8; Mark 10:14, 41; 14:4; Luke 13:14. Spicq (1994: 1.7) suggests that the use in the Gospels always carries a sense of anger rather than mere displeasure.

17. Spicq's (1994: 1.7) suggestion that the word at 2 Cor. 7:11 communicates the idea of the Corinthians being "distraught" at their own blindness seems to be pure speculation.

NIV, NRSV). One might be tempted to interpret the use in our passage as referring to a deep "respect," another possible meaning of the word, especially used with reference to someone acting in an official capacity. Yet, when we consider the five other uses of φόβος in the Corinthian correspondence, we find that two have to do with the fear of God (2 Cor. 5:11; 7:1) and the other three seem to refer to an emotional state of being afraid or anxious, or at least deeply sobered by a situation. In fact, in two of those three occurrences, φόβος is paired with "trembling" (τρόμος, tromos; 1 Cor. 2:3; 2 Cor. 7:15). A few verses later, in 2 Cor. 7:15, the Corinthians are said to have received Titus with "fear and trembling." Thus it seems best to translate the word here with "fear," in the sense of anxiety, rather than "alarm."

Paul has already mentioned their "longing" or "deep desire" (ἐπιπόθησις, epipothēsis) in 7:7,[18] and in both passages he may have in mind the Corinthians' longing to see him personally and to know that all was well in their relationship with their apostle. This deep desire to see someone is often the sense of the cognate verb in the NT (Rom. 1:11; 2 Cor. 9:14; Phil. 1:8; 2:26; 1 Thess. 3:6; 2 Tim. 1:4). Further, the word translated as "enthusiasm" (ζῆλος, zēlos) also appears at 7:7, speaking of the enthusiastic concern they have now shown on Paul's behalf. Again, this word has to do with "intense positive interest in something . . . marked by a sense of dedication" (BDAG 427).

Finally, to cap off this string of terms describing the Corinthians' response during Titus's visit, the apostle lists "justice" (ἐκδίκησις, ekdikēsis). The word could refer to "retaliation" or "vengeance," but these seem out of step with the general ethos of Paul's dealing with the offender in Corinth (e.g., 2:6–8). Rather, ἐκδίκησις probably refers here to the dispensing of justice or the handing down of a punishment. Paul has already mentioned the punishment of the wrongdoer doled out by the congregation (2:6), and that sense probably is again in play here.

In summary, the seven responses listed in 7:11 had clearly demonstrated a shift in the posture of this wayward congregation toward their wounded apostle. He sums up his assessment of their change of heart with "In every way you have shown yourselves to be innocent in this matter." The phrase rendered "In every way" (ἐν παντί, en panti) speaks of this tremendous variety of indicators that the church had taken the apostle's concerns seriously and were now committed to him as they should be. Further, by engaging Paul's concerns, the Corinthians had demonstrated (συνεστήσατε, synestēsate)[19] that they were "innocent" in the difficult situation: they had repented and carried out actions in keeping with their repentance in the matter. They had recognized their complicity in the matter of failing to deal

18. These are the only two occurrences of the term in the NT.
19. Paul has already used this verb four times in the book, at 3:1; 4:2; 5:12; 6:4. In every case, with perhaps the exception of 6:4, the word carries the sense of "recommending" or "commending." The use at 6:4 seems nearer to our present context, which tends toward the sense of "demonstrate." The NLT[2] translates 6:4a as, "In everything we do, we show that we are true ministers of God."

with the wrongdoer, and they had taken responsibility for it (Harris 2005: 543). Thus they were "innocent" (ἁγνός, *hagnos*, pure), not in the sense of never having done wrong (contra Barrett 1973: 212), but in the sense of having made things right.

7:12–13a   Finally, in verse 12 Paul makes clear his motives in writing the harsh letter, but his explanation begins in a way that is unexpected. Whenever Paul begins a sentence with ἄρα (*ara*), the particle communicates an inference drawn from what has gone before: "consequently" (BDAG 127). Yet how can Paul's intention in writing the letter also be the consequence of the letter's outcome? A couple points can be offered as an answer. First, when the apostle writes "although I wrote to you," he is structurally marking a return to the point at which he started this particular unit (7:8–13a)—with a reference to the harsh letter. As in the current verse, verse 8 begins with a connector (ὅτι, *hoti*) followed by εἰ καί (*ei kai*): "For even though I upset you by my letter." So in verse 12 Paul again mentions the harsh letter (indeed, this is the last time he will do so in the book), in effect returning to the question of his role in sending it. The εἰ καί construction, in other words, connects back to a point at which Paul was discussing his feelings about communicating with the church in the way he had. Second, however, Paul now sees the ultimate purpose of his letter (from the standpoint of God's providence?) as having to do with the impact it had on the Corinthians. As explained by Margaret Thrall (1994: 495–96), when Paul writes, "I did not write because of the wrongdoer, nor for the sake of the person who was wronged," we should not take these as absolute negations, but rather as Hebraic expressions whereby a comparison is made to stress the greater importance of the alternative. Thus, what we have is "a comparison of three purposes" (Harris 2005: 544), with emphasis placed on the last. Paul's *main* reason for writing was not to deal with the wrongdoer, nor for the sake of the one wronged (probably himself), but rather that the Corinthians' devotion might be made clear. The word φανερόω (*phaneroō*) has to do with something being "revealed," "publicly exposed," "shown," or "disclosed." God delights in displaying truth, spiritual realities, through authentic Christian ministry (e.g., 2 Cor. 4:11; 5:11; 11:6). What Paul's harsh letter disclosed to the Corinthians themselves (πρὸς ὑμᾶς, *pros hymas*, to you) was the deep devotion they had to the apostle. We have already noted that the term σπουδή (*spoudē*) can refer to haste, especially when preceded by μετά (*meta*, with) (Mark 6:25; Luke 1:39). Yet, as was the case in verse 11, the word here communicates the idea of "eager commitment" or "diligence" in carrying out an obligation (BDAG 939). The Corinthians have now shown such diligence ὑπὲρ ἡμῶν (*hyper hēmōn*), "on our behalf" or "to us," Paul writes. In other words, they had gotten behind Paul and his mission. Moreover, they had done so "before God" (ἐνώπιον τοῦ θεοῦ, *enōpion tou theou*), a concept that for the apostle speaks of a right posture spiritually, whereby a person or community lives in an awareness of their obligation to the God, who is ever present (Rom. 3:20; 14:22; 1 Cor. 1:29; 2 Cor. 4:2; 8:21; Gal. 1:20; 1 Tim. 2:3;

5:4, 21; 6:13; 2 Tim. 2:14; 4:1).[20] The fact that this intention for the letter was accomplished has encouraged Paul greatly.

3. Titus's Joy (7:13b–16)

The third and final movement (7:13b–16) of this section speaks of Titus's joy in the face of his encounter with the Corinthians. He was refreshed by his time with them and found that the positive statements Paul had made about the Corinthians had proved true (7:13b–14). The whole situation has resulted in Titus's increased affection toward the church, and Paul celebrates the confidence he has in this group of brothers and sisters (7:15–16).

The encouragement Paul felt was enhanced by Titus's joy. Thus far in this section of 2 Corinthians (7:5–16), Paul primarily has focused on his own emotions and motives, as well as the effect his actions have had on the Corinthians. Yet Titus's role in the interface between Paul and the church has been significant, the young fellow worker having deftly negotiated the rocky terrain of the strained relationship between the apostle and the congregation. Thus Paul's own joy was enhanced by Titus's experience of joy in the situation. The terms περισσοτέρως μᾶλλον (*perissoterōs mallon*) express a heightened degree, captured well by the translation "We were *especially* delighted to see how happy Titus was" (NLT[2], NIV). Paul had experienced joy at the response of the Corinthians, but the joy was increased by Titus's own response of joy to the situation. Encouragement and joy are contagious and can have a ripple effect in community. Paul remarks on the source of Titus's joy, that the church had "refreshed" the young worker's "spirit."[21] The term ἀναπαύω (*anapauō*) can speak of the kind of rest that comes from being allowed relief from some difficult work (e.g., 1 Chron. 22:18 LXX; Matt. 11:28). This nuance of "relief" is reflected, for instance, in the NLT[2] and NRSV, both of which say that Titus's mind was set at ease by the encounter. Yet in cases as here where an encounter with another person(s) brings revitalization of some type (e.g., 1 Cor. 16:18; Philem. 7, 20), perhaps the translation "refreshed" is preferred (so the HCSB, NASB, NET, ESV, NIV). The perfect form of the verb underscores that Titus's experience of refreshment was initiated by his encounter with the church yet had continued to the present, from Paul's perspective.

7:13b

Further, Paul has "boasted a bit" to Titus (τι αὐτῷ ὑπὲρ ὑμῶν κεκαύχημαι, *ti autō hyper hymōn kekauchēmai*) about the Corinthians. He speaks of boasting a good deal in his letters, not least in his writings to this congregation.[22]

7:14

20. At 2:17 and 12:19 he uses the less common phrase κατέναντι θεοῦ (*katenanti Theou*, before God).
21. More lit., "His spirit has been refreshed by all of you."
22. See καυχάομαι in Rom. 2:17, 23; 5:2–3, 11; 1 Cor. 1:29, 31 (2x); 3:21; 4:7; 13:3; 2 Cor. 5:12; 7:14; 9:2; 10:8, 13, 15, 16, 17 (2x); 11:12, 16, 18 (2x), 30 (2x); 12:1, 5 (2x), 6, 9; Gal. 6:13–14; Eph. 2:9; Phil. 3:3. Paul uses the verb thirty-five times, including twenty times in 2 Corinthians, marking it as a very important concept for the apostle in this letter. Only two NT uses appear outside the Pauline literature, both of these in James (1:9; 4:16).

As mentioned earlier in the comments on 1:12, the act of "boasting" or being "proud" (καύχησις, *kauchēsis*) of someone or something could, in the ancient world, be looked down upon,[23] as it often is today. Yet we must bring into play use of the term in the Greek version of the Jewish Scriptures (LXX), where on the one hand this verb and its cognate noun are used to describe foolish pride in human activities (e.g., Judg. 7:2; 1 Sam. 2:3; Jer. 12:13; Ezek. 24:25; cf. 2 Cor. 5:12), and on the other hand an appropriate, verbal celebration of the Lord's character and works (e.g., 1 Chron. 16:35; 29:13; Ps. 5:12 [5:11 ET]; Prov. 16:31). Thus Paul's boast about the Corinthians, his pride in them, was ultimately a boast about the work God was doing in the church, rather than a statement of pride in their personal accomplishments or character. Paul's boasts always related to the work of Christ (cf. Gal. 6:14), and he also wanted the Corinthians to take appropriate pride in the work of Christ in and through his ministry (2 Cor. 5:12).

Further, boasting about the work of God in the lives of any group can be risky, tinged as we all are by the fall (as was so apparent with the Corinthians themselves: e.g., 1 Cor. 1:10; 3:1). It was entirely possible that Paul's boast to Titus could have been made to look vapid if the Corinthians had behaved badly upon Titus's arrival. The term καταισχύνω (*kataischynō*) can refer to being disgraced or put to shame (e.g., Luke 13:17; 2 Cor. 9:4; 1 Pet. 3:16), as well as a milder feeling of disappointment. The former probably is in view here. In a culture of honor/shame, the term carries a weightiness beyond our modern emotion of embarrassment. Paul would have been shamed by having represented the Corinthians in a positive light only to have had them make him look the fool, but thankfully this did not happen.[24]

"Rather, just as everything we said to you was true, so our boasting to Titus about you turned out to be true as well" (7:14b). Early on in 2 Corinthians, Paul defends himself as having written and spoken truthfully to the church (1:12–22), and such a defense indicates that the apostle had been sharply criticized by some in the church as being unreliable, questionable in terms of character. Yet, Paul reiterates here in chapter 7 that everything he had said to the Corinthians was true: his ministry to them had been one of complete integrity (e.g., 4:2; 6:3–4, 6–8). So too, what Paul had communicated to Titus *about* the Corinthians also turned out to be true. They had come through with flying colors, living out the response Paul anticipated they would give in this difficult moment in relation to their apostle. Thus the apostle was shown to be consistent in communicating what was true in a variety of situations.

7:15–16 Given this experience, Titus has grown in his affection for the Corinthians as he remembered the Corinthians' obedience. Paul characterizes this obedience as

---

23. For the wide-ranging, pejorative uses of this term and its cognates in Greco-Roman literature, see Spicq 1994: 2.295–302. Keener (2005: 159) notes that boasting was frowned upon unless properly justified (see also Roetzel 2007: 130).

24. John Chrysostom (*Hom. 2 Cor.* 16.1) declares, "It is high praise when a teacher boasts that his pupils have not put him to shame. Paul even adds that after he had boasted about the Corinthians to Titus they had not let him down" (Bray 1999: 268).

the church receiving his young fellow worker "with fear and trembling." They took his role seriously and the situation he addressed seriously. The apostle concludes by again affirming the Corinthians in strong terms.

Paul repeats the expression of confidence in the Corinthians he has stated at 7:4, the two passages forming parallel conclusions of the successive units. Elsewhere in 2 Corinthians the apostle uses the term θαρρέω (tharreō) to speak of the courage or boldness he has in the face of challenging situations, whether death (2 Cor. 5:6, 8) or the dicey relational mix in the church at Corinth (10:1–2). Here, however, Paul speaks of his confidence in the Corinthians (ἐν ὑμῖν, en hymin, in you, v. 16), a convention found elsewhere in his writings (e.g., Rom. 15:14; 2 Cor. 9:1–2; Gal. 5:10; 2 Thess. 3:4; Philem. 21). Such expressions of confidence in the ancient world were used strategically to persuade the recipients and encourage them to follow a certain course of response or action (e.g., P.Oxy. 1064; P.Ryl. 696).[25]

Reflection

The passage before us begins with trouble, conflicts, and fear, yet it ends in joy. Paul's distress at not finding Titus in Macedonia gives way to his relief, encouragement, and elation at his young associate's arrival and report. The real hinge upon which the section turns, however, is not primarily the presence of Titus, although his presence encouraged Paul greatly. Rather, the section turns on the particular grief experienced by the Corinthians: a godly grief, which leads to repentance.

Already in 2 Corinthians we have encountered God's redemption of suffering, certainly a key theme of the book (e.g., 2 Cor. 1:4, 8; 2:4; 4:17; 6:4; 8:2, 13). But here we have a different form of grief, not caused by persecution or various trials but by one's own sinfulness and need for repentance. This is a grief born of being confronted concerning our sins, working through the confrontation, and finding forgiveness and restoration as we come out on the other side of the experience. It is a sweet grief that leads us back to God and right relationship with others in the body of Christ.

Writing of the joy of repentance, Mathewes-Green (2004: 95) declares: "Repentance is the doorway to the spiritual life, the only way to begin. It is also the path itself, the only way to continue. Anything else is foolishness and self-delusion. Only repentance is both brute-honest enough, and joyous enough, to bring us all the way home. But how repentance could be either joyous or vibrantly true is a foreign idea to most of us." She explains that the joyous nature of repentance—a sad joy to be sure—flows from

25. On expressions of confidence and their uses in the ancient world, see Olson 1985; J. White 1972: 103–4. Olson states that we should not speak of formulas of confidence, because ways of expressing confidence vary, but rather in terms of functional parallels. Yet NT expressions of confidence normally have in common three elements: (a) a first-person subject expressed in verb or pronoun, or in an antecedent to a participle; (b) the term(s) for confidence; and (c) a reference to the addresses as those in whom the writer has confidence, making use of the second-person plural pronoun. All three are present in 2 Cor. 7:16.

the transformation that is possible when one turns to God. Quoting Abba Isaiah, she writes, "The sadness according to God, on the other hand, is joy, the joy of seeing yourself in God's will. . . . Sadness according to God does not weigh on the soul, but says to it, 'Do not be afraid! Up! Return!' God knows that man is weak, and strengthens him" (2004: 97).

In other words, we find joy from the depths of grief because we find God in a fresh way. And we give joy to others in the body of Christ, who see our spiritual agony, but also the repentance it produces, and bear witness that something other than worldly grief has taken place. We can rejoice in all things that have their source in heaven.

Additional Notes

7:5. Digressions were strategically used in ancient communication to organize material, both to focus the hearer's attention in certain directions and to refresh the hearer in the midst of a logically developing argument. Quintilian (*Inst.* 4.3.14–17) writes of the effectiveness of digressions in speeches (see the quote in the introduction to 2:14–7:4). Of course 2 Corinthians is not a speech, but it would have been read aloud in the congregation, and Paul would have considered the rhetorical impact of his organization of material in the letter. Thus the shift in focus, as Paul leaves his travel narrative after 2:13 and resumes it at 7:5, may be read as rhetorically strategic.[26]

7:5. The manuscripts 𝔓⁴⁶ F G B K read the aorist ἔσχεν rather than the more difficult ἔσχηκεν (ℵ C 33 D Ψ 0243 1739 1881 𝔐). The former probably was due either to scribal error (by the dropping of the middle syllable) or a scribal correction to what would seem the more appropriate tense (Martin 1986: 213; Thrall 1994: 487). In 2 Corinthians Paul uses both the aorist and the perfect forms of ἔχω sparingly, but ἔσχηκεν seems the better reading here and is aoristic in use, since Paul has now found relief from his troubles (Harris 2005: 525).

7:5. The plural form here is preferred over the singular found in 𝔓⁴⁶ pc syᵖ Tert, not least because it balances the plural μάχαι.

7:8. As attested by the bracketing of γάρ, the judgment call on the shape of the text at this point is difficult. The majority of witnesses include the conjunction (ℵ C D¹ F G Ψ 0243 33 1739 1881 𝔐 sy bo), yet its omission (𝔓⁴⁶ᶜ B D* it sa) is both the more difficult reading and a harsher rendering of Paul's thoughts (𝔓⁴⁶* softens the expression a bit by the inclusion of the participle βλέπων). The harshness seems to be out of place in the current context. Metzger notes that the majority of the editorial committee preferred the reading βλέπω γάρ based on external attestation; the variants were understandable if copyists, seeing εἰ καὶ μετεμελόμην as initiating a new movement in the discourse, sought to smooth the expression in various ways. Yet a minority on the committee suggested that the well-attested βλέπω, if seen as standing alone, would present a typically Pauline anacoluthon, and copyists would have felt the need to adjust the syntax by making βλέπω a participle or by adding the conjunction γάρ. The committee, based on the uncertainty of which option seemed best, retained the conjunction but within brackets (Metzger 1994: 512).

---

26. In modern, Western culture, we tend to think of digressions negatively, as getting off point and mentioning things that are less important than other elements of a discourse. Yet in ancient literary and oratorical contexts, digressions could be used to rivet attention, to focus the hearer or reader on certain points, which is the case with Paul's embedded discourse that runs from 2 Cor. 2:14–7:4.

7:10. The reading κατεργάζεται ($\mathfrak{P}^{99}$ $\aleph^2$ F G Ψ 0243 0296 1739 1881 𝔐; Eus Did) should be rejected on two bases. Its external attestation is much inferior to the more difficult ἐργάζεται ($\mathfrak{P}^{46}$ $\aleph^*$ B C D P 81 1175 *pc* [33: h.t.]; Clem), and its presence can be explained as brought about by the more common complex form κατε- in the following sentence.

7:11. The witnesses that omit ὑμᾶς following λυπηθῆναι ($\mathfrak{P}^{46}$ $\aleph^*$ B C F G 0243 33 81 630 1739 1881 2464* *pc* b r ρ; Ambst) are much stronger than those that include it in the text ($\aleph^2$ D Ψ 𝔐 ar f vg; Cl Pel).

III. The Ministry of Giving (8:1–9:15)

The span of 2 Corinthians extending from 8:1 to 9:15 has three main movements. In the first, 8:1–15, the apostle presents the Macedonians as an example of exceptional giving (8:1–5), exhorts the Corinthians to follow the example of the Macedonians and Christ and finish the collection for God's people in Jerusalem (8:6–7), and clarifies both the tone and motives for his exhortation (8:8–15). The second movement, 8:16–9:5, focuses squarely on Titus's mission to Corinth. Paul relates Titus's eagerness to travel to Corinth again, and he introduces two unnamed brothers who traveled with Titus as envoys from the churches of Macedonia (8:16–24). The last segment of this second movement provides details concerning the purpose of this mission (9:1–5), especially that the Corinthians might have their part of the collection ready when Paul and others from Macedonia arrive in Corinth. Then 2 Cor. 9:6–15 constitutes the third and final movement of chapters 8–9. Paul wraps up his treatment of "The Ministry of Giving" with reflections on various results of giving, as well as God's elaborate resources that enable faithful believers to give in such a way that other believers are blessed and God receives glory and thanks.

The Ministry of Giving (8:1–9:15)
A. Paul's Exhortation to Finish the Collection (8:1–15)
B. Titus's Mission (8:16–9:5)
C. Reflections on Resources for Giving and the Results (9:6–15)

A. Paul's Exhortation to Finish the Collection (8:1–15)

In 2 Cor. 8–9 Paul addresses the topic of giving, specifically the need for the Corinthians to do their part in raising funds to support the saints in Jerusalem.[1] In the first verses of chapter 8, the apostle lays a firm foundation for his exhortation by using two effective rhetorical techniques: a positive example (the Macedonians; 8:1–5) and an affirmation of what the Corinthians are already doing well (8:7). In responding well to Titus's leadership in the matter (8:6), they will be building on and continuing in healthy spiritual patterns already evident in their congregations. So Paul exhorts the Corinthians to give (8:7). The balance of the section finds the apostle clarifying his tone and motives in offering this exhortation (8:8–15).

From a thematic standpoint, we could identify a transition following verse 5, for the first five verses of chapter 8 focus squarely on the example of the Macedonian churches, and the verses that follow shift to Titus's role in the collection from the Corinthians (8:6) and a direct exhortation to the Corinthians to complete this ministry of giving (8:7). The problem with placing a break after verse 5, however, is twofold, having to do both with grammar and key themes. As to grammar, in spite of the fact that most translations place a period at the end of verse 5 (CEV, HCSB, NET, ESV, NIV, NLT[2], and our own translation), the sentence continues in verse 6 with a result clause (εἰς τὸ παρακαλέσαι ἡμᾶς Τίτον, *eis to parakalesai hēmas Titon*, As a result we encouraged Titus), which is grammatically dependent on ἔδωκαν (*edōkan, they gave*) in verse 5. Consequently, the first six verses of the chapter constitute one complete sentence. So from a grammatical standpoint it seems that this unit should extend at least through verse 6, and some have ended the unit there. Supporting this approach, the conjunction ἀλλ' (*all'*) at the beginning of verse 7 starts a new sentence, and verse 7 could be seen as an appropriate heading for the following verses, focusing as it does on the Corinthians' involvement in the ministry of giving.

Yet there is one more piece of evidence suggesting that verse 7 also should be seen as integrated with these first six verses, and that evidence has to do with key motifs that tie the first seven verses of the chapter together. Notice that throughout these verses we have three interrelated concepts, all used with reference to the act of giving:

---

1. On the collection for the saints in Jerusalem, see Georgi 1992; Nickle 1966; and esp. D. E. Watson (2006), who argues that the collection was a normal aspect of Jewish piety, consisting of giving to the poor, whether locally or at a distance.

References to χάρις (*charis*, gift, vv. 1, 4, 6, 7)
An emphasis on the act of giving (forms of δίδωμι, *didōmi*, vv. 1, 5 [understood in vv. 3, 7])
References to περισσεύω (*perisseuō*, spillover, excel, vv. 2, 7a, 7d) or its cognate περισσεία (*perisseia*, effusive, v. 2)

Consider that after verse 7 χάρις occurs only once, at 8:9 (but not with reference to giving), and then not again until verse 16, δίδωμι (but not with reference to the act of giving of financial resources) occurs only once, at 8:10, and then not again until verse 16, and περισσεύω and its cognate do not occur in the remainder of the chapter. Thus these three concepts give a very high level of lexical cohesion to the first seven verses of the chapter. Now it may be that verse 7 functions as an overlapping transition (see Guthrie 1994: 102–4), functioning both as the concluding thought of verses 1–6 and the introductory thought for what follows. Yet Paul crafts smooth transitions here, so the exact delineation of the units is not critical, but we should notice the thematic cohesiveness of these first seven verses of the chapter. Consequently, we place a break *after* verse 7.

This section can be outlined as follows:

1. Excel in giving like the Macedonians (8:1–7)
2. Paul clarifies the tone and motives for his exhortation (8:8–15)

Exegesis and Exposition

[1]Now we want you to be aware, brothers and sisters, of God's grace that has been given in connection with the Macedonian churches, [2]that during a severe test involving affliction, their effusive joy and extreme poverty spilled over in ⌜extravagant⌝ generosity; [3]I can confirm this—they voluntarily gave according to their resources, even ⌜beyond their resources⌝, [4]begging us most emphatically for the privilege of being able to join in this ministry to God's people. [5]And confounding our expectations, they gave themselves preeminently to the Lord and also to us by God's will. [6]As a result we encouraged Titus that since he started work on this gracious gift, he should be the one to bring it to completion among you also. [7]Now then, just as you excel in all kinds of ways—in faith and speech and knowledge and with the highest degree of enthusiasm and ⌜in the love we inspired among you⌝—excel also in this gracious gift.

[8]I am not ordering you to do this. Rather, using the enthusiasm of others as an example, I am ⌜seeking to verify⌝ the genuineness of your own love as well. [9]For you know the grace demonstrated by our Lord Jesus ⌜Christ⌝: though he was rich, he became poor for ⌜your⌝ sake, so that by his poverty you might become rich. [10]I am giving my advice on the matter, for this course of action is to your advantage. After all, you are the ones who took the initiative beginning last year, not only in action, but also in wanting to do something! [11]Now finish what you started, in order that,

out of your resources, the completed task might be brought in line with the eager desire to help! [12]For, since this eager desire exists, the gift, rather than being judged deficient due to limited resources, is deemed acceptable on the basis of what is available. [13]So I don't mean to offer others relief ⌐ ⌐ by burdening you! Rather, it is a matter of equality. [14]This is how equality works: at present your oversupply can be used to meet their shortfall, so that at some point in the future their oversupply might be used to address your shortfall. [15]As it is written, "The person who had much didn't have too much, and the person who had little didn't have too little."

1. Excel in Giving Like the Macedonians (8:1–7)

Paul affectionately addresses the "brothers and sisters"[2] in Corinth, declaring, "We want you to be aware . . . of God's grace that has been given in connection with the Macedonian churches." Paul has used this term ἀδελφός (*adelphos*) earlier to address the whole congregation at 1:8, where he writes, "Now brothers and sisters, we do not want you to take lightly [Οὐ γὰρ θέλομεν ὑμᾶς ἀγνοεῖν, *ou gar thelomen hymas agnoein*, more directly, "We do not want you to be ignorant of"] the tremendous affliction that happened to us in Asia." There too his exhortation has to do with "knowing about" or "being aware of" (here γνωρίζω, *gnōrizō*) an event that has taken place, so the apostle points to these happenings, hoping to motivate the congregation in some way. It is the apostle's way of saying, "Pay attention now! This is an important event for you to consider as you think about your response to me!"

Here in 8:1 he wants them to be aware of a very specific expression of "God's grace" (τὴν χάριν τοῦ θεοῦ, *tēn charin tou theou*). The term χάρις, of course, had a broad semantic range in the first century,[3] being used variously to communicate the concepts of "attractiveness," "charm,"[4] "winsomeness," "thanks," "thankfulness," "grace," "gift," "benefit," "generosity," "favor," "help," and a number of other ideas (BDAG 1079–80; *EDNT* 3:457–60). In terms of "benefit," it carries the sense of "any gift, present, pardon, or concession that is granted freely, out of one's goodness" (Spicq 1994: 3.503). So χάρις became a cornerstone for the early Christians as they talked about God's good work in the world and especially his expressions of favor toward believers

8:1

---

2. The term ἀδελφός occurs 343 times in the NT. The idea of tribal kinship in the OT literature lays the foundation for the broader figurative use of "family" at times in play in the NT. In the Gospels, Jesus builds on that tradition by declaring that those who do God's will, obeying his word, are his brothers and sisters and mother—that is, his true family (Mark 3:31–35; Matt. 12:46–50; Luke 8:19–21). In the Qumran literature, the equivalent אָח (*'āḥ*) takes on the figurative sense of a member of the community (e.g., 1QS 6.22; 1QSa 1.18), and this is a common sense of the term in Paul's writings (e.g., Rom. 8:29, where the Son is said to be the firstborn among many "brothers"). Thus it carries the sense of "siblings" (*EDNT* 1:29–30).

3. The term χάρις occurs 156 times in the NT, with 100 of these in Paul's writings. The word is used 18 times in 2 Corinthians: 1:2, 12, 15; 2:14; 4:15; 6:1; 8:1, 4, 6–7, 9, 16, 19; 9:8, 14–15; 12:9; 13:13. Used seven times in chap. 8, the word presents a dominant motif in the chapter.

4. Plutarch, e.g., speaks of the "charm" of language (*Aem.* 2.2), and the *Palatine Anthology* (9.666) refers to the "charm" of a garden.

(Rom. 12:6; 15:15; 1 Cor. 1:4; *NIDNTT* 2:118–23). Paul uses the term 100 of the 156 times in the NT. The term as used in this chapter and the next has various nuances, including these four:

God's *kindness, favor,* or *enablement* (8:1; 9:8, 14),

the *privilege* of participating in the collection (8:4),

the collection itself (referred to as "this gift") as an expression of God's grace (8:6, 7, 19), and

a *verbal expression of thanks* (8:16; 9:15).[5]

In 8:1 Paul clarifies the word χάρις in two ways. First, it is grace "from God,"[6] the giver of good gifts being the *source* of the favor given. Second, this grace from God "has been given in connection with the Macedonian churches," meaning the churches at Philippi, Thessalonica, and Berea. The theological passive τὴν δεδομένην (*tēn dedomenēn,* that has been given) confirms that "from God" should be read as a genitive of source, and the perfect form of this participle may indicate that the churches involved continue in a state of grace: God, the source of all good things, continues to grant his favor to them.

Yet how should we understand the Greek phrase ἐν ταῖς ἐκκλησίαις τῆς Μακεδονίας (*en tais ekklēsiais tēs Makedonias*)? The preposition ἐν might simply be understood spatially as "in" or "among" (so CEV, ESV, NASB, Message). Or, as with our translation, perhaps we have here the preposition as a "marker denoting the object to which something happens or in which something shows itself, or by which something is recognized," translated as "to," "by," or "in connection with" (BDAG 329; so HCSB, NET, NIV, NLT[2]). The translation "in connection with the Macedonian churches" keeps the focus on God as the prime giver and makes it clear that the Macedonians are not the terminus of the gift. Thus Paul gives a heading or introduction to these first seven verses of 2 Cor. 8 by offering the Macedonians as an example of how God has manifested his grace by doing a great work in, but also through, their churches. This nuance becomes even more clear as we move to verse 2.

But before going there, we might pause and reflect on whether our own churches are a context in which the grace of God is being manifest. Further,

---

5. Harris (2005: 559–60) identifies six distinct ideas, including God's unconditional kindness or enablement (8:1; 9:8, 14), the privilege or favor of participating in the collection (8:4), the collection itself as a charitable act (8:6), the act of sharing (the "grace of giving") (8:7), the offering as an expression and proof of goodwill (8:19), and a verbal expression of thanks (8:16; 9:15), although the distinction between the third and fourth of these is quite thin. Yet it should be noted that the third, fourth, and fifth of these all refer to "this gift" (χάρις + the feminine form of οὗτος [*houtos,* this]) and can be understood as referring to the collection for the saints.

6. The phrase "the grace of God" is used twelve times in Paul: Rom. 5:15; 1 Cor. 1:4; 3:10; 15:10; 2 Cor. 6:1; 8:1; Gal. 2:21; Eph. 3:2, 7; Col. 1:6; 2 Thess. 1:12; Titus 2:11. God, in his nature, is gracious, giving good gifts to his people.

are we appropriately dependent on God as the source for the ministry taking place among us? Or are our resources such that dependence on God for what goes on is not that necessary? One of the great spiritual poverties in the Western church has to do with our wealth of material resources: we are drowning in wealth. It lulls us to depend on that rather than on the Lord. Finally, we might ask whether the grace of God is manifested among us in a way that bears witness to those outside of our immediate location, denomination, or cultural context. Might we be used as an edifying example to those not in our immediate circles?

In verses 2–5 the apostle now goes into a more detailed explanation of how **8:2** God's grace was manifested among the Macedonian churches, focusing on the elaborate generosity of these exemplars.[7] Verse 2 provides a general statement concerning the circumstances and effusiveness of their giving, while verses 3–5 elaborate by focusing on the manner in which the collection was raised and the extent to which they gave.

The chapter's second verse has been crafted[8] in the form of an epexegetical ὅτι (*hoti*, that) clause, which further describes the display of God's grace through the Macedonians, mentioned in the previous verse: "that during a severe test involving affliction their effusive joy and extreme poverty spilled over in extravagant generosity." Two main points come through, both of which focus on the character of the Macedonians, rather than on their financial resources. First, *the Macedonians gave under difficult circumstances.* We are not told the exact nature of the "test" or "ordeal" (δοκιμή, *dokimē*)[9] they experienced, but we do know that it was "severe" since the term πολλή (*pollē*) points to something extensive. We also know that it involved "affliction" (θλίψεως, *thlipseōs*),[10] a life experience with which the Macedonians were quite familiar (Acts 17:5–8; Phil. 1:28–30;

---

7. On the handling of money in the churches of the first century, see Talbert 1989.

8. Note also the triple occurrence of αὐτῶν and the alliteration in 8:2 built on the repetition of the letter π (*p*):

ὅτι ἐν (*hoti en*, that during)	πολλῇ (*pollē*, a severe)
δοκιμῇ θλίψεως ἡ (*dokimē thlipseōs hē*, test involving affliction the)	περισσεία (*perisseia*, effusive)
τῆς χαρᾶς αὐτῶν καὶ ἡ κατὰ βάθους (*tēs charas autōn kai hē kata bathous*, joy of them and extreme)	πτωχεία (*ptōcheia*, poverty)
αὐτῶν (*autōn*, of them)	ἐπερίσσευσεν (*eperisseusen*, spilled over)
εἰς τὸ (*eis to*, in)	πλοῦτος (*ploutos*, extravagant)
τῆς (*tēs*, the)	ἁπλότητος (*haplotētos*, generosity)
αὐτῶν (*autōn*, of them).	

9. The word, as here, can refer to the process of testing or can be used with special emphasis on the character that results from a test (BDAG 256).

10. The genitive here is read as a genitive of apposition, sometimes called an epexegetical genitive (see D. Wallace 1996: 95). Harris (2005: 561) suggests, rather, that we have here a subjecting genitive, "brought about by affliction."

---

1 Thess. 1:6; 2:14; 3:3–4; 2 Thess. 1:4–7). Paul has used *thlipsis* and its cognates a number of times in the book to describe persecution and other harsh difficulties surrounding his mission.[11] In 2 Corinthians the apostle goes to great lengths to demonstrate that authentic Christianity in its glory is often displayed on the stage of difficulty and suffering. Rather than suggesting that something must be wrong with a church or minister, "affliction" may well be a mark of authenticity or at least a common context in which the Christian movement goes forward. Those of us in the Western church should reflect deeply on how well we grasp this fact. Do we give primarily out of our context of comfort, or do we give extensively, even under severe circumstances?

Second, *the Macedonians gave joyfully and extravagantly in spite of their poverty*. The compound subjects of this sentence are laid out according to a balanced cadence and express seemingly contrasting realities, joy mixed with poverty:

ἡ πε-ρισ-σεί-α τῆς χα-ρᾶς αὐ-τῶν	καὶ
ἡ κα-τὰ βά-θους πτω-χεί-α αὐ-τῶν	
hē pe-ris-sei-a tēs cha-ras au-tōn	*kai*
hē ka-ta ba-thous ptō-chei-a au-tōn	
their effusive joy	and
their extreme poverty	

The first of these subjects notes "the abundance" or "surplus" of the Macedonians' joy: the term περισσεία (*perisseia*) speaks of something beyond what would normally be expected (BDAG 805). Accordingly, our translation "effusive" communicates the sense of a joy that is overflowing.[12] Several years ago I heard about a practice in some churches in Africa, where congregants literally dance down the aisles to present their offerings to God in worship. We should ask ourselves whether our giving to God flows from such an effusive joy, regardless of how that joy is expressed. The love and commitments of our hearts are seen through the window of our joy.

The second subject provides further insight into the Macedonians' situation: they gave out of their "extreme poverty."[13] The term πτωχεία (*ptōcheia*, poverty) only occurs twice elsewhere in the NT: at 2 Cor. 8:9, where Paul speaks of Christ becoming poor so that the Corinthians' might become rich; and at Rev. 2:9, where Jesus speaks to the church at Smyrna, saying, "I know your

---

11. For the noun: 2 Cor. 1:4, 8; 2:4; 4:17; 6:4; 7:4; 8:2, 13. For the verb 2 Cor. 1:6; 4:8; 7:5. See discussion of the concept in the comments on 1:4, 6.

12. In this case the genitive τῆς χαρᾶς can be read as an attributed genitive, the head noun functioning almost adjectivally.

13. Opinions are mixed concerning why the Macedonians were so poor. Some attribute this to the general economic condition, especially of rural people. Others, however, suggest that conversion to Christianity had economic implications for those in the church. For a discussion of the matter, see Thrall 2000: 522–23.

affliction and poverty, yet you are rich" (Rev. 2:9 HCSB). So the term clearly stands in contrast to a state of being rich or having abundant resources. As noted by Deborah E. Watson (2006: 171–72),

> In the Graeco-Roman world, giving was the purview of the wealthy, whose giving is attested as largely benefiting fellow elites who had passed a stringent "worthiness" test. In the Jewish world, everyone who could was responsible to aid the poor, and the giving was in proportion to one's means. Here (in Macedonia) we have people from the Graeco-Roman world acting out of character for their natural heritage, but very much in character with respect to their adopted (i.e., Jewish) heritage. A profound shift had taken place in them.
>
> Beyond what in Jewish terms might be expected, the Macedonians' giving was more than proportional, and it was proactively voluntary—they *asked* to be part of the collection. This may mean that their circumstances were perceived by Paul as so difficult that he had not asked them to give, making their eager and extravagant participation even more impressive (vv. 3–4).

In fact, the Macedonians' poverty was "extreme"—κατὰ βάθους (*kata bathous*, abysmal), the word βάθος (*bathos*) having to do with depth, or something far removed from the ordinary.[14] The word could be used positively to represent the intensity or greatness of something, such as the depths of God, or the knowledge or mysteries of God (Rom. 11:33; 1 Cor. 2:10; see 1QS 11.19; 1QM 10.11), but it also could be used of an extremely difficult circumstance, as here, and at several points in ancient literature is used to describe dire poverty, what Barrett (1973: 216) translates as "rock-bottom poverty." The Macedonians, then, gave joyfully out of a very great lack of material resources, and the Corinthians could not attribute their generosity to a booming economic situation among the churches of Macedonia.

Yet this mix of abundant joy and abundant poverty "spilled over in extravagant generosity." Paul uses the word περισσεύω (*perisseuō*) ten times in 2 Corinthians, three times here in chapter 8 and thrice again in chapter 9 (1:5 [2x]; 3:9; 4:15; 8:2, 7 [2x]; 9:8 [2x], 12). The term has to do with abundance or having such a wealth of something that it spills over, overflows. The result of this superabundance of joy and poverty among the Corinthians was "extravagant generosity" (εἰς τὸ πλοῦτος τῆς ἁπλότητος αὐτῶν, *eis to ploutos tēs haplotētos autōn*, more directly, "unto the wealth of their generosity"), the term τὸ πλοῦτος (= wealth) being clarified by τῆς ἁπλότητος (= generosity). It is not simply that the result of their joy and poverty was material "wealth" (τὸ πλοῦτος), but rather a "wealth of generosity," or as we have translated it, "extravagant generosity," and this places the emphasis on the character, or spiritual health, of the Macedonians. Thus the genitive form τῆς ἁπλότητος functions as an "attributed genitive," where the head noun (in this case τὸ

---

14. The word βάθος could be used more literally, e.g., of the depth of soil (Matt. 13:5; Mark 4:5; Josephus, *Ant.* 8.63) or the depth of the sea or of deep water (Ps. 68:3 [69:2 ET]; Amos 9:3; Mic. 7:19).

πλοῦτος), in its relation to the genitive, functions like an attributive adjective (D. Wallace 1996: 89).[15] So the giving of resources that took place among the Macedonian churches stemmed from a posture of integrity. In the upside-down world of God's kingdom values, monetary help from the Macedonian churches flowed not from a reservoir of monetary wealth, but from joy-filled, integrity-infused, poverty. They were a "rich poor" church that in spite of their impoverished condition refused to turn inward (Garland 1999: 367) and poured out what was needed by others at that moment. A few verses later Paul writes that this pattern emulates the Lord Jesus himself, who in an extravagant expression of grace "became poor, so that by His poverty you might become rich" (2 Cor. 8:9 HCSB). Paul has already used the term ἁπλότητος, which normally speaks of a single-hearted, rigorous integrity or frankness,[16] at 1:12, and he will use it thrice more in the book, at 9:11, 13 and 11:3. In 1:12 he writes, "We have lived a pattern of life in the world, and especially toward you, which is characterized by straightforwardness [ἐν ἁπλότητι, en haplotēti] and sincerity that come from God." Thus the term speaks of a spiritual openness and health that is the opposite of a divided or corrupted or closed heart. Out of such a singleness of heart and purpose for God, ministry can be elaborate in openness both to God and to others. As Spicq (1994: 1.171) explains this term, "Simplicity is thus total involvement and the unreserved giving of the self." This then relates to the use of one's resources, the sense of the term at points in ancient literature (e.g., T. Iss. 3.8; Josephus, *Ant.* 7.332), as well as in Paul's own writing (e.g., at Rom. 12:8, where the exhortation is to give with generosity, and it seems to be the sense here as well).

8:3–4   Beginning at 8:3 and extending through 8:6, we have a second ὅτι (*hoti*, that) clause, which parallels the ὅτι clause of verse 2, elaborating extensively on the extravagant generosity spotlighted in 8:2. The focus remains on the topic of "giving," expressed most overtly with the aorist verb ἔδωκαν (*edōkan*, they gave)[17] in verse 5. Yet in verses 3–4 the grammatical construction builds around an understood ἔδωκαν rather than the verb in verse 5.[18] The layout of

15. Although Furnish (1984: 400), e.g., takes the genitive as epexegetical, "describing the Macedonians' wealth as their generosity."

16. Spicq (1994: 1.169–70) writes of the concept,

> This is not just a dictionary entry but an entire spirituality. This faultless innocence, this uncompromising rectitude, is blessed by God (Prov 2:7; 10:29; 11:20; 28:10) and is the way of salvation (Prov 28:18). It is the virtue of the servants of God (Deut 18:13; Ps 19:13; 25:21 [18:14; 24:21 LXX]; Prov 13:6), or better, a deep-seated purpose, a condition of the soul. As opposed to duplicitous people, those with divided hearts, those who are simple have no other concern than to do the will of God, to observe his precepts; their whole existence is an expression of this disposition of heart, this rectitude: "Let us all die in our simplicity" (1 Macc 2:37). In the first century BC, *haplotēs*, so exalted in the Wisdom writings, is considered the supreme virtue of the patriarchs.

17. It probably should be understood as a constative aorist, viewing the action as a whole or in summary fashion (D. Wallace 1996: 557).

18. On whether or not the clauses of 8:3–4 anticipate the verb ἔδωκαν of verse 5, see the additional note on 8:3–5.

the grammar might look something like this, with the brackets showing the verb as understood:

> according to their resources,
> I can confirm this—[they voluntarily gave]
> even beyond their resources,
>
> most emphatically
> begging us
> for the privilege
> of being able to join in
> this ministry
> to God's people.

So, how does Paul elaborate on the Macedonians' generosity?

1. *The Macedonians gave voluntarily, even beyond their resources.* They gave "according to their resources" (κατὰ δύναμιν, *kata dynamin*), "even beyond their resources." With a word in the accusative case, the preposition κατά can communicate the idea of a standard, speaking of an action in this case that corresponds to something. The idea here is that the Macedonians' giving corresponded with what they had to give: "according to their resources." So they did not skimp on their giving, just winking stingily at the need of the moment. No, they gave in line with what they were capable of giving; here the term δύναμις speaks of their ability or capability, and the context suggests Paul has in mind their financial resources. What pastor of a church today would not be thrilled with a congregation, or network of congregations, that gave according to what they had the ability to give?! This contrasts sharply with the kind of giving that merely tosses God the leftovers of one's resources!

Yet what surprised the apostle—and his parenthetical statement, "I can confirm this" (μαρτυρῶ, *martyrō*, I bear witness), shows that he anticipated a bit of incredulity on the part of the Corinthians!—was that the Macedonians gave to an extent that was "even beyond their resources" (καὶ παρὰ δύναμιν, *kai para dynamin*). We might say today that they gave "above and beyond" what would normally be expected of them. And rather than being coerced into doing so, they gave "voluntarily" (αὐθαίρετοι, *authairetoi*). The only other use of this term in the NT comes at 8:17, where Paul says of Titus, "He accepted our urging and, being very diligent, went out to you *by his own choice*" (HCSB). So the term points to a voluntary action, and the Macedonians' volunteerism impressed Paul.

Paul elaborates on the generosity of the Macedonians in a second point.

2. *The Macedonians gave, begging for the opportunity to be involved in the ministry to fellow believers.* In verse 4 the verb δέομαι (*deomai*) means "to ask," or "request," but the context can add a note of urgency. Especially prevalent in Luke-Acts, the word is often used in the NT of someone either praying or making an urgent request that would have some benefit for the one

doing the asking (e.g., Luke 5:12; 8:28; 9:38; 21:36). Paul also uses the word when speaking both of prayer (1 Thess. 3:10) and of earnest entreaties made to his churches (2 Cor. 5:20; 10:2; Gal. 4:12;). The irony, of course, is that the "givers" in such an exchange often are being begged to give or respond, but here it is the "beggars"—those making the request—who insist on participating as "givers," and they are insisting rather energetically!

The preposition μετά plus the genitive points to the circumstances surrounding the act of begging. They were begging "with much encouragement" (μετὰ πολλῆς παρακλήσεως, *meta pollēs paraklēseōs*) and the phrase could be translated more smoothly as "earnestly" (ESV), "urgently" (NIV), or as we have rendered it, "most emphatically." Paul has tapped the theme of "encouragement" a good deal thus far in the book, speaking of it as coming from God (1:3–7), as being appropriate to relationships in the congregation (2:7–8), as being offered by the apostle in the form of exhortation (5:20; 6:1), and as stemming from the good report that Titus brought about the Corinthians' recent response to the apostle's communication (7:4–13). Now the Macedonians are said to have "encouraged" him with "much" (πολλῆς) encouragement to allow them to participate in the ministry of giving. In other words, the Macedonians were exuberant, both eager and excited about the opportunity to give to this work of ministry, and insisted on participating. Their eagerness obviously caught Paul off guard and delighted him.

At the end of verse 4 the apostle refers to "this ministry to God's people" (τῆς διακονίας τῆς εἰς τοὺς ἁγίους, *tēs diakonias tēs eis tous hagious*), meaning the charitable collection for the saints in Jerusalem; the word διακονία (ministry) is used as a technical term for financial relief among the congregations (Acts 11:29; 12:25; Rom. 15:31; Harris 2005: 567) as they "ministered" to each other, sharing resources. The Macedonians saw this ministry as a "privilege"; here Paul capitalizes on one of the nuances of the term χάρις (*charis*), which he has already used variously in the book to speak of "grace," "benefit," and the giving of "thanks" (1:2, 12, 15; 2:14; 4:15; 6:1; 8:1).[19] So the opportunity of giving to the saints is a gift or expression of God's grace. In other words, the Macedonians considered the opportunity to give as not only a grace *through* them (8:1), but also a grace *to* them as they had the resources to help other members of Christ's church. It was a privilege, moreover, as they were "able to join in this ministry" (καὶ τὴν κοινωνίαν τῆς διακονίας, *kai tēn koinōnian tēs diakonias*).[20] The rich word κοινωνία connotes "close association," "fellowship," "sharing," or "joining in" an activity because of a "close relationship" (BDAG 552–53). When Christ-followers share their resources to build up needy brothers and sisters in Christ, this both expresses and builds *koinōnia*.

8:5   Now in verse 5, as he continues to elaborate on the Macedonians' generosity, Paul offers a third point.

---

19. For more on Paul's use of the term χάρις, see the comments on 8:1.

20. The construction τὴν χάριν καὶ τὴν κοινωνίαν (8:4) can be read as a hendiadys (lit., "one through two"), which expresses a focal concept through two separate terms joined by καί.

3. *The Macedonians gave personally and in a manner beyond what their apostle had expected.* The καί (*kai*, and) at the beginning of verse 5 stands as conjunctive, as Paul continues to paint, point by point, the compelling picture of enthusiastic, sacrificial giving among the Macedonian churches. In elaborating on the extravagant generosity noted in verse 2, he has already shown that the Macedonians gave voluntarily, beyond their resources (v. 3), even begging to be involved in this ministry to God's people (v. 4). He now states that they gave personally, beyond what might have been anticipated, offering themselves as first priority to the Lord and then to his representatives.

Paul describes the giving of the Macedonians as "confounding our expectations" (οὐ καθὼς ἠλπίσαμεν, *ou kathōs ēlpisamen*), or not in line with what he had dared to hope from this poor, persecuted group. He has already pointed out that the amount they gave was elaborate, given their circumstances (vv. 2–3), and he has hinted that such extravagance flowed from Christian character and commitment of the highest order, but now the underlying commitments come out. In contrast (ἀλλά, *alla*) to what Paul had dared to hope in response to his request for monetary support for the saints in Jerusalem, the Macedonians had recommitted themselves (not just their possessions) to the Lord and the Lord's work through Paul's mission. This is quite significant given the broader intention of 2 Corinthians, in which Paul calls the Corinthians to a renewed commitment to him and his ministry.

Thus the pronoun ἑαυτούς (*heautous*, themselves), as the object of the Macedonians' giving, occurs at the front of the clause following ἀλλά, placed there for emphasis. This act of self-giving seems to have both stunned and delighted the apostle. He knew that if the Lord has a person's heart, he has that person's resources as well. In fact, as seen throughout the biblical literature, the sacrifice of possessions is always secondary to the personal, spiritual commitments of the offerer. "To obey is better than sacrifice" (1 Sam. 15:22). Proper commitment to "lordship" lays the appropriate foundation for "stewardship."

Yet there is more to be said about this act of self-giving on the part of the Macedonians, as indicated by the adverb πρῶτον (*prōton*). The term should not be read as merely temporal, as if the point primarily is one of sequence in time (i.e., "to Christ first, then to us"). Rather, the adverb speaks of priority or prominence, submission to the lordship of Christ positioned as foundational, as utmost in importance, and then issuing in a consequential commitment to Paul and his mission. Thus commitment to Paul's mission is an expression, or outflow, of the deeper commitment to Christ, before whom Paul carries out his ministry (e.g., 2:17). The phrase "by God's will" (διὰ θελήματος θεοῦ, *dia thelēmatos theou*) can be understood grammatically as relating both to the Macedonians' giving of themselves "to the Lord" and to their commitment to Paul and his mission, and truly it was God's will that the Macedonians submit themselves to Christ. But since the apostle normally and particularly uses the phrase "by God's will" to describe his ministry (Rom. 15:32; 1 Cor. 1:1; 2 Cor. 1:1; 8:5; Eph. 1:1; Col. 1:1; 2 Tim. 1:1), it may be that "by God's will" here should be seen as a special expression describing the Macedonians' commitment to the apostle's mission.

As we look at how Paul uses the example of the Macedonians to challenge the Corinthians to give, we might reflect for a moment on how instructive, on a number of levels, that example is for us in the modern church, especially as we struggle with lackluster giving in our churches. First, notice that commitment to the lordship of Christ stands as the preeminent foundation stone for a robust, joy-infused, sacrificial giving. Thus giving to any ministry should find its primary impetus in a commitment to Christ. Do you want a congregation to grow in giving? Then lead them to a large view of Christ's lordship. Second, on the other hand, such a commitment to the lordship of Christ will naturally lay the foundation for support of those ministries that are sacrificial in ministering under that lordship. When a ministry is seen as self-serving, rather than Christ-serving, the motives for giving lie elsewhere. Could it be that huckster ministers loom large, having greatest influence, only where there is a small view of Christ's lordship? Third, giving of oneself should be seen as foundational for a robust giving of one's possessions. The goal is not to get people to open their resources but to open their hearts. This is why, later in the book, Paul writes, "I am not seeking what is yours, but you" (2 Cor. 12:14 HCSB). The apostle knows that if he has the hearts of the Corinthians, their giving will follow. Finally, the Macedonians show us that this level of giving must be seen as an expression of God's grace, a manifestation of the presence and work of God among his people.

8:6   Having put the Macedonian churches before the Corinthians as exemplars of the grace of giving, Paul now moves to the point. The Corinthians themselves need to get on board with that same ministry so beautifully exemplified in the Macedonian congregations. Consequently, his time among the Macedonians has emboldened the apostle to exhort Titus concerning a fresh effort for the collection: "As a result we encouraged Titus that since he started work on this gracious gift, he should be the one to bring it to completion among you also." As reflected in the translation, the first clause of the verse communicates a result (εἰς τὸ παρακαλέσαι ἡμᾶς, *eis to parakalesai hēmas*, As a result we encouraged).[21] Given his extensive use of the theme, "encouragement" certainly was on the apostle's mind as he wrote 2 Corinthians,[22] and at times this encouragement takes the form of exhortation, as here. In terms of the book's development, Paul establishes an atmosphere of encouragement in the first chapter, grounded in the encouragement that God offers to his people. The apostle especially reiterates that orientation in chapter 7 as he continues his travel narrative, speaking of the encouragement he received upon his rendezvous with Titus in Macedonia.

---

21. The pronoun ἡμᾶς, acc. in form, functions as the subject of the infinitive.
22. Thus far in the book the verb has occurred at 1:4, 6; 2:7–8; 5:20; 6:1; 7:6–7, 13; and the noun at 1:3–7; 7:4, 7, 13; 8:4.

As the apostle contemplated renewing efforts to get the Corinthian collection moving again, Titus was a natural choice for the task in at least two ways. We saw in 2 Cor. 7 that Titus has just returned to Paul from a successful time among the Corinthians; they had responded well to his ministry (7:7, 13–15). Moreover, Titus was the one who had initiated the collection among the Corinthians, which we find out as 8:6 continues. The ἵνα (*hina*, that) clause that fills out the rest of the verse communicates why[23] Paul encouraged his young protégé to take up the task, and the clause divides into two parts, introduced by "just as" (καθώς, *kathōs*) and "so also" (οὕτως καί, *houtos kai*).[24] The Greek construction suggests a correspondence between the two parts, communicating some idea of accordance or logical relationship:[25]

"since he started" (καθὼς προενήρξατο, *kathōs proenēzato*)
"he should . . . finish" (οὕτως καὶ ἐπιτελέσῃ, *houtōs kai epitelesē*)

We have translated the first part as "since" (so NIV) because Paul's point is probably not that Titus should continue the ministry of collection among the Corinthians in the same way, "just as" (so NET), he had started it, but rather that Titus should continue that same ministry *because* he had started it.[26] The Greek term ἐνάρχομαι (*enarchomai*) means "to begin." The cognate form used in this verse (with the prefix προ-, *pro-*) communicates that something had been started in the past (BDAG 868) and in the NT only occurs here and in the parallel passage four verses later (8:10). The contrasting verb ἐπιτελέω (*epiteleō*), on the other hand, means "to finish something" or bring it "to completion."[27] In short, Paul thinks that since Titus started the collection among the Corinthians, he would be the logical choice of one who could bring this project to a good conclusion.

The phrase εἰς ὑμᾶς (*eis hymas*) probably relates grammatically to ἐπιτελέσῃ and may be translated as communicating a location or place: "among you" (BDAG 288–89). Since the beginning of chapter 8, Paul has been speaking of the collection among the Macedonians, here referred to as "this gracious gift"

23. The use of ἵνα here, rather than epexegetical (so Barnett 1997: 400), communicates purpose.

24. For use of various forms of καθώς + a correlative, see Robertson 1934: 968.

25. As usual, καθώς is a comparative, second only to ὡς (*hōs*, as) in frequency.

26. A number of ETs leave this ambiguous by translating καθώς with "as" (so HCSB, NASB⁹⁵, NRSV). With regard to the collection, in verse 10 Paul notes that the Corinthians themselves had taken "the initiative beginning last year." So, how do we reconcile that Titus "started work on this gracious gift" and the Corinthians took the initiative on the work? What we have here are two sides of the same coin. Titus led in starting the work on behalf of the apostolic team. The Corinthians expressed desire for the work and acted on it. Almost certainly the collection came from the apostle's mission, not from the Corinthians themselves, but in verse 10 Paul means that the church, once confronted (by Titus) with the need, expressed their desire to be involved and set to work on the task.

27. The word occurs ten times in the NT, three times here in 2 Cor. 8; and in Rom. 15:28; 2 Cor. 7:1; 8:6, 11 (2x); Gal. 3:3; Phil. 1:6; Heb. 8:5; 9:6; 1 Pet. 5:9.

(τὴν χάριν ταύτην, *tēn charin tautēn*).[28] Now the focus has shifted to the Corinthians and their need to take up the ministry; so, speaking to the Corinthians, he states that the collection needs to be finished "among you also," with the καί (*kai*) following ὑμᾶς understood as adjunctive: "also."[29]

8:7   After introducing the primary purpose for Titus's latest trek to Corinth, Paul then offers a direct exhortation to the Corinthians; the implicit need intimated in verse 6 is now made explicit: "Now then, just as you excel in all kinds of ways—in faith and speech and knowledge and with the highest degree of enthusiasm and in the love we inspired among you—excel also in this gracious gift." The conjunction ἀλλά (*alla*, so, then) can be used as here both to draw out an inference and to bolster an imperative, strengthening a command (BDAG 45). Furnish (1984: 403), for instance, reads the ἵνα (*hina*) clause at the end of the verse as imperatival in function. It certainly is a mild form of exhortation, more appropriate to a wish, and fits well with the rhetorical finesse demonstrated in the verse; the apostle gives strong encouragement before baldly stating his exhortation (Thrall 2000: 529; Verbrugge 1992: 251). That encouragement he introduces with "just as you excel in all kinds of ways" (ὥσπερ ἐν παντὶ περισσεύετε, *hōsper en panti perisseuete*), drawing a parallel between the positive patterns he has witnessed in their lives and the positive response he hopes to arouse. In responding well to Titus's resumption of the collection, the Corinthians would be building on and continuing in healthy spiritual patterns already evident among them.

What then were those patterns? Paul uses the term περισσεύω (*perisseuō*) throughout the book to speak of something that overflows, increases, or excels, and the double use of it here in verse 7 forms somewhat a "bookends" structure with the use of the verb and its cognate noun in 8:2 (as in 1:5; 3:9; 4:15; 8:2, 7; 9:8, 12). The ἐν παντί, moreover, certainly doesn't mean that they already excel in *everything*, for they have yet to step up and excel in participation in the collection! Rather, Paul means that the many areas in which they do excel—"in faith, and speech, and knowledge, and with the highest degree of enthusiasm, and in the love we inspired among you"—provide a solid foundation on which to build. The positive patterns in their lives indicate that they have the spiritual resources to "excel also in this gracious gift."

"Faith" (πίστει, *pistei*), "speech" (λόγῳ, *logō*), and "knowledge" (γνώσει, *gnōsei*) all call to mind gifts or attributes celebrated in 1 Corinthians. "Faith" could refer to a special endowment by God to trust him for miracles (1 Cor. 12:9; 13:2); but throughout 1 and 2 Corinthians, Paul primarily uses "faith" in a more general way to speak of one's posture of trust or Christian commitment

---

28. On the various uses of χάρις in 2 Corinthians, see the comments on 8:1.

29. In 8:6 the use of adjunctive καί probably does not allude to a previous ministry of Titus among the Corinthians, perhaps the successful ministry completed on Titus's previous trip to Corinth, reported in chap. 7 (so Harris 2005: 572; Thrall 2000: 528). The primary ministry in view is the collection as taken up in so exemplary a fashion by the Macedonians, so the καί may be read as primarily relating to the pronoun ὑμᾶς (i.e., "you also").

before God (1 Cor. 2:5; 13:13; 15:14, 17; 16:13; 2 Cor. 1:24; 4:13; 5:7; 8:7; 10:15; 13:5). "Speech" and "knowledge," on the other hand, bring to mind 1 Cor. 1:5, where Paul says that the Corinthians "were enriched in everything—in all speech and all knowledge" (HCSB). The former could refer to special gifts of speaking like prophecy and tongues (e.g., 1 Cor. 12:10), but Paul also mentions a "message of wisdom" and a "message of knowledge" in 1 Cor. 12:8, both using this same term, λόγος. With reference to the latter, "knowledge" is mentioned often in the Corinthian correspondence (1 Cor. 1:5; 8:1, 7, 10–11; 12:8; 13:2, 8; 14:6; 2 Cor. 2:14; 4:6; 6:6; 8:7; 10:5; 11:6), speaking of one's grasp of some aspect of Christian truth. As for the Corinthians excelling in their ministry "with the highest degree of enthusiasm" (πάσῃ σπουδῇ, *pasē spoudē*; 8:7), in the previous chapter (7:11) the apostle has already celebrated their passionate zeal for him, and for making things right with him. Last of all, he mentions "the love we inspired among you" (τῇ ἐξ ἡμῶν ἐν ὑμῖν ἀγάπῃ, *tē ex hēmōn en hymin agapē*).[30] At a number of places Paul notes his love for this wayward church (6:11–12; 11:11; 12:15), but there is no overt mention of their love for him (Barnett 1997: 403); and this certainly is a roundabout way of speaking of their love! The phrase ἐξ ἡμῶν (from us) shows clearly the context of love, which the apostle now celebrates as excellent among the Corinthians, has its impetus in Paul's mission.[31] Nevertheless, this celebration of love caps off an admirable list of praiseworthy qualities that Paul uses to good rhetorical effect in preparing them to participate in the collection for the saints. These excellent manifestations of God's grace have laid a good foundation for them to "excel also in this gracious gift" (καὶ ἐν ταύτῃ τῇ χάριτι περισσεύητε, *kai en tautē tē chariti perisseuēte*).

As we have seen at numerous places in 2 Corinthians, Paul knows how to make a skillful appeal. In these first seven verses of chapter 8, he uses two of the most common means of exhortation in the first-century world: a positive example and sincere praise. As we appeal to people in our churches, exhorting them to participate in ministries that advance the cause of Christ in the church and the world—not to mention their own spiritual lives!—we need to do so skillfully, and we can follow Paul's pattern here of using good examples and praising what is praiseworthy. Both forms of encouragement provide a strong basis for next steps in Christian obedience.

2. Paul Clarifies the Tone and Motives for His Exhortation (8:8–15)

One of the challenges of written communication has to do with the lack of auditory and visual clues that accompany a face-to-face conversation. In this unit Paul clarifies both the tone and the motives behind his exhortation just

---

30. See the additional notes for a discussion of the textual variant in 8:7, which reads τῇ ἐξ ὑμῶν ἐν ἡμῖν ἀγάπῃ (*tē ex hymōn en hēmin agapē*, your love for us).

31. Although he says they excel in this Paul-inspired love, in the very next verse (8:8) he says that their opportunity to participate in the collection will serve as a test for the sincerity of their love.

given in 8:7. He first assures the Corinthians that he is not commanding them to get busy with the collection for Jerusalem. He wants their giving to be voluntary. But he is trying to spur them on through the example of the Macedonians and especially the example of Jesus. The impetus to give ultimately is grounded in the gospel. Since the Corinthians have taken the initiative the previous year, both in terms of their desire to be involved and their start at raising funds, Paul advises them that it will be to their advantage to follow through. But he also assures them that they should give proportionately, based on the resources they have. He is not trying to hurt them, but he wants them to grasp the biblical principle of equality, with God using the surplus of one group of Christ-followers to meet the needs of others in the body.

8:8–9   Paul now clarifies the tone and motivation of the exhortation given in verse 7. That he feels the need to clarify—he does not want them to receive his words as an authoritarian mandate—may hint at the note of tension that remains in the Corinthians' relationship with their apostle.

The term ἐπιταγή (*epitagē*) could be used in the first century to speak of an "authoritative directive," a "command," an "order," or an "injunction." The NT authors use the term to speak of a command, an authoritative word that comes ultimately from God (Rom. 16:26; 1 Tim. 1:1; Titus 1:3), especially in relation to apostolic authority (Titus 2:15; BDAG 383; *EDNT* 2:41).[32] Here Paul makes clear he is not playing "the authority card," as if his exhortation that the Corinthians proceed with the collection for the saints is a directive straight from God. He does not want to be read as a religious "dictator" bent on "removing the elements of free choice and warm spontaneity from" the Corinthians' response (Harris 2005: 576). He simply states, "I am not ordering you to do this," because he wants them to give voluntarily, as an expression of God's grace at work among them.[33] Perhaps he has been accused by some of being authoritarian (1:24); later in the letter, Paul will return to the topic of authority (e.g., 10:8). Yet here he wants to make clear the difference between his challenge to them concerning the collection and an authoritative word from God. His exhortation to get to work on the collection does not carry the force of a divine directive.

So what is Paul doing in the first part of this chapter? "Rather," he says, "using the enthusiasm of others as an example, I am seeking to verify the genuineness of your own love as well." In other words, to help the Corinthians respond appropriately, he would rather use "friendly emulation" (Bruce 1971: 222) than a harsh injunction. The conjunction ἀλλά (*alla*, but, rather) draws a sharp line of contrast between an authoritarian posture and Paul's true

---

32. Paul uses the same word in 1 Corinthians to draw a contrast between a word of encouragement and a directive from the Lord. At 1 Cor. 7:6, speaking of his preference for singleness over marriage, he states, "I say the following as a concession, not as a command," and later in that same chapter, at verse 25, he writes, "About virgins: I have no command from the Lord, but I do give an opinion as one who by the Lord's mercy is trustworthy" (HCSB).

33. Keener (2005: 204) states that commanding was seen as inappropriate for deliberative rhetoric seeking a favor.

intention expressed here. In relation to 8:1–5, we have already noticed that the Macedonian churches are held up before the eyes of the Corinthians as a stellar example of extravagant giving. Without using this exact term, Paul has marked the Macedonians' σπουδή (*spoudē*), their "enthusiasm"—a word he has used to describe the Corinthians three times in the broader context (7:11–12; 8:7)—when in 8:2–4 he speaks of the Macedonians' "effusive joy," their "extravagant generosity," the extent of their giving, which was "beyond their resources," and their act of "begging . . . most emphatically for the privilege of being able to join in this ministry to God's people." As he states clearly in 8:7, the apostle thinks the Corinthians are appropriately enthusiastic about a number of things, but he wants to spur them on to a higher degree of σπουδή for the collection, challenging them via (διά, *dia*) the σπουδή of the Macedonians for that ministry.

Further, Paul describes his exhortation as "seeking to verify the genuineness of your own love as well" (καὶ τὸ τῆς ὑμετέρας ἀγάπης γνήσιον δοκιμάζων, *kai to tēs hymeteras agapēs gnēsion dokimazōn*). The conjunction καί (also, as well) is adjunctive and relates most directly to the phrase "your own love" (τῆς ὑμετέρας ἀγάπης), again contrasting the current posture of the Corinthians with that of the Macedonians in terms of the collection for the saints. The Macedonians' love is clear by their commitment to that ministry of grace. Although Paul has just affirmed the excellent love of the Corinthians in verse 7, we noted that his wording did not amount to a ringing endorsement ("in the love we inspired among you")! What would make their love clear would be enthusiastic participation in the collection for the saints.

Moreover, two Greek words are used to express that Paul is "seeking to verify the genuineness" of their love. The word δοκιμάζω (cf. the cognate in 2:9), here in the form of a present active participle, has to do with examination, testing, or determining the genuineness of something.[34] The object of the participle, γνήσιον, originally was used in the ancient world to speak of a legitimate child. Correspondingly, in the introductions of 1 Timothy (1:2) and Titus (1:4), Paul speaks of these fellow workers as "true" or "legitimate" (γνησίῳ, *gnēsiō*) sons. In the rest of the NT the word speaks more broadly of something that is valid, legitimate, true, or sincere (BDAG 202; *EDNT* 1:255). So in 2 Cor. 8:8 Paul says he is seeking to "verify the genuineness" of the Corinthians' love. That verification will come when they follow the lead of the Macedonians, stepping up to the task of finishing the collection for the saints in Jerusalem.

But the Macedonians are not the only example of sacrificial, voluntary giving, or even the most significant! Indeed, the preeminent example is the Lord Jesus himself: "For you know the grace demonstrated by our Lord Jesus

---

34. The story of God giving the Israelites manna in the wilderness, from which Paul takes the quotation at 8:15, is also explained as a context of "testing" (Exod. 16:4 LXX: ὅπως πειράσω αὐτούς, so that I might test them), though another Greek term is used. In that case God was testing his people concerning whether they would walk in his instructions. Here Paul says he is testing the Corinthians' love.

Christ: though he was rich, he became poor for your sake, so that by his poverty you might become rich." The apostle has already reported that the "poor" Macedonians had responded to the financial need of the Jerusalem church in a "rich" way. He now shows a divine basis for such a ministry. The overarching framework for Paul's thought involves a "divine interchange" similar to other Pauline texts (Matera 2003: 191). For instance, 2 Cor. 5:21 states, "The One who has never known sin, he made sin on our behalf, in order that we might become the righteousness of God in him." Similarly, here the logic is based on parallels of interchange:

> Christ was rich
>   [implied: and you were poor.]
> Christ became poor
>   so you could become rich.

When the apostle says, "though he was rich," he probably has in mind Christ's preincarnate state. He became "poor" by the incarnation, and especially his suffering, in order to bring salvation to those who would follow him in the new covenant.[35] John Chrysostom (*Hom. 2 Cor.* 17.1) comments on this interchange: "If you do not believe that poverty is productive of great wealth, think of the case of Jesus and you will be persuaded otherwise. For if he had not become poor, you would not have become rich" (Bray 1999: 272).

In pointing to this interchange, Paul appeals to the Corinthians on the basis of the gospel, an expression of grace that they "know" (γινώσκω, *ginōskō*) very well, since they have experienced this spiritual interchange by which their spiritual poverty was turned to spiritual riches. In short, he sees the gospel also as a basis for right Christian response to the needs of others. The grace demonstrated by Jesus becomes a fitting foundation for the Corinthians to express grace through "this gracious gift" of which Paul has been speaking (8:7). The Corinthians can be like Jesus in meeting the need of the moment. They can embrace the magnanimity of Christ's spirit, deny themselves, even as Jesus did in the incarnation, and meet the need of the saints in Jerusalem (Hafemann 2000: 337–38).

Following Christ on the path of discipleship turns out to be following a path of extravagant, grace-filled giving. To say it from another perspective, if we are going to call people to extravagant giving of their resources, we need to call them first to embrace the gospel and its implications. This is the only firm basis for any type of radical lifestyle of self-sacrifice on behalf of others. Verses 8–9 show that people need to see the grace of God incarnated or manifested plainly in the lives of others. As with the Macedonians, fellow believers may serve as stellar examples in this regard. When people see Jesus

---

35. Paul's emphasis is not primarily on literal poverty, although the status of Christ's birth and his identification with the poor are noteworthy. Further, the aorist verb here probably should be read as ingressive, he "began to be poor" (with the incarnation), with his "poverty" referring to the whole of his earthly life culminating in crucifixion (Thrall 2000: 534).

more clearly through the clear presentation of the gospel, they can be called to grace-filled, sacrificial giving. Yet, as the apostle demonstrates, the tone with which we call people to consider these examples is important.

Paul further clarifies that he is not commanding the Corinthians to participate **8:10–11** in the collection by saying, "I am giving my advice on the matter" (καὶ γνώμην ἐν τούτῳ δίδωμι, *kai gnōmēn en toutō didōmi*). Used nine times in the NT,[36] the word translated "advice" (γνώμη) could refer to a person's intention, decision, judgment on a matter, perspective, mind-set, opinion, or approval/ consent (BDAG 202–3; *EDNT* 1:255). Here it speaks of Paul's considered opinion concerning their involvement in the collection, which he refers to as ἐν τούτῳ (in this, on this matter). Thus he is offering (δίδωμι) them his "advice" (NLT², NRSV, NIV), or "serious, apostolic counsel" under the direction of the Holy Spirit (Furnish 1984: 405). This is similar to the way he uses the word γνώμη in 1 Cor. 7:25, 40, where he shares his advice on marriage and single-ness. So the tone of his exhortation in this chapter is one of appealing to the Corinthians and offering them advice, rather than commanding them to act.

When Paul points out that the Corinthians' involvement in the collection would be to their "advantage" or "benefit" (ὑμῖν συμφέρει, *hymin sympherei*),[37] he takes up an aspect of rhetoric, or public oratory, common to his day: appealing to what would benefit the audience.[38] So in what way would it be advantageous for them to participate in the collection? The grammatical relationship of this statement with the somewhat awkward relative clause that follows (οἵτινες[39] οὐ μόνον τὸ ποιῆσαι ἀλλὰ καί, *hoitines ou monon to poiēsai alla kai*; lit., who not only acted but also), suggests that our answer

36. See γνώμη in Acts 20:3; 1 Cor. 1:10; 7:25, 40; 2 Cor. 8:10; Philem. 14; Rev. 17:13, 17 (2x).

37. Harris (2005: 581) translates the word as "fitting." He agrees that there is expediency implied in the term but says, "The expediency implied by συμφέρει . . . did not involve some benefit that would accrue to the Corinthians if they completed their collection, but rather was an appropriate or advantageous action that Paul himself was taking in the case of the Corinthians" (ὑμῖν, *hymin*, in your case). But the problem with this interpretation is at least twofold. First, almost universally in the NT the verb refers to an action that is "better" or "advantageous," not "fitting" (Matt. 5:29–30; 18:6; 19:10; John 11:50; 16:7; 18:14; Acts 20:20; 1 Cor. 6:12; 10:23; 12:7; 2 Cor. 8:10; 12:1; Heb. 12:10). An exception here is Acts 19:19, where the term means "to bring together." Indeed, elsewhere in the Corinthian correspondence the sense of "beneficial" seems to be the sense. Harris himself translates the word as "beneficial" at 12:1 (Harris 2005: 828). Second, however, when Paul says in 8:10, "This [τοῦτο, *touto*] would be to your advantage," the word echoes the use of the same pronoun in the previous clause, where Paul gives his advice "on this matter" (ἐν τούτῳ, *en toutō*), referring to the collection for the saints (see 8:6–7, where the pronoun also refers to the collection). So it is the Corinthians' participation in the collection that would be advantageous, not Paul's action.

38. Deliberative rhetoric was speech designed to persuade the audience to take a certain course of action or to warn against a course of action. Appeal was often made to what was most advantageous to the audience. Furnish (1984: 405) points to Aristotle's description of exhortation as recommending that some action will be beneficial to the hearers (*Rhet.* 1.3.3–5).

39. As Harris (2005: 582) points out, the relative pronoun ὅστις (*hostis*) can carry a qualitative ("being of such a character as to") or a causal meaning ("inasmuch as"). The latter seems best in this case.

is found in the relative clause: completing the collection would actually bring to fruition the desires of the Corinthians themselves. The "not only . . . but also" construction draws special attention to the Corinthians' desire to act. The apostle states that they have had a vital role in the collection, being the first church to initiate (προενήρξασθε, *proenērxasthe*) their participation. The verb προενάρχομαι (*proenarchomai*) has to do with beginning something in the past, and the verb here is explained with ἀπὸ πέρυσι (*apo perysi*, from last year, [or] in the last year). This may be a reference to the time the Corinthians had received Paul's instructions in 1 Cor. 16:1–4,[40] since they would have begun acting on the collection at that time. We take the ἀπό as communicating an initiation point: "beginning last year."

Yet, more significant for Paul at this point, they were the first to *want* to be involved. Whereas the infinitive τὸ ποιῆσαι (*to poiēsai*) is aorist (viewing the action as a completed whole), the tense of the infinitive τὸ θέλειν (*to thelein*) is present, in context suggesting that their desire has been ongoing, steady perhaps even to the time Paul writes these words in 2 Corinthians, as the apostle also states plainly in the next verse. The action on the collection "last year" seems to have been interrupted and needed to be taken up again, but Paul hints at their constant desire to be involved. It is "better" or "advantageous" in this case to follow up on one's desire and bring it to completion. Then their "wants" and their "acts" could be fully integrated, which is the point of the next verse. So it is "better" or "advantageous" for the church to now act on their desires in the sense that they would be more fully integrated people in relation to the collection. Paul's words here remind us that a great deal of ministry involves challenging people to align their expressed desires with their actions. Any number of dynamics can cause a stall in moving from the first to the second—laziness, excuses, procrastination, confusion over how to proceed—but not acting on what one knows to be right constitutes a spiritual problem. In this regard we are called to shepherd people, and ourselves, in being "doers of the Word" (James 1:22).

Further, in the following verses Paul goes on to explain that the gift given with the right spirit and in the right way is considered "acceptable," and giving now will put them in a relationship of "equality" with the church in Jerusalem, so that in the future, when the Corinthians themselves have the need, their needs can be met by the body of Christ elsewhere (see the comments on 8:12–15). This too will be to their advantage.

Accordingly, Paul encourages them (v. 11): "Now finish what you started" (νυνὶ δὲ καὶ τὸ ποιῆσαι ἐπιτελέσατε, *nyni de kai to poiēsai epitelesate*; lit., but now also finish the to do!). In verse 10 the apostle has just referred to the Corinthians' actions and desires in relation to the collection "last year." The

---

40. The passage reads, "Now about the collection for the saints: You should do the same as I instructed the Galatian churches. On the first day of the week, each of you is to set something aside and save in keeping with how he prospers, so that no collections will need to be made when I come. When I arrive, I will send with letters those you recommend to carry your gracious gift to Jerusalem. If it is suitable for me to go as well, they can travel with me" (1 Cor. 16:1–4 HCSB).

adverb νυνί (now), at the beginning of verse 11, rivets attention back on the present moment of opportunity, and the conjunction καί (also) is adjunctive, helping to communicate the idea that a present response needs to be added to the past acts and intentions. What the Corinthians need to do is to "finish," or "complete," or "fulfill" (ἐπιτελέσατε, epitelesate, aorist active imperative) the collection begun last year. This is the only imperative verb in chapters 8–9, which draws special attention to the use here. When Paul refers to this "action" that is to be finished, he uses the same aorist infinitive used in the previous verse (τὸ ποιῆσαι), which can mean "to do" something, or "to accomplish" or "carry out" something. So in essence the apostle wants them to complete the activity they previously started.

Now he explains why they should do so: "in order that [ὅπως, hopōs][41] . . . the completed task might be brought in line with the eager desire to help!" There are two complementary parts of the clause in the Greek text:

> just as the eager desire to help
> (καθάπερ ἡ προθυμία τοῦ θέλειν,
> *kathaper hē prothymia tou thelein*),
> so also the completed task
> (οὕτως καὶ τὸ ἐπιτελέσαι,
> *houtōs kai to epitelesai*).

The "just as . . . so also" construction connotes alignment, and Paul's idea is that the Corinthians must follow through on the task, bringing their actions in line with their desires. In the first part, the word προθυμία, which the apostle uses three other times in the following verses (2 Cor. 8:12, 19; 9:2), has to do with an "eagerness," "goodwill," or "willingness" to be of service (*EDNT* 3:156). Here it is used with a substantival infinitive, τοῦ θέλειν (lit., of the to want), answering the question "Eagerness for what?" So the construction speaks of an "eager desire to help."

In the second part of this construction of alignment, the apostle picks up the same verb with which he exhorted the church to "finish" (ἐπιτελέω, epiteleō) the task at the beginning of verse 11. Expressed here as another substantival infinitive, τὸ ἐπιτελέσαι reiterates the idea of a task being accomplished. It too is qualified, but this time with a final prepositional phrase involving yet another substantival infinitive. The Corinthians are to bring the collection to completion ἐκ τοῦ ἔχειν (*ek tou echein*), "out of the resources" they have. In other words, he is not encouraging them to go out and find new resources for the work, or to live up to the high standard set by the Macedonians, who gave "even beyond their resources" (8:3; Barnett 1997: 412), but rather to draw from their resources at hand. It is not that Paul is lowering the bar but that he wants the Corinthians to see that what he asks them to do is immediately attainable.

---

41. The adverb ὅπως can express the manner in which something is done, or serve as a marker indicating the purpose of an event or state (BDAG 718). In this case it does the latter.

8:12 So the apostle next explains (γάρ) that it is one's desire and proportional giving that count, not the amount of resources a person might have available. Even though Paul doesn't speak of the Corinthian church as poor, some in that community may have objected to the collection, saying in effect, "We really can't give a significant amount—so perhaps we need to wait until our resources are more substantial!" In the first-century world of Corinth, status was gained publicly by generous donations. Some in the church may have shrunk back from participation in the collection out of pride, fearing the shame that would come from contributing only a small amount. Paul wants to quash that idea and push his readers to a more biblical perspective.

The verse begins with the first part (the protasis) of a conditional sentence: εἰ γὰρ ἡ προθυμία πρόκειται (*ei gar hē prothymia prokeitai*, For since this eager desire exists).[42] In this case, the protasis of the conditional sentence is clearly true: Paul has already made clear that the Corinthians' desire (ἡ προθυμία, *hē prothymia*) exists (vv. 10–11). This being the case, (1) we translate εἰ with "since" ("since this eager desire exists"),[43] and (2) we render the article as anaphoric ("this"),[44] intentionally referring back to the "eager desire" (ἡ προθυμία) noted by Paul in the previous verse.

The remainder of the verse (the apodosis) is stated as somewhat a generalized truth: "the gift, rather than being judged deficient due to limited resources, is deemed acceptable on the basis of what is available." The Greek text is nicely balanced.

> καθὸ ἐὰν ἔχῃ (*katho ean echē*, according to what one might have)
> εὐπρόσδεκτος (*euprosdektos*, acceptable)
> οὐ καθὸ οὐκ ἔχει (*ou katho ouk echei*, not according to what one does not have)

We understand here that Paul is referring to the gift given (the "gift" is not mentioned in the Greek text), and the double use of the verb ἔχω (*echō*) harks back to the use of the same verb at the very end of the previous verse, where Paul refers to the Corinthians' resources. A key point here is that one give "in proportion to" (καθό, *katho*) what one has, rather than the arbitrary measurement of what one does not have.

The term εὐπρόσδεκτος has to do with what is "very acceptable," and a great deal of attention in Scripture is paid to gifts that were acceptable or

42. This is a first-class conditional sentence, which communicates that if something is true (and let's assume it is), then what follows is true or will occur. The first part of the sentence (since . . .) is called the protasis, and the second part is called the apodosis.
43. Understandably, many versions prefer "if" (e.g., ESV, HCSB, NASB, NRSV, NET, NIV), leaving the wording as expressing an open condition, and this certainly fits the whole of the verse as an aphorism. However, the idea that here we are dealing with an aphorism, a generalized pithy saying, does not override the strong connotations of the context at this point. It may be that the apodosis of the sentence (the remainder of the verse) should be read as the aphorism. So Paul would be saying, "Since you do have this eager desire, as the saying goes, 'The gift, rather than being judged deficient due to limited resources . . .'"
44. "Anaphoric" means that reference is made to something mentioned previously.

unacceptable before God. In the LXX, προσδεκτός (*prosdektos*) is used a handful of times for what is "acceptable" (Prov. 11:20; 16:15; Wis. 9:12), and δεκτός (*dektos*) especially is used of gifts and sacrifices that are "acceptable" as they are brought before the Lord in worship (e.g., Exod. 28:38; Lev. 1:3–4; 17:4; 19:5; 22:21; 23:11; Prov. 15:8; Mal. 2:13; Isa. 56:7; Jer. 6:20). The form εὐπρόσδεκτος found in our passage is intensified ("very acceptable" or "easily acceptable," BDAG 410) and is found five times in the NT, four of these in Paul's writings (Rom. 15:16, 31; 2 Cor. 6:2; 8:12; 1 Pet. 2:5); at Rom. 15:31 Paul prays that the gift he intends to bring to the church in Jerusalem might be "very acceptable" to the believers there, and 1 Pet. 2:5 calls believers a "holy priesthood" appointed to offer spiritual sacrifices "very acceptable" to God.

The upshot of the statement in 2 Cor. 8:12 is clear: "As long as giving is proportionate to one's means, the gift is acceptable whether it be large or small" (Thrall 2000: 538). This concept of proportionate giving was not unknown in broader Judaism. Speaking of such giving in the apocryphal book that carries his name, Tobit remembers money he has laid away and teaches his son Tobias about the proper use of those resources:

> If you have many possessions, make your gift from them in proportion; if few, do not be afraid to give according to the little you have. So you will be laying up a good treasure for yourself against the day of necessity. For almsgiving delivers from death and keeps you from going into the Darkness. Indeed, almsgiving, for all who practice it, is an excellent offering in the presence of the Most High. (Tob. 4:8–11 NRSV)

In a similar vein, Paul wants the Corinthians to draw out of the resources they have to give proportionately to the fund for the Jerusalem church. Generally speaking, the church in Corinth was probably more wealthy than their counterpart in Macedonia.[45] Corinth was the capital of Achaia and thriving economically, and Paul does not specifically mention the Corinthians' poverty.[46] Nevertheless, as the next verses make clear, the biblical goal is not extravagant giving but giving that works for equality in resources. This has the effect of dealing with excuses that might arise. Speaking of this verse, Calvin (1964: 112) expounds:

> The flesh is always ingenious in devising excuses, and some plead that they have families it would be unkind to neglect, and some use the fact that they cannot give much as an excuse for giving nothing. . . . Paul takes away all excuses of this

45. Following Riesner (1998: 376–77), Keener (2005: 203) notes, "Although Philippi was relatively prosperous and Macedonia's economy had been growing, the prosperity failed to affect most of the poor, many of whom were unemployed. Much of the urban proletariat depended on benefactors' generosity for the grain dole."

46. It may be, however, that with the statement of 8:12, Paul was being especially sensitive to the poorer members of the church. Slaves in the congregation, e.g., would have had little to give and would have been saving up for their manumission, and perhaps the apostle wants to make clear that he does not expect egregious giving from them (Barclay 1991: 179–80; Garland 1999: 381–82).

kind by telling them that each of them should contribute according to his ability and he adds, as his reason, that God looks not at the amount but at the heart.

8:13   Anticipating objections that might arise, in verse 13 Paul clarifies his perspective. He does so by making two statements, one negative and one positive, first describing what he is *not* trying to do (οὐ . . . ἵνα, *ou . . . hina*) and then explaining positively the end-goal of biblical giving. He begins, "So I don't mean to offer others relief by burdening you!" Following on the concept of proportionate giving in verses 11–12, Paul draws an inference (γάρ, *gar*, so),[47] placing the concept of proportionate giving in contrast here with egregious giving. The "others" (ἄλλοις, *allois*)[48] Paul has in mind are the believers in Jerusalem to whom the collection eventually will be sent. We render ἄνεσις (*anesis*) as "relief." The word can connote "rest," or "relaxation," but here speaks of the removal of a situation that is onerous or troublesome. It is the same word Paul uses at 2:15 and 7:5 to speak of the apostle's troublesome lack of "rest" in his spirit (2:13) and body (7:5) when he came to Macedonia. In 8:13 it stands in contrast to θλῖψις (*thlipsis*), which could be translated as "trouble," "distress," or "affliction," but we render with the idea of being "burdened." In the LXX the noun (or its verbal cognate) is often used of "situations of extreme need or misery for the people of Israel" (e.g., Exod. 3:9; 4:31; *EDNT* 2:152). Throughout the book Paul has spoken of the θλῖψις encountered in his ministry (2 Cor. 1:8; 2:4; 4:17; 6:4; 7:4), and earlier in chapter 8 (8:2) he writes of the "severe test involving affliction" (ἐν πολλῇ δοκιμῇ θλίψεως, *en pollē dokimē thlipseōs*) experienced by the Macedonians.

Yet the Macedonians' affliction is not a pattern that must be emulated. The apostle is not calling for a change of economic conditions between the Corinthians and their brothers and sisters in Jerusalem—"economic comfort for the Corinthians and economic distress for the Jerusalem church," replaced by, "relief for them, hardship for you." Rather (ἀλλ᾽, *all᾽*), he aims for the biblical principle of "equality" (ἰσότητος, *isotētos*). In the ancient world, the term had to do with a state of being fair or balanced. This noun and its cognate adjective (ἴσος, *isos*, equal) were used in the realms of arithmetic and geometry to refer to equal sums or measurements, equal rights or justice in the political realm, or equal sums of money in accounting (Spicq 1994: 2.223–28). In the NT, the noun is only found in the present context (here and in the next verse) and at Col. 4:1, where Paul writes, "Masters, treat your slaves with justice and *fairness*, because you know that you also have a master in heaven" (Col. 4:1 NET).

8:14–15   In verse 14 Paul explains what he means by "equality" in relation to the collection: "This is how equality works: at present your oversupply can be used to meet their shortfall, so that at some point in the future their oversupply might be used to address your shortfall." The first statement in our translation,

---

47. At times, γάρ serves as a marker of inference, best translated as "certainly, by all means, so, then" (BDAG 190).

48. This is a dative of interest showing advantage, and the ὑμῖν (*hymin*, [to] you) that follows is a dative of interest showing disadvantage.

"This is how equality works," actually translates the last clause in the Greek text: ὅπως γένηται ἰσότης (hopōs genētai isotēs, in order that there might be equality). In this case the word ὅπως functions as a conjunction expressing the purpose for an event or state of affairs: "in order that" (BDAG 718; ὅπως alternates with ἵνα, hina). Paul says in effect, "This is how things are done to bring about equality."

The apostle's description of how things should be done contrasts two dynamics: the present time over against a future time, and a situation of surplus over against a condition of need. At present (ἐν τῷ νῦν καιρῷ, en tō nyn kairō)[49] the Corinthians have an "oversupply" (περίσσευμα, perisseuma) that can be used to answer the "shortfall" (ὑστέρημα, hysterēma) presently experienced by those in the Jerusalem church. The noun περίσσευμα finds expression three times in the NT outside this immediate context to speak of an "overflow" of the heart coming out of a wicked person's mouth (Matt. 12:34; Luke 6:45) and the "leftovers" gathered after the feeding of the four thousand (Mark 8:8).[50] As described in the introduction, Corinth of the mid-first century was a city of extraordinary wealth, and we know that at least some of the members of the church had access to significant resources.

The contrasting term ὑστέρημα speaks of a "need" or "lack" in the present context. Later, in 11:9, Paul writes of the brothers who, when Paul was in Corinth, met his needs (ὑστέρημα) so he would not be a burden to the church. So Paul says that the blessing of the Corinthians' surplus can go to meet a current need of the church at Jerusalem. But Paul also envisions a future time (communicated simply with an adjunctive use of καί, "also") when the tables are turned, when the church in Jerusalem has a surplus (τὸ ἐκείνων περίσσευμα, to ekeinōn perisseuma) and the Corinthians are in a position of need (εἰς τὸ ὑμῶν ὑστέρημα, eis to hymōn hysterēma).

The concept of patronal reciprocity was very important in the Greco-Roman world of the first century, and Paul at times makes appeals based on some form of reciprocity, though there is a question if those instances can be described as patronal. In patronal reciprocity a relationship exists between a social superior and an inferior. The superior is committed to meeting some need(s) of the inferior, offering protection, services, or benefits of some sort. The inferior is then obligated, as a matter of honor, to render what services he can, to show gratitude, and to be available for future points of need (P. Marshall 1987: 143). Cicero (Off. 1.48) writes, "To fail to repay [a favor] is not permitted to a good man" (quoted in Horsley 1997: 96).

But what is described in 2 Cor. 8:14 is not the reciprocity of Paul's culture. With the cultural reciprocity of the day, there most often was inequality in the

49. Some (e.g., Barnett 1997: 415) have interpreted the phrase eschatologically, which is possible (see Rom. 3:26; 8:18). But the problem with this position is that Paul uses the term in contrast to an implied "future time" when the Corinthians themselves might be in need. Also, the phrase was good Greek for referring to a time of crisis (Danker 1989: 128–29).

50. Paul has used the cognate verb seven times thus far in 2 Corinthians: 1:5 (2x); 3:9; 4:15; 8:2, 7 (2x).

relationship between the two parties. Here Paul appeals to the equality that exists between brothers and sisters in Christ, and he reinforces the idea with Scripture. Verse 15 begins with Paul's standard formula for introducing an OT text: καθὼς γέγραπται (kathōs gegraptai), "as it is written." The quotation then reads, "The person who had much didn't have too much, and the person who had little didn't have too little." The text comes from Exod. 16:18, located in a passage on God's provision of food for the Israelites during the time of the wilderness wanderings. In Exod. 16 they grumble against the Lord and his chosen leaders, Moses and Aaron, saying they missed the meat and bread of Egypt (16:2–3). God promises to rain bread from heaven but says that this will be a test (cf. 2 Cor. 8:8) as to whether they will walk in his instructions (Exod. 16:4). So in the evening the Lord sends them quail to eat (16:13), and in the morning the manna appears (16:13–15). Each one is to gather as much manna as that person can eat, an omer per person, and not seek to hoard the food. "When they measured with an omer, the one who gathered much had nothing left over, and the one who gathered little lacked nothing; each one had gathered what he could eat" (Exod. 16:18 NET).

Paul's point is to illustrate an equality that has been ordained by God for the people of God, which implicitly speaks against a posture of hoarding resources. This "Israelite ideal" that lay behind the distribution of food among the wilderness wanderers—and such institutions as the Sabbatical Year and the Year of Jubilee—lays a foundation in principle for how God's people are to treat one another in the new-covenant era. The sharing is based on brotherhood and the principle of equality, not social obligation (Spicq 1994: 2.230–31). God has given more to some parts of the body of believers, not so they can spend their resources on themselves, but so they can share their resources with brothers and sisters in need (Garland 1999: 386). With reference to this passage, Calvin (1964: 114) reflects:

> The Lord has not prescribed to us an omer or any other measure of the food we have each day, but He has commended to us frugality and temperance and has forbidden anyone from going to excess because of his abundance. Thus those who have riches, whether inherited or won by their own industry and labour, are to remember that what is left over is meant not for intemperance or luxury but for relieving the needs of the brethren.

Reflection

How then are we to respond today to Paul's words in 2 Cor. 8:1–15? First, handling resources (including money) well and giving to those in need were part of broader Jewish and Christian teachings of Paul's time. These teachings were grounded in both OT Scripture and the teaching of Jesus (see esp. Blomberg 1999: 111–239). Paul himself warns against greed (e.g., Rom. 1:29; 1 Cor. 5:10–11; 6:10; Eph. 5:3, 5; Col. 3:5) and instructs believers to give to those in need (e.g., Rom. 12:13; 2 Cor. 9:8; Gal. 6:6–10; Eph. 4:28; 2 Thess. 3:13). Our money and resources are integrated with our spiritual lives, and we need to take our stewardship of these resources seriously as an aspect of Christian discipleship.

Second, in 2 Cor. 8:8–15 Paul gives admonitions concerning a specific area of need (needy fellow believers in the Jerusalem church) but draws from general principles concerning giving.[51] Although the collection is for the saints in Jerusalem (rather than the poor generally), Paul appeals to the example of Jesus (8:9) and to a general principle from the OT (8:15; Exod. 16:18), both of which may be applied appropriately to the need for giving among believers in the modern church. The twin principles of giving from a position of being "rich" (8:9) and giving out of one's surplus (8:14–15) are clear and, I think, directly applicable to Christ-followers today. In a world where approximately one billion people will go to bed hungry tonight and millions of children die each year of malnutrition and water-related diseases, certainly many of our fellow believers around the world suffer due to a lack of resources. In the United States alone, it is estimated that approximately 49 million people struggle with hunger. Paul's words in this passage call us to examine our stewardship of resources in light of the desperate needs elsewhere in our cities, our nation, and the world. We should give as an act of solidarity with other parts of the body of Christ at home and around the world, and as a witness to the "giving" nature of God in the gospel.

Third, however, Paul does not exhort by appealing to guilt. Rather, the apostle's exhortation in 2 Cor. 8:8–15 calls for giving that is voluntary, grace-infused, and proportionate to one's resources. Giving is to be a joy and an expression of grace as God's Spirit works in us. At the same time, it should be proportionate to the resources we have. We should examine our "surplus" against the "needs" of others. The concepts of "surplus" and "need" are vital to our understanding of the relevance of Paul's words for us at this point. In context, "surplus" does not mean whatever you happen to have left over after you have spent lavishly on yourself. Rather, "surplus" refers to the resources one has after basic needs in life are met. At the same time "need" or "shortfall" refers to a lack in basic needs for life. What would happen if the body of Christ in the United States began to give in accordance with Paul's exhortation to the Corinthians?

Additional Notes

8:2. The reading τὸ πλοῦτος ($\mathfrak{P}^{46\,99}$ א* B C P 0243 6 33 81 104 1175 1739 2464 *pc*) is preferred to the masculine form τὸν πλοῦτον (א 2 D F G Ψ 1881 𝔐). Although Paul uses the masculine form in

---

51. Some have suggested that Paul's focus on the collection for Jerusalem was based on an obligation owed the "mother church" by the Gentile Christians. But, although it is true that the Gentiles owe a debt to the Jews (Rom. 15:27), it is a spiritual debt. Garland (1999: 387–90) suggests that the collection was rather an expression both of solidarity between Gentiles and their Jewish counterparts and a witness to non-Christian Jews that OT prophecies telling of a day when Gentiles would send gifts to Zion had been fulfilled.

Romans (2:4; 9:23; 11:33), he has the neuter form in Phil. 4:19, and the manuscript evidence heavily favors τὸ πλοῦτος.

8:3. The reading ὑπέρ δύναμιν (Ψ 𝔐) has the same essential meaning as the preferred παρὰ δύναμιν (𝔓⁹⁹ ℵ B C D F G 0243 6 33 81 1175 1739 1881 2464 pc); manuscript evidence clearly favors the latter. Although ὑπέρ . . . is the more common expression, it seems to be a scribal correction.

8:3–5. On the grammatical structure of these verses, Harris (2005: 566) disagrees with Barnett (1997: 395), who suggests that the participle δεόμενοι is dependent on an implied ἔδωκαν in verse 2, and with Furnish (1984: 401), who posits that the participle relates directly to the ἔδωκαν of verse 5. Harris rightly notes that the καί at the beginning of verse 5 signals a fresh grammatical movement and makes Furnish's position unlikely. However, Harris's suggestion that the participle stands in for a finite verb form of δέομαι can also be challenged, since the first clause of verse 5—"confounding our expectations"—would with Harris's rendering seem a continuation of the idea of "begging" rather than "giving," when "giving" is demanded by the context. Nevertheless, in fairness to Harris, his translation correctly captures the sense of the passage, since he begins verse 5 with "And their giving was not what we expected." But it seems better to allow the participle of verse 4 to function as a participle, delimiting an understood ἔδωκαν, perhaps at the beginning of verse 3, as with our translation: "they voluntarily gave according to their resources." Thus it seems better to allow this understood verb to hold verses 3–4 together conceptually, and this motif continues in verse 5 with use of the verb ἔδωκαν.

8:7. Toward the end of this unit we find one of its more significant variants. The text either should read (1) τῇ ἐξ ἡμῶν ἐν ὑμῖν ἀγάπη (𝔓⁴⁶ B 0243 6 104 630 1175 1739 1881 pc r syᵖ co; Ambst), which we have translated as "in the love we inspired among you"; or (2) τῇ ἐξ ὑμῶν ἐν ἡμῖν ἀγάπη (ℵ C D F G Ψ [33] 𝔐 lat syʰ), which means "your love for us." In the context Paul is speaking about the Corinthians' attributes, and that fact seems to favor the second reading, as does the wide circulation of this reading in the early church. In favor of the first reading, the manuscript evidence is strong, and it seems to be the more difficult reading. Likely a scribe changed the first reading to the second, based on the context. On this basis, Metzger (1994: 512–13) notes that the UBS committee was divided but slightly favored the first reading.

8:8. Instead of δοκιμάζων a few witnesses read δοκιμάζω (D* F G). Since the participle is coordinate with the verb λέγω in the first clause of the sentence, one can see why a scribe would be induced to drop the final ν. The more difficult reading, and thus the one preferred, is the one that has the participle.

8:9. Here B sa omit Χριστοῦ. It seems the desire to make the implications of Christ becoming poor read more inclusively led to the reading ἡμᾶς (C K 6 323 614 al; Eus Didᵖᵗ; i.e., "for all of us") in place of the much more strongly supported ὑμᾶς (𝔓⁴⁶ ℵ B D F G L P al). Metzger (1994: 513) comments, "Since in later Greek the vowels η and υ came to be pronounced alike, scribes sometimes confused the two, writing ἡμᾶς instead of ὑμᾶς. Furthermore, homiletic or devotional application of the statement to Christian believers in general would have fostered the adoption of the reading ἡμᾶς."

8:13. A number of manuscripts (ℵ² D F G Ψ 𝔐 lat syʰ; Cl Ambst) have δέ following ὑμῖν, a seeming attempt to clarify the contrast between the hypothetical burden placed on the Corinthians and the relief to the "others." Omission of the δέ, supported by ℵ* B C 048 0243 33 81 323 1739 1881 pc d ρ; Cyp, is preferred since it is the more difficult reading stylistically.

8:15. The form of Paul's quotation differs slightly from the LXX reading:

Exod. 16:18 LXX	2 Cor. 8:15
οὐκ ἐπλεόνασεν ὁ τὸ πολύ, καὶ ὁ τὸ ἔλαττον οὐκ ἠλαττόνησεν.	ὁ τὸ πολὺ οὐκ ἐπλεόνασεν, καὶ ὁ τὸ ὀλίγον οὐκ ἠλαττόνησεν.
ouk epleonasen ho to poly, kai ho to elatton ouk ēlattonēsen.	*ho to poly ouk epleonasen, kai ho to oligon ouk ēlattonēsen.*

Notice that the apostle has moved ὁ τὸ πολύ (the person who had much) to the front of the first line, probably to enhance the parallelism between the two lines (Harris 2005: 593). In the second line, the apostle replaces τὸ ἔλαττον (small, little) with the rough synonym τὸ ὀλίγον (little, few, small), perhaps enhancing the parallelism still further by the matching omicron sound in the first syllable of both πολύ in the first line and ὀλίγον in the second.

B. Titus's Mission (8:16–9:5)

The section on Titus's mission to Corinth extends from 8:16 to 9:5 and has two primary movements. The first (8:16–24) introduces Titus as the lead envoy on the mission team with two unnamed brothers traveling with him. Paul explains why each of the three are making the trip and heads off possible criticism that could be raised against them. The second movement (9:1–5) turns to focus on the purpose of this mission. Paul again admits the Corinthians' eagerness in terms of their intentions, but he is not so sure about their follow-through on the collection they had previously promised. So he sends these three brothers to get them organized and ready for the apostle's subsequent arrival; for if they are still not prepared when he and a delegation from Macedonia arrive, the situation will be humiliating for both him and the church. In the end, he wants them to get the collection ready as a generous, openhanded gift rather than an expression of stinginess. The section may be outlined as follows:

1. Titus and the appointed brother (8:16–19)
2. Paul's motive for organizing the delegation (8:20–21)
3. The reputation and integrity of the delegation (8:22–24)
4. The purpose of the mission (9:1–5)

Exegesis and Exposition

[8:16]Now, thanks be to God, ⌜who placed⌝ in Titus's heart the same enthusiasm I have for you! [17]For he accepted our request and was so eager to act on it that he voluntarily is leaving for his visit with you. [18]Along with him we are sending the brother who is universally praised throughout all the churches for his gospel work. [19]Not only that, but also he has been appointed by the churches to be our traveling companion ⌜in relation to⌝ this gift being delivered by us for the glory of the Lord ⌜himself⌝ and to show our readiness to help. [20]We are organizing things in this way so that no one can criticize us over this large sum of money we are administering. [21]For we are giving careful consideration not only to what is noble in the Lord's eyes but also what is noble in the eyes of people. [22]And we are sending with them our brother whose diligence we have often proved in many ways and who now is much more eager than ever because of his great confidence in you. [23]If anyone raises a question about Titus, he is my partner and coworker in our ministry to you. Or if a question comes up about our brothers, they are the churches' envoys, Christ's glory. [24]Therefore, ⌜display⌝ openly before the churches the proof of your love and the accuracy of our boast to them about you.

⁹:¹Now on the one hand it is ⌜redundant⌝ for me to write to you further about this ministry to God's people, ²for I know how eager you are—on your behalf I keep boasting about it to the Macedonians!: "Achaia has been anxious to participate since last year." And ⌜ ⌝ ⌜your zeal⌝ has stirred up most of them. ³Nevertheless, I am sending the brothers in order that in this particular instance our boast on your behalf might not be made empty of meaning—in order that you might be prepared, as I kept telling them you would be. ⁴In ⌜this undertaking⌝, we (not ⌜to mention⌝ you!) would be so humiliated if Macedonians come with me and find you unprepared! ⁵Consequently, I have thought it necessary to encourage the brothers to travel on ahead to you and organize in advance your previously promised generous gift, in order that it might thus be ready as a generous gift and not as an expression of stinginess.

As Paul continues with this broader section on giving (8:1–9:15), he now explains Titus's current mission to Corinth (8:16–9:5); here in 8:16–24 he begins by telling who is involved in the trip. Of course, at the time the letter is being read to the church in Corinth, those participating in this ministry to the Corinthians are obvious! Yet Paul, through the words in this unit, seeks to support their efforts by the way he describes each of the participants. He first writes about Titus, detailing his eagerness to visit the Corinthians again and especially how he volunteered to be involved (8:16–17). With Titus, Paul is sending an unnamed brother, whom he describes as having an outstanding reputation for Christian ministry among the churches (8:18) and as having been appointed by the churches to participate in the collection for Jerusalem (8:19). The apostle further notes that the appointment of this brother as his traveling companion has been arranged to avoid public criticism, safeguarding the reputation of the mission by building in a strong measure of accountability. He wants to make clear to all that his motives are noble (8:20–21). With Titus and this brother, Paul sends a second anonymous brother, probably a close associate of his, who has a strong track record in ministry and who also is eager to visit the Corinthians (8:22). Finally, Paul anticipates that some could raise questions about these three envoys. He cuts short objections to them by clearly stating his close working relationship with Titus and by affirming the special role of these two brothers: they are the churches' envoys and thus give glory to Christ (8:23). The unit closes in 8:24 with Paul exhorting the Corinthians to make their acceptance of this ministry team public by participating in the collection for the saints, validating the confidence Paul has shown in them.

1. Titus and the Appointed Brother (8:16–19)

Thus far Titus has figured prominently in chapters 7 and 8; the apostle recounts various ways the young minister, his main liaison with the Corinthians at this point in the mission, has played a significant role. In 7:5–7, at the resumption of Paul's travel narrative (picking up the narrative paused after 2:13), he reports that Titus brought exceptional encouragement to his mentor at a moment of stress and turmoil. He goes on to say that Titus was wonderfully

8:16–17

refreshed by his visit with the Corinthians and had grown in his affection for them (7:13b–15). Earlier in chapter 8 Paul mentions that Titus was the logical choice for someone to resume an emphasis on the collection among the Corinthians and that he was encouraged to do so (8:6). Now in 8:16–24 Paul reflects not only on Titus as an envoy to Corinth, sent to lead in resumption of the collection, but he also introduces two other envoys who are joining Titus on the trek.

Verse 16 reads, "Now, thanks be to God, who placed in Titus's heart the same enthusiasm I have for you!" The phrase "Now, thanks be to God" (Χάρις δὲ τῷ θεῷ, *Charis de tō theō*) echoes the same exclamation, offered at 2:14, where the word order is Τῷ δὲ θεῷ χάρις (*Tō de theō charis*). In four of the six occurrences of this expression of thanks in the NT (always in Paul), τῷ θεῷ follows χάρις as it does here in 8:16.[1] As seen in the commentary already (2 Cor. 1:2, 12, 15; 2:14; 4:15; 6:1; 8:1, 4, 6–7, 9), the word χάρις had a broad range of meanings in the first century, and here in chapter 8 the apostle has used the word variously to refer to God's kindness, favor, or enablement (8:1), the privilege of participating in the collection (8:4), and the collection itself (referred to as "this gift," 8:6–7, 19). Here in 8:16 Paul is thankful that God has placed enthusiasm for the Corinthians in the heart of Titus. The statement shows that Titus's attitude was an act of grace and God's initiation, for God worked on Titus, putting (δόντι, *donti*)[2] an eagerness "in Titus's heart" (ἐν τῇ καρδίᾳ Τίτου, *en tē kardia Titou*; cf. 1:22).[3] As Matera remarks, "Although Paul is not formally developing a theology of grace in this chapter, one cannot but notice that here and throughout the chapter God is the one who inspires and enables the good that humans do" (Matera 2003: 196).

The word rendered "enthusiasm" we have seen before (2 Cor. 7:11–12; 8:7–8); the term variously connotes "eagerness," "willingness," "diligence," or "earnest commitment in discharge of an obligation" (BDAG 939). God had made Titus enthusiastic about ministry to the Corinthians, which is not surprising given the enthusiasm of his mentor. We have translated the words here as "the same enthusiasm I have for you!" but the Greek text simply reads,

---

1. The phrase occurs in various configurations at Rom. 6:17; 7:25; 1 Cor. 15:57; 2 Cor. 2:14; and 9:15, each expressing gratefulness for some aspect of God's work. At 1 Cor. 15:57 and 2 Cor. 2:14, the order of wording is reversed when compared to 8:16. Moving τῷ θεῷ forward could be for emphasis, but the order may simply be literary variation. It is difficult to discern a comparatively heightened emphasis on God at 2:14 and 1 Cor. 15:57. Rather, the phrase as a whole, in whichever configuration, communicates an expression of thankfulness to God.

2. This is an aorist active participle of δίδωμι (*didōmi*, I give, cause, place). The participle can be read as epistolary, choosing to speak of the event from the standpoint of those reading the letter in Corinth.

3. Perhaps most significant for the present context, Paul has identified the transformed heart as the seat of authentic ministry (5:12; so Scott 1998: 182). Paul has used "heart" imagery a number of times in the book: 2 Cor. 1:22; 2:4; 3:2–3, 15; 4:6; 5:12; 6:11; 7:3. The word καρδία speaks of the seat and source of a person's inner life, thus the seat of the understanding, knowledge, and will. The 157 occurrences of the word are found in all the writings of the NT except Titus, Philemon, 2–3 John, and Jude (*EDNT* 2:250).

τὴν αὐτὴν σπουδὴν ὑπὲρ ὑμῶν (*tēn autēn spoudēn hyper hymōn*), "the same enthusiasm for you." However, the word rendered "same" suggests a relationship in which this enthusiasm of Titus is closely related to the enthusiasm held by someone else for the Corinthians. From the context Paul seems to be the most likely candidate; thus our translation (so also, ESV, NLT[2], NRSV, NIV, NET; Barrett 1973: 227; Plummer 1915: 247).[4] Further, Paul makes clear that Titus's enthusiasm is for the Corinthians themselves ("for you") rather than their money (P. Hughes 1962: 311). Such a simple phrase reminds us that the attitude and motivations of a Christian minister are vital. Ministry must be done from the heart and for the people.

This enthusiasm in the heart of Titus had been manifested in two ways, both communicated in the explanatory ὅτι (*hoti*, for) clause of verse 17. First, as already discussed at 8:6, Paul made a request that Titus take leadership in the matter of the collection. We have marked the term παράκλησις (*paraklēsis*) and its cognate verb (παρακαλέω, *parakaleō*) as among Paul's favorites in the book.[5] Yet as at 8:4, the nuance of the noun here is slightly different from its more common sense in 2 Corinthians (i.e., "encouragement"), communicating that Paul has made a "request," or "appeal." To Paul's delight, Titus "received," or "accepted" the request (aorist active of δέχομαι, *dechomai*). Given the turmoil between the church at Corinth and the mission of Paul, this is no small matter, and here we catch a glimpse of the apostle's deep appreciation for his younger colleague (Barnett 1997: 418). Certainly Titus had been greatly encouraged by his previous visit and had grown in his affection for the Corinthians (7:15), but the younger minister has taken up a challenging task and run with it, as we see in the balance of the verse.

Thus as a second manifestation of his enthusiasm, Titus voluntarily left for Corinth: "and was so eager to act on it that he voluntarily is leaving for his visit with you." The word σπουδαιότερος (*spoudaioteros*, so eager to act on it), a comparative adjective[6] used only here and twice later in 8:22,[7] was employed in the broader culture to describe a heightened sense of civic duty. Originally having to do with haste or rapidity, the word group to which this term belongs came to be associated with diligence, conscientious effort, and zealousness. Speaking of Paul's use here in 8:17, Spicq highlights the connotations of someone being virtuous or especially diligent in action but notes in his broader discussion that the word also carries the sense of eagerness or zealousness.[8] So more than mere emotional excitement, Titus was spurred to

---

4. Windisch and Strecker (1970: 261) interpret the statement to be referring to the same enthusiasm the Corinthians have for Paul and his mission (8:7).

5. The noun: 1:3–7; 7:4, 7, 13; 8:4, 17. The verb: 1:4, 6; 2:7–8; 5:20; 6:1; 7:6–7, 13; 8:6; 9:5; 10:1; 12:8, 18; 13:11.

6. The use here is elative (= "extremely earnest"; Furnish 1984: 422).

7. As noted above, the noun form has been used by Paul at 2 Cor. 7:11–12; 8:7–8.

8. Speaking of the use in 2 Cor. 8:17, Spicq (1994: 3.276–85) writes,

> We have every right to think that in choosing the adjective *spoudaios*, he also gave it the connotations "good, excellent, virtuous" that are implied in other NT usages and

act by an admirable, conscientious diligence that put a holy fire under his feet and set him on the road to Corinth. Paul describes this leaving for Greece with "he voluntarily is leaving for his visit with you" (αὐθαίρετος ἐξῆλθεν πρὸς ὑμᾶς, *authairetos exēlthen pros hymas*). The aorist active indicative verb form, ἐξῆλθεν (from ἐξέρχομαι, *exerchomai*, to go out), may be read as an epistolary aorist[9] ("is leaving" rather than "left;" so, e.g., ESV, NRSV, NIV, NET), since Titus was still with Paul at the time of writing, and Paul notes that Titus's trip to the Corinthians (πρὸς ὑμᾶς, *pros hymas*, to you) is voluntary. At 8:3 the apostle has already used the word αὐθαίρετος (*authairetos*) to describe how the Macedonians "voluntarily" (αὐθαίρετοι, *authairetoi*) gave according to their resources and beyond their resources. So rather than being compelled or coerced in some way, Titus, of his own volition, decided to embark on the trip. Such volunteerism certainly would endear the young minister to the Corinthians even more, while Paul's initial request would also give the trip a necessary note of the apostle's endorsement.

8:18–19 Paul explains that there were two fellow workers traveling with Titus. He does not name them[10] (their names would have been well known to the Corinthians by the time they were reading the letter!) but describes each. The first he calls "the brother" (τὸν ἀδελφόν, *ton adelphon*) and the second "our brother" (τὸν ἀδελφὸν ἡμῶν, *ton adelphon hēmōn*; 8:22). In both cases the use of the term translated as "brother" could simply be a way of referring to these persons as fellow believers in Christ. But in this context, the term also could be understood as a technical term for Christian workers, those appointed by the churches to accompany Paul on mission (8:19).[11] Supporting this interpretation, in both cases he also describes them as being "sent," again using an epistolary aorist,

---

which were so common in the Koine, that a Roman epitaph uses this word to sum up all the virtues of "Crispina, wife of Procopius, *spoudaia* [industrious], loving the law" (*CIJ* 132). This moral meaning of *spoudaios* comes especially from Aristotle, who probably borrowed it from Antisthenes (Diogenes Laertius, *Phil.* 6.104–5). On the one hand, *spoudaios* means "serious, conscientious"; on the other hand, "meticulous, done well, virtuous." (1994: 3.282)

9. The epistolary aorist occurs where the author "self-consciously describes his letter from the time frame of the audience." This is a matter of courtesy: such use of the aorist describes action that is "contemporaneous or future at the time of writing but will be past when the letter is read" (Harris 2005: 599–600; D. Wallace 1996: 562–63).

10. For the various theories as to why the brothers are not named, see Garland 1999: 392–93. Barnett (1997: 422) speculates that the unnamed brothers in this section are two of those noted in Acts as having traveled with Paul to Jerusalem after his final visit to Corinth. The three Macedonians named in Acts 20:4 are Sopater of Berea and Aristarchus and Secundus from Thessalonica. This suggestion seems most reasonable. Martin (1986: 275) names other candidates in the history of interpretation, including Luke, Barnabas, Aristarchus, and Apollos.

11. So Ellis (1978: 15), who states, "When used in the plural with an article, 'the brothers' in Pauline literature fairly consistently refers to a relatively limited group of workers, some of whom have the Christian mission and/or ministry as their primary occupation." With regard to 2 Cor. 8:18, Ellis explains, "This is clear in the case of those appointed by the churches to accompany Paul." While it is true that the form of the word in this case is singular, two "brothers" are mentioned in context.

συνεπέμψαμεν (*synepempsamen*), "we are sending." He "requested" Titus to go to Corinth but is sending these brothers (Thrall 2000: 547) in some official capacity as envoys or at least as helpers to Titus.

The first brother Paul describes as "universally praised throughout all the churches for his gospel work." The description has three parts. First, in the NT world the noun ἔπαινος (*epainos*) could refer to something that is "praise-worthy" (e.g., Phil. 4:8), or as here to "approval," "praise," or "recognition" (BDAG) offered with reference to God or people (Rom. 2:29; 13:3; 1 Cor. 4:5; Eph. 1:6, 12, 14; Phil. 1:11; 1 Pet. 1:7; 2:14). With the relative pronoun[12] that opens this clause (οὗ ὁ ἔπαινος, *hou ho epainos*), a direct translation would be something like "of whom the praise." We might say the brother was celebrated or widely approved; the key idea probably is that everywhere he went, people spoke well of him. He had a good reputation.

Second, his reputation was tied in some way to the gospel, as indicated by the phrase ἐν τῷ εὐαγγελίῳ (*en tō euangeliō*), "in the gospel." Almost certainly this does not mean that the brother was praised in a written Gospel account, for that use of the term "gospel" probably was not yet known (Martin 1986: 274). More likely he was praised either for his proclamation of the gospel (e.g., ESV, Message, NLT[2], NRSV; so Thrall 2000: 548), or more generally in connection with his work of gospel (i.e., "Christian") ministry (cf., Phil. 1:5; 4:3; 1 Thess. 2:4; so NIV, NET, HCSB). Finally, the phrase διὰ πασῶν τῶν ἐκκλησιῶν (*dia pasōn tōn ekklēsiōn*) further defines the good reputation of this brother, describing the extent to which he was celebrated: "throughout[13] all the churches."

Verse 19 continues the description: "Not only that, but also he has been appointed by the churches to be our traveling companion in relation to this gift being delivered by us." The "not only . . . but also" (οὐ μόνον δέ, ἀλλὰ καί, *ou monon de, alla kai*) construction shows that Paul's thought here builds on the description just given, perhaps now moving to an even more important point:[14] the "praised" brother's appointment as a traveling companion for Paul in relation to the gift. There are two sides to this appointment, the choosing and the sending. The brother's good reputation has led to him being chosen by the churches for this important ministry. The verb χειροτονέω (*cheirotoneō*), only found here and at Acts 14:23,[15] has to do with choosing or appoint-ing someone for a given task. We see this pattern elsewhere in relation to

---

12. The genitive relative pronoun could be understood as a genitive of reference ("praise with reference to whom") or perhaps an objective genitive, the brother to whom the pronoun makes reference being the object of praise.

13. The use of διά + the genitive can function spatially as a "marker of extension through an area or object" (BDAG 223; *EDNT* 1:296).

14. In this construction the "not only" refers back to the previous point, and the contrast-ing "but also" (with καί being adjunctive) anticipates the fuller description to follow (contra Barnett 1997: 421n30).

15. "When they had appointed elders in every church and prayed with fasting, they committed them to the Lord in whom they had believed" (Acts 14:23 HCSB). According to Furnish (1984: 422), the word originally connoted "to elect by a show of hands" and later simply "to elect."

Paul's mission, when the apostle sends to Jerusalem those chosen by the local churches, and the Corinthians were familiar with the arrangement. At 1 Cor. 16:3 we read, "Then, when I arrive, I will send those whom you approve with letters of explanation to carry your gift to Jerusalem" (1 Cor. 16:3 NET). As with our passage under consideration, the churches choose and Paul sends, sanctioning the appointment of the brother with apostolic authority. Thus the "sending" of this Christian minister from Macedonia to Corinth is not the terminus of the trip, for his role was to be Paul's "traveling companion" (συνέκδημος, *synekdēmos*) as they traveled with "this gift" (τῇ χάριτι ταύτῃ, *tē chariti tautē*), the collection for the church in Jerusalem (8:4, 6–7; 9:12–13). So, the ultimate destination is Jerusalem.

Further, Paul describes this gift as "being administered" by himself and his mission. At 8:4 he has already referred to the collection itself as a "this ministry" (τῆς διακονίας, *tēs diakonias*), and here we have the cognate verb in the form of a present participle (τῇ διακονουμένῃ, *tē diakonoumenē*). As pointed out in the comments on 3:3, the verb διακονέω (*diakoneō*) generally communicates the idea of providing a service or help to someone (e.g., Matt. 25:44). Especially the help can take the form of the person functioning as an intermediary, an agent serving as a go-between (e.g., 1 Pet. 1:12), and that sense seems clear in the present context since Paul is delivering the collection to Jerusalem on behalf of the churches. His ministry at this point consists of administering the collection, seeing it delivered appropriately and safely to Jerusalem.

As the description of this brother continues, Paul notes two purposes[16] for the collection: Paul and companions administer it "for the glory of the Lord himself" and "to show our readiness to help." The Lord's glory is utmost in Paul's mind, for to bring glory to the Lord is the ultimate purpose of an authentic, new-covenant ministry (2 Cor. 3:7–11, 18; 4:6, 15); consequently, "for the glory of the Lord himself" underscores again that Paul's motives are pure with regard to the collection. He only wants to see people give thanks and glory to God as the gift makes it into needy hands in Jerusalem (9:11–13; Harris 2005: 604–5).

As for the second stated purpose, at 8:11–12 we have already encountered the Corinthians' "eager desire" to help in the collection, and the same word is used here. However, there are several ways καὶ προθυμίαν ἡμῶν (*kai prothymian hēmōn*, and our readiness to help) could be read in relation to the preposition πρός (*pros*).[17] Thrall (2000: 550) suggests two possibilities: (a) that the preposition communicates "in accordance with" or (b) that it indicates

---

It was not used of ordination until a later period. The participial form here (where we would expect a finite verb) is an example of anacoluthon.

16. The preposition πρός (*pros*) + the acc. at this point indicates the intended purpose for which something is done (BDAG 874).

17. Since πρός governs both nouns in this construction, it normally would carry the same sense in relation to both nouns.

result—the appointment of the brother has resulted in a heightening of Paul's eagerness for the collection. She opts for the second.

Yet it is also possible to read the phrase in terms of purpose.[18] Just as Paul's mission carries out the administration of the collection, for the purpose of manifesting glory to the Lord, so also that administration has the purpose of manifesting Paul's goodwill toward the church in Jerusalem: "to show our readiness to help."[19] At times in his ministry Paul was suspected of undermining Judaism, and some had read his work as being at cross-purposes with the church in the holy city. Yet, if we take the record of Acts and Galatians seriously, Paul was in harmony with the church leaders in Jerusalem (Acts 21:18–26; Gal. 2:7–10) and was working in accord with their ministry. The collection certainly would make clear Paul's exemplary goodwill, his "readiness to help" the church in Jerusalem (Matera 2003: 197).

2. Paul's Motive for Organizing the Delegation (8:20–21)

After explaining twin purposes for the collection, the apostle now makes clear an important motive for the brother's appointment as a traveling companion: "We are organizing things in this way so that no one can criticize us over this large sum of money we are administering." The NT is clear concerning the spiritual dangers surrounding money (Matt. 6:24; 21:12; Mark 6:8; Luke 3:14; 9:3; 16:11; Acts 4:37; 8:18, 20; 1 Tim. 6:10; 2 Tim. 3:2; Heb. 13:5), and church leaders especially are exhorted to keep money in perspective and handle it properly (1 Tim. 3:8; Titus 1:7; 1 Pet. 5:2). Paul has elected not to claim his right for financial support from the Corinthians (1 Cor. 9:4–18; 2 Cor. 11:9–12), perhaps with the aim of making a clear distinction between himself and his opponents, "hucksters who peddle the Word of God to make money" (2:17). At the same time, his unusual posture toward money would certainly have raised suspicions about his motives, especially since he was supervising a very large sum of money ostensibly being collected for disbursement among strangers who lived a great distance from Corinth! Normally public speakers worked and acted for the benefaction of the city in which they were teaching.[20]

The participle (στελλόμενοι, *stellomenoi*) at the beginning of verse 20 grammatically continues the thought of the previous two verses, but the exact sense of the term in this context is debatable.[21] First-century authors could use the verb στέλλω (*stellō*)—which originally meant "to put something in its right place" (Harris 2005: 606)—to mean "to stay away" or "keep one's distance"

8:20

---

18. Similarly, Windisch and Strecker (1970: 264) understand the apostle to say that the motive has been "zur Erhöhung unserer Freudigkeit [for the increasing of our joy]."

19. Thus many versions: ESV, HCSB, NASB, NLT[2], NRSV, NIV, NET.

20. Winter (2002: 166–68) suggests that Paul's opponents were Sophists, who eschewed common labor, often promised elaborate gifts to their city of residence, and charged their pupils for their teaching.

21. Yet the participle itself should be regarded as independent, used in place of a finite verb (Harris 2005: 605; Robertson 1934: 1039; D. Wallace 1996: 653).

from someone or something.[22] Similarly, the word could carry the sense of "to avoid"[23] or "shun" (BDAG 942), an idea that a number of current English versions communicate as "taking precaution" (e.g., HCSB, NASB, NET). Furnish (1984: 423) notes that Philo (*Emb.* 216) uses the word "for the annual 'dispatching' of envoys with the offerings of Diaspora Jews for the Temple treasury,"[24] which certainly seems to parallel our current context.[25] Yet it may be best to understand the word here as meaning "prepare," or "organize" (so Thrall 2000: 551; Martin 1986: 276), setting up matters related to the collection as described in verses 18–19. On this understanding, τοῦτο (*touto*, this) functions as the object of the participle and refers back to the arrangement of the "praised" brother as Paul's traveling companion: "We are organizing things in this way."

The apostle explains that this setup has been designed as a precaution against someone accusing him of mishandling the collection: "so that no one can criticize us over this large sum of money we are administering." In the NT, the term μωμάομαι (*mōmaomai*) occurs only here and at 6:3;[26] it has to do with "criticism," "finding fault," or "blame" (BDAG 663) or perhaps "mocking" (*EDNT* 2:449). Further, he refers to the collection as τῇ ἁδρότητι ταύτῃ (*tē hadrotēti tautē*, this abundance), assuming that when the Corinthians' contribution is added to that of the Macedonians, he will be administering a "lavish" or "large sum of money." So Paul wants to avoid anyone being able to find fault with the way he and his mission handle such a generous gift.

8:21 Consequently, the apostle reinforces his posture of integrity, expressing his commitment with a biblical principle taken directly from Prov. 3:4 LXX: "For we are giving careful consideration not only to what is noble in the Lord's eyes but also what is noble in the eyes of people." At Rom. 12:17 Paul also alludes to the same verse from Proverbs, there woven into a series of miscellaneous exhortations. Here the apostle reinforces the travel arrangement involving the

---

22. E.g., 2 Thess. 3:6 reads, "Keep away [στέλλεσθαι, *stellesthai*] from every brother who walks irresponsibly and not according to the tradition received from us" (HCSB).

23. E.g., Mal. 2:5 LXX reads in part, "that he avoid the presence of my name" (NETS; ἀπὸ προσώπου ὀνόματός μου στέλλεσθαι αὐτόν, *apo prosōpou onomatos mou stellesthai auton*).

24. Philo writes, "For every year envoys were dispatched for the sacred purpose of conveying to the temple a great quantity of gold and silver amassed from the first-fruits, and these envoys travel over the pathless, trackless, endless routes which seem to them good highroads because they feel that they lead them to piety" (*Emb.* 216; Colson 1971: 113). The same sense is found in *Emb.* 312: "where men . . . subscribed the annual first-fruits to pay for the sacrifices which they offer and commissioned sacred envoys to take them to the temple in Jerusalem" (Colson 1971: 157). On the use of escorts used in the transport of money in a religious context in the first century, see D. E. Watson 2006: 142.

25. If this is the sense, however, it is not clear why Paul follows with the neuter τοῦτο (*touto*, in this way) rather than a pronoun referring back to the brother.

26. "We make it a point not to offend anyone in any way, so that the ministry won't be criticized" (6:3).

brother, presenting it as a form of accountability with regard to the collection.[27] To enhance his application of this text for this end, he adjusts the wording slightly to make the relevance of the principle more clear.

	2 Cor. 8:21	Prov. 3:4 LXX
Focused attention	προνοοῦμεν γάρ (*pronooumen gar*, For we are giving careful consideration to)	καὶ προνοοῦ (*kai pronoou*, And think of)
The object	καλά (*kala*, what is noble)	καλά (*kala*, what is noble)
The audience	οὐ μόνον ἐνώπιον κυρίου ἀλλὰ καὶ ἐνώπιον ἀνθρώπων (*ou monon enōpion kyriou alla kai enōpion anthrōpōn*, not only in the Lord's eyes but also in the eyes of people).	ἐνώπιον κυρίου καὶ ἀνθρώπων (*enōpion kyriou kai anthrōpōn*, in the sight of the Lord and of people). (NETS)

The conjunction καί from the LXX passage has become an explanatory γάρ in Paul's adaptation since he uses the proverb to clarify the biblical principle underlying the collection arrangement. Paul changes the present imperative verb of Prov. 3:4 LXX into present active indicative in 2 Cor. 8:21 as a way of bearing witness to the actions being carried out by his mission. Meaning "to give careful thought to," or "to think about beforehand," the verb προνοέω (*pronoeō*), used elsewhere in the NT at Rom. 12:17 and 1 Tim. 5:8, describes well the safeguards already put in place for delivering the generous offering being collected. The object of the verb, καλά, a neuter plural adjective functioning as a substantive in this case, speaks of something that is "noble" or of high moral quality, what is "right" (HCSB, NRSV, NIV, NET), "honorable" (ESV, NLT[2], NEB), or "aboveboard" (Phillips). Finally, in both the LXX and 2 Corinthians two audiences are in view, "the Lord" and "people." Yet Paul frames these in a "not only . . . but also" (οὐ μόνον . . . ἀλλὰ καί) construction and repeats ἐνώπιον, placing the word before ἀνθρώπων to heighten attention on the human audience. Paul makes clear that he carries out his ministry with the Lord as his primary audience (2 Cor. 2:17; 12:19; cf. 2 Kings 3:14; Ps. 56:13). Consequently, he wants to carry out the collection in a way that is morally beautiful "in the Lord's eyes" (ἐνώπιον κυρίου; lit., before the Lord). However, the travel arrangements surrounding the collection are put in place out of a desire to be aboveboard "in the eyes of people" (ἐνώπιον ἀνθρώπων), who can't look at the heart and could mistake the motives. John Chrysostom (*Hom. 2 Cor.* 18.1) writes, "Who is there who can be compared with Paul? For he did whatever he thought was right without ignoring those who might doubt his intentions. On the contrary, he was concerned not to appear to be doing wrong even in the eyes of the weak" (Bray 1999: 277).

27. Financial propriety was a value in the broader Greco-Roman world at the time. In Judaism, financial integrity and the avoidance of financial scandals is noted, e.g., in Josephus (*Ant.* 18.81–84) and other Jewish texts of the period, and especially with reference to the temple tax from the Diaspora (*m. Šeqal.* 3.2; Keener 2005: 210).

3. The Reputation and Integrity of the Delegation (8:22–24)

8:22	Thus far Paul has spoken of two members of the delegation to Corinth, Titus and the "praised" brother of 8:18–19. In 8:22 a second unnamed[28] brother is introduced: "And we are sending with them our brother whose diligence we have often proved in many ways and who now is much more eager than ever because of his great confidence in you." As in 8:18, the aorist verb συνεπέμψα-μεν (*synepempsamen*, we are sending with) can be read as epistolary: Paul describes the current state of affairs at the time of writing, but doing so with the time frame of the reading audience in mind.[29] The apostle describes this second brother in three ways.

First, he is "our" (ἡμῶν, *hēmōn*) brother, as distinct from "the brother" (τὸν ἀδελφόν, *ton adelphon*) in 8:18. The personal pronoun probably means that Paul had a closer relationship with this second anonymous brother, but that cannot be certain. As with the previously mentioned "brother," the designation simply is a means by which Paul refers to him as a fellow Christian, not a blood relative. Second, this brother has been tested often and in a variety of circumstances and found to be "diligent." There are at least two primary ways Paul uses the verb δοκιμάζω (*dokimazō*) in his writings. At times the term has to do with examination, testing the genuineness of a person or thing. This is the sense at 8:8, where the apostle says his exhortation to involvement in the collection serves to test the genuineness of the Corinthians' love; this sense also occurs at 13:5, where the apostle writes, "Test yourselves to see if you are in the faith. *Examine* [δοκιμάζετε, *dokimazete*] yourselves" (2 Cor. 13:5 HCSB). At other points the word has to do with discernment, coming to a conclusion about something, approving or proving it (e.g., Rom. 1:28; 2:18; 12:2; 14:22), which is the sense here in 8:22.[30] Furthermore, this brother's character has been proved ἐν πολλοῖς πολλάκις (*en pollois pollakis*), "often, in many ways," so he probably is not a novice in the ministry but rather has served Paul's mission consistently and in a variety of circumstances.

We have seen the adjective σπουδαῖος (*spoudaios*) already in its comparative form at 8:17, where it is used to describe the exceptional eagerness of Titus. Here the word speaks of the brother being proved to be "diligent" (HCSB, Tyndale, NASB), or perhaps "eager" (NLT[2], NRSV) or "zealous" (NIV). And Paul has sprinkled the cognate noun σπουδή (*spoudē*) throughout 2 Cor. 7 and 8, describing the eagerness of the Corinthians and the Macedonians (7:11–12; 8:7–8, 16). In 8:22 the adjective is a predicate of the present participle ὄντα

---

28. Again, it is likely that the brothers are not named since Titus would introduce them upon arrival in Corinth; because they probably were unknown to the Corinthians at the time of writing, their names would not mean anything to the church.

29. The epistolary aorist is used as a courtesy, presenting the time frame of certain actions from the perspective of the readers at the time the letter is read.

30. An interesting parallel exists in 1 Corinthians when, speaking of the collection for Jerusalem, the apostle writes, "Then, when I arrive, I will send those whom you approve with letters of explanation to carry your gift to Jerusalem" (1 Cor. 16:3 NET). There the term seems to connote a recommendation (so HCSB).

(*onta*, being), which supplements[31] the action of the main verb ἐδοκιμάσαμεν (*edokimasamen*): "whom we have proved . . . being diligent," or more smoothly, "whose diligence we have proved."

Third, this brother "now is much more eager than ever because of his great confidence in" the Corinthians. At 7:7–13a Paul has already noted that he was greatly encouraged by the Corinthians' response to Titus's recent visit, and the young minister himself was refreshed and had grown in his affection for the Corinthians through the experience (7:13b–15). Perhaps this unnamed brother had been with Paul during the very difficult period when his conflict with the Corinthians was at its worst (Matera 2003: 198). Obviously the state of the Corinthian church would have been discussed with those who were chosen to minister to that church, and this brother, perhaps hearing of the Corinthians' response to Titus's visit, had become "much more eager" as he had become more confident of the Corinthians. The term rendered "more eager" (σπουδαιότερον, *spoudaioteron*) translates the same adjective we rendered as "diligence" earlier in the verse, and as at 8:17, it occurs now in a comparative form (BDF 126–27). In fact, Paul accents the word with the addition of "much" (πολὺ, *poly*). Whereas this brother has been tested and found a ready participant in the Pauline mission in various contexts in the past, the opportunity to minister to the Corinthians, as a part of this trip, has brought him to a new level of eagerness. In light of the next two verses, Paul almost certainly intends this bit of information to be rhetorical in effect, laying the groundwork for a positive first encounter between the Corinthians and this diligent brother.

8:23–24 Since 7:7 Paul has been quite upbeat about the Corinthians' posture toward him and his ministry team, but this does not mean that pockets of opposition to the apostle's mission have dissipated completely, as will become clear with chapter 10 and following. So Paul concludes this unit, which tells of those involved in the current trip to Corinth, by anticipating and blocking criticism that might arise concerning these envoys. He begins with Titus: "If anyone raises a question about Titus . . ." The double use of εἴτε (*eite*) occurs with a series of conditional statements, as here: "if . . . or if" (BDAG 279). The Greek text has no verbs in the verse; in fact, the clause in our translation, "anyone raises a question," supplies what is implied by the context, filling in the semantic gap left by an ellipsis in Paul's conditional clause, the Greek text reading simply, εἴτε ὑπὲρ[32] Τίτου (*eite hyper Titou*), "if concerning Titus." In this clipped-off manner, Paul anticipates someone questioning Titus's qualifications and then answers such questioning in an equally terse, almost poetic way: κοινωνὸς ἐμὸς καὶ εἰς ὑμᾶς συνεργός (*koinōnos emos kai eis hymas synergos*, he is my partner and coworker in our ministry to you). The Greek here is perfectly balanced in terms of syllables and sounds:

---

31. On the supplementary use of the participle, see BDF 214–15.

32. In 2 Corinthians, ὑπέρ often functions as a "marker of general content" meaning "about" or "concerning" (BDAG 1031).

κοινωνὸς
ἐμὸς
καὶ
εἰς
ὑμᾶς
συνεργός

The statement affirms two things about Titus: his close relationship with Paul and his ministry role vis-à-vis the Corinthians. Both carry a strong sense that Titus is Paul's *representative* in this ministry he brings to Corinth (Barnett 1997: 426). A κοινωνός could simply be someone who had a share in some experience, action, or thing (e.g., Matt. 23:30; 1 Cor. 10:18, 20; 2 Cor. 1:7), but the term carries more a note of intimacy or familiarity here—a sharing *with* someone—speaking of Titus as the apostle's "companion" or "partner" and thus his representative in the ministry (Martin 1986: 277).[33] Moreover, the younger man was a συνεργός (coworker), a favorite term Paul uses when speaking about those with whom he was involved in advancing the cause of Christ (Rom. 16:3, 9, 21; 1 Cor. 3:9; 2 Cor. 1:24; 8:23; Phil. 2:25; 4:3; Col. 4:11; 1 Thess. 3:2; Philem. 1, 24). At 1 Cor. 3:9 Paul calls himself "God's coworker," and earlier in 2 Corinthians he speaks of himself and his ministry team as coworkers for the Corinthians' joy (1:24). So Paul wants the Corinthians to be clear about Titus's standing, and he affirms the close working relationship he has with the young minister in no uncertain terms. He is both companion and coworker with Paul, representing him in this task of carrying forward the collection for the saints, and the apostle hopes to avert anyone raising unnecessary objections to the younger man's work in Corinth.

Next, the apostle continues by addressing any questions that might be raised concerning the other two brothers traveling with Titus: "Or if a question comes up about our brothers, they are the churches' envoys, Christ's glory." Again, as was the case with Titus in the first part of the verse, the clause begins with a correlative use of the conditional particle εἴτε (*eite*, or if), and we have two descriptions of these men. First, they are called ἀπόστολοι ἐκκλησιῶν (*apostoloi ekklēsiōn*), which can be translated directly as "apostles of the churches." However, the use of the term "apostle" here is quite different from Paul's use at 1:1, where he refers to himself as an apostle, or "official representative." Paul and the twelve apostles stand in a distinct category as those directly commissioned by the Lord Jesus for a unique, authoritative role in the early church (Harris 2005: 128; 1 Cor. 9:1; 15:3–9; Gal. 1:17). The term can also be used in a semitechnical sense of those who are associates of Paul or the Twelve, who hold significant support positions in the church.[34] Yet here

33. Using the term, Luke 5:10 speaks of James and John as Simon's partners; and at Philem. 17 Paul appeals to his addressee as a "companion."
34. Examples include Barnabas (1 Cor. 9:5–6), Andronicus and Junia[s] (Rom. 16:7), James brother of the Lord (1 Cor. 15:7; Gal. 1:19), and perhaps Apollos (1 Cor. 4:6–9).

in 2 Cor. 8:23 we find a third use of the term ἀπόστολος as referring to a messenger or a representative chosen to carry out a specific task (cf. John 13:16; Phil. 2:25). In this sense Paul speaks of these brothers as "the churches' envoys." Given the description of the second brother in 8:22, it may be that Paul chose that brother to accompany Titus and the brother elected for the task by the churches of Macedonia. Nevertheless, as Paul's choice of one who would also make the trip, the second brother would be recognized as the churches' envoy, since Paul and the Macedonians were of one mind concerning the collection.

Second, Paul describes these brothers as "the glory of Christ" (δόξα Χριστοῦ, *doxa Christou*).[35] The word δόξα is important for Paul, used eighteen times in the book (1:20; 3:7–11 [8x], 18 [2x]; 4:4, 6, 15, 17; 6:8; 8:19, 23) in at least three distinct ways:

1. Fame or honor given, whether to God (1:20; 4:15; 8:19) or a person (6:8)
2. The Shekinah glory manifesting God's presence (3:7–11, 18; 4:4, 6)
3. The state of being in the afterlife, in God's glorious presence (4:17)

Here at 8:23, in the final use of the word in 2 Corinthians, the term carries the sense of the first of these three options. These brothers are being celebrated as bringing honor or fame to Christ,[36] making him known by the way they carry out Christian ministry (Garland 1999: 395).

Based on these glowing credentials (οὖν, *oun*, therefore), in verse 24 Paul exhorts the Corinthians, "display openly before the churches the proof of your love and the accuracy of our boasts to them about you." The apostle communicates the main verbal idea in the form of a present participle, ἐνδεικνύμενοι (*endeiknymenoi*), which should be read as imperatival[37] in force and imperfective in aspect—an open-ended exhortation. In the first century the word ἐνδείκνυμι (*endeiknymi*) could mean "to direct attention to or cause something

---

35. It could be that the phrase δόξα Χριστοῦ delimits ἐκκλησιῶν (*ekklēsiōn*), that is, the "churches" as the "glory of Christ" (Barnett 1997: 427), but this seems less than likely based both on grammar (which would be awkward if read in this way) and the way the parallelism is crafted in 8:23.

> If anyone raises a question about Titus,
>   he is my   partner and
>   coworker in our ministry to you. Or
> if a question comes up about our brothers,
>   they are   the churches' envoys,
>   Christ's glory.

The double description of the brothers structurally matches the double description of Titus. Thus, "Christ's glory" should be read as a description of the brothers rather than a description of the churches.

36. Thus Χριστοῦ (*Christou*) would be an objective genitive—they glorified "Christ."

37. On the use of the participle in place of a finite verb, see BDF 245. This use normally carries an imperatival sense. Also, many ancient scribes understood this to be the sense of the participle, replacing it with the imperative form of the verb. Discussion on this textual variant may be found in the additional note on 8:4.

to become known," that is, "to show" or "to demonstrate" something (BDAG 331). This participle has a main object and a phrase describing the manner in which the exhortation is to be carried out. Concerning the former, the Corinthians are to show "proof" (ἔνδειξιν, *endeixin*), with Paul using a cognate noun of the participle. Similarly using cognate words in English, we might say they are to "prove the proof," or "demonstrate the demonstration," or "manifest the manifestation" (Plummer 1915: 251). The noun could carry the sense of a "sign" (e.g., Phil. 1:28), but here it communicates more the nuance of a "demonstration" or "proof" (e.g., Rom. 3:25) by which someone would be compelled to accept something. Philo (*Creat.* 45), for instance, uses the term to speak of a "demonstration" of God's power in creation.

In relation to the delegation sent by Paul, the Corinthians are "to show the proof" of two things. First, they are to demonstrate the proof of their "love," which could be a reference to the love they have for Christ, or perhaps the love they have for others in the body of Christ, or more specifically, the love they have for these delegates. Ambrosiaster (*Comm. Paul's Ep.*, 2 Cor. 8:25), for example, understands Paul to be exhorting the Corinthians to show love to these brothers: "Paul is urging the Corinthians to demonstrate their love by the way they treat those he is sending to them" (Bray 1999: 277). Yet this probably is not the correct reading of the text at this point. Although there is no stated object of the love mentioned in the Greek text, the reference to love here can be read in light of Paul's earlier statement at 8:8, "I am seeking to verify the genuineness of your own love as well," a statement he makes with reference to the collection for the saints. The Corinthians were to follow the Macedonians' example of Christian love by participating in the collection.

Similarly, they are to demonstrate that the apostle's boast—that the Corinthians are in a sound place spiritually and ready to be obedient to God with regard to the collection—is accurate. Thus both the "love" they are to show and the verification of Paul's boast have to do with the collection for the saints in Jerusalem. Finally, as to manner, they are to demonstrate such realities "openly before the churches" (εἰς πρόσωπον τῶν ἐκκλησιῶν, *eis prosōpon tōn ekklēsiōn*; lit., before the face of the churches). Paul consistently underscores the importance of living openly before the Lord and others (e.g., 2:17). Yet at this point what he wants from the Corinthians is a very public display of their acceptance of these envoys and thus an endorsement of their mission. They could fulfill Paul's wishes by no better means than an enthusiastic participation in the offering to be delivered to Jerusalem.

4. The Purpose of the Mission (9:1–5)

With 9:1–5 Paul continues to write about the collection for the saints in Jerusalem, and he admits that this may seem redundant (9:1). But in these first five verses of chapter 9, the apostle clarifies exactly why he feels compelled to send Titus and the two brothers (all three now simply referred to as "the brothers") on ahead to them. In short, he wants to make sure the Corinthians are completely prepared, having gathered the collection; for if Paul comes with a delegation from Macedonia (perhaps with the Macedonian collection in hand), only to find the Corinthians disorganized and still defaulting on their previously promised gift, all of the apostle's boasting about their "eagerness" (9:2–3) will fall flat, and the situation will be humiliating for both Paul and the Corinthian church (9:4). So he sends the brothers on ahead to put things in order so that their generous gift might be ready when Paul arrives (9:5).

The three words that begin this chapter, Περὶ μὲν γάρ (*Peri men gar*), stand at the center of a considerable debate on the origin of chapters 8 and 9 and thus the integrity of the book as a whole. Hans Dieter Betz, for instance, suggests that these two chapters constitute separate administrative letters of the apostle,[38] and he presents Περὶ μὲν γάρ as an important piece of evidence for his theory (Betz and MacRae 1985: 90). He reasons that Περὶ μὲν γάρ must be distinguished from περὶ δέ (*peri de*), which serves to introduce movements of a discourse within a larger work (e.g., 1 Cor. 7:1, 25; 8:1; 12:1; 16:1; 1 Thess. 4:9; 5:1). Betz argues that the inclusion of μέν in a sense neutralizes the explanatory effect of γάρ, since μέν is correlative with δέ at the beginning of verse 3 ("on the one hand . . . nevertheless"; Furnish 1984: 426).[39] In this case, he reasons, the conjunction γάρ need not be read in relation to what has gone before but, rather, refers to what follows.[40] On this basis Betz suggests that 2 Cor. 9 originally was an independent letter (Betz and MacRae 1985: 90).

9:1-2

However, this approach has been soundly answered by Stanley Stowers, who investigates ninety uses of Περὶ μὲν γάρ outside the NT. Stowers (1990: 347–48) concludes that use of these words at 2 Cor. 9:1 is very much in line with conventional uses of the day, by which these three words connote a close connection to what has just been stated in the broader discourse. Thus Paul writes in 9:1 with reference to what he has just stated in chapter 8, and this makes a great deal of sense in context. Generally, having dealt with the "who" of the trip in 8:16–24, the words of 9:1–5 offer an explanation of "why" he is sending these brothers on ahead to deal with the collection, here referred to as τῆς διακονίας τῆς εἰς τοὺς ἁγίους (*tēs diakonias tēs eis tous hagious*, this ministry to God's people). Paul has already referred to the collection as "this ministry to God's people" at 8:4, where he reports that the Macedonians have been "begging us most emphatically for the privilege of being able to join in." More specifically, however, at 8:24 he exhorts the Corinthians to demonstrate "the accuracy of" Paul's "boast." At 9:1 the apostle's boasting is reiterated and indeed stands at the heart of Paul's concern expressed in 9:3–5

---

38. The position of Betz and MacRae (1985) is reflected in the work's subtitle: *A Commentary on Two Administrative Letters of the Apostle Paul.*

39. At times the correlation "does not emphasize a contrast, but separates one thought from another in a series, so that they may be easily distinguished" (BDAG 630). Yet this seems to be a case where a note of contrast is present, as indicated by the ET of δέ with "nevertheless" at the beginning of 9:3.

40. It is true that the conjunction γάρ at times indicates a new thought or movement (e.g., Heb. 5:1). But in such cases, it nonetheless serves as a discourse marker.

(Hafemann 2000: 363). He does not want his boast to be emptied of meaning by their lack of preparation. Thus, reading 9:1–5 as a natural continuation and development of 8:16–24 seems well founded (Barrett 1973: 232; Stowers 1990: 347–48).

Given the extensive treatment of the collection in chapter 8, Paul realizes that his explanation here in 9:1–5 might seem a bit redundant, and this is why in verse 1 he begins this new movement as he does: "Now . . . it is redundant for me to write to you further about this ministry to God's people." The term περισσόν (*perisson*) has already been used by Paul (in a comparative form, περισσοτέρᾳ) at 2:7 to speak of "excessive" or "overwhelming" sadness. Writers of the first century could use the word to speak of something as being "extraordinary" (e.g., Matt. 5:47), or "remarkable" as to the amount of something, thus "abundant" or "profuse" (e.g., John 10:10), or in a comparative sense of "more" or "going beyond a certain point" (e.g., Matt. 5:37; BDAG 805). Here Paul uses the word in the sense of "superfluous," and a number of English translations thus render the term with the sense of "unnecessary" (e.g., HCSB, NLT², NRSV, NET, NIV, Goodspeed). But I suggest that the translation "redundant" captures the superfluity of Paul continuing to drive home his subject, while alluding to the fact that he has already been addressing the issue at length! Further, the present active infinitive γράφειν (*graphein*), with its imperfective aspect, carries the sense "to keep on writing."[41] Indeed a number of concepts or topics in this unit repeat points covered in the previous chapter about "this ministry to God's people," including the eagerness of the Corinthians to be involved (8:10–11), the reference to "last year" (8:10), Paul's boast about the Corinthians (8:24), the sending of the brothers (8:16–24), the need for preparation (8:20), and the need for organization (8:19). Thus the apostle begins this new movement by acknowledging that it could be a bit tedious to continue on the topic of the collection. Yet 9:1–5 has a distinct purpose in the developing discourse: to explain why the apostle is sending the brothers ahead to deal with the collection prior to his coming.

Before getting to that purpose, however, in 9:2 he underscores why it is redundant for him to continue addressing the collection for the saints: the Corinthians' eagerness has already been noted in the previous section (8:10–11). Paul is walking a fine line here. He wants to acknowledge and affirm what can be affirmed, while at the same time offering appropriate encouragement to get on with the process. He writes, "For I know how ready you are to help—on your behalf I keep boasting about it to the Macedonians!: 'Achaia has been anxious to participate since last year.'" As we have noted previously, in the ancient world the word προθυμία (*prothymia*) connoted "eagerness," "goodwill," or "willingness" to be of service (*EDNT* 3:156). The term has been used three times thus far in 2 Corinthians, all in chapter 8 and all in relation to the

---

41. D. Wallace (1996: 519) refers to this type of present as "extending-from-past present," by which "the present tense may be used to describe an action which, begun in the past, continues in the present."

collection (2 Cor. 8:11–12, 19). At 8:19 the administration of the collection by Paul not only brings the Lord glory but also serves as a demonstration of the apostle's "readiness to help." But earlier in that chapter, at 8:11–12 Paul applauds the Corinthians' "eager desire" to help through the collection. Now in 9:2 he reiterates their eager desire, their readiness to be involved in this ministry. He "knows," οἶδα (*oida*), meaning he "grasps" or "recognizes" their eagerness, affirming that their hearts are in the right place.

In fact, "on behalf of" the Corinthians the apostle has been "boasting about it to the Macedonians!" This clause begins with a relative pronoun (ἥν, *hēn*), which has the term προθυμία (the eagerness that) as its referent, and continues with the apostle's declaration of his constant boasting to the Macedonians.[42] Besides two occurrences in James, Paul is the only NT author to use the verb καυχάομαι (*kauchaomai*), which he does thirty-five times.[43] As mentioned earlier in the comments on 1:12 (where the cognate noun is used), in the ancient world the act of "boasting" could be looked upon positively or negatively.[44] In the Greek OT, the verb or its cognate noun could be used to speak of a wrongheaded pride in human achievement (e.g., Judg. 7:2; 1 Sam. 2:3; Jer. 12:13; Ezek. 24:25; cf. 2 Cor. 5:12); or this family of words could be used of appropriately celebrating the Lord's character and works (e.g., 1 Chron. 16:35; 29:13; Ps. 5:12 [5:11 ET]; Prov. 16:31). Paul's boast to the Macedonians about the Corinthians expresses his enthusiasm about what God has been doing in their midst. As emphasized at several points thus far in Paul's treatment of the collection, the stirring of enthusiasm for this ministry ultimately stands as a manifestation of God's grace (8:1, 9, 16). The present-tense form of the verb communicates an imperfective aspect and seems to indicate in context that Paul's boasting is a current affair.

The apostle further defines the act of boasting as "on your behalf" (ὑπὲρ ὑμῶν, *hyper hymōn*). Although the phrase could be understood as communicating general content (i.e., "about you," so ESV, HCSB, Message, NASB, NRSV),[45] this would make the phrase quite redundant, following as it does on the heels of the possessive ὑμῶν just three words earlier. In that case the sense of the translation would be an awkward "I know about your eagerness—about you I keep boasting about it to the Macedonians." It seems better to hear the phrase as communicating Paul's boasting as being in the interest of the Corinthians ("on your behalf"; Harris 2005: 619).

---

42. The relative pronoun serves as the object of the verb καυχῶμαι (*kauchōmai*, I keep boasting; 9:2).

43. Rom. 2:17, 23; 5:2–3, 11; 1 Cor. 1:29, 31 (2x); 3:21; 4:7; 13:3; 2 Cor. 5:12; 7:14; 9:2; 10:8, 13, 15–17 (4x); 11:12, 16, 18 (2x), 30 (2x); 12:1, 5–6 (3x), 9; Gal. 6:13–14; Eph. 2:9; Phil. 3:3. Most of the occurrences in 2 Corinthians are in chaps. 10–12. Paul also uses the related verb κατακαυχάομαι in Rom. 11:18, a term James takes up in 2:13 and 3:14.

44. For the wide-ranging, pejorative uses of this term and its cognates in Greco-Roman literature, see Spicq 1994: 2.295–302. Keener (2005: 159) notes that boasting was frowned upon unless properly justified (see also Roetzel 2007: 130).

45. NIV seems to simply drop the phrase. NET reads it as a reiteration of "your eagerness" earlier in the sentence.

What then has the apostle been boasting to the Macedonians? He tells us with a content (ὅτι, *hoti*) clause: "Achaia has been eager to participate since last year." He has affirmed this same thing to the Corinthians at 8:10: "You are the ones who took the initiative beginning last year, not only in action, but also in wanting to do something!" Much ink has been spilled suggesting reasons why Paul refers to "Achaia" here rather than "Corinth."[46] Yet it should be remembered that from the very first words of the letter, Paul has been addressing "God's church in Corinth, along with all the saints throughout Achaia" (1:1). Certainly those living in Corinth have been the focus (e.g., 6:11), but the letter has always had the broader province in mind, and at 11:10 he again speaks of the province in relation to his boasting.[47]

The greater difficulty has to do with the perfect verb παρεσκεύασται (*pareskeuastai*, has been ready), since Paul's rebuke in chapter 8, not to mention 9:3–5, which comes on the heels of this statement—both suggest that the Corinthians as yet are *not* ready to have the collection taken! (Furnish 1984: 430). Philip Hughes (1962: 323–24) seeks to solve the problem by making a distinction between two types of "readiness": a readiness of "intention" and a readiness of "completion." Consistently the apostle has celebrated their readiness in terms of *eagerness*, not in terms of thoroughness in the task itself, and this seems to be the case here as well. Indeed, it is their eagerness or "zeal" (ζῆλος, *zēlos*) that the apostle says has "stirred up most of them" (ἠρέθισεν τοὺς πλείονας, *ērethisen tous pleionas*). The verb ἐρεθίζω (*erethizō*), found only here and at Col. 3:21 in the NT,[48] means "to arouse" or "provoke."[49] So, even though the Corinthians have yet to act on their own eagerness, that zeal has been productive, used by the apostle to encourage the Macedonians in the collection. At 8:1–5 Paul uses the Macedonians as an example to motivate the Corinthians. Now he mentions that he has already worked the other way around, using the eagerness of the Corinthians to "stir up" the Macedonians (Garland 1999: 402). As Theodoret of Cyr (*Comm. 2 Cor.* 333) said, "Paul holds up the Macedonians to the Corinthians and the Corinthians to the Macedonians as examples to imitate" (Bray 1999: 279). According to Belleville (1996: 231), "A contagious enthusiasm is a very effective way to rouse a congregation to action," which seems to have been a part of Paul's strategy.

9:3–4 As noted in our discussion of Περὶ μὲν γάρ (*Peri men gar*) at the beginning of verse 1, the μέν there functions correlatively with δέ (*de*) at the beginning of verse 3. The correlation marks an "on the one hand . . . on the other hand" relationship between verses 1–2 and 3–4, making a distinction between two

46. For the various suggestions, see Harris 2005: 618–20.

47. Some see the geographical designation "Achaia," the Roman province established in 146 BC with Corinth as its capital, as corresponding to the reference to "Macedonians" (so Hafemann 2000: 363).

48. "Fathers, do not provoke your children, so they will not become disheartened" (Col. 3:21 NET).

49. Deut. 21:20 LXX uses the word to refer to a son who is "contentious," and Proverbs LXX uses it with the sense of provocation (19:7; 25:23).

somewhat contrasting points. On the one hand, given the eagerness of the Corinthians, he readily acknowledges that it is a bit redundant for him to keep writing about the collection (9:1–2).[50] On the other hand, he *obviously* continues to write about this ministry, and he does so because he wants to explain *why* he is sending the brothers on ahead to Corinth (9:3–4). Thus at the beginning of verse 3 we mark the correlation, bringing in that note of contrast, by translating δέ as "nevertheless." The sentence begun here continues through verse 4.

With the verb ἔπεμψα (*epempsa*) we again have an epistolary aorist, translated as present tense, and the verb takes as its object "the brothers" (τοὺς ἀδελφούς, *tous adelphous*) introduced in 8:16–24: "I am sending the brothers" (9:3).[51] But now that he has introduced both of the unnamed brothers and Titus, initially making subtle distinctions between Titus and the other two, the young minister is now included in the broad designation, being referred to simply as one of "the brothers."[52] In the form of a pair of contrasting purpose clauses (ἵνα . . . ἵνα, *hina . . . hina*, in order that . . . in order that), Paul gets to the twin reasons he is sending the envoys on ahead (9:3):

> in order that in this particular instance our boast on your behalf might not be made empty of meaning—
> in order that you might be prepared, as I kept telling them you would be

Paul wants to avoid the travesty described in the first clause by making sure the Corinthians will follow through on the preparedness described in the second.

"Our boast" (τὸ καύχημα ἡμῶν, *to kauchēma hēmōn*), here in noun form (cf. 2 Cor. 1:14; 5:12), refers back to the "boasting" mentioned in verse 2, where Paul celebrates the eagerness of the Corinthians for the collection. As in verse 2, the apostle's boast in verse 3 is presented as "on your behalf" (τὸ ὑπὲρ ὑμῶν, *to hyper hymōn*). Here too the phrase could be read in terms of content ("about you"), but given the clear reiteration of the "boasting" mentioned in verse 2, it seems best to render the phrase consistently as referring to something done in the interest of the Corinthians ("on your behalf").

The apostle's concern is that this boast on behalf of the Corinthians might be "made empty" (κενωθῇ, *kenōthē*) of meaning. In the ancient world, the verb κενόω (*kenoō*) meant "to empty," or "evacuate," and could be used with the sense of "to purge," or "to annihilate" (Spicq 1994: 2.308–9). Paul, who alone among the NT authors employs the word, mostly uses it to speak of something being nullified (Rom. 4:14; 1 Cor. 1:17; 9:15).[53] So here Paul

---

50. The construction was more characteristic of classical style and during the first century was on the decline (see BDF 231–32).

51. See the discussion above at 8:16–17. If chap. 9 is a separate letter, the aorist would not be read as epistolary (Martin 1986: 284; Thrall 2000: 567).

52. See esp. the discussion in Thrall 2000: 570.

53. The one exception is the "hymnic" material at Phil. 2:7, which says, "he emptied himself" (ἑαυτὸν ἐκένωσεν, *heauton ekenōsen*).

expresses a concern that the boast he has made on behalf of the Corinthians could be nullified, shattered, emptied of meaning if they are not prepared with the collection. In short, his boasting would fall flat. The final phrase of the Greek clause, ἐν τῷ μέρει τούτῳ (en tō merei toutō), means "in this matter," or "in this affair." With Moffatt we render it "in this particular instance." Some English versions present the phrase as delimiting Paul's "boast" (e.g., HCSB, NIV), but it is better to understand the phrase as clarifying the verb κενωθῇ (kenōthē, be made empty): "in order that in this particular instance our boast on your behalf might not be made empty of meaning."

With a second ἵνα clause, Paul explains how the Corinthians might avoid such an embarrassing situation: "in order that you might be prepared, as I kept telling them you would be." The perfect middle participle, παρεσκευασμένοι (pareskeuasmenoi), plus the present subjunctive of εἰμί (eimi, appearing as ἦτε, ēte) forms a periphrastic perfect subjunctive construction that amounts to "(so that) you may be in a state of having prepared yourselves" (lit.; Harris 2005: 624), that is, "in order that you might be prepared." The present subjunctive verb of being indicates that the preparation Paul has in mind is still in the future at the time of writing. As we see in the previous verse, the apostle has just used the verb παρασκευάζω (paraskeuazō) to affirm a type of readiness on the part of those in Achaia. But as discussed in the comments at that point, such preparation was a declaration of intent that had not yet been consummated by an action of completion (so P. Hughes 1962: 324). A full-orbed preparation would mean that the collection was in hand, ready to be forwarded to Jerusalem. Only this type of preparation would be in accordance with (καθώς, kathōs, just as) what Paul consistently has been telling (ἔλεγον, elegon)[54] the Macedonians and would keep his boast from being vacuous.

Grammatically verse 4 continues the sentence begun with verse 3, but the Greek text needs a bit of unpacking to sort out the clausal relationships. Two purpose clauses, flip sides of the same coin, delimit ἔπεμψα (epempsa, I am sending). Paul is sending the brothers (a) so that his boast on behalf of the Corinthians might not be emptied of meaning, and (b) so that the Corinthians might be fully prepared.

The content of verse 4 further defines this second purpose clause: if the Corinthians are "prepared," then they can avert an embarrassing situation.[55] The negative μή plus the enclitic particle πώς (pōs, somehow, perhaps) expresses misgiving in a somewhat tentative manner and at times is translated as "lest" (so KJV, Tyndale) or "otherwise" (ESV, NASB[95], NRSV). The main verbal idea to which this misgiving relates is καταισχυνθῶμεν ἡμεῖς (kataischynthōmen hēmeis, we might be humiliated). Paul has already used the term καταισχύνω

---

54. The imperfect verb is iterative in force: "I kept telling them."

55. Harris understands μή πως . . . καταισχυνθῶμεν ἡμεῖς (mē pōs . . . kataischynthōmen hēmeis, lest we be so humiliated) to be a third purpose clause relating to the verb ἔπεμψα. However, Paul's concern about the Corinthians being "unprepared" (ἀπαρασκευάστους, aparaskeuastous) upon his arrival with "Macedonians" relates very directly to the periphrastic construction "that you might be prepared" (παρεσκευασμένοι ἦτε) in the second ἵνα clause of 9:3.

(*kataischynō*) in relation to boasting at 7:14.[56] The term can refer to being shamed or humiliated by some action, as well as a milder feeling of disappointment.[57] For Greco-Roman culture, in which honor and shame shaped a significant framework for relationships at all levels of society, the term connoted more than our modern concept of embarrassment. Paul expresses concern that having boasted so about the preparedness of the Corinthians, the possibility that they could humiliate him was real. Further, the Corinthians themselves would share in the humiliation. The clause ἵνα μὴ λέγω ὑμεῖς (*hina mē legō hymeis*) is potently parenthetical, meaning "not to mention you!" Betz reports that those from the broader culture who defaulted on their public pledges had their names published in the Athenian Agora, an action intended to shame publicly. In the early Christian movement one cannot help but think of Ananias and Sapphira (Acts 5:1–11) at this point (Betz and MacRae 1985: 96; Garland 1999: 403). To fail in following through on a pledge brought humiliation or worse.

What would lead to such humiliation?: "if Macedonians come with me and find you unprepared!" Clearly, Paul expected to follow Titus's mission team to Corinth (see 12:14; 13:1), and he raises at least the possibility that the Corinthians might not be prepared. Paul's impending visit, therefore, presents the Corinthians with a form of accountability (cf. Philem. 22). The conjunction ἐάν (*ean*), which relates to both of the aorist subjunctive verbs (ἔλθωσιν, *elthōsin*, come; εὕρωσιν, *heurōsin*, find) can speak of a probability or just a possibility, and this is somewhat ambiguous in context. Yet from the context it seems that Paul intends to bring along fellow travelers from Macedonia—at least that is a real possibility. The lack of the article in front of Μακεδόνες (*Makedones*) suggests an indefinite number are in mind, simply speaking of "Macedonians," supposedly from among those who would have heard Paul boasting on a consistent basis about the readiness of the Corinthians (9:2). Paul's exhortation takes seriously that the unpreparedness (ἀπαρασκευάστους, *aparaskeuastous*) of the Corinthians is also a distinct possibility. If they remain unprepared, they and their apostle will be humiliated.

Finally, the last phrase of the verse reads, ἐν[58] τῇ ὑποστάσει ταύτῃ (*en tē hypostasei tautē*); the key sticking point concerns how to translate the word ὑπόστασις (*hypostasis*), which occurs only five times in the NT (2 Cor. 9:4; 11:17; Heb. 1:3; 3:14; 11:1). In secular Greek the word generally had the sense of the "basis" of something (lit., something that stands under) and was rendered variously as "foundation support, guarantee, possession, existence, deposit" (*EDNT* 3:407). In terms of property, it could speak variously of the contents of a house or a title deed (Spicq 1994: 3.421–22). Given the context of 2 Cor. 9:4, many interpreters opt for the traditional translation as "confidence" (ESV,

---

56. "For if I have boasted a bit to him about you, I was not shamed by your response" (2 Cor. 7:14a).

57. See καταισχύνω in Luke 13:17; Rom. 5:5; 9:33; 10:11; 1 Cor. 1:27; 11:4–5, 22; 2 Cor. 7:14; 9:4; 1 Pet. 2:6; 3:16.

58. In this case the preposition ἐν marks a circumstance or condition under which something takes place.

Message, NASB, NIV, NET, NEB; e.g., Wendland 1968: 222–23;[59] Spicq 1994: 3.422), but that understanding has been vigorously challenged by Thrall (1994: 568–70) and others (following H. Köster, *TDNT* 8:584) as not supportable in biblical or extrabiblical literature (BDAG 1040–41; e.g., NRSV; Furnish 1984: 427–28). Instead, these scholars understand the term to refer to a "plan," "undertaking," or "endeavor," or even a "situation" or "condition."[60] Here Paul seems to be speaking of the collection as a "project" or "undertaking," which he calls "this [ταύτῃ, *tautē*] undertaking." Considering all these points, the sense of Paul's thoughts in verse 4 may be rendered thus: "In this undertaking, we (not to mention you!) would be so humiliated if Macedonians come with me and find you unprepared!"

9:5   Paul continues in verse 5: "Consequently, I think it necessary to encourage the brothers to travel on ahead to you and organize in advance your previously promised generous gift, in order that it might thus be ready as a generous gift and not as an expression of stinginess." The sentence rounds out the unit (9:1–5), providing a nice summary explanation of why Paul is sending the delegation ahead to Corinth. The summary falls into three parts: the necessity of the trip, the practical organization Paul intends the brothers to accomplish, and the ultimate effect—that the Corinthians' generous gift, which they have previously promised, might be ready and given with the right attitude.

He first mentions the necessity of the trip. The conjunction οὖν (*oun*), which may be translated as "Consequently," indicates that the content of verse 5 is inferred from the concern expressed by Paul in verse 4. To avoid the potential humiliation mentioned there, the apostle thinks (ἡγησάμην, *hēgēsamēn*) it "necessary" (ἀναγκαῖον, *anankaion*) to attempt a prevention. Authors of the first century could use the word ἡγέομαι (*hēgeomai*) to refer to the act of leading or guiding, or to a person in a leadership role,[61] but here the term means to "consider," "think," or "regard" (BDAG 433–34).[62] What Paul thinks at this point is that the situation is serious and needs to be addressed (thus ἀναγκαῖον, necessary); he senses that the need is great to encourage the brothers to make their way to Corinth and help get things ready. As Paul has encouraged Titus to reengage in helping the Corinthians proceed with the collection (8:6), so here he says that he has encouraged (παρακαλέσαι, *parakalesai*) all three of "the brothers" (τοὺς ἀδελφούς, *tous adelphous*)[63] to go ahead of him to the

59. With the translation "beschämt dastehen mit dieser Erwartung [to shame with this expectation]."

60. See the discussion in the comments on 11:17.

61. As, e.g., at Ezek. 43:7; Sir. 17:17; 41:17; 1 Macc. 9:30; 2 Macc. 14:16; Matt. 2:6; Acts 7:10; Heb. 13:7, 17, 24.

62. As with several previous aorists in the context, this one too can be read as epistolary and thus presented as present tense in meaning (so, e.g., TCNT, Knox). See the parallel in Phil. 2:25, where Paul "considers it necessary" (ἀναγκαῖον δὲ ἡγησάμην, *anankaion de hēgēsamēn*) to send Epaphroditus to the Philippians.

63. The mention of "the brothers" harks back to 9:3, where Paul speaks of "sending the brothers," using the designation for the first time to speak of all three of the envoys.

Corinthians (προέλθωσιν εἰς ὑμᾶς, *proelthōsin eis hymas*, travel on ahead to you).[64] The aorist active subjunctive verb προέλθωσιν (travel ahead) begins a series of three terms with the προ- prefix, stressing collectively the need for the Corinthians to "work ahead" in preparation for the apostle's arrival:

προέλθωσιν (*proelthōsin*, travel ahead)

προκαταρτίσωσιν (*prokatartisōsin*, organize in advance)

προεπηγγελμένην (*proepēngelmenēn*, previously promised)

The second of these terms brings us to a second emphasis of this verse. Note the practical organization Paul intends the brothers to accomplish. By traveling on ahead, they would "organize in advance" the Corinthians' "previously promised generous gift." The verb καταρτίζω (*katartizō*) can mean "to put in order," "restore," or "prepare" (e.g., Matt. 4:21; 21:16; Mark 1:19; Luke 6:40; Rom. 9:22; 1 Cor. 1:10; 2 Cor. 13:11). So with the προ- prefix, the term can be understood as meaning "to get ready" or "make arrangements" ahead of time (BDAG 871). What they are to "get ready" is their "previously promised generous gift" (προεπηγγελμένην εὐλογίαν, *proepēngelmenēn eulogian*). This brings us to the third emphasis of the verse, the ultimate effect Paul is after: that the Corinthians' generous gift, which they have previously promised, might be ready and given with the right attitude. The perfect middle participle, προεπηγγελμένην, functions as the direct object of the verb, and in the NT this word occurs only here and at Rom. 1:2, where Paul describes the gospel as *promised beforehand* through his prophets in the holy scriptures" (NET). So Paul here refers to the Corinthian offering as "previously promised." Indeed, the Corinthians' interest in the collection predates 1 Corinthians (see Paul's answer to a question they had raised about the offering at 1 Cor. 16:1–4), and the discussion since 2 Cor. 8:1 has made clear that by the time 2 Corinthians is being written, they have already committed themselves to the collection for Jerusalem. Titus has begun the work among them (8:6), and they have made a good start the previous year (8:10–11) and have made clear their eagerness to help (9:2).

Here Paul refers to the collection itself as "your blessing" or "your generous gift" (εὐλογίαν ὑμῶν, *eulogian hymōn*). At 1 Cor. 16:1 the apostle refers to the "collection" with the term λογεία (περὶ δὲ τῆς λογείας τῆς εἰς τοὺς ἁγίους, *peri de tēs logeias tēs eis tous hagious*, now concerning the collection for the saints), and it may be that his reference to the offering as a εὐλογία at this point crafts a play on words (Furnish 1984: 428). Of course, εὐλογία has a rich biblical backdrop, referring in part to some significant benefit given by God or people (BDAG 408), and Josh. 15:19 LXX, for instance, uses the term with this sense of a generous gift: "And [Achsa] said to him, 'Give me a

---

64. The ἵνα (*hina*) clause in 9:5, rather than indicating purpose, provides the content of Paul's encouragement: "encourage the brothers to travel on ahead to you" (ἵνα προέλθωσιν εἰς ὑμᾶς, *hina proelthōsin eis hymas*).

blessing, since you have placed me in the land of Nageb; give me Golathmain.'
And Chaleb gave her upper Golathmain and lower Golathmain" (NETS; see
also 2 Kings 5:15 LXX). But what Paul seems most interested in at this point
is to set up a contrast with an attitude that is opposite to one that generously
blesses others. He wants their collection for Jerusalem "to be ready" (ἑτοίμην
εἶναι, *hetoimēn einai*) as a "generous gift" rather than "as an expression of
stinginess."

The term πλεονεξία (*pleonexia*) speaks of "greediness," "wanting more than
one's due," "covetousness," or "avarice." In short it constitutes a self-centered,
stingy attitude that is "ever ready to sacrifice one's neighbor to oneself in all
things" (Plummer 1915: 256, quoting J. B. Lightfoot on Rom. 1:29). According
to Jesus, such self-consumption defiles a person (Mark 7:22) and should be
guarded against vigorously (Luke 12:15). Elsewhere in Paul πλεονεξία turns
up in lists of nasty vices that characterize ungodliness (Rom. 1:29; Eph. 4:19;
5:3; Col. 3:5). Now some understand the word here to speak of "extortion"
on the part of Paul and his team—he wants the offering to be a "generous
gift" on the part of the Corinthians, not funds that Paul and company need
to "extort" from them, forcing them to give up what they want to keep (so in
various forms by NRSV, Moffatt, ESV, HCSB, NET). However, in light of the
clear contrast with "as a generous gift" (ὡς εὐλογίαν, *hōs eulogian*), which
describes an offering of right attitude, ὡς πλεονεξίαν (*hōs pleonexian*) should
be read as a contrasting attitude on the part of the Corinthians (Keener 2005:
212): "as an expression of stinginess." This interpretation also fits very well
with Paul's words that follow in 9:6–11 on the blessings of giving, where he
begins by contrasting sowing "sparingly" and sowing "generously."

Reflection

Paul's words speak with profundity and relevance into contemporary ministry contexts, for where a large amount of money, given for ministry, is in
play, there too lies the possibility of suspicion and public criticism—at times
well deserved. Cicero (*Off.* 2.21.75) wrote, "But the main thing in all public
administration and public service is to avoid even the slightest suspicion of
avarice" (as cited by Martin 1986: 279). Not only in financial situations, but
also in areas such as sexuality, leadership, and communication, forethought
should be given to safeguarding attitudes, postures, and actions that are
noble and morally beautiful before the Lord and before people. The high
level of integrity expressed in Prov. 3:4 and embodied by Paul in the collection for Jerusalem needs to be embraced and lived by Christian ministers
in a wide variety of contemporary contexts. We should ask ourselves with
regard to our handling of resources and our public witness, "Do we act with
such sterling integrity that we allay suspicion of our motives and promote
a positive witness before both a watching world and our God?"

In fact, the theme of integrity permeates this passage, and it is a coin with
two sides. Paul is keen to make sure that his ministry team, and the whole

handling of the gift for Jerusalem, rings with such a clear public integrity that actions and processes match the purported intent and impact of the ministry. Paul has thought carefully about what is noble before the Lord (2:17) and before people, choosing representatives who have a known record of gospel work well done. But the apostle also challenges the Corinthians themselves to respond with integrity. They are to embrace these good ministers (8:23–24), for you can tell a great deal about a church by observing whom they embrace (11:4, 19!). But Paul has sent these brothers to ensure that the Corinthians follow through with their commitments. In other words, he facilitates a response of integrity from the Corinthians. This constitutes wise leadership. Help people succeed. Help them establish patterns of integrity. But this can only be done from an unquestionable posture of integrity. We must establish the pattern of integrity in ourselves and our ministry team before we try to lead others there.

Additional Notes

8:16. The difference in meaning between the aorist participle δόντι (supported by $\mathfrak{P}^{46}$ $\aleph^2$ D F G L 6 323 326 1241 1505 *al* lat sy bo; Ambst) and the present participle διδόντι ($\aleph^*$ B C I^{vid} Ψ 0243 (33) 1739 1881 $\mathfrak{M}$ sa) is negligible if the aorist is understood as either gnomic or epistolary. The aorist form has slightly stronger external attestation. Perhaps a scribe, missing the "epistolary" perspective that Paul seems to embrace in this unit (the immediate context is characterized by the aorist form), adjusted the form to present tense, thinking to make the sense more immediate in context. It seems likely, therefore, that the aorist was the original reading.

8:19. Witnesses are divided as to which preposition, σύν or ἐν, originally preceded the phrase τῇ χάριτι. The former, supported by $\mathfrak{P}^{46}$ $\aleph$ D F G Ψ $\mathfrak{M}$ ar b ρ, is the more difficult reading since τῇ χάριτι is an impersonal object. The more common preposition in such a phrase, ἐν (B C P 0225 0243 6 33 81 104 365 630 1175 1739 1881 2464 *al* f vg co; Ambst), has already been used with the same phrase (though in slightly different configuration) at 8:7. Thus, as the more difficult reading, σύν seems the more likely candidate (Harris 2005: 597; Thrall 2000: 549).

8:19. The reading αὐτοῦ ($\aleph$ D^1 Ψ 1881* $\mathfrak{M}$ sy [$\mathfrak{P}^{46}$ 33: h.t.]) is uncertain and was considered "least unsatisfactory" by the editorial committee of the UBS text (Metzger 1994: 513). The witnesses omitting the word (B C D* F G L 81 104 326 365 629 1175 2464 *al* lat co; Ambst) are a bit stronger, but this is the easier reading and thus suspect. A third variant, αὐτήν, has the weakest external evidence (P 0243 630 1739 1881^c *pc* vg^{ms}) and is an obvious conformation to the article τήν. Harris (2005: 597) points to Barrett's suggestion (1973: 217) that the apostle first wrote αὐτοῦ, and then, wishing to avoid ambiguity, added τοῦ κυρίου.

8:24. The witnesses are fairly balanced between the participle ἐνδεικνύμενοι (B D* F G 33 *pc* b ρ vg^{ms}) and the imperative form ἐνδείξασθε ($\aleph$ C D^2 Ψ 0225 0243 1739 1881 $\mathfrak{M}$ lat). However, the use of the participle form in place of the imperative is a commonly recognized Semitic idiom, and it is difficult to imagine why a scribe would alter the imperative of a finite verb to read as a participle. The reverse, on the other hand, is readily understandable.

9:1. $\mathfrak{P}^{46}$ and g have the comparative περισσότερον rather than περισσόν, but this probably constitutes an assimilation to the comparative form found in the Corinthian correspondence to this point (see 1 Cor. 12:23–24; 2 Cor. 2:7). It is clearly a scribal correction.

9:2. Two text-critical matters are in play with the phrase τὸ ὑμῶν ζῆλος. The first involves the variant ἐξ that occurs before ὑμῶν in D F G Ψ 0209 𝔐 vg^ms sy^h. Manuscripts 𝔓^46 ℵ B C P 0243 6 33 81 326 630 1175 1739 1881 *pc* lat sy^p co; Ambst have ὑμῶν alone. Since in context Paul is talking about both the Macedonians and those from Achaia, a scribe probably added the preposition to reduce ambiguity about whose zeal was in mind, the ἐξ making it clear that the zeal of the Corinthians has stirred up the Macedonians.

Second, some manuscripts read the gender of ζῆλος as neuter (𝔓^46 ℵ B 33 1175 *pc*), others as masculine (C D F G Ψ 0243 1739 1881 𝔐). Classical Greek always has the word as masculine, but Hellenistic Greek had either masculine or neuter (Harris 2005: 616); the masculine is also the most common form in Paul, though Phil. 3:6 has the neuter, and questions can be raised due to ambiguity at a number of points (e.g., Rom. 13:13; 2 Cor. 11:2; see Thrall 2000: 566). Yet the neuter has the stronger external evidence and is probably original; a scribe likely adjusted it to the more common masculine form.

9:4. The reading ταύτῃ (𝔓^46 ℵ* B C D* F G 048 0243 33 81 629 1739 1881 2464 latt co) is preferred since the addition of τῆς καυχήσεως (ℵ² D² K L P [Ψ] 0209 104 365 630 1175 1241 1505 𝔐 sy^(p)) has weaker external attestation and almost certainly is a scribal clarification offered under the influence of a similar phrase at 11:17 (so Harris 2005: 617).

9:4. The majority of the editorial committee of the UBS text preferred the reading λέγω (𝔓^46 C* D F G 048 ar ρ vg^mss sa^ms; Ambst) to λέγωμεν (ℵ B C² Ψ 0209 0243 33 1739 1881 𝔐 f vg sy sa^mss bo) due to the predominance of the first-person singular in the immediate context (vv. 1, 2, 3, 5). They read the first-person plural as a scribal assimilation to καταισχυνθῶμεν ἡμεῖς (Metzger 1994: 514).

▸ The Ministry of Giving (8:1–9:15)
  A. Paul's Exhortation to Finish the Collection (8:1–15)
  B. Titus's Mission (8:16–9:5)
  C. Reflections on Resources for Giving and the Results (9:6–15)

C. Reflections on Resources for Giving and the Results (9:6–15)

As the apostle moves toward wrapping up his extended exhortation on giving, he lays before the Corinthians certain principles—giving should be generous and cheerful, for instance—and his focus rests especially on God, whose elaborate resources lie behind the believer's ability to give extravagantly, meeting the needs of brothers and sisters in Christ. God gives to givers so they might keep on giving in a way that will give glory and thanks to God, as well as prompt a greater solidarity between those who give and those who receive their gifts. The section can be analyzed as follows:

1. Give generously and cheerfully (9:6–7)
2. God blesses generous givers (9:8–11)
3. Giving evokes responses to God (9:12–15)

Garland (1999: 400) has pointed out an extensive inclusio bracketing the beginning and end of 8:1–9:15. To his list of five elements we add four others:[1]

τὴν χάριν τοῦ θεοῦ, *tēn charin tou theou* (8:1; 9:14)
δίδωμι/δωρεά, *didōmi/dōrea* (8:1; 9:15)
δοκιμή, *dokimē* (8:2; 9:13)
ἡ περισσεία/περισσεύω, *perisseia/perisseuō* (8:2; 9:12)
ἁπλότης, *haplotēs* (8:2; 9:11, 13)
κοινωνία, *koinōnia* (8:4; 9:13)
διακονία, *diakonia* (8:4; 9:12–13)
δέησις/δέομαι, *deēsis/deomai* (8:4; 9:14)
ἅγιος, *hagios* (8:4; 9:12)

As noted in the introduction, these extensive parallels provide further evidence of the literary unity of 2 Cor. 8–9.

Exegesis and Exposition

⁶Now, think about this. The person who sows sparingly will also reap sparingly, and the one who sows generously will also reap generously. ⁷Each person should give the amount he has resolved in his heart to give—not motivated by sad feelings or

---

1. In his list Garland does not include the following (with two parallels based on cognate relationships): δίδωμι/δωρεά, *didōmi/dōrea* (8:1; 9:15); δέησις/δέομαι, *deēsis/deomai* (8:4; 9:14); ἅγιος, *hagios* (8:4; 9:12); κοινωνία, *koinōnia* (8:4; 9:13). See the section ETs.

pressure!—because God loves the cheerful giver. ⁸And God ⌐has the ability⌐ to lavish you with all kinds of grace, in order that always having everything you need in every situation you may have plenty of resources for every good work. ⁹As it stands written,

> He distributed.
> He gave to the poor.
> His righteousness remains forever.

¹⁰Now the One who provides the sower with ⌐seed⌐ and bread to eat ⌐will supply⌐ and ⌐greatly multiply⌐ your seed and ⌐will increase⌐ the harvest of your righteousness. ¹¹You will be enriched in every way, resulting in every kind of generosity, which through us is producing thanksgiving to God; ¹²for the ministry fulfilling this service not only is meeting the needs of God's people but also is having a broader effect through many thanks being offered up to God. ¹³Because of this ministry's proven character, they will glorify God in response to the obedience flowing from your confession of the gospel of Christ and the generous way you have shared with them and everyone else. ¹⁴And they will feel deep affection for you as they pray on your behalf, because God's extraordinary grace rests on you. ¹⁵Thanks be to God for his indescribable gift!

1. Give Generously and Cheerfully (9:6–7)

9:6–7 Paul concludes his explanation on why he was sending the team of Titus and the two brothers on ahead of him (9:1–5) by implicitly encouraging the Corinthians to give in a "blessed" way, rather than with an attitude of abject stinginess (9:5). In 9:6–15 he now reinforces that implicit exhortation to generosity by providing both the theological basis (God as a giving God of grace) and purpose (for God's glory) of the collection for God's people (Hafemann 2000: 366). The apostle begins by offering a highly crafted principle: "Now, think about this. The person who sows sparingly will also reap sparingly, and the one who sows generously will also reap generously." The complex, beautifully balanced structure of the passage may be depicted as follows:[2]

Τοῦτο δέ (*Touto de*, Now [think about] this).	
ὁ σπείρων (*ho speirōn*, The person who sows)	A
φειδομένως (*pheidomenōs*, sparingly)	B
φειδομένως (*pheidomenōs*, sparingly)	B′
καὶ θερίσει (*kai therisei*, will also reap),	C
καὶ (*kai*, and)	
ὁ σπείρων (*ho speirōn*, the one who sows)	A′
ἐπ' εὐλογίαις (*ep' eulogiais*, generously)	D
ἐπ' εὐλογίαις (*ep' eulogiais*, generously)	D′
καὶ θερίσει (*kai therisei*, will also reap).	C′

2. This roughly follows the lead of Barnett 1997: 436. The rhetorical pattern is called *symploche* or *koinotēs* (same word repeated, sharing in common; Keener 2005: 213).

The Τοῦτο δέ (*touto de*, Now this) with which the passage begins is transitional, assuming what has just been said and anticipating what the apostle says next. It is also elliptical, and the ellipsis probably has in mind an understood verb akin to φημί (*phēmi*, I say; Thrall 2000: 573; so KJV, NASB). Paul uses τοῦτο δέ φημι twice in 1 Corinthians (7:29; 15:50), and on both occasions, as here, he is introducing an important principle or teaching. Τοῦτο δέ, therefore, seems crafted for the purpose of focusing the readers'/hearers' attention;[3] the apostle wants them to pay close attention to what he is about to say—"Now think about this"—a fitting opening for a beautifully stated axiom.[4]

This proverbial statement on reaping what one sows comes from a common stock of OT and Jewish Wisdom literature (Prov. 22:8; Hosea 8:7; Job 4:8; Sir. 7:3; Philo, *Conf.* 21, 152; *Dreams* 2.76; Scott 1998: 186). Gentiles also used images of "sowing and reaping" to describe benefaction and reciprocity (e.g., Aristotle, *Rhet.* 3.3.4; Cicero, *De or.* 2.65.261; Keener 2005: 213; Thrall 2000: 575). The thought divides evenly into two chiastic movements, and at the heart of the twin chiastic structures lies the contrast: a sowing and reaping described as "sparingly" versus a sowing and reaping done "generously." The term φειδομένως (*pheidomenōs*), used only here in the biblical literature, has a cognate verb, φείδομαι (*pheidomai*), which means "to refrain," or "to spare," that is, "to save from loss of some kind" (BDAG 1051). Our word is adverbial, describing the manner in which the sowing and harvesting are carried out: "sparingly," or using "little" seed (so Tyndale), a sowing that is "tightfisted." If little seed is sown, a small harvest will result.[5] Ambrosiaster (*Comm. Paul's Ep.*, 2 Cor. 9:6) notes, "Paul is referring to misers when he talks about people who sow sparingly. He says this here because the Corinthians had promised to send something and had subsequently backtracked" (Bray 1999: 279).

The contrasting phrase, ἐπ' εὐλογίαις (*ep' eulogiais*), picks up on the reference to the "generous gift" (εὐλογίαν) mentioned twice in verse 5. The preposition plus the dative plural probably carries the sense of "upon the basis of blessings" (i.e., "liberally," "generously") or out of a heart's desire to bless others. Here is a sowing that is generous, openhanded, which will lead to a lavish, ungrudging harvest. God blesses the blesser. The point rests not on the *amount* one gives but on the manner and heart attitude (Hafemann 2000: 366).

Paul makes the point by painting a clear agricultural word picture. The agrarian economy of the biblical world offered rich imagery taken up by the biblical

3. Thus Τοῦτο δέ, or perhaps with the same intended effect as κατανοήσατε (*katanoēsate*, consider; second-person plural aorist imperative from κατανοέω, *katanoeō*) in Heb. 3:1.
4. Most English versions opt similarly for "The point is this" (ESV, NRSV, NET) or "Remember this" (HCSB, NLT[2], NIV). Barrett (1973: 235) comments, "Paul is about to set forth a proposition which he is sure will be accepted by his readers and should determine their attitude."
5. Garland (1999: 405) explains,

> No farmer considers sowing as a loss of seed because the harvest will provide the seed for the next season. Consequently, no sower begrudges the seed he casts upon the ground or tries to scrimp by with sowing as little as possible. He willingly sows all that he can and trusts that God will bless the sowing with a bountiful harvest. If the farmer, for some reason, stints on the sowing, he will cheat himself of that harvest. The more he sows, the greater the harvest he will reap and the more he will have for sowing for the next harvest.

authors, who at points use the image of "sowing" to depict engaging in specific kinds of activities, whether righteous and loving (e.g., Prov. 11:18; Eccles. 11:1; Hosea 10:12) or evil (Job 4:8; Prov. 6:14, 19; 16:28; 22:8). The "sowing" metaphor is often tied to "harvesting," the point being that particular actions have proportionate or at least related consequences (DBI 809).[6] Through this word picture of sowing and harvesting, applied to financial giving in the church, Paul wants the Corinthians to grasp an important principle. Those who give grudgingly and little will receive a tightfisted return. By contrast, generous, openhanded giving leads to lavish blessings in return. Of course those blessings come from God, for God as the ultimate giver is at the very heart of Paul's thought here. The passage is quite theocentric (Matera 2003: 208), and this is made overt in the next verse.

With verse 7 the apostle now makes the application very specific, extending the thoughts just presented in proverbial form by writing of the manner and motive of appropriate giving: "Each person should give the amount he has resolved in his heart to give—not motivated by sad feelings or pressure!—because God loves the cheerful giver."

ἕκαστος [διδότω] (hekastos [didotō], Each person should give)
καθὼς προῄρηται τῇ καρδίᾳ (kathos proērētai tē kardia, the
    amount he has resolved in his heart),
μὴ ἐκ λύπης ἢ (mē ek lypēs ē, not motivated by sad feelings or)
ἐξ ἀνάγκης· (ex anankēs, pressure);

ἱλαρὸν γὰρ δότην ἀγαπᾷ ὁ θεός (hilaron gar dotēn agapa ho theos,
    for God loves a cheerful giver).

With verse 7 we are confronted with yet another ellipsis, but given the context it is clear that the apostle speaks about giving. Thus we can supply the sense of διδότω (didotō, present active imperative of δίδωμι), "let each one give." Notice that Paul places an emphasis on "each" (ἕκαστος, hekastos) member of the community giving (Stegman 2009: 212). This is not just a ministry for the well-to-do! Further, the manner of giving is to be according to "the amount he has resolved in his heart to give" (καθὼς προῄρηται τῇ καρδίᾳ, kathōs proērētai tē kardia). The adverb καθώς can indicate comparison or accordance ("just as he has resolved"), and most translations appropriately opt for this sense (e.g., ESV, HCSB, Tyndale, NIV, NRSV). But with a slightly different nuance, the adverb also can mark the extent or degree to which something is done (BDAG 493), which seems fitting here (cf. Acts 11:29);[7] thus "as much as

6. At Gal. 6:8–9, e.g., the apostle contrasts sowing "to the flesh" with sowing "to the Spirit," each of which lead to a certain kind of harvest. There are cases, however, where the image is used differently. At points "one sows and another reaps" (see Job 31:8; Mic. 6:15; cf. John 4:37), showing that the results of sowing might not be experienced personally or immediately; or "those who sow in tears reap in joy" (see Ps. 126:5; Prov. 22:8), suggesting a paradox of the spiritual life—pain sometimes is followed by joy.

7. "So the believers in Antioch decided to send relief to the brothers and sisters in Judea, everyone giving as much as they could [καθὼς εὐπορεῖτό τις, kathōs euporeito tis]" (Acts 11:29 NLT²).

he has decided" (Harris 2005: 631), that is, "the amount he has resolved in his heart to give." The verb προαιρέω (*proaireō*),[8] here in perfect middle indicative form, means to "choose for oneself," "determine," "make up one's mind," or "commit oneself to," so "to resolve." The phrase τῇ καρδίᾳ (*tē kardia*), "in the heart," indicates that Paul has in mind each member of the congregation processing privately how much they should give, perhaps under the guidance of the Spirit (3:3).[9] In other words, the amount one gives is not to be a public decision, nor is it to be publicly flaunted (Belleville 1996: 237), but it should be a matter of private conviction.

This conviction of the heart stands in contrast to two motivations: "not motivated by sad feelings or pressure!" (μὴ ἐκ λύπης ἢ ἐξ ἀνάγκης, *mē ek lypēs ē ex anankēs*). In both cases the preposition ἐκ indicates especially that we are dealing with an unacceptable *motive* (BDAG 296.3) for giving that must not (μή) be embraced. Paul has already used the term λύπη five times in the book to speak of "grief" or "sorrow," a painful state of mind (2:1, 3, 7; 7:10 [2x]). It has to do with being sad or distressed and was used in ancient literature as the opposite of happiness, joy, or elation (Spicq 1994: 2.417–22). In short, in making up their minds about what to give to the collection, he does not want the Corinthians to be motivated by grief or made to feel bad. Neither does he want them to be driven by "pressure" (ἀνάγκη, *anankē*), another word speaking of distress, but now the distress is from being constrained, forced to do something. The term often speaks of necessity or compulsion (e.g., Matt. 18:7; Luke 14:18; 21:23; Rom. 13:5; 1 Cor. 7:26, 37; 9:16). So the apostle does not want the Corinthians' giving driven by externally imposed, negative emotions, and he perhaps echoes the sentiments of Deut. 15:10 (so Hafemann 2000: 366), a passage on giving to others among the people of God during the "Sabbath year of remission": "Giving you shall give to him, and you shall lend him a loan whatever he needs, and you shall not be grieved in your heart when you give to him, because through this thing the Lord your God will bless you in all your works and in all to which you may put your hand" (NETS).

Why are bad feelings and pressure inappropriate motives for giving?: "because [γάρ] God loves the cheerful giver" (ἱλαρὸν γὰρ δότην ἀγαπᾷ ὁ θεός, *hilaron gar dotēn agapa ho theos*). The key term—emphasized by its pride of place in the sentence—is the word ἱλαρόν, which means "cheerful."[10] The apostle paraphrases part of Prov. 22:8 LXX, which, as does our current context in 2 Corinthians, speaks of "sowing" and "reaping."

8. Only here in the NT does προαιρέω appear, but it occurs fourteen times in the LXX: Gen. 34:8; Deut. 7:6–7; 10:15; Jdt. 13:15; 2 Macc. 6:9; 3 Macc. 2:30; 6:10; 7:2; Prov. 1:29; 21:25; Wis. 7:10; 9:7; Isa. 7:15. In a number of places it has to do with God's election of his people (e.g., Deut. 7:6–7; 10:15), but in other places has to do with the choices a person makes (2 Macc. 6:9; 3 Macc. 2:30; 6:10; 7:2; Prov. 1:29; 21:25; Isa. 7:15).

9. Paul uses the image of "the heart" in 2 Corinthians to speak of the internal life (2 Cor. 1:22; 2:4; 3:2–3, 15; 4:6; 5:12; 6:11; 7:3; 8:16; 9:7).

10. Used only here in the NT, the term finds expression six times in the LXX: Add. Esth. 15:5; 3 Macc. 6:35; Prov. 19:12; 22:8; Sir. 13:26; 26:4.

> He who sows what is cheap will reap what is bad
> and will complete the impact of his deeds.
> God blesses a cheerful and generous man. (Prov. 22:8 NETS)

The wording of the last statement has been adjusted by the apostle.

> ἄνδρα ἱλαρὸν καὶ δότην εὐλογεῖ ὁ θεός. (Prov. 22:8b LXX)
> *andra hilaron kai dotēn eulogei ho theos.*
> God blesses a cheerful man and a giver.

> ἱλαρὸν γὰρ δότην ἀγαπᾷ ὁ θεός. (2 Cor. 9:7b)
> *hilaron gar dotēn agapa ho theos.*
> God loves a cheerful giver.

The "blesses" (εὐλογεῖ) of Prov. 22:8 has been changed to "loves" (ἀγαπᾷ) as God's active response to the cheerful giver.[11] The proverb speaks of a "cheerful man" (ἄνδρα ἱλαρόν) who is also a "giver" (δότην), while Paul simply shortens the description to a "cheerful giver" (ἱλαρὸν . . . δότην). Paul's intent could not be more clear. God loves the person who gives cheerfully, and this should motivate the Corinthians to examine their motives for giving. It is not that God loves *only* the cheerful giver: this is not a warning. Rather, these are words of encouragement to those who give liberally (Thrall 2000: 577). Rather than being pressured to give, or being spurred on by being made to feel bad, they should be motivated to give cheerfully by this affirmation of God's response of love. In his *Sermon 71 on Fasting and Almsgiving*, Maximus of Turin offers a fitting reflection on the contrast between Christian giving and a "giving" that is forced:

> Joyful, therefore, and cheerful is the one who attends to the poor. Quite clearly he is joyful, because for a few small coins he acquires heavenly treasures for himself; on the contrary, the person who pays taxes is always sad and dejected. Rightly is he sad who is not drawn to payment by love but forced by fear. Christ's debtor, then, is joyful, and Caesar's sad, because love urges the one to payment, and punishment constrains the other; the one is invited by rewards, the other compelled by penalties. (Bray 1999: 280)

2. God Blesses Generous Givers (9:8–11)

9:8–9 In verses 6 and 7 the apostle has laid down basic principles for giving, especially emphasizing that giving should be generous and cheerful. Now he elaborates on the idea that generous "sowing" leads to a generous "harvest"; much of what follows in verses 8–11 reinforces the biblical truth that God richly blesses those who give elaborately. Accordingly, with verse 8 we come to one of the richest statements in all of Scripture on God's abundant provision for a generous people.

11. This is perhaps under the influence of Prov. 22:11 LXX, which says that "the Lord loves pure hearts" (ἀγαπᾷ κύριος ὁσίας καρδίας, *agapa kyrios hosias kardias*).

At least two stylistic features of this verse are striking. First, Paul crafts the statement by using alliteration, built on words beginning with π: πᾶσαν, περισσεῦσαι, παντί, πάντοτε, πᾶσαν, περισσεύητε, πᾶν (*pasan, perisseusai, panti, pantote, pasan perisseuēte, pan*). As you can see, especially prominent are forms of the word πᾶς (*pas*, all). Second, the verse consists of a main clause celebrating God's ability to lavish the giver with grace ("And God has the ability to lavish you with all kinds of grace") and a purpose clause focusing on the resulting abundance in the life of the giver ("in order that always having everything you need in every situation you may have plenty of resources for every good work").[12] Yet, the words in these two clauses have been arranged beautifully and, following the opening declaration of God's ability, somewhat chiastically to highlight certain concepts.

> δυνατεῖ δὲ ὁ θεὸς (*dynatei de ho theos*)
> A πᾶσαν χάριν (*pasan charin*)
>   B περισσεῦσαι εἰς ὑμᾶς (*perisseusai eis hymas*),
>   C ἵνα ἐν παντὶ (*hina . . . en panti*)
>   D πάντοτε (*pantote*)
>   C′ πᾶσαν αὐτάρκειαν ἔχοντες (*pasan autarkeian echontes*)
>   B′ περισσεύητε εἰς (*perisseuēte eis*)
> A′ πᾶν ἔργον ἀγαθόν (*pan ergon agathon*)

> And God has the ability
> A with all kinds of grace
>   B to lavish you,
>   C in order that in every situation
>   D always
>   C′ having everything you need
>   B′ you may have plenty of resources for
> A′ every good work.

Paul grounds the passage in a confession about God's ability; the verb δυνατέω (*dynateō*) means "to display capability, be effective, be able" (BDAG 264). One of the great threads through Scripture has to do with God's capability to act on behalf of his people, providing for their needs through displays of his

---

12. Here is 2 Cor. 9:8 from UBS[4]:
> δὲ
> ὁ θεὸς δυνατεῖ . . .περισσεῦσαι > πᾶσαν χάριν
>   εἰς ὑμᾶς,
>   ἵνα . . .   ἔχοντες > πᾶσαν > αὐτάρκειαν
>   ἐν παντὶ
>   πάντοτε
>   . . . περισσεύητε
>   εἰς πᾶν ἔργον ἀγαθόν

power.[13] Indeed, the story of redemption serves as one grand story of God's provision for his people. More specifically, God provides the daily resources needed by those who follow his ways in giving to others.

The apostle builds the framework for this celebration of God's ability on the double use of the verb περισσεύω (perisseuō),[14] which he has employed previously at 1:5; 3:9; 4:15; 8:2, 7. As we have noted elsewhere in the commentary, the word has to do with something being "present in superabundance," "being extremely rich," "being left over," "abounding." When the verb is used transitively, as in the first of the two occurrences in 9:8, it means "to cause something to exist in abundance" or "to make extremely rich" (BDAG 805; EDNT 3:76–77). So the aorist infinitive with πᾶσαν χάριν as the object means "to cause all grace to be abundant to you," or "to lavish you with all kinds of grace." The second use of the word serves as the main verb of the purpose clause: "in order that . . . you might abound," or "might have plenty of resources." The phrase εἰς πᾶν ἔργον ἀγαθόν (eis pan ergon agathon) tells the "advantage" gained by such resources: believers use God's blessings "for every good work." So the framework for Paul's confession of God's ability in 2 Cor. 9:8 is "God has the ability to lavish you with all kinds of grace . . . so that you may have plenty of resources for every good work." At the heart of God's blessings, therefore, stands a purpose for those blessings. Rather than lavishing believers with expansive expressions of grace so that they might glut themselves on God's gifts, the resources are to be used "for every good work."

Once this framework is identified, three other elements in the middle of the verse stand out as elaborating on the main verb in the purpose clause (περισσεύητε, you may have plenty of resources): ἐν παντὶ πάντοτε πᾶσαν αὐτάρκειαν ἔχοντες (en panti pantote pasan autarkeian echontes, in every situation, always, having everything you need). These three phrases speak to the circumstances, time frame, and extent of God's provision. The first phrase, ἐν παντί, is rather ambiguous and can simply be translated as "in all things" (ESV, NIV) or "in everything" (NASB), but it may be understood as referring to varied circumstances of life, thus "in every situation." In other words, the encouragement here declares that God's resources are not subject to the ebbs and flows of life. Whatever comes, God has the ability to provide abundantly.

Second, πάντοτε (always) sets the time frame for God's provision as unlimited. Provision is always available to God's people. Third, the participle clause πᾶσαν αὐτάρκειαν ἔχοντες (having everything you need) tells the extent of God's provision. Although the term αὐτάρκεια (autarkeia) can refer to a state of contentment[15] attained by a degree of self-sufficiency (1 Tim. 6:6),

---

13. E.g., Exod. 15:3, 6–8, 10–12; Num. 11:23; 23:20; Deut. 3:24; 7:21; 11:2; 32:39; Josh. 4:24; 1 Sam. 2:6–8, 10; 14:6; 2 Sam. 22:13, 16; 1 Chron. 29:11–12; 2 Chron. 14:11; 16:9; 20:6; 25:8–9; Ezra 8:22; Neh. 1:10.

14. Notice that in both cases, forms of the verb are followed by εἰς (eis, with, for).

15. The apostle uses the cognate noun αὐτάρκης (autarkēs) at Phil. 4:11 to speak of contentment: "I am not saying this because I am in need, for I have learned to be content in any circumstance" (NET).

here it speaks of having what is entirely adequate (BDAG 152). Two points should be made in relation to this term, however. First, the context makes clear that Paul's focus is on a "God-sufficiency" rather than self-dependent "self-sufficiency." The Stoics and Cynics of Paul's day pointed to self-sufficiency as a high virtue, a way of showing moral superiority; the ideal was being self-sufficient so as to avoid dependence on others. But this is opposite to what Paul has in mind. His point is that God's person is dependent on God's resources for God's ministry to others. Thus for the apostle, God's abilities and God's glory are at the heart of the sufficiency he has in mind (Hafemann 2000: 368; Witherington 1995: 427).

Second, the apostle has in mind a form of sufficiency that is not self-centered and consumerist but rather elaborate in giving to others (Harris 2005: 638). Again, the giver will have "plenty of resources," not for an elaborate lifestyle but "for every good work."

In verse 9 the apostle reinforces this final thought about the generosity of God's giver with an OT quotation taken from Ps. 112:9a (111:9a LXX): "As it stands written, 'He distributed. He gave to the poor. His righteousness remains forever.'"[16] As with the quotation at 8:15, Paul uses a standard introductory formula, καθὼς γέγραπται (kathōs gegraptai), "As it stands written." Psalm 112, originally an extended acrostic poem in Hebrew, sings of the "blessed" man[17] who lives out a reverent fear of God (v. 1). Of this man we read, "Glory and riches are in his house" (v. 3 NETS), but his riches are used in accordance with his "righteousness," for he is a person of mercy and compassion (vv. 4–5). Not afraid of evil circumstances, he puts his hope in the Lord (vv. 7–8). This righteous person stands in sharp contrast to the "sinner," whose "desire will come to nothing" (v. 10 NETS). Paul's quotation comes just before this final contrast and consists of three affirmations about the blessed man. First, "he distributed" (ἐσκόρπισεν, eskorpisen), an aorist active indicative from σκορπίζω (skorpizō), which means variously "to scatter" or "disperse," or "to distribute." In a negative sense it could be used of scattering in a destructive manner (e.g., Matt. 12:30; John 10:12), but here, read in light of the context and especially the reference to giving that immediately follows, the connotations are positive, referring to distribution. This certainly seems to be the way Paul, who has trumpeted "sowing generously" in verse 6, understands the passage. In fact, some interpret σκορπίζω and the second affirmation, ἔδωκεν (edōken, he gave), which immediately follows, as a hendiadys, the expression of a single idea by using two verbs (or nouns). For instance, the NIV renders the passage, "He has scattered abroad his gifts to the poor." Since the beginning of chapter 8, such a distribution, giving to the poor, is exactly what the apostle has been vying for, exhorting the Corin-

16. The final part of the verse, "His horn will be exalted in glory" (Ps. 111:9b NETS [112:9b ET]), is not quoted by Paul.

17. Some interpreters (e.g., Barnett 1997: 440) understand Paul to use the psalm with reference to God. However, the place of the quotation, both in its original and its applied contexts, argues against this.

thians to engage fully in the collection for God's people in Jerusalem. Such giving certainly can be celebrated as an expression of "righteousness" (ἡ δικαιοσύνη, hē dikaiosynē; cf. Matt. 6:1–4), which will "last forever" (μένει εἰς τὸν αἰῶνα, menei eis ton aiōna). This is the kind of life that endures—the person has a lasting character—and constitutes the third affirmation about God's generous giver (Belleville 1996: 238–39).[18]

9:10 With verses 10–11—and combining what has been said in verses 6–9 concerning "sowing" and God's abundant provision—Paul now comes to a climactic statement about the magnanimous ways God blesses those who give generously. Verse 10 reads, "Now the One who provides the sower with seed and bread to eat will supply and greatly multiply your seed and will increase the harvest of your righteousness." This confession picks up the key images from the proverbial principle about the laws of sowing and harvesting stated in verse 6. Yet here in verse 10 the apostle moves back a step in the process of sowing and reaping, answering the question, "If one is to sow elaborately, from where does the supply of seed come, and who stands behind these dynamics of sowing and harvesting?" His answer is both theocentric (Matera 2003: 207) and biblically grounded.

God surely stands behind and above the whole process of sowing and reaping and thus, as just noted in verse 8, is the ultimate source of giving, for no one would have anything to give apart from him. He provides the seed for the sower to sow and thus bread to eat (cf. Matt. 6:11). The words in verse 10 almost certainly are an overt allusion to Isa. 55:10b LXX, which in the NETS reads, "and [rain or snow has] given seed to the sower and bread for food" (καὶ δῷ σπέρμα τῷ σπείροντι καὶ ἄρτον εἰς βρῶσιν, kai dō sperma tō speironti kai arton eis brōsin).[19] In context, the prophetic word presents the inevitable productivity of the Word of God, drawing an analogy with rain and snow that falls from heaven. Just as rain and snow bridge the gap between heaven and earth, saturating the earth, causing plants to spring up and blossom, providing seed for sowing and bread for food, so also God's Word bridges the gap between heaven and earth, revealing God's ways and thoughts and accomplishing his will. The apostle's allusion to the passage in the prophet seizes specifically on God as the source, the provider. Thus Paul begins quite literally (as does the passage in Isaiah) with God as the ultimate author of agriculture, "the One who provides the sower with seeds." The verb ἐπιχορηγέω (epichorēgeō), found in four other places in the NT (Gal. 3:5; Col. 2:19; 2 Pet. 1:5, 11; only at Sir. 25:22 in the LXX), could be used variously with the sense "to give," "grant," "supply," or "support." In the broader Greco-Roman world, the word and its

---

18. Some understand the passage to refer to the righteousness of God or of right standing before God, rather than moral uprightness (Furnish 1984: 448–49; Harris 2005: 640–41).

19. There are differences between the Greek version of the Isaiah passage and Paul's appropriation of the latter part of Isa. 55:10. In Isaiah the rain and snow are the "actors" that "give" (aorist subjunctive of δίδωμι [didōmi] rather than Paul's use of ἐπιχορηγέω [epichorēgeō, provide]) the seed, and Isaiah uses the word σπέρμα (sperma, seed) rather than Paul's σπόρον (sporon, seed).

cognates seem to have been associated with generous public service (BDAG 386–87). Even so, God is a provider by nature.

Paul now moves from the general agricultural principle to the specific application, in which the "seed" has taken on a figurative meaning: "will supply and greatly multiply your seed." The analogy is clear. The same God "who provides the sower with seed . . . will supply" (χορηγήσει, *chorēgēsei*, found also at 1 Pet. 4:11)[20] the Corinthians with "seed," that is, the resources needed to give elaborately in ministering to the poor in Jerusalem. Yet God will do more than just supply the bare essentials needed for this ministry. He will "greatly multiply" (πληθυνεῖ, *plēthynei*) their resources, just as a farmer, who starts with a limited number of seeds, can with a healthy crop significantly multiply his seeds for the next planting.

Moreover, the apostle adds a parallel statement, expounding on the blessings of giving, proclaiming that God "will increase the harvest of your righteousness" (αὐξήσει τὰ γενήματα τῆς δικαιοσύνης ὑμῶν, *auxēsei ta genēmata tēs dikaiosynēs hymōn*). The increase of the harvest continues the analogy with the agricultural principle, but now Paul alludes to another OT passage that uses the twin images of "sowing" and "harvesting," Hosea 10:12:[21]

> Sow for yourselves unto justice;
>> reap unto the fruit of life;
> enlighten yourselves with the light of knowledge.
>> Seek the Lord until the produce of justice comes to you. (NETS)

Again, there exists a slight difference in the wording between the LXX and Paul's adaptation:

Hosea 10:12 LXX	2 Cor. 9:10
γενήματα δικαιοσύνης ὑμῖν	τὰ γενήματα τῆς δικαιοσύνης ὑμῶν
genēmata dikaiosynēs hymin	*ta genēmata tēs dikaiosynēs hymōn*
a harvest of righteousness [comes] to you	the harvest of your righteousness

The apostle adds articles in front of γενήματα and δικαιοσύνης, which does not change the meaning of these terms; and the personal pronoun, which functions as an indirect object in Hosea, is expressed as further defining "righteousness" in Paul.

But what does he mean by "the harvest of your righteousness"? Several possible interpretations exist. If understood as a "genitive of production," it would mean "the righteousness produced by you," or the expression of a moral way of living rightly for God. If we are correct to take the allusion to

20. A difference between the complex version of the word and the simplex used here is not discerned.
21. It may be that the Isaiah passage and this verse from Hosea were brought together by Paul (or some earlier interpreter) on the basis of "verbal analogy," both passages referring to "sowing" and calling for the reader to "seek" the Lord/God (Isa. 55:6).

Ps. 112:9a (111:9a LXX) in the previous verse as referring to the righteous giver, this comports well with understanding "your righteousness" as the righteous living of the Corinthians. Or might it be better to read the phrase as a "genitive of possession," a righteousness that the Corinthians have, which constitutes a right standing with God and has been bestowed by him in response to the giver's generosity? After all, in the Hosea (10:12) passage, the "harvest of righteousness" (γενήματα δικαιοσύνης, *genēmata dikaiosynēs*) *comes to* persons who have sown righteousness (ὑμῖν, to you). Or is it a combination of the result of righteous acts and a bestowed righteousness, as suggested by Barnett (1997: 442)? From the context, this may be the best way of reading the phrase, since multifaceted results of the Corinthians' giving have been the focus of Paul's thoughts from verse 6 onward, and this focus continues in the following verse.

9:11   Paul concludes his treatment of the blessings of giving with verse 11: "You will be enriched in every way, resulting in every kind of generosity, which through us is producing thanksgiving to God." Three happy results are expressed. First, the Corinthians "will be enriched in every way." Although the Greek verb, here presented as a present participle (πλουτιζόμενοι, *ploutizomenoi*), could refer to making a person materially wealthy (Gen. 14:23; Sir. 11:21; Josephus, *Ant.* 17.147), Paul probably has in mind material resources that will lead to spiritual enrichment. The phrase "in every way" (ἐν παντί, *en panti*) may mean that he has both kinds of riches in mind, and the two are interrelated. Similarly, the sense of the verb seems to have both material and spiritual connotations at 2 Cor. 6:10, where the apostle says his poverty (i.e., lack of material resources) has enriched many (i.e., provided them with spiritual resources). At 1 Cor. 1:5, however, the wording provides an especially apt parallel to our passage under consideration: "that by Him you were enriched in everything—in all speech and all knowledge" (HCSB). As with 2 Cor. 9:11, the phrase ἐν παντί in 1 Cor. 1:5 precedes a form of πλουτίζω (*ploutizō*) and refers to spiritual riches. In 2 Cor. 9:11, however, a specific purpose is expressed, which makes clear that both material and spiritual resources are in view: εἰς πᾶσαν ἁπλότητα (*eis pasan haplotēta*, for all generosity). Again, the blessing of the Corinthians financially by God is so that they might be a blessing to others. As noted in the comments at 8:2, the term ἁπλότης (*haplotēs*) normally speaks of a single-hearted, rigorous integrity or frankness, a "singleness of mind and heart" in their commitment to God's program (Stegman 2009: 217), and God's program has to do with giving to poor brothers and sisters in need.

Finally, Paul further defines their generosity with the clause "which through us is producing thanksgiving to God." That their giving is "through" Paul and his mission (δι' ἡμῶν, *di' hēmōn*) refers to Paul's role in the collection, since he functions as an intermediary administering the giving done by the churches. The giving, moreover, is producing "thanksgiving to God" as those in need receive God's provision through the churches, and this statement is made in confidence, as if the collection is already an accomplished fact (Furnish 1984:

450). The thanksgiving brought about by the collection is elaborated as the apostle continues.

3. Giving Evokes Responses to God (9:12–15)

Although 2 Cor. 9:6–11 and 9:12–15 are of one piece, a shift of emphasis appears as we move to the final four verses of the chapter. Whereas the first movement focuses squarely on God's vast resources that lie behind Christian giving, verses 12–15 celebrate the results of such giving, mentioning three responses directed toward God: thanksgiving (9:12), glory given (9:13), and prayer offered for the Corinthians (9:14). Verse 12 begins with the apostle once again making reference to the collection for the saints in Jerusalem, writing, "for the ministry fulfilling this service." The conjunction ὅτι (*hoti*, for) indicates that what follows is in some sense a continuation of what has gone before. In context the conjunction seems either causal (so NET: "*because* the service of this ministry") or perhaps explanatory, indicating that the content of verse 12 is an elaboration on the "thanksgiving to God" at the end of verse 11. In either case, the translation "for" serves well; the line between "cause" and "explanation" is rather thin, for an explanation may involve clarifying a cause.

9:12

Twice since the beginning of chapter 8 Paul has referred to the collection for Jerusalem as "the ministry to God's people" (8:4; 9:1), and thrice as "this gift" (8:6, 7, 19). But here he uses a bit different wording: ἡ διακονία τῆς λειτουργίας ταύτης (*hē diakonia tēs leitourgias tautēs*; lit., the ministry of this service). The semantic ranges of the two nouns overlap, since both could be used to mean "service" or "assistance" of some kind. The term διακονία perhaps carries more a sense of administration and λειτουργία brings more cultic overtones. In this case, it seems the latter is intended to give greater definition to the former in some way. In the ancient world λειτουργία could refer generally to a form of public service either to the society or to the gods. In the LXX it was taken up as a term associated with priestly ministry in the tabernacle (e.g., Exod. 37:19; Num. 4:24, 27–28, 33; 7:5, 7–8; 8:22, 25; 16:9) and later the temple (e.g., 1 Chron. 28:20–21; 2 Chron. 8:14; 31:2, 4, 16; 35:10, 15–16; Ezra 7:19). The word could also be used in a popular, nontechnical sense as personal "help" or "assistance" (as at Phil. 2:30; BDAG 230, 591). Our translation, "the ministry fulfilling this service," reads the genitive as an objective genitive,[22] understanding "the ministry" to refer to the whole of the endeavor of raising and delivering the funds to Jerusalem, and "this service" as the active fulfillment of that ministry in aiding the Jerusalem church.

The apostle notes that this ministry has two important effects, expressed in a "not only . . . but also" (οὐ μόνον . . . ἀλλὰ καί, *ou monon . . . alla kai*) construction.

1. Obviously the financial collection of money for the saints in Jerusalem will serve to "meet the needs of God's people" (τὰ ὑστερήματα τῶν ἁγίων, *ta*

---

22. So Barrett 1973: 239; Harris 2005: 648; Martin 1986: 287. The other option would be to take the word as an epexegetical genitive (Betz and MacRae 1985: 87; Plummer 1915: 265).

hysterēmata tōn hagiōn). The verb προσαναπληρόω (prosanaplēroō) means to "supply" or "fill up" something that is lacking.[23] Later in 2 Corinthians, Paul uses the term to speak of the brothers meeting his needs: "When I was with you and was in need, I was not a burden to anyone, for the brothers who came from Macedonia fully supplied my needs" (τὸ γὰρ ὑστέρημά μου προσανεπλήρωσαν, to gar hysterēma mou prosaneplērōsan; 2 Cor. 11:9 NET). In 9:12 as well it is the gap constituting "the needs of God's people" that is being "filled up" or "met," and the language echoes Paul's earlier reflections on Exod. 16:18 at 8:14–15, where he posits that equality in Christian community means the need (ὑστέρημα) of those who lack should be met by those who have surplus.

2. Second, however, the "ministry fulfilling this service" also "is having a broader effect through many thanks being offered up to God." The participle περισσεύουσα (perisseuousa), rendered here as "is having a broader effect," means more directly, "overflowing," or "abounding." We have seen various forms of the verb at a number of places thus far in the book (1:5; 3:9; 4:15; 8:2, 7; 9:8). The apostle's point is that the impact of the collection is bigger than what might seem apparent at first, and he says this to encourage the Corinthians. The broader effect is happening "through" (διά, dia) many expressions of thanks being offered up to God (πολλῶν εὐχαριστιῶν τῷ θεῷ, pollōn eucharistiōn tō theō). In this case the preposition διά plus the genitive points to a circumstance by which something is accomplished or brought about (BDAG 224). The "spilling over" effect of the ministry is the stimulus for the "thanksgiving to God" response of those who witness the generosity of the Corinthians. So the collection does more than "just" meet practical needs; it also prompts people to turn to God in thanksgiving, and that response of thanks is having a ripple effect, drawing attention to the work of God in the world.

9:13   With verse 13 Paul elaborates on this thought, now giving various reasons why people are responding positively to God in light of the collection. He begins with "Because of this ministry's proven character, they will glorify God." Although a less common use, διά (dia) plus the genitive, with which the verse begins, seems to be causal in context (BDAG 225). It is because of "this ministry's" proven character (τῆς δοκιμῆς, tēs dokimēs) that people will glorify God. The word δοκιμή could be used to refer to a "test," an "ordeal," or the "proven character" that results from a test, the manifestation that something that has been tested is of high quality. Earlier in this section, using the term at 8:2, the apostle notes that the Macedonians had given during a "severe test involving affliction" (ἐν πολλῇ δοκιμῇ θλίψεως, en pollē dokimē thlipseōs), and they had given elaborately. Earlier in the book, at 2:9, Paul tells the Corinthians why he had written to them concerning the person who had brought

---

23. The only use in the LXX is at Wis. 19:4, where the text speaks of "filling up" what was lacking in punishment for the wicked: "For the fate they deserved drew them on to this end and made them forget the things that had happened in order that they might fill up the punishment that their torments still lacked" (NETS).

grief to the congregation: "For I also wrote to test you" (ἵνα γνῶ τὴν δοκιμὴν ὑμῶν, *hina gnō tēn dokimēn hymōn*), more literally, "that I might know your character." In that verse he continues, "to see the extent of your obedience." So the apostle ties proven character to "obedience," and this he does also at 9:13. But here it is the proven character of the ministry itself, which is in view, and this ministry has "stood the test," proved its quality.

As the verse continues, Paul specifically mentions two ways the quality of the ministry has been manifested, and it is because of these two manifestations that people will glorify God. First, they will glorify God "in response to the obedience flowing from your confession of the gospel of Christ." For Paul, the Corinthians' giving to the collection is an act of "obedience" (τῇ ὑποταγῇ, *tē hypotagē*), and their obedience has elicited a response (ἐπί, *epi*)[24] from those observing it. Moreover, the obedience itself flows from the Corinthians' "confession of the gospel of Christ" (τῆς ὁμολογίας ὑμῶν εἰς τὸ εὐαγγέλιον τοῦ Χριστοῦ, *tēs homologias hymōn eis to euangelion tou Christou*). In this case the genitive τῆς ὁμολογίας is understood as a genitive of producer (see D. Wallace 1996: 104–6), the confession of the gospel prompting the obedience. The apostle had already written at 8:9, "For you know the grace demonstrated by our Lord Jesus Christ: though he was rich, he became poor for your sake, so that by his poverty you might become rich," and challenged the Corinthians to follow the pattern of the Messiah, marked out in the gospel. Thus, ultimately, the Corinthians' robust participation in the collection for the saints at Jerusalem was a manifestation of their confession of the gospel. The ministry of the collection, therefore, shows its quality as a sacrificial, gospel-grounded ministry. People whose lives have been truly touched by the transforming power of Christ's gospel do extraordinary things that bring glory to God.

Second, people will glorify God in response to "the generous way you have shared with them and everyone else." Their involvement in giving demonstrates ἁπλότητι τῆς κοινωνίας (*haplotēti tēs koinōnias*), straightforwardly, "a generosity of fellowship." As discussed earlier in the commentary (at 1:12; 8:2; 9:11), the word ἁπλότης (*haplotēs*) could refer to an openness, either in attitude ("frankness," "sincerity," "simplicity," "uprightness"), or with one's resources ("generosity," "liberality"). At 9:11, Paul uses the same term: "You will be enriched in every way, resulting in every kind of *generosity*." Since the broader context of our statement has to do with God blessing the financial resources of the Corinthians, that context points in the direction of interpreting the word as referring to the giving done through the collection. Yet this is called a generosity "of fellowship" (τῆς κοινωνίας), and the phrase may be understood either as perhaps another genitive of producer, "a generosity stemming from fellowship," or as an attributed genitive ("generous fellowship"), or more smoothly, "the generous way you have shared with them and everyone else."

---

24. This is a case where ἐπί (*epi*) is used "after verbs which express feelings, opinions, etc.," meaning "at" or "because of" (BDAG 365).

9:14–15   There is yet another response to the Corinthians' participation in the collection, however: Paul anticipates that others will be prompted to pray for the Corinthians. The prayers, first of all, will be with "deep affection" (αὐτῶν . . . ἐπιποθούντων ὑμᾶς, *autōn . . . epipothountōn hymas*). The pronoun αὐτῶν plus the participle can be taken as forming a genitive absolute clause, with the present participle ἐπιποθούντων standing in for a finite verb (so Harris 2005: 657). In the biblical literature the term ἐπιποθέω (*epipotheō*) could be used with various shades of meaning, communicating both positive and negative emotions. The NT authors use the word, referring to a strong desire or longing for someone or something (e.g., Rom. 1:11; Phil. 2:26; 1 Thess. 3:6; 2 Tim. 1:4; James 4:5; 1 Pet. 2:2), but Paul also takes up the word with the sense of having "tender affection," possessing a "fervent tenderness . . . that grips the heart" (Spicq 1994: 2.60; Phil. 1:8), and that seems to be the meaning here. The dative δεήσει (*deēsei*), could be translated as communicating means ("by prayer"), location ("in prayer"), or the circumstance in which the tender affection will be expressed ("as they pray"). The last of these options seems best in context. So the sense of the whole clause has to do with the recipients of the collection feeling tender affection for the Corinthians in the context of prayer. Thus our translation, "They will feel deep affection for you as they pray on your behalf."

In the latter half of verse 14, the apostle explains why (διά + the acc.) the recipients of the Corinthians' generosity will be moved to prayerful affection: "because God's extraordinary grace rests on you." As already noted in the commentary, the theme of χάρις (*charis*) has formed a constant refrain throughout chapters 8 and 9 (8:1, 4, 6–7, 9, 16, 19; 9:8), used variously to refer to God's *kindness*, *favor*, or *enablement* (8:1; 9:8, 14), the *privilege* of participating in the collection (8:4), *the collection itself* (referred to as "this gift") as an expression of God's grace (8:6, 7, 19), and a *verbal expression of thanks* (8:16; 9:15; see the discussion above at 8:1). As noted in the introduction to our unit under discussion, the use at 9:14–15 plays a special part in forming an inclusio with the use in 8:1, where Paul writes of "God's grace that has been given in connection with the Macedonian churches." In the context, of course, he is speaking of that grace as manifested through their giving. Now at the end of his minidiscourse on giving (2 Cor. 8–9), Paul anticipates that the same grace will be manifested by the Corinthians' giving, a grace that he says rests "upon" (ἐφ', *eph'*) them. Yet Paul describes this grace upon the Corinthians as τὴν ὑπερβάλλουσαν, "extraordinary," a term he also uses at 3:10, which means "to go beyond, surpass, outdo" (BDAG 1032). The grace expressed by their giving shows a work of God in the lives of the Corinthians that is above and beyond what might have normally been expected.

In verse 15 the chapter (and the section) concludes with an exclamatory expression of thanks to God, the "grace" manifested in the Corinthians, reverberating back in "thanks" to God. God's grace, poured out among his people, comes back to him in the form of thanks from his people (9:11–12), and Paul quite naturally responds to God with χάρις (thanks).[25] Thus the long embedded discourse comes full circle, presenting the "grace-giving God" and the manifestation of that grace through the giving of his people.

Here Paul thanks God "for his indescribable gift" (ἐπὶ τῇ ἀνεκδιηγήτῳ αὐτοῦ δωρεᾷ, *epi tē anekdiēgētō autou dōrea*), but what is that gift? Ἀνεκδιηγήτῳ, the term translated "indescribable" (so HCSB, NASB, NRSV, NIV, NET), occurs only here in the biblical literature. Clement of Rome uses the word, for example, of God's power or judgments (1 Clem. 20.5; 61.1). A positive term, it means something "too wonderful for words." So what "gift" of God might be described in that way? Plummer (1915: 267–68) suggests that the apostle gives thanks for "the glorious picture" of loving unity between Gentile and Jewish Christians, painted by the contribution of the former to the latter. Furnish (1984: 452), on the other hand, sees God's grace, at work among the Macedonians and (anticipated!) among the Corinthians, as the gift prompting Paul to give thanks. Yet certainly underlying that grace is the gift of God's redemptive, gospel work through his Son (e.g., Martin 1986: 295; Matera 2003: 210);[26] hence many commentators see the Son himself as the ultimate gift Paul has in mind (8:9), one "too wonderful for words" (Barrett 1973: 241; Garland 1999: 415; Harris 2005: 660).[27] Thus ends Paul's extended appeal to the Corinthians to join in the collection for the people of God in Jerusalem. From Rom. 15:26–27 it seems that his appeal was successful and his confident outlook throughout these two chapters was merited.

Reflection

Keller (2009: 65) makes a helpful distinction between "surface idols" and "deep idols." Surface idols simply are idolatrous areas of life that facilitate the fulfillment of deeper idols, like the need for power over our lives or the lives of others, a sense of self-worth, social status, or security. Keller points out that a surface treatment of how we deal with the surface idol of money won't do. We have to push to deeper issues. He explains:

> Some people want lots of money as a way to control their world and life. Such people usually don't spend much money and live very modestly. They keep it all safely saved and invested, so they can feel completely secure in the world. Others want money for access to social circles and to make themselves beautiful and attractive. These people *do* spend their money on themselves in lavish ways. Other people want money because it gives them so much power

---

25. This is the third time in the book that Paul has given "thanks to God," using the words (in various configurations) χάρις τῷ θεῷ (*charis tō theō*; 2:14; 8:16). God acts, and his action elicits an appropriate response from the apostle.

26. Matera (2003: 210) notes that δωρεᾷ (*dōrea*) is used of the "gift" of salvation elsewhere in Paul at Rom. 5:15, 17; Eph. 3:7; 4:7.

27. So also John Chrysostom (*Hom. 2 Cor.* 20.2), who states, "Or it refers to the inexpressible gift which Christ bestowed liberally on the whole world by his incarnation, . . . [which] seems to be the more likely meaning" (Bray 1999: 282).

over others. In every case, money functions as an idol and yet, because of various deep idols, it results in very different patterns of behavior.

It is clear from the whole of 2 Cor. 8–9 that Paul was interested in more than the "surface" actions of the Corinthians; he cared about the condition of their hearts and how their response to the collection for the saints in Jerusalem reflected that condition. He did not want their gift to be "an expression of stinginess" (9:5). He wanted them to follow the example of the Macedonians, who "gave themselves" (8:5). He wanted them to excel in giving as an expression of grace and love (8:7–8).

Biblical principles, over time, should shape our hearts to conform to the beauty of God's values and ways, and here in 9:6–15 the apostle has given the Corinthians, and us, much to guide us in how we think about and use our material resources. Rather than focusing on external measurements (e.g., "the standard for giving is *this* amount"), notice how Paul addresses the condition of our hearts and the health of our relationships:

1. Christ-followers should be generous (9:6), meeting the needs of others.
2. Christ-followers should trust the principle of the harvest—that givers benefit from giving (9:6, 10).
3. Christ-followers should be cheerful in their giving, rather than giving under compulsion (9:7).
4. Christ-followers should trust God, the ultimate Giver, to meet their needs, for he supplies his people with what they need to carry on his work (9:8–9).
5. Since God is the one who ultimately supplies resources to meet the needs of every person, giving results in thanks being given to God (9:11–12).
6. Giving is a sign of obedience to God's gospel (9:13).
7. Giving builds fellowship between different groups of Christ-followers (9:14).

Nothing addresses the "deep idols" fed by various forms of money-idolatry more powerfully than generosity nurtured in community with God and others.

Additional Notes

9:8. The external evidence for δυνατεῖ is quite strong ($\mathfrak{P}^{46}$ ℵ B C* D* F G 104 t vg; Ambst), and it is probably due to the rare use of δυνατέω (only three times in the NT; here, 13:3; Rom. 14:4) that two other variants exist: the adjective δυνατός (C² D² Ψ 048 0243 1739 1881 𝔐 b) and the common verb δύναται (33 *pc* f g ρ vg^ms).

9:10. The reading σπόρον ($\mathfrak{P}^{46}$ B D* F G 1175 *pc*) seems to be preferred on the following bases. As pointed out by Harris (2005: 632), it occurs in strong Western uncials (D* F G) and proto-Alexandrian witnesses ($\mathfrak{P}^{46}$ B). It parallels τὸν σπόρον later in the verse, and the use of the cognates σπέρμα τῷ σπείροντι occur in the LXX at Isa. 55:10, making σπόρον the more difficult reading. A scribe, probably wishing to bring Paul's text in line with the LXX reading of Isa. 55:10, presented the reading σπέρμα (ℵ C D¹ Ψ 048 0209 0243 33 1739 1881 𝔐).

9:10. It seems likely that some scribes did not like the future indicative readings χορηγήσει ... πληθυνεῖ ... αὐξήσει ([$\mathfrak{P}^{46}$ 104: -σαι] ℵ* B C D* P 33 81 326 1175 2464 *pc* latt), perhaps thinking the apostle could be misunderstood as being presumptuous and substituting the aorist optative forms (ℵ² D² Ψ 0209 0243 1739 1881 𝔐; "May God"). The change could also be due to scribal error or atticizing tendencies (Thrall 2000: 585).

IV. Paul Confronts the Malignant Ministry of His Opponents (10:1–13:13)

In 2 Corinthians, following the letter opening (1:1–2) and prologue (1:3–11), Paul carries out an extensive defense of his apostolic ministry (1:12–7:16). Highlighting the nature of authentic Christian ministry, Paul demonstrates why the Corinthians should have discerned the integrity of their apostle's activities (e.g., 6:4–13) and commended him before his detractors (5:12; cf. 12:11). The section ends with Paul making a heartfelt appeal (6:11–13), offering an exhortation to separate from those who stand against the work of the true gospel (6:14–7:4), and then resuming the travel narrative at 7:5–16, which gives the apostle the opportunity to celebrate the repentance of the faithful majority. In the letter's next section, he builds on that hopeful sign by calling the Corinthians to resume the collection for the saints in Jerusalem (chaps. 8–9). Against this backdrop, Paul in chapters 10–13 now turns to confront the recalcitrant minority, who persist in opposing his ministry.[1]

As theorized by some, perhaps Paul wrote 2 Cor. 1–9 over a period of time as he traveled, and then, receiving distressing news from Corinth, penned this final movement of the book (so Harris 2005: 30–31, 50–51, 104–5). But rather, it may be that the apostle held in reserve a very direct and confrontive word to the opponents until the very end of the letter and did so for the rhetorical impact. As noted in the introduction, something very similar is seen, for example, in Demosthenes (*Ep.* 2.26). In any case, these final chapters of the book confront the opponents in biting language and with an eloquent flair, and they do so in three main movements. First, in 10:1–18 Paul defends himself against certain accusations made against him by the opponents. Second, provoked by his opponents, Paul boasts about his apostleship in 11:1–12:13. Third, the book closes in 12:14–13:10 with the apostle anticipating his third visit to Corinth (Scott 1998: 193). As noted in the introduction, the beginning and ending of the section is bracketed with an inclusio built around the themes of "presence" and "absence" (10:1, 11; 13:2, 10).

---

1. On 2 Cor. 10–13, see Garland 1989; Holland 1993; Kee 1980; Lambrecht 1996; Murphy-O'Connor 1991a; Neyrey 1997; Peterson 1998a; Sampley 1988; Timmis 1993; Wanamaker 2003; F. Watson 1984; Welborn 1995b.

Paul Confronts the Malignant Ministry of His Opponents (10:1–13:13)
A. Present or Absent, Paul's Authority Is the Same (10:1–11)
B. Proper and Improper Boasting (10:12–18)
C. Paul Boasts Like a Fool to Stop the False Apostles (11:1–12:13)
D. Preparation for the Third Visit (12:14–13:10)
E. Closing Exhortations, Greetings, and Benediction (13:11–13)

A. Present or Absent, Paul's Authority Is the Same (10:1–11)

The apostle's ministry in Corinth illustrates the reality of spiritual warfare, and with 10:1 the battle is fully joined. Paul begins by appealing to the Corinthians that they address his opponents so that he will not need to act with bold confidence when he arrives in the city (10:1), but he anticipates having to take such action (v. 2). These opponents have leveled the accusation against him that his public personae lack integrity since he presents himself as an intimidating bully when writing letters from a distance but a pathetic "pushover" when face-to-face with the Corinthians (vv. 1–2, 9–11). Paul points out that the opponents, who judge him on the basis of human standards (vv. 2–3), have misread him and his ministry, seeing as "weakness" what should be understood as Christ's powerful "meekness." Evidently, some of the Corinthians themselves have joined in this misstep by judging him according to outward appearances (10:7a). Yet, using warfare language, Paul assures them that the boldness with which he writes will match the power of God, displayed in action in his face-to-face ministry with the Corinthians (vv. 2, 11). Those who stand against him will be punished (v. 6). But he is not trying to intimidate the church; rather, his boldness is meant for their spiritual good (vv. 8–9). Nevertheless, they will only be built up as they submit themselves in full obedience to his leadership (v. 6). The unit may be outlined as follows:

1. Meekness not weakness (10:1–2)
2. Spiritual warfare according to God's standards (10:3–7a)
3. The apostle's claim to authority (10:7b–11)

Exegesis and Exposition

[1]Now I, Paul, personally appeal to you by the leniency and clemency of Christ—I who am "pitiful" when face-to-face among you but "confident" toward you when I am absent—[2]when I am with you, please don't force me to act with bold confidence, which I think I will dare to use against certain people, who evaluate us on the (false) assumption that we conduct ourselves according to human standards. [3]For although we conduct our lives in these human bodies, we do not wage war according to human standards. [4]For our weapons used in ⌜warfare⌝ are not merely human but, rather, powerful in God's service to the end that fortresses are destroyed. We tear down arguments [5]and every rampart raised up in opposition to knowledge about God and take captive every thought, resulting in obedience to Christ. [6]And we stand ready to

punish every disobedient act once your obedience is complete. [7]You are looking at things as they appear on the surface!

If anyone ⌐has convinced himself⌐ that he is from Christ, he ⌐personally⌐ should consider again the fact that just as he is from Christ, so are we! [8]For ⌐even⌐ if ⌐I boast⌐ a bit more about our authority, which ⌐the Lord⌐ gave for the purpose of building you up and not for tearing you down, I will not be ashamed of it. [9]In order that I won't seem to be trying to terrify you with my letters—[10]to quote a certain person, "His letters are intimidating and make a big impression, but he is a pushover in person, and his public speaking is disgraceful"—[11]such a person should consider this: what we are in word, by writing letters when away, we will be in action when present!

1. Meekness Not Weakness (10:1–2)

10:1 From the first words of chapter 10, we sense a shift in tone and rhetorical strategy, and we witness how deeply personal this appeal is to the apostle. He begins, "Now I, Paul, personally appeal to you" (Αὐτὸς δὲ ἐγὼ Παῦλος παρακαλῶ ὑμᾶς, *Autos de egō Paulos parakalō hymas*). The δέ could be read as marking a continuation of what has gone before ("then"), and some have put forward the case that these beginning words of the chapter flow from the thanksgiving of 9:12–15 (Garland 1999: 425; Witherington 1995: 432).[1] As Harris (2005: 666) notes, however, δέ may simply be loosely resumptive, as often the case in Paul. Two more common phrases Paul uses to refer to himself—αὐτός ἐγώ (I myself; e.g., Rom. 7:25; 9:3; 15:14; 2 Cor. 12:13) and ἐγὼ Παῦλος (I Paul; Gal. 5:2; Eph. 3:1; Col. 1:23; Philem. 19)—have been combined in the words Αὐτὸς . . . ἐγὼ Παῦλος, with the sense, "I, Paul, personally." The wording is emphatic and underscores that what follows constitutes a firsthand cry of Paul's heart. This is a critical juncture in the life of this church, as their apostle addresses his opponents head-on.[2] The apostle puts himself on the line. Rather than locking arms with his coworkers, as elsewhere in 2 Corinthians (e.g., 1:1, 19), Paul steps forward to stand and make his case alone. Poignantly, Garland (1999: 426) states, "He is defending *his* authority, explaining the theological significance of *his* weakness, and warning of *his* power and willingness to discipline the disobedient vigorously when *he* comes."[3] Paul has been personally attacked, and he offers a first-person, heartfelt answer to the Corinthians generally, but it is an answer directed at his detractors.

---

1. The thought here is that παρακαλῶ (10:1) sometimes is preceded by doxologies or thanksgivings (9:12–15).

2. The emphatic form of self-reference parallels similar wording in Gal. 5:2: Ἴδε ἐγὼ Παῦλος λέγω ὑμῖν (*Ide egō Paulos legō hymin*, Pay attention; I Paul say to you), which comes at a critical moment of confrontation in Galatians. Matera (2003: 220) observes how the wording here suggests "that Paul has come to a critical juncture in this letter when he must finally deal with the intruding apostles who have called into question the style and perhaps the content of his apostolic ministry." And Keener (2005: 216) points out that going on the offensive was standard practice in defense speeches.

3. The personal nature of the appeal is not unlike Paul's shift to first person at 1:23–2:13, where Paul makes a highly personal defense of his actions to the Corinthians.

Yet the apostle frames his answer in a striking way. Rather than "commanding" the Corinthians, wielding his authority, he appeals to them (παρακαλῶ ὑμᾶς, *parakalō hymas*) and does so "by the leniency and clemency of Christ" (διὰ τῆς πραΰτητος καὶ ἐπιεικείας τοῦ Χριστοῦ, *dia tēs prautētos kai epieikeias tou Christou*). As noticed throughout the commentary, thus far Paul has employed the verb παρακαλέω (*parakaleō*) extensively in this book (1:4, 6; 2:7–8; 5:20; 6:1; 7:6–7, 13; 8:6; 9:5). In Paul's era it could be used variously with the sense "to encourage," "to invite in," "to comfort" or "cheer up," "to request," or "to call to one's side" (BDAG 764–65). Here it means "to urge" or "to appeal to." Paul sees himself as God's agent, pleading with the Corinthians for the sake of their spiritual well-being (cf. 5:20).

The words διὰ τῆς πραΰτητος καὶ ἐπιεικείας τοῦ Χριστοῦ further define the posture by which the apostle makes his appeal. The dissenters characterize Paul as being "pitiful" when present and "confident" when absent. Here the absent Paul says that he anticipates acting with bold confidence when he arrives in Corinth—if repentance is not forthcoming. He would like to be lenient with them, but he will not spare those who are unrepentant (13:2). The use of διά plus the genitive probably communicates here the personal agency by which Paul is acting, or perhaps Paul phrases this as he does to make an urgent request (Rom. 12:1; 1 Cor. 1:10; BDAG 224). Paul thus makes his appeal "through" the dynamics of Christ's gospel.[4] The terms are not exact synonyms, but they do overlap semantically a great deal, both communicating the idea of "leniency" or "clemency" (D. Walker 2002: 38–90).[5] Πραΰτης (*prautēs*) belongs to a family of words found especially in Greek literature, which are "opposed to roughness and severity," "speak of a calm and soothing disposition," and are often used in contrast to rage, wrath, or vengeance. Plutarch (*Cor.* 15.4) often praises heroes for their deliberateness and mildness, and Epictetus (*Disc.* 3.20.9) underscores that a trainer must help an athlete learn to be calm, patient, and mild. But most pertinent to our context, the word describes the virtue of a person who, through self-mastery, moderation, and flexibility, can deal graciously with other people in conflictual situations (Spicq 1994: 3.161–63). So, based on the posture of Christ toward people, Paul offers the unrepentant "leniency," which he will reiterate at the beginning of chapter 13. The idea of "sparing," the work of Christ, and being present/absent here and in 13:1–10 form an inclusio that marks off chapters 10–13 as a major unit.[6] He is lenient, but his leniency will come to an end if repentance does not take place. When he arrives, he will not "spare" those who continue in disobedience.

Ἐπιείκεια (*epieikeia*), on the other hand, speaks of "the quality of making allowances despite facts that might suggest reason for a different reaction,"

---

4. The genitive τοῦ Χριστοῦ (*tou Christou*, of Christ) is understood as an attributed genitive: these characteristics are attributed to Christ.

5. D. Walker (2002: 89) suggests that these terms can be understood as a hendiadys, the two terms driving home a single idea of "leniency" or "clemency."

6. On Jesus as the meek king in dealing with people, see Good 1999.

that is, "clemency, gentleness, graciousness, courtesy, indulgence," or "tolerance" (BDAG 371). Given the warfare language that follows, the translation "clemency" works well (D. Walker 2002: 89). Thus Paul draws on the very character of Christ in setting the tone for the confrontation he pens in the following chapters, and it is critical to understand this tone if we are to understand these final chapters of 2 Corinthians. He implies that the meekness of nature that some accuse him of showing (in the latter part of the verse) is actually very much in line with the posture of Christ toward sinful people, and contrary to the contrarians, his letter, rather than "bold" in a presumptuous sense, is communicated from the standpoint of graciousness; his authority is grounded in the gospel of Christ. The opponents have miscalculated Paul's "meekness" as "weakness," as we see in the balance of the verse. Yet, depicted preeminently in the person and ministry of Christ, great power and graciousness can go together. Christ's ministry was marked by a power-backed boldness against his opponents, even while he lived in humble submission to the Father, effecting grace for new-covenant people. This is why there is no contradiction between Paul's boldness toward the opponents and the graciousness with which he addresses the church generally (Hafemann 2000: 394).

Now the apostle adopts a more ironic tone, a tone that marks these last four chapters of the book (Matera 2003: 218). The latter part of 10:1, which offers a parenthetical statement, embodies the first of two accusations made against Paul. The first accusation is that he is ταπεινός (*tapeinos*), "abject," "pitiful" (ESV, HCSB, NRSV), or "timid" (NLT[2], NIV) when "face-to-face" (κατὰ πρόσωπον, *kata prosōpon*) and "confident" or "bold" (θαρρῶ, *tharrō*)[7] when "away" (ἀπών, *apōn*), the latter a reference to Paul's communication through letters (10:10). Paul probably quotes the opponents at this point, who have labeled him as a waffler, in turns "pitiful" or "confident" depending on the circumstances.[8] Calvin (1964: 126) writes that the opponents "were making out that the vehemence with which he thundered in his letters was . . . the bravado of a cowardly braggart." In short, the opponents disparage Paul for being a very unimpressive person when in Corinth—he has no public presence—and for playing "the confident leader" only when he is writing letters from a distance (i.e., when he doesn't have to stand toe-to-toe with those opposing him in Corinth). The fuller form of this accusation comes out in 10:10: "to quote a certain person, 'His letters are intimidating and make a big impression, but he is a pushover in person, and his public speaking is disgraceful!'" If the opponents are correctly identified with the Sophist movement (Winter 2002), the accusation fits a particular set of cultural values, for the Sophists placed a great deal of emphasis on both a leader's public presence and ability as a

---

7. The verb θαρρέω (*tharreō*) has to do with having confidence, courage, or boldness in a matter (Spicq 1994: 2.188–92).

8. Thus the quotation marks around the rendering of these terms in our ET (as with the NIV; Scott 1998: 194).

public speaker.[9] Even today it is easy to fall into the trap of equating public presence and presentation with spiritual power and authenticity of ministry. The false teachers were attractive in part because they fit the cultural norms of Corinth.

So in the first verse the apostle sets the tone for his appeal and reveals one of the accusations made against him. Paul begins the second verse by making his appeal specific, asking the Corinthians to take action so he will not need to prove that accusation of "bold when away" wrong by being bold when he arrives: "Please don't force me to act with bold confidence when I am with you." The δέ (de) again can be read as resumptive ("Now" in NET), picking up on the apostle's posture of "request" and the themes of presence and boldness in the previous verse; but this dynamic, continuing the thought of the previous verse, seems clear if we set off the parenthetical statement of verse 1 with em dashes:[10] "Now I, Paul, personally appeal to you by the leniency and clemency of Christ—I who am 'pitiful' when face-to-face among you, but 'confident' toward you when I am absent—²when I am with you, please don't force me to act with bold confidence." The verb δέομαι (deomai) introduces the specific content of Paul's appeal and can be rendered variously as "ask," "beg," or "implore"; the term has to do with making a request in a way that involves pleading. Normally in English we communicate the idea by asking someone to "please" do something or to "please" refrain from doing something. Here Paul asks the Corinthians, "Please don't force me to act boldly." The articular infinitive τὸ μὴ . . . θαρρῆσαι (to mē . . . tharrēsai) serves as the direct object of δέομαι. In light of the accusation alluded to in verse 1, that Paul was only "bold" when away, the apostle is in effect pleading with the Corinthians, "Don't make me prove wrong those who are being critical of me!" Of course that could only happen when Paul is "present" (παρών, parōn, being present),[11] thus when he arrives, and it is clear that he anticipates being with them soon (9:4–5; 12:14, 20–21; 13:1–2, 10).[12] In fact, the promise of his impending arrival stands as a rhetorical strategy, a form of accountability, that Paul uses at points (e.g., 2 Cor. 9:4–5; Philem. 22).

The apostle further underscores the posture of "boldness" or "confidence" communicated through the articular infinitive with (a) the phrase τῇ πεποιθήσει (tē pepoithēsei), "with confidence"; and (b) the verbal heart of the relative clause ᾗ λογίζομαι τολμῆσαι (hē logizomai tolmēsai), which we translate with "which I think I will dare to use." The phrase τῇ πεποιθήσει is adverbial, further defining τὸ μὴ . . . θαρρῆσαι, and speaks of the manner

9. See Savage 1996: 65; and esp. Keener 2005: 216–19, who writes, "People of status demanded appropriate appearance, gestures, and voice intonation as important components of good oratory. It was effective delivery that made sound reasoning rhetorically effective" (218). For primary sources, see Pliny the Younger, *Ep.* 1.23.2; Cicero, *Brut.* 55.203.

10. The majority of ETs don't render δέ at all (e.g., ESV, HCSB, NIV, NRSV, NASB). The KJV interprets the conjunction as adversative ("but").

11. The participle is adverbial, modifying the infinitive: "to be bold when present."

12. Paul at times uses his impending arrival as a form of accountability, as, e.g., at Philem. 22.

in which the boldness might be exercised: "to be bold *with confidence.*"
Yet the two can be conflated as "confident boldness" (Barrett 1973: 243) or
"bold confidence," as in our translation. The relative clause further defines
this confidence and combines the verb λογίζομαι—which means variously
"to think," "reckon," "evaluate," "consider," or "to be of a certain opinion"
(BDAG 597)—with the complementary aorist infinitive τολμῆσαι. The verb
τολμάω (*tolmaō*) is another word having to do with courage or boldness. In
the infinitive it means "to dare," "have the courage," "presume," "be bold," or
"be brave enough" to do something (BDAG 1010). Here, as in 10:12 and 11:21,
it refers to a boundary line of behavior, which may or may not be crossed. In
this case the apostle is concerned that the Corinthians are pushing him over
that line. So Paul asks of the Corinthians, "Please don't force me to act with
bold confidence," and of this bold confidence he says, "which I think I will
dare to use." This resolute boldness is grounded in "his conviction that as
a divinely appointed apostle he had a God-given right to exercise discipline
within his churches if the need arose (cf. 10:8; 13:10)" (Harris 2005: 672). Paul
is not playing power games or posturing in the face of naysayers in Corinth.
Rather, God's agenda and God's authority lay behind his confrontation of
the problem group in Greece.

Thus, this bold confidence will be brought to bear "against certain people,
who evaluate us as conducting ourselves according to human standards."
Here we have the apostle's first overt mention in chapter 10 of the opposition
group that constitutes the focus of these final chapters of 2 Corinthians. He
refers to them simply as "certain people, who evaluate" (τινας τοὺς λογιζομένους, *tinas tous logizomenous*), and it is "against" (ἐπί, *epi*)[13] this group
that he is considering standing with a bold, confident public posture.[14] First,
these opponents of the apostle have been evaluating him. Paul has just used
the word λογίζομαι (*logizomai*)[15] to declare that he is considering bringing
a bold confidence to bear in a public confrontation with his opponents at
Corinth. Yet the word also can convey the sense of "evaluation," which
seems to be the nuance here. Second, the opponents have been evaluating
the apostle (and his mission) *as conducting his ministry according to human
standards* (ὡς κατὰ σάρκα περιπατοῦντας, *hōs kata sarka peripatountas*).
In this case the particle ὡς serves as a "marker introducing the perspective
from which a person, thing, or activity is viewed or understood as to character, function, or role" and may be translated "on the (false) assumption
that" (BDAG 1104, see esp. 3.a.β and 3.c). The opponents have misread the
situation by assuming that Paul should be evaluated on their terms, namely,

13. Here ἐπί + the acc. could be translated as "toward" (NIV), or "before" (as in a legal
setting), but it probably is best to reflect the element of hostility given the context ("against,"
so ESV, NASB, Tyndale, NET; see BDAG 366).

14. Paul could be referring to the interlopers (Furnish 1984: 48), or to the group of local Corinthians infected with their disdain for Paul (Barnett 1997: 462), or to both (Lambrecht 1999: 154).

15. The word is important in the immediate context (2 Cor. 10:2, 7, 11; 11:5; 12:6).

by their Sophist standards of public presentation and leadership.[16] Paul describes these standards as κατὰ σάρκα περιπατοῦντας, literally, "walking[17] according to the flesh."

Generally in Paul, σάρξ (*sarx*) has various connotations, some morally or spiritually neutral and others quite negative.[18] Here he seems to be crafting a play on words (Martin 1986: 300), and unraveling the specific use of the prepositions is critical. What does he mean by κατὰ σάρκα (*kata sarka*, twice in 10:2–3), over against Ἐν σαρκί (*En sarki*, 10:3). He admits to conducting his life ἐν σαρκί (a concessive use of the participle περιπατοῦντες, *peripatountes*; lit., although we walk ἐν σαρκί) but denies that he "wages war" (10:3) or conducts himself (10:2) κατὰ σάρκα. Although the phrase ἐν σαρκί can refer to a carnal existence apart from God and the work of the Spirit (e.g., Rom. 8:8–9), it more often in Paul refers to being in a human body or experiencing human life on earth (e.g., Rom. 2:28; Gal. 2:20; 6:12; Eph. 2:11; Phil. 1:22; Col. 2:1), which seems to be the case here (P. Hughes 1962: 349; Keener 2005: 215; Thrall 2000: 607). Paul thus concedes that he is a normal human being.

What he denies is that his conduct and ministry are κατὰ σάρκα, and this phrase has been assessed in various ways,[19] but by far the most common are the criticism (1) that the apostle lacked the power of the Spirit or was unspiritual in some way (Barnett 1997: 462; Hafemann 2000: 392; Matera 2003: 222), or (2) that he did not measure up to a certain set of human standards or have the necessary human resources for ministry (Furnish 1984: 454, 461; Garland 1999: 434; Keener 2005: 215; Scott 1998: 195; Winter 2002: 174, 212; Witherington 1995: 433–34). While the two are undoubtedly related, the emphasis here seems to be on the latter. The apostle apparently finds himself positioned over against his opponents in a public speaking and leadership competition (Judge 1968: 47). Thus, in verse 2 Paul implicitly denies that his conduct of ministry is κατὰ σάρκα, according to "human standards."

16. Calvin (1964: 128) reads this as judging the situation in terms of "external pomp or show," and "warring according to the flesh" points to a reliance on worldly resources.

17. For the image of "walking" as referring to conduct of life, see the comments on 2 Cor. 4:2; 5:7; and the use of the word at 12:18. The image of "walking" is one of Paul's favorites for describing patterns of life: Rom. 6:4; 8:4; 13:13; 14:15; 1 Cor. 3:3; 7:17; 2 Cor. 12:18; Gal. 5:16; Eph. 2:2, 10; 4:1, 17; 5:2, 8, 15; Phil. 3:17–18; Col. 1:10; 2:6; 3:7; 4:5; 1 Thess. 2:12; 4:1, 12; 2 Thess. 3:6, 11.

18. Equivalent with the Hebrew term בָּשָׂר (*bāśār*, flesh, body), Paul often uses σάρξ to speak of the human person as a whole (e.g., Rom. 3:20; Gal. 1:16) but can use the term to speak specifically of the human body as a whole (e.g., 1 Cor. 6:16; 2 Cor. 7:1; 12:7; Gal. 4:13). At times the apostle uses the word neutrally to refer to human life or human nature (e.g., Rom. 4:1; 8:3; 9:8; 1 Cor. 1:29), but at other times the term carries a negative connotation, referring to human existence as independent of God or opposed to God and the Spirit (Rom. 7:5; 8:8; 13:14; Gal. 5:13–18; Moo 1996: 47).

19. For a wide range of interpretations that have been offered, see Thrall 2000: 605–6. R. J. Erickson (*DPL* 305) has noted that when Paul uses κατὰ σάρκα + a verb (as here), the use is morally negative; but when he uses κατὰ σάρκα + a noun, it is morally neutral.

2. Spiritual Warfare according to God's Standards (10:3–7a)

10:3   In verse 3 the apostle asserts that he does not "wage war" κατὰ σάρκα, according to such standards.[20] The verb στρατεύω (*strateuō*) occurs in the NT seven times, meaning either to serve as a soldier or to engage in battle (Luke 3:14; 1 Cor. 9:7; 2 Cor. 10:3; 1 Tim. 1:18; 2 Tim. 2:4; James 4:1; 1 Pet. 2:11), and the latter is in play in the present context. Paul likes to use word pictures drawn from the work of a soldier or warfare (Rom. 13:12; 1 Cor. 9:7; 2 Cor. 6:7; Eph. 6:11–17; Phil. 2:25; 1 Thess. 5:8; 1 Tim. 1:18; 6:12; 2 Tim. 2:3–4; 4:7; Philem. 2), and with Roman soldiers ever present in the Mediterranean world, use of such language would have been effective with Paul's audiences (Malherbe 1983). The use of "warfare" language was common: "Philosophers and orators often used military imagery to describe their battle against rival ideologies" or "false opinions" (Keener 2005: 217; Seneca the Younger, *Lucil.* 109.8–9; Seneca the Elder, *Controv.* 9, pref. 4; Tacitus, *Dial.* 32, 34, 37; Diogenes of Sinope, *Cyn. Ep.* 10).

Yet two points are striking about the use of the language in 10:3–6. First, although Paul normally uses military word pictures to make a point about living the Christian life victoriously in the face of spiritual forces, or partnership in Christian ministry, the imagery here is directed pointedly *against the apostle's opponents* at Corinth. He portrays himself as in a battle for the hearts and minds of the Corinthians, and the false ministers in Corinth clearly are seen as the enemy. Second, the imagery used in these verses seems to cluster around a specific aspect of battle in the ancient world: *siege warfare*, by which walls are torn down (Harris 2005: 676).[21]

10:4a–b   As he continues his extended word picture of siege warfare, Paul first offers a description of the weapons he uses in battle (10:4a–b) and then moves to the effectiveness of the weapons (10:4c–5). Verse 4 opens with the conjunction γάρ (*gar*), which serves to provide clarification of the statement in the previous verse, "We do not wage war according to human standards." The apostle explains more of what he means by waging war according to human standards, contrasting "human" weaponry and the weapons of authentic Christian ministry: "For our weapons used in warfare are not merely human but, rather, powerful in God's service to the end that fortresses are destroyed."

The word ὅπλα (*hopla*), which Bruce (1971: 230) identifies specifically as "siege engines," really is a more general term referring to a wide range of tools or weapons. Yet, of the sixty-seven uses of the word in the LXX, almost all clearly refer to "weapons," as do at least four of the other five uses in the NT.[22]

---

20. On the warfare imagery used by Paul at this point, see Bagalawis 2000.

21. For the various suggestions made for a wide range of terms used in this unit, see Harris 2005: 676. Especially apt are the terms καθαίρεσις (*kathairesis*, demolition, v. 4), ὀχύρωμα (*ochyrōma*, fortress, v. 4), ὕψωμα ἐπαιρόμενον (*hypsōma epairomenon*, rampart raised up, v. 5), and αἰχμαλωτίζω (*aichmalōtizō*, take captive/prisoner, v. 5).

22. In the NT the word is almost always used with the sense of "weapon" (John 18:3; Rom. 6:13; 13:12; 2 Cor. 6:7; 10:4). The one exception might be Rom. 6:13, where it may be

In any case, the attributive genitive, τῆς στρατείας[23] (*tēs strateias*, of warfare; cf. 1 Tim. 1:18), speaks of a military campaign and makes clear that Paul has battle weaponry in mind. Given the image of tearing down fortress walls that follows, Bruce may be right that Paul specifically is thinking of siege engines, tools (sometimes towers) brought against an enemy wall either to get over it or break it down. That the apostle describes the warfare as "our" (ἡμῶν, *hēmōn*) warfare, provides an overt allusion to his work of Christian ministry and that of his mission as they combat false teachers in Corinth.

In answer to the opponents' criticism that Paul seems to be a weak and ineffective leader, he declares that the "weapons" he uses in ministry are not to be evaluated as "merely human" (οὐ σαρκικά, *ou sarkika*),[24] a term that can be used of something associated with the physical realm, thus "physical," "human," or "material" (Rom. 15:27; 1 Cor. 9:11). Yet the word also can refer to something that is "fleshly," carrying a more negative tone, to represent that which is "worldly" or "merely human." In his *Homilies on 2 Corinthians*, John Chrysostom (*Hom. 2 Cor.* 21.2) suggests that Paul has in mind "worldly weapons" like "wealth, glory, power, loquaciousness, cleverness, half-truths, flatteries, hypocrisies and so on" (Bray 1999: 284). Human beings often behave in a way that is disappointing or spiritually lacking (1 Cor. 3:3; 1 Pet. 2:11), attempting to use such forces for their own advancement, or at least in clear contrast to God's wisdom and works. In both cases where this word is used in 2 Corinthians (here and at 1:12), Paul makes it clear that the work of an authentic Christian minister is not σαρκικός (*sarkikos*), "merely human," but rather draws on God's wisdom and resources for ministry.

Further, by contrast (ἀλλά, *alla*, but, rather), the work of an authentic Christian minister is δυνατὰ τῷ θεῷ (*dynata tō theō*, powerful for God). To speak of something as "powerful," the apostle uses the word δυνατός (*dynatos*) three times in 2 Corinthians, all in this final movement of the book (2 Cor. 10–13). At 12:10 he makes his famous statement, ὅταν γὰρ ἀσθενῶ, τότε δυνατός εἰμι (*hotan gar asthenō, tote dynatos eimi*), "For when I am weak, then I am powerful!" And later in the letter, at 13:9, he refers to the Corinthians themselves as "strong" in contrast to the weakness inherent in human ministers.[25] The dative τῷ θεῷ in 10:4 could be interpreted as a dative of advantage ("for God"), agency ("by God"), or perhaps cause ("because of God"). In the words that follow, since Paul crafts a word picture of himself as a soldier doing battle on behalf of God—he attacks the ramparts raised against the knowledge of God, making thoughts captive and bringing them

interpreted as "instruments": "Do not present your members to sin as instruments to be used for unrighteousness, but present yourselves to God as those who are alive from the dead and your members to God as instruments to be used for righteousness" (NET).

23. But see the additional note on the variants here.

24. The words σαρκικά and δυνατά are predicate adjectives delimiting ὅπλα.

25. "In fact, we rejoice when we are weak and you are strong [δυνατοί, *dynatoi*]. We also pray that you become fully mature" (2 Cor. 13:9 HCSB).

into submission to Christ—the first of these options seems most probable and may be read as "in God's service" (so Harris 2005: 664; Thrall 2000: 609).[26]

These powerful ministry "weapons," moreover, work "to the end that fortresses are destroyed" (πρὸς καθαίρεσιν ὀχυρωμάτων, *pros kathairesin ochyrōmatōn*; lit., to the destruction of fortresses). An ὀχύρωμα (*ochyrōma*) is either a prison,[27] or a military installation, stronghold, or fortress.[28] Unless one has overwhelming numbers, in the ancient world having a secure fortification was essential to survival in warfare. Correspondingly, the key to victory over a city or a fortress is destruction of such a stronghold's walls, which must be pulverized, torn down, or scaled. Paul draws a word picture of Christian ministry as bringing about the "destruction" (καθαίρεσιν) or "dismantling" (BDAG 487) of a particular kind of fortress—arguments built up by his opponents. It is the same term he uses later at 10:8 and 13:10 to speak of his ministry to the Corinthians as "building up" rather than "tearing down" (καθαίρεσιν).

10:4c–5 The standard Greek texts present 10:3–6 as a single sentence, probably due to the fact that the only finite verb in these verses is στρατευόμεθα (*strateuometha*, we wage war) in verse 3. The three parallel participles that follow (καθαιροῦντες, αἰχμαλωτίζοντες, ἔχοντες, *kathairountes, aichmalōtizontes, echontes*, tearing down, taking captive, standing), however, can be read as standing in for finite verbs. Via these three participles, the apostle presents three stages of "waging war": tearing down the enemies' walls, capturing enemy soldiers, and prosecuting those soldiers.

Paul first proclaims that *"walls" must be torn down*: "We tear down arguments and every rampart raised up in opposition to knowledge about God." In the first century, the participle καθαιροῦντες (*kathairountes*), a cognate of the noun καθαίρεσις used earlier in the verse, could mean to "take down" or "bring down" to a lower level, as with kings being toppled from their thrones (e.g., Luke 1:52), or Jesus being taken down from the cross (Mark 15:36, 46; Luke 23:53; Acts 13:29). But here the word carries the related meanings of "tear down," "break down," or "destroy," as with the foolish rich man of Luke 12:18: "Then he said, 'I will do this: I will *tear down* my barns and build bigger ones'" (NET; BDAG 287–88). Following up on the siege-warfare imagery he has already introduced, Paul says the powerful weapons of ministry warfare dismantle "arguments," walls of wrong thinking that stand in opposition to right Christian teaching. The participle, in fact, has two objects. The first,

---

26. In the Corinthian correspondence, Paul consistently speaks of God's power as foundational for ministry (1 Cor. 1:18, 24; 2:5; 4:20; 6:14; 12:28; 15:24; 2 Cor. 4:7; 6:7; 13:4). Yet the wording here varies from the norm, both in the use of θεός (*theos*, God) in the dative case and in the use of the adjective δυνατός. We probably do not have an "instrumental" or "dative of agency" here, since the instrumental usually would be preceded by the preposition ἐν (*en*, in; BDF 118).

27. As with the Joseph story in the LXX (Gen. 39:20; 40:14; 41:14).

28. As in most uses in the LXX aside from the Joseph story (e.g., Judg. 6:2; 9:46, 49; 2 Sam. 22:2; 2 Kings 8:12; 1 Macc. 1:2; 4:61; 5:9, 11, 27, 29–30, 65; 6:61–62; Ps. 88:41 [89:40 ET]; Prov. 10:29; 12:11–12; 21:22; 30:28; Amos 5:9; Mic. 5:10 [5:11 ET]; Nah. 3:12, 14; Hab. 1:10; Zech. 9:3, 12; Isa. 22:10; 23:14; 24:22). Here Paul uses the image in line with the common LXX usage.

λογισμούς (*logismous*), refers to "thoughts," "calculations," "reasonings," or "reflections," thus "arguments" in our translation. The apostle probably has in mind the patterns of thinking being set forward by his opponents in Corinth.

The second object of the participle, πᾶν ὕψωμα ἐπαιρόμενον κατὰ τῆς γνώσεως τοῦ θεοῦ (*pan hypsōma epairomenon kata tēs gnōseōs tou theou*), can be translated, "every rampart raised up in opposition to knowledge about God." The term ὕψωμα (*hypsōma*) refers to something "high" or "exalted"; its cognate verb can refer to something being lifted up spatially, or in a figurative sense, a person being "exalted" in terms of honor, position, fame, or fortune. Here Paul seems to speak figuratively of a "rampart," a defensive wall of a city or fortress, "raised up" (ἐπαιρόμενον) to fend off an assault. Thus the "thoughts" of his opponents are depicted as an enemy wall standing against a true knowledge of God; authentic Christian ministry tears down such thoughts and makes clear the gospel.[29]

Once the walls are torn down, the second stage of "waging war" in Paul's ministry involves *the capture of enemy soldiers*, who, because the wall has been dismantled, are vulnerable. The present active participle[30] (αἰχμαλωτίζοντες, *aichmalōtizontes*) stems from the verb αἰχμαλωτίζω (*aichmalōtizō*), which refers to securing someone as a prisoner of war (Luke 21:24; 1 Macc. 10:33), as with Judg. 5:12 LXX: "Strengthen, arise, Barak, and, Debbora, strengthen Barak. Take captive your captives, O son of Abineem" (NETS).[31] Yet Paul uses the word figuratively (cf. Rom. 7:23; 2 Tim. 3:6) to speak of taking "every thought" (πᾶν νόημα, *pan noēma*) as a prisoner of war. So having torn down the "arguments" and mental "ramparts" raised up against a true knowledge of God (2 Cor. 10:4c–5a), the apostle now speaks of taking captive "every thought." Roughly synonymous with λογισμούς in 10:4c, νόημα could refer to a "thought," "design," or the "mind" or "understanding" by which a thought is processed (BDAG 675). Earlier, in 4:4, Paul declares that the god of this age has blinded "the minds" (τὰ νοήματα, *ta noēmata*) of the unbelieving, and at 11:3 he mentions his fear that "the minds" (τὰ νοήματα, *ta noēmata*) of the Corinthians will be led off course by the false apostles. Clearly Paul sees the mind as a spiritual battleground. Consequently, with the true gospel, Paul binds up all (πᾶν, every) wrong thinking, bringing it into submission to Christ.

29. Bruce (1971: 230) speculates that Paul has in mind either the perversion of the true gospel, which his opponents replace with another teaching, or an attack on Paul's apostolic status. He further comments that these "fortresses" and "high towers which vaunt themselves against the divine revelation may reflect a spiritual interpretation of the tower of Babel, described by Philo as 'the stronghold' (Gk *ochyrōma*, as here) built through persuasiveness of speech . . . to divert and deflect the mind from honouring God" (*Conf.* 129). The Philo reference is also discussed by Thrall 2000: 611.

30. The present tense may be read as gnomic in context.

31. The word αἰχμαλωτίζω occurs eighteen times in the LXX (Judg. 5:12; 1 Kings 8:46 [2x]; 2 Kings 24:14; 2 Chron. 28:8, 17; 30:9; Jdt. 16:9; Tob. 1:10; 14:15; 1 Macc. 1:32; 5:13; 8:10; 10:33; 15:40; Pss. 70:1 [not in MT/ET]; 105:46 [106:46 ET]; Lam. 1:1) and four times in the NT (Luke 21:24; Rom. 7:23; 2 Cor. 10:5; 2 Tim. 3:6). With the exception of Jdt. 16:9, the uses in the LXX speak literally of being taken captive. In the NT, Luke 21:24 uses the term literally of warfare.

The genitive τοῦ Χριστοῦ (*tou Christou*) may be read as an objective genitive: these schemes are made to obey the Lord Christ. In other words, Paul's siege warfare imagery "is a highly figurative way of saying, 'We . . . preach Jesus Christ *as Lord*' (4:5)" (Barnett 1997: 466).

10:6–7a   So in siege warfare there is the breaking down of walls and the capturing of enemy soldiers. Third, *captured enemy soldiers must be prosecuted*. In 10:6 the apostle writes, "And we stand ready to punish every disobedient act once your obedience is complete." Here we have the last of the three parallel nominative plural participles (ἔχοντες, *echontes*) that seem to function as finite verbs in the passage. The adjective ἕτοιμος (*hetoimos*, ready), has already been used by Paul at 9:5 to speak of the need for the Corinthians to have their generous gift "ready" when he comes to collect it.[32] Here the preposition, the dative form of the word, and the present participle (ἐν ἑτοίμῳ ἔχοντες, *en hetoimō echontes*) convey the sense, "we stand ready," paralleling the similarly worded ἑτοίμως ἔχω (*hetoimōs echō*, I am ready) at 12:14, where the cognate adverb (ἑτοίμως) is used. Paul is poised, in other words, to act when he comes to Corinth. What he intends to do is "punish every disobedient act." The aorist infinitive ἐκδικῆσαι (*ekdikēsai*) means to bring to bear a penalty for a wrong having been done, thus "to punish," and the punishment is for "every disobedient act" (πᾶσαν παρακοήν, *pasan parakoēn*, every disobedience), thus underscoring the comprehensiveness of the apostle's work. He will tear down "every rampart" (πᾶν ὕψωμα, v. 5a), take captive "every thought" (πᾶν νόημα, v. 5b), and deal with "every disobedient act." Yet a condition is stated. Paul will be able to deal fully with his opponents when the Corinthians themselves are fully obedient: "once your obedience is complete" (ὅταν πληρωθῇ ὑμῶν ἡ ὑπακοή, *hotan plērōthē hymōn hē hypakoē*). In other words, it is only when the Corinthians have fully brought themselves back wholeheartedly under the authority of Paul's apostolic work that the opponent problem will be resolved.[33] As with his delay in coming to them (2:1), his writing such a confrontational letter is intended to give the Corinthians an opportunity to come to full repentance, bringing the whole church back together in unity under his leadership (Hafemann 2000: 396).

Thus with verses 3–6 Paul paints a word picture to describe the struggle for leadership of the church. It is like a war in which he is prepared to "attack" the position of the opponents, laying siege to their so-called ministry in Corinth, "capturing" errant thinking, and "prosecuting" those who have shown themselves as the enemies of sound Christian teaching. He will bring God's power to bear, like a siege engine, dismantling the schemes and wrong thinking built up by these false teachers, forcing their ideas into submission to Christ and Christ's gospel. He is ready to do so but again raises the question of the readiness of the Corinthians themselves.

32. Using the same term, Titus 3:1 exhorts believers to be "ready for every good work."
33. John Chrysostom (*Hom. 2 Cor.* 21.3) notes Paul's pastoral skill at this point. The apostle uses restraint, continuing to counsel and appeal to the Corinthians generally before a showdown with the opponents (Bray 1999: 285).

Paul's final statement in this movement of the passage,[34] Τὰ κατὰ πρόσωπον βλέπετε (*Ta kata prosōpon blepete*), can be read either as an imperative
("Notice what is staring you in the face!"), or as an indicative ("You are looking at things as they appear on the surface!"). The latter offers a rebuke. The
former exhorts to action. Yet there are at least two reasons for reading βλέπετε
as indicative (so NASB, NIV, NET). At 5:12 Paul speaks of those who boast
inappropriately in outward appearance (πρὸς τοὺς ἐν προσώπῳ καυχωμένους,
pros tous en prosōpō kauchōmenous), and this concern with an evaluation
of leaders on inadequate bases is also reflected in the present context. Also,
while it is true that all other uses of the inflected form βλέπετε in Paul are
imperatives (1 Cor. 1:26; Eph. 5:15; Phil. 3:2; Col. 2:8), in every one of those
instances the verb begins the clause. It may be that Paul, in our present case,
has shifted Τὰ κατὰ πρόσωπον forward for emphasis, as Harris (2005: 687) and
others suggest, but the change from Paul's normal pattern of placing βλέπετε
at the beginning of the sentence may indicate a different use of the form. In
keeping with the context, Paul seems to be rebuking the Corinthians for buying in to a surface appraisal of himself and his ministry: "You are looking at
things as they appear on the surface!" This fits the context well and makes a
nice transition to the following sentence, in which the apostle issues a call to
affirm the authenticity of his relationship with Christ.

The church in the West stands under the most grave attacks in terms of
spiritual warfare, an attack in some ways worse than the physical and social
persecution faced by our brothers and sisters around the world. False gospels
offered by false teachers thrive in a context of biblical and theological illiteracy.
Paul understood what was at stake for the church. The question is, Do we?

3. The Apostle's Claim to Authority (10:7b–11)

Three primary thoughts make up 2 Cor. 10:7b–11, and it takes some work to
piece together the apostle's logic as we move from one to another. The first
(10:7b) offers a clear call for his detractors to consider in a fresh way Paul's
relationship to Christ. The second thought (10:8) asserts that Paul will not

10:7b–8

34. Some read the statement as belonging with what follows (as with the paragraph division
in NA[28]). If the statement is read as an indicative, it is seen as contrasting with the balance of
10:7, with its exhortation to personally consider Paul from a deeper perspective. If the sentence
is read as an imperative, what follows in verse 7 is understood as reinforcement by means of
further encouragement. However, there are three reasons for understanding this brief sentence
as the capstone of 10:1–6. First, the reference to seeing things κατὰ πρόσωπον (as they look on
the surface) certainly picks up a thought on "outward appearance" (ἐν προσώπῳ, *en prosōpō*) at
5:12, but it also may be understood as forming an inclusio (bracket) with the same phrase, κατὰ
πρόσωπον, in 10:1 and as continuing an emphasis on evaluation from outward appearances at
10:2. In other words, the Corinthians are falling into a pattern set by the interlopers, evaluating Paul on surface issues rather than deeper, spiritual criteria. Second, if Τὰ κατὰ πρόσωπον
βλέπετε is read as concluding 10:1–7a, then the main clause in 10:7b, τοῦτο λογιζέσθω, and the
repeating of that clause at 10:11, may also be taken as an inclusio bracketing 10:7b–11. Finally,
the shift from second person (βλέπετε) in 10:7a to third person (τις πέποιθεν) in 10:7b serves
as another key discourse marker.

be ashamed of boasting about his position of authority in relation to the Corinthians, even if it comes across to the Corinthians as a bit overdone. The third main thought comes in 10:11 and, mirroring certain aspects of the first thought in 10:7b, again calls for consideration of something about Paul—that the way he acts out his authority in person will match the authoritative statements he has communicated in his letters. With the repetition of τοῦτο λογιζέσθω (*touto logizesthō*) in the first and third of these thoughts (10:7b, 11), we have an inclusio, a bracket structure, that ties this submovement of chapter 10 together. All three points in this unit focus on *the apostle's claim to authority*.

The apostle begins, "If anyone has convinced himself that he is from Christ, he personally should consider again the fact that just as he is from Christ, so are we!" The conditional clause almost certainly reflects a statement made by one of Paul's opponents—perhaps their ringleader—who was bolstering a claim to leadership by saying, "I am sent from Christ!" The verb at the heart of the conditional clause, πέποιθεν (*pepoithen*), is perfect in form and means "to be convinced or certain of something" (BDAG 792). Furthermore, the prepositional phrase with the reflexive pronoun ἐφ᾽ ἑαυτοῦ (*eph' heautou*) can be read in this case as suggesting presumptuousness on the part of the interloper (i.e., "in his own mind" or "personally"; see Lambrecht 1999: 153). What the false teacher has convinced himself of is that he is "from Christ" (Χριστοῦ εἶναι, *Christou einai*), having been sent on Christ's business to the church at Corinth. This reading understands Χριστοῦ as a genitive of source.

Yet a number of other possibilities have been offered by commentators.[35] The genitive Χριστοῦ could simply be equivalent to "be a Christian," referring to a person who belongs to Christ (perhaps a genitive of possession), but this interpretation is unlikely in a context in which Paul defends not his relationship with Christ but rather his authority as an apostle. Or it could be that the opponents attack the apostle as not belonging to the "Christ group" mentioned at 1 Cor. 1:12; yet it would not make sense for Paul, in the next breath, to assert in essence, "I am too!" since he clearly has decried such Corinthian cliques! As another possible interpretation, it could be that "to be of Christ" is understood as a reference to firsthand knowledge of the earthly Jesus (P. Hughes 1962: 356), or perhaps the interlopers were claiming a unique spiritual relationship with Jesus to which Paul was not privy.

Nevertheless, the most likely interpretation based on the broader context, is that these "false apostles" (11:13), who were claiming to be "servants of Christ" (11:23), were appealing to their authority as leaders of the church, as having been sent "from Christ." They were claiming to be authoritative representatives sent from the Messiah and thus the Corinthians' true leaders. The claim was meant to supplant Paul. This interpretation, focused on the issue of authority over the congregation, comports well with the flow of thought in this section of the book and fits nicely with the next verse.

35. For detailed overviews, see esp. Harris 2005: 688–89; Thrall 2000: 620–22.

Verse 8 reads, "For even if I boast a bit more about our authority, which the Lord gave for the purpose of building you up and not for tearing you down, I will not be ashamed of it." Here the apostle clearly states the topic that forms the focus for the letter from this point all the way through chapter 12: Paul boasts about his apostolic authority. As noted already in the commentary, although at points he speaks of an inappropriate form of boasting, when Paul himself boasts, he boasts in the Lord, focusing on the character and work of God.[36] Yet he realizes that he might be misunderstood at this point and characterized as boasting inappropriately, claiming more than he should, given his status.[37] The tension between appropriate and inappropriate boasting will heighten as the theme develops.

Thus far in the letter Paul has used the verb καυχάομαι (kauchaomai, boast) three times (5:12; 7:14; 9:2), the cognate noun καύχημα (kauchēma, boasting) three times (1:14; 5:12; 9:3), and the similar καύχησις (kauchēsis, boasting) four times (1:12; 7:4, 14; 8:24), so "boasting" constitutes a significant theme for 2 Corinthians. In 5:12 the verb has been used to speak negatively of those who "boast" in outward appearance, and at 7:14 and 9:2 we find Paul boasting about the work of God among the Corinthians to others. From this point onward, the apostle boasts "a bit more" (περισσότερόν τι, perissoteron ti),[38] weaving an important topical thread, the apostle uses the verb no fewer than sixteen times over the next two and a half chapters (10:13, 15, 16, 17 [2x]; 11:12, 16, 18 [2x], 30 [2x]; 12:1, 5 [2x], 6, 9)!

Two key points can be made about the topic of boasting as Paul develops the theme in this final movement of the book. First, the verb καυχάομαι and its cognates are conceptually related in 2 Corinthians to the verb συνίστημι, "to recommend" (3:1; 4:2; 5:12; 6:4; 7:11; 10:12, 18; 12:11), and the two words are used in the same general context at 5:12; 7:11–14, 10:12–13, 16–18; and

36. The Jewish Scriptures speak of two types of boasting (kauch-, verb and nouns): the first is a foolish pride in human abilities or accomplishments (e.g., Judg. 7:2; 1 Sam. 2:3; Jer. 12:13; Ezek. 24:25); the second is a celebration of the Lord's character and works (e.g., 1 Chron. 16:35; 29:13; Ps. 5:12 [5:11 ET]; Prov. 16:31). James 4:16 constitutes an example of the negative use: "But as it is, you boast in your arrogance. All that kind of boasting is evil." Only two of the ten uses of the verb in Paul are overtly negative in tone (Rom. 3:27; 2 Cor. 11:17). Paul uses this verb to speak of "boasting" in the Lord (1 Cor. 1:29, 31; 2 Cor. 10:17) or in the Lord's cross (Gal. 6:14).
37. Dewey (1985: 209) describes this type of boasting: "Boasting represents the action of a person who, in the eyes of those he has challenged socially and in view of the larger public audience, has gone beyond the limits of his perceived status."
38. This rendering understands περισσότερον as adverbial, delimiting the verb καυχήσωμαι (kauchēsōmai), and made indefinite by τι (ti, some, a bit; so HCSB, NASB, NET; cf. Luke 12:4). An adverbial interpretation also could be rendered as "somewhat freely" (NIV) or as communicating excess, "too much" (NLT[2], NRSV, ESV). The other option is to take περισσότερον as adjectival, with the περισσότερόν τι functioning as the direct object of the verb, meaning to make a "further boast"; for Barrett (1973: 258) this means "beyond the boast that I and 'Christ's. . . .'" Also Thrall (2000: 624) suggests that περισσότερον probably should be taken adjectivally, to boast of "something more," pointing out that Paul more often uses περισσοτέρως (perissoterōs, especially), the true adverbial form (e.g., 2 Cor. 1:12; 2:4; 7:13, 15). Yet she admits that reading the term here as adverbial is easier.

12:9–11. Among these passages, 5:12 and 10:16–18 present the clearest association of the terms:

> It is not *really* that *we are recommending ourselves* to you again; rather, we are giving you an opportunity *to boast* on our behalf, in order that you might have something for those *boasting* in appearance and not in heart. (5:12)

> . . . so that we can preach the gospel in the regions beyond you. For we do not want *to boast* about work already done in someone else's territory. But, "Let the one who *boasts boast* in the Lord." For it is not the one who *commends* himself who is approved, but the one whom the Lord *commends*. (2 Cor. 10:16–18 NIV)

So the act of commending stands in close association with the act of boasting. From our most ancient examples of letters of recommendation, the writer, in supporting the person of whom the letter speaks, seeks to "'bear witness' to their qualities or abilities" (Spicq 1994: 3.343). Thus to commend someone is to boast about them. As noted at 5:12, Paul practically equates "recommending" with "boasting." On the surface, he seems to be denying that he is practicing self-recommendation, but as we have suggested, this denial actually has behind it an action that would easily be mistaken for the apostle participating in self-recommendation! The association of the two concepts is even more clear in 10:16–18, where boasting about one's work parallels commending oneself, and boasting in the Lord is closely associated with being commended by the Lord. Similarly, here in 10:8 Paul speaks of boasting about his authority. This reference to boasting leads almost immediately into the discussion of how the false leaders "recommend themselves" (10:12) and "boast beyond certain limits" (10:13).

Second, the emphasis here and in the following chapters rests on appropriate boasting over against inappropriate boasting. Throughout the book the act of boasting seems to rest a bit uneasily on the apostle since he opens himself to the accusation of boasting beyond appropriate limits. He does not want to be associated with those who boast inappropriately, focusing on human standards and their own accomplishments (e.g., 10:12–13). Rather than self-exaltation, Paul's boasting serves to underscore his apostolic authority. The double use of εἰς (*eis*) in 10:8 indicates the purpose of his authority: "for the purpose of building you up and not for tearing you down." Paul often uses the metaphor of "building up" to describe a ministry of edification, enhancing the spiritual life of churches or individual believers (e.g., Rom. 14:19; 15:2; 1 Cor. 3:9; 14:3, 5, 12, 26; 2 Cor. 12:19; 13:10; Eph. 2:21; 4:12, 16, 29).[39]

---

39. The language relates in part to believers as God's temple (e.g., 1 Cor. 3:9; Eph. 2:21), or a body (Eph. 4:16), but in this context, which also focuses on the new-covenant minister (2 Cor. 3:6) as "tearing down" walls of opposition to God, it may specifically allude to Jer. 31:27–28 (so Hafemann 2000: 398–99): "'The days are coming'—this is the Lord's declaration—'when I will sow the house of Israel and the house of Judah with the seed of man and the seed of beast. Just as I watched over them to uproot and to tear them down, to demolish and to destroy, and to cause disaster, so will I be attentive to build and to plant them,' says the Lord" (Jer. 31:27–28 HCSB).

This is why he shamelessly boasts in the following chapters. He "will not be ashamed" (οὐκ αἰσχυνθήσομαι, *ouk aischynthēsomai*) because his boasting, which might be considered audacious, even foolish (11:1, 16–17, 21; 12:11), serves the purpose of compelling the Corinthians to acknowledge his apostolic authority (12:11, 19) so that they might submit to that authority. If it takes a bit of foolishness to get the Corinthians to a point of spiritual health, Paul is not above such a course of action.

This raises a very important question for those of us in modern ministry. Is it ever appropriate for us to "boast in the Lord," commending our ministries to others? How might we stay on the right side of that fine line between boasting in the Lord and boasting in oneself, according to human standards? When should we allow others to praise us, rather than pointing to the fruit of our ministries?

At least one critical aspect of Paul's ministry needs to be taken into consideration as we answer such questions. Paul was an apostle and the person who had laid down the gospel foundation under this church, and the church was in danger of departing from the gospel and thus facing spiritual ruin. In part the apostle uses extreme measures for extreme circumstances. Thus as we consider whether it is appropriate to call attention to our accomplishments or calling, we might well ask ourselves, "Is my boasting truly for the sake of this congregation, or am I boasting for my own exaltation or advancement?" And also ask, "Is the effect of my boasting to make much of Christ, to give glory to God, or is the effect to make much of myself in the eyes of people?"

With 10:9–11 Paul returns to the accusation that he was "'pitiful' when face-to-face among" the Corinthians but "'confident' toward" them when away (10:1). Now it becomes clear that the charge was leveled at the supposed contrast between his ministry in Corinth and his ministry of letter writing when away. The syntax of verse 9, which begins with a seemingly abrupt ἵνα (*hina*, in order that) clause, has generated a good deal of discussion. Does it relate grammatically to αἰσχυνθήσομαι, the verb that immediately precedes it? The result of this position seems strained at best, reading something like, "I will not be shamed into seeming not to terrify you with my letters" (Young and Ford 1987: 272). Perhaps, rather, we are confronted with some form of ellipsis. For example, Furnish (1984: 465, 467–68) supplies βούλωμαι (*boulōmai*) with ὡς ἄν (*hos an*), "—lest I should seem as if I wanted to be scaring you with my letters." Harris (2005: 697), on the other hand, adds τοῦτο λέγω (*touto legō*, I say this) at the beginning of the clause: "I say this so that I may not seem as if I am trying to terrify you with my letters," with "this" referring back to Paul's assertion in verse 8 that the authority given him by God was not meant to destroy the Corinthians. Yet, as a standard grammar (BDF 255) explains, at times a ἵνα clause may be put ahead of the main clause, stating the purpose of the following clause.[40] If this is the case with 2 Cor. 10:9–11, the ἵνα clause

10:9–11

---

40. The difficulty here is that we would normally expect a δέ (as in some MSS) or καί, not an asyndetic clause (Harris 2005: 697).

of 10:9 delimits the main clause in verse 11: "In order that I won't seem to be trying to terrify you with my letters, . . . such a person should consider this." On this reading of the text, verse 10 stands as a parenthetical statement (thus the em dashes around verse 10 in our translation), with Paul quoting an opponent as saying, "His letters are intimidating and make a big impression, but he is a pushover in person, and his public speaking is disgraceful."

So Paul begins in verse 9 by stating that he does not want his letters to be perceived as weapons of terror. The negation of the aorist subjunctive verb δόξω (doxō, seem) plus ὡς (hōs, as) makes clear that the apostle speaks of a perception, not wanting to be perceived as having a sinister motive behind his letter writing. The verb ἐκφοβέω (ekphobeō) in verse 9, used only here in the NT,[41] means to cause intense fear or terror. So Paul does not want to be perceived as terrorizing the congregation through his letters. Momentarily we address how this thought relates to the main clause in verse 11.

But before completing this thought, Paul offers the parenthetical statement in verse 10: "to quote a certain person, 'His letters are intimidating and make a big impression, but he is a pushover in person, and his public speaking is disgraceful'—." So clearly his statement about terrorizing the Corinthians through his letters has been made in response to a false accusation made by an opponent.[42] The statement that Paul's letters are "intimidating and make a big impression" is well balanced and rhythmic in Greek: βα-ρεῖ-αι καὶ ἰ-σχυ-ραί (ba-rei-ai kai i-schy-rai). The first of these words, βαρύς (barys), can refer to something vitally important (Matt. 23:23),[43] yet it often refers to something burdensome because of demands or threats, or troublesome, even something fierce or cruel (BDAG 167). Here the opponents probably are accusing Paul's letters of being severe or intimidating. The second term, ἰσχυρός (ischyros), normally translates as "strong" (ESV, NASB[95], Tyndale, NRSV), "powerful" (KJV, HCSB), or "forceful" (NLT[2], NIV, NET). This common word could refer to physical, mental, or spiritual strength, but it also could speak of something loud, violent, or impressive (BDAG 483–84). Even in modern English we refer to a "strong speech," meaning that the speech was forceful or impressive. The accusation seems to be that Paul's letters are forceful or impressive in contrast to his physical presence (ἡ . . . παρουσία τοῦ σώματος, hē . . . parousia tou sōmatos) and his speaking ability. The former the opponent describes as ἀσθενής (asthenēs), "weak" or "unimpressive." In terms of leadership ability, Paul was considered a "pushover," one who did not have the strength to lead. To make matters worse, his public speaking, a skill so highly valued in that

41. The word ἐκφοβέω finds expression fourteen times in the LXX: Lev. 26:6; Jdt. 16:25; 1 Macc. 14:12; 4 Macc. 9:5; Job 7:14; 33:16; Wis. 11:19; 17:18; Mic. 4:4; Nah. 2:12; Zeph. 3:13; Ezek. 32:27; 34:28; 39:26.

42. The verb φησίν (phēsin, he says; a third-person singular present active indicative; 10:10) and singular forms in the main clause of 10:11 (λογιζέσθω ὁ τοιοῦτος, logizesthō ho toioutos, such a person should consider) seem to indicate that Paul has a particular person in mind.

43. The verse refers to "the more important matters of the law" (τὰ βαρύτερα τοῦ νόμου, ta barytera tou nomou).

culture, was tagged as ἐξουθενημένος (*exouthenēmenos*), the perfect passive participle of ἐξουθενέω (*exoutheneō*) being used to describe Paul's oratory as having no merit, being contemptible or worthy of disdain. The opponent considered Paul's public speaking not just as weak, but also as disgraceful, beneath serious consideration!

Consequently, in the final verse of this unit, Paul calls for a change of perspective: "Such a person should consider this: what we are in word, by writing letters when away, we will be in action when present!" Paul does not name the opponent he has just quoted in the previous verse, referring to him as "such a person" (ὁ τοιοῦτος, *ho toioutos*). Earlier, in verses 2 and 7, the apostle has used the verb λογίζομαι (*logizomai*) to speak of the act of evaluating, or putting forth an opinion about, Paul and his ministry. Using this verb at 10:2, the apostle himself "thinks" he will "dare" (λογίζομαι τολμῆσαι, *logizomai tolmēsai*) to use bold confidence against those who evaluate (λογιζομένους, *logizomenous*) him and his ministry team as living according to human standards. In verse 7 he challenges his opponent to consider (λογιζέσθω, *logizesthō*) the fact that Paul's apostleship has been given him by Christ. Now in verse 11 Paul challenges the opponent to adjust his thinking about the relationship between the apostle's public ministry in Corinth and his ministry of writing letters to the congregation. The accusation suggests that the forcefulness of Paul's persona in his letters does not coincide with his public presence and public speaking in Greece. In other words, Paul doesn't have the leadership moxie, nor the skills, to follow through on his written words! But the apostle counters that when he arrives in Corinth, there will be an absolute correspondence between the words he has written and the actions he will take. The integration of the two is expressed in a parallel ("just as . . . so also") grammatical construction as follows:

οἷοί ἐσμεν	τῷ λόγῳ	δι᾽ ἐπιστολῶν	ἀπόντες,
τοιοῦτοι καὶ	τῷ ἔργῳ		παρόντες
hoioi esmen	*tō logō*	*di᾽ epistolōn*	*apontes,*
toioutoi kai	*tō ergō*		*parontes*
What we are	in word,	by writing letters	when away,
we will be	in action		when present!

The apostle has already stated that he does not wage spiritual warfare on the basis of human standards or weapons. Rather, the validity of his apostolic leadership has been and will be manifested through God's power. This seems to mean that he will bring to bear the power of God in holding the opponent(s) accountable. The apostle returns to this idea at the end of the section (and the letter), stating,

> When I was there the second time, I warned those who sinned before and all the rest, and although I am absent right now, I warn them again. When I return I will not spare you, since you are demanding proof that Christ is speaking

through me—Christ, who is not weak in dealing with you but demonstrates his power among you. For indeed, he was crucified as a result of weakness, but he lives as a result of God's power. For also we ourselves are weak by virtue of our relationship with him, but we will live with him as a result of God's power, which is manifested in dealing with you. (13:2–4)

Paul's authority does not consist of mere words. The power of the living God undergirds his position and will be manifested in dealing with opposition.

So how does this assertion relate to the purpose clause in verse 9? Paul has been accused of a ministry that is out of balance. His letters are intimidating, while his public presence is unimpressive. He suggests that he is being misread on both counts, and the opponents have greatly underestimated him. In fact, the power that will be manifested in dealing with his opponents will be very much in line with his claims to apostolic authority in his letters. Rather than being tools of terror, his letters speak simply of the reality of a role given him by God. They are not meant to intimidate. Rather, they make clear the nature of his ministry to the Corinthians. On the other hand, the meekness of his public persona is not a manifestation of a weakness of character or a lack of leadership skills. Rather, his meekness manifests the character of Christ (10:1) and thus the true nature of Christian ministry. All this will be made abundantly clear to everyone when Paul again arrives in Corinth. The spiritual power behind his apostleship will be brought to bear in dealing with his opponents, but that power will be wielded in humble submission to Christ and for Christ's cause in the church. This is the power of a person humbly submitted to God.

Reflection

In *Knowing God*, Packer (1973: 239) states, "Opposition is a fact: the Christian who is not conscious of being opposed had better watch himself, for he is in danger." Truth will be opposed by what is false, and the truth must oppose what is false. Paul's ministry in Corinth bears witness to both sides of this truism. Paul opposes the false teachers at Corinth and thus draws opposition to himself and his mission. Opposition by its very nature is conflictual and, for many of us, uncomfortable. The challenge is not to use false means to combat false men and women who pervert the gospel. Human standards of engagement alone are both inadequate and potentially destructive in dealing with conflict in the church, for we are dealing with spiritual conditions that must be addressed by spiritual means and to spiritual ends. Spiritual weapons must be used so that fortresses are destroyed, arguments are torn down, and thoughts are taken captive. But the end result is key to assessing whether our warfare works by the Spirit of God or the spirit of the age. Does the warfare result in obedience to Christ? Is authority wielded in a way that people are built up rather than torn down? Authority must be wielded in the "humility and graciousness of Christ" and for the health of the community. Too often ministers in the modern world exercise a worldly authority, in worldly ways, with worldly results. We should reevaluate the standards by which we purportedly fight for the truth.

Additional Notes

10:4. The variant preferred by the UBS[4] and NA[27], στρατείας (B[2] [F G: -τίας] Ψ 33 81 104 365 630 1505 1739 *pm*), which connotes a military campaign, makes the most sense in the context but has weaker external support than does forms of στρατιᾶς (from στρατιά, army) especially when unaccented (D[2] K L 1175 1241 1881 *al* [𝔓[46] ℵ B* C D* P 2464 without the accent]). In any case, the word στρατιά could at times be used with the same sense as στρατείας (BDAG 948), so it is possible that this was Paul's choice of terms. However, the dropping of the ε in στρατείας could be a scribal error, itacism, since the ει and ι were pronounced identically. Regardless, Paul's metaphor seems clear.

10:7. In place of πέποιθεν, B alone has δοκεῖ πεποιθέναι, perhaps to make the presumptuousness of Paul's opponent clearer (so Harris 2005: 665; Thrall 2000: 619). Perhaps also the scribe of B employs the verb δοκέω (also used in v. 9) in light of the statement in the previous sentence (v. 7a): the Corinthians are being duped in part by appearances.

10:7. The reading ἐφ᾽ ἑαυτοῦ (lit., based on himself) has very strong attestation (𝔓[46] ℵ B L 1175 1505 *pc*) over against ἀφ᾽ ἑαυτοῦ (C D F G H Ψ 0209 0243 33 1739 1881 𝔐 sy). The latter, which communicates a similar meaning, probably resulted due to similar pronunciation.

10:8. Although τε is included following ἐάν and prior to γάρ at the beginning of verse 8 in a number of strong witnesses (ℵ C D Ψ [0209] 𝔐 f [r] vg sy; Ambst), its omission also enjoys extensive support (𝔓[46] B F G H 0243 6 33 365 630 1175 1739 1881 *pc* it vg[mss]). Nevertheless, it probably should be read as original, since it is unlikely that a scribe would have added it to the more common γάρ (Thrall 2000: 623). The particle adds a nuanced note that is ascensive in nature, rendered in our translation as "even."

10:8. In terms of proper grammar, with ἐάν we would expect the subjunctive form καυχήσωμαι (B C D F G Ψ 1739 1881[c] 𝔐), but a number of witnesses have the indicative form καυχήσομαι (ℵ L P 0209 0243 6 104 326 1175 1241 1505 1881* *al* [g]), perhaps reflecting that Paul has already been boasting and is in the process of doing so. In addition to grammatical form, however, the latter as an early scribal error seems indicated by 𝔓[46] conflating the two readings in καυχήσωμαι, καυχήσομαι.

10:8. The addition of ἡμῖν as a clarifying element either before (P Ψ 629 1505 1881 *pc* it) or after (ℵ[2] D[2] F G [0209] 𝔐 sy[h]) ὁ κύριος is understandable (cf. μοι at 13:10), but its omission is much better attested (𝔓[46] ℵ* B C D* H 0243 33 81 365 630 1175 1739 2464 *pc* b vg[st]).

B. Proper and Improper Boasting (10:12–18)

In the previous unit Paul categorically denies that he and his mission team conduct ministry according to human standards (10:2–3). Although he admits to boasting, he boasts appropriately, according to the authority given him by the Lord and for the building up of the church (10:8). Now at 10:12–18 the apostle focuses on various dimensions of "inappropriate boasting" carried out by the interlocutors, offering us tantalizing details on the activities of this problem group. In contrast to Paul, they conduct their ministries according to human standards, comparing themselves to one another, and they thus boast inappropriately. Simply rendered, the outline of the passage may be depicted as follows:

1. We don't engage in carnal comparisons (10:12)
2. We don't overstep ministry boundaries (10:13–15a)
3. We hope to extend the mission (10:15b–16)
4. We boast in the Lord (10:17–18)

Another way of envisioning the flow of the passage, however, depicts it in a chiastic structure, with the first and last point speaking of self-recommendation over against the Lord's commendation; the second and fourth focusing on the act of boasting about work accomplished by someone else; and the third point, offered in twin, terse, independent clauses, pointing out that Paul and his mission did not overextend themselves but rather had reached the Corinthians with the gospel.

  A We don't dare to use ourselves as their standard of measurement for ministry (like those commending themselves) (10:12).
    B We don't boast outside of proper limits (10:13).
      C We don't overextend ourselves (10:14a).
      C′ We reached as far as you with the gospel of Christ (10:14b).
    B′ i. not boasting in the work accomplished by someone else but (10:15a).
        ii. hoping   to enlarge our area of ministry (10:15b).
                  to evangelize the area beyond you.
                  not to boast in work already accomplished by someone else.
  A′ Proper boasting is "in the Lord" who alone sets the standards for ministry (10:17–18).

Tightly cohering around repeated terms,[1] the passage also presents Paul's categorical denials (see the repetition of the negative οὐ, *ou*, not), which drive home what he sees as appropriate activities of God's ministers. Also, the topic of "boundaries" raises the issue of Paul's ministry boundaries being extended once the Corinthians respond appropriately to the current crisis (10:15–16). The apostle has already been thinking about next steps in the mission, and he sees the partnership with the Corinthians as important to those next steps.

Exegesis and Exposition

[12]For we wouldn't dare to classify or compare ourselves with any of those who are commending themselves. Here's the difference: when they measure themselves, using themselves as the standard, and compare themselves with one another, ⌜they are clueless. [13]We, on the other hand⌝, refuse to boast beyond proper limits but boast within the boundaries of the assignment God has given us, boundaries that reach even as far as you. [14]For we are not overextending ourselves (which we would be doing if our ministry does not extend to you). Indeed, we reached even as far as you with the good news about Christ. [15]Neither do we boast beyond appropriate limits by boasting of hard work done by others. But we do hope that as your faith continues to grow, our ministry, in accordance with our assignment, will be extended tremendously by you. [16]We hope for this so that we might preach the good news in the regions beyond you, instead of boasting about work already accomplished in another person's sphere of ministry. [17]Rather, *"The one who boasts should boast in the Lord!"* [18]For it is not the one commending himself who passes the test, but the one whom the Lord commends!

1. We Don't Engage in Carnal Comparisons (10:12)

In 2 Cor. 10:12 Paul takes up the topic of "boasting" mentioned in 10:8 and reflects on a key distinction between his biblical form of boasting (10:17–18) and the worldly boasting carried out by his opponents.[2] Thus the γάρ (*gar*, for) at the beginning of the verse is a marker of clarification (BDAG 189). The apostle boasts—he is about to do so extensively in the remainder of the letter—but his boasting must not be associated with the boasting of his opponents. He writes, "For we wouldn't dare to classify or compare ourselves with any of those who are commending themselves." The Οὐ . . . τολμῶμεν (*Ou . . . tolmōmen*, we wouldn't dare) underscores Paul's conviction concerning the

10:12

---

1. Especially συγκρίνω (*synkrinō*, compare; and cognate forms), ἑαυτοῦ (*heautou*, oneself), συνίστημι (*synistēmi*, commend), καυχάομαι (*kauchaomai*, boast), ἄμετρος (*ametros*, beyond limits) and μέτρον (*metron*, within limits), κανών (*kanōn*, limits), and ἐφικνέομαι (*ephikneomai*, extend).

2. For the important textual variant at 10:12–13, see the additional notes. For a discussion of the variant in the history of Catholic interpretation, see Hennig 1946.

inappropriateness of the boasting he sees among the Corinthian opponents.[3] Used earlier at 10:2 and later at 11:21, the verb τολμάω (*tolmaō*) speaks in the present context of a line of behavior that the apostle refuses to cross (cf. Rom. 15:18; Jude 9)—to arrogantly put himself forward as superior (Martin 1986: 319). He will dare to use bold confidence against his opponents (10:2), but he won't dare to join in their games of ministry evaluation—a posture potently ironic. The opponents have tagged him as "a pushover in person," and as a "disgraceful" public speaker (10:10). No doubt they think Paul is beneath them in ability and not in their league. Ironically, he agrees that he should not go toe-to-toe with these braggarts. But his read of the situation could not be more different from theirs.

The twin complementary aorist infinitives ἐγκρῖναι (*enkrinai*, to classify) and συγκρῖναι (*synkrinai*, to compare) form a play on words (notice the *-krinai* they have in common) and specifically define that behavior. The first, a rare word,[4] means "to make a judgment about something and classify it in a specific group" (BDAG 274). The second, used by Paul at 1 Cor. 2:13,[5] connotes drawing a conclusion by making a comparison (BDAG 953).[6] Drawing comparisons, referred to as *synkrisis*, was a prominent rhetorical technique in discourses and debates of the ancient world (Keener 2005: 220).[7] In the political sphere, vicious smear campaigns sought to demobilize the influence of rival leaders in light of one's own strengths. Referencing the work of Stansbury (1990: 278), Garland (1999: 452) explains, "In the cutthroat competition for plaudits and pupils, one had to advertise oneself publicly with audacious praise while impugning the qualities of other contenders for honor. People were constantly vying with others to attain elusive glory and engaged in a constant game of one-upmanship."[8] Thus one way to move up in the world was to tear down

3. On the use of boasting and comparison in Hellenistic rhetoric, see Forbes 1986.

4. A hapax in the biblical literature, it finds expression in Philo once and in the Pseudepigrapha once (Let. Aris. 228). Philo (*Post.* 96), in a passage about the importance of numbers and classification, uses this word in a context that includes the term δόκιμος (*dokimos*, approved), which Paul uses at 10:18.

5. Used with the sense of "explaining": "We speak about these things, not with words taught us by human wisdom, but with those taught by the Spirit, explaining spiritual things to spiritual people" (1 Cor. 2:13 NET).

6. Philo (*Post.* 105), e.g., who uses the word twenty-two times, writes, "It is not appropriate to compare [συγκρίνειν, *synkrinein*] the music of man with that of any other animal, since a human being has a special privilege with which he has been honoured, namely, being able to articulate distinctly when speaking."

7. Hebrews, e.g., uses comparison extensively but quite differently from what is implied in the present context. In Hebrews, comparison is drawn, not to denigrate angels or Moses (Heb. 1:5–14; 3:1–6), e.g., but to build on the appropriate respect the audience had for angels and Moses to vie for the greater honor and veneration due Jesus.

8. Following Forbes (1986: 8), Garland relates how Lucian pokes fun at sham teachers who built their own reputations by elaborately comparing themselves with others. Lucian has a veteran instruct a pupil on how to be successful: "Make marvelous assertions about yourself, be extravagant in your self-praise, and make yourself a nuisance to him" (*Rhet. praec.* 13.21). As Lucian's satire demonstrates, such boasting was not universally applauded. Keener points out

an opponent, using the opponent's shredded image as a step stool to greater status. Paul refuses to get caught up in such worldly competition, classifying and comparing himself or the members of his mission (ἑαυτούς, *heautous*, ourselves) with the false teachers in Corinth.

He refers to the opponents in mind as "any of those who are commending themselves." We have noted that in speaking of "commendation," Paul seems to walk a fine line. He does commend himself (3:1; 4:2; 5:12; 6:4), pointing out all the characteristics of authenticity that mark his ministry. Yet the act of recommending himself seems to sit uneasily with the apostle. In a sense he is being forced to do so because the Corinthians have not stepped in the gap, stood up to the opposition, and strongly recommended their apostle (12:11)! Paul is not ashamed of boasting (10:8) because his boasting is fundamentally different from that of his opponents; essentially, he boasts in the Lord, not in human ability or achievement (10:17–18). Self-recommendation, done with proper motives and in submission to God, is not wrong in and of itself, but self-recommendation, done apart from a proper boasting about God's work, drifts into unhealthy attitudes and behaviors. Specifically, the opponents commend themselves, boasting of what they have to offer, not by pointing to the works of God but by classifying and comparing themselves to one another. Paul writes, "Here's the difference: when they measure themselves using themselves as the standard, and compare themselves with one another, they are clueless." So it is a form of self-recommendation that works by tearing down another person.

The contrastive ἀλλά (*alla*) in verse 12, which we translate as "Here's the difference," highlights the distinction between Paul's spiritual posture as he boasts in God and that of the opponents, who seek to build themselves up in the eyes of people by classification and comparison. To the thought he now introduces the present participle of μετρέω (*metreō*), "to measure" or, better in this context, "to evaluate" (BDAG 643). The false teachers are evaluating themselves "by themselves" (ἐν ἑαυτοῖς, *en heautois*),[9] that is, "using themselves as the standard" of measurement. And they "compare themselves with one another" (συγκρίνοντες ἑαυτοὺς ἑαυτοῖς, *synkrinontes heautous heautois*).[10] This is "ministry as contest," and Paul labels the activity as "clueless" (οὐ συνιᾶσιν, *ou syniasin*), or more literally, "They don't understand." Used broadly in the ancient world, the word συνίημι (*syniēmi*) occurs twenty-six times in the NT, mostly in the Synoptic Gospels and Acts, and speaks especially of spiritual understanding or discernment.[11] Both Jesus (Matt. 13:14–15; Mark

---

that many prominent rhetoricians of the Greco-Roman world looked down on self-praise and warned against it (e.g., Plutarch, *Plat. Q.* 1.2, *Cic.* 24.1–2). At the same time, it was appropriate to appeal to one's deeds in the face of criticism; this was a form of apologetic self-recommendation (e.g., Demosthenes, *Cor.* 299–300; *False Emb.* 174; Cicero, *Fam.* 5.12.8; see Keener 2005: 220–21).

9. Here the preposition ἐν is used of a standard, "according to the standard of."

10. The first ἑαυτούς is a direct object; the second, the dative plural ἑαυτοῖς, is a dative of reference, "with reference to themselves."

11. Matt. 13:13–15, 19, 23, 51; 15:10; 16:12; 17:13; Mark 4:12; 6:52; 7:14; 8:17, 21; Luke 2:50; 8:10; 18:34; 24:45; Acts 7:25 (2x); 28:26–27; Rom. 3:11; 15:21; 2 Cor. 10:12; Eph. 5:17.

4:12; Luke 8:10) and Paul (in the narrative at Acts 28:26–27) quote Isa. 6:9–10 as a foundational passage about spiritual perceptiveness over against spiritual denseness, and our verb stands at the heart of this prophetic word:

> Go, and say to this people: "You will listen by listening, but you will not understand [οὐ μὴ συνῆτε, *ou mē synēte*], and looking you will look, but you will not perceive." For this people's heart has grown fat, and with their ears they have heard heavily, and they have shut their eyes so that they might not see with their eyes and hear with their ears and understand [συνῶσιν, *synōsin*] with their heart and turn—and I would heal them. (NETS)

But, as will become clear with the apostle's allusion to Jer. 9:23–24 (9:22–23 LXX) at 10:17, the origin of his accusation that the opponents "are clueless" stems especially from that passage on boasting in the Lord: ἀλλ' ἢ ἐν τούτῳ καυχάσθω ὁ καυχώμενος, συνίειν καὶ γινώσκειν ὅτι ἐγώ εἰμι κύριος (*all' ē en toutō kauchasthō ho kauchōmenos, syniein kai ginōskein hoti egō eimi kyrios*; 9:23 LXX), "but let him who boasts boast in this: that he *understands* and knows that I am the Lord" (NETS).

So Paul strongly asserts that the opponents, who carry on "ministry" by classifying one another, comparing themselves to one another, and evaluating performances using one another as the standard of measurement, demonstrate that they simply are spiritual dullards, clueless about what constitutes true Christian ministry. Here, of course, the apostle himself carries out a bit of classification and comparison, and he will offer further comparison as the letter continues (e.g., 11:22)! But there is a profound difference between what he writes and how the opponents size him up! Paul does not judge ministries or missions by the standards of men. Rather, he evaluates his own ministry and that of others on the basis of a set standard—whether ministry is carried out under the lordship of Christ, faithfully, and according to the assignment given by God.

2. We Don't Overstep Ministry Boundaries (10:13–15a)

10:13 Paul's opponents have embraced a second major error by offering themselves as ministers to the church at Corinth, inappropriately invading an area of ministry that had been assigned by God to Paul. The boasting of the opponents was "out of bounds" in that they boasted about a ministry they had neither started nor nurtured. His first main point (v. 13a) asserts that *Paul and his ministry team only boast about ministry given them by God*. Paul writes, "We, on the other hand, refuse to boast beyond proper limits but boast within the boundaries of the assignment God has given us." A contrastive use of δέ (*de*, on the other hand) links this statement with the previous verse, as the apostle continues to explain the difference between his mission and the opponents' so-called ministry. He has been speaking of "commending" (συνιστανόντων, *synistanontōn*) in the previous verse, but the focus now turns overtly back to the related concept of "boasting" (various forms of καυχάομαι, *kauchaomai*), and again the emphasis is on appropriate over against inappropriate behavior.

The pronoun ἡμεῖς (*hēmeis*, we) at the beginning of the verse adds emphasis to the contrast between the opponents' actions and those of Paul's mission. The negated future indicative verb (οὐκ καυχησόμεθα, *ouk kauchēsometha*, we will not boast) states a solemn commitment.[12] Sandwiched between the pronoun/conjunction at the beginning of the verse and the verb, we find the phrase εἰς τὰ ἄμετρα (*eis ta ametra*, beyond proper limits), which expresses the extent of boasting Paul avoids. At 10:12 he has already spoken of the opponents who "measure themselves" (ἑαυτοὺς μετροῦντες, *heautous metrountes*), and here in verse 13 he uses four other terms built on the same root:

εἰς τὰ **ἄμετρα**
καυχησόμεθα ἀλλὰ
κατὰ τὸ **μέτρον** τοῦ κανόνος
οὗ **ἐμέρισεν** ἡμῖν ὁ θεὸς **μέτρου**

The first of these, ἄμετρα, could be used to mean "excessively" (or with εἰς τά, to an excessive degree, with εἰς being a marker of degree). For instance, Epictetus in his *Enchiridion* (33) uses the cognate adverb to warn a person involved in conversations at a party against "mentioning frequently and excessively" (ἐπὶ πολὺ καὶ ἀμέτρως μεμνῆσθαι, *epi poly kai ametrōs memnēsthai*) their own adventures. But Paul crafts a play on words here, and the terms speak not just of moderation in speech but primarily of boasting beyond certain limits (Thrall 2000: 644). In other words, the opponents boast about things that for them should have been off limits. Thus they boast "beyond proper limits."

Paul and his coworkers, on the other hand "boast within the boundaries of the assignment God has given" them (ἀλλὰ κατὰ τὸ μέτρον τοῦ κανόνος οὗ ἐμέρισεν ἡμῖν ὁ θεὸς μέτρου, *alla kata to metron tou kanonos hou emerisen hēmin ho theos metrou*). That Paul and his team boast κατὰ τὸ μέτρον τοῦ κανόνος communicates the idea of boasting "according to the limits of the assignment," or as with our translation, "within the boundaries of the assignment." The term μέτρον can refer to an instrument used to measure something, or the quantity or number assessed by the act of measuring (BDAG 644). From the context we discern that what is measured out in this case are the boundaries of Paul's ministry. Although κανών (*kanōn*) commonly means a "rule" or "standard" (this eventually will lead to our English word "canon"), here it refers to Paul's "assignment,"[13] or "jurisdiction" (Furnish 1984: 465),

12. This may be an example of an imperatival future, which offers a timeless statement of solemn force, often a very strong command or guideline by which one is to live. Most of the examples in the NT are OT quotations and stem generally from the legal literature of the Pentateuch (e.g., Matt. 19:18; 22:37; see D. Wallace 1996: 569). If we are reading the form correctly, it adds a degree of solemnity to Paul's declaration.

13. Translations of the word at 10:13 have included "rule" (KJV), "influence" (ESV), "area of ministry" (HCSB), "sphere" (NEB, NASB), "measure" (Tyndale), "field" (NRSV, TEV, NIV⁸⁴),

especially the geographical area he is to visit in his travels.[14] What this says is that in ministering to the Corinthians, Paul has gone where God told him to go and was ministering to those to whom God had sent him. In boasting of his missionary activity in Corinth, therefore, he is boasting of work initiated and built up by God himself. This constitutes boasting that is appropriate (10:17–18). The apostle further describes this assignment as that which "God has given us" or which "God himself has assigned to us" (οὗ ἐμέρισεν ἡμῖν ὁ θεὸς μέτρου, *hou emerisen hēmin ho theos metrou*; more lit., of which measure God assigned to us). In his *Commentary on Paul's Epistles* (2 Cor. 10:12), Ambrosiaster puts the contrast between Paul and his opponents in this way:

> People who commend themselves are those who wish to dominate, claiming authority for their own name. A person who is sent on a mission lays claim to power, not on his own behalf but on behalf of the one who sent him. Here Paul is saying that he has been chosen as a steward of the Lord. By not presuming to anything beyond what has been granted to him, he is not associating himself with those who preach without a commission. (Bray 1999: 286)

Thus Paul again underscores God's role in staking out the extent of his ministry. Those boundaries, of course, reach as far as the Corinthians themselves: "boundaries that reach even[15] as far as you" (ἐφικέσθαι ἄχρι καὶ ὑμῶν, *ephikesthai achri kai hymōn*). The aorist infinitive ἐφικέσθαι[16] (reach) complements the verb ἐμέρισεν in the relative clause, showing more specifically the measure of the assignment: God has *assigned* the boundaries *to extend* as far as the church at Corinth.

10:14–15a   In verse 14 the apostle builds on the negative assertion he has just made in verse 13 by making another one. In verse 13 Paul denies that he boasts "out of bounds," and in the next verse he denies that he ministers "out of bounds." Whereas in verse 13 Paul asserts that he will not boast in an undisciplined manner by boasting about ministry not assigned to him, he now denies categorically that he and his mission, in ministering to the Corinthians, have trespassed on another person's territory: "For we are not overextending ourselves" (οὐ

"service" (NIV), "work" (NET), "line" (YLT). A use similar to Paul's is found in 1 Clem. 41.1, which speaks of not overstepping one's κανών (*kainōn*) of ministry (τῆς λειτουργίας αὐτοῦ κανόνα, *tēs leitourgias autou kanona*, the designated rule of his ministry). James Strange (1983: 168) points to an inscription from Galatia, which came to light in 1976. It is an edict by the governor of Galatia, Sotidius (ca. AD 13–15), and concerns the need for the citizens of Sagalassus to provide public transportation for officials of the empire. Our word is used in terms of the services provided within certain territorial limits. The inscription has been published in *NewDocs* 1:36–45. For the sense of the word as "standard" in this context, see Dewey 1985: 214.

14. For the "missionary concordat" of Gal. 2:7–9 as part of the backdrop for Paul being assigned the Gentile area that included Corinth, see Harris 2005: 712.

15. This is an ascensive use of καί (Robertson 1934: 1181). At this point the Corinthians are near the outer boundaries of Paul's mission (he has not yet been beyond them to Rome). But even though they are on the frontier, his ministry has reached them and included them.

16. The verb ἐφικνέομαι (*ephikneomai*) is used in the NT only here and in the next verse.

γὰρ . . . ὑπερεκτείνομεν ἑαυτούς, *ou gar . . . hyperekteinomen heautous*). Whereas the common word ἐκτείνω (*ekteinō*) means "to stretch out," this rare intensification, ὑπερεκτείνω (*hyperekteinō*), means "to stretch out beyond" or "overextend" (BDAG 1033). The ὡς (*hōs*) clause, placed between the οὐ γὰρ and the ὑπερεκτείνομεν ἑαυτούς, presents an analogous circumstance (BDAG 1104). If Paul and his mission are "overextending" themselves, the apostle implies, that would be inferred from the corresponding thought that their ministry assignment did not reach as far as the Corinthians (μὴ ἐφικνούμενοι εἰς ὑμᾶς, *mē ephiknoumenoi eis hymas*). The fact is, however, that they are *not* overextending their ministry because the Corinthians *are* a part of the ministry God has given Paul to do. Thus the parenthetical ὡς clause amounts to "which we would be doing if our ministry does not extend to you."

Paul further underscores the point by writing, "Indeed, we reached even as far as you with the good news about Christ." The conjunction γάρ (*gar*) sometimes is repeated when the statement it introduces confirms the previous statement, and this is the case here; so we translate the conjunction as "Indeed" to clarify the conjunction's role in underscoring the statement just made. As with the similar construction at the end of verse 13, the καί, on the other hand, is ascensive, meaning "even" (Tyndale; Robertson 1934: 1181) and works with ἄχρι . . . ὑμῶν (*achri . . . hymōn*) to communicate, "even as far as you." In his second mission endeavor, the apostle had "reached" (ἐφθάσαμεν, *ephthasamen*)[17] as far as Corinth (Acts 18:1–11), though no farther west. He had brought the good news to the Corinthians, telling them about Christ, and we read the τοῦ Χριστοῦ (*tou Christou*) as an objective genitive. Consequently, Paul was the Corinthians' spiritual father in the faith. Accordingly, at 1 Cor. 4:15 the apostle writes, "For you can have 10,000 instructors in Christ, but you can't have many fathers. For I became your father in Christ Jesus through the gospel" (HCSB). It was absurd for some to suggest that the ministry of the one who founded this church in Corinth was trespassing on someone else's ministry.

With verse 15 comes another denial: "Neither do we boast beyond appropriate limits by boasting of hard work done by others." We have already seen the phrase εἰς τὰ ἄμετρα (*eis ta ametra*) in 10:13 and made the point there that although the term ἄμετρα could speak of something as "excessive" (i.e., "boasting on and on of [something]"), Paul probably uses the word in this context to mean "beyond appropriate limits." This accusation obviously constitutes a slap at the opponents, even though the apostle poses the statement as defending his own mission. Paul has made clear that he and his mission are the legitimate apostolic ministry, placed in Corinth by God. The apostle had done "hard work" (κόποις, *kopois*) during his initial eighteen months among the Corinthians. The noun κόπος (*kopos*, here in the plural) and its cognate verb could be used generally of labor that was burdensome (e.g., Deut. 25:18; Ps. 6:7 [6:6 ET]; 1 Sam. 17:39; Luke 5:5), but in Paul's case, "this labor comes

17. For the interpretation of this term as "reached first," see Barrett 1973: 266–67; Thrall 2000: 648–49.

to encompass more and more all of the efforts, cares, constraints, austerities, and labors of the apostolic ministry" (Spicq 1994: 2.322–29), which were abundant and characterized by hardship (2 Cor. 11:27). So the opponents were bragging about ministry whose foundation had been dug with the calluses and sweat of Paul and his coworkers.

3. We Hope to Extend the Mission (10:15b–16)

10:15b   Paul now presents an envisioned counteraction (δέ, *de*) to boasting in the work accomplished by someone else. In verses 13–15a he has been speaking a good deal about ministry boundaries, and at the end of verse 14 he has just made the point that the boundaries of his ministry reach as far as the Corinthians. Yet he hopes for more: "But we do hope that as your faith continues to grow, our ministry, in accordance with our assignment, will be extended tremendously by you." Paul points out that the Corinthians' response to the current crisis with the interlopers has implications that reach beyond Corinth, for the apostle dreams of using Corinth as a base for ministry to the west, much as he will later speak of the Roman church in the letter addressed to that congregation (Rom. 15:24, 28).

He expresses "hope" (ἐλπίδα δὲ ἔχοντες, *elpida de echontes*, but having hope), with the participle expressing a contrast to the "boasting" mentioned in the previous participial clause. The essence of Paul's hope is that "our ministry . . . will be extended" (μεγαλυνθῆναι, *megalynthēnai*). This verb (μεγαλύνω, *megalynō*), here in an aorist passive infinitive form, could be used figuratively to refer to speaking highly of someone or exalting them, but in this context it speaks of making something larger, increasing its size (BDAG 623). The subject of the infinitive is understood from the context as referring to the boundaries of the apostle's ministry. Specifically Paul has in mind the expansion of his mission's reach. In his Letter to the Romans he comments briefly on his desire to go to Spain (15:24, 28), and it seems that at least a beginning to that longing was already on Paul's mind as he wrote this letter to the Corinthians. This infinitive is the first of three infinitives that express the content of the apostle's hope:

> to enlarge (μεγαλυνθῆναι, *megalynthēnai*)
>> so that we might preach the good news (εἰς τὰ . . . εὐαγγελίσα-
>> σθαι, *eis ta . . . euangelisasthai*)
>> instead of boasting (οὐκ . . . καυχήσασθαι, *ouk . . . kauchēsasthai*)

The first infinitive is epexegetical, functioning adjectivally to clarify the nature of the hope held by Paul. The other two are grammatically parallel. These contrasting adverbial infinitives show the purpose of the first infinitive.[18]

---

18. The suggestions concerning the grammatical functions of these infinitives vary widely, but a key is to understand the first as adjectival and the other two as adverbial. See the discussion under 10:16 below.

Four other elements delimit the first of these infinitives, and these elements can be diagrammed as follows:

αὐξανομένης τῆς πίστεως ὑμῶν (*auxanomenēs tēs pisteōs hymōn*)
ἐν ὑμῖν (*en hymin*)
μεγαλυνθῆναι (*megalynthēnai*)
κατὰ τὸν κανόνα ἡμῶν (*kata ton kanona hēmōn*)
εἰς περισσείαν (*eis perisseian*)

As your faith continues to grow,
by you
[our ministry] will be extended
in accordance with our assignment
tremendously.

1. The participial clause, a genitive absolute, may be read as circumstantial, and the present passive participle indicates imperfective aspect, that is, that the action is seen as ongoing or "in process." Whereas μεγαλύνω means "to cause to grow," the verb αὐξάνω (*auxanō*) means "to grow," "to become larger," or "to increase" (BDAG 151). As the faith[19] of the Corinthians increases, there will be a corresponding effect in the expansion of the mission. On the other hand, by implication, if the Corinthians fail to respond well to the current crisis, allowing the opponents' deleterious influence to continue, the movement of the gospel westward will be hobbled.

2. In fact, Paul hopes for a strong partnership with the Corinthians as their faith increases. The phrase ἐν ὑμῖν has been understood by many as local, either suggesting that the Corinthians' faith might increase "among" themselves (see Tyndale), or that the Pauline work might be increased "among" the Corinthians (so ESV, NLT[2], NRSV, NIV, NET). However, given the context, Paul's emphasis clearly rests on the work being expanded *beyond* the Corinthians, not among them, and their *role* in that expansion seems to be in play at this point. Thus it seems best to read ἐν ὑμῖν as communicating agency: Paul tells the Corinthians that he hopes the ministry will be extended "by you" (so NASB, KJV).

3. We have already noticed that the term κανόνα (*kanona*), used in 10:13, refers to the "assignment" that God has given the apostle, the geographical sphere to be encompassed by Paul's mission. Then κατά plus the accusative may in this case be read as denoting accordance: "in accordance with our ministry assignment." Paul only boasts "within the boundaries of the assignment God has given" to him (10:13) and ministers within those boundaries. As his mission expands, it will only do so according to God's will and direction.

4. Finally, the apostle notes the degree to which he hopes the mission will move forward—εἰς περισσείαν, "tremendously," more literally, "to an

---

19. For the view that πίστεως here refers to the Corinthians' "faithfulness," see Martin 1986: 323–24. It seems best to stay with the normal Pauline usage.

unexpected degree," the εἰς being used as a marker of extension. The term περισσεία (*perisseia*) occurs only four times in the NT, twice in 2 Corinthians (Rom. 5:17; 2 Cor. 8:2; 10:15; James 1:21), but the cognate verb περισσεύω (*perisseuō*) has been peppered throughout the letter (1:5; 3:9; 4:15; 8:2, 7 [2x]; 9:8 [2x], 12). The noun form used here speaks of "that which is beyond the regular or expected amount, surplus, abundance" (BDAG 804–5), and at 8:2 the apostle has already used the word to describe the effusiveness of the Macedonians' joy (ἡ περισσεία τῆς χαρᾶς αὐτῶν, *hē perisseia tēs charas autōn*). Paul's hope is that the mission will expand dynamically, not simply showing modest growth but extending the work in surprising ways.

10:16 Parallel and contrasting purpose clauses (εἰς τά + the infinitive) make up verse 16.[20]

εἰς τὰ ὑπερέκεινα ὑμῶν	εὐαγγελίσασθαι,
	οὐκ
	ἐν ἀλλοτρίῳ κανόνι
εἰς τὰ ἕτοιμα	καυχήσασθαι.
eis ta hyperekeina hymōn	*euangelisasthai,*
	ouk
	en allotriō kanoni
eis ta hetoima	*kauchēsasthai.*

The first part of verse 16 describes the purpose of the expansion: "We hope for this so that we might preach the good news in the regions beyond you." The apostle hopes that the boundaries of his mission's ministry assignment will be extended by the Corinthians so that he and his ministry team "might preach the good news in the regions beyond" Corinth. Preaching the good news of the gospel about Christ constitutes the focus of his ministry, and he almost always uses this term εὐαγγελίζω (*euangelizō*) to refer to "preach[ing] the gospel" about Christ (Rom. 1:15; 10:15; 15:20; 1 Cor. 1:17; 9:16, 18; 15:1–2; 2 Cor. 10:16; 11:7; Gal. 1:8–9, 11, 16, 23; 4:13; Eph. 2:17; 3:8).[21] Geographically, Paul's ministry has worked from east to west, with Greece roughly forming the western boundary of his mission thus far. The preposition ὑπερέκεινα means "beyond" and in this case refers to the regions to the west of Corinth. So Paul wants to extend the mission by preaching the gospel in regions that are as yet unreached.

Now comes the contrast, effected by negating the infinitive καυχήσασθαι. With this contrast Paul again makes a jab at the opponents for invading another person's ministry assignment: "instead of boasting about work already accomplished in another person's sphere of ministry" (οὐκ ἐν ἀλλοτρίῳ κανόνι εἰς τὰ ἕτοιμα καυχήσασθαι, *ouk en allotriō kanoni eis ta hetoima kauchēsasthai*). The apostle expresses the contrast between two modes of ministry. The first

---

20. Harris (2005: 722–23) reads the second of the purpose clauses as delimiting the first.

21. The one exception seems to be 1 Thess. 3:6, where Paul speaks of the good news about the Thessalonians related to Paul by Timothy.

approach expands a ministry by outreach in a new area. The second expands by exploiting the ministry work "already" (εἰς τὰ ἕτοιμα, *eis ta hetoima*) accomplished in another person's "sphere of ministry" (κανόνι; see 10:13, 15 above).

4. We Boast in the Lord (10:17–18)

Now Paul brings his train of thought in 10:12–18 full circle. In verse 12 he launched the unit by focusing on the interlopers' foolish commendation of themselves (τῶν ἑαυτοὺς συνιστανόντων, *tōn heautous synistanontōn*), and labels as "cluelessness" (οὐ συνιᾶσιν, *ou syniasin*) the form of boasting by which his opponents classify and compare ministries, using themselves as the standard of measure. In the intervening verses he has written a good deal about inappropriate boasting (10:13–16). Clearly associating these twin concepts of "commending" and "boasting," Paul now points out that there is only one form of commendation that counts—that which comes from the Lord and is given to those who boast in the Lord: "Rather,[22] '*The one who boasts should boast in the Lord!*' For it is not the one commending himself who passes the test, but the one whom the Lord commends!" (2 Cor. 10:17–18). What Paul presents as appropriate boasting ("boasting in the Lord") is underscored with an allusion to Jer. 9:23–24 (9:22–23 LXX).[23] Here Paul finds the basis upon which boasting should be evaluated, for the Jeremiah passage also presents a contrast between appropriate and inappropriate boasting. The full context reads,

10:17

> This is what the Lord says: Let not the wise boast in his wisdom, and let not the mighty boast in his might, and let not the wealthy boast in his wealth, but let him who boasts boast in this: that he understands and knows that I am the Lord when I do mercy and justice and righteousness in the earth, because in these things is my will, says the Lord. (NETS)

When we compare the LXX rendering of the passage to the apostle's wording in 2 Cor. 10:17, we find that he takes from Jeremiah the words about boasting and then sums up the remainder of the passage succinctly in the phrase ἐν κυρίῳ:

Jer. 9:24 (9:23 LXX)	2 Cor. 10:17
ἀλλ᾽ ἢ ἐν τούτῳ **καυχάσθω ὁ καυχώμενος**, συνίειν καὶ γινώσκειν ὅτι ἐγώ εἰμι κύριος (*all' ē en toutō kauchasthō ho kauchōmenos, syniein kai ginōskein hoti egō eimi kyrios*).	Ὁ δὲ **καυχώμενος** ἐν κυρίῳ **καυχάσθω** (*ho de kauchōmenos en kyriō kauchasthō*).

22. The conjunction δέ (*de*, rather) at the beginning of 10:17 highlights a mild contrast with the second infinitival clause of verse 16. The alternative to boasting in the work already accomplished in another person's sphere of ministry is to boast in the Lord. For this use of δέ, see, e.g., Wis. 2:11; 4:9; 7:6; 2 Macc. 4:5; 5:6; 3 Macc. 2:24; 3:15; Matt. 6:33; Luke 10:20; Acts 12:9, 14; Rom. 3:4; Eph. 4:15; Heb. 4:13, 15; 6:12; 9:12; BDAG 213.

23. In an earlier letter to the Corinthians, Paul used this same passage to speak of the "foolish" wisdom of God, which determines that no person can boast in God's presence (1 Cor. 1:29–31). Interestingly, Paul's paraphrase in that passage matches his paraphrase here at 2 Cor. 10:17.

In Paul's version the conjunction has been changed from ἀλλ' ἤ (*all' ē*, but rather) to the milder δέ (*de*), and the substantival participle ὁ καυχώμενος has been moved forward in the sentence, probably to place emphasis on "the one boasting" (Paul's focus throughout the unit). Finally, the ἐν τούτῳ (*en toutō*, in this) of the LXX has been replaced with ἐν κυρίῳ (*en kyriō*, in the Lord) in Paul's wording, encapsulating in one word the content of an appropriate boast, according to Jeremiah, which is "to understand and know that I am the Lord." In speaking of "the Lord," Paul almost certainly has Christ in mind rather than just a general reference to God.[24] Note particularly that according to Jer. 9:23 LXX the person who boasts appropriately should boast that "he understands" (συνίειν, *syniein*) the Lord, and here we find the origin of Paul's wording in 10:12, where he says that his opponents "do not understand" (οὐ συνιᾶσιν, "are clueless" in our translation) the Lord when they carry on their game of ministry evaluation.

So let's review what Paul has said thus far in chapter 10 about boasting. Anticipating his discussion in 10:12–18, at 10:8 he states that he is not averse to boasting about the authority the Lord has given him for building up the Corinthians. Yet as he comes to 10:12–18, it immediately becomes clear that two kinds of boasting are in the air at Corinth. On the one hand there is the kind of boasting of which Paul is not ashamed. His form of boasting is disciplined, only boasting about the ministry assignment given to him by God (10:13), and he refuses to boast in work accomplished by someone else (10:15–16). His opponents, on the other hand, boast about work accomplished in a ministry assignment given to someone else (10:13–16). But what Paul counters here in 10:17–18 is the object of their boasting: they boast by commending themselves, classifying, comparing, and measuring themselves while using themselves as the standard (10:12). In other words, they boast *in themselves*, demonstrating clearly that their form of boasting about ministry is self-focused and self-validating.

10:18   Thus Paul makes clear that this form of boasting in ministry won't do, "For it is not the one commending himself who passes the test, but the one whom the Lord commends!" (10:18). In other words, and according to the principle laid down in Jer. 9:24 (9:23 LXX), Paul boasts with *the Lord* as the object of his boasting, and he looks only to the Lord for the validation, the commendation,[25] of his ministry. Thus the conjunction γάρ (*gar*) connecting verses 17 and 18 points to what follows as an inference; the apostle is communicating the implications of the passage of Scripture to which he has just alluded. That the

---

24. So Furnish 1984: 474; Harris 2005: 725–26; Thrall 2000: 652–53. The phrase ἐν κυρίῳ in Paul often refers to Christ (Rom. 14:14; 16:2, 8, 11–13, 22; 1 Cor. 16:19; 2 Cor. 2:12; Gal. 5:10; Eph. 4:17; 5:8; 6:1; Phil. 2:19, 24, 29; 3:1; 4:1–2, 4, 10; Col. 3:18, 20; 4:7; 1 Thess. 3:8; 5:12; 2 Thess. 3:4, 12; Philem. 16, 20), and the object of boasting at 1 Cor. 1:31, where the apostle uses the same allusion to Jer. 9:23 LXX, seems to be Christ. Moreover, Paul at times applies OT "Lord" passages to Christ (e.g., Isa. 28:16 at Rom. 9:33; Isa. 45:23 at Phil. 2:10–11; Joel 2:32 at Rom. 10:12–13).

25. On the concept of "commending," see the comments on 3:1.

opponents commend themselves counts for nothing. Only the person whom the Lord commends has truly "passed the test" of authentic, God-ordained ministry. In every other occurrence of the noun δόκιμος (*dokimos*)[26] in Paul, the word may be read as connoting a ministry that is "approved," that has measured up to certain standards (Rom. 14:18; 16:10; 1 Cor. 11:19; 2 Cor. 13:7; 2 Tim. 2:15). For instance, at 2 Tim. 2:15 we read, "Be diligent to present yourself approved to God, a worker who doesn't need to be ashamed, correctly teaching the word of truth" (HCSB).

So does Paul commend himself? This question can be answered similarly to the question of whether Paul boasts. The answer to both is "yes and no!" We have shown that Paul boasts but does so appropriately, with the Lord as the object of his boasting. Similarly, Paul commends himself and even suggests that the Corinthians should have commended him (2 Cor. 12:11). However, his form of self-recommendation amounts to pointing to the call and work of God. In other words, rather than self-focused, his "self" commendation is thoroughly God-centered.

Reflection

Many dynamics in the modern, Western church lend themselves to ministers falling into the error of the opponents as described by Paul in 2 Cor. 10:12–18. The competitiveness and love of advancement in spheres such as business, sports, and academia can fuel an atmosphere of classification and evaluation that can dull ministry spiritually, transforming the wine of ministry into the water of a talent contest. The exaltation of public ministers and ministries to pedestals of fame and influence can prove harmful both to the minister and to those who are the recipients of that ministry. This does not mean that visibility and influence are inherently bad. Some ministers have had profoundly productive, visible ministries and have carried out those ministries with great integrity.

We must ask ourselves some key questions. Do we carry out our ministries, constantly assessing, in contrast to others, how we are doing in terms of influence, applause, nickels and noses in our churches, book sales, speaking engagements, and social media? Do we evaluate how others are doing by comparing the fruit of their ministries with ours? Or is God really the primary reference point by which we carry out and evaluate our ministries? Do we do our ministries "before God" (2:17), looking to God to assess how we are doing and evaluating the ministries of others from a mature spiritual vantage point? We must not use the world's standards of measurement for our ministries. That path is the path of spiritual vapidity and fruitlessness, no matter the statistics surrounding our ministries.

Moreover, often in our consumerist cultural context in the United States, we think little of the boundaries of our ministry outreach; "more" and "farther" may be deemed always better. If we can attract people to our

---

26. The cognate verb δοκιμάζω (*dokimazō*, verify, prove) was used at 8:8, 22.

ministries, that is justification enough, and our growing numbers are seen as validating our work. It may even be that, unlike the ministry carried out by Paul's opponents, which seems to have been tainted by false teaching, our ministries are doctrinally sound and sincerely executed. Yet we may need to think more about this concept of ministry boundaries. Are our churches "consumers" of "consumers," snatching up as many people as we may attract to our impressive ministries, regardless of the other ministries we trample? Is it possible that at times we transgress the ministry territory that the Lord has given others in the body of Christ?

Years ago in Franklin, Tennessee, a large, wealthy church was reaching out to the disadvantaged families and their children in the poorer part of town. They brought gifts and took the children on outings. One day Scott Roley, a staff member from that church, thought to step inside the much smaller Baptist church in the heart of that poorer section of the community. Scott met the Baptist pastor, Denny Denson, who said, "You can come down here and buy off these kids, but when they get shot in the middle of the night, they are going to call me." The conversation led to tears, repentance, and ultimately a deep friendship and ministry partnership that lasted until Denny's death. Scott realized that his church had transgressed the boundaries of another church's ministry, and he repented of his lack of sensitivity. The partnership resulted in much greater ministry impact and laid the foundation for a profound, wide-reaching, intercultural ministerial fellowship in that community.

Additional Notes

10:12. Verse 12 is artistically crafted, twice using chiastic structure to shape the expressions:

Οὐ γὰρ τολμῶμεν . . .
A συγκρῖναι
  B ἑαυτούς
    τισιν τῶν
  B′ ἑαυτοὺς
A′ συνιστανόντων,
    ἀλλὰ
αὐτοὶ . . .
A ἐν ἑαυτοῖς
  B ἑαυτοὺς
    C μετροῦντες καὶ
    C′ συγκρίνοντες
  B′ ἑαυτοὺς
A′ ἑαυτοῖς
οὐ συνιᾶσιν.

10:12–13. A major variant occurs at 10:12–13, with two possible readings. The longer reading, which includes the words οὐ συνιᾶσιν. ἡμεῖς δέ is preferred by most commentators and translations and by the editors of NA[27] and UBS[4] (with a B rating). The witnesses for this reading are strong ($\mathfrak{P}^{46}$ $\aleph^a$ B H[vid] 1739 0243 33 81 104 330 451 1881 Augustine Euthalius Theodoret). The UBS committee suggests that the shorter, weaker (D* F G ar b [vg]; Ambst) reading, which omits οὐ συνιᾶσιν. ἡμεῖς δέ, "is doubtless the result of an accident in transcription, when the eye of a copyist passed from οὐ to οὐκ and omitted the intervening words" (Metzger 1994: 514). The shorter reading has Paul measuring and comparing himself with himself, which seems odd in context. For the conceptual problems created by the shorter reading, see Harris 2005: 705; Thrall 2000: 637–40.

C. Paul Boasts Like a Fool to Stop the False Apostles (11:1–12:13)

The span of 2 Corinthians running from 11:1 to 12:13 presents us with one of the most fascinating, rhetorically charged, and discussed parts of this complex letter. Through much of the book, Paul has restrained his self-recommendation, his godly boasting, holding himself in tenuous check so that he might not be misunderstood as engaging the false teachers of Corinth on their own terms, using their questionable tactics. Now, pushed to extremities, he *seems* to plunge into boasting at full throttle. Yet this "braggart" form of boasting gets turned on its head as the apostle "brags" about things that highlight his weaknesses rather than his strengths. The section develops in six movements: the first three movements form a lengthy introduction to the "Fool's Speech" (11:1–4, 5–15, 16–21), movements four and five embody the speech itself (11:22–29; 11:30–12:10), and the last movement forms an epilogue to the whole section (12:11–13).

1. Bear with Me, Not Them (11:1–4)

At 11:1–4 we gain a bit more clarity on Paul's specific concerns about the interlopers in Corinth. An inclusio brackets the unit: Paul begins and ends with references to "bearing with" someone. Notice that as with 10:1–11 and 10:12–18 the face-off between Paul and his opponents is front and center. He begins with a wish that the Corinthians would bear with him as he exercises a bit of foolishness, foreshadowing the "foolish" boasting he undertakes later in the chapter (11:17, 21). The unit ends with the reflection that the Corinthians "bear with" the interlopers (too!) well as they offer a different Jesus, a different spirit, indeed a different gospel. Thus the apostle continues to employ a good bit of irony in this section of the book. What has driven Paul to foolish boasting is nothing less than the seduction of the Corinthian church. He is jealous about the Corinthians with a godly jealousy. Having promised them as a pure virgin to Christ as husband, he now fears that their thinking is being ruined, moved away from a sincere, pure relationship with Christ, and that calls for Paul to raise the level of his rhetoric. What we see in 11:1–4 is the heart of Paul's reason for entering into "foolish boasting." He undertakes what seems to be an uncomfortable posture for him in order to save the Corinthian congregation from being ruined spiritually. The unit may be outlined as follows:

a. A plea: Bear with me! (11:1)
b. Paul's godly jealousy (11:2–3)
c. (The foolishness of) bearing with false teachers (11:4)

Exegesis and Exposition

¹I wish you would bear with me in a little ⌜bit of foolishness⌝; yes, do bear with me! ²For I am jealous about you with a jealousy from God, since I promised you in marriage to one husband, to present you as a pure virgin to Christ. ³But I am afraid that just as the snake deceived Eve by his chicanery, your thought processes might be ruined, steered away ⌜from a sincere, pure devotion⌝ to Christ. ⁴As a matter of fact, if an interloper preaches another Jesus than the Jesus we preached, or if you receive a different spirit than the Spirit you received, or a different gospel than the one you espoused, ⌜you bear with it⌝ splendidly!

a. A Plea: Bear with Me! (11:1)

Paul begins with a wish: "I wish you would bear with me in a little bit of foolishness" (Ὄφελον ἀνείχεσθέ μου μικρόν τι ἀφροσύνης, *Ophelon aneichesthe*

11:1

mou mikron ti aphrosynēs). Ὄφελον, an aorist active participle (ἐστίν [*estin*, is] is understood; BDF 37; cf. 1 Cor. 4:8; Gal. 5:12; Rev. 3:15), often expresses a wish that something had taken place in the past or would take place in the future. Used with an imperfect verb, as here, the time frame is present (Epictetus, *Disc.* 2.22.12; Dio Chrysostom, *Or.* 21 [38].47; BDAG 743), and though marked by irony,[1] Paul clearly is expressing a wish for a particular response from the Corinthians as they hear this letter read. That imperfect verb, ἀνέχω (*anechō*), speaks of tolerance, "putting up with" or "bearing with" someone or something (e.g., Philo, *Sacr.* 79; *Post.* 135). Paul writes that he wants the Corinthians to bear with him (μου, me)[2] in "a little bit of foolishness" (μικρόν τι ἀφροσύνης),[3] a reference to the apostle's boasting in this movement of the book (11:1–12:10). Paul calls that boasting "foolishness" (ἀφροσύνης), a term that communicates "lacking sense, prudence, or good judgment" (BDAG 159). As "foolishness," what follows in 11:5–12:10 is not the ideal course of argument, but rather what the Corinthians have forced on him by their lack of defending their apostle against the interlopers (12:1, 11). By boasting in the way he does in the following verses, he skirts close to the opponents' boasting according to human standards (10:12–13; 11:18–19), taking the focus off Christ and placing it on human leadership (Matera 2003: 240). But at this point Paul feels the need to "fight fire with fire," and so he indulges in boasting. By thus playing the fool, the apostle "models" the utter foolishness of the interlopers' ministry style. As Garland (1999: 458) observes, "If he stoops to their level by boasting, he is a fool. But if he does not defend himself, he might lose the congregation to even greater fools."[4]

The second half of 11:1, ἀλλὰ καὶ ἀνέχεσθέ μου (*alla kai anechesthe mou*), can be read in two ways, primarily. The first understands ἀνέχεσθε as an

1. The context of each use of ὄφελον in the NT (here; 1 Cor. 4:8; Gal. 5:12; Rev. 3:15) suggests an ironic tone (Harris 2005: 732). Quintilian (*Inst.* 9.1.29) notes that using forms of *dissimulatio* is "the most effective of all means of stealing into people's minds and a very attractive device as long as we adopt a conversational rather than controversial tone" (cited by Witherington 1995: 443). For Paul's use of irony, see Spencer (1981), who calls irony "the queen of indirectness" (349) and observes that since the Corinthians are unreceptive, Paul resorts to an ironic posture, pretended ignorance, humor, and indirectness. The irony here is sardonic (bitterly ironic) but not sarcastic (cutting, caustic, and taunting) (351).

2. Rather than μου being understood as relating most directly to ἀφροσύνης (i.e., "my foolishness"; so Martin 1986: 327, 331; Thrall 2000: 658), its position in this first use in the sentence and the use of ἀνέχεσθέ μου (*anechesthe mou*) at the end of 11:1 suggest that the pronoun should be understood as relating to ἀνείχεσθε: "bear with me."

3. The μικρόν τι is an acc. of reference, and the genitive ἀφροσύνης may be read as partitive. Barrett (1973: 271) notes, "Christians have not always been as successful as Paul in distinguishing between regrettable and unnecessary folly, regrettable but necessary folly, and divine wisdom."

4. Further, by labeling the boasting he is about to do as "foolishness," the apostle in effect apologizes in advance for this boasting! Thus the passage drips with irony. Harris (2005: 734) notes that such apology in advance was referred to as *prodiorthōsis* (Robertson 1934: 1199). In fact, the whole of this section has been described as "an ironic parody of self-praise and comparison of [Paul's] opponents" (Forbes 1986: 16–17).

imperative (so ESV, HCSB, NLT[2], NRSV, NIV, KJV; Barrett 1973: 270–71; Lambrecht 1999: 172; Matera 2003: 239; Thrall 2000: 656): "Yes, do bear with me!" The other approach reads the verb as an indicative (NASB, NET; Barnett 1997: 496, 498): "Actually, you already are bearing with me." Although either is possible, the former seems the better. Read as an imperative, the repetition of ἀνέχεσθέ μου underscores the urgency that seems to drive the apostle at this point. Further, in the following verses he explains *why* he has this sense of urgency, and his explanations read best as following on the heels of an exhortation (Robertson 1934: 1186).[5]

b. Paul's Godly Jealousy (11:2–3)

Now, in two movements, Paul explains (γάρ, *gar*, for) why he is urgent about the Corinthians bearing with him, and the two reasons given are interrelated: (1) like a father presenting his daughter to an intended husband, Paul is jealous for the Corinthians' doctrinal purity (11:2–3), and (2) the Corinthians already are bearing with teachers who are theologically dangerous (11:4).

11:2

Thus he first speaks as a "jealous" father, being jealous (ζηλῶ, *zēlō*) for the Corinthians with a particular kind of jealousy. In English the term "jealousy" connotes strong negative emotions about the success or possessions of another person, or concerning the unwelcome attention paid toward one's love interest by another person. In the ancient world the verb ζηλόω (*zēloō*) could be used of negative emotions, as when the patriarchs were jealous of their brother Joseph, or when Rachel was envious of her sister Leah (Gen. 26:14; 30:1; Acts 7:9). Yet in the biblical literature, as well as the broader literatures of the Greco-Roman world, the word could also speak very positively of intense desire or dedication (Wis. 1:12; Sir. 51:18; Aristotle, *Rhet.* 2.9.5–11.7), or of being deeply interested in someone and seeking their favor (Prov. 23:17; 24:1; Gal. 4:17).[6] Thus Furnish (1984: 484, 486) translates the verb here as "I care deeply."

Paul particularly qualifies the type of jealousy he has in mind as "about you" (ὑμᾶς, *hymas*), the pronoun functioning as an adverbial accusative of respect referring to the Corinthians, and θεοῦ ζήλῳ (*theou zēlō*), "with a jealousy from God." This translation renders the term θεοῦ as a genitive of source, since "jealousy" is a character trait of God, and Paul's very appropriate

---

5. If ἀνέχεσθε is read as an indicative, one would almost need to read the second half of 11:1 as a parenthetical statement (which is not impossible!), since the explanations that follow do not as readily flow from a simple statement of fact. However, we have already noted Paul's ironic tone in this section. Such a parenthetical statement would present a clash between his ironic wish and the admission that his listeners have already been doing what he is wishing they would do! If we have correctly interpreted the clause as imperatival, the ἀλλὰ καί that heads the clause is emphatic ("yes"; see Rom. 6:5; Phil. 1:18; D. Wallace 1996: 673).

6. Note the earlier use in 2 Corinthians of the cognate ζῆλος (*zēlos*) with the sense of "zeal" (2 Cor. 7:7, 11; 9:2). The word at times can also be translated as "jealousy" (e.g., 2 Cor. 12:20; Gal. 5:20).

jealousy for the Corinthians originates in the character of God himself.[7] John Chrysostom (*Hom. 2 Cor.* 23.1) writes of 2 Cor. 11:2:

> Paul uses a word here which is far stronger than mere love. Jealous souls burn ardently for those whom they love, and jealousy presupposes a strong affection. Then, in order that they should not think that Paul is after power, wealth or honor, he adds that his jealousy is "divine." For God is said to be jealous, not in a human way but so that everyone may know that he claims sovereign rights over those whom he loves and does what he does for their exclusive benefit. Human jealousy is basically selfish, but divine jealousy is both intense and pure. (Bray 1999: 289–90)

At the giving of the Ten Commandments, God describes himself as a God who is "jealous" (קַנָּא, *qannāʾ*; LXX: ζηλωτής, *zēlōtēs*; Exod. 20:5), and Exod. 34:14 even states that God's name (i.e., his very nature) is "Jealous" (יְהוָה קַנָּא שְׁמוֹ, *yhwh qannāʾ šĕmô*, Yahweh, his name is Jealous).[8] Further, when Paul says he is jealous with a divine jealousy, the language particularly calls to mind Num. 25:11–13, where Phinehas, the son of Eleazar the priest, stopped God's wrath against the Israelites when they defected to the worship of Baal:

> Phinees son of Eleazar son of Aaron the priest has put a stop to my wrath from Israel's sons when I was jealous with jealousy among them [ἐν τῷ ζηλῶσαί μου τὸν ζῆλον ἐν αὐτοῖς, *en tō zēlōsai mou ton zēlon en autois*], and I did not utterly destroy the sons of Israel in my jealousy. Thus I said, "Behold, I am giving him a covenant of peace. And there shall be for him and for his offspring after him an everlasting covenant of priesthood, because he was zealous for his God [ὧν ἐζήλωσεν τῷ θεῷ αὐτοῦ, *hōn ezēlōsen tō theō autou*] and made atonement for the sons of Israel." (LXX, NETS)

The phrases ἐν τῷ ζηλῶσαί μου τὸν ζῆλον ἐν αὐτοῖς could be understood as communicating that Phinees (Phinehas) stopped God's wrath "by being jealous with my jealousy among them." Similarly, Paul shares God's jealousy toward the church, for, as becomes clear in verse 4, by defecting to the interlopers' teaching, the Corinthians are defecting from the real Jesus and receiving another spirit and another gospel. So, in being seduced away from Paul's ministry, the Corinthians are ultimately being seduced away from a pure relationship with Christ himself.

---

7. This also could be considered a genitive of quality since the emphasis seems to be on the quality of the jealousy (Furnish 1984: 486), or even a genitive of association, since Paul is jealous by virtue of his association with God as God's apostle.

8. Or perhaps, God is "jealous for his name." The pentateuchal context presents God's jealousy as a reaction to idolatry, a theme that threads its way through the OT (e.g., Ezek. 8:3; 16:38; 23:25, where God is provoked to jealousy by his people's worship of idols). God's jealousy is grounded in God's love for his people, and that jealous love brings about judgment (Deut. 6:14–15; Josh. 24:19–20; Ps. 78:58–64; Zeph. 1:18; 1 Cor. 10:22; *NDBT* 570).

The apostle, using betrothal imagery grounded in the OT, presents a picture of God as the Lover and God's people as the betrothed. The word picture, of course, picks up on a rich OT backdrop and expresses the covenant commitment between God and his people. As here, the prophets often use the marriage imagery to challenge a lack of covenant faithfulness (e.g., Hosea 1:1–2:2; Ezek. 23:5–8; Jer. 2:2; 3:6; Isa. 54:6–7; *DBI* 538–39). Moreover, Paul presents himself as either the matchmaker who has arranged the relationship, or the father of the bride (the church).[9] The latter probably is the preferable interpretation, since Paul speaks of himself as the spiritual "father" of the Corinthians elsewhere (1 Cor. 4:15), and "jealousy" fits the father image better (Keener 2005: 226; Matera 2003: 241).[10] During the betrothal period, it was the father's responsibility to watch over his daughter, guarding her sexual integrity.[11] As their apostle, and during this time of betrothal, between their conversion and the second coming of Christ, Paul bears this unique responsibility toward the Corinthians. He guards their theological integrity so they can be presented appropriately to Christ.[12] The problem is that the church, toying with the leadership of the interlopers, seems on the verge of jilting Christ, to whom, at their conversion, they have already been committed for marriage. Thus Paul explains (the γάρ [*gar*, since] again is explanatory) the reason for his jealousy: "since I promised you in marriage to one husband" (ἡρμοσάμην γὰρ ὑμᾶς ἑνὶ ἀνδρὶ, *hērmosamēn gar hymas heni andri*). In short, Paul wants "to present" the Corinthians "as a pure virgin to Christ" (παρθένον ἁγνὴν παραστῆσαι τῷ Χριστῷ, *parthenon hagnēn parastēsai tō Christō*), rather than as a "bride" that has been compromised.[13] Pure doctrine serves as the basis for

9. Contra Martin (1986: 332), who sees the image as "the friend of the groom" or "best man" (John 3:29). A betrothal contract could be arranged between a suitor and the woman's parents, or between two fathers (*DJBP* 92). Some later Jewish works present Moses as the matchmaker between God and his people (Batey 1971: 16–17; Keener 2003: 311).

10. In fact, Deut. 22:13–21, which deals with a father bringing proof of his daughter's virginity to the city's elders in a contested situation, provides a fitting backdrop for the imagery as used by the apostle here: "Then the father of the girl and her mother, having taken them, shall bring the proofs of the girl's virginity to the council of elders at the gate" (Deut. 22:15 NETS).

11. Matera (2003: 241) further notes Sir. 42:9–10, which reads, "A daughter is a hidden sleeplessness to a father, and anxiety about her takes away sleep—in her youth, lest she become past her prime, and having married, lest she be hated, in virginity, lest she be defiled and she become pregnant in her father's house, being with a man, lest she transgress and having married, lest she be barren" (Sir. 42:9–10 NETS).

12. The NT has taken this marriage image up into Christ's relationship with the church as his bride (Eph. 5:25–27; Rev. 19:7). In first-century Judaism, betrothal, as with marriage, could only be broken by the death of a partner or divorce.

13. John Chrysostom (*Hom. 2 Cor.* 23.1) notes, "In the world, a woman is a virgin before her marriage, when she loses her virginity. But in the church, those who were anything but virgins before they turned to Christ acquire virginity in him. As a result, the whole church is a virgin" (Bray 1999: 290). As Harris (2005: 737) points out, "The juxtaposition in the passage of the plural ὑμᾶς [*hymas*, you] and the singulars ἡρμοσάμην [*hērmosamēn*, I promised], ἑνὶ ἀνδρί [*heni andri*, to one husband] and παρθένον ἁγνήν [*parthenon hagnēn*, pure virgin] is dramatic. It was the entire Corinthian church, regarded corporately and as representative of all believers (cf. Eph. 5:32), which was the betrothed bride of Christ."

pure commitment, and this stands as Paul's primary concern in the current crisis, for he now shifts his imagery to the seduction of Eve in the garden of Eden: "But I am afraid that just as the snake deceived Eve by his chicanery, your thought processes might be ruined, steered away from a sincere, pure devotion to Christ."[14]

11:3 Paul fears (φοβοῦμαι, *phoboumai*)[15] the satanic[16] scheme to pervert the sound teaching of the gospel among the Corinthians. Indeed, at 11:13–15 he draws the analogy between Satan,[17] who disguises himself as an angel of light, and his servants, the interlopers at Corinth, who disguise themselves as apostles, as servants of righteousness. Deception ranks as one of Satan's chief abilities, and Paul points to this character quality by recalling the tempting of Eve (ὡς ὁ ὄφις ἐξηπάτησεν Εὕαν, *hōs ho ophis exēpatēsen Heuan*, "as the snake deceived Eve"). The verb ἐξαπατάω (*exapataō*), which means "to deceive," "to cheat," or "to cause someone to accept false ideas" (BDAG 345), is used six times in the NT (here; Rom. 7:11; 16:18; 1 Cor. 3:18; 2 Thess. 2:3; 1 Tim. 2:14), most often with reference to someone being drawn into sin. At 1 Tim. 2:14 the word also expresses Eve's temptation with "And Adam was not deceived, but the woman was deceived and transgressed" (HCSB).

Further, Satan's deception is accomplished "by his chicanery," his "cunning," or "trickery" (πανουργία, *panourgia*), a dative of means. The word was used in antisophistic polemic of the first century (Betz 1972: 105), and Paul's concern is that the false teachers, employing the tricks of their master, might steer the minds of the Corinthians down destructive paths. Just as the Edenic snake, through a perversion of thoughts, wreaked havoc on the first marriage, so Paul fears false teaching could prove devastating to the Corinthians' relationship with God (Harvey 1996: 97–98).

So, as with 10:1–11, Paul's fight clearly lies in the realm of ideas, teachings that contradict the gospel of Christ. Eve's downfall was in listening to the twisted logic that called into question the word of God; so too the Corinthians are in dangerous territory, toying with or entertaining tantalizing teachers who

---

14. The parallels between our passage and 4 Macc. 18:7–9 are striking. Alluding to the tempting of Eve, the text speaks of the mother of seven sons, who tells her children that she was a "pure virgin" (παρθένος ἁγνή, *parthenos hagnē*) and "took care of the built-up rib. No destroyer of the desert [or ravisher (φθορεύς, *phthoreus*) of the plain] injured me; nor did the destructive, deceitful, snake [ἀπάτης ὄφις, *apatēs ophis*] make spoil of my chaste virginity [μου τὰ ἁγνὰ τῆς παρθενίας, *mou ta hagna tēs parthenias*]; and I remained with my husband during the period of my prime."

15. The imperfective aspect suggests that this is a current state of affairs for him. The phrase μή πως (*mē pōs*) may be rendered lit. as "lest somehow."

16. As Harris (2005: 741) reports, the snake was the archetypal unclean animal in Jewish thought and symbolized opposition to God. Thus the snake came to be identified with Satan. Although the identification of the serpent of Eden (Gen. 3) with the devil or Satan occurs in the NT only at Rev. 12:9 and 20:2, the parallels between our passage and 2 Cor. 11:14–15 are suggestive.

17. On the identification of the snake of Gen. 3 with Satan, see Wis. 2:24; Rev. 12:9 (Keener 2005: 226).

---

sound good but are devastatingly evil. The perverted ministry of the interlopers could lead to the destruction of the Corinthians' minds, and the apostle warns the church that their "thought processes" (τὰ νοήματα, *ta noēmata*) "might be ruined" (φθαρῇ, *phtharē*), a term that could refer to breaking a set of rules but here has more to do with corruption, something that is spoiled or destroyed, turned to a wrong path. Interestingly, in the ancient world the term was used at times of a virgin being seduced and robbed of her virginity (e.g., Josephus, *Ant.* 4.252; BDAG 1054), and in context this fits the traditions that understood Satan as having seduced Eve, robbing her of her virginity (Ellis 1981: 62; see the rabbinic source *b. Yeb.* 103b).

So Paul plays on the analogy of the Corinthians, who have been promised in marriage to Christ as a pure virgin, being drawn away into giving up their theological virginity in relation to the gospel preached by their apostle. Thus they risk being "steered away from a sincere, pure devotion to Christ" (ἀπὸ τῆς ἁπλότητος [καὶ τῆς ἁγνότητος] τῆς εἰς τὸν Χριστόν, *apo tēs haplotētos [kai tēs hagnotētos] tēs eis ton Christon*). Paul has already used the word ἁπλότης (*haplotēs*) several times in the book; the three uses in chapters 8–9 have the sense of "generosity" (8:2; 9:11, 13). The use in our current context is more in line with that at 1:12, where the apostle says his pattern of life is upright, "characterized by straightforwardness [ἁπλότητι, *haplotēti*] and sincerity that come from God." The apostle wants this church to follow him in pure devotion to Christ, and his concern has to do with right teaching about Christ, which becomes even clearer with verse 4.

c. (The Foolishness of) Bearing with False Teachers (11:4)

Whereas verses 2–3 present a first reason why Paul pleads with the Corinthians to bear with him, now, in verse 4, the apostle gives a second main reason he asks the Corinthians to bear with him: they are putting up with false teachers. His accusations against the ministry of the interlopers are laid out in three parallel thoughts. This verse at once provides some clarity concerning the problem of the false teachers and yet does not give us all the information we could wish. The structure of the passage may be presented as follows:

11:4

As a matter of fact,				
	if an interloper		preaches	
		another Jesus		than the Jesus we preached, or
	if you	a different spirit	receive	than the Spirit you received, or
		a different gospel		than the one you espoused,
you bear with it splendidly!				

The μὲν γάρ (*men gar*, for in fact, as a matter of fact) makes the transition from verses 2–3 to verse 4 and marks the thought here as building on what has been stated in verses 2–3. Notice that the complex conditional clause contains two present-tense verbs: "if an interloper preaches," and "you receive." Thus the aspect is imperfective, and the conditional clause, followed by the present-tense verb ἀνέχεσθε (*anechesthe*), assumes a present reality. In other words, this state of affairs is currently in place among the Corinthians. What the interloper(s) (more literally, "the one coming," ὁ ἐρχόμενος, *ho erchomenos*) preaches is "another[18] Jesus" (ἄλλον Ἰησοῦν, *allon Iēsoun*), and consequently, what the Corinthians are in the process of receiving is a "different spirit" and "a different gospel."

Harris (2005: 744), following Windisch (and Strecker 1970: 326–27), notes that the triad of Jesus-Spirit-gospel provides an appropriate summary of the Christian faith. Paul preached Christ as crucified and raised from the dead (1 Cor. 1:23; 15:1–4; 1 Thess. 4:14), the Spirit as given to those who believe (Rom. 8:9; 2 Cor. 1:22), and the good news of forgiveness from sins and reconciliation with God (Rom. 1:16; 2 Cor. 5:19). The real Jesus, the Spirit, and the gospel are inseparably linked. As many note, to preach "another Jesus" inevitably results in the reception of a "different spirit" and a "different gospel." Although we can't know the exact content of the interlopers' teaching,[19] from Paul's perspective they clearly are teaching an aberrant theology, a perversion of the true gospel, which stems from a false Jesus and leads to a spirit other than the Holy Spirit. They may use the right language and claim to be ministers sent from God, but their preaching of Jesus is skewed, their gospel is unsound, and the spirit received as a result of their preaching is a spirit other than the Holy Spirit.

We certainly could wish for more here, and commentators disagree on whether we are dealing with a heretical form of Christology,[20] or primarily a difference in ministry style. In fact, it is impossible to treat the exact *content* of the false teaching. The problem is that Paul does not explain what is aberrant in the opponents' preaching about Jesus. Nevertheless, given the other dominant concerns Paul has about his opponents, it may well have to do with focusing on a gospel of power and status enhancement, rather than on the suffering of Jesus. Elsewhere in the letter are indications that suggest the opponents were not comfortable with a humble, suffering apostle, and perhaps they also played down a humble, suffering Messiah. Witherington (1995: 442) writes that the opponents "do not accept his vision of ministry, that is, its cruciform, Christlike, and servant shape." Martin (1986: 341) describes the problem this way:

18. In this case the ἄλλον (another) should be seen as roughly synonymous with ἕτερον (*heteron*, different), and the shift from the first to the second as merely stylistic variation.

19. Certainly attempts have been made to pinpoint the exact teaching of the false apostles in Corinth. For a summary of suggestions, see Furnish 1984: 500–502; Thrall 2000: 667–70.

20. Pelagius (*Comm. 2 Cor.* 11), e.g., suggests that the false teachers were preaching that the gospel was added to the OT and that it was necessary still to keep the law of Moses (Bray 1999: 291).

The Christ they proclaimed is κατὰ σάρκα (5:16) which means that the power on display is visible and self-centered. The πνεῦμα is manifest in a spirit of ἐξουσία, which they construed as lordly power which in turn leads to a posture of καυχᾶσθαι, "boasting." . . . The "gospel" is branded as a false message since it contradicts Paul's message of the cross and of the Christ who "did not please himself" (Rom 15:3). They glory in outward appearance (5:12), because they have no place for the hiddenness of Christ's weak demeanor (10:1; 13:3, 4) and the life based on "faith" (5:7). . . . "Another Jesus" for the opponents is the wonderworking Jesus, rather than Paul's crucified and risen Lord. The alien "spirit" is the spirit of power and ecstasy which these messengers claimed to possess and embody in their ministry, rather than the Spirit of Christ which Paul exemplified. The new "gospel" is the message of power and present glory, based on demonstrable tokens of the divine and evidences of authority in their lives as Christ's servants ([11:]13), rather than Paul's kerygma of the suffering Christ whose power is displayed incognito and in patient love (13:3, 4). Above all, the contrast is seen in the way the rival preachers overlooked, and Paul expounded, the truth that the "true apostle" not only is a proclaimer of the passion story; he also lives it out.

This "gospel" that the interlopers are preaching—Paul considers it to be a false gospel, "totally other" than his gospel (Harris 2005: 745).

In 11:1 Paul pleads with the Corinthians to bear with him. Now, in the main clause of verse 4, he suggests that they are bearing with the interlopers' teaching splendidly![21] The word we have translated "splendidly"; the common Greek adverb καλῶς (kalōs), can simply refer to something that has been done "well," "beautifully," "appropriately," "acceptably," or "commendably." Obviously, Paul's words continue to drip with irony, since in no way does he find the Corinthians' tolerance toward the false teachers acceptable. Our choice to render καλῶς as "splendidly" is meant to highlight this irony. In reality, this ironic commendation stands as a firm rebuke, and at 11:19 he reiterates this rebuke: "Wise as you are, you gladly put up with fools!" So in light of Paul's plea that the Corinthians "bear with" him in 11:1, the passage comes full circle. Paul vies for the attention of the Corinthians, who at present are "bearing with" the wrong party.

It takes little imagination to think of widely varying approaches to "preaching Jesus" today in our Western cultural contexts. For instance, Wax (2011) explores six perversions of the gospel in contemporary Western culture, each of which downplay particular aspects of "good news" theology. For instance, the "therapeutic gospel" downplays the serious effects of the fall and attempts to point people to their full potential. The "judgmentless gospel" downplays

---

21. But is the whole church doing so, or just a subgroup? Barnett (1997: 506) suggests that since the church would have been made up of households, it is likely that only a subgroup within the congregation extended hospitality to the false teachers, reasoning that since the newcomers are Hebrews (2 Cor. 11:22), the hosts probably are Jews, perhaps those who have hosted Cephas earlier (1 Cor. 1:12; 3:22; 9:5). Yet that a subgroup played host to the interlopers is not expressly stated in the text.

the consequences of sin. The "moralist gospel" focuses on personal willpower and "being good people." Wax goes on to discuss the "quietist gospel," the "activist gospel," and "the churchless gospel." We could add that some are so anxious to preach a triumphant Christ, who always gives us health and wealth, that the suffering of the Christian life suffers for attention. Paul's words in 2 Cor. 11:1–4 offer us a strong warning. Ministries that preach a gospel different from the Pauline gospel actually preach another Jesus. In other words, Paul says that such an approach to ministry constitutes more than merely preaching the same Jesus a different way; it constitutes preaching another Jesus, the receiving of a different spirit than the Holy Spirit, and embracing a different gospel than the true gospel.

As noted in the comments, we cannot be dogmatic about the exact content of the false teaching offered by Paul's opponents at Corinth. Yet we can stress that it is dangerous to make any move away from the gospel as clearly preached by Paul.

Reflection

True tolerance is at once an essential aspect of healthy relationships and inherently intolerant of dynamics that destroy the other persons in one's sphere. Paul exhorts the Corinthians to "bear with" him, to tolerate his act of foolish boasting. He asks them, in other words, to *listen*, to *follow the logic* embodied in his masterful rhetoric (disguised as foolish boasting), to *open themselves up* to him. At the same time, the apostle chastises them for their tolerance of the interlopers and their false teaching. They have opened themselves to ideas that are steering them away from a healthy relationship with Christ, and that makes Paul appropriately, anxiously jealous. Their tolerance—the Corinthians' listening to false teachers, embracing false logic fed to them by vapid rhetoric, opening themselves to another Jesus, another spirit, another gospel—constitutes a destructive sort of tolerance.

We need to lead people to discern the difference between a godly, gospel-centered tolerance and a worldly, spiritually devastating tolerance. Carson (2012) has sorted these out for us very well. Speaking of the superiority of the "old tolerance" in Western culture, Carson (2012: 163) writes that to hold to an appropriate tolerance is "to keep reserving a place for truth, not only in our own hearts and minds, but [also] in our interaction with the broader culture." Gospel truth then leads us to true biblical tolerance, in which we interact with people redemptively, and redemption is grounded in God's revealed truth. This is Paul's agenda and the reason why his spiritual warfare centers on "arguments" set in opposition to "the knowledge of God" and "thoughts" that must be taken captive if "obedience to Christ" is to follow (10:4–5). He knows that misplaced tolerance leads into the way of mother Eve, away from God and his Christ, to spiritual destruction.

Additional Notes

11:1. There is outstanding external support for the inclusion of τι in the text (𝔓⁴⁶ ℵ B D Ψ 0121 0243 6 33 365 1739 1881 *al* f t vg syʰ), although some scribes omitted it, perhaps deeming it unnecessary (F G H 𝔐 it; Lcf Ambst). Perhaps these witnesses misread the τι as an article (witnesses F G 6 81 630 1175 *pc* add the article, and H 𝔐 present the dative τῇ ἀφροσύνῃ), for instance reading τη for τι (so Thrall 2000: 657). However, strong external witnesses align in support of ἀφροσύνης being anarthrous (𝔓⁴⁶ᵛⁱᵈ ℵ B D P Ψ 0243 33 1739 1881 *pc*).

11:3. The significant textual turbulence in verse 3 presents us with two primary options (the reading with ἀπὸ τῆς ἁγνότητος preceding καὶ τῆς ἁπλότητος is supported only by D* itᵈ Epiphanius), a longer reading, ἀπὸ τῆς ἁπλότητος καὶ τῆς ἁγνότητος, supported by 𝔓⁴⁶ ℵ* B D⁽²⁾ F G 33 81 104 (326) *pc* ar r syʰ** co; Pel, and a shorter reading, ἀπὸ τῆς ἁπλότητος, found in ℵ² H Ψ 0121 0243 1739 1881 𝔐 (b) f* vg syᵖ; Julᶜˡ. Although several variants can be read as modifications of the shorter of these two readings, the standard texts opt for the longer reading. As Metzger (1994: 514) notes, "The external evidence and the transcriptional probabilities are susceptible of quite diverse interpretations." The reasons for retaining the longer reading include the superior external support, the supposition that the shorter reading is due to homoeoteleuton, the scribe's eye skipping the second word ending in -οτητος, and contextual considerations (Harris 2005: 731; Thrall 2000: 663). Thus the longer reading prevailed primarily on the strength of its external witnesses. However, because of the diverse interpretations made possible by the readings, the UBS editorial committee presented καὶ τῆς ἁγνότητος in brackets (Metzger 1994: 515). See the proposal by Kurek-Chomycz (2007), who suggests that the brackets should be removed.

11:4. The external evidence is fairly balanced between the imperfect form ἀνείχεσθε (𝔓³⁴ ℵ D² F G H [Ψ *al*: ην-] 0121 0243 0278 1739 1881 𝔐 lat sy) and the present ἀνέχεσθε (𝔓⁴⁶ B D* 33 *pc* r sa). The imperfect, given its grammatical relationship to the two present-tense verbs in the conditional clause (κηρύσσει, λαμβάνετε), is the more difficult reading, and it seems more likely that a scribe would have accidentally omitted the ι than that a scribe would have added the vowel. Also, the present-tense form could have found expression here under pressure from the same form at the end of 11:1 and in 11:19–20. Nevertheless, the present-tense reading is more likely original. First, as to the form, the imperfect could have arisen in light of the initial use in the passage at the beginning of 11:1, and it is not beyond question that scribal error could have been involved. In fact, a scribe may have altered the form to remove the sense that the Corinthians had already capitulated to the false teachers (Furnish 1984: 489). Second, the imperfect, which would point away from the reality of a current situation in Corinth, would lessen the impact (Harris 2005: 731), and the parallel thoughts in 11:19–20 are expressed forcefully with the present tense. In short, the context, in combination with the strength of the external evidence, leads to the present form being preferable.

2. Paul and the "Superapostles" (11:5–15)

The conflict between Paul and the opponents has been anything but subtle in 10:1–11:4, but both the accusations leveled against the apostle and his defense of himself against those accusations become strikingly overt in 11:5–15. As with the previous unit, Paul here brackets his thoughts with an inclusio, referring to the false apostles at 11:5 and 11:13,[1] although some interpreters question whether the "superapostles" mentioned in 11:5 refer to Paul's opponents. The apostle begins by categorically denying that he is inferior to these ministers. Then follow two points on which Paul has been criticized: (1) he is not a trained public speaker, and (2) he has not accepted compensation from the Corinthians for his services. These criticisms, of course, are interrelated, for a professional public speaker in that culture was compensated for his work. He answers the first accusation by pointing out that his knowledge (of the gospel and of God) is without question. The second, that he has humbled himself by preaching the gospel free of charge, he answers by affirming that fact. Yes, that is exactly what he has done; in fact, his preaching for free constitutes a "boast" that will continue to ring out through Achaia, if Paul has anything to do with it. Paul will keep right on ministering to the Corinthians for free, boasting about his humility, until the spiritual threat from the opponents is eradicated; for they are merely pretend apostles, not real ones, masquerading as servants of righteousness.

An analysis of the passage can be depicted as follows:

   a. Accusation 1: Paul is an inferior public speaker (11:5–6)
   b. Accusation 2: Paul preaches free of charge (11:7–9b)
   c. Paul's commitment to his pattern of ministry (11:9c–12)
   d. The deceitful character of the false apostles (11:13–15)

Exegesis and Exposition

⁵I do not consider myself ⌜ ⌝ to be the least bit inferior to these "superapostles!" ⁶Even if I am an "amateur" in public speaking, I certainly am not an amateur when it comes to knowledge; indeed, ⌜this has been clear to you in every way⌝, on all occasions.

---

1. The closing of an inclusio at times occurred near the end of a unit, rather than in a final statement. As the commentary below discusses, some interpreters believe the "superapostles" referred to at 11:5 point to the pillar apostles in Jerusalem rather than the false teachers in Corinth. However, the beginning and ending of the unit, with overt references to "apostles," can be read as one point in favor of understanding the "superapostles" as meaning the false teachers who have invaded the church.

[7]Or did I commit a sin by humbling ⌜myself⌝, by preaching God's gospel to you free of charge, so that your position might be enhanced? [8]I requisitioned the resources of other churches by receiving support from them, so that I could serve you! [9]And when I was with you and needed something, I did not burden anyone, for the brothers arriving from Macedonia provided whatever I needed. In every way I kept myself from being a burden to you, and I will keep doing so. [10]As surely as Christ's truth is in me, *this* particular boast of mine, as far as I am concerned, will not be silenced in the regions of Achaia. [11]Why? Because I don't love you? God knows I do!! [12]And what I am doing I will keep on doing in order to eliminate the opportunity of those who want a chance to be considered our equals in the things about which they boast. [13]For such people are false apostles, deceitful workers disguising themselves as apostles of Christ. [14]And no ⌜wonder⌝! For Satan himself masquerades as an angel of light. [15]Therefore, it is no great surprise that his servants also masquerade as ministers of righteousness. But their fate will be in accordance with their actions.

a. Accusation 1: Paul Is an Inferior Public Speaker (11:5–6)

Paul begins by categorically denying that he is inferior to the interloping **11:5** ministers at Corinth: "I do not consider myself to be the least bit inferior to these 'superapostles!'" The conjunction γάρ (*gar*) makes the transition from the previous unit, and some interpret the conjunction as marking a continuation of Paul's reasons for asking the Corinthians to bear with him (11:1).[2] However, it is also possible to read verse 5 as turning to a new though related topic,[3] and so take the γάρ as a simple signal marking the "next point" in the discourse (thus it may even be left untranslated).[4] Paul still has in mind "the interloper" (lit., the one coming, ὁ ἐρχόμενος, *ho erchomenos*) mentioned in verse 4, who preaches "another Jesus," for in verse 6 he will boast that his own "knowledge" of the true gospel is beyond question. But with verse 5 he changes from his accusation against the interloper's ministry, to accusations the interlopers have made against him, namely, that he is "inferior" in terms of ministry skills.

The word ὑστερέω (*hystereō*), here in a perfect active infinitive form, could mean "to miss," "fail to reach," "to lack," "to have a deficiency," or "to be inferior to" (BDAG 1043–44). Paul's opponents accuse him of being deficient

2. The repetition of γάρ at 11:2a and 11:4 marks succeeding explanations for why Paul pleads with the Corinthians to bear with him. The use of γάρ at 11:2b seems to play a different role, tagging its clause as explaining the statement at the beginning of 11:2, "For I am jealous about you with a jealousy from God."

3. At 11:5 MS B reads δέ instead, perhaps recognizing a mild shift in the argument (see additional notes). In any case, 2 Cor. 11:1–4 coheres around the idea of "bearing with" a leader, while 11:5–15 shifts to a focus on two interrelated accusations leveled against the apostle Paul. As with 11:1–4, so also verses 5–15 seem to have a bracket structure, or inclusio: Paul begins and ends with overt references to the false teachers. Thus these successive units may be seen as distinct yet meaningfully connected steps in Paul's discourse.

4. As does Furnish (1984: 489), who suggests that the conjunction "has no clear causal force and seems to function merely as a connective"; also Matera 2003: 245.

in certain ministry skills, of being inferior to τῶν ὑπερλίαν ἀποστόλων[5] (*tōn hyperlian apostolōn*, the superapostles), but Paul denies this, saying that he is "not the least bit"[6] (μηδέν, *mēden*) inferior to them. Based on what will be said in the following verses, the main sticking point seems to have to do with Paul's lack of public speaking ability.

Several suggestions have been made concerning the identity of these "superapostles,"[7] but it seems best to read the reference as meaning the "false apostles" mentioned in the same context at 11:13 (Barnett 1997: 512; Thrall 2000: 671, 675–76).[8] Scholars have offered at least three primary points in favor of this position. The word ὑπερλίαν obviously drips with harsh irony (Matera 2003: 247), and it is unlikely that the apostle would use the tone with reference to Peter, James, and John (or the twelve Jerusalem apostles as a whole). Second, if Paul was conceding inferiority to the Jerusalem apostles, it most certainly would not be with reference to public speaking in Greek (see Acts 4:13)! Third, Paul uses the title τῶν ὑπερλίαν ἀποστόλων again at 12:11, at the conclusion of his span of "foolish boasting." In fact, the whole context from 11:4–12:10 has the interloping false teachers in view, and a comparison between Paul and that group is also the topic of 10:12–18 (Barnett 1997: 522–23; Furnish 1984: 502–5; Garland 1999: 469; Thrall 2000: 674; Windisch and Strecker 1970: 330). Thus it seems best to understand τῶν ὑπερλίαν ἀποστόλων as a reference to the false teachers in Corinth.

Yet Paul does not "consider," "reckon," or "think of" himself (λογίζομαι, *logizomai*) as deficient when compared to those being put forward as exceptional in their skills. As noted elsewhere in the commentary, the verb translated "consider" has to do with perspective, thinking carefully about a matter from a particular vantage point, and all the uses of the word in 2 Corinthians, except one (5:19), have to do with Paul's reflection on his own ministry, how his opponents should think about his ministry, or how he thinks about their ministry (2 Cor. 3:5; 10:2, 7, 11; 11:5; 12:6). So the apostle is appropriately reflective on the nature and practice of Christian ministry,

---

5. The genitive functions here as an ablatival genitive of comparison.

6. Here μηδείς (*mēdeis*) functions emphatically (Barrett 1973: 277) and as an "acc. of inner object" meaning "not," "not in the least," "not at all" (cf. Acts 4:21; 10:20; 11:12; James 1:6; Rev. 2:10). Verbs of thinking call for a form of μή (*mē*, not; BDF 222).

7. Paul uses "superapostles" again at 12:11: "I have made a fool of myself; you yourselves drove me to it. Actually, I should have been commended by you, since I lack nothing in comparison to the 'superapostles'—even though I am nothing." In the letter fifteen times Paul uses compound words formed with the preposition ὑπέρ- (*hyper-*, super, excessively; 1:8; 3:10; 4:7, 17 [2x]; 7:4; 9:14; 10:14, 16; 11:5, 23; 12:7 [3x], 11). P. Marshall (1987: 214) tags Paul's opponents as "hybrists" who provoke Paul to use a "vocabulary of hybris" in response.

8. The other main view is that the reference is to the Jerusalem apostles (so Barrett 1971; 1973: 278; Harris 2005: 746–47; Martin 1986: 342; John Chrysostom, *Hom. 2 Cor.* 23.2; cf. Gal. 2:9, "pillar apostles"). For arguments in favor of this view, see the summary by Thrall 2000: 671–72. The theory is that the interlopers in Corinth claim support, perhaps letters of recommendation (3:1) from the Jerusalem apostles, or that Paul here attacks the exalted view of the Twelve held by "the false apostles."

and here he reflects his confidence concerning the skills God has given him to carry out his ministry well.

Yet Paul also begins verse 6 with a concession, "Even if I am an 'amateur' in public speaking" (εἰ δὲ καὶ ἰδιώτης τῷ λόγῳ, *ei de kai idiōtēs tō logō*). The word ἰδιώτης could be used with a range of meanings (Winter 2002: 224–25). Generally, a person who was ἰδιώτης lacked experience or training in a particular field of knowledge (e.g., government, military, medicine, oratory, etc.; cf. Acts 4:13) and therefore was an amateur or layperson as compared to a specialist of some kind. The word could be used pejoratively of a "common" person belonging to a low social class, but it often was used to distinguish an untrained person, or a "beginner," over against a professional or expert (Spicq 1994: 2.213). For instance, Hyperides (*Lyc.* 20) writes,

11:6

> I am a fellow-citizen of yours, an *amateur* unused to speaking, on trial now with the risk not only of losing my life—a minor consideration to men with a proper sense of values—but also of being cast out after death, without even the prospect of a grave in my own country. So if you will give the word, gentlemen of the jury, I will call an advocate. Will you please come up, Theophilus, and say what you can in my defense? The jury asks you to do so.

Thus the speaker asks for a professional orator to speak for him, since he is not a public speaker by experience.

However, Winter (2002: 224–25) makes the interesting observation that the word also could be used of those trained in rhetoric but who choose not to function as public orators or teachers of rhetoric. Thus "'non-orators' may indeed possess some knowledge of rhetoric, but they have abandoned ἀπάτη [*apatē*, fraud, trickery] in their practice of it." Indeed, Philo (*Agr.* 143) can use ἰδιώτης of those highly trained in rhetoric, and Isocrates (*Antid.* 201, 204) celebrates those so trained but who choose to use their skills for the good of the community rather than for personal advancement. Ambrosiaster (*Comm. Paul's Ep.*, 2 Cor. 11:6) seems to reflect this understanding of Paul's modest assessment of himself at this point:

> Paul did not mean by this that he did not know how to speak but that commendation did not depend on mere eloquence. A person of little eloquence is not guilty before God, but someone who does not know God is liable to be charged with ignorance, because it was a sin to be ignorant of what is conducive to salvation. It was not eloquence which would commend Paul's message but the power to save which accompanied it. (Bray 1999: 291–92)

Given the broader context of 2 Cor. 11:6, τῷ λόγῳ (in word) clearly refers to public speaking. Thus Paul admits that he is not engaged professionally as a public orator. Indeed, some commentators have suggested that Paul's response here "corresponds to the way philosophers in the Socratic tradition typically attacked the pretentiousness of the Sophists" (Furnish 1984: 490, following Betz 1972: 66). The "professional" skill to which Paul alludes is the affected, or "ornamental," style of the Sophists (Witherington 1995: 447), rather than classical Greek rhetoric. He "admits" that he does not possess their "skill" in professional speaking—but this is not an admission that Paul was ignorant of Greek rhetoric,[9] for his letters point to a knowledge of the art (Winter 2002: 225–27); indeed, "he must have had the basic training in rhetoric available to highly educated individuals in Greco-Roman cities" (Keener 2005: 227); even this section of 2 Corinthians shows a detailed knowledge of rhetorical argument (Witherington 1995: 447)! Thus, rather than a humble admission of inadequacy, the apostle continues to speak somewhat tongue in cheek.

Moreover, Paul adds, "I certainly am not an amateur when it comes to knowledge; indeed, this has been clear to you in every way, on all occasions." The ἀλλ᾽ οὐ (all' ou, but not) effects the contrast between τῷ λόγῳ (in public speaking) in the previous clause and the phrase τῇ γνώσει (tē gnōsei, in knowledge).[10] Both of these phrases delimit ἰδιώτης. Most commentators understand the "knowledge" of which Paul speaks in one of two ways. Either he denies that he is an "amateur" when it comes to knowledge about Jesus, the Spirit, and the gospel (11:4; Barnett 1997: 507), or he denies that he lacks "knowledge" in terms of "spiritual insight" (Furnish 1984: 490; cf. 6:6; 8:7; 1 Cor. 12:8). Between the two, and given Paul's protestations about "a different gospel" in verse 4 and the preached gospel in verse 7, he most likely speaks of an understanding of the good news and right Christian teaching, that is, knowledge of God and God's gospel (cf. 2:14; 4:6; 10:5).[11]

He further asserts that his knowledge of right Christian teaching should be obvious to the Corinthians. The second ἀλλ᾽ (all') in verse 6 may be considered rhetorically ascensive[12] ("indeed"), building on Paul's assertion that

9. As a parallel example, Dio Chrysostom (Or. 12.15) claims to be "unskilled" in comparison to the Sophists.

10. Both of these datives may be considered datives of respect.

11. Yet, in line with Winter's insights noted above, a third option is that Paul speaks here of knowledge about rhetoric. In effect, he states that he does not assume the role of a public orator, but that this does not mean he is uneducated. He may be "trained in rhetoric but not living the professional life of a public orator or teacher" (Winter 2002: 228). In this light the act of Paul humbling himself in 11:7 is his decision not to play the role of public orator for hire, and this makes good sense in context. The earlier criticism of Paul (in 10:10) is an attack on his public presentations, judged inadequate in terms of the "professional public speaker." How is his choice of ministry approach an act of "humbling" if he has no skills and thus no other option for the conduct of his ministry (and no other option for support of himself except by working with his hands)? Rather, if Paul is knowledgeable of forensic rhetoric but has chosen not to use that knowledge in his preaching and teaching, his choice to support himself rather by manual labor could be interpreted as "humbling." This interpretation of Paul's knowledge also flows well into his discussion of "ministry" freely given. However, a difficulty with this position is Paul's use of the word "knowledge" elsewhere in the book (2 Cor. 2:14; 4:6; 10:5) and the claim that this knowledge has been manifested "in every way, on all occasions," a description more fit for Paul's focus on the gospel itself.

12. Harris (2005: 749), on the other hand, reads this use as contrastive, "on the contrary."

he is knowledgeable and driving home the Corinthians' obligation to open their eyes to certain truths that are tacitly obvious! The apostle's knowledge of the true gospel has been "clear" or "made plain" (φανερώσαντες, *phanerōsantes*) to the Corinthians "in every way, on all occasions" (ἐν παντί . . . ἐν πᾶσιν, *en panti . . . en pasin*). The first phrase, a common expression in the letter (1:4; 2:14; 4:8; 6:4; 7:5, 11, 16; 8:7; 9:8, 11; 11:9; 12:12), normally is read as referring to the various "ways" Paul's knowledge has been demonstrated to the Corinthians. The second "all" is plural and may be read as masculine (so P. Hughes 1962: 382; Plummer 1915: 300), with the sense, "among all people." However, the adjective probably should be understood as neuter, perhaps underscoring the multiple circumstances in which Paul's knowledge of right teaching has shone brightly (see the same two phrases at Phil. 4:12): "on all occasions." In other words, Paul has always presented himself as knowledgeable of right teaching, even if he has not assumed the role of "professional speaker."

b. Accusation 2: Paul Preaches Free of Charge (11:7–9b)

Now comes the rub. Those opposing Paul make a second, interrelated accusation against the apostle: he preaches the gospel free of charge! "Or did I commit a sin by humbling myself, by preaching God's gospel to you free of charge?" The conjunction ἤ (*ē*) is sometimes used to introduce rhetorical questions (BDAG 432), and this rhetorical question anticipates a negative answer. In effect, Paul insists that, in taking a nonmonetized approach to ministry in Corinth, he has not sinned. Very rarely does Paul speak of an individual "sin" (the only other exception is Rom. 4:8; Matera 2003: 249); the word in the singular most often refers to "sin" as a power in the world or in the life of a person.[13] It seems that, again with an ironic tone, Paul uses "sin" here as equivalent to "a wrong against you." From his statements at 11:11 and 12:13, it is clear that because he is refusing pay, he is being accused of acting in a way that is unloving and hurtful toward the Corinthians.

11:7

Paul characterizes this approach to ministry in several ways. First, by not taking pay from the Corinthians, he "humbles" himself (ἐμαυτὸν ταπεινῶν, *emauton tapeinōn*) while correspondingly enhancing the position of the Corinthians. The OT Scriptures celebrate God's exaltation of those who have humbled themselves (e.g., 1 Sam. 2:7; Job 5:11; Ezek. 17:24; 21:26), and the theme echoes through the NT as well (Matt. 23:12; Luke 14:11; 18:14; James 4:10; 1 Pet. 5:6; Phil. 2:5–11; Furnish 1984: 491). Perhaps due to their cultural context, this biblical value has escaped the apostle's opponents and has blurred the vision of the socially elite church members in Corinth. Paul's work at tentmaking (Acts 18:3) was unclean since it involved working with leather, and this manual form of labor would have offended the elite. Indeed, given

13. See Rom. 3:9, 20; 5:12–13, 20–6:2; 6:6–7, 10–14, 16–18, 20, 22–23; 7:7–9, 11, 13–14, 17, 20, 23, 25; 8:2–3, 10; 14:23; 1 Cor. 15:56; 2 Cor. 5:21; Gal. 2:17; 3:22.

the cultural context, for their apostle to work with his hands would have been considered humiliating![14] Hock (2007: 60) explains:

> In the social world of a city like Corinth, Paul would have been a weak figure, without power, prestige, and privilege. . . . To those of wealth and power, the appearance (σχῆμα [*schēma*]) of the artisan was that befitting a slave (δουλοπρεπής [*douloprepēs*]). It is no wonder then that Paul thought it necessary to defend his practice of supporting himself by his work at a trade (1 Cor. 9:1–27) . . . and that the dominant theme of this defense was whether he was free or slavish (vv. 1, 19). To Corinthians who, relative to Paul, appeared to be rich, wise, powerful, and respected (cf. 4:8, 10), their lowly apostle seemed to have enslaved himself with his plying a trade (cf. 9:19).

In short, Paul's manual labor embarrasses them and is taken as a slap against their public status and dignity. As Savage (1996: 87) notes, "An impoverished leader was a contradiction in terms."

Yet for Paul, living with limited means and performing manual labor serves the end that his hearers may become spiritually rich (Barrett 1973: 282; 2 Cor. 6:10; 9:11; 1 Cor. 1:5). This he explains eloquently in 1 Cor. 9:12. After proclaiming his "right" to remuneration, he continues, "However, we have not made use of this right; instead we endure everything so that we will not hinder the gospel of Christ" (1 Cor. 9:12 HCSB). How might the gospel be hindered? By Paul having a heightened obligation to one or more patrons. Therefore, instead of being obligated to a few (by receiving pay), he has enslaved himself to all people, even the weak, so that he might win as many people as possible (1 Cor. 9:19–22). This is the nature of his "humiliation." So he reminds the Corinthians that humble service, a ministry that does the opposite of self-exaltation, serves as the means for others to move up and move on in their relationship to God. Consequently, the effect of Paul's "humiliation" is that the Corinthians are exalted!

So the Corinthians have felt hurt that Paul preached the gospel to them "free of charge," but Paul was committed to offering the gospel as "gift" rather than "goods" (Witherington 1995: 448). The term "freely" in this case speaks of something "freely given, as a gift, without payment, gratis" (BDAG 266; see Matt. 10:8; 2 Thess. 3:8; Rev. 21:6). Paul echoes an approach to ministry reflected in the ministry of Jesus himself: "Heal the sick, raise the dead, cleanse those with skin diseases, drive out demons. You have received free of charge; give free of charge" (Matt. 10:8 HCSB; 2 Cor. 8:9).

11:8   Second, Paul serves the Corinthians by drawing on the resources of other churches. The verb συλάω (*sylaō*), here in its aorist active indicative form, is

---

14. See, e.g., Cicero, *Off.* 1.42; 1.150; 2.225. A teacher of the era could get financial support in a number of ways, such as charging fees for instruction, joining a patron's household as a tutor to the patron's sons, begging, accepting gifts from followers, or doing physical labor (Hock 2007: 52–59; P. Marshall 1987: 226–30, 296–98).

found only in this passage in the NT and only at Let. Jer. 17 LXX (18 ET)[15] in the LXX. Philo uses the word to speak of thieves ransacking a city (*Conf.* 47; *Decal.* 136), but he can also use it figuratively of being robbed of the ability to think well (*Alleg.* 3.20). In the papyri the term especially refers to theft by violently breaking and entering (P.Stras. 296, verso 10), yet it could be used more mildly of being deprived of something (e.g., P.Oxf. 19.7).[16] So Paul says he has "requisitioned the resources of" other churches in order to serve the Corinthians. The choice of the term may have been to dispel any notion that he has chosen the patronage of another congregation in preference to the Corinthians (so Furnish 1984: 484, 492). We know from Phil. 4:15–17 that Paul received "missionary funds" from the Philippians,[17] but as Matera points out, that "sharing" of ministry with the Philippians was distinctly different from the remuneration offered in Corinth. The Macedonian church had partnered with Paul in extending the reach of the gospel through missionary enterprise. The Corinthians, on the other hand, were offering pay for services rendered to them as a church and, given their patron-client cultural framework, would have obligated Paul to those providing him with wages (Matera 2003: 250–51). Nevertheless, it would have rankled that he received missionary funding from the Corinthians' "poor cousins" in Macedonia (11:9; Phil. 4:15–17) but refused local support from the wealthy and socially well-situated elite in Corinth.

The term rendered "support" (ὀψώνιον, *opsōnion*) could refer generally to "pay" (e.g., Josephus, *Ant.* 12.28) or perhaps "provisions" given as compensation (e.g., 1 Macc. 14:32; Caragounis 1974). At times in the NT it is used of a military context, either literally or figuratively, in which a soldier serves for pay (Luke 3:14; 1 Cor. 9:7), but it also can be used generally of compensation (e.g., Rom. 6:23; see BDAG 747).[18] Among the Corinthians Paul's practice of ministering without pay (Acts 18:3; 1 Cor. 4:12) was culturally awkward in three ways: (1) public speakers normally were paid; (2) those to whom they spoke expected to pay (indeed, could effect a closer bond of relationship by paying!); and (3) those who worked with their hands were accorded a lower social status (Barnett 1997: 513; Martin 1986: 344–45). Perhaps Paul has especially angered the socially elite in the church by refusing their patronage.

---

15. "The priests make their temples secure with doors and locks and bars, in order that they may not be plundered [συληθῶσι, *sylēthōsi*] by robbers" (Let. Jer. 18 NRSV [17 LXX]).

16. However, Spicq (1994: 3.315–16) points out that συλάω also could refer to an official seizure of property in retaliation for a wrong committed, which he takes to be the primary image on which Paul draws at this point. Yet the idea of retaliation does not really fit Paul's purpose at this point. Rather, his ministry for free models a countercultural posture to the Corinthians and avoids the impression that he is just another itinerant Sophist preacher.

17. "And as you Philippians know, at the beginning of my gospel ministry, when I left Macedonia, no church shared with me in this matter of giving and receiving except you alone. For even in Thessalonica on more than one occasion you sent something for my need. I do not say this because I am seeking a gift. Rather, I seek the credit that abounds to your account" (Phil. 4:15–17 NET).

18. On ministers in the early church receiving pay, see Ellis 1978: 10–13. But, for the opinion that such a system of pay was not in place in the early church, see P. Marshall 1987: 218–20.

This may be the reason why the interlopers were embraced by a portion of the community—they fit the norms and expectations of the culture. Paul, on the other hand, has angered the elite by refusing their patronage—thereby also avoiding the demand of indebtedness and reciprocity to a patron!

11:9a–b Third, the apostle relieved the Corinthians from the "burden" of his financial needs, depending instead on the Macedonian brothers to meet his needs. The verb καταναρκάω (*katanarkaō*),[19] used in the NT only here and twice in 12:13–14, connotes "being a burden" to someone; according to Keener, this concept also was used in the context of patron-client relationships, in which one person was obligated socially to another.[20] By choosing not to accept pay from the wealthy at Corinth, Paul avoided being socially dependent on, or obligated to, a particular faction within the Corinthian church, yet he also avoided the charge of exploiting them (Keener 2005: 229; Peterman 1997: 159, 169, 201–4).[21] So Paul chose rather to depend on the services of the "brothers" coming from Macedonia. "Brothers" could refer to the Macedonian coworkers who came to Corinth (8:18, 22–23; 9:3, 5) but more likely refers to Silas and Timothy (1:1, 19), who joined the apostle in the Greece mission after Paul had initiated ministry there (Acts. 18:5).

Harris sets out the following plausible scenario. Paul brought with him to Corinth financial and/or other resources as ministry support from Macedonia (11:8). According to Acts 18:3 Paul, partnering with Priscilla and Aquila (1 Cor. 4:11–12; Acts 18:2–3), supported himself by making tents from the time he arrived in Corinth. There was a time when his funds ran low or out (11:9), but he refused to take money from the Corinthians (11:9). However, after Silas and Timothy arrived from Macedonia with renewed resources, Paul's need was met, and he was able to give his full attention to preaching (Acts 18:5; 2 Cor. 11:9). So Paul changed his work pattern upon the arrival of his fellow workers from the north, and it is reasonable that they had brought helpful resources from Philippi (Phil. 4:15–16) and perhaps other towns in Macedonia (Harris 2005: 761–62). Paul says these brothers "provided whatever I needed." The word προσανεπλήρωσαν (*prosaneplērōsan*) could mean "supplemented" (Barnett 1997: 517) but more likely simply means "supplied."

Here Paul's words pose a question we might consider in terms of ground-breaking mission work today. Barnett (1997: 518) comments, "While Paul

---

19. The word καταναρκάω belonged to medical terminology in Greek literature. Hippocrates (*Epid.* 6.7.3), e.g., could speak of a person being "benumbed" (καταναναρκωμένους, *katanenarkōmenous*) or perhaps "anesthetized" (Spicq 1994: 2.267).

20. Seneca, *Ben.* 2.21.3; and Lucian (*Dep. Schol.* 20) states,

[The prospective employer] calls for the intervention of one of the company: let him name a sum, at once worthy of your [the prospective dependent scholar's] acceptance, and not burden-some to his purse, which has so many more urgent calls upon it. "Sir," says this officious old gentleman, who has been a toady from his youth, "Sir, you are the luckiest man in Rome. Deny it if you can! You have gained a privilege which many a man has longed for, and is not like to obtain at Fortune's hands."

21. See the very helpful summary by Garland 1999: 479–82.

insists that the local and permanent teacher in the church be paid, it may be that his apostolic ministry, 'free of charge,' provides a useful paradigm for pioneer missionaries in subsequent generations. The minister engaged in groundbreaking evangelism, who expects remuneration from those he evangelizes, runs the risk of portraying his ministry as venal." In most cultures of the world today, the suspicion of greed on the part of those coming to an area to minister certainly presents a pause of caution to those wishing to present the gospel effectively. Yet Paul's concern also seems to be that remuneration obligates the minister uniquely to those of status and wealth. This should encourage us to reflect on the influence in our churches. Can influence be bought by "the highest bidder"?

c. Paul's Commitment to His Pattern of Ministry (11:9c–12)

In the face of the Corinthian faction hammering against his pattern of ministry, Paul plants his feet firmly in resistance, making it clear that he has no intention of changing. His words at the end of verse 9, καὶ τηρήσω (*kai tērēsō*),[22] "and I will keep doing so," form a simple declaration of commitment. In this context the verb carries the basic sense of "keeping" something undisturbed, but it can also carry nuances of "guarding" or "persisting in obedience" (BDAG 1002).

11:9c–10

Paul's firmness on the matter of how he conducts his ministry does not constitute a stubborn streak or inborn inflexibility; when he writes, "As surely as Christ's truth is in me" (ἔστιν ἀλήθεια Χριστοῦ ἐν ἐμοί, *estin alētheia Christou en emoi*), this is no empty oath. "Christ's truth" forms the foundation for everything the apostle does, including his commitment to ministry without pay. Here Χριστοῦ should probably be understood as a subjective genitive,[23] that is, "truth given by Christ" (Harris 2005: 763), and perhaps Paul's Damascus road encounter with the exalted Lord forms the ultimate backdrop here (Barnett 1997: 519). All of the apostle's life—everything he does in his ministry—stems from a profound orientation to the truth that Christ lives and has given Paul a clear mission to accomplish in the world. Thus the statement as a whole serves as a solemn affirmation of the apostle's commitment to the truth, undergirded by his relationship with the truth-giving Christ. Therefore the "oath" also forms a statement of resolute commitment to the truth given by Christ.

The apostle expresses that commitment with "this boasting of mine . . . will not be stopped in the regions of Achaia." Paul speaks of his "boast" here, using the noun form καύχησις (*kauchēsis*), a word used consistently but somewhat sparsely earlier in the book (1:12; 7:4, 14; 8:24) and only twice in chapters 10–12 (11:10, 17). More common, especially in chapters 10–12, is the cognate verb καυχάομαι (*kauchaomai*; 2 Cor. 5:12; 7:14; 9:2; 10:8, 13, 15–17; 11:12, 16, 18, 30; 12:1, 5–6, 9), and by considering this noun and verb together, we develop a clear idea about the substance of Paul's boasting. In this broader

---

22. This is a predictive future, which states that something will take place in the future.
23. If taken as an objective genitive, it would read "truth about Christ," that is, the gospel.

section he lays a foundation by boasting about his authority (10:8) and about the ministry he has accomplished (10:13, 15–17). He has been drawn into such boasting by the boasting of his opponents (11:18, 21); yet in the balance of chapter 11 and then in 12:1–10, Paul strikes a masterful rhetorical stroke. In each of these movements he begins by listing strengths about which he might boast (11:22–23a; 12:1–5a) and then transitions—without drawing attention to the transition—to boasting about weaknesses (11:23b–33; 12:5b–10)! Thus the focus rests on the celebration of the apostle's weaknesses.

Accordingly, when at 11:10 Paul speaks of "this boast" (ἡ καύχησις αὕτη, *hē kauchēsis hautē*), he has in mind the particular "weakness" that has been under discussion in 11:7–9, namely, ministering for free, the "humble" approach to ministry that some have found culturally jarring. In no uncertain terms Paul declares that he will not be deterred from this approach. He will not change. This boast "will not be silenced in the regions of Achaia." The verb φράσσω (*phrassō*) means "to shut" or "close," as in the act of shutting human mouths (Rom. 3:19) or the mouths of lions (Heb. 11:33). So the term here could be rendered with the sense of Paul's boast being "silenced" (e.g., ESV, NRSV), but it has also been understood as the boast being "blocked" or "quashed," that is, "stopped" (e.g., HCSB, NASB, NLT², NIV, NET, KJV). Regardless, the effect is the same. Paul will not allow his "boast" of humble service without pay to be "shut up," nor his working without pay to be shut down. The parenthetical "as far as I am concerned" (εἰς ἐμέ, *eis eme*) means, in effect, "not if I have anything to do with it!" The preposition plus the accusative ἐμέ communicates reference (lit., with reference to me).

11:11 In verses 11 and 12, the apostle first heads off a misguided explanation of his resistance to giving up this pattern of ministry (11:11) and then explains why he feels compelled to minister free of charge (11:12). He begins by asking, διὰ τί; (*dia ti?*), a common way of framing the question "Why?"[24] Paul then provides the wrong answer to the question, an answer that some undoubtedly were talking up: ὅτι οὐκ ἀγαπῶ ὑμᾶς; (*hoti ouk agapō hymas?* Because I don't love you?). This answer is posed as a question. Paul asks in effect, "Is this what you think? That I don't take your money because I don't love you?" As already explained, given the cultural context, the apostle's refusal to accept pay would have been read as a rejection of friendship with those making the offer. Thus Paul has been accused of being unloving. Yet the apostle denies this, countering, ὁ θεὸς οἶδεν (*ho theos oiden*), simply put, "God knows!"[25] which means here "God knows I do!!" Paul appeals to God's knowledge of all things and specifically God's knowledge of the apostle's motives and truthfulness (cf. the

24. More lit., "Because of what?" The διά with the acc. speaks of cause, and the construction used here in 11:11 (or the alternate διατί) is a common way of framing the question "Why?" (Matt. 9:11, 14; 13:10; Mark 2:18; 11:31; Luke 5:30; 19:23, 31; 20:5; 24:38; John 7:45; 8:43, 46; 12:5; 13:37; Acts 5:3; 1 Cor. 6:7; Rev. 17:7). As here, at Rom. 9:32 we have simply διὰ τί (BDAG 225).

25. The affirmation will be repeated at 11:31 and twice more in 12:2–3. Furnish (1984: 493) understands our present occurrence as an abbreviation of the more extended oath formula at 11:31.

double use of ὁ θεὸς οἶδεν [*ho theos oiden*, God knows] at 2 Cor. 12:2–3). God knows that Paul loves the Corinthians, regardless of the way his actions might be read from a particular cultural perspective.

With verse 12 Paul explains his true motive in the matter: "And what I am **11:12** doing I will keep on doing in order to eliminate the opportunity of those who want a chance to be considered our equals in the things about which they boast." This declaration begins with Ὃ δὲ ποιῶ, καὶ ποιήσω (*ho de poiō, kai poiēsō*). The first occurrence of ποιέω (*poieō*, I do) is present tense in form and refers to the apostle's current pattern of ministry. The second use of ποιέω is future in form and refers to Paul's approach to ministry from this point in his life onward. Thus the pattern of ministry currently in place will continue into the future. Paul will not change his approach due to pressure from his opponents at Corinth.

He goes on to explain this commitment, understanding his approach to ministry as critical for dealing with the interlopers in Corinth. The conjunction ἵνα (*hina*, in order that) introduces the purpose clause, and the clause reads, literally, "in order that I might eliminate the opportunity of those wanting an opportunity" (ἐκκόψω τὴν ἀφορμὴν τῶν θελόντων ἀφορμήν, *ekkopsō tēn aphormēn tōn thelontōn aphormēn*). The aorist active subjunctive verb ἐκκόψω could be used by authors to speak of chopping something down. For instance, Deut. 20:19 LXX commands that in siege warfare trees are not to be cut down (ἐκκόψεις) but rather kept for their fruit.[26] In other places the word refers to cutting something off, as at Rom. 11:24, where the Gentiles are said to be "cut off" from a wild olive tree in order to be grafted in to God's people, or at Matt. 5:30 and 18:8, where Jesus hyperbolically speaks of cutting off one's hand. By extension ἐκκόπτω means "to eliminate" or "do away with" something, and that more figurative sense is what Paul has in mind here. He wants to "cut off" or "eliminate" the "opportunity of those who want a chance" to gain a form of ministry credibility with the Corinthians. The term ἀφορμή (*aphormē*), used twice in this verse, speaks of a "circumstance from which other action becomes possible, such as the starting point or base of operations for an expedition" or "a set of convenient circumstances for carrying out some purpose." In other words, the term connotes an "opportunity" or "occasion" or a "chance" to accomplish something (Rom. 7:8, 11; 2 Cor. 5:12; Gal. 5:13; 1 Tim. 5:14; BDAG 158). So Paul wants to block any opportunity for the interlopers to accomplish their desired ends among the Corinthians.

The apostle expresses those desired ends as "to be considered our equals in the things about which they boast." This language seems somewhat strange since the interlopers have put themselves forward as Paul's superiors, rather than his equals (11:5)! But the latter part of the infinitival clause provides the key. A wooden rendering of this part of the verse might run, "In order that in what they are boasting they might be found [to be] just as also we [are]"

26. See also Herodotus, *Hist.* 9.97; 1 En. 26.1; Pss. Sol. 12.3; Josephus, *Ant.* 10.52; Matt. 3:10; 7:19; Luke 3:9.

(ἵνα ἐν ᾧ καυχῶνται εὑρεθῶσιν καθὼς καὶ ἡμεῖς, *hina en hō kauchōntai heurethōsin kathōs kai hēmeis*). In other words, Paul says, the interlopers want "to be considered our equals." He refers to the part of their boasting that asserts, "We are offering you the same type of ministry that Paul has on offer." Their claim, of course, is that they can do that ministry more effectively (e.g., 10:10). Yet their foot in the door would begin by claiming to be replacements for Paul in doing essentially the same ministry he was doing. Paul intends to quash this illusion by sticking to a pattern of ministry that stands in stark contrast to these charlatans. They receive pay for their ministry services. He does not. As long as Paul takes this course of ministry, the clear line between his ministry and that of the interlopers is unmistakable. Thus, whatever their claims, their "ministry" in Corinth is not the same as Paul's; they should not "be considered our equals," Paul insists. They are not true apostles, as he makes clear in 11:13–15.

d. The Deceitful Character of the False Apostles (11:13–15)

11:13   In blunt and confrontational terms, Paul now explains (γάρ, *gar*, for) his determination to block any opportunity for the interlopers to present their ministry in Corinth as on an equal footing with his apostolic ministry: "For such people are false apostles, deceitful workers disguising themselves as apostles of Christ." The adjective οἱ . . . τοιοῦτοι (*hoi . . . toioutoi*, such people),[27] used here as a substantive referring specifically to the interlopers, forms the subject of the sentence and refers back to "those wanting a chance" (τῶν θελόντων ἀφορμήν) in the previous verse.[28] These opportunists at Corinth are then described in two primary ways that mirror one another, as ψευδαπόστολοι (*pseudapostoloi*, false apostles) and as ἐργάται δόλιοι μετασχηματιζόμενοι εἰς ἀποστόλους Χριστοῦ (*ergatai dolioi metaschēmatizomenoi eis apostolous Christou*, deceitful workers disguising themselves as apostles of Christ).[29] On this reading, "deceitful workers disguising themselves as apostles of Christ" is an appositional expansion of "false apostles" (as with the NLT[2]).

27. This use with the article is somewhat common and points to a class or group of people (BDF 143).

28. The absence of the main verb (ellipsis, likely of the verb εἰσίν, they are) in 11:13 probably is stylistic. Notice the article, followed by the repetition of the -οι ending:

οἱ   γὰρ
τοιοῦτοι
ψευδαπόστολοι
ἐργάται δόλιοι
μετασχηματιζόμενοι

Thus the ellipsis allows for an almost uninterrupted repetition of the -οι sound.

29. The editors of our standard Greek texts place a comma after δόλιοι, thus reading the participle μετασχηματιζόμενοι as a substantival participle offering a third description of the false teachers. Yet it is also possible, as with our ET, to read the participle as attributive and related most directly to δόλιοι (see the description of the attributive participle in D. Wallace 1996: 617–18).

Using a word that he probably coins himself (so Harris 2005: 772), the apostle Paul first labels them ψευδαπόστολοι (*pseudapostoloi*, false apostles). Elsewhere in the NT we are warned extensively about the danger of "false prophets" (Matt. 7:15; 24:11, 24; Mark 13:22; Luke 6:26; Acts 13:6; 2 Pet. 2:1; 1 John 4:1; Rev. 16:13; 20:10), cautioned about "false messiahs" (Matt. 24:24; Mark 13:22) and "false teachers" (2 Pet. 2:1), and told about "false brothers" (i.e., Jewish teachers; 2 Cor. 11:26; Gal. 2:4). But only at Rev. 2:2b do we find a comparable reference to "apostles" who are "false": "You have tested those who call themselves apostles [ἀποστόλους, *apostolous*] and are not, and you have found them to be false [ψευδεῖς, *pseudeis*]." For Paul, these so-called apostles are "false" because they teach a false Jesus, are ambassadors associated with a false spirit, proclaim a false gospel (11:4), and promote a false form of righteousness (11:15); they peddle the Word of God for profit (2:17) and reflect values that are out of line with authentic Christian ministry (e.g., 10:12; 11:18–20). Ultimately they show their falsity by opposing God's true apostle to the Corinthians, inappropriately invading his ministry territory (10:13–16).

Second, however, Paul expands on the fraud of these so-called apostles by focusing on their mendaciousness, describing them as "deceitful workers disguising themselves as apostles of Christ." The tradition of "ministers" being referred to as "workers" goes back to Jesus (Matt. 9:37–38; 10:10; Luke 10:2, 7), and Paul uses the word similarly in 1 Timothy (5:18; 2 Tim. 2:15). In line with our present context, at Phil. 3:2 he also exhorts the Philippians to "watch out for . . . evil workers," who are equated with "dogs" (i.e., false teachers) and "those who mutilate the flesh" (i.e., the circumcision party). But the adjective in our present context is δόλιοι, a term found only here in the NT, although it is quite common in the LXX; the word connotes the idea of being "deceitful" or "treacherous" (BDAG 256),[30] and Paul describes their deceitfulness by use of the graphic verb μετασχηματίζω (*metaschēmatizō*; here as a present middle participle). The term can mean to transform or change something (Plutarch, *Ages.* 603 [14.2]; *Mor.* 426e; T. Sol. 20.13; T. Reu. 5.6; Philo, *Etern.* 79; Josephus, *Ant.* 7.257), like the transformation that will come with the resurrection from the dead (Phil. 3:21). Here, used with the preposition εἰς (*eis*, as), the word connotes, "to disguise oneself" or "to pretend to be what one is not" (4 Macc. 9:22; T. Job 17.2; BDAG 641). Thus, the fake apostles wrap themselves in a guise meant to mislead. They say they are apostles, but they are not.

Paul, the true apostle, repeats the term μετασχηματίζω two other times in verses 14–15 as he goes on to explain that these charlatan workers simply   **11:14–15**

---

30. For δόλιος, *EDNT* 1:343 lists the meaning as "malicious, insidious," but the word is used extensively in the LXX, most often meaning "deceitful" or "treacherous" and often referring to "lips" or "tongues" (Pss. 5:7; 11:3–4; 16:1; 30:19; 42:1; 51:6; 108:2; 119:2–3 [5:6; 12:2–3; 17:1; 31:18; 43:1; 52:4; 109:2; 120:2–3 ET]; Prov. 11:1; 12:6, 17, 24, 27; 13:9, 13; 14:25; 20:23; Sir. 11:29; 22:22; 27:25; Pss. Sol. 4.23; 12.1; Zeph. 3:13; Jer. 9:7 [9:8 ET]). Also see the cognates δολιόω (*dolioō*, deceive), δόλος (*dolos*, deceit), and δολόω (*doloō*, falsify), all of which have to do with deceit and cunning.

act in accordance with patterns of behavior modeled by their master, Satan. Thus their deceptiveness should not be a shock, as verse 14 states, "And no wonder! For Satan himself masquerades as an angel of light." The verse begins simply, καὶ οὐ θαῦμα (*kai ou thauma*); and θαῦμα could refer to a marvel (so Tyndale, KJV) or even a miracle, but it could also refer to a state of "wondering" because one is amazed or extraordinarily impressed.[31] In effect, Paul says the fact that the interlopers act deceptively should not be surprising (NLT[2]). Thus modern translations tend to render the clause "and no wonder!" (ESV, HCSB, NASB, NRSV, NIV, NET).

The remainder of verse 14 and the first part of verse 15 explain why the character of the false teachers should be no surprise. Paul crafts two statements that are parallel with the description of the false apostles already offered in verse 13:

11:13	ἐργάται δόλιοι,	μετασχηματιζόμενοι	εἰς ἀποστόλους Χριστοῦ
	ergatai dolioi,	*metaschēmatizomenoi*	*eis apostolous Christou*
	deceitful workers,	disguising themselves	as apostles of Christ
11:14	αὐτὸς γὰρ ὁ σατανᾶς	μετασχηματίζεται	εἰς ἄγγελον φωτός.
	autos gar ho satanas	*metaschēmatizetai*	*eis angelon phōtos.*
	For Satan himself	masquerades	as an angel of light.
11:15	οἱ διάκονοι αὐτοῦ	μετασχηματίζονται	ὡς διάκονοι δικαιοσύνης
	hoi diakonoi autou	*metaschēmatizontai*	*hōs diakonoi dikaiosynēs*
	his servants also	masquerade	as ministers of righteousness.

Earlier, in verse 3, Paul mentioned that "the snake deceived Eve by his chicanery," and here he draws an analogy to "Satan himself" (αὐτὸς . . . ὁ σατανᾶς), who "masquerades as an angel of light." We have already noted that the verb μετασχηματίζω means "to disguise oneself" or "to pretend to be what one is not," thus "to masquerade." In the pseudepigraphical work Testament of Job, Satan disguises himself as a beggar (6.4), the king of the Persians (17.2), and later as a baker (23.1), and this same verb is used.[32] A number of Jewish traditions also present Satan as transforming himself into an angel or an angel of light in order to get the better of those he tempts. For instance, Paul may have been aware of a passage in Life of Adam and Eve (9.1) in which Satan tempts Eve again after the fall: "Then Satan was angry and transformed himself into the brightness of angels and went away to the Tigris River to Eve and found her weeping" (M. D. Johnson, *OTP* 2:260; see Furnish 1984: 495). Whether Paul plays off this extrabiblical literature or coins the image

---

31. Its cognate verb θαυμάζω (*thaumazō*) means "to be extraordinarily impressed or disturbed by something" or "to wonder" or "be amazed" (BDAG 444). Our noun and the verb are brought together at Rev. 17:6: "I saw that the woman was drunk with the blood of the saints and the blood of those who testified to Jesus. I was greatly astounded when I saw her" (NET; lit., "I was astounded at [ἐθαύμασα, *ethaumasa*] a great wonder [θαῦμα, *thauma*]").

32. See, e.g., T. Job 6.4: "And while I was inside, Satan, having disguised himself as a beggar, knocked on the door" (R. P. Spittler, *OTP* 1:841–42); T. Job 23.1: "And Satan, knowing this, was transformed into a bread seller" (R. P. Spittler, *OTP* 1:848).

himself (Harris 2005: 774), the point is clear. Satan, who is associated with darkness (6:14–15), presents himself in a way out of line with his true nature, and this is the same point that Paul wants to make about the false teachers: "Therefore, it is no great surprise" that they "also"[33] masquerade. The οὐ μέγα εἰ (*ou mega ei*, not great that) parallels οὐ θαῦμα (*ou thauma*, no wonder) at the beginning of verse 14 and carries the sense of "it is not surprising that."[34] What is not surprising is that these false apostles "masquerade as ministers of righteousness" (ὡς διάκονοι δικαιοσύνης).[35] The genitive could be understood as an objective genitive, "ministers who produce righteousness." Yet the point probably is not that they pretend to live righteously but don't; instead, they themselves are not truly righteous. Thus it might be better to interpret the word as an attributive genitive, "righteous ministers" (so Barrett 1973: 287). The implication, of course, is that they are "unrighteous ministers," wicked servants of Satan.

Therefore, Paul speaks a word of judgment over them: "But their fate will be in accordance with their actions." The relative pronoun ὧν (*hōn*, of whom) refers to the οἱ διάκονοι (*hoi diakonoi*), Satan's ministers. Their τέλος (*telos*, end, fate) will accord with (κατά, *kata*)[36] τὰ ἔργα αὐτῶν (*ta erga autōn*, their works). Paul has already pointed out numerous ways the false teachers have sinned. They promote Satan's work, not God's, teaching another Jesus, promoting a false spirit, and proclaiming a false gospel (11:4). They have attacked God's true apostle and have borne false witness against him (e.g., 10:12; 11:18–20), and they have invaded his ministry territory (10:13–16). Because of their unrighteousness, they will be judged by God. Thus the implications of this judgment should be clear to the Corinthians still siding with the false teachers: to align themselves with such people constitutes more than a preference for one minister over another; it involves an entanglement in the work of Satan and a destiny of destruction.

Aspects of the cultural values reflected in 2 Corinthians—performance, ability in public speaking, fame, celebration of achievements, pay scale as an indication of status—fit so well our contemporary values in the modern, Western church. We measure ministers on the basis of their abilities in speaking and writing. We celebrate the renowned.

33. In 11:15 the use of καί is adjunctive (*kai*, also), supporting the logical relationship established by οὖν (*oun*, therefore) and pointing back to the assertion just made about Satan in 11:14.

34. This is similar to the idiom in American English when we say something is "not a big deal," meaning the circumstance is not of great importance. As for the use of εἰ in this case, the conditional serves as a marker of content (BDAG 277–78). Robertson (1934: 965) explains that "verbs of emotion in classical Greek sometimes used εἰ (conceived as an hypothesis) rather than ὅτι ([*hoti*, that] a direct reason)" in this way. Thus we translate εἰ as "that."

35. At 3:9 Paul described his own ministry as a ἡ διακονία τῆς δικαιοσύνης (*ha diakonia tēs dikaiosynēs*): "For if in the ministry characterized by condemnation there was glory, to a much greater degree *the ministry characterized by righteousness* overflows with glory."

36. Here κατά serves as a marker of homogeneity, "in accordance with," "in conformity to."

Reflection

There are at least two dynamics reflected in our passage that caused serious difficulties for Paul's ministry in Corinth, and they strike close to home in our modern church contexts. First, at least some church members in Corinth evaluated Paul's ministry (and correspondingly devalued his message) based on a particular skill set. Paul did not measure up, according to some, in the area of professional public speaking. As noted in the comments, it is likely that Paul had rhetorical training but refused to employ that training in the manipulative way of his opponents. His "failure" to match their style was considered to be a weakness by some. Thus his "weakness" pitted against the "strength" of his opponents in this particular skill set justified the rejection of the apostle's ministry as a whole and his message. Paul asserts that his "knowledge" (of God's gospel) has been the foundation of his ministry, not a particular style of public speaking. In this regard, John Chrysostom (*Hom. 2 Cor.* 23.3), a skilled preacher himself, comments, "The false apostles obviously had the gift of eloquence which Paul lacked. But that means nothing as far as the substance of the preaching is concerned and may even cast a shadow over the glory of the cross, which is anything but superficially attractive" (Bray 1999: 292).

As we think about modern church ministry, do we elevate particular skills above a minister's theological foundations or grasp of the gospel? Or even worse, do we celebrate highly "effective" speaking even when it is vapid theologically? If we are not careful, "powerful" public speaking, strong leadership skills, or some other outstanding attribute can be the be-all and end-all of a church that feels it has a particular need in a pastor or public speakers. Yet how many churches have failed to assess well the theological grounding of a ministerial candidate—to their long-term detriment? We need to think carefully about which skills we elevate and make the ability to lead the church in theological foundation-building chief among them. If there is no true gospel at the center of a ministry, all the eloquence or leadership ability in the world will lead nowhere in terms of kingdom effectiveness.

Second, Paul works on the basis of a principle that runs counter to a cultural value held dear by the Corinthians, and they read his countercultural pattern as unloving. Ambrosiaster (*Comm. Paul's Ep.*, 2 Cor. 11:7) captures Paul's pattern well: "Paul refused payment for two reasons. He would not resemble the false apostles who were preaching for their own advantage and not for the glory of God, nor would he allow the vigor of his message to become sluggish. For the person who accepts payment from sinners loses the authority to censor them" (Bray 1999: 292).

This principle, that he will not have particular patrons who support his ministry in a local church, has set him up for ridicule among the status-conscious Corinthians. Paul's principle has been offensive to those who want to support him. The manual labor he has taken up to support himself would have been seen as socially degrading. Yet Paul places biblical principle in priority over a cultural value, since that value inherently would have worked against him living out his ministry fully under the lordship of Christ and for the health of the church. This raises a question for us: are we more governed by biblical principles or by cultural or personal pressures? We must, of course, work with cultural sensitivity in our ministries. But is the gospel shaping our cultural contexts and our personal values, or are our ministries and values being shaped by the values of the culture?

Additional Notes

11:5. In place of γάρ, B reads δέ. Perhaps a scribe sensed a break from the repetition of explanatory γάρ in verses 2–4 and a move to a new topic in verse 5. It may be also that the scribe wished to craft a μέν ... δέ correlation between the beginning of verse 4 and the beginning of verse 5.

11:6. A good bit of textual turbulence exists in the latter half of this verse. Due to scribal error, 𝔓⁴⁶ omits ἀλλ' ἐν παντὶ φανερώσαντες ἐν πᾶσιν εἰς ὑμᾶς altogether. Although NA²⁷ and NA²⁸ read φανερώσαντες (an aorist active participle), based on the strength of that reading's witnesses (ℵ* B F G 33 *pc*), some scribes were apparently unsettled by the lack of an object following the active participle (so Harris 2005: 731). Thus 0121 0243 630 1739 1881 *pc* add ἑαυτούς. Others read with a passive participle φανερωθέντες (𝔓³⁴ ℵ² D² Ψ 0278 𝔐 r [vgᶜˡ]) or φανερωθείς (D*).

11:7. Given the context, the first-person singular reflexive ἐμαυτόν (𝔓³⁴ ⁴⁶ ℵ B Ψ 0121 0278 33 1739 1881 𝔐 sy) is the appropriate reading over against ἕαυτον (D F G K* L P 365 *pc*), which probably resulted from an accidental dropping of the μ.

11:14. The external evidence for reading θαῦμα (𝔓⁴⁶ ℵ B D* F G P 098 0243 0278 6 33 81 326 365 630 1175 1739 1881 2464 *pc*; Or) is greatly superior to that for the variant θαυμαστόν (D¹ Ψ 0121 𝔐). The latter was a much more common word, used forty-one times in the LXX and six times in the NT (Matt. 21:42; Mark 12:11; John 9:30; 1 Pet. 2:9; Rev. 15:1, 3); θαῦμα was used but rarely in the biblical literature (here and at Rev. 17:6 in the NT; and at Job 17:8; 18:20 in the LXX). Thus a scribe may have opted for the more familiar term.

3. Embracing Fools (11:16–21)

At this point in 2 Corinthians, Paul is about to do something that is awkward, something that embarrasses him. As we have seen, at the beginning of chapter 11 he broaches the topic of foolishness (ἀφροσύνη, *aphrosynē*), begging the Corinthians to bear with him. The successive units at 11:1–4 and 11:5–15 function as the first two steps in setting up the bit of "foolish" boasting the apostle takes up in 11:22–12:10, and 11:16–21 is the third and final preparatory step before he launches into his speech. In fact, these three units, 11:1–4; 11:5–15; and 11:16–21 form a "ring" structure, with elements of 11:16–21 echoing elements of 11:1–4 and with 11:5–15 forming the center. In both 11:1–4 and 11:16–21 there are at least five corresponding pieces:

a reference to "foolishness" at the beginning of each unit (ἀφροσύνη, 11:1; ἄφρων, 11:16)[1]

"a little" (μικρόν, 11:1, 16) at the beginning of each unit

the idea of "putting up with" at the beginning and ending of the first unit and at the end of the second (ἀνέχω, 11:1, 4, 19–20)

forms of δέχομαι at 11:4 ("espoused," or "adopted") and 11:16 ("embrace")

a conditional clause (εἰ +) at the end of each unit, reflecting a real situation in the church: false teachers are leading inappropriately (11:4, 20)

These structural dynamics suggest that 11:16–21 intentionally comes back around to and reiterates themes from 11:1–4 in order to frame the whole of Paul's introduction (11:1–21) to "The Fool's Speech" (11:22–12:10). The center unit (11:5–15), on the other hand, focuses on the contrast between Paul's humble "boast" about ministering free of charge and the superapostles' foolish boasting (11:12). As Matera (2003: 256) explains, "A consequence of this ring pattern is that Paul encloses his 'boast' of not accepting financial support from the Corinthians between two subunits that disclose his awareness of the foolishness of boasting." In addition, the ring pattern also underscores that in their foolish "wisdom" the Corinthians are "putting up with" rank abuses by the interlopers, abuses both theological and personal. So Paul's goal is to cut off the opportunity for these charlatans to make further inroads in the Corinthian church, indeed, to cut them out of influence in Corinth altogether (11:12). This very great need has pushed

---

1. Paul uses the noun form ἀφροσύνη (*aphrosynē*, foolishness) at 2 Cor. 11:1, 17, 21. The adjectival form ἄφρων (*aphrōn*, fool, foolish) is used at 2 Cor. 11:16, 19; 12:6, 11.

Paul in a "foolish" direction: he has been brought to the extreme measure of matching the interlopers' boasting, and 11:16–21 offers us a final preparatory step before we come to the speech itself.

This unit drips with sarcasm and has four basic movements: (1) Hoping to gain a hearing, Paul asks the Corinthians to embrace him as a fool (11:16). (2) He makes clear that the boasting he is about to employ is not the Lord's way of doing things (11:17–18). (3) The apostle goads the Corinthians about their idiotic "tolerance" of the abusive false teachers (11:18–20). Finally (4) he proclaims his intention to boast in spite of his weaknesses. So the passage can be outlined as follows:

a. "Please, embrace me like a fool!" (11:16)
b. Paul adopts a foolish strategy (11:17–18)
c. The Corinthians' foolish tolerance (11:19–20)
d. Paul dares to boast—in spite of his "weakness"! (11:21)

Further, 11:16–21 is marked out as a unit by an inclusio, for these verses begin and end with a combination of τις (*tis*, a certain person, 11:16, 20), εἰ (*ei*, if, 11:16, 20), κἀγώ (*kagō*, I too, 11:16, 21), λέγω (*legō*, I say, 11:16–17, 21), and ἄφρων/ἀφροσύνη (*aphrōn/aphrosynē*, foolish/foolishness, 11:16–17, 21).[2]

Finally, some have suggested that our unit under consideration be labeled an *insinuatio*, by which Paul would be trying to induce a favorable attitude on the part of the Corinthians (see Thrall 2000: 709). But 11:16–21 really presents us with a final apologia for the boasting Paul is about to do at 11:22–12:10 (Keener 2005: 231). Here he takes another overt swipe at his opponents and does everything he can to position this exercise in foolishness as distinct from the foolish boasting carried out by them.

Exegesis and Exposition

[16]I repeat: a certain person must not suppose me to be a fool! But if that person does think of me that way, you, at least, embrace me as you would a fool, so that I too might boast a bit. [17]In this boasting stratagem, the way I am speaking is not the ⌜Lord's⌝ way of doing things, but, as it were, an exercise in foolishness. [18]Since many are boasting according to ⌜human standards⌝, I too will boast. [19]For you cheerfully put up with fools—you wise people, you! [20]Indeed, you put up with it if a certain person enslaves you, if a certain person eats up your resources, if a certain person

2. Commentaries commonly end the unit at 11:21a and view 11:21b (Ἐν ᾧ δ' ἄν τις τολμᾷ, ἐν ἀφροσύνῃ λέγω, τολμῶ κἀγώ, *En hō d' an tis tolma, en aphrosynē legō, tolmō kagō*, Nevertheless, whatever a certain person dares to boast about—I am talking like a fool!—I too dare to boast about that!) as the introduction to the Fool's Speech that follows. While it is possible that the parallels we have noted form "parallel introductions," Paul seems more given to using inclusio as a means of marking out units. Therefore, it seems best to allow all of 11:21 to wrap up the introduction to the Fool's Speech and to present the speech itself as beginning with verse 22.

kidnaps you, if a certain person puts on airs around you, if a certain person slaps you in the face! [21]I am ashamed to admit that ⌜we have been weak by comparison⌝! Nevertheless, whatever a certain person dares to boast about—I am talking like a fool!—I too dare to boast about that!

a. "Please, Embrace Me Like a Fool!" (11:16)

11:16   With the words Πάλιν λέγω (*Palin legō*, I repeat), Paul picks up a thread about "foolishness" from 11:1. The apostle begins by denying that he is a fool, even while assuming the role of a "fool." The words μή τίς με δόξῃ ἄφρονα εἶναι (*mē tis me doxē aphrona einai*) are normally translated along the lines of "Let no one think me foolish" (ESV) or "a fool" (the adjective is read as a substantive: NASB, NRSV, NIV, NET), the third-person singular aorist subjunctive δόξῃ being read as communicating an intense desire that none of those hearing the letter read should think him foolish.[3] Whereas μή plus a second-person aorist subjunctive normally would be read as a prohibitive subjunctive, that is, as an imperative (so NLT[2]), Harris (2005: 779) suggests that with the third-person subject (τις, *tis*, someone, a certain person), "the tone is less peremptory," perhaps due to the indefinite referent of the pronoun.

Yet we notice that the language here is actually quite strong and peremptory. At times Paul has used the indefinite pronoun to refer in a vague (thus derogatory) way to his opponents at Corinth (2 Cor. 2:5, 10; 3:1; 8:20; 10:2, 7, 12; cf. 1 Cor. 16:11; 2 Thess. 2:3), and this is clearly the case in the immediate context at 11:20–21;[4] thus here we may have another instance of the apostle alluding to an opponent in a way that is insulting, and Paul demands that such a person should not be allowed to characterize him as a fool. Further, the construction (μή plus the aorist subjunctive) should be read as prohibitive in a stronger sense than a mere wish. That sense, then, might be rendered, "A certain person must not suppose me to be a fool!" Furthermore, it is obvious from this opening salvo and Paul's repeated interjections in what follows (11:21, 23)[5] that the apostle is intensely embarrassed by the "foolishness" he is about to undertake, and he doesn't want the *appearance* of foolishness to be mistaken as indicative of his true character.

Paul continues, "But if that person does think of me that way . . ." The conjunction δέ (*de*, but) is mildly contrastive, and εἰ . . . μή γε (*ei . . . mē ge*; the particle γε intensifies the negative) has the sense, "if this is not to be," that

---

3. See D. Wallace 1996: 464, 469 on the nuances of the hortatory subjunctive over against the prohibitive subjunctive, which often uses μή (*mē*, not), as here.

4. So Barnett 1997: 529. To make this more explicit, 2 Cor. 11:20–21 could be rendered: "Indeed, you put up with it if *a certain person* enslaves you, if *a certain person* eats up your resources, if *someone* kidnaps you, if *someone* acts presumptuously toward you, if *someone* slaps you in the face! I am ashamed to admit that we have been weak by comparison! Nevertheless, whatever *any* of them dares to boast about—I am talking like a fool!—I too dare to boast about that!" It is also possible to read the construction using the indefinite pronoun in this way at 1 Cor. 16:11 and 2 Thess. 2:3.

5. "I am talking like a fool!" (11:21); "I must be out of my mind to talk like this!" (11:23).

is, if Paul doesn't have his way and that "certain person,"[6] the real fool himself, insists on supposing the apostle to be a fool. So the contrast stands between Paul's demand and the distinct possibility that his demand will go unheeded.

In that case, if the true fool has his way in portraying Paul as a fool, the apostle exhorts the Corinthians, "You, at least, embrace me as you would a fool, so that I too might boast a bit." In other words, he insists that if his opponents are allowed to hold him up as a fool, the Corinthians should "at least" (κἄν, *kan*; a word formed by crasis from καί and ἐάν) do him the courtesy of embracing him as a fool, for that would give him a platform to communicate with them. After all, they have a pattern of listening to fools! The κἀγώ (*kagō*) means "I also," or "I too," alluding to the fact that the opponents in Corinth are already boasting like fools (10:12–18).

The apostle does not plan on boasting a lot, but just enough to make his point. Paul says that he wants the Corinthians to embrace him so he might boast "a bit" (μικρόν τι, *mikron ti*; another repetition harking back to 11:1). Thus he assumes the role of a fool to accomplish two very specific objectives. First, he wants to have a platform from which he can address those Corinthians still balking at his apostolic authority in hope that they will repent and again embrace his mission.[7] Second, by acting "the fool," he lampoons the opponents' foolish boasting, taking up their method of boasting but using it to showcase weaknesses rather than strengths (see below on 11:22–33).

b. Paul Adopts a Foolish Strategy (11:17–18)

Yet Paul wants to make it blatantly clear that the boasting he is about to undertake is not a pattern of ministry appropriate for an authentic minister of Christ: "In this boasting stratagem, the way I am speaking is not the Lord's way of doing things, but, as it were, an exercise in foolishness." The structure of the passage is as follows:

11:17

> οὐ κατὰ κύριον (*ou kata kyrion*)
> λαλῶ > ὃ λαλῶ (*lalō > ho lalō*)
>   ἀλλ' (*all'*)
>   ὡς ἐν ἀφροσύνῃ (*hōs en aphrosynē*)
>   ἐν ταύτῃ τῇ ὑποστάσει τῆς καυχήσεως (*en tautē tē hypostasei tēs kauchēseōs*)

At the heart of the sentence stands the main verb λαλῶ (I speak), which has the relative clause ὃ λαλῶ (what I speak) as its direct object[8]: thus literally, "I

---

6. Contra Barnett (1997: 529), who suggests that the clause refers to the Corinthians and should be translated, "Otherwise, if you must." But the contingency refers back to the first part of the verse and the "certain person" to whom Paul has just referred.

7. The rhetorical exercise of assuming a particular character and arguing from that vantage point was referred to as prosopopoeia (Keener 2005: 231).

8. The relative pronoun ὅ is neuter singular acc.

speak what I speak." So Paul in some way refers to his own communication; but in mentioning his manner of speaking, the apostle does not mean his pattern of communication in general, for at the end of the sentence he delimits the main verb λαλῶ (I speak) with the phrase ἐν ταύτῃ τῇ ὑποστάσει τῆς καυχήσεως, a phrase we have translated as "In this boasting stratagem,"[9] referring to the "Fool's Speech" that will follow in 11:22–12:10. A key interpretive question concerns τῇ ὑποστάσει. Some translations still render the noun as "confidence" (e.g., ESV, NASB, NRSV, NET, KJV; and, e.g., Barrett 1973: 288) or "self-confident" (NIV; e.g., Barnett 1997: 530), referring to a self-assured posture of boasting, though there is no evidence for this meaning of the word in the first century.[10] Yet the word ὑπόστασις (hypostasis) has a broad and interesting semantic range, referring variously to something's nature, essence, or reality; or it could refer to a plan of action, a project, an undertaking, endeavor, a situation, a condition, or even a title deed (BDAG 1040–41; Spicq 1994: 3.421–23). We suggest that in our current context, Paul uses the term to speak of his "undertaking" or, as we have rendered it, his "stratagem"[11] of boasting (τῆς καυχήσεως, an attributive genitive). Thus the phrase ἐν ταύτῃ τῇ ὑποστάσει (in this stratagem) would as its referent have the "boasting stratagem" that Paul is about to embark upon in 11:22–2:10.

What remains of the sentence consists of a balanced contrast (ἀλλ')[12] between two ways of speaking. First, Paul says that in the boasting he is about to undertake, he is *not* speaking "according to the Lord" (κατὰ κύριον), meaning, "according to the manner approved of by the Lord" (so Thrall 2000: 713), that is, "the Lord's way of doing things."[13] In other words, such self-focused boasting is not "boasting in the Lord" (10:17; Jer. 9:23–24). So Paul considers this pattern of foolish boasting to be unbiblical, outside the normal patterns of communication and conduct appropriate for an authentic minister who is submitted to Christ as Lord. It is incongruous for a minister who does ministry "before God" (2:17) and boasts "in the Lord" (10:17) to put himself forward by bragging about his own work! As 11:18 makes clear, the opposite of speaking "according to the Lord" seems to be to speak or minister "according to the flesh" (κατὰ σάρκα; cf. 1:17; 5:16; 10:2–3; 11:18), a reference to

9. Note that in 11:17 the ἐν ταύτῃ τῇ ὑποστάσει τῆς καυχήσεως is not parallel structurally with ἐν ἀφροσύνῃ, as if it were a continuation of the ὡς clause. Rather, the second prepositional phrase stands in direct grammatical relationship with the main verb.

10. BDAG 1040–41 has now dropped this definition. See Thrall 2000: 568–70. Paul's normal word for "confidence" in 2 Corinthians is πεποίθησις (pepoithēsis; 1:15; 3:4; 8:22; 10:2).

11. Similarly, Matera (2003: 254) translates ὑπόστασις as "project," Harris (2005: 781) suggests "undertaking," and Thrall (2000: 714) prefers "plan," "project," or "intention." The ET "stratagem," however, carries the nuance of "tactic," appropriate to a context in which a battle is being fought and a specific objective is the goal.

12. Notice the structural balance in 11:17 between οὐ κατὰ κύριον, which precedes λαλῶ, and ἀλλ' ὡς ἐν ἀφροσύνῃ, which follows the verb.

13. Other possible renderings are "with the Lord's authority" (RSV, NRSV), "according to the Lord's ways" (Tyndale), as received "from the Lord" (NLT², Message), "the way the Lord would" (HCSB, NET, NIV).

doing ministry according to merely human standards, rather than according to Christ's direction and enablement.

Rather than speaking as the Lord would have him communicate, the apostle's mode of communication laid out in 11:22–12:10 is ὡς ἐν ἀφροσύνῃ (as it were, an exercise in foolishness). Here ὡς functions as a "marker introducing the perspective from which a person, thing, or activity is viewed or understood as to character" (BDAG 1104), for the nature of this activity of inappropriate boasting is in view. Furthermore, the preposition ἐν can be read as a marker of the circumstance or condition under which something takes place (i.e., "in foolishness"), or a marker of means or the instrument by which something takes place (i.e., "with" or "by foolishness"; BDAG 326–30). In this case the former might be preferable, since Paul is focused on a unique circumstance, one that involves foolishness. The opponents have pushed him to participate in an activity he would prefer to avoid. Regardless, he wants to make perfectly clear that he considers his opponents' choice of rhetorical tactics as sheer idiocy and his own "boasting" as appropriate only in a circumstance where foolishness seems to win the day.

Yet, to beat them, he must join them. In verse 18 he explains why he takes up this idiotic activity: "Since many are boasting according to human standards, I too will boast." The lead clause in the sentence is causal, introduced by the conjunction ἐπεί (epei, since, because, for). Paul says that there are "many" (πολλοί, polloi)[14] who are boasting κατὰ σάρκα (kata sarka; lit., according to the flesh),[15] boasting "according to human standards," in contrast to speaking κατὰ κύριον (kata kyrion; 11:17), as the Lord would have a minister speak. This, in tandem with the Corinthians' willingness to listen to such fools (11:19), has driven the apostle to action. He states tersely, κἀγὼ καυχήσομαι (kagō kauchēsomai, I too will boast). The clause approximates a part of verse 16, where Paul asks the Corinthians to embrace him as a fool, in order that κἀγὼ μικρόν τι καυχήσωμαι (kagō mikron ti kauchēsōmai, I too might boast a bit). Here the conjunction κἀγώ (I too) is repeated, but the form of καυχάομαι (kauchaomai) has changed from an aorist subjunctive in verse 16 to a future indicative here; Paul is alerting the Corinthians to the boasting he is about to take up in 11:22–12:10. So he will boast but he clearly distinguishes himself from the intruders at Corinth by openly declaring that such boasting is mere foolishness.

It seems that the worldly boasting of Paul's opponents (and the Corinthians' willingness to listen to them) has forced the apostle to think creatively about how he might regain the ear of those in Corinth still skeptical about his ministry (12:11). To some extent, the opponents, who must have been a dominant

11:18

14. Furnish (1984: 511) suggests that πολλοί is used in a derogatory manner: the vague reference is a way of "diminishing their stature in the eyes of the Corinthians."

15. Paul uses the phrase κατὰ σάρκα six times in the book (1:17; 5:16 [2x]; 10:2–3; 11:18), and every case can be interpreted as referring to a "worldly" activity, or something done according to "human standards," as opposed to a godly approach to life or ministry.

voice in the conversation about Paul's ministry, were using their rhetorical skills to elevate their own stock and diminish Paul's. Thus Paul decides to fight fire with fire—but as we will see, he turns the tables on his opponents in the process, for his boasting is not "according to human standards" after all.

c. The Corinthians' Foolish Tolerance (11:19–20)

11:19   Of course the worldly boasting of the opponents would have fallen flat if the Corinthians had denied them an audience. Thus verse 19 points to the other reason Paul is forced to take up "foolish boasting": it seems that the Corinthians, in their "wisdom," like listening to fools! As Harris (2005: 777) notes, "In a sense, his converts rather than his rivals had dictated his *modus operandi*." Paul wants them to listen to him and is willing the play the role of a fool if that is what it takes to gain their ear: "For you cheerfully put up with fools—you wise people, you!" The γάρ (*gar*, for) marks the sentence as explanatory. At 11:1, 4 Paul has already used the verb ἀνέχω (*anechō*) to observe that the Corinthians "put up with" those preaching a different Jesus, offering a different spirit, and proclaiming a different gospel, and he uses the same verb here. They "put up with" or "tolerate" those acting foolishly (τῶν ἀφρόνων, *tōn aphronōn*; here again the adjective is used as a substantive), and moreover they do so "cheerfully" (ἡδέως, *hēdeōs*), a word placed at the beginning of the sentence for emphasis. The term here may speak of some in Corinth "being pleased with" or "enjoying" the public speaking on offer by Paul's opponents (cf. Mark 6:20; 12:37). The apostle sarcastically points to such "tolerance" as a mark of the Corinthians' wisdom, and such mock praise was common in Greco-Roman rhetoric.[16] The present participle ὄντες (*ontes*), together with the predicate adjective φρόνιμοι (*phronimoi*, wise), delimits the main verb, indicating the condition that facilitated their tolerance. Their form of foolish "wisdom" has enabled the opponents' platform of foolishness. Paul's words here might cause us to reflect on the "wise" forms of tolerance today that give an inappropriate platform to "foolishness" in the church. What do we "put up with," not out of biblical motives but because of cultural accommodation?

11:20   At the beginning of verse 20, Paul repeats both the verb ἀνέχεσθε (*anechesthe*, you put up with; 11:19) from the previous verse and the postpositive conjunction γάρ (*gar*, indeed),[17] expounding on the inappropriate "tolerance" the Corinthians have toward the interlopers. Delivered in a repetitive form[18] and with a driving rhythm, the apostle uses five conditional clauses that detail ways the false teachers have abused the church at Corinth; his main point is that the

16. See Keener 2005: 231. Cf. 1 Cor. 4:10, where Paul also contrasts his own foolishness and the Corinthians' wisdom.

17. Twice in a series of clauses, γάρ occurs either to introduce several arguments for the same assertion or, as here, to have one clause confirm or expound on the other (Jdt. 5:23; 7:27; 1 Macc. 11:10; Matt. 10:19–20; Luke 8:29; John 5:21–22, 46; Acts 2:15; Rom. 6:14; 8:2–3; BDAG 189).

18. In 11:20, the repetition at the beginning of each clause is called anaphora.

Corinthians have tolerated such abuse, and the posture depicted here is the opposite of Paul's christocentric posture of leniency (see 10:1).

ἀνέχεσθε γὰρ (*anechesthe gar*)
 εἴ τις ὑμᾶς καταδουλοῖ (*ei tis hymas katadouloi*),
 εἴ τις κατεσθίει (*ei tis katesthiei*),
 εἴ τις λαμβάνει (*ei tis lambanei*),
 εἴ τις ἐπαίρεται (*ei tis epairetai*),
 εἴ τις εἰς πρόσωπον ὑμᾶς δέρει (*ei tis eis prosōpon hymas derei*).

Indeed, you put up with it
 if a certain person enslaves you,
 if a certain person eats you up,
 if a certain person kidnaps you,
 if a certain person puts on airs around you,
 if a certain person slaps you in the face!

Each clause consists of εἴ τις (*ei tis*, if a certain person) followed by a present-tense verb in the indicative mood. When the subordinate conjunction εἴ is used with the indicative in this way, the construction marks a real condition, so Paul writes about a real, rather than a hypothetical, situation going on in the church. Furthermore, as noted in the comments on 11:16, Paul uses the indefinite pronoun τις as a derogatory allusion to his opponents (or perhaps a chief rival) at Corinth (e.g., 2 Cor. 2:5, 10; 3:1; 8:20; 10:2, 7, 12), not affording them the dignity of being mentioned by name (thus our translation, "a certain person"). Finally, notice that the first and last of these subordinate clauses include the same direct object, the pronoun ὑμᾶς (*hymas*, you), framing the whole description of the abuse and making clear that the Corinthians themselves are the ones being misused. This will be important to keep in mind as we sort out the possible meanings of the specific abuses listed.

The descriptors that Paul uses to speak of the false teachers' abusive "ministry" are striking and, according to Welborn (2009), taken from a common "stock" character in Greco-Roman comedy and satire: the pompous, loathsome parasite who arrogantly abuses his hosts and other guests alike.[19] Such an association would have been unmistakable to the Corinthians, and this powerful rhetorical device not only further discredits Paul's opponents; it also presents a strong rebuke to those embracing such unsavory characters.

19. Welborn (2009) draws a composite portrait of this stock character from the comedies of Alexis, Antiphanes, Plautus, and Terence, as well as from Lucian's satirical work *The Parasite*, where he satirically argues that parasitism is the highest art form. Such works also use terms such as καταδουλόω (*katadouloō*, take advantage of), κατεσθίω (*katesthiō*, eat up), and λαμβάνω (*lambanō*, take) to describe the artful social parasite.

In the first of these clauses, the term καταδουλόω (*katadouloō*; Gal. 2:4) means "to enslave" someone, or to reduce a person to the status of slave. In the ancient world, slavery and the threat of being enslaved were part of the social and cultural fabric of the age. For instance, a person might be enslaved if they were taken captive in war, or if they could not pay their debts. The word occurs ten times in the LXX to speak of people being forced into, or burdened under, slavery in one form or another (Gen. 47:21; Exod. 1:14; 6:5; Ezra 7:24; 1 Macc. 8:10, 18; 3 Macc. 2:6; Jer. 15:14; Ezek. 29:18; 34:27). At Gal. 2:4, the only other use of this verb in the NT, Paul employs the term figuratively in a fashion similar to our current context. There he speaks of the false brothers who slipped covertly into the Galatian community in order to spy on the freedom that Paul and company experience in Christ; Paul says they did so "to make us slaves" (NET). Thus the imagery connotes a loss of one's freedom and, perhaps in our current context, complete subservience to another. By contrast, instead of enslaving the Corinthians (cf. 2 Cor. 1:24), Paul has made himself their slave (4:5).

The second description of the false teachers' abuse states that the Corinthians put up with it "if a certain person [lit.] eats you up." The compound verb κατεσθίω (*katesthiō*) could speak literally of ravenous eating (e.g., Matt. 13:4; Mark 4:4; Rev. 10:9–10), but by extension the rich image could be used to speak of a person being consumed by zeal (T. Sim. 4.9; John 2:17; cf. Ps. 69:10 [68:9 ET]), of something being destroyed, for instance, by fire (Rev. 11:5; 20:9), of resources being wasted, as with the prodigal son (Luke 15:30), of one person robbing or exploiting another (Mark 12:40; Luke 20:47), or of one person tearing another person to pieces through conflict (Gal. 5:15). Of course, for one person to "eat up" another communicates some form of violence, but the terseness of the use here in 2 Cor. 11:20 makes it difficult to choose among these options. Nevertheless, given that financial remuneration, or other compensation, stands near the heart of Paul's differences with his opponents (11:5–15), the idea of exploitation of "resources" probably is not far from the mark. The opponents gobble up the community's resources as they stand by in idle approval. By contrast, Paul refuses to even be compensated for his ministry among them.

Third, Paul says his opponents have "kidnapped" the Corinthians (lit., if a certain person takes [you]). The common word λαμβάνω (*lambanō*) has a broad semantic range. Basically, it can mean to grab hold of someone or something, but also can connote "to take something away" or "to acquire something" (BDAG 583). In the current context, and underlining the previously mentioned abuses, Paul can mean that the interlopers are grabby, that they snatch whatever goods they can; so some translations read, "takes advantage of you"[20]

---

20. BDAG 584 uses our passage to suggest "takes advantage of you" as a possible meaning for λαμβάνω, but the only other passage offered in support ("in a related vein") is 2 Cor. 12:16, where δόλῳ ὑμᾶς ἔλαβον may be read as "catch someone by a trick" (ibid.). Thus this most popular rendering among modern English versions actually has little to commend it.

(ESV, NASB, NLT², NRSV, NIV, NET). Similarly, *The Message* reads, "steals you blind." But as noted above, the pronoun ὑμᾶς (you) probably should be understood here; thus the Corinthians themselves are the object of the verb. Accordingly, Paul might be talking about the Corinthians themselves being "taken" or "kidnapped" (HCSB: "captures you").

Fourth, the word ἐπαίρω (*epairō*) could be used to speak of lifting something up, such as a staff (Exod. 10:13 LXX), hands in prayer or blessing (Neh. 8:6 [2 Esd. 18:6]; Ps. 133:2 [134:2 ET]; Luke 24:50; 1 Tim. 2:8), or one's eyes (Gen. 13:10; 1 Chron. 21:16). By extension it can refer to a person who "lifted" himself up, who was presumptuous or put on airs (Aristophanes, *Nub.* 810; Sir. 11:4; 32:1; 1 Macc. 2:63). For instance, Sir. 11:4 warns, "Do not exalt yourself in the day of glory" (ἐν ἡμέρα δόξης μὴ ἐπαίρου, *en hēmera doxēs mē epairou*); and 1 Macc. 2:62–63 reads, "And do not fear on account of the words of a sinner, because their glory will become dung and worms. Today they will be elevated [ἐπαρθήσεται, *eparthēsetai*], but tomorrow they will not be found" (NETS). At 2 Cor. 10:5 the apostle, using warfare imagery, speaks of tearing down "every rampart raised up [ἐπαιρόμενον, *epairomenon*] in opposition to knowledge about God." In this list of abuses, the word probably refers to the opponents putting on airs (so ESV, NRSV, NIV), exalting themselves (the word is reflexive; so NASB, Tyndale, KJV) acting arrogantly (presumptuously) toward the Corinthians (NET). By contrast, Paul has ministered to the Corinthians "by the leniency and clemency of Christ" (10:1).

Finally, Paul states that the false teachers have been slapping the Corinthians "in the face" (εἰς πρόσωπον ὑμᾶς δέρει); he would be hard pressed to find a more offensive image, or one that communicates the concept of abuse more forcefully. Elsewhere in the NT, the term speaks of "beating up" another person (Matt. 21:35; Mark 12:3, 5; Luke 20:10–11; 22:63), or of someone being flogged or beaten as a punishment (Mark 13:9; Luke 12:47–48; Acts 5:40; 16:37). At 1 Cor. 9:26 Paul uses the term to say that he is not like a boxer "beating the air" (ὡς οὐκ ἀέρα δέρων, *hōs ouk aera derōn*). So, speaking either literally or figuratively, Paul says the false teachers at Corinth have slapped or punched the Corinthians in the face! Among Jews (11:22), to slap a person's face—especially the right cheek with the back of the hand—was to humiliate them (cf. Job 16:10; Lam. 3:30). As Harris (2005: 786) points out, Paul perhaps speaks figuratively here of outrageous verbal abuse, but we cannot assume that, for religious leaders of the day at times punished offenders by slapping them (John 18:22; Acts 23:2) or bullying them physically in some other way. So Paul's opponents at Corinth may even have resorted to physical forms of abuse. By contrast, Paul has ministered to the Corinthians with patience, benevolence, and love (6:6).

At 7:2 Paul writes, "We haven't mistreated anyone; we haven't corrupted anyone; we haven't taken advantage of anyone." Clearly Paul's opponents in Corinth cannot say the same. We know from literature of the era that the Sophists at times were accused of outlandish behavior fit for lesser-skilled rhetors, behavior that included abuse of their audience and each other (Winter 2002:

243–45; Witherington 1995: 449–50; Dio Chrysostom, *Or.* 8.9; Philo, *Worse* 32–34). Thus, acting contrary to all sound pastoral care, the false teachers have taken the Corinthians' freedom, eaten up their resources, snatched them away from their true apostle, presumptuously imposed themselves on the community, and humiliated them in the most egregious terms. The parasites have treated the Corinthians dishonorably and abused them terribly. But the Corinthians have embraced them and taken the abuse admirably! Paul clearly depicts both his rivals' actions and the Corinthians' tolerance of the abuse as blatantly shameful.

d. Paul Dares to Boast—in Spite of His "Weakness"! (11:21)

11:21 In 11:21, maintaining his sarcastic tone, the apostle says he is the one who is "ashamed": "I am ashamed to admit that we have been weak by comparison!" (κατὰ ἀτιμίαν λέγω, ὡς ὅτι ἡμεῖς ἠσθενήκαμεν, *kata atimian legō, hōs hoti hēmeis ēsthenēkamen*). Here we have a mock "confession" by Paul, with both ὡς (used redundantly) and ὅτι introducing the content of his confession (i.e., "that we live in a state of weakness").[21] This confession of "weakness" plays a significant role as the apostle transitions to "the Fool's Speech," for though he begins as might be expected with his heritage (11:22), his countercultural "boasting" quickly turns to focus especially on an extensive set of validating "weaknesses" experienced in the course of his ministry (11:30). Paul shows the bullying "strength" of the interlopers to be destructive abuse, and he places their "ministry" in stark contrast to his, a ministry in which he has suffered for Christ. Thus he has turned the cultural values of "strength" (which would accord with honor) and "weakness" (which would accord with shame) on their heads by trumpeting "weakness" as the defining characteristic of his ministry. When he says he is "ashamed" (κατὰ ἀτιμίαν), therefore, he means nothing of the sort. Rather, Paul has carried out his mission and ministry of gentle leadership in ways that are authentic, even if those ways are out of step with cultural norms.

Earlier in 2 Corinthians, Paul lambastes his opponents for evaluating ministries on the basis of comparison, stating that he would have no part of it: "For we wouldn't dare to classify or compare ourselves with any of those who are commending themselves. Here's the difference: when they measure themselves, using themselves as the standard, and compare themselves with one another, they are clueless" (10:12). He further criticizes the false missionaries for "boasting" about ministry not assigned to them by the Lord, implying that such boasting was not "boasting in the Lord" (10:13, 15, 17). Yet here, on his

---

21. The perfect tense has stative aspect, focusing on the state of the action communicated by the verb. In this case, Paul's emphasis is not on the pattern of weakness in the past but rather that his whole ministry is permeated with weakness and thus characterized by it. This "confession" of weakness sets the tone for the speech, since Paul repeatedly says that he is boasting about his weaknesses. In his writings, Paul uses ὡς ὅτι (*hōs hoti*) three times to introduce content (2 Cor. 5:19; 11:21; 2 Thess. 2:2). See similar use, introduced by λέγω (*legō*, say), in Philo, *Dreams* 2.115.

own terms, Paul "boasts" about his "weak" ministry and makes comparisons between himself and the rivals. The apostle turns their inappropriate modes of operation inside out, forcing the Corinthians to compare the sham ministry of the opponents with his authentic ministry of suffering with Christ.

Paul continues by writing, "Nevertheless, whatever a certain person dares to boast about—I am talking like a fool!—I too dare to boast about that!" The δέ (*de*) tying 21b to the first half of the verse presents a mild contrast ("Nevertheless") with the weakness mentioned there. In other words, Paul may be weak when compared to his opponents, but he will go toe-to-toe with them. The relative clause Ἐν ᾧ δ' ἄν τις τολμᾷ (*En hō d' an tis tolma*), continues the pattern of referring to the interlopers vaguely (τις, *tis*, a certain person).[22] The Ἐν ᾧ means "in that which," but the particle ἄν plus the present subjunctive form of the verb that follows adds a note of contingency or indefiniteness, like one would expect in a conditional sentence (BDAG 56). The "in that which" points to the content of the opponents' boast, and Paul probably has in mind the claims that follow, namely, the claim to being Hebrews, Israelites, descendants of Abraham, and Christian ministers. In "whatever" the opponents "dare" (τολμᾷ) to boast about, Paul will match them, but he will focus especially on the final claim.

The apostle has used the verb τολμάω (*tolmaō*) twice earlier in the letter, at 10:2 and 10:12. At 10:2 he speaks of the boldness he might "dare" to use against those opposing him, and at 10:12 he writes that he would not "dare" to join in the false teachers' game of classification and comparison. Yet now he does "dare," stating, "I too dare to boast about that!" (τολμῶ κἀγώ, *tolmō kagō*). The apostle does not mention "boasting" overtly in 11:21b, but it is implied clearly by the context (see 11:18), which is why most English versions render the thought "dare to boast" (e.g., ESV, HCSB, NLT², NRSV, NIV, NET). In between the relative clause that begins 2 Cor. 11:21b and the "daring" proclamation that ends it, Paul inserts the parenthetical statement, "I am talking like a fool!" (ἐν[23] ἀφροσύνῃ λέγω, *en aphrosynē legō*), clearly uncomfortable with the "fool's" approach he has now embarked upon. That he is speaking "in foolishness" refers to the vapid idiocy of a minister boasting about himself and his work.

Reflection

At first glance, the passage before us seems to depict the extremity to which the apostle has been pushed in dealing with the foolishness being embraced in Corinth. Now he seems willing to fight fire with fire, to be buying into the opponents' methods of engagement, their unprincipled "boasting" according to human standards. The passage drips with sarcasm, and we

---

22. Contra Barrett (1973: 292), who suggests that τις be translated "anyone else" as a reference to the Jerusalem leaders who supposedly placed their stamp of approval on the misguided missionaries in Corinth.

23. The preposition probably marks a state or condition (BDAG 327).

need to hear that sarcasm to begin to pick up on Paul's real intent here, for sarcasm turns the surface words in a statement on their head. In fact, the apostle really subverts the methods of the interlopers by overtly labeling this "boastful" move as idiocy and not how the Lord would do things, and by pointing out the abuse the Corinthians are experiencing as they embrace their foolish false leaders. So, through sarcasm Paul tips off all who read the book that he takes up this foolish boasting reluctantly but in a way that is intended to subvert the foolish boasting of his opponents. He turns their ministry inside out to show that it is diametrically opposed to authentic Christian ministry, which does things the Lord's way and for the good of those on the receiving end of the ministry.

Michael Card wrote a song called "God's Own Fool," which he says has gotten him in a lot of trouble through the years. It is scandalous to label God and his ways as "foolish." Yet, playing off Paul's words in 1 Cor. 1:20–25, Card writes,

> When we in our foolishness thought we were wise,
> He played the fool and He opened our eyes.
> When we in our weakness believed we were strong,
> He became helpless to show we were wrong.
> And so, we follow God's own fool, for only the foolish can tell.
> Believe the unbelievable and come be a fool as well.[24]

©1985 Mole End Music

From an eternal perspective, the power structures and power plays of this world are inherently weak and destructive. Yet from an eternal perspective, the weakness of the gospel message and Christian ministry are inherently strong. Paul will go to any length to keep the Corinthians tethered to the "foolish," "weak" message of the gospel. He even reverts to sarcasm, draping himself momentarily with the "foolishness" of his opponents, but he does so to undo that foolishness completely.

Additional Notes

11:17. The evidence in favor of the strong reading κύριον ($\mathfrak{P}^{46}$ ℵ B D F G Ψ 075 098 0121 Basil Chrysostom et al.) shows clearly that the alternate readings of θεόν (*l* 170 Origen[lat2/3] Ambrosiaster Pelagius Augustine) and ἄνθρωπον (69) are due to scribal error.

11:18. Paul's common phrase κατὰ σάρκα finds expression twenty times in the apostle's writings (Rom. 1:3; 4:1; 8:4–5, 12–13; 9:3, 5; 1 Cor. 1:26; 10:18; 2 Cor. 1:17; 5:16 [2x]; 10:2–3; 11:18; Gal. 4:23, 29; Eph. 6:5; Col. 3:22), six of these in 2 Corinthians. At 11:18 some witnesses include the article (τήν) before σάρκα (ℵ² B D¹ Ψ 0121 1739ᶜ 1881ᶜ 𝔐), and since Paul elsewhere includes the article only for the similar phrase at Gal. 5:17 (but with the genitive form, κατὰ τῆς σαρκός, with the meaning,

---

24. Michael Card, "God's Own Fool," from the album *Scandalon* (Brentwood, TN: Sparrow Records, 1985).

"against the flesh"), the reading has the standard of "most difficult" in its favor. Yet, since Paul never departs from the common form of the phrase, including the other five occurrences in 2 Corinthians, most scholars prefer the reading without the article ($\mathfrak{P}^{46}$ $\aleph$* D* F G H 098 0278 33 81 104 365 629 1175 1505 1739* 1881* *al*).

11:21. On the basis of external evidence, the perfect form ἠσθενήκαμεν ($\mathfrak{P}^{46}$ $\aleph$ B H 0243 0278 33 81 1175 1739* 1881 *pc*) is preferred to the aorist ἠσθενήσαμεν (D F G l^vid Ψ 0121 1739^c 𝔐) (so Metzger 1994: 515). Not catching Paul's sarcasm, some scribes may have been uncomfortable with Paul's admission of ongoing weakness in comparison to his opponents. A similar clarification may be behind D's inclusion of the phrase ἐν τούτῳ τῷ μέρει (in this matter), from a scribe wishing to clarify that Paul's weakness was only in relation to the abuse offered by the false teachers (so Harris 2005: 778).

4. Paul's Countercultural "Fool's Speech," Part 1 (11:22–29)

We finally come to Paul's "boasting"[1] (11:22–12:10), which many now refer to as "The Fool's Speech" (Zmijewski 1978). Barnett (1997: 529) calls the boast "a daring countercultural exercise," for Paul almost certainly boasts in a way that runs counter to the emphases in his opponents' rhetoric. Specifically, boasting about one's trials,[2] for which there was precedent in broader Greco-Roman oratory,[3] did not fit the Sophists' triumphal rhetoric of successful "power" leadership (10:10; 11:6), nor the cultural expectations of those of high social status in Corinth.[4] Thus there was a gaping divide between Paul's vision of the Christian minister as a "suffering servant" and the interlopers' view of ministry as triumphal, strong-armed leadership; this gap finds clear expression in Paul's foolish speech.[5] Here we have "a ruthless parody of the pretensions of his opponents" (Forbes 1986: 18).

1. The form of Paul's speech follows a general pattern of recounting praiseworthy "accomplishments," although Paul turns this approach on its head, boasting about hardships. An example of boasting on behalf of another in the Greco-Roman context is found, e.g., in the Duilius Inscription to the consul Gaius Duilius, in honor of his naval victory over the Carthaginians at Mylae in 260 BC:

> The Segestaeans . . . he [Duilius] delivered from blockade; and all the Carthaginian hosts and their most mighty chief after nine days fled in broad daylight from their camp; and he took their town Macela by storm. And in the same command he as a consul performed an exploit in ships at sea, the first [*primos*] Roman to do so; the first [*primos*] he was to equip and train crews and fleets of fighting ships; and with these ships he defeated in battle all the most mighty troops of the Carthaginians in the presence of Hannibal their commander-in-chief. And by main force he captured ships with their crews, to wit: one septireme, 30 quinqueremes and triremes; 13 he sank. Gold taken: 3,600 (and more) pieces. Silver taken, together with that derived from booty: 100,000 . . . pieces. Total sum taken, reduced to Roman money: . . . 2,100,000. . . . He also was the first [*primos*] to bestow on people a gift of booty from a sea-battle, [and the first (*primosque*)] to lead native free-born Carthaginians in triumph. (Warmington 1935: 129)

2. On the hardship list, see Andrews 1995; Barré 1975: 519–26; Hodgson 1983; Lambrecht 1997.

3. In the literature of the period, philosophers might underscore what they had suffered to uphold their teachings; e.g., Stoics could point to their endurance in suffering as a mark of their moral character. Further, statesmen might celebrate their trials for the good of the state; heroes faced dangers to win honor. See the discussion in Garland 1999: 491–92; Keener 2005: 233.

4. This interpretation runs counter to, e.g., Fitzgerald 1988: 44–51; for the Sophists' form of boasting in light of the Corinthian correspondence, see Winter 2002: 187–95.

5. As noted below, some scholars suggest that the opponents at Corinth also boasted about their sufferings in ministry, for nowhere here does the apostle deny that they have worked, or have been imprisoned, or that they have been beaten or faced death, etc. However, 11:30 should be seen as a key to understanding Paul's approach, for there he states, "If I have to boast, I will

The apostle's approach, moreover, is to draw his audience in by beginning his boast with something that might be expected—boasting about the fact that he is a true Hebrew, an Israelite, of the seed of Abraham, and thus of God's chosen people. Paul is glad to stand on equal footing with his opponents on this point. But when he comes to the question of Christian ministry (11:23), he no longer concedes equality; indeed, the apostle insists on his superiority, but it is a "superiority" based on weakness! And this constitutes the unexpected shift in his rhetoric. After pulling his audience along in a way that might be expected, he turns the tables and begins emphasizing the difficulties and suffering of ministry as badges of authenticity.

Some scholars take the references to weakness as only referring to the latter half of the speech, specifically the ignoble escape from Damascus (11:32–33) and the thorn in the flesh of chapter 12 (12:7b–9). These scholars understand the hardship list of 11:23b–29 as a list of strengths. After all, the hardships—imprisonment, hard work, braving dangers of various forms, and circumstantial difficulties—demonstrate the apostle's great fortitude and endurance!

But this reading of the hardship list will not do for at least three reasons. First, many of the hardships listed in this passage would have been deemed deficiencies or social weaknesses in the broader Greco-Roman culture, including the elite in Corinth. We have already noted that manual labor was seen as slave's work, and the public shame of imprisonment, beatings, stonings, and various deprivations such as hunger, thirst, and exposure to the elements—these would have been deemed to be indicators of failure, as "weakness" rather than strength. In battling against the cultural value of strength-and-wisdom religion at Corinth, Paul framed his whole ministry in terms of "weakness" (1 Cor. 1:18–31), contrasting the Corinthians' strength and "superiority," about which they were boasting, with the "inferiority" of apostolic ministry, which involved condemnation to death, weakness, dishonor, manual labor, hunger, thirst, being poorly clothed and treated brutally (1 Cor. 4:6–13). In other words, Paul in 1 Corinthians lists many of the same hardships found in 2 Cor. 11 as examples of "weakness" (1 Cor. 4:10): "We are weak, but you are strong." He concludes that passage with "We are the world's dirt and scum" (NET). So Paul presents his hardships as weaknesses, not strengths.

Second, the whole of the Fool's Speech (11:22–12:10) is capped off at 12:10 with a summary of all that has been described since 11:23. Here Paul mentions "weaknesses," "insults," "persecutions," and "difficulties" endured "for the sake of Christ," and all of these are tagged by the apostle with "for when I am weak, then I am strong!" Thus "weakness" serves as an

---

boast about things that display my weakness!" Hence I suggest that he marks boasting about "weakness" as a key distinction between his approach and that of the opponents. His point here is not simply that he has suffered more than his opponents. Rather, these sufferings form a primary aspect of his "commendation" as an authentic minister (6:4).

overarching category that includes hardships the apostle had listed earlier in his speech.

Third, the concluding statement in 12:10 plays an important role in framing the whole of the speech with references to "weakness." Notice the following references to weakness, which are evenly distributed throughout the speech (and just before it):

2 Cor.	Greek	Weakness	Boasting
11:16			that I may *boast*
11:18			I will *boast.*
11:21a	ἡμεῖς ἠσθενήκαμεν *hēmeis ēsthenēkamen*	We are *weak*!	
11:29–30	τίς ἀσθενεῖ καὶ οὐκ ἀσθενῶ; *tis asthenei kai ouk asthenō?*	Who is *weak* and I am not *weak*?	
			If *boasting* is necessary, I will *boast* about
	τὰ τῆς ἀσθενείας μου *ta tēs astheneias mou*	things that display my *weakness*!	
12:1			It is necessary to *boast,*
12:5			I will not *boast,* except
	ἐν ταῖς ἀσθενείαις. *en tais astheneiais.*	about my *weaknesses.*	
12:6			If I wish to *boast* . . .
12:9a	ἡ γὰρ δύναμις ἐν ἀσθενείᾳ τελεῖται *hē gar dynamis en astheneia teleitai*	for power is made perfect in *weakness.*	
12:9b–10			Therefore, I will *boast* most gladly
	ἐν ταῖς ἀσθενείαις μου *en tais astheneiais mou*	about my *weaknesses.*	
	εὐδοκῶ ἐν ἀσθενείαις *eudokō en astheneiais*	I delight in *weaknesses.*	
	ὅταν γὰρ ἀσθενῶ, τότε δυνατός εἰμι. *hotan gar asthenō, tote dynatos eimi.*	When I am *weak,* then I am strong.	

The speech has been introduced with a confession of weakness in 11:21a. Here we find the true heading of the Fool's Speech, for Paul's main intent is to boast about weaknesses. The reference to weakness at 11:29 concludes the list of hardships and anticipates the proclamation of 11:30, the hinge between the list of hardships and the two specific examples that comprise the remainder of the list. At the end of the second of these examples, the heavenly vision Paul experienced, the apostle again reiterates his commitment to boasting only about weaknesses (12:5). He goes on to explain how even this great "strength," perhaps the most amazing experience of the apostle's amazing life, led to a "weakness," his thorn in the flesh; at the conclusion of his explanation, he declares that "power is made perfect in weakness." Finally, the speech concludes in 12:9b–10 with Paul saying that he is glad to boast about his weaknesses, that he delights in his weaknesses, and the summary thought that when he is weak, then he is strong.

The speech falls into two primary movements: 2 Cor. 11:22–29 focuses on trials experienced in Paul's missionary activities, and 2 Cor. 11:30–12:10 makes a transition and then recounts two specific examples of his weaknesses. He tells of an escape from Damascus early in his ministry (11:32–33), and about his "visions and revelations" (12:1) and how these led to a "thorn in the flesh" (12:7). Tucked strategically between these two movements is a transitional "hinge" at 11:30–31, which both summarizes the hardship list of 11:23–29 and anticipates the specific examples in 11:32–12:10.

The span that we first consider, 11:22–29, has six embedded movements, the headings of which also provide our subheadings for the commentary:

a. Introduction: Questions of identity (11:22–23b)
   Are they Hebrews? So am I!
   Are they Israelites? So am I!
   Are they descendants of Abraham? So am I!
   [the primary question] Are they Christ's ministers? (I must be out of my mind to talk like this!)
   [Paul's "thesis"] I am superior to them in this regard!
b. General characterization of trials 1 (11:23c)
   In much more difficult work,
   in many more imprisonments,
   in much worse beatings,
   often staring death in the face.
c. Enumeration of specific trials (11:24–25)
   On five occasions I received forty lashes minus one from Jewish leaders.
   Three times I was beaten with rods.
   Once I was pummeled with stones.
   Three times I was shipwrecked.
   A night and a day I have been adrift in the open sea.
d. A list of dangers (11:26)
   Often in my travels, I have experienced
   dangers from rivers,
   dangers from bandits,

dangers from my own people,
dangers from Gentiles,
dangers in the city,
dangers in the wilderness,
dangers at sea,
dangers among false brothers,
e. General characterization of trials 2 (11:27)
    in exhausting work and hard labor,
    often going without sleep,
    in hunger and thirst,
    often doing without food,
    in cold temperatures and without adequate clothing.
f. Anxiety about the churches (11:28–29)
    Apart from other things I could mention, pressure—my anxiety
    about all the churches—weighs me down every day.
    Who is weak and I am not weak?
    Who is led into sin and I am not livid?

Exegesis and Exposition

[22]Are they Hebrews? So am I!

Are they Israelites? So am I!

Are they descendants of Abraham? So am I!

[23]Are they Christ's ministers? (I must be out of my mind to talk like this!) I am superior to them in this regard! In much more difficult work, ⌜in many more imprisonments, in much worse beatings⌝, often staring death in the face.

[24]On five occasions I received forty lashes minus one from Jewish leaders.

[25]Three times I was beaten with rods.

Once I was pummeled with stones.

Three times I was shipwrecked.

A night and a day I have been adrift in the open sea.

[26]Often during my travels, I have experienced

dangers from rivers,

dangers from bandits,

dangers from my own people,

dangers from Gentiles,

dangers in the city,

dangers in the wilderness,

dangers at sea,

dangers among false brothers,

[27]⌜ ⌝ in exhausting work and hard labor,

often going without sleep,

in hunger and thirst,

often doing without food,

in cold temperatures and without adequate clothing.

²⁸Apart from other things I could mention, ⌜pressure⌝—⌜my⌝ anxiety about all the churches—weighs me down every day.
²⁹Who is weak and I am not weak?
Who is led into sin and I am not livid?

a. Introduction: Questions of Identity (11:22–23b)

As he begins his boasting, Paul presents a series of four "identity" questions   **11:22–23b** with four corresponding answers. The questions almost certainly reflect specific claims made by the interlopers, or those commending the interlopers (3:1), as to their qualifications for ministry.[6] In the rhetoric of the Greco-Roman world, appeal could be made to "good breeding," and here the emphasis seems to be on one coming from "good Jewish stock" (Betz 1972: 97; Furnish 1984: 534). Notice, however that the four questions are framed with Paul's disclaimer that this kind of boasting is foolishness (11:21b, 23b). Paul prefers to boast about his weakness, which his opponents detest as unworthy of a leader; his opponents prefer to boast about qualifications, which Paul decries as foolishness and unworthy of an apostle (Hafemann 2000: 438)!

The first three questions and their answers have to do with ethnic identity:

Ἑβραῖοί εἰσιν;	κἀγώ.
hebraioi eisin?	*kagō.*
Are they Hebrews?	So am I!
Ἰσραηλῖταί εἰσιν;	κἀγώ.
Israēlitai eisin?	*kagō.*
Are they Israelites?	So am I!
σπέρμα Ἀβραάμ εἰσιν;	κἀγώ.
sperma Abraam eisin?	*kagō.*
Are they descendants of Abraham?	So am I!

The term Ἑβραῖος (*hebraios*, Hebrew) could be used either as an ethnic/racial designation, perhaps a title of honor (Furnish 1984: 514), to distinguish Israelites from other people groups (cf. Phil. 3:5, "Hebrew of Hebrews"; Eusebius, *Eccl. Hist.* 2.4.2 in reference to Philo of Alexandria), or as a linguistic label to differentiate a Hebrew/Aramaic-speaking Israelite from an Israelite who primarily spoke Greek (Acts 6:1).[7] The latter probably is ruled out by the fact that Paul's opponents seem to be fluent in Greek, and the triple question here

6. In terms of qualifications, it is striking what Paul does not bring to his boasting. He certainly could appeal to superior credentials, the converts won across the Mediterranean world, and the number of churches he has planted in the past decade (Bruce 1971: 241–42). But these would not be matching his opponents (the program of the moment), and they would be buying into the kind of foolish boasting that Paul intends to subvert by a focus rather on weaknesses.

7. In this sense Paul is a Hellenistic Jew who probably has taught in the Greek-speaking synagogues in Jerusalem (Barnett 1997: 536; Hengel and Deines 1991: 54–61). Barnett suggests that these false apostles may have been "drawn from the same 'Hellenist' group as Paul, [people] who first bitterly opposed Stephen and then Paul himself (cf. Acts 6:9–11; 9:29)."

seems to focus more on an honorable aspect of identity rather than ability. Therefore ethnic identity almost certainly is in mind.

That the false teachers are "Israelites" (Ἰσραηλῖται, *Israēlitai*), while somewhat synonymous, connotes the Hebrews as God's covenant people who shared in a particular history, heritage, and tradition (2 Cor. 3:7, 13; Rom. 9:4–5; 11:1). Note especially that the speeches in Acts to Jewish audiences are often addressed to "Men, Israelites" (Acts 2:22; 3:12; 5:35; 13:16; 21:28; Barnett 1997: 537). Thus the designation "Israelites" is also roughly synonymous with "seed/descendants of Abraham" (σπέρμα Ἀβραάμ, *sperma Abraham*; see esp. Rom. 11:1; 4 Macc. 18:1), which points to Abraham's offspring as children of the promise (Gen. 17:7).[8] So the three labels together sum up what it means to be a religiously devoted Jew.[9]

A fourth identity question—the primary question Paul means to address—concerns the opponents' claim that they are "Christ's ministers." Here stands the hinge[10] on which his whole program of boasting turns, for it strikes at the heart of whom should be embraced by the Corinthians. Paul's main question is not whether he or the opponents are *better* as Christ's ministers (it is

8. Paul uses σπέρμα Ἀβραάμ elsewhere to speak specifically of Jesus as the promised Messiah (Gal. 3:16, 19). Here, however, all three of these designations emphasize Paul's "genuine Jewishness" (Harris 2005: 795–96).

9. Furnish (1984: 534) suggests that the emphasis on Abraham might indicate that the false teachers are Hellenistic-Jewish Christians.

10. There are two lexical dynamics that demonstrate the "hinge" nature of this fourth identity question: (1) Of the 208 uses of the conjunction καί (*kai*, and) in 2 Corinthians, Paul uses the contraction κἀγώ (*kagō* [καί + ἐγώ, *kai* + *egō*], and, I) only 9 times, and only 7 of these as adjunctive (= "I also"): the use at 2:10 and the 6 uses in 11:16–22. These 6 uses drum home Paul's "demand" that he be given equal time to boast (11:16, 18, 21) and that he be considered side by side with his opponents in terms of identity qualifications (3 times in 11:22). But this pattern abruptly breaks with the fourth identity question (11:23):

11:16	κἀγώ
11:18	κἀγώ
11:21	κἀγώ
11:22	κἀγώ
	κἀγώ
	κἀγώ
11:23	ὑπὲρ ἐγώ

So the pattern is "I also, I also, I also, I also, I also, I also, I more so." (2) In 11:16–21 Paul refers to "foolishness" or being "foolish" (ἄφρων/ἀφροσύνη, *aphrōn/aphrosynē*) 5 times. But this pattern breaks, again with the fourth identity question (11:23):

11:16	ἄφρονα
	ἄφρονα
11:17	ἀφροσύνη
11:19	ἀφρόνων
11:21	ἀφροσύνη
11:23	παραφρονῶν

In other words, with the fourth identity question, Paul makes a sudden turning, distinguishing himself from his opponents, on the one hand, and moving for the moment from speaking about "foolishness" (which will resume at 12:6, 11) to a confession of being out of his mind.

they who are speaking in terms of "equality"; 11:12).[11] He has already made clear that they are "servants" of Satan, "false apostles, deceitful workers" (11:13–15). Rather, Paul asserts that he is "better" only to join them for the moment in their game of comparison, but he quickly demonstrates that their idea of what constitutes authentic ministry and his idea do not line up. With the fourth identity question, which concerns identity as a Christian minister, Paul suddenly and dramatically takes an unexpected course: he boasts about weaknesses!

The foolish boasting, by which Paul points to himself and his qualifications, is so out of line with what the apostle considers appropriate to a real Christian minister that he says, "I must be out of my mind to talk like this!" (παραφρονῶν λαλῶ, *paraphronōn lalō*). The language of this exclamation constitutes a decided step up from his earlier admission of "foolishness" (11:17, 21); now he suggests that he speaks as if he has lost his mind; the term πα-ραφρονέω (*paraphroneō*), used only here in the NT, refers to being "besides oneself" or "irrational" (BDAG 772). Nevertheless, on the basis of his own ministry activities, Paul claims superiority to the interlopers. They have been labeled "superior apostles" (superapostles, τῶν ὑπερλίαν ἀποστόλων, *tōn hyperlian apostolōn*; 2 Cor. 11:5), but Paul's ministry activities make clear that he is the one who is "superior" (ὑπὲρ ἐγώ, *hyper egō*);[12] yet his superiority is shown by his sufferings.

b. General Characterization of Trials 1 (11:23c)

Now comes Paul's third hardship list in 2 Corinthians (see 4:8–11; 6:4b–10),   **11:23c** and the apostle begins this list in chapter 11 with generalizations about his sufferings,[13] generalizations that he will unpack in the following verses (see esp. Barnett 1997: 541; Martin 1986: 369). At two points in this third of Paul's lists we find generalizations about his sufferings (each introduced by the preposition ἐν; 11:23c, 27), and a number of these elements echo items from his earlier lists of hardships in the book.

11. Since Paul has already called the opponents "servants of Satan," some ask whether he contradicts himself here by admitting that the interlopers, at least in some sense, are "Christ's ministers" (see the discussion in Thrall 2000: 731–33). After all, he does not categorically deny them the label. But it should be kept in mind that Paul answers their "boasting," their claims, on their terms for the moment. He allows them the title "ministers" in order to set their so-called ministry over against his. But what follows shows that Paul is superior in the sense of being in a different class or category from his opponents at Corinth.

12. BDAG 1031 notes this as a rare case of an adverbial use of ὑπέρ. Yet it may be that an acc. noun is understood ("superior to them") and the preposition interpreted as a "marker of a degree beyond" the opponents in regard to ministry.

13. Garland (1999: 496), following E. A. Judge (1968), points out that Paul's list of personal disasters hits home because he is a man of rank and has been voluntarily involved in activities that put him in harm's way. In comparison to the earlier lists in 2 Corinthians, Paul now extends his list of hardships, becoming very specific and repetitive, giving the impression that these trials are simply common experiences for him and representative of other sufferings.

2 Cor. 11:23c, 27	6:4–10	4:8–10
difficult work,	in hard work,	
imprisonments,	being put in jail,	
beatings,	beatings,	
staring death in the face.	as dying (v. 9)	carrying around the dying of Jesus in our bodies
exhausting work and hard labor,	[in hard work]	
often going without sleep,	in sleepless nights,	
hunger and thirst,	in times of hunger,	
doing without food,		
in cold temperatures and without adequate clothing		

As demonstrated in the table above, Paul has already mentioned the first four generalizations, found in 11:23c, earlier in the book. These refer to the normal patterns the apostle experienced in his mission activity. The specific pattern for each of these four phrases is the preposition ἐν (*en*) + a noun + an adverb:[14]

ἐν κόποις περισσοτέρως (*en kopois perissoterōs*),

ἐν φυλακαῖς περισσοτέρως (*en phylakais perissoterōs*),

ἐν πληγαῖς ὑπερβαλλόντως (*en plēgais hyperballontōs*),

ἐν θανάτοις πολλάκις (*en thanatois pollakis*).

At 6:5 Paul stated that his ministry has been conducted ἐν κόποις (*en kopois*, in labors), which at 11:23 has been elevated to ἐν κόποις περισσοτέρως (cf. 1 Cor. 15:10), the comparative adverb proclaiming either that the apostle has done "more difficult" work than his opponents, or simply has been engaged in more work. The noun κόπος can speak of discomfort, distress, or trouble, but Paul most likely prefers to speak of hard work (cf., 1 Cor. 3:8; 15:58; 2 Cor. 10:15; 1 Thess. 1:3; 2 Thess. 3:8). The combination of ancient travel in a variety of both rural and urban contexts, supporting himself through manual labor as a tentmaker, battling opponents, and overseeing a variety of fledgling churches across the Mediterranean world—all of this would have made his work onerous at times. The strain of cross-cultural ministry, relationship building and maintenance, evangelistic proclamation and conflict; theological training of converts, church leaders, and fellow workers; correspondence with the churches, not to mention his theological battles with opponents such as those at Corinth—all would have taken their toll. We agree with Furnish (1984: 515) that there is no reason contextually to limit Paul's reference to work here either to his manual labor or to his "ministry" (as do Thrall 2000: 734–35; Barrett 1973: 295). Of course all of Paul's labors were done in the context of missionary activity.

14. In this case the preposition functions to mark a circumstance (BDAG 329).

"In many more imprisonments" (ἐν φυλακαῖς περισσοτέρως) and "in much worse beatings" (ἐν πληγαῖς ὑπερβαλλόντως) speak of common aspects of persecution for the early church. Luke reports in Acts that beatings, attacks by mobs, and being put into prison were normal hazards of missionary work (Acts 13:50; 14:19; 16:22–23; 17:5; 18:12; 19:29–30; 21:30–36; 23:35), as religious and cultural forces opposed the advance of the gospel. Yet, by the time 2 Corinthians is being written, Acts has mentioned only one imprisonment for Paul (Acts 16:23–40), that at Philippi, which suggests that Luke has telescoped his Pauline travel narratives a great deal.

Evidently Paul has already been in prison many times for the sake of the gospel.[15] In the first-century world, prison was not a building for long-term detention but, rather, a holding place for a person awaiting trial or execution (Rapske 1994: 288–97). Imprisonment also was a matter of physical hardship and social shame, and in countercultural strokes, both Acts and Paul's Letters demonstrate extensive reflection on imprisonment as a badge of ministry honor and a means of advancing God's work in the world.[16] In the next verse the apostle elaborates on his "beatings" (πληγαῖς), but here he notes that they were ὑπερβαλλόντως, probably meaning that they were "excessive." Finally, he states that he was ἐν θανάτοις πολλάκις, "often in death," or as we have translated it, "often staring death in the face." At the beginning of 2 Corinthians, Paul mentioned the "brush with death" he experienced in Asia (1:8–10). The list that follows in 11:24–33 shows that the experience was not unusual for the apostle.

c. Enumeration of Specific Trials (11:24–25)

The second movement in the hardship list enumerates specific types of persecution, as well as Paul's trials involving ship travel.   **11:24**

> On five occasions I received forty lashes minus one from Jewish leaders.
>
> Three times I was beaten with rods.
>
> Once I was pummeled with stones.

15. One reasonable suggestion is that Paul was in prison for a time in Ephesus, perhaps in relation to the severe trial faced in Asia (1:8–11; so Bruce 1971: 242).

16. On Christian responses to imprisonment, see Rapske's article on "Prison, Prisoner" (*DNTB* 827–30), where he explains:

> The damage of going into custody, the rigors and restrictions of being in custody and the shame and dishonor of being a prisoner resulted in significant theological reflection, particularly for Luke and Paul. Acts shows that not only is Paul unflaggingly for the Lord, but also the Lord is decidedly for his imprisoned apostle. Paul is moved to account for his imprisonments and bonds to individuals and to churches, demonstrating that his status, credibility and effectiveness as missionary accommodates to and shows the divine purpose of these trials. This is demonstrable in Paul's terminology of self-designation (Eph 3:1; 4:1; 6:20; Philem 1, 9), his reflections on suffering and mission (Phil 1:12–13, 16, 29; Col 1:24; Philem 13; cf. Eph 4:7–13) and the terminology with which he affirms those who courageously continue to support and help him in his bonds (Col 4:10; Philem 23; cf. Rom 16:7).

> Three times I was shipwrecked.
> A night and a day I have been adrift in the open sea.

The apostle begins by mentioning that on "five occasions" (πεντάκις, *pentakis*, five times) he received "forty lashes minus one" (τεσσεράκοντα παρὰ μίαν, *tesserakonta para mian*) from "Jews" (ὑπὸ Ἰουδαίων, *hypo Ioudaiōn*), that is, at the hands of[17] Jewish synagogue officials. This punishment originated with Deut. 25:2–3, which speaks of giving a violator up to forty lashes; the flogging was to be proportionate to the level of the offense. The passage points out that more than forty lashes would degrade or dishonor (וְנִקְלָה, *wĕniqlâ*) a brother. By the first century, tradition had adjusted the "forty" to "forty minus one" (Josephus, *Ant.* 4.238, 248), perhaps to guard against the law being violated by accident (Plummer 1915: 324), or perhaps reflecting an interpretation of the Hebrew text as reading "by number forty," that is, "a number near to forty" (Harris 2005: 801). According to the rabbis (*m. Mak.* 3.10–15; *makkôt* = stripes), this punishment was to be administered with a strap of three hide thongs, two-thirds on the back and one-third on the front of the offender (Bruce 1971: 242). Local synagogues throughout the Mediterranean world were the context for this punishment; for synagogues, among other purposes, served as the convening place for local Jewish courts.

Jesus had told his first followers that Jewish councils would scourge them in the synagogues (Matt. 10:17), and Paul himself probably participated in such beatings during his days as a persecutor of believers (Acts 22:19). We are not told why Paul himself repeatedly faced the thirty-nine lashes, but since this was the maximum penalty allowed by the law, his offenses must have been considered severe. In his interaction with the Gentiles, Paul certainly broke Sabbath observance and food laws (*m. Mak.* 3.2), as well as other aspects of ritual purity. His opposition to circumcision among the Gentiles (e.g., Gal. 5:11) would have engendered a strong reaction from devout Jews. Among the most probable reasons Paul was repeatedly punished as a Jew by Jewish leaders, Harris (2005: 802) points to blasphemy, "dishonoring God and his people" by proclaiming Christ crucified and vindicated as deity.[18]

In spite of receiving this severe punishment numerous times, Paul continued to go to the Jewish synagogue first in his missionary work, for he shared both common authority (the Scriptures) and a common hope with those worshipers (Acts 13:14–15, 43; 14:1; 17:1–2, 10, 17; 18:4, 7–8, 19, 26; 19:8). Paul celebrates his Jewish heritage (11:22) and continues to proclaim the gospel to his fellow Jews. His persistence in ministry to the synagogues in spite of such persecution bears witness to his understanding of his calling, his courage, and his physical

---

17. The preposition ὑπό + the genitive communicates agency.

18. At Acts 21:21, Paul was warned by church leaders in Jerusalem that Jewish converts "have been told about you that you teach all the Jews who are among the Gentiles to abandon Moses, by telling them not to circumcise their children or to walk in our customs" (Acts 21:21 HCSB); and later, Acts 21:28 records that Jews from the province of Asia shout against Paul, "This is the man who teaches everyone everywhere against our people, our law, and this place" (HCSB).

stamina, for such beatings did sometimes lead to death. Ironically, this form of punishment also indicates that synagogue leaders of this period consider him a wayward brother rather than an apostate, which normally would have resulted in expulsion from the synagogue (Matera 2003: 267).

Second, Paul writes that on three occasions (τρίς, *tris*) he "was beaten with rods" (ἐρραβδίσθην, *errabdisthēn*), a Roman form of punishment. In carrying out a sentence, a lictor, the attendant of a magistrate, carried before the magistrate a bundle of elm or birch rods and an axe. Criminals were flogged with the rods, and at times the axe was used for beheadings (see esp. the excursus by Thrall 2000: 739–42). Acts 16 recounts that the apostle and Silas, while ministering in the Roman colony of Philippi, were beaten with such rods by Roman officials in that city. Having cast a demon out of a fortune-telling slave girl, the missionaries were dragged before the city's chief magistrates (στρατηγοί, *stratēgoi*) as Jewish disturbers of the peace (16:20). The magistrates had Paul and Silas stripped and ordered them to be "beaten with rods" (ῥαβδίζειν, *rhabdizein*; 16:22). "When they had laid many blows [or wounds] on them" (πολλάς τε ἐπιθέντες αὐτοῖς πληγάς, *pollas te epithentes autois plēgas*), they threw them into jail (16:23).

11:25

Luke goes on to tell of their miraculous deliverance and the salvation of the Philippian jailer and his household (Acts 16:25–34). But what happens next reflects a particular aspect of Roman law. On the next day when the magistrates sent word for Paul and Silas to be released, Paul refused to go quietly:

> But Paul said to them, "They beat us in public without a trial, although we are Roman citizens, and threw us in jail. And now are they going to smuggle us out secretly? Certainly not! On the contrary, let them come themselves and escort us out!"
>
> Then the police reported these words to the magistrates. They were afraid when they heard that Paul and Silas were Roman citizens. So they came and apologized to them, and escorting them out, they urged them to leave town. (16:37–39 HCSB)

Luke's narrative reflects both the Lex Porcia, a Roman law that forbade the scourging of a Roman citizen (Livy, *Hist. Rom.* 10.9.4–5; Barrett 1973: 297; Furnish 1984: 516), and the Lex Julia, under which the citizen could make an appeal to Rome. So a citizen was protected from a trial by magistrates, as well as from being punished without trial. Yet there were exceptions[19] when a citizen could be beaten legally, as when flagrant disobedience had taken place (Thrall 2000: 740). But this clearly was not the case in Paul's beating in Philippi, and the magistrates' apology was warranted. Thus Luke gives us one account of Paul being beaten with rods. We have no knowledge of the other two occurrences.

---

19. Before the Jewish War in AD 66, e.g., Gessius Florus had two Roman citizens, who were Jews, flogged and crucified (Josephus, *J.W.* 2.308; Scott 1998: 218).

Third, Paul says that once he was pummeled with stones (ἅπαξ ἐλιθάσθην, *hapax elithasthēn*), a form of capital punishment prescribed in Deuteronomy (17:5–7; 22:22–24). Among the violations that could lead to stoning were apostasy (Lev. 20:2; Deut. 13:10–11; 17:2–7), blasphemy (Lev. 24:14, 16, 23), sorcery (Lev. 20:27), breaking the Sabbath (Num. 15:35–36), disobedience as a son (Deut. 21:21), and adultery by a bride (Deut. 22:21, 24). At several points in his tenure as the Israelites' leader, Moses was threatened with being stoned (Exod. 17:4; Num. 14:10; Scott 1998: 218). In the early Christian movement, Stephen was stoned for speaking against the temple and the law of Moses (Acts 6:13–14; 7:58–59). However, the stoning that Paul mentions at 2 Cor. 11:25, recounted in Acts 14:19–20, may have been more a mob action than the carrying out of a sentence by a Jewish synagogue council. At this point in Luke's narrative, the apostle and Barnabas have just healed a lame man in Lystra. Hailed by the crowds as Zeus and Hermes, the apostles barely keep the enthusiastic Lystrans from offering sacrifices to them. Then Jews arrive from Antioch and Iconium, win over the crowds, and stone Paul, leaving him for dead. Undaunted, the apostle got up and marched back into the city!

Finally, Paul notes that he had been "shipwrecked" (ἐναυάγησα, *enauagēsa*) three times and had spent "a night and a day . . . adrift in the open sea" (νυχθήμερον ἐν τῷ βυθῷ πεποίηκα, *nychthēmeron en tō bythō pepoiēka*). In some ways travel by sea, usually limited to the months of May through October,[20] was greatly preferred to travel overland. Normally it was much faster and much more comfortable than walking, riding a mule, or riding in a carriage (Casson 1974: 149–50). Yet the hazards of the sea, and the ancients' fear of this mode of travel, are well documented (e.g., Seneca, *Leis.* 8.4; Epictetus, *Disc.* 2.6.20),[21] and vessels did not carry lifeboats (Casson 1974: 149–57). We know from Acts that Paul traveled this way extensively (Acts 13:4, 13; 14:25–26; 16:11; 17:14–15; 18:18–22, 27; 2 Cor. 2:1), and yet the one account of the apostle being shipwrecked (Acts 27) would have happened after he wrote 2 Corinthians. This is just another reminder of how little Acts tells us of Paul's experiences on his journeys!

What the apostle tells us here is that he was "in the deep sea" (ἐν τῷ βυθῷ), that is, out "in the open sea," and Paul probably was clinging to floating debris from one of the three shipwrecks mentioned. The term νυχθήμερον (*nychthēmeron*), a compound of νύξ (*nyx*, night) and ἡμέρα (*hēmera*, day), refers to a twenty-four-hour period—an egregious amount of time to be adrift in open water. Thus Paul ends his list of enumerated persecutions and trials with one of the terrors of ancient travel, and this reference to travel makes a nice transition to the list of travel dangers in the next verse.

---

20. This was due both to the violence of winter weather and cloudiness, since ancient sailors plotted their courses by landmarks, the sun, and the stars (Casson 1974: 150).

21. "Those who sail the sea describe its danger, and we marvel at the reports of our ears" (Sir. 43:24 NETS).

d. A List of Dangers (11:26)

Thus, next in Paul's list we find a series of "dangers" (κίνδυνος, *kindynos*),   **11:26**
life-threatening situations, groups, or contexts that the apostle experienced
in his travels. In the ancient world the term could be used to refer to various
kinds of risky situations, or to things that were inherently dangerous in some
way. Also from Paul's hand, Rom. 8:35 offers us the only other place the word
occurs in the NT, "Who will separate us from the love of Christ? Will trouble,
or distress, or persecution, or famine, or nakedness, or danger [κίνδυνος], or
sword?" (Rom. 8:35 NET). But it finds expression a dozen times in the LXX,
where, for example, it refers to the hazards of pregnancy (Tob. 4:4), politics
and warfare (1 Macc. 11:23; 14:29), dangers to the soul (4 Macc. 3:15), and
the danger of dying (Ps. 114:3 [116:3 ET]).[22] Emphasis often rests on the noble
or courageous character of the person willing to undergo such dangers for
other people or for the nation.

At the head of the list stands the phrase ὁδοιπορίαις πολλάκις (*hodoiporiais
pollakis*), "Often during my travels." The feminine plural dative noun (from
ὁδοιπορία, *hodoiporia*, journey) may be read as a dative of time ("during"), or
perhaps a dative of sphere ("in"),[23] and the adverb πολλάκις (*pollakis*, often)
simply speaks to the frequency of these types of experiences for Paul. As Paul
in his ministry was "often [πολλάκις][24] staring death in the face" (11:23),
now he mentions that he often was in danger during his missionary travels.
Further, three things should be noted about the form of this list of dangers.
First, the recurrence of the dative plural κινδύνοις (*kindynois*) in verse 26 is
called anaphora, a rhetorical device that drives home a point by rhythmic
repetition (cf. πίστις, *pistis*, in Heb. 11). The effect impresses the reader with
the varied abundance of evidence available on the topic. Paul means to drive
home to the Corinthians the pervasiveness of the risks he has taken in his
mission. Second, the multiple uses of the dative plural form κινδύνοις can be
interpreted as datives of sphere, defining the various contexts that proved risky
for Paul and his mission (i.e., "in dangers").[25] Finally, there are several ways
of understanding Paul's crafting of this list of eight dangers. At first blush,
noticing the prepositions (or lack thereof) gives a certain shape to the list,
with the first two items speaking of specific dangers related to travel in open
country, the second two (introduced by the preposition ἐκ, *ek*) pointing out
dangers "from" two primary people groups, and the last four (introduced by

22. See κίνδυνος in Add. Esth. 14:3 [14:4 ET]; Tob. 4:4; 1 Macc. 11:23; 14:29; 2 Macc. 1:11;
3 Macc. 6:26; 4 Macc. 3:15; 13:15; Ps. 114:3 [116:3 ET]; Wis. 18:9; Sir. 3:26; 43:24.
23. On the dative of sphere and its relation to the dative of place and dative of reference,
see D. Wallace 1996: 144–46, 153–55.
24. These references to Paul "often" being in danger of harm or death frame the list of
specifically enumerated trials mentioned in 11:24–25.
25. The words "I have experienced" in our ET are not in the Greek text but have been added
to facilitate the sense. More lit., the text reads, "Often during travels in dangers from rivers,
dangers from bandits." Thus Paul says he has been "in dangers" of various kinds. In English
we might simply say, "We experienced dangers from . . ."

the preposition ἐν, *en*) offering contexts "in" which persecution took place. Some have identified four pairs, with the last four divided into "dangers in the city/wilderness" and "dangers at sea/among false brothers." However, Thrall (2000: 742) may be right in dividing the final four into the triad of city-wilderness-sea, with "dangers among false brothers," the great fight Paul wages with this letter, serving as a climax to the whole.

κινδύνοις ποταμῶν, *kindynois potamōn*, dangers from rivers

κινδύνοις λῃστῶν, *kindynois lēstōn*, dangers from bandits

κινδύνοις ἐκ γένους, *kindynois ek genous*, dangers from my own people

κινδύνοις ἐξ ἐθνῶν, *kindynois ex ethnōn*, dangers from Gentiles

κινδύνοις ἐν πόλει, *kindynois en polei*, dangers in the city

κινδύνοις ἐν ἐρημίᾳ, *kindynois en erēmia*, dangers in the wilderness

κινδύνοις ἐν θαλάσσῃ, *kindynois en thalassē*, dangers at sea

κινδύνοις ἐν ψευδαδέλφοις, *kindynois en pseudadelphois*, dangers among false brothers

The first two dangers, ποταμῶν (from rivers) and λῃστῶν (bandits) are genitives of source. The "dangers from rivers" refers to the hazards associated with crossing rivers in remote areas where bridges were scarce. The power of a river suddenly swollen with floodwaters is terrifying and life threatening. Paul's trip crossing the Taurus Mountains, between Perga and Pisidian Antioch (Acts 13:14; 14:24; 15:41–16:6), may be in mind, for the region was notorious for cascading rivers as well as bandits (Harris 2005: 806). The term λῃστής (*lēstēs*) could refer to revolutionaries or insurrectionists but here speaks of thieves, highway bandits (BDAG 594), pirates who inhabited the coast of the Mediterranean,[26] or gangs of violent outlaws in the mountains. The Romans were able to greatly reduce the numbers of such robbers under the Pax Romana but they were never eradicated completely. The literature of the period consistently points to the dangers posed to travelers by such brigands (e.g., Josephus, *J.W.* 2.125, 228; Juvenal, *Sat.* 10.22). Epictetus writes, "When traveling, it is especially upon falling into the hands of brigands that we say we are isolated" (*Disc.* 3.13.3); "It is said that the route is infested with brigands. . . . Where to hide? How to get through without being robbed? . . . If my traveling companion himself turns against me and becomes my robber?" (4.1.91–98) (Spicq 1994: 2.389–94).

With the next pair Paul mentions "dangers from my own people, dangers from Gentiles," which is another way of saying, "dangers from all people," for

---

26. "If anyone has not fallen into the hands of pirates, it is because they have been spared by shipwreck" (Seneca, *Ben.* 6.9.2).

the two terms are all-inclusive. The term γένους (*genous*) could refer to family members or relatives (Josephus, *Ant.* 17.22; 18.127; Acts 7:13), or a class or kind of species, such as plants or animals (Wis. 19:21; 1 Cor. 12:10, 28). But here the word refers to the Jewish people as a whole, Paul's fellow Israelites (Mark 7:26; Acts 4:36; 18:2, 24; BDAG 194–95). The word ἔθνος (*ethnos*), on the other hand, here refers to those who are not Jews, meaning unbelievers from the nations of the world, thus most "Gentiles."[27] Already in the previous three verses he has mentioned his "imprisonments," "beatings," "forty lashes minus one from Jewish leaders," the three times he "was beaten with rods" by Roman officials. Jesus had said that his followers would be persecuted by the various power structures they encountered in spreading the good news of the kingdom (e.g., John 15:20), and Paul's life bears ample witness to the truth of his Lord's words.

For instance, following his conversion in Damascus and in response to his powerful proclamation of Jesus as Messiah, Jews there "conspired to kill him" (Acts 9:20–25), and persecution by his fellow Israelites would dog him through his missionary activities around the Mediterranean world (e.g., 13:45–50; 14:2–7, 19–20; 17:5–9, 13; 18:6–13).[28] Yet, though not with as much focus, Acts also recounts persecution Paul faced at the hands of Gentiles. We have already mentioned the uproar at Philippi, when Paul and Silas were beaten with rods by the city officials and imprisoned (16:16–24). Later, in Ephesus, "a great disturbance took place concerning the Way" (19:23 NET), instigated by a silversmith named Demetrius, and Paul was forced to terminate his long stay there (19:24–20:1).

The next three "dangers" in the hardships list form a triad of "contexts" where various persecutions and challenges took place (Thrall 2000: 743): "dangers in the city, dangers in the wilderness, dangers at sea." Just as "my own people" and "Gentiles" sum up all the people Paul would have encountered in his mission work, so "city," "wilderness," and "sea" sum up all possible places he would have gone in his work and constitute another, dramatic way of saying that he has been in constant danger throughout his missionary travels. As presented by Acts, Paul's work often focused on preaching in urban centers, and all of the dangers from the Jews and Gentiles mentioned above took place

---

27. The term ἔθνος can also be used to refer to a particular nation or people group (Acts 8:9), or Gentile believers in Christ (Rom. 16:4; Gal. 2:12; Eph. 3:1), but in 2 Cor. 11:26 Paul uses the term for Gentiles who are not Christ-followers.

28. After Paul wrote 2 Corinthians, he continued to be persecuted by Jewish leaders, and a significant turning point in Acts comes at 21:27. Accused of disparaging the Jewish people, the law, and the temple, the apostle is attacked in the temple in Jerusalem (21:27–31), saved only by being taken into Roman custody. The plot escalates as Paul first makes a defense before the mob (22:1–23) and then is brought before the Sanhedrin (22:30–23:10). Conspirators plot the apostle's death (23:12–15). Saved only by Roman incarceration in Caesarea (23:16–35), Paul stays in Roman custody through the tenure of the governor Felix. When Festus takes Felix's place, the Jewish leaders again plot to ambush and kill Paul (25:1–5), and to escape their hands, he is ultimately compelled to make an appeal to stand trial before Caesar (25:11–12). Thus "dangers from" Paul's "own people" were a constant threat throughout the remainder of his ministry.

in cities. Further, "dangers from rivers" and "dangers from bandits" would have been largely associated with "the wilderness" (ἐρημία, erēmia),[29] though the "bandits," as we have noted, could also refer to pirates on the sea. Finally, in verse 25 Paul has already mentioned how dangerous sea travel could be.

Strategically, Paul ends his list of "dangers" by stating he has been "among[30] false brothers" (ψευδαδέλφοις, pseudadelphois). Perhaps the apostle's reference is not limited to the Corinthian interlopers, but they certainly are included, and the conflict-weary minister associates them with other dangers to Christ's mission. Paul uses the term ψευδάδελφος (pseudadelphos), elsewhere only at Gal. 2:4: "This issue arose because of *false brothers* smuggled in, who came in secretly to spy on the freedom that we have in Christ Jesus, in order to enslave us" (HCSB). This does not mean that the false teachers of Corinth should be identified with the same Judaizing error confronted in Paul's ministry, but the nature of the threat was the same. The "false brothers," or "false believers" (NIV) of Corinth constituted the most insidious danger of all. Whereas all the other dangers in this subset of Paul's hardships were external forces brought to bear against him personally, the "dangers among false brothers" would include both persecution against Paul and the mission, yet would also involve infiltration of the churches (cf. 2 Cor. 11:28–29). The local churches were in danger of being compromised by false teaching, which could work as a cancer from within, even while it was disguised as Christian "ministry."

e. General Characterization of Trials 2 (11:27)

11:27   The next subset of hardships in the list (11:27), consisting of five parts, speaks of challenges faced in daily living conditions, especially relating to the lack of resources. This list displays another balanced literary shape:

κόπῳ καὶ μόχθῳ, *kopō kai mochthō,*	in exhausting work and hard labor,
ἐν ἀγρυπνίαις πολλάκις, *en agrypniais pollakis,*	often going without sleep,
ἐν λιμῷ καὶ δίψει, *en limō kai dipsei,*	in hunger and thirst,
ἐν νηστείαις πολλάκις, *en nēsteiais pollakis,*	often doing without food,
ἐν ψύχει καὶ γυμνότητι, *en psychei kai gymnotēti,*	in cold temperatures and without adequate clothing.

Notice two things about the structure of the passage. First, as with the previous list of dangers in verse 26, the first pair of items, κόπῳ καὶ μόχθῳ, have no preceding preposition, while Paul introduces the rest of these conditions,

29. At times ἐρημία is used in contrast to πόλις (as Ezek. 35:4; Josephus, *Ant.* 2.24; 6.11).

30. Although the preposition ἐν (*en*, in) with city, wilderness, and sea indicates places, the ἐν prior to a group of people, while still local, has more relational overtones (BDAG 326–27). Thus our ET's "among."

presented in four phrases, with the preposition ἐν (*en*), the same preposition, used four times, at the end of the list in verse 26. Thus a literary continuity exists as we move from verse 26 to verse 27. Second, notice that lines 1, 3, and 5 match in our list, presenting two nouns joined by καί (*kai*, and). Lines 2 and 4, on the other hand, consist of a single noun introduced by the preposition ἐν and followed by the adverb πολλάκις (*pollakis*, often). Perhaps line 2 expands on line 1, and line 4 expands on line 3, but more on that in a moment.

The first two items in the list, κόπῳ καὶ μόχθῳ (*kopō kai mochthō*) are roughly synonymous, both referring to grueling or exhausting work—the depletion of Paul's physical and perhaps temporal resources.[31] Used eighteen times in the NT,[32] and earlier in the book at 6:5; 10:15; and 11:23, the word κόπος (*kopos*) in Greek literature often is associated with fatigue (Hippocrates, *Aph.* 2.5; Plato, *Resp.* 7.537b), and in the LXX it is used with reference to exhaustion (e.g., Gen. 31:42) or especially suffering, misery, or trouble (Spicq 1994: 2.323). Thus it speaks of burdensome, tiring or "hard work" (so NET) or "toil" (e.g., ESV, NRSV). Paul specifically uses the term with reference to Christian ministry at 1 Cor. 3:8; 15:58; 2 Cor. 10:15; 11:23; 1 Thess. 1:3; 2:9; 3:5. At 1 Cor. 15:58 the apostle writes, "Therefore, my dear brothers, be steadfast, immovable, always excelling in the Lord's work, knowing that your labor [ὁ κόπος, *ho kopos*] in the Lord is not in vain" (1 Cor. 15:58 HCSB).

A related term, μόχθος (*mochthos*) is used twenty-two times in the LXX to speak of "fatigue, misery, adversity, evil." The pairing of the terms (or their cognates), occurs in a variety of literatures of the period (T. Jud. 18.4; T. Job 24.2; Philo, *Mos.* 1.284; Spicq 1994: 2.526). Further, presented together in the forms we have here, the words have a poetic ring to them, due to the assonance (syllables that sound alike) of the *k* (κ, χ) and *ō* (ῳ) sounds in each of the Greek forms.[33] So Paul speaks of his doings in Christian ministry as "exhausting work and hard labor."[34]

Second, Paul says he was "often going without sleep" (ἐν ἀγρυπνίαις πολλάκις, *en agrypniais pollakis*), more literally, "often in sleeplessness." As with κόπος, this condition occurs in the hardship list of 6:4–10 (6:5), its only other occurrence in the NT. The word here speaks of not sleeping as a deprivation of some kind (cf., Plutarch, *Mor.* 135e). The lack of sleep may be due to diligent work (e.g., 2 Macc. 2:26; Sir. prologue 30;[35] 38:27), but it

---

31. The two terms are also used together at 1 Thess. 2:9; 2 Thess. 3:8.

32. See κόπος in Matt. 26:10; Mark 14:6; Luke 11:7; 18:5; John 4:38; 1 Cor. 3:8; 15:58; 2 Cor. 6:5; 10:15; 11:23, 27; Gal. 6:17; 1 Thess. 1:3; 2:9; 3:5; 2 Thess. 3:8; Rev. 2:2; 14:13.

33. At one point in Charles Dickens's novel *Little Dorrit*, Mr. Pancks, the rent collector in the Bleeding Heart Yard neighborhood near the Marshalsea Prison, asks, "What has my life been? Fag and grind. Fag and grind. Turn the wheel! Turn the wheel!" (Dickens 1998: 757). His exclamation, "Fag and grind," two words referring to grueling work, roll off the tongue because of the *g* sound in both. Both the synonymy and the assonance between these words are analogous to Paul's expression, translated here as "grueling labor and exhausting work."

34. The *h* sound in "exhausting" and "hard" in our ET mirrors assonance in the construction.

35. "I myself too made it a most compulsory task to bring some speed and industry to the translating of this tome, meanwhile having contributed much sleeplessness and skill, with the

also might be caused by anxiety of some type (e.g., Sir. 42:9).[36] Paul could have either cause in mind here. From the testimony of Acts, we know that the apostle experienced sleepless nights due to late hours of ministry, as in Troas when he preached until midnight and then talked until daylight (20:7–12), or in ministry to the household of the Philippian jailer (16:25–35). Yet his daily anxiety about the churches certainly weighed on him, as he mentions next in 2 Cor. 11 (vv. 28–29), and that anxiety could have produced nights of tossing, turning, and prayer. Ambrosiaster (*Comm. Paul's Ep.*, 2 Cor. 11:27) notes, "Some of Paul's sleepless nights were voluntary, but others were forced on him. When he was in dire straits, he had to stay awake and seek God's help" (Bray 1999: 299).

The next pair of terms, ἐν λιμῷ καὶ δίψει (*en limō kai dipsei*) refers to yet other conditions in which resources were lacking: "in hunger and thirst." Although the word λιμός (*limos*) can be used to refer to famine (e.g., Gen. 12:10 LXX; Luke 4:25), and there are passages in the LXX in which δίψος (*dipsos*) might be interpreted as "drought" (e.g., Deut. 28:48; 32:10; Hosea 2:5 [2:3 ET]; Isa. 50:2), here they mean "hunger and thirst," for Paul speaks of personal deprivations related to ongoing ministry. Similarly, at 1 Cor. 4:11 he writes, "Up to the present hour we are both hungry and thirsty [διψῶμεν, *dipsōmen*]; we are poorly clothed, roughly treated, homeless" (HCSB). In the Mediterranean world of the first century, extensive travel over land and sea demanded that one carry extensive provisions: hunger and thirst could be constant threats or companions (Casson 1974: 153).

In the hardship list in 2 Cor. 6 Paul has written of going hungry (6:5), and the same word, νηστεία (*nēsteia*, hunger), occurs again here. Elsewhere in the LXX and the NT, the word almost always refers to "fasting" as a religious discipline (e.g., 2 Sam. 12:16; 1 Kings 20:9 [21:9 ET], 12; 2 Chron. 20:3; 1 Esd. 8:49, 70 [8:50, 73 ET]; Ezra 8:21; Neh. 9:1; Tob. 12:8; Luke 2:37; Acts 14:23; 27:9), and it probably should be interpreted that way here. Given the context in which Paul writes about various deprivations, ἐν νηστείαις πολλάκις (*en nēsteiais pollakis*, often doing without food) may well speak of times when Paul went hungry voluntarily,[37] perhaps in order to accomplish certain ministry goals (Harris 2005: 809–10). But fasting as a spiritual discipline certainly would be a normal part of Paul's preparation for ministry (e.g., Acts 13:1–2). He has already mentioned "hunger" in the previous phrase, and it seems redundant for him simply to reiterate the thought of "lacking food" here. Further, we

---

aim of bringing the book to completion and to publish it also for those living abroad if they wish to become learned" (Sir. prologue 30 NETS).

36. "A daughter is a hidden sleeplessness to a father, and anxiety about her takes away sleep" (Sir. 42:9 NETS).

37. Philo (*Migr.* 204), e.g., uses νηστεία at points in a nonreligious sense to mean abstaining from something: "the mind is labouring under a famine, as, on the contrary, when the outward senses are fasting, the mind is feasting" (ταῖς γὰρ τῶν αἰσθήσεων εὐωχίαις λιμὸν ἄγει διάνοια, ὡς ἔμπαλιν ταῖς νηστείαις εὐφροσύνας, *tais gar tōn aisthēseōn euōchiais limon agei dianoia, hōs empalin tais nēsteiais euphrosynas*). Notice that λιμός also occurs in this context.

have already noticed that the phrase ἐν ἀγρυπνίαις πολλάκις (often going without sleep) matches perfectly the phrase under consideration in terms of form, and the reference to "in sleepless nights" at 6:5 immediately precedes the term νηστεία there, so there seems to be a connection between these two forms of going without food. That connection could be that the deprivation in each case is voluntary and for the sake of greater productivity in ministry. All points considered, "doing without food" probably refers to fasting as a spiritual discipline, since this constitutes the almost universal use of the word in the biblical literature, and the adverb πολλάκις (often) indicates that the practice constitutes a normal pattern in Paul's ministry.

Finally, verse 27 concludes with the interrelated pair "in cold temperatures and without adequate clothing"[38] (ἐν ψύχει καὶ γυμνότητι, *en psychei kai gymnotēti*). At times the rare term ψῦχος (*psychos*) in the LXX is associated with ice or frost (Ps. 147:6 [147:17 ET]; Job 37:9; Zech. 14:6; Dan. 3:69 [Pr. Azar. 46 ET]), and it generally speaks of discomforting conditions, such as cold weather, in which a fire would be called for (so John 18:18; Acts 28:2). One can imagine various situations (e.g., Acts 16:22) in which Paul would have been ἐν . . . γυμνότητι, "naked" (NRSV, NIV), or "without adequate clothing" (cf. Rom. 8:35; Rev. 3:18) in the face of the elements. In this hardship list he has already mentioned being imprisoned, being in the wilderness, dealing with rivers, being shipwrecked, and being at sea, all of which involve periods of intense cold as well as wet, tattered, or otherwise inadequate clothing. Once again, Paul's point is that authentic ministry bears a tremendous cost in terms of hardship and is not for those given to leisure and comfort.

f. Anxiety about the Churches (11:28–29)

After crafting his long list of hardships, Paul now comes to a climactic point—   **11:28–29**
one that strikes at the heart of his current relationship with the Corinthian church: "Apart from other things I could mention, pressure—my anxiety about all the churches—weighs me down every day." Up to this point the list has ranged through a variety of persecutions, difficulties, dangers, and adverse conditions related to the ongoing work of Paul's mission. Many of these challenges constitute physical threats or deprivations, which certainly could take a toll on the apostle's emotional well-being, though he has not mentioned his emotional state to this point.

Now the hardship list culminates in the emotional weight, the anxiety Paul bears on a daily basis as he thinks about problems in the churches throughout the Mediterranean world. The adverb χωρίς (*chōris*), used as a preposition, works with the genitive plural neuter article to mean "apart from things," and παρεκτός (*parektos*, from παρά + ἐκ; cf. Matt. 5:32; Acts 26:29), another adverb, pertains "to being different and in addition to something else." As a whole the phrase carries the sense "apart from other matters" or "apart from other things I could mention" (so variously, ESV, HCSB, NLT[2], NRSV, NIV, NET)

---

38. The pair could be rendered as a hendiadys: "in cold due to lack of adequate clothing."

and is not referring to "external" hardships over against internal struggles (so NASB, Tyndale, KJV). Such a bridge from the detailed list of 11:23c–27, to Paul's mention of his anxiety for the churches, serves rhetorically to give the impression that even this varied, extensive account of his ministry challenges does not capture the full picture. The price he has paid to be God's true minister in the world has been beyond even what has been told here: "Apart from other things I could mention . . ."

Apart from those other things, on a daily basis (καθ'[39] ἡμέραν, *kath' hēmeran*, every day) Paul faced ἡ ἐπίστασις (*hē epistasis*), the burden of responsibility, that is, the personal (μοι,[40] *moi*) "pressure" or "weight" of caring deeply about what is going on in "the churches." Due to the parallel forms and their relationship as roughly synonymous, ἡ μέριμνα (*hē merimna*), "the anxiety" or "care," can be read as epexegetical and appositional to ἡ ἐπίστασις: "the daily weight, that is my anxiety" about all the churches. This can be smoothed in translation to read, "pressure—my anxiety about all the churches—weighs me down every day," and that anxiety stems from Paul's responsibility πασῶν τῶν ἐκκλησιῶν (*pasōn tōn ekklēsiōn*), "about all the churches" (this may be read as an objective genitive). So the list of hardships has moved from a wide variety of challenges that would have occurred periodically in the course of Paul's mission to a climactic burden—indeed the primary burden—that he carries on a daily basis.

Paul puts the emotional freight of his daily responsibility into words with the parallel rhetorical questions of verse 29:

Who is weak and I am not weak?
Who is led into sin and I am not livid?

The first of these rhetorical questions amounts to the statement "I am weak when anyone in the churches experiences weakness" and calls to mind his references to the "weak brothers" he mentions elsewhere (e.g., 1 Cor. 8:7–13; Rom. 14:1–23; see Bruce 1971: 244). Thus Paul confesses his identification with the weaker brothers and sisters in the church.

The first time Paul used the verb ἀσθενέω (*astheneō*)[41] in 2 Corinthians was in 11:21, his ironic exclamation in response to the interlopers' strong-armed abuse of the church: "I am ashamed to admit that we have been weak!" He famously uses the same verb later at 12:10 where he writes, "For when I am weak, then I am strong!" The verb can refer to being sick (e.g., Matt. 25:39;

---

39. Used distributively, "day by day" (as in Matt. 26:55; Mark 14:49; Luke 16:19; 22:53; Acts 3:2; 16:5; 17:11; 19:9; 1 Cor. 15:31; Heb. 7:27; 10:11).

40. The dative μοι should probably be read as communicating disadvantage (i.e., "against me").

41. The verb ἀσθενέω is used later at 2 Cor. 12:10; 13:3. The noun ἀσθένεια (*astheneia*, weakness) plays an important role in this section of the book as well (11:30; 12:5, 9–10; 13:4). The adjective ἀσθενής (*asthenēs*) only occurs at 10:10, where Paul's opponents are quoted, saying his physical presence is "weak" or "a pushover."

Luke 7:10 v.l.; John 4:46; 11:1, 2, 3, 6; Phil. 2:26–27; 2 Tim. 4:20; James 5:14; P.Oxy. 725) or to being in need of resources (Acts 20:35), or it could refer to some limitation or incapacity, such as the inability to do something, or fear, timidity, or uncertainty (e.g., Rom. 8:3; 14:2; 2 Cor. 13:3). One might wonder if synonymous parallelism is in play with the next line, in which case Paul would be alluding to someone falling into sin, but this cannot be the meaning. Paul is not suggesting that when a person in one of the churches falls into sin, he does too! The apostle really doesn't give us enough to know what he specifically has in mind, but the kernel is clear. When a person in one of the churches is in need, whether in terms of spiritual peril, material resources, illness, or some other limitation, their apostle is burdened. The needs in the churches affect him, and he is aware of and attentive to those needs. This "weakness," this willingness to suffer for the sake of the gospel, lies at the heart of authentic Christian ministry and sets Paul apart from his opponents.

The second line, "Who is led into sin and I am not livid?" may be read as a particular example of the general "weakness" mentioned in the previous line. In any case, Paul now speaks of a person in the churches as being "led into sin." Used twenty-six times in the Gospels,[42] the verb σκανδαλίζω (*skandalizō*) occurs in Paul only here and twice at 1 Cor. 8:13 (although see the variant at Rom. 14:21), where he writes of not causing a brother or sister to stumble by eating meat that has been offered to an idol. The word carries two primary meanings in the NT literature (BDAG 926). First, it can refer to causing offense, anger, or shock, as at Matt. 15:12: "Then the disciples came up and told Him, 'Do You know that the Pharisees took offense [ἐσκανδαλίσθησαν] when they heard this statement?'" (Matt. 15:12 HCSB). Second, the word can speak of being led astray, caused to experience a spiritual downfall, or led into sin. For instance, one writer prays, "Rule over me, O God, from wicked sin and from every evil woman who causes the foolish to stumble" (Pss. Sol. 16.7 NETS). Similarly, at Matt. 5:29, Jesus says, "If your right eye causes you to sin [σκανδαλίζει], gouge it out and throw it away. For it is better that you lose one of the parts of your body than for your whole body to be thrown into hell" (Matt. 5:29 HCSB). This second meaning probably is what Paul intends at 11:29. Earlier in the chapter, at verse 3, he expressed his fear of the Corinthians being steered away from pure devotion to Christ by false teaching, even as Eve was deceived by the serpent and led into sin. The danger is much more than the Corinthians, or any other believer in Paul's ministry, being offended. Rather, he is burdened when a person falls into sin (cf. 2:6–11).

Such a situation makes him "livid" (πυροῦμαι, *pyroumai*), very angry. The Greek word could be used of something "burning," "being on fire," or being made "hot" (Job 22:25; Pss. 12:6; 66:10 [11:7; 65:10 LXX]; Prov. 10:20; Eph. 6:16; 2 Pet. 3:12; Philo, *Alleg.* 1.67), or it could be used figuratively to speak of

---

42. See σκανδαλίζω in Matt. 5:29–30; 11:6; 13:21, 57; 15:12; 17:27; 18:6, 8–9; 24:10; 26:31, 33 (2x); Mark 4:17; 6:3; 9:42, 43, 45, 47; 14:27, 29; Luke 7:23; 17:2; John 6:61; 16:1.

burning with desire (e.g., 1 Cor. 7:9; Sir. 23:16 [23:17 LXX]) or, as here, to be inflamed with some emotion, whether thanks, sympathy, anger, or indignation (e.g., 2 Macc. 4:38; 10:35; 14:45; 3 Macc. 4:2; Philo, *Alleg.* 1.84; see BDAG 899).[43]

These are glimpses into the anxiety, the emotional weight Paul carries for the churches. In fact, the letter as a whole carries a tremendous sense of Paul's burden as he vies for the hearts, the minds, and the spiritual future of this particular church. If his battle for the Corinthian church, as reflected in 2 Corinthians, is any indication, his anxiety over the dozens of churches around the Mediterranean world must have been great indeed. John Chrysostom (*Hom. Gen.*, homily 57) writes:

> What wonderful affection in a pastor! Others' falls, he is saying, accentuate my grief, others' obstacles inflame the fire of my suffering. Let all those entrusted with the leadership of rational sheep imitate this and not prove inferior to the shepherd who for many years cares for irrational sheep. In that case no harm ensues even if some negligence occurs, but in our case if only one rational sheep is lost or falls to predators, the loss is extreme; the harm, terrible; the punishment, unspeakable. After all, if our Lord did not forbear to pour out his own blood for him, what excuse would such a person deserve for allowing himself to neglect the one so esteemed by the Lord and not making every effort on his part to care for the sheep. (Bray 1999: 299–300)

Reflection

As stated in our introduction to this section, Paul's speech should be read as "a daring countercultural exercise" (Barnett 1997: 529), intended to both highlight and celebrate his weaknesses. The speech thus stands diametrically opposed to what would be deemed appropriate leadership in Corinthian culture. Paul parodies the opponents' ministry, even while giving a clear picture of suffering as inherent to the authentic ministry to which he has been called by God. Having begun with the question of ethnic identity, he then turns to a fourth identity question, which concerns what it means to be identified as a Christian minister. It is on this identity question that the speech turns, for Paul powerfully turns the speech upside down from what might have been expected among the culturally elite in Corinth—he boasts about weaknesses!

The hardship list communicates an overriding theme, a clear thread that runs through the whole and challenges our concepts of why we do what we do in ministry: cost. Authentic ministry, carried out under the lordship of Christ, is costly. There was a cost attached to the ministry of Paul's opponents in Corinth, but the cost was on the side of the church: financial cost, emotional and relational cost, theological cost. The ministry of the interlopers benefited themselves and cost the Corinthians. Paul's ministry, on the other hand, was costly to him personally, and he gladly paid the price to

---

43. Contra Barré (1975: 518), who understands the term to refer to "burning" in the fires of an eschatological ordeal.

carry out his ministry. Speaking on the "false brothers" of 11:26, Augustine (*Letter 208 to Felicia*) says there are two kinds of pastors:

> There are some who occupy the pastoral chair in order to care for the flock of Christ, but there are others who sit in it to gratify themselves by temporal honors and worldly advantages. These are the two kinds of pastors, some dying, some being born, who must needs continue in the Catholic church itself until the end of the world and the judgment of the Lord. If there were such men in the times of the apostles, whom the apostle lamented as false brothers when he said: "Perils from false brothers," yet whom he did not proudly dismiss but bore with them and tolerated them, how much more likely is it that there should be such men in our times. (Bray 1999: 299)

We might examine ourselves and ask, Which kind of minister am I? Whom is my ministry costing? Do I see it as a means of my advancement in the world? Or as a costly means of advancing Christ's agenda in the world? The two approaches to ministry are diametrically opposed.

Additional Notes

11:23. In this verse are four ἐν phrases, and our manuscript evidence shows much turbulence in the word order. The options are as follows:

a. ἐν φυλακαῖς περισσοτέρως, ἐν πληγαῖς ὑπερβαλλόντως (𝔓[46] B D* [2] [0243] 33 629 630. [1739 1881] *pc* lat; Ambst)

b. ἐν πληγαῖς περισσοτέρως, ἐν φυλακαῖς ὑπερβαλλόντως (ℵ* F G; Or)

c. ἐν φυλακαῖς ὑπερβαλλόντως, ἐν πληγαῖς περισσοτέρως (P)

d. ἐν πληγαῖς ὑπερβαλλόντως, ἐν φυλακαῖς περισσοτέρως (ℵ[2] D[1] H Ψ 0121 𝔐 sy[p])

e. ἐν πληγαῖς ὑπερβαλλόντως (Cl)

The final three readings have weak external attestation. Option *a* has the strongest manuscript support; three possible reasons a scribe may have altered this reading as in option *b* emerge. With Harris (2005: 792) and Thrall (2000: 734), perhaps the scribe wanted to highlight a perceived gradation of the severity of each persecution, feeling that imprisonments should follow beatings (whether imprisonments were more severe than beatings is another matter!). Second, the order of imprisonments following beatings is in line with the same two persecutions in the hardship list of chapter 6 (6:5), and the adjustment may have been made under the influence of the earlier list. Third, in reading *b*, the first syllable in each pair share a sound (the π in the first pair; the υ in the second pair), and this phonetic association may have been crafted by a scribe who rearranged the words. In the case of the second and third possibilities, it would be less likely that the scribe would adjust the word order, moving from the form of *b* to *a*. Thus, on both external and internal evidence, reading *a* is preferred.

11:27. The addition of ἐν at the beginning of verse 27 (ℵ[2] H 0121 33 1881 𝔐 lat; Ambst) clearly has been added to bring the lead phrase (κόπῳ καὶ μόχθῳ) into conformity with the prepositional phrases that follow, and perhaps under the influence of 6:5, where the preposition also precedes κόπος. The reading without ἐν (𝔓[46] ℵ* B D F G Ψ 0243 1739 *pc*) has the stronger external support and is the more difficult reading.

11:28. At 11:28 ἐπίστασις (𝔓⁴⁶ ⁹⁹ ℵ B D F G H* 0243 0278 33 81 326 1175 1739 1881 *pc*) is preferred over ἐπισύστασις (Hᶜ lᵛⁱᵈ Ψ 0121 𝔐) on the basis of external evidence (cf. the same variant at Acts 24:12).

11:28. The reading μοι (𝔓⁴⁶ ℵ* B F G H 0278 33 81 1175 *pc* b d) is preferred over μου (ℵ² D Ψ 0121 0243 1739 1881 𝔐 lat; Ambst) on the basis of external support. A scribe may have mistakenly read υ for ι or may have understood Paul to refer to the responsibility embraced by Paul ("my responsibility"), rather than the pressure bearing down "on" him.

5. Paul's Countercultural "Fool's Speech," Part 2 (11:30–12:10)

As noted above, the speech falls into two primary movements. In the first part, 2 Cor. 11:22–29, Paul focuses on trials experienced in his missionary activities. In this second part, 11:30–12:10, the apostle makes a transition (11:30–31) and then recounts three specific experiences from his past. The first and third of these offer striking examples of his weakness. First, he tells of an escape from Damascus early in his ministry, certainly an ignoble (read, "weak") way to leave a city (11:32–33). Then he moves to an account of his "visions and revelations" (12:1) and explains how even these have led to another example of weakness, a "thorn in the flesh" (12:7).

It is clear from the parallel statements at 11:30 and 12:1 that "boasting" continues to be the main theme as the apostle continues the Fool's Speech in part 2.

2 Cor. 11:30	2 Cor. 12:1
Εἰ καυχᾶσθαι δεῖ, τὰ τῆς ἀσθενείας μου καυχήσομαι.	Καυχᾶσθαι δεῖ.
Ei kauchasthai dei, ta tēs astheneias mou kauchēsomai.	*Kauchasthai dei.*
If I have to boast, I will boast about things that display my weakness!	It is necessary to continue boasting.

Yet Paul continues to boast only in his weaknesses. The unit is capped off at 12:10 with a summary of all that has been described since 11:23. Here Paul mentions "weaknesses," "insults," "persecutions," and "difficulties" endured "for the sake of Christ," and all of these are tagged by the apostle with the exclamatory "for when I am weak, then I am strong!" This movement of the Fool's Speech may be outlined as follows:

a. A midpoint transition and an oath (11:30–31)
b. Paul's escape in Damascus (11:32–33)
c. Snatched up to paradise of the third heaven (12:1–4)
d. Boasting only in weaknesses (12:5–6)
e. Paul's thorn in the flesh (12:7–9)
f. Conclusion to the Fool's Speech (12:10)

Exegesis and Exposition

11:30If I have to boast, I will boast about things that display my weakness! 31The God and Father of the Lord Jesus, who is blessed forever, knows that I am not lying.

³²When I was in Damascus, the governor under King Aretas was guarding the city of the Damascenes in order to arrest me ⌜ ⌝, ³³but I was let down in a basket through a window in the city wall and escaped his hands.

¹²:¹⌜It is necessary⌝ to continue boasting. ⌜Although it is not helpful⌝, ⌜nevertheless⌝ I will move on to visions and revelations from the Lord. ²I know a person in Christ who, fourteen years ago—whether in the body or out of the body, I do not know; God knows—was snatched up to the third heaven. ³And I know that such a person— whether in the body or ⌜apart from⌝ the body, I do not know; God knows—⁴was snatched up into paradise and heard words too sacred to tell, words that a person is not permitted to speak. ⁵I will boast on behalf of such a person, but I will not boast on my own behalf, except with regard to weaknesses ⌜ ⌝. ⁶Now, if I want to boast, I will not be acting foolishly, for I will be telling the truth. But I am refraining from doing so in order that a certain person may not evaluate me beyond what he sees in me or ⌜anything⌝ he hears from me. ⁷And due to the extraordinary character of the revelations, ⌜therefore⌝, so that I might not become consumed with self-importance, a thorn in the flesh was given to me, a messenger of Satan, in order that it might beat me, ⌜so that I might not become consumed with self-importance⌝. ⁸I pleaded with the Lord three times about this, so that it might be kept away from me. ⁹But he answered me, "My grace is entirely sufficient for you, for ⌜ ⌝ power is perfected in weakness." Therefore I will boast all the more gladly about ⌜my⌝ weaknesses, so that the power of Christ might take up residence on me. ¹⁰For this reason, I am delighted in weaknesses, in indignities, in crises, in persecutions and troubles for Christ's sake. For when I am weak, then I am strong.

a. A Midpoint Transition and an Oath (11:30–31)

11:30   Having finished his highly crafted list of hardships (11:23–29), Paul now forms a brief summary, or a special transition in the Fool's Speech (11:22–12:10): "If I have to boast, I will boast about things that display my weakness!" We have seen these themes of "boasting" and "weakness" before. He begins, Εἰ καυχᾶσθαι δεῖ (*Ei kauchasthai dei*, If I have to boast), alluding to the fact that the openness of the Corinthians to the opponent missionaries has necessitated that the apostle take extreme measures in the community's spiritual defense. The verb δεῖ speaks here of what Paul feels he must do given the situation. Εἰ plus the present active indicative of this verb assumes this necessity to be a fact: Paul is not stating a hypothetical situation.

Further, Paul has been building up to his boasting (καυχᾶσθαι)[1] via the Fool's Speech since 10:8, mentioning boasting at numerous points along the way (10:13, 15–17; 11:12, 16, 18). His point here comprises his main point for the speech: If he must boast, he will focus his boasting on τὰ τῆς ἀσθενείας (*ta tēs astheneias*), "things that display" the apostle's (μου, *mou*, my) "weakness." The article is neuter plural as an accusative of reference in relation to

---

1. This present infinitive is complementary, completing δεῖ, "it is necessary to boast," or as with our ET, "If I have to boast."

the future indicative verb καυχήσομαι (*kauchēsomai*), "I will boast about the things." The genitive singular τῆς ἀσθενείας may be read as a descriptive genitive, "things characterized by weakness." So all together his main point is that if he is compelled to join the false teachers in boasting, he will boast in his own countercultural way, focusing on various aspects of his ministry that display his weakness. As noted in the introduction to this section of the commentary, 11:30 serves as an important transition between the long list of hardships and two very specific examples of weakness found in 11:32–12:9. Further, references to weakness occur at each major seam or transition point in the speech.

This transition is followed in verse 31 by a doxology combined with a solemn   **11:31** oath: "The God and Father of the Lord Jesus, who is blessed forever, knows that I am not lying." Very early in this letter, at the beginning of his praise to God for encouragement (1:3–7), Paul has blessed "The God and Father of our Lord Jesus Christ" (Εὐλογητὸς ὁ θεὸς καὶ πατὴρ τοῦ κυρίου ἡμῶν Ἰησοῦ Χριστοῦ, *Eulogētos ho theos kai patēr tou kyriou hēmōn Iēsou Christou*), and the doxology here is similar to other such blessings in Paul's writings (cf. Rom. 1:25; 9:5). As in Paul's opening praise of God, the blessing here is offered in a context of reflection on suffering in the cause of Christ. As in 2 Cor. 1:3–7, benediction flows from a reservoir of redemption theology: God works in and through the very hardships Paul has been describing thus far in his speech. Blessing (εὐλογητός, *eulogētos*) has to do with God being "worthy of praise or commendation" (*GELNT* 430) and formed a common aspect of Jewish prayers of the era, the בְּרָכָה (*bĕrākâ*, blessing), such as the Eighteen Benedictions (the Shemoneh Esreh; lit., Eighteen), which repeats "Blessed art Thou, O Lord."[2] In Paul's blessing of 11:31, God is blessed "forever" (εἰς τοὺς αἰῶνας, *eis tous aiōnas*), meaning "into all eternity" (BDAG 32). Thus Paul's ministry of hardship, and the integrity of that ministry, is grounded in a relationship with the eternally blessed God. The temporal finds its stability in the Eternal One. Further, God is "the God and Father of our Lord Jesus," and this confession makes the blessing christologically oriented (cf. Eph. 1:3–14; 1 Pet. 1:3–12). Thus, in the middle of his "boasting" about his sufferings, Paul models for the Corinthians authentic Christian ministry, a ministry profoundly related to God in Christ and profoundly sacrificial in its commitment to Christ's mission (Welborn 2001: 57–59).

Yet Paul knits this blessing with an oath. Earlier in the letter, at 1:23, Paul had called upon God as a witness to the truthfulness of his reason why he has failed to visit the Corinthians as earlier planned; and at 11:10–11, Paul has solemnly declared his resolute commitment to sticking with his established pattern of ministry to the Corinthians. Here, when the apostle says, "God . . . knows that I am not lying," he appeals to Truth himself as the ultimate

---

2. With Barrett (1973: 58), it is somewhat immaterial whether we read the blessing as indicative or optative, though the Jewish liturgical context would favor the former. As Barrett notes, a blessing is a blessing.

verifier of his statement (cf. Rom. 9:1; 1 Tim. 2:7). This is a strong way of solemnly assuring the Corinthians of the truthfulness of what he is saying. But of what specifically does he speak? Some understand this solemn assurance to relate to the account in the next two verses of his escape from Damascus (Witherington 1995: 458). Others understand it to relate to the list of Paul's hardships already mentioned in the speech (Windisch and Strecker 1970: 362). Still others see the oath as related to the proclamation of 11:30, that Paul only boasts in his weaknesses (Martin 1986: 384; Scott 1998: 220; Thrall 2000: 762–63), or perhaps a combination of this boast with the weaknesses that follow (Harris 2005: 818).

If we agree with those who suggest that the oath primarily relates to verse 30, we will not be far from the mark, for that proclamation of boasting in weakness, as we have demonstrated, is a structural feature that reaches both backward and forward in the speech, playing a significant role in tying the whole together.[3] Thus, what Paul solemnly assures the Corinthians is that this posture of boating in weakness is Paul's true posture for his ministry, and the posture plays out in his willingness to suffer for the cause of Christ, including the example Paul now gives of his near escape in Damascus.[4]

b. Paul's Escape in Damascus (11:32–33)

11:32–33   Now Paul offers a very specific illustration of his weakness, recounting an event from the earliest days of his ministry and riveting attention on the place of his call to ministry.[5] In 11:32–33 he writes, "When I was in Damascus the governor under King Aretas was guarding the city of the Damascenes in order to arrest me, but I was let down in a basket through a window in the city wall and escaped his hands." The relationship between this story and the hardship list of 11:23b–29 is not one of contrast, with the strengths of the list now counterbalanced by a glaring weakness (contra Matera 2003: 273). Rather, the brief account builds on the listed weaknesses by giving the first of two specific examples from the apostle's "weak" ministry.

Paul was converted on the road to Damascus (Δαμασκός, *Damaskos*; Acts 9:1–8) and spent his first days as a believer and Christian minister there (Acts 9:9–24). We know from Gal. 1:17 that he left Damascus for Arabia, that is, Nabatea, probably preaching the Word of God there, as he had done in Damascus. "After many days had gone by" in Acts 9:23 probably refers to the period that Paul spent away from Damascus. After returning to that city from

---

3. As pointed out in the comments on 12:1, the repetition of καυχᾶσθαι δεῖ (*kauchasthai dei*, it is necessary to boast) and ὁ θεὸς οἶδεν (*ho theos oiden*, God knows) at 11:30–31 and 12:1–3 provides parallel introductions to the accounts of the Damascus deliverance and the ascent to heaven.

4. Belleville (1996: 295) whimsically calls this "Daring Escapades."

5. In the Greek text, the words rendered "in Damascus" (ἐν Δαμασκῷ, *en Damaskō*) stand first in the sentence for emphasis. In this way, Paul rivets attention on the place of his conversion and call to ministry (Hafemann 2000: 444).

Nabatea, he then had to flee by being let down in a basket through the wall (Acts 9:25; 2 Cor. 11:32–33).

Although Acts focuses on "the Jews" who conspired to kill the apostle, keeping watch on the city gates (9:23–24), Paul writes here that an official serving under King Aretas was guarding the city in order to arrest him. This was Aretas IV, who ruled the desert kingdom east, south, and southwest of the Dead Sea from about 9 BC to AD 40 and had his capital in Petra.[6] As explained below, during this period in Paul's ministry Aretas's power may have reached far north to Damascus, and it may be that Paul's preaching of the Messiah prompted an aggressive response from the king.

The term ἐθνάρχης (*ethnarchēs*) could be interpreted as "governor," but some doubt that the Nabateans had control of Damascus at this period (Harding 1993). Yet Douglas Campbell (2002: 285, 287–98) has pointed out that in AD 36 Aretas successfully defeated Antipas and probably gained control of Damascus for a brief time. Moreover, it has been shown from inscriptional evidence that Nabatean leaders could hold several titles, and thus Aretas may have appointed a Nabatean chieftain to be "governor" of Damascus after its annexation. The primary alternative, therefore, is to read ἐθνάρχης (*ethnarchēs*) as referring to the head of the ethnic community of Nabateans in Damascus, acting under the direction of King Aretas. It is entirely possible that the Nabateans were working with the local Jewish leaders to address a mutual "enemy." In both the Acts account and here in 2 Cor. 11, the city gates were guarded (ἐφρούρει τὴν πόλιν, *ephrourei tēn polin*), prompting Paul's escape through a window in the wall of the city.[7] He was let down "in a basket" (ἐν σαργάνῃ, *en sarganē*), which would have been a large basket, or a woven or netted workbag, for carrying hay, straw, or wool (Bruce 1971: 245).

But how is this event so significant that Paul recounts it here? Basically, escape as a fugitive from a city, by night, and in a basket would be an ignoble form of transportation, a position of "weakness," standing in stark contrast to the position of status and "authority" with which he had set out for Damascus (Acts 9:1–2)! The "honor" of being commissioned by the high priest in Jerusalem, had turned to the "shame" of being a fugitive for Christ. The persecutor had become the persecuted (Hafemann 2000: 443–44). Some have suggested that being let down from the wall would then lead to Paul's account of being lifted up to heaven in the next unit, and this may be the case as well.

6. Aretas's daughter was married to Herod Antipas, who divorced her to marry the former wife of his brother Philip (Matt. 14:3–4). Aretas had a border dispute with Antipas in AD 36 and defeated Antipas's army, thus for a brief time putting the Nabatean ruler in conflict with Rome (Josephus, *Ant.* 18.109–26; Harris 2005: 821).

7. Holland (1993: 250) notes the parallels with OT accounts of Josh. 2:8–15 and 1 Sam. 19:12, but these do not seem to be alluded to specifically. Even less certain is that Paul has in mind an inversion of the Roman military honor called the *corona muralis*, the "wall crown," given to the first Roman soldier to scale the wall in an attack on an enemy city (contra Witherington 1995: 458–59).

c. Snatched Up to Paradise of the Third Heaven (12:1–4)

The passage now before us stands as one of the most debated in Pauline literature, due in part to the uncertainty surrounding a number of interpretive variables. For instance, since it appears to be a "strength" rather than a "weakness," why does Paul include this vision/revelation experience in his Fool's Speech? What is the nature of the experience? Is it a vision and/or a revelation *from* the Lord or *about* the Lord? Does the apostle speak of his own experience, the experience of one of his associates in ministry, or an experience about which his opponents have boasted (and thus a parody)? If this tells us of Paul's experience, why does he speak of "such a person," rather than mentioning himself directly? If this is Paul's experience, do we have other references to this experience in Scripture? What is the "third heaven" and "paradise," and what (if we can know anything about the experience at all) did Paul see or hear? Last but not least, what was Paul's "thorn in the flesh," that "messenger of Satan" that God used to keep him from becoming consumed with his own self-importance? Having sorted out these questions and their possible answers, we also will want to ask about the relevance of Paul's account for those who want to be engaged in authentic Christian ministry today.

12:1   This verse begins with Καυχᾶσθαι δεῖ (*Kauchasthai dei*), "It is necessary to continue boasting." At four points in this section of 2 Corinthians, Paul makes clear that only under compulsion does he join the foolish boasting[8] of his opponents: in the introduction to the speech (11:18–19), just following its conclusion (12:11), at the seam separating the hardship list from the account of Paul's escape from Damascus (11:30), and here at the seam separating the account of the escape from Damascus and Paul's ascent to heaven (12:1). Clearly the apostle's words on the necessity of his foolish boast seem strategically placed for emphasis.

The assertion here at 12:1 matches the words from the conditional clause at 11:30. In addition, each of these expressions of necessity are followed by "God knows" (ὁ θεὸς . . . οἶδεν (*ho theos . . . oiden*):

11:30	Εἰ καυχᾶσθαι δεῖ	If I have to boast
11:31	ὁ θεὸς . . . οἶδεν.	God . . . knows.
12:1	Καυχᾶσθαι δεῖ.	It is necessary to continue boasting.
12:2, 3	ὁ θεὸς οἶδεν. (2x)	God knows.

As noted in our discussion on the structure of this section, the repetition of καυχᾶσθαι δεῖ serves to mark key turning points in the speech,[9] specifically

---

8. On the biblical concept of "boasting" and its function in 2 Corinthians, see the comments on 10:8.

9. Runge (2010: 151) writes that if a discourse orienter is repeated in the middle of a speech, one function of such a placement is "to mark the introduction of a new point within the same reported speech."

forming "parallel introductions"[10] to each of Paul's more specific illustrations of his weakness. These parallel introductions, moreover, reiterate the main theme of the apostle's speech, "boasting about weakness."

Here, as with the use of δεῖ at 11:30, the verb speaks of necessity, what Paul feels he needs to do given the current threat to the Corinthians posed by the interlopers. In rhetoric, "'necessity' was a major justification for deeds otherwise considered inappropriate" (Hermogenes, *Issues* 7.6–19, as cited in Keener 2005: 237). Since the false teachers are boasting "according to human standards" (lit., the flesh; 11:18) and being embraced by at least some in the Corinthian church (11:19), Paul feels compelled to join in boasting. As with our translation, the complementary present infinitive can be read as progressive, "to *continue* boasting," since Paul speaks about the "boast" as an ongoing activity in which he is currently involved (i.e., he is in the middle of this "boasting" speech). This "seam" in the structure of the speech constitutes a momentary "coming up for air" as the apostle marks a transition to a new topic—the "visions and revelations from the Lord."

But though boasting is necessary, Paul again makes clear his assessment of such a foolish form of boasting (as opposed to "boasting in the Lord," 10:17), qualifying the "boasting stratagem" (11:17) with οὐ συμφέρον μέν (*ou sympheron men*), "Although it is not helpful." The negated (οὐ) present participle is concessive ("Although"), and together with the μεν . . . δέ construction, means "Although . . . nevertheless." In this context the verbal idea communicated by the participle means "to be useful," or "helpful," or advantageous in some way (1 Cor. 6:12; 10:23; 2 Cor. 8:10). At 1 Cor. 6:12 he had written the Corinthians, "'All things are lawful for me'–but not everything is *beneficial* [συμφέρει, *sympherei*]" (NET). So, even though boasting is not really advantageous, or beneficial, "nevertheless" Paul "will move on to visions and revelations from the Lord." Why? Because "much more could be lost if Paul does not somehow cancel out the seductive megalomania of his rivals" (Garland 1999: 508), and taking the Fool's Speech to its climactic and "thorny" conclusion will serve Paul's strategy. The future indicative ἐλεύσομαι (*eleusomai*, from ἔρχομαι, *erchomai*, come, go) speaks of movement, in this case proceeding or "moving on to" (εἰς, *eis*; so Furnish 1984: 513) the next point in the speech.

The terms rendered as "visions" (ὀπτασίας, *optasias*) and "revelations" (ἀποκαλύψεις, *apokalypseis*) are plural, and thus the apostle may be providing a general heading, which will then be followed by a specific example, the ascent to heaven. "Visions" involve the intersection of the heavenly and earthly realms in some way and, in the NT for instance, can speak of the appearance[11]

10. On parallel introductions, see Guthrie 1994: 104–5.
11. In the LXX (Add. Esth. 14:16; Sir. 43:2, 16; Mal. 3:2) ὀπτασία has to do with an "appearance" of some sort, natural or supernatural. Another term, ὅρασις (*horasis*), which can speak of a "seeing" event, is much more common in the OT and also occurs in the NT (Acts 2:17; Rev. 4:3; 9:17); and ὅραμα (*horama*, vision) is also common in the NT (Matt. 17:9; Acts 7:31; 9:10, 12; 10:3, 17, 19; 11:5; 12:9; 16:9–10; 18:9).

of angelic beings (Luke 1:22; 24:23), or, as with Paul's apocalyptic encounter on the road to Damascus, an encounter with the exalted Christ (Acts 26:19). Visions were common in both the prophetic (e.g., Ezek. 1:1; Isa. 6:1; Jer. 1:11; Dan. 7:1; 10:5–7) and the apocalyptic literatures (e.g., 1 En. 1.2; 2 Bar. 81.4), and according to Joel 2//Acts 2:17 are a characteristic experience of God's people "in the last days."[12] Some of the visions Paul had seen by this point in his ministry are recorded in Acts, including his vision of Ananias laying hands on him (9:11–12), the vision of the man from Macedonia asking for help (16:9–10), a vision of encouragement during his early days in Corinth (!) (18:9–10), and a visionary experience during a visit to the temple in Jerusalem (22:17–21). Other visions would occur later (Acts 23:11; 27:23–24).

The term "revelations" refers to a "disclosure" of some kind (Luke 2:32; Rom. 2:5; 8:19; 16:25; 1 Cor. 1:7; 14:6, 26; 2 Thess. 1:7; 1 Pet. 1:7, 13), and it is clear from what follows that words were "disclosed" to Paul in the specific encounter he has in mind (see 12:4). In fact, such "revelations" seem to be the focus in verse 7. The genitive κυρίου (*kyriou*) relates both to "visions" and "revelations," but should we understand Jesus as the source of the visions and revelations ("from the Lord")? Or is κυρίου an objective genitive ("of the Lord"), with Jesus as the object or focus of the visions and revelations? In line with the latter interpretation, Paul saw the risen Lord at his conversion (1 Cor. 9:1; 15:8; Gal. 1:16; Lambrecht 1999: 200). But it is equally true that at each revelatory encounter the Lord disclosed information to him (Gal. 1:12–16), and as Harris (2005: 833) notes, elsewhere in Paul when ἀποκάλυψις (*apokalypsis*) is followed by the genitive (Rom. 2:5; 8:19; 1 Cor. 1:7; Gal. 1:12), the genitive speaks of the content of the revelation. Certainly an emphasis is placed on content for this particular experience as Paul's account continues (12:4, 7, 9). After considering all the evidence, Paul in some way recognized where he was during his transport (i.e., to "the third heaven," "paradise"), and thus it may be arbitrary to set what Paul saw over against what he heard in his various "visions and revelations."[13] Both what was seen and what was heard must have been overwhelming.

12:2–4   With verse 2 Paul provides a specific example of these "visions and revelations from the Lord," recounting, "I know a person in Christ who, fourteen years ago—whether in the body or out of the body, I do not know; God knows— was snatched up to the third heaven." In validating his own experiences and motives in this letter, Paul has appealed both to what he knows (e.g., 1:7; 4:14; 5:1, 6, 11, 16) and what God knows or is aware of (1:23; 2:17; 4:2; 5:11; 7:1, 12; 11:11, 31) at several points thus far. Now he writes, "I know a person in Christ" (οἶδα ἄνθρωπον ἐν Χριστῷ, *oida anthrōpon en Christō*). The verb οἶδα had a range of meanings in the first century, including to "respect," "honor," "recall," "be aware of," "understand," "recognize," "experience,"

---

12. On "visions" in Greco-Roman and Jewish writers of the era, see Keener 2005: 170–71.

13. It is also possible to interpret "visions" and "revelations" as a hendiadys, something like "visionary revelations" or "revelatory visions" (Lambrecht 1999: 200).

"understand how" something is done, "be intimately acquainted with," or "to have information about" someone or something (BDAG 693–94). The apostle may simply mean that he is "aware of" a certain person, or that he "has information about" that person, but the nature of the acquaintance as described in the following sentences speaks of intimacy or close personal relationship. Further, what Paul knows (A), what he does not know (B), and what God knows (C) form the highly crafted, structural backbone of 12:2–3 (similar to Barnett 1997: 559–60). The translation here is a bit more straightforward to mark the parallels more accurately:

> A I know a *person* in Christ
> >   who, fourteen years ago—
> > >   whether in the body
> >   B¹ I do not know
> > >   or out of the body,
> >   B² I do not know;
> >   C God knows—
> > >   *such was snatched up to the third heaven.*
> A And I know that *such a person*—
> >   whether in the body or apart from the body,
> >   B I do not know;
> >   C God knows—
> > >   *was snatched up into paradise and*
> > >   heard words too sacred to tell,
> > > >   words that are not appropriate
> >   for a *person* to speak.

Notice in this structure (a) the ABCABC pattern; (b) the triple reference to "a person" (ἄνθρωπος, *anthrōpos*), found at the beginning, middle, and end; (c) the parallel references to "such" (τὸν τοιοῦτον, *ton toiouton*); (d) the parallel statements, "whether in the body or out of/apart from the body," each of which precede (e) the parallel statements about being "snatched/caught up" to "the third heaven/paradise." The significance of this parallelism will become more clear momentarily.

But of whom does Paul speak? He describes the person (ἄνθρωπον, *anthrōpon*) simply as "in Christ" (ἐν Χριστῷ, *en Christō*), a common Pauline phrase that here is equivalent to affirming that the person is a "Christian."[14] Scholars have offered three main options for this person's identity:

1. *Paul speaks of a ministry partner who had a vision experience.* In this case, he uses the experience of a fellow Christian as an example since he himself was more oriented to "revelations" and was suspicious of

---

14. The dative is understood as a dative of relationship, "in relationship with Christ."

visionary experiences as potentially manipulative when used in ministry contexts (Goulder 1994b: 53).[15]

2. *Paul offers a parody of the visionary experience of his opponents*, presenting the experience of words as ending with a lack of communication (Furnish 1984: 533), just as the following request for divine healing ends without healing (Betz 1972: 72–100).[16]

3. *Paul speaks of his own experience*, although in a strikingly reserved and unusual way.[17]

There are at least two main reasons for accepting this third position as the correct reading of the passage. First, the whole context concerns Paul's own boast about aspects of his ministry, and "moving on to visions and revelations" fits the flow of Paul's boasting more naturally if it refers to his own experience. Second, the purpose of the "thorn," to keep Paul from becoming self-consumed (12:7), only makes sense if the ascent to heaven was Paul's own experience and thus a temptation to pride.

If this is the correct position, we still need to ascertain why Paul speaks of his experience in the third person. Certainly this mode of reference gives a sense of distance between Paul and the event as described, but this hardly means that he does not see the visionary experience as relevant to his apostolic ministry (as with Furnish 1984: 544; Lincoln 1979: 210), for Paul most certainly has a reason for sharing it here! It is relevant that such a third-person approach to relating one's own experience was used at points in rhetoric to deflect attention from oneself, thus reducing the offense of boasting about oneself (Keener 2005: 238), and Paul's whole posture in his "boasting" involves humbly focusing attention on the Lord and not on himself. He would have been aware of the great exemplars of faith who had been snatched up to the heavens, and he doesn't want to be seen as claiming a place of honor among them (Garland 1999: 511). Furthermore, in such ecstatic experiences the visionary at times has a profound sense of "self-transcendence," of being apart from oneself and observing oneself as the event unfolds (e.g., 3 Bar. 17.3; Thrall 2000: 782), and his own experience of "self-transcendence" could have affected Paul's mode of narrating the ascent. All of these insights offer reasonable explanations.

But primarily it seems that the apostle uses the technique as a way simultaneously (a) to note a "strength" that gives rise to the account of a major

---

15. For astute criticism of Goulder's position, see Thrall 2000: 779.

16. See esp. Betz's classification of the passage as parody (1972: 84). The reference to the person as "in Christ" does not necessarily rule out this position, for the parody could include the opponents' claim to be followers of Jesus. However, it seems questionable whether parody is the appropriate genre for understanding the account (so Garland 1999: 511; Matera 2003: 276).

17. Betz's (1972: 84) "parody" position is rejected, e.g., by W. Baird (1985: 658, 661–62), who suggests that Paul refuses to base his authority on his own visionary experiences, even though he has had such experiences about which he could boast. His sufferings are the only credentials Paul embraces as validating his ministry.

weakness,[18] his "thorn in the flesh"; and (b) to distance himself at the moment from that experience in order to keep the focus on his weaknesses. Thus Paul's main interest in even mentioning his ascent to heaven is that it affords him an opportunity to talk about the thorn. But since he chooses to mention the extraordinary encounter with God, he insists on talking about it in a way that makes clear he is not inappropriately boasting about one of the most amazing spiritual experiences of his life.[19]

That Paul speaks of a personal experience is further supported by his knowledge of the exact date of the event: "fourteen years ago" (πρὸ ἐτῶν δεκατεσσάρων, *pro etōn dekatessarōn*). When referring to time, the preposition πρό usually refers to a point in time "before" or "earlier" than a specified event (BDAG 864), but here it seems to mean "fourteen years ago" (so, e.g., ESV, HCSB, NASB, NIV, NLT², NRSV, NET; cf. John 12:1; BDF 114 for the temporal usage).[20] This would place Paul's heavenly ascent at about AD 40–42, during his time of ministry in Syria and Cilicia; considering Paul's other letters and the account of his ministry in Acts, we have no known record of this particular experience elsewhere.[21] This reference to "fourteen years" may be the apostle's way of underscoring both the event as a fact in his personal history, but also (especially if he had never mentioned the experience before) the long period of silence that he now is breaking (so Harris 2005: 837). After all, he had "heard words too sacred to tell, words that a person is not permitted to speak." This may be Paul's way of explaining why he has never mentioned the ascent to the Corinthians before, but admittedly this reading assumes that now, given the circumstances at Corinth, the Lord has granted him permission to at least communicate the event, if not the specific words he heard. Nevertheless, it also seems clear that Paul does not want to be evaluated on the basis of such an experience, as we will see momentarily (12:6).

Here and in verse 4 the apostle explains that he was "snatched up." Both the aorist passive participle[22] in verse 2 and the aorist passive indicative in verse 4 are from ἁρπάζω (*harpazō*), a word that could mean taking something away suddenly, as in the case of a person being grabbed and taken away by a wild animal (e.g., Gen. 37:33; Ps. 7:3 [7:2 ET]), or a thief stealing someone's property (Matt. 12:29). The term could also refer to a person suddenly being

---

18. I agree with Gooder (2006: 213), who writes, "One thing is clear: ascent is not the primary purpose of the passage here. Paul's interest is the true nature of apostleship not the correct attitude to ascent. Indeed the matter of ascent seems of little interest to the apostle. In contrast to the message about the true nature of apostleship the issue of ascent into heaven seems to fade into insignificance."

19. It may well be that the opponents have been boasting in their own revelatory experiences (Barrett 1973: 306; Georgi 1986: 282; Martin 1986: 403; Matera 2003: 276).

20. At Gal. 2:1 Paul notes that "after fourteen years" (διὰ δεκατεσσάρων ἐτῶν, *dia dekatessarōn etōn*) of ministry in Syria and Cilicia, he went up again to Jerusalem.

21. See the helpful chart in Harris (2005: 836–37) lining out the visions or revelations of Paul recorded in Scripture. Gooder (2006: 8) notes that among the visionary experiences mentioned in the NT, the event recounted here is unique among those by and about Paul.

22. This is a "theological passive," and God as the "actor" is understood (Harris 2005: 837).

taken away in supernatural movement, as when Philip was "snatched up" by the Spirit (Acts 8:39), or when at the end of the age believers will be "caught up" to be with the Lord in the air (1 Thess. 4:17). In John's apocalyptic vision, the Christ was "caught up" to God's throne (Rev. 12:5). Such movement between heaven and earth is perhaps the most distinguishing feature of apocalyptic literature of the era (e.g., 1 En. 39.3–4; 52.1; Wis. 4:10–11; Apoc. Mos. 37.3). Thus Paul's experience involved suddenly being "snatched up," transported to the very presence of God in "the third heaven" and "paradise."[23]

Scholars often suggest that there existed various Jewish cosmologies in the first century, literatures of the day making reference to three, four, seven, and even ten "heavens."[24] Although it seems that some views of multiple heavens may have existed in the first century, what is not clear is how widespread or how developed these views were. The highly developed cosmologies often referred to, from such texts as 2 Enoch, may have been earlier but most likely were from a period after Paul's time. It may well be that this reference from Paul to the "third heaven" (12:2) is "one of the few indications of a multiple-heavens cosmology that we can confidently date to the first-century CE" (Pennington 2007: 129).[25] A recent study by Gooder (2006), moreover, concludes that beyond the general narrative of a living person ascending to a multilevel heaven, the similarities between Paul's account in 2 Cor. 12 and other ascent narratives are nonexistent.[26]

Yet there are good reasons for understanding Paul's reference to "the third heaven" as speaking of the highest heavenly realm, God's throne room in the heavenly temple's holy of holies, and that this "third heaven" has a direct relationship to "paradise" mentioned in verse 4.[27] The word "paradise"

23. In 12:2 the occurrence of τὸν τοιοῦτον (ton toiouton, such a person) probably is due to the participle being so far removed from its subject, ἄνθρωπον (anthrōpon, person), these words being separated by the parenthetical statement (εἴτε . . . οἶδεν, eite . . . oiden, whether . . . knows). Notice that the term occurs in each of the clauses having to do with being caught/snatched up to the heavenly realm.

24. See, e.g., Lincoln 1979: 212–13. Pennington (2007: 99–103) points out that the belief in multiple levels of heaven, found in the later rabbinic and apocalyptic literatures, does not have its source in the MT or the LXX (particularly references to "the heavens of the heavens"), as some have supposed.

25. Collins (1995: 46) writes, "The familiar pattern of ascent through a numbered series of heavens, usually seven, is not attested in Judaism before the Christian era. . . . For a Jewish writer who claims to have ascended to heaven (apart from 4QM), we must wait until St. Paul."

26. Gooder (2006: 212–13) notes that none of the major motifs found in other ascent accounts (e.g., angelic guides, vision of a throne, fear, a specific revelation) are found here. However, Gooder concludes that Paul was familiar with ascent traditions in other literatures and subverts the tradition to make a point. Yet Paul's ascent is a failed ascent, since it ends in the thorn. J. Wallace (2011: 166, 169–230, 289–331), on the other hand, agrees that Paul does not replicate other ascent traditions found in Greco-Roman and Jewish literatures of the day, but he understands Paul's ascent experience as having a positive spiritual message for the Corinthians; such experiences must lead to humility, which in turn leads to power, a power grounded in a direct experience of God.

27. Some have understood Paul to refer to two different ascents here, one to the third heaven and another to paradise. Plummer notes, e.g., that patristic authors generally seem to read in

(παράδεισος, *paradeisos*) originally was used of parks belonging to the Persian king and his nobles, and it was picked up by the LXX with reference to the garden of Eden (Thrall 2000: 792; Gen. 2:8; 13:10; Ezek. 28:13; 31:8). Thus it came to be identified with God's transcendent place of blessedness (1 En. 32.3; cf. 20.7; T. Levi 18.10). In both Apoc. Mos. 37.5 and 2 En. 8.1 the paradise is identified with the third heaven. Morray-Jones (1993: 268) has shown, moreover, that paradise in some traditions was associated with the holy of holies in the heavenly temple and thus the very presence of God.[28] It may be, therefore, that Paul was taken into the very presence of God in the heavenly holy of holies.

In parallel fashion (2 Cor. 12:2–3) the apostle confesses ignorance as to whether he was "in the body" or "out of the body" when the vision took place. At 5:8, grappling with his mortality, Paul writes that he, "would rather be away from the body and at home with the Lord." Perhaps this earlier experience of ascent to heaven had encouraged him in that direction! Yet there is an ambiguity to this ascent. In some Jewish apocalyptic texts, it seems that only the soul goes into the heavenly realm, but in others the person still seems to be in "the body" (Thrall 2000: 787–88). The point is that since such an event is so outside the realm of normal experience, Paul could not be sure exactly what happened to him in this regard. Rowland (1982: 383) writes that Paul's reference to his agnosticism about the particulars of the event is "an indication of the overwhelming impact the experience had on the apostle, with the result that he was at a loss to explain adequately how he had experienced the ascent." He did not know for sure whether he was taken to heaven in his body or apart from it. But God knows.

The only aspect of Paul's experience we are told about is that he "heard words too sacred to tell, words which a person is not permitted to speak" (12:4). The paradoxical nature of the encounter is illustrated by Paul saying he heard ἄρρητα ῥήματα (*arrēta rhēmata*), "unutterable words," in part a slap at the audacity of "boasting" about the things of God (Keener 2005: 239). The term ἄρρητος (*arrētos*) could refer either to something that *cannot* be expressed, since the words are beyond human ability, or to something that *must not* be expressed because they are too holy to speak and thus forbidden (BDAG 134). The relative clause that follows, ἃ οὐκ ἐξὸν ἀνθρώπῳ λαλῆσαι (*ha ouk exon anthrōpō lalēsai*, that a person is not permitted to speak), seems to clarify matters. The key term here is ἐξόν (*exon*), from ἔξεστιν (*exestin*). Although the word could refer to something being in the realm of possibility (e.g., Acts 2:29), the dominant use in the first century seems to have been to

---

the account either two ascents or one ascent in two stages, and Plummer (1915: 344) himself prefers the two-ascents position. Still others understand Paul to say he passed through the third heaven on his way to paradise. It is better, however, to understand the third heaven and paradise as associated in some way.

28. Hood (2011: 363, 365) suggests that the tripartite conception of heaven parallels the triadic sanctuary arrangements adumbrated by the garden of Eden, the tabernacle, the temple. Hood proposes that Paul saw not only the enthroned Christ but also the church enthroned with him.

refer to something that is right, permitted, or authorized (BDAG 349).[29] Thus Paul was not allowed to reveal the words that had been spoken to him.

d. Boasting Only in Weaknesses (12:5–6)

12:5 In telling of his heavenly ascent (12:2–4), Paul has briefly departed from the speech's resolute focus on boasting in weakness. For this astounding spiritual experience certainly would qualify as a "strength," that is, a powerful validation of Paul's apostleship. By sharing the account in the third person, however, the apostle has objectified the experience to a certain extent, maintaining a sense of distance between himself and his experience, as if he was detached from the experience and looking on. But he now puts the account in perspective, orienting it to his larger program of boasting (Barnett 1997: 563), restating his commitment to boasting only in his weaknesses (12:5b).

Verse 5 presents nicely balanced clauses in Greek:

ὑπὲρ τοῦ τοιούτου καυχήσομαι (*hyper tou toioutou kauchēsomai*)
ὑπὲρ δὲ ἐμαυτοῦ οὐ καυχήσομαι (*hyper de emautou ou kauchēsomai*)

I will boast on behalf of such a person,
but I will not boast on my own behalf.

As we saw in the previous unit, the "such a person" (τοῦ τοιούτου) really refers to Paul himself, but Paul presented as an objectified third party; again, this is a device by which the apostle maintains some distance between his present program of boasting and his ascent to heaven. When he says, "I will boast," the future-tense verb communicates a gnomic idea, by which such boasting is stated generically.[30] Paul in effect says, "I am willing to boast on behalf of such a person." With both uses of ὑπέρ (*hyper*, on behalf of) in verse 5, the preposition functions as "a marker indicating that an activity or event is in some entity's interest" (BDAG 1030), and the δέ (*de*, but) separating the two main clauses in the verse sets up a contrast between that about which the apostle will boast and that about which he is not willing to boast. He will boast on behalf of the person in the ascent narrative (i.e., himself), and he won't boast on behalf of himself. Rather than contradictory, the contrast embodies Paul's strategy in the Fool's Speech, as demonstrated by the qualification he adds: "except with regard to weaknesses" (εἰ μὴ ἐν ταῖς ἀσθενείαις, *ei mē en*

---

29. The NT Gospels use ἔξεστιν to speak of what is "unlawful" (Matt. 12:2, 4, 10, 12; 14:4; 19:3; 20:15; 22:17; 27:6; Mark 2:24, 26; 3:4; 6:18; 10:2; 12:14; Luke 6:2, 4, 9; 14:3; 20:22; John 5:10; 18:31). In Acts it also is used with reference to what is legal or permissible (16:21; 21:37; 22:25). The two occasions where it is used earlier in the Corinthian correspondence, the term carries the sense of what is "permissible" (1 Cor. 6:12; 10:23). There are other apocalyptic encounters in which the visionary is not allowed to speak what has been revealed (e.g., Dan. 12:4).

30. He is not stating his intention to boast about the ascent in the future (predictive). Nor is it "deliberative" (asking a question) or "imperatival" (giving a command). On the rare gnomic future, see D. Wallace 1996: 571.

tais astheneiais).[31] His present program will not permit him to use his experience of the ascent to heaven as an item for boasting (but he astutely has let the Corinthians know about it nonetheless!). He has shared that experience for another purpose, to introduce one of the great weaknesses of his life, his thorn in the flesh.

Nevertheless, at the beginning of verse 6 he points out that even if he wanted   **12:6**
to boast about the experience, it would not constitute foolishness, for he would simply be recounting an experience that really happened: "Now, if I want to boast, I will not be acting foolishly, for I will be telling the truth." Both uses of the conjunction γάρ (*gar*) are explanatory but with slightly different nuances. The first gives clarification[32] ("Now") in light of Paul's commitment to boasting only in his weaknesses (12:5). Paul clarifies that boasting about the ascent experience would not be wrong, on the level with the "foolishness" on offer from his opponents. Thus, if he preferred (θελήσω, *thelēsō*) to boast about it at some point in the future,[33] he would not be "acting foolishly" (οὐκ ἔσομαι ἄφρων, *ouk esomai aphrōn*; lit., I will not be foolish) as the opponents have been doing (11:19), acting out of line with prudence or good judgment (BDAG 159). He has already made clear that not all boasting is foolish (10:17–18), and if Paul boasts about the ascent, we can assume that he does so appropriately, "boasting in the Lord."

    The second γάρ offers an explanation of why boasting about his ascent to heaven will not constitute foolishness if he decides to boast in that experience. He writes simply, "For I will be telling the truth."[34] The future tense verb (ἐρῶ, *erō*, from λέγω) is predictive and stated as a fact. If in the event that Paul wishes to tell about the experience of his ascent to heaven, the telling will reflect his commitment to the truth (ἀλήθεια, *alētheia*). Earlier in the letter the apostle has already made clear that he lives before God and commends himself to every person's conscience "by public proclamation of the truth" (4:2; cf. 6:7). Further, Paul is a truth teller (7:14), not a liar, and all he does in his ministry stems from a profound commitment to the truth as he has received it from Christ (11:10). This reference to truth at 12:6, moreover, certainly has to do with content (he speaks of an event that really happened) but more than mere content. The import is not just that Paul has his facts straight, but rather that he speaks truthfully or dependably (cf. 7:14; 1 Cor. 5:8), a posture that stands in contrast to speaking foolishly.

---

31. The prepositional phrase introduced by ἐν communicates the idea, "with reference to."

32. This is a case in which γάρ is fairly synonymous with δέ (*de*; BDAG 190) and is therefore interpreted similarly to Lambrecht (1999: 202), who reads the conjunction as adversative.

33. The construction in 12:6 is ἐάν (*ean*, if) + the aorist subjunctive (θελήσω, *thelēsō*, I want) + an aorist complementary infinitive (καυχήσασθαι, *kauchēsasthai*, to boast). The clause functions as a generalized statement comparable to "If in the event that I want to boast about the ascent . . ." In the apodosis the use of the future tense probably indicates that Paul is thinking of some point in the future.

34. This may be a swipe at the opponents, implying that their boasted spiritual experiences were not really true (see Barrett 1971: 245; 1973: 73).

Paul further explains his rationale for that commitment to only boast in his weaknesses—he doesn't want to be evaluated on the basis of an experience like the ascent but rather on the basis of what may be observed in a face-to-face ministry encounter (v. 6b). The term φείδομαι (*pheidomai*) can refer to sparing someone from trouble, as it does at 1:23 (similarly, Acts 20:29; Rom. 8:32; 11:21; 1 Cor. 7:28), but here the verb means "to refrain" from doing something: "But I am refraining from doing so" (φείδομαι δέ, *pheidomai de*). The mild contrast inherent in this use of δέ (*de*) refers to the "boasting" mentioned at the beginning of verse 6. Paul could boast about his ascent experience, *but* he chooses not to, and he tells us why: "in order that a certain person may not evaluate me beyond what he sees in me or hears from me" (μή τις εἰς ἐμὲ λογίσηται ὑπὲρ ὃ βλέπει με ἢ ἀκούει [τι] ἐξ ἐμοῦ, *mē tis eis eme logisētai hyper ho blepei me ē akouei [ti] ex emou*). The use of μή is unusual, since it functions as a conjunction (not a negative particle) that introduces a strongly worded, negative purpose clause (so Harris 2005: 849; Robertson 1934: 988).

Paul clearly feels strongly about being evaluated inappropriately. But by whom? We have already noted that in this broader context, τις (*tis*) has been used consistently to refer to Paul's opponent(s) (2 Cor. 2:5, 10; 3:1; 8:20; 10:2, 7, 12; cf. 1 Cor. 16:11; 2 Thess. 2:3). Further, the apostle has used the verb λογίζομαι (*logizomai*)[35] five times since the beginning of chapter 10, and in every case, the "evaluation" mentioned has had something to do with the Corinthian interlopers (2 Cor. 10:2, 7, 11; 11:5). Thus we suggest that he particularly does not want to be evaluated by the false teachers at Corinth on the basis of anything but the daily practice of ministry. In the prepositional phrase εἰς ἐμέ (*eis eme*), εἰς serves as a marker of a point of reference, and the phrase means "with reference to me." Also, ὑπέρ, with the neuter accusative relative pronoun (ὅ, *ho*), in this context carries the sense "beyond" (BDAG 1031). Therefore this part of the clause communicates, "in order that a certain person may not evaluate (with reference to) me beyond . . ." Paul doesn't want to be evaluated "beyond" a particular set of evidence, which he describes as "what he sees in me or anything he hears from me." The content of this relative clause parallels two main ways of evaluating a person:

βλέπει	με	ἤ	(*blepei me ē*)
ἀκούει [τι]	ἐξ	ἐμοῦ	(*akouei [ti] ex emou*)

The "certain person" (τις, *tis*) is the subject of both verbs. The pronoun με (*me*) is an accusative of reference ("sees with reference to me"), which best comes over into English as "sees in me" (Barrett 1973: 313). The clause continues with an alternative, "or hears from me." Clearly ἐξ ἐμοῦ carries the idea of source,

---

35. The term λογίζομαι (*logizomai*) could be used in a mathematical sense, "to count," "calculate," or with the sense of an evaluation or estimation based on a calculation, as elsewhere in 2 Corinthians (3:5; 5:19; 10:2, 7, 11; 11:5; BDAG 597). Several English versions render the verb here as "think well of" or "think better of" (e.g., ESV, NLT², NRSV, NIV), but Paul seems to use the word more with the sense of critical evaluation.

but the uncertain textual variant (on which see the additional note on 12:6) τι (*ti*) is somewhat puzzling. If the standard Greek texts have its placement correct, as following ἀκούει, it probably should be understood as paralleling the sense of "reference" or "respect" in the accusative pronoun με—"with respect to anything he hears from me," or more simply, "anything he hears from me." Harris (2005: 850) explains, "Seeing and hearing encompass the two primary ways in which an evaluation of a person can be undertaken—by observing conduct and by listening to what is said. In Paul's case the reference would be to all his behavior as a person and as a missionary-pastor, and to all his preaching and teaching." Impressive heavenly visions and revelations, as authentic as they are, and as significant as they are, are not what makes for authentic ministry. Rather, Paul suggests authentic ministry is shaped and verified in the nitty-gritty of day-to-day ministry.

In effect, then, 12:5–6 constitutes a "seam" in the speech, a transition from the account of the ascent to heaven to the account of how this "strength" led to unremitting ministry "weakness," Paul's thorn in the flesh. In this perspective-setting turn in the speech, these two verses underscore the main theme around which the speech is built, "boasting in weakness" (11:21a, 29–30; 12:1, 9a, 9b–10), and also reiterate—albeit in a roundabout way—Paul's assessment of boasting apart from the Lord as "foolishness." The apostle declares that if he chose to boast in the experience, it would not constitute foolish boasting since he would be telling the truth (v. 6a); but he is committed not to go that route, instead sticking to his "boasting stratagem" of focusing on weaknesses.

e. Paul's Thorn in the Flesh (12:7–9)

In verse 7 we finally come to Paul's famous "thorn in the flesh," his climactic illustration of "weakness" in this wide-ranging and "foolish" boast (11:21–12:10). A term most often rendered as "thorn" in English translations, σκόλοψ (*skolops*), could refer to something sharp or pointed, such as a splinter or a stake (see Park 1980), but against the LXX backdrop, the translation "thorn" seems appropriate (Num. 33:55; Hosea 2:6; Ezek. 28:24). There the image speaks of forms of opposition, something incessantly painful and thus irritating or vexing. Paul defines this thorn as "in the flesh" (τῇ σαρκί, *tē sarki*), probably a dative of place, though some have taken it as a dative of disadvantage, reading it as a thorn "against the flesh."

12:7

But before turning to the nature of the thorn itself, we must first discern the function of the verse's initial segment: καὶ τῇ ὑπερβολῇ τῶν ἀποκαλύψεων (*kai tē hyperbolē tōn apokalypseōn*, and due to the extraordinary character of the revelations). There are two primary options as to its grammatical relationship to the other clauses that surround it. As option 1, with the standard Greek texts, we can read these words as the final part of the previous sentence (so, e.g., HCSB, NLT[2], NIV, NET; Furnish 1984: 513; Zmijewski 1978: 355). In this case the καί at the beginning of verse 7 is read variously as ascensive (e.g.,

NRSV, HCSB),[36] concessive (e.g., NLT²),[37] contrastive (NIV),[38] or epexegetic (e.g., Furnish 1984: 528).[39] There is a grammatical point to be made for and against this position. In its favor διό (*dio*, therefore), which immediately follows our segment under question, almost always in Paul comes at the beginning of a sentence, and this is the case if this clause ends the previous sentence (begun in v. 6).[40] On the other hand, as demonstrated by the multifarious interpretations of καί (i.e., the varied understandings of how this segment makes sense as an extension of what goes before it), our segment sits quite uncomfortably in grammatical relationship to what precedes it.

Other scholars have suggested, therefore, that it makes more sense as a bridge to what follows, which offers a second option on the grammatical function of 12:7a (so e.g., ESV, NASB, KJV; Harris 2005: 852–53; P. Hughes 1962: 449; Matera 2003: 275; Thrall 2000: 772). This second option seems preferable; with this interpretation, καί normally is read as a simple connective, and the dative τῇ ὑπερβολῇ (the surpassing) as either instrumental (e.g., RSV,[41] NKJV, Darby) or as a dative of reference (e.g., NAB), or most commonly as causal (e.g., ESV,[42] NASB⁹⁵), as with our translation: "And due to the extraordinary character of the revelations . . ."

The apostle has already used the term ὑπερβολή four times in 2 Corinthians, once when speaking of the "extraordinary degree" (καθ᾽ ὑπερβολήν, *kath' hyperbolēn*) to which he had been oppressed in Asia (1:8), and again at 4:7 to write of God's "extraordinary power." Paul uses the term twice in 4:17 (καθ᾽ ὑπερβολὴν εἰς ὑπερβολήν, *kath' hyperbolēn eis hyperbolēn*) to convey thoughts on the "eternal tonnage of glory" that far outweighs the momentary, light trouble faced in the present age. Thus the word describes something that is extraordinary in character and here makes a nice bridge from the end of verse 6, lexically playing off the preposition ὑπέρ (in v. 6b). Paul insists that he not be evaluated "beyond" (ὑπέρ) what he says and does in ordinary, everyday ministry, and he proclaims, in fact, that it was because of extraordinary (τῇ ὑπερβολῇ) revelations that he has received his thorn.

Moreover, τῇ ὑπερβολῇ is delimited by τῶν ἀποκαλύψεων (*tōn apokalypseōn*), an attributed genitive,[43] the "extraordinary character" serving as an attribute

36. "What is seen in me or heard from me, even considering the exceptional character of the revelations" (12:6–7 NRSV); "What he sees in me or hears from me, especially because of the extraordinary revelations" (HCSB).

37. "What they can see in my life or hear in my message, even though I have received such wonderful revelations" (12:6–7 NLT²).

38. "By what I do or say, or because of these surpassingly great revelations" (12:6–7 NIV).

39. "What one may see me doing or hear from me, specifically, because of the extraordinary character of the revelations" (Furnish 1984: 528).

40. See διό in Rom. 1:24; 2:1; 4:22; 13:5; 15:7, 22; 1 Cor. 12:3; 14:13; 2 Cor. 1:20; 2:8; 4:16; 5:9; 6:17; 12:7, 10; Gal. 4:31; Eph. 2:11; 3:13; 4:8, 25; 5:14; Phil. 2:9; 1 Thess. 3:1; 5:11; Philem. 8. Yet cf. 2 Cor. 4:13, which admittedly is within a quotation.

41. "Too elated by the abundance of revelations" (12:7 RSV).

42. "Because of the surpassing greatness" (12:7 ESV).

43. Contra Harris (2005: 853), who labels the genitive as possessive. On the attributed genitive, see D. Wallace 1996: 89–91.

"of the revelations" of which Paul speaks. Only twice in his writings does the apostle use ἀποκάλυψις in the plural form, here and earlier in the chapter, at 12:1. In both cases the plural may be used as a category description to refer to "revelations" in general, of which the ascent recounted in 12:2–4 is a specific example (so Thrall 2000: 806). If this is the case, the thorn was given not just in relation to this specific ascent, but also in relation to Paul's revelatory experiences in general.

The inferential conjunction διό (*dio*, for this reason, therefore) is somewhat redundant[44] if the previous phrase is taken as causal, which may be one reason the variant is omitted in a number of manuscripts (see the first additional note on 12:7). Yet the conjunction may be understood as playing a part in underscoring the very specific cause of Paul's thorn in the flesh, bridging the cause stated at the beginning of verse 7 onward to the purpose clause that follows διό.

In the words that follow in verses 7–8 we are told six more things about the thorn:

1. It was given so that the apostle would not become consumed with self-importance.
2. It was given to Paul (by the Lord).
3. It was a thorn "in the flesh."
4. It was a messenger of Satan.
5. It "beat" him repeatedly.
6. Paul pleaded three times that it would be taken away.

We consider these in the order in which they occur in the text and then try to determine the nature of "the thorn."

First, Paul's thorn in the flesh was given to him "so that" he "might not become consumed with self-importance" (ἵνα μὴ ὑπεραίρωμαι, *hina mē hyperairōmai*). Repeated verbatim at the end of verse 7, this purpose clause brackets Paul's description of the thorn in the flesh, thus underscoring its purpose, emphasizing the redemptive nature of this troublesome, painful "gift."[45] The negative particle μή plus the present subjunctive may be rendered, "so that *I might not*," and the aspect of the present-tense form is "imperfective" or seen as in process: Paul is dealing with an ongoing situation. The word ὑπεραίρω (*hyperairō*) finds expression in the NT only here and at 2 Thess. 2:4, which says that the "man of lawlessness . . . opposes and *exalts* [ὑπεραιρόμενος, *hyperairomenos*] himself above every so-called god or object of worship" (NET).[46] Accordingly, the word at 12:7 has to do with being full of

---

44. Philip Hughes (1962: 449) calls it an "emphatic redundancy."

45. Some MSS omit the repeated ἵνα (*hina*, so that) clause at the end of the verse. See the second additional note on 12:7.

46. However, Paul uses a cognate of ὑπεραίρω at 11:20, where he describes the interloper as one who "puts on airs" (ἐπαίρεται, *epairetai*) around the Corinthians. In the LXX the word at times has a positive meaning of something or someone being "lifted up" in a positive way (e.g., 2 Chron. 32:23; Ps. 72:16 [71:16 ET]; Prov. 31:29).

oneself or becoming "consumed with self-importance." So for Paul the thorn plays an important role in keeping his self-perception from being skewed by the extraordinary revelations he has received.

Second, the thorn has been "given" to the apostle; this was no "accident," or the machination of evil people, or something Paul has taken upon himself. The apostle describes the thorn as a "gift." The aorist passive of δίδωμι (*didōmi*), ἐδόθη (*edothē*), could be read as having "Satan" as its agent. However, the tone surrounding the thorn seems positive and redemptive, suggesting rather that the verb should be understood as a divine passive, with God as the "giver." Ultimately the thorn was for Paul's spiritual good and the display of God's power. We are not told when the thorn was given, just that it was given in response to "the revelations."

Third, it was a thorn "in the flesh," which we understand to refer to the persecution the apostle experienced at the hands of opponents (on which see the comments on 12:8).

Fourth, although the thorn was redemptive and ultimately from God, Paul also describes it as "a messenger of Satan" (ἄγγελος σατανᾶ, *angelos satana*), words in direct apposition to σκόλοψ τῇ σαρκί (*skolops tē sarki*, a thorn in the flesh). The genitive σατανᾶ could be a genitive of source ("from Satan") or possession ("belonging to Satan"), but regardless, Paul sees Satan's "messenger" (ἄγγελος) as directly involved in his thorny situation. Paradoxically, the thorn was both a "gift" from God and a "goad" from Satan.

Fifth, the thorn was given in order that it might "beat" Paul (ἵνα με κολαφίζῃ, *hina me kolaphizē*). Writers in the first century could use the verb κολαφίζω (*kolaphizō*) to speak of hitting someone with a hand or fist. For instance, at Matt. 26:67 we read that those interrogating Jesus on the night before his crucifixion "spat in his face and *struck him with their fists* [ἐκολάφισαν, *ekolaphisan*]" (NET). Thus the word tells of being treated roughly (1 Cor. 4:11) or beaten (1 Pet. 2:20); by extension, Paul probably uses the word figuratively here to speak of being tormented, again with the present-tense form to communicate that this torment is ongoing.

As noted above, the purpose clause ἵνα μὴ ὑπεραίρωμαι (*hina mē hyperairōmai*, so that I might not become consumed with self-importance) is repeated at the end of verse 7 for emphasis. But it also may put the whole of this thorn back into perspective as a good gift from God.

12:8   Finally, sixth, Paul writes, "I pleaded with the Lord three times about this, so that it might be kept away from me." Quite common in the NT,[47] and used eighteen times in 2 Corinthians, the verb παρακαλέω (*parakaleō*) plays a significant part in crafting an "encouragement" motif in the letter.[48] Yet here the word carries a different force, that of calling on someone (especially God) for help (e.g., Epictetus, *Disc.* 3.21.12; Josephus, *Ant.* 6.25; Matt. 26:53), or urgently imploring someone for something (e.g., Matt. 8:5; 18:32; Mark 1:40;

---

47. The verb appears 109 times in the NT, 18 of these in 2 Corinthians. See comments on 1:4.
48. On the cognate παράκλησις (*paraklēsis*, encouragement), see comments on 1:3.

2 Cor. 12:18; BDAG 764–65). The urgency of Paul's request can be seen in that he cried out to God "three times" (τρίς, *tris*).[49] His plea to God was that the thorn would be "taken away" or perhaps "kept away" from him (ἵνα ἀποστῇ ἀπ᾽ ἐμοῦ, *hina apostē ap' emou*). The translation we choose depends in part on our interpretation of the "thorn in the flesh."

In general three main categories encompass the suggestions on the thorn's identity.[50]

1. *Physical illness of some kind.* Suggestions include malarial fever, epilepsy, severe headaches (Tertullian, *On Modesty* 13), a pathology of the eyes (Gal. 4:13–15),[51] a speech impediment (2 Cor. 10:10; Barrett 1973: 315), perhaps a socially debilitating disease or disfigurement (P. Marshall 1983: 315–16), or some unspecified personal illness (Hafemann 2000: 462, following Heckel 1993).[52]

2. *A psychological malady.* Suggestions include anxiety disorders, pangs of conscience over persecuting the church, deep suffering over his ineffectiveness in reaching the Jews with the gospel, depression, and sexual temptation (yet see 1 Cor. 7:7 and Furnish 1984: 548; see also the discussion and counterarguments in Thrall 2000: 809–11).

3. *Opposition.* Suggestions include conflict with the Judaizers, specific opponents such as Alexander the coppersmith (John Chrysostom),[53] opposition in general (Keener 2005: 240), a specific opponent at Corinth (Mullins 1957), and even the church at Corinth itself (McCant 1988).

Understandably, a host of commentators remain agnostic on the matter (e.g., Garland 1999: 521; P. Hughes 1962: 442; Matera 2003: 284), and we may do best to honor Paul's decision not to name his thorn (Hafemann 2000: 463–64). However, if one were forced to choose, the two strongest positions are options

---

49. At three other points in the NT, τρίς is used: where Paul speaks of being beaten three times with rods (2 Cor. 11:25), at the triple crowing of the rooster upon Peter's denials (Matt. 26:34, 75; Mark 14:30, 72; Luke 22:34, 61; John 13:38), and in the account of Peter's triple vision of the descending "sheet" of animals (Acts 10:16; 11:10). The closest parallels in the LXX are perhaps the story of Elijah calling out to God to restore a boy who had died (1 Kings 17:21) and Daniel's practice of praying to God three times a day (Dan. 6:10, 13 [Old Greek via NETS: 6:5, 8, 10–11, 13, 16]).

50. See the extensive overview by Thrall 2000: 809–18.

51. Against this, Keener (2005: 240) notes, "Treating another as dearer than one's eyes was a figure of speech (e.g., Catullus 3–5; 14.1–3; 82.1–4; Sipre Deut. 313.1.4)."

52. Concerning physical illness, Paul's physical stamina through the long list of hardships mentioned in 11:23b–33 count against the interpretation, at least to some extent. As Martin (1986: 415) states, the apostle seems to be in "robust health" and to have "a strong constitution."

53. Rejecting the view that the "thorn" refers to headaches brought on by Satan, John Chrysostom (*Hom. 2 Cor.* 26.2) states, "What Paul means is that God would not allow the preaching of the gospel to go forward, so that his proud thoughts might be checked. Instead, Paul was attacked by adversaries like Alexander the coppersmith, the party of Hymenaeus and Philetus and all the opponents of the Word. These were the messengers of Satan." A similar interpretation is offered by Theodoret of Cyr (*Comm. 2 Cor.* 34.9; Bray 1999: 305).

1 and 3 above, with perhaps a slight edge being given to the option 3. Arguments in favor of the thorn being the intense opposition faced by Paul in his ministry are as follows: (1) The thorn would need to be consonant with the list of hardships Paul has already provided in the speech, and the list is permeated with references to opposition (while there is no reference to physical illness). (2) The "thorn" may be read as alluding to OT passages that use the image for opposition to God's people (Num. 33:55; Ezek. 28:24). Note that the "thorn" in Ezekiel is singular but refers to "those all around them" (NETS).[54] (3) The reference to the "messenger of Satan" at least shares verbal analogy with the servants of "Satan" to whom Paul refers at 11:14–15. (4) Paul has used the term κολαφίζω (kolaphizō) in his First Letter to the Corinthians with reference to being harshly treated (4:11). (5) The conclusion to the speech at 12:10 has a focus on persecution, and Paul describes his weaknesses as being embraced "for Christ's sake."

As recognized above, Paul's use of the plural in speaking of "visions and revelations" (12:1, 7) may tip us off that here we have a label referring to his revelatory experiences in general. If this is the case, the thorn may be understood as given, not specifically as a result of the experience of fourteen years prior, but more generally in relation to a life and ministry in which "revelations" occurred periodically. Indeed, associated with Paul's Damascus road encounter with Christ (remember that he has just told us of his escape from Damascus!), are Jesus's words, "I will show him how much he must suffer for my name's sake" (Acts 9:16). If this reading is correct, then the specific example of the ascent to heaven in 12:2–4 is just that—a stirring example. But Paul's reflections on the thorn relate to his revelatory experiences as a whole.

12:9 So Paul asked that he might be relieved of this "thorn," the incessant persecution he faces in the course of his ministry. Yet the apostle's request was denied. The καί (kai) at the beginning of verse 9 is contrastive ("But"), setting Paul's plea over against God's answer (εἴρηκέν μοι, eirēken moi, he answered me),[55] which was, "My grace is entirely sufficient for you, for power is perfected in weakness." In 2 Corinthians the word χάρις (charis) serves as a staple of Paul's lexicon (1:2, 12, 15; 2:14; 4:15; 6:1; 8:1, 4, 6–7, 9, 16, 19; 9:8, 14–15; 12:9; 13:13), with the apostle drawing on various meanings across the word's semantic range (BDAG 1079–80; EDNT 3:457–60).[56] Here God speaks of

54. "And the house of Israel shall no longer have a thorn of bitterness [σκόλοψ πικρίας, skolops pikrias] or a prick of pain from those all around them [ἀπὸ πάντων τῶν περικύκλῳ αὐτῶν, apo pantōn tōn perikyklō autōn], who dishonor them, and they shall know that I am the Lord" (Ezek. 28:24 NETS). This seems to answer those who suggest Paul's "thorn," since it is singular, could not refer to multiple opponents.

55. The perfect-tense form can be read as aoristic (historical), giving vividness to Paul's memory of the occasion. The "three times" Paul has pleaded with the Lord grounds the dialogue in a concrete event. But the apostle also may have used the perfect, with its stative aspect, to underscore the ongoing relevance of God's proclamation, this Word of God constantly ringing in the apostle's ears, reverberating through all of his trials and sufferings.

56. E.g., χάρις as "kindness, favor, or enablement" (1:2, 12; 8:1; 9:8, 14), "benefit" (1:15), "privilege" (8:4), "thanks" (8:16; 9:15), the collection for the saints as a "gift" or expression of

his (μου, *mou*, my) grace,[57] his "enabling" Paul to deal with the thorn, as "entirely sufficient" (ἀρκεῖ, *arkei*) for the apostle (σοι, *soi*, for you; a dative of advantage); the present active verb means "to be adequate," "enough" (BDAG 131–32).[58] The verb's placement at the beginning of God's answer is for emphasis: "*completely* adequate." Thus God told Paul in effect, "You do not really need the thorn removed. All you need is my grace to deal with it."

God goes on to explain (γὰρ, *gar*, for) why the thorn needs to stay in place: "power is perfected in weakness" (δύναμις ἐν ἀσθενείᾳ τελεῖται, *dynamis en astheneia teleitai*). The principle presents the synergetic relationship between apparently antithetical concepts. At 6:7 Paul has already noted that his ministry stems from the "power (δύναμις, *dynamis*) of God," and, similar to the point made here, 4:7 celebrates the fact that God's "power" comes in fragile "jars of clay," containers made of earth, "in order that this extraordinary power might be seen for what it is, power that comes from God and not from us" (cf. 13:4). But Paul has also used this word for the "ability" or "strength" to cope with an overwhelming situation (1:8) and for the Macedonians' ability to give beyond their "resources" (8:3). At 12:12 he will use the term again, there referring to "miracles" (plural). So, to what does Paul refer here?

In the next sentence, the apostle tells us he is talking about "Christ's power" (ἡ δύναμις τοῦ Χριστοῦ, *hē dynamis tou Christou*), which is synonymous with "God's power" (6:7; 4:7), and in the letter each time Paul speaks of "God's power," he is dealing with a dynamic that characterizes his ministry. The power manifested in his ministry comes from God. So the principle that "power is perfected in weakness" (12:9) has to do with God's power manifested in Paul's ministry.

As Paul has talked about "weakness" in the broader context—the subject is almost exclusively dealt with in the Fool's Speech[59]—it seems clear that various kinds of trials are in mind. The apostle does not seem to be speaking about "weakness" in terms of a lack of ministry skill or ineptitude of some sort. Further, we have suggested that in some way the thorn itself refers to these trials (or at least a particular trial) experienced in the context of ongoing ministry. So, how might we understand God's power to be "perfected" (τελεῖται, *teleitai*) "in weakness"? First, the preposition ἐν (*en*) could be understood as instrumental ("by weakness"), but it also may connote sphere ("in the context of weakness"). The verb τελέω (*teleō*) in this context means to "bring something to a desired end." So when God says that power is "perfected" in weakness, he

---

God's "grace" (8:6, 7, 19), etc. The term occurs 156 times in the NT, 100 of these occurring in Paul's writings, and 18 of these occurring in 2 Corinthians.

57. Probably a genitive of source: "the grace you receive from me."

58. E.g., LXX: Num. 11:22; Josh. 17:16; 1 Kings 8:27; also Matt. 25:9. When used as a passive, ἀρκέω (*arkeō*) speaks of being content or satisfied (e.g., 2 Macc. 5:15).

59. The noun occurs in 2 Cor. 11:30; 12:5; the verb at 11:21, 29; 12:10; 13:3–4, 9; and the adjective at 10:10. Thus in this letter, with the exception of the occurrences in chap. 13 (which play a part in drawing the Fool's Speech into the section's conclusion) and the adjective at 10:10, Paul speaks about "weakness" only in the immediate context of the Fool's Speech.

means that the power of God has its intended effect or fulfillment in contexts of weakness, that is, in trials and persecutions. This is quite similar to 4:7, where persecuted "terra-cotta" manifests the "treasure" of the gospel and thus the power of God. The Corinthian interlopers, by contrast, have attempted to play their "strengths," their "power" Christianity, over against Paul's weaknesses. Yet God proclaims that his true power, and thus authentic ministry, does not work from a power orientation, but rather from a position of weakness.

Paul concludes verse 9 with "Therefore, I will boast all the more gladly about my weaknesses, so that the power of Christ might rest on me." We have followed his theme of "boasting in weakness" from the beginning and through key turning points of the Fool's Speech (11:21, 29–30; 12:5; see the table in the introduction to 11:22–29).[60] Based on the principle that "power is perfected in weakness" (12:9b), the apostle now adds two additional reflections on this posture in boasting.

First, in light of God's explanation for why the thorn would not be taken away (οὖν, *oun*, therefore), Paul says he will boast in his weaknesses "all the more gladly" (ἥδιστα οὖν μᾶλλον, *hēdista oun mallon*). We have already seen the word rendered "gladly" (ἥδιστα, *hēdista*) earlier at 11:19, where Paul says that the Corinthians "gladly" put up with fools. The only other point where he employs the term in the book is at 12:15, where he tells the Corinthians he will "gladly" "spend and be spent" for them as he carries out his ministry to them. So the word refers to doing something "with pleasure."[61]

The word μᾶλλον could be used to mark an alternative (i.e., "rather"), and if read that way (so BDAG 614; e.g., NASB, KJV) would be in response to God's negative answer to Paul's plea ("God turned me down, so I will *rather* boast gladly in my weaknesses"). But the term can also be read as referring to something being done to a greater degree than it had been done before (so ESV, HCSB, NIV, NET; e.g., Luke 5:15; John 5:18; 19:8; Acts 5:14; 22:2; 2 Cor. 7:7), and this seems to be the sense here: Paul will boast "all the more gladly."

Second, the apostle says he will take this great pleasure in boasting about his weaknesses, "so that the power of Christ might take up residence on" him (ἵνα ἐπισκηνώσῃ ἐπ᾽ ἐμὲ ἡ δύναμις τοῦ Χριστοῦ, *hina episkēnōsē ep' eme hē dynamis tou Christou*). Later in the letter, the apostle writes that Christ "was crucified as a result of weakness, but he lives as a result of God's power. For also we ourselves are weak by virtue of our relationship with him, but we will live with him as a result of God's power, which is manifested in dealing with you" (2 Cor. 13:4). In other words, God's power has been manifested in his Son, Jesus Christ, and Paul, who is in relationship with Christ, identifies with Christ's weakness. He also, through Christ, participates in the manifestation of God's power. Here the apostle expresses this as Christ's power "taking up

---

60. For more on the concepts of "boasting" and "weakness," see the comments on verses where those terms appear in 2 Corinthians.

61. This adverb can be used, e.g., of someone enjoying a speaker (Mark 6:20; 12:37) or taking pleasure in a gift or someone's company (Spicq 1994: 2.172).

residence on"[62] him (ἐπισκηνώσῃ ἐπ᾽ ἐμέ). This is the only use of the verb ἐπισκηνόω (*episkēnoō*) in the NT, but it is cognate with the common term σκηνή (*skēnē*), which can refer to a tent, a temporary shelter, or the OT tabernacle.[63] Accordingly, our verb means "to use a place for lodging, take up quarters, take up one's abode" (BDAG 378), but the connection to OT tabernacle/temple imagery probably is in mind. Paul rests content in his weaknesses so Christ's power might be at home, "take up residence on," him.

f. Conclusion to the Fool's Speech (12:10)

Playing off his reflections on his weaknesses and Christ's power in verse 9, Paul concludes the speech with (1) the apostle expressing delight in his unabashed "weaknesses" about which he has boasted in this foolish discourse and then (2) an explanation for why such onerous experiences prove a source of delight: "For this reason, I am delighted in weaknesses, in indignities, in crises, in persecutions and troubles for Christ's sake. For when I am weak, then I am strong." Paul makes use of the conjunction διό (*dio*, For this reason) at nine points in 2 Corinthians (1:20; 2:8; 4:13 [2x], 16; 5:9; 6:17; 12:7, 10) and here employs it to introduce an inference from the previous verse. In fact, the inferential conjunction bridges parallel ideas in 12:9b and 12:10:

12:10

2 Cor. 12:9b	2 Cor. 12:10
Therefore	For this reason,
I will boast all the more gladly about my weaknesses,	I am delighted in weaknesses, in indignities, in crises, in persecutions and troubles for Christ's sake.
so that the power of Christ might take up residence on me.	For when I am weak, then I am strong.

In verse 9 the apostle writes that he will "boast all the more gladly" (ἥδιστα . . . μᾶλλον καυχήσομαι, *hēdista . . . mallon kauchēsomai*) about the weaknesses inherent in his ministry; in the parallel of verse 10 he expresses, "I am delighted in weaknesses," using the verb εὐδοκέω (*eudokeō*, delight). Generally NT authors use this verb to speak of taking pleasure or delight in something and thus approving of it. This is the term, for instance, used by the Gospel writers to express the "delight" the Father has in the Son at the baptism (Matt. 3:17) and then again at the transfiguration (17:5). Elsewhere Paul uses the word to speak of God's pleasure in saving the lost through the foolishness of preaching (1 Cor. 1:21), or God's pleasure in revealing his Son in Paul (Gal. 1:15–16). Earlier in 2 Corinthians the apostle comments on his preference[64] for being out of the body and present with the Lord (5:8). Furnish

---

62. The preposition ἐπί (*epi*) is used of a power or condition coming upon a person.

63. See σκηνή in Matt. 17:4; Mark 9:5; Luke 9:33; 16:9; Acts 7:43–44; 15:16; Heb. 8:2, 5; 9:2–3, 6, 8, 11, 21; 11:9; 13:10; Rev. 13:6; 15:5; 21:3.

64. In 5:8–9 Paul uses the word to craft a play on words between "preferring" (εὐδοκοῦμεν, *eudokoumen*) to be with Christ and the desire to be "pleasing" (εὐάρεστοι, *euarestoi*) to Christ.

(1984: 531) suggests that it means "something less than 'take delight in,'" but that is the dominant meaning in the NT (Matt. 3:17; 12:18; 17:5; Mark 1:11; Luke 3:22; 12:32; Rom. 15:26–27; 1 Cor. 1:21; 2 Cor. 5:8; Gal. 1:15; Col. 1:19; 1 Thess. 2:8; Heb. 10:6, 8, 38; 2 Pet. 1:17), and it is appropriate here. Paul proclaims that the onerous experiences he has described in the Fool's Speech can be viewed as a source of delight because of their outcome (cf. James 1:2–4): power in ministry.

In this concluding list of hardships, "in weaknesses" (ἐν ἀσθενείαις, en astheneiais)[65] serves as a general heading stamped on the whole speech. Paul has employed the term four other times since the beginning of the speech, twice as singular (11:30; 12:9b) and twice as plural (12:5, 9c). Both the singular form and the plural form can refer to the content of Paul's boast (11:30; 12:5, 9),[66] as is the case here. "In indignities" (ἐν ὕβρεσιν, en hybresin), on the other hand, points to a subcategory of "weaknesses." The noun ὕβρις can refer to a disaster or hardship generally (e.g., Acts 27:10; 3 Macc. 3:25; Jos. Asen. 7.5; Josephus, Ant. 1.60), and this could be the sense in the present case, or as with our English term "hubris," it could point to an attitude of arrogance or insolence (LXX: Prov. 11:2; 29:23; Isa. 9:8 [9:9 ET]; Philo, Spec. Laws 3.186). In the present context, however, Paul may have in mind the times he has been mistreated, shamed, or insulted, as when he was beaten or stoned (e.g., 11:23–25).

The apostle has used the word we translate as "crises" (ἐν ἀνάγκαις, en anankais) at 9:7, where he insists that giving should be done freely, not motivated by a person being put under "pressure" (ἐξ ἀνάγκης, ex anankēs). Accordingly, ἀνάγκη can refer to some form of compulsion, constraint, or necessity (e.g., Matt. 18:7; 1 Cor. 7:37; Heb. 7:27; 9:16). Yet the present context parallels the use in an earlier hardship list at 6:4, which probably communicates the sense of "crises" or "difficulties" (cf. 1 Cor. 7:26; BDAG 61).

Fourth in this summary list, the apostle mentions "persecutions" (ἐν διωγμοῖς, en diōgmois), and fifth, "stressful situations" (στενοχωρίαις, stenochōriais). Used ten times in the NT (Matt. 13:21; Mark 4:17; 10:30; Acts 8:1; 13:50; Rom. 8:35; 2 Cor. 12:10; 2 Thess. 1:4; 2 Tim. 3:11 [2x]), διωγμός[67] (diōgmos) speaks of persecution, "a program or process designed to harass and oppress someone" (BDAG 253). Jesus promised his followers that they would face persecution (Mark 10:30), and Paul himself has been involved in oppressing and even killing Christ-followers (Acts 8:1). As noted in his foolish speech (2 Cor. 11:23–25), the apostle felt the sting of persecution in his travels (e.g., Acts. 13:50); when he later wrote his Letter to the

65. The preposition ἐν connotes the idea "with respect to." Paul takes delight with respect to these hardships because of the resulting power for ministry.

66. The exceptions seem to be the singular forms at 12:9a, where weakness is presented as a general concept over against "power," and later at 13:4, where the crucifixion specifically is in mind.

67. The cognate διώκτης (diōktēs) refers to a "persecutor," and the related verb, διώκω (diōkō), means "to run after, pursue," or "to harass, persecute."

Romans, he celebrated persecution's inability to separate the believer from Christ (Rom. 8:35).

Also referred to at Rom. 8:35 and earlier in the hardship list of 2 Cor. 6:4–10, στενοχωρία (*stenochōria*) presents yet another general term for distress, difficulties, anguish, or troubles (BDAG 943). Rendering the LXX, NETS speaks of the "desperate straits" that the Israelites would suffer under when tormented by their enemies (Deut. 28:53, 55, 57) or the "anguish" or "distress" experienced in times of great difficulty (e.g., Add. Esth. 11:8; 14:1; 1 Macc. 2:53; 13:3; 3 Macc. 2:10; Wis. 5:3). The word fits well the lengthy and varied list of "troubles" the apostle experienced in the course of his ministry.

All of these hardships Paul suffers "for Christ's sake" (ὑπὲρ Χριστοῦ, *hyper Christou*), or "on Christ's behalf," the preposition ὑπέρ + the genitive communicating the idea of "advantage," or something done in Christ's interest. Throughout 2 Corinthians one of the key aspects of authentic ministry concerns motive. Paul does not minister for personal profit (e.g., 2:17), but rather out of obedience and obligation to Christ and for his glory. Paul seeks to advance the kingdom of Christ and God, not his own kingdom. Only such a posture could undergird the endurance depicted in the Fool's Speech. But God's divine proclamation concerning the purpose of his "thorn" (12:9) has also helped Paul keep his hardships in perspective.

Accordingly, Paul explains (γάρ, *gar*, for) that this is why such onerous experiences prove a source of delight, because "weaknesses" lead to "strength," that is, empowerment for ministry. At 12:9 we are told God's response to Paul's request that his thorn be removed, and Paul records that response in the form of a general principle: "for power is perfected in weakness" (ἡ γὰρ δύναμις ἐν ἀσθενείᾳ τελεῖται, *hē gar dynamis en astheneia teleitai*). Paul now personalizes the principle with "For when I am weak, then I am strong" (ὅταν γὰρ ἀσθενῶ, τότε δυνατός εἰμι, *hotan gar asthenō, tote dynatos eimi*). The nouns of the general principle have now become a verb (ἀσθενῶ, I am weak) and a predicate adjective (δυνατός, powerful) working with the verb of being (εἰμι, I am). When used in the ancient world of a person, the adjective could refer to the person being "powerful," or "capable," or even of someone who was particularly "competent"[68] or "skilled." Paul's point, playing off the principle he has received from God, is that the weaknesses, indignities, crises, persecutions, and troubles he has faced for the cause of Christ—these actually put him in a position of being more effective in ministry.

Reflection

The latter part of Paul's "Fool's Speech" focuses on two events from the apostle's life that put his weakness on display: his escape from Damascus and his thorn in the flesh. Ironically, these weaknesses form the climax of his foolish, boastful speech. Even the apostle's experience of being "snatched up to the third heaven" (12:2) serves as a lamp by which he draws attention

---

68. Cf. the use of ἱκανός (*hikanos*, qualified) at 2 Cor. 3:5.

to the thorn in the flesh, for it is the thorn, that weakness that facilitates the gracious perfection of God's power, that interests Paul the most at this point. God has used the thorn to beat against Paul's sense of self-importance. Paul celebrates weakness and the unique power it brings. He delights in indignities, crises, and persecutions. These paradoxical responses to weakness are grounded in a particular, cruciform vision of authentic ministry. Yet this vision runs counter to our celebration of strength, skill, excellence, position, status, and power in Western culture. We want to be the best and do the best. But the secret of Paul's excellence—an excellence borne witness to by the legacy of his ministry—is his weakness. He knows that all the suffering and trials he has faced are the seedbed for kingdom fruitfulness. God delights in using the brokenness of weakness to accomplish his purposes.

In 1958 John Stott led a university outreach in Sydney, Australia. He received word of his father's death the day before the final meeting and at the same time was beginning to lose his voice. He describes the final day of outreach as follows:

> It was already late afternoon within a few hours of the final meeting of the mission, so I didn't feel I could back away at that time. I went to the great hall and asked a few students to gather round me. I asked one of them to read . . . "My grace is sufficient for you, for my strength is made perfect in weakness" (2 Corinthians 12:8–9). A student read these verses and then I asked them to lay hands on me and . . . pray that those verses might be true in my own experience.
>
> When time came for me to give my address, I preached on the [broad and narrow ways from Matt. 7]. I had to get within half an inch of the microphone, and I croaked the gospel like a raven. I couldn't exert my personality. I couldn't move. I couldn't use any inflections in my voice. I croaked the gospel in monotone. Then when the time came to give the invitation, there was an immediate response, larger than any other meeting during the mission, as students came flocking forward.

Reflecting on the impact of that experience, Stott reports, "I've been back to Australia about ten times since 1958, and on every occasion somebody has come up to me and said, 'Do you remember that final meeting in the university in the great hall?' 'I jolly well do,' I reply. 'Well,' they say, 'I was converted that night.'" He concludes, "The Holy Spirit takes our human words, spoken in great weakness and frailty, and he carries them home with power to the mind, the heart, the conscience, and the will of the hearers in such a way that they see and believe" (Knowles 2007: 137–38).

Additional Notes

11:32. Adding θέλων to πιάσαι με (ℵ D² [F G 1739 transpose the order] H Ψ 0121 0243 0278^vid· 33 1881 𝔐 sy^h bo) seems clearly to be a scribal addition. The variant may have been for stylistic reasons, to make the infinitive complementary to the participle ("wanting to arrest me") and thus smoother. It also may have been included to support the fact, revealed in the next verse, that the arrest failed and thus remained a "wish" (so Harris 2005: 817). As noted by the UBS editorial committee, the quality of the reading without the participle, while not extensive, is strong (B D* it$^{d, ar}$ vg syr^p cop^{sa} arm), and the omission of θέλων, if not original, would be difficult to explain (Metzger 1994: 515–16).

12:1. Based on both external evidence and the principle that the more difficult reading is to be preferred, δεῖ ($\mathfrak{P}^{46}$ B D² F G H L P 0243 0278 6 33 81 104 365 629 630 1175 1241 1739 1881 2464 *pm* latt sy sa bo^{ms}) seems original against either δέ (ℵ D* Ψ bo; [Ambst]), which avoids asyndeton (Harris 2005: 828), or δή (K 0121 945 1505 *pm*).

12:1. The reading συμφέρον μέν ($\mathfrak{P}^{46}$ ℵ B F G [P: -ρει] 0243 0278 33 1175 1739 *pc* [f vg] co) has far superior external evidence than συμφέρει (D* 81) or συμφέρει μοι (D¹ H Ψ 1881 𝔐 it vg^{ms} sy^h; Ambst Pel).

12:1. The μέν following συμφέρον anticipates the δέ that follows ἐλεύσομαι, and the reading δέ has much stronger and varied manuscript support ($\mathfrak{P}^{46}$ ℵ F G H P 0243 0278 33 81 1175 1739 2464 *pc* lat) than δὲ καί (B) or γάρ (D Ψ 1881 𝔐 sy). Seemingly these latter two variants read μέν as a marker of contrast and, perhaps, as the end of the thought, letting a new sentence start with ἐλεύσομαι.

12:3. Almost certainly ἐκτός (ℵ D² F G H Ψ 0121 0243 0278 33 1739 1881 𝔐 latt) has replaced χωρίς ($\mathfrak{P}^{46}$ B D*) in some manuscripts due to pressure from the parallel use of ἐκτός in the previous verse. Given that parallel, χωρίς is the more difficult reading and preferred.

12:5. Probably for the sake of clarification, some witnesses add μου following ἀσθενείαις (ℵ D² F G Ψ 0121 1881 𝔐 lat; Ambst). But, given the presence of ἐμαυτοῦ earlier in the sentence, the pronoun is not necessary, and the reading that omits it ($\mathfrak{P}^{46}$ B D* 0243 0278 6 33 1175 1739 *pc* sy co) is almost certainly original.

12:6. Although the reading with τι following ἀκούει is quite difficult and has strong external support ($\mathfrak{P}^{46}$ ℵ² D* Ψ 0243 0278 1881 𝔐 f vg^{cl} sy^h; Ambst), external support for the shorter reading that omits τι is strong as well (ℵ* B D² F G I 6 33 81 1175 1739 *pc* ar b vgst co). The editorial committee for the UBS text retains the word, enclosed within square brackets, noting both the syntactical difficulty of the reading that retains it but also acknowledging the strength of the external attestation for omitting it (Metzger 1994: 516). If retention is correct, Harris's suggestion (2005: 850), that τι may be considered "an accusative of respect ('in any respect') that is parallel to the preceding με," seems reasonable and better than theories that τι was displaced from its original position in the text (e.g., Thrall 2000: 801).

12:7. As noted in the comments, if understood as coming in the middle of the sentence, the inclusion of διό breaks with Paul's normal pattern of having the inferential conjunction at the beginning of sentences. So, due to the interpretive turbulence in this part of the passage (particularly the role of καὶ τῇ ὑπερβολῇ τῶν ἀποκαλύψεων), it is understandable that some manuscripts retain διό (ℵ A B F G 0243 33 81 1175 1739 *pc* sy^h bo) while others omit it ($\mathfrak{P}^{46}$ D Ψ 1881 𝔐 lat sa; Ir^{lat}). The former reading has strong external support and is the more difficult reading, and the omission can be explained on the basis of interpretive difficulties surrounding the verse. On the other hand, if the omission of the conjunction was original, scribes may have added it, interpreting καὶ τῇ ὑπερβολῇ τῶν ἀποκαλύψεων as going with what precedes it and feeling the necessity for a transitional conjunction at the beginning of the next sentence. All in all, the reading that retains διό is preferred based on external support and the difficulty of the reading.

12:7. It is understandable why scribes would have dropped the final clause in verse 7 (ἵνα μὴ ὑπεραίρωμαι), thinking it redundant (ℵ* A D F G 33 629* *pc* lat; Ir^{lat}). But its inclusion has strong support ($\mathfrak{P}^{46}$ ℵ² B I^{vid} Ψ 0243 0278 1739 [1881] 𝔐 ar sy co; Cyp Ambst) (Metzger 1994: 517); as noted in the comments, the clause plays an important role in framing Paul's description of the thorn, underscoring its redemptive purpose.

12:9. The possessive pronoun μου occurs in the following witnesses: ℵ² A^c D¹ K L P Ψ 0243 0278 33 81 104 365 630 1175 1241 1505 1739 1881 2464 𝔐 sy bo^pt; Ir^arm. However, in the history of transmission, this addition probably came from a scribe who wished to make overt the implicit idea that it was *God's* power in view here. Although the reading that omits this occurrence of the pronoun (𝔓^46vid ℵ* A* B D* F G latt sa bo^pt; Ir^lat) is almost certainly original, the clarifying addition of "my" in an English translation at this point in the verse occurs often (e.g., ESV, NET, Message, NLT², NIV) and is by no means inappropriate.

12:9. Some manuscripts omit the μου following ἀσθενείαις (B 6 81 1175* 1739 *pc* sy^h bo; Ir), perhaps under influence from its omission at 12:5, while a slightly stronger group of witnesses retain it (ℵ A D F G Ψ 0278 33 1881 𝔐 latt sy^p sa). The latter reading is preferred.

6. Epilogue to the "Fool's Speech" (12:11–13)

In a brief epilogue to the speech, Paul returns to several themes covered in 11:5–15, an important movement that set up Paul's delivery of the speech (see the comments on 11:5–15). Now the apostle sums up the impetus for his foolish boasting, to which the Corinthians have driven him. They should not have been comparing him to the so-called "superapostles," for all the signs of an authentic apostle have been performed among them. Paul has not treated them poorly by failing to accept patronage, so they have sadly misjudged the situation and put him in the awkward position of commending himself to them when *they* should have been commending Paul.

Exegesis and Exposition

[11]I have made a fool of myself ⌜ ⌝; you yourselves drove me to it. Actually, I should have been commended by you, since ⌜ ⌝ I lack nothing in comparison to the "superapostles"—even though I am nothing. [12]The signs of the apostle were performed among you with utmost endurance— ⌜yes, signs⌝, wonders, and miracles. [13]In what way, then, were you treated worse than the other churches, except that I myself did not burden you? Forgive me for this injustice!

In a brief epilogue[1] to the speech, Paul revisits a number of prominent themes already covered in the book. Verse 11 reads, "I have made a fool of myself; you yourselves drove me to it. Actually, I should have been commended by you, since I lack nothing in comparison to the 'superapostles'—even though I am nothing." First, the apostle reiterates that the extensive boast he has just completed (11:21–12:10) was an exercise in foolishness. At 11:1 Paul alerts the Corinthians to the fact that foolishness is coming, and he begs their tolerance of it. At 11:16 he insists that a certain person not be allowed to cast him as a fool, but immediately Paul turns around and pleads with the Corinthians to embrace him as a fool, since they are so good at embracing fools (11:19). At the very front door of his speech, he admits he is "speaking foolishly" (11:21). So it is no surprise that, after finishing the "foolish" speech, he admits (in 12:11), "I have made a fool of myself" (Γέγονα ἄφρων, *Gegona aphrōn*; lit., I have become foolish). The perfect active indicative verb perhaps may be interpreted as consummative, the emphasis being on the speech as a completed action from which the present state of "foolishness" emerges. This is the last time Paul mentions "fool" or "foolishness" in the letter; the concept seems to be tied most particularly to the speech itself.

12:11–13

---

1. This is *epidiorthōsis*, rhetorically justifying what one has just written (Keener 2005: 241).

But Paul insists that his foolish boast was under compulsion, and in Greco-Roman rhetoric, boasting was justified if it had been forced on the public speaker (so Keener 2005: 241; Quintilian, *Inst.* 11.1.17–19; Cicero, *Fam.* 5.12.8; Pliny the Younger, *Ep.* 1.8.6).[2] The Corinthians have forced the necessity on their apostle: "you yourselves drove me to it" (ὑμεῖς με ἠναγκάσατε, *hymeis me ēnankasate*). The verb ἀναγκάζω (*anankazō*), here in an aorist active indicative form, could be used by ancient writers to mean "urge" or "press" someone to do something (P.Oxy. 1069.2, 20; Matt. 14:22; Mark 6:45; Luke 14:23), but Paul probably intends the stronger sense of "to compel" or "to force" a person to act in a particular manner (BDAG 60). For instance, in 1 and 2 Maccabees, the word is used of the Greeks forcing Jews to participate in actions that violate the law of God (1 Macc. 2:25; 2 Macc. 6:1, 7, 18; 7:1). The book of 1 Esdras also speaks of wine compelling people to certain types of behavior (1 Esd. 3:24) and of farmers being compelled to bring levies to the king (4:6). The Corinthians have not "urged" Paul to boast. Rather, their dangerous dalliance with the false itinerant teachers has compelled Paul to take up foolish boasting, a course of action that is "not helpful" but has become "necessary"[3] (12:1).

The apostle continues, "Actually, I should have been commended by you" (ἐγὼ γὰρ ὤφειλον ὑφ᾽ ὑμῶν συνίστασθαι, *egō gar ōpheilon hyph᾽ hymōn synistasthai*). In this case the conjunction γάρ marks a clarification, for Paul intimates that if they had done what they should (i.e., commending him and rejecting the false teachers), he would not have needed to make a "fool" of himself by the boastful speech. As we have seen, the "commendation" motif serves as one of the main threads weaving its way through 2 Corinthians (3:1; 4:2; 5:12; 6:4; 7:11; 10:12, 18; 12:11; see the introduction and the comments at 3:1), and here our thread comes to an end. This terminus seems significant, marking the "boast" Paul has just completed as a form of self-recommendation. If the Corinthians had commended him, he would not have felt the need to commend himself. Yet, since they did not, his boasting—recommending himself again so that they would reject the interlopers and embrace him—became a necessity.[4]

Further, Paul explains (γάρ, *gar*, since) that they should have commended him, "since I lack nothing in comparison to the 'superapostles'—even though I am nothing" (οὐδὲν γὰρ ὑστέρησα τῶν ὑπερλίαν ἀποστόλων εἰ καὶ οὐδέν εἰμι, *ouden gar hysterēsa tōn hyperlian apostolōn ei kai ouden eimi*). He has already

2. Duane Watson (2003: 89) explains that Paul is justifying and tempering his boasting, as advised by Quintilian: "I do not mean to deny that there are occasions when an orator may speak of his own achievements, as Demosthenes himself does in his defense of Ctesiphon. But . . . he qualified his statements in such a way as to show that he was compelled by necessity to do so, and to throw the odium attaching to such a proceeding on the man who had forced him to it" (*Inst.* 11.1.23).

3. Also, the cognate adjective ἀναγκαῖος (*anankaios*, necessary) is used at 9:5.

4. As noted in the comments, the themes of boasting and commendation begin to be interwoven at 10:12–18. There is a form of self-recommendation of which Paul approves (e.g., in which self-recommendation is done "as God's ministers" [6:4], "in God's sight," and by an "open display of the truth" [4:2]). This is why boasting about the ascent to heaven—if Paul chose to take it up—would not be inappropriate (12:6). It would be true and done "in God's sight."

used the label ὑπερλίαν ἀποστόλων (*hyperlian apostolōn*), "superapostles,"[5] at 11:5, where he says, "I do not consider myself to be the least bit inferior to these 'superapostles!'" (Λογίζομαι γὰρ μηδὲν ὑστερηκέναι τῶν ὑπερλίαν ἀποστόλων, *Logizomai gar mēden hysterēkenai tōn hyperlian apostolōn*). Though the wording is slightly different, the meaning is essentially the same here.

As noted at 11:5, Paul's opponents see him as lacking in particular leadership skills and thus inferior to them in a number of ways. As they play their game of comparison (10:12), boasting about their abilities and accomplishments (10:13–16), they read the apostle as "lacking" and have communicated this to the Corinthians. But Paul denies that he fails to measure up, saying that he lacks nothing (οὐδὲν . . . ὑστέρησα)[6] in comparison to the false teachers (12:11),[7] and thus the Corinthians should have commended their apostle and confronted the interlopers regarding their public denouncement of Paul. Nevertheless, Paul ends the thought humbly with "even though I am nothing" (εἰ καὶ οὐδέν εἰμι). After a negative statement, εἰ καί (*ei kai*) functions to communicate a concession ("although," "even though"). Again he puts the discussion back into perspective. Even though he "lacks nothing" when measured against the opponents, in himself he has "nothing" to offer in terms of ministry (cf. 3:4–6); indeed, he is nothing. Paul makes no claims to personal adequacy. The only way he can boast, therefore, is "in the Lord" (10:17–18).

Supporting his contention that he lacks nothing in comparison to the "superapostles,"[8] Paul continues in verse 12, "The signs of the apostle were performed among you with utmost endurance—yes, signs, wonders, and miracles." On the day of Pentecost, Peter proclaimed that Jesus's ministry had been validated in part by "signs":[9] "Men of Israel, listen to these words: Jesus the Nazarene, a man clearly attested to you by God with powerful deeds, wonders, and miraculous signs [σημείοις, *sēmeiois*] that God performed among you

---

5. Here too the genitive plural "superapostles" is comparative (12:11).

6. At 11:5 μηδείς (*medeis*) functions emphatically (Barrett 1973: 277) and as an "acc. of inner object" meaning, "not," "not in the least," "not at all" (cf. Acts 4:21; 10:20; 11:12; James 1:6; Rev. 2:10). Verbs of thinking call for a form of μή (*me*, not; BDF 222). Here οὐδέν may also be understood as an acc. of inner object.

7. For a discussion of the "superapostles" as a label referring to the false teachers in Corinth, see the comments on 11:5.

8. The particle μέν (*men*) at the beginning of 12:12 does not mark a correlation but can be read either as marking a contrast with "even though I am nothing" at the end of verse 11 or perhaps as a continuation of the thought that Paul lacked nothing in comparison with the false apostles. The latter seems more likely since Paul follows a reference to the "superapostles" with the comment on the "signs of the apostle" that accompany his ministry.

9. Generally the word "signs" (σημεῖον, *sēmeion*) carries a negative connotation in the Synoptic Gospels, referring to the demand for miracles by unbelievers (Matt. 12:38–39; 16:1, 4; Mark 8:11–12; Luke 11:16, 29; 23:8) or the signs performed by false leaders (Matt. 24:24; Mark 13:22). But the term can also refer to eschatological events (Matt. 16:3; 24:3, 30; Mark 13:4; Luke 21:7, 11, 25); and in Luke's Gospel, Jesus himself can be referred to as a "sign" (Luke 2:12, 34; 11:30). John's Gospel readily uses the term for Jesus's "miracles" (2:11, 23; 3:2; 4:54; 6:2, 14, 26; 7:31; 9:16; 10:41; 11:47; 12:18, 37; 20:30).

through him, just as you yourselves know" (Acts 2:22 NET). Accordingly, the apostles themselves performed "many wonders and signs"[10] (πολλά τε τέρατα καὶ σημεῖα, *polla te terata kai sēmeia*) that awed the crowds of Jerusalem (2:43), and the Sanhedrin was concerned that such abilities would convince the people of the apostles' validity (4:16, 22). In short, signs and wonders done through the hands of the apostles were seen as accomplished through God extending his hand among his people (4:30; 5:12). When God set the apostle Paul on his missionary journeys, the Lord "testified to the message" he preached, in part by "miraculous signs and wonders" (14:3), and the signs and wonders that accompanied the ministry of Paul and Barnabas even played a role in validating their ministry among the Gentiles (Acts 15:12). Specifically for Paul, his apostolic preaching of the gospel of Christ, by the power of the Holy Spirit, involved "signs and wonders" as a key mark of authenticity (Rom. 15:18–20), and Paul appeals that mark in 2 Cor. 12:12.

At the end of the verse he adds to "signs" and "wonders" (τέρασιν, *terasin*), a third term, "miracles" (δυνάμεσιν, *dynamesin*, from δύναμις), that is, "powers," a word (though used here in a different way) to which Paul has already appealed in speaking about the power of God manifested in a "weak" ministry (2 Cor. 4:7; 6:7; 8:3; 12:9). These three terms, "signs," "wonders," and "miracles" are found together in Bar. 2:11 LXX and at five points in the NT, especially in Acts and Paul.[11] As Harris (2005: 875) notes, the three labels probably do not refer to three categories of miracles, but rather three vantage points from which God's powerful works might be considered: "signs" offer validation, "wonders" elicit awe, and "miracles" display God's power.

Thus Paul tells the Corinthians that the signs of "the apostle" (τοῦ ἀποστόλου, *tou apostolou*), that is, "signs that may be attributed to a true apostle,"[12] "were performed" (κατειργάσθη, *kateirgasthē*)[13] or accomplished among them. We have no record from Acts of Paul performing "signs" when he established the church in Corinth; instead, the emphasis rested on his interaction with fellow believers, as well as his opponents from among the Jews (Acts 18:1–11).

Nevertheless, Paul writes that these signs were performed "with utmost endurance" (ἐν πάσῃ ὑπομονῇ, *en pasē hypomonē*). What might this mean? The term πᾶς (*pas*) in this case marks the highest degree of something (cf. 2 Cor. 9:8b; Eph. 6:18c). Similarly, at 2 Cor. 1:3 Paul refers to God as the (lit.) "God of every possible encouragement" (θεὸς πάσης παρακλήσεως, *theos*

---

10. "Signs and wonders" are a pair of terms found together many times in the LXX to speak of God's powerful works (e.g., Exod. 7:3, 9; 11:9–10; Deut. 4:34; 6:22; 7:19; 11:3; 13:2–3; 26:8; 28:46; 29:2 [29:3 ET]; 34:11; Add. Esth. 10:9; Pss. 77:43; 104:27; 134:9 [78:43; 105:27; 135:9 ET]; Wis. 8:8; 10:16; Isa. 8:18; 20:3; Jer. 39:20–21 [32:20–21 ET]; Bar. 2:11; Dan. 4:37 [not in MT/ET]).

11. Acts 2:22; 6:8; Rom. 15:19; 2 Cor. 12:12; 2 Thess. 2:9; Heb. 2:4.

12. In this case the article is generic, referring to "apostleship," and the genitive can be read as attributive: what is characteristic of an apostle.

13. The verb κατεργάζομαι (*katergazomai*), used twenty times in Paul, refers to something being done or accomplished (BDAG 531).

pasēs paraklēseōs). Here in 12:12 he speaks of the highest degree of ὑπομονή (*hypomonē*), which refers to holding up in the face of difficulties and could be rendered as "patience," "fortitude," "perseverance," or "endurance" (BDAG 1039). The apostle considers endurance in the face of opposition—so extensively borne witness to by the hardship list of 11:21–12:10—to be a defining mark of authentic ministry, the substance by which he can "commend" himself to every person's conscience (6:4). By definition, authentic, apostolic ministry involves suffering and thus demands endurance, both from the minister and those to whom the apostle ministers (1:6).

With verse 13 the letter returns to perhaps the main bone of contention that some at Corinth had with Paul: he would not take pay for his ministry. At 11:5–15, a key movement leading up to the Fool's Speech (11:21–12:10), Paul asserts that he is in no way inferior to the "superapostles," and then proceeds to defend his practice of not taking compensation for his ministry among the Corinthians. That pattern he revisits here. Having proclaimed that he lacks nothing in comparison to the superapostles (12:11–12), the apostle now poses a rhetorical question (v. 13a–b), sarcastically asks their "forgiveness" (v. 13c), informs them that he is about to visit them again and will maintain his practice of not receiving payment for his ministry (v. 14a), proclaims that he is interested in them and not in their money (v. 14b), draws on a proverb (v. 14c), proclaims that he gladly will spend and be spent for their sakes (v. 15a), and asks a final rhetorical question (v. 15b). As with 11:5–15, he uses a mix of vivid imagery and rhetorical questions, focusing on the concept of "burdening" the Corinthians; and he assures them that he will not give up this pattern of ministry.

Paul begins with the rhetorical question of 12:13a: "In what way,[14] then, were you treated worse than the other churches, except that I myself did not burden you?" At 11:8 Paul writes that he has "requisitioned the resources of other churches" (by receiving their financial support) so that he could serve the Corinthians. They have been blessed, treated well in relation to "the other churches" (τὰς λοιπὰς ἐκκλησίας, *tas loipas ekklēsias*; 12:13a). Here Paul has just pointed out that apostolic "signs," "wonders," and "miracles" have been performed among them (ἐν ὑμῖν, *en hymin*, among you; 12:12), and that his ministry in Corinth has been carried out "with utmost endurance" (ἐν πάσῃ ὑπομονῇ), that is, amid great difficulties and opposition. The account reflected in verse 12, to which the Corinthians no doubt have to admit as true, raises the question (γάρ, *gar*)[15] of how they can perceive themselves as being treated poorly. The verb ἐσσόομαι (*hessoomai*), found only here in the biblical literature (although see the uses of the similar term ἡττάομαι [*hēttaomai*] in 2 Pet. 2:19–20), means "to be worse off than," or "to be inferior to" (BDAG 397). In some way, then, the Corinthians understood Paul's actions to have

14. Τί . . . ἐστιν ὅ (*ti . . . estin ho*) can be rendered more lit. as "What is it with reference to which . . . ?" reading the relative pronoun as an acc. of reference.
15. The conjunction γάρ can be used in questions and either left untranslated or reflected with "then," "pray," or a prefix like "What!" (BDAG 189).

been mistreatment, or to have made them seem inferior to the other churches. His actions have put them in a bad light by comparison. So not only were the trespassing leaders in Corinth playing comparison games, so were the church members under their influence! They were comparing Paul's interaction with them to the interaction he was having with the rest of the churches. Of course, Paul's rhetorical question anticipates a negative answer: "You weren't mistreated!"

Nevertheless, he goes on to offer a qualification: "except that I myself did not burden you?" (εἰ μὴ ὅτι αὐτὸς ἐγὼ οὐ κατενάρκησα ὑμῶν; *ei mē hoti autos egō ou katenarkēsa hymōn?*). At 11:9 we noticed that the term καταναρκάω (*katanarkaō*) was used in the context of patron-client relationships, with one person "being a burden" or being socially obligated to another. By choosing not to accept pay from the wealthy at Corinth, Paul has avoided being socially dependent on, or obligated to, a particular faction within the Corinthian church (Keener 2005: 229; Peterman 1997: 159, 169, 201–4). Contextually, then, the most likely explanation for Paul's offense seems to concern his refusal of compensation. Given the Corinthians' cultural values, Paul's refusal of pay has been received as a social slap in the face. Given the social status of some of the church members, one can understand how they feel slighted. Yet Paul intimates that they are acting like spoiled children, provided with all that is good and pouting about it. So he concludes his response to their perceived wrong with an ironic request for forgiveness: "Forgive me for this injustice!" (χαρίσασθέ μοι τὴν ἀδικίαν ταύτην, *charisasthe moi tēn adikian tautēn*). To call Paul's loving, sacrificial service of the Corinthians ἀδικίαν (*adikian*, injustice), something that violates standards of right conduct, and thus is "wickedness," or an "injustice" (BDAG 20–21), seems tacitly ridiculous, and that is Paul's point. His request for forgiveness (χαρίζομαι, *charizomai*)[16] is offered with his tongue very firmly in his cheek.

Additional Notes

12:11. The participle καυχώμενος has been added by Ψ 0243 1881 𝔐 b sy[(p)], probably to reiterate the theme of "foolish boasting" that permeates the context. But the external support for its omission is overwhelming (𝔓[46] ℵ A B D F G K 6 33 81 629 1175 1739 2464 *al* lat co).

12:11. It could be that τι (in anything) originally followed γάρ (B 𝔓[46]), with scribes omitting the word as superfluous. But it also could be that B and 𝔓[46] have added the indefinite for greater clarification (i.e., "in any aspect of ministry").

12:12. The reading with σημείοις τε has strong external support (𝔓[46] ℵ* B [F G] 0243 0278 33 81 326 630 1175 1739 1881 2464 *pc* g) but evidently was read as an awkward or unclear construction by scribes, some of whom dropped the enclitic particle τέ (A D* *pc* lat; Ambst Pel), while others adjusted the reading to ἐν σημείοις (ℵ² D² Ψ [1505] 𝔐 vg[cl]), perhaps clarifying the idea of "means" inherent in the dative and building continuity with the earlier uses of ἐν in the verse.

---

16. The verb χαρίζομαι, a cognate of χάρις (*charis*, grace [et al.]), can connote giving something graciously, to cancel (forgive) a debt or graciously forgive a wrongdoing (BDAG 1078).

Paul Confronts the Malignant Ministry of His Opponents (10:1–13:13)
A. Present or Absent, Paul's Authority Is the Same (10:1–11)
B. Proper and Improper Boasting (10:12–18)
C. Paul Boasts Like a Fool to Stop the False Apostles (11:1–12:13)
D. Preparation for the Third Visit (12:14–13:10)
E. Closing Exhortations, Greetings, and Benediction (13:11–13)

D. Preparation for the Third Visit (12:14–13:10)

As one of Paul's many rhetorical tools in his letters, the mention of an impending visit perhaps offers the greatest sense of imminent accountability. This final movement of 2 Corinthians consists of two subunits, each introduced by mention of the apostle's promised "third visit":[1]

12:14–21	Pay attention! I am ready to make this third trip to you. (12:14)
13:1–10	This will be my third trip to you. (13:1)

On his first visit, in AD 50, Paul founded the church at Corinth. His second visit, in spring of 54, was the impromptu "sorrowful visit" mentioned at 2:1. So now, writing in the autumn/winter of 54/55, Paul mentions a third trip to this conflicted church.

In the first of these units (12:14–21), Paul appeals to his "family" relationship with the Corinthians (12:14–15) and the integrity of his mission (12:16–18). Then in 12:19 the apostle clarifies his purpose for writing. Correctly considered, this letter has not been a defense of Paul and his mission. Rather, it has been ministry carried out before God, in relationship with Christ, and for the edification of the church. So Paul turns the spotlight on the Corinthians themselves. His concern is that patterns of sin in the church may not have been addressed (12:20–21). In other words, Paul is not on the defense, but there are some in the church who will be held accountable for their immorality!

The second unit (13:1–10) continues the theme of accountability. Paul will not spare those who have not repented (13:2)—the power of God will be manifested among them (13:3–4)! So the Corinthians should examine themselves to see whether they really are in the faith (13:5). Other themes in this unit round off the whole of 2 Cor. 10–13 by again emphasizing Paul's absence over against his presence (10:1–2, 10; 13:10), the apostle's authority for building up the church (10:8; 13:10), and weakness over against power (10:4, 10; 11:21, 29; 12:10; 13:3–4, 9).

---

1. This special form of transition may be referred to as a "parallel introduction" and occurs elsewhere in 2 Corinthians at 4:1 and 4:16; 11:30–31 and 12:1, 2–3. On the use of parallel introductions, see Guthrie 1994: 104–5.

---

1. Concerns Related to the Third Visit (12:14–21)

Confrontation constitutes one of the most difficult aspects of a healthy relationship. In this long and complex letter, Paul has confronted the Corinthians in various ways, but now he prepares to meet them again face-to-face, and in preparing for that encounter, he raises a number of issues he wants them to consider. First, he appeals to them as a spiritual parent to his children (12:14–16a), reiterating that he will not be a burden to them, because parents are supposed to spend themselves for their children. Rather than posing a professional relationship, Paul frames his relationship with the church as one of familial love, and the Corinthians should respond in love. Second, Paul appeals to the Corinthians on the basis of his integrity and the integrity of the fellow workers he has sent to them (12:16b–18). Responding to the charge that he has taken them in by fraud (perhaps in relation to the collection for Jerusalem), Paul points out that they have never been cheated by him or others on his mission team. Third, the apostle puts his letter in perspective. It may have sounded like he was mounting a defense to the Corinthians (and he has been commending himself to them), but the letter primarily should be considered an act of edifying ministry, carried out before God, in relation to Christ (and thus by his authority; 12:19). Finally, Paul expresses his concern that some of the Corinthians may not be morally and spiritually prepared for his visit, forcing the apostle to respond in a way they will not like (12:20–21).

Given these four themes in 12:14–21, the outline of this unit may be depicted as follows:

a. To spend and be spent (12:14–16a)
b. The integrity of Paul's mission (12:16b–18)
c. A misunderstanding (12:19)
d. Further concerns (12:20–21)

Exegesis and Exposition

¹⁴Pay attention! I am ready to make this third trip to you, and I will not be a burden; for I want you yourselves, not your possessions! Children ought not to save up for their parents, but parents for their children. ¹⁵So I will be more than happy to spend and be spent for your souls' sake. ⌜If⌝ ⌜I love⌝ you more, am I to be loved less? ¹⁶So be it; I ⌜haven't burdened you⌝ with your obligation to me! But rather, devious me, I "bamboozled" you by "fraud!" ¹⁷Did I cheat you through any of the men I sent to

you? [18]I encouraged Titus to visit you, and I sent the brother with him. Surely Titus didn't cheat you, did he? Did we not walk by the same Spirit, in the same footsteps? [19]Have you been thinking ⌜all this time⌝ that we are defending ourselves to you? No. We are speaking ⌜before God⌝, in Christ. And everything, dear friends, is for your edification. [20]For I am afraid that perhaps when I come I will find you to be not the sort of "you" I want you to be, and I myself will be found by you to be the sort of "me" that you do not want me to be. I am afraid that perhaps there might be ⌜dissension⌝, ⌜jealousy⌝, fits of rage, selfish ambitions, slanderous words, gossiping, swelled heads, and chaos. [21]I am also afraid that ⌜when I come my God may make me ashamed again in my relationship with you⌝ and that I will grieve over many, who have persisted in their previous patterns of sinning and have not repented in response to the uncleanness and sexual immorality and the rank promiscuity in which they participated.

a. To Spend and Be Spent (12:14–16a)

With verse 14 Paul turns attention to his upcoming third visit to Corinth. The particle ἰδού (*idou*, behold, pay attention; 5:17; 6:2, 9; 7:11), coupled with Paul anticipating his third[1] visit, may be used here to grab the Corinthians' attention in a fresh way as he turns the letter toward its final phase: "Pay attention! I am ready to make this third trip to you."[2] One of Paul's main purposes for this letter is to prepare the Corinthians for an impending visit to their city, a visit to which he has alluded a number of times (2:1, 3; 9:4; 10:6), and the visit becomes an oft-mentioned topic in this last movement of the book (12:20–21; 13:1–2, 10). He speaks of the upcoming visit to offer a measure of accountability to the church; the apostle wants to make sure they are ready for his arrival. Paul wants them to have joy at his coming (2:3), but he also wants them to have the offering for Jerusalem ready (9:4). Moreover, it is clear that he plans to deal straightforwardly with his opponents in the city (10:2, 6), as well as any church members who are rebelling against God's ways (12:20–21; 13:1–2, 10).

12:14

---

1. Twice (12:14; 13:1) Paul mentions that this is the "third" visit he will make to Corinth. His first visit was in AD 50, when he established the church and spent eighteen months ministering among them (Acts 18:1–11). The second visit, referred to as the "painful visit" (2 Cor. 2:1–2), was in response to a disturbing visit that Timothy had made to the city: Paul traveled to Corinth during the spring of AD 54 and clashed with members of the church. Paul will make this third visit (cf. Acts 20:2–3) shortly after 2 Corinthians is completed and spend three months in their midst.

2. The statement here and the restatement at 13:1 may be considered "parallel introductions," introducing successive units. On parallel introductions, see Guthrie 1994: 104. The heart of the main clause in 12:14a is ἑτοίμως ἔχω ἐλθεῖν (*hetoimōs echō elthein*, I am ready to come). The verb ἔχω (*echō*, I have) + the adverb ἑτοίμως (*hetoimōs*, readily, willingly) means "I am ready," or "I am willing," and some versions suggest that the text means that this is the third time Paul is ready to visit them. E.g., the ESV reads, "Here for the third time I am ready to come to you" (similarly, NASB, NET, KJV). In this case, staying closer to the word order of the Greek text is misleading in terms of the author's intent. Rather, Paul means that he has now finished preparing for the trip and is ready to travel to them on a third visit (so HCSB, NRSV, NIV).

At 12:14 he mentions the upcoming third visit so that they might be crystal clear about his unflinching stance on receiving pay for his ministry among them.[3] If they harbor hopes that he might abandon his commitment to working without compensation, they will be sorely disappointed. The apostle states flatly, "I will not be a burden" (οὐ καταναρκήσω, *ou katanarkēsō*). Again, in this case the verb rendered "burden" refers to receiving wages (see comments on 11:9) and was commonly used in patron-client relationships of the dependence of one party on the other (and thus obligation to the patron). Paul sticks by his program of not receiving the pay for his "work" among the Corinthians.

He explains why in parallel sentences, each sentence crafted to highlight a contrast.[4]

For I don't want	your possessions—but you!	[lit.]
Children	ought not to save up	for their parents, but
parents		for their children.

The first sentence clarifies (γάρ, *gar*, for) Paul's motives for refusing pay. In his interaction with the church at Corinth, the apostle, unlike his opponents (2:17; 11:20), is not driven by material gain. The word ζητέω (*zēteō*) can be used variously as meaning "to seek," "look for," "investigate," "consider," or "deliberate," but here it communicates the concept to "strive for, aim (at), try to obtain, desire, wish (for)" (BDAG 428). "Not" (οὐ, *ou*) has pride of place at the beginning of the sentence, making it more emphatic. Paul doesn't want—is not striving to obtain—the Corinthians' "possessions" (τὰ ὑμῶν, *ta hymōn*; lit., the things that belong to you),[5] but rather (ἀλλά, *alla*)[6] the Corinthians themselves. His commitment is to relationship, not financial reward; he wants only what is good for them spiritually, not their goods.

The second sentence offers a truism explaining (γάρ, *gar*) the first sentence, that is, why Paul is interested in them rather than their possessions. Normally[7]

3. As Barnett (1997: 882) comments, it may seem strange to us that, having addressed the issue so straightforwardly at 11:9–12, Paul feels the need to raise the issue again. Yet the reiteration underscores "the sensitivity and centrality of the issue in Paul's relation with the church and is an indication of the influence of his opponents' strategy of seeking to discredit him in the eyes of the Corinthians by pointing to his waiver of an apostolic right as proof of his counterfeit apostleship."

4. The parallelism is seen best in the Greek text of 12:14b:

οὐ γὰρ ζητῶ	τὰ	ὑμῶν ἀλλὰ	
		ὑμᾶς.	
οὐ γὰρ ὀφείλει	τὰ	τέκνα τοῖς γονεῦσιν	θησαυρίζειν ἀλλὰ
	οἱ	γονεῖς τοῖς τέκνοις.	
Ou gar zētō	*ta*	*hymōn alla*	
		hymas.	
Ou gar opheilei	*ta*	*tekna tois goneusin*	*thēsaurizein alla*
	hoi	*goneis tois teknois.*	

5. The genitive is possessive.

6. The conjunction is contrastive.

7. Paul is not stating a hard-and-fast rule. Children often do care for their parents in old age, and Paul has already made clear that other churches have supported him in his mission (2 Cor. 11:8–9; Phil. 4:15–16).

it is the case that parents are obligated to save up and provide financially for their children, not the other way around. In the Greco-Roman world, parents were celebrated as the benefactors of their children (Seneca, *Ben.* 2.11.4–5; 3.11.2; Keener 2005: 242–43), and Paul has already appealed to the Corinthians as his children (1 Cor. 4:14–15; 2 Cor. 6:13). So, instead of patrons in Corinth serving as his benefactors, he, as the "father" of this church, functions as their benefactor, which makes them obligated to him! Given cultural norms, children are supposed to show gratitude, offering love and honor to a sacrificial parent (Xenophon, *Cyr.* 8.1.1; P. Marshall 1987: 248); obviously the Corinthians are falling far short in the relationship! Nevertheless Paul is deeply committed to the principle of providing for his spiritual children and is willing to do whatever it might take to meet their needs. From a spiritual standpoint, they need Paul to buck the cultural currents of Corinth and minister to them outside of the patronage system for traveling public speakers, and Paul draws on the deeper cultural value of parents providing for their children as a way to make his point.

That is why in verse 15 he concludes from this principle, "So[8] I will be more than happy to spend and be spent for your souls' sake." At least a faction among the Corinthians have been concerned about Paul's refusal to take compensation for the public ministry he has carried out among them, but he has explained that his approach serves as part of a strategy to rob his opponents of their opportunity for "ministry" advancement in Corinth (11:7–12). But not only does he refuse to benefit by receiving resources from patrons in Corinth; he also expresses his readiness to "spend and be spent" on behalf of the church. The term δαπανάω (*dapanaō*)[9] could be used in the ancient world to mean "wear out" or "destroy," but given the focus on financial and/or material resources given in compensation for work, Paul uses it to refer to "spending," or "spending freely" one's resources (BDAG 212). The word occurs, for example, in the story of the woman with the flow of blood, who spent all she had on doctors (Mark 5:26), and the parable of the prodigal son, who spent all his resources (Luke 15:14). The compound form of the word that follows also means to spend,[10] and the compound perhaps intensifies the sense a bit. Therefore, the future passive (ἐκδαπανηθήσομαι, *ekdapanēthēsomai*) means "to be spent" or "exhausted"; Paul is speaking of pouring himself out in ministry to the Corinthians. So the apostle expresses his readiness not only to spend his own

12:15

---

8. The conjunction δέ (*de*) in 12:15 draws a simple connection to the principle in verse 14, but based on the context it is appropriate to present Paul's readiness to spend and be spent as grounded in that principle ("So," NIV).

9. Since the future tense form used here expresses a commitment on Paul's part, rather than a prediction of specific actions in the future, it seems more gnomic in nature, referring to a timeless truth.

10. Josephus (*Ant.* 15.117), e.g., uses this term (an aorist active participle) to speak of the Jewish freedom fighters "spending" their courage on their enemies: "For as the Jews had spent [ἐκδαπανήσαντες] their courage upon their known enemies, and were about to enjoy themselves in quietness after their victory, they were easily beaten by these that attacked them afresh."

resources in ministering to the Corinthians, but also to be poured out himself. The thought mirrors somewhat the admirable posture of the Macedonians, who not only gave of their resources generously, but also "gave themselves" in the cause of Christ (8:3–5), and both Paul and the Macedonians surely show themselves to be followers of the one who served and gave his life for many (Mark 10:45).

For Paul's part, he will be ἥδιστα (hēdista, more than happy)[11] to spend and be spent for the Corinthians. The phrase ὑπὲρ τῶν ψυχῶν ὑμῶν (hyper tōn psychōn hymōn, for your souls' sake) speaks of advantage for the Corinthian believers. Ironically, the Corinthians read Paul's refusal of compensation as hurting them (11:11), but the apostle is only wanting to help them, to benefit them spiritually. The word ψυχή (psychē) had a broad semantic range in the first century. It could refer to the "lives" of the Corinthians, but here it probably refers to their "souls," the center of one's life (cf. 2 Cor. 1:23).[12]

Naturally, this spending and being spent should be understood as a profound expression of love, and the Corinthians' ironic, negative response to it is not lost on Paul: "If I love you more, am I to be loved less?" (εἰ περισσοτέρως ὑμᾶς ἀγαπῶ[ν], ἧσσον ἀγαπῶμαι; ei perissoterōs hymas agapō[n], hēsson agapōmai?). The rhetorical question begins with an interrogative use of εἰ, an unusual construction for Paul (BDAG 278). The descriptor περισσοτέρως (perissoterōs) has already been used several times in the letter to speak of something "more," or done to a greater degree (1:12; 2:4; 7:13, 15; 11:23). Paul does not mean he is "loving" (ἀγαπῶ[ν], agapō[n])[13] the Corinthians "more" than other churches, nor that he loves them "more" than his opponents do. Rather, περισσοτέρως balances ἧσσον (hēsson, less), the apostle asserting, "I am loved[14] less" (Harris 2005: 886–87). In essence, Paul asks, "As my love increases, does yours decrease?" One would expect that increasing expressions of love on the apostle's part would engender a greater response of love, honor, and commitment from the Corinthians, but the opposite seems true. The more he gives himself in sacrificial love, the less they love him, the less they commit themselves to him in honor and gratitude! Thus the irony of the rhetorical question.

12:16a In answer to his own question he simply responds (v. 16a), "So be it" (Ἔστω δέ, Estō de).[15] Verse 16 begins with Ἔστω, a present imperative of εἰμί (eimi) that can be translated, "Let it be." Although the verb could be introducing what

---

11. Paul has already said that the Corinthians "cheerfully [gladly] put up with fools" (11:19) and that he "will boast all the more gladly about" his "weaknesses" (12:9).

12. Paul's uses of ψυχή (13x) show a range of meanings (Rom. 2:9; 11:3; 13:1; 16:4; 1 Cor. 15:45; 2 Cor. 1:23; 12:15; Eph. 6:6; Phil. 1:27; 2:30; Col. 3:23; 1 Thess. 2:8; 5:23).

13. The present participle is conditional.

14. The present passive indicative from ἀγαπάω (agapaō, love) has an imperfective aspect: Paul refers to an ongoing situation in his relationship with the Corinthians.

15. The δέ draws a simple connection to the previous sentence and does not need to be translated.

follows (e.g., HCSB, NLT², NRSV),[16] it probably refers back to the rhetorical question that precedes it, with Paul in essence saying, "If I love you more, am I to be loved less? *So be it!*"

He continues, "I haven't burdened you with your obligation to me!" (ἐγὼ οὐ κατεβάρησα ὑμᾶς, *egō ou katebarēsa hymas*). The aorist verb κατεβάρησα could be reiterating Paul's earlier statements on not "burdening" the Corinthians by taking pay from them (11:9; 12:13–14), but the verb the apostle employs here is different and quite rare; we should ask if the change is significant. Granted, Paul may simply be using a synonym for literary variety, but a different interpretation is possible. As noted in the comments at 11:9, the verb καταναρκάω (*katanarkaō*) could be used of the patron-client relationship. Paul has refused to "burden" wealthy patrons at Corinth, thus avoiding being socially dependent on them, or obligated to a particular faction within the Corinthian church (Keener 2005: 229; Peterman 1997: 159, 169, 201–4). But now he uses the verb καταβαρέω (*katabareō*), which means "to weigh heavily on," or "to be a burden to" (BDAG 514), and appears only here in the biblical literature.[17]

Josephus (*Ant.* 2.83), for instance, uses a related term in a retelling of Joseph's interpretation of Pharaoh's dream: "I saw seven ears of corn growing out of one root, having their heads *borne down* [καρηβαροῦντας, *karēbarountas*] by the weight of the grains." Similarly, Plutarch (*Cleom.* 2.27.2) employs our word of wrestlers becoming "tired down" in the course of a match, and Epictetus (*Disc.* 2.22.18) says that friends, country, family, and justice all give way before selfishness and thus are "weighed down by what is personally advantageous" (καταβαρούμενα ὑπὸ τοῦ συμφέροντος, *katabaroumena hypo tou sympherontos*). So the word speaks of fatigue, being loaded down with an egregious weight.

Perhaps the use of a different verb for a similar concept signals that Paul crafts a play on words in response to the Corinthians' ironic response to his ministry. Employing a nice bit of irony, he says in effect, "Your love decreases as I love you more? So be it; I don't mean to weigh you down under the obligation of responding appropriately to my love!" He has not "burdened them" by receiving pay for his services; but neither has he "burdened them" with the obligation of responding well to his love.

b. The Integrity of Paul's Mission (12:16b–18)

That the apostle is speaking tongue-in-cheek is blatantly clear as he continues in the second half of verse 16: "But rather, devious me, I 'bamboozled' you by 'fraud!'" The conjunction (ἀλλά, *alla*, but) draws a sharp contrast and is rhetorically ascensive (imagine Paul's tone of voice rising). The contrast stands

12:16b

---

16. "Now granted, I have not burdened you" (2 Cor. 12:16 HCSB); "Some of you admit I was not a burden to you" (NLT²); "Let it be assumed that I did not burden you" (NRSV).

17. See, however, the similar verb, καταβαρύνω (*katabarynō*), in Mark 14:40; 2 Sam. 13:25; 14:26; Joel 2:8.

between what Paul has not done (i.e., burdening them by pressing their obligation to love him in response to his ministry; see 6:13) and what some say he has done (i.e., tricked them into commitment to his ministry and perhaps the collection for Jerusalem). The latter probably reflects an accusation made by Paul's opponents,[18] who accuse him of being devious in his dealings with the Corinthians. Dripping with sarcasm, then, the second half of verse 16 presents a blunt denial that Paul has acted with anything but the utmost integrity.

The term πανοῦργος (panourgos) means "crafty," "sly," thus "devious," and serves as a predicate adjective related to the verb of being ὑπάρχων (hyparchōn; lit., being crafty; or as with our translation, "devious me"). How was Paul's craftiness supposedly manifested? He "bamboozled" (ἔλαβον, elabon) the Corinthians; in this case the verb λαμβάνω (lambanō, take, receive) is used to speak of "taking someone in," that is, taking advantage of or defrauding a person. Paul has used the term earlier at 11:20 of the false teachers "kidnapping" the Corinthians. Here the emphasis seems to be that Paul hoodwinked or bamboozled the church in some way. Perhaps he has been accused of pulling a fast one on the Corinthians in terms of the collection for Jerusalem (8:20). By what means did he do so? "By fraud" (δόλῳ, dolō), the word referring to "taking advantage through craft and underhanded methods," "by deceit" or "treachery" (BDAG 256). If the collection for the saints in Jerusalem is in mind, we again are confronted with a great irony: the Corinthians whine that Paul won't receive compensation for his ministry among them, even as some accuse him of cheating them with regard to the collection for the saints!

Yet the apostle has repeatedly asserted his own integrity and the foundational nature of integrity for authentic Christian ministry. Speaking sarcastically, he has just denied that he is "devious" (πανοῦργος). Using the cognate term πανουργία (panourgia) at 4:2, Paul proclaims that he and his ministry team do not "live by tricks"; and at 11:3 he writes that it is Satan the deceiver, the master of the false teachers at Corinth (11:14–15), who misled Eve "by his chicanery" (ἐν τῇ πανουργίᾳ αὐτοῦ, en tē panourgia autou). Elsewhere in the letter the apostle appeals to his good conscience (1:12; 4:2; 5:11) as he lives out his ministry with a God-given sincerity (1:12). He has not misled them or spoken falsely about his plans to visit them (1:18–23). Unlike his opponents, the apostle is no huckster, peddling God's Word for his own profit, for all he does he does "before God" (2:17; 12:19) and in the fear of God (7:1), commending himself to the conscience of others (4:2; 6:4).

12:17–18   In verse 17 he begins to press them on the matter, challenging the Corinthians to put meat on the bones of this accusation of deviousness, if they can. He asks, "Did I cheat you through any of the men I sent to you?" (μή τινα ὧν ἀπέσταλκα πρὸς ὑμᾶς, δι' αὐτοῦ ἐπλεονέκτησα ὑμᾶς; mē tina hōn apestalka pros hymas, di' autou epleonektēsa hymas?). Paul's question may clarify the accusation a bit for us, pointing in the direction of the collection for the saints. First, the verb πλεονεκτέω (pleonekteō), employed in the NT only by Paul and

---

18. Thus the ET's quotation marks around the words "bamboozled" and "fraud."

only once outside of the four occurrences in 2 Corinthians (1 Thess. 4:6), could be used to speak of exploiting, defrauding, or cheating others (BDAG 824). Earlier in 2 Corinthians, at 2:11, Paul uses the word of Satan's exploitative schemes, and at 7:2 he strongly denies that he has cheated anyone, taking up the word in conjunction with his denial that he has mistreated (ἠδικήσαμεν, *ēdikēsamen*) or corrupted (ἐφθείραμεν, *ephtheiramen*) people. As we look to the two passages in which this word occurs in the LXX, the nuances related to greedy gain become more apparent. At Hab. 2:9 we read, "Ah he who gains [πλεονεκτῶν, *pleonektōn*] an evil gain for his house" (NETS), and Ezek. 22:27 laments concerning the leaders of Israel and sinful Jerusalem, "Its rulers in its midst were like wolves catching prey to shed blood so that they gain through greed [πλεονεξίᾳ πλεονεκτῶσιν, *pleonexia pleonektōsin*]" (NETS). So the word can refer to unjust material gain.[19]

Second, however, Paul's question focuses specifically on the men he has sent (ὧν ἀπέσταλκα, *hōn apestalka*)[20] to the Corinthians. In chapter 8 he writes, explaining that he sends Titus and the brothers to make sure that the collection for Jerusalem is administered properly (8:16–24). In our current context Titus and "the brother" are mentioned at 12:18, with Paul reiterating that he has urged Titus to visit them (παρεκάλεσα Τίτον, *parekalesa Titon*; cf. 8:16–17), sending with him "the brother" (καὶ συναπέστειλα τὸν ἀδελφόν, *kai synapesteila ton adelphon*; cf. 8:18). These references tie the concerns at 12:16–18 to Paul's earlier explanation of how the collection for Jerusalem is to be conducted *to maintain the utmost integrity*. Further, the μή (*mē*) that introduces the rhetorical question of verse 17 anticipates a negative answer and thus constitutes a denial on Paul's part. The fact is, Paul asserts, Titus and the brother have acted with complete integrity while among the Corinthians. This is underscored with "Surely Titus didn't cheat you, did he?" (μήτι ἐπλεονέκτησεν ὑμᾶς Τίτος; *mēti epleonektēsen hymas Titos?*). Again, μήτι stands as a marker that invites a negative answer to the question.

Following on the heels of this denial comes a confident assertion (the twice-used negative οὐ anticipates a positive answer), again in the form of yet another pair of rhetorical questions. The first reads: "Did we not walk by the same Spirit?" (οὐ τῷ αὐτῷ πνεύματι περιεπατήσαμεν; *ou tō autō pneumati periepatēsamen?*). At several points Paul has already used the idiom of "walking" to refer to living according to a certain pattern of life (4:2; 5:7; 10:2–3), and the first-person plural ("we") refers to Titus and the apostle. Here that pattern of life is more specifically defined as "by the same Spirit." He made

---

19. Josephus also uses the word consistently of greedy gain (e.g., *Ant.* 1.66; 2.260; 3.29; 4.225; 17.277; 18.172).

20. Rather than an "aoristic perfect" (so), the use of the perfect in 12:17 may reflect the "state" of those sent as still being with the Corinthians (thus, perhaps, an extensive perfect). The construction of the sentence is a bit awkward since Paul begins by referring to the one sent with μή τινα ὧν (*mē tina hōn*, any of whom) and then shifts to δι' αὐτοῦ (*di' autou*, through him). Barrett (1973: 318) works the awkwardness out with "Any of those I have sent to you—did I defraud you through him?"

the point earlier that the false teachers in Corinth came, bringing with them "a different spirit than the Spirit" the Corinthians have received (see comments at 11:4). By contrast, Paul and Titus conduct their lives and ministries by the same (τῷ αὐτῷ) Spirit. The phrase τῷ αὐτῷ πνεύματι has been interpreted primarily in two ways. Some read "spirit" anthropologically as referring to the spiritual dimension of a person (i.e., "by the same spirit"), or perhaps a common disposition (e.g., ESV, HCSB, NASB, NLT², NRSV, NET; BDAG 833). In support of this view, the second rhetorical question in our verse, "in the same footsteps?" (οὐ τοῖς αὐτοῖς ἴχνεσιν; *ou tois autois ichnesin?*), presents the figurative use of "in the same footsteps," which also refers to a pattern of life (Rom. 4:12; 1 Pet. 2:21), in parallel relationship with "in the same spirit," suggesting to some that with "spirit" Paul refers to a common approach, or course, to life and ministry (Harris 2005: 892). They see life the same way and thus live by the same principles and patterns. The apostle does employ the word πνεῦμα anthropologically at several points in the letter (2:13; 4:13; 7:1, 13).

On the other hand, there are reasons for reading the reference to πνεῦμα as referring to the Holy Spirit (see esp. the argument in Fee 1994: 357–59). At Rom. 8:4 Paul speaks of walking "according to the Spirit" (κατὰ πνεῦμα, *kata pneuma*) and, even more closely resembling our passage at hand, Gal. 5:16 exhorts believers to "walk by the Spirit" (πνεύματι περιπατεῖτε, *pneumati peripateite*). Both contexts can be read as speaking of the Holy Spirit. Further, at 1 Cor. 12:9 he also uses the phrase "by the same Spirit" (ἐν τῷ αὐτῷ πνεύματι, *en tō autō pneumati*), referring to the Holy Spirit, and in the other places in 2 Corinthians where ministry is clearly in view, πνεῦμα seems to refer consistently to the Holy Spirit (2 Cor. 3:3, 6, 8, 17–18; 5:5). As Fee (1994: 359) explains, "in the same footsteps," while parallel to "in the same Spirit" in terms of word-crafting, picks up and specifically reinforces the concept of "walking." Thus it is possible to read "walking . . . in the same footsteps" in life and ministry as being facilitated by the power of the Spirit. Paul and Titus have ministered according to the same patterns and principles because they are empowered by the same Spirit.

c. A Misunderstanding (12:19)

12:19   The first sentence in verse 19 can be read either as a statement of fact or a question. Since Paul has been peppering the Corinthians with questions since 12:13, the latter may be intended: "Have you been thinking all this time that we are defending ourselves to you?" The Corinthians have been "supposing" (δοκεῖτε, *dokeite*) something about Paul and his ministry team. In other words, Paul discerns that their perception of him and his mission has been running in a certain vein,[21] and this has been going on for a while. Πάλαι (*Palai*) can refer to a time in the past ("formerly, long ago"; e.g., Heb. 1:1), or be roughly

---

21. The present-tense form, with its imperfective aspect, may be considered as reflecting an ongoing activity that is "extending-from-past" (D. Wallace 1996: 519).

equivalent to "already" (ἤδη, *ēdē*, though normally referring to a longer period of time; e.g., Mark 15:44). But here the word pertains to looking back from the present to a point in the past (i.e., "for a long time," "for a while now"; BDAG 751). The Corinthians have been thinking something about him "all this time," beginning perhaps with the tattering of relationships between Paul and others in Corinth, or perhaps referring to the beginning of the letter (i.e., they have been thinking about him a certain way from the start of this correspondence; see, e.g., 1:12–20).

The content (ὅτι, *hoti*) of their thought is that Paul has been defending himself and his mission before the Corinthians[22] (ὅτι ὑμῖν ἀπολογούμεθα, *hoti hymin apologoumetha*, that we are defending ourselves to you; 12:19). The verb ἀπολογέομαι (*apologeomai*) belongs to legal settings, in which a person defends himself publicly (Luke 12:11; 21:14; Acts 19:33; 24:10; 25:8; 26:1–2, 24; Rom. 2:15). Certainly a defensive tone can be read at a number of points throughout the letter (e.g., 1:12–20, 23–24; 3:1, 4–6; 6:3, 12; 7:2; 8:20; 10:9–10; 11:6–8). Here again we have a situation in which Paul may be perceived as doing something from a certain perspective, but perceived as not doing it from another angle. At points in 2 Corinthians Paul can be read as "commending" himself (3:1; 4:2; 6:4), but he seems reticent to embrace that perspective (3:1; 5:12). At other points he "boasts" (7:14; 10:8, 17; 11:12, 16; 12:9)—but he also does not want to boast in a worldly way (10:13; 11:12, 18, 21; 12:5). He mounts a defense of himself and his mission, but here the apostle suggests that such a perspective fails to do justice to the reality of the situation.

Echoing what he wrote earlier, at 2:17, Paul proclaims that his words are spoken "before God, in Christ" (κατέναντι θεοῦ ἐν Χριστῷ, *katenanti theou en Christō*). The words he has written in this letter are not motivated by "winning" a debate with the opponents, mounting a defense before the Corinthians (ὑμῖν, *hymin*, to you) as if to a jury. Rather his words are profoundly grounded in his posture before God and in his relationship with Christ.

Although the phrase κατέναντι θεοῦ (*katenanti theou*) occurs elsewhere in the book only at 2 Cor. 2:17,[23] the concept has a rich backdrop in biblical theology (see the comments at 2:17) and serves as a constant in Paul's self-understanding reflected in 2 Corinthians. Paul carries out his ministry with a gravity of posture, a profound sense of accountability to the One True God, who has called him and commissioned him (Rom. 3:20; 14:22; 1 Cor. 1:29; 2 Cor. 4:2; 8:21; Gal. 1:20; 1 Tim. 2:3; 5:4, 21; 6:13; 2 Tim. 2:14; 4:1). Thus he does not speak or act to impress people but rather to please God.

---

22. The dative plural pronoun ὑμῖν could be considered an indirect object, with the implied "ourselves" inherent in the verb read as the implied object. Yet, given the contrasting parallel with κατέναντι (*katenanti*, before) in the next sentence, ὑμῖν may be read as speaking of posture ("before you").

23. The LXX, e.g., uses variously the prepositions ἀπέναντι, ἐνώπιον, ἐναντίον, πρός (*apenanti, enōpion, enantion, pros* + acc.), or the words πρὸ προσώπου (*pro prosōpou*) in phrases that speak of someone being "before God." The NT renderings of the concept are equally varied.

Paul also speaks ἐν Χριστῷ, using a Pauline staple phrase that has strong relational overtones. At points the apostle uses the phrase to speak of corporate solidarity ("in the body of Christ"), but here he seems to speak more from the standpoint of his personal relationship. We may understand it as a dative of association, "in relation to Christ." Paul not only preaches *about* Christ Jesus; he not only preaches by the authority of Christ; he also preaches grounded in a profound relationship *with Christ*.

This posture before God and relationship with Christ keeps Paul's motives pure in relation to the Corinthians: "And everything, dear friends, is for your edification" (τὰ δὲ πάντα, ἀγαπητοί, ὑπὲρ τῆς ὑμῶν οἰκοδομῆς, *ta de panta, agapētoi, hyper tēs hymōn oikodomēs*). The "everything" (τὰ . . . πάντα) refers comprehensively to all that Paul has been doing and saying in his ministry to the Corinthians. The affectionate term "dear friends" (ἀγαπητοί), found earlier at 7:1, is one that Paul often uses in the plural to address his churches (Rom. 1:7; 11:28; 12:19; 1 Cor. 10:14; 15:58; Phil. 2:12; 4:1; 1 Thess. 2:8; 1 Tim. 6:2); this address takes a bit of the edge off the ironic tone that permeates much of what has been communicated since 12:11. Perhaps as he turns once more to the coming "third trip," the apostle hints at the bond he has with the Corinthians—a bond by which he intends to hold them accountable (12:20–21). It is because they are dear to him that he does what he does and says what he says. His ministry exists only for their edification (ὑπὲρ τῆς ὑμῶν οἰκοδομῆς).[24] Paul has already used the word οἰκοδομή (*oikodomē*) of the resurrection body as "the building" made by God (5:1), an image taken from the term's literal use to speak of a building or the process of construction of a building (BDAG 696–97). But the figurative uses at 10:8 and 13:10 correspond more directly with the use here at 12:19. In chapters 10 and 13 the apostle speaks overtly about "edification" as the purpose of his authority. At 10:8 he declares that he will not be ashamed to boast about his authority, and at 13:10 he writes that he does not want to need to deal harshly with the Corinthians when he arrives. In both cases Paul reminds the Corinthians that the exercise of his apostolic authority works to build them up, not to tear them down. Certainly the latter can be mistaken for the former. Being "built up" sometimes feels like being "torn down," especially when the edification comes wrapped in confrontation and correction.

Yet at 12:19 Paul intimates that the Corinthians are misunderstanding him in another way, reading his words in the letter thus far as though Paul is defending himself to them. Paul corrects them. Rather than securing their affirmation of him as an end in itself, the apostle intends to secure their spiritual well-being through everything he says and does. In other words, Paul is not on the defense in 2 Corinthians—he is on the offense. He wants the Corinthians to embrace him fully as their apostle, so that they will be rightly related to God and God's gospel.

24. The preposition ὑπέρ with the genitive serves as a marker of the "edification" being carried out in their interest, for their benefit.

d. Further Concerns (12:20–21)

The mention of "edification" at the end of verse 19 brings to the apostle's **12:20–21** mind, in a fresh way, the Corinthians' very great need of being built up from their current spiritual state. Consequently, in verses 20–21 Paul names three fears burdening him as he anticipates this third visit to the city:[25]

1. He and the Corinthians might disappoint one another (v. 20a).
2. He might find the Corinthians to be dysfunctional in relationships (v. 20b).
3. He might be ashamed again when he needs to confront blatant immorality in the church (v. 21).

Early in 2 Corinthians Paul writes that he had adjusted his travel plans, delaying his visit to Corinth, to "spare" the Corinthians, not wishing to cause them (and himself) emotional turmoil (1:23–2:1). He also had written to this effect in the "sorrowful letter," the composition of which was "gut-wrenching" (2:3–4). Rather than the rantings of an overlord, such confrontations are an expression of the apostle's love (1:24; 2:4b). Yet clearly, Paul did not relish conflict in Corinth.

Accordingly, as the third trip approaches, the apostle has misgivings. Although the Corinthians have responded positively to Titus's recent visit, especially with regard to the person who had sinned (7:7–11, 13b–16), there still was a great deal of work to do. He confesses, "For I am afraid that perhaps when I come I will find you to be not the sort of 'you' I want you to be, and I myself will be found by you to be the sort of 'me' that you do not want me to be." In other words, *he is afraid that he and the Corinthians will disappoint one another*. This is the first concern he expresses.

The conjunction γάρ (*gar*, for) picks up on the concept of edification (οἰκοδομῆς, *oikodomēs*) at the end of verse 19, perhaps moving from that general concept to specific examples of the need for spiritual upbuilding in the Corinthian congregation. The mention of the apostle's deep concern (φοβοῦμαι, *phoboumai*, fear)[26] functions as the heading for all of 12:20–21, and the repeated conjunction μή πως (*mē pōs*, perhaps) highlights a negative perspective, expressing Paul's misgivings (BDAG 901).[27] What Paul fears, first of all, is that "when[28] he comes" (ἐλθών, *elthōn*), he could be disappointed with

---

25. The structure of 12:20–21 builds around the initial verb:

φοβοῦμαι	. . . μή πως	ἐλθών	(*phoboumai . . . mē pōs elthōn*, I am afraid that perhaps when I come)
	. . . μή πως		(*mē pōs*, perhaps there might be)
	. . . μὴ πάλιν	ἐλθόντος μου	(*mē palin elthontos mou*, that when I come again)

26. The term φοβοῦμαι communicates in context deep concern or apprehension, rather than terror (e.g., Josephus, *Ant.* 10.8; Acts 23:10; 27:17).
27. This is a case in which μή πως is in an object clause after a verb of apprehension.
28. The aorist participle is temporal.

the Corinthians. The aorist subjunctive εὕρω (*heurō*, I might find) expresses a degree of uncertainty concerning what Paul will encounter upon arrival in Corinth. The apostle writes his concern tactfully, rather than dogmatically, but he thinks it probable that he will find them to be "not[29] the sort of 'you'[30] I want you to be" (οὐχ οἵους θέλω, *ouch hoious thelō*; lit., not such as I wish),[31] and the remainder of the letter details the "sort" they might turn out to be. Correspondingly[32] (κἀγώ, *kagō*, and I myself), if they are behaving badly when he arrives, they are sure to find Paul (κἀγὼ εὑρεθῶ ὑμῖν, *kagō heurethō hymin*; lit., and I will be found by you) to be the sort of person they do not wish to have confronting them.

Second, Paul *fears that he will find the Corinthians to be dysfunctional in relationships*. Prior to his list of specific concerns (v. 20b), Paul reiterates his "fear" by repeating μή πως (*mē pōs*, perhaps), with the φοβοῦμαι (*phoboumai*, I fear) being understood at this point. What the apostle fears specifically is "that perhaps there might be dissension, jealousy, fits of rage, selfish ambitions, slanderous words, gossiping, swelled heads, and chaos." The relational breakdown with their apostle (and thus with God) manifests itself in fragmentation and harmful interpersonal dynamics in the community. Found at times in lists of vices, ἔρις (*eris*) refers to quarrels[33] or conflict over certain positions taken by different parties, that is, "controversy" or "dissension" (Rom. 1:29; 13:13; Gal. 5:20; Phil. 1:15; 1 Tim. 6:4; Titus 3:9); since they are driven by fleshly desires, the Corinthians have been torn by dissension for some time (1 Cor. 1:11; 3:3). At times ζῆλος (*zēlos*, jealousy, envy) occurs in the same vice lists as ἔρις (Rom. 13:13; 1 Cor. 3:3; Gal. 5:20), with ζῆλος perhaps giving rise to ἔρις. Earlier in the book Paul uses the term positively to speak of the Corinthians' deep "concern" (7:7, 11), their "enthusiasm" for participating in the collection for Jerusalem (9:2), and Paul's own godly "jealousy" toward the Corinthians (11:2). Yet clearly here the word refers to a vice about which the apostle is concerned. These first two terms are singular. The remaining six are plural.

The third specific concern Paul mentions, θυμοί (*thymoi*) joins the first two vices in the list at Gal. 5:20. Referring to stoked passions, in the NT it

---

29. Harris (2005: 897) correctly points out that the versions rendering the verse as "that I will not find" (e.g., HCSB, NIV[84], NIV, NET, KJV) err. Paul's concern is with what he will find, specifically, that the Corinthians are "not the sort" he hopes.

30. This also can be rendered appropriately as "not the sort of people."

31. The correlative pronoun οἷος (*hoios*) pertains to someone or something belonging to a certain class or group. In this case, it relates to the pronoun ὑμᾶς (*hymas*, you), "the sort of persons I wish you to be," or "the sort of 'you' I want you to be."

32. Paul expresses the concepts with a chiastic structure:

   A οὐχ οἵους θέλω (*ouch hoious thelō*, not the sort I want)

     B εὕρω ὑμᾶς (*heurō hymas*, I may find you)

       C κἀγὼ (*kagō*, and I myself)

     B′ εὑρεθῶ ὑμῖν (*heurethō hymin*, may be found by you)

   A′ οἷον οὐ θέλετε (*hoion ou thelete*, [to be] the sort that you do not want [me to be])

33. In the LXX, Sir. 28:11 proverbially proclaims, "A quarrel [ἔρις] being hastened kindles a fire, and strife in a hurry sheds blood" (NETS).

can speak of God's intense anger or wrath (Rom. 2:8; Rev. 14:10; 15:1, 7; 16:1, 19; 19:15), or intensely passionate immorality (Rev. 14:8; 18:3), but in the context of human relationships the term communicates rage, intense anger, or indignation (Luke 4:28; Acts 19:28; Gal. 5:20; Eph. 4:31; Col. 3:8; Heb. 11:27). With the NIV, we translate the plural form as "fits of rage." Of questionable meaning, the fourth term in this vice list (ἐριθεῖαι, *eritheiai*) is also found at Gal. 5:20; it is almost nonexistent in ancient literature outside the NT. In Aristotle, the word connotes "self-seeking pursuit of a political office by unfair means,"[34] and in the NT it probably means something to the effect of "selfish ambition" (Rom. 2:8; Gal. 5:20; Phil. 1:17; 2:3; James 3:14, 16), or in the plural, "selfish ambitions."

The next two terms, καταλαλιαί (*katalaliai*) and ψιθυρισμοί (*psithyrismoi*), refer to sins of speech. The first, found only here and at 1 Pet. 2:1 in the NT, refers to "slander" or "abusive language" about or to another person (e.g., Polybius, *Hist*. 27.13.2). Philo uses the word, for instance, of Miriam "speaking against" Moses (*Alleg*. 2.66) and of the Israelites "speaking against" the Lord (*Alleg*. 2.78). In the plural it can be rendered as "slanderous words." Ψιθυρισμός (*psithyrismos*), on the other hand, carries more a note of secrecy about it. For example, Eccles. 10:11 LXX[35] uses the word of the "whispers" of a snake charmer, and Plutarch employs it to describe a student "whispering" to another person during a lecture.[36] In the type of conflictual context Paul describes, the word refers to "derogatory information about someone that is offered in a tone of confidentiality," that is, "gossip" (BDAG 1098). The plural perhaps refers to a pattern of behavior, thus, "gossiping."

Our final two terms in Paul's list of concerns are φυσιώσεις (*physiōseis*) and ἀκαταστασίαι (*akatastasiai*). The first, a hapax in the biblical literature and rarely outside it, refers to "swelled-headedness" (BDAG 1070), or as we might say in English idiom, "having the big head." In the plural we render it with "swelled heads" (so Message). Using another term, at 11:20 Paul describes the interlopers as behaving arrogantly, and their attitude seems to have spread. Further, it may be that the word ἀκαταστασία (*akatastasia*) sums up the effect of all these other interpersonal problems, for it speaks of disorder or "chaos," especially as it relates to established authority (BDAG 35).[37] Paul has used the word earlier, at 6:5, to refer to riots or mob actions. Yet Prov. 26:28 LXX employs the term to speak of the havoc caused by a flattering mouth. Using this

34. The statement in BDAG 392 that "before NT times" ἐριθεία is found only in Aristotle (*Pol*. 5.3–4) is incorrect, for it also occurs in a third-century BC papyrus, P.Sorb. 1.34, which nevertheless does nothing to clarify the word's meaning.
35. This is the sole use in the LXX. It occurs in the Pseudepigrapha twice in the vice lists of 3 Baruch (8.5; 13.4).
36. "And so in the particular case of a lecture, not only frowning, a sour face, a roving glance, twisting the body about, and crossing the legs, are unbecoming, but even nodding, whispering to another [ψιθυρισμὸς πρὸς ἕτερον], smiling, sleepy yawns, bowing down the head, and all like actions, are culpable and need to be carefully avoided" (Plutarch, *Rect. rat. aud*. 1.13; Babbitt 1927: 243–45).
37. Thus P.Mich. 8.477 uses the word in tandem with θόρυβος (*thorybos*, confusion) of a city.

term earlier, in 1 Cor. 14:33 Paul has written to the Corinthians, "for God is not characterized by *disorder* but by peace" (NET), and James observes, "For where there is jealousy and selfishness, there is *disorder* and every evil practice" (3:16 NET). Thus the term refers to the relational upheaval, or chaos, caused by sinful patterns of behavior.

With verse 21, the apostle moves to yet a third main concern that plagues him as his third visit to Corinth draws near: *He is afraid that he might be ashamed again upon having to confront blatant immorality in the church.* The content of verse 21 falls in two main movements,[38] crafted around the verbs ταπεινώσῃ (*tapeinōsē*, he may humble) and πενθήσω (*penthēsō*, I may grieve). As we saw in verse 20, the initial verb φοβοῦμαι (*phoboumai*, I am afraid) is understood as carrying over to verse 21 as well, and the successive uses of μή πως (*mē pōs*, perhaps) in verse 20 mark successive movements in Paul's thought, highlighting two of his concerns about returning to Corinth. Accordingly, as verse 21 begins, φοβοῦμαι is understood, and now, instead of μή πως we have μή alone marking a third concern the apostle wishes to communicate.[39]

First, he is concerned that *God may cause him to be ashamed again* (πάλιν . . . ταπεινώσῃ με ὁ θεός μου, *palin . . . tapeinōsē me ho theos mou*, my God may make me ashamed again). As detailed in our historical backdrop of

38. The structure may be depicted as follows (cf. ET at unit opening):

<pre>
                          πάλιν
                          ἐλθόντος μου
[φοβοῦμαι] μή   > ταπεινώσῃ με ὁ θεός μου
                          πρὸς ὑμᾶς
                     καὶ
                     πενθήσω
                          πολλοὺς τῶν   προημαρτηκότων καὶ
                                         μὴ μετανοησάντων
                                                ἐπὶ τῇ ἀκαθαρσίᾳ καὶ
                                                    πορνείᾳ καὶ
                                                    ἀσελγείᾳ ᾗ ἔπραξαν.

                     palin
                     elthontos mou
[phoboumai] mē   >tapeinōsē me ho theos mou
                          pros hymas
                  kai
                  penthēsō
                     pollous tōn   proēmartēkotōn kai
                                    mē metanoēsantōn
                                         epi tē akatharsia kai
                                             porneia kai
                                             aselgeia hē epraxan.
</pre>

39. Thus μή again functions as a conjunction after a verb of fearing (BDF 188). It may be, as Harris (2005: 901) speculates, that μή alone rather than μή πως suggests that Paul believes the humiliation mentioned in 12:21 to be even more likely to materialize than the concerns mentioned in verse 20.

2 Corinthians (see the introduction), Paul's "sorrowful visit" in the spring of AD 54 was deeply disturbing to the apostle. Paul was publicly confronted and verbally abused by a vitriolic church member (2:1–5), who was supported by a minority of the church, while the majority stood by in silence, failing to defend the apostle (2:5; 7:12). The experience, which made painfully clear the continued spiritual immaturity of the Corinthian church, left Paul emotionally bruised and discouraged as he traveled back to Ephesus (Garland 1999: 95–96). His "sorrowful letter" soon followed.

Understandably, a return visit (when I come, ἐλθόντος μου, *elthontos mou*)[40] to the place of deep distress and embarrassment was somewhat unsettling, and Paul here reflects that a repeat of that type of experience would make him ashamed "again."[41] The verb ταπεινόω (*tapeinoō*) could be used by writers in the first century to mean "to cause someone to lose prestige or status," in the sense of "to shame" or "humiliate" (so, e.g., HCSB, NASB, NET), and this probably is what Paul intends here.[42] He has already mentioned that he has "humbled" himself by working without pay (11:7), and his manual labor has been considered "shameful" or "humiliating" by the socially elite in Corinth.[43] Now the apostle faces the probability[44] that, as he expresses it, "my God may make me ashamed again in my relationship with you" (ταπεινώσῃ με ὁ θεός μου πρὸς ὑμᾶς, *tapeinōsē me ho theos mou pros hymas*). That "God" would make Paul ashamed is equivalent to Paul experiencing shame "before God." The apostle wants to present the Corinthians as a pure bride to Christ (11:2), and the failure to do so would be a cause of shame. Further, πρός plus the accusative pronoun ὑμᾶς can speak of intimacy of relationship (i.e., "in my relationship with you").[45] Why God might cause him to be ashamed becomes clear as the passage continues. If the apostle returns to Corinth and some in the church continue to be embroiled in sexual immorality, it will constitute a shameful situation before God.

Thus the second half of the verse reads, "and that I will grieve over many, who have persisted in their previous patterns of sinning and have not repented

40. The participle with μου forms a genitive absolute used temporally.

41. The word πάλιν (*palin*, again) has been moved forward in the sentence for emphasis, but it almost certainly belongs with the verb ταπεινόω (*tapeinoō*, make ashamed) rather than with the participle ἐλθόντος (*elthontos*, when I come).

42. Of course, the word can also be used with the nuance of "be humble" or "choose to humble oneself before God," which is by far the most common use in the NT (Matt. 18:4; 23:12; Luke 14:11; Phil. 2:8; James 4:10; 1 Pet. 5:6) and an ET embraced by most English versions (e.g., ESV, NLT², NRSV, NIV).

43. See the comments on 11:7, where the use of the term has overtones of "shame"; Paul engages in manual labor and does not assert his rights as a professional public speaker.

44. At this point the aorist subjunctive communicates probability.

45. Some English versions render πρός ὑμᾶς as "before you" (e.g., ESV, NASB, NRSV, NIV, NET), but Paul's point is not that he will be ashamed "before" the Corinthians but that he will be ashamed of them. Better is the ET, "in your presence" (HCSB, NLT²) or "among you" (Message, KJV), but again, he could be ashamed among them without being ashamed of them. Specifically, he is ashamed that in his role as their apostle, he has failed to move them to a place of spiritual maturity.

in response to the uncleanness and sexual immorality and the rank promiscuity in which they participated." The probable humbling that Paul anticipates, if it materializes, will occur simultaneously with him grieving over those who are the source of the shame. We render the aorist active subjunctive verb πενθήσω (*penthēsō*)[46] as "I will grieve" (so HCSB, NLT[2], NIV, NET) rather than "I may grieve" since the note of probability ("may") has already been sounded in the translation of the previous aorist active subjunctive verb and is still in effect here. Paul sees these two verbs as an interrelated pair. If God makes the apostle ashamed by what he finds in Corinth, then there is no question that simultaneously he *will* grieve over the situation. Used in the NT at nine other places (Matt. 5:4; 9:15; Mark 16:10; Luke 6:25; 1 Cor. 5:2; James 4:9; Rev. 18:11, 15, 19), the verb πενθέω (*pentheō*) speaks of a sadness brought on by some condition or circumstance, thus "to mourn" or "grieve." With an accusative of person, as here (πολλούς, *pollous*, many), the word may be rendered "grieve over" (BDAG 795; BDF 82; Robertson 1934: 475); in the biblical literature the expression often is used for mourning the dead (Gen. 23:2; 37:34; 50:3) but also for mourning in the face of sin and/or sin's consequences (Num. 14:39; 1 Sam. 6:19; 15:35–16:1; 1 Esd. 8:69 [8:72 ET]). Accordingly, Paul grieves over "many," suggesting that those in mind were more than a few in number.

The apostle describes this grief-giving group as those "who have persisted in their previous patterns of sinning" (τῶν προημαρτηκότων, *tōn proēmartēkotōn*). Rather than partitive (i.e., "many of the ones"),[47] the genitive form of the sub-stantive participle is appositional: "the many, that is, those who have." The verb προαμαρτάνω (*proamartanō*; also in 13:2) means "to sin beforehand," and the perfect participle form here, given the context, expresses a state of having sinned in the past and continuing that pattern. Thus they have "persisted in their previous patterns of sinning" (Furnish 1984: 562; Harris 2005: 903). The emphasis on the group's continued pattern of sin becomes even clearer with the second participle,[48] καὶ μὴ μετανοησάντων (*kai mē metanoēsantōn*), translated as "and have not repented."[49] With this second participle, Paul has shifted to an aorist form, the aspect of which simply views the action (or the failure to act in this case) as a whole. Rather than referring to their failure to repent at some particular time in the past, the negated aorist participle probably means something equivalent to the sinners never having repented.

---

46. It seems likely that the form should be read as aorist subjunctive rather than future indicative, for the verbs are grammatically parallel and temporally concurrent, and a measure of uncertainty (though probability) hangs over both.

47. Obviously Paul would be grieved not just for a portion of those who have been living in sexual sin!

48. The article (τῶν, *tōn*) before προημαρτηκότων governs both participles, indicating that both describe the same group of people.

49. It may be that Paul uses the perfect form to emphasize the pattern of life that the group has continued to embrace, perhaps thinking the aorist more appropriate to an action in which they have not engaged.

"Repenting from" something can be expressed with μετανοέω (*metanoeō*) plus the preposition ἀπό (*apo*; Acts 8:22), or in Revelation with ἐκ (*ek*; 2:21–22; 9:20–21; 16:11), and in English idiom we are used to speaking of a person repenting "from" or "of" sin. English translations almost universally translate ἐπί (*epi*) plus the dative here as "of" (so ESV, HCSB, NASB, NLT², NRSV, NIV, NET). Yet Paul probably uses the preposition ἐπί[50] to mark the basis for the action of repenting, that is, "in response to" their sins, or "in the face of the sins" (BDAG 364.6). Sins should prompt repentance. Paul's point is that since the first time this sexually immoral group was confronted with their sins, they have failed to respond properly.

Those sins are given triple expression with "the uncleanness and sexual immorality and the rank promiscuity in which they participated" (τῇ ἀκαθαρσίᾳ καὶ πορνείᾳ καὶ ἀσελγείᾳ ᾗ ἔπραξαν, *tē akatharsia kai porneia kai aselgeia hē epraxan*). All three words are also found at Gal. 5:19, and since in our passage they are bound together with a single article, the apostle conceives of them as closely interrelated; all three are sexual in nature. The word ἀκαθαρσία (*akatharsia*) could be used in the ancient world to refer to refuse of any type, anything filthy or dirty (e.g., P.Oxy. 912.26). The vast majority of the sixty-two uses in the LXX relate to being ceremonially unclean (e.g., Lev. 5:3; 7:21; 15:3, 25; Judg. 13:7; 2 Sam. 11:4; 2 Chron. 29:16; Ezra 6:21; 1 Macc. 13:48; Jer. 19:13; Ezek. 4:14), but the figurative sense of being morally filthy forms the more immediate backdrop for Paul's concern, and employment of the term with the sense of "immorality" was common in the literatures of the first century (Epictetus, *Disc.* 4.11.5, 8; Philo, *Alleg.* 1.52; 2.29; *Plant.* 95, 99). Most often Paul seems to use ἀκαθαρσία as a label for forms of sexual sin (e.g., Rom. 1:24; 6:19; Eph. 4:19; 5:3; Col. 3:5; 1 Thess. 4:7); generally the word is the opposite of "holiness," as in 1 Thess. 4:7, where Paul writes, "For God did not call us to *impurity* but in holiness" (NET).

The second term, πορνεία (*porneia*), has even stronger sexual overtones, referring to unlawful forms of sexual intercourse such as prostitution or fornication. The Jerusalem Council warned the first Gentile believers against "sexual immorality" (Acts 15:20, 29; 21:25), and Paul addressed the problem of πορνεία extensively in 1 Corinthians (5:1; 6:13, 18; 7:2), but his admonitions apparently fell on deaf ears to some extent. The third word, ἀσέλγεια (*aselgeia*) speaks of "rank promiscuity" or debauchery in which people throw off all constraints of social or religious boundaries,[51] abandoning themselves

---

50. Harris (2005: 903) follows Plummer, who, for instance, in his ICC volume (1915: 370) points out that μετανοέω + ἐπί is not uncommon in the LXX. Yet the cases where this construction occurs (Odes 12.7 [not in MT/ET]; Amos 7:3, 6; Joel 2:13; Jon. 3:10; 4:2) refer to God repenting of certain forms of judgment.

51. Plutarch (*Mar.* 44.6) uses ἀσέλγεια with broader connotations than just sexual sin but illustrates well the abandonment suggested by the term: "The people were most distressed, however, by the wanton licence [ἀσέλγεια] of the Bardyaei, as they were called, who butchered fathers of families in their houses, outraged their children, violated their wives, and could not be checked in their career of rapine and murder until Cinna and Sertorius, after taking counsel

to their lusts (BDAG 141).[52] Clearly some of the converts in Corinth were still caught up in the sexual depravity that marked the city, and this moral failure on the part of some church members is deeply distressing to their apostle, calling for confrontation, to which Paul turns in the book's final chapter.

Reflection

Accountability is one of the most important aspects of life in the community of faith—and one of the most difficult. Striking the balance between a hovering authoritarianism and a laissez-faire individualism can only be achieved when accountability is carried out under the lordship of Christ, with a commitment to love, and for the edification of the other. Writing of the importance of accountability, Augustine states in his *Confessions* (10.4.5),

> To such people I will reveal myself. They will take heart from my good traits, and sigh with sadness at my bad ones. My good points are instilled by you and are your gifts. My bad points are my faults and your judgements on them. Let them take heart from the one and regret the other. Let both praise and tears ascend in your sight from brotherly hearts, your censers. But you Lord, . . . Make perfect my imperfections. (Chadwick 2009: 181)

Here we have healthy community. The foundation for such a relationship must be built on receptive hearts, hearts that want the Lord's best for the Lord's glory in the world. Paul's challenge is that certain immature (or unregenerate) members of the Corinthian church are not willing to be held accountable, and our challenge in ministry today is at least twofold.

First, we must make sure our hearts really are hearts of integrity. We must carry out the ministry of accountability, making sure that we ourselves are accountable to God and others in Christ. To whom are we accountable? To whom do we "reveal" ourselves, in Augustine's words? Whether we have a Wesleyan type small group, or a heart friend among our associates, are we characterized by *being* accountable in the healthiest sense of the word?

Second, we must not shirk our responsibility to foster accountability in our communities of faith. To have a hands-off posture, often cloaked in an excuse that "we must extend grace," actually turns people over to sin in a way that is anything but gracious, and it certainly is not being responsible as Christ's ministers. Rather, we must learn to do the hard thing of holding people accountable in loving, edifying ways. We must be willing, like our mentor Paul, to go into the "tunnel" of conflict to rescue those who are caught in the snares of sin and selfishness. May God give us the grace to carry out this ministry in redemptive ways.

---

together, fell upon them as they were asleep in their camp, and transfixed them all with javelins" (Perrin 1920: 591). In the *Republic* 4.424e Plato presents a dialogue in which changing modes of music in a culture can tear down society with its laws by ἀσέλγεια until all things public and private are destroyed!

52. Cf. Mark 7:22; Rom. 13:13; Gal. 5:19; Eph. 4:19; 1 Pet. 4:3; 2 Pet. 2:2, 7, 18; Jude 4.

Additional Notes

12:15. The reading εἰ (𝔓⁴⁶ ℵ* A B F G 33 81* *pc* co) has stronger attestation than does either εἰ καί (ℵ² D¹ Ψ 0243 1739 1881 𝔐 f vg sy) or the omission of both words from Western witnesses (D* ar g r; Ambst). The omission could be due to scribes wanting to state Paul's love for the church more emphatically. Metzger (1994: 517), who gives the reading εἰ a B rating, suggests that καί was added by scribes for emphasis (perhaps, "if indeed").

12:15. The external support for the participle ἀγαπῶν is strong and widely distributed (𝔓⁴⁶ ℵ² B D F G Ψ 0243 1739 1881 𝔐 latt), and it is the more difficult reading since the reader has to supply the finite verb εἰμί (Metzger 1994: 517). So it is preferred over ἀγαπῶ (ℵ* A 33 104* 1241 1505 *pc*). Scribes may have accidentally dropped the ν before η.

12:16. The reading οὐ κατεβάρησα ὑμᾶς (A B D² Ψ 0243 33 1739 𝔐) as original offers the best explanation for either οὐκ ἐβάρησα ὑμᾶς (𝔓⁴⁶ D*) or οὐ κατενάρκησα ὑμῶν (ℵ F G 81 104 326 629 1881 *pc*), which has arisen under pressure from the same phrase in 12:13.

12:19. Based on external attestation, the reading πάλαι (ℵ* A B F G 0243 6 33 81 365 1175 1739 1881 *pc* lat) is preferred over the much more common πάλιν (ℵ² D Ψ 0278 𝔐 g vg^mss sy bo); the latter reading probably arose from other uses in the broader context (2 Cor. 10:7; 11:16; 12:21; 13:2) and with the similar idea of Paul "commending" himself "again" (3:1; 5:12). 𝔓⁴⁶ adds οὐ in front of πάλαι, making the clause a question anticipating an affirmative answer.

12:19. Clearly the reading κατέναντι θεοῦ has much stronger attestation (𝔓⁴⁶ ℵ A B F G 0243 0278 6 33 81 365 630 1175 1739^txt 1881 2464 *pc*) than κατενώπιον τοῦ θεοῦ (D [* P: -τ.] Ψ 𝔐) or ἐνώπιον τοῦ θεοῦ καὶ ἐναντίον τοῦ θεοῦ (1739^mg; Or).

12:20. Both the singular ἔρις (𝔓⁴⁶ ⁹⁹vid ℵ A 0243 33 326 945 1505 1739 1881 *al* sy^p bo?) and singular ζῆλος (𝔓⁴⁶ ⁹⁹ A B D* F G 33 326 *pc* sy^p bo^ms) should be read as original; their plural counterparts (ἔρεις: B D F G Ψ 𝔐 latt sy^h sa bo?; and ζῆλοι: ℵ D¹ Ψ 0243 1739 1881 𝔐 latt sy^h sa bo?) have arisen under the influence of the plural forms that follow in the sentence (Metzger 1994: 518).

12:21. The genitive absolute construction ἐλθόντος μου plus the word order ταπεινώσῃ με ὁ θεός μου πρὸς ὑμᾶς has strong external attestation (𝔓⁴⁶ ℵ* A B F G P 81 326 *pc*), although some MSS (𝔓⁴⁶ B D F G L P 6 33 81 104 365 1175 1241 2464 *pm*) have ταπεινώσει (future indicative) rather than the preferred ταπεινώσῃ (ℵ* A B 326; aorist subjunctive); Thrall (2000: 865) suggests that the future, however, "is either an accidental error or . . . an adaptation to the following πενθήσω, understood as a future." Thus ἐλθόντος μου with the specified word order is preferred over ἐλθόντα με ταπεινώσῃ ὁ θεός μου πρὸς ὑμᾶς (ℵ² Ψ 0243 0278 33 1739 [1881] 𝔐 lat?) or ἐλθόντα με πρὸς ὑμᾶς ταπεινώσῃ με ὁ θεός μου (D^[1] sy^p). The inferior readings probably arose in an attempt to correct a supposed grammatical mistake in relating the μου of the genitive absolute to the με later in the sentence (Harris 2005: 894).

2. The Third Visit as Stern Accountability (13:1–10)

Early in 2 Corinthians, Paul defends his chosen travel plans (1:15–23), and travel narrative frames the center section of the letter (2:12–13; 7:5–7). As he moves toward the letter's close, the apostle clearly anticipates being back with the church at Corinth. He has sent Titus and the brothers to make sure the Corinthians are prepared for his imminent return, that they would be ready with a generous donation to the collection (9:3–4). As chapter 10 begins with reflections on being "present" and "absent" (reflections renewed in 13:2), Paul anticipates a confrontation with those who misread him as ministering according to human standards (10:2, 11). Closer to our current context, at 12:14 he announces that he is now prepared for his third trip to Corinth, and at 12:20–21 the apostle speaks bluntly of his concerns about finding the community fragmented, dysfunctional, and harboring recalcitrant, unrepentant, immoral members. So, echoing through this lengthy letter we find notes of anticipation about the coming trip, as if Paul is poised, ready for the return but somewhat anxious about it as well. Among other things, 2 Cor. 13:1–10 communicates a resounding note of accountability. The apostle wants the Corinthians to examine themselves (13:5), desiring them to be rightly related to God (13:7). He does not want to deal with them harshly when he arrives (13:10), but if that is what it takes for the truth to be advanced and for the Corinthians to become "fully qualified" (13:8–9), he will use his authority to build them up. This unit may be analyzed as follows:

a. The "testimony" of the third visit (13:1)
b. Warning: Christ will deal with you powerfully! (13:2–4)
c. Authentication of faith (13:5–7)
d. Edification: The purpose of Paul's letter (13:8–10)

Exegesis and Exposition

[1]This will be my third trip to you. *Every accusation must be validated on the testimony of two or three witnesses.* [2]When I was there the second time, I warned those who sinned before and all the rest, and although I am absent right now, I warn them again. When I return, I will not spare you, [3]since you are demanding proof that Christ is speaking through me—Christ, who is not weak in dealing with you but demonstrates his power among you. [4]For indeed ⌐ ¬, he was crucified as a result of weakness, but he lives as a result of God's power. For also we ourselves are weak by virtue of our relationship

⌜with⌝ him, but we will live with him as a result of God's power, which is manifested in dealing ⌜with you⌝.

⁵Test yourselves to see whether you are in the faith! Examine yourselves! Do you not grasp the fact that Jesus Christ is in you?—unless, of course, you don't qualify. ⁶And I hope that you will realize that we are not unqualified. ⁷Now we pray to God that you will not do anything evil, not so that we may be recognized as qualified, but in order that you might do what is right, even though we may seem to be unqualified. ⁸For we cannot do anything against the truth but only in support of the truth. ⁹We rejoice when we are weak and you are strong. Indeed, this is what we pray for—your restoration. ¹⁰This is why I am writing these things while absent, so that when I am there with you, I may not have to deal harshly with you, acting according to the authority the Lord gave me for building up, not tearing down.

a. The "Testimony" of the Third Visit (13:1)

As he begins our chapter 13, the apostle mentions the third trip again, writing, **13:1** "This will be my third trip to you" (Τρίτον τοῦτο ἔρχομαι πρὸς ὑμᾶς, *Triton touto erchomai pros hymas*).[1] Paul's first trip to Corinth, in AD 50, involved the founding of the church and an eighteen-month stint of ministry in the city (Acts 18:1–11). The second, the "sorrowful visit" mentioned in 2 Cor. 2:1–2, was in the spring of 54, growing out of Timothy's troublesome report on his recent visit to Corinth. Now Paul will[2] take "this third"[3] trip to the Corinthians (to you, πρὸς ὑμᾶς, *pros hymas*), to receive the collection for Jerusalem, to address charges that have been made against him, and to confront those who are still living in blatant sin.

Without any introductory formula (e.g., "It is written"), the apostle abruptly reinforces this third important purpose for the trip with a passage of Scripture: "Every accusation must be validated on the testimony of two or three witnesses" (ἐπὶ στόματος δύο μαρτύρων καὶ τριῶν σταθήσεται πᾶν ῥῆμα, *epi stomatos dyo martyrōn kai triōn stathēsetai pan rhēma*). Paul takes the passage from Deut. 19:15, and the changes from the LXX are minor:

2 Cor. 13:1b	Deut. 19:15 LXX
ἐπὶ στόματος δύο μαρτύρων	ἐπὶ στόματος δύο μαρτύρων
καὶ	καὶ ἐπὶ στόματος
τριῶν σταθήσεται	τριῶν μαρτύρων σταθήσεται
πᾶν ῥῆμα.	πᾶν ῥῆμα.

1. Earlier, at 12:14, he notes he is "ready" (ἑτοίμως ἔχω, *hetoimōs echō*) to make his third trip to Corinth. The two mentions of the "this third trip" (τρίτον τοῦτο, *triton touto*) may be read as "parallel introductions," a way of crafting the beginning of successive units to mark those units in the developing discourse (see Guthrie 1994: 104).

2. The present indicative verb ἔρχομαι may be considered a futuristic present, "I will come." The futuristic present is often used in situations where immediacy and certainty are in view (see D. Wallace 1996: 535–37).

3. Τρίτον (*triton*) is used as an adverb, delimiting the verb ἔρχομαι, with the concept of "time" understood (Josephus, *Ant.* 8.371; Mark 14:41; Luke 23:22; John 21:17; BDAG 1016).

The form of Paul's quotation simply drops the redundant elements, ἐπὶ στόματος and μαρτύρων, from the LXX text,[4] but there is not a change in meaning. In its OT context, the passage comes in a section on life in the promised land. Specifically, stipulations are given concerning witnesses against a person who has been accused of sinning (Deut. 19:15–21). Witnesses against a person must be neither too few (i.e., a single person) nor false, harming a person by bearing false witness (Deut. 19:16–21; cf. Exod. 20:16). The requirement that there be "two witnesses and three" means "at least two witnesses, or[5] more if possible" for conviction, and this legal demand was unique in the ancient world, found neither in Greek nor Roman law (Vliet 1958).

The heart of this Jewish legal requirement asserts, "Every accusation must be validated" (σταθήσεται πᾶν ῥῆμα). The term ῥῆμα was used earlier, at 12:4, where Paul spoke of the "words too sacred to tell" (ἄρρητα ῥήματα, *arrēta rhēmata*), and the word thus can be used to refer to "words" or "statements of any kind." But ῥῆμα also can mean a "matter" or an "event" spoken about (e.g., Luke 1:37, 2:15; Acts 10:37; BDAG 905). Given the legal context of the OT text, the term has the sense of an "accusation" or perhaps a "case," and "every" (πᾶν) accusation "must be validated" (σταθήσεται, *stathēsetai*), with the future[6] passive indicative from ἵστημι (*histēmi*) communicating the idea of something being "established," "upheld," that is, shown to be true (BDAG 482). Translations render the text variously as,

ESV	"Every charge must be established."
GNT	"Any accusation must be upheld."
NASB	"Every fact is to be confirmed."
NLT[2]	"The facts of every case must be established."
NRSV	"Any charge must be sustained."
NET	"Every matter will be established."

This commentary offers the translation, "Every accusation must be validated." How then is an accusation to be validated? "On the testimony of two or three witnesses." The preposition ἐπί (*epi*) plus the genitive means "in consideration of," or "on the basis of," and accusations are to be validated on the basis of the στόματος (*stomatos*), literally, "the mouth," in this case "the utterance" (e.g., Luke 19:22; 21:15) or what the mouth speaks. This utterance is particularized further by specifying that there be at least two μαρτύρων (*martyrōn*, witnesses; see the discussion above).

But to what "witnesses" does Paul refer? Some have understood the apostle to speak quite literally of witnesses (e.g., God, Timothy, Titus, or church

---

4. The LXX mirrors the MT closely. A shortened version similar to Paul's quotation here is found at Matt. 18:16.

5. The conjunction καί joining the "two witnesses" and "three" in Paul's version is equivalent to ἤ (*ē*, or; BDAG 494; James 4:13).

6. The future is an imperative future; when it appears in the NT, it is almost always in OT quotations (D. Wallace 1996: 569–70).

members in Corinth; Garland 1999: 541; Welborn 2010) who will be called forward formally as Paul answers the charges brought against him and/or brings charges against those needing church discipline (cf. Matt. 18:16; 1 Tim. 5:19). Yet one must ask of this latter position, would the concerns Paul expresses at 12:20–21 have needed the validation of witnesses? Would not the chaos of the community bear witness to these sins in its own public way? And as to the suggestion that Paul will be mounting a formal defense against the accusations brought against him, his tone in this section of the book seems anything but defensive (12:19)—he is on the offense! He will not "stand trial" before the Corinthians. Rather, he intends to bring those needing church discipline to account.

Even more pertinent, however, the "two and three" (lit.) from the quotation parallel the "third trip" mentioned earlier in 13:1 and the "second time" mentioned in 13:2.[7] Consequently, the legal text from Deuteronomy can be read metaphorically as referring either to Paul's "two warnings" (given on the previous trip and the coming trip) mentioned in verse 2, or the three trips themselves (two in the past and a third coming), or perhaps the combination of the three trips with their two accompanying warnings (Harris 2005: 908); this seems to be the most straightforward interpretation. These trips and warnings by Paul bear ample witness against the guilty in Corinth.

b. Warning: Christ Will Deal with You Powerfully! (13:2–4)

Paul underscores the legal stipulation of "at least two witnesses" by crafting our verse 2 around two warnings, two places, and two groups, all knit together under the proclamation that when he returns, the sinners will not be spared: "When I was there the second time, I warned those who sinned before and all the rest, and although I am absent right now, I warn them again. When I return I will not spare you."[8] The verse begins with προείρηκα καὶ προλέγω (*proeirēka kai prolegō*), the first a perfect active indicative form and the second a present active indicative, both from προλέγω, a verb meaning "to say something in advance." Given the context, Paul clearly uses the word with the sense of "to

13:2

---

7. The Greek terms are:
   Τρίτον (*Triton*, third)   δύο (*dyo*, two)
   τριῶν (*triōn*, three)   δεύτερον (*deuteron*, second)
8. The structure of the passage is as follows:

προείρηκα καὶ (*proeirēka kai*)	Two warnings:
προλέγω, (*prolegō*)	"I warned," "I warn"
ὡς παρὼν τὸ δεύτερον καὶ (*hōs parōn to deuteron kai*)	Paul in two places: "there the second time,"
ἀπὼν νῦν, (*apōn nyn,*)	"absent now"
τοῖς προημαρτηκόσιν καὶ (*tois proēmartēkosin kai*)	Two groups: "those who sinned before,"
τοῖς λοιποῖς πᾶσιν, (*tois loipois pasin,*)	"all the rest"
ἐὰν ἔλθω εἰς τὸ πάλιν (*ean elthō eis to palin*)	Same content:
ὅτι . . . οὐ φείσομαι (*hoti . . . ou pheisomai*)	"when I return, I will not spare"

warn" (so, e.g., ESV, HCSB, NLT², NIV).⁹ The two warnings correspond to two points in time. The first warning, expressed with the perfect-tense verb,¹⁰ was given upon Paul's second visit (τὸ δεύτερον, *to deuteron*), when he was present (ὡς παρών, *hōs parōn*), or "there" with the Corinthians. The second warning, expressed with the present-tense form, he gives now as he writes, when he is absent (ἀπὼν νῦν, *apōn nyn*). The second warning does not replace the first but reinforces it; they are not merely successive but especially cumulative in their force. These warnings also are directed at two groups within the church. He has already mentioned "those who sinned before" (τοῖς προημαρτηκόσιν, *tois proēmartēkosin*) at 12:21 (on which see the comments), that is, those who, in spite of being warned "have persisted in their previous patterns of sinning." But Paul adds another group here, to whom he refers as "all the rest" (τοῖς λοιποῖς πᾶσιν, *tois loipois pasin*). This ambiguous reference could be addressing variously those who have fallen into sin since Paul's second visit, those who have been sinning but have not been confronted personally by Paul, those under the influence of the false missionaries, or all the rest of the Corinthian congregation, who have not sinned but need the stiff warning to keep from falling into sin (Harris 2005: 909–10). On this view, the whole congregation comes under Paul's warning.

The apostle expresses the content (ὅτι, *hoti*, that) of the warning with "When I return I will not spare you." Ἐάν (*ean*, when) plus the aorist subjunctive ἔλθω (*elthō*) suggests what Paul expects to happen (BDF 188), and used temporally here, it means "when I come," for Paul has made clear his intentions to join them shortly. Moreover, the verb ἔρχομαι (*erchomai*) plus εἰς τὸ πάλιν¹¹ (*eis to palin*), means "to come again" or "to return." Thus Paul alerts the Corinthians as to what will happen when he returns to their city. What will happen, the apostle suggests, is that he will not "spare" them. The verb φείδομαι (*pheidomai*) can be used variously to mean "to spare" someone of something, or to refrain from doing something (as at 12:6), and he at times uses the word in contexts having to do with judgment of some kind (e.g., Rom. 8:32; 11:21). Paul has already used φείδομαι¹² with the first of these meanings at 1:23, where he writes concerning a change in his travel plans, "Now, I call upon God as my witness, the reason I did not return to Corinth was to spare you."¹³ In other words, the apostle earlier avoided confronting the Corinthians with apostolic discipline, sensing that the timing was not right, but now the time for discipline approaches and

---

9. The sense of "warn" in the broader Greco-Roman literature had long been established by Paul's time (see, e.g., Thucydides, *Pel. War* 1.138.6; Aeschines, *Or.* 3.5; 3.177).

10. In one sense the perfect tense προείρηκα in 13:2 may be considered "dramatic," referring to a "state" created by the warning given on Paul's second trip. Yet that "state" has remained in force to the moment Paul writes about it here in the letter, so the perfect can be considered "intensive."

11. The phrase εἰς τὸ πάλιν = πάλιν (BDAG 289).

12. Here in 13:2 the future tense φείσομαι is predictive.

13. He also uses the word at 12:6, where he says that he is "refraining" (φείδομαι, *pheidomai*) from boasting about his revelatory experiences.

will constitute a focal purpose for this third trip. Paul does not offer details of the punishment he will bring to bear, but clearly it will be severe (13:10). Harris (2005: 911) suggests that the discipline could involve removing those who do not repent from association with the church (1 Cor. 5:13), or handing the sinners over to Satan "for the destruction of their flesh" (5:5), perhaps referring to an illness that could lead to death (cf. 11:30).

With verse 3 Paul explains that the punishment he will bring against those who are living unrepentant lives has been prompted not only by ongoing patterns of sin in the community (12:20–21), but also by the call by some for a validation of his ministry. Certainly Paul will hold the sinners accountable for the sake of the community's spiritual health, but the community's health also depends on the Corinthians being rightly related to God's true apostle—and accordingly, their rejection of the false apostles. So Paul sees the coming spiritual showdown as also serving the purpose (ἐπεί, *epei*, because, since; 13:3) of displaying Christ's power and therefore demonstrating that Christ really speaks through him.[14] Thus the sentence continues, "since you are demanding proof that Christ is speaking through me—Christ, who is not weak in dealing with you but demonstrates his power among you."

13:3–4

That Paul is competing for the affections of the Corinthian church comes through clearly here, for some are "demanding"[15] (ζητεῖτε, *zēteite*) "proof," that is, some form of validation for the authoritative underpinnings of Paul's ministry. As we have seen earlier in the letter (2:9; 8:2; 9:13), the term δοκιμή (*dokimē*) can be used to speak of a "test" or "ordeal" of some kind, but also can refer to the result of a test, the "proof" of one's character (Rom. 5:4; Phil. 2:22; BDAG 256; Spicq 1994: 1.360). More specifically, Paul tells us that the Corinthians have asked for "proof that Christ is speaking through" him (τοῦ ἐν ἐμοὶ λαλοῦντος Χριστοῦ, *tou en emoi lalountos Christou*). The genitive construction τοῦ . . . Χριστοῦ gives the content ("that," or in some translations, "of") of the proof they are demanding. They want to know that it truly is Christ speaking "by" or "through" Paul. The preposition ἐν, in this case, may be understood as communicating the agent (i.e., Paul) of the communication, rather than the place of the communication (i.e., Christ speaking "in" the apostle). Thus the emphasis rests on the authoritative source of Paul's teaching/preaching/apostolic ministry, rather than the quality of his personal interaction with the Lord. We are not told what this demanding group has in mind—perhaps a more polished rhetorical performance from Paul (10:10–11), or an account of a visionary experience (12:1–6), or a miraculous sign (12:12)—but the apostle will give them more than they bargained for! He will bring the power of the

---

14. In missiology this is sometimes referred to as a "power encounter," in which the display of God's power bears witness to the validity of the message preached.

15. Although ζητέω (*zēteō*) can be used with the milder sense of "seek," "examine," or "consider," the context of 13:3 suggests a more combative posture on the part of the Corinthian faction; thus the ET's "demanding" seems appropriate (so NIV, NET; cf. Sir. 7:4; 28:3; 1 Esd. 8:50; Tob. 4:18; Mark 8:11; Luke 11:16; 12:48; see BDAG 428).

living Christ to bear in a confrontation with those who are hurting the church. Paul reminds them that he is not the main person to whom they answer or with whom they interact. They ultimately answer to the Lord Christ.

Having acknowledged their demand for such proof, therefore, Paul reminds the Corinthians that the living Christ manifests his power among his people: "Christ, who is not weak in dealing with you but demonstrates his power among you." This second part of verse 3 introduces a brief span of prose (13:3b–4) beautifully crafted by use of parallelism. The structure may be depicted as follows:[16]

(A) [Christ,] who
     a in dealing with you
       b is not weak but
       b demonstrates his <u>power</u>
     a among you.

(B) For indeed,
     a he was crucified
       b as a result of weakness, but
     a he lives
       b as a result of God's <u>power</u>.

(C) For also
     a we ourselves are weak
       b by virtue of our relationship with him, but
     a we will live
       b with him
         c as a result of God's <u>power</u>,
           d which is manifested in dealing with you.

The passage can be assessed from various vantage points:

    the contrast of weakness and power presented in three movements
    the parallel between Christ's weakness and power and the weakness and power of Paul
    the interplay of past, present, and future, and the implications of each in dealing with the present crisis in Corinth
    the quadrangle of God-Christ-Paul-Corinthians for noting the flow of power as Paul discusses his ministry to the church

All three movements—A, B, and C—contrast weakness and power. This contrast plays off Paul's earlier reflections on power being perfected in weakness,

---

16. The Greek text of this diagram is given in the additional notes.

his boast in weakness, and his contentment in weakness. Weakness makes for powerful ministry (12:9–10). The first movement (A) is not really a contrast as much as a form of parallelism, for "not weak" = "demonstrates his power." The effectiveness of Christ's power, expressed with a present active indicative form of the verb δυνατέω (*dynateō*, is effective, capable), almost certainly refers to the manifestation of power in Paul's past encounters with the Corinthians but also anticipates the manifestation of power in his confrontation of those opposing him in Corinth (see 10:4–6, 11). So "weak" (ἀσθενέω, *astheneō*) here, by contrast, refers to being "ineffective" or "impotent" due to a lack of power. Christ is not impotent but effective in his dealing with his church.

Further, notice that the references to "you" (εἰς ὑμᾶς/ἐν ὑμῖν, *eis hymas/ en hymin*, with you/among you) bracket the reflections on Christ's effectiveness in this first cluster, but the whole wraps up at the end of verse 4 with a third reference to "you." The first of these prepositional phrases can be read as communicating reference ("with reference to you"), or it may simply be spatial ("toward you"). Our translation, "in dealing with you," which takes the latter approach, gets at the nuance of interpersonal relationship in this delicate, dangerous dance that Paul portrays. The second phrase also seems to be spatial, referring to Christ's power "among" the members of the community (rather than "in" each individual).

The second cluster of clauses (B) begins with καὶ γάρ (*kai gar*, for indeed; 13:4), both continuing the previous thought and expanding on it.[17] The first part of this expansion points to the crucifixion as related to Christ's weakness: "For indeed, he was crucified as a result of weakness." The aorist passive verb is constative, making a historical reference to Christ's crucifixion, and the phrase ἐξ ἀσθενείας (*ex astheneias*) points to the crucifixion as occurring "because of," or "as a result of" the "weakness" of Christ. That weakness has been variously understood to refer to physical weakness, meaning human frailty, or defenselessness before the Jewish and Roman systems. But Harris (2005: 914–15) seems correct when he points to Christ's *posture* of nonretaliation, his willingness to follow the thread of obedience all the way to the point of death (Phil. 2:5–11). This form of "weakness" then would parallel Paul's own posture of meekness in the face of his Corinthian opponents. Rather than overpower the Corinthians, he appeals to them "by the leniency and clemency of Christ" (10:1). Yet the crucifixion, carried through as a result of Christ choosing vulnerability, did not have the final say, for here we have a contrasting statement: "he lives as a result of God's power." This certainly points to the resurrection, yet it also directs the attention of the Corinthians to the living Lord of the universe, who rules his church.

The third set of clauses (C) takes what has been said about the weakness and power of Christ and draws parallels to Paul's ministry. He opens once more with καὶ γάρ (*kai gar*, for also), again both drawing from what has just been

---

17. In 13:4 the added textual variant εἰ, if original, would add a concessive note ("although"), as with BDF 239. See the first additional note on 13:4.

said in the previous pair of clauses about Christ (γάρ) and adding reflections on the correspondences with the apostle's life and ministry. In this case we translate the conjoined conjunctions with "For also." In set C, Paul follows the *abab* pattern found in B and then extends it (*ababcd*). Just as Christ's crucifixion was a result of weakness, Paul, by virtue of his relationship[18] with Christ, is weak, choosing a posture of humble obedience before God rather than a power posture that exerts control through power (10:1). Paul doesn't "dominate" the Corinthians in terms of their faith (1:24).

"But" (ἀλλά, *alla*)[19] just as Christ lives by God's resurrection power, that same power will raise Paul from the dead: "but we will live with him as a result[20] of God's power" (ἀλλὰ ζήσομεν σὺν αὐτῷ ἐκ δυνάμεως θεοῦ, *alla zēsomen syn autō ek dynameōs theou*). So the resurrection power of God is operative in Paul's life. Paul's "weakness" flows from the "weakness" of Christ. He carries around the death of Christ in his mortal body (4:10–11). But this is so that God's resurrection power and life, demonstrated preeminently in the resurrection of Christ, might be manifested in Paul's ministry (e.g., 5:7, 10–11). This is why the same power that will raise Paul from the dead in the future resurrection is what God demonstrates now in Paul's dealing with the Corinthians (εἰς ὑμᾶς, *eis hymas*, with you).

Thus far in this beautifully crafted span (13:3b–4), we have noted the contrast of weakness and power in each of the three submovements and the parallel between Christ's weakness and power on one hand, and the weakness and power of Paul on the other hand. Notice the flow of Paul's thought. On the topic of "weakness," Paul moves from "Christ is not weak" (i.e., Christ works powerfully among you), to stating that this powerful Christ has manifested "weakness" as a foundation stone of his ministry ("crucified as a result of weakness"), to declaring that weakness is inherent in the apostle's relationship with Christ.

Christ is not weak.

▼

Christ was crucified as a result of weakness.

▼

We are weak in relationship with him.

Thus Paul cannot be faulted for "weakness," for weakness is inherent both in his relationship with Christ and in a Christlike ministry.

18. If the ἐν is original in 13:4, it can be read as communicating relationship, corresponding to a common use of Paul's "in Christ," taken up seventy-six times by the apostle (e.g., Rom. 3:24; 6:11, 23; 8:1–2, 39; 9:1; 12:5; 15:17; 16:3, 7, 9–10; 1 Cor. 1:2, 4, 30; 3:1; 4:10, 15, 17; 15:18–19, 31; 16:24; 2 Cor. 2:17; 3:14; 5:17, 19; 12:2, 19; Gal. 1:22; 2:4, 17). Some scribes apparently wanted to make this sense of relationship clearer and replaced the preposition ἐν with σύν. See the second additional note on 13:4.

19. Both uses of ἀλλά (*alla*, however) in 13:4 are strongly contrastive and play an important role in the crafting of parallelism at this point.

20. The preposition ἐκ expresses result.

Second, notice the step-by-step development of the apostle's thoughts on power. Christ demonstrates his power among the Corinthians, Christ lives as a result of God's power, Paul will live with Christ as a result of God's power, and that power is manifested among the Corinthians. On the last point, that the power will be manifested through Paul seems to be implied.

Christ demonstrates his power among you.

▼

Christ lives as a result of God's power.

▼

Paul will live with Christ as a result of God's power,

▼

manifested to you [through Paul].

Notice that the manifestation of the power of Christ/God among the Corinthians brackets the passage. Thus Paul ties the authenticity of his apostolic ministry not to a power inherent in himself, but ultimately to the power of God, which was preeminently demonstrated in the resurrection of Christ. Thus, when we consider the relational quadrangle and the flow of power through these relationships, we find that God's power underlies all that Paul proclaims here. God's power was manifested in the resurrection of Christ in the past, will be manifested in Paul's resurrection in the future, and presently manifests itself in Paul's christocentric ministry to the Corinthians at present. Paul, in relationship with Christ, manifests the power of the living God in the church. There can be no greater authentication for Paul's ministry.

Figure 13 **God's Power Manifested in the Past, Present, and Future**

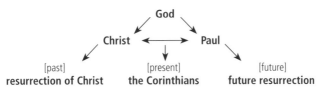

c. Authentication of Faith (13:5–7)

Some in the Corinthian church have demanded proof of the authoritative source of Paul's ministry and message, and as we have seen, the apostle points to the manifestation of resurrection power in their midst as proof. Now Paul turns the tables on the Corinthians, suggesting that they need to examine themselves! If it turns out that they qualify as true Christ-followers, their spiritual authenticity will point to the authenticity of the apostle's ministry as well, for his ministry will have been shown to produce true Christians. He writes in verses 5–6: "Test yourselves to see whether you are in the faith! Examine yourselves! Do you not grasp the fact that Jesus Christ is in you?—unless, of course, you don't qualify. And I hope that you will realize that we are not unqualified."

13:5–6

The first two main clauses are parallel exhortations; the repetition underscores the great need: "Test yourselves. . . . Examine yourselves." Paul normally uses the first of these verbs, πειράζετε (*peirazete*, a present active imperative), to speak of temptation to sin (1 Cor. 7:5; 10:13; Gal. 6:1; 1 Thess. 3:5), although at 1 Cor. 10:9 he employs the word with the sense of Christ being put on trial by the wilderness generation. To "test" in this latter sense is "to endeavor to discover the nature or character of something" (BDAG 792), and once God's will has been made known, people should not "test" him in this way (Exod. 17:2, 7; Num. 14:22; Isa. 7:12; Ps. 77:41, 56 [78:41, 56 ET]; Wis. 1:2; Acts 5:9; 15:10; Heb. 3:9). Yet Paul calls for the Corinthians to test themselves, probing their own nature or character. With this sense, the word is roughly synonymous to the second term, δοκιμάζετε (*dokimazete*, also a present active imperative), which we have already seen twice in chapter 8. There Paul writes of verifying the Corinthians' love (8:8) and of the brother whom he had "proved," that is, "put to the test and validated" many times (8:22). As used here in 2 Cor. 13:5, the verb speaks of making a critical examination of something to determine its genuineness, thus, "to put to the test," or "examine" (BDAG 255). So the apostle calls for the Corinthians to examine themselves.

Specifically, they are to test themselves to see "whether" (εἰ, *ei*)[21] they really "are in the faith" (ἐστὲ ἐν τῇ πίστει, *este en tē pistei*). Now this condition, together with the qualification that occurs at the end of verse 5 ("unless . . . you don't qualify"), points to the lack of absolute certainty, from a human perspective, when it comes to any person's relationship with Christ. Although the Holy Spirit "bears witness with our spirit that we are the children of God" (Rom. 8:16), human discernment on the status of another person, or even on the status of one's own spiritual condition, has its limitations. Any pastor, and any believer for that matter, depends on the outward manifestations of spiritual life to point to the reality of that spiritual life (e.g., Matt. 7:15–23; James 2:14–26). We do not have perfect knowledge when it comes to spiritual realities, and when certain manifestations come up in our lives, it is entirely appropriate for us to examine ourselves. In the case of the Corinthians, their flirtation with false apostles and immoral living constitute question marks over their spiritual condition, whether they are "in the faith,"[22] that is, in a state of right belief, right convictions, and true devotion to Christ. To be

21. As usual in 13:5, εἰ with the indicative is used "to express a condition thought of as real or to denote assumptions relating to what has already happened" (BDAG 277; e.g., Matt. 4:3; 6:23; 8:31; Acts 5:39; Rom. 2:17).

22. Paul uses the term πίστις (*pistis*) with the article some sixty-seven times, but he often refers to "the faith" with the sense of the beliefs, convictions, and practice surrounding trust in Christ as Lord of one's life and community (e.g., Rom. 14:1; 1 Cor. 16:13; Gal. 1:23; Eph. 4:13; Phil. 1:25, 27; Col. 1:23; 1 Tim. 3:9; 4:1; 5:8; 6:10, 12, 21; 2 Tim. 3:8; 4:7; Titus 1:13). In this sense one can be "weak" in the faith (Rom. 14:1), or "firm" in the faith (1 Cor. 16:13). When Paul tells us in Gal. 1:23 that he once tried to destroy "the faith," it was not merely believers' individual trust in Christ that is in view, but their whole practice of following Christ.

rightly "in the faith" is not just an individual posture but also a community's spiritual condition, since a community claiming to follow Christ as Lord is called to live appropriately in covenant with the living Christ. Paul wants the Corinthians to assess their spiritual condition, to see whether their beliefs, convictions, and practice of Christ-following lines up with the true, apostolic teaching he has delivered to them.

For, if they are to be an authentic Christian community, devoted, new-covenant members of Christ's people, they must not only be "in Christ" but also have Christ "in you": "Do you not grasp the fact that Jesus Christ is in you?"[23] Paul, using a rhetorical question, pushes the Corinthians a bit with regard to their basic understanding of what it means to be people of "the faith." He probes, "Do you[24] not know," or "Do you not grasp the fact that Christ is in you?" The verb ἐπιγινώσκω (*epiginōskō*) can refer to having a complete or thorough knowledge of something, but here may simply mean "to know" (= γινώσκω) or "understand." Paul may be asking concerning the Corinthians' grasp of basic Christian teaching, but his rhetorical question seems, rather, to be probing their experience of the faith; he may be asking whether they know for sure that Christ indeed lives "in" (ἐν, *en*)[25] them, and this seems likely given the qualification at the end of verse 6. For them to fail to "qualify" concerns their spiritual condition more than the rudiments of their theological knowledge, though the latter certainly is foundational for the former. In other words, Paul wants the Corinthians to ask questions about their relationship to Christ.

There are a number of points in Paul's writings at which he makes a statement of fact about the spiritual condition of those to whom he writes and then qualifies the statement.[26] For instance, consider the following:

> You, however, are not in the flesh but in the Spirit, *if indeed* the Spirit of God lives in you. (Rom. 8:9 NET)

> And if children, then heirs (namely, heirs of God and also fellow heirs with Christ)–*if indeed* we suffer with him so we may also be glorified with him. (Rom. 8:17 NET)

---

23. The particle ἤ (*ē*) with which the sentence begins in 13:5c is often used to introduce a rhetorical question such as this one (Matt. 26:53; Rom. 3:29; 6:3; 7:1; 11:2; 1 Cor. 6:9, 16, 19; BDAG 432.d.α). Since its function is not really contrastive, we choose to leave the particle untranslated.

24. The acc. ἑαυτοὺς (*heautous*) probably should be read as an acc. of reference (i.e., "with reference to yourselves") and is somewhat redundant, given the use of the second-person pronoun in the prepositional phrase that ends the question.

25. The preposition could be rendered "among" you, but Paul probably has in mind Christ as indwelling believers.

26. For more on this type of conditional sentence, see Guthrie (1998: 134–36, on the construction at Heb. 3:6, 14) and the more extensive treatment by Buist Fanning in Bateman 2007: 207–18. Fanning distinguishes between conditional clauses that are "cause-to-effect" and those that are evidence-to-inference in which "(1) a proposed situation (the protasis) that is known to be the effect or evidence of (2) a prior condition that causes it and so can be inferred from it (the apodosis)" (210).

Consider therefore the kindness and sternness of God: sternness to those who fell, but kindness to you, *provided that* you continue in his kindness. Otherwise, you also will be cut off. (Rom. 11:22 NIV)

But now he has reconciled you by Christ's physical body through death to present you holy in his sight, without blemish and free from accusation—*if* you continue in your faith, established and firm, and do not move from the hope held out in the gospel. (Col. 1:22–23 NIV)

Here at 2 Cor. 13:5, we see a similar approach. Paul, via his rhetorical question, asserts that Christ is "in" the Corinthians, but then he qualifies the assertion with εἰ μήτι ἀδόκιμοί ἐστε (*ei mēti adokimoi este*, unless, of course, you don't qualify). The term ἀδόκιμος (*adokimos*), used as a predicate adjective, speaks of something that does not stand up under testing and thus doesn't qualify, or is worthless. In OT imagery the word can be used of dross, the worthless extract from a precious metal (Prov. 25:4; Isa. 1:22). At 1 Cor. 9:27 Paul writes that he does not want to be "disqualified," and 2 Tim. 3:8 speaks of those who are "disqualified" with regard to the faith.

So at 2 Cor. 13:5 the apostle makes a statement about the spiritual condition of those in the church at Corinth—"Jesus Christ is in you"—but he cannot know the true spiritual condition of everyone in the congregation and does not want to give an unqualified assessment of their spiritual condition. It may be that upon examination some will discern that they are not "in the faith."

But the question some have kept up in the air at Corinth is whether Paul himself is qualified to be their apostle. So in verse 6 he writes, "And I hope that you will realize that we are not unqualified." The conjunction δέ (*de*, and) builds on and adds to the previous thought about lacking qualification as Paul expresses this "hope" (ἐλπίζω, *elpizō*)[27] that the Corinthians will "realize" (γνώσεσθε, *gnōsesthe*), or "comprehend," that he has not failed the test as their apostle.[28] Undoubtedly, the questions raised about his ministry have to do with matters such as his character (particularly, for instance, concerning his waffling on travel plans [1:12–22]), the tenor of his leadership (e.g., 1:24), his motives with regard to the collection for Jerusalem (e.g., 8:20), and his public speaking ability (e.g., 10:1, 10–11; 11:6). But Paul hopes that his

---

27. While the verb ἐλπίζω can carry a note of trepidation, it normally connotes the expectation of something good, to place confidence or trust in someone, especially God. In the LXX, God most commonly is the object of hope (e.g., Pss. 83:13; 145:5 [84:12; 146:5 ET]; cf. Sir. 14:2; Jer. 17:7). Overwhelmingly in the rest of the NT, the word is used theologically to speak of hope in God and his salvation through Christ (Spicq 1994: 1.480–92), and this constitutes the way Paul uses the word about half of the time (Rom. 8:24–25; 15:12; 1 Cor. 13:7; 15:19; 2 Cor. 1:10; 13:6; 1 Tim. 4:10; 5:5; 6:17). Yet, as here in 2 Cor. 13:6, the word can be used of personal desire that something will come to pass, and Paul makes use of the word this way, especially when speaking of interpersonal relationships (Rom. 15:24; 1 Cor. 16:7; 2 Cor. 1:13; 5:11; 8:5; Phil. 2:19, 23; 1 Tim. 3:14; Philem. 22).

28. In 13:7 the question of the apostle's qualification stands in direct relationship to the Corinthians' behavior, and this seems to point in the direction of interpreting the qualification as related to his ministry.

qualifications as their apostle will be self-evident as he continues to work with them. He has expressed a similar hope early in the letter at 1:13–14, where he writes, "I hope that you really will understand us completely, just as you have understood us partially, so that you will be proud of us."

He continues to speak of his "qualification" in verse 7: "Now we pray to God   **13:7** that you will not do anything evil, not so that we may be recognized as qualified, but in order that you might do what is right, even though we may seem to be unqualified." The motivational bottom line stands as one of the great tests of authentic ministry. Is the minister more concerned about the spiritual condition of the church, or how he or she is perceived in the public eye? With 13:7 Paul places before the Corinthians the bottom line, the bedrock of his motives with regard to his relationship with them. Notice that the content of Paul's prayer is expressed in the first of the four clauses. The final three clauses clarify the apostle's motive for praying this prayer to God. The four clauses, moreover, are crafted around parallel ideas.[29]

Figure 14 **Synonymous and Contrasting Parallels in 13:7**

Now we pray to God:

content:	that	you	**will not do anything evil,**	
denial:	not so that	we	*may be recognized as* qualified, but	
restatement:	in order that	you	**might do what is right,**	
qualification:	even though	we	*may seem to be* unqualified.	

The first line constitutes the main content of Paul's prayer:[30] "that you will not do anything evil." Generally speaking, κακός (*kakos*, evil, bad) in Paul is the opposite of what is morally right or good, often with interpersonal or social connotations (thus, "harmful" or "pernicious").[31] Paul prays that the Corinthians will choose a course of action that aligns them with his ministry and his teaching, in short, with him as their apostle. This thought of not doing evil runs parallel (α) and is synonymous with the thought expressed in the third line: "in order that you might do what is right." This purpose clause (ἵνα, *hina*, in order that) expresses the bottom line of Paul's motives. He wants them to refrain from evil in order that they might do what is "right" (καλός, *kalos*), what is morally good or praiseworthy. Paraphrasing Prov. 3:4 LXX, Paul has used this term earlier, at 8:21, pointing to the importance of him maintaining a blameless reputation with regard to the collection for Jerusalem.

---

29. The diagram is based roughly on Barnett 1997: 923.

30. The imperfective aspect of the present indicative verb εὐχόμεθα (*euchometha*, we pray) suggests either that this is an ongoing prayer Paul prays for the Corinthians or that he is in the process of praying the prayer even as he writes.

31. See κακός in Rom. 1:30; 2:9; 3:8; 7:19, 21; 12:17, 21; 13:3–4, 10; 14:20; 16:19; 1 Cor. 10:6; 13:5; 15:33; 2 Cor. 13:7; Phil. 3:2; Col. 3:5; 1 Thess. 5:15; 1 Tim. 6:10; 2 Tim. 4:14; Titus 1:12.

But this third line also parallels (β) the second line (they are both ἵνα clauses), while expressing a contrast (οὐχ ἵνα . . . , ἀλλ' ἵνα, *ouch hina . . . , all' hina*, not so that we may be recognized as qualified, but in order that . . .). The apostle does not want the Corinthians to think that he prays for their right behavior so that he might fare well as to public opinion of his ministry. The verb φαίνω (*phainō*), used only here in 2 Corinthians, can mean "to shine," "to become visible," or "to seem," but in the passive it also can mean "to be recognized," "to be revealed," or "to be apparent" (BDAG 1047). Further, as we saw at 10:18,[32] δόκιμος (*dokimos*) refers to something "approved," something that has been put to the test and shown to be genuine. In our current context it stands over against someone being ἀδόκιμος (*adokimos*), that is, "unqualified," "worthless," shown to have failed the test. So Paul asserts that he prays that the Corinthians will not do evil, not so that he might be recognized as the truly qualified apostle he is, but so that they might do what is right. After all, Paul's goal for his ministry to the Corinthians is to present them to Christ as "a pure virgin" (11:2). He only wants to build them up in the faith (12:19) and grieves over their continued stumbling into various forms of immorality (12:20–21). Certainly their spiritual condition reflects on his apostleship, but he definitely cares more about their spiritual condition than his own reputation.

This priority he makes clear with the final qualification, which offers yet another parallel contrast with the second line (γ): "even though we may seem to be unqualified" (ἡμεῖς δὲ ὡς ἀδόκιμοι ὦμεν, *hēmeis de hōs adokimoi ōmen*). This qualifying statement alludes to the apostolic power Paul will bring to bear if the Corinthians don't repent. They have demanded proof. Proof will come, by Christ's power, in the form of Paul bringing his apostolic authority to bear against those who are still living in sin (13:1–3). Although such a display of apostolic power would clearly and publicly demonstrate the authenticity of Paul's apostolic ministry among the Corinthians, he says it would be much better for them to repent. He prefers for them to do the right thing, even if that means he and his ministry team might be perceived ὡς ἀδόκιμοι, "as unqualified."

d. Edification: The Purpose of Paul's Letter (13:8–10)

13:8–9   At verses 8–9, with a pair of clauses introduced by γάρ (*gar*, for), the apostle explains further his desire that the Corinthians would do what is "right" rather than what is "evil." The first of these reads, "For we cannot do anything against the truth but only in support of the truth." Rather than taking this bold assertion as a lofty aphorism, our interpretation of Paul's thought here must be guided by the immediate context, specifically by what he has been saying about the disciplinary action he will bring to bear if those who should repent don't, and calling for the better course of repentance and right action. In short, Paul's power-filled authority will be brought to bear against

---

32. "For it is not the one commending himself who passes the test [ἐστιν δόκιμος, *estin dokimos*], but the one whom the Lord commends!" (10:18).

the Corinthians if they do not repent. But if they do repent, he will not act against them.

Paul explains that he is not able (οὐ γὰρ δυνάμεθα, *ou gar dynametha*) to act against the truth (κατὰ τῆς ἀληθείας, *kata tēs alētheias*).[33] As Christ's apostle, he has openly proclaimed the truth (4:2) and speaks truthfully in his ministry (6:7; 7:14; 12:6). Indeed, the truth of Christ is in him (11:10), that is, he has received the truth from Christ himself, beginning with his encounter on the Damascus road. Thus his whole life and ministry focuses on work that is "in support of the truth" or "in the interest of the truth" (ὑπὲρ τῆς ἀληθείας, *hyper tēs alētheias*).[34] It is not in him to fight against it. Consequently, if those in Corinth who need to repent do so, standing in the truth of the gospel, Paul will not act against them, but will be aligned with them as companions in the truth.

As we have seen elsewhere in 2 Corinthians, the conjunction γάρ (*gar*) at times occurs two or more times in a series of thoughts supporting an idea, or providing further explanation or clarification of an idea. Introduced by γάρ, verse 9 continues Paul's clarification of his desire that the Corinthians might do what is right, and thus the interpretation here must also rest on the flow of the apostle's thought in context. He writes, "We rejoice when we are weak and you are strong." This too relates to the Corinthians making right spiritual choices at this point in their relationship with the apostle.

Paul has had a good bit to say about the "weak" and the "strong" in the Corinthian correspondence.[35] At 1 Cor. 1:25–27 the apostle describes the "weakness" of the Christ crucified over against the perceived "strength" of worldly wisdom. The Corinthians who have responded to the gospel are not wise, or powerful, or of high social status, but God has chosen the weak and foolish of the world to shame the strong, the wise. So at the beginning of 1 Corinthians, Paul uses the images of "weakness" and "strength" to speak of human perceptions of the gospel's foolishness over against the values of power, wisdom, and position embraced by the world. Christ calls people to a gospel of "weakness," bringing them to a place where they only "boast in the Lord" (1:31); here the apostle quotes Jer. 9:24, as he does at 2 Cor. 10:17. Similar to our passage under consideration, 1 Cor. 4:10 draws a contrast between Paul (and more generally, the apostles) as weak, over against the Corinthians, who appear to be strong. In that passage, weakness again parallels foolishness, and strength parallels wisdom. In terms of the normal values of the world, the apostles don't measure up well. They are not distinguished in the eyes of the world but rather are condemned to die, dishonored, suffer from harsh living

---

33. As here in 13:8a, κατά + the genitive can be used to express actions taken against someone (e.g., Matt. 5:23; Mark 9:40; 11:25; Rom. 8:31).

34. This is the antithesis of working κατά + the genitive, against someone. So ὑπὲρ τῆς ἀληθείας, thus ὑπέρ + the genitive, communicates the idea of doing something that is in the interest of the truth (13:8b).

35. See 1 Cor. 1:25, 27; 4:10; 8:7, 9–12; 9:22; 11:30; 12:22; 2 Cor. 10:10; 11:21, 29; 12:10; 13:3–4, 9.

conditions, do manual labor, are abused and lied about. In short, the apostles are the dirt and scum of the world (4:13). Thus weakness here refers to being a "fool" for Christ (thus the opposite of "wise person"), a fool who holds no respect or status in the value system of the world. Elsewhere in 1 Corinthians, Paul uses the image of weakness to speak of a person's weak conscience (8:7, 9–12; 9:22?), someone who is sick (11:30), and those who seem to be less significant from the standpoint of their spiritual giftedness (12:22).

As we have seen in the comments, Paul uses the image of weakness extensively in 2 Corinthians, all in chapters 10–13. In addition to the uses of the verb (ἀσθενέω; 2 Cor. 11:21, 29; 12:10; 13:3–4, 9), we have the adjective (ἀσθενής; 10:10) and the cognate noun (ἀσθένεια; 11:30; 12:5, 9, 10; 13:4), and note that in 2 Corinthians the topic occurs from chapter 10 onward. Paul uses the concept of weakness to speak variously of his own public persona as unimpressive (10:10), his refusal to strong-arm the Corinthians (11:21), the apostle's burden when a person in one of the churches is in need (whether in terms of spiritual danger, material resources, illness, or some other limitation) (11:29), his struggle with persecution and other difficulties (12:10), ineffectiveness (13:3), and a posture of vulnerability and nonretaliation (13:4). Given our current context, when at 13:9 Paul writes "We rejoice when we are weak," he speaks most in line with the use of the verb at 13:4. In essence Paul celebrates (χαίρομεν, chairomen, rejoice) when he does not have to wield apostolic authority in disciplining the Corinthians, when he can be meek in dealing with them (P. Hughes 1962: 483). By contrast, the Corinthians' strength here refers to their moral and spiritual vigor once they have come to a place of repentance and are aligned with the truth.

The pronoun τοῦτο (touto, this; 13:9) functions as an accusative of reference ("We pray [εὐχόμεθα, euchometha] with reference to this") and may be read either as retrospective, referring back to the just-mentioned spiritual strength of the Corinthians (13:9a), but also could be prospective, anticipating the hoped-for restoration mentioned in the next breath (τὴν ὑμῶν κατάρτισιν, tēn hymōn katartisin, your restoration). The term κατάρτισις (katartisis) occurs only here in the biblical literature. Yet the word is cognate with the verb καταρτίζω (katartizō, to put in order, restore, prepare), used just two verses later in 13:11, and the noun καταρτισμός (katartismos, equipping; Eph. 4:12). The latter term could be used in a medical context to speak of setting a bone (BDAG 526). Paul probably uses the word κατάρτισις here to refer to the Corinthians being put in order, that is, their "restoration." This is that for which the apostle prays. He wants them to move beyond the spiritual muddle caused by the interloping and false teachers and the Corinthians' bad, immoral choices. Then their community will be put in order and restored to a healthy progress in the faith.

13:10   Paul continues in verse 10, "This is why I am writing these things while absent, so that when I am there with you, I may not have to deal harshly with you, acting on the authority the Lord gave me for building up, not tearing down." Paul's references to "being absent" over against "being present" in chapters 10–13 are structurally significant, framing the first and the last main movements of this distinct and much-discussed section of the book. The four occurrences of this contrast between the apostle's absence over against his presence are as follows:

2 Cor. 10:1–2	2 Cor. 10:11	2 Cor. 13:2	2 Cor. 13:10
Now I, Paul, personally appeal to you by the leniency and clemency of Christ—I who am "pitiful"			
when *face-to-face among you,*		When *I was there* the second time, I warned those who sinned before and all the rest,	
but "confident" toward you when I am *absent*—	such a person should consider this: what we are in word, by writing letters when *away,*	and although I am *absent* right now, I warn them again.	This is why I am writing these things while *absent,*
when I am *with you.*	we will be in action when *present*!		so that when *I am there with you,* I may not have to deal harshly with you.

We suggest that the first two form an inclusio marking the first movement and the final two form an inclusio marking the final main movement of the section. Further, it seems to be no coincidence that Paul begins and ends the section with references to his presence among the Corinthians over against his absence from them. This fits the tenor of a book so marked by travel narrative and so shaped by an emphasis on Paul's imminent visit to the city. It also concludes the book with the anticipation of the apostle's arrival and the accountability that his time among the Corinthians will bring.

Significantly, here in 13:10 Paul clearly states why he wrote the book (i.e., these things, ταῦτα, *tauta*); the phrase διὰ τοῦτο (*dia touto*, for this reason, this is why) points to why Paul is "writing" (γράφω, *graphō*) this letter while "absent" (ἀπών, *apōn*). Correspondingly, he follows with a purpose clause: ἵνα παρὼν μὴ ἀποτόμως χρήσωμαι (*hina parōn mē apotomōs chrēsōmai*, so that when I am there with you, I may not have to deal harshly with you). Paul is on his way to Corinth and thus will be "with" or "present" (παρών) among the Corinthians soon. The rebellion against Paul's leadership, particularly the dalliance of some false teachers and the continuing immorality among those who have not repented, will be dealt with one way or another. In writing what we have as 2 Corinthians, Paul hopes to lead the unrepentant to renewal before he arrives. The apostle does not want the visit to be a confrontation marked by humiliation, grief, and a display of power (12:20–13:3). In short, he does not want "to deal harshly with" (μὴ ἀποτόμως χρήσωμαι, *mē apotomōs chrēsōmai*) the unrepentant. The verb χράομαι (*chraomai*), here an aorist subjunctive negated by μή (*mē*), can be used to mean making use of something, acting in a particular manner, or treating a person in a certain way (BDAG 1088). Moreover, the adverb ἀποτόμως (*apotomōs*) speaks of something done "rigorously," "relentlessly," or "severely," and in context refers to action that is harsh.[36] So Paul does not want to confront the Corinthians harshly, and he hopes his letter will prevent such, removing the need.

Although rebuking the Corinthians harshly would be an unpleasant encounter for both Paul and the Corinthians (e.g., 1:23; 2:1–2), such a chastising would be entirely appropriate and "according to the authority" (κατὰ τὴν ἐξουσίαν, *kata tēn exousian*)[37] the apostle has been given by the Lord. Paul has been "appointed" to his ministry among the Corinthians (10:13) as a true "apostle," thus an authorized representative "of Christ Jesus by God's will" (1:1). He acts by God's authority for the good of the Corinthian church. The language here echoes a similar statement at 10:8: "For even if I boast a bit more about our authority, which the Lord gave for the purpose of building you up and not for tearing you down, I will not be ashamed of it." There too the authority is said to have a very specific purpose. It is not for "tearing down" καθαίρεσις (*kathairesis*), siege-warfare language reserved for the dismantling of the opponents' false teaching and activity (10:4). Rather, the authority given Paul by the Lord is "for building up" (εἰς οἰκοδομήν, *eis oikodomēn*), a word picture of construction or building used with the figurative sense of edification or spiritual strengthening (e.g., Rom. 14:19; 15:2; 1 Cor. 14:3, 26; Eph. 4:29).

Reflection

In our reflection on 12:14–21 I noted that "we must learn to do the hard thing of holding people accountable in loving, edifying ways." At 13:1–10 Paul models for us a number of healthy practices that make for a loving, edifying form of accountability, one that is "for building up, not tearing down" (13:10). Notice that, playing off Deut. 19:15, the apostle speaks of *validation of an accusation* in 13:1. Exercising accountability in the community has serious implications for a person's life and therefore must not be approached lightly. Paul has worked with the unrepentant over time. So the accountability he brings is not a rush job to resolve tension in the church.

36. E.g., Plutarch (*Crass.* 3.1) tells of a man who, once his loan to a person came due, would demand repayment relentlessly. The only other uses of the term in the biblical literature are at Wis. 5:22, where in a scene of judgment we are told "the water of the sea will rage against them, and rivers will overwhelm them relentlessly [ἀποτόμως]"; and at Titus 1:13, which has affinities with Paul's usage in 2 Cor. 13:10. In Titus, Paul exhorts the young minister to rebuke "sharply" (ἀποτόμως) rebellious people who are misled by false teachers, so that they might be healthy when it comes to the faith.

37. The use of κατά + the acc. can be used, as here in 13:10, to introduce a norm that governs a particular action (BDAG 512).

His repeated trips and encounters with believers in Corinth have served to validate that those who need to be confronted are in destructive patterns of behavior. Validation serves to slow the rush to judgment on matters of importance. Second, in a related vein, *Paul offers warnings and therefore opportunities for change.* Warnings in a sense give a person caught in a pattern of sin the space to make a change of direction. Third, not depending merely on human stratagems or abilities, *Paul's form of accountability is christocentrically powerful.* Whatever the manifestation of the power of Christ he has in mind, it is clear that the apostle depends on Christ's power to deal with the situation in Corinth. We should approach the ministry of accountability in much prayer, filled with the Holy Spirit, asking Christ to intervene in helping brothers and sisters come to needed repentance. Fourth, *Paul challenges those caught in sin to assess their spiritual condition.* He does not assume that their association with the church equals their regeneration spiritually. At times we need to challenge the hardened, unrepentant sinner to consider whether they really are in the faith. Fifth, *the apostle vies for what is right and true rather than the affirmation of his position.* This is not about Paul. It is about the spiritual well-being of those at Corinth, and Paul rejoices in their spiritual well-being. For Paul's authentic ministry always keeps in clear view that the purpose of the ministry is to build up, not tear down the church. These principles can go a long way to helping us shape an appropriate, loving, edifying form of accountability in our ministries.

Additional Notes

13:3b–4. Below is the Greek of the diagram presented in my comments on 13:3–4:

(A) [Χριστοῦ] ὃς
  a εἰς ὑμᾶς
    b οὐκ ἀσθενεῖ ἀλλὰ
    b δυνατεῖ
  a ἐν ὑμῖν.

(B) καὶ γὰρ
  a ἐσταυρώθη
    b ἐξ ἀσθενείας, ἀλλὰ
  a ζῇ
    b ἐκ δυνάμεως θεοῦ.

(C) καὶ γὰρ
  a ἡμεῖς ἀσθενοῦμεν
    b ἐν αὐτῷ, ἀλλὰ
  a ζήσομεν
    b σὺν αὐτῷ
      c ἐκ δυνάμεως θεοῦ
        d εἰς ὑμᾶς.

13:4. The added textual variant εἰ (ℵ^{2} A D^{1} Ψ 1881 𝔐 lat sy; Ambst), if original, would add a concessive note ("although"), as with BDF 239. Yet the evidence for omission is much stronger (𝔓^{46vid} ℵ* B D* F G K P 0243 33 81 104 365 1241 1739 co; Eu) and to be preferred. The εἰ probably was a scribal addition to weaken Paul's bold proclamation of Christ's weakness!

13:4. The strongly attested reading ἐν αὐτῷ (B D K L P Ψ 0243 0278 33 81 104 365 630 1175 1241 1505 1739 1881 2464 𝔐 ar vg sy^{h} sa; Ambst) has been replaced by σὺν αὐτῷ in some witnesses (ℵ A F G r sy^{p} bo) under the influence of the σὺν αὐτῷ that occurs in the final clause of the verse (Metzger 1994: 518). The ἐν in original form can be read as communicating relationship, expressing a common use of Paul's "in Christ" motif.

13:4. The phrase εἰς ὑμᾶς is omitted by some witnesses (B D^{2} it^{r} vg^{ms} arm Chrysostom), probably because a scribe saw the addendum as awkward (does it delimit ζήσομεν or ἐκ δυνάμεως θεοῦ? so Metzger 1994: 519). For the same reason, others retain the phrase but reposition it before ἐκ δυνάμεως (*l* 1441). Yet the occurrence of the phrase at the end of the verse has a wealth of support and is preferred (𝔓^{46vid} ℵ A D* F G Ψ 075 0150 0243 *Byz* [K L P]).

E. Closing Exhortations, Greetings, and Benediction (13:11–13)

These final verses of the book are introduced by "finally" (λοιπόν, *loipon*) and consist of a series of brief, rapid-fire exhortations, greetings, and a benediction, common elements in the closing of the NT writings (1 Thess. 5:16–28; 2 Thess. 3:16–18; 1 Cor. 16:19–24; Heb. 13:20–25; 1 Pet. 5:12–14), as well as letters of the broader Greco-Roman world (Barnett 1997: 615). Some scholars, understanding chapters 10–13 to be a separate letter, regard what we have here as the particular conclusion of these chapters. Others who consider 2 Corinthians a unity read 13:11–13 as the conclusion to the whole. The content of the exhortations fits well the themes that have been on Paul's mind as he has moved toward the book's ending, but some find the shift to an affectionate and conciliatory tone too abrupt, suggesting that the conclusion must have originally belonged elsewhere (see the discussion on unity in the introduction). Yet as noted above, the patterns here fit other writings of the period, and the shift in tone should not be taken as an indication of literary fragmentation (Garland 1999: 552). Rather, Paul appropriately brings his letter to a conclusion embodying hope that the Corinthians will respond well to his admonitions.

Exegesis and Exposition

[11]Finally, brothers and sisters, rejoice, be restored, be encouraged, be of one mind, live in peace, and then the God of love and peace will be with you. [12]Greet one another with a holy kiss. All God's people send their greetings. [13]The grace of the Lord Jesus Christ and the love of God and the fellowship of the Holy Spirit be with all of you. ⌐ ⌐

Paul affectionately addresses the Corinthians as ἀδελφοί (*adelphoi*, brothers and sisters) as he does elsewhere at 1:8 and 8:1.[1] He then follows with a list of five present imperatives:

13:11-13

χαίρετε (*chairete*)	rejoice
καταρτίζεσθε (*katartizesthe*)	be restored
παρακαλεῖσθε (*parakaleisthe*)	be encouraged
τὸ αὐτὸ φρονεῖτε (*to auto phroneite*)	be of one mind
εἰρηνεύετε (*eirēneuete*)	live in peace

1. The familial address is also used in 2 Corinthians of Paul's coworkers (2 Cor. 1:1; 2:13; 8:18, 22–23; 9:3, 5; 11:9; 12:18).

The first exhortation is to "rejoice" (χαίρετε),[2] a common theme in Paul's writings, with the verb used twenty-nine times.[3] Elsewhere in 2 Corinthians, Paul states that he has handled communication with the Corinthians in a particular way "in order that when I arrive, I might not be made sad by the ones who ought to *give me joy*" (2:3). The apostolic ministry is characterized by being sorrowful "but constantly rejoicing" (6:10), and Paul has been made to rejoice over Titus's report on his recent visit (7:7, 9, 13, 16). Finally, in 13:9 Paul has just written the Corinthians, "We rejoice when we are weak and you are strong." So in a nuanced way his admonition for the Corinthians to rejoice shows how Paul wants the Corinthians to join him in a particular response to life that marks his ministry. He does not want the heavy tone of the latter part of the letter to leave a cloud over the church. Rather, he hopes for a good response from the church, a response that will give them—as well as him—joy.

We encountered the cognate noun of the second exhortation, καταρτίζεσθε (*katartizesthe*, be restored), at 13:9 (κατάρτισιν, *katartisin*) and translated the noun as referring to the Corinthians' "restoration." Further, at the beginning of our extant Corinthian correspondence is a passage parallel in thought to 13:11. It reads, "I appeal to you, brothers and sisters, in the name of our Lord Jesus Christ, that all of you agree with one another in what you say and that there be no divisions among you, but that you be perfectly united [κατηρτισμένοι, *katērtismenoi*] in mind and thought" (1 Cor. 1:10 NIV). In the 1 Corinthians passage, the perfect participle form of our verb means not allowing divisions, an emphasis also found in 2 Cor. 13:11 (τὸ αὐτὸ φρονεῖτε, *to auto phroneite*, be of one mind), and the nuanced thought shows that Paul wants the divided Corinthians (1 Cor. 1:10–17) to "be restored" to a community of unity. In any case, the idea clearly relates to the church being put into proper order, which relates very directly to being unified in mind and purpose. This, for Paul, would be an answer to prayer (13:9).

Paul's third exhortation in this list, παρακαλεῖσθε (*parakaleisthe*), a present passive imperative, reiterates one of 2 Corinthians' main themes—encouragement.[4] In fact, here we have a theme that ties the ending of 2 Corinthians back to the introduction of the book. Although the word could be translated as "be comforted" (e.g., ESV, NASB, Tyndale, KJV), we render it with the sense of "be encouraged" (so HCSB, NLT[2], NIV, NET; BDAG 765), that is, "allow yourself to be exhorted."[5] Any pastor who has dealt with a difficult

2. The NRSV and NIV[84] read χαίρετε as "farewell" and "good-by" respectively (similarly, KJV with "farewell"; Tyndale, "fare ye well"). Yet Paul uses the word throughout his letters as a comment on or exhortation to rejoicing.

3. See χαίρω in Rom. 12:12, 15 (2x); 16:19; 1 Cor. 7:30 (2x); 13:6; 16:17; 2 Cor. 2:3; 6:10; 7:7, 9, 13, 16; 13:9, 11; Phil. 1:18 (2x); 2:17–18, 28; 3:1; 4:4 (2x), 10; Col. 1:24; 2:5; 1 Thess. 3:9; 5:16.

4. The theme is found elsewhere throughout 2 Corinthians and is used most extensively in chaps. 1; 7; and 8; plus 1:3–7; 2:7–8; 5:20; 6:1; 7:4–13; 8:4, 6, 17; 9:5; 10:1; 12:8, 18; 13:11. In Paul's other writings, the noun occurs nine times, and the verb thirty-six times (see the note under my comments on 1:3).

5. For more on the use of the verb and its cognates in 2 Corinthians, see comments on 1:3.

and morally entrenched person or group in a church knows the frustration, the "wall" thrown up by those who will not receive exhortation. Resistance sets in, and progress in the faith suffers. So Paul exhorts the Corinthians to be open to his words and God's ways for their spiritual well-being.

The fourth exhortation, "be of one mind" (τὸ αὐτὸ φρονεῖτε, *to auto phroneite*), constitutes another common Pauline theme (Rom. 12:16; 15:5; Gal. 5:10; Phil. 2:2, 5; 3:15; 4:2). The apostle wants members of Christ's community to "think" the same way and thus be unified. The juxtaposition of "comfort" (that is, encouragement, παρακλήσεως, *parakleseōs*) and "unity" (τὸ αὐτὸ φρονεῖν ἐν ἀλλήλοις, *to auto phronein en allēlois*) also occur at Rom. 15:5: "Now may the God of endurance and comfort give you unity with one another in accordance with Christ Jesus" (Rom. 15:5 NET).[6] As is obvious from 1 Corinthians, the Corinthian church, at least for several years, has been marred by relational fragmentation, with the church splintering into pods gathered around particular leaders (1 Cor. 1:10–17). Further, key points of 2 Corinthians reek of disunity. For example: the accusation that Paul, by changing his travel itinerary, manifests a wishy-washy character (2 Cor. 1:17–18); conflict with a key figure in the community, who has opposed Paul publicly while much of the church was standing by (2:5–11); the question of whether Paul needs to go through the process of recommending himself to the Corinthians (3:1); the tolerance of interloping teachers, who bring an impressive public style of "ministry," while bearing a false gospel and an alien "spirit" (11:4); and differences regarding genuine spirituality (10:2–7) and Paul's apostolic ministry (11:1–12:14; Barnett 1997: 616). In 12:20 Paul mentions that when he arrives in Corinth, he is afraid that he might find the community locked in "dissension, jealousy, fits of rage, selfish ambitions, slanderous words, gossiping, swelled heads, and chaos," all destroyers of church unity.

The absence of unity relates closely to a lack of relational "peace," an ancient and pervasive Jewish value and a widely published exhortation in the NT literature. In offering final words to the chaotic Corinthians, whose recent relationship with Paul has been so marked by tension, his exhortation "Live in peace" fails to surprise. The apostle longs for them to be at peace with one another and with him. The result[7] (καί, *kai*, and then) of living in peace will be that "the God of love and peace will be with you" (ὁ θεὸς τῆς ἀγάπης καὶ εἰρήνης ἔσται μεθ᾽ ὑμῶν, *ho theos tēs agapēs kai eirēnēs estai meth᾽ hymōn*). When God's children live at peace with one another, they manifest the Father's character and are given the blessing of the Father's presence. God himself is not a God of disorder, but rather a God characterized by peace (1 Cor. 14:33). Thus he is called the "God of peace" at several points in the NT (Rom. 15:33; 16:20; Phil. 4:9; 1 Thess. 5:23), and, as noted in the comments at 1:2, the blessings of "grace" and "peace" are widely used in the NT letters as a form of

---

6. Interestingly, these exhortations also occur in the context of references to the "strong" and the "weak" (Rom. 15:1).

7. The use of καί (*kai*) at the beginning of this assertion introduces a result that stems from what precedes.

greeting (Rom. 1:7; 1 Cor. 1:3; Gal. 1:3; Eph. 1:2; Phil. 1:2; Col. 1:2; 2 Thess. 1:2; 1 Tim. 1:2; 2 Tim. 1:2; Titus 1:4; Philem. 3; 2 John 3). By contrast, God is called "the God of love" only here, although 1 John notes twice that "God is love" (1 John 4:8, 16), and the NT bears witness extensively and eloquently to the "love of God" (John 5:42; Rom. 5:5; 8:39; 2 Thess. 3:5; 1 John 2:5; 3:17; 4:9; 5:3; Jude 21), which Paul mentions in the next verse.

Paul continues in verse 12: "Greet one another with a holy kiss. All God's people send their greetings" (Ἀσπάσασθε ἀλλήλους ἐν ἁγίῳ φιλήματι. Ἀσπάζονται ὑμᾶς οἱ ἅγιοι πάντες, *Aspasasthe allēlous en hagiō philēmati. Aspazontai hymas hoi hagioi pantes*).[8] Greetings were often offered in Greco-Roman letters, and exchanging kisses was common, both in Judaism and the broader culture. A kiss could express respect, or a simple form of greeting or parting between friends or relatives, or a sign of brotherhood in a religious context (Thrall 2000: 912). Yet to describe the kiss of greeting as "holy" seems to have originated with Paul (Rom. 16:16; 1 Cor. 16:20; 1 Thess. 5:26),[9] since, as far as we know, such a description did not exist in the broader Greco-Roman world; it seems to have been born in the extended-family context of the early church.[10] The convention marked Jesus's first followers as a distinct subculture, one that manifested the kind of affection that might be found in a family. In Paul's use, the kiss as "holy" could speak of proper and pure motives, but it also represented unity in the church (Weima 1994: 113–14). Thus Paul's exhortation to greet brothers and sisters with "a holy kiss" was an especially apt exhortation for such a fragmented church. "A holy kiss" is also appropriate for those who are part of that larger communion of people referred to as "holy ones." Thus Paul sends greetings from "all the saints," that is, "all God's people" (οἱ ἅγιοι πάντες, *hoi hagioi pantes*), supposedly referring to those in Macedonia. Elsewhere Paul sends greetings from those who share a common geographical heritage, but here the greeting is more general, highlighting the universal bond of all believers.

Paul ends the letter with a beautiful, balanced, tripartite blessing, which has been celebrated as the most robust expression on the interworking of the Trinity in the NT:

Ἡ	χάρις	τοῦ κυρίου Ἰησοῦ Χριστοῦ	καὶ
ἡ	ἀγάπη	τοῦ θεοῦ	καὶ
ἡ	κοινωνία	τοῦ ἁγίου πνεύματος	
			μετὰ πάντων ὑμῶν.

8. As Harris (2005: 935) notes, the shift to the aorist ἀσπάσασθε here (from the present imperative verbs used previously) probably is not significant since the aorist imperative is common in prayers and greetings.

9. In each of these other references, the word order is different from this exhortation in 2 Cor. 13. The exhortations in Romans, 1 Corinthians, and 1 Thessalonians read ἐν φιλήματι ἁγίῳ (*en philēmati hagiō*, with a holy kiss).

10. In the context of the other three exhortations to greet one another with a holy kiss, Paul sends greetings from "all the churches" (Rom. 16:16), from "all the brothers and sisters" (1 Cor. 16:20), and encourages the Thessalonians to "greet the brothers and sisters with a holy kiss."

Hē	charis	tou kyriou Iēsou Christou	kai
hē	agapē	tou theou	kai
hē	koinōnia	tou hagiou pneumatos	
			meta pantōn hymōn.
The	grace	of the Lord Jesus Christ	and
the	love	of God	and
the	fellowship	of the Holy Spirit	
			be with all of you.

Paul's wish is that grace, love, and fellowship, each initiated by a member of the Trinity, might "be[11] with all of" the Corinthians.

The benediction at the end of 1 Corinthians states more simply, "The grace of the Lord Jesus be with you" (ἡ χάρις τοῦ κυρίου Ἰησοῦ μεθ᾽ ὑμῶν, hē charis tou kyriou Iēsou meth᾽ hymōn) and then adds, "My love be with all of you in Christ Jesus" (ἡ ἀγάπη μου μετὰ πάντων ὑμῶν ἐν Χριστῷ Ἰησοῦ, hē agapē mou meta pantōn hymōn en Christō Iēsou). Yet here in 2 Cor. 13:13 Paul expands on his normal, more basic benediction to point to God as the source of love and the Spirit as the true source of fellowship.

The closing of the letter begins with the most common element of Pauline benedictions, the "grace" (Ἡ χάρις, hē charis) of the Lord Jesus Christ.[12] The apostle may start with the grace offered through Christ, since it is foundational to the believers' relationship with God (Harris 2005: 938), but it may also be that, as the most common element of Paul's benediction when writing his churches, the "grace" of Christ most naturally comes to mind first. Further, Paul has started his letter with the blessing of "grace and peace" (1:2) and

11. The verb, probably the optative of εἰμί (eimi, am; here supply εἴη, eiē, be; cf. Rom. 15:5; 15:13; 1 Thess. 3:11; 3:12–13; 5:23), is understood.

12. References to "grace" are found in all of the Pauline Letters, and Paul's benedictions generally include wish(es), the divine source(s), and those addressed (see Weima 1994: 78–83). Pauline benedictions in his letters to churches outside the Corinthian correspondence include the following (translation mine):

Romans	"The grace of our Lord Jesus be with you." (16:20)
Galatians	"The grace of our Lord Jesus Christ be with your spirit." (6:18)
Ephesians	"May the brothers and sisters have peace, and love with faith, from God the Father and the Lord Jesus Christ. Grace be with all who love our Lord Jesus Christ with a love that doesn't die." (6:23–24)
Philippians	"The grace of the Lord Jesus Christ be with your spirit." (4:23)
Colossians	"Grace be with you." (4:18c)
1 Thessalonians	"Now may the God of peace himself make you completely holy and may your spirit and soul and body be kept blamelessly whole at the coming of our Lord Jesus Christ. . . . . . . The grace of our Lord Jesus Christ be with you." (5:23, 28)
2 Thessalonians	"Now may the Lord of peace himself give you peace at all times and in every way. The Lord be with you all. . . . . . . The grace of our Lord Jesus Christ be with you all." (3:16, 18)

speaks of various manifestations of God's grace through Christ throughout the letter (2 Cor. 1:12; 4:15; 6:1; 8:1, 9; 9:8, 14–15; 12:9; 13:13). At 8:9 Paul celebrates "the grace of our Lord Jesus Christ" (τὴν χάριν τοῦ κυρίου ἡμῶν Ἰησοῦ Χριστοῦ, *tēn charin tou kyriou hēmōn Iēsou Christou*), who manifested his grace by the incarnation: "though he was rich, he became poor for your sake, so that by his poverty you might become rich." Accordingly, most commentators take the genitive, τοῦ κυρίου Ἰησοῦ Χριστοῦ, as a subjective genitive, pointing to Christ as the initiator of the grace.[13] Moreover, the apostolic benediction wishes a continuous supply of grace for the believers, for God's ongoing generosity and favor constitute an ongoing need (e.g., 9:8; 12:9).

The second element of the benediction wishes for the Corinthians "the love of God" (cf. John 5:42; Rom. 5:5; 8:39; 2 Thess. 3:5; 1 John 2:5; 3:17; 4:9; 5:3; Jude 21). The apostle has just mentioned the "God of love" in verse 11. We face the question as to whether the genitive here (ἡ ἀγάπη τοῦ θεοῦ, *hē agapē tou theou*) is subjective (i.e., love given by God) like the first element of the benediction, or objective (i.e., "love for God"). Its close proximity to "the God of love" in verse 11 and the fact that Paul wishes on the Corinthians a blessing from God—both call for the former, "God's love." The Corinthians, in their fractious state, desperately need love from God the Father to be manifested among them.

Although the third element of the benediction, "the fellowship of the Holy Spirit" (ἡ κοινωνία τοῦ ἁγίου πνεύματος) could be read as an objective genitive (believers embracing a relationship with the Spirit),[14] I suggest that the parallelism in the benediction, in which the first two elements almost certainly are subjective genitives, along with the emphasis on the need for church unity in the book's broader context—both point to this third element also being a subjective genitive, that is, a fellowship among members of the church that is prompted by the Holy Spirit. Once the Spirit fell on the earliest church, "fellowship" formed a foundational element of the Christian community (Acts 2:42). In 2 Corinthians, Paul does not want the Corinthians to have fellowship with unbelievers (6:14) but rather to participate in fellowship among the saints, for instance, in the sharing of resources (8:4; 9:13). That fellowship stems in part from the presence and work of the Spirit in the hearts of believers (1:22; 3:3; 5:5). An alien "spirit" produces chaos (11:4), but the life-giving Spirit produces unity.

As Harris (2005: 938) points out, these three gifts—grace, love, and fellowship—should not be seen as exclusive to the respective members of the Trinity here. For instance, elsewhere Paul speaks of the "grace of God" (1 Cor. 1:4), the "love of Christ" (2 Cor. 5:14), and "the fellowship of Jesus Christ" (1 Cor. 1:9).

---

13. Remember, however, that in the letter's opening, both "God our Father and the Lord Jesus Christ" are named as the source of "grace and peace" (1:2).

14. In support of this view, Thrall (2000: 917–18) notes, e.g., that in the NT when a genitive form follows the word κοινωνία, the genitive is almost always an objective genitive (e.g., 1 Cor. 10:16, "participation in the blood of Christ, . . . participation in the body of Christ"; see also 1 Cor. 1:9; Phil. 3:10). For the rest of the argument, see Thrall 2000: 917–18.

Further, this concise trinitarian statement, which speaks of Jesus Christ and the Spirit in parallel with God the Father, pulls together in a concise statement the cooperative working within the Godhead manifested throughout the letter.

Reflection

At the end of this letter, we recognize that in 2 Corinthians Paul offers a profoundly God-centered solution to the problems at Corinth. Ultimately, the church's struggle with their apostle manifests an underlying dysfunction in their relationship with God. The answer, then, has to do with the Corinthians being restored to right relationship with God through a proper understanding of the gospel and an obedience to the implications of the gospel for their various relationships with each other, with other believers, with the false teachers, and with Paul himself, but ultimately with God through the Lord Jesus. Perseverance in the faith always stems from a clarity with which we see Jesus and what he has accomplished on our behalf. If we lose a clear picture of the Christ and lose a grasp of the gospel, that leads to chaos in community. As Paul demonstrates, God uses authentic ministers of the gospel to project a clear picture of Christ and the gospel, through both their words and lives.

In closing, dear readers, I echo the apostle:

> The grace of the Lord Jesus Christ
> and
> the love of God
> and
> the fellowship of the Holy Spirit
> be with all of you.

Additional Note

13:13. Some manuscripts include a closing ἀμήν (ℵ² D K L P Ψ 104 365 1505 2464 𝔐 lat sy bo), but the evidence for its omission is much stronger ($\mathfrak{P}^{46}$ ℵ* A B F G 0243 6 33 81 630 1175 1241 1739 1881 sa bo^ms; Ambst).

Works Cited

Abernathy, D.

2000   "Exegetical Problems in 2 Corinthians 3." *Notes on Translation* 14:44–56.

Adewuya, J. A.

2003   *Holiness and Community in 2 Cor 6:14–7:1: Paul's View of Communal Holiness in the Corinthian Correspondence.* Studies in Biblical Literature 40. New York: Lang.

Allison, D. C., Jr.

2003   *Testament of Abraham.* Commentaries on Early Jewish Literature. Berlin: de Gruyter.

Anderson, L.

2004   "Mystery Martyrs." *Men of Integrity,* February 17.

Andrews, S. B.

1995   "Too Weak Not to Lead: The Form and Function of 2 Cor 11.23b–33." *New Testament Studies* 41:263–76.

ANRW   *Aufstieg und Niedergang der römischen Welt: Geschichte und Kultur Roms im Spiegel der neueren Forschung,* vol. 2.7.1. Edited by H. Temporini and W. Haase. Berlin: de Gruyter, 1979.

Babbitt, F. C.

1927   *Plutarch: Moralia,* vol. 1: *The Education of Children*; et al. Loeb Classical Library. Cambridge, MA: Harvard University Press/London: Heinemann.

1931   *Plutarch: Moralia,* vol. 3: *Sayings of Kings and Commanders*; et al. Loeb Classical Library. Cambridge, MA: Harvard University Press/London: Heinemann.

Bagalawis, M. A.

2000   "Ministry as Warfare: An Exegesis of 2 Corinthians 10:2b–6." *Asian Journal of Pentecostal Studies* 3:5–18.

Baird, W.

1985   "Visions, Revelation, and Ministry: Reflections on 2 Cor 12:1–5 and Gal 1:11–17." *Journal of Biblical Literature* 104:651–62.

Baird, W. R., Jr.

1961   "Letters of Recommendation: A Study of II Cor 3:1–3." *Journal of Biblical Literature* 80:166–72.

Baker, W. R.

2000   "Did the Glory of Moses' Face Fade? A Reexamination of *Katargeō* in 2 Corinthians 3:7–18." *Bulletin for Biblical Research* 10:1–15.

Barclay, J. M. G.

1987   "Mirror-Reading a Polemical Letter: Galatians as a Test Case." *Journal for the Study of the New Testament* 31:73–93.

1991   "Paul, Philemon and the Dilemma of Christian Slave-Ownership." *New Testament Studies* 37:161–86.

Barnett, P.

1997   *The Second Epistle to the Corinthians.* New International Commentary on the New Testament. Grand Rapids: Eerdmans.

2008   *Paul: Missionary of Jesus.* After Jesus 2. Grand Rapids: Eerdmans.

Barré, M. L.

1975   "Paul as Eschatologic Person: A New Look At 2 Cor 11:29." *Catholic Biblical Quarterly* 37:500–526.

Barrett, C. K.
1971   "Paul's Opponents in II Corinthians." *New Testament Studies* 17:233–54.
1973   *The Second Epistle to the Corinthians.* Black's New Testament Commentary. London: Black. Reprinted Peabody, MA: Hendrickson, 1997.
1978   *The Gospel according to St John: An Introduction with Commentary and Notes on the Greek Text.* 2nd ed. London: SPCK.
1982   *Essays on Paul.* London: SPCK.

Barrier, J. W.
2005   "Visions of Weakness: Apocalyptic Genre and the Identification of Paul's Opponents in 2 Corinthians 12:1–6." *Restoration Quarterly* 47:33–42.

Bateman, H. W.
1997   *Early Jewish Hermeneutics and Hebrews 1:5–13: The Impact of Early Jewish Exegesis on the Interpretation of a Significant New Testament Passage.* New York: Lang.
2007   *Four Views on the Warning Passages in Hebrews.* Grand Rapids: Kregel.

Batey, R. A.
1971   *New Testament Nuptial Imagery.* Leiden: Brill.

Bauckham, R.
1999   *God Crucified: Monotheism and Christology in the New Testament.* Didsbury Lectures 1996. Grand Rapids: Eerdmans.
2008   *Jesus and the God of Israel:* God Crucified *and Other Studies on the New Testament's Christology of Divine Identity.* Grand Rapids: Eerdmans.

Baxter, R.
1821   *The Reformed Pastor: Shewing the Nature of Pastoral Work.* New York: J. C. Totten.
1998   *Richard Baxter: The Pastor's Pastor; Autobiography.* Reprinted Fearn, Ross-shire, UK: Christian Focus.

BDAG   *A Greek-English Lexicon of the New Testament and Other Early Christian Literature.* By W. Bauer, F. W. Danker, W. F. Arndt, and F. W. Gingrich. 3rd ed. Chicago: University of Chicago Press, 2000.

BDF   *A Greek Grammar of the New Testament and Other Early Christian Literature.* By F. Blass and A. Debrunner. Translated and revised by R. W. Funk. Chicago: University of Chicago Press, 1961.

Beale, G. K.
1989   "The Old Testament Background of Reconciliation in 2 Corinthians 5–7 and Its Bearing on the Literary Problem of 2 Corinthians 6.14–7.1." *New Testament Studies* 35:550–81.

Beard, M.
2007   *The Roman Triumph.* Cambridge, MA: Belknap Press of Harvard University Press.

Becker, E.-M.
2004   *Letter Hermeneutics in 2 Corinthians.* Edinburgh: T&T Clark.

Becker, J.
1989   *Paulus: Der Apostel der Völker.* 2nd ed. Tübingen: Mohr (Siebeck).

Beker, J. C.
1980   *Paul the Apostle: The Triumph of God in Life and Thought.* Philadelphia: Fortress.

Belleville, L. L.
1989   "A Letter of Apologetic Self-Commendation: 2 Cor. 1:8–7:16." *Novum Testamentum* 31:142–63.
1991   *Reflections of Glory: Paul's Polemical Use of the Moses-Doxa Tradition in 2 Corinthians 3.1–18.* Journal for the Study of the New Testament: Supplement Series 52. Sheffield: JSOT Press.
1996   *2 Corinthians.* IVP New Testament Commentary Series. Downers Grove, IL: InterVarsity.

Belz, J.
2006   "Tender Toughness." *World Magazine,* July 22.

Best, E.
1987   *Second Corinthians.* Interpretation. Atlanta: John Knox.

Betz, H. D.
1972   *Der Apostel Paulus und die sokratische Tradition: Eine exegetische Untersuchung zu seiner Apologie 2 Korinther 10–13.* Tübingen: Mohr.
1973   "2 Cor 6:14–7:1: An Anti-Pauline Fragment?" *Journal of Biblical Literature* 92:88–108.

Betz, H. D., and G. W. MacRae
1985   *2 Corinthians 8 and 9: A Commentary on Two Administrative Letters of the Apostle Paul.* Hermeneia. Philadelphia: Fortress.

Bieringer, R.
1994   "Paul's Understanding of DIAKONIA in 2 Corinthians 5,18." Pp. 413–28 in *Studies on 2 Corinthians.* Edited by

R. Bieringer and J. Lambrecht. Bibliotheca ephemeridum theologicarum lovaniensium 112. Louvain: Leuven University Press/Peeters.

1996a   *The Corinthian Correspondence.* Bibliotheca ephemeridum theologicarum lovaniensium 125. Louvain: Leuven University Press/Peeters.

1996b   "Teilungshypothesen zum 2. Korintherbrief: Ein Forschungsüberblick." Pp. 67–105 in *The Corinthian Correspondence.* Edited by R. Bieringer. Bibliotheca ephemeridum theologicarum lovaniensium 125. Louvain: Leuven University Press/Peeters.

Bieringer, R., and J. Lambrecht
1994   *Studies on 2 Corinthians.* Bibliotheca ephemeridum theologicarum lovaniensium 112. Louvain: Leuven University Press/Peeters.

Bieringer, R., E. Nathan, and D. Kurek-Chomycz
2008   *2 Corinthians: A Bibliography.* Louvain: Peeters.

Bird, M. F.
2008   *Introducing Paul: The Man, His Mission, and His Message.* Downers Grove, IL: InterVarsity.

Block, D. I.
1997   *The Book of Ezekiel: Chapters 1–24.* New International Commentary on the Old Testament. Grand Rapids: Eerdmans.

1998   *The Book of Ezekiel: Chapters 25–48.* New International Commentary on the Old Testament. Grand Rapids: Eerdmans.

Blomberg, C.
1989   "The Structure of 2 Corinthians 1–7." *Criswell Theological Review* 4:3–20.

1999   *Neither Poverty nor Riches: A Biblical Theology of Material Possessions.* Grand Rapids: Eerdmans.

Boers, H.
2002   "2 Corinthians 5:14–6:2: A Fragment of Pauline Christology." *Catholic Biblical Quarterly* 64:527–47.

Boismard, M. E.
1999   *Our Victory over Death: Resurrection.* Collegeville, MN: Liturgical Press.

Bornkamm, G.
1965   *Die Vorgeschichte des sogenannten zweiten Korintherbriefes.* Heidelberg: Carl Winter.

Bowersock, G. W.
1969   *Greek Sophists in the Roman Empire.* Oxford: Clarendon.

Boyarin, D.
1994   *A Radical Jew: Paul and the Politics of Identity.* Berkeley: University of California Press.

Bray, G. (ed.)
1999   *1–2 Corinthians.* Ancient Christian Commentary on Scripture: New Testament 7. Edited by T. C. Oden. Downers Grove, IL: InterVarsity.

Breytenbach, C.
1989   *Versöhnung: Eine Studie zur paulinischen Soteriologie.* Wissenschaftliche Monographien zum Alten und Neuen Testament 60. Neukirchen-Vluyn: Neukirchener Verlag.

1990   "Paul's Proclamation and God's 'THRIAMBOS' (Notes on 2 Corinthians 2:14–16b)." *Neotestamentica* 24:257–71.

Bruce, F. F.
1971   *1 and 2 Corinthians.* Greenwood, SC: Attic.

1977   *Paul, Apostle of the Heart Set Free.* Grand Rapids: Eerdmans.

1990   *The Acts of the Apostles: The Greek Text with Introduction and Commentary.* 3rd ed. Grand Rapids: Eerdmans/Leicester, UK: Apollos.

Bultmann, R.
1910   *Der Stil der paulischen Predigt und die kynisch-stoische Diatribe.* Göttingen: Vandenhoeck & Ruprecht.

Bultmann, R., and E. Dinkler
1985   *The Second Letter to the Corinthians.* Minneapolis: Augsburg.

Burchard, C.
1970   *Der dreizehnte Zeuge: Traditions- und kompositionsgeschichtliche Untersuchungen zu Lukas Darstellung der Frühzeit des Paulus.* Göttingen: Vandenhoeck & Ruprecht.

Calvin, J.
1964   *The Second Epistle of Paul the Apostle to the Corinthians and the Epistles to Timothy, Titus and Philemon.* Calvin's Commentaries 10. Edinburgh: Oliver & Boyd.

Campbell, C.
2012   *Paul and Union with Christ: An Exegetical and Theological Study.* Grand Rapids: Zondervan.

Campbell, D. A.
2002   "An Anchor for Pauline Chronology: Paul's Flight from 'the Ethnarch of King Aretas' (2 Corinthians 11:32–33)." *Journal of Biblical Literature* 121:279–302.

Capes, D. B., R. Reeves, and E. R. Richards
2007   *Rediscovering Paul: An Introduction to His World, Letters, and Theology.* Downers Grove, IL: IVP Academic/Nottingham, UK: Apollos.

Caragounis, C. C.
1974   "Ὀψώνιον: A Reconsideration of Its Meaning." *Novum Testamentum* 16:35–57.

Carson, D. A.
2012   *The Intolerance of Tolerance.* Grand Rapids: Eerdmans.

Carter, W.
2000   "Evoking Isaiah: Matthean Soteriology and an Intertextual Reading of Isaiah 7–9 and Matthew 1:23 and 4:15–16." *Journal of Biblical Literature* 119:503–20.

Casson, L.
1974   *Travel in the Ancient World.* London: Allen & Unwin.

Chadwick, H.
2009   *Augustine: Confessions.* Oxford World's Classics. New York: Oxford University Press.

Chapple, A.
2013   "Paul and Illyricum." *Reformed Theological Review* 72:20–35.

Chen, K.
2013   *Eschatological Sanctuary in Exodus 15:17 and Related Texts.* Studies in Biblical Literature 154. New York: Lang.

Cherniss, H. F., and W. C. Helmbold
1957   *Plutarch: Moralia,* vol. 12: *Concerning the Face Which Appears in the Orb of the Moon*; et al. Loeb Classical Library. Cambridge, MA: Harvard University Press.

Ciampa, R. E.
2011   "Paul's Theology of the Gospel." Pp. 180–91 in *Paul as Missionary: Identity, Activity, Theology, and Practice.* Edited by T. J. Burke and B. S. Rosner. London: T&T Clark.

Ciampa, R. E., and B. S. Rosner
2010   *The First Letter to the Corinthians.* Grand Rapids: Eerdmans/Nottingham, UK: Apollos.

Clarke, A. D.
1993   *Secular and Christian Leadership in Corinth: A Socio-Historical and Exegetical Study of 1 Corinthians 1–6.* Arbeiten zur Geschichte des antiken Judentums und des Urchristentums 18. Leiden: Brill.

CNTUOT *Commentary on the New Testament Use of the Old Testament.* Edited by G. K. Beale and D. A. Carson. Grand Rapids: Baker Academic/Nottingham, UK: Apollos, 2007.

Collange, J. F.
1972   *Énigmes de la deuxième épître de Paul aux Corinthiens: Étude exégétique de 2 Cor. 2:14–7:4.* Society for New Testament Studies Monograph Series 18. Cambridge: Cambridge University Press.

Collins, A. Y.
1995   "A Throne in the Heavens: Apotheosis in Pre-Christian Judaism." Pp. 43–58 in *Death, Ecstasy, and Other Worldly Journeys.* Edited by J. J. Collins and M. Fishbane. New York: State University of New York Press.

Colson, F. H.
1941   *Philo: With an English Translation,* vol. 9: *Every Good Man Is Free,* et al. Loeb Classical Library. Cambridge, MA: Harvard University Press.
1971   *Philo in Ten Volumes (and Two Supplementary Volumes),* vol. 10: *The Embassy to Gaius,* et. al. Loeb Classical Library. Cambridge, MA: Harvard University Press/London: Heinemann.

Craigie, P. C.
1976   *The Book of Deuteronomy.* New International Commentary on the Old Testament. Grand Rapids: Eerdmans.

Cranfield, C. E. B.
1982   "Changes of Person and Number in Paul's Epistles." Pp. 280–89 in *Paul and Paulinism: Essays in Honour of C. K. Barrett.* Edited by M. D. Hooker and S. G. Wilson. London: SPCK.

Crossan, J. D., and J. L. Reed
2005   *In Search of Paul: How Jesus' Apostle Opposed Rome's Empire with God's Kingdom: A New Vision of Paul's Words and World.* London: SPCK.

Croy, N. C.
1998   *Endurance in Suffering: Hebrews 12:1–13 in Its Rhetorical, Religious,*

and Philosophical Context. Cambridge: Cambridge University Press.

Cullmann, O.
2000   *Immortality of the Soul or Resurrection of the Dead? The Witness of the New Testament*. Reprinted Eugene, OR: Wipf & Stock.

Cyprian, B.
2009   "The Mystery of the Rapture: The Deifying Experience of the 'Rapture' of the Apostle Paul 'to the Third Heaven,' That Is, 'to Paradise' (II Corinthians 12:2–4)." *Orthodox Tradition* 26:5–28.

Dalton, W. J.
1987   "Is the Old Covenant Abrogated (2 Cor 3.14)?" *Australian Biblical Review* 35:88–94.

Danker, F. W.
1988   "2 Corinthians." *Journal of Biblical Literature* 107:550–53.
1989   *II Corinthians*. Minneapolis: Augsburg.
1991   "Paul's Debt to the *De corona* of Demosthenes: A Study of Rhetorical Techniques in Second Corinthians." Pp. 262–80 in *Persuasive Artistry: Studies in New Testament Rhetoric in Honor of George A. Kennedy*. Edited by D. F. Watson. Journal for the Study of the New Testament: Supplement Series 50. Sheffield: JSOT Press.

DBI   *Dictionary of Biblical Imagery*. Edited by L. Ryken, J. Wilhoit, and T. Longman. Downers Grove, IL: InterVarsity, 1998.

Derrett, J.
1978   "2 Cor 6:14: A Midrash on Dt 22:10." *Biblica* 59:231–50.

Dewey, A.
1985   "A Matter of Honor: A Social-Historical Analysis of 2 Corinthians 10." *Harvard Theological Review* 78:209–17.

De Witt, N. W., and N. J. De Witt
1949   *Demosthenes*, vol. 7: *Funeral Speech, Erotic Essay, Exordia and Letters*. Loeb Classical Library. London: Heinemann/ Cambridge, MA: Harvard University Press.

Dickens, C.
1998   *Little Dorrit*. Wordsworth Classics. Ware, Hertfordshire, UK: Wordsworth Editions.
2003   *Barnaby Rudge*. Edited by Gordon W. Spence. Penguin Classics. New York: Penguin Random House.

DJBP   *Dictionary of Judaism in the Biblical Period: 450 B.C.E. to 600 C.E.* Edited by J. Neusner and W. S. Green. New York: Macmillan Library Reference, 1996.

DJG   *Dictionary of Jesus and the Gospels*. Edited by J. B. Green, S. McKnight, and I. H. Marshall. Downers Grove, IL: InterVarsity, 1992.

DNTB   *Dictionary of New Testament Background*. Edited by C. A. Evans and S. E. Porter. IVP Bible Dictionary Series. Downers Grove, IL: IVP Academic, 2000.

DPL   *Dictionary of Paul and His Letters*. Edited by G. F. Hawthorne, R. P. Martin, and D. G. Reid. Downers Grove, IL: InterVarsity, 1993.

Dubis, M.
2002   *Messianic Woes in First Peter: Suffering and Eschatology in 1 Peter 4:12–19*. Studies in Biblical Literature 33. New York: P. Lang.

Dudley-Smith, T.
1999   *John Stott: The Making of a Leader*. Leicester, UK: Inter-Varsity.

Duff, P. B.
1991   "Metaphor, Motif, and Meaning: The Rhetorical Strategy behind the Image 'Led in Triumph' in 2 Corinthians 2:14." *Catholic Biblical Quarterly* 53:79–92.
2004   "Glory in the Ministry of Death: Gentile Condemnation and Letters of Recommendation in 2 Cor 3:6–18." *Novum Testamentum* 46:313–37.

Dumbrell, W. J.
1986   "Paul's Use of Exodus 34 in 2 Corinthians 3." Pp. 179–94 in *God Who Is Rich in Mercy: Essays Presented to Dr. D. B. Knox*. Edited by P. T. O'Brien and D. Peterson. Homebush, AUS: Lancer Books.
2002   "The Newness of the New Covenant: The Logic of the Argument in 2 Corinthians 3." *Reformed Theological Review* 61:61–84.

Dunn, J. D. G.
1970   "2 Corinthians 3:17: The Lord Is the Spirit." *Journal of Theological Studies* 21:309–20.

Dupont, J.
1949   "Le chrétien: Miroir de la gloire divine d'après 2 Cor 3:18." *Revue biblique* 56:392–411.

EDNT   *Exegetical Dictionary of the New Testament*. Edited by H. R. Balz and G. Schneider. Grand Rapids: Eerdmans, 1990.

Edwards, J.

1825   *A Treatise concerning Religious Affections*. Edited by D. Young. Glasgow: Chalmers & Collins.

Egan, R. B.

1977   "Lexical Evidence on Two Pauline Passages." *Novum Testamentum* 19:34–62.

Elliot, J.

1978   *The Journals of Jim Elliot*. Edited by E. Elliot. Grand Rapids: Revell.

Elliott, J. K.

2003   "The Divine Names in the Corinthian Letters." Pp. 3–15 in *Paul and the Corinthians: Studies on a Community in Conflict; Essays in Honour of Margaret Thrall*. Edited by T. J. Burke and J. K. Elliott. Leiden: Brill.

Elliott, M.

2006   *Faithful Feelings: Rethinking Emotion in the New Testament*. Grand Rapids: Kregel.

Ellis, E. E.

1960   "II Corinthians V.1–10 in Pauline Eschatology." *New Testament Studies* 6/3:211–24.

1978   *Prophecy and Hermeneutic in Early Christianity: New Testament Essays*. American Paperback ed. Grand Rapids: Eerdmans.

1981   *Paul's Use of the Old Testament*. Grand Rapids: Baker.

Engels, D. W.

1990   *Roman Corinth: An Alternative Model for the Classical City*. Chicago: University of Chicago Press.

Fee, G. D.

1978   "Χάρις in II Corinthians 1:15: Apostolic Parousia and Paul-Corinth Chronology." *New Testament Studies* 24:533–38.

1987   *The First Epistle to the Corinthians*. Grand Rapids: Eerdmans.

1994   *God's Empowering Presence: The Holy Spirit in the Letters of Paul*. Peabody, MA: Hendrickson.

Ferguson, S. B.

1996   *The Holy Spirit*. Downers Grove, IL: InterVarsity.

Fitzgerald, J. T.

1988   *Cracks in an Earthen Vessel: An Examination of the Catalogues of Hardships in the Corinthian Correspondence*. SBL Dissertation Series 99. Atlanta: Scholars Press.

Fitzmyer, J. A.

1961   "Qumrân and the Interpolated Paragraph in 2 Cor 6:14–7:1." *Catholic Biblical Quarterly* 23:271–80.

1981   "Glory Reflected on the Face of Christ (2 Cor 3:7–4:6) and a Palestinian Jewish Motif." *Theological Studies* 42:630–44.

Fletcher-Louis, C.

2002   *All the Glory of Adam: Liturgical Anthropology in the Dead Sea Scrolls*. Studies on the Texts of the Desert of Judah 42. Leiden: Brill.

Forbes, C.

1986   "Comparison, Self-Praise and Irony: Paul's Boasting and the Conventions of Hellenistic Rhetoric." *New Testament Studies* 32:1–30.

Fredrickson, D. E.

2000   "Paul's Sentence of Death (2 Corinthians 1:9)." *Word & World* 4:99–107.

Frey, J.

2008   "Paul's Jewish Identity." Pp. 285–321 in *Jewish Identity in the Greco-Roman World*. Edited by J. Frey, D. R. Schwartz, and S. Gripentrog. Leiden: Brill.

Friesen, S. J.

2010   "The Wrong Erastus: Ideology, Archaeology, and Exegesis." Pp. 231–56 in *Corinth in Context: Comparative Studies on Religion and Society*. Edited by S. J. Friesen, D. N. Schowalter, and J. C. Walters. Leiden: Brill.

Funk, R. W.

1967   "The Apostolic *Parousia*: Form and Significance." Pp. 249–69 in *Christian History and Interpretation: Studies Presented to John Knox*. Edited by W. R. Farmer, C. F. D. Moule, and R. R. Niebuhr. Cambridge: Cambridge University Press.

Furnish, V. P.

1984   *II Corinthians: A New Translation with Introduction and Commentary*. Anchor Bible. Garden City, NY: Doubleday.

1988   "Corinth in Paul's Time: What Can Archaeology Tell Us?" *Biblical Archaeology Review* 14/3:14–27.

Garland, D. E.

1989   "Paul's Apostolic Authority: The Power of Christ Sustaining Weakness (2 Corinthians 10–13)." *Review & Expositor* 86:371–89.

1999   *2 Corinthians*. New American Commentary 29. Nashville: Broadman & Holman.

2003   *1 Corinthians*. Baker Exegetical Commentary on the New Testament. Grand Rapids: Baker Academic.

Garrett, D. A.
2010   "Veiled Hearts: The Translation and Interpretation of 2 Corinthians 3." *Journal of the Evangelical Theological Society* 53:729–72.

GELNT   *Greek-English Lexicon of the New Testament: Based on Semantic Domains.* Edited by J. P. Louw and Eugene Nida. 2nd ed. New York: United Bible Societies, 1989.

Georgi, D.
1986   *The Opponents of Paul in Second Corinthians: A Study of Religious Propaganda in Late Antiquity.* Philadelphia: Fortress.
1992   *Remembering the Poor: The History of Paul's Collection for Jerusalem.* Nashville: Abingdon.

Gerson, M. J.
2008   *Heroic Conservatism: Why Republicans Need to Embrace America's Ideals (and Why They Deserve to Fail If They Don't).* 2007. Reprinted New York: HarperOne.

Gignilliat, M. S.
2007   *Paul and Isaiah's Servants: Paul's Theological Reading of Isaiah 40–66 in 2 Corinthians 5:14–6:10.* London: T&T Clark.

Gill, D. W. J.
1994   "Achaia." Pp. 433–53 in *The Book of Acts in Its Graeco-Roman Setting.* Edited by D. W. J. Gill and C. H. Gempf. Grand Rapids: Eerdmans/Carlisle, UK: Paternoster.

Gillman, J.
1988   "A Thematic Comparison: 1 Cor 15:50–57 and 2 Cor 5:1–5." *Journal of Biblical Literature* 107:439–54.

Goldsworthy, G.
2000   "Biblical Theology and the Shape of Paul's Mission." Pp. 7–18 in *The Gospel to the Nations: Perspectives on Paul's Mission; in Honour of Peter T. O'Brien.* Edited by P. Bolt and M. Thompson. Downers Grove, IL: InterVarsity.

Good, D. J.
1999   *Jesus the Meek King.* Harrisburg, PA: Trinity.

Gooder, P.
2006   *Only the Third Heaven? 2 Corinthians 12.1–10 and Heavenly Ascent.* Library

of New Testament Studies 313. London: T&T Clark.

Goulder, M. D.
1994a   "2 Cor 6:14–7:1 as an Integral Part of 2 Corinthians." *Novum Testamentum* 36:47–57.
1994b   "Vision and Knowledge." *Journal for the Study of the New Testament* 56:53–71.

Grabbe, L. L.
2000   *Judaic Religion in the Second Temple Period: Belief and Practice from the Exile to Yavneh.* London: Routledge.

Greenwood, L. H. G.
1953   *Cicero: The Verrine Orations*, vol. 2. Rev. ed. Loeb Classical Library 293. Cambridge, MA: Harvard University Press/London: Heinemann.

Gregory, T. E.
1993   *The Corinthia in the Roman Period: Including the Papers Given at a Symposium Held at the Ohio State University on 7–9 March, 1991.* Ann Arbor, MI: Journal of Roman Archaeology.

Grindheim, S.
2001   "The Law Kills but the Gospel Gives Life: The Letter-Spirit Dualism in 2 Corinthians 3.5–18." *Journal for the Study of the New Testament* 84:97–115.

Guthrie, G. H.
1994   *The Structure of Hebrews: A Text-Linguistic Analysis.* Supplements to Novum Testamentum 73. Leiden: Brill.
1998   *Hebrews.* NIV Application Commentary. Grand Rapids: Zondervan.
2004   "Hebrews in Its First-Century Contexts: Recent Research." Pp. 414–43 in *The Face of New Testament Studies: A Survey of Recent Research.* Edited by S. McKnight and G. R. Osborne. Grand Rapids: Baker Academic.
2015   "Paul's Triumphal Procession Imagery (2 Cor 2.14–16a): Neglected Points of Background." *New Testament Studies* 61:79–91.

Hafemann, S. J.
1986   *Suffering and the Spirit: An Exegetical Study of II Cor. 2:14–3:3 within the Context of the Corinthian Correspondence.* Wissenschaftliche Untersuchungen zum Neuen Testament 2/19. Tübingen: Mohr.
1990a   "'Self-Commendation' and Apostolic Legitimacy in 2 Corinthians: A Pauline Dialectic?" *New Testament Studies* 36:66–88.

1990b   *Suffering and Ministry in the Spirit: Paul's Defense of His Ministry in II Corinthians 2:14–3:3.* Grand Rapids: Eerdmans.

1992   "The Glory and Veil of Moses in 2 Cor 3:7–14: An Example of Paul's Contextual Exegesis of the OT; A Proposal." *Horizons in Biblical Theology* 14:31–49.

1994   "Adam Christology as the Exegetical and Theological Substructure of 2 Corinthians 4:7–5:21." *Journal of Biblical Literature* 113:346–49.

1995   *Paul, Moses, and the History of Israel: The Letter/Spirit Contrast and the Argument from Scripture in 2 Corinthians 3.* Wissenschaftliche Untersuchungen zum Neuen Testament 81. Tübingen: Mohr (Siebeck).

1996   "Paul's Argument from the Old Testament and Christology in 2 Cor 1–9: The Salvation-History/Restoration Structure of Paul's Apologetic." Pp. 277–303 in *The Corinthian Correspondence.* Edited by R. Bieringer. Bibliotheca ephemeridum theologicarum lovaniensium 125. Louvain: Leuven University Press/Peeters.

2000   *2 Corinthians.* NIV Application Commentary. Grand Rapids: Zondervan.

Hall, D. R.
2003   *The Unity of the Corinthian Correspondence.* London: T&T Clark.

Hamilton, J. M.
2010   *God's Glory in Salvation through Judgment: A Biblical Theology.* Wheaton, IL: Crossway.

Hanson, A. T.
1965   *Jesus Christ in the Old Testament.* London: SPCK.

1980   "The Midrash in 2 Corinthians 3: A Reconsideration." *Journal for the Study of the New Testament* 9:2–28.

1987   *The Paradox of the Cross in the Thought of St Paul.* Journal for the Study of the New Testament: Supplement Series 17. Sheffield: JSOT Press.

Hanson, R. P. C.
1961   *The Second Epistle to the Corinthians: Introduction and Commentary.* Torch Bible Commentaries. London: SCM.

Harding, M.
1993   "On the Historicity of Acts: Comparing Acts 9.23–5 with 2 Corinthians 11.32–3." *New Testament Studies* 39:518–38.

Harris, M. J.
2005   *The Second Epistle to the Corinthians: A Commentary on the Greek Text.* New International Greek Testament Commentary. Grand Rapids: Eerdmans.

2008   "2 Corinthians." Vol. 11 / pp. 415–545 in *The Expositor's Bible Commentary.* Edited by T. Longman and D. E. Garland. Rev. ed. Grand Rapids: Zondervan.

Harrison, J. R.
2009   "Paul and the Roman Ideal of Glory in the Epistle to the Romans." Pp. 329–69 in *The Letter to the Romans.* Edited by U. Schnelle. Louvain: Peeters.

Harvey, A. E.
1996   *Renewal through Suffering: A Study of 2 Corinthians.* Studies of the New Testament and Its World. Edinburgh: T&T Clark.

Hasitschka, M.
1999   "'Diener eines neuen Bundes': Skizze zum Selbstverständnis des Paulus in 2 Kor 3,4–4,6." *Zeitschrift für katholische Theologie* 121:291–99.

Hausrath, A.
1870   *Der Vier-Capitel-Brief des Paulus an die Korinther.* Heidelberg: Bassermann.

Hawthorne, N.
2008   *The Scarlet Letter.* Rockville, MD: Arc Manor.

Hays, R. B.
1989   *Echoes of Scripture in the Letters of Paul.* New Haven: Yale University Press.

HBD   *Holman Bible Dictionary.* Edited by T. C. Butler. Nashville: Holman Bible Publishers, 1991.

Heckel, U.
1993   "Der Dorn im Fleisch die Krankheit des Paulus in 2 Kor 12,7 und Gal 4,13f." *Zeitschrift für die neutestamentliche Wissenschaft* 84:65–92.

Hemer, C. J.
1972   "A Note on 2 Corinthians 1:9." *Tyndale Bulletin* 23:103–7.

Hengel, M., and R. Deines
1991   *The Pre-Christian Paul.* London: SCM/Philadelphia: Trinity.

Hengel, M., and A. M. Schwemer
1997   *Paul between Damascus and Antioch: The Unknown Years.* London: SCM.

Hennig, J.
1946   "The Measure of Man: A Study of 2 Cor. 10:12." *Catholic Biblical Quarterly* 8:332–43.

Héring, J.
1958   *La seconde épître de saint Paul aux Corinthiens*. Neuchatel: Delachaux & Niestlé.

Hoad, J.
1957   "Some New Testament References to Isaiah 53." *Expository Times* 68:254–55.

Hock, R. F.
2007   *The Social Context of Paul's Ministry: Tentmaking and Apostleship*. Minneapolis: Fortress.

Hodge, C.
1994   *Commentary on the Second Epistle to the Corinthians*. Grand Rapids: Eerdmans.

Hodgson, R.
1983   "Paul the Apostle and First Century Tribulation Lists." *Zeitschrift für die neutestamentliche Wissenschaft* 74:59–80.

Holland, G. S.
1993   "Speaking Like a Fool: Irony in 2 Corinthians 10–13." Pp. 250–64 in *Rhetoric and the New Testament: Essays from the 1992 Heidelberg Conference*. Edited by S. E. Porter and T. H. Olbricht. Journal for the Study of the New Testament: Supplement Series 90. Sheffield: Sheffield Academic Press.

Hood, J. B.
2011   "The Temple and the Thorn: 2 Corinthians 12 and Paul's Heavenly Ecclesiology." *Bulletin for Biblical Research* 21:357–70.

Hooker, M. D.
2003   *Paul: A Short Introduction*. Oxford: Oneworld.
2008   "On Becoming the Righteousness of God: Another Look At 2 Cor 5:21." *Novum Testamentum* 50:358–75.

Hooker, R.
1888   "A Learned Discourse of Justification, Works, and How the Foundation of Faith Is Overthrown." Vol. 3 / pp. 483–547 in *The Works of That Learned and Judicious Divine Mr. Richard Hooker*. Edited by J. Keble. Revised by R. W. Church and F. Paget. 7th ed. Oxford: Clarendon.

Horrell, D. G.
2006   *An Introduction to the Study of Paul*. 2nd ed. London: T&T Clark.

Horsley, R. A.
1997   *Paul and Empire: Religion and Power in Roman Imperial Society*. Harrisburg, PA: Trinity.

Horton, M. S.
2008   *People and Place: A Covenant Ecclesiology*. Louisville: Westminster John Knox.

Hughes, P. E.
1962   *Paul's Second Epistle to the Corinthians: The English Text with Introduction, Exposition and Notes*. New International Commentary on the New Testament. Grand Rapids: Eerdmans.

Hughes, R. K.
2006   *2 Corinthians: Power in Weakness*. Preaching the Word. Wheaton, IL: Crossway.

Hunter, A. M.
1980   *The Fifth Evangelist*. London: SCM.

Hunter, J. D.
2010   *To Change the World: The Irony, Tragedy, and Possibility of Christianity in the Late Modern World*. New York: Oxford University Press.

Hurd, J. C.
1965   *The Origin of I Corinthians*. London: SPCK.

Hurtado, L. W.
1998   *One God, One Lord: Early Christian Devotion and Ancient Jewish Monotheism*. 2nd ed. Edinburgh: T&T Clark.
2003   *Lord Jesus Christ: Devotion to Jesus in Earliest Christianity*. Grand Rapids: Eerdmans.

Hyldahl, N.
1986   *Die paulinische Chronologie*. Leiden: Brill.

Instone-Brewer, D.
2003   "The Eighteen Benedictions and the Minim before 70 CE." *Journal of Theological Studies* 54:25–44.
2004   *Traditions of the Rabbis from the Era of the New Testament*. Grand Rapids: Eerdmans.

Jeremias, J.
1971   *New Testament Theology*, vol. 1: *The Proclamation of Jesus*. London: SCM.

Jewett, R.
1978   *The Redaction of 1 Corinthians and the Trajectory of the Pauline School*. Journal of the American Academy of Religion: Supplement Series 44.4. N.p.: American Academy of Religion.

1979a   A Chronology of Paul's Life. Philadelphia: Fortress.
1979b   Dating Paul's Life. London: SCM.
2003   "Paul, Shame, and Honor." Pp. 551–74 in Paul in the Greco-Roman World: A Handbook. Edited by J. P. Sampley. Harrisburg, PA: Trinity.

Jewett, R., and R. D. Kotansky
2007   Romans: A Commentary. Hermeneia. Minneapolis: Fortress.

Johnson, L. A.
2006   "Paul's Epistolary Presence in Corinth: A New Look at Robert W. Funk's Apostolic Parousia." Catholic Biblical Quarterly 68:481–501.

Johnson, S.
2003   Selected Essays. Edited with an introduction and notes by D. Womersley. Penguin Classics. London: Penguin Books.

Jones, H. L., and J. R. S. Sterrett
1954   Strabo: Geography, vol. 5: Books X–XII. Loeb Classical Library. Cambridge, MA: Harvard University Press/London: Heinemann.

Judge, E. A.
1966   "The Conflict of Educational Aims in New Testament Thought." Journal of Christian Education 9:32–45.
1968   "Paul's Boasting in Relation to Contemporary Professional Practice." Australian Biblical Review 16:37–50.

Junger, S.
2009   The Perfect Storm: A True Story of Men against the Sea. New York: Norton.

Käsemann, E.
1942   "Die Legitimität des Apostels: Eine Untersuchung zu II Korinther 10–13." Zeitschrift für die neutestamentliche Wissenschaft 41/1:33–71.

Kayama, H.
1990   "The Doxa of Moses and Jesus (2 Cor. 3:7–18 and Luke 9:28–32)." Bulletin of the Christian Research Institute, Meiji Gakuin University 23:23–48.

Kee, D.
1980   "Who Were the 'Super-Apostles' of 2 Corinthians 10–13?" Restoration Quarterly 23:65–76.

Keener, C. S.
2003   The Gospel of John: A Commentary. 2 vols. Peabody, MA: Hendrickson.
2005   1–2 Corinthians. New Cambridge Bible Commentary. Cambridge: Cambridge University Press.

2012   Acts: An Exegetical Commentary, vol. 1: Introduction and 1:1–2:47. Grand Rapids: Baker Academic.

Keller, T.
2009   Counterfeit Gods: The Empty Promises of Money, Sex, and Power, and the Only Hope That Matters. New York: Dutton.

Kerr, A. J.
1988   "Arrabōn." Journal of Theological Studies, n.s., 39:92–97.

Keyes, C. W.
1935   "The Greek Letter of Introduction." American Journal of Philology 56:28–44.

Kierkegaard, S.
1956   Kierkegaard's Attack upon "Christendom," 1854–1855. Boston: Beacon.

Kim, S.
1985   The Origin of Paul's Gospel. 2nd ed. Tübingen: Mohr.
1997   "2 Cor 5:11–21 and the Origin of Paul's Concept of 'Reconciliation.'" Novum Testamentum 39:360–84.
2002   Paul and the New Perspective: Second Thoughts on the Origin of Paul's Gospel. Wissenschaftliche Untersuchungen zum Neuen Testament 140. Tübingen: Mohr Siebeck.

Klauck, H.-J., and D. P. Bailey
2006   Ancient Letters and the New Testament: A Guide to Context and Exegesis. Waco: Baylor University Press.

Klausner, J., and W. F. Stinespring
1946   From Jesus to Paul. London: Allen & Unwin.

Knowles, M. P.
2007   The Folly of Preaching: Models and Methods. Grand Rapids: Eerdmans.
2008   We Preach Not Ourselves: Paul on Proclamation. Grand Rapids: Brazos.

Koenig, J.
1979   Jews and Christians in Dialogue: New Testament Foundations. Philadelphia: Westminster.

Kruse, C. G.
1987   The Second Epistle of Paul to the Corinthians: An Introduction and Commentary. Tyndale New Testament Commentaries. Leicester, UK: InterVarsity/Grand Rapids: Eerdmans.

Kurek-Chomycz, D. A.
2007   "Sincerity and Chastity for Christ: A Textual Problem in 2 Cor 11:3 Reconsidered." Novum Testamentum 49:54–84.

Lambrecht, J.
1983 "Transformation in 2 Cor 3:18." *Biblica* 64:243–54.
1994a "Structure and Line of Thought in 2 Cor 2:14–4:6." Pp. 257–94 in *Studies on 2 Corinthians*. Edited by R. Bieringer and J. Lambrecht. Louvain: Leuven University Press.
1994b "Transformation in 2 Corinthians 3,18." Pp. 295–307 in *Studies on 2 Corinthians*. Edited by R. Bieringer and J. Lambrecht. Louvain: Leuven University Press.
1996 "Dangerous Boasting: Paul's Self-Commendation in 2 Corinthians 10–13." Pp. 325–46 in *The Corinthian Correspondence*. Edited by R. Bieringer. Louvain: Leuven University Press.
1997 "Strength in Weakness." *New Testament Studies* 43:285–90.
1999 *Second Corinthians*. Sacra pagina. Collegeville, MN: Liturgical Press.

Landon, M. E.
2003 "Beyond Peirene: Toward a Broader View of Corinthian Water Supply." Pp. 43–62 in *Corinth, the Centenary, 1896–1996*. Edited by C. K. Williams and N. Bookidis. Princeton: American School of Classical Studies at Athens.

Lane, W.
1982 "Covenant: The Key to Paul's Conflict with Corinth." *Tyndale Bulletin* 33:3–29.

Lewis, C. S.
2001 *Mere Christianity: A Revised and Amplified Edition, with a New Introduction, of the Three Books Broadcast Talks, Christian Behaviour and Beyond Personality*. New York: Harper One.
2009 *The Weight of Glory*. New York: HarperCollins.

Licona, M.
2010 *The Resurrection of Jesus: A New Historiographical Approach*. Downers Grove, IL: InterVarsity.

Lincoln, A. T.
1979 "Paul the Visionary: The Setting and Significance of the Rapture to Paradise in II Corinthians 12:1–10." *New Testament Studies* 25:204–20.
1981 *Paradise Now and Not Yet: Studies in the Role of the Heavenly Dimension in Paul's Thought with Special Reference to His Eschatology*. Society for New Testament Studies Monograph Series

43. Cambridge: Cambridge University Press.

Lohmann, H.
2013 "Der Diolkos von Korinth—Eine antike Schiffsschleppe?" Pp. 207–30 in *The Corinthia and the Northeast Peloponnese: Topography and History from Prehistoric Times until the End of Antiquity*. Edited by W. Niemeier. Munich: Hirmer.

Long, F. J.
2004 *Ancient Rhetoric and Paul's Apology: The Compositional Unity of 2 Corinthians*. Society for New Testament Studies 131. Cambridge: Cambridge University Press.

Loubser, J. A.
1991 "Winning the Struggle (or: How to Treat Heretics) (2 Corinthians 12:1–10)." *Journal of Theology for Southern Africa* 75:75–83.

Lyons, G.
1985 *Pauline Autobiography: Toward a New Understanding*. Atlanta: Scholars Press.

MacDonald, G.
1867 "The Imagination: Its Functions and Its Culture." *British Quarterly Review* 46/91:45–70.

Malherbe, A. J.
1983 "Antisthenes and Odysseus, and Paul at War." *Harvard Theological Review* 76:143–73.

Malina, B. J.
1983 *The New Testament World: Insights from Cultural Anthropology*. London: SCM.

Marshall, I. H.
1978 "The Meaning of 'Reconciliation.'" Pp. 117–32 in *Unity and Diversity in New Testament Theology: Essays in Honor of George E. Ladd*. Edited by R. A. Guelich. Grand Rapids: Eerdmans.

Marshall, P.
1983 "A Metaphor of Social Shame: *Thriambeuein* in 2 Cor 2:14." *Novum Testamentum* 25:302–17.
1987 *Enmity in Corinth: Social Conventions in Paul's Relations with the Corinthians*. Wissenschaftliche Untersuchungen zum Neuen Testament 23. Tübingen: Mohr.

Martin, R. P.
1986 *2 Corinthians*. Word Biblical Commentary. Waco: Word.

Martyn, J. L.
1997   "Epistemology at the Turn of the
        Ages." Pp. 89–110 in *Theological Issues
        in the Letters of Paul*. Studies of the
        New Testament and Its World. Edin-
        burgh: T&T Clark.

Matera, F. J.
2003   *II Corinthians: A Commentary*. New
        Testament Library. Louisville: Westmin-
        ster John Knox.

Mathewes-Green, F.
2004   "Both Door and Path." Pp. 93–98
        in *The Best Christian Writing 2004*.
        Edited by J. Wilson. San Francisco:
        Jossey-Bass.

McCant, J. W.
1988   "Paul's Thorn of Rejected Apostle-
        ship." *New Testament Studies*
        34:550–72.

Meeks, W. A.
1983   *The First Urban Christians: The Social
        World of the Apostle Paul*. New Haven:
        Yale University Press.

Merrill, E. H.
1994   *Deuteronomy*. New American Com-
        mentary. Nashville: Broadman &
        Holman.

Metzger, B. M.
1975   *A Textual Commentary on the Greek
        New Testament*. New York: United
        Bible Societies.
1994   *A Textual Commentary on the Greek
        New Testament*. 2nd ed. Stuttgart:
        United Bible Societies.

Millis, B. W.
2010   "The Social and Ethnic Origins of the
        Colonists in Early Roman Corinth." Pp.
        13–35 in *Corinth in Context: Compara-
        tive Studies on Religion and Society*.
        Edited by S. J. Friesen, D. N. Schowalter,
        and J. C. Walters. Leiden: Brill.

Mitchell, M. M.
1991   *Paul and the Rhetoric of Reconcilia-
        tion: An Exegetical Investigation of the
        Language and Composition of 1 Corin-
        thians*. Hermeneutische Untersuchun-
        gen zur Theologie 28. Tübingen: Mohr.
1992   "New Testament Envoys in the Context
        of Greco-Roman Diplomatic and Epis-
        tolary Conventions: The Example of
        Timothy and Titus." *Journal of Bibli-
        cal Literature* 111:641–62.
2000   *The Heavenly Trumpet: John Chrysos-
        tom and the Art of Pauline Interpreta-
        tion*. Tübingen: Mohr Siebeck.

Moberly, R. W. L.
1983   *At the Mountain of God: Story and
        Theology in Exodus 32–34*. Sheffield:
        JSOT Press.

Molière, J. B. P.
1879   *The Dramatic Works of Molière*. Ren-
        dered into Engl. by H. van Laun with a
        prefatory memoir. Vol. 2. Philadelphia:
        Gebbie & Barrie.

Moo, D. J.
1996   *The Epistle to the Romans*. New In-
        ternational Commentary on the New
        Testament. Grand Rapids: Eerdmans.

Morgan, C. W.
2010   "Toward a Theology of the Glory of
        God." Pp. 153–87 in *The Glory of God*.
        Edited by C. W. Morgan and R. A.
        Peterson. Wheaton, IL: Crossway.

Morray-Jones, C. R. A.
1993   "Paradise Revisited (2 Cor 12:1–12):
        The Jewish Mystical Background of
        Paul's Apostolate." *Harvard Theo-
        logical Review* 86:265–92.

Motyer, J. A.
1993   *The Prophecy of Isaiah*. Leicester, UK:
        Inter-Varsity.

Moule, C. F. D.
1959   *An Idiom Book of New Testament
        Greek*. 2nd ed. Cambridge: Cambridge
        University Press.

Mullins, T. Y.
1957   "Paul's Thorn in the Flesh." *Journal of
        Biblical Literature* 76:299–303.

Munck, J.
1959   *Paul and the Salvation of Mankind*.
        London: SCM.

Murphy-O'Connor, J.
1983   *St. Paul's Corinth: Texts and Archaeol-
        ogy*. Good News Studies 6. Wilming-
        ton, DE: Michael Glazier.
1985   "Paul and Macedonia: The Connection
        between 2 Corinthians 2:13 and 2:14."
        *Journal for the Study of the New Testa-
        ment* 25:99–103.
1991a   "The Date of 2 Corinthians 10–13."
        Australian Biblical Review 39:31–43.
1991b   *The Theology of the Second Letter to
        the Corinthians*. Cambridge: Cam-
        bridge University Press.
2010   *Keys to Second Corinthians: Revisiting
        the Major Issues*. Oxford: Oxford Uni-
        versity Press.

Nayak, I.
2002   "The Meaning of *Katoptrizomenoi* in
        2 Cor 3,18." *Euntes docete* 55:33–44.

NBD   *New Bible Dictionary.* Edited by J. D. Douglas et al. 3rd ed. Leicester, UK: Inter-Varsity/Downers Grove, IL: InterVarsity, 1996.

NDBT   *New Dictionary of Biblical Theology.* Edited by T. D. Alexander and B. S. Rosner. Leicester, UK: Inter-Varsity/Downers Grove, IL: InterVarsity, 2000.

NewDocs   *New Documents Illustrating Early Christianity: A Review of the Greek Inscriptions and Papyri Published in 1976.* Edited by G. H. R. Horsley. North Ryde, NSW: Ancient History Documentary Research Centre, Macquarie University, 1981–.

Neyrey, J. H.
1997   "Paul's Use of Ethos, Pathos, and Logos in 2 Corinthians 10–13." *Catholic Biblical Quarterly* 59:375–76.

Nickle, K. F.
1966   *The Collection: A Study in Paul's Strategy.* Studies in Biblical Theology 48. London: SCM.

NIDNTT   *The New International Dictionary of New Testament Theology.* Edited by C. Brown and D. Townsley. Rev. ed. Exeter, Devon, UK: Paternoster, 1986.

O'Brien, P. T.
1977   *Introductory Thanksgivings in the Letters of Paul.* Supplements to Novum Testamentum 49. Leiden: Brill.

O'Collins, G. G.
1971   "Power Made Perfect in Weakness: 2 Cor 12:9–10." *Catholic Biblical Quarterly* 33:528–37.

Oldfather, W. A.
1925   *Epictetus,* vol. 1: *The Discourses as Reported by Arrian, the Manual, and Fragments.* Loeb Classical Library. Cambridge, MA: Harvard University Press/London: Heinemann.

Olley, J. W.
1998   "A Precursor of the NRSV? 'Sons and Daughters' in 2 Cor 6.18." *New Testament Studies* 44:204–12.

Ollrog, W.-H.
1979   *Paulus und seine Mitarbeiter: Untersuchungen zu Theorie und Praxis der paulinischen Mission.* Neukirchen-Vluyn: Neukirchener Verlag.

Olson, S. N.
1985   "Pauline Expressions of Confidence in His Addressees." *Catholic Biblical Quarterly* 47:282–95.

Orlov, A. A.
2007   "Vested with Adam's Glory: Moses as the Luminous Counterpart of Adam in the Dead Sea Scrolls and the Macarian Homilies." Pp. 327–44 in *From Apocalypticism to Merkabah Mysticism: Studies in the Slavonic Pseudepigrapha.* Journal for the Study of Judaism: Supplement Series 114. Leiden: Brill.

Oster, R. E.
1992   "Use, Misuse and Neglect of Archaeological Evidence in Some Modern Works on 1 Corinthians (1 Cor 7,1–5; 8,10; 11,2–16; 12,14–26)." *Zeitschrift für die neutestamentliche Wissenschaft* 83:52–73.

Oswalt, J.
1998   *The Book of Isaiah.* New International Commentary on the Old Testament. Grand Rapids: Eerdmans.

OTP   *The Old Testament Pseudepigrapha.* Edited by J. H. Charlesworth. 2 vols. Garden City, NY: Doubleday, 1983–85.

Packer, J. I.
1961   *Evangelism and the Sovereignty of God.* Downers Grove, IL: InterVarsity.
1973   *Knowing God.* Downers Grove, IL: InterVarsity.

Park, D. M.
1980   "Paul's Σκόλοψ τῇ Σαρκί: Thorn or Stake? (2 Cor. XII 7)." *Novum Testamentum* 22:179–83.

Pate, C. M.
1991   *Adam Christology as the Exegetical and Theological Substructure of 2 Corinthians 4:7–5:21.* Lanham, MD: University Press of America.
1995   *The End of the Age Has Come: The Theology of Paul.* Grand Rapids: Zondervan.

Pennington, J. T.
2007   *Heaven and Earth in the Gospel of Matthew.* Supplements to Novum Testamentum 126. Leiden: Brill.

Perrin, B.
1920   *Plutarch: The Parallel Lives,* vol. 9: *Demetrius and Antony; Pyrrhus and Gaius Marius.* Loeb Classical Library. Cambridge, MA: Harvard University Press/London: Heinemann.
1921   *Plutarch: The Parallel Lives,* vol. 10: *Agis and Cleomenes; Tiberius and Gaius Gracchus; Philopoemen and Flamininus.* Loeb Classical Library.

Cambridge, MA: Harvard University Press/London: Heinemann.

Peterman, G. W.
1997　*Paul's Gift from Philippi: Conventions of Gift-Exchange and Christian Giving.* Cambridge: Cambridge University Press.

Peterson, B. K.
1998a　"Conquest, Control, and the Cross: Paul's Self-Portrayal in 2 Corinthians 10–13." *Interpretation* 52:258–70.
1998b　*Eloquence and the Proclamation of the Gospel in Corinth.* Society of Biblical Literature Dissertation Series 163. Atlanta: Scholars Press.

Pettegrew, D. K.
2011　"The Diolkos of Corinth." *American Journal of Archaeology* 115:549–74.

PG　　Patrologia graeca. Edited by J.-P. Migne. 161 vols. Paris, 1857–66.

Philpot, J. M.
2013　"Exodus 34:29–35 and Moses' Shining Face." *Bulletin for Biblical Research* 23:1–11.

Pickett, R.
1997　*The Cross in Corinth: The Social Significance of the Death of Jesus.* Journal for the Study of the New Testament: Supplement Series 143. Sheffield: Sheffield Academic Press.

Plummer, A.
1915　*A Critical and Exegetical Commentary on the Second Epistle of St. Paul to the Corinthians.* International Critical Commentary. Edinburgh: T&T Clark.

Pogoloff, S. M.
1992　*Logos and Sophia: The Rhetorical Situation of 1 Corinthians.* Society of Biblical Literature Dissertation Series 134. Atlanta: Scholars Press.

Polaski, S. H.
2008　"2 Corinthians 12:1–10: Paul's Trauma." *Review & Expositor* 105:279–84.

Pollock, J. C.
1972　*George Whitefield and the Great Awakening.* London: Hodder & Stoughton.

Price, R. M.
1980　"Punished in Paradise (an Exegetical Theory on 2 Corinthians 12:1–10)." *Journal for the Study of the New Testament* 7:33–40.

Randrianarimalala, R.
1996　"'The Lord Is the Spirit,' 2 Cor 3:17a." *Hekima Review* 15:29–36.

Rapske, B.
1994　*The Book of Acts and Paul in Roman Custody.* Grand Rapids: Eerdmans/Carlisle, UK: Paternoster.

Renan, E.
1869　*St. Paul.* Translated by I. Lockwood. New York: Carleton.

Renwick, D. A.
1991　*Paul, the Temple, and the Presence of God.* Brown Judaic Studies 224. Atlanta: Scholars Press.

Richards, E. R.
2004　*Paul and First-Century Letter Writing: Secretaries, Composition, and Collection.* Downers Grove, IL: InterVarsity.

Riesner, R.
1998　*Paul's Early Period: Chronology, Mission Strategy, Theology.* Grand Rapids: Eerdmans.

Robertson, A. T.
1934　*A Grammar of the Greek New Testament in the Light of Historical Research.* Nashville: Broadman.

Roetzel, C. J.
2007　*2 Corinthians.* Abingdon New Testament Commentaries. Nashville: Abingdon.

Rosner, B. S.
2011　"The Glory of God in Paul's Missionary Theology and Practice." Pp. 158–68 in *Paul as Missionary: Identity, Activity, Theology, and Practice.* Edited by T. J. Burke and B. S. Rosner. London: T&T Clark.

Rowland, C.
1982　*The Open Heaven: A Study of Apocalyptic in Judaism and Early Christianity.* London: SPCK.

Runge, S. E.
2010　*Discourse Grammar of the Greek New Testament: A Practical Introduction for Teaching and Exegesis.* Peabody, MA: Hendrickson/Edinburgh: Alban.

Russell, D. A.
2002　*Quintilian: The Orator's Education,* vol. 2: *Books 3–5.* Loeb Classical Library. Cambridge, MA: Harvard University Press.

Saake, H.
1973　"Paulus als Ekstatiker: Pneumatologische Beobachtungen zu 2 Kor 12:1–10." *Novum Testamentum* 15:153–60.

Sampley, J. P.
1988   "Paul, His Opponents in 2 Corinthians 10–13, and the Rhetorical Handbooks." Pp. 162–77 in *Social World of Formative Christianity and Judaism: Essays in Tribute to Howard Clark Kee*. Edited by J. Neusner. Philadelphia: Fortress.

Sanders, E. P.
1977   *Paul and Palestinian Judaism: A Comparison of Patterns of Religion*. London: SCM.

Sandnes, K. O.
1991   *Paul—One of the Prophets? A Contribution to the Apostle's Self-Understanding*. Wissenschaftliche Untersuchungen zum Neuen Testament 2/43. Tübingen: Mohr (Siebeck).

Savage, T. B.
1996   *Power through Weakness: Paul's Understanding of the Christian Ministry in 2 Corinthians*. Society for New Testament Studies Monograph Series 86. Cambridge: Cambridge University Press.

Sayers, D. L., and R. Jellema
1969   *Christian Letters to a Post-Christian World: A Selection of Essays*. Grand Rapids: Eerdmans.

Schmeller, T.
2013   "No Bridge over Troubled Water? The Gap between 2 Corinthians 1–9 and 10–13." *Journal for the Study of the New Testament* 36:73–84.

Schulz, S.
1958   "Die Decke des Moses: Untersuchungen zu einer vorpaulinischen Überlieferung in 2 Cor 3:7–18." *Zeitschrift für die neutestamentliche Wissenschaft* 49:1–30.

Scott, J. M.
1992   *Adoption as Sons of God: An Exegetical Investigation into the Background of Huiothesia in the Pauline Corpus*. Wissenschaftliche Untersuchungen zum Neuen Testament 2/48. Tübingen: Mohr (Siebeck).
1996   "The Triumph of God in 2 Cor 2.14: Additional Evidence of Merkabah Mysticism in Paul." *New Testament Studies* 42:260–81.
1998   *2 Corinthians*. New International Biblical Commentary. Peabody, MA: Hendrickson/Carlisle, UK: Paternoster.

Segalla, G.
1988   "Struttura letteraria e unità della 2 Corinzi." *Teologia* 13:189–218.

Seitz, C. R.
1994   "The Book of Isaiah 40–66." Vol. 6 / pp. 307–552 in *The New Interpreter's Bible*. Edited by L. E. Keck. Nashville: Abingdon.

Semler, J. S.
1776   *D. Io. Sal. Semleri paraphrasis ii. epistolae ad Corinthios: Accessit latina vetus translatio et lectionum varietas*. Halle: Hemmerde.

Sinnott, A. M.
2005   *The Personification of Wisdom*. Society for Old Testament Study Monographs. Aldershot: Ashgate.

Sloan, R. B.
1995   "2 Corinthians 2:14–4:6 and 'New Covenant Hermeneutics': A Response to Richard Hays." *Bulletin for Biblical Research* 5:129–54.

Smith, G. V.
2009   *Isaiah 40–66*. New American Commentary. Nashville: Broadman & Holman.

Solzhenitsyn, A.
1974   *The Gulag Archipelago, 1918–1956: An Experiment in Literary Investigation*. Edited by T. P. Whitney and H. T. Willetts. London: Collins & Harvill.

Spencer, A. B.
1981   "The Wise Fool (and the Foolish Wise): A Study of Irony in Paul." *Novum Testamentum* 23:349–60.

Spicq, C.
1965   *Agapē in the New Testament*. Translated by M. A. McNamara and M. H. Richter. St. Louis: Herder.
1994   *Theological Lexicon of the New Testament*. Translated and edited by J. Ernest. 3 vols. Peabody, MA: Hendrickson.

Spurgeon, C. H.
1954   *Lectures to My Students*. London: Marshall, Morgan & Scott.
1960   *An All-Round Ministry: Addresses to Ministers and Students*. London: Banner of Truth Trust.

Stanley, C. D.
1992   *Paul and the Language of Scripture: Citation Technique in the Pauline Epistles and Contemporary Literature*. Society for New Testament Studies 74. Cambridge: Cambridge University Press.

Stansbury, H.
1990   "Corinthian Honor, Corinthian Conflict: A Social History of Early Roman

Corinth and Its Pauline Community."
PhD diss., University of California.

Starnitzke, D.
1999   "Der Dienst des Paulus: Zur Interpreta-
        tion von Ex 34 im 2 Kor 3." *Wort und
        Dienst* 25:193–207.

Stegemann, E. W.
1986   "Der neue Bund im Alten: Zum Schrift-
        verständnis des Paulus im 2 Kor 3."
        Theologische Zeitschrift 42:97–114.

Stegman, T. D.
2007   "Ἐπίστευσα, διὸ ἐλάλησα (2 Corin-
        thians 4:13): Paul's Christological Read-
        ing of Psalm 115:1a LXX." *Catholic
        Biblical Quarterly* 69:725–45.
2009   *Second Corinthians*. Catholic Com-
        mentary on Sacred Scripture. Grand
        Rapids: Baker Academic.

Stirewalt, M. L.
2003   *Paul, the Letter Writer*. Grand Rapids:
        Eerdmans.

Stockhausen, C. K.
1989   *Moses' Veil and the Glory of the New
        Covenant: The Exegetical Substructure
        of II Cor. 3,1–4,6*. Analecta biblica 116.
        Rome: Pontifical Biblical Institute Press.

Stott, J. R. W.
1971   *Basic Christianity*. 2nd ed. London:
        Inter-Varsity.
1992   *The Contemporary Christian: Applying
        God's Word to Today's World*. Downers
        Grove, IL: InterVarsity.

Stowers, S. K.
1990   "*Peri Men Gar* and the Integrity of
        2 Cor. 8 and 9." *Novum Testamentum*
        32:340–48.

Strange, J. F.
1983   "2 Corinthians 10:13–16 Illuminated by
        a Recently Published Inscription." *Bibli-
        cal Archaeologist* 46:167–68.

Sumney, J. L.
1990   *Identifying Paul's Opponents: The
        Question of Method in 2 Corinthians*.
        Journal for the Study of the New Testa-
        ment: Supplement Series 40. Sheffield:
        JSOT Press.
1999   *"Servants of Satan," "False Brothers"
        and Other Opponents of Paul*. Journal
        for the Study of the New Testament:
        Supplement Series 188. Sheffield: Shef-
        field Academic Press.

Talbert, C. H.
1989   "Money Management in Early Medi-
        terranean Christianity: 2 Corinthians
        8–9." *Review & Expositor* 86:359–70.

2002   *Reading Corinthians: A Literary and
        Theological Commentary*. Macon, GA:
        Smyth & Helwys.

Taylor, N. H.
1991   "The Composition and Chronology of
        Second Corinthians." *Journal for the
        Study of the New Testament* 44:67–87.

TDNT   *Theological Dictionary of the New Testa-
        ment*. Edited by G. Kittel and G. Friedrich.
        Translated and edited by G. W. Bromi-
        ley. 10 vols. Grand Rapids: Eerdmans,
        1964–76.

Thierry, J. J.
1962   "Der Dorn im Fleische (2 Kor 12:7–9)."
        Novum Testamentum 5:301–10.

Thiselton, A. C.
2000   *The First Epistle to the Corinthians: A
        Commentary on the Greek Text*. New
        International Greek Testament Com-
        mentary. Grand Rapids: Eerdmans.

Thrall, M. E.
1962   *Greek Particles in the New Testament:
        Linguistic and Exegetical Studies*.
        Leiden: Brill.
1967   "The Pauline Use of ΣΥΝΕΙΔΗΣΙΣ."
        New Testament Studies 14:118–25.
1976   "2 Corinthians 1:12: ΑΓΙΟΤΗΤΙ or
        ΑΠΛΟΤΗΤΙ." Pp. 366–72 in *Studies in
        New Testament Language and Text:
        Essays in Honour of George D. Kilpat-
        rick on the Occasion of His Sixty-fifth
        Birthday*. Edited by F. S. Kilpatrick.
        Supplements to Novum Testamentum
        44. Leiden: Brill.
1977   "Problem of II Cor 6:14–7:1 in Some
        Recent Discussion." *New Testament
        Studies* 24:132–48.
1981   "'Putting On' or 'Stripping Off' in
        2 Corinthians 5:3." Pp. 221–37 in *New
        Testament Textual Criticism: Its Signifi-
        cance for Exegesis; Essays in Honor of
        Bruce M. Metzger*. Edited by E. J. Epp
        and G. D. Fee. Oxford: Clarendon.
1982   "A Second Thanksgiving Period in
        II Corinthians." *Journal for the Study
        of the New Testament* 16:101–24.
1994   *A Critical and Exegetical Com-
        mentary on the Second Epistle to the
        Corinthians*, vol. 1: *Introduction and
        Commentary on II Corinthians I–VII*.
        International Critical Commentary.
        Edinburgh: T&T Clark.
2000   *A Critical and Exegetical Com-
        mentary on the Second Epistle to the
        Corinthians*, vol. 2: *Commentary on*

II Corinthians VIII–XIII. International Critical Commentary. London: T&T Clark.

Thyen, H.
1955   *Der Stil der jüdisch-hellenistischen Homilie*. Forschungen zur Religion und Literatur des alten und neuen Testaments 47. Göttingen: Vandenhoeck & Ruprecht.

Timmis, S.
1993   "Power: Playing according to Satan's Rules? Some Reflections on 2 Corinthians 10–13." *Evangel* 11:54–61.

Tozer, A. W.
1961   *The Knowledge of the Holy: The Attributes of God and Their Meaning in the Christian Life*. New York: Harper & Row.

Tripp, P. D.
2002   *Instruments in the Redeemer's Hands: People in Need of Change Helping People in Need of Change*. Resources for Changing Lives. Phillipsburg, NJ: P&R.

Turner, D. L.
1989   "Paul and the Ministry of Reconciliation in 2 Cor 5:11–6:2." *Criswell Theological Review* 4:77–95.

Twain, M.
2009   *Adventures of Huckleberry Finn*. Mineola, NY: Dover.

Ulonska, H.
1966   "Die *Doxa* des Mose: Zum Problem des alten Testaments in 2 Kor 3:1–16." *Evangelische Theologie* 26:378–88.

Unnik, W. C. van
1963   "With Unveiled Face: An Exegesis of 2 Corinthians 3:12–18." *Novum Testamentum* 6:153–69.

Vander Broek, L. D.
2002   *Breaking Barriers: The Possibilities of Christian Community in a Lonely World*. Grand Rapids: Brazos.

Vegge, I.
2008   *2 Corinthians—a Letter about Reconciliation: A Psychagogical, Epistolographical, and Rhetorical Analysis*. Wissenschaftliche Untersuchungen zum Neuen Testament 239. Tübingen: Mohr Siebeck.

Verbrugge, V. D.
1992   *Paul's Style of Church Leadership Illustrated by His Instructions to the Corinthians on the Collection*. San Francisco:

Mellen Research University Press/Lewiston, NY: Edwin Mellen.

Verhoef, E.
1996   "The Senders of the Letters to the Corinthians and the Use of 'I' and 'We.'" Pp. 417–25 in *The Corinthian Correspondence*. Edited by R. Bieringer. Louvain: Leuven University Press.

Versnel, H. S.
1970   *Triumphus: An Inquiry into the Origin, Development and Meaning of the Roman Triumph*. Leiden: Brill.

Vliet, H. van
1958   *No Single Testimony: A Study on the Adoption of the Law of Deut. 19:15 Par. into the New Testament*. Studia theologica rheno-traiectina 4. Utrecht: Kemink & Zoon.

Walker, D. D.
2002   *Paul's Offer of Leniency (2 Cor 10,1): Populist Ideology and Rhetoric in a Pauline Letter Fragment*. Wissenschaftliche Untersuchungen zum Neuen Testament 2/152. Tübingen: Mohr Siebeck.

Walker, P. W. L.
2012   "Revisiting the Pastoral Epistles: Part I." *European Journal of Theology* 21:4–16.

Wallace, D. B.
1996   *Greek Grammar beyond the Basics: An Exegetical Syntax of the New Testament*. Grand Rapids: Zondervan.

Wallace, J. B.
2011   *Snatched into Paradise (2 Cor. 12:1–10): Paul's Heavenly Journey in the Context of Early Christian Experience*. Beihefte zur Zeitschrift für die neutestamentliche Wissenschaft 179. Berlin: de Gruyter.

Wanamaker, C. A.
2003   "By the Power of God": Rhetoric and Ideology in 2 Corinthians 10–13." Pp. 194–221 in *Fabrics of Discourse: Essays in Honor of Vernon K. Robbins*. Edited by D. B. Gowler, L. G. Bloomquist, and D. F. Watson. Harrisburg, PA: Trinity.

Warmington, E. H.
1935   *Remains of Old Latin: Archaic Inscriptions*, vol. 4. Edited by J. Henderson. Loeb Classical Library. London: Heinemann/Cambridge, MA: Harvard University Press.

Watson, D. E.
2006   "Paul's Collection in Light of Motivations and Mechanisms for Aid to the

Poor in the First-Century World." PhD diss., University of Durham.

Watson, D. F.
2003   "Paul and Boasting." Pp. 77–100 in *Paul in the Greco-Roman World: A Handbook*. Edited by J. P. Sampley. Harrisburg, PA: Trinity.

Watson, F.
1984   "2 Cor 10–13 and Paul's Painful Letter to the Corinthians." *Journal of Theological Studies* 35:324–46.
2004   *Paul and the Hermeneutics of Faith*. London: T&T Clark.

Wax, T.
2011   *Counterfeit Gospels: Rediscovering the Good News in a World of False Hope*. Chicago: Moody.

Webb, W. J.
1993   *Returning Home: New Covenant and Second Exodus as the Context for 2 Corinthians 6.14–7.1*. Journal for the Study of the New Testament: Supplement Series 85. Sheffield: Sheffield Academic Press.

Weima, J. A. D.
1994   *Neglected Endings: The Significance of the Pauline Letter Closings*. Journal for the Study of the New Testament: Supplement Series 101. Sheffield: JSOT Press.

Weiss, J.
1894   "Review of A. Halmel, *Der Viercapitelbrief im zweiten Korintherbrief des Apostels Paulus* (Essen: Baedeker, 1894)." *Theologische Literaturzeitung* 19:513–14.

Welborn, L. L.
1995a   "The Dangerous Double Affirmation: Character and Truth in 2 Cor 1,17." *Zeitschrift für die neutestamentliche Wissenschaft* 86:34–52.
1995b   "The Identification of 2 Corinthians 10–13 with the 'Letter of Tears.'" *Novum Testamentum* 37:138–53.
1996   "Like Broken Pieces of a Ring: 2 Cor 1.1–2.13; 7.5–16 and Ancient Theories of Literary Unity." *New Testament Studies* 42:559–83.
2001   "Paul's Appeal to the Emotions in 2 Corinthians 1.1–2.13; 7.5–16." *Journal for the Study of the New Testament* 82:31–60.
2009   "Paul's Caricature of His Chief Rival as a Pompous Parasite in 2 Corinthians 11.20." *Journal for the Study of the New Testament* 32:39–56.

2010   "'By the Mouth of Two or Three Witnesses': Paul's Invocation of a Deuteronomic Statute." *Novum Testamentum* 52:207–20.

Wendland, H. D.
1968   *Die Briefe an die Korinther*. 11th ed. Das Neue Testament deutsch 7. Göttingen: Vandenhoeck & Ruprecht.

Wenham, D.
1986   "2 Corinthians 1:17, 18: Echo of a Dominical Logion." *Novum Testamentum* 28:271–79.

Wevers, J. W.
1990   *Notes on the Greek Text of Exodus*. Atlanta: Scholars Press.

White, H.
1912   *Appian: Roman History*, vol. 1: *Books I–VIII.1*. Loeb Classical Library. London: Heinemann/Cambridge, MA: Harvard University Press.

White, J. L.
1972   *The Form and Function of the Body of the Greek Letter: A Study of the Letter-Body in the Non-literary Papyri and in Paul the Apostle*. Society of Biblical Literature Dissertation Series. Missoula, MT: Scholars Press.

White, T. H.
1977   *The Book of Merlyn: The Unpublished Conclusion to the Once and Future King*. Austin: University of Texas Press.

Williams, C. K.
1993   "Roman Corinth as a Commercial Center." Pp. 31–46 in *The Corinthia in the Roman Period: Including the Papers Given at a Symposium Held at the Ohio State University on 7–9 March, 1991*. Edited by T. E. Gregory. Ann Arbor, MI: Journal of Roman Archaeology.

Williamson, L.
1968   "Led in Triumph: Paul's Use of *Thriambeuō*." *Interpretation* 22:317–32.

Windisch, H., and G. Strecker
1970   *Der zweite Korintherbrief*. Kritisch-exegetischer Kommentar über das Neue Testament. Göttingen: Vandenhoeck & Ruprecht.

Winter, B. W.
1999   "Gallio's Ruling on the Legal Status of Early Christianity (Acts 18:14–15)." *Tyndale Bulletin* 50:213–24.

2001   *After Paul Left Corinth: The Influence of Secular Ethics and Social Change.* 2nd ed. Grand Rapids: Eerdmans.

2002   *Philo and Paul among the Sophists: Alexandrian and Corinthian Responses to a Julio-Claudian Movement.* Grand Rapids: Eerdmans.

Witherington, B.

1995   *Conflict and Community in Corinth: A Socio-Rhetorical Commentary on 1 and 2 Corinthians.* Grand Rapids: Eerdmans/Carlisle, UK: Paternoster.

Wong, E.

1985   "The Lord Is the Spirit (2 Cor 3,17a)." *Ephemerides theologicae lovanienses* 61:48–72.

Wright, N. T.

1995   *Following Jesus: Biblical Reflections on Discipleship.* Grand Rapids: Eerdmans.

2003   *The Resurrection of the Son of God.* Christian Origins and the Question of God 3. Philadelphia: Augsburg Fortress.

Yancey, P.

1990   *Where Is God When It Hurts?* Rev. and expanded ed. Grand Rapids: Zondervan.

Yates, R.

1981   "Paul's Affliction in Asia: 2 Corinthians 1:8." *Evangelical Quarterly* 53:241–45.

Young, F. M., and D. Ford

1987   *Meaning and Truth in 2 Corinthians.* London: SPCK.

Zerwick, M.

1963   *Biblical Greek: Illustrated by Examples.* English ed. adapted from the 4th Latin ed. by J. Smith. Scripta pontificii instituti biblici 114. Rome: Pontifical Biblical Institute Press.

Zmijewski, J.

1978   *Der Stil der paulinischen "Narrenrede": Analyse der Sprachgestaltung in 2 Kor 11,1–12,10 als Beitrag zur Methodik von Stiluntersuchungen neutestamentlicher Texte.* Bonner biblische Beiträge 52. Cologne: Hanstein.

Index of Subjects

Abba 66
Abraham 111
accountability 380–81, 646–47
Achaian League 10
Acrocorinth 13
Adam-Christology 275n3
affections 344–46
Alciphron 13n12
ambassadors 311–12
Ambrosiaster 80, 447, 492, 517, 530
"amen," use in worship 111–13
apocalyptic Judaism 75
apostle 8–9, 55–56, 61, 161
apostolic ministry 43–44
Aquila 6n4, 8, 19, 79
Aristotle 621
asceticism 15n13
Augustine 364, 569, 626
Augustus 11
authoritarianism 626

Barclay, John 41n62
Barnett, Paul 8, 84, 189n15, 290, 610n3
Barrett, C. K. 159–60, 282n22, 312, 336
Basil 137
Bauckham, Richard 60n19
Baxter, Richard 203, 251
Beale, G. K. 355n25
Beliar 352–53
Belleville, Linda 181
Beltz, Joe 28n41, 129
benediction 62, 65–66
Berry, Wendell 291
Best, E. 94
Betz, Hans Dieter 433, 439
Bieringer, R. 309n14
blameless reputation 641–42
Block, D. I. 192
boasting 93–94, 98, 185–86, 298–99, 437, 479–81, 487–500, 504–5

Boers, H. 293n1
Bruce, F. F. 475n29
Bultmann, Rudolf 27, 293n1

calling 195–96, 234–35
Calvin, John 216n35, 256, 411, 414, 471n16
Campbell, Douglas 575
Carson, D. A. 512
Cenchreae 58
cheating 614–15
Christian leadership 152–54, 243–44
church
   as bride of Christ 507–8, 623
   conflicts in 300–301
   discipline in 130–38
   as eschatological Israel 58
   establishment of 9
   influence of 499–500
   as marked by suffering 74–75
   unity within 58
church planting 8–9
Cicero 160, 208
Clarke, Andrew 15
clean/unclean imagery 347–48, 356–60
commendation motif 601–7
communication
   and authentic ministry 119, 128–29, 150–51
   letter formats of 53–55
   use of envoys 371–72
   use of media imagery 191–92
condemnation 216–17
conscience 93–95, 295, 297
Corinth 1–4, 9–14, 411–12
Corinthian church
   accountability within 609–13
   call to rejoice 650–51
   foolish tolerance of 538–42
   fundraising from 388–415
   generous giving of 456–61
   immorality within 619–26

leadership values of 14–19
letter of recommendation from 187–89
openness of 342–46, 361–64
purity within 346–61, 505–9
response to harsh letter 376–84
spiritual immaturity in 189n15
countercultural Christianity 364, 542
countercultural glory 208–9
covenants. *See also* new covenant; old covenant
   continuum of old and new 198–201, 358–59
   faithfulness to 507
   promises of 359–60
   veiled vs. unveiled 217–32
Cranfield, C. E. B. 36
Crispus 8, 19
Cullmann, Oscar 276, 278n13

David 111
death 168–74, 205–17, 258–61, 283–84, 555–56
deceivers 335–36
deliverance 84–88, 257, 318
despair 256–57
Dewey, A. 479n37
Diolkos 12n8
disembodied state 282–83
doubt 67, 82, 257
Duff, P. B. 159
Dumbrell, W. J. 214n29, 214n32

edification 642–46
Edwards, Jonathan 341
Eighteen Benedictions 64, 84
election 58
Elliot, Jim 365
Ellis, E. E. 275n3
encouragement 63–73
Ephesus 20, 101
Epictetus 183, 560
Erastus 4, 6

tolerance 512, 538–42
Tolkien, J. R. R. 155
Tozer, A. W. 88
transfiguration 228
Trinity 57
triumphal-procession imagery
157–74, 239
triumphal procession metaphor
170–74
Troas 142, 144–47
Turner, D. L. 312

unbelief 226
unbelievers 349–51
unrepentance 633–34

validation of accusations 630–32
Versnel, H. S. 157–58, 166
visions 577–84

Wallace, Daniel 190
Watson, D. F. 93n4, 395, 602n2
Watson, Francis 199, 210n18
weapons of righteousness 333–34
Weiss, Johannes 24
Welborn, L. L. 65, 108, 539
Wevers, J. W. 221n44
White, T. H., 99
Whitefield, George 378
Windisch, Hans 293n1
Winter, Bruce 45, 242, 517

wisdom 334, 532–33
Witherington, B. 510
Word of God
authentic proclamation of 153–54
distortion of 236–38
productivity of 454–55
as salvation or devastation 174
works 287–90
world
evaluations based on 306–8
seeking affirmation from 155–56
worship 347
Wright, N. T. 88, 287

Xenophon 226–27

Index of Authors

Index of Greek Words

Index of Scripture and Other Ancient Writings

Old Testament

Genesis
1:3 244
1:26 246
2:7 253n8, 253n10
2:8 583
3 508n16, 508n17
3:1 240
3:7 283n23
3:10–11 283n23
3:16 122, 123
3:17 123
3:19 253n10, 254
5:29 123
8:21 167, 167n18
9:26 64
12:3 111
12:10 564
13:10 541, 583
13:16 358
14:20 64
14:23 456
17:5–6 358
17:7 552
18:18 111
23:2 624
24:27 64
24:31 64
26:14 505
27:27 169
28:15 257n20
30:1 505
31:42 563
34:8 449n8
37:33 581
37:34 624
38:18 115
39:20 474n27
40:14 474n27
41:14 474n27
41:42 115
47:21 540
50:3 624

Exodus
1:14 540
3:9 412
3:11 195
4:10 195
4:11–12 195
4:31 412
5:21 169
6:5 540
7:3 604n10
7:9 604n10
9:14 271n5
10:13 541
11:9–10 604n10
14:18 209

14:29–30 228
15:3 452n13
15:6–8 452n13
15:9 122
15:10–12 452n13
16 414
16:2–3 414
16:4 405n34, 414
16:7 209
16:13 414
16:13–15 414
16:18 414, 415, 417, 458
17:2 638
17:4 558
17:7 638
18:10 64
19:12 207
20:5 506
20:16 630
21:12 207
21:14–17 207
21:28–19 207
22:2 207
22:19 207
23:15 316
24:12 207
24:15–18 225
24:16–17 209

25:16 207
28:38 411
28:41 114
29:7 114
29:18 167n18
29:25 167n18
29:41 167n18
30:31–35 168
31:3 225
31:14–15 207
31:18 193, 193n23, 207
32 221, 309n14
32–34 193n23, 210n18, 221n43, 222
32:15 193n23, 207
33 221
33:3 225
33:7–11 225
33:9–11 226
33:12–23 221n43
33:16 221, 221n44
33:16–17 221, 221n44
33:18 209
33:19 221n43
34 204n2, 215, 220, 225, 240

34 LXX 153
34:1 193n23, 207, 232
34:1–9 209
34:4 193n23
34:6–7 213, 221n43
34:7 213
34:14 506
34:20 316
34:28 232
34:29 207, 209, 210, 215, 221n44
34:29–30 204
34:29–35 204, 205, 206, 212, 213, 217
34:30 210n18, 215, 219
34:30–32 210n18
34:33–35 204, 219
34:34 197, 211n18, 225, 225n53
34:34–35 210n18
34:35 204, 210n18, 211, 213, 215, 216, 221n44
35:2 213
35:31 225

New Testament

Old Testament Apocrypha

Old Testament Pseudepigrapha

Rabbinic Writings

Qumran/Dead Sea Scrolls

Papyri and Inscriptions

Josephus

Philo

Classical Writers

Church Fathers